D0075935

Operating Systems

A Concept-Based Approach

Dhananjay M. Dhamdhere

Professor of Computer Science & Engineering
Indian Institute of Technology, Bombay

The McGraw·Hill Companies

OPERATING SYSTEMS: A CONCEPT-BASED APPROACH

Published by McGraw-Hill, a business unit of The McGraw-Hill Companies, Inc., 1221 Avenue of the Americas, New York, NY 10020.

This book is printed on acid-free paper.

1 2 3 4 5 6 7 8 9 0 DOC/DOC 0 9 8

ISBN 978-0-07-295769-3
MHID 0-07-295769-7

Global Publisher: *Raghothaman Srinivasan*
Director of Development: *Kristine Tibbetts*
Freelance Developmental Editor: *Melinda Bilecki*
Project Coordinator: *Melissa M. Leick*
Lead Production Supervisor: *Sandy Ludovissy*
Designer: *Laurie B. Janssen*
(USE) Cover Image: *S. Solum/PhotoLink/Getty Images, RF*
Compositor: *Newgen*
Typeface: *10/12 Times*
Printer: *R. R. Donnelley Crawfordsville, IN*

Library of Congress Cataloging-in-Publication Data

Dhamdhere, Dhananjay M.
Operating systems : a concept-based approach / Dhananjay M. Dhamdhere. – 1st ed.
p. cm.
Includes bibliographical references and index.
ISBN 978-0-07-295769-3 — ISBN 0-07-295769-7 (hard copy : alk. paper) 1. Operating systems (Computers) I. Title.

QA76.76.O63D5 2009
005.4′3–dc22 2007041510

www.mhhe.com

Dedication

To my wife Snehalata

Brief Contents

Contents

Chapter 6

Process Synchronization 165

Chapter 7

Scheduling 228

Chapter 10

Part 3

Chapter 11

Chapter 14

Implementation of File Operations 543

Chapter 15

Security and Protection 605

Chapter 18

Distributed Control Algorithms 714

Chapter 19

Recovery and Fault Tolerance 743

Chapter 20

Distributed File Systems 760

Chapter 21

Distributed System Security 785

Preface

OBJECTIVE

The main objective of a first course in operating systems is to develop an understanding of the fundamental concepts and techniques of operating systems. Most of the students are already exposed to diverse information on operating systems as a result of practical exposure to operating systems and literature on the Internet; such students have a lot of information but few concepts about operating systems. This situation makes teaching of operating systems concepts a challenging task because it is necessary to retrofit some concepts to the information possessed by these students without boring them, yet do it in a manner that introduces concepts to first-time learners of operating systems without intimidating them. This book presents operating system concepts and techniques in a manner that incorporates these requirements.

GENERAL APPROACH

The book begins by building a core knowledge of what makes an operating system tick. It presents an operating system as an intermediary between a computer system and users that provides good service to users and also achieves efficient use of the computer system. A discussion of interactions of an operating system with the computer on one hand and with user computations on the other hand consolidates this view and adds practical details to it. This approach demystifies an operating system for a new reader, and also relates to the background of an experienced reader. It also emphasizes key features of computer architecture that are essential for a study of operating systems.

The rest of the book follows an analogous approach. Each chapter identifies fundamental concepts involved in some functionality of an operating system, describes relevant features in computer architecture, discusses relevant operating system techniques, and illustrates their operation through examples. The highlights of this approach are:

- Fundamental concepts are introduced in simple terms.
- The associations between techniques and concepts are readily established.
- Numerous examples are included to illustrate concepts and techniques.
- Implementation details and case studies are organized as small capsules spread throughout the text.

- Optional sections are devoted to advanced topics such as deadlock characterization, kernel memory allocation, synchronization and scheduling in multiprocessor systems, file sharing semantics, and file system reliability.

The key benefit of this approach is that concepts, techniques, and case studies are well integrated, so many design and implementation details look "obvious" by the time the reader encounters them. It emphasizes the most important message an operating systems text can give to students: A concept-based study of operating systems equips a computer professional to comprehend diverse operating system techniques readily.

PEDAGOGICAL FEATURES

Preview of the Book The last section of the first chapter is a brief preview of the book that motivates study of each chapter by describing its importance within the overall scheme of the operating system, the topics covered in the chapter, and its relationships with other chapters of the book.

Part Introduction Each part of the book begins with an introduction that describes its contents and provides a road map of the chapters in the part.

Chapter Introduction The chapter introduction motivates the reader by describing the objectives of the chapter and the topics covered in it.

Figures and Tables Each chapter has concept-based figures that illustrate fundamental concepts and techniques of a specific OS functionality. These figures are a vital part of the book's pedagogy. Other figures are used for traditional purposes such as depicting practical arrangements or stepwise operation of specific techniques. Tables play a crucial role in the pedagogy by providing overviews and summaries of specific topics.

Examples Examples demonstrate the key issues concerning concepts and techniques being discussed. Examples are typeset in a different style to set them apart from the main body of the text, so a reader can skip an example if he does not want the flow of ideas to be interrupted, especially while reading a chapter for the first time.

Program Code Program code is presented in an easy-to-understand pseudocode form.

Snapshots of Concurrent Systems Students have difficulty visualizing concurrent activities in a software system, which leads to an inadequate understanding of process synchronization. A snapshot depicts the state of different activities and their data to provide a holistic view of activities in a concurrent system.

Case Studies Case studies are included in a chapter to emphasize practical issues, arrangements, and trade-offs in the design and implementation of a specific OS functionality. We draw freely from operating systems of the Unix, Linux, Solaris, and Windows families—we refer to them simply as Unix, Linux, Solaris, and Windows, respectively, except when features of a specific version such as Linux 2.6 or Windows Vista are being discussed.

Tests of Concepts A set of objective and multiple-choice questions is provided at the end of each chapter so that the reader can test his grasp of concepts presented in the chapter.

Exercises Exercises are included at the end of each chapter. These include numerical problems based on material covered in the text, as well as challenging conceptual questions that test understanding and also provide deeper insights.

Summaries The summary included at the end of each chapter highlights the key topics covered and their interrelationships.

Instructor Resources A detailed solutions manual and slides for classroom usage are provided.

ORGANIZATION OF THE BOOK

The study of conventional operating systems is organized into four parts. The fifth part is devoted to distributed operating systems. The structure of the first four parts and interdependency between chapters is shown overleaf. Details of the parts are described in the following.

- **Part 1: Overview** Part 1 consists of four chapters. The introduction discusses how user convenience, efficient use of resources, and security and protection are the fundamental concerns of an operating system and describes the tasks involved in implementing them. It also contains a preview of the entire book. Chapter 2 describes how an OS uses features in a computer's hardware to organize execution of user programs and handle requests made by them. Chapter 3 describes the different classes of operating systems, discusses the fundamental concepts and techniques used by each of them, and lists those of their techniques that are employed in modern operating systems as well. Chapter 4 describes operating system design methodologies that enable an OS to adapt to changes in computer architecture and the computing environment in which it is used.
- **Part 2: Process Management** An operating system uses the concepts of *process* and *thread* to manage execution of programs—informally, both process and thread represent an execution of a program. The OS contains many processes at any time and services them in an overlapped manner to provide good user service and achieve efficient use of resources. Part 2 consists of six chapters describing issues relating to management of processes and threads. Chapter 5 describes how processes and threads are created, how they interact with one another to jointly achieve a goal, and how they are controlled by the operating system. The remaining five chapters deal with specifics in process management—process synchronization, scheduling, deadlocks, message passing, and synchronization and scheduling in multiprocessor operating systems.

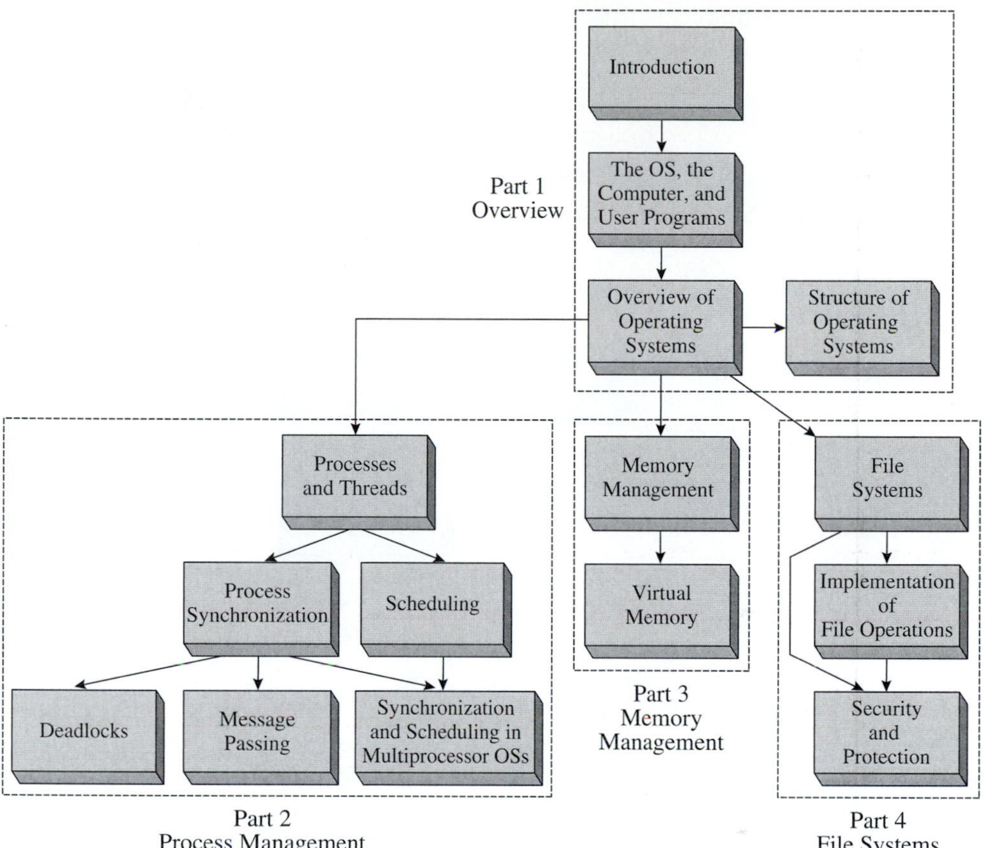

- **Part 3: Memory Management** Two chapters are devoted to allocation and sharing of memory between processes. Chapter 11 deals with the fundamentals of memory management—the problem of *memory fragmentation*, which is a situation in which an area of memory is unusable because it is too small, and techniques that address memory fragmentation. Chapter 12 discusses implementation of *virtual memory*, which overcomes the problem of memory fragmentation and also supports execution of large programs.
- **Part 4: File Systems** This part consists of three chapters. Chapter 13 describes facilities for creation, access, sharing and reliable storage of files. Chapter 14 discusses I/O devices and describes how operations on files are implemented in an efficient manner. Chapter 15 discusses how security and file protection techniques together prevent illegal forms of access to files.
- **Part 5: Distributed Operating Systems** A distributed operating system differs from a conventional one in that the resources, processes and control operations of the OS are spread across individual computer systems contained in the distributed system. This difference gives rise to a host of issues concerning performance, reliability, and security of computations and the OS itself. Part 5 contains six chapters that discuss these issues.

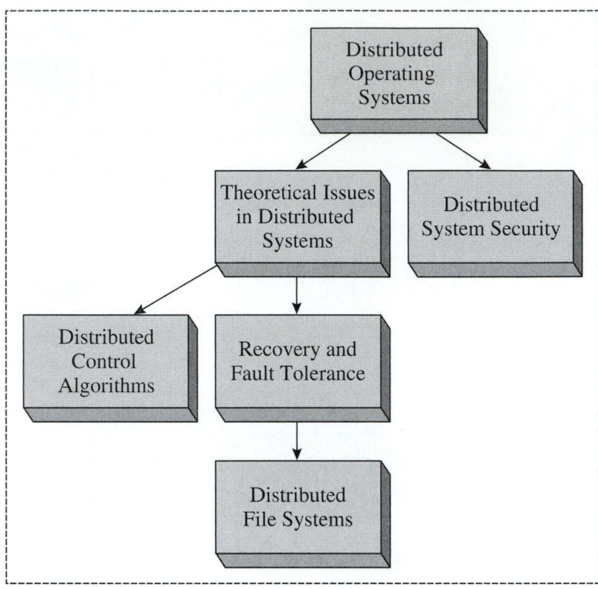

Part 5
Distributed Operating Systems

USING THIS BOOK

Apart from an introduction to computing, this book does not assume the reader to possess any specific background, so instructors and students are likely to find that it contains a lot of introductory material that students already know. This material has been included for one very important reason: As mentioned at the start of the preface, students know many *things* on their own, but often lack *concepts*. So it is useful for students to read even familiar topics that are presented in a concept-based manner. For the same reason, it is essential for instructors to cover Chapters 2 and 3, particularly the following topics, in class:

- Section 2.2: Memory hierarchy, input/output and interrupts
- Section 2.3: Interrupt servicing and system calls
- Section 3.5: Multiprogramming systems, particularly program mix and priority.

All topics included in this text cannot be covered in a quarter or semester length course on operating systems. An instructor may wish to omit some of the advanced topics or the chapters on structure of operating systems, message passing, and synchronization and scheduling in multiprocessor operating systems, and some of the chapters devoted to distributed operating systems.

part 1

Overview

An operating system controls use of a computer system's resources such as CPUs, memory, and I/O devices to meet computational requirements of its users. Users expect convenience, quality of service, and a guarantee that other persons will not be able to interfere with their activities; whereas system administrators expect efficient use of the computer's resources and good performance in executing user programs. These diverse expectations can be characterized as *user convenience*, *efficient use*, and *security* and *protection*; they form the primary goals of an operating system. The extent to which an operating system provides user convenience or efficient use depends on its *computing environment*, i.e., the computer system's hardware, its interfaces with other computers, and the nature of computations performed by its users.

Different classes of operating systems were developed for different computing environments. We discuss the fundamental concepts and techniques used in each class of operating systems, and the flavor of user convenience and efficient use provided by it. A modern operating system has elements of several classes of operating systems, so most of these concepts and techniques are found in modern operating systems as well.

Road Map for Part 1

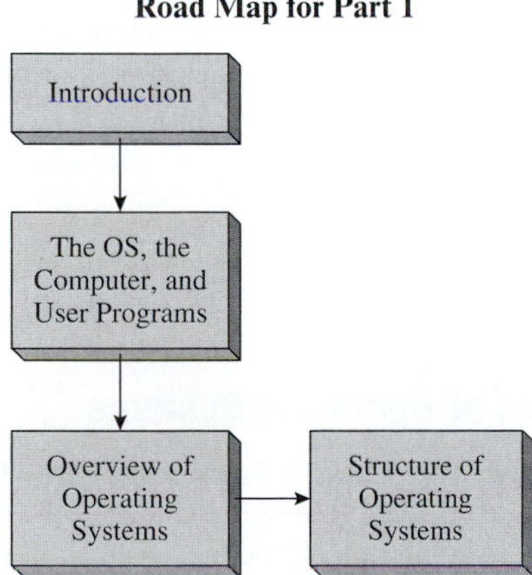

Schematic diagram showing the order in which chapters of this part should be covered in a course.

A modern operating system has to be used on computer systems with different architectures; it also has to keep pace with evolution of its computing environment. We discuss operating system design methodologies that enable an operating system to be implemented on different computer architectures, and to evolve with its computing environment.

Chapter 1: Introduction

This chapter discusses how users perceive *user convenience*, how an operating system achieves *efficient use* of resources, and how it ensures *security* and *protection*. It introduces the notion of *effective utilization* of a computer system as the combination of user convenience and efficient use that best suits a specific computing environment. It also describes the fundamental tasks involved in management of programs and resources, and in implementing security and protection. The last section of this chapter is a preview of the entire book that describes the concepts and techniques discussed in each chapter and their importance in the operating system.

Chapter 2: The OS, the Computer, and User Programs

This chapter presents hardware features of a computer system that are relevant for operation and performance of an operating system (OS). It describes how an OS uses some of the hardware features to control execution of user programs and perform I/O operations in them, and how user programs use features in the hardware to interact with the OS and obtain the services they need.

Chapter 3: Overview of Operating Systems

This chapter deals with the fundamental principles of an operating system; it is a key chapter in the book. It discusses the nature of computations in different kinds of computing environments and features of operating systems used in these environments, and follows up this discussion with the notions of efficiency, system performance, and user service. Later sections discuss five classes of operating systems—*batch processing, multiprogramming, time-sharing, real-time*, and *distributed operating systems*—and describe the principal concepts and techniques they use to meet their goals. The last section discusses how a modern OS draws upon the concepts and techniques used in these operating systems.

Chapter 4: Structure of Operating Systems

The structure of an operating system has two kinds of features—those that contribute to simplicity of coding and efficiency of operation; and those that contribute to the ease with which an OS can be implemented on different computer systems, or can be enhanced to incorporate new functionalities. This chapter discusses three methods of structuring an operating system. The *layered structure* of operating systems simplifies coding, the *kernel-based structure* provides ease of implementation on different computer systems, and the *microkernel-based structure* permits modification of an operating system's features to adapt to changes in the computing environment and also provides ease of implementation on different computer systems.

Chapter 1

Introduction

The way you would define an operating system probably depends on what you expect from your computer system. Each user has his own personal thoughts on what the computer system is for. In technical language, we would say that an individual user has an *abstract view* of the computer system, a view that takes in only those features that the user considers important.

The operating system, or OS, as we will often call it, is the intermediary between users and the computer system. It provides the services and features present in abstract views of *all* its users through the computer system. It also enables the services and features to evolve over time as users' needs change.

People who design operating systems have to deal with three issues: efficient use of the computer system's resources, the convenience of users, and prevention of interference with users' activities. Efficient use is more important when a computer system is dedicated to specific applications, and user convenience is more important in personal computers, while both are equally important when a computer system is shared by several users. Hence, the designer aims for the right combination of efficient use and user convenience for the operating system's environment. Prevention of interference is mandatory in all environments.

We will now take a broad look at what makes an operating system work—we will see how its functions of *program management* and *resource management* help to ensure efficient use of resources and user convenience, and how the functions of *security* and *protection* prevent interference with programs and resources.

1.1 ABSTRACT VIEWS OF AN OPERATING SYSTEM

A question such as "What is an OS?" is likely to evoke different answers, depending on the user's interest. For example,

- To a school or college student, the OS is the software that permits access to the Internet.
- To a programmer, the OS is the software that makes it possible to develop programs on a computer system.

- To a user of an application package, the OS is simply the software that makes it possible to use the package.
- To a technician in, say, a computerized chemical plant, the OS is the invisible component of a computer system that controls the plant.

A user perceives an OS as simply a means of achieving an intended use of a computer system. For the student, the sole purpose of the computer system is to get onto the Internet; the OS helps in achieving this. Hence the student thinks of the operating system as the means for Internet browsing. The programmer, the user of a package, and the technician similarly identify the OS with their particular purposes in using the computer. Since their purposes are different, their perceptions of the OS are also different.

Figure 1.1 illustrates the four views of an OS we have just considered. They are *abstract views*, because each focuses on those characteristics considered essential from the perspective of the individual viewer—it includes some elements of reality but ignores other elements. The student, the application user, and the technician are end users of the OS; their views do not contain any features of the OS. The programmer's view is that of a software developer. It includes features of the OS for software development.

An OS designer has his own abstract view of the OS, which shows the structure of an OS and the relationship between its component parts. Figure 1.2

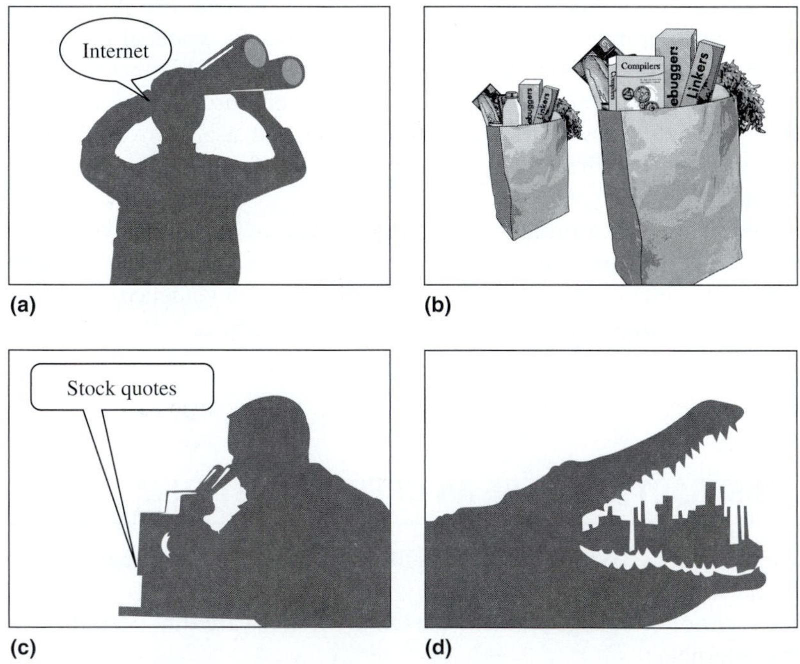

Figure 1.1 Abstract views of an OS: a student's, a programmer's, an application user's and a technician's.

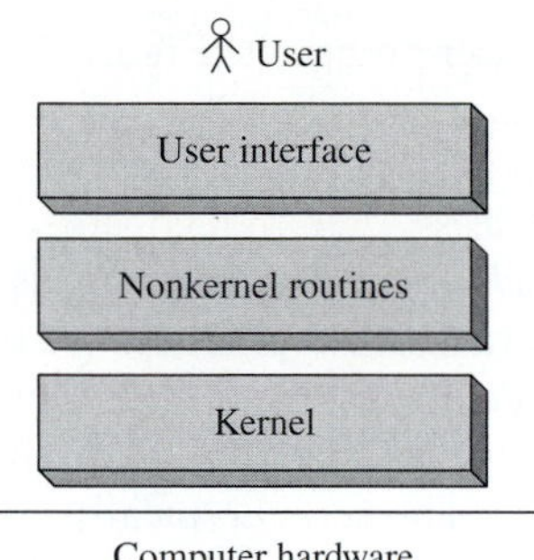

Figure 1.2 A designer's abstract view of an OS.

illustrates this view. Each part consists of a number of routines. The typical functionalities of these parts are as follows:

- *User interface:* The user interface accepts commands to execute programs and use resources and services provided by the operating system. It is either a command line interface, as in Unix or Linux, which displays a command prompt to the user and accepts a user command, or is a graphical user interface (GUI), as in the Windows operating system, which interprets mouse clicks on icons as user commands.
- *Nonkernel routines:* These routines implement user commands concerning execution of programs and use of the computer's resources; they are invoked by the user interface.
- *Kernel:* The kernel is the core of the OS. It controls operation of the computer and provides a set of functions and services to use the CPU, memory, and other resources of the computer. The functions and services of the kernel are invoked by the nonkernel routines and by user programs.

Two features of an OS emerge from the designer's view of an OS shown in Figure 1.2. The OS is actually a collection of routines that facilitate execution of user programs and use of resources in a computer system. It contains a hierarchical arrangement of layers in which routines in a higher layer use the facilities provided by routines in the layer below it. In fact, each layer takes an abstract view of the layer below it, in which the next lower layer is a machine that can understand certain commands. The fact that the lower layer is a set of routines rather than a whole computer system makes no difference to the higher layer. Each higher layer acts as a more capable machine than the layer below it. To the user, the user interface appears like a machine that understands commands in the command language of the OS.

Throughout this book, we will use abstract views to present the design of OS components. This has two key benefits:

- *Managing complexity:* An abstract view of a system contains only selected features of the system. This property is useful in managing complexity during design or study of a system. For example, an abstract view of how an OS organizes execution of user programs (Figure 1.3 illustrates such a view later in this chapter), focuses only on handling of programs; it simplifies a study of this aspect of the OS by *not* showing how the OS handles other resources like memory or I/O devices.

- *Presenting a generic scheme:* An *abstraction* is used to present a generic scheme that has many variants in practice. We see two examples of this use in the designer's abstract view of Figure 1.2. The user interface is an abstraction, with a command line interface and a graphical user interface (GUI) as two of its many variants. The kernel typically presents an abstraction of the computer system to the nonkernel routines so that the diversity of hardware, e.g., different models of CPUs and different ways of organizing and accessing data in disks, is hidden from view of the nonkernel routines.

1.2 GOALS OF AN OS

The fundamental goals of an operating system are:

- *Efficient use:* Ensure efficient use of a computer's resources.
- *User convenience:* Provide convenient methods of using a computer system.
- *Noninterference:* Prevent interference in the activities of its users.

The goals of efficient use and user convenience sometimes conflict. For example, emphasis on quick service could mean that resources like memory have to remain allocated to a program even when the program is not in execution; however, it would lead to inefficient use of resources. When such conflicts arise, the designer has to make a trade-off to obtain the combination of efficient use and user convenience that best suits the environment. This is the notion of *effective utilization* of the computer system. We find a large number of operating systems in use because each one of them provides a different flavor of effective utilization. At one extreme we have OSs that provide fast service required by command and control applications, at the other extreme we have OSs that make efficient use of computer resources to provide low-cost computing, while in the middle we have OSs that provide different combinations of the two.

Interference with a user's activities may take the form of illegal use or modification of a user's programs or data, or denial of resources and services to a user. Such interference could be caused by both users and nonusers, and every OS must incorporate measures to prevent it.

In the following, we discuss important aspects of these fundamental goals.

1.2.1 Efficient Use

An operating system must ensure efficient use of the fundamental computer system resources of memory, CPU, and I/O devices such as disks and printers. Poor efficiency can result if a program does not use a resource allocated to it, e.g., if memory or I/O devices allocated to a program remain idle. Such a situation may have a snowballing effect: Since the resource is allocated to a program, it is denied to other programs that need it. These programs cannot execute, hence resources allocated to them also remain idle. In addition, the OS itself consumes some CPU and memory resources during its own operation, and this consumption of resources constitutes an *overhead* that also reduces the resources available to user programs. To achieve good efficiency, the OS must minimize the waste of resources by programs and also minimize its own overhead.

Efficient use of resources can be obtained by monitoring use of resources and performing corrective actions when necessary. However, monitoring use of resources increases the overhead, which lowers efficiency of use. In practice, operating systems that emphasize efficient use limit their overhead by either restricting their focus to efficiency of a few important resources, like the CPU and the memory, or by not monitoring the use of resources at all, and instead handling user programs and resources in a manner that guarantees high efficiency.

1.2.2 User Convenience

User convenience has many facets, as Table 1.1 indicates. In the early days of computing, user convenience was synonymous with bare necessity—the mere ability to execute a program written in a higher level language was considered adequate. Experience with early operating systems led to demands for better service, which in those days meant only fast response to a user request.

Other facets of user convenience evolved with the use of computers in new fields. Early operating systems had *command-line interfaces*, which required a user to type in a command and specify values of its parameters. Users needed substantial training to learn use of the commands, which was acceptable because most users were scientists or computer professionals. However, simpler interfaces were needed to facilitate use of computers by new classes of users. Hence *graphical user interfaces* (GUIs) were evolved. These interfaces used *icons* on a screen to represent programs and files and interpreted mouse clicks on the icons and associated menus as commands concerning them. In many ways, this move can be compared to the spread of car driving skills in the first half of

Table 1.1 Facets of User Convenience

Facet	Examples
Fulfillment of necessity	Ability to execute programs, use the file system
Good Service	Speedy response to computational requests
User friendly interfaces	Easy-to-use commands, graphical user interface (GUI)
New programming model	Concurrent programming
Web-oriented features	Means to set up Web-enabled servers
Evolution	Add new features, use new computer technologies

the twentieth century. Over a period of time, driving became less of a specialty and more of a skill that could be acquired with limited training and experience.

Computer users attacked new problems as computing power increased. New models were proposed for developing cost-effective solutions to new classes of problems. Some of these models could be supported by the compiler technology and required little support from the OS; modular and object-oriented program design are two such models. Other models like the concurrent programming model required specific support features in the OS. Advent of the Internet motivated setting up of Web-enabled servers, which required networking support and an ability to scale up or scale down the performance of a server in response to the amount of load directed at it.

Users and their organizations invest considerable time and effort in setting up their applications through an operating system. This investment must be protected when new application areas and new computer technologies develop, so operating systems need to evolve to provide new features and support new application areas through new computer technologies.

1.2.3 Noninterference

A computer user can face different kinds of interference in his computational activities. Execution of his program can be disrupted by actions of other persons, or the OS services which he wishes to use can be disrupted in a similar manner. The OS prevents such interference by allocating resources for exclusive use of programs and OS services, and preventing illegal accesses to resources. Another form of interference concerns programs and data stored in user files.

A computer user may collaborate with some other users in the development or use of a computer application, so he may wish to share some of his files with them. Attempts by any other person to access his files are illegal and constitute interference. To prevent this form of interference, an OS has to know which files of a user can be accessed by which persons. It is achieved through the act of *authorization*, whereby a user specifies which collaborators can access what files. The OS uses this information to prevent illegal accesses to files.

1.3 OPERATION OF AN OS

The primary concerns of an OS during its operation are execution of programs, use of resources, and prevention of interference with programs and resources. Accordingly, its three principal functions are:

- *Program management:* The OS initiates programs, arranges their execution on the CPU, and terminates them when they complete their execution. Since many programs exist in the system at any time, the OS performs a function called *scheduling* to select a program for execution.

- *Resource management:* The OS allocates resources like memory and I/O devices when a program needs them. When the program terminates, it deallocates these resources and allocates them to other programs that need them.
- *Security and protection:* The OS implements noninterference in users' activities through joint actions of the security and protection functions. As an example, consider how the OS prevents illegal accesses to a file. The *security* function prevents nonusers from utilizing the services and resources in the computer system, hence none of them can access the file. The *protection* function prevents users other than the file owner or users authorized by him, from accessing the file.

Table 1.2 describes the tasks commonly performed by an operating system. When a computer system is switched on, it automatically loads a program stored on a reserved part of an I/O device, typically a disk, and starts executing the program. This program follows a software technique known as *bootstrapping* to load the software called the *boot procedure* in memory—the program initially loaded in memory loads some other programs in memory, which load other programs, and so on until the complete boot procedure is loaded. The boot procedure makes a list of all hardware resources in the system, and hands over control of the computer system to the OS.

A system administrator specifies which persons are registered as users of the system. The OS permits only these persons to log in to use its resources and services. A user authorizes his collaborators to access some programs and data. The OS notes this information and uses it to implement protection. The OS also performs a set of functions to implement its notion of effective utilization. These functions include scheduling of programs and keeping track of resource status and resource usage information.

Table 1.2 **Common Tasks Performed by Operating Systems**

Task	When performed
Construct a list of resources	During booting
Maintain information for security	While registering new users
Verify identity of a user	At login time
Initiate execution of programs	At user commands
Maintain authorization information	When a user specifies which collaborators can acces what programs or data
Perform resource allocation	When requested by users or programs
Maintain current status of resources	During resource allocation/deallocation
Maintain current status of programs and perform scheduling	Continually during OS operation

The following sections are a brief overview of OS responsibilities in managing programs and resources and in implementing security and protection.

1.3.1 Program Management

Modern CPUs have the capability to execute program instructions at a very high rate, so it is possible for an OS to interleave execution of several programs on a CPU and yet provide good user service. The key function in achieving interleaved execution of programs is *scheduling*, which decides which program should be given the CPU at any time. Figure 1.3 shows an abstract view of scheduling. The *scheduler*, which is an OS routine that performs scheduling, maintains a list of programs waiting to execute on the CPU, and selects one program for execution. In operating systems that provide fair service to all programs, the scheduler also specifies how long the program can be allowed to use the CPU. The OS takes away the CPU from a program after it has executed for the specified period of time, and gives it to another program. This action is called *preemption*. A program that loses the CPU because of preemption is put back into the list of programs waiting to execute on the CPU.

The scheduling policy employed by an OS can influence both efficient use of the CPU and user service. If a program is preempted after it has executed for only a short period of time, the overhead of scheduling actions would be high because of frequent preemption. However, each program would suffer only a short delay before it gets an opportunity to use the CPU, which would result in good user service. If preemption is performed after a program has executed for a longer period of time, scheduling overhead would be lesser but programs would suffer longer delays, so user service would be poorer.

1.3.2 Resource Management

Resource allocations and deallocations can be performed by using a resource table. Each entry in the table contains the name and address of a resource unit and its present status, indicating whether it is free or allocated to some program. Table 1.3 is such a table for management of I/O devices. It is constructed by the boot procedure by sensing the presence of I/O devices in the system, and updated by the operating system to reflect the allocations and deallocations made by it. Since any part of a disk can be accessed directly, it is possible to treat different parts

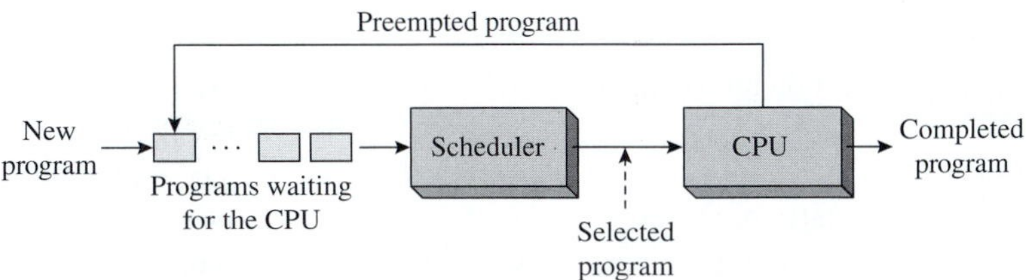

Figure 1.3 A schematic of scheduling.

Table 1.3 Resource Table for I/O Devices

Resource name	Class	Address	Allocation status
printer1	Printer	101	Allocated to P_1
printer2	Printer	102	Free
printer3	Printer	103	Free
disk1	Disk	201	Allocated to P_1
disk2	Disk	202	Allocated to P_2
cdw1	CD writer	301	Free

of a disk as independent devices. Thus the devices disk1 and disk2 in Table 1.3 could be two parts of the same disk.

Two resource allocation strategies are popular. In the *resource partitioning* approach, the OS decides *a priori* what resources should be allocated to each user program, for example, it may decide that a program should be allocated 1 MB of memory, 1000 disk blocks, and a monitor. It divides the resources in the system into many *resource partitions*, or simply *partitions*; each partition includes 1 MB of memory, 1000 disk blocks, and a monitor. It allocates one resource partition to each user program when its execution is to be initiated. To facilitate resource allocation, the resource table contains entries for resource partitions rather than for individual resources as in Table 1.3. Resource partitioning is simple to implement, hence it incurs less overhead; however, it lacks flexibility. Resources are wasted if a resource partition contains more resources than what a program needs. Also, the OS cannot execute a program if its requirements exceed the resources available in a resource partition. This is true even if free resources exist in another partition.

In the *pool-based* approach to resource management, the OS allocates resources from a common pool of resources. It consults the resource table when a program makes a request for a resource, and allocates the resource if it is free. It incurs the overhead of allocating and deallocating resources when requested. However, it avoids both problems faced by the resource partitioning approach—an allocated resource is not wasted, and a resource requirement can be met if a free resource exists.

Virtual Resources A *virtual resource* is a fictitious resource—it is an illusion supported by an OS through use of a real resource. An OS may use the same real resource to support several virtual resources. This way, it can give the impression of having a larger number of resources than it actually does. Each use of a virtual resource results in the use of an appropriate real resource. In that sense, a virtual resource is an abstract view of a resource taken by a program.

Use of virtual resources started with the use of virtual devices. To prevent mutual interference between programs, it was a good idea to allocate a device exclusively for use by one program. However, a computer system did not possess many real devices, so virtual devices were used. An OS would create a virtual device when a user needed an I/O device; e.g., the disks called disk1 and disk2 in

Table 1.3 could be two virtual disks based on the real disk, which are allocated to programs P_1 and P_2, respectively. Virtual devices are used in contemporary operating systems as well. A print server is a common example of a virtual device. When a program wishes to print a file, the print server simply copies the file into the print queue. The program requesting the print goes on with its operation as if the printing had been performed. The print server continuously examines the print queue and prints the files it finds in the queue. Most operating systems provide a virtual resource called *virtual memory*, which is an illusion of a memory that is larger in size than the real memory of a computer. Its use enables a programmer to execute a program whose size may exceed the size of real memory.

Some operating systems create *virtual machines* (VMs) so that each machine can be allocated to a user. The advantage of this approach is twofold. Allocation of a virtual machine to each user eliminates mutual interference between users. It also allows each user to select an OS of his choice to operate his virtual machine. In effect, this arrangement permits users to use different operating systems on the same computer system simultaneously (see Section 4.5).

1.3.3 Security and Protection

As mentioned in Section 1.2.3, an OS must ensure that no person can illegally use programs and resources in the system, or interfere with them in any manner. The *security* function counters threats of illegal use or interference that are posed by persons or programs outside the control of an operating system, whereas the *protection* function counters similar threats posed by its users. Figure 1.4 illustrates how security and protection threats arise in an OS.

In a classical stand-alone environment, a computer system functions in complete isolation. In such a system, the security and protection issues can be handled easily. Recall that an OS maintains information that helps in implementing the security and protection functions (see Table 1.2). The identity of a person wishing to use a computer system is verified through a password when the person logs in. This action, which is called *authentication*, ensures that no person other

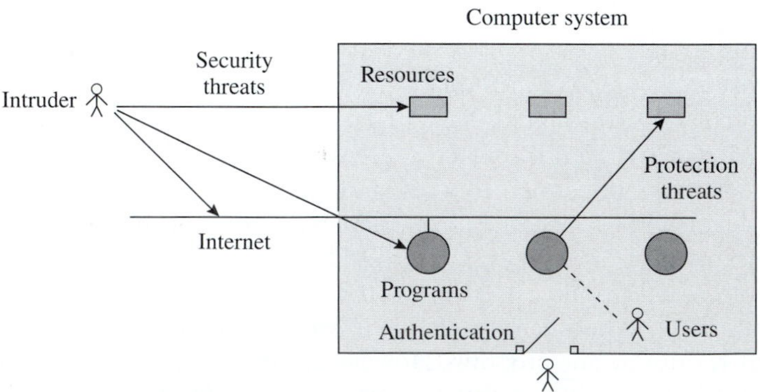

Figure 1.4 Overview of security and protection threats.

than a registered user can use a computer system. Consequently, security threats do not arise in the system if the authentication procedure is foolproof. In this environment, the forms of interference mentioned earlier in Section 1.2.3 are all protection threats. The OS thwarts disruption of program executions and OS services with the help of hardware features such as *memory protection*. It thwarts interference with files by allowing a user to access a file only if he owns it or has been authorized by the file's owner to access it.

When a computer system is connected to the Internet, and a user downloads a program from the Internet, there is a danger that the downloaded program may interfere with other programs or resources in the system. This is a security threat because the interference is caused by some person outside the system, called an *intruder*, who either wrote the downloaded program, or modified it, so that it would interfere with other programs. Such security threats are posed either through a *Trojan horse*, which is a program that has a known legitimate function and a well-disguised malicious function, or a *virus*, which is a piece of code with a malicious function that attaches itself to other programs in the system and spreads to other systems when such programs are copied. Another class of security threats is posed by programs called *worms*, which replicate by themselves through holes in security setups of operating systems. Worms can replicate at unimaginably high rates and cause widespread havoc. The Code Red worm of 2001 spread to a quarter of a million computer systems in 9 hours.

Operating systems address security threats through a variety of means—by using sophisticated authentication techniques, by plugging security holes when they are discovered, by ensuring that programs cannot be modified while they are copied over the Internet, and by using Internet *firewalls* to filter out unwanted Internet traffic through a computer system. Users are expected to contribute to security by using passwords that are impossible to guess and by exercising caution while downloading programs from the Internet.

1.4 PREVIEW OF THE BOOK

A computer system, the services it provides to its users and their programs, and its interfaces with other systems all make up the *computing environment*. Operating systems are designed to provide *effective utilization* of a computer system in its computing environment, which is the appropriate combination of efficient use of resources and good user service in the computing environment, and to ensure noninterference in the activities of its users. Parts 1–4 of this book primarily discuss operating systems for conventional computing environments characterized by use of a single computer system having a single CPU; only Chapter 10 discusses operating systems for the multiprocessor computing environment. Operating systems for the distributed computing environment are discussed in the chapters of Part 5.

All through this book, we will use abstract views to present the design and implementation of operating systems because, as discussed in Section 1.1, abstract views help in managing complexity and presenting generic concepts or ideas.

1.4.1 Introduction to Operating Systems

Part 1 of the book consists of Chapters 1–4, of which the present chapter is Chapter 1. We begin the study of operating systems in Chapter 2 with a discussion of how an operating system interacts with the computer and with user programs.

Events and Interrupts An OS interleaves execution of several user programs on the CPU. While a user program is in execution, some situations concerning its own activity, or concerning activities in other programs, may require attention of the OS. Hence, occurrence of an *event*, which is any situation that requires attention of the OS, causes control of the CPU to be passed to the operating system. The operating system uses the CPU to execute instructions that analyze the event and perform appropriate actions. When an event has been attended to, the OS schedules a user program for execution on the CPU. Hence operation of the OS is said to be *event driven*. For example, if an I/O operation ends, the OS informs the program that had requested the I/O operation and starts another I/O operation on the device, if one is pending; if a program requests a resource, the OS allocates the resource if it is available. In either case, it performs scheduling to select the program to be executed next. Figure 1.5 is an abstract view, also called a *logical view*, of the functioning of an operating system.

The end of an I/O operation or the making of a resource request by a program actually causes an *interrupt* in the computer system. The CPU is designed to recognize an interrupt and divert itself to the OS. This physical view, which is the foundation for a study of operating systems, is developed in Chapter 2.

Effective Utilization of a Computer System Computing environments evolved in response to advances in computer architecture and new requirements of computer users. Each computing environment had a different notion of effective utilization, so its OS used a different set of techniques to realize it. A modern computing environment contains features of several classical computing environments, such as noninteractive, time-sharing, and distributed computing environments, so techniques employed in these environments are used in modern OSs as well. Chapter 3 discusses these techniques to form the background for a detailed study of operating systems.

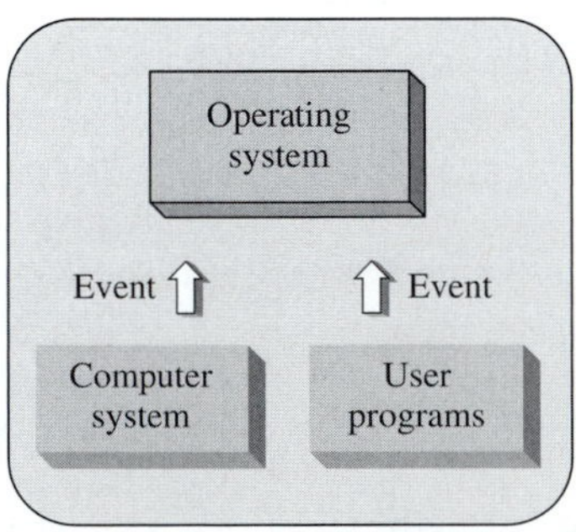

Figure 1.5 An operating system in its computing environment.

Portability and Extensibility of Operating Systems Early operating systems were developed for specific computer systems, so they were tightly integrated with architectures of specific computer systems. Modern operating systems such as Unix and Windows pose two new requirements—the operating system has to be *portable*, that is, it should be possible to implement it on many computer architectures, and it should be *extensible* so that it can meet new requirements arising from changes in the nature of its computing environment. Chapter 4 discusses the operating system design techniques for portability and extensibility.

1.4.2 Managing User Computations

Chapters 5–10, which constitute Part 2 of the book, discuss various facets of the program management function. Chapter 5 lays the foundation of this study by discussing how the operating system handles execution of programs.

Processes and Threads A *process* is an execution of a program. An OS uses a process as a unit of computational work—it allocates resources to a process and schedules it for servicing by the CPU. It performs *process switching* when it decides to preempt a process and schedule another one for servicing by the CPU (see Figure 1.3). Process switching involves saving information concerning the preempted process and accessing information concerning the newly scheduled process; it consumes some CPU time and constitutes *overhead* of the operating system. The notion of a *thread* is introduced to reduce the OS overhead. Switching between threads requires much less information to be stored and accessed compared with switching between processes. However, processes and threads are similar in other respects, so we use the term *process* as a generic term for both a process and a thread, except while discussing the implementation of threads.

Process Synchronization Processes that have a common goal must coordinate their activities so that they can perform their actions in a desired order. This requirement is called *process synchronization*. Figure 1.6 illustrates two kinds of process synchronization. Figure 1.6(a) shows processes named *credit* and *debit* that access the balance in a bank account. Their results may be incorrect if both processes update the balance at the same time, so they must perform their updates strictly one after another. Figure 1.6(b) shows a process named *generate* that

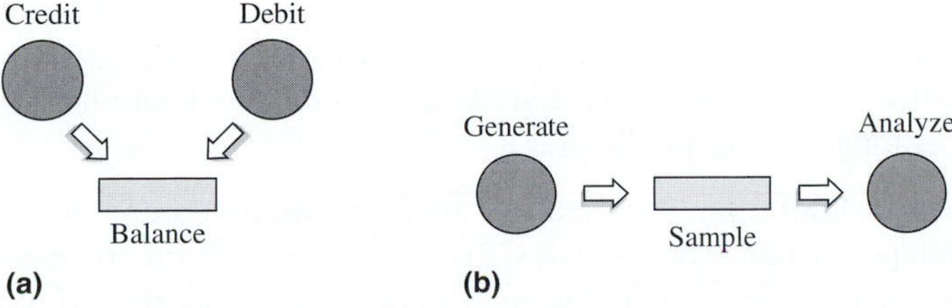

Figure 1.6 Two kinds of process synchronization.

produces some data and puts it into a variable named *sample*, and the process named *analyze* that performs analysis on the data contained in variable *sample*. Here, process *analyze* should not perform analysis until process *generate* has deposited the next lot of data in *sample*, and process *generate* should not produce the next lot of data until process *analyze* has analyzed the previous data. Programming languages and operating systems provide several facilities that processes may use for performing synchronization. Chapter 6 describes these facilities, their use by processess and their implementation in an OS.

Message Passing Processes may also interact through *message passing*. When a process sends some information in a message to another process, the operating system stores the message in its own data structures until the destination process makes a request to receive a message. Unlike the situation in Figure 1.6(b), synchronization of sender and destination processes is performed by the operating system—it makes the destination process wait if no message has been sent to it by the time it makes a request to receive a message. Details of message passing are described in Chapter 9.

Scheduling The nature of a computing environment decides whether effective utilization of a computer system implies efficient use of its resources, high user convenience, or a suitable combination of both. An OS realizes effective utilization through a scheduling policy that shares the CPU among several processes. This way, many processes make progress at the same time, which contributes to quick service for all users, and hence to high user convenience. The manner in which the CPU is shared among processes governs the use of resources allocated to processes, so it governs efficient use of the computer system. In Chapter 7, we discuss the classical scheduling policies, which aimed either at efficient use of a computer system, or at high user convenience, and scheduling policies used in modern operating systems, which aim at suitable combinations of efficient use and user convenience.

Deadlocks User processes share a computer system's resources. If a resource requested by some process P_i is currently allocated to process P_j, P_i has to wait until P_j releases the resource. Such waits sometimes cause a *deadlock*, which is a situation in which processes wait for other processes' actions indefinitely. Figure 1.7 illustrates such a situation. The arrow drawn from process P_i to P_j indicates that process P_i is waiting because it requested a resource that is currently allocated to process P_j. Processes P_j and P_k similarly wait for resources that are currently allocated to processes P_k and P_i, respectively. Hence the three processes are in a deadlock. A deadlock adversely affects performance of a system because processes involved in the deadlock cannot make any progress and resources allocated to them are wasted. We discuss deadlock handling techniques used in operating systems in Chapter 8.

Multiprocessor Operating Systems A multiprocessor computer system can provide high performance because its CPUs can service several processes simultaneously. It can also speed up operation of a computer application if its processes are scheduled simultaneously on several CPUs. To realize these advantages, the

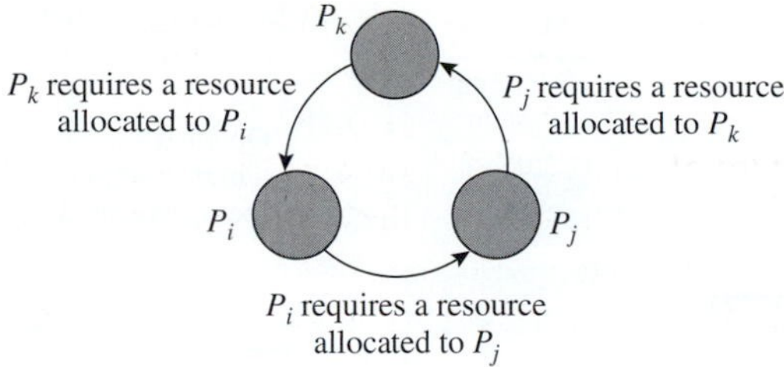
P_k
P_k requires a resource allocated to P_i
P_j requires a resource allocated to P_k
P_i
P_j
P_i requires a resource allocated to P_j

Figure 1.7 A deadlock involving three processes.

operating system has to use special scheduling and synchronization techniques to ensure that processes can operate efficiently and harmoniously on the CPUs. We discuss these techniques in Chapter 10.

1.4.3 Management of Memory

Memory management involves efficient allocation, release and reuse of memory to meet requests of processes. In the classical model of memory allocation, a single contiguous area of memory is allocated to a process. This model does not support reuse of a memory area that is not large enough to accommodate a new process, so the kernel has to use the technique of *compaction* to combine several free areas of memory into one large free area of memory; it incurs substantial overhead. The *noncontiguous memory allocation model* allows many disjoint areas of memory to be allocated to a process, which enables direct reuse of several small areas of memory. We describe memory reuse techniques and the model of noncontiguous memory allocation in Chapter 11. The kernel uses special techniques to meet its own memory requirements efficiently. These techniques are also discussed in this chapter.

Virtual Memory Modern operating systems provide *virtual memory*, which is a storage capability that is larger than the actual memory of a computer system. The OS achieves it by storing the code and data of a process on a disk, and loading only some portions of the code and data in memory. This way, a process can operate even if its size exceeds the size of memory.

The operating system employs the noncontiguous memory allocation model to implement virtual memory. It maintains a table of memory allocation information to indicate which portions of the code and data of a process are present in memory, and what their memory addresses are. During operation of the process, the CPU passes each instruction address or data address used by it to a special hardware unit called the *memory management unit* (MMU), which consults the memory allocation information for the process and computes the address in memory where the instruction or data actually resides. If the required instruction or data does not exist in memory, the MMU causes a "missing from memory" interrupt. The operating system now loads the portion that contains the required instruction or data in memory—for which it might have to remove some other

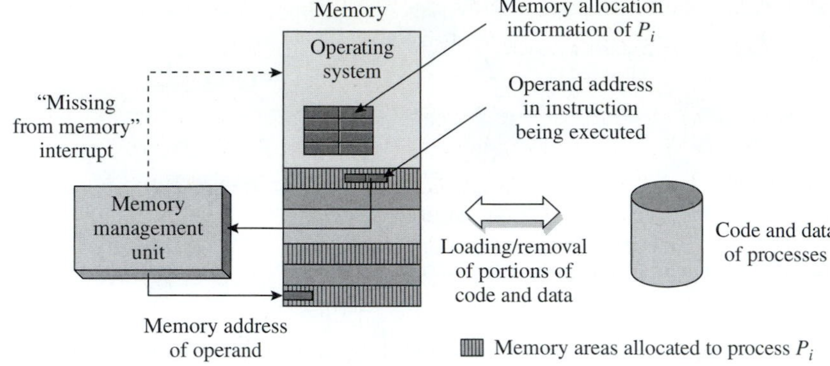

Figure 1.8 A schematic of virtual memory operation.

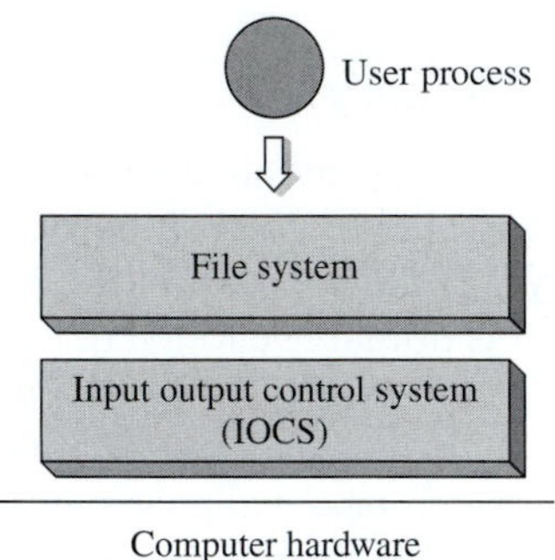

Figure 1.9 An overview of file system and input output control system (IOCS).

portion from memory—and resumes operation of the process. Figure 1.8 is a schematic diagram of virtual memory when a process P_i is in operation.

A "missing from memory" interrupt slows down progress of a process, so the operating system has to make two key decisions to ensure a low rate of these interrupts: *how many* and *which* portions of the code and data of a process should it keep in memory. The techniques used in making these decisions are described in Chapter 12.

1.4.4 Management of Files and I/O Devices

A file system has to meet several expectations of its users—provide fast access to a file, protect the file against access by unauthorized persons, and provide reliable operation in the presence of faults such as faulty I/O media or power outages—and also ensure efficient use of I/O devices. A file system uses a layered organization to separate the various issues involved in fulfilling these expectations; Figure 1.9 shows an abstract view. The upper layer, which is the file system itself, permits a user to share his files with some other users, implements file protection and provides reliability. To implement an operation on a file, the file system invokes the lower layer, which contains the *input output control system* (IOCS). This layer ensures fast access to files by a process, and efficient use of I/O devices.

File System The file system provides each user with a logical view in which the user has a *home directory* at an appropriate place in the directory structure of the file system. The user can create directories, or folders, as they are called in the Windows operating system, in his home directory, and other directories or folders in these directories, and so on. A user can authorize some collaborators to access a file by informing the file system of the names of collaborators and the name of the file. The file system uses this information to implement file protection. To ensure reliability, the file system prevents damage to the data in a file, and to its own data such as a directory, which is called the *metadata*, due to faults like faulty I/O media or power outages. All these features of file systems are discussed in Chapter 13.

Input Output Control System (IOCS) The IOCS implements a file operation by transferring data between a process and a file that is recorded on an I/O device. It ensures efficient implementation of file operations through three means—by reducing the time required to implement a data transfer between a process and an I/O device, by reducing the number of times data has to be transferred between a process and an I/O device, and by maximizing the number of I/O operations that an I/O device can complete in a given period of time. Its techniques are discussed in Chapter 14.

Security and Protection Security and protection threats, and the arrangement used to implement security and protection, were described earlier in Section 1.3.3. The OS encrypts the password data through an encryption function known only to itself. Encryption strengthens the security arrangement because an intruder cannot obtain passwords of users except through an exhaustive search, which would involve trying out every possible string as a password. Various security and protection threats, the technique of encryption, and various methods used to implement protection are described in Chapter 15.

1.4.5 Distributed Operating Systems

A distributed computer system consists of several computer systems, each with its own memory, connected through networking hardware and software. Each computer system in it is called a *node*. Use of a distributed computer system provides three key advantages: speeding up of a computer application by scheduling its processes in different nodes of the system simultaneously, high reliability through redundancy of computer systems and their resources, and resource sharing across node boundaries. To realize these advantages, a distributed OS must tackle the following fundamental issues:

- Networking causes delays in the transfer of data between nodes of a distributed system. Such delays may lead to an inconsistent view of data located in different nodes, and make it difficult to know the chronological order in which events occurred in the system.

- Control functions like scheduling, resource allocation, and deadlock detection have to be performed in several nodes to achieve computation speedup and provide reliable operation when computers or networking components fail.
- Messages exchanged by processes present in different nodes may travel over public networks and pass through computer systems that are not controlled by the distributed operating system. An intruder may exploit this feature to tamper with messages, or create fake messages to fool the authentication procedure and masquerade as a user of the system (see Figure 1.4).

The chapters of part 5 present various facets of a distributed operating system. Chapter 16 discusses the model of a distributed computer system, networking hardware and software, and distributed computation paradigms, which permit parts of a computation to be performed in different nodes. Chapter 17 discusses the theoretical issues that arise from networking delays, and the methods of tackling them. Chapter 18 discusses how the OS performs its control functions in a distributed manner. Chapter 19 describes the reliability techniques of *fault tolerance* and *recovery*, which enable a distributed system to provide continuity of operation when failures occur. Chapter 20 describes the reliability and performance improvement techniques employed in distributed file systems, while Chapter 21 discusses the security issues in distributed systems and the techniques employed to address them.

1.5 SUMMARY

A computer user's requirements are determined by a computer's role in fulfilling his need. For some users, computing is merely a means to fulfilling a need like Internet browsing or sending of e-mails, whereas for some others it directly satisfies their needs like running programs to perform data processing or scientific computations. An operating system has to meet the needs of *all* its users, so it has diverse functionalities.

A modern computer has an abundance of resources like memory and disk space, and it also has a powerful CPU. To ensure that computer users benefit from this abundance, the operating system services many programs simultaneously by distributing its resources among them and interleaving their execution on the CPU. The OS has to satisfy three requirements to ensure effectiveness of computing:

- *Efficient use:* Ensure efficient use of a computer's resources.
- *User convenience:* Provide convenient methods of using a computer system.
- *Noninterference:* Prevent interference in the activities of its users.

An operating system meets these requirements by performing three primary functions during its operation—management of programs, management of resources, and security and protection. An OS is a complex software system that may contain millions of lines of code, so we use abstraction to master the complexity of studying its design. Abstraction helps us to focus on a specific aspect of a system, whether a hardware system like a computer, a software system like an operating system, or a real-life system like the urban transportation network, and ignore details that are not relevant to this aspect. We will use abstraction throughout the book to study different aspects of design and operation of operating systems.

The plan of the book is as follows: We begin by discussing how an operating system interacts with a computer system to control its operation. We then study how the operating system manages execution of programs, allocation of memory, and use of files by programs and ensures security and protection. This is followed by the study of distributed operating systems, which control operation of several computer systems that are networked.

TEST YOUR CONCEPTS

1.1 Classify each of the following statements as true or false:

a. The boot procedure is used to initiate a user program.

b. The technique of preemption is employed to share the CPU among user programs.

c. Resources may be wasted if an OS employs pool-based resource allocation.

d. Assignment of virtual resources to processes prevents mutual interference between them.

e. Threats posed by an authenticated user are security threats.

1.2 Indicate whether each of the following techniques/arrangements provides (i) user convenience and (ii) efficient use of a computer system:

a. Virtual memory

b. File protection

c. Noncontiguous memory allocation

1.3 Classify the following into security lapses and protection lapses:

a. Scribbling your password on a piece of paper

b. Authorizing everybody to perform read and write operations on your file

c. Leaving your monitor unattended in the middle of a session

d. Downloading a program that is known to contain a virus

EXERCISES

1.1 A computer can operate under two operating systems, OS_1 and OS_2. A program P always executes successfully under OS_1. When executed under OS_2, it is sometimes aborted with the error "insufficient resources to continue execution," but executes successfully at other times. What is the reason for this behavior of program P? Can it be cured? If so, explain how, and describe its consequences. (*Hint:* Think of resource management policies.)

1.2 A time-sharing operating system uses the following scheduling policy: A program is given a limited amount of CPU time, called the *time slice*, each time it is selected for execution. It is preempted at the end of the time slice, and it is considered for execution only after all other programs that wish to use the CPU have been given an opportunity to use the CPU. Comment on (a) user service and (b) efficiency of use, in a time-sharing system.

1.3 If a computer has a very fast CPU but a small memory, few computer programs can fit into its memory at any time and consequently the CPU is often idle because of lack of work. *Swapping* is a technique of removing an inactive program from memory and loading a program that requires use of the CPU in its place so that the CPU can service it. Does swapping improve (a) user service and (b) efficiency of use? What is its effect on OS overhead?

1.4 Comment on validity of the following statement: "Partitioned resource allocation provides more user convenience but may provide poor efficiency."

1.5 A program is in a dormant state if it is not engaged in any activity (e.g., it may be waiting for an action by a user). What resources does a dormant program consume? How can this resource consumption be reduced?

1.6 An OS creates virtual devices when it is short of real devices. Does creation of virtual devices improve (a) user service, (b) efficiency of use?

1.7 Can deadlocks arise in the following situations?

a. A system performs partitioned allocation of resources to programs.

b. A set of programs communicate through message passing during their execution.

1.8 A user wishes to let his collaborators access some of his files, but expects the OS to prevent his collaborators from accessing his other files, and also prevent noncollaborators from accessing any of his files. Explain how it is achieved jointly by the user and the OS.

BIBLIOGRAPHY

The view of an OS as the software that manages a computer system is usually propounded in most operating systems texts. Tanenbaum (2001), Nutt (2004), Silberschatz et al. (2005), and Stallings (2005) are some of the recent texts on operating systems.

Berzins et al. (1986) discusses how the complexity of designing a software system can be reduced by constructing a set of abstractions that hide the internal working of a subsystem. Most books on software engineering discuss the role of abstraction in software design. The paper by Parnas and Siewiorek (1975) on the concept of transparency in software design is considered a classic of software engineering. The book by Booch (1994) discusses abstractions in object oriented software development.

The concept of virtual devices was first used in the spooling system of the Atlas computer system developed at Manchester University. It is described in Kilburn et al. (1961).

Ludwig (1998) and Ludwig (2002) describe different kinds of viruses, while Berghel (2001) describes the Code Red worm that caused havoc in 2001. Pfleeger and Pfleeger (2003) is a text on computer security. Garfinkel et al. (2003) discusses security in Solaris, Mac OS, Linux, and FreeBSD operating systems. Russinovich and Solomon (2005) discusses security features in Windows.

1. Berghel, H. (2001): "The Code Red worm," *Communications of the ACM*, **44** (12), 15–19.
2. Berzins, V., M. Gray, and D. Naumann (1986): "Abstraction-based software development," *Communications of the ACM*, **29** (5), 403–415.
3. Booch, G. (1994): *Object-Oriented Analysis and Design*, Benjamin-Cummings, Santa Clara.
4. Garfinkel, S., G. Spafford, and A. Schwartz (2003): *Practical UNIX and Internet Security*, 3rd ed., O'Reilly, Sebastopol, Calif.
5. Kilburn, T., D. J. Howarth, R. B. Payne, and F. H. Sumner (1961): "The Manchester University Atlas Operating System, Part I: Internal Organization," *Computer Journal*, **4** (3), 222–225.
6. Ludwig, M. A. (1998): *The Giant Black Book of Computer Viruses*, 2nd ed., American Eagle, Show Low.
7. Ludwig, M. A. (2002): *The Little Black Book of Email Viruses*, American Eagle, Show Low.
8. Nutt, G. (2004): *Operating Systems—A Modern Perspective*, 3rd ed., Addison-Wesley, Reading, Mass.
9. Parnas, D. L., and D. P. Siewiorek (1975): "Use of the concept of transparency in the design of hierarchically structured systems," *Communications of the ACM*, **18** (7), 401–408.
10. Pfleeger, C. P., and S. Pfleeger (2003): *Security in Computing*, Prentice Hall, Englewood Cliffs, N.J.
11. Russinovich, M. E., and D. A. Solomon (2005): *Microsoft Windows Internals*, 4th ed., Microsoft Press, Redmond, Wash.
12. Silberschatz, A., P. B. Galvin, and G. Gagne (2005): *Operating System Principles*, 7th ed., John Wiley, New York.
13. Stallings, W. (2005): *Operating Systems—Internals and Design Principles*, 5th ed., Pearson Education, New York.
14. Tanenbaum, A. S. (2001): *Modern Operating Systems*, 2nd ed., Prentice Hall, Englewood Cliffs, N.J.

Chapter 2

The OS, the Computer, and User Programs

As we saw in Chapter 1, the operating system performs many tasks like program initiation and resource allocation repetitively. We call each of these tasks a *control function*. Since the operating system is a collection of routines, and not a hardware unit, it performs control functions by executing instructions on the CPU. Thus, the CPU services both user programs and the operating system. A key aspect of understanding how an operating system works is knowing how it interacts with the computer system and with user programs—what the arrangement is by which it gets control of the CPU when it needs to perform a control function, and how it passes control to a user program.

We use the term *switching of the CPU* for an action that forces the CPU to stop executing one program and start executing another program. When the kernel needs to perform a control function, the CPU must be switched to execution of the kernel. After completing the control function, the CPU is switched to execution of a user program.

We begin this chapter with an overview of relevant features of a computer, particularly how an *interrupt* switches the CPU to execution of the kernel when the kernel needs to perform a control function. In a later section we discuss how *interrupt servicing* and the operating system concept of *system calls* facilitate interaction of the operating system with user programs.

2.1 FUNDAMENTAL PRINCIPLES OF OS OPERATION

Before we discuss features of operating systems in Chapter 3, and their design in later chapters, it is important to have a functional understanding of the operation of an OS—what features of a modern computer system are important from the OS viewpoint, how the OS uses these features during its operation to control user programs and resources and implement security and protection, and how user programs obtain services from the OS.

As discussed in Section 1.1, the *kernel* of the operating system is the collection of routines that form the core of the operating system. It controls operation of the computer by implementing the tasks discussed in Section 1.3, hence we call each of these tasks a *control function*. It also offers a set of services to user programs. The kernel exists in memory during operation of the OS, and executes instructions on the CPU to implement its control functions and services. Thus, the CPU is used by both user programs and the kernel.

For efficient use of a computer, the CPU should be executing user programs most of the time. However, it has to be diverted to execution of the kernel code whenever a situation requiring the kernel's attention arises in the system, e.g., when an I/O operation ends or a timer interrupt occurs, or when a program requires some service of the kernel. In Section 1.4, we used the term *event* for such a situation. Accordingly, we need to grasp the following details to understand how the OS operates:

- How the kernel controls operation of the computer.
- How the CPU is diverted to execution of kernel code when an event occurs.
- How a user program uses services offered by the kernel.
- How the kernel ensures an absence of mutual interference among user programs and between a user program and the OS.

In this chapter we discuss elements of computer system architecture and describe how the kernel uses features of computer architecture to control operation of a computer. We then discuss how the notion of an *interrupt* is used to divert the CPU to execution of the kernel code, and describe how a special kind of interrupt called a *software interrupt* is used by programs to communicate their requests to the kernel.

The absence of mutual interference among user programs and between a user program and the OS is ensured by having two modes of operation of the CPU. When the CPU is in the *kernel mode*, it can execute all instructions of the computer. The kernel operates with the CPU in this mode so that it can control operations of the computer. When the CPU is in the *user mode*, it cannot execute those instructions that have the potential to interfere with other programs or with the OS if used indiscriminately. The CPU is put in this mode to execute user programs. A key issue in understanding how an OS operates is knowing how the CPU is put in the kernel mode to execute kernel code, and how it is put in the user mode to execute user programs.

2.2 THE COMPUTER

Figure 2.1 is a schematic of a computer showing the functional units that are relevant from the viewpoint of an operating system. The CPU and memory are directly connected to the bus, while the I/O devices are connected to the bus through device controllers and the DMA. If the CPU and I/O devices try to access the memory at the same time, the bus permits only one of them to proceed. The other accesses are delayed until this access completes. We describe important details of the functional units in the next few sections. In a later section, we discuss how the OS uses features of a computer to control the operation of

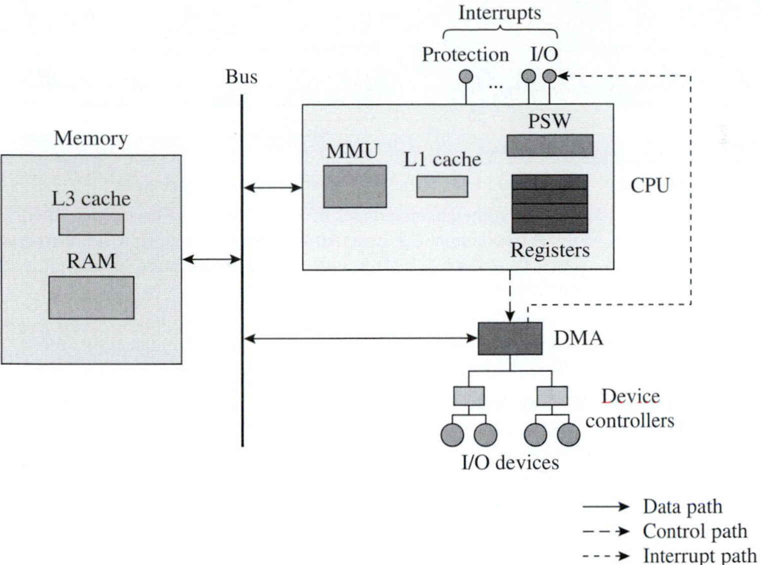

Figure 2.1 Schematic of a computer.

the computer and execution of user programs on it. Discussions in this chapter are restricted to computers with a single CPU; features of multiprocessor and distributed computer systems are described in later chapters.

2.2.1 The CPU

General-Purpose Registers (GPRs) and the Program Status Word (PSW) Two features of the CPU are visible to user programs or the operating system. The first is those registers that are used to hold data, addresses, index values, or the stack pointer during execution of a program. These registers are variously called *general-purpose registers* (GPRs) or *program-accessible registers*; we prefer to call them GPRs. The other feature is a set of *control registers*, which contain information that controls or influences operation of the CPU. For simplicity, we will call the collection of control registers the *program status word* (PSW), and refer to an individual control register as a *field* of the PSW.

Figure 2.2 describes the fields of the PSW. Two fields of the PSW are commonly known to programmers: The *program counter* (PC) contains the address of the next instruction to be executed by the CPU. The *condition code* (CC) contains a code describing some characteristics of the last arithmetic or logical result computed by the CPU (e.g., whether the result of an arithmetic operation is 0, or the result of a comparison is "not equal"). These characteristics are often stored in a set of discrete flags; however, we will view them collectively as the *condition code* field or a field called *flags*. Contents and uses of other control registers are described later in this section.

Program counter (PC)	Condition code (CC)	Mode (M)	Memory protection information (MPI)	Interrupt mask (IM)	Interrupt code (IC)

Field	Description
Program counter	Contains address of the next instruction to be executed.
Condition code (flags)	Indicates some characteristics of the result of the last arithmetic or logical instruction, e.g., whether the result of an arithmetic instruction was < 0, $= 0$, or > 0. This code is used in execution of a conditional branch instruction.
Mode	Indicates whether the CPU is executing in kernel mode or user mode. We assume a single-bit field with the value 0 to indicate that the CPU is in kernel mode and 1 to indicate that it is in user mode.
Memory protection information	Memory protection information for the currently executing program. This field consists of subfields that contain the *base register* and *size register*.
Interrupt mask	Indicates which interrupts are enabled (that is, which interrupts can occur at present) and which ones are masked off.
Interrupt code	Describes the condition or event that caused the last interrupt. This code is used by an interrupt servicing routine.

Figure 2.2 Important fields of the program status word (PSW).

Kernel and User Modes of CPU Operation The CPU can operate in two modes, called *user mode* and *kernel mode*. The CPU can execute certain instructions only when it is in the kernel mode. These instructions, called *privileged instructions*, implement special operations whose execution by user programs would interfere with the functioning of the OS or activities of other user programs; e.g., an instruction that changes contents of the *memory protection information* (MPI) field of the PSW could be used to undermine memory protection in the system (Section 2.2.3 contains an example). The OS puts the CPU in kernel mode when it is executing instructions in the kernel, so that the kernel can execute special operations, and puts it in user mode when a user program is in execution, so that the user program cannot interfere with the OS or other user programs. We assume the *mode* (M) field of the PSW to be a single-bit field that contains a 0 when the CPU is in kernel mode and a 1 when it is in user mode.

State of the CPU The general-purpose registers and the PSW together contain all the information needed to know what the CPU is doing; we say that this information constitutes the *state* of the CPU. As discussed in Section 1.3.1, the kernel may preempt the program that is currently using the CPU (see Figure 1.3). To ensure that the program can resume its execution correctly when scheduled in future, the kernel saves the state of the CPU when it takes away the CPU from the program, and simply reloads the saved CPU state into the GPRs and the PSW when execution of the program is to be resumed. Example 2.1 illustrates how saving and restoring the state of the CPU suffices to correctly resume execution of a program.

State of the CPU

Example 2.1

Figure 2.3(a) shows an assembly language program for a hypothetical computer whose CPU has two data registers A and B, an index register X, and the stack pointer register SP. Each assembly language instruction in this program corresponds to either an instruction in the CPU or a directive to the assembler; e.g., the last statement declares ALPHA to be a memory location that contains the value 1. The first instruction moves the value of ALPHA into register A. The second instruction compares the value in register A with the value 1; this comparison sets an appropriate value in the *condition code* field (also called the *flags* field). The third instruction, which has the operation code BEQ, is a conditional branch instruction that transfers control to the instruction with label NEXT if the result of the comparison is "equal." We assume that the result of the COMPARE instruction was "equal," and that condition code 00 corresponds to this result.

If the kernel decides to take away the CPU from the program after the program has executed the COMPARE instruction, it saves the state of the CPU, which is shown in Figure 2.3(b). The state consists of the contents of the PSW, and the registers A, B, X, and SP. The PC contains 150, which is the address of the next instruction to be executed. The condition code field contains 00 to indicate that the values that were compared were equal. The MPI field contains memory protection information for the program, which we shall discuss in Section 2.2.3. If this CPU state is loaded back into the CPU, the program will resume its execution at the BEQ instruction that exists in the memory location with the address 150. Since the condition code field contains 00, implying "equal," the BEQ instruction will transfer control to the instruction labeled NEXT. Thus, the program would execute correctly when resumed.

Address		Instruction	
0142		MOVE	A, ALPHA
0146		COMPARE	A, 1
0150		BEQ	NEXT
		...	
0192	NEXT		
		...	
0210	ALPHA	DCL_CONST	1

(a)

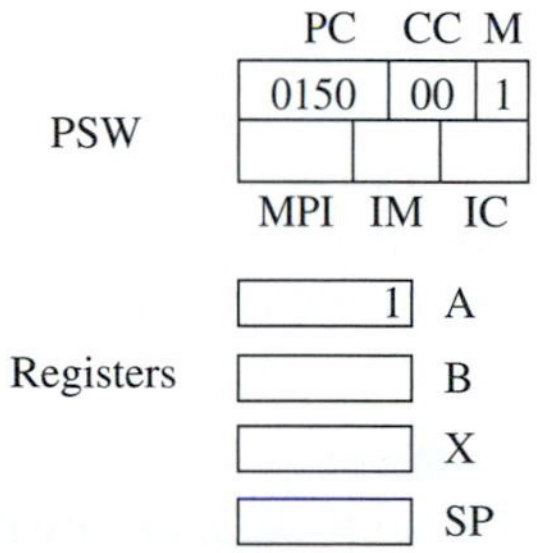

PSW:

PC	CC	M
0150	00	1
MPI	IM	IC

Registers:

A	1
B	
X	
SP	

(b)

Figure 2.3 (a) Listing of an assembly language program showing address assigned to each instruction or data; (b) state of the CPU after executing the COMPARE instruction.

2.2.2 Memory Management Unit (MMU)

As mentioned in Section 1.3.2, *virtual memory* is an illusion of a memory that may be larger that the real memory of a computer. As described in Section 1.4.3, an OS implements virtual memory by using noncontiguous memory allocation and the MMU (Figure 1.8). The OS allocates a set of memory areas to a program, and stores information concerning these areas in a table of memory allocation information. During the execution of the program, the CPU passes the address of a data or instruction used in the current instruction to the MMU. This address is called a *logical address*. The MMU uses the memory allocation information to find the address in memory where the required data or instruction actually resides. This address is called the *physical address*, and the process of obtaining it from a logical address is called *address translation*. In the interest of simplicity, we do not describe details of address translation here; they are described in Chapter 12.

2.2.3 Memory Hierarchy

A computer system should ideally contain a large enough and fast enough memory, so that memory accessing will not slow down the CPU. However, fast memory is expensive, so something that can provide the same service as a large and fast memory but at a lower cost is desirable. The solution is a memory hierarchy containing a number of memory units with differing speeds. The fastest memory in the hierarchy is the smallest in size; slower memories are larger in size. The CPU accesses only the fastest memory. If the data (or instruction) needed by it is present in the fastest memory, it is used straightaway; otherwise the required data is copied into the fastest memory from a slower memory, and then used. The data remains in the fastest memory until it is removed to make place for other data. This arrangement helps to speed up accesses to repeatedly used data. Other levels in the memory hierarchy are used analogously—if data is not present in a faster memory, it is copied there from a slower memory, and so on. The effective memory access time depends on how frequently this situation arises in a faster memory.

Figure 2.4 shows a schematic of a simple memory hierarchy. The hierarchy contains three memory units. The cache memory is fast and small. Main memory, which is also called *random access memory* (RAM), is slow and large; we will simply call it *memory*. The disk is the slowest and largest unit in the hierarchy. We discuss operation of this memory hierarchy before discussing memory hierarchies in modern computers.

Cache Memory The cache memory holds some instructions and data values that were recently accessed by the CPU. To enhance cache performance, the memory hardware does not transfer a single byte from memory into the cache; it always loads a block of memory with a standard size into an area of the cache called a *cache block* or *cache line*. This way, access to a byte in close proximity of a recently accessed byte can be implemented without accessing memory. When the CPU writes a new value into a byte, the changed byte is written into the cache.

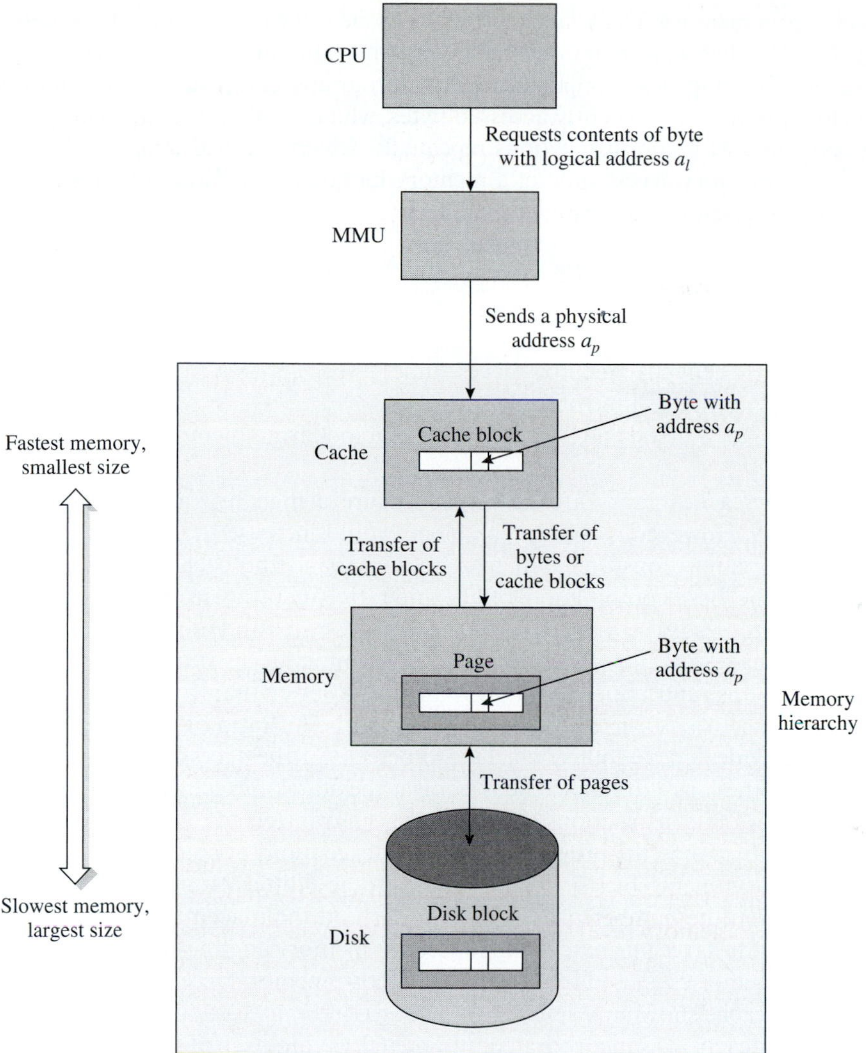

Figure 2.4 Operation of a memory hierarchy.

Sooner or later it also has to be written into the memory. Different schemes have been used for writing a byte into memory; a simple one is to write the byte into the cache and the memory at the same time. It is called the *write-through* scheme.

For every data or instruction required during execution of a program, the CPU performs a cache lookup by comparing addresses of the required bytes with addresses of bytes in memory blocks that are present in the cache. A *hit* is scored if the required bytes are present in memory, in which case the bytes can be accessed straightaway; otherwise, a *miss* is scored and the bytes have to be loaded into the cache from memory. The *hit ratio* (h) of the cache is the fraction of bytes accessed by the CPU that score a hit in the cache. High hit ratios are obtained in practice as a result of an empirical law called *locality*—programs tend to access bytes located in close proximity of recently accessed bytes, which is called *spatial locality*, and access some data and instructions repeatedly, which is called *temporal locality*. Effective memory access time of a memory hierarchy consisting of a cache and memory is given by the formula

$$
\begin{aligned}
t_{ema} &= h \times t_{cache} + (1 - h) \times (t_{tra} + t_{cache}) \\
&= t_{cache} + (1 - h) \times t_{tra} \qquad \textbf{(2.1)}
\end{aligned}
$$

where t_{ema} = effective memory access time,
t_{cache} = access time of cache, and
t_{tra} = time taken to transfer a cache block from memory to cache.

Larger cache blocks are needed to ensure a high hit ratio through spatial locality. However, a large cache block would increase t_{tra}, hence advanced memory organizations are used to reduce t_{tra}, and the cache block size that provides the best combination of the hit ratio and t_{tra} is chosen. The Intel Pentium processor uses a cache block size of 128 bytes and a memory organization that makes t_{tra} only about 10 times the memory access time. If we consider t_{cache} = 10 ns, and a memory that is 10 times slower than the cache, we have $t_{tra} = 10 \times (10 \times 10)$ ns = 1000 ns. With a cache hit ratio of 0.97, this organization provides t_{ema} = 40ns, which is 40 percent of the access time of memory. Note that the hit ratio in a cache is poor at the start of execution of a program because few of its instructions or data have been transferred to the cache. The hit ratio is higher when the program has been in execution for some time.

Memory hierarchies in modern computers differ from that shown in Figure 2.4 in the number of cache memories and the placement of the MMU. Because of the large mismatch in the speeds of memory and the cache, a hierarchy of cache memories is used to reduce the effective memory access time instead of the single cache shown in Figure 2.4. As shown in Figure 2.1, an L1 cache—that is, a level 1 cache—is incorporated into the CPU chip itself. The CPU chip may also contain another cache called the level 2 or L2 cache which is slower but larger than the L1 cache. A much larger and slower L3 cache is typically external to the CPU. We show it to be associated with memory as in Figure 2.1. All these cache levels help to improve the effective memory access time. To determine how much, just substitute the transfer time of a block from the lower cache level in place of t_{tra} in Eq. (2.1), and use the equation analogously to account for a cache miss in the lower cache level during the transfer (see Exercise 2.9). Another difference is that the MMU is replaced by a parallel configuration of the MMU and the L1 cache. This way, a logical address is sent to the L1 cache, rather than a physical address. It eliminates the need for address translation before looking up the L1 cache, which speeds up access to the data if a hit is scored in the L1 cache. It also permits address translation performed by the MMU to overlap with lookup in the L1 cache, which saves time if a cache miss occurs in the L1 cache.

Memory As a part of the memory hierarchy, operation of memory is analogous to operation of a cache. The similarities are in transferring a block of bytes—typically called a *page*—from the disk to memory when a program refers to some byte in the block, and transferring it from memory to the disk to make place for other blocks that are needed in memory. The difference lies in the fact that the management of memory and transfer of blocks between memory and the disk are performed by the software, unlike in the cache, where it is performed by the hardware. The memory hierarchy comprising the memory management unit (MMU), memory, and the disk is called the *virtual memory*. Virtual memory is discussed in Chapter 12; elsewhere in the book, for simplicity, we ignore the role of the MMU and disks.

Memory Protection Many programs coexist in a computer's memory, so it is necessary to prevent one program from reading or destroying the contents of memory used by another program. This requirement is called *memory protection*; it is implemented by checking whether a memory address used by a program lies outside the memory area allocated to it.

Two control registers are used to implement memory protection. The *base register* contains the start address of the memory area allocated to a program, while the *size register* (also called the *limit register*) contains the size of memory allocated to the program. Accordingly, the last byte of memory allocated to a program has the address

$$\text{Address of last byte} = \text{<base>} + \text{<size>} - 1$$

where <base> and <size> indicate contents of the base register and size register, respectively. Before making any memory access, say access to a memory location with address *aaa*, the memory protection hardware checks whether *aaa* lies outside the range of addresses defined by contents of the base and size registers. If so, the hardware generates an interrupt to signal a memory protection violation and abandons the memory access. As described in a later section, the kernel aborts the erring program in response to the interrupt. The *memory protection information* (MPI) field of the PSW (see Figure 2.2) contains the base and size registers. This way the memory protection information also becomes a part of the CPU state and gets saved or restored when the program is preempted or resumed, respectively.

Fundamentals of Memory Protection

Example 2.2

Program P_1 is allocated the 5000-byte memory area 20000 to 24999 by the kernel. Figure 2.5 illustrates memory protection for this program using the base and size registers. The start address of the allocated area (i.e., 20000) is loaded in the base register, while the number 5000 is loaded in the size register. A memory protection violation interrupt would be generated if the instruction being executed by the CPU uses an address that lies outside the range 20000–24999, say, the address 28252.

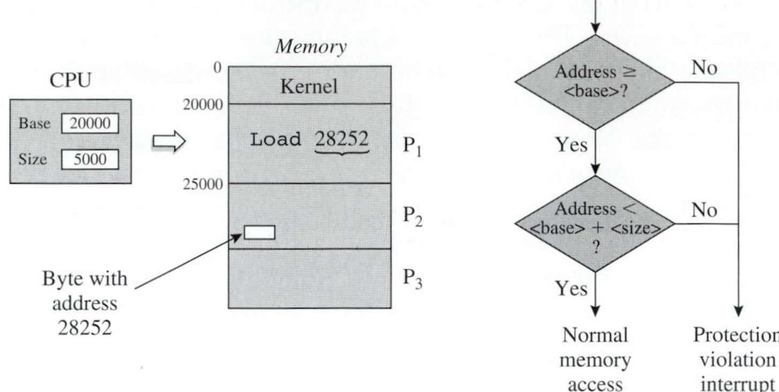

Figure 2.5 Memory protection using the *base* and *size* registers.

A program could undermine the memory protection scheme by loading information of its choice in the base and size registers. For example, program P_1 could load the address 0 in the base register and the size of the computer's memory in the size register and thereby get itself a capability of modifying contents of any part of memory, which would enable it to interfere with the OS or other user programs. To prevent this, instructions to load values into the base and size registers are made privileged instructions. Since the CPU is in the user mode while executing a user program, this arrangement prevents a user program from undermining the memory protection scheme.

Memory protection in a cache memory is more complex. Recall from the earlier discussion that the L1 cache is accessed by using logical addresses. A program of size n bytes typically uses logical addresses $0, \ldots, n-1$. Thus, many programs may use the same logical addresses, so a check based on a logical address cannot be used to decide whether a program may access a value that exists in the cache memory. A simple approach to memory protection would be to *flush* the cache, i.e., to erase contents of the entire cache, whenever execution of a program is initiated or resumed. This way, the cache would not hold contents of memory areas allocated to other programs. However, any parts of the program that were loaded in the cache during its execution in the past would also be erased. Hence, execution performance of the program would suffer initially because of a poor cache hit ratio. In an alternative scheme, the id of the program whose instructions or data are loaded in a cache block is remembered, and only that program is permitted to access contents of the cache block. It is implemented as follows: When a program generates a logical address that is covered by contents of a cache block, a cache hit occurs only if the program's id matches the id of the program whose instructions or data are loaded in the cache block. This scheme is preferred because it does not require flushing of the cache and does not affect execution performance of programs.

2.2.4 Input/Output

An I/O operation requires participation of the CPU, memory, and an I/O device. The manner in which the data transfer between memory and the I/O device

Table 2.1 Modes of Performing I/O Operations

I/O mode	Description
Programmed I/O	Data transfer between the I/O device and memory takes place through the CPU. The CPU cannot execute any other instructions while an I/O operation is in progress.
Interrupt I/O	The CPU is free to execute other instructions after executing the I/O instruction. However, an interrupt is raised when a data byte is to be transferred between the I/O device and memory, and the CPU executes an interrupt servicing routine, which performs transfer of the byte. This sequence of operations is repeated until all bytes get transferred.
Direct memory access (DMA)-based I/O	Data transfer between the I/O device and memory takes place directly over the bus. The CPU is not involved in data transfer. The DMA controller raises an interrupt when transfer of all bytes is complete.

is implemented determines the data transfer rates and the extent of the CPU's involvement in the I/O operation. The I/O organization we find in modern computers has evolved through a sequence of steps directed at reducing the involvement of the CPU in an I/O operation. Apart from providing higher data transfer rates, it also frees the CPU to perform other activities while an I/O operation is in progress.

We assume that operands of an I/O instruction indicate the address of an I/O device and details of I/O operations to be performed. Execution of the I/O instruction by the CPU initiates the I/O operation on the indicated device. The I/O operation is performed in one of the three modes described in Table 2.1. In the *programmed I/O mode*, data transfer is performed through the CPU. Hence data transfer is slow and the CPU is fully occupied with it. Consequently, only one I/O operation can be performed at a time. The *interrupt mode* is also slow as it performs a byte-by-byte transfer of data with the CPU's assistance. However, it frees the CPU between byte transfers. The *direct memory access (DMA) mode* can transfer a block of data between memory and an I/O device without involving the CPU, hence it achieves high data transfer rates and supports concurrent operation of the CPU and I/O devices. The interrupt and DMA modes permit I/O operations on several devices to be performed simultaneously.

DMA operations are actually performed by the *DMA controller*, which is a special-purpose processor dedicated to performing I/O operations; however, for simplicity we will not maintain this distinction in this chapter, and refer to both simply as DMA. In Figure 2.1, the I/O organization employs a DMA. Several I/O devices of the same class are connected to a device controller; a few device controllers are connected to the DMA. When an I/O instruction is executed, say a *read* instruction on device *d*, the CPU transfers details of the I/O operation to the DMA. The CPU is not involved in the I/O operation beyond this point; it is free to execute instructions while the I/O operation is in progress. The DMA passes on details of the I/O operation to the device controller, which initiates the *read* operation on device d. The device transfers the data to the device controller; transfer of data between the device controller and memory is organized by the DMA. Thus the CPU and the I/O subsystem can operate concurrently. At the end of the data transfer, the DMA generates an *I/O interrupt*. As described in the next section, the CPU switches to execution of the kernel when it notices the interrupt. The kernel analyzes the cause of the interrupt and realizes that the I/O operation is complete.

2.2.5 Interrupts

An *event* is any situation that requires the operating system's attention. The computer designer associates an *interrupt* with each event, whose sole purpose is to report the occurrence of the event to the operating system and enable it to perform appropriate event handling actions. It is implemented using the following arrangement: In the instruction execution cycle of the CPU, it performs four steps repeatedly—fetching the instruction whose address is contained in the program counter (PC), decoding it, executing it, and checking whether an interrupt has occurred during its execution. If an interrupt has occurred, the CPU performs an *interrupt action* that saves the CPU state, that is, contents of the PSW and the GPRs, and loads new contents into the PSW and the GPRs, so that the CPU starts executing instructions of an *interrupt servicing routine*, often called ISR, in the kernel. Sometime in the future, the kernel can resume execution of the interrupted program simply by loading back the saved CPU state into the PSW and GPRs (see Example 2.1). The computer designer associates a numeric priority with each interrupt. If several interrupts occur at the same time, the CPU selects the highest-priority interrupt for servicing. Other interrupts remain pending until they are selected.

Classes of Interrupts Table 2.2 describes three classes of interrupts that are important during normal operation of an OS. An *I/O interrupt* indicates the end of an I/O operation, or occurrence of exceptional conditions during the I/O operation. A *timer interrupt* is provided to implement a timekeeping arrangement in an operating system. It is used as follows: A *clock tick* is defined as a specific fraction of a second. Now, an interrupt can be raised either periodically, i.e., after a predefined number of ticks, or after a programmable interval of time, i.e., after occurrence of the number of ticks specified in a special *timer register*, which can be loaded through a privileged instruction.

A *program interrupt*, also called a *trap* or an *exception*, is provided for two purposes. The computer hardware uses the program interrupt to indicate occurrence of an exceptional condition during the execution of an instruction, e.g., an overflow during arithmetic, or a memory protection violation (see Section 2.2.3). User programs use the program interrupt to make requests to the kernel for resources or services that they are not allowed to provide for themselves. They achieve it by using a special instruction provided in the computer whose sole

Table 2.2 **Classes of Interrupts**

Class	Description
I/O interrupt	Caused by conditions like I/O completion and malfunctioning of I/O devices.
Timer interrupt	Raised at fixed intervals or when a specified interval of time elapses.
Program interrupt	(1) Caused by exceptional conditions that arise during the execution of an instruction, e.g., arithmetic exceptions like overflow, addressing exceptions, and memory protection violations. (2) Caused by execution of a special instruction called the *software interrupt instruction*, whose sole purpose is to cause an interrupt.

purpose is to raise a program interrupt so that control gets transferred to the kernel. The operation code of this instruction machine-specific, e.g., it is called `int` in the Intel Pentium, `trap` in Motorola 68000, and `syscall` in MIPS R3000. Generically, we assume that a computer provides an instruction called a *software interrupt instruction* with the operation code SI, and call the interrupt raised by it a *software interrupt*.

Interrupt Code When an interrupt of some class occurs, the hardware sets an interrupt code in the *interrupt code* (IC) field of the PSW to indicate which specific interrupt within that class of interrupts has occurred. This information is useful for knowing the cause of the interrupt. For example, if a program interrupt occurs, the interrupt code would help to decide whether it was caused by an overflow condition during arithmetic or by a memory protection violation.

Interrupt codes are machine-specific. For an I/O interrupt, the interrupt code is typically the address of the I/O device that caused the interrupt. For a program interrupt, a computer assigns distinct codes for exceptional conditions such as overflow and memory protection violation, and reserves a set of interrupt codes for software interrupts. Typically, the software interrupt instruction (SI instruction) has a small integer as an operand; it is treated as the interrupt code when the interrupt occurs. If a computer does not provide an operand in the SI instruction, an operating system has to evolve its own arrangement, e.g., it may require a program to push a software interrupt number on the stack before executing the SI instruction to cause a software interrupt.

Interrupt Masking The *interrupt mask* (IM) field of the PSW indicates which interrupts are permitted to occur at the present moment of time. The IM field may contain an integer m to indicate that only interrupts with priority $\geq m$ are permitted to occur. Alternatively, it may contain a bit-encoded value, where each bit in the value indicates whether a specific kind of interrupt is permitted to occur. Interrupts that are permitted to occur are said to be *enabled*, and others are said

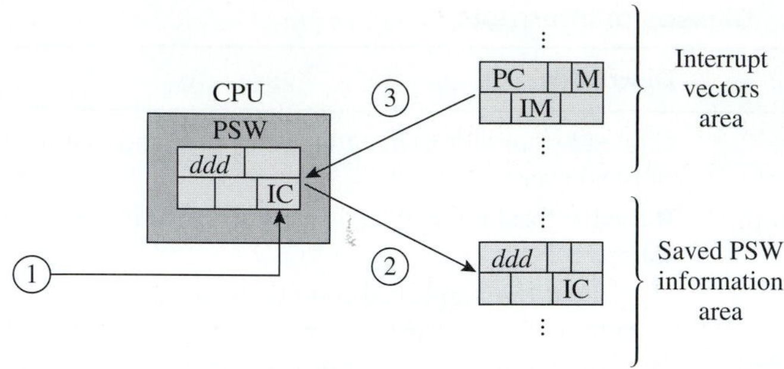

Step	Description
1. Set interrupt code	The interrupt hardware forms a code describing the cause of the interrupt. This code is stored in the *interrupt code* (IC) field of the PSW.
2. Save the PSW	The PSW is copied into the *saved PSW information* area. In some computers, this action also saves the general-purpose registers.
3. Load interrupt vector	The interrupt vector corresponding to the interrupt class is accessed. Information from the interrupt vector is loaded into the corresponding fields of the PSW. This action switches the CPU to the appropriate interrupt servicing routine of the kernel.

Figure 2.6 The interrupt action.

to be *masked* or *masked off*. If an event corresponding to a masked interrupt occurs, the interrupt caused by it is not lost; it remains pending until it is enabled and can occur.

Interrupt Action After executing every instruction, the CPU checks for occurrence of an interrupt. If an interrupt has occurred, the CPU performs the interrupt action, which saves the state of the CPU in memory and switches the CPU to an interrupt servicing routine in the kernel.

As shown in the schematic of Figure 2.6, the interrupt action consists of three steps. Step 1 sets the interrupt code in the *interrupt code* (IC) field of the PSW according to the cause of the interrupt. Step 2 of the interrupt action saves contents of the PSW in memory so that the kernel can form the CPU state of the interrupted program (see Figure 2.3), which it can use to resume execution of the program at a later time. The *saved PSW information* area, where the PSW of the interrupted program is stored, is either a reserved area in memory or an area on the stack. Step 3 of the interrupt action switches the CPU to execution of the appropriate interrupt servicing routine in the kernel as follows: The *interrupt vectors* area contains several interrupt vectors; each interrupt vector is used to control interrupt servicing for one class of interrupts. Depending on which class an interrupt belongs to, the interrupt action chooses the correct interrupt vector and loads its contents into PSW fields. An interrupt vector contains the following information:

1. Address of an interrupt servicing routine.
2. An interrupt mask indicating which other interrupts can occur while this interrupt is being processed.
3. A 0 or 1 to indicate whether the CPU should be in kernel or user mode, respectively, while executing the interrupt servicing routine. Typically 0 is chosen so that the interrupt servicing routine, which is a part of the kernel, can use privileged instructions.

For simplicity, we assume that an interrupt vector has the same format as a PSW and contains these three items of information in the *program counter* (PC), *interrupt mask* (IM), and *mode* (M) fields, respectively. Thus, Step 3 of the interrupt action loads information from the relevant interrupt vector into the *program counter*, *interrupt mask* and *mode* fields of the PSW, which puts the CPU in the kernel mode and switches it to the interrupt servicing routine.

2.3 OS INTERACTION WITH THE COMPUTER AND USER PROGRAMS

To respond readily to events, an OS uses an arrangement in which every event causes an interrupt. In this section, we discuss how the OS interacts with the computer to ensure that the state of an interrupted program is saved, so that its execution can be resumed at a later time, and how an interrupt servicing routine obtains information concerning the event that had caused an interrupt, so that it can perform appropriate actions. We also discuss how a program invokes the services of the OS through a software interrupt. A *system call* is the term used for this method of invoking OS services.

2.3.1 Controlling Execution of Programs

To control execution of user programs, the OS has to ensure that various fields of the PSW contain appropriate information at all times when user programs are in execution, which includes the time when a new program's execution is initiated, and also times when its execution is resumed after an interruption. From the discussion in Section 2.2, the key points in this function are:

1. At the start of execution of a user program, the PSW should contain the following information:
   a. The *program counter* field (PC field) should contain the address of the first instruction in the program.
   b. The *mode* field (M field) should contain a 1 such that the CPU is in the user mode.

   c. The *memory protection information* field (MPI field) should contain information about the start address and size of the memory area allocated to the program.
   d. The *interrupt mask* field (IM field) should be set so as to enable all interrupts.
2. When a user program's execution is interrupted, the CPU state—which consists of the contents of the PSW and the general-purpose registers—should be saved.
3. When execution of an interrupted program is to be resumed, the saved CPU state should be loaded into the PSW and the general-purpose registers.

The OS maintains a table to contain information relevant to this function. For now, we will use the generic name *program table* for it—in later chapters we will discuss specific methods of organizing this information such as the *process control block* (PCB). Each entry in the table contains information pertaining to one user program. One field in this entry is used to store information about the CPU state. The kernel puts information mentioned in item 1 into this field when the program's execution is to be initiated, and saves the CPU state into this field when the program's execution is interrupted—it achieves this by copying information from the *saved PSW information* area when the program is interrupted. Information stored in this field is used while resuming operation of the program. Effectively, relevant fields of the PSW would contain the information mentioned in items 1(b)–1(d) whenever the CPU is executing instructions of the program.

2.3.2 Interrupt Servicing

As mentioned in Section 2.2.5, for simplicity, we assume that an interrupt vector has the same format as the PSW. The kernel forms the interrupt vectors for various classes of interrupts when the operating system is booted. Each interrupt vector contains the following information: a 0 in the *mode* (M) field to indicate that the CPU should be put in the kernel mode, the address of the first instruction of the interrupt servicing routine in the *program counter* (PC) field, a 0 and the size of memory in the *memory protection information* (MPI) field—so that the interrupt servicing routine would have access to the entire memory—and an interrupt mask in the *interrupt mask* (IM) field that either disables other interrupts from occurring or enables only higher-priority interrupts to occur, in accordance with the philosophy of nested interrupt servicing employed in the operating system (we discuss details of this philosophy later in this section).

Figure 2.7 contains a schematic of operation of the kernel—it gets control only when an interrupt occurs, so its operation is said to be *interrupt-driven*. The interrupt action actually transfers control to an appropriate *interrupt servicing routine*, also called an ISR, which perform the actions shown in the dashed box. It first saves information about the interrupted program in the *program table*, for use when the program is scheduled again. This information consists of the PSW

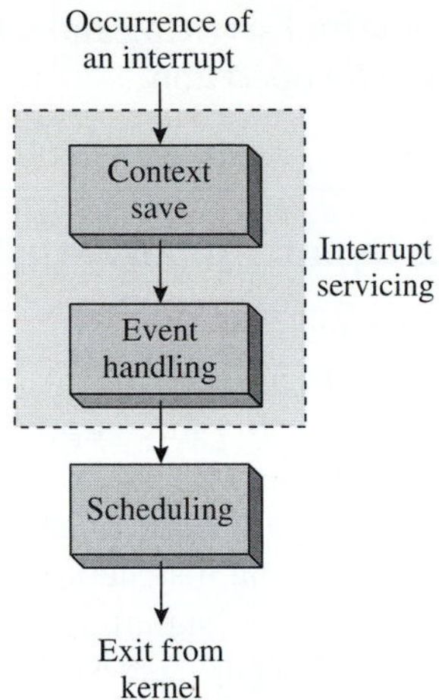

Figure 2.7 Interrupt-driven operation of the kernel.

Table 2.3 Event Handling Actions of the Kernel

Interrupt	Event handling action
Arithmetic exception	Abort the program.
Memory protection violation	Abort the program.
Software interrupt	Satisfy the program's request if possible; otherwise, note it for future action.
End of I/O operation	Find which program had initiated the I/O operation and note that it can now be considered for scheduling on the CPU. Initiate a pending I/O operation, if any, on the device.
Timer interrupt	(1) Update the time of the day. (2) Take appropriate action if a specified time interval has elapsed.

saved by the interrupt action, contents of GPRs, and information concerning memory and resources used by the program. It is called the execution context, or simply *context*, of a program; the action that saves it is called the *context save* action. The interrupt servicing routine now takes actions appropriate to the event that had caused the interrupt. As mentioned in Section 2.2.5, the *interrupt code* field of the saved PSW provides useful information for this purpose. Table 2.3 summarizes these actions, which we call the *event handling* actions of the kernel.

The *scheduling* routine selects a program and switches the CPU to its execution by loading the saved PSW and GPRs of the program into the CPU. Depending on the event that caused the interrupt and the state of other programs, it may be the same program that was executing when the interrupt occurred, or it may be a different program.

Example 2.3 illustrates interrupt servicing and scheduling when an interrupt occurs signaling the end of an I/O operation.

Example 2.3 Interrupt Servicing in a Hypothetical Kernel

Figure 2.8(a) shows the arrangement of interrupt vectors and interrupt servicing routines in memory, while Figure 2.8(b) shows contents of the PSW at various times during servicing of an I/O interrupt. The interrupt vectors are formed by the OS boot procedure. Each interrupt vector contains the address of an interrupt servicing routine, an interrupt mask and a 0 in the *mode* field. A user program is about to execute the instruction that exists at the address *ddd* in memory when an interrupt occurs signaling the end of an I/O operation on device d_1. The leftmost part of Figure 2.8(b) shows the PSW contents at this time.

Step 1 of the interrupt action puts d_1 in the IC field of the PSW and saves the PSW in the *saved PSW information* area. The saved PSW contains a 1 in the *mode* field, *ddd* in the PC field, and d_1 in the IC field. The contents of the interrupt vector for the I/O completion interrupt are loaded into the PSW. Effectively, the CPU is put in the kernel mode of operation, and control is transferred to the routine that has the start address *bbb*, which is the I/O interrupt servicing routine (see the arrow marked Ⓐ in Figure 2.8(a), and the PSW contents shown in Figure 2.8(b)).

The I/O interrupt servicing routine saves the PSW and contents of the GPRs in the *program table*. It now examines the IC field of the saved PSW, finds that device d_1 has completed its I/O operation, and notes that the program that had initiated the I/O operation can be considered for scheduling. It now transfers control to the scheduler (see the arrow marked Ⓑ in Figure 2.8(a)). The scheduler happens to select the interrupted program itself for execution, so the kernel switches the CPU to execution of the program by loading back the saved contents of the PSW and GPRs (see arrow marked Ⓒ in Figure 2.8(a)). The Program would resume execution at the instruction with the address *ddd* (see the PSW contents in the rightmost part of Figure 2.8(b)).

Nested Interrupt Servicing Figure 2.9(a) diagrams the interrupt servicing actions of Example 2.3 in the simplest form: interrupt servicing routine "a" handles the interrupt and the scheduler selects the interrupted program itself for execution. If another interrupt occurs, however, while interrupt servicing routine "a" is servicing the first interrupt, it will lead to identical actions in the hardware and software. This time, execution of interrupt servicing routine "a" is the "program" that will be interrupted; the CPU will be switched to execution of another interrupt servicing routine, say, interrupt servicing routine "b" (see Figure 2.9(b)). This situation delays servicing of the first interrupt, and it also requires careful coding

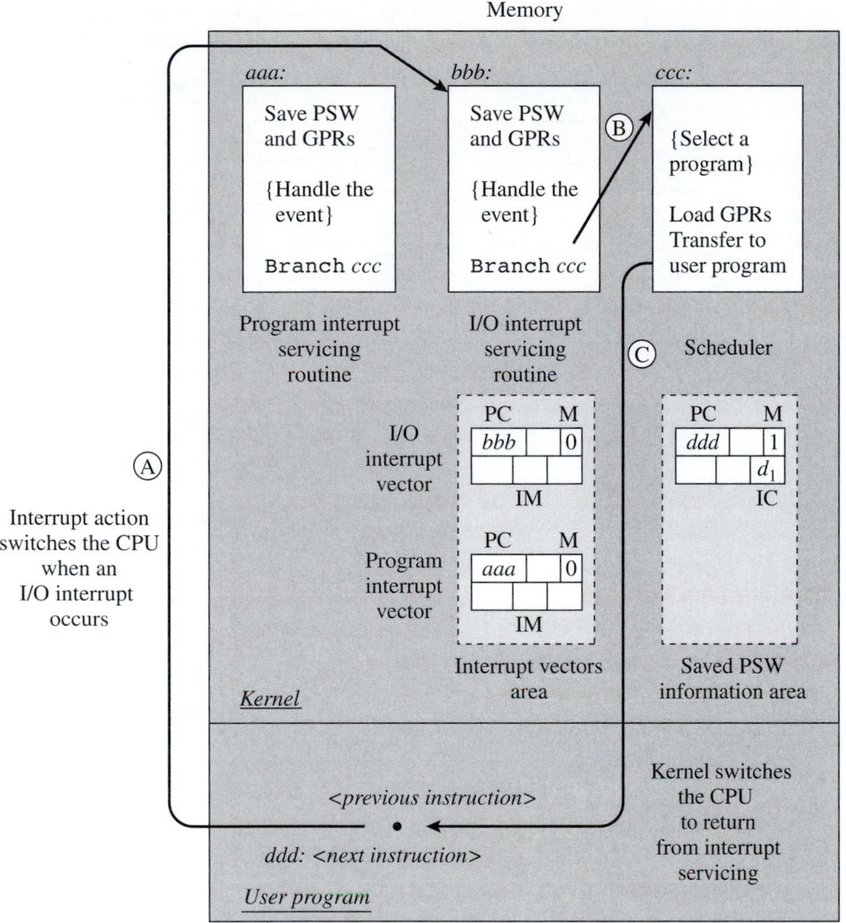

(a) Interrupt vectors and interrupt servicing routines.

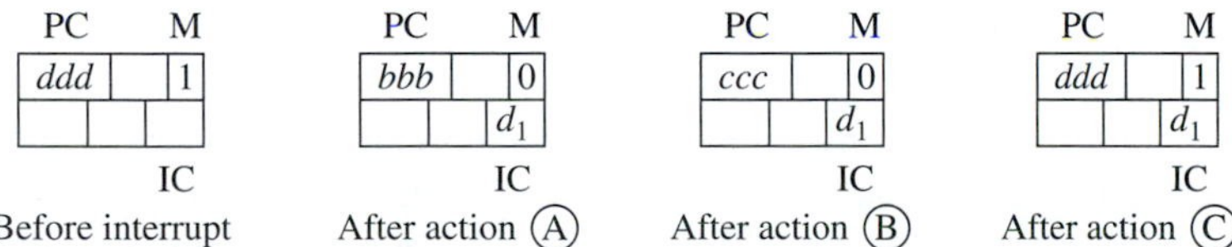

(b) PSW contents at various times.

Figure 2.8 Servicing of an I/O interrupt and return to the same user program.

of the kernel to avoid a mix-up if the same kind of interrupt were to arise again (also see Exercise 2.6). However, it enables the kernel to respond to high-priority interrupts readily.

Operating systems have used two approaches to nested interrupt servicing. Some operating systems use the interrupt mask (IM) field in the interrupt vector

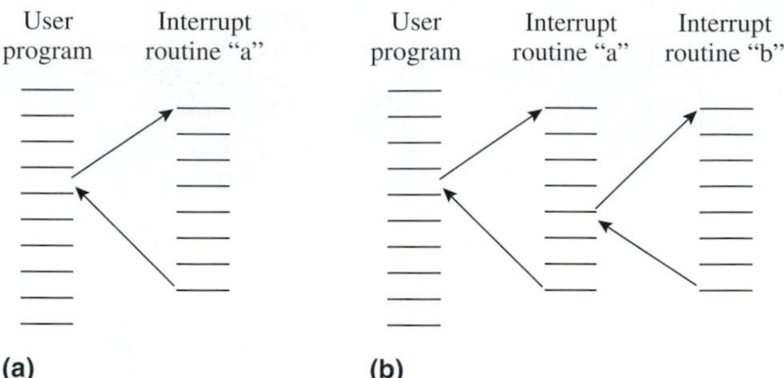

Figure 2.9 Simple and nested interrupt servicing.

to mask off *all* interrupts while an interrupt servicing routine is executing (see Figure 2.8). This approach makes the kernel noninterruptible, which simplifies its design because the kernel would be engaged in servicing only one interrupt at any time. However, noninterruptibility of the kernel may delay servicing of high-priority interrupts. In an alternative approach, the kernel sets the interrupt mask in each interrupt vector to mask off less critical interrupts; it services more critical interrupts in a nested manner. Such a kernel is called an *interruptible kernel* or a *preemptible kernel*. Data consistency problems would arise if two or more interrupt servicing routines activated in a nested manner update the same kernel data, so the kernel must use a locking scheme to ensure that only one interrupt processing routine can access such data at any time.

User Program Preemption In the scheme of Figure 2.7, preemption of a user program occurs implicitly when an interrupt arises during its execution and the kernel decides to switch the CPU to some other program's execution. Recall from Example 2.3 that the interrupted program's context is stored in the *program table*, so there is no difficulty in resuming execution of a preempted program when it is scheduled again.

2.3.3 System Calls

A program needs to use computer resources like I/O devices during its execution. However, resources are shared among user programs, so it is necessary to prevent mutual interference in their use. To facilitate it, the instructions that allocate or access critical resources are made privileged instructions in a computer's architecture. This way, these instructions cannot be executed unless the CPU is in the kernel mode, so user programs cannot access resources directly; they must make requests to the kernel, and the kernel must access resources on their behalf. The kernel provides a set of services for this purpose.

In a programmer view, a program uses a computer's resources through statements of a programming language. The compiler of a programming language implements the programmer view as follows: While compiling a program, it

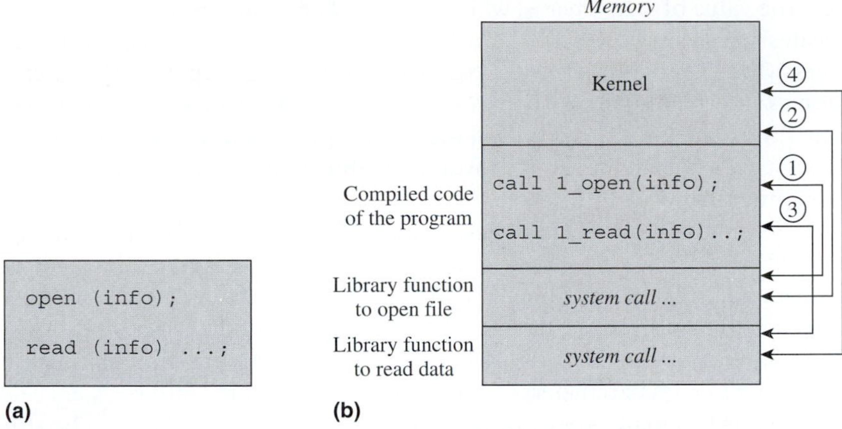

Figure 2.10 A schematic of system calls: (a) a program and (b) an execution time arrangement.

replaces statements concerning use of computer resources by calls on library functions that implement use of the resources. These library functions are then linked with the user program. During execution, the user program calls a library function and the library function actually uses the resource through a kernel service. We still need a method by which a library function can invoke the kernel to utilize one of its services. We will use *system call* as a generic term for such methods.

Figure 2.10 shows a schematic of this arrangement. The program shown in Figure 2.10(a) opens file `info` and reads some data from it. The compiled program has the form shown in Figure 2.10(b). It calls a library function to open the file; this call is shown by the arrow marked ①. The library function invokes the kernel service for opening a file through a system call (see the arrow marked ②). The kernel service returns to the library function after opening the file, which returns to the user program. The program reads the file analogously through a call on a library function, which leads to a system call (see arrows marked ③ and ④).

A system call is actually implemented through the interrupt action described earlier, hence we define it as follows:

Definition 2.1 System Call A request that a program makes to the kernel through a software interrupt.

We assume that the software interrupt instruction mentioned in Section 2.2.5 has the format

SI <*int_code*>

where the value of *<int_code>*, which is typically an integer in the range 0–255, indicates which service of the kernel is being requested. A program interrupt occurs when a program executes this instruction, and Step 1 of the interrupt action as shown in Figure 2.6 copies *<int_code>* into the *interrupt code* (IC) field of the PSW. The interrupt servicing routine for program interrupts analyzes the interrupt code field in the saved PSW information area to know the request made by the program.

A system call may take parameters that provide relevant information for the invoked kernel service, e.g., the system call to open a file in Figure 2.10 would take the filename `info` as a parameter, and the system call to read data would take parameters that indicate the filename, number of bytes of data to be read, and the address in memory where data is to be delivered, etc. Several different methods can be used to pass parameters—parameters can be loaded into registers before the system call is made, they can be pushed on the stack, or they can be stored in an area of memory and the start address of the memory area can be passed through a register or the stack.

The next example describes execution of a system call to obtain the current time of day.

Example 2.4 System Call in a Hypothetical OS

A hypothetical OS provides a system call for obtaining the current time. Let the code for this time-of-day service be 78. When a program wishes to know the time, it executes the instruction `SI 78`, which causes a software interrupt. 78 is entered in the interrupt code field of the PSW before the PSW is saved in the saved PSW information area. Thus the value d_1 in the IC field of the saved PSW in Figure 2.8 would be 78. As shown in Figure 2.8, the interrupt vector for program interrupts contains *aaa* in its PC field. Hence the CPU is switched to execution of the routine with the start address *aaa*. It finds that the interrupt code is 78 and realizes that the program wishes to know the time of the day. According to the conventions defined in the OS, the time information is to be returned to the program in a standard location, typically in a data register. Hence the kernel stores this value in the entry of the *program table* where the contents of the data register were saved when the interrupt occurred. This value would be loaded into the data register when the CPU is switched back to execution of the interrupted program.

In accordance with the schematic of Figure 2.10, we will assume that a program written in a programming language like C, C++, or Java calls a library function when it needs a service from the OS, and that the library function actually makes a system call to request the service. We will use the convention that the name of the library function is also the name of the system call. For example, in Example 2.4, a C program would call a library function `gettimeofday` to obtain the time of day, and this function would make the system call *gettimeofday* through the instruction `SI 78` as described in Example 2.4.

Table 2.4 Some Linux System Calls

Call number	Call name	Description
1	exit	Terminate execution of this program
3	read	Read data from a file
4	write	Write data into a file
5	open	Open a file
6	close	Close a file
7	waitpid	Wait for a program's execution to terminate
11	execve	Execute a program
12	chdir	Change working directory
14	chmod	Change file permissions
39	mkdir	Make a new directory
74	sethostname	Set hostname of the computer system
78	gettimeofday	Get time of day
79	settimeofday	Set time of day

An operating system provides system calls for various purposes like initiation and termination of programs, program synchronization, file operations, and obtaining information about the system. The Linux operating system provides close to 200 system calls; some of these calls are listed in Table 2.4. These system calls can also be invoked in a C or C++ program through the call names mentioned in Table 2.4; an assembly language program can invoke them directly through the SI instruction.

2.4 SUMMARY

As mentioned in the first chapter, a modern OS can service several user programs simultaneously. The OS achieves it by interacting with the computer and user programs to perform several control functions. In this chapter we described relevant features of a computer and discussed how they are used by the OS and user programs.

The operating system is a collection of routines. The instructions in its routines must be executed on the CPU to realize its control functions. Thus the CPU should execute instructions in the OS when a situation that requires the operating system's attention occurs, whereas it should execute instructions in user programs at other times. It is achieved by sending a special signal, called an *interrupt*, to the CPU. Interrupts are sent at the occurrence of a situation such as completion of an I/O operation, or a failure of some sort. A software interrupt known as a *system call* is sent when a program wishes to use a kernel service such as allocation of a resource or opening of a file.

The CPU contains a set of *control registers* whose contents govern its functioning. The *program status word* (PSW) is the collection of control registers of the CPU; we refer to each control register as a field of the PSW. A program whose execution was interrupted should be resumed at a later time. To facilitate this, the kernel saves the *CPU state* when an interrupt occurs. The CPU state consists of the PSW and program-accessible registers, which we call general-purpose registers (GPRs). Operation of the interrupted program is resumed by loading back the saved CPU state into the PSW and GPRs.

The CPU has two modes of operation controlled by the *mode* (M) field of the PSW. When the CPU is in the *user mode*, it cannot execute sensitive instructions like those that load information into PSW fields like the *mode* field, whereas it can execute all instructions when it is in the *kernel mode*. The OS puts the CPU in the user mode while it is executing a user program, and puts the CPU in the kernel mode while it is executing instructions in the kernel. This arrangement prevents a program from executing instructions that might interfere with other programs in the system.

The memory hierarchy of a computer provides the same effect as a fast and large memory, though at a low cost. It contains a very fast and small memory called a *cache*, a slower and larger random access memory (RAM)—which we will simply call memory—and a disk. The CPU accesses only the cache. However, the cache contains only some parts of a program's instructions and data. The other parts reside in memory; the hardware associated with the cache loads them into the cache whenever the CPU tries to access them. The effective memory access time depends on what fraction of instructions and data accessed by the CPU was found in the cache; this fraction is called the *hit ratio*.

The input-output system is the slowest unit of a computer; the CPU can execute millions of instructions in the amount of time required to perform an I/O operation. Some methods of performing an I/O operation require participation of the CPU, which wastes valuable CPU time. Hence the input-output system of a computer uses *direct memory access* (DMA) technology to permit the CPU and the I/O system to operate independently. The operating system exploits this feature to let the CPU execute instructions in a program while I/O operations of the same or different programs are in progress. This technique reduces CPU idle time and improves system performance.

TEST YOUR CONCEPTS

2.1 Classify each of the following statements as true or false:

- **a.** The condition code (i.e., flags) set by an instruction is not a part of the CPU state.
- **b.** The state of the CPU changes when a program executes a no-op (i.e., no operation) instruction.
- **c.** The software interrupt (SI) instruction changes the mode of the CPU to kernel mode.
- **d.** Branch instructions in a program may lead to low spatial locality, but may provide high temporal locality.
- **e.** When a DMA is used, the CPU is involved in data transfers to an I/O device during an I/O operation.
- **f.** A memory protection violation leads to a program interrupt.
- **g.** The kernel becomes aware that an I/O operation has completed when a program makes a system call to inform it that the I/O operation has ended.

2.2 Which of the following should be privileged instructions? Explain why.

- **a.** Put the CPU in kernel mode
- **b.** Load the size register
- **c.** Load a value in a general-purpose register
- **d.** Mask off some interrupts
- **e.** Forcibly terminate an I/O operation

EXERCISES

2.1 What use does the kernel make of the interrupt code field in the PSW?

2.2 The CPU should be in the kernel mode while executing the kernel code and in the user mode while executing a user program. Explain how it is achieved during operation of an OS.

2.3 The kernel of an OS masks off all interrupts during interrupt servicing. Discuss the advantages and disadvantages of such masking.

2.4 A computer system has the clock-tick-based timer arrangement described in Section 2.2.5. Explain how this arrangement can be used to maintain the time of day. What are the limitations of this approach?

2.5 An OS supports a system call *sleep*, which puts the program making the call to sleep for the number of seconds indicated in the argument of the *sleep* call. Explain how this system call is implemented.

2.6 A computer system organizes the saved PSW information area as a stack. It pushes contents of the PSW onto this stack during Step 2 of the interrupt action (see Figure 2.6). Explain the advantages of a stack for interrupt servicing.

2.7 If the request made by a program through a system call cannot be satisfied straightaway, the kernel informs the scheduling component that the program should not be selected for execution until its request is met. Give examples of such requests.

2.8 A hypothetical OS provides a system call for requesting allocation of memory. An experienced programmer offers the following advice: "If your program contains many requests for memory, you can speed up its execution by combining all these requests and making a single system call." Explain why this is so.

2.9 A computer has two levels of cache memories, which provide access times that are 0.01 and 0.1 times the access time of memory. If the hit ratio in each cache is 0.9, the memory has an access time of 10 microseconds, and the time required to load a cache block is 5 times the access time of the slower memory, calculate the effective memory access time.

2.10 A computer has a CPU that can execute 10 million instructions per second and a memory that has a transfer rate of 100 million bytes/second. When interrupt I/O is performed, the interrupt routine has to execute 50 instructions to transfer 1 byte between memory and an I/O device. What is the maximum data transfer rate during I/O operations implemented by using the following I/O modes: (a) interrupt I/O and (b) DMA-based I/O.

2.11 Several units of an I/O device that has a peak data transfer rate of 10 thousand bytes/second and operates in the interrupt I/O mode are connected to the computer in Exercise 2.10. How many of these units can operate at full speed at the same time?

2.12 A hypothetical OS supports two system calls for performing I/O operations. The system call *init_io* initiates an I/O operation, and the system call *await_io* ensures that the program would execute further only after the I/O operation has completed. Explain all actions that take place when the program makes these two system calls. (*Hint:* When none of the programs in the OS can execute on the CPU, the OS can put the CPU into an infinite loop in which it does nothing. It would come out of the loop when an interrupt occurs.)

BIBLIOGRAPHY

Smith (1982) and Handy (1998) describe cache memory organizations. Przybylski (1990) discusses cache and memory hierarchy design. Memory hierarchy and I/O organization are also covered in most books on computer architecture and organization, e.g., Hayes (1997), Patterson and Hennessy (2005), Hennessy and Patterson (2002), Hamacher et al. (2002), and Stallings (2003).

Most books on operating systems discuss the system calls interface. Bach (1986) contains a useful synopsis of Unix system calls. O'Gorman (2003) describes interrupt processing in Linux. Beck et al. (2002), Bovet and Cesati (2005), and Love (2005) contain extensive discussions of Linux system calls. Mauro and McDougall (2006) describes system calls in Solaris, while Russinovich and Solomon (2005) describes system calls in Windows.

1. Bach, M. J. (1986): *The Design of the Unix Operating System*, Prentice-Hall, Englewood Cliffs, N.J.
2. Beck, M., H. Bohme, M. Dziadzka, U. Kunitz, R. Magnus, C. Schroter, and D. Verworner (2002): *Linux Kernel Programming*, 3rd ed., Pearson Education, New York.
3. Bovet, D. P., and M. Cesati (2005): *Understanding the Linux Kernel*, 3rd ed., O'Reilly, Sebastopol.
4. O'Gorman, J. (2003): *Linux Process Manager: The internals of Scheduling, Interrupts and Signals*, John Wiley, New York.
5. Hamacher, C., Z. Vranesic, and S. Zaky (2002): *Computer Organization*, 5th ed., McGraw-Hill, New York.
6. Handy, J. (1998): *The Cache Memory Book*, 2nd ed., Academic Press, New York.
7. Hayes, J. (1997): *Computer Architecture and Organization*, 3rd ed., McGraw-Hill, New York.
8. Hennessy, J., and D. Patterson (2002): *Computer Architecture: A Quantitative Approach*, 3rd ed., Morgan Kaufmann, San Mateo, Calif.
9. Love, R. (2005): *Linux Kernel Development*, 2nd ed., Novell Press.
10. Mauro, J., and R. McDougall (2006): *Solaris Internals*, 2nd ed., Prentice Hall, Englewood Cliffs, N.J.
11. Patterson, D., and J. Hennessy (2005): *Computer Organization and Design: The Hardware/Software Interface*, 3rd ed., Morgan Kaufman, San Mateo, Calif.
12. Przybylski, A. (1990): *Cache and Memory Hierarchy Design: A Performance-Directed Approach*, Morgan Kaufmann, San Mateo, Calif.
13. Russinovich, M. E., and D. A. Solomon (2005): *Microsoft Windows Internals*, 4th ed., Microsoft Press, Redmond, Wash.
14. Smith, A. J. (1982): "Cache memories," *ACM Computing Surveys*, **14**, 473–530.
15. Stallings, W. (2003): *Computer Organization and Architecture*, 6th ed., Prentice Hall, Upper Saddle River, N.J.
16. Tanenbaum, A. (1998): *Structured Computer Organization*, 4th ed., Prentice Hall, Englewood Cliffs, N.J.

Chapter 3

Overview of Operating Systems

When we want to describe a *computing environment*, we need to look at both the computer system and its users: How is the computer system built? How is it installed to work with other systems? What are the services it provides to its users? All these features of a computing environment influence the design of an operating system because the OS has to provide a suitable combination of efficient use of the computer's resources and convenience of its users—what we called the notion of *effective utilization* of a computer system in Chapter 1—and also prevent interference in the activities of its users.

Throughout the history of computing, computing environments have changed as computer architecture and users' expectations have changed. New notions of effective utilization emerged with each new computing environment, so a new class of operating systems was developed, which used new concepts and techniques to achieve effective utilization.

Modern computing environments support diverse applications, so they possess features of several of the classical computing environments. Consequently, many of the concepts and techniques of the classical computing environments can be found in the strategies modern operating systems employ. To simplify the study of modern operating systems, in this chapter we present an overview of the concepts and techniques of the classical computing environments and discuss which of them find a place in a modern operating system.

3.1 COMPUTING ENVIRONMENTS AND NATURE OF COMPUTATIONS

A *computing environment* consists of a computer system, its interfaces with other systems, and the services provided by its operating system to its users and their programs. Computing environments evolve continuously to provide better quality of service to users; however, the operating system has to perform more complex tasks as computer systems become more powerful, their interfaces with I/O devices and with other computer systems become more complex, and its users demand new services.

The nature of computations in a computing environment, and the manner in which users realize them, depends on features of the computing environment. In a typical modern computing environment, a user initiates diverse activities simultaneously; e.g., he may run a mail handler, edit a few files, initiate computations, listen to music or watch a video, and browse the Internet at the same time. The operating system has to provide the resources required by each of these activities, such as the CPU and memory, and I/O devices located either within the same computer system or in another computer system that can be accessed over the Internet, so that the activities progress to the user's satisfaction.

We will begin the discussion of operating systems by taking a quick look at how computing environments evolved to their present form.

Noninteractive Computing Environments These are the earliest forms of computing environments. In these environments, a user submits both a computation in the form of a program and its data together to the operating system. The computation is performed by the operating system and its results are presented back to the user. The user has no contact with the computation during its execution. Hence these computations can be viewed as passive entities, to be interpreted and realized by the operating system. Examples of noninteractive computations are scientific computations involving number crunching and database updates performed overnight. In these computing environments, the operating system focuses on efficient use of resources.

Computations used in a noninteractive environment are in the form of a *program* or a *job*. A program is a set of functions or modules that can be executed by itself. A job is a sequence of programs that together achieve a desired goal; a program in a job is executed only if previous programs in the job have executed successfully. For example, consider compilation, linking, and execution of a C++ program. A job to achieve these actions would consist of execution of a C++ compiler, followed by execution of a linker to link the program with functions from libraries, followed by execution of the linked program. Here, linking is meaningful only if the program is compiled successfully, and execution is meaningful only if linking is successful.

Interactive Computing Environments In these computing environments, a user may interact with a computation while it is in progress. The nature of an interaction between a user and his computation depends on how the computation is coded; e.g., a user may input the name of a data file to a computation during its execution, or may directly input some data to it, and the computation may display a result after processing the data. The operating system focuses on reducing the average amount of time required to implement an interaction between a user and his computation.

A user also interacts with the OS to initiate a computation, typically each user command to the OS calls for separate execution of a program. Here the notion of a job is not important because a user would himself consider the dependence of programs while issuing the next command. For example, if a C++ program is to be compiled, linked, and executed, a user would attempt linking only if

Table 3.1 Computations in an OS

Computation	Description
Program	A *program* is a set of functions or modules, including some functions or modules obtained from libraries.
Job	A *job* is a sequence of programs that together achieve a common goal. It is not meaningful to execute a program in a job unless previous programs in the job have been executed successfully.
Process	A *process* is an execution of a program.
Subrequest	A *subrequest* is the presentation of a computational requirement by a user to a process. Each subrequest produces a single response, which consists of a set of results or actions.

the program had compiled successfully. Hence operating systems for interactive environments deal exclusively with execution of programs, not jobs. OS literature uses the term *process* for an execution of a program in an interactive environment. In principle, the term *process* is applicable in both noninteractive and interactive environments. However, we will follow the convention and use it only in the context of interactive computing environments.

A user's interaction with a process consists of presentation of a computational requirement—a *subrequest*—by the user to the process, and a response by the process. Depending on the nature of a subrequest, the response may be in the form of a set of results, or a set of actions such as file operations or database updates. Table 3.1 describes the program, job, process, and subrequest computations.

Real-Time, Distributed, and Embedded Environments Some computations have special requirements, hence special computing environments are developed to service them. A *real-time computation* is one that works under specific time constraints, so its actions are effective only if they are completed within a specified interval of time. For example, a computation that periodically samples the data from an instrument and stores the samples in a file must finish storing a sample before it is due to take the next sample. The operating system in a real-time environment uses special techniques to ensure that computations are completed within their time constraints. The *distributed computing environment* enables a computation to use resources located in several computer systems through a network. In the *embedded computing environment*, the computer system is a part of a specific hardware system, such as a household appliance, a subsystem of an automobile, or a handheld device such as a personal digital assistant (PDA), and runs computations that effectively control the system. The computer is typically an inexpensive one with a minimal configuration; its OS has to meet the time constraints arising from the nature of the system being controlled.

Modern Computing Environments To support diverse applications, the computing environment of a modern computer has features of several of the computing environments described earlier. Consequently, its operating system has to employ complex strategies to manage user computations and resources; e.g., it has to reduce the average amount of time required to implement an interaction between a user and a computation, and also ensure efficient use of resources.

We study the strategies used in modern operating systems in two stages: In this chapter, we first study the operating system strategies used in each of the computing environments mentioned earlier, and then see which of them are useful in a modern computing environment. In later chapters, we discuss the design of the strategies used in modern operating systems.

3.2 CLASSES OF OPERATING SYSTEMS

Classes of operating systems have evolved over time as computer systems and users' expectations of them have developed; i.e., as computing environments have evolved. As we study some of the earlier classes of operating systems, we need to understand that each was designed to work with computer systems of its own historical period; thus we will have to look at architectural features representative of computer systems of the period.

Table 3.2 lists five fundamental classes of operating systems that are named according to their defining features. The table shows when operating systems of each class first came into widespread use; what fundamental effectiveness criterion, or prime concern, motivated its development; and what key concepts were developed to address that prime concern.

Computing hardware was expensive in the early days of computing, so the batch processing and multiprogramming operating systems focused on efficient use of the CPU and other resources in the computer system. Computing environments were noninteractive in this era. In the 1970s, computer hardware became cheaper, so efficient use of a computer was no longer the prime concern and the focus shifted to productivity of computer users. Interactive computing environments were developed and time-sharing operating systems facilitated

Table 3.2 Key Features of Classes of Operating Systems

OS class	Period	Prime concern	Key concepts
Batch processing	1960s	CPU idle time	Automate transition between jobs
Multiprogramming	1960s	Resource utilization	Program priorities, preemption
Time-sharing	1970s	Good response time	Time slice, round-robin scheduling
Real time	1980s	Meeting time constraints	Real-time scheduling
Distributed	1990s	Resource sharing	Distributed control, transparency

better productivity by providing quick response to subrequests made to processes. The 1980s saw emergence of real-time applications for controlling or tracking of real-world activities, so operating systems had to focus on meeting the time constraints of such applications. In the 1990s, further declines in hardware costs led to development of distributed systems, in which several computer systems, with varying sophistication of resources, facilitated sharing of resources across their boundaries through networking.

The following paragraphs elaborate on key concepts of the five classes of operating systems mentioned in Table 3.2.

Batch Processing Systems In a batch processing operating system, the prime concern is CPU efficiency. The batch processing system operates in a strict one-job-at-a-time manner; within a job, it executes the programs one after another. Thus only one program is under execution at any time. The opportunity to enhance CPU efficiency is limited to efficiently initiating the next program when one program ends, and the next job when one job ends, so that the CPU does not remain idle.

Multiprogramming Systems A multiprogramming operating system focuses on efficient use of both the CPU and I/O devices. The system has several programs in a state of partial completion at any time. The OS uses *program priorities* and gives the CPU to the highest-priority program that needs it. It switches the CPU to a low-priority program when a high-priority program starts an I/O operation, and switches it back to the high-priority program at the end of the I/O operation. These actions achieve simultaneous use of I/O devices and the CPU.

Time-Sharing Systems A time-sharing operating system focuses on facilitating quick response to subrequests made by *all* processes, which provides a tangible benefit to users. It is achieved by giving a fair execution opportunity to each process through two means: The OS services all processes by turn, which is called *round-robin scheduling*. It also prevents a process from using too much CPU time when scheduled to execute, which is called *time-slicing*. The combination of these two techniques ensures that no process has to wait long for CPU attention.

Real-Time Systems A real-time operating system is used to implement a computer application for controlling or tracking of real-world activities. The application needs to complete its computational tasks in a timely manner to keep abreast of external events in the activity that it controls. To facilitate this, the OS permits a user to create several processes *within* an application program, and uses *real-time scheduling* to interleave the execution of processes such that the application can complete its execution within its time constraint.

Distributed Systems A distributed operating system permits a user to access resources located in other computer systems conveniently and reliably. To enhance convenience, it does not expect a user to know the location of resources in the system, which is called *transparency*. To enhance efficiency, it may execute parts of a computation in different computer systems at the same time. It uses *distributed control*; i.e., it spreads its decision-making actions across different computers in the system so that failures of individual computers or the network does not cripple its operation.

In Sections 3.4–3.8, we will examine each of the five fundamental OS classes in greater detail.

3.3 EFFICIENCY, SYSTEM PERFORMANCE, AND USER SERVICE

Measurement provides a method of assessing selected aspects of an operating system's functioning. In Chapter 1, we defined efficiency of use and user convenience as two of the fundamental goals of an OS. However, to a system administrator the performance of a system in its environment is more important than merely efficiency of use, hence in this section we discuss measures of efficiency, system performance, and user service. Table 3.3 summarizes these measures.

Efficiency The way to evaluate efficiency of use of a resource is to see how much of the resource is unused or wasted, and, in the amount of resource that is used, check how much of it is put to productive use. As an example of efficiency, consider use of the CPU. Some amount of CPU time is wasted because the CPU does not have enough work to do. This happens when all user processes in the system are either performing I/O operations or waiting for the users to supply data. Of the CPU time that is used, some amount of time is used by the OS itself in performing interrupt servicing and scheduling. This constitutes the *overhead* of OS operation. The remaining CPU time is used for executing user processes. To evaluate efficiency of CPU use, we should consider what fraction or percentage of the total CPU time is used for executing user processes. Efficiency of use of other resources such as memory and I/O devices can be similarly determined: Deduct the amount of unused resource and the OS overhead from the total resource and consider what fraction or percentage the result is of the total resource.

Using the notion of efficiency of use, we briefly discuss the fundamental trade-off between efficiency of use and user convenience: A multiprogramming system has several user programs at any time and switches between them to obtain efficient use of both the CPU and I/O devices. The CPU is given to the

Table 3.3 Measures of Efficiency, System Performance, and User Service

Aspect	Measure	Description
Efficiency of use	CPU efficiency	Percent utilization of the CPU
	Memory efficiency	Percent utilization of memory
System performance	Throughput	Amount of work done per unit time
User service	Turnaround time	Time to complete a job or a process
	Response time	Time to implement one subrequest

highest-priority program in the system whenever it wants, and it can use the CPU for as long as it wants. A time-sharing system, however, restricts the amount of CPU time a scheduled process can use. It preempts a process that uses too much CPU time and schedules another process. The preempted process may be scheduled again sometime in future. This feature increases the OS overhead in interrupt servicing and scheduling, thereby affecting efficiency of CPU use. However, it provides good response times to all processes, which is a feature desired by users of the OS.

System Performance Once we decide on the suitable combination of CPU efficiency and user service, it is important to know how well the OS is performing. The notion of performance depends on the computing environment and indicates the rate at which a computer system accomplishes work during its operation.

An operating system typically uses a measure of efficiency to tune its functioning for better performance. For example, if memory efficiency is low, the operating system may load more user programs in memory. In turn, it may lead to better performance of the system by increasing the rate at which the system completes user computations. If CPU efficiency is low, the operating system may investigate its causes—either too few programs in memory or programs spending too much time in waiting for I/O to complete—and take corrective actions where possible.

System performance is characterized as the amount of work done per unit time. It is typically measured as *throughput*.

Definition 3.1 Throughput The average number of jobs, programs, processes, or subrequests completed by a system in unit time.

The unit of work used for measuring throughput depends on the computing environment. In a noninteractive environment, throughput of an OS is measured in terms of the number of jobs or programs completed per unit time. In an interactive environment, it may be measured in terms of the number of subrequests completed per unit time. In a specialized computing environment, performance may be measured in terms meaningful to the application; for example, in a banking environment, it could be the number of transactions per unit time. Throughput can also be used as a measure of performance for I/O devices. For example, the throughput of a disk can be measured as the number of I/O operations completed per unit time or the number of bytes transferred per unit time.

User Service Some aspects of user convenience are intangible and thus impossible to measure numerically; e.g., a feature like user friendly interfaces cannot be quantified. However, there are some measurable aspects of user convenience, so we can define appropriate measures for them. *User service*, which indicates how quickly a user's computation has been completed by the OS, is one such aspect. We define two measures of user service—*turnaround time*, in noninteractive computing environments, and *response time*, in interactive computing environments. A smaller turnaround time or response time implies better user service.

Definition 3.2 Turnaround Time The time from submission of a job, program, or process by a user to the time its results become available to the user.

Definition 3.3 Response Time The time from submission of a subrequest by a user to the time a process responds to it.

Specialized measures of user service may be defined for use in specific computing environments. Two such examples are *deadline overrun* in a real-time operating system and *computation speedup* in a distributed operating system. Deadline overrun indicates by how much time the OS was late in completing the execution of a computation with time constraints, so a negative deadline overrun indicates good user service. Computation speedup indicates by what factor the execution of an application was speeded up because its processes were executed at the same time in different computers of a distributed system; a larger value of computation speedup implies better user service.

3.4 BATCH PROCESSING SYSTEMS

Computer systems of the 1960s were noninteractive. Punched cards were the primary input medium, so a job and its data consisted of a deck of cards. A computer operator would load the cards into the card reader to set up the execution of a job. This action wasted precious CPU time; batch processing was introduced to prevent this wastage.

A *batch* is a *sequence* of user jobs formed for processing by the operating system. A computer operator formed a batch by arranging a few user jobs in a sequence and inserting special marker cards to indicate the start and end of the batch. When the operator gave a command to initiate processing of a batch, the *batching kernel* set up the processing of the first job of the batch. At the end of the job, it initiated execution of the next job, and so on, until the end of the batch. Thus the operator had to intervene only at the start and end of a batch.

Card readers and printers were a performance bottleneck in the 1960s, so batch processing systems employed the notion of virtual card readers and printers (described in Section 1.3.2) through magnetic tapes, to improve the system's throughput. A batch of jobs was first recorded on a magnetic tape, using a less powerful and cheap computer. The batch processing system processed these jobs from the tape, which was faster than processing them from cards, and wrote their results on another magnetic tape. These were later printed and released to users. Figure 3.1 shows the factors that make up the turnaround time of a job.

User jobs could not interfere with each other's execution directly because they did not coexist in a computer's memory. However, since the card reader was the only input device available to users, commands, user programs, and data were all derived from the card reader, so if a program in a job tried to read more data than provided in the job, it would read a few cards of the following job! To protect against such interference between jobs, a batch processing system required

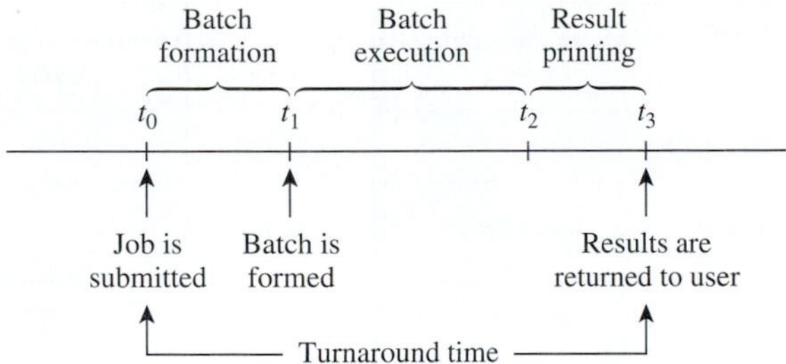

Figure 3.1 Turnaround time in a batch processing system.

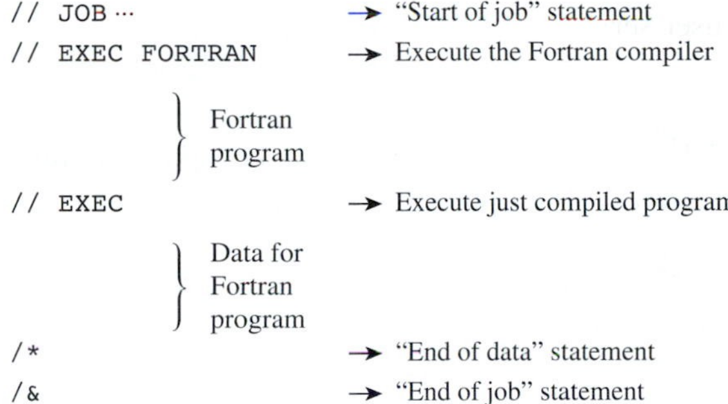

Figure 3.2 Control statements in IBM 360/370 systems.

a user to insert a set of *control statements* in the deck of cards constituting a job. The *command interpreter*, which was a component of the batching kernel, read a card when the currently executing program in the job wanted the next card. If the card contained a control statement, it analyzed the control statement and performed appropriate actions; otherwise, it passed the card to the currently executing program. Figure 3.2 shows a simplified set of control statements used to compile and execute a Fortran program. If a program tried to read more data than provided, the command interpreter would read the `/*`, `/&` and `// JOB` cards. On seeing one of these cards, it would realize that the program was trying to read more cards than provided, so it would abort the job.

A modern OS would not be *designed* for batch processing, but the technique is still useful in financial and scientific computation where the same kind of processing or analysis is to be performed on several sets of data. Use of batch processing in such environments would eliminate time-consuming initialization of the financial or scientific analysis separately for each set of data.

3.5 MULTIPROGRAMMING SYSTEMS

Multiprogramming operating systems were developed to provide efficient resource utilization in a noninteractive environment. A multiprogramming OS

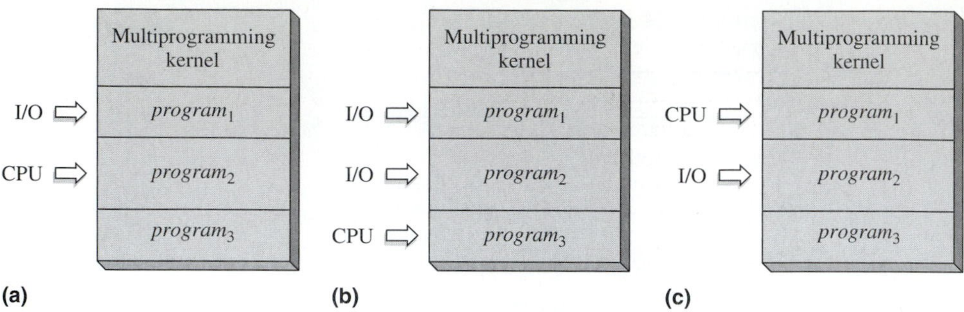

Figure 3.3 Operation of a multiprogramming system: (a) *program*$_2$ is in execution while *program*$_1$ is performing an I/O operation; (b) *program*$_2$ initiates an I/O operation, *program*$_3$ is scheduled; (c) *program*$_1$'s I/O operation completes and it is scheduled.

has many user programs in the memory of the computer at any time, hence the name *multiprogramming*. It employs the DMA mode of I/O (see Section 2.2.4), so it can perform I/O operations of some program(s) while using the CPU to execute some other program. This arrangement makes efficient use of both the CPU and I/O devices. The I/O and computational activities in several programs are in progress at any time, so it also leads to high system performance. We discuss this aspect in Section 3.5.1.

Figure 3.3 illustrates operation of a multiprogramming OS. The memory contains three programs. An I/O operation is in progress for *program*$_1$, while the CPU is executing *program*$_2$. The CPU is switched to *program*$_3$ when *program*$_2$ initiates an I/O operation, and it is switched to *program*$_1$ when *program*$_1$'s I/O operation completes. The multiprogramming kernel performs scheduling, memory management and I/O management. It uses a simple scheduling policy, which we will discuss in Section 3.5.1, and performs simple partitioned or pool-based allocation of memory and I/O devices. Since several programs are in memory at the same time, the instructions, data, and I/O operations of a program should be protected against interference by other programs. We shall shortly see how it is achieved.

A computer must possess the features summarized in Table 3.4 to support multiprogramming (see Section 2.2). The DMA makes multiprogramming feasible by permitting concurrent operation of the CPU and I/O devices. Memory protection prevents a program from accessing memory locations that lie outside the range of addresses defined by contents of the *base register* and *size register* of the CPU. The kernel and user modes of the CPU provide an effective method of preventing interference between programs. Recall from Section 2.2 that the OS puts the CPU in the user mode while executing user programs, and that instructions that load an address into the base register and a number into the size register of the CPU, respectively, are privileged instructions. If a program tries to undermine memory protection by changing contents of the base and size registers through these instructions, a program interrupt would be raised because

Table 3.4 Architectural Support for Multiprogramming

Feature	Description
DMA	The CPU initiates an I/O operation when an I/O instruction is executed. The DMA implements the data transfer involved in the I/O operation without involving the CPU and raises an I/O interrupt when the data transfer completes.
Memory protection	A program can access only the part of memory defined by contents of the *base register* and *size register*.
Kernel and user modes of CPU	Certain instructions, called *privileged instructions*, can be performed only when the CPU is in the kernel mode. A program interrupt is raised if a program tries to execute a privileged instruction when the CPU is in the user mode.

the CPU is in the user mode; the kernel would abort the program while servicing this interrupt.

The turnaround time of a program is the appropriate measure of user service in a multiprogramming system. It depends on the total number of programs in the system, the manner in which the kernel shares the CPU between programs, and the program's own execution requirements.

3.5.1 Priority of Programs

An appropriate measure of performance of a multiprogramming OS is *throughput*, which is the ratio of the number of programs processed and the total time taken to process them. Throughput of a multiprogramming OS that processes n programs in the interval between times t_0 and t_f is $n/(t_f - t_0)$. It may be larger than the throughput of a batch processing system because activities in several programs may take place simultaneously—one program may execute instructions on the CPU, while some other programs perform I/O operations. However, actual throughput depends on the nature of programs being processed, i.e., how much computation and how much I/O they perform, and how well the kernel can overlap their activities in time.

The OS keeps a sufficient number of programs in memory at all times, so that the CPU and I/O devices will have sufficient work to perform. This number is called the *degree of multiprogramming*. However, merely a high degree of multiprogramming cannot guarantee good utilization of both the CPU and I/O devices, because the CPU would be idle if each of the programs performed I/O operations most of the time, or the I/O devices would be idle if each of the programs performed computations most of the time. So the multiprogramming OS employs the two techniques described in Table 3.5 to ensure an overlap of CPU and I/O activities in programs: It uses an appropriate *program mix*, which ensures that some of the programs in memory are *CPU-bound programs*, which are programs that

Table 3.5 Techniques of Multiprogramming

Technique	Description
Appropriate *program mix*	The kernel keeps a mix of CPU-bound and I/O-bound programs in memory, where • A *CPU-bound program* is a program involving a lot of computation and very little I/O. It uses the CPU in long bursts—that is, it uses the CPU for a long time before starting an I/O operation. • An *I/O-bound program* involves very little computation and a lot of I/O. It uses the CPU in small bursts.
Priority-based preemptive scheduling	Every program is assigned a priority. The CPU is always allocated to the highest-priority program that wishes to use it. A low-priority program executing on the CPU is preempted if a higher-priority program wishes to use the CPU.

involve a lot of computation but few I/O operations, and others are *I/O-bound programs*, which contain very little computation but perform more I/O operations. This way, the programs being serviced have the potential to keep the CPU and I/O devices busy simultaneously. The OS uses the notion of *priority-based preemptive scheduling* to share the CPU among programs in a manner that would ensure good overlap of their CPU and I/O activities. We explain this technique in the following.

Definition 3.4 Priority A tie-breaking criterion under which a scheduler decides which request should be scheduled when many requests await service.

The kernel assigns numeric priorities to programs. We assume that priorities are positive integers and a large value implies a high priority. When many programs need the CPU at the same time, the kernel gives the CPU to the program with the highest priority. It uses priority in a preemptive manner; i.e., it preempts a low-priority program executing on the CPU if a high-priority program needs the CPU. This way, the CPU is always executing the highest-priority program that needs it. To understand implications of priority-based preemptive scheduling, consider what would happen if a high-priority program is performing an I/O operation, a low-priority program is executing on the CPU, and the I/O operation of the high-priority program completes—the kernel would immediately switch the CPU to the high-priority program.

Assignment of priorities to programs is a crucial decision that can influence system throughput. Multiprogramming systems use the following priority assignment rule: *An I/O-bound program should have a higher priority than a CPU-bound program.* Example 3.1 illustrates operation of this rule.

Execution of Programs in a Multiprogramming System

Example 3.1

A multiprogramming system has $prog_{iob}$, an I/O-bound program, and $prog_{cb}$, a CPU-bound program. Its operation starts at time 0. In Figure 3.4, the CPU and I/O activities of these programs are plotted in the form of a timing chart in which the x axis shows time and the y axis shows CPU and I/O activities of the two programs. Cumulative CPU and I/O activities are shown at the bottom of the chart. Note that the chart is not to scale; the CPU activity of $prog_{iob}$ has been exaggerated for clarity.

Program $prog_{iob}$ is the higher priority program. Hence it starts executing at time 0. After a short burst of CPU activity, it initiates an I/O operation (time instant t_1). The CPU is now switched to $prog_{cb}$. Execution of $prog_{cb}$ is thus concurrent with the I/O operation of $prog_{iob}$. Being a CPU-bound program, $prog_{cb}$ keeps the CPU busy until $prog_{iob}$'s I/O completes at t_2, at which time $prog_{cb}$ is preempted because $prog_{iob}$ has a higher priority. This sequence of events repeats in the period 0–t_6. Deviations from this behavior occur when $prog_{cb}$ initiates an I/O operation. Now both programs are engaged in I/O operations, which go on simultaneously because the programs use different I/O devices, and the CPU remains idle until one of them completes its I/O operation. This explains the CPU-idle periods t_6–t_7 and t_8–t_9 in the cumulative CPU activity. I/O-idle periods occur whenever $prog_{iob}$ executes on the CPU and $prog_{cb}$ is not performing I/O (see intervals $0 - t_1$, t_2–t_3, and t_4–t_5). But the CPU and the I/O subsystem are concurrently busy in the intervals t_1–t_2, t_3–t_4, t_5–t_6, and t_7–t_8.

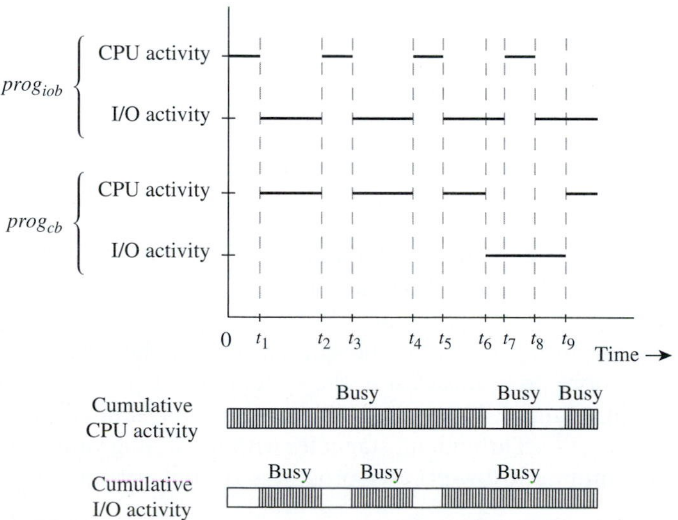

Figure 3.4 Timing chart when I/O-bound program has higher priority.

Table 3.6 Effect of Increasing the Degree of Multiprogramming

Action	Effect
Add a CPU-bound program	A CPU-bound program (say, $prog_3$) can be introduced to utilize some of the CPU time that was wasted in Example 3.1 (e.g., the intervals t_6–t_7 and t_8–t_9). $prog_3$ would have the lowest priority. Hence its presence would not affect the progress of $prog_{cb}$ and $prog_{iob}$.
Add an I/O-bound program	An I/O-bound program (say, $prog_4$) can be introduced. Its priority would be between the priorities of $prog_{iob}$ and $prog_{cb}$. Presence of $prog_4$ would improve I/O utilization. It would not affect the progress of $prog_{iob}$ at all, since $prog_{iob}$ has the highest priority, and it would affect the progress of $prog_{cb}$ only marginally, since $prog_4$ does not use a significant amount of CPU time.

We can make a few observations from Example 3.1: The CPU utilization is good. The I/O utilization is also good; however, I/O idling would exist if the system contained many devices capable of operating in the DMA mode. Periods of concurrent CPU and I/O activities are frequent. $prog_{iob}$ makes very good progress because it is the highest-priority program. It makes very light use of the CPU, and so $prog_{cb}$ also makes very good progress. The throughput is thus substantially higher than if the programs were executed one after another as in a batch processing system. Another important feature of this priority assignment is that system throughput can be improved by adding more programs. Table 3.6 describes how addition of a CPU-bound program can reduce CPU idling without affecting execution of other programs, while addition of an I/O-bound program can improve I/O utilization while marginally affecting execution of CPU-bound programs. The kernel can judiciously add CPU-bound or I/O-bound programs to ensure efficient use of resources.

When an appropriate program mix is maintained, we can expect that an increase in the degree of multiprogramming would result in an increase in throughput. Figure 3.5 shows how the throughput of a system actually varies with the degree of multiprogramming. When the degree of multiprogramming is 1, the throughput is dictated by the elapsed time of the lone program in the system. When more programs exist in the system, lower-priority programs also contribute to throughput. However, their contribution is limited by their opportunity to use the CPU. Throughput stagnates with increasing values of the degree of multiprogramming if low-priority programs do not get any opportunity to execute.

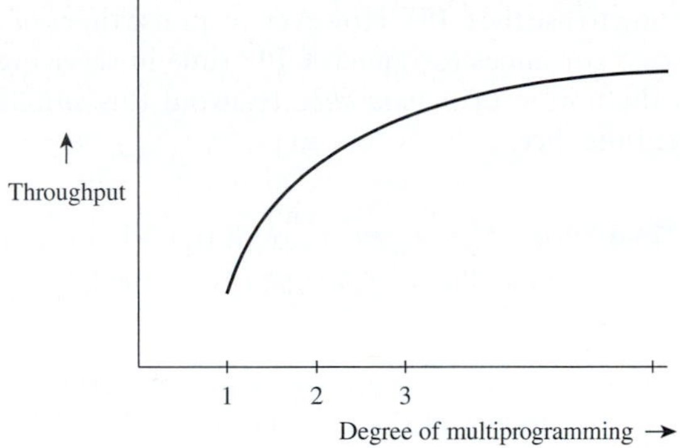

Figure 3.5 Variation of throughput with degree of multiprogramming.

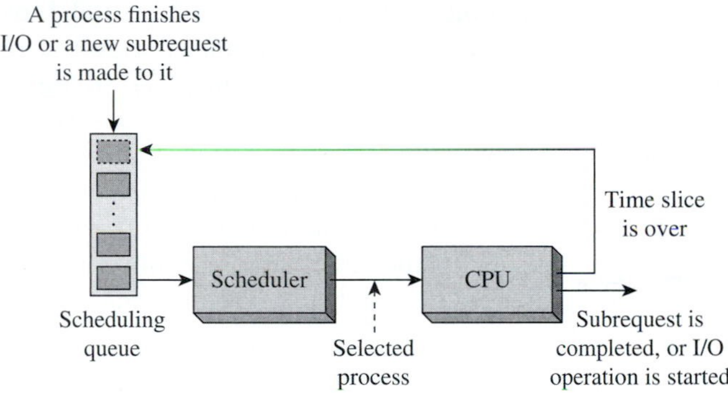

Figure 3.6 A schematic of round-robin scheduling with time-slicing.

3.6 TIME-SHARING SYSTEMS

In an interactive computing environment, a user submits a computational requirement—a subrequest—to a process and examines its response on the monitor screen. A time-sharing operating system is designed to provide a quick response to subrequests made by users. It achieves this goal by sharing the CPU time among processes in such a way that each process to which a subrequest has been made would get a turn on the CPU without much delay.

The scheduling technique used by a time-sharing kernel is called *round-robin scheduling with time-slicing*. It works as follows (see Figure 3.6): The kernel maintains a *scheduling queue* of processes that wish to use the CPU; it always schedules the process at the head of the queue. When a scheduled process completes servicing of a subrequest, or starts an I/O operation, the kernel removes it from the queue and schedules another process. Such a process would be added at the end of the queue when it receives a new subrequest, or when its I/O operation completes. This arrangement ensures that all processes would suffer comparable delays before getting to use the CPU. However, response times of processes would degrade if a process consumes too much CPU time in servicing its subrequest. The kernel uses the notion of a *time slice* to avoid this situation. We use the notation δ for the time slice.

Definition 3.5 Time Slice The largest amount of CPU time any time-shared process can consume when scheduled to execute on the CPU.

If the time slice elapses before the process completes servicing of a subrequest, the kernel preempts the process, moves it to the end of the scheduling queue, and schedules another process. The preempted process would be rescheduled when it reaches the head of the queue once again. Thus, a process may have to be scheduled several times before it completes servicing of a subrequest. The kernel employs a timer interrupt to implement time-slicing (see Section 2.2.5 and Table 2.2).

The appropriate measure of user service in a time-sharing system is the time taken to service a subrequest, i.e., the response time (rt). It can be estimated in the following manner: Let the number of users using the system at any time be n. Let the complete servicing of each user subrequest require exactly δ CPU seconds, and let σ be the *scheduling overhead*; i.e., the CPU time consumed by the kernel to perform scheduling. If we assume that an I/O operation completes instantaneously and a user submits the next subrequest immediately after receiving a response to the previous subrequest, the response time (rt) and the CPU efficiency (η) are given by

$$rt = n \times (\delta + \sigma) \tag{3.1}$$

$$\eta = \frac{\delta}{\delta + \sigma} \tag{3.2}$$

The actual response time may be different from the value of rt predicted by Eq. (3.1), for two reasons. First, all users may not have made subrequests to their processes. Hence rt would not be influenced by n, the total number of users in the system; it would be actually influenced by the number of active users. Second, user subrequests do not require exactly δ CPU seconds to produce a response. Hence the relationship of rt and η with δ is more complex than shown in Eqs. (3.1) and (3.2).

Example 3.2 illustrates round-robin scheduling with time-slicing, and how it results in interleaved operation of processes.

Example 3.2 Operation of Processes in a Time-Sharing System

Processes P_1 and P_2 follow a cyclic behavior pattern. Each cycle contains a burst of CPU activity to service a subrequest and a burst of I/O activity to report its result, followed by a wait until the next subrequest is submitted to it. The CPU bursts of processes P_1 and P_2 are 15 and 30 ms, respectively, while the I/O bursts are 100 and 60 ms, respectively.

Figure 3.7 shows operation of the processes in a time-sharing system using a time slice of 10 ms. The table in the top half of Figure 3.7 shows the scheduling list and scheduling decisions of the kernel, assuming scheduling overhead to be negligible, while the timing chart shows the CPU and I/O activities of the processes. Both processes have to be scheduled a few times before they can complete the CPU bursts of their execution cycle and start I/O. Process P_1 uses the CPU from time 0 to 10 ms and P_2 uses the CPU from 10 to 20 ms without completing the CPU bursts of their execution cycles. P_1 is scheduled once again at 20 ms and starts an I/O operation at 25 ms. Now P_2 gets two consecutive time slices. However, these time slices are separated by the scheduling overhead because the OS preempts process P_2 at 35 ms and schedules it again, since no other process in the system needs the CPU. P_1's I/O operation completes at 125 ms. P_2 starts an I/O operation at 45 ms, which completes at 105 ms. Thus, the response times are 125 ms and 105 ms, respectively.

3.6.1 Swapping of Programs

Throughput of subrequests is the appropriate measure of performance of a time-sharing operating system. The time-sharing OS of Example 3.2 completes two subrequests in 125 ms, hence its throughput is 8 subrequests per second over the period 0 to 125 ms. However, the throughput would drop after 125 ms if users do not make the next subrequests to these processes immediately. The CPU is

Time	Scheduling list	Scheduled program	Remarks
0	P_1, P_2	P_1	P_1 is preempted at 10 ms
10	P_2, P_1	P_2	P_2 is preempted at 20 ms
20	P_1, P_2	P_1	P_1 starts I/O at 25 ms
25	P_2	P_2	P_2 is preempted at 35 ms
35	P_2	P_2	P_2 starts I/O at 45 ms
45	–	–	CPU is idle

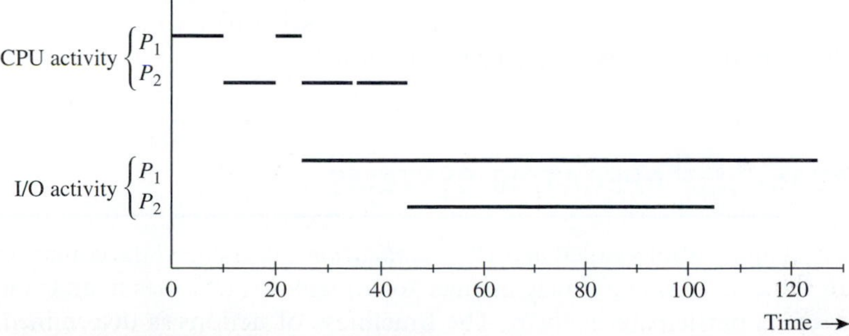

Figure 3.7 Operation of processes P_1 and P_2 in a time-sharing system.

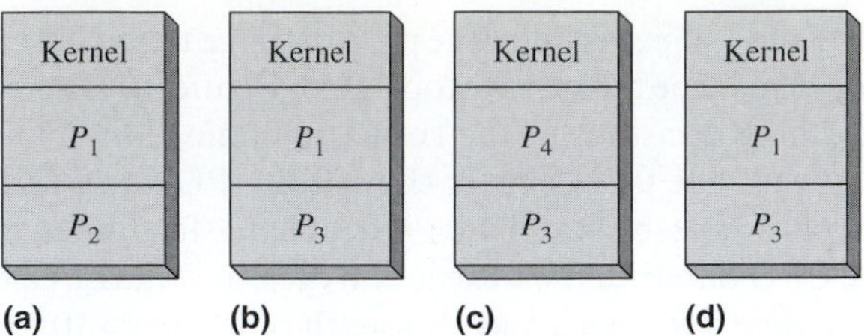

Figure 3.8 Swapping: (a) processes in memory between 0 and 105 ms; (b) P_2 is replaced by P_3 at 105 ms; (c) P_1 is replaced by P_4 at 125 ms; (d) P_1 is swapped in to service the next subrequest made to it.

idle after 45 ms because it has no work to perform. It could have serviced a few more subrequests, had more processes been present in the system. But what if only two processes could fit in the computer's memory? The system throughput would be low and response times of processes other than P_1 and P_2 would suffer. The technique of *swapping* is employed to service a larger number of processes than can fit into the computer's memory. It has the potential to improve both system performance and response times of processes.

Definition 3.6 Swapping The technique of temporarily removing a process from the memory of a computer system.

The kernel performs a *swap-out* operation on a process that is not likely to get scheduled in the near future by copying its instructions and data onto a disk. This operation frees the area of memory that was allocated to the process. The kernel now loads another process in this area of memory through a *swap-in* operation. The kernel would overlap the swap-out and swap-in operations with servicing of other processes on the CPU, and a swapped-in process would itself get scheduled in due course of time. This way, the kernel can service more processes than can fit into the computer's memory. Figure 3.8 illustrates how the kernel employs swapping. Initially, processes P_1 and P_2 exist in memory. These processes are swapped out when they complete handling of the subrequests made to them, and they are replaced by processes P_3 and P_4, respectively. The processes could also have been swapped out when they were preempted. A swapped-out process is swapped back into memory before it is due to be scheduled again, i.e., when it nears the head of the scheduling queue in Figure 3.6.

3.7 REAL-TIME OPERATING SYSTEMS

In a class of applications called *real-time applications*, users need the computer to perform some actions in a timely manner to control the activities in an external system, or to participate in them. The timeliness of actions is determined by the time constraints of the external system. Accordingly, we define a real-time application as follows:

Definition 3.7 Real-Time Application A program that responds to activities in an external system within a maximum time determined by the external system.

If the application takes too long to respond to an activity, a failure can occur in the external system. We use the term *response requirement* of a system to indicate the largest value of response time for which the system can function perfectly; a timely response is one whose response time is not larger than the response requirement of the system.

Consider a system that logs data received from a satellite remote sensor. The satellite sends digitized samples to the earth station at the rate of 500 samples per second. The application process is required to simply store these samples in a file. Since a new sample arrives every two thousandth of a second, i.e., every 2 ms, the computer must respond to every "store the sample" request in less than 2 ms, or the arrival of a new sample would wipe out the previous sample in the computer's memory. This system is a real-time application because a sample must be stored in less than 2 ms to prevent a failure. Its response requirement is 1.99 ms. The *deadline* of an action in a real-time application is the time by which the action should be performed. In the current example, if a new sample is received from the satellite at time t, the deadline for storing it on disk is $t + 1.99$ ms.

Examples of real-time applications can be found in missile guidance, command and control applications like process control and air traffic control, data sampling and data acquisition systems like display systems in automobiles, multimedia systems, and applications like reservation and banking systems that employ large databases. The response requirements of these systems vary from a few microseconds or milliseconds for guidance and control systems to a few seconds for reservation and banking systems.

3.7.1 Hard and Soft Real-Time Systems

To take advantage of the features of real-time systems while achieving maximum cost-effectiveness, two kinds of real-time systems have evolved. A *hard real-time system* is typically *dedicated* to processing real-time applications, and provably meets the response requirement of an application under all conditions. A *soft real-time system* makes the best effort to meet the response requirement of a real-time application but cannot guarantee that it will be able to meet it under all conditions. Typically, it meets the response requirements in some probabilistic manner, say, 98 percent of the time. Guidance and control applications fail if they cannot meet the response requirement, hence they are serviced by hard real-time systems. Applications that aim at providing good quality of service, e.g., multimedia applications and applications like reservation and banking, do not have a notion of failure, so they may be serviced by soft real-time systems—the picture quality provided by a video-on-demand system may deteriorate occasionally, but one can still watch the video!

3.7.2 Features of a Real-Time Operating System

A real-time OS provides the features summarized in Table 3.7. The first three features help an application in meeting the response requirement of a system as follows: A real-time application can be coded such that the OS can execute its parts concurrently, i.e., as separate processes. When these parts are assigned priorities and priority-based scheduling is used, we have a situation analogous to multiprogramming *within* the application—if one part of the application initiates an I/O operation, the OS would schedule another part of the application. Thus, CPU and I/O activities of the application can be overlapped with one another, which helps in reducing the duration of an application, i.e., its running time. *Deadline-aware scheduling* is a technique used in the kernel that schedules processes in such a manner that they may meet their deadlines.

Ability to specify *domain-specific events* and event handling actions enables a real-time application to respond to special conditions in the external system promptly. *Predictability* of policies and overhead of the OS enables an application developer to calculate the worst-case running time of the application and decide whether the response requirement of the external system can be met. The predictability requirement forces a hard real-time OS to shun features such as *virtual memory* whose performance cannot be predicted precisely (see Chapter 12). The OS would also avoid shared use of resources by processes, because it can lead to delays that are hard to predict and unbounded, i.e., arbitrarily large.

A real-time OS employs two techniques to ensure continuity of operation when faults occur—*fault tolerance* and *graceful degradation*. A fault-tolerant computer system uses redundancy of resources to ensure that the system will keep functioning even if a fault occurs; e.g., it may have two disks even though the application actually needs only one disk. Graceful degradation is the ability of a system to fall back to a reduced level of service when a fault occurs and to revert to normal operations when the fault is rectified. The programmer can

Table 3.7 Essential Features of a Real-Time Operating System

Feature	Explanation
Concurrency within an application	A programmer can indicate that some parts of an application should be executed concurrently with one another. The OS considers execution of each such part as a process.
Process priorities	A programmer can assign priorities to processes.
Scheduling	The OS uses priority-based or deadline-aware scheduling.
Domain-specific events, interrupts	A programmer can define special situations within the external system as events, associate interrupts with them, and specify event handling actions for them.
Predictability	Policies and overhead of the OS should be predictable.
Reliability	The OS ensures that an application can continue to function even when faults occur in the computer.

assign high priorities to crucial functions so that they would be performed in a timely manner even when the system operates in a degraded mode.

3.8 DISTRIBUTED OPERATING SYSTEMS

A distributed computer system consists of several individual computer systems connected through a network. Each computer system could be a PC, a multiprocessor system (see Chapter 10), or a *cluster*, which is itself a group of computers that work together in an integrated manner (see Section 16.2). Thus, many resources of a kind, e.g., many memories, CPUs and I/O devices, exist in the distributed system. A distributed operating system exploits the multiplicity of resources and the presence of a network to provide the benefits summarized in Table 3.8. However, the possibility of network faults or faults in individual computer systems complicates functioning of the operating system and necessitates use of special techniques in its design. Users also need to use special techniques to access resources over the network. We discuss these aspects in Section 3.8.1.

Resource sharing has been the traditional motivation for distributed operating systems. A user of a PC or workstation can use resources such as printers over a local area network (LAN), and access specialized hardware or software resources of a geographically distant computer system over a wide area network (WAN).

A distributed operating system provides *reliability* through redundancy of computer systems, resources, and communication paths—if a computer system or a resource used in an application fails, the OS can switch the application to another computer system or resource, and if a path to a resource fails, it can utilize another path to the resource. Reliability can be used to offer high *availability* of resources and services, which is defined as the fraction of time a resource or service is operable. High availability of a data resource, e.g., a file, can be provided by keeping copies of the file in various parts of the system.

Computation speedup implies a reduction in the duration of an application, i.e., in its running time. It is achieved by dispersing processes of an application

Table 3.8 **Benefits of Distributed Operating Systems**

Benefit	Description
Resource sharing	Resources can be utilized across boundaries of individual computer systems.
Reliability	The OS continues to function even when computer systems or resources in it fail.
Computation speedup	Processes of an application can be executed in different computer systems to speed up its completion.
Communication	Users can communicate among themselves irrespective of their locations in the system.

to different computers in the distributed system, so that they can execute at the same time and finish earlier than if they were to be executed in a conventional OS.

Users of a distributed operating system have user ids and passwords that are valid throughout the system. This feature greatly facilitates *communication* between users in two ways. First, communication through user ids automatically invokes the security mechanisms of the OS and thus ensures authenticity of communication. Second, users can be mobile within the distributed system and still be able to communicate with other users through the system.

3.8.1 Special Techniques of Distributed Operating Systems

A distributed system is more than a mere collection of computers connected to a network—functioning of individual computers must be integrated to achieve the benefits summarized in Table 3.8. It is achieved through participation of all computers in the control functions of the operating system. Accordingly, we define a distributed system as follows:

Definition 3.8 Distributed System A system consisting of two or more nodes, where each node is a computer system with its own clock and memory, some networking hardware, and a capability of performing some of the control functions of an OS.

Table 3.9 summarizes three key concepts and techniques used in a distributed OS. *Distributed control* is the opposite of centralized control—it implies that the control functions of the distributed system are performed by several computers in the system in the manner of Definition 3.8, instead of being performed by a single computer. Distributed control is essential for ensuring that failure of a single computer, or a group of computers, does not halt operation of the entire system. *Transparency* of a resource or service implies that a user should be able to access it without having to know which node in the distributed system contains it. This feature enables the OS to change the position of a software resource or service to optimize its use by applications. For example, in a system providing

Table 3.9 Key Concepts and Techniques Used in a Distributed OS

Concept/Technique	Description
Distributed control	A control function is performed through participation of several nodes, possibly *all* nodes, in a distributed system.
Transparency	A resource or service can be accessed without having to know its location in the distributed system.
Remote procedure call (RPC)	A process calls a procedure that is located in a different computer system. The RPC is analogous to a procedure or function call in a programming language, except that the OS passes parameters to the remote procedure over the network and returns its results over the network.

transparency, a distributed file system could move a file to the node that contains a computation using the file, so that the delays involved in accessing the file over the network would be eliminated. The *remote procedure call* (RPC) invokes a procedure that executes in another computer in the distributed system. An application may employ the RPC feature to either perform a part of its computation in another computer, which would contribute to computation speedup, or to access a resource located in that computer.

3.9 MODERN OPERATING SYSTEMS

Users engage in diverse activities in a modern computing environment. Hence a modern operating system cannot use a uniform strategy for all processes; it must use a strategy that is appropriate for each individual process. For example, as mentioned in Section 3.1, a user may open a mail handler, edit a few files, execute some programs, including some programs in the background mode, and watch a video at the same time. Here, operation of some of the programs may be interactive or may involve activities in other nodes of a distributed computer system, whereas rendering of a video is a soft real-time activity. Hence the OS must use round-robin scheduling for program executions, use priority-based scheduling for processes of the video application, and implement remote procedure calls (RPC) to support activities in another node. Thus, a modern OS uses most concepts and techniques that we discussed in connection with the batch processing, multiprogramming, time-sharing, real-time, and distributed operating systems. Table 3.10 shows typical examples of how the earlier concepts are drawn upon.

To handle diverse activities effectively, the OS employs strategies that adapt to the situations encountered during their operation. Some examples of such strategies are:

- The kernel employs priority-based scheduling; however, instead of assigning fixed priorities to all processes as in a multiprogramming system, it assigns fixed high priorities only to processes with real-time constraints, and changes current priorities of other processes to suit their recent behavior—increases the priority of a process if it has been engaged in an interaction or an I/O operation recently, and reduces its priority if it has not been.
- A modern OS typically uses the feature called *virtual memory*, whereby only some of the parts of a process are held in memory at any time and other parts are loaded when needed. The kernel considers the recent behavior of a process to decide how much memory it should allocate to the process—it allocates less memory if the process had used only a few of its parts recently, and allocates more memory if the process had used several of its parts.
- The kernel provides a *plug-and-play* capability whereby I/O devices could be connected to the computer at any time during its operation, and the kernel would select appropriate methods of handling them.

We will see several instances of adaptive strategies in the following chapters.

Table 3.10 Use of Classical OS Concepts in Modern Computing Environments

Concept	Typical example of use
Batch processing	To avoid time-consuming initializations for each use of a resource; e.g., database transactions are batch-processed in the back office and scientific computations are batch-processed in research organizations and clinical laboratories.
Priority-based preemptive scheduling	To provide a favored treatment to high-priority applications, and to achieve efficient use of resources by assigning high priorities to interactive processes and low priorities to noninteractive processes.
Time-slicing	To prevent a process from monopolizing the CPU; it helps in providing good response times.
Swapping	To increase the number of processes that can be serviced simultaneously; it helps in improving system performance and response times of processes.
Creating multiple processes in an application	To reduce the duration of an application; it is most effective when the application contains substantial CPU and I/O activities.
Resource sharing	To share resources such as laser printers or services such as file servers in a LAN environment.

3.10 SUMMARY

A *computing environment* consists of a computer system, its interfaces with other systems, and the services provided by its operating system to its users and their programs. Computing environments evolved with advances in computer technology and computer applications. Each environment desired a different combination of efficient use and user service, so it was serviced by a separate class of operating systems that employed its own concepts and techniques. In this chapter, we discussed the concepts and techniques used in the fundamental classes of operating systems.

The batch processing operating systems focused on automating processing of a collection of programs, which reduced CPU idle times between programs. Development of the direct memory access (DMA) technology enabled the CPU to execute instructions while an I/O operation was in progress. Operating systems exploited this feature to service several programs simultaneously by overlapping an I/O operation within one program with execution of instructions in another program. A multiprogramming operating system assigned high *priorities* to I/O-bound programs and performed *priority-based scheduling* to achieve good system performance.

User convenience became important when the cost of computing hardware declined. Accordingly, the time-sharing operating systems focused on providing fast response to user programs. It was achieved through *round-robin* scheduling with *time-slicing*, which serviced all programs by turn and limited the amount of CPU time a program could use when it was its turn to use the CPU.

A real-time computer application has to satisfy time constraints specified by an external system. *Hard real-time systems* such as mission control systems require their time constraints to be satisfied in a guaranteed manner, whereas *soft real-time systems* such as multimedia systems can tolerate occasional failure to meet their time constraints. Real-time operating systems support concurrency *within* an application program and employ techniques such as *priority-based scheduling* and *deadline-aware scheduling* to help meet the time constraints.

A distributed operating system controls a group of computer systems that are networked; it performs its control functions in several of these computers. It achieves efficient use of resources of all computers by letting programs share them over the network, speeds up execution of a program by running its parts in different computers at the same time, and provides reliability through redundancy of resources and services.

A modern operating system controls a diverse computing environment that has elements of all the classic computing environments, so it has to use different techniques for different applications. It employs an adaptive strategy that selects the most appropriate techniques for each application according to its nature.

TEST YOUR CONCEPTS

3.1 Programs A, B, C, and D have similar structure—each of them consists of a single loop that contains n statements that perform some processing on each element of a single dimensioned array Z. Other features of these programs are as follows:

Program A: $n = 4$ and Z is a huge array.
Program B: $n = 100$ and Z is a huge array.
Program C: $n = 4$ and Z is a small array.
Program D: $n = 100$ and Z is a small array.

These programs are executed in a batch processing system. List these programs in the descending order by cache hit ratio.

3.2 A multiprogramming system is used to execute a collection of programs C. The system has enough memory to accommodate a large number of programs. The programs in C are executed several times, each time with a different degree of multiprogramming, and throughput of the system and CPU efficiency are plotted against the degree of multiprogramming. In each of the following cases, what inference can you draw about the nature of programs in C?

a. Throughput changes only marginally with the degree of multiprogramming
b. Throughput increases almost linearly with the degree of multiprogramming
c. CPU efficiency changes only marginally with the degree of multiprogramming
d. CPU efficiency increases linearly with the degree of multiprogramming

3.3 Classify each of the following statements as true or false:

a. Because of presence of the cache memory, a program requires more CPU time to execute in a multiprogramming or time-sharing system than it would require if it were to be executed in a batch processing system.
b. To achieve high throughput, a multiprogramming OS assigns a higher priority to CPU-bound programs.
c. If a multiprogramming kernel finds that the CPU efficiency is low, it should remove an I/O-bound program from memory.
d. If the time slice in a time-sharing system is too large, processes will complete their operation in the same order in which they were initiated.
e. Two persons using the same time-sharing system at the same time might receive widely different response times.
f. It is incorrect to use masking of interrupts in a real-time operating system.

EXERCISES

3.1 A system is described as overloaded if more work is directed at it than its capacity to perform work. It is considered underloaded if some of its capacity is going to waste. The following policy is proposed to improve the throughput of a batch processing system: Classify jobs into small jobs and long jobs depending on their CPU time requirements. Form separate batches of short and long jobs. Execute a batch of long jobs only if no batches of short jobs exist. Does this policy improve the throughput of a batch processing system that is: (a) underloaded? (b) overloaded?

3.2 The kernel of a multiprogramming system classifies a program as CPU-bound or I/O-bound and assigns an appropriate priority to it. What would be the consequence of a wrong classification of programs for throughput and turnaround times in a multiprogramming system? What would be the effect of a wrong classification on the plot of throughput *versus* degree of multiprogramming of Figure 3.5?

3.3 The CPU of a multiprogramming system is executing a high-priority program when an interrupt signaling completion of an I/O operation occurs. Show all actions and activities in the OS following the interrupt if

a. The I/O operation was started by a lower-priority program

b. The I/O operation was started by a higher-priority program.

Illustrate each case with the help of a timing chart.

3.4 A multiprogramming OS has programs $prog_{iob}$ and $prog_{cb}$ in memory, with $prog_{cb}$ having a higher priority. Draw a timing chart for the system analogous to Figure 3.4, and show that the throughput is less than for the system of Figure 3.4.

3.5 Draw a timing chart for a system containing two CPU-bound programs and two I/O-bound programs when (a) CPU-bound programs have a higher priority, (b) I/O-bound programs have a higher priority.

3.6 A program consists of a single loop that executes 50 times. The loop contains a computation that consumes 50 ms of CPU time, followed by an I/O operation that lasts for 200 ms. The program is executed in a multiprogramming OS with negligible overhead. Prepare a timing chart showing the CPU and I/O activities of the program and compute its elapsed time in the following cases:

a. The program has the highest priority in the system.

b. The program is multiprogrammed with n other programs with identical characteristics and has the lowest priority. Consider cases (i) $n = 3$, (ii) $n = 4$, and (iii) $n = 5$.

3.7 A multiprogramming operating system has a negligible overhead. It services programs that are identical in size. Each program contains a loop that has n iterations, where each iteration contains computations that consume t_c ms of CPU time, followed by I/O operations that require t_{io} ms. The programs are of two classes; values of n, t_c, and t_{io} for these two classes are:

Class	n	t_c	t_{io}
A	5	15	100
B	6	200	80

The system has sufficient memory to accommodate only two programs. Ten programs arrive in the system at time 0, five each of classes A and B. Draw a timing chart showing operation of programs in the system until two programs complete their operation. Find their turnaround times.

3.8 A program is said to "make progress" if either the CPU is executing its instructions or its I/O operation is in progress. The *progress coefficient* of a program is the fraction of its lifetime in the system during which it makes progress. Compute progress coefficients of the programs in Exercise 3.6(b).

3.9 Comment on the validity of the following statement: "A CPU-bound program always has a very low progress coefficient in a multiprogramming system."

3.10 A multiprogramming system uses a degree of multiprogramming (m) $\gg$ 1. It is proposed to double the throughput of the system by augmentation/replacement of its hardware components. Would any of the following three proposals achieve the desired result?

time, followed by an I/O operation that lasts for t_{io} seconds, and has to produce a response within t_d seconds. What is the largest value of δ for which the time-sharing system can satisfy the response requirements of the real time application?

3.21 An application program is being developed for a microprocessor-based controller for an automobile. The application is required to perform the following functions:

i. Monitor and display the speed of the automobile

ii. Monitor the fuel level and raise an alarm, if necessary

iii. Display the fuel efficiency, i.e., miles/gallon at current speed

iv. Monitor the engine condition and raise an alarm if an unusual condition arises

v. Periodically record some auxiliary information like speed and fuel level (i.e., implement a "black box" as in an airliner.)

Answer the following questions concerning the application:

a. Is this a real-time application? Justify your answer.

b. Would creation of multiple processes reduce the response time of the application? If so, what should be the processes in it? What should be their priorities?

c. Is it necessary to define any domain-specific events and interrupts? If so, specify their priorities.

3.22 If two independent events e_1 and e_2 have the probabilities of occurrence pr_1 and pr_2, where both pr_1 and $pr_2 < 1$, the probability that both events occur at the same time is $pr_1 \times pr_2$. A distributed system contains two disks. The probability that both disks fail is required to be <0.0001. What should be the probability of failure of a disk?

3.23 To obtain computation speedup in a distributed system, an application is coded as three parts to be executed on three computer systems under control of a distributed operating system. However, the speedup obtained is <3. List all possible reasons for the poor speedup.

BIBLIOGRAPHY

Literature on batch processing, multiprogramming, and time-sharing systems dates back to the 1970s. Zhao (1989) and Liu (2000) are good sources for real-time systems. Most operating systems texts cover the classes of operating systems described in this chapter; some recent OS texts are Tanenbaum (2001), Bic and Shaw (2003), Nutt (2004), Silberschatz et al. (2005), and Stallings (2005). Several comprehensive bibliographies on operating systems are available on the Internet.

Tanenbaum and Renesse (1985) is a good starting point for a study of distributed operating systems. It discusses the major design issues in distributed operating systems and contains a survey of some distributed operating systems. Tanenbaum (1995) discusses some well-known distributed operating systems in detail. Coulouris et al. (2001) discusses the concepts and design of distributed systems.

Several books describe specific modern operating systems. Bach (1986) and Vahalia (1996) describe the Unix operating system. Beck et al. (2002), Bovet and Cesati (2005), and Love (2005) discuss the Linux operating system, while Stevens and Rago (2005) describes Unix, Linux, and BSD operating systems. Mauro and McDougall (2006) discusses Solaris. Russinovich and Solomon (2005) describes the Windows operating systems.

1. Bach, M. J. (1986): *The Design of the Unix Operating System*, Prentice Hall, Englewood Cliffs, N.J.
2. Beck, M., H. Bohme, M. Dziadzka, U. Kunitz, R. Magnus, C. Schroter, and D. Verworner (2002): *Linux Kernel Programming*, 3rd ed., Pearson Education, New York.
3. Bic, L., and A. C. Shaw (2003): *Operating Systems Principles*, Prentice Hall, Englewood Cliffs, N.J.
4. Bovet, D. P., and M. Cesati (2005): *Understanding the Linux Kernel*, 3rd ed., O'Reilly, Sebastopol.

a. Replace the CPU by a CPU with twice the speed.
b. Expand the memory to twice its present size.
c. Replace the CPU by a CPU with twice the speed and expand the memory to twice its present size.

3.11 Programs being serviced in a multiprogramming system are named $P_1, \ldots, P_m$, where m is the degree of multiprogramming, such that priority of program P_i > priority of program P_{i+1}. All programs are cyclic in nature, with each cycle containing a burst of CPU activity and a burst of I/O activity. Let b_{cpu}^i and b_{io}^i be the CPU and I/O bursts of program P_i. Comment on the validity of each of the following statements:
a. CPU idling occurs if $b_{io}^h > \Sigma_{j \neq h}(b_{cpu}^j)$, where P_h is the highest-priority program.
b. Program P_m is guaranteed to receive CPU time if $b_{io}^i < (b_{cpu}^{i+1} + b_{io}^{i+1})$ and $b_{io}^i > \Sigma_{j=i+1 \ldots m}(b_{cpu}^j)$ for all values of $i = 1, \ldots, m - 1$,

3.12 A program is said to *starve* if it does not receive any CPU time. Which of the following conditions implies starvation of the lowest-priority program in a multiprogramming system? (The notation is the same as in Exercise 3.11.)
a. For some program P_i, $b_{io}^i < \Sigma_{j=i+1 \ldots m}(b_{cpu}^j)$.
b. For some program P_i, $b_{io}^i < \Sigma_{j=i+1 \ldots m}(b_{cpu}^j)$ and $b_{cpu}^i > b_{io}^j$ for all $j > i$.

3.13 A time-sharing system contains n identical processes, each executing a loop that contains a computation requiring t_p CPU seconds and an I/O operation requiring t_{io} seconds. Draw a graph depicting variation of response time with values of the time slice δ. (*Hint:* Consider cases for $t_p < \delta$, $\delta < t_p < 2 \times \delta$, and $t_p > 2 \times \delta$.)

3.14 Comment on the validity of the following statement: "Operation of a time-sharing system is identical with operation of a multiprogramming system executing the same programs if δ exceeds the CPU burst of every program."

3.15 Answer the following with full justifications:
a. Does swapping improve or degrade the efficiency of system utilization?
b. Can swapping be used in a multiprogramming system?

3.16 A computer is operated under a time-sh OS. It is proposed to add a second CP the computer to improve its throughput. U what conditions would addition of the ond CPU improve throughput only if me ory is increased? Under what conditions wou it improve throughput even if memory is n increased?

3.17 A time-sharing system uses swapping as the fundamental memory management technique. It uses the following lists to govern its actions: a scheduling list, a swapped-out list containing processes that are swapped out, a being-swapped-out list containing processes to be swapped out, and a being-swapped-in list containing processes to be swapped in. Explain when and why the time-sharing kernel should put processes in the being-swapped-out and being-swapped-in lists.

3.18 A time-sharing system uses a time slice of 100 ms. Each process has a cyclic behavior pattern. In each cycle, it requires an average of 50 ms of CPU time to compute the result of a subrequest and an average of 150 ms to print it on the user's screen. A process receives a new subrequest 1 second after it has finished printing results of the previous subrequest. The operating system can accommodate 10 processes in memory at any time; however, it has enough I/O devices for 25 processes. The swap-in and swap-out times of each process are t_s ms each. Calculate the average throughput of the system over a 10-second period in each of the following cases:
a. The operating system contains 10 processes.
b. The operating system contains 20 processes and t_s is 750 ms.
c. The operating system contains 20 processes and t_s is 250 ms.

3.19 A real-time application requires a response time of 2 seconds. Discuss the feasibility of using a time-sharing system for the real-time application if the average response time in the time-sharing system is (a) 20 seconds, (b) 2 seconds, or (c) 0.2 seconds.

3.20 A time-sharing system services n processes. It uses a time slice of δ CPU seconds, and requires t_s CPU seconds to switch between processes. A real-time application requires t_c seconds of CPU

5. Coulouris, G., J. Dollimore, and T. Kindberg (2001): *Distributed Systems—Concepts and Design,* 3rd ed., Addison-Wesley, New York.
6. Crowley, C. (1997): *Operating Systems—A Design Oriented Approach*, McGraw-Hill, New York.
7. Denning, P. J. (1971): "Third generation operating systems," *Computing Surveys*, **4** (1), 175–216.
8. Fortier, P. J. (1988): *Design of Distributed Operating Systems*, McGraw-Hill, New York.
9. Goscinski, A. (1991): *Distributed Operating Systems—The Logical Design*, Addison-Wesley, New York.
10. Liu, J. W. S. (2000): *Real-Time systems*, Pearson Education, New York.
11. Love, R. (2005): *Linux Kernel Development,* 2nd ed., Novell Press.
12. Mauro, J., and R. McDougall (2006): *Solaris Internals,* 2nd ed., Prentice Hall.
13. Nutt, G. (2004): *Operating Systems—A Modern Perspective,* 3rd ed., Addison-Wesley, Reading, Mass.
14. Russinovich, M. E., and D. A. Solomon (2005): *Microsoft Windows Internals,* 4th ed., Microsoft Press, Redmond, Wash.
15. Silberschatz, A., P. B. Galvin, and G. Gagne (2005): *Operating System Principles,* 7th ed., John Wiley, New York.
16. Singhal, M., and N. G. Shivaratri (1994): *Advanced Concepts in Operating Systems*, McGraw-Hill, New York.
17. Sinha, P. K. (1997): *Distributed Operating Systems*, IEEE Press, New York.
18. Smith, A. J. (1980): "Multiprogramming and memory contention," *Software—Practice and Experience*, **10** (7), 531–552.
19. Stallings, W. (2005): *Operating Systems—Internals and Design Principles,* 5th ed., Pearson Education, New York.
20. Stevens, W. R., and S. A. Rago (2005): *Advanced Programming in the Unix Environment,* 2nd ed., Addison-Wesley Professional.
21. Tanenbaum, A. S. (2003): *Computer Networks,* 4th ed., Prentice Hall, Englewood Cliffs, N.J.
22. Tanenbaum, A. S. (2001): *Modern Operating Systems,* 2nd ed., Prentice Hall, Englewood Cliffs, N.J.
23. Tanenbaum, A. S., and R. Van Renesse (1985): "Distributed Operating Systems," *Computing Surveys*, **17** (1), 419–470.
24. Tanenbaum, A. S. (1995): *Distributed Operating Systems*, Prentice Hall, Englewood Cliffs, N.J.
25. Vahalia, U. (1996): *Unix Internals: The New Frontiers*, Prentice Hall, Englewood Cliffs, N.J.
26. Wirth, N. (1969): "On multiprogramming, machine coding, and computer organization," *Communications of the ACM*, **12** (9), 489–491.
27. Zhao, W. (1989): "Special issue on real-time operating systems," *Operating System Review*, **23**, 7.

4

Chapter

Structure of Operating Systems

During the lifetime of an operating system, we can expect several changes to take place in computer systems and computing environments. To adapt an operating system to these changes, it should be easy to implement the OS on a new computer system, and to add new functionalities to it. These requirements are called *portability* and *extensibility* of an operating system, respectively.

Early operating systems were tightly integrated with the architecture of a specific computer system. This feature affected their portability. Modern operating systems implement the core of an operating system in the form of a *kernel* or a *microkernel*, and build the rest of the operating system by using the services offered by the core. This structure restricts architecture dependencies to the core of the operating system, hence portability of an operating system is determined by the properties of its kernel or microkernel. Extensibility of an OS is determined by the nature of services offered by the core.

The structure of an operating system concerns the nature of the OS core and other parts of the operating system, and their interactions with one another. We describe different philosophies concerning the structure of an operating system and discuss their influence on portability and extensibility of operating systems.

4.1 OPERATION OF AN OS

When a computer is switched on, the *boot procedure* analyzes its configuration—CPU type, memory size, I/O devices, and details of other hardware connected to the computer (see Section 1.3). It then loads a part of the OS in memory, initializes its data structures with this information, and hands over control of the computer system to it.

Figure 4.1 is a schematic diagram of OS operation (see Section 2.3). An event like I/O completion or end of a time slice causes an interrupt. When a process makes a *system call*, e.g., to request resources or start an I/O operation, it too leads to an interrupt called a *software interrupt*. The interrupt

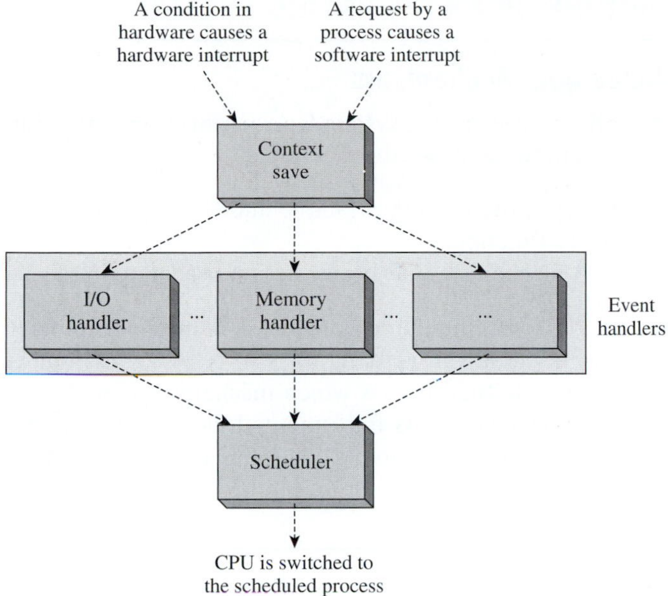

Figure 4.1 Overview of OS operation.

Table 4.1 Functions of an OS

Function	Description
Process management	Initiation and termination of processes, scheduling
Memory management	Allocation and deallocation of memory, swapping, virtual memory management
I/O management	I/O interrupt servicing, initiation of I/O operations, optimization of I/O device performance
File management	Creation, storage and access of files
Security and protection	Preventing interference with processes and resources
Network management	Sending and receiving of data over the network

action switches the CPU to an interrupt servicing routine. The interrupt servicing routine performs a *context save* action to save information about the interrupted program and activates an *event handler*, which takes appropriate actions to handle the event. The scheduler then selects a process and switches the CPU to it. CPU switching occurs twice during the processing of an event—first to the kernel to perform event handling and then to the process selected by the scheduler.

The functions of an OS are thus implemented by event handlers when they are activated by interrupt servicing routines. Table 4.1 summarizes these functions, which primarily concern management of processes and resources, and prevention of interference with them.

4.2 STRUCTURE OF AN OPERATING SYSTEM

4.2.1 Policies and Mechanisms

In determining how an operating system is to perform one of its functions, the OS designer needs to think at two distinct levels:

- *Policy:* A policy is the guiding principle under which the operating system will perform the function.
- *Mechanism:* A mechanism is a specific action needed to implement a policy.

A policy decides *what* should be done, while a mechanism determines *how* something should be done and actually does it. A policy is implemented as a decision-making module that decides which mechanism modules to call under what conditions. A mechanism is implemented as a module that performs a specific action. The following example identifies policies and mechanisms in round-robin scheduling.

Example 4.1 Policies and Mechanisms in Round-Robin Scheduling

In scheduling, we would consider the round-robin technique (Section 3.6) to be a *policy*. The following mechanisms would be needed to implement the round-robin scheduling policy:

Maintain a queue of ready processes
Switch the CPU to execution of the selected process (this action is called *dispatching*).

The priority-based scheduling policy, which is used in multiprogramming systems (see Section 3.5.1), would also require a mechanism for maintaining information about ready processes; however, it would be different from the mechanism used in round-robin scheduling because it would organize information according to process priority. The dispatching mechanism, however, would be common to all scheduling policies.

Apart from mechanisms for implementing specific process or resource management policies, the OS also has mechanisms for performing housekeeping actions. The context save action mentioned in Section 4.1 is implemented as a mechanism.

4.2.2 Portability and Extensibility of Operating Systems

The design and implementation of operating systems involves huge financial investments. To protect these investments, an operating system design should have a lifetime of more than a decade. Since several changes will take place in computer architecture, I/O device technology, and application environments during this time, it should be possible to adapt an OS to these changes. Two features are important in this context—portability and extensibility.

Porting is the act of adapting software for use in a new computer system. *Portability* refers to the ease with which a software program can be ported—it is inversely proportional to the porting effort. *Extensibility* refers to the ease with which new functionalities can be added to a software system.

Porting of an OS implies changing parts of its code that are architecture-dependent so that the OS can work with new hardware. Some examples of architecture-dependent data and instructions in an OS are:

- An interrupt vector contains information that should be loaded in various fields of the PSW to switch the CPU to an interrupt servicing routine (see Section 2.2.5). This information is architecture-specific.
- Information concerning memory protection and information to be provided to the memory management unit (MMU) is architecture-specific (see Sections 2.2.2 and 2.2.3).
- I/O instructions used to perform an I/O operation are architecture-specific.

The architecture-dependent part of an operating system's code is typically associated with mechanisms rather than with policies. An OS would have high portability if its architecture-dependent code is small in size, and its complete code is structured such that the porting effort is determined by the size of the architecture-dependent code, rather than by the size of its complete code. Hence the issue of OS portability is addressed by separating the architecture-dependent and architecture-independent parts of an OS and providing well-defined interfaces between the two parts.

Extensibility of an OS is needed for two purposes: for incorporating new hardware in a computer system—typically new I/O devices or network adapters—and for providing new functionalities in response to new user expectations. Early operating systems did not provide either kind of extensibility. Hence even addition of a new I/O device required modifications to the OS. Later operating systems solved this problem by adding a functionality to the boot procedure. It would check for hardware that was not present when the OS was last booted, and either prompt the user to select appropriate software to handle the new hardware, typically a set of routines called a *device driver* that handled the new device, or itself select such software. The new software was then loaded and integrated with the kernel so that it would be invoked and used appropriately. Modern operating systems go a step further by providing a *plug-and-play* capability, whereby new hardware can be added even while an OS is in operation. The OS handles the interrupt caused by addition of new hardware, selects the appropriate software, and integrates it with the kernel.

Lack of extensibility leads to difficulties in adapting an OS to new user expectations. Several examples of such difficulties can be found in the history of operating systems. In 1980s and 1990s, PC users desired a new feature for setting up several sessions with an operating system at the same time. Several well-known operating systems of that time, e.g., MS-DOS, had difficulties providing it because they lacked sufficient extensibility. A similar difficulty was experienced by the Unix operating system while supporting multiprocessor computer systems. We discuss provisions for extensibility in Section 4.7.

4.3 OPERATING SYSTEMS WITH MONOLITHIC STRUCTURE

An OS is a complex software that has a large number of functionalities and may contain millions of instructions. It is designed to consist of a set of software modules, where each module has a well-defined *interface* that must be used to access any of its functions or data. Such a design has the property that a module cannot "see" inner details of functioning of other modules. This property simplifies design, coding and testing of an OS.

Early operating systems had a *monolithic* structure, whereby the OS formed a single software layer between the user and the bare machine, i.e., the computer system's hardware (see Figure 4.2). The user interface was provided by a command interpreter. The command interpreter organized creation of user processes. Both the command interpreter and user processes invoked OS functionalities and services through system calls.

Two kinds of problems with the monolithic structure were realized over a period of time. The sole OS layer had an interface with the bare machine. Hence architecture-dependent code was spread throughout the OS, and so there was poor portability. It also made testing and debugging difficult, leading to high costs of maintenance and enhancement. These problems led to the search for alternative ways to structure an OS. In the following sections we discuss three methods of structuring an OS that have been implemented as solutions to these problems.

- *Layered structure:* The layered structure attacks the complexity and cost of developing and maintaining an OS by structuring it into a number of layers (see Section 4.4). The THE multiprogramming system of the 1960s is a well-known example of a layered OS.
- *Kernel-based structure:* The kernel-based structure confines architecture dependence to a small section of the OS code that constitutes the kernel (see Section 4.6), so that portability is increased. The Unix OS has a kernel-based structure.

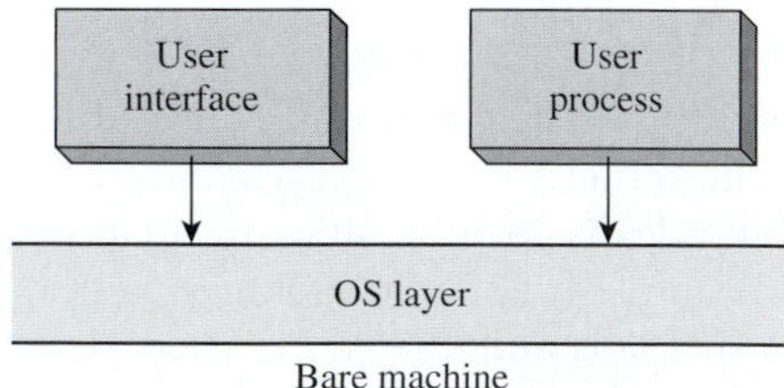

Figure 4.2 Monolithic OS.

- *Microkernel-based OS structure:* The microkernel provides a minimal set of facilities and services for implementing an OS. Its use provides portability. It also provides extensibility because changes can be made to the OS without requiring changes in the microkernel (see Section 4.7).

4.4 LAYERED DESIGN OF OPERATING SYSTEMS

The monolithic OS structure suffered from the problem that all OS components had to be able to work with the bare machine. This feature increased the cost and effort in developing an OS because of the large *semantic gap* between the operating system and the bare machine.

Definition 4.1 Semantic Gap The mismatch between the nature of operations needed in the application and the nature of operations provided in the machine.

The semantic gap can be illustrated as follows: A machine instruction implements a machine-level primitive operation like arithmetic or logical manipulation of operands. An OS module may contain an algorithm, say, that uses OS-level primitive operations like saving the context of a process and initiating an I/O operation. These operations are more complex than the machine-level primitive operations. This difference leads to a large semantic gap, which has to be bridged through programming. Each operation desired by the OS now becomes a *sequence* of instructions, possibly a routine (see Figure 4.3). It leads to high programming costs.

The semantic gap between an OS and the machine on which it operates can be reduced by either using a more capable machine—a machine that provides instructions to perform some (or all) operations that operating systems have to perform—or by *simulating* a more capable machine in the software. The former approach is expensive. In the latter approach, however, the *simulator*, which is a

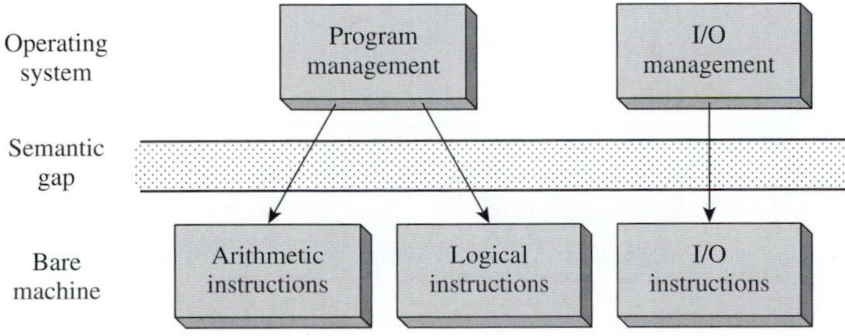

Figure 4.3 Semantic gap.

program, executes on the bare machine and mimics a more powerful machine that has many features desired by the OS. This new "machine" is called an *extended machine*, and its simulator is called the extended machine software. Now the OS interfaces with the extended machine rather than with the bare machine; the extended machine software forms a layer between the OS and the bare machine.

The basic discipline in designing a layered OS is that the routines of one layer must use only the facilities of the layer directly below it—that is, no layer in the structure can be bypassed. Further, access to routines of a lower layer must take place strictly through the interface between layers. Thus, a routine situated in one layer does not "know" addresses of data structures or instructions in the lower layer—it only knows how to invoke a routine of the lower layer. This property, which we will call *information hiding*, prevents misuse or corruption of one layer's data by routines situated in other layers of the OS. During debugging, localization of errors becomes easy since the cause of an error in a layer, e.g., an incorrect value in its data element, must lie within that layer itself. Information hiding also implies that an OS layer may be modified without affecting other layers. These features simplify testing and debugging of an OS.

Figure 4.4 illustrates a two-layered OS. The extended machine provides operations like context save, dispatching, swapping, and I/O initiation. The operating system layer is located on top of the extended machine layer. This arrangement considerably simplifies the coding and testing of OS modules by separating the algorithm of a function from the implementation of its primitive operations. It is now easier to test, debug, and modify an OS module than in a monolithic OS. We say that the lower layer provides an *abstraction* that is the extended machine. We call the operating system layer the *top layer* of the OS.

The layered structures of operating systems have been evolved in various ways—using different abstractions and a different number of layers. Example 4.2 describes the THE multiprogramming OS, which uses a multilayered structure and provides a process as an abstraction in the lowest layer.

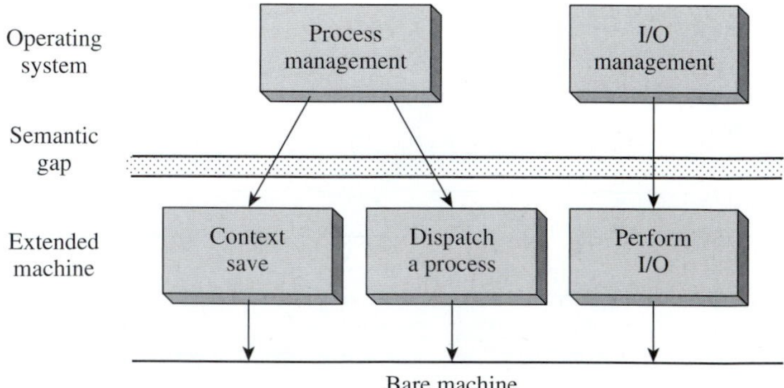

Figure 4.4 Layered OS design.

Structure of the THE Multiprogramming System

Example 4.2

The THE multiprogramming system was developed at Technische Hogeschool Eindhoven in the Netherlands by Dijkstra and others using a layered design. Table 4.2 shows the hierarchy of layers in the THE system.

Layer 0 of the system handles processor allocation to implement multiprogramming. This function involves keeping track of process states and switching between processes, using priority-based scheduling. Layers above layer 0 need not concern themselves with these issues. In fact, they can be oblivious to the presence of multiple processes in the system.

Layer 1 performs memory management. It implements a memory hierarchy consisting of the memory and a drum, which is a secondary storage device (see Section 2.2.3). Details of transfer between the memory and the drum need not concern the rest of the OS.

Layer 2 implements communication between a process and the operator's console by allocating a virtual console to each process. Layer 3 performs I/O management. Intricacies of I/O programming (see Section 14.4) are thus hidden from layer 4, which is occupied by user processes.

The layered approach to OS design suffers from three problems. The operation of a system may be slowed down by the layered structure. Recall that each layer can interact only with adjoining layers. It implies that a request for OS service made by a user process must move down from the highest numbered layer to the lowest numbered layer before the required action is performed by the bare machine. This feature leads to high overhead.

The second problem concerns difficulties in developing a layered design. Since a layer can access only the immediately lower layer, all features and facilities needed by it must be available in lower layers. This requirement poses a problem in the ordering of layers that require each other's services. This problem is often solved by splitting a layer into two and putting other layers between the two halves. For example, a designer may wish to put process handling functions in one layer and memory management in the next higher layer. However, memory allocation is required as a part of process creation. To overcome this difficulty, process handling can be split into two layers. One layer would perform process management functions like context save, switching, scheduling, and process synchronization.

Table 4.2 Layers in the THE Multiprogramming System

Layer	Description
Layer 0	Processor allocation and multiprogramming
Layer 1	Memory and drum management
Layer 2	Operator–process communication
Layer 3	I/O management
Layer 4	User processes

This layer would continue to be lower than the memory management layer. The other layer would perform process creation. It would be located above the memory management layer.

The third problem concerns stratification of OS functionalities. Stratification occurs because each functionality has to be divided into parts that fit into different layers of a layered OS. These parts must use interfaces between the various layers to communicate with one another. For example, consider a certain functionality F of the OS that consists of two modules, F_{l_1} and F_{l_2}, belonging to layers l_1 and l_2 respectively. If layer l_2 can be entered only through an interrupt, F_{l_1} must cause an interrupt to communicate with F_{l_2}. This fact can lead to a complex design and a loss of execution efficiency. Stratification also leads to poor extensibility because addition of a new functionality requires new code to be added in many layers of the OS, which, in turn, may require changes in the layer interfaces.

It may be noted that the design of a multilayered OS does not focus on separating architecture-dependent parts of OS code; for example, four out of the five layers of the THE multiprogramming system described in Table 4.2 contain architecture-dependent parts. Thus, a layered structure does not guarantee high portability.

4.5 VIRTUAL MACHINE OPERATING SYSTEMS

Different classes of users need different kinds of user service. Hence running a single OS on a computer system can disappoint many users. Operating the computer under different OSs during different periods is not a satisfactory solution because it would make accessible services offered under only one of the operating systems at any time. This problem is solved by using a *virtual machine operating system* (VM OS) to control the computer system. The VM OS creates several *virtual machines*. Each virtual machine is allocated to one user, who can use any OS of his own choice on the virtual machine and run his programs under this OS. This way users of the computer system can use different operating systems at the same time. We call each of these operating systems a *guest OS* and call the virtual machine OS the *host OS*. The computer used by the VM OS is called the *host machine*.

A *virtual machine* is a virtual resource (see Section 1.3.2). Let us consider a virtual machine that has the same architecture as the host machine; i.e., it has a virtual CPU capable of executing the same instructions, and similar memory and I/O devices. It may, however, differ from the host machine in terms of some elements of its configuration like memory size and I/O devices. Because of the identical architectures of the virtual and host machines, no semantic gap exists between them, so operation of a virtual machine does not introduce any performance loss (contrast this with the use of the extended machine layer described in Section 4.4); software intervention is also not needed to run a guest OS on a virtual machine.

The VM OS achieves concurrent operation of guest operating systems through an action that resembles process scheduling—it selects a virtual machine and arranges to let the guest OS running on it execute its instructions on the CPU. The guest OS in operation enjoys complete control over the host machine's environment, including interrupt servicing. The absence of a software layer between the host machine and guest OS ensures efficient use of the host machine. A guest OS remains in control of the host machine until the VM OS decides to switch to another virtual machine, which typically happens in response to an interrupt. The VM OS can employ the timer to implement time-slicing and round-robin scheduling of guest OSs.

A somewhat complex arrangement is needed to handle interrupts that arise when a guest OS is in operation. Some of the interrupts would arise in its own domain, e.g., an I/O interrupt from a device included in its own virtual machine, while others would arise in the domains of other guest OSs. The VM OS can arrange to get control when an interrupt occurs, find the guest OS whose domain the interrupt belongs to, and "schedule" that guest OS to handle it. However, this arrangement incurs high overhead because of two context switch operations—the first context switch passes control to the VM OS, and the second passes control to the correct guest OS. Hence the VM OS may use an arrangement in which the guest OS in operation would be invoked directly by interrupts arising in its own domain. It is implemented as follows: While passing control to a guest operating system, the VM OS replaces its own interrupt vectors (see Section 2.2.5) by those defined in the guest OS. This action ensures that an interrupt would switch the CPU to an interrupt servicing routine of the guest OS. If the guest OS finds that the interrupt did not occur in its own domain, it passes control to the VM OS by making a special system call "invoke VM OS." The VM OS now arranges to pass the interrupt to the appropriate guest OS. When a large number of virtual machines exists, interrupt processing can cause excessive shuffling between virtual machines, hence the VM OS may not immediately activate the guest OS in whose domain an interrupt occurred—it may simply note occurrence of interrupts that occurred in the domain of a guest OS and provide this information to the guest OS the next time it is "scheduled."

Example 4.3 describes how IBM VM/370—a well-known VM OS of the 1970s—operates.

Example 4.3

Structure of VM/370

Figure 4.5 shows three of the guest OSs supported by VM/370. The Conversational Monitor System (CMS) is a single-user operating system, while the OS/370 and DOS/370 are multiprogramming operating systems. A user process is unaware of the presence of the VM/370—it sees only the guest OS that it uses. To prevent interference between the guest OSs, the CPU is put in the user mode while executing a guest OS. Initiation of I/O operations, which involves use of privileged instructions, is handled as follows: When the kernel of a guest OS executes an I/O instruction, it appears as an attempt to execute a privileged instruction while the CPU is in the user mode, so it causes a program interrupt. The interrupt is directed to the VM/370 rather than to the guest OS. The VM/370 now initiates the I/O operation by executing the I/O instruction that had caused the interrupt.

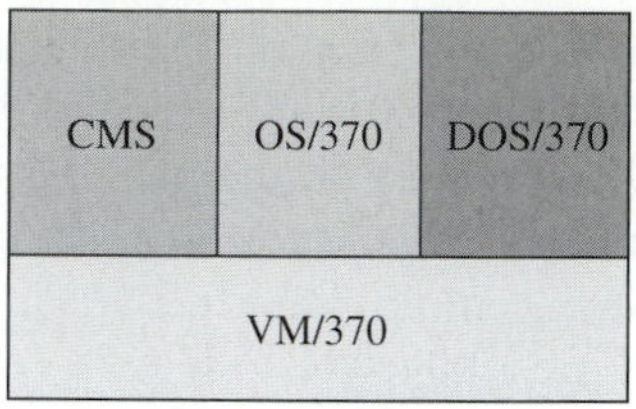

Figure 4.5 Virtual machine operating system VM/370.

Distinction between kernel and user modes of the CPU causes some difficulties in the use of a VM OS. The VM OS must protect itself from guest OSs, so it must run guest OSs with the CPU in the user mode. However, this way both a guest OS and user processes under it run in the user mode, which makes the guest OS vulnerable to corruption by a user process. The Intel 80x86 family of computers has a feature that provides a way out of this difficulty. The 80x86 computers support four execution modes of the CPU. Hence the host OS can run with the CPU in the kernel mode, a guest OS can execute processes running under it with the CPU in the user mode but can itself run with the CPU in one of the intermediate modes.

Virtualization is the process of mapping the interfaces and resources of a virtual machine into the interfaces and resources of the host machine. Full virtualization would imply that the host machine and a virtual machine have identical capabilities, hence an OS can operate identically while running on a bare machine and on a virtual machine supported by a VM OS. However, full virtualization may weaken security. In Example 4.3, we saw how VM/370 lets a guest OS execute a privileged instruction, but its execution causes an interrupt and VM/370 itself executes the instruction on behalf of the guest OS. This arrangement is insecure because VM/370 cannot determine whether use of the privileged instruction is legitimate—it would be legitimate if a guest OS used it, but illegitimate if a user process used it.

Modern virtual machine environments employ the technique of *paravirtualization* to overcome the problems faced in full virtualization. Paravirtualization replaces a nonvirtualizable instruction, i.e., an instruction that cannot be made available in a VM, by easily virtualized instructions. For example, the security issue in VM/370 could be resolved through paravirtualization as follows: The privileged instructions would not be included in a virtual machine. Instead, the virtual machine would provide a special instruction for use by a guest OS that wished to execute a privileged instruction. The special instruction would cause a software interrupt and pass information about the privileged instruction the guest OS wished to execute to the VM OS, and the VM OS would execute the privileged instruction on behalf of the guest OS. The host OS, guest OS, and user processes would use different execution modes of the CPU so that the host OS would know whether the special instruction in the virtual machine was used by a guest OS or by a user process—the latter usage would be considered illegal. Paravirtualization has also been used to enhance performance of a host OS.

The kernel of an OS typically puts the CPU into an *idle loop* when none of the user processes in the OS wishes to use the CPU. However, CPU time of the host machine would be wasted when a guest OS enters into an idle loop. Hence paravirtualization could be employed to provide a special instruction in the virtual machine to notify this condition to the host OS, so that the host OS could take away the CPU from the guest OS for a specified period of time.

Use of paravirtualization implies that a virtual machine would differ from the host machine, so the code of a guest OS would have to be modified to avoid use of nonvirtualizable instructions. It can be done by *porting* a guest OS to operate under the VM OS. Alternatively, it can be achieved by employing the technique of *dynamic binary translation* for the kernel of a guest OS, which replaces a portion of kernel code that contains nonvirtualizable instructions by code that does not contain such instructions. To reduce the overhead of this arrangement, the modified kernel code is cached so that binary translation does not have to be repeated often.

Virtual machines are employed for diverse purposes:

- To use an existing server for a new application that requires use of a different operating system. This is called *workload consolidation*; it reduces the hardware and operational cost of computing by reducing the number of servers needed in an organization.
- To provide security and reliability for applications that use the same host and the same OS. This benefit arises from the fact that virtual machines of different applications cannot access each other's resources.
- To test a modified OS (or a new version of application code) on a server concurrently with production runs of that OS.
- To provide disaster management capabilities by transferring a virtual machine from a server that has to shut down because of an emergency to another server available on the network.

A VM OS is large, complex and expensive. To make the benefits of virtual machines available widely at a lower cost, virtual machines are also used without a VM OS. Two such arrangements are described in the following.

Virtual Machine Monitors (VMMs) A VMM, also called a *hypervisor*, is a software layer that operates on top of a host OS. It virtualizes the resources of the host computer and supports concurrent operation of many virtual machines. When a guest OS is run in each virtual machine provided by a VMM, the host OS and the VMM together provide a capability that is equivalent of a VM OS. VMware and XEN are two VMMs that aim at implementing hundreds of guest OSs on a host computer while ensuring that a guest OS suffers only a marginal performance degradation when compared to its implementation on a bare machine.

Programming Language Virtual Machines Programming languages have used virtual machines to obtain some of the benefits discussed earlier. In the 1970s, the

Pascal programming language employed a virtual machine to provide portability. The virtual machine had instructions called *P-code instructions* that were well-suited to execution of Pascal programs. It was implemented in the software in the form of an interpreter for P-code instructions. A compiler converted a Pascal program into a sequence of P-code instructions, and these could be executed on any computer that had a P-code interpreter. The virtual machine had a small number of instructions, so the interpreter was compact and easily portable. This feature facilitated widespread use of Pascal in the 1970s. However, use of the VM incurred a substantial performance penalty due to the semantic gap between P-code instructions and instructions in the host computer.

The Java programming language employs a virtual machine to provide security and reliability. A Java program consists of objects, whose structure and behavior is specified in classes. Each class is compiled into a *bytecode* form, where the bytecode is a sequence of instructions for the Java virtual machine (JVM). During execution of an application coded in Java, the class loader is activated whenever an object of a new class is encountered. The loader fetches the bytecode form of the class, either from a library or from the Internet, and verifies that the class conforms to the security and reliability standards—that it has a valid *digital signature* (see Section 21.3.2), and does not use features such as pointer arithmetic. The application would be aborted if a class file fails any of these checks. If several Java applications run on the same host, each of them would execute in its own virtual machine, hence their operation cannot cause mutual interference. The performance penalty implicit in use of the virtual machine can be offset by implementing the JVM in the hardware.

4.6 KERNEL-BASED OPERATING SYSTEMS

Figure 4.6 is an abstract view of a kernel-based OS. The *kernel* is the core of the OS; it provides a set of functions and services to support various OS functionalities. The rest of the OS is organized as a set of *nonkernel routines*, which implement operations on processes and resources that are of interest to users, and a *user*

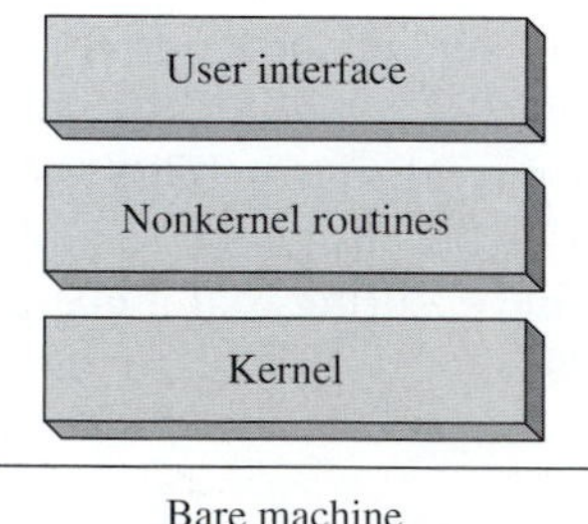

Figure 4.6 Structure of a kernel-based OS.

interface. Recall from Section 4.1 and Figure 4.1 that the operation of the kernel is interrupt-driven. The kernel gets control when an interrupt such as a timer interrupt or an I/O completion interrupt notifies occurrence of an event to it, or when the software-interrupt instruction is executed to make a *system call*. When the interrupt occurs, an interrupt servicing routine performs the *context save* function and invokes an appropriate *event handler*, which is a nonkernel routine of the OS.

A system call may be made by the user interface to implement a user command, by a process to invoke a service in the kernel, or by a nonkernel routine to invoke a function of the kernel. For example, when a user issues a command to execute the program stored in some file, say file `alpha`, the user interface makes a system call, and the interrupt servicing routine invokes a nonkernel routine to set up execution of the program. The nonkernel routine would make system calls to allocate memory for the program's execution, open file `alpha`, and load its contents into the allocated memory area, followed by another system call to initiate operation of the process that represents execution of the program. If a process wishes to create a child process to execute the program in file `alpha`, it, too, would make a system call and identical actions would follow.

The historical motivations for the kernel-based OS structure were portability of the OS and convenience in the design and coding of nonkernel routines. Portability of the OS is achieved by putting architecture-dependent parts of OS code—which typically consist of *mechanisms*—in the kernel and keeping architecture-independent parts of code outside it, so that the porting effort is limited only to porting of the kernel. The kernel is typically monolithic to ensure efficiency; the nonkernel part of an OS may be monolithic, or it may be further structured into layers.

Table 4.3 contains a sample list of functions and services offered by the kernel to support various OS functionalities. These functions and services provide a set of abstractions to the nonkernel routines; their use simplifies design and coding of nonkernel routines by reducing the semantic gap faced by them (see Section 4.4). For example, the I/O functions of Table 4.3 collectively implement the abstraction of virtual devices (see Section 1.3.2). A process is another abstraction provided by the kernel.

A kernel-based design may suffer from stratification analogous to the layered OS design (see Section 4.4) because the code to implement an OS command may contain an architecture-dependent part, which is typically a *mechanism* that would be included in the kernel, and an architecture-independent part, which is typically the implementation of a *policy* that would be kept outside the kernel. These parts would have to communicate with one another through system calls, which would add to OS overhead because of interrupt servicing actions. Consider the command to initiate execution of the program in a file named `alpha`. As discussed earlier, the nonkernel routine that implements the command would make four system calls to allocate memory, open file `alpha`, load the program contained in it into memory, and initiate its execution, which would incur considerable overhead. Some operating system designs reduce OS overhead by including the architecture-independent part of a function's code also in the kernel.

Table 4.3 Typical Functions and Services Offered by the Kernel

OS functionality	Examples of kernel functions and services
Process management	Save context of the interrupted program, dispatch a process, manipulate scheduling lists
Process communication	Send and receive interprocess messages
Memory management	Set memory protection information, swap-in/ swap-out, handle page fault (that is, "missing from memory" interrupt of Section 1.4)
I/O management	Initiate I/O, process I/O completion interrupt, recover from I/O errors
File management	Open a file, read/write data
Security and protection	Add authentication information for a new user, maintain information for file protection
Network management	Send/receive data through a message

Thus, the nonkernel routine that initiated execution of a program would become a part of the kernel. Other such examples are process scheduling policies, I/O scheduling policies of device drivers, and memory management policies. These inclusions reduce OS overhead; however, they also reduce portability of the OS.

Kernel-based operating systems have poor extensibility because addition of a new functionality to the OS may require changes in the functions and services offered by the kernel.

4.6.1 Evolution of Kernel-Based Structure of Operating Systems

The structure of kernel-based operating systems evolved to offset some of its drawbacks. Two steps in this evolution were dynamically loadable kernel modules and user-level device drivers.

To provide *dynamically loadable kernel modules*, the kernel is designed as a set of modules that interact among themselves through well-specified interfaces. A *base kernel* consisting of a core set of modules is loaded when the system is booted. Other modules, which conform to interfaces of the base kernel, are loaded when their functionalities are needed, and are removed from memory when they are no longer needed. Use of loadable modules conserves memory during OS operation because only required modules of the kernel are in memory at any time. It also provides extensibility, as kernel modules can be modified separately and new modules can be added to the kernel easily. Use of loadable kernel modules has a few drawbacks too. Loading and removal of modules fragments memory, so the kernel has to perform memory management actions to reduce its memory requirement. A buggy module can also crash a system. Loadable kernel modules are used to implement device drivers for new I/O devices, network adapters, or new file systems, which are simply device drivers in many operating systems; and to add new system calls to the kernel. The Linux and Solaris systems have incorporated support for dynamically loadable kernel modules (see Sections 4.8.2 and 4.8.3).

A *device driver* handles a specific class of I/O devices. Device drivers constitute the most dynamically changing part of an OS as a result of rapid changes in the I/O device interfaces, hence the ease with which they could be tested and added to an OS would determine the reliability and extensibility of the OS. Dynamic loading of device drivers enhances both these aspects; however, it is not adequate because a device driver would operate with the privileges of the kernel, so a buggy device driver could disrupt operation of the OS and cause frequent boot-ups. Enabling a device driver to operate in the user mode would overcome this difficulty. Such a device driver is called a *user-level device driver*.

User-level device drivers provide ease of development, debugging, and deployment and robustness, since both the code of the kernel and its operation are unaffected by presence of the user-level driver. However, they pose performance problems. Early user-level drivers were found to cause a drop in the I/O throughput or an increase in the CPU time consumed by I/O operations. Both of these resulted from the large number of system calls needed to implement an I/O operation, e.g., the device driver had to make system calls to set up and dismantle the DMA for the I/O operation, to wake up the user process waiting for the I/O operation to complete, and to return control to the kernel at the end of its operation. Later hardware and software developments have overcome the performance problems through a variety of means. The setting up and dismantling actions have been simplified by presence of the IOMMU unit, and system calls have been speeded up through fast system call support.

4.7 MICROKERNEL-BASED OPERATING SYSTEMS

Putting all architecture-dependent code of the OS into the kernel provides good portability. However, in practice, kernels also include some architecture-independent code. This feature leads to several problems. It leads to a large kernel size, which detracts from the goal of portability. It may also necessitate kernel modification to incorporate new features, which causes low extensibility. A large kernel supports a large number of system calls. Some of these calls may be used rarely, and so their implementations across different versions of the kernel may not be tested thoroughly. This compromises reliability of the OS.

The *microkernel* was developed in the early 1990s to overcome the problems concerning portability, extensibility, and reliability of kernels. A microkernel is an essential core of OS code, thus it contains only a subset of the mechanisms typically included in a kernel and supports only a small number of system calls, which are heavily tested and used. This feature enhances portability and reliability

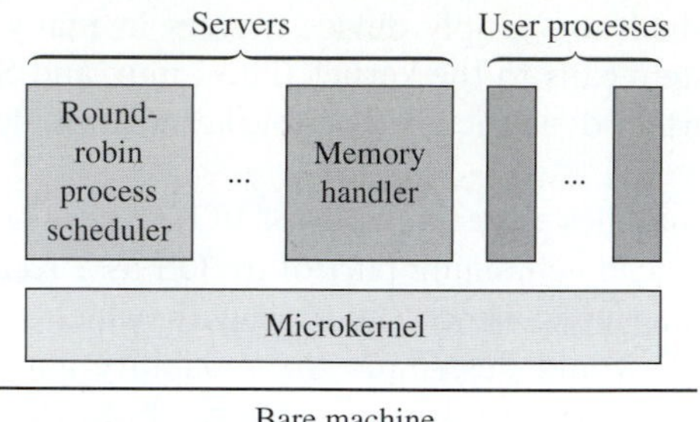

Figure 4.7 Structure of microkernel-based operating systems.

of the microkernel. Less essential parts of OS code are outside the microkernel and use its services, hence these parts could be modified without affecting the kernel; in principle, these modifications could be made without having to reboot the OS! The services provided in a microkernel are not biased toward any specific features or policies in an OS, so new functionalities and features could be added to the OS to suit specific operating environments.

Figure 4.7 illustrates the structure of a microkernel-based OS. The microkernel includes mechanisms for process scheduling and memory management, etc., but does not include a scheduler or memory handler. These functions are implemented as *servers*, which are simply processes that never terminate. The servers and user processes operate on top of the microkernel, which merely performs interrupt handling and provides communication between the servers and user processes.

The small size and extensibility of microkernels are valuable properties for the embedded systems environment, because operating systems need to be both small and fine-tuned to the requirements of an embedded application. Extensibility of microkernels also conjures the vision of using the same microkernel for a wide spectrum of computer systems, from palm-held systems to large parallel and distributed systems. This vision has been realized to some extent. The Mach microkernel has been used to implement several different versions of Unix. The distributed operating system Amoeba uses an identical microkernel on all computers in a distributed system ranging from workstations to large multiprocessors.

Just what is the "essential core of OS code" has been a matter of some debate, and as a result considerable variation exists in the services included in a microkernel. For example, IBM's implementation of the Mach microkernel leaves the process scheduling policy and device drivers outside the kernel—these functions run as servers. The QNX microkernel includes interrupt servicing routines, process scheduling, interprocess communication, and core network services. The L4 microkernel includes memory management and supports only seven system calls. Both QNX and L4 are only 32 KB in size, where 1 KB is 1024 bytes. Despite such variation, it can be argued that certain services *must* be provided by a microkernel. These include memory management support, interprocess communication and interrupt servicing. Memory management and interprocess communication would be invoked by higher-level modules in the OS code that exist outside the microkernel. The interrupt servicing routine would accept interrupts and pass them to higher-level modules for processing.

Operating systems using first-generation microkernels suffered up to 50 percent degradation in throughput compared to operating systems that did not use microkernels. This problem has its origin in the fact that some functionalities of a conventional kernel are split between a microkernel and an OS implemented by using the microkernel—the familiar stratification problem again. For example, a kernel includes the complete process management function, which performs creation, scheduling, and dispatching of processes, whereas a microkernel might include only process creation and dispatching, and process scheduling might run as a server under the microkernel. Communication between the two parts would require use of the interprocess communication (IPC) facility. Researchers found that up to 73 percent of the performance penalty was due to IPC. The L4 microkernel, which is a second-generation microkernel, made IPC more efficient by eliminating validity and rights checking by default, and by tuning the microkernel to the hardware being used. These actions made IPC 20 times faster than in the first-generation microkernels. Paging activities related to virtual memory management were also moved out of the microkernel and into the operating system built by using the microkernel. After these improvements, microkernel-based operating systems were found to suffer only 5 percent degradation in throughput compared to operating systems that did not use a microkernel.

The *exokernel* uses a radically different philosophy of structuring an OS to reduce performance degradation: Resource management need not be centralized; it can be performed by applications themselves in a distributed manner. Accordingly, an exokernel merely provides efficient multiplexing of hardware resources, but does not provide any abstractions. Thus an application process sees a resource in the computer system in its raw form. This approach results in extremely fast primitive operations, 10–100 times faster than when a monolithic Unix kernel is used. For example, data that is read off an I/O device passes directly to the process that requested it; it does not go through the exokernel, whereas it would have gone through the Unix kernel. Since traditional OS functionalities are implemented at the application level, an application can select and use an OS from a library of operating systems. The OS executes as a *process* in the nonkernel mode and uses features of the Exokernel.

4.8 CASE STUDIES

Previous sections discussed the structure of an operating system, that is, arrangement of its parts, and properties of these arrangements. In this section, we discuss both structure and *architecture* of some modern operating systems, where architecture concerns the structure of the operating system as well as functionalities of its components and relationships between them. Design and implementation features of specific OS components are described in relevant chapters of Parts 2–4 of this text.

4.8.1 Architecture of Unix

Unix is a kernel-based operating system. Figure 4.8 is a schematic diagram of the Unix kernel. It consists of two main components—process management and file management. The process management component consists of a module for interprocess communication, which implements communication and synchronization between processes, and the memory management and scheduling modules. The file management component performs I/O through device drivers. Each device driver handles a specific class of I/O devices and uses techniques like disk scheduling to ensure good throughput of an I/O device. The buffer cache is used to reduce both the time required to implement a data transfer between a process and an I/O device, and the number of I/O operations performed on devices like disks (see Section 1.4.4).

The process management and file management components of the kernel are activated through interrupts raised in the hardware, and system calls made by processes and nonkernel routines of the OS. The user interface of the OS is a command interpreter, called a *shell*, that runs as a user process. The Unix kernel cannot be interrupted at any arbitrary moment of time; it can be interrupted only when a process executing kernel code exits, or when its execution reaches a point at which it can be safely interrupted. This feature ensures that the kernel data structures are not in an inconsistent state when an interrupt occurs and another process starts executing the kernel code, which considerably simplifies coding of the kernel (see Section 2.3.2).

The Unix kernel has a long history of over four decades. The original kernel was small and simple. It provided a small set of abstractions, simple but powerful features like the pipe mechanism, which enabled users to execute several programs concurrently, and a small file system that supported only one file organization called the *byte stream* organization. All devices were represented as files, which unified the management of I/O devices and files. The kernel was

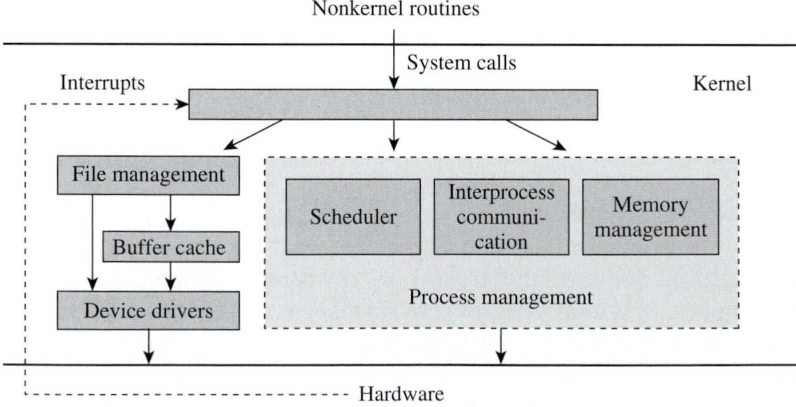

Figure 4.8 Kernel of the Unix operating system.

written in the C language and had a size of less than 100 KB. Hence it was easily portable.

However, the Unix kernel was monolithic and not very extensible. So it had to be modified as new computing environments, like the client–server environment, evolved. Interprocess communication and threads were added to support client–server computing. Networking support similarly required kernel modification.

A major strength of Unix was its use of open standards. It enabled a large number of organizations ranging from the academia to the industry to participate in its development, which led to widespread use of Unix, but also led to the development of a large number of variants because of concurrent and uncoordinated development. The kernel became bulky, growing to a few million bytes in size, which affected its portability. Around this time, a feature was added to dynamically load kernel modules in memory. It enabled kernel modules to be loaded only when needed. This feature reduced the memory requirement of the kernel, but not its code size. Hence it did not enhance its portability.

Several efforts have been made to redesign the Unix kernel to make it modular and extensible. The Mach kernel, which has a specific emphasis on multiprocessor systems, is an example of this trend. Later Mach developed into a microkernel-based operating system.

4.8.2 The Kernel of Linux

The Linux operating system provides the functionalities of Unix System V and Unix BSD; it is also compliant with the POSIX standard. It was initially implemented on the Intel 80386 and has since been implemented on later Intel processors and several other architectures.

Linux has a monolithic kernel. The kernel is designed to consist of a set of individually loadable modules. Each module has a well-specified interface that indicates how its functionalities can be invoked and its data can be accessed by other modules. Conversely, the interface also indicates the functions and data of other modules that are used by this module. Each module can be individually loaded into memory, or removed from it, depending on whether it is likely to be used in near future. In principle, any component of the kernel can be structured as a loadable module, but typically device drivers become separate modules.

A few kernel modules are loaded when the system is booted. A new kernel module is loaded dynamically when needed; however, it has to be integrated with the kernel modules that already existed in memory so that the modules can collectively function as a monolithic kernel. This integration is performed as follows: The kernel maintains a table in which it records the addresses of functions and data that are defined in the modules existing in memory. While loading a new module, the kernel analyzes its interface and finds which functions and data of other modules it uses, obtains their addresses from the table, and inserts them in appropriate instructions of the new module. At the end of this step, the kernel updates its table by adding the addresses of functions and data defined in the new module.

Use of kernel modules with well-specified interfaces provides several advantages. Existence of the module interface simplifies testing and maintenance of the kernel. An individual module can be modified to provide new functionalities or enhance existing ones. This feature overcomes the poor extensibility typically associated with monolithic kernels. Use of loadable modules also limits the memory requirement of the kernel, because some modules may not be loaded during an operation of the system. To enhance this advantage, the kernel has a feature to automatically remove unwanted modules from memory—it produces an interrupt periodically and checks which of its modules in memory have not been used since the last such interrupt. These modules are delinked from the kernel and removed from memory. Alternatively, modules can be individually loaded and removed from memory through system calls.

The Linux 2.6 kernel, which was released in 2003, removed many of the limitations of the Linux 2.5 kernel and also enhanced its capabilities in several ways. Two of the most prominent improvements were in making the system more responsive and capable of supporting embedded systems. Kernels up to Linux 2.5 were non-preemptible, so if the kernel was engaged in performing a low-priority task, higher-priority tasks of the kernel were delayed. The Linux 2.6 kernel is preemptible, which makes it more responsive to users and application programs. However, the kernel should not be preempted when it is difficult to save its state, or when it is performing sensitive operations, so the kernel disables and enables its own preemptibility through special functions. The Linux 2.6 kernel can also support architectures that do not possess a memory management unit (MMU), which makes it suitable for embedded systems. Thus, the same kernel can now be used in embedded systems, desktops and servers. The other notable feature in the Linux 2.6 kernel is better scalability through an improved model of threads, an improved scheduler, and fast synchronization between processes; these features are described in later chapters.

4.8.3 The Kernel of Solaris

Early operating systems for Sun computer systems were based on BSD Unix; however, later development was based on Unix SVR4. The pre-SVR4 versions of the OS are called SunOS, while the SVR4-based and later versions are called Solaris. Since the 1980s, Sun has focused on networking and distributed computing; several networking and distributed computing features of its operating systems have become industry standards, e.g., remote procedure calls (RPC), and a file system for distributed environments (NFS). Later, Sun also focused on multiprocessor systems, which resulted in an emphasis on multithreading the kernel, making it preemptible (see Section 2.3.2), and employing fast synchronization techniques in the kernel.

The Solaris kernel has an abstract machine layer that supports a wide range of processor architectures of the SPARC and Intel 80x86 family, including multiprocessor architectures. The kernel is fully preemptible and provides real-time capabilities. Solaris 7 employs the kernel-design methodology of dynamically loadable kernel modules (see Section 4.6.1). The kernel has a core module that is always loaded; it contains interrupt servicing routines, system calls, process and memory management, and a virtual file system framework that can support different file systems concurrently. Other kernel modules are loaded and unloaded dynamically. Each module contains information about other modules on which it depends and about other modules that depend on it. The kernel maintains a symbol table containing information about symbols defined in currently loaded kernel modules. This information is used while loading and linking a new module. New information is added to the symbol table after a module is loaded and some information is deleted after a module is deleted.

The Solaris kernel supports seven types of loadable modules:

- Scheduler classes
- File systems
- Loadable system calls
- Loaders for different formats of executable files
- Streams modules
- Bus controllers and device drivers
- Miscellaneous modules

Use of loadable kernel modules provides easy extensibility. Thus, new file systems, new formats of executable files, new system calls, and new kinds of buses and devices can be added easily. An interesting feature in the kernel is that when a new module is to be loaded, the kernel creates a new thread for loading, linking, and initializing working of the new module. This arrangement permits module loading to be performed concurrently with normal operation of the kernel. It also permits loading of several modules to be performed concurrently.

4.8.4 Architecture of Windows

Figure 4.9 shows architecture of the Windows OS. The *hardware abstraction layer* (HAL) interfaces with the bare machine and provides abstractions of the I/O interfaces, interrupt controllers, and interprocessor communication mechanisms in a multiprocessor system. The kernel uses the abstractions provided by the HAL to provide basic services such as interrupt processing and multiprocessor synchronization. This way, the kernel is shielded from peculiarities of a specific architecture, which enhances its portability. The HAL and the kernel are together equivalent to a conventional kernel (see Figure 4.6). A *device driver* also uses the abstractions provided by the HAL to manage I/O operations on a class of devices.

The kernel performs the process synchronization and scheduling functions. The *executive* comprises nonkernel routines of the OS; its code uses facilities in the kernel to provide services such as process creation and termination, virtual memory management, an interprocess message passing facility for client–server communication called the *local procedure call* (LPC), I/O management and a *file cache* to provide efficient file I/O, and a *security reference monitor* that performs

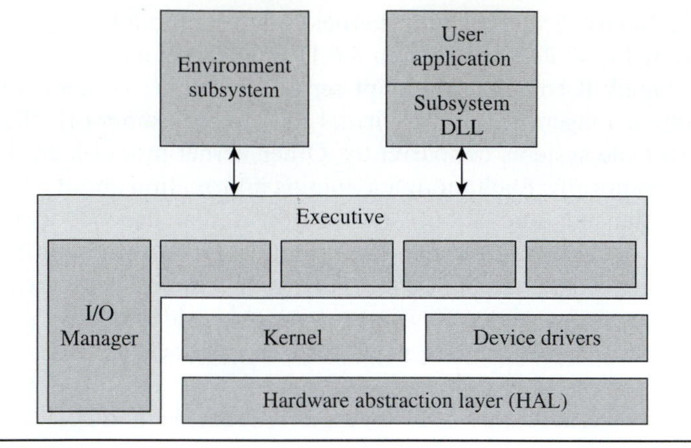

Figure 4.9 Architecture of Windows.

file access validation. The *I/O manager* uses device drivers, which are loaded dynamically when needed. Many functions of the executive operate in the kernel mode, thus avoiding frequent context switches when the executive interacts with the kernel; it has obvious performance benefits.

The environment subsystems provide support for execution of programs developed for other operating systems like MS-DOS, Win32, and OS/2. Effectively, an environment subsystem is analogous to a guest operating system within a virtual machine OS (see Section 4.5). It operates as a process that keeps track of the state of user applications that use its services. To implement the interface of a guest OS, each environment subsystem provides a *dynamic link library* (DLL) and expects a user application to invoke the DLL when it needs a specific system service. The DLL either implements the required service itself, passes the request for service to the executive, or sends a message to the environment subsystem process to provide the service.

4.9 SUMMARY

Portability of an operating system refers to the ease with which the OS can be implemented on a computer having a different architecture. *Extensibility* of an operating system refers to the ease with which its functionalities can be modified or enhanced to adapt it to a new computing environment. Portability and extensibility have become crucial requirements because of long life-spans of modern operating systems. In this chapter we discussed different ways of structuring operating systems to meet these requirements.

An OS functionality typically contains a *policy*, which specifies the principle that is to be used to perform the functionality, and a few *mechanisms* that perform actions to implement the functionality. Mechanisms such as dispatching and context save interact closely with the computer, so their code is inherently architecture-dependent; policies are architecture-independent. Hence portability and extensibility of an OS depends on how the code of its policies and mechanisms is structured.

Early operating systems had a *monolithic* structure. These operating systems had poor portability because architecture-dependent code was spread throughout the OS. They also suffered from high design complexity. The *layered design* of operating systems used the principle of abstraction to control complexity of designing the OS. It viewed the OS as a hierarchy of layers, in which each layer provided a set of services to the layer above it, and itself used the services in the layer below it. Architecture dependencies were often restricted to lower layers in the hierarchy; however, the design methodology did not guarantee it.

The *virtual machine operating system* (VM OS) supported operation of several operating systems on a computer simultaneously, by creating a *virtual machine* for each user and permitting the user to run an OS of his choice in the virtual machine. The VM OS interleaved operation of the users' virtual machines on the host computer through a procedure analogous to scheduling. When a virtual machine was scheduled, its OS would organize execution of user applications running under it.

In a *kernel-based* design of operating systems, the *kernel* is the core of the operating system, which invokes the *nonkernel routines* to implement operations on processes and resources. The architecture-dependent code in an OS typically resides in the kernel; this feature enhances portability of the operating system.

A *microkernel* is the essential core of OS code. It is small in size, contains a few mechanisms, and does not contain any policies. Policy modules are implemented as *server* processes; they can be changed or replaced without affecting the microkernel, thus providing high extensibility of the OS.

TEST YOUR CONCEPTS

4.1 Classify each of the following statements as true or false:

- **a.** Mechanisms of the OS are typically architecture-independent.
- **b.** A layered OS organization reduces the semantic gap between the top layer of the OS and the bare machine.
- **c.** In a virtual machine OS, each user can run an OS of his choice.
- **d.** A kernel-based OS structure provides extensibility.
- **e.** In a microkernel-based OS, the process scheduler may run as a user process.

4.2 Classify each of the following functions performed by an OS as a policy or a mechanism (refer to relevant sections of Chapters 1 and 3):

- **a.** Preempting a program
- **b.** Priority-based scheduling used in multiprogramming systems
- **c.** Loading a swapped-out program into memory
- **d.** Checking whether a user program can be permitted to access a file

4.3 Which of the following operating systems has the highest portability?

- **a.** An OS with a monolithic structure.
- **b.** An OS with a layered structure.
- **c.** A virtual machine OS.
- **d.** A kernel-based OS.

EXERCISES

4.1 The scheduling mechanism "manipulate scheduling lists" (see Table 4.3) is invoked to modify scheduling lists in response to events in the system and actions of the scheduler. Describe the functions this mechanism should perform for (a) round-robin scheduling and (b) priority-based scheduling (as used in a multiprogramming OS).

4.2 Justify the following statement: "Secure operation of a virtual machine operating system requires less-than-full virtualization of its resources; however, it may degrade efficiency of operation of a guest OS."

4.3 What are the consequences of merging nonkernel routines with (a) the user interface, (b) the kernel? (*Hint:* Refer to Section 1.1.)

4.4 List the differences between a kernel employing dynamically loadable modules and (a) a monolithic kernel and (b) a microkernel.

BIBLIOGRAPHY

Dijkstra (1968) describes the structure of the THE multiprogramming system. The virtual machine operating system VM/370 is based on CP/67, and is described in Creasy (1981). The XEN and VMware virtual machine products are described in Barham et al. (2003) and Sugarman et al. (2001), respectively. The May 2005 issue of *IEEE Computer* is a special issue on virtualization technologies. Rosenblum and Garfinkel (2005) discusses trends in the design of virtual machine monitors.

Warhol (1994) discusses the strides made by microkernels in the early 1990s while Liedtke (1996) describes the principles of microkernel design. Hartig et al. (1997) describes porting and performance of the Linux OS on the L4 microkernel. Engler et al. (1995) discusses design of an Exokernel. Bach (1986), Vahalia (1996), and McKusick et al. (1996) describe the Unix kernel. Beck et al. (2002), Bovet and Cesati (2005), and Love (2005) describe the Linux kernel, while Mauro and McDougall (2006) describes the kernel of Solaris. Tanenbaum (2001) describes microkernels of the Amoeba and Mach operating systems. Russinovich and Solomon (2005) describes architecture of Windows.

1. Bach, M. J. (1986): *The Design of the Unix Operating System*, Prentice Hall, Englewood Cliffs, N.J.
2. Barham, P., B. Dragovic, K. Fraser, S. Hand, T. Harris, A. Ho, R. Neugebauer, I. Pratt, and A. Warfield (2003): "XEN and the art of virtualization," *ACM Symposium on Operating System Principles*, 164–177.
3. Beck, M., H. Bohme, M. Dziadzka, U. Kunitz, R. Magnus, C. Schroter, and D. Verworner (2002): *Linux Kernel Programming*, 3rd ed., Pearson Education, New York.
4. Bovet, D. P., and M. Cesati (2005): *Understanding the Linux Kernel*, 3rd ed., O'Reilly, Sebastopol.
5. Creasy, R. J. (1981): "The origin of the VM/370 time-sharing system," *IBM Journal of Research and Development*, **25** (5), 483–490.
6. Dijkstra, E. W. (1968): "The structure of THE multiprogramming system," *Communications of the ACM*, **11**, 341–346.
7. Engler D. R., M. F. Kasshoek, and J. O'Toole (1995): "Exokernel: An operating system architecture for application-level resource management," *Symposium on OS Principles*, 251–266.
8. Hartig, H., M. Hohmuth, J. Liedtke, S. Schonberg, and J. Wolter (1997): "The performance of microkernel-based systems," *16th ACM Symposium on Operating System Principles*.
9. Liedtke J. (1996): "Towards real microkernels," *Communications of the ACM*, **39** (9), 70–77.
10. Love, R. (2005): *Linux Kernel Development*, 2nd ed., Novell Press.
11. Mauro, J., and R. McDougall (2006): *Solaris Internals,* 2nd ed., Prentice Hall, Englewood Cliffs, N.J.

12. McKusick, M. K., K. Bostic, M. J. Karels, and J. S. Quarterman (1996): *The Design and Implementation of the 4.4 BSD Operating System*, Addison-Wesley, Reading, Mass.
13. Meyer, J., and L. H. Seawright (1970): "A virtual machine time-sharing system," *IBM Systems Journal*, **9** (3), 199–218.
14. Rosenblum, M., and T. Garfinkel (2005): "Virtual machine monitors: current technology and future trends," *IEEE Computer*, **38** (5), 39–47.
15. Russinovich, M. E., and D. A. Solomon (2005): *Microsoft Windows Internals*, 4th ed., Microsoft Press, Redmond, Wash.
16. Sugarman, J., G. Venkitachalam, and B. H. Lim (2001): "Virtualizing I/O devices on VMware workstation's hosted virtual machine monitor," *2001 USENIX Annual Technical Conference*.
17. Tanenbaum, A. S. (2001): *Modern Operating Systems*, 2nd ed., Prentice Hall, Englewood Cliffs, N.J.
18. Vahalia, U. (1996): *UNIX Internals—the New Frontiers*, Prentice-Hall, Englewood Cliffs, N.J.
19. Warhol, P. D. (1994): "Small kernels hit it big," *Byte*, January 1994, 119–128.

Chapter 5: Processes and Threads

This chapter begins by discussing how an application creates processes through system calls and how the presence of many processes achieves concurrency and parallelism within the application. It then describes how the operating system manages a process—how it uses the notion of *process state* to keep track of what a process is doing and how it reflects the effect of an event on states of affected processes. The chapter also introduces the notion of *threads*, describes their benefits, and illustrates their features.

Chapter 6: Process Synchronization

Processes of an application work toward a common goal by sharing data and coordinating with one another. The key concepts in process synchronization are the use of *mutual exclusion* to safeguard consistency of shared data and the use of *indivisible operations* in coordinating activities of processes. This chapter discusses the synchronization requirements of some classic problems in process synchronization and discusses how they can be met by using synchronization features such as *semaphores* and *monitors* provided in programming languages and operating systems.

Chapter 7: Scheduling

Scheduling is the act of selecting the next process to be serviced by a CPU. This chapter discusses how a scheduler uses the fundamental techniques of *priority-based scheduling, reordering* of requests, and variation of *time slice* to achieve a suitable combination of user service, efficient use of resources, and system performance. It describes different scheduling policies and their properties.

Chapter 8: Deadlocks

A deadlock is a situation in which processes wait for one another indefinitely due to resource sharing or synchronization. This chapter discusses how deadlocks can arise and how an OS performs *deadlock handling* to ensure an absence of deadlocks, either through *detection* and *resolution* of deadlocks, or through resource allocation policies that perform *deadlock prevention* or *deadlock avoidance*.

Chapter 9: Message Passing

Processes exchange information by sending *interprocess messages*. This chapter discusses the semantics of message passing, and OS responsibilities in buffering and delivery of interprocess messages. It also discusses how message passing is employed in higher-level protocols for providing electronic mail facility and in providing intertask communication in parallel or distributed programs.

part 2

Process Management

A *process* is an execution of a program. An application may be designed to have many processes that operate concurrently and interact among themselves to jointly achieve a goal. This way, the application may be able to provide a quicker response to the user.

An OS contains a large number of processes at any time. Process management involves creating processes, fulfilling their resource requirements, *scheduling* them for use of a CPU, implementing *process synchronization* to control their interactions, avoiding *deadlocks* so that they do not wait for each other indefinitely, and terminating them when they complete their operation. The manner in which an OS schedules processes for use of a CPU determines the response times of processes, resource efficiency, and system performance.

A *thread* uses the resources of a process but resembles a process in all other respects. An OS incurs less overhead in managing threads than in managing processes. We use the term *process* as generic to both processes and threads.

Road Map for Part 2

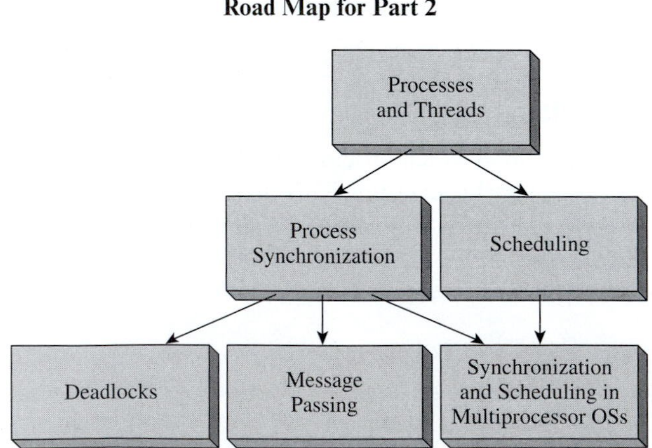

Schematic diagram showing the order in which chapters of this part should be covered in a course.

Chapter 10: Synchronization and Scheduling in Multiprocessor OSs

Presence of many CPUs in a multiprocessor computer system holds the promise of high throughput and fast response to applications. This chapter discusses different kinds of multiprocessor systems, and describes how the OS achieves high throughput and fast response by using special techniques of structuring its kernel, so that many CPUs can execute kernel code in parallel, and of synchronizing and scheduling processes.

Chapter 5

Processes and Threads

The concept of a *process* helps us understand how programs execute in an operating system. A process is *an* execution of a program using a set of resources. We emphasize "an" because several executions of the same program may be present in the operating system at the same time; these executions constitute different processes. That happens when users initiate independent executions of the program, each on its own data. It also happens when a program that is coded with concurrent programming techniques is being executed. The kernel allocates resources to processes and schedules them for use of the CPU. This way, it realizes execution of sequential and concurrent programs uniformly.

A *thread* is also an execution of a program but it functions in the environment of a process—that is, it uses the code, data, and resources of a process. It is possible for many threads to function in the environment of the same process; they share its code, data, and resources. Switching between such threads requires less overhead than switching between processes.

In this chapter, we discuss how the kernel controls processes and threads—how it keeps track of their *states*, and how it uses the state information to organize their operation. We also discuss how a program may create concurrent processes or threads, and how they may interact with one another to achieve a common goal.

5.1 PROCESSES AND PROGRAMS

A program is a passive entity that does not perform any actions by itself; it has to be executed if the actions it calls for are to take place. A *process* is an execution of a program. It actually performs the actions specified in a program. An operating system shares the CPU among processes. This is how it gets user programs to execute.

5.1.1 What Is a Process?

To understand what is a process, let us discuss how the OS executes a program. Program P shown in Figure 5.1(a) contains declarations of a file `info` and a variable `item`, and statements that read values from `info`, use them to perform some calculations, and print a result before coming to a halt. During execution,

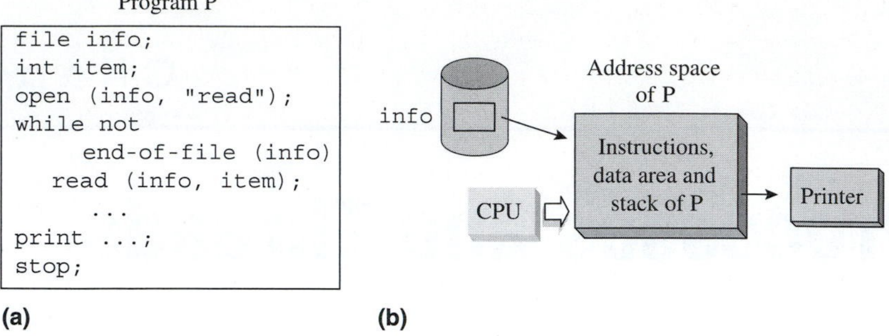

Program P
file info;
int item;
open (info, "read");
while not
end-of-file (info)
read (info, item);
...
print ...;
stop;
info
Address space
of P
Instructions,
data area and
stack of P
CPU
Printer
(a)
(b)

Figure 5.1 A program and an abstract view of its execution.

instructions of this program use values in its data area and the stack to perform the intended calculations. Figure 5.1(b) shows an abstract view of its execution. The instructions, data, and stack of program P constitute its *address space*. To realize execution of P, the OS allocates memory to accommodate P's address space, allocates a printer to print its results, sets up an arrangement through which P can access file `info`, and schedules P for execution. The CPU is shown as a lightly shaded box because it is not always executing instructions of P—the OS shares the CPU between execution of P and executions of other programs.

Following the above discussion, we can define a process as follows:

Definition 5.1 Process An execution of a program using resources allocated to it.

When a user initiates execution of a program, the OS creates a new process and assigns a unique id to it. It now allocates some resources to the process—sufficient memory to accommodate the address space of the program, and some devices such as a keyboard and a monitor to facilitate interaction with the user. The process may make system calls during its operation to request additional resources such as files. We refer to the address space of the program and resources allocated to it as the address space and resources of the process, respectively.

Accordingly, a process comprises six components:

$$(id, code, data, stack, resources, CPU\ state) \tag{5.1}$$

where *id* is the unique id assigned by the OS
code is the code of the program (it is also called the *text* of a program)
data is the data used in the execution of the program, including data from files
stack contains parameters of functions and procedures called during execution of the program, and their return addresses

resources is the set of resources allocated by the OS
CPU state is composed of contents of the PSW and the general-purpose registers (GPRs) of the CPU (we assume that the stack pointer is maintained in a GPR)

The CPU state (Section 2.2.1) contains information that indicates which instruction in the code would be executed next, and other information—such as contents of the *condition code* field (also called the *flags* field) of the PSW—that may influence its execution. The CPU state changes as the execution of the program progresses. We use the term *operation of a process* for execution of a program. Thus a process operates when it is scheduled.

5.1.2 Relationships between Processes and Programs

A program consists of a set of functions and procedures. During its execution, control flows between the functions and procedures according to the logic of the program. Is an execution of a function or procedure a process? This doubt leads to the obvious question: what is the relationship between processes and programs?

The OS does not know anything about the nature of a program, including functions and procedures in its code. It knows only what it is told through system calls. The rest is under control of the program. Thus functions of a program may be separate processes, or they may constitute the code part of a single process. We discuss examples of these situations in the following.

Table 5.1 shows two kinds of relationships that can exist between processes and programs. A one-to-one relationship exists when a single execution of a sequential program is in progress, for example, execution of program P in Figure 5.1. A many-to-one relationship exists between many processes and a program in two cases: Many executions of a program may be in progress at the same time; processes representing these executions have a many-to-one relationship with the program. During execution, a program may make a system call to request that a specific part of its code should be executed concurrently, i.e., as a separate activity occurring at the same time. The kernel sets up execution of the specified part of the code and treats it as a separate process. The new process and the process representing execution of the program have a many-to-one relationship with the program. We call such a program a *concurrent program*.

Processes that coexist in the system at some time are called *concurrent processes*. Concurrent processes may share their code, data and resources with other

Table 5.1 Relationships between Processes and Programs

Relationship	Examples
One-to-one	A single execution of a sequential program.
Many-to-one	Many simultaneous executions of a program, execution of a concurrent program.

processes; they have opportunities to interact with one another during their execution.

5.1.3 Child Processes

The kernel initiates an execution of a program by creating a process for it. For lack of a technical term for this process, we will call it the *primary process* for the program execution. The primary process may make system calls as described in the previous section to create other processes—these processes become its *child processes*, and the primary process becomes their *parent*. A child process may itself create other processes, and so on. The parent–child relationships between these processes can be represented in the form of a *process tree*, which has the primary process as its root. A child process may inherit some of the resources of its parent; it could obtain additional resources during its operation through system calls.

Typically, a process creates one or more child processes and delegates some of its work to each of them. It is called *multitasking* within an application. It has the three benefits summarized in Table 5.2. Creation of child processes has the same benefits as the use of multiprogramming in an OS—the kernel may be able to interleave operation of I/O-bound and CPU-bound processes in the application, which may lead to a reduction in the duration, i.e., running time, of an application. It is called *computation speedup*. Most operating systems permit a parent process to assign priorities to child processes. A real-time application can assign a high priority to a child process that performs a critical function to ensure that its response requirement is met. We shall elaborate on this aspect later in Example 5.1.

The third benefit, namely, guarding a parent process against errors in a child process, arises as follows: Consider a process that has to invoke an untrusted code.

Table 5.2 Benefits of Child Processes

Benefit	Explanation
Computation speedup	Actions that the primary process of an application would have performed sequentially if it did not create child processes, would be performed concurrently when it creates child processes. It may reduce the duration, i.e., running time, of the application.
Priority for critical functions	A child process that performs a critical function may be assigned a high priority; it may help to meet the real-time requirements of an application.
Guarding a parent process against errors	The kernel aborts a child process if an error arises during its operation. The parent process is not affected by the error; it may be able to perform a recovery action.

If the untrusted code were to be included in the code of the process, an error in the untrusted code would compel the kernel to abort the process; however, if the process were to create a child process to execute the untrusted code, the same error would lead to the abort of the child process, so the parent process would not come to any harm. The OS command interpreter uses this feature to advantage. The command interpreter itself runs as a process, and creates a child process whenever it has to execute a user program. This way, its own operation is not harmed by malfunctions in the user program.

Example 5.1 illustrates how the data logging system of Section 3.7 benefits from use of child processes.

Child Processes in a Real-Time Application

Example 5.1

The real-time data logging application of Section 3.7 receives data samples from a satellite at the rate of 500 samples per second and stores them in a file. We assume that each sample arriving from the satellite is put into a special register of the computer. The primary process of the application, which we will call the *data_logger* process, has to perform the following three functions:

1. Copy the sample from the special register into memory.
2. Copy the sample from memory into a file.
3. Perform some analysis of a sample and record its results into another file used for future processing.

It creates three child processes named *copy_sample*, *record_sample*, and *housekeeping*, leading to the process tree shown in Figure 5.2(a). Note that a process is depicted by a circle and a parent–child relationship is depicted by an arrow. As shown in Figure 5.2(b), *copy_sample* copies the sample from the register into a memory area named *buffer_area* that can hold, say, 50 samples. *record_sample* writes a sample from *buffer_area* into a file. *housekeeping* analyzes a sample from *buffer_area* and records its results in another file. Arrival of a new sample causes an interrupt, and a programmer-defined interrupt servicing routine is associated with this interrupt. The kernel executes this routine whenever a new sample arrives. It activates *copy_sample*.

Operation of the three processes can overlap as follows: *copy_sample* can copy a sample into *buffer_area*, *record_sample* can write a previous sample to the file, while *housekeeping* can analyze it and write its results into the other file. This arrangement provides a smaller worst-case response time of the application than if these functions were to be executed sequentially. So long as *buffer_area* has some free space, only *copy_sample* has to complete before the next sample arrives. The other processes can be executed later. This possibility is exploited by assigning the highest priority to *copy_sample*.

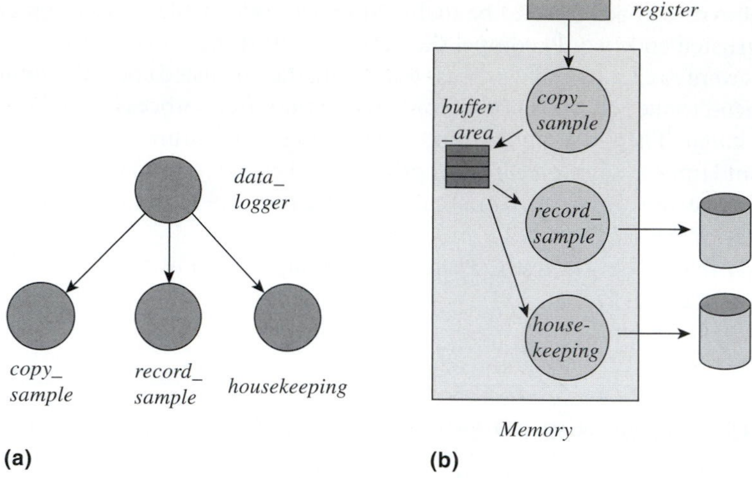

Figure 5.2 Real-time application of Section 3.7: (a) process tree; (b) processes.

To facilitate use of child processes, the kernel provides operations for:

1. Creating a child process and assigning a priority to it
2. Terminating a child process
3. Determining the status of a child process
4. Sharing, communication, and synchronization between processes

Their use can be described as follows: In Example 5.1, the *data_logger* process creates three child processes. The *copy_sample* and *record_sample* processes share *buffer_area*. They need to synchronize their operation such that process *record_sample* would copy a sample out of *buffer_area* only after process *copy_sample* has written it there. The *data_logger* process could be programmed to either terminate its child processes before itself terminating, or terminate itself only after it finds that all its child processes have terminated.

5.1.4 Concurrency and Parallelism

Parallelism is the quality of occurring at the same time. Two events are parallel if they occur at the same time, and two tasks are parallel if they are performed at the same time. *Concurrency* is an illusion of parallelism. Thus, two tasks are concurrent if there is an illusion that they are being performed in parallel, whereas, in reality, only one of them may be performed at any time.

In an OS, concurrency is obtained by interleaving operation of processes on the CPU, which creates the illusion that these processes are operating at the same time. Parallelism is obtained by using multiple CPUs, as in a multiprocessor system, and operating different processes on these CPUs.

How does mere concurrency provide any benefits? We have seen several examples of this earlier in Chapter 3. In Section 3.5 we discussed how the throughput of a multiprogramming OS increases by interleaving operation of processes on a CPU, because an I/O operation in one process overlaps with a computational activity of another process. In Section 3.6, we saw how interleaved operation of processes created by different users in a time-sharing system makes each user think that he has a computer to himself, although it is slower than the real computer being used. In Section 5.1.2 and in Example 5.1, we saw that interleaving of processes may lead to computation speedup.

Parallelism can provide better throughput in an obvious way because processes can operate on multiple CPUs. It can also provide computation speedup; however, the computation speedup provided by it is qualitatively different from that provided through concurrency—when concurrency is employed, speedup is obtained by overlapping I/O activities of one process with CPU activities of other processes, whereas when parallelism is employed, CPU and I/O activities in one process can overlap with the CPU and I/O activities of other processes.

Computation speedup of an application through concurrency and parallelism would depend on several factors:

- *Inherent parallelism within the application:* Does the application have activities that can progress independently of one another?
- *Overhead of concurrency and parallelism:* The overhead of setting up and managing concurrency should not predominate over the benefits of performing activities concurrently, e.g., if the chunks of work sought to be performed concurrently are too small, the overhead of concurrency may swamp its contributions to computation speedup.
- *Model of concurrency and parallelism supported by the OS:* How much overhead does the model incur, and how much of the inherent parallelism within an application can be exploited through it.

We have so far discussed one model of concurrency and parallelism, namely the *process* model. In Section 5.3, we introduce an alternative model called the *thread* model, and discuss its properties.

5.2 IMPLEMENTING PROCESSES

In the operating system's view, a process is a unit of computational work. Hence the kernel's primary task is to control operation of processes to provide effective utilization of the computer system. Accordingly, the kernel allocates resources to a process, protects the process and its resources from interference by other processes, and ensures that the process gets to use the CPU until it completes its operation.

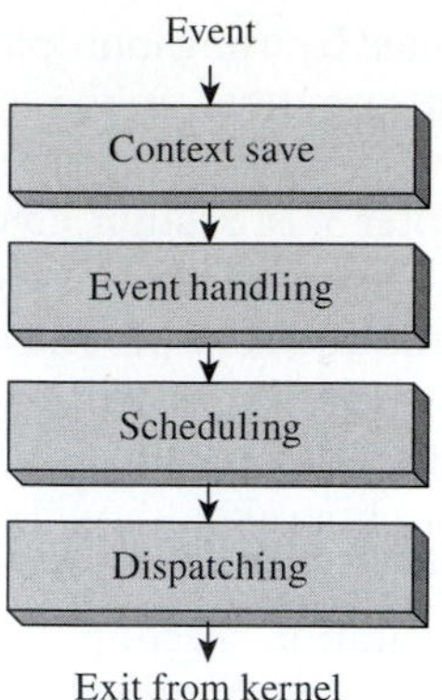

Figure 5.3 Fundamental functions of the kernel for controlling processes.

The kernel is activated when an *event*, which is a situation that requires the kernel's attention, leads to either a hardware interrupt or a system call (see Section 2.3). The kernel now performs four fundamental functions to control operation of processes (see Figure 5.3):

1. *Context save:* Saving CPU state and information concerning resources of the process whose operation is interrupted.
2. *Event handling:* Analyzing the condition that led to an interrupt, or the request by a process that led to a system call, and taking appropriate actions.
3. *Scheduling:* Selecting the process to be executed next on the CPU.
4. *Dispatching:* Setting up access to resources of the scheduled process and loading its saved CPU state in the CPU to begin or resume its operation.

The kernel performs the context save function to save information concerning the interrupted process. It is followed by execution of an appropriate event handling routine, which may inhibit further operation of the interrupted process, e.g., if this process has made a system call to start an I/O operation, or may enable operation of some other process, e.g., if the interrupt was caused by completion of its I/O operation. The kernel now performs the scheduling function to select a process and the dispatching function to begin or resume its operation.

As discussed earlier in Sections 3.5.1 and 3.6, to perform scheduling an operating system must know which processes require the CPU at any moment. Hence the key to controlling operation of processes is to monitor all processes and know what each process is doing at any moment of time—whether executing on the CPU, waiting for the CPU to be allocated to it, waiting for an I/O operation to complete, or waiting to be swapped into memory. The operating system monitors the *process state* to keep track of what a process is doing at any moment.

Here in Section 5.2, we will see what is meant by a process state, and we will look at the different states of a process; and the arrangements by which the operating system maintains information about the state of a process. We do not discuss scheduling in this chapter. It is discussed later in Chapter 7.

5.2.1 Process States and State Transitions

An operating system uses the notion of a *process state* to keep track of what a process is doing at any moment.

Definition 5.2 Process state The indicator that describes the nature of the current activity of a process.

The kernel uses process states to simplify its own functioning, so the number of process states and their names may vary across OSs. However, most OSs use the four fundamental states described in Table 5.3. The kernel considers a process to be in the *blocked* state if it has made a resource request and the request is yet to be granted, or if it is waiting for some event to occur. A CPU should not be allocated to such a process until its wait is complete. The kernel would change the state of the process to *ready* when the request is granted or the event for which it is waiting occurs. Such a process can be considered for scheduling. The kernel would change the state of the process to *running* when it is dispatched. The state would be changed to *terminated* when execution of the process completes or when it is aborted by the kernel for some reason.

A conventional computer system contains only one CPU, and so at most one process can be in the *running* state. There can be any number of processes in the *blocked*, *ready*, and *terminated* states. An OS may define more process states to simplify its own functioning or to support additional functionalities like swapping. We discuss this aspect in Section 5.2.1.1.

Table 5.3 Fundamental Process States

State	Description
Running	A CPU is currently executing instructions in the process code.
Blocked	The process has to wait until a resource request made by it is granted, or it wishes to wait until a specific event occurs.
Ready	The process wishes to use the CPU to continue its operation; however, it has not been dispatched.
Terminated	The operation of the process, i.e., the execution of the program represented by it, has completed normally, or the OS has aborted it.

Process State Transitions A *state transition* for a process P_i is a change in its state. A state transition is caused by the occurrence of some event such as the start or end of an I/O operation. When the event occurs, the kernel determines its influence on activities in processes, and accordingly changes the state of an affected process.

When a process P_i in the *running* state makes an I/O request, its state has to be changed to *blocked* until its I/O operation completes. At the end of the I/O operation, P_i's state is changed from *blocked* to *ready* because it now wishes to use the CPU. Similar state changes are made when a process makes some request that cannot immediately be satisfied by the OS. The process state is changed to *blocked* when the request is made, i.e., when the request event occurs, and it is changed to *ready* when the request is satisfied. The state of a *ready* process is changed to *running* when it is dispatched, and the state of a *running* process is changed to *ready* when it is preempted either because a higher-priority process became ready or because its time slice elapsed (see Sections 3.5.1 and 3.6). Table 5.4 summarizes causes of state transitions.

Figure 5.4 diagrams the fundamental state transitions for a process. A new process is put in the *ready* state after resources required by it have been allocated. It may enter the *running, blocked*, and *ready* states a number of times as a result of events described in Table 5.4. Eventually it enters the *terminated* state.

Example 5.2 **Process State Transitions**

Consider the time-sharing system of Example 3.2, which uses a time slice of 10 ms. It contains two processes P_1 and P_2. P_1 has a CPU burst of 15 ms followed by an I/O operation that lasts for 100 ms, while P_2 has a CPU burst of 30 ms followed by an I/O operation that lasts for 60 ms. Execution of P_1 and P_2 was described in Figure 3.7. Table 5.5 illustrates the state transitions during operation of the system. Actual execution of programs proceeds as follows: System operation starts with both processes in the *ready* state at time 0. The scheduler selects process P_1 for execution and changes its state to *running*. At 10 ms, P_1 is preempted and P_2 is dispatched. Hence P_1's state is changed to *ready* and P_2's state is changed to *running*. At 20 ms, P_2 is preempted and P_1 is dispatched. P_1 enters the *blocked* state at 25 ms because of an I/O operation. P_2 is dispatched because it is in the *ready* state. At 35 ms, P_2 is preempted because its time slice elapses; however, it is dispatched again since no other process is in the *ready* state. P_2 initiates an I/O operation at 45 ms. Now both processes are in the *blocked* state.

5.2.1.1 *Suspended Processes*

A kernel needs additional states to describe the nature of the activity of a process that is not in one of the four fundamental states described earlier. Consider a

Table 5.4 Causes of Fundamental State Transitions for a Process

State transition	Description
ready → *running*	The process is dispatched. The CPU begins or resumes execution of its instructions.
blocked → *ready*	A request made by the process is granted or an event for which it was waiting occurs.
running → *ready*	The process is preempted because the kernel decides to schedule some other process. This transition occurs either because a higher-priority process becomes *ready*, or because the time slice of the process elapses.
running → *blocked*	The process in operation makes a system call to indicate that it wishes to wait until some resource request made by it is granted, or until a specific event occurs in the system. Five major causes of blocking are: • Process requests an I/O operation • Process requests a resource • Process wishes to wait for a specified interval of time • Process waits for a message from another process • Process waits for some action by another process.
running → *terminated*	Execution of the program is completed. Five primary reasons for process termination are: • *Self-termination:* The process in operation either completes its task or realizes that it cannot operate meaningfully and makes a "terminate me" system call. Examples of the latter condition are incorrect or inconsistent data, or inability to access data in a desired manner, e.g., incorrect file access privileges. • *Termination by a parent:* A process makes a "terminate P_i" system call to terminate a child process P_i, when it finds that execution of the child process is no longer necessary or meaningful. • *Exceeding resource utilization:* An OS may limit the resources that a process may consume. A process exceeding a resource limit would be aborted by the kernel. • *Abnormal conditions during operation:* The kernel aborts a process if an abnormal condition arises due to the instruction being executed, e.g., execution of an invalid instruction, execution of a privileged instruction, arithmetic conditions like overflow, or memory protection violation. • *Incorrect interaction with other processes:* The kernel may abort a process if it gets involved in a deadlock.

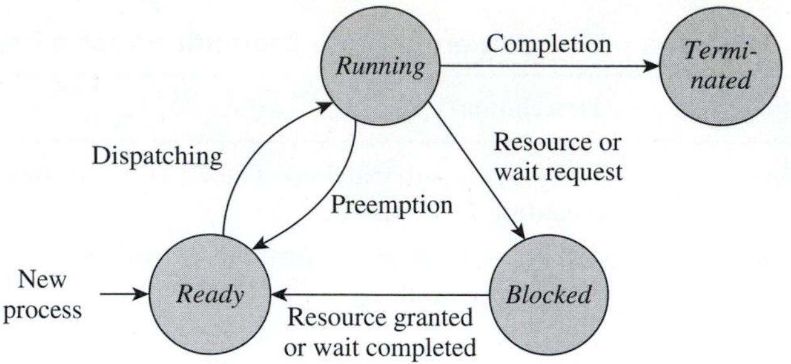

Figure 5.4 Fundamental state transitions for a process.

Table 5.5 Process State Transitions in a Time-Sharing System

Time	Event	Remarks	New states P_1	New states P_2
0		P_1 is scheduled	*running*	*ready*
10	P_1 is preempted	P_2 is scheduled	*ready*	*running*
20	P_2 is preempted	P_1 is scheduled	*running*	*ready*
25	P_1 starts I/O	P_2 is scheduled	*blocked*	*running*
35	P_2 is preempted	—	*blocked*	*ready*
		P_2 is scheduled	*blocked*	*running*
45	P_2 starts I/O	—	*blocked*	*blocked*

process that was in the *ready* or the *blocked* state when it got swapped out of memory. The process needs to be swapped back into memory before it can resume its activity. Hence it is no longer in the *ready* or *blocked* state; the kernel must define a new state for it. We call such a process a *suspended process*. If a user indicates that his process should not be considered for scheduling for a specific period of time, it, too, would become a suspended process. When a suspended process is to resume its old activity, it should go back to the state it was in when it was suspended. To facilitate this state transition, the kernel may define many *suspend* states and put a suspended process into the appropriate suspend state.

We restrict the discussion of suspended processes to swapped processes and use two suspend states called *ready swapped* and *blocked swapped*. Accordingly, Figure 5.5 shows process states and state transitions. The transition *ready* $\rightarrow$ *ready swapped* or *blocked* $\rightarrow$ *blocked swapped* is caused by a swap-out action. The reverse state transition takes place when the process is swapped back into memory. The *blocked swapped* $\rightarrow$ *ready swapped* transition takes place if the request for which the process was waiting is granted even while the process is in a suspended state, for example, if a resource for which it was blocked is granted to it. However, the process continues to be swapped out. When it is swapped back into memory, its state changes to *ready* and it competes with other *ready* processes for

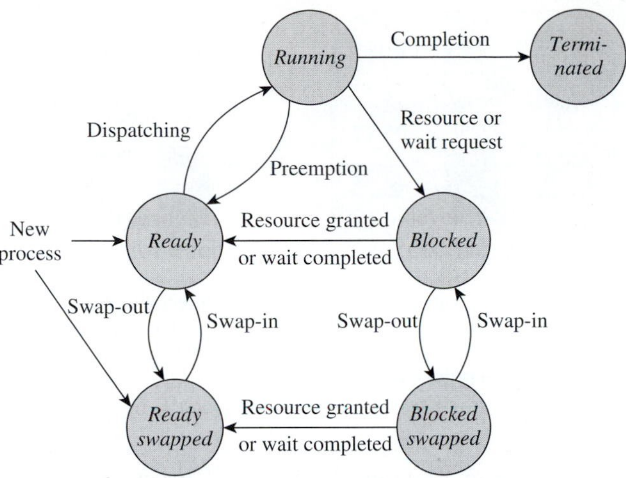

Figure 5.5 Process states and state transitions using two swapped states.

the CPU. A new process is put either in the *ready* state or in the *ready swapped* state depending on availability of memory.

5.2.2 Process Context and the Process Control Block

The kernel allocates resources to a process and schedules it for use of the CPU. Accordingly, the kernel's view of a process consists of two parts:

- Code, data, and stack of the process, and information concerning memory and other resources, such as files, allocated to it.
- Information concerning execution of a program, such as the process state, the CPU state including the stack pointer, and some other items of information described later in this section.

These two parts of the kernel's view are contained in the *process context* and the *process control block* (PCB), respectively (see Figure 5.6). This arrangement enables different OS modules to access relevant process-related information conveniently and efficiently.

Process Context The process context consists of the following:

1. *Address space of the process:* The code, data, and stack components of the process (see Definition 5.1).
2. *Memory allocation information:* Information concerning memory areas allocated to a process. This information is used by the memory management unit (MMU) during operation of the process (see Section 2.2.2).
3. *Status of file processing activities:* Information about files being used, such as current positions in the files.

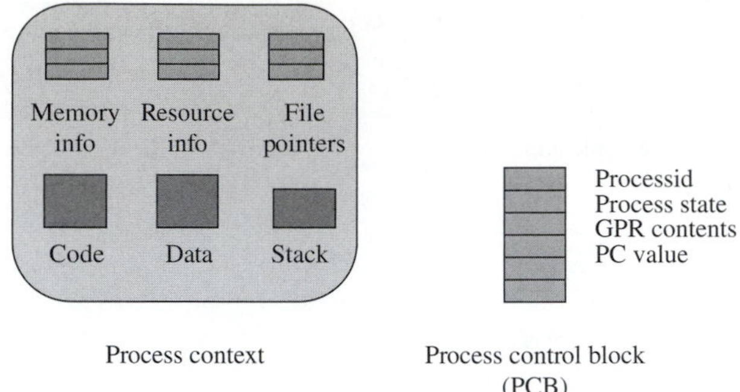

Figure 5.6 Kernel's view of a process.

4. *Process interaction information:* Information necessary to control interaction of the process with other processes, e.g., ids of parent and child processes, and interprocess messages sent to it that have not yet been delivered to it.
5. *Resource information:* Information concerning resources allocated to the process.
6. *Miscellaneous information:* Miscellaneous information needed for operation of a process.

The OS creates a process context by allocating memory to the process, loading the process code in the allocated memory and setting up its data space. Information concerning resources allocated to the process and its interaction with other processes is maintained in the process context throughout the life of the process. This information changes as a result of actions like file open and close and creation and destruction of data by the process during its operation.

Process Control Block (PCB) The *process control block* (PCB) of a process contains three kinds of information concerning the process—identification information such as the process id, id of its parent process, and id of the user who created it; process state information such as its state, and the contents of the PSW and the general-purpose registers (GPRs); and information that is useful in controlling its operation, such as its priority, and its interaction with other processes. It also contains a pointer field that is used by the kernel to form PCB lists for scheduling, e.g., a list of *ready* processes. Table 5.6 describes the fields of the PCB data structure.

The priority and state information is used by the scheduler. It passes the id of the selected process to the dispatcher. For a process that is not in the *running* state, the *PSW* and *GPRs* fields together contain the *CPU state* of the process when it last got blocked or was preempted (see Section 2.2.1). Operation of the process can be resumed by simply loading this information from its PCB into the CPU. This action would be performed when this process is to be dispatched.

When a process becomes *blocked*, it is important to remember the reason. It is done by noting the cause of blocking, such as a resource request or an

Table 5.6 Fields of the Process Control Block (PCB)

PCB field	Contents
Process id	The unique id assigned to the process at its creation.
Parent, child ids	These ids are used for process synchronization, typically for a process to check if a child process has terminated.
Priority	The priority is typically a numeric value. A process is assigned a priority at its creation. The kernel may change the priority dynamically depending on the nature of the process (whether CPU-bound or I/O-bound), its age, and the resources consumed by it (typically CPU time).
Process state	The current state of the process.
PSW	This is a snapshot, i.e., an image, of the PSW when the process last got blocked or was preempted. Loading this snapshot back into the PSW would resume operation of the process. (See Fig. 2.2 for fields of the PSW.)
GPRs	Contents of the general-purpose registers when the process last got blocked or was preempted.
Event information	For a process in the *blocked* state, this field contains information concerning the event for which the process is waiting.
Signal information	Information concerning locations of signal handlers (see Section 5.2.6).
PCB pointer	This field is used to form a list of PCBs for scheduling purposes.

I/O operation, in the *event information* field of the PCB. Consider a process P_i that is blocked on an I/O operation on device d. The *event information* field in P_i's PCB indicates that it awaits end of an I/O operation on device d. When the I/O operation on device d completes, the kernel uses this information to make the transition *blocked* $\rightarrow$ *ready* for process P_i.

5.2.3 Context Save, Scheduling, and Dispatching

The context save function performs housekeeping whenever an event occurs. It saves the CPU state of the interrupted process in its PCB, and saves information concerning its context (see Section 5.2.2). Recall that the interrupted process would have been in the *running* state before the event occurred. The context save function changes its state to *ready*. The event handler may later change the interrupted process's state to *blocked*, e.g., if the current event was a request for I/O initiation by the interrupted process itself.

The scheduling function uses the process state information from PCBs to select a *ready* process for execution and passes its id to the dispatching function. The dispatching function sets up the context of the selected process, changes its state to *running*, and loads the saved CPU state from its PCB into the CPU.

To prevent loss of protection, it flushes the address translation buffers used by the memory management unit (MMU). Example 5.3 illustrates the context save, scheduling, and dispatching functions in an OS using priority-based scheduling.

Example 5.3 Context Save, Scheduling, and Dispatching

An OS contains two processes P_1 and P_2, with P_2 having a higher priority than P_1. Let P_2 be *blocked* on an I/O operation and let P_1 be *running*. The following actions take place when the I/O completion event occurs for the I/O operation of P_2:

1. The context save function is performed for P_1 and its state is changed to *ready*.
2. Using the *event information* field of PCBs, the event handler finds that the I/O operation was initiated by P_2, so it changes the state of P_2 from *blocked* to *ready*.
3. Scheduling is performed. P_2 is selected because it is the highest-priority *ready* process.
4. P_2's state is changed to *running* and it is dispatched.

Process Switching Functions 1, 3, and 4 of Example 5.3 collectively perform switching between processes P_1 and P_2. Switching between processes also occurs when a running process becomes blocked as a result of a request or gets preempted at the end of a time slice. An event does not lead to switching between processes if occurrence of the event either (1) causes a state transition only in a process whose priority is lower than that of the process whose operation is interrupted by the event or (2) does not cause any state transition, e.g., if the event is caused by a request that is immediately satisfied. In the former case, the scheduling function selects the interrupted process itself for dispatching. In the latter case, scheduling need not be performed at all; the dispatching function could simply change the state of the interrupted process back to *running* and dispatch it.

Switching between processes involves more than saving the CPU state of one process and loading the CPU state of another process. The process context needs to be switched as well. We use the term *state information of a process* to refer to all the information that needs to be saved and restored during process switching. Process switching overhead depends on the size of the state information of a process. Some computer systems provide special instructions to reduce the process switching overhead, e.g., instructions that save or load the PSW and all general-purpose registers, or flush the address translation buffers used by the memory management unit (MMU).

Process switching has some indirect overhead as well. The newly scheduled process may not have any part of its address space in the cache, and so it may perform poorly until it builds sufficient information in the cache (see Section 2.2.3). Virtual memory operation is also poorer initially because address translation buffers in the MMU do not contain any information relevant to the newly scheduled process.

5.2.4 Event Handling

The following events occur during the operation of an OS:

1. *Process creation event:* A new process is created.
2. *Process termination event:* A process completes its operation.
3. *Timer event:* The timer interrupt occurs.
4. *Resource request event:* Process makes a resource request.
5. *Resource release event:* A process releases a resource.
6. *I/O initiation request event:* Process wishes to initiate an I/O operation.
7. *I/O completion event:* An I/O operation completes.
8. *Message send event:* A message is sent by one process to another.
9. *Message receive event:* A message is received by a process.
10. *Signal send event:* A signal is sent by one process to another.
11. *Signal receive event:* A signal is received by a process.
12. *A program interrupt:* The current instruction in the *running* process malfunctions.
13. *A hardware malfunction event:* A unit in the computer's hardware malfunctions.

The timer, I/O completion, and hardware malfunction events are caused by situations that are external to the running process. All other events are caused by actions in the *running* process. We group events 1–9 into two broad classes for discussing actions of event handlers, and discuss events 10 and 11 in Section 5.2.6. The kernel performs a standard action like aborting the *running* process when events 12 or 13 occur.

Events Pertaining to Process Creation, Termination, and Preemption When a user issues a command to execute a program, the command interpreter of the user interface makes a *create_process* system call with the name of the program as a parameter. When a process wishes to create a child process to execute a program, it itself makes a *create_process* system call with the name of the program as a parameter.

The event handling routine for the *create_process* system call creates a PCB for the new process, assigns a unique process id and a priority to it, and puts this information and id of the parent process into relevant fields of the PCB. It now determines the amount of memory required to accommodate the address space of the process, i.e., the code and data of the program to be executed and its stack, and arranges to allocate this much memory to the process (memory allocation techniques are discussed later in Chapters 11 and 12). In most operating systems, some standard resources are associated with each process, e.g., a keyboard, and standard input and output files; the kernel allocates these standard resources to the process at this time. It now enters information about allocated memory and resources into the context of the new process. After completing these chores, it sets the state of the process to *ready* in its PCB and enters this process in an appropriate PCB list.

When a process makes a system call to terminate itself or terminate a child process, the kernel delays termination until the I/O operations that were initiated by the process are completed. It now releases the memory and resources allocated to it. This function is performed by using the information in appropriate fields of the process context. The kernel now changes the state of the process to *terminated*. The parent of the process may wish to check its status sometime in future, so the PCB of the terminated process is not destroyed now; it will be done sometime after the parent process has checked its status or has itself terminated. If the parent of the process is already waiting for its termination, the kernel must activate the parent process. To perform this action, the kernel takes the id of the parent process from the PCB of the terminated process, and checks the *event information* field of the parent process's PCB to find whether the parent process is waiting for termination of the child process (see Section 5.2.2).

The process in the *running* state should be preempted if its time slice elapses. The context save function would have already changed the state of the running process to *ready* before invoking the event handler for timer interrupts, so the event handler simply moves the PCB of the process to an appropriate scheduling list. Preemption should also occur when a higher-priority process becomes *ready*, but that is realized implicitly when the higher-priority process is scheduled so an event handler need not perform any explicit action for it.

Events Pertaining to Resource Utilization When a process requests a resource through a system call, the kernel may be able to allocate the resource immediately, in which case event handling does not cause any process state transitions, so the kernel can skip scheduling and directly invoke the dispatching function to resume operation of the interrupted process. If the resource cannot be allocated, the event handler changes the state of the interrupted process to *blocked* and notes the id of the required resource in the *event information* field of the PCB. When a process releases a resource through a system call, the event handler need not change the state of the process that made the system call. However, it should check whether any other processes were blocked because they needed the resource, and, if so, it should allocate the resource to one of the blocked processes and change its state to *ready*. This action requires a special arrangement that we will discuss shortly.

A system call to request initiation of an I/O operation and an interrupt signaling end of the I/O operation lead to analogous event handling actions. The state of the process is changed to *blocked* when the I/O operation is initiated and the cause of blocking is noted in the *event information* field of its PCB; its state is changed back to *ready* when the I/O operation completes. A request to receive a message from another process and a request to send a message to another process also lead to analogous actions.

Event Control Block (ECB) When an event occurs, the kernel must find the process whose state is affected by it. For example, when an I/O completion interrupt occurs, the kernel must identify the process awaiting its completion. It can achieve this by searching the *event information* field of the PCBs of all

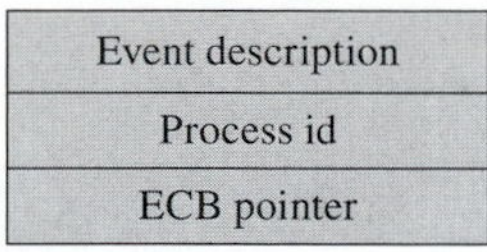

Figure 5.7 Event control block (ECB).

processes. This search is expensive, so operating systems use various schemes to speed it up. We discuss a scheme that uses *event control blocks* (ECBs).

As shown in Figure 5.7, an ECB contains three fields. The *event description* field describes an event, and the *process id* field contains the id of the process awaiting the event. When a process P_i gets blocked for occurrence of an event e_i, the kernel forms an ECB and puts relevant information concerning e_i and P_i into it. The kernel can maintain a separate ECB list for each class of events like interprocess messages or I/O operations, so the *ECB pointer* field is used to enter the newly created ECB into an appropriate list of ECBs.

When an event occurs, the kernel scans the appropriate list of ECBs to find an ECB with a matching event description. The *process id* field of the ECB indicates which process is waiting for the event to occur. The state of this process is changed to reflect the occurrence of the event. The following example illustrates use of ECBs for handling an I/O completion event; their use in handling interprocess messages is described in Section 9.2.2. The *event information* field of the PCB now appears redundant; however, we retain it because the kernel may need to know which event a process is blocked on, for example, while aborting the process.

Use of ECB for Handling I/O Completion

Example 5.4

The actions of the kernel when process P_i requests an I/O operation on some device d, and when the I/O operation completes, are as follows:

1. The kernel creates an ECB, and initializes it as follows:
   a. Event description := end of I/O on device d.
   b. Process awaiting the event := P_i.
2. The newly created ECB (let us call it ECB_j) is added to a list of ECBs.
3. The state of P_i is changed to *blocked* and the address of ECB_j is put into the "Event information" field of P_i's PCB (see Figure 5.8).
4. When the interrupt 'End of I/O on device d' occurs, ECB_j is located by searching for an ECB with a matching event description field.
5. The id of the affected process, i.e., P_i, is extracted from ECB_j. The PCB of P_i is located and its state is changed to *ready.*

Summary of Event Handling Figure 5.9 illustrates event handling actions of the kernel described earlier. The *block* action always changes the state of the process that made a system call from *ready* to *blocked*. The *unblock* action finds a process whose request can be fulfilled now and changes its state from *blocked*

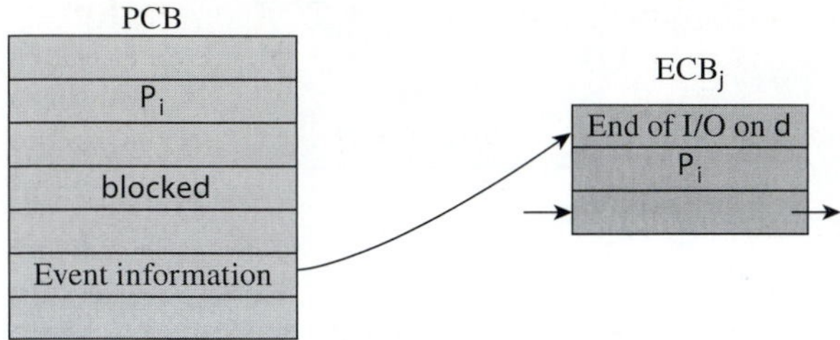

Figure 5.8 PCB-ECB interrelationship.

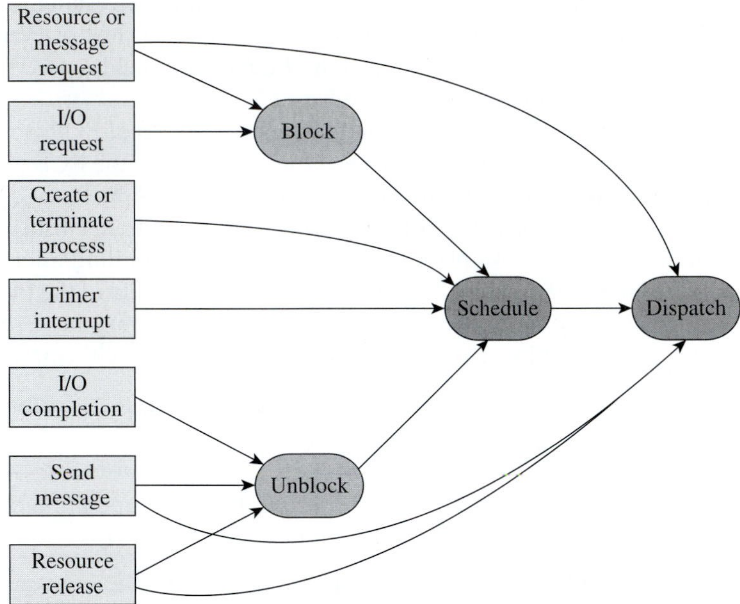

Figure 5.9 Event handling actions of the kernel.

to *ready*. A system call for requesting a resource leads to a *block* action if the resource cannot be allocated to the requesting process. This action is followed by scheduling and dispatching because another process has to be selected for use of the CPU. The block action is not performed if the resource can be allocated straightaway. In this case, the interrupted process is simply dispatched again. When a process releases a resource, an *unblock* action is performed if some other process is waiting for the released resource, followed by scheduling and dispatching because the unblocked process may have a higher priority than the process that released the resource. Again, scheduling is skipped if no process is unblocked because of the event.

5.2.5 Sharing, Communication, and Synchronization Between Processes

Processes of an application need to interact with one another because they work toward a common goal. Table 5.7 describes four kinds of process interaction. We summarize their important features in the following.

Data Sharing A shared variable may get inconsistent values if many processes update it concurrently. For example, if two processes concurrently execute the statement `a:= a+1`, where `a` is a shared variable, the result may depend on the way the kernel interleaves their execution—the value of `a` may be incremented by only 1! (We discuss this problem later in Section 6.2.) To avoid this problem, only one process should access shared data at any time, so a data access in one process may have to be delayed if another process is accessing the data. This is called *mutual exclusion*. Thus, data sharing by concurrent processes incurs the overhead of mutual exclusion.

Message Passing A process may send some information to another process in the form of a message. The other process can copy the information into its own data structures and use it. Both the sender and the receiver process must anticipate the information exchange, i.e., a process must know when it is expected to send or receive a message, so the information exchange becomes a part of the convention or protocol between processes.

Synchronization The logic of a program may require that an action a_i should be performed only after some action a_j has been performed. Synchronization between processes is required if these actions are performed in different processes—the process that wishes to perform action a_i is made to wait until another process performs action a_j.

Signals A signal is used to convey an exceptional situation to a process so that it may handle the situation through appropriate actions. The code that a process wishes to execute on receiving a signal is called a *signal handler*. The signal mechanism is modeled along the lines of interrupts. Thus, when a signal

Table 5.7 Four Kinds of Process Interaction

Kind of interaction	Description
Data sharing	Shared data may become inconsistent if several processes modify the data at the same time. Hence processes must interact to decide when it is safe for a process to modify or use shared data.
Message passing	Processes exchange information by sending messages to one another.
Synchronization	To fulfill a common goal, processes must coordinate their activities and perform their actions in a desired order.
Signals	A signal is used to convey occurrence of an exceptional situation to a process.

is sent to a process, the kernel interrupts operation of the process and executes a signal handler, if one has been specified by the process; otherwise, it may perform a default action. Operating systems differ in the way they resume a process after executing a signal handler.

Example 5.5 illustrates sharing, communication, and synchronization between processes in the real-time application of Example 5.1. Implementation of signals is described in Section 5.2.6.

Example 5.5 **Process Interaction in a Real-time Data Logging Application**

In the real-time data logging application of Example 5.1, *buffer_area* is shared by processes *copy_sample* and *record_sample*. If a variable *no_of_samples_in_buffer* is used to indicate how many samples are currently in the buffer, both these processes would need to update *no_of_samples_in_buffer*, so its consistency should be protected by delaying a process that wishes to update it if another process is accessing it. These processes also need to synchronize their activities such that a new sample is moved into an entry in *buffer_area* only after the previous sample contained in the entry is written into the file, and contents of a buffer entry are written into the file only after a new sample is moved into it.

These processes also need to know the size of the buffer, i.e., how many samples it can hold. Like *no_of_samples_in_buffer*, a variable *size* could be used as shared data. However, use as shared data would incur the overhead of mutual exclusion, which is not justified because the buffer size is not updated regularly; it changes only in exceptional situations. Hence these processes could be coded to use the size of the buffer as a *local* data item *buf_size*. Its value would be sent to them by the process *data_logger* through messages. Process *data_logger* would also need to send signals to these processes if the size of the buffer has to be changed.

5.2.6 Signals

A signal is used to notify an exceptional situation to a process and enable it to attend to it immediately. A list of exceptional situations and associated signal names or signal numbers are defined in an OS, e.g., CPU conditions like overflows, and conditions related to child processes, resource utilization, or emergency communications from a user to a process. The kernel sends a signal to a process when the corresponding exceptional situation occurs. Some kinds of signals may also be sent by processes. A signal sent to a process because of a condition in its own activity, such as an overflow condition in the CPU, is said to be a *synchronous* signal, whereas that sent because of some other condition is said to be an *asynchronous* signal.

To utilize signals, a process makes a *register_handler* system call specifying a routine that should be executed when a specific signal is sent to it; this routine is called a *signal handler*. If a process does not specify a signal handler for a signal, the kernel executes a *default handler* that performs some standard actions like dumping the address space of the process and aborting it.

A process P_i wishing to send a signal to another process P_j invokes the library function `signal` with two parameters: id of the destination process, i.e., P_j, and the signal number. This function uses the software interrupt instruction *<SI_instrn> <interrupt_code>* to make a system call named *signal*. The event handling routine for the *signal* call extracts the parameters to find the signal number. It now makes a provision to pass the signal to P_j and returns. It does not make any change in the state of the sender process, i.e., P_i.

Signal handling in a process is implemented along the same lines as interrupt handling in an OS. In Section 2.2 we described how the interrupt hardware employs one interrupt vector for each class of interrupts, which contains the address of a routine that handles interrupts of that class. A similar arrangement can be used in each process. The signal vectors area would contain a signal vector for each kind of signal, which would contain the address of a signal handler. When a signal is sent to a process, the kernel accesses its signal vectors area to check whether it has specified a signal handler for that signal. If so, it would arrange to pass control to the handler; otherwise, it would execute its own default handler for that signal.

Signal handling becomes complicated if the process to which a signal is sent is in the *blocked* state. The kernel would have to change its state temporarily to *ready* so that it could execute a signal handler, after which it would have to change the state back to *blocked*. Some operating systems prefer a simpler approach that merely notes the arrival of a signal if the destination process is in the *blocked* state, and arranges to execute the signal handler when the process becomes *ready* and gets scheduled.

Example 5.6 illustrates how a signal is handled by a process.

Signal Handling

Example 5.6

Figure 5.10 illustrates the arrangement used for handling signals. The code of process P_i contains a function named `sh1`, whose last instruction is a "return from function" instruction, which pops an address off the stack and passes control to the instruction with this address. Process P_i makes a library call `register_handler(sig1,sh1)` to register `sh1` as the signal handler for signal `sig1`. The library routine `register_handler` makes the system call *register_handler*. While handling this call, the kernel accesses the PCB of P_i, obtains the start address of the signal vectors area, and enters the address `sh1` in the signal vector of signal `sig1`. Control now returns to P_i. The solid arrows in Figure 5.10(a) indicate addresses in the kernel's data structures, while the dashed arrows indicate how the CPU is switched to the kernel when the system call is made and how it is switched back to P_i.

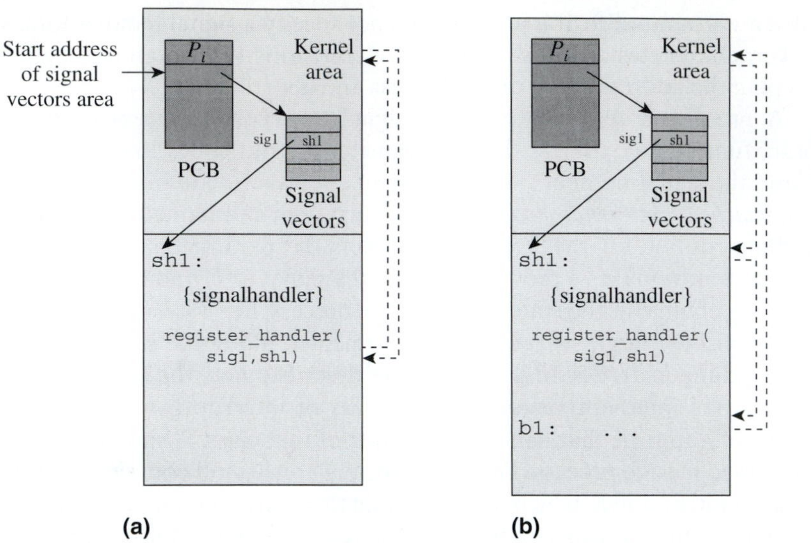

Figure 5.10 Signal handling by process P_i: (a) registering a signal handler; (b) invoking a signal handler.

Let process P_i get preempted when it was about to execute the instruction with address `b1`. A little later, some process P_j makes the system call `signal` (P_i, `sig1`). The kernel locates the PCB of P_i, obtains the address of its signal vectors area and locates the signal vector for `sig1`. It now arranges for process P_i to execute the signal handler starting at address `sh1` before resuming normal execution as follows: It obtains the address contained in the *program counter* (PC) field of the saved state of P_i, which is the address `b1` because P_i was about to execute the instruction with this address. It pushes this address on P_i's stack, and puts the address `sh1` in the program counter field of the saved state of P_i. This way, when process P_i is scheduled, it would execute the signal handler function with the start address `sh1`. The last instruction of `sh1` would pop the address `b1` off the stack and pass control to the instruction with address `b1`, which would resume normal operation of process P_i. In effect, as shown by the broken arrows in Figure 5.10(b), P_i's execution would be diverted to the signal handler starting at address `sh1`, and it would be resumed after the signal handler is executed.

5.3 THREADS

Applications use concurrent processes to speed up their operation. However, switching between processes within an application incurs high process switching overhead because the size of the process state information is large (see Section 5.2.3), so operating system designers developed an alternative model of execution of a program, called a *thread,* that could provide concurrency within an application with less overhead.

To understand the notion of threads, let us analyze process switching overhead and see where a saving can be made. Process switching overhead has two components:

- *Execution related overhead:* The CPU state of the running process has to be saved and the CPU state of the new process has to be loaded in the CPU. This overhead is unavoidable.
- *Resource-use related overhead:* The process context also has to be switched. It involves switching of the information about resources allocated to the process, such as memory and files, and interaction of the process with other processes. The large size of this information adds to the process switching overhead.

Consider child processes P_i and P_j of the primary process of an application. These processes inherit the context of their parent process. If none of these processes have allocated any resources of their own, their context is identical; their state information differs only in their CPU states and contents of their stacks. Consequently, while switching between P_i and P_j, much of the saving and loading of process state information is redundant. Threads exploit this feature to reduce the switching overhead.

Definition 5.3 Thread An execution of a program that uses the resources of a process.

A process creates a thread through a system call. The thread does not have resources of its own, so it does not have a context; it operates by using the context of the process, and accesses the resources of the process through it. We use the phrases "thread(s) of a process" and "parent process of a thread" to describe the relationship between a thread and the process whose context it uses. Note that threads are not a substitute for child processes; an application would create child processes to execute different parts of its code, and each child process can create threads to achieve concurrency.

Figure 5.11 illustrates the relationship between threads and processes. In the abstract view of Figure 5.11(a), process P_i has three threads, which are represented by wavy lines inside the circle representing process P_i. Figure 5.11(b) shows an implementation arrangement. Process P_i has a context and a PCB. Each thread of P_i is an execution of a program, so it has its own stack and a *thread control block* (TCB), which is analogous to the PCB and stores the following information:

1. Thread scheduling information—thread id, priority and state.
2. CPU state, i.e., contents of the PSW and GPRs.
3. Pointer to PCB of parent process.
4. TCB pointer, which is used to make lists of TCBs for scheduling.

Use of threads effectively splits the process state into two parts—the resource state remains with the process while an execution state, which is the CPU state, is

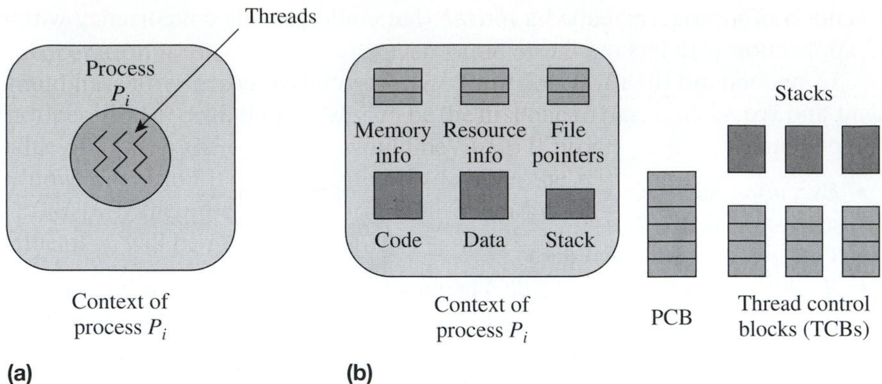

Figure 5.11 Threads in process P_i: (a) concept; (b) implementation.

associated with a thread. The cost of concurrency within the context of a process is now merely replication of the execution state for each thread. The execution states need to be switched during switching between threads. The resource state is neither replicated nor switched during switching between threads of the process.

Thread States and State Transitions Barring the difference that threads do not have resources allocated to them, threads and processes are analogous. Hence thread states and thread state transitions are analogous to process states and process state transitions. When a thread is created, it is put in the *ready* state because its parent process already has the necessary resources allocated to it. It enters the *running* state when it is dispatched. It does not enter the *blocked* state because of resource requests, because it does not make any resource requests; however, it can enter the *blocked* state because of process synchronization requirements. For example, if threads were used in the real-time data logging application of Example 5.1, thread *record_sample* would have to enter the *blocked* state if no data samples exist in *buffer_area*.

Advantages of Threads over Processes Table 5.8 summarizes the advantages of threads over processes, of which we have already discussed the advantage of lower overhead of thread creation and switching. Unlike child processes, threads share the address space of the parent process, so they can communicate through shared data rather than through messages, thereby eliminating the overhead of system calls.

Applications that service requests received from users, such as airline reservation systems or banking systems, are called *servers*; their users are called *clients*. (Client–server computing is discussed in Section 16.5.1.) Performance of servers can be improved through concurrency or parallelism (see Section 5.1.4), i.e., either through interleaving of requests that involve I/O operations or through use of many CPUs to service different requests. Use of threads simplifies their design; we discuss it with the help of Figure 5.12.

Figure 5.12(a) is a view of an airline reservation server. The server enters requests made by its clients in a queue and serves them one after another. If

Table 5.8 Advantages of Threads over Processes

Advantage	Explanation
Lower overhead of creation and switching	Thread state consists only of the state of a computation. Resource allocation state and communication state are not a part of the thread state, so creation of threads and switching between them incurs a lower overhead.
More efficient communication	Threads of a process can communicate with one another through shared data, thus avoiding the overhead of system calls for communication.
Simplification of design	Use of threads can simplify design and coding of applications that service requests concurrently.

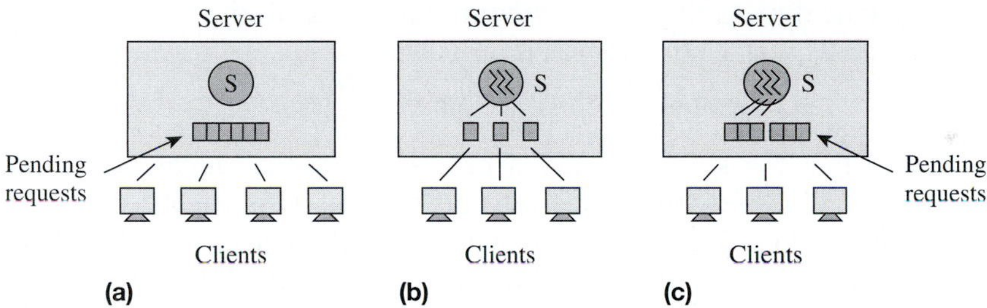

Figure 5.12 Use of threads in structuring a server: (a) server using sequential code; (b) multithreaded server; (c) server using a thread pool.

several requests are to be serviced concurrently, the server would have to employ advanced I/O techniques such as asynchronous I/O, and use complex logic to switch between the processing of requests. By contrast, a multithreaded server could create a new thread to service each new request it receives, and terminate the thread after servicing the request. This server would not have to employ any special techniques for concurrency because concurrency is implicit in its creation of threads. Figure 5.12(b) shows a multithreaded server, which has created three threads because it has received three requests.

Creation and termination of threads is more efficient than creation and termination of processes; however, its overhead can affect performance of the server if clients make requests at a very high rate. An arrangement called *thread pool* is used to avoid this overhead by reusing threads instead of destroying them after servicing requests. The thread pool consists of one primary thread that performs housekeeping tasks and a few worker threads that are used repetitively. The primary thread maintains a list of pending requests and a list of idle worker threads. When a new request is made, it assigns the request to an idle worker thread, if one exists; otherwise, it enters the request in the list of pending requests. When a worker thread completes servicing of a request, the primary thread either assigns a new request to the worker thread to service, or enters it in the list of idle worker threads. Figure 5.12(c) illustrates a server using a thread pool. It contains three worker threads that are busy servicing three service requests, while three service requests are pending. If the thread pool facility is implemented in the OS, the OS would provide the primary thread for the pool, which would simplify coding of the server because it would not have to handle concurrency explicitly. The OS could also vary the number of worker threads dynamically to provide adequate concurrency in the application, and also reduce commitment of OS resources to idle worker threads.

Coding for Use of Threads Threads should ensure correctness of data sharing and synchronization (see Section 5.2.5). Section 5.3.1 describes features in the POSIX threads standard that can be used for this purpose. Correctness of data sharing also has another facet. Functions or subroutines that use static or global data to carry values across their successive activations may produce incorrect results when invoked concurrently, because the invocations effectively share the global or static data concurrently without mutual exclusion. Such routines are said to be *thread unsafe*. An application that uses threads must be coded in a *thread safe* manner and must invoke routines only from a thread safe library.

Signal handling requires special attention in a multithreaded application. Recall that the kernel permits a process to specify signal handlers (see Section 5.2.6). When several threads are created in a process, which thread should handle a signal? There are several possibilities. The kernel may select one of the threads for signal handling. This choice can be made either statically, e.g., either the first or the last thread created in the process, or dynamically, e.g., the highest-priority thread. Alternatively, the kernel may permit an application to specify which thread should handle signals at any time.

A synchronous signal arises as a result of the activity of a thread, so it is best that the thread itself handles it. Ideally, each thread should be able to specify which synchronous signals it is interested in handling. However, to provide this feature, the kernel would have to replicate the signal handling arrangement of Figure 5.6 for each thread, so few operating systems provide it. An asynchronous signal can be handled by any thread in a process. To ensure prompt attention to the condition that caused the signal, the highest-priority thread should handle such a signal.

5.3.1 POSIX Threads

The ANSI/IEEE Portable Operating System Interface (POSIX) standard defines the pthreads application program interface for use by C language programs. Popularly called POSIX threads, this interface provides 60 routines that perform the following tasks:

- *Thread management:* Threads are managed through calls on thread library routines for creation of threads, querying status of threads, normal or abnormal termination of threads, waiting for termination of a thread, setting of scheduling attributes, and specifying thread stack size.
- *Assistance for data sharing:* Data shared by threads may attain incorrect values if two or more threads update it concurrently. A feature called *mutex* is

provided to ensure mutual exclusion between threads while accessing shared data, i.e., to ensure that only one thread is accessing shared data at any time. Routines are provided to begin use of shared data in a thread and indicate end of use of shared data. If threads are used in Example 5.5, threads *copy_sample* and *record_sample* would use a mutex to ensure that they do not access and update *no_of_samples_in_buffer* concurrently.

- *Assistance for synchronization: Condition variables* are provided to facilitate coordination between threads so that they perform their actions in the desired order. If threads are used in Example 5.5, condition variables would be used to ensure that thread *copy_sample* would copy a sample into *buffer_area* before *record_sample* would write it from there into the file.

Figure 5.13 illustrates use of pthreads in the real-time data logging application of Example 5.1. A pthread is created through the call

`pthread_create`(< *data structure* >, < *attributes* >,
< *start routine* >, < *arguments* >)

where the thread data structure becomes the de facto thread id, and attributes indicate scheduling priority and synchronization options. A thread terminates through a `pthread_exit` call which takes a thread status as a parameter. Synchronization between the parent thread and a child thread is performed through the `pthread_join` call, which takes a thread id and some attributes as parameters. On issuing this call, the parent thread is blocked until the thread indicated in the call has terminated; an error is raised if the termination status of the thread does not match the attributes indicated in the `pthread_join` call. Some thread implementations require a thread to be created with the attribute "joinable" to qualify for such synchronization. The code in Figure 5.13 creates three threads to perform the functions performed by processes in Example 5.1. As mentioned above, and indicated through comments in Figure 5.13, the threads would use the mutex `buf_mutex` to ensure mutually exclusive access to the buffer and use condition variables `buf_full` and `buf_empty` to ensure that they deposit samples into the buffer and take them out of the buffer in the correct order. We do not show details of mutexes and condition variables here; they are discussed later in Chapter 6.

5.3.2 Kernel-Level, User-Level, and Hybrid Threads

These three models of threads differ in the role of the process and the kernel in the creation and management of threads. This difference has a significant impact on the overhead of thread switching and the concurrency and parallelism within a process.

5.3.2.1 Kernel-Level Threads

A kernel-level thread is implemented by the kernel. Hence creation and termination of kernel-level threads, and checking of their status, is performed

```
#include <pthread.h>
#include <stdio.h>
int size, buffer[100], no_of_samples_in_buffer;
int main()
{
   pthread_t id1, id2, id3;
   pthread_mutex_t buf_mutex, condition_mutex;
   pthread_cond_t buf_full, buf_empty;
   pthread_create(&id1, NULL, move_to_buffer, NULL);
   pthread_create(&id2, NULL, write_into_file, NULL);
   pthread_create(&id3, NULL, analysis, NULL);
   pthread_join(id1, NULL);
   pthread_join(id2, NULL);
   pthread_join(id3, NULL);
   pthread_exit(0);
}
void *move_to_buffer()
{
   /* Repeat until all samples are received */
   /* If no space in buffer, wait on buf_full */
   /* Use buf_mutex to access the buffer, increment no. of samples */
   /* Signal buf_empty */
   pthread_exit(0);
}
void *write_into_file()
{
   /* Repeat until all samples are written into the file */
   /* If no data in buffer, wait on buf_empty */
   /* Use buf_mutex to access the buffer, decrement no. of samples */
   /* Signal buf_full */
   pthread_exit(0);
}
void *analysis()
{
   /* Repeat until all samples are analyzed */
   /* Read a sample from the buffer and analyze it */
   pthread_exit(0);
}
```

Figure 5.13 Outline of the data logging application using POSIX threads.

through system calls. Figure 5.14 shows a schematic of how the kernel handles kernel-level threads. When a process makes a *create_thread* system call, the kernel creates a thread, assigns an id to it, and allocates a thread control block (TCB). The TCB contains a pointer to the PCB of the parent process of the thread.

When an event occurs, the kernel saves the CPU state of the interrupted thread in its TCB. After event handling, the scheduler considers TCBs of all threads and selects one *ready* thread; the dispatcher uses the PCB pointer in its

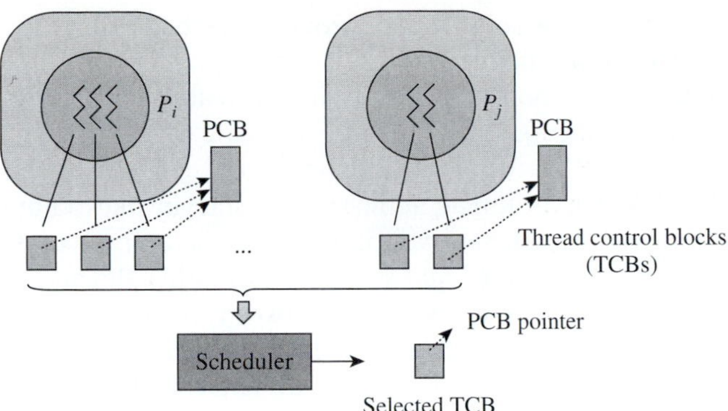

Figure 5.14 Scheduling of kernel-level threads.

TCB to check whether the selected thread belongs to a different process than the interrupted thread. If so, it saves the context of the process to which the interrupted thread belongs, and loads the context of the process to which the selected thread belongs. It then dispatches the selected thread. However, actions to save and load the process context are skipped if both threads belong to the same process. This feature reduces the switching overhead, hence switching between kernel-level threads of a process could be as much as an order of magnitude faster, i.e., 10 times faster, than switching between processes.

Advantages and Disadvantages of Kernel-Level Threads A kernel-level thread is like a process except that it has a smaller amount of state information. This similarity is convenient for programmers—programming for threads is no different from programming for processes. In a multiprocessor system, kernel-level threads provide parallelism (see Section 5.1.4), as many threads belonging to a process can be scheduled simultaneously, which is not possible with the user-level threads described in the next section, so it provides better computation speedup than user-level threads.

However, handling threads like processes has its disadvantages too. Switching between threads is performed by the kernel as a result of event handling. Hence it incurs the overhead of event handling even if the interrupted thread and the selected thread belong to the same process. This feature limits the savings in the thread switching overhead.

5.3.2.2 User-Level Threads

User-level threads are implemented by a *thread library*, which is linked to the code of a process. The library sets up the thread implementation arrangement shown in Figure 5.11(b) without involving the kernel, and itself interleaves operation of threads in the process. Thus, the kernel is not aware of presence of user-level threads in a process; it sees only the process. Most OSs implement the pthreads application program interface provided in the IEEE POSIX standard (see Section 5.3.1) in this manner.

An overview of creation and operation of threads is as follows: A process invokes the library function *create_thread* to create a new thread. The library function creates a TCB for the new thread and starts considering the new thread for "scheduling." When the thread in the *running* state invokes a library function to perform synchronization, say, wait until a specific event occurs, the library function performs "scheduling" and switches to another thread of the process. Thus, the kernel is oblivious to switching between threads; it believes that the *process* is continuously in operation. If the thread library cannot find a ready thread in the process, it makes a "block me" system call. The kernel now blocks the process. It will be unblocked when some event activates one of its threads and will resume execution of the thread library function, which will perform "scheduling" and switch to execution of the newly activated thread.

Scheduling of User-Level Threads Figure 5.15 is a schematic diagram of scheduling of user-level threads. The thread library code is a part of each process. It performs "scheduling" to select a thread, and organizes its execution. We view this operation as "mapping" of the TCB of the selected thread into the PCB of the process.

The thread library uses information in the TCBs to decide which thread should operate at any time. To "dispatch" the thread, the CPU state of the thread should become the CPU state of the process, and the process stack pointer should point to the thread's stack. Since the thread library is a part of a process, the CPU is in the user mode. Hence a thread cannot be dispatched by loading new information into the PSW; the thread library has to use nonprivileged instructions to change PSW contents. Accordingly, it loads the address of the thread's stack

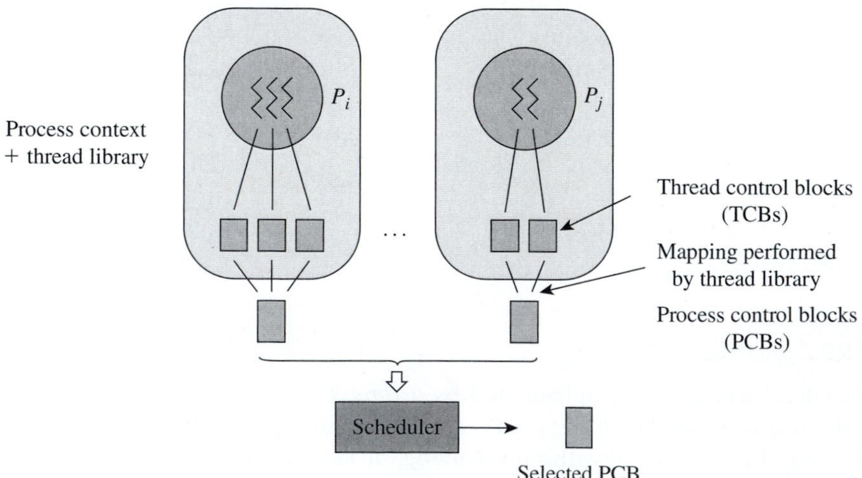

Figure 5.15 Scheduling of user-level threads.

into the stack address register, obtains the address contained in the *program counter* (PC) field of the thread's CPU state found in its TCB, and executes a branch instruction to transfer control to the instruction which has this address. The next example illustrates interesting situations during scheduling of user-level threads.

Scheduling of User-Level Threads

Example 5.7

Figure 5.16 illustrates how the thread library manages three threads in a process P_i. The codes N, R, and B in the TCBs represent the states *running*, *ready*, and *blocked*, respectively. Process P_i is in the *running* state and the thread library is executing. It dispatches thread h_1, so h_1's state is shown as N, i.e. *running*. Process P_i is preempted sometime later by the kernel. Figure 5.16(a) illustrates states of the threads and of process P_i. Thread h_1 is in the *running* state, and process P_i is in the *ready* state. Thread h_1 would resume its operation when process P_i is scheduled next. The line from h_1's TCB to P_i's PCB indicates that h_1's TCB is currently mapped into P_i's PCB. This fact is important for the dispatching and context save actions of the thread library.

Thread h_2 is in the *ready* state in Figure 5.16(a), so its TCB contains the code R. Thread h_3 awaits a synchronization action by h_1, so it is in the *blocked* state. Its TCB contains the code B, and h_1 to indicate that it is awaiting an event that is a synchronization action by h_1. Figure 5.16(b) shows the situation when the kernel dispatches P_i and changes its state to *running*.

The thread library overlaps operation of threads using the timer. While "scheduling" h_1, the library would have requested an interrupt after a small interval of time. When the timer interrupt occurs, it gets control through the event handling routine of the kernel for timer interrupts, and decides to preempt h_1. So it saves the CPU state in h_1's TCB, and "schedules" h_2. Hence the state codes in the TCB's of h_1 and h_2 change to R and N, respectively (Figure 5.16(c)). Note that thread scheduling performed by the thread library is invisible to the kernel. All through these events, the kernel sees process P_i in the *running* state.

A user thread should not make a blocking system call; however, let us see what would happen if h_2 made a system call to initiate an I/O operation on device d_2, which is a blocking system call. The kernel would change the state of process P_i to *blocked* and note that it is blocked because of an I/O operation on device d_2 (Figure 5.16(d)). Some time after the I/O operation completes, the kernel would schedule process P_i, and operation of h_2 would resume. Note that the state code in h_2's TCB remains N, signifying the *running* state, all through its I/O operation!

Advantages and Disadvantages of User-Level Threads Thread synchronization and scheduling is implemented by the thread library. This arrangement avoids

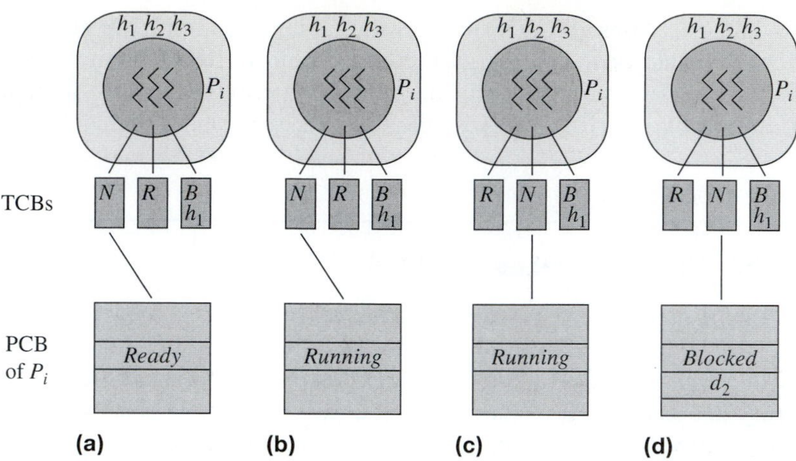

Figure 5.16 Actions of the thread library (N, R, B indicate *running*, *ready*, and *blocked*).

the overhead of a system call for synchronization between threads, so the thread switching overhead could be as much as an order of magnitude smaller than in kernel-level threads. This arrangement also enables each process to use a scheduling policy that best suits its nature. A process implementing a real-time application may use priority-based scheduling of its threads to meet its response requirements, whereas a process implementing a multithreaded server may perform round-robin scheduling of its threads. However, performance of an application would depend on whether scheduling of user-level threads performed by the thread library is compatible with scheduling of processes performed by the kernel. For example, round-robin scheduling in the thread library would be compatible with either round-robin scheduling or priority-based scheduling in the kernel, whereas priority-based scheduling would be compatible only with priority-based scheduling in the kernel.

Managing threads without involving the kernel also has a few drawbacks. First, the kernel does not know the distinction between a thread and a process, so if a thread were to block in a system call, the kernel would block its parent process. In effect, *all* threads of the process would get blocked until the cause of the blocking was removed—In Figure 5.16(d) of Example 5.7, thread h_1 cannot be scheduled even though it is in the *ready* state because thread h_2 made a blocking system call. Hence threads must not make system calls that can lead to blocking. To facilitate this, an OS would have to make available a nonblocking version of each system call that would otherwise lead to blocking of a process. Second, since the kernel schedules a process and the thread library schedules the threads within a process, at most one thread of a process can be in operation at any time. Thus, user-level threads cannot provide parallelism (see Section 5.1.4), and the concurrency provided by them is seriously impaired if a thread makes a system call that leads to blocking.

5.3.2.3 Hybrid Thread Models

A hybrid thread model has *both* user-level threads and kernel-level threads and a method of associating user-level threads with kernel-level threads. Different methods of associating user- and kernel-level threads provide different combinations of the low switching overhead of user-level threads and the high concurrency and parallelism of kernel-level threads.

Figure 5.17 illustrates three methods of associating user-level threads with kernel-level threads. The thread library creates user-level threads in a process and associates a *thread control block* (TCB) with each user-level thread. The kernel creates kernel-level threads in a process and associates a *kernel thread control block* (KTCB) with each kernel-level thread. In the many-to-one association method, a single kernel-level thread is created in a process by the kernel and all user-level threads created in a process by the thread library are associated with this kernel-level thread. This method of association provides an effect similar to mere user-level threads: User-level threads can be concurrent without being parallel, thread switching incurs low overhead, and blocking of a user-level thread leads to blocking of all threads in the process.

In the one-to-one method of association, each user-level thread is permanently mapped into a kernel-level thread. This association provides an effect similar to mere kernel-level threads: Threads can operate in parallel on different CPUs of a multiprocessor system; however, switching between threads is performed at the kernel level and incurs high overhead. Blocking of a user-level thread does not block other user-level threads of the process because they are mapped into different kernel-level threads.

The many-to-many association method permits a user-level thread to be mapped into different kernel-level threads at different times (see Figure 5.17(c)). It provides parallelism between user-level threads that are mapped into different kernel-level threads at the same time, and provides low overhead of switching

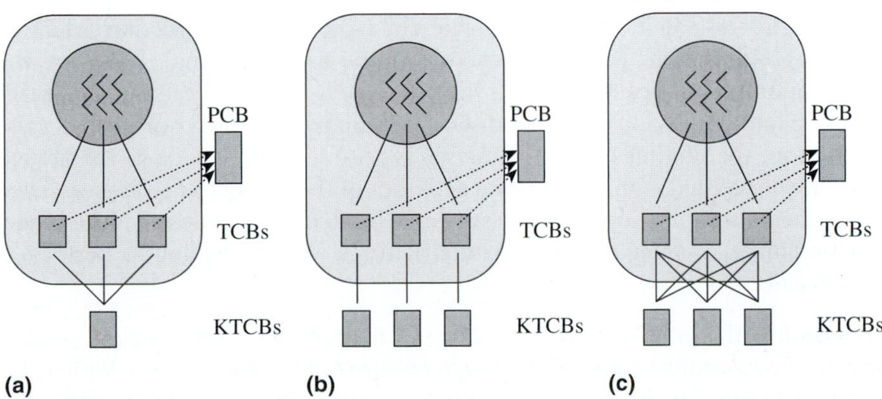

Figure 5.17 (a) Many-to-one; (b) one-to-one; (c) many-to-many associations in hybrid threads.

between user-level threads that are scheduled on the same kernel-level thread by the thread library. However, the many-to-many association method requires a complex implementation. We shall discuss its details in Section 5.4.3 when we discuss the hybrid thread model that was used in the Sun Solaris operating system until Solaris 8.

5.4 CASE STUDIES OF PROCESSES AND THREADS

5.4.1 Processes in Unix

Data Structures Unix uses two data structures to hold control data about processes:

- *proc structure:* Contains process id, process state, priority, information about relationships with other processes, a descriptor of the event for which a blocked process is waiting, signal handling mask, and memory management information.
- *u area* (stands for "user area"): Contains a process control block, which stores the CPU state for a blocked process; pointer to *proc* structure, user and group ids, and information concerning the following: signal handlers, open files and the current directory, terminal attached to the process, and CPU usage by the process.

These data structures together hold information analogous to the PCB data structure discussed in Section 5.2. The *proc* structure mainly holds scheduling related data while the *u area* contains data related to resource allocation and signal handling. The *proc* structure of a process is always held in memory. The *u area* needs to be in memory only when the process is in operation.

Types of Processes Two types of processes exist in Unix—user processes and kernel processes. A *user process* executes a user computation. It is associated with the user's terminal. When a user initiates a program, the kernel creates the primary process for it, which can create child processes (see Section 5.1.2). A *daemon process* is one that is detached from the user's terminal. It runs in the background and typically performs functions on a systemwide basis, e.g., print spooling and network management. Once created, daemon processes can exist throughout the lifetime of the OS. *Kernel processes* execute code of the kernel. They are concerned with background activities of the kernel like swapping. They are created automatically when the system is booted and they can invoke kernel functionalities or refer to kernel data structures without having to perform a system call.

Process Creation and Termination The system call *fork* creates a child process and sets up its context (called the *user-level context* in Unix literature). It allocates a *proc* structure for the newly created process and marks its state as *ready*, and also allocates a *u area* for the process. The kernel keeps track of the parent–child relationships using the *proc* structure. *fork* returns the id of the child process.

The user-level context of the child process is a copy of the parent's user-level context. Hence the child executes the same code as the parent. At creation, the program counter of the child process is set to contain the address of the instruction at which the *fork* call returns. The fork call returns a 0 in the child process, which is the only difference between parent and child processes.A child process can execute the same program as its parent, or it can use a system call from the *exec* family of system calls to load some other program for execution. Although this arrangement is cumbersome, it gives the child process an option of executing the parent's code in the parent's context or choosing its own program for execution. The former alternative was used in older Unix systems to set up servers that could service many user requests concurrently.

The complete view of process creation and termination in Unix is as follows: After booting, the system creates a process *init*. This process creates a child process for every terminal connected to the system. After a sequence of *exec* calls, each child process starts running the login shell. When a programmer indicates the name of a file from the command line, the shell creates a new process that executes an *exec* call for the named file, in effect becoming the primary process of the program. Thus the primary process is a child of the shell process. The shell process now executes the *wait* system call described later in this section to wait for end of the primary process of the program. Thus it becomes blocked until the program completes, and becomes active again to accept the next user command. If a shell process performs an *exit* call to terminate itself, *init* creates a new process for the terminal to run the login shell.

A process P_i can terminate itself through the exit system call *exit* (*status_code*), where *status_code* is a code indicating the termination status of the process. On receiving the *exit* call the kernel saves the status code in the *proc* structure of P_i, closes all open files, releases the memory allocated to the process, and destroys its *u area*. However, the *proc* structure is retained until the parent of P_i destroys it. This way the parent of P_i can query its termination status any time it wishes. In essence, the terminated process is dead but it exists, hence it is called a *zombie* process. The *exit* call also sends a signal to the parent of P_i. The child processes of P_i are made children of the kernel process *init*. This way *init* receives a signal when a child of P_i, say P_c, terminates so that it can release P_c's *proc* structure.

Waiting for Process Termination A process P_i can wait for the termination of a child process through the system call *wait* (*addr*(...)), where *addr*(...) is the address of a variable, say variable xyz, within the address space of P_i. If process P_i has child processes and at least one of them has already terminated, the *wait* call stores the termination status of a terminated child process in xyz and immediately returns with the id of the terminated child process. If more terminated child processes exist, their termination status will be made available to P_i only when it repeats the *wait* call. The state of process P_i is changed to *blocked* if it has children but none of them has terminated. It will be unblocked when one of the child processes terminates. The *wait* call returns with a "−1" if P_i has no children. The following example illustrates benefits of these semantics of the *wait* call.

Example 5.8 Child Processes in Unix

Figure 5.18 shows the C code of a process that creates three child processes in the `for` loop and awaits their completion. This code can be used to set up processes of the real-time data logging system of Example 5.1. Note that the *fork* call returns to the calling process with the id of the newly created child process whereas it returns to the child process with a 0. Because of this peculiarity, child processes execute the code in the `if` statement while the parent process skips the `if` statement and executes a `wait` statement. The wait is satisfied whenever a child process terminates through the `exit` statement. However, the parent process wishes to wait until the last process finishes, so it issues another `wait` if the value returned is anything other than −1. The fourth `wait` call returns with a −1, which brings the parent process out of the loop. The parent process code does not contain an explicit `exit()` call. The language compiler automatically adds this at the end of `main()`.

Waiting for Occurrence of Events A process that is blocked on an event is said to *sleep* on it; e.g., a process that initiates an I/O operation would sleep on its completion event. Unix uses an interesting arrangement to activate processes sleeping on an event. It does not use event control blocks (ECBs) described earlier in Section 5.2.4; instead it uses *event addresses*. A set of addresses is reserved in the kernel, and every event is mapped into one of these addresses. When a process wishes to sleep on an event, the address of the event is computed, the state of the process is changed to *blocked*, and the address of the event is put in its process structure. This address serves as the description of the event awaited by the process. When the event occurs, the kernel computes its event address and activates all processes sleeping on it.

```
main()
{
        int saved_status;
        for (i=0; i<3; i++)
        {
              if (fork()==0)
              { /* code for child processes */
                    ...
                    exit();
              }
        }
        while (wait(&saved_status) !=-1);
                /* loop till all child processes terminate */
}
```

Figure 5.18 Process creation and termination in Unix.

This arrangement incurs unnecessary overhead in some situations. For example, consider several processes sleeping on the same event as a result of data access synchronization. When the event occurs, all these processes are activated but only one process gains access to the data and the other processes go back to sleep. This is analogous to the *busy wait* situation, which we will discuss in the next chapter. The method of mapping events into addresses adds to this problem. A hashing scheme is used for mapping, and so two or more events may map into the same event address. Now occurrence of any one of these events will activate all processes sleeping on *all* these events. Each activated process would now have to check whether the event on which it is sleeping has indeed occurred, and go back to sleep if this is not the case.

Interrupt Servicing Unix avoids interrupts during sensitive kernel-level actions by assigning each interrupt an *interrupt priority level* (*ipl*). Depending on the program being executed by the CPU, an interrupt priority level is also associated with the CPU. When an interrupt at a priority level l arises, it is handled only if l is larger than the interrupt priority level of the CPU; otherwise, it is kept pending until the CPU's interrupt priority level becomes $< l$. The kernel uses this feature to prevent inconsistency of the kernel data structures by raising the *ipl* of the CPU to a high value before starting to update its data structures and lowering it after the update is completed.

System Calls When a system call is made, the system call handler uses the system call number to determine which system functionality is being invoked. From its internal tables it knows the address of the handler for this functionality. It also knows the number of parameters this call is supposed to take. However, these parameters exist on the user stack, which is a part of the process context of the process making the call. So these parameters are copied from the process stack into some standard place in the *u area* of the process before control is passed to the handler for the specific call. This action simplifies operation of individual event handlers.

Signals A signal can be sent to a process, or to a group of processes. This action is performed by the *kill* system call *kill* (*<pid>*, *<signum>*), where *<pid>* is an integer value that can be positive, zero, or negative. A positive value of *<pid>* is the id of a process to which the signal is to be sent. A 0 value of *<pid>* implies that the signal is to be sent to some processes within the same process tree as the sender process, i.e., some processes that share an ancestor with the sender process. This feature is implemented as follows: At a *fork* call, the newly created process is assigned a group id that is the same as the process group number of its parent process. A process may change its group number by using the *setpgrp* system call. When *<pid>*= 0, the signal is sent to all processes with the same group number as the sender. A negative value of *<pid>* is used to reach processes outside the process tree of the sender. We will not elaborate on this feature here.

A process specifies a signal handler by executing the statement

```
oldfunction = signal (<signum>, <function>)
```

where `signal` is a function in the C library that makes a *signal* system call, <*signum*> is an integer, and <*function*> is the name of a function within the address space of the process. This call specifies that the function <*function*> should be executed on occurrence of the signal <*signum*>. The `signal` call returns with the previous action specified for the signal <*signum*>. A user can specify `SIG_DFL` as <*function*> to indicate that the default action defined in the kernel, such as producing a core dump and aborting the process, is to be executed on occurrence of the signal, or specify `SIG_IGN` as <*function*> to indicate that the occurrence of the signal is to be ignored.

The kernel uses the *u area* of a process to note the signal handling actions specified by it, and a set of bits in the *proc* structure to register the occurrence of signals. Whenever a signal is sent to a process, the bit corresponding to the signal is set to 1 in the *proc* structure of the destination process. The kernel now determines whether the signal is being ignored by the destination process. If not, it makes provision to deliver the signal to the process. If a signal is ignored, it remains pending and is delivered when the process specifies its interest in receiving the signal (either by specifying an action or by specifying that the default action should be used for it). A signal remains pending if the process for which it is intended is in a *blocked* state. The signal is delivered when the process comes out of the blocked state. In general, the kernel checks for pending signals when a process returns from a system call or interrupt, after a process gets unblocked, and before a process gets blocked on an event.

Invocation of the signal handling action is implemented as described earlier in Section 5.2.6. A few anomalies exist in the way signals are handled. If a signal occurs repeatedly, the kernel simply notes that it has occurred, but does not count the number of its occurrences. Hence the signal handler may be executed once or several times, depending on when the process gets scheduled to execute the signal handler. Another anomaly concerns a signal sent to a process that is blocked in a system call. After executing the signal handler, such a process does not resume its execution of the system call. Instead, it returns from the system call. If necessary, it may have to repeat the system call. Table 5.9 lists some interesting Unix signals.

Table 5.9 **Interesting Signals in Unix**

Signal	Description
SIGCHLD	Child process died or suspended
SIGFPE	Arithmetic fault
SIGILL	Illegal instruction
SIGINT	Tty interrupt (Control-C)
SIGKILL	Kill process
SIGSEGV	Segmentation fault
SIGSYS	Invalid system call
SIGXCPU	CPU time limit is exceeded
SIGXFSZ	File size limit is exceeded

Process States and State Transitions There is one conceptual difference between the process model described in Section 5.2.1 and that used in Unix. In the model of Section 5.2.1, a process in the *running* state is put in the *ready* state the moment its execution is interrupted. A system process then handles the event that caused the interrupt. If the running process had itself caused a software interrupt by executing an <*SI_instrn*>, its state may further change to *blocked* if its request cannot be granted immediately. In this model a user process executes only user code; it does not need any special privileges. A system process may have to use privileged instructions like I/O initiation and setting of memory protection information, so the system process executes with the CPU in the kernel mode.

Processes behave differently in the Unix model. When a process makes a system call, the process itself proceeds to execute the kernel code meant to handle the system call. To ensure that it has the necessary privileges, it needs to execute with the CPU in the kernel mode. A mode change is thus necessary every time a system call is made. The opposite mode change is necessary after processing a system call. Similar mode changes are needed when a process starts executing the interrupt servicing code in the kernel because of an interrupt, and when it returns after servicing an interrupt.

The Unix kernel code is made reentrant so that many processes can execute it concurrently. This feature takes care of the situation where a process gets blocked while executing kernel code, e.g., when it makes a system call to initiate an I/O operation, or makes a request that cannot be granted immediately. To ensure reentrancy of code, every process executing the kernel code must use its own kernel stack. This stack contains the history of function invocations since the time the process entered the kernel code. If another process also enters the kernel code, the history of its function invocations will be maintained on its own kernel stack. Thus, their operation would not interfere. In principle, the kernel stack of a process need not be distinct from its user stack; however, distinct stacks are used in practice because most computer architectures use different stacks when the CPU is in the kernel and user modes.

Unix uses two distinct *running* states. These states are called *user running* and *kernel running* states. A user process executes user code while in the *user running* state, and kernel code while in the *kernel running* state. It makes the transition from *user running* to *kernel running* when it makes a system call, or when an interrupt occurs. It may get blocked while in the *kernel running* state because of an I/O operation or nonavailability of a resource. When the I/O operation completes or its resource request is granted, the process returns to the *kernel running* state and completes the execution of the kernel code that it was executing. It now leaves the kernel mode and returns to the user mode. Accordingly, its state is changed from *kernel running* to *user running*.

Because of this arrangement, a process does not get blocked or preempted in the *user running* state—it first makes a transition to the *kernel running* state and then gets blocked or preempted. In fact, *user running* → *kernel running* is the only transition out of the *user running* state. Figure 5.19 illustrates fundamental process states and state transitions in Unix. As shown there, even process termination occurs when a process is in the *kernel running* state. This happens because the

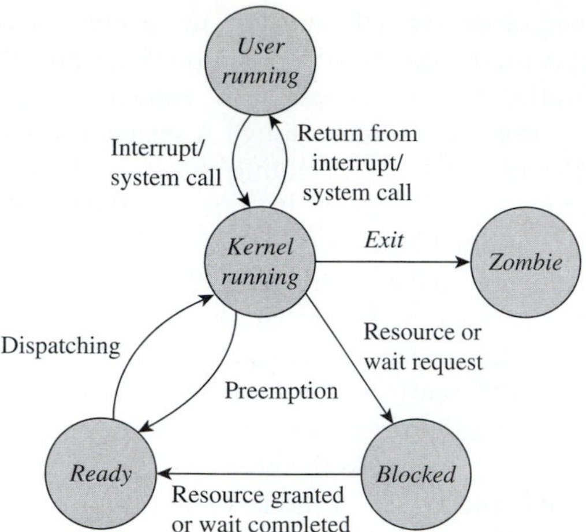

Figure 5.19 Process state transitions in Unix.

process executes the system call *exit* while in the *user running* state. This call changes its state to *kernel running*. The process actually terminates and becomes a *zombie* process as a result of processing this call.

5.4.2 Processes and Threads in Linux

Data Structures The Linux 2.6 kernel supports the 1 : 1 threading model, i.e., kernel-level threads. It uses a *process descriptor*, which is a data structure of type `task_struct`, to contain all information pertaining to a process or thread. For a process, this data structure contains the process state, information about its parent and child processes, the terminal used by the process, its current directory, open files, the memory allocated to it, signals, and signal handlers. The kernel creates substructures to hold information concerning the terminal, directory, files, memory and signals and puts pointers to them in the process descriptor. This organization saves both memory and overhead when a thread is created.

Creation and Termination of Processes and Threads Both processes and threads are created through the system calls *fork* and *vfork*, whose functionalities are identical to the corresponding Unix calls. These functionalities are actually implemented by the system call *clone*, which is hidden from the view of programs. The *clone* system call takes four parameters: start address of the process or thread, parameters to be passed to it, flags, and a child stack specification. Some of the important flags are:

`CLONE_VM`	Shares the memory management information used by the MMU
`CLONE_FS`	Shares the information about root and current working directory

`CLONE_FILES`	Shares the information about open files
`CLONE_SIGHAND`	Shares the information about signals and signal handlers

The organization of `task_struct` facilitates selective sharing of this information since it merely contains pointers to the substructures where the actual information is stored. At a *clone* call, the kernel makes a copy of `task_struct` in which some of these pointers are copied and others are changed. A thread is created by calling *clone* with all flags set, so that the new thread shares the address space, files and signal handlers of its parent. A process is created by calling *clone* with all flags cleared; the new process does not share any of these components.

The Linux 2.6 kernel also includes support for the Native POSIX Threading Library (NPTL), which provides a number of enhancements that benefit heavily threaded applications. It can support up to 2 billion threads, whereas the Linux 2.4 kernel could support only up to 8192 threads per CPU. A new system call *exit_group*( ) has been introduced to terminate a process and all its threads; it can terminate a process having a hundred thousand threads in about 2 seconds, as against about 15 minutes in the Linux 2.4 kernel. Signal handling is performed in the kernel space, and a signal is delivered to one of the available threads in a process. Stop and continue signals affect an entire process, while fatal signals terminate the entire process. These features simplify handling of multithreaded processes. The Linux 2.6 kernel also supports a fast user-space mutex called *futex* that reduces the overhead of thread synchronization through a reduction in the number of system calls.

Parent–Child Relationships Information about parent and child processes or threads is stored in a `task_struct` to maintain awareness of the process tree. `task_struct` contains a pointer to the parent and to the deemed parent, which is a process to which termination of this process should be reported if its parent process has terminated, a pointer to the youngest child, and pointers to the younger and older siblings of a process. Thus, the process tree of Figure 5.2 would be represented as shown in Figure 5.20.

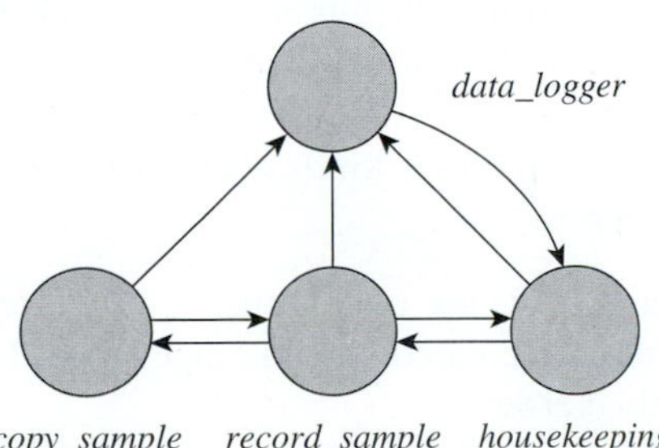

Figure 5.20 Linux process tree for the processes of Figure 5.2(a).

Process States The *state* field of a process descriptor contains a flag indicating the state of a process. A process can be in one of five states at any time:

TASK_RUNNING	The process is either scheduled or waiting to be scheduled.
TASK_INTERRUPTIBLE	The process is sleeping on an event, but may receive a signal.
TASK_UNINTERRUPTIBLE	The process is sleeping on an event, but may not receive a signal.
TASK_STOPPED	The operation of the process has been stopped by a signal.
TASK_ZOMBIE	The process has completed, but the parent process has not yet issued a system call of the *wait*-family to check whether it has terminated.

The TASK_RUNNING state corresponds to one of *running* or *ready* states described in Section 5.2.1. The TASK_INTERRUPTIBLE and TASK_UNINTERRUPTIBLE states both correspond to the *blocked* state. Splitting the *blocked* state into two states resolves the dilemma faced by an OS in handling signals sent to a process in the *blocked* state (see Section 5.2.6)—a process can decide whether it wants to be activated by a signal while waiting for an event to occur, or whether it wants the delivery of a signal to be deferred until it comes out of the *blocked* state. A process enters the TASK_STOPPED state when it receives a SIGSTOP or SIGTSTP signal to indicate that its execution should be stopped, or a SIGTTIN or SIGTTOU signal to indicate that a background process requires input or output.

5.4.3 Threads in Solaris

Solaris, which is a Unix 5.4-based operating system, originally provided a hybrid thread model that actually supported all three association methods of hybrid threads discussed in Section 5.3.2.3, namely, many-to-one, one-to-one, and many-to-many association methods. This model has been called the $M \times N$ *model* in Sun literature. Solaris 8 continued to support this model and also provided an alternative 1 : 1 implementation, which is equivalent to kernel-level threads. The support for the $M \times N$ model was discontinued in Solaris 9. In this section we discuss the $M \times N$ model, and the reasons why it was discontinued.

The $M \times N$ model employs three kinds of entities to govern concurrency and parallelism within a process.

- *User threads:* User threads are analogous to user-level threads discussed in Section 5.3.2.2; they are created and managed by a thread library, so they are not visible to the kernel.
- *Lightweight processes:* A *lightweight process* (LWP) is an intermediary between user threads and a kernel thread. Many LWPs may be created for

a process; each LWP is a unit of parallelism within a process. User threads are mapped into LWPs by the thread library. This mapping can be one-to-one, many-to-one, many-to-many, or a suitable combination of all three. The number of LWPs for a process and the nature of the mapping between user threads and LWPs is decided by the programmer, who makes it known to the thread library through appropriate function calls.

- *Kernel threads:* A kernel thread is a kernel-level thread. The kernel creates one kernel thread for each LWP in a process. It also creates some kernel threads for its own use, e.g., a thread to handle disk I/O in the system.

Figure 5.21 illustrates an arrangement of user threads, LWPs, and kernel threads. Process P_i has three user threads and one LWP, so a many-to-one mapping exists between them. Process P_j has four user threads and three LWPs. One of these user threads is exclusively mapped into one of the LWPs. The remaining three user threads and two LWPs have a many-to-many mapping; this way each of the three threads can operate in any of the two LWPs.

LWPs can operate in parallel because each of them has a kernel thread associated with it. The kernel creates an LWP control block for each LWP, and a *kernel thread control block* (KTCB) for each kernel thread. In addition, the thread library maintains a thread control block for each user thread. The information in this control block is analogous to that described in Section 5.3.2.2. The scheduler examines the KTCBs and, for each CPU in the system, selects a kernel thread that is in the *ready* state. The dispatcher dispatches the LWP corresponding to this kernel thread. The thread library can switch between user threads mapped into this LWP to achieve concurrency between user threads. The number of LWPs

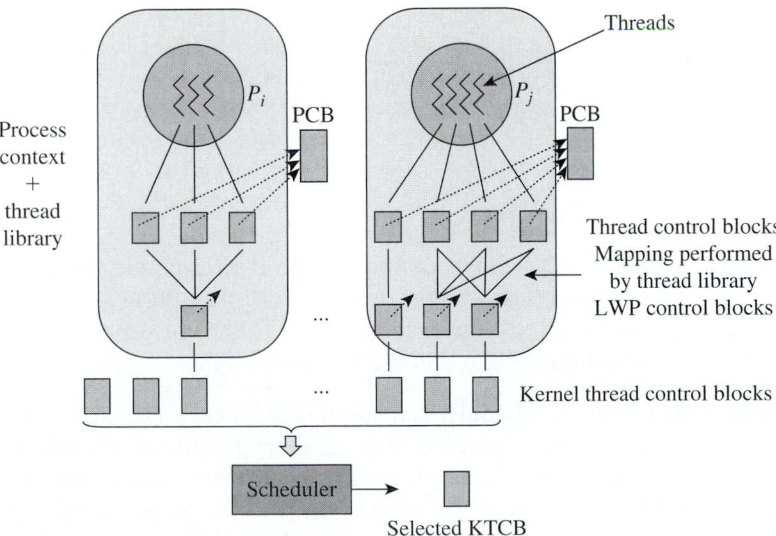

Figure 5.21 Threads in Solaris.

per process and the association of user threads with LWPs is decided by the programmer, thus both parallelism and concurrency within a process are under the programmer's control. An n-way parallelism would be possible within a process if the programmer created n LWPs for a process, $1 \leq n \leq p$, where p is the number of CPUs. However, the degree of parallelism would reduce if a user thread made a blocking system call during its operation, because the call would block the LWP in which it is mapped. Solaris provides *scheduler activations*, described later in this section, to overcome this problem.

A complex arrangement of control blocks is used to control switching between kernel threads. The kernel thread control block contains the kernel registers of the CPU, stack pointer, priority, scheduling information, and a pointer to the next KTCB in a scheduling list. In addition, it contains a pointer to the LWP control block. The LWP control block contains saved values of user registers of the CPU, signal handling information, and a pointer to the PCB of the owner process.

Signal Handling Signals generated by operation of a thread, such as an arithmetic condition or a memory protection violation, are delivered to the thread itself. Signals generated by external sources, such as a timer, have to be directed to a thread that has enabled its handling. The $M \times N$ model provided each process with an LWP that was dedicated to signal handling. When a signal was generated, the kernel would keep it pending and notify this LWP, which would wait until it found that some thread that had enabled handling of that specific signal was running on one of the other LWPs of the process, and would ask the kernel to direct the pending signal to that LWP.

States of Processes and Kernel Threads The kernel is aware only of states of processes and kernel threads; it is oblivious to existence of user threads. A process can be in one of the following states:

`SIDL`	A transient state during creation
`SRUN`	Runnable process
`SONPROC`	Running on a processor
`SSLEEP`	Sleeping
`SSTOP`	Stopped
`SZOMB`	Terminated process

The `SRUN` and `SSLEEP` states correspond to the *ready* and *blocked* states of Section 5.2.1. A kernel thread has states `TS_RUN`, `TS_ONPROC`, `TS_SLEEP`, `TS_STOPPED`, and `TS_ZOMB` that are analogous to the corresponding process states. A kernel thread that is free is in the `TS_FREE` state.

Scheduler Activations A scheduler activation is like a kernel thread. The kernel uses scheduler activations to perform two auxiliary functions: (1) When some LWP of the process becomes blocked, the kernel uses a scheduler activation to create a new LWP so that other runnable threads of the process could operate. (2) When an event related to the operation of the thread library occurs, the kernel uses a scheduler activation to notify the thread library.

Consider a many-to-one mapping between many user threads and an LWP, and a user thread that is currently mapped into the LWP. A kernel thread is associated with the LWP, so the user thread operates when the kernel thread is scheduled. If the user thread makes a blocking system call, the kernel thread would block. Effectively, the LWP with which it is associated would block. If some of the other threads that are mapped into the same LWP are runnable, we have a situation where a runnable user thread cannot be scheduled because the LWP has become blocked.

In such situations, the kernel creates a scheduler activation when the user thread is about to block, provides the activation to the thread library, and makes an *upcall* to it. The upcall is implemented as a signal sent to the thread library. The thread library now executes its signal handler, using the activation provided by the kernel. The signal handler saves the state of the user thread that is about to block, releases the LWP that was used by it, and hands it over to the kernel for reuse. It now schedules a new user thread on the new activation provided by the kernel. In effect, the user thread that was about to block is removed from an LWP and a new user thread is scheduled in a new LWP of the process. When the event for which the user thread had blocked occurs, the kernel makes another upcall to the thread library with a scheduler activation so that it can preempt the user thread currently mapped into the LWP, return the LWP to the kernel, and schedule the newly activated thread on the new activation provided by the kernel.

Switchover to the 1:1 Implementation The $M \times N$ model was developed in the expectation that, because a context switch by the thread library incurred significantly less overhead than a context switch by the kernel, user-level scheduling of threads in the thread library would provide good application performance. However, as mentioned in Section 5.3.2.2, it is possible only when schedulers in the thread library and in the kernel work harmoniously. The 1 : 1 implementation in Solaris 8 provided efficient kernel-level context switching. Use of the 1 : 1 model led to simpler signal handling, as threads could be dedicated to handling of specific signals. It also eliminated the need for scheduler activations, and provided better scalability. Hence the $M \times N$ model was discontinued in Solaris 9.

5.4.4 Processes and Threads in Windows

The flavor of processes and threads in Windows differs somewhat from that presented earlier in this chapter—Windows treats a process as a unit for resource allocation, and uses a thread as a unit for concurrency. Accordingly, a Windows process does not operate by itself; it must have at least one thread inside it. A resource can be accessed only through a *resource handle*. A process inherits some resource handles from its parent process; it can obtain more resource handles by opening new resources. The kernel stores all these handles in a handles table for each process. This way, a resource can be accessed by simply specifying an offset into the handles table.

Windows uses three control blocks to manage a process. An *executive process block* contains fields that store the process id, memory management information, address of the handle table, a kernel process block for the process, and address of the process environment block. The *kernel process block* contains scheduling information for threads of the process, such as the processor affinity for the process, the state of the process and pointers to the kernel thread blocks of its threads. The executive process block and the kernel process block are situated in the system address space. The *process environment block* contains information that is used by the loader to load the code to be executed, and by the heap manager. It is situated in the user address space.

The control blocks employed to manage a thread contain information about its operation, and about the process containing it. The *executive thread block* of a thread contains a *kernel thread block*, a pointer to the executive process block of its parent process and impersonation information. The kernel thread block contains information about the kernel stack of the thread and the thread-local storage, scheduling information for the thread, and a pointer to its *thread environment block*, which contains its id and information about its synchronization requirements.

Windows supports the notion of a *job* as a method of managing a group of processes. A job is represented by a job object, which contains information such as handles to processes in it, the jobwide CPU time limit, per process CPU time limit, job scheduling class that sets the time slice for the processes of the job, processor affinity for processes of the job, and their priority class. A process can be a member of only one job; all processes created by it automatically belong to the same job.

Process Creation The *create* call takes a parameter that is a handle to the parent of the new process or thread. This way, a *create* call need not be issued by the parent of a process or thread. A server process uses this feature to create a thread in a client process so that it can access resources with the client's access privileges, rather than its own privileges.

Recall from Section 4.8.4 that the environment subsystems provide support for execution of programs developed for other OSs like MS-DOS, Win 32, and OS/2. The semantics of process creation depend on the environment subsystem used by an application process. In the Win/32 and OS/2 operating environments, a process has one thread in it when it is created; it is not so in other environments supported by the Windows OS. Hence process creation is actually handled by an environment subsystem DLL that is linked to an application process. After creating a process, it passes the id of the new process or thread to the environment subsystem process so that it can manage the new process or thread appropriately.

Creation of a child process by an application process in the Win/32 environment proceeds as follows: The environment subsystem DLL linked to the application process makes a system call to create a new process. This call is handled by the executive. It creates a process object, initializes it by loading the image of the code to be executed, and returns a handle to the process object. The environment subsystem DLL now makes a second system call to create a thread, and passes the handle to the new process as a parameter. The executive creates a thread in the new process and returns a handle to it. The DLL now sends a message to the environment subsystem process, passing it the process and thread handles, and the id of their parent process. The environment subsystem process enters the process handle in the table of processes that currently exist in the environment and enters the thread handle in the scheduling data structures. Control now returns to the application process.

Thread States and State Transitions Figure 5.22 shows the state transition diagram for threads. A thread can be in one of following six states:

1. *Ready*: The thread can be executed if a CPU is available.
2. *Standby*: This is a thread that has been selected to run next on a specific processor. If its priority is high, the thread currently running on the processor would be preempted and this thread would be scheduled.
3. *Running*: A CPU is currently allocated to the thread and the thread is in operation.
4. *Waiting*: The thread is waiting for a resource or event, or has been suspended by the environment subsystem.
5. *Transition*: The thread's wait was satisfied, but meanwhile its kernel stack was removed from memory because it had been waiting for long. The thread would enter the *ready* state when the kernel stack is brought back into memory.
6. *Terminated*: The thread has completed its operation.

Thread Pools Windows provides a thread pool in every process. As described in Section 5.3, the pool contains a set of worker threads and an arrangement

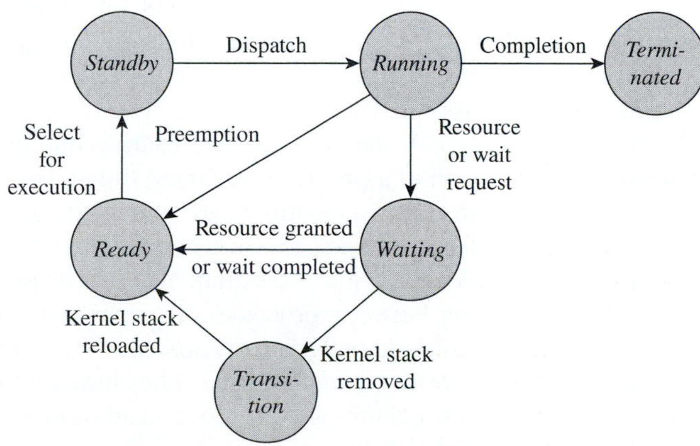

Figure 5.22 Thread state transitions in Windows.

of lists of pending services and idle worker threads. The threads of a pool can be used to perform work presented to the pool, or can be programmed to perform specific tasks either at specific times or periodically or when specific kernel objects become signaled. The number of worker threads is adapted to the pool's workload dynamically. Threads are neither created nor destroyed if the rate at which service requests are made to the pool matches the rate at which worker threads complete servicing of requests. However, new threads are created if the request rate exceeds the service rate, and a thread is destroyed if it is idle for more than 40 seconds. Windows Vista supports several thread pools in a process.

5.5 SUMMARY

A computer user and the operating system have different views of execution of programs. The user is concerned with achieving execution of a program in a sequential or concurrent manner as desired, whereas the OS is concerned with allocation of resources to programs and servicing of several programs simultaneously, so that a suitable combination of efficient use and user service may be obtained. In this chapter, we discussed various aspects of these two views of execution of programs.

Execution of a program can be speeded up through either *parallelism* or *concurrency*. Parallelism implies that several activities are in progress within the program at the same time. Concurrency is an illusion of parallelism—activities appear to be parallel, but may not be actually so.

A *process* is a model of execution of a program. When the user issues a command to execute a program, the OS creates the primary process for it. This process can create other processes by making requests to the OS through system calls; each of these processes is called its *child process.* The OS can service a process and some of its child processes concurrently by letting the same CPU execute instructions of each one of them for some time, or service them in parallel by executing their instructions on several CPUs at the same time. The processes within a program must work harmoniously toward a common goal by sharing data or by coordinating their activities with one another. They achieve this by employing the *process synchronization* means provided in the operating system.

The operating system allocates resources to a process and stores information about them in the *process context* of the process. To control operation of the process, it uses the notion of a *process state*. The process state is a description of the current activity within the process; the process state changes as the process operates. The fundamental process states are: *ready, running, blocked, terminated*, and *suspended.* The OS keeps information concerning each process in a *process control block* (PCB). The PCB of a process contains the process state, and the CPU state associated with the process if the CPU is not currently executing its instructions. The scheduling function of the kernel selects one of the *ready* processes and the dispatching function switches the CPU to the selected process through information found in its process context and the PCB.

A *thread* is an alternative model of execution of a program. A thread differs from a process in that no resources are allocated to it. This difference makes the overhead of switching between threads much less than the overhead of switching between processes. Three models of threads, called *kernel-level threads, user-level threads*, and *hybrid threads*, are used. They have different implications for switching overhead, concurrency, and parallelism.

TEST YOUR CONCEPTS

5.1 An application comprises several processes—a primary process and some child processes. This arrangement provides computation speedup if
   a. The computer system contains many CPUs
   b. Some of the processes are I/O bound
   c. Some of the processes are CPU bound
   d. None of the above

5.2 Classify each of the following statements as true or false:
   a. The OS creates a single process if two users execute the same program.
   b. The state of a process that is blocked on a resource request changes to *running* when the resource is granted to it.
   c. There is no distinction between a terminated process and a suspended process.
   d. After handling an event, the kernel need not perform scheduling before dispatching if none of the process states has changed.
   e. When a user-level thread of a process makes a system call that leads to blocking, all threads of the process become blocked.
   f. Kernel-level threads provide more concurrency than user-level threads in both uniprocessor and multiprocessor systems.
   g. When a process terminates, its termination code should be remembered until its parent process terminates.

5.3 Which of the following state transitions for a process can cause the state transition *blocked* → *ready* for one or more other processes?
   a. A process starts an I/O operation and becomes *blocked*.
   b. A process terminates.
   c. A process makes a resource request and becomes *blocked*.
   d. A process sends a message.
   e. A process makes the state transition *blocked* → *blocked swapped*.

EXERCISES

5.1 Describe the actions of the kernel when processes make system calls for the following purposes:
   a. Request to receive a message
   b. Request to perform an I/O operation
   c. Request for status information concerning a process
   d. Request to create a process
   e. Request to terminate a child process

5.2 Describe the conditions under which a kernel may perform dispatching without performing scheduling.

5.3 Give an algorithm to implement a Unix-like *wait* call using the PCB data structure shown in Table 5.6. Comment on comparative lifetimes of a process and its PCB.

5.4 Describe how each signal listed in Table 5.9 is raised and handled in Unix.

5.5 A process is in the *blocked swapped* state.
   a. Give a sequence of state transitions through which it could have reached this state.
   b. Give a sequence of state transitions through which it can reach the *ready* state.

   Is more than one sequence of state transitions possible in each of these cases?

5.6 The designer of a kernel has decided to use a single *swapped* state. Give a diagram analogous to Figure 5.5 showing process states and state transitions. Describe how the kernel would perform swapping and comment on the effectiveness of swapping.

5.7 Compare and contrast inherent parallelism in the following applications:
   a. An online banking application which permits users to perform banking transactions through a Web-based browser.
   b. A Web-based airline reservation system.

5.8 An airline reservation system using a centralized database services user requests concurrently. Is it preferable to use threads rather than processes in this system? Give reasons for your answer.

5.9 Name two system calls a thread should avoid using if threads are implemented at the user level, and explain your reasons.

5.10 As described in Example 5.7 and illustrated in Figure 5.16, if a process has user-level threads, its own state depends on states of all of its threads. List the possible causes of each of the fundamental state transitions for such a process.

5.11 Explain whether you agree with the following statement on the basis of what you read in this chapter: "Concurrency increases the scheduling overhead without providing any speedup of an application program."

5.12 On the basis of the Solaris case study, write a short note on how to decide the number of user threads and lightweight processes (LWPs) that should be created in an application.

5.13 An OS supports both user-level threads and kernel-level threads. Do you agree with the following recommendations about when to use user-level threads and when kernel-level threads? Why, or why not?

a. If a candidate for a thread is a CPU-bound computation, make it a kernel-level thread if the system contains multiple processors; otherwise, make it a user-level thread.

b. If a candidate for a thread is an I/O-bound computation, make it a user-level thread if the process containing it does not contain a kernel-level thread; otherwise, make it a kernel-level thread.

5.14 Comment on computation speedup of the following applications in computer systems having (i) a single CPU and (ii) many CPUs.

a. Many threads are created in a server that handles user requests at a large rate, where servicing of a user request involves both CPU and I/O activities.

b. Computation of an expression $z := a * b + c * d$ is performed by spawning two child processes to evaluate $a * b$ and $c * d$.

c. A server creates a new thread to handle every user request received, and servicing of each user request involves accesses to a database.

d. Two matrices contain m rows and n columns each, where m and n are both very large. An application obtains the result of adding the two matrices by creating m threads, each of which performs addition of one row of the matrices.

5.15 Compute the best computation speedup in the real-time data logging application of Example 5.1 under the following conditions: The overhead of event handling and process switching is negligible. For each sample, the *copy_sample* process requires 5 microseconds (μs) of CPU time, and does not involve any I/O operation, *record_sample* requires 1.5 ms to record the sample and consumes only 1 μs of CPU time, while *housekeeping* consumes 200 μs of CPU time and its write operation requires 1.5 ms.

CLASS PROJECT: IMPLEMENTING A SHELL

Write a program in C/C++, which will act as a shell in a Unix or Linux system. When invoked, the program will display its own prompt to the user, accept the user's command from the keyboard, classify it, and invoke an appropriate routine to implement it. The command "system" should not be used in implementing any command other than the `ls` command. The shell must support the following commands:

Command	Description
`cd` *<directory_name>*	Changes current directory if user has appropriate permissions.
`ls`	Lists information about files in the current directory.
`rm`	Deletes indicated files. Supports options `-r`, `-f`, `-v`.
`history` *n*	Prints the most recent *n* commands issued by the user, along with their serial numbers. If *n* is omitted, prints all commands issued by the user.
`issue` *n*	Issues the *n*th command in the history once again.
<program_name>	Creates a child process to run *<program_name>*. Supports the redirection operators > and < to redirect the input and

	output of the program to indicated files.
<program_name> `&`	The child process for *<program_name>* should be run in the background.
`quit`	Quits the shell.

After implementing a basic shell supporting these commands, you should add two advanced features to the shell:

1. Design a new command that provides a useful facility. As an example, consider a command `rmexcept` *<list_of_files>* which removes all files except those in *<list_of_files>* from the current directory.
2. Support a command *<program_name> m* that creates a child process to execute *program_name*, but aborts the process if it does not complete its operation in *m* seconds. (*Hint:* Use an appropriate routine from the library to deliver a SIGALRM signal after *m* seconds, and use a signal handler to perform appropriate actions.)

BIBLIOGRAPHY

The process concept is discussed in Dijkstra (1968), Brinch Hansen (1973), and Bic and Shaw (1974). Brinch Hansen (1988) describes implementation of processes in the RC 4000 system.

Marsh et al. (1991) discusses user-level threads and issues concerning thread libraries. Anderson et al. (1992) discusses use of scheduler activations for communication between the kernel and a thread library. Engelschall (2000) discusses how user-level threads can be implemented in Unix by using standard Unix facilities, and also summarizes properties of other multithreading packages.

Kleiman (1996), Butenhof (1997), Lewis and Berg (1997), and Nichols et al. (1996) discuss programming with POSIX threads. Lewis and Berg (2000) discusses multithreading in Java.

Bach (1986), McKusick (1996), and Vahalia (1996) discuss processes in Unix. Beck et al. (2002) and Bovet and Cesati (2005) describes processes and threads in Linux. Stevens and Rago (2005) describes processes and threads in Unix, Linux, and BSD; it also discusses daemon processes in Unix. O'Gorman (2003) discusses implementation of signals in Linux. Eykholt et al. (1992) describes threads in SunOS, while Vahalia (1996) and Mauro and McDougall (2006) describe threads and LWPs in Solaris. Custer (1993), Richter (1999), and Russinovich and Solomon (2005) describe processes and threads in Windows. Vahalia (1996) and Tanenbaum (2001) discuss threads in Mach.

1. Anderson, T. E., B. N. Bershad, E. D. Lazowska, and H. M. Levy (1992): "Scheduler activations: effective kernel support for the user-level management of parallelism," *ACM Transactions on Computer Systems*, **10** (1), 53–79.
2. Bach, M. J. (1986): *The Design of the Unix Operating System*, Prentice Hall, Englewood Cliffs, N.J.
3. Beck, M., H. Bohme, M. Dziadzka, U. Kunitz, R. Magnus, C. Schroter, and D. Verworner (2002): *Linux Kernel Programming,* 3rd ed., Pearson Education, New York.
4. Bic, L., and A. C. Shaw (1988): *The Logical Design of Operating Systems,* 2nd ed., Prentice Hall, Englewood Cliffs, N.J.
5. Brinch Hansen, P. (1970): "The nucleus of a multiprogramming system," *Communications of the ACM*, **13**, 238–241, 250.
6. Brinch Hansen, P. (1973): *Operating System Principles*, Prentice Hall, Englewood Cliffs, N.J.
7. Bovet, D. P., and M. Cesati (2005): *Understanding the Linux Kernel,* 3rd ed., O'Reilly, Sebastopol.
8. Butenhof, D. (1997): *Programming with POSIX threads*, Addison-Wesley, Reading, Mass.
9. Custer, H. (1993): *Inside Windows/NT*, Microsoft Press, Redmond, Wash.
10. Dijkstra, E. W. (1968): "The structure of THE multiprogramming system," *Communications of the ACM*, **11**, 341–346.
11. Engelschall, R. S. (2000): "Portable Multithreading: The signal stack trick for user-space thread creation," *Proceedings of the 2000 USENIX Annual Technical Conference*, San Diego.

12. Eykholt, J. R, S. R. Kleiman, S. Barton, S. Faulkner, A. Shivalingiah, M. Smith, D. Stein, J. Voll, M. Weeks, and D. Williams (1992): "Beyond multiprocessing: multithreading the SunOS kernel," *Proceedings of the Summer 1992 USENIX Conference*, 11–18.
13. Kleiman, S., D. Shah, and B. Smaalders (1996): *Programming with Threads*, Prentice Hall, Englewood Cliffs, N.J.
14. Lewis, B., and D. Berg (1997): *Multithreaded Programming with Pthreads*, Prentice Hall, Englewood Cliffs, N.J.
15. Lewis, B., and D. Berg (2000): *Multithreaded Programming with Java Technology*, Sun Microsystems.
16. Mauro, J., and R. McDougall (2006): *Solaris Internals,* 2nd ed., Prentice Hall, Englewood Cliffs, N.J.
17. Marsh, B. D., M. L. Scott, T. J. LeBlanc, and E. P. Markatos (1991): "First-class user-level threads," *Proceedings of the Thirteenth ACM Symposium on Operating Systems Principles*, October 1991, 110–121.
18. McKusick, M. K., K. Bostic, M. J. Karels, and J. S. Quarterman (1996): *The Design and Implementation of the 4.4 BSD Operating System*, Addison Wesley, Reading, Mass.
19. Nichols, B., D. Buttlar, and J. P. Farrell (1996): *Pthreads Programming*, O'Reilly, Sebastopol.
20. O'Gorman, J. (2003): *Linux Process Manager: The internals of Scheduling, Interrupts and Signals*, John Wiley, New York.
21. Richter, J. (1999): *Programming Applications for Microsoft Windows,* 4th ed., Microsoft Press, Redmond, Wash.
22. Russinovich, M. E., and D. A. Solomon (2005): *Microsoft Windows Internals,* 4th ed., Microsoft Press, Redmond, Wash.
23. Silberschatz, A., P. B. Galvin, and G. Gagne (2005): *Operating System Principles,* 7th ed., John Wiley, New York.
24. Stevens, W. R., and S. A. Rago (2005): *Advanced Programming in the Unix Environment,* 2nd ed., Addison-Wesley, Reading, Mass.
25. Tanenbaum, A. S. (2001): *Modern Operating Systems,* 2nd ed., Prentice Hall, Englewood Cliffs, N.J.
26. Vahalia, U. (1996): *Unix Internals—The New Frontiers*, Prentice Hall, Englewood Cliffs, N.J.

Chapter 6

Process Synchronization

Interacting processes are concurrent processes that share data or coordinate their activities with respect to one another. *Data access synchronization* ensures that shared data do not lose consistency when they are updated by interacting processes. It is implemented by ensuring that processes access shared data only in a mutually exclusive manner. *Control synchronization* ensures that interacting processes perform their actions in a desired order. Together, these two kinds of synchronization make up what we refer to as *process synchronization*. Computer systems provide *indivisible instructions* (also called *atomic instructions*) to support process synchronization.

We discuss *critical sections*, which are sections of code that access shared data in a mutually exclusive manner, and indivisible *signaling operations*, which are used to implement control synchronization, and show how both are implemented by using indivisible instructions. Following this discussion, we introduce some classic problems of process synchronization, which are representative of synchronization problems in various application domains. We analyze their synchronization requirements and study important issues involved in fulfilling them.

In the remainder of the chapter, we discuss *semaphores* and *monitors*, which are the primary facilities for synchronization in programming languages and operating systems. We will see how they offer ways to fulfill the process synchronization requirements of the classic problems.

6.1 WHAT IS PROCESS SYNCHRONIZATION?

In this chapter, we use the term *process* as a generic term for both a process and a thread. Applications employ concurrent processes either to achieve computation speedup (see Table 5.2), or to simplify their own design, as in multithreaded servers (see Section 5.3). As summarized in Table 5.7, processes of an application interact among themselves to share data, coordinate their activities, and exchange messages or signals. We use the following notation to formally define the term *interacting processes*:

- $read\_set_i$ — set of data items read by process P_i and interprocess messages or signals received by it
- $write\_set_i$ — set of data items modified by process P_i and interprocess messages or signals sent by it

We use the term "update of a data item" for a modification of the data item's value that is based on its own previous value, e.g., $x := x + 1$ is an update, whereas $x := 5$ is not.

Definition 6.1 Interacting Processes Processes P_i and P_j are interacting processes if the *write_set* of one of the processes overlaps the *write_set* or *read_set* of the other.

The nature of interaction between processes when the *write_set* of one overlaps the *read_set* of another is obvious—the first process may set the value of a variable which the other process may read. The situation when the *write_sets* of two processes overlap is included in Definition 6.1 because the manner in which the processes perform their write operations can lead to incorrect results, so the processes must cooperate to avoid such situations. Processes that do not interact are said to be *independent processes*; they can execute freely in parallel.

Two kinds of requirements arise in interacting processes:

- A process should perform a specific operation op_i only when some condition concerning shared data holds. The process must be delayed if these requirements are not met when it wishes to perform operation op_i, and it must be allowed to resume when these requirements have been met.
- A process should perform an operation op_i only after some other process performs another specific operation op_j. This requirement is met by using some shared data to note whether operation op_j has been performed, so that the process can be delayed and resumed as described above.

Process synchronization is a generic term for the techniques used to delay and resume processes to implement process interactions. The execution speed of a process, or the relative execution speeds of interacting processes, cannot be known in advance because of factors such as time-slicing, priorities of processes, and I/O activities in processes. Hence a process synchronization technique must be designed so that it will function correctly irrespective of the relative execution speeds of processes.

Throughout this chapter, we will use the conventions shown in Figure 6.1 in the pseudocode for concurrent processes.

6.2 RACE CONDITIONS

In Section 5.2.5, we mentioned that uncoordinated accesses to shared data may affect consistency of data. To see this problem, consider processes P_i and P_j that update the value of a shared data item d_s through operations a_i and a_j, respectively.

$$\text{Operation } a_i: \quad d_s := d_s + 10;$$
$$\text{Operation } a_j: \quad d_s := d_s + 5;$$

- The control structure **Parbegin** <*list of statements*> **Parend** encloses code that is to be executed in parallel. (Parbegin stands for parallel-begin, and Parend for parallel-end.) If <*list of statements*> contains n statements, execution of the **Parbegin–Parend** control structure spawns n processes, each process consisting of the execution of one statement in <*list of statements*>. For example, **Parbegin** S_1, S_2, S_3, S_4 **Parend** initiates four processes that execute S_1, S_2, S_3 and S_4, respectively.

  The statement grouping facilities of a language such as **begin–end**, can be used if a process is to consist of a block of code instead of a single statement. For visual convenience, we depict concurrent processes created in a **Parbegin–Parend** control structure as follows:

Parbegin				
	S_{11}	S_{21}	...	S_{n1}
	$\vdots$	$\vdots$		$\vdots$
	S_{1m}	S_{2m}	...	S_{nm}
Parend				
	Process P_1	*Process* P_2		*Process* P_n

  where statements $S_{11} \cdots S_{1m}$ form the code of process P_1, etc.
- Declarations of shared variables are placed before a **Parbegin**.
- Declarations of local variables are placed at the start of a process.
- Comments are enclosed within braces "{ }".
- Indentation is used to show nesting of control structures.

Figure 6.1 Pseudocode conventions for concurrent programs.

Let $(d_s)_{\text{initial}}$ be the initial value of d_s, and let process P_i be the first one to perform its operation. The value of d_s after operation a_i will be $(d_s)_{\text{initial}} + 10$. If process P_j performs operation a_j now, the resulting value of d_s will be $(d_s)_{\text{new}} = ((d_s)_{\text{initial}} + 10) + 5$, i.e., $(d_s)_{\text{initial}} + 15$. If the processes perform their operations in the reverse order, the new value of d_s would be identical.

If processes P_i and P_j perform their operations concurrently, we would expect the result to be $(d_s)_{\text{initial}} + 15$; however, it is not guaranteed to be so. This situation is called a *race condition*. This term is borrowed from electronics, where it refers to the principle that an attempt to examine a value, or make measurements on a waveform, while it is changing can lead to wrong results.

The race condition can be explained as follows: Operation a_i is typically implemented by using three machine instructions. The first instruction loads the value of d_s in a data register, say, register r_1, the second instruction adds 10 to the contents of r_1, and the third instruction stores the contents of r_1 back into the location assigned to d_s. We call this sequence of instructions the *load-add-store* sequence. Operation a_j is similarly implemented by a *load-add-store* sequence. The result of performing operations a_i and a_j would be wrong if both a_i and a_j operated on the old value of d_s. This could happen if one process were engaged in performing the load-add-store sequence, but the other process was performing a load instruction before this sequence was completed. In such a case the value of d_s at the end of both the operations would be either $(d_s)_{\text{initial}} + 5$ or $(d_s)_{\text{initial}} + 10$, depending on which of the operations completed later.

We define a race condition formally as follows: Let function $f_i(d_s)$ represent the operation a_i on d_s, i.e., for a given value of d_s, $f_i(d_s)$ indicates the value d_s would have after executing operation a_i. Function $f_j(d_s)$ analogously represents the operation a_j on d_s. Let process P_i be the first one to perform its operation. The value of d_s after the operation would be $f_i(d_s)$. If process P_j performs operation a_j now, operation a_j will operate on $f_i(d_s)$, so the resulting value of d_s will be $f_j(f_i(d_s))$. If the processes perform their operations in the reverse order, the new value of d_s will be $f_i(f_j(d_s))$.

Definition 6.2 Race Condition A condition in which the value of a shared data item d_s resulting from execution of operations a_i and a_j on d_s in interacting processes may be different from both $f_i(f_j(d_s))$ and $f_j(f_i(d_s))$.

The next example illustrates a race condition in an airline reservation application and its consequences.

Example 6.1 Race Condition in an Airline Reservation Application

The left column in the upper half of Figure 6.2 shows the code used by processes in an airline reservation application. The processes use identical code, hence a_i and a_j, the operations performed by processes P_i and P_j, are identical. Each of these operations examines the value of *nextseatno* and updates it by 1 if a seat is available. The right column of Figure 6.2 shows the machine instructions corresponding to the code. Statement S_3 corresponds to three instructions $S_3.1$, $S_3.2$ and $S_3.3$ that form a load-add-store sequence of instructions for updating the value of *nextseatno*.

The lower half of Figure 6.2 is a timing diagram for the applications. It shows three possible sequences in which processes P_i and P_j could execute their instructions when *nextseatno* = 200 and *capacity* = 200. In case 1, process P_i executes the **if** statement that compares values of *nextseatno* with *capacity* and proceeds to execute instructions $S_2.1$, $S_3.1$, $S_3.2$ and $S_3.3$ that allocate a seat and increment *nextseatno*. When process P_j executes the **if** statement, it finds that no seats are available so it does not allocate a seat.

In case 2, process P_i executes the **if** statement and finds that a seat can be allocated. However, it gets preempted before it can execute instruction $S_2.1$. Process P_j now executes the **if** statement and finds that a seat is available. It allocates a seat by executing instructions $S_2.1$, $S_3.1$, $S_3.2$ and $S_3.3$ and exits. *nextseatno* is now 201. When process P_i is resumed, it proceeds to execute instruction $S_2.1$, which allocates a seat. Thus, seats are allocated to both requests. This is a race condition because when *nextseatno* = 200, only one seat should be allocated.

In case 3, process P_i gets preempted after it loads 200 in reg_j through instruction $S_3.1$. Now, again both P_i and P_j allocate a seat each, which is a race condition.

	Code of processes		**Corresponding machine instructions**
S_1	**if** *nextseatno* ≤ *capacity*	$S_1.1$	Load *nextseatno* in reg_k
		$S_1.2$	If reg_k > *capacity* goto $S_4.1$
	then		
S_2	*allotedno:=nextseatno;*	$S_2.1$	Move *nextseatno* to *allotedno*
S_3	*nextseatno:=nextseatno+1;*	$S_3.1$	Load *nextseatno* in reg_j
		$S_3.2$	Add 1 to reg_j
		$S_3.3$	Store reg_j in *nextseatno*
		$S_3.4$	Go to $S_5.1$
	else		
S_4	*display "sorry, no seats available"*	$S_4.1$	Display "*sorry,* · · ·"
S_5	. . .	$S_5.1$	. . .

Some execution cases

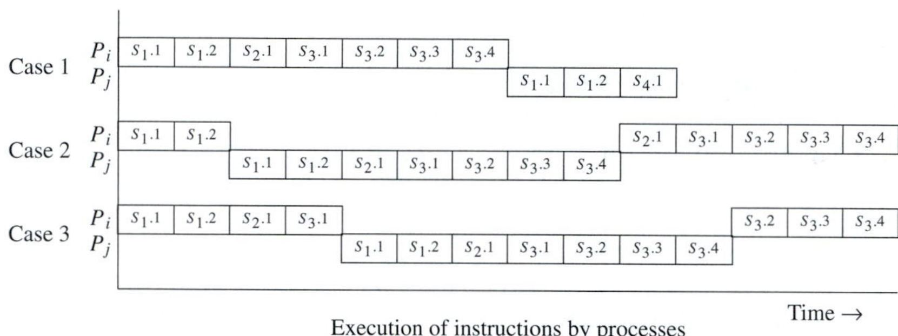

Figure 6.2 Data sharing by processes of a reservation application.

A program containing a race condition may produce correct or incorrect results depending on the order in which instructions of its processes are executed. This feature complicates both testing and debugging of concurrent programs, so race conditions should be prevented.

Data Access Synchronization Race conditions are prevented if we ensure that operations a_i and a_j of Definition 6.2 do not execute concurrently—that is, only one of the operations can access shared data d_s at any time. This requirement is called *mutual exclusion*. When mutual exclusion is ensured, we can be sure that the result of executing operations a_i and a_j would be either $f_i(f_j(d_s))$ or $f_j(f_i(d_s))$. *Data access synchronization* is coordination of processes to implement mutual exclusion over shared data. A technique of data access synchronization is used to delay a process that wishes to access d_s if another process is currently accessing d_s, and to resume its operation when the other process finishes using d_s.

To prevent race conditions, we first check if the logic of processes in an application causes a race condition. We use the following notation for this purpose:

update_set$_i$ set of data items updated by process P_i, that is, the set of data items whose values are read, modified, and written back by process P_i

The logic of a pair of processes P_i and P_j causes a race condition if $update\_set_i \cap update\_set_j \neq \emptyset$ i.e., if some variable is updated by both P_i and P_j. The logic of processes P_i and P_j in the airline reservation application of Example 6.1 causes a race condition because $update\_set_i = update\_set_j = \{nextseatno\}$. Once we know the data item whose updates cause a race condition, we use data access synchronization techniques to ensure that this data item is used in a mutually exclusive manner. The next section discusses a conceptual basis for data access synchronization.

6.3 CRITICAL SECTIONS

Mutual exclusion between actions of concurrent processes is implemented by using *critical sections* of code. A critical section is popularly known by its acronym CS.

Definition 6.3 Critical Section A critical section for a data item d_s is a section of code that is designed so that it cannot be executed concurrently either with itself or with other critical section(s) for d_s.

If some process P_i is executing a critical section for d_s, another process wishing to execute a critical section for d_s will have to wait until P_i finishes executing its critical section. Thus, a critical section for a data item d_s is a mutual exclusion region with respect to accesses to d_s.

We mark a critical section in a segment of code by a dashed rectangular box. Note that processes may share a single copy of the segment of code that contains one critical section, in which case only a single critical section for d_s exists in the application. In all other cases, many critical sections for d_s may exist in the application. Definition 6.3 covers both situations. A process that is executing a critical section is said to be "in a critical section." We also use the terms "enter a critical section" and "exit a critical section" for situations where a process starts and completes an execution of a critical section.

Figure 6.3(a) shows the code of a process that contains several critical sections. The process has a cyclic behavior due to the statement **repeat forever**. In each iteration, it enters a critical section when it needs to access a shared data item. At other times, it executes other parts of code in its logic, which together constitute "remainder of the cycle." For simplicity, whenever possible, we use the simple process form shown in Figure 6.3(b) to depict a process. The following example illustrates the use of a critical section to avoid race conditions.

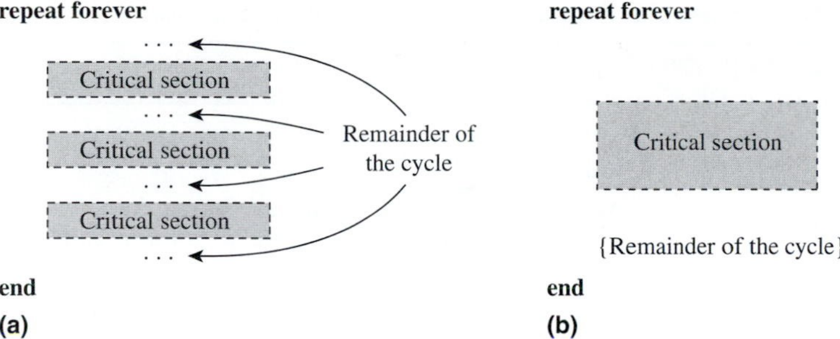

Figure 6.3 (a) A process with many critical sections; (b) a simpler way of depicting this process.

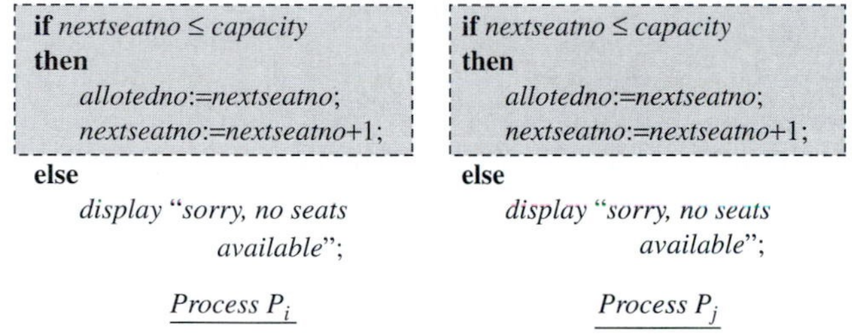

Figure 6.4 Use of critical sections in an airline reservation system.

Preventing a Race Condition through a Critical Section

Example 6.2

Figure 6.4 shows use of critical sections in the airline reservation system of Figure 6.2. Each process contains a critical section in which it accesses and updates the shared variable *nextseatno*. Let $f_i(nextseatno)$ and $f_j(nextseatno)$ represent the operations performed in critical sections of P_i and P_j, respectively. If P_i and P_j attempt to execute their critical sections concurrently, one of them will be delayed. Hence, the resulting value of *nextseatno* will be either $f_i(f_j(nextseatno))$ or $f_j(f_i(nextseatno))$. From Definition 6.2, a race condition does not arise.

Use of critical sections causes delays in operation of processes. Both processes and the kernel must cooperate to reduce such delays. A process must not execute for too long inside a critical section and must not make system calls that might put it in the *blocked* state. The kernel must not preempt a process that is engaged in executing a critical section. This condition requires the kernel to know whether a process is inside a critical section at any moment, and it cannot be met if processes implement critical sections on their own, i.e., without involving the kernel. Nevertheless, in this chapter we shall assume that a process spends only a short time inside a critical section.

Table 6.1 Essential Properties of a CS Implementation

Property	Description
Mutual exclusion	At any moment, at most one process may execute a CS for a data item d_s.
Progress	When no process is executing a CS for a data item d_s, one of the processes wishing to enter a CS for d_s will be granted entry.
Bounded wait	After a process P_i has indicated its desire to enter a CS for d_s, the number of times other processes can gain entry to a CS for d_s ahead of P_i is bounded by a finite integer.

6.3.1 Properties of a Critical Section Implementation

When several processes wish to use critical sections for a data item d_s, a critical section implementation must ensure that it grants entry into a critical section in accordance with the notions of correctness and fairness to all processes. Table 6.1 summarizes three essential properties a critical section implementation must possess to satisfy these requirements. The *mutual exclusion* property guarantees that two or more processes will not be in critical sections for d_s simultaneously, which is the crux of Definition 6.3. It ensures correctness of the implementation. The second and third property of Table 6.1 together guarantee that no process wishing to enter a critical section will be delayed indefinitely; i.e., *starvation* will not occur. We discuss this aspect in the following.

The *progress* property ensures that if some processes are interested in entering critical sections for a data item d_s, one of them will be granted entry if no process is currently inside any critical section for d_s—that is, use of a CS cannot be "reserved" for a process that is not interested in entering a critical section at present. However, this property alone cannot prevent starvation because a process might never gain entry to a CS if the critical section implementation always favors other processes for entry to the CS. The *bounded wait* property ensures that this does not happen by limiting the number of times other processes can gain entry to a critical section ahead of a requesting process P_i. Thus the progress and bounded wait properties ensure that every requesting process will gain entry to a critical section in finite time; however, these properties do not guarantee a specific limit to the delay in gaining entry to a CS.

6.4 CONTROL SYNCHRONIZATION AND INDIVISIBLE OPERATIONS

Interacting processes need to coordinate their execution with respect to one another, so that they perform their actions in a desired order. This requirement is met through *control synchronization*.

{Perform operation a_i only after P_j performs operation a_j}	Perform operation a_j ...
Process P_i	*Process P_j*

Figure 6.5 Processes requiring control synchronization.

```
var
        operation_aj_performed : boolean;
        pi_blocked : boolean;
begin
        operation_aj_performed := false;
        pi_blocked := false;

Parbegin
        ...                                      ...
        if operation_aj_performed = false        {perform operation a_j}
        then                                     if pi_blocked = true
            pi_blocked := true;                  then
            block (P_i);                             pi_blocked := false;
        {perform operation a_i}                      activate (P_i);
        ...                                      else
        ...                                          operation_aj_performed := true;
        ...                                      ...
Parend;
end.

              Process P_i                             Process P_j
```

Figure 6.6 A naive attempt at signaling through boolean variables.

Figure 6.5 shows a pseudocode for processes P_i and P_j, wherein process P_i would perform an operation a_i only after process P_j has performed an operation a_j. *Signaling* is a general technique of control synchronization. It can be used to meet the synchronization requirement of Figure 6.5 as follows: When process P_i reaches the point where it wishes to perform operation a_i, it checks whether process P_j has performed operation a_j. If it is so, P_i would perform operation a_i right away; otherwise, it would block itself waiting for process P_j to perform operation a_j. After performing operation a_j, process P_j would check whether P_i is waiting for it. If so, it would signal process P_i to resume its operation.

Figure 6.6 shows a naive attempt at signaling. The synchronization data consists of two boolean variables: *operation_aj_performed* is a flag that indicates whether process P_j has performed operation a_j, and *pi_blocked* is a flag which indicates whether process P_i has blocked itself waiting for process P_j to execute operation a_j. Both these flags are initialized to *false*. The code makes system calls to block and activate processes to achieve the desired control synchronization.

Before performing operation a_i, process P_i consults the variable *operation_aj_performed* to check whether process P_j has already performed operation a_j. If so, it goes ahead to perform operation a_i; otherwise, it sets

Table 6.2 Race Condition in Process Synchronization

Time	Actions of process P_i	Actions of process P_j
t_1	**if** *action_aj_performed* = *false*	
t_2		{*perform action* a_j}
t_3		**if** *pi_blocked* = *true*
t_4		*action_aj_performed* :=*true*
⋮		
t_{20}	*pi_blocked* :=*true*;	
t_{21}	*block* (P_i);	

pi_blocked to *true* and makes a system call to block itself. Process P_j performs operation a_j and checks whether process P_i has already become blocked to wait until it has performed operation a_j. If so, it makes a system call to activate P_i; otherwise, it sets *operation_aj_performed* to *true* so that process P_i would know that it has performed operation a_j.

However, this naive signaling arrangement does not work because process P_i may face indefinite blocking in some situations. Table 6.2 shows such a situation. Process P_i checks the value of *operation_aj_performed* and finds that operation a_j has not been performed. At time t_2, it is poised to set the variable *pi_blocked* to *true*, but at this time it is preempted. Process P_j is now scheduled. It performs operation a_j and checks whether process P_i is blocked. However, *pi_blocked* is *false*, so P_j simply sets *operation_aj_performed* to *true* and continues its execution. P_i is scheduled at time t_{20}. It sets *pi_blocked* to *true* and makes a system call to block itself. Process P_i will sleep for ever!

In the notation of Section 6.2, consider the **if** statements in processes P_i and P_j to represent the operations f_i and f_j on the state of the system. The result of their execution should have been one of the following: process P_i blocks itself, gets activated by P_j and performs operation a_i; or process P_i finds that P_j has already performed a_j and goes ahead to perform operation a_i. However, in the execution shown in Table 6.2, process P_i blocks itself and is never activated. From Definition 6.2, this is a race condition.

The race condition has two causes—process P_i can be preempted after finding *operation_aj_performed* = *false* but before setting *pi_blocked* to *true*, and process P_j can be preempted after finding *pi_blocked* = *false* but before setting *operation_aj_performed* to *true*. The race condition can be prevented if we could ensure that processes P_i and P_j would not be preempted before they set the respective flags to *true*. An *indivisible operation* (also called an *atomic operation*) is the device that ensures that processes can execute a sequence of actions without being preempted.

Definition 6.4 Indivisible Operation An operation on a set of data items that cannot be executed concurrently either with itself or with any other operation on a data item included in the set.

```
procedure check_aj
begin
    if operation_aj_performed=false
     then
         pi_blocked:=true;
         block (P_i)
end;

procedure post_aj
begin
    if pi_blocked=true
     then
         pi_blocked:=false;
         activate(P_j)
    else
          operation_aj_performed:=true;
end;
```

Figure 6.7 Indivisible operations *check_a*$_j$ and *post_a*$_j$ for signaling.

Since an indivisible operation cannot be performed concurrently with any other operation involving the same data, it must be completed before any other process accesses the data. The situation shown in Table 6.2 would not arise if the **if** statements in Figure 6.6 were implemented as indivisible operations on data items *operation_aj_performed* and *pi_blocked*, because if process P_i found *operation_aj_performed* = *false*, it would be able to set *pi_blocked* = *true* without being preempted, and if process P_j found *pi_blocked* to be *false*, it would be able to set *operation_aj_performed* to *true* without being preempted. Accordingly, we define two indivisible operations *check_aj* and *post_aj* to perform the **if** statements of processes P_i and P_j, respectively, and replace the **if** statements by invocations of these indivisible operations. Figure 6.7 shows details of the indivisible operations *check_aj* and *post_aj*. When *operation_aj_performed* is *false*, indivisible operation *check_aj* is deemed to be complete after process P_i is blocked; it would enable process P_j to perform operation *post_aj*.

An indivisible operation on the set of data items $\{d_s\}$ is like a critical section on $\{d_s\}$. However, we differentiate between them because a critical section has to be explicitly implemented in a program, whereas the hardware or software of a computer system may provide some indivisible operations among its primitive operations.

6.5 SYNCHRONIZATION APPROACHES

In this section we discuss how the critical sections and indivisible operations required for process synchronization can be implemented.

6.5.1 Looping versus Blocking

A critical section for $\{d_s\}$ and an indivisible signaling operation on $\{d_s\}$ have the same basic requirement—processes should not be able to execute some sequences of instructions concurrently or in parallel. Hence both could be implemented through mutual exclusion as follows:

while (some process is in a critical section on $\{d_s\}$ or
is executing an indivisible operation using $\{d_s\}$)
{ do nothing }

Critical section or indivisible operation using $\{d_s\}$

In the **while** loop, the process checks if some other process is in a critical section for the same data, or is executing an indivisible operation using the same data. If so, it keeps looping until the other process finishes. This situation is called a *busy wait* because it keeps the CPU busy in executing a process even as the process does nothing! The busy wait ends only when the process finds that no other process is in a critical section or executing an indivisible operation.

A busy wait in a process has several adverse consequences. An implementation of critical sections employing busy waits cannot provide the bounded wait property because when many processes are in a busy wait for a CS, the implementation cannot control which process would gain entry to a CS when the process currently in CS exits. In a time-sharing OS, a process that gets into a busy wait to gain entry to a CS would use up its time slice without entering the CS, which would degrade the system performance.

In an OS using priority-based scheduling, a busy wait can result in a situation where processes wait for each other indefinitely. Consider the following situation: A high-priority process P_i is blocked on an I/O operation and a low-priority process P_j enters a critical section for data item d_s. When P_i's I/O operation completes, P_j is preempted and P_i is scheduled. If P_i now tries to enter a critical section for d_s using the **while** loop described earlier, it would face a busy wait. This busy wait denies the CPU to P_j, hence it is unable to complete its execution of the critical section and exit. In turn, this situation prevents P_i from entering its critical section. Processes P_i and P_j now wait for each other indefinitely. Because a high-priority process waits for a process with a low priority, this situation is called *priority inversion*. The priority inversion problem is typically addressed through the *priority inheritance protocol*, wherein a low-priority process that holds a resource temporarily acquires the priority of the highest-priority process that needs the resource. In our example, process P_j would temporarily acquire the priority of process P_i, which would enable it to get scheduled and exit from its critical section. However, use of the priority inheritance protocol is impractical in these situations because it would require the kernel to know minute details of the operation of processes.

To avoid busy waits, a process waiting for entry to a critical section should be put into the *blocked* state. Its state should be changed to *ready* only when it can be allowed to enter the CS. This approach can be realized through the following outline:

if (some process is in a critical section on $\{d_s\}$ or
is executing an indivisible operation using $\{d_s\}$)
then *make a system call to block itself;*

Critical section or indivisible operation using $\{d_s\}$

In this approach, the kernel must activate the blocked process when no other process is operating in a critical section on $\{d_s\}$ or executing an indivisible operation using $\{d_s\}$.

When a critical section or an indivisible operation is realized through any of the above outlines, a process wishing to enter a CS has to check whether any other process is inside a CS, and accordingly decide whether to loop (or block). This action itself involves executing a few instructions in a mutually exclusive way to avoid a race condition (see Section 6.4), so how is that to be done? Actually, it can be done in two ways. In the first approach, called the *algorithmic approach*, a complex arrangement of checks is used in concurrent processes to avoid race conditions. We shall discuss the features of this approach, and its drawbacks, in Section 6.8. The second approach uses some features in computer hardware to simplify this check. We discuss this approach in the next section.

6.5.2 Hardware Support for Process Synchronization

Process synchronization involves executing some sequences of instructions in a mutually exclusive manner. On a uniprocessor system, this can be achieved by disabling interrupts while a process executes such a sequence of instructions, so that it will not be preempted. However, this approach involves the overhead of system calls to disable interrupts and enable them again, and also delays processing of interrupts, which can lead to undesirable consequences for system performance or user service. It is also not applicable to multiprocessor systems. For these reasons, operating systems implement critical sections and indivisible operations through *indivisible instructions* provided in computers, together with shared variables called *lock variables*. In this section, we use illustrations of the looping approach to process synchronization; however, the techniques discussed here are equally applicable to the blocking approach to process synchronization. Note that indivisible instructions merely assist in implementing critical sections; the properties of CS implementation summarized in Table 6.1 have to be ensured separately by enabling processes to enter CS in an appropriate manner (see Exercise 6.12).

Indivisible Instructions Since the mid-1960s, computer systems have provided special features in their hardware to prevent race conditions while accessing a memory location containing shared data. The basic theme is that all accesses to a memory location made by one instruction should be implemented without permitting another CPU to access the same location. Two popular techniques used for this purpose are locking the memory bus during an instruction (e.g., in Intel 80x86 processors) and providing special instructions that perform some specific operations on memory locations in a race-free manner (e.g., in IBM/370 and M68000 processors). We will use the term *indivisible instruction* as a generic term for all such instructions.

Use of a Lock Variable A *lock variable* is a two-state variable that is used to bridge the semantic gap (see Definition 4.1) between critical sections or indivisible operations, on the one hand, and indivisible instructions provided in a computer system, on the other. To implement critical sections for a data item d_s, an application associates a lock variable with d_s. The lock variable has only two possible values—open and closed. When a process wishes to execute a critical section for d_s, it tests the value of the lock variable. If the lock is open, it closes the lock, executes the critical section, and opens the lock while exiting from the critical section. To avoid race conditions in setting the value of the lock variable, an indivisible instruction is used to test and close the lock. Lock variables assist in implementing indivisible operations in a similar manner.

Figure 6.8 illustrates how a critical section or an indivisible operation is implemented by using an indivisible instruction and a lock variable. The indivisible instruction performs the actions indicated in the dashed box: if the lock is closed, it loops back to itself; otherwise, it closes the lock. In the following, we illustrate use of two indivisible instructions—called *test-and-set* and *swap* instructions—to implement critical sections and indivisible operations.

Test-and-Set (TS) Instruction This indivisible instruction performs two actions. It "tests" the value of a memory byte and sets the *condition code* field (i.e., the *flags* field) of the PSW to indicate whether the value was zero or nonzero. It also sets all bits in the byte to 1s. No other CPU can access the memory byte until both actions are complete. This instruction can be used to implement the statements enclosed in the dashed box in Figure 6.8.

Figure 6.9 is a segment of an IBM/370 assembly language program for implementing a critical section or an indivisible operation. `LOCK` is a lock variable used with the convention that a nonzero value implies that the lock is closed, and a zero implies that it is open. The first line in the assembly language program declares `LOCK` and initializes it to 0. The `TS` instruction sets the condition code according to the value of `LOCK` and then sets the value of `LOCK` to *closed*. Thus, the condition code indicates if the lock was closed before the `TS` instruction was executed. The branch instruction `BC 7, ENTRY_TEST` checks the condition code and loops

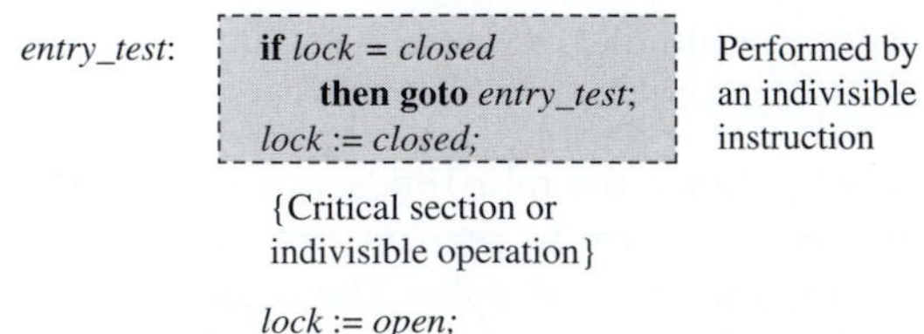

Figure 6.8 Implementing a critical section or indivisible operation by using a lock variable.

```
LOCK          DC    X'00'           Lock is initialized to open
ENTRY_TEST    TS    LOCK            Test-and-set lock
              BC    7, ENTRY_TEST   Loop if lock was closed

              ...                   { Critical section or
                                      indivisible operation }

              MVI   LOCK, X'00'     Open the lock(by moving 0s)
```

Figure 6.9 Implementing a critical section or indivisible operation by using test-and-set.

```
TEMP          DS    1               Reserve one byte for TEMP
LOCK          DC    X'00'           Lock is initialized to open
              MVI   TEMP, X'FF'     X'FF' is used to close the lock
ENTRY_TEST    SWAP  LOCK, TEMP
              COMP  TEMP, X'00'     Test old value of lock
              BC    7, ENTRY_TEST   Loop if lock was closed

              ...                   { Critical section or
                                      indivisible operation }

              MVI   LOCK, X'00'     Open the lock
```

Figure 6.10 Implementing a critical section or indivisible operation by using a swap instruction.

back to the `TS` instruction if the lock was closed. This way a process that finds the lock closed would execute the loop in a busy wait until lock was opened. Thc `MVI` instruction puts 0s in all bits of `LOCK`; i.e., it opens the lock. This action would enable only one of the processes looping at `ENTRY_TEST` to proceed.

Swap Instruction The swap instruction exchanges contents of two memory locations. It is an indivisible instruction; no other CPU can access either of the locations during swapping. Figure 6.10 shows how a critical section or an indivisible operation can be implemented by using the swap instruction. (For convenience, we use the same coding conventions as used for the `TS` instruction.) The temporary location `TEMP` is initialized to a nonzero value. The SWAP instruction swaps its contents with LOCK. This action closes the lock. The old value of `LOCK` is now available in `TEMP`. It is tested to find whether the lock was already closed. If so, the process loops on the swap instruction until the lock is opened. The process executing the critical section or indivisible operation opens the lock at the end of the operation. This action enables one process to get past the `BC` instruction and enter the critical section or the indivisible operation.

Many computers provide a *Compare-and-swap* instruction. This instruction has three operands. If the first two operands are equal, it copies the third operand's value into the second operand's location; otherwise, it copies the second operand's value into the first operand's location. It is easy to rewrite the program of Figure 6.10 by using the instruction `Compare-and-swap first_opd, LOCK, third_opd` where the values of `first_opd` and `third_opd` correspond to the open and closed values of the lock. In effect, this instruction closes the lock and puts its old value in `first_opd`.

6.5.3 Algorithmic Approaches, Synchronization Primitives, and Concurrent Programming Constructs

Historically, implementation of process synchronization has gone through three important stages—algorithmic approaches, synchronization primitives, and concurrent programming constructs. Each stage in its history solved practical difficulties that were faced in the previous stage.

Algorithmic approaches were largely confined to implementing mutual exclusion. They did not use any special features in computer architecture, programming languages, or the kernel to achieve mutual exclusion; instead they depended on a complex arrangement of checks to ensure that processes accessed shared data in a mutually exclusive manner. Thus the algorithmic approaches were independent of hardware and software platforms. However, correctness of mutual exclusion depended on correctness of these checks, and was hard to prove because of logical complexity of the checks. This problem inhibited development of large applications. Since the algorithmic approaches worked independently of the kernel, they could not employ the blocking approach to process synchronization (see Section 6.5.1), so they used the looping approach and suffered from all its drawbacks.

A set of *synchronization primitives* were developed to overcome deficiencies of the algorithmic approach. Each primitive was a simple operation that contributed to process synchronization; it was implemented by using indivisible instructions in the hardware and support from the kernel for blocking and activation of processes. The primitives possessed useful properties for implementing both mutual exclusion and indivisible operations, and it was hoped that these properties could be used to construct proofs of correctness of a concurrent program. However, experience showed that these primitives could be used haphazardly, a property that caused its own difficulties with correctness of programs. Most modern operating systems provide the *wait* and *signal* primitives of *semaphores*; however, they are employed only by system programmers because of the problems mentioned above.

The next important step in the history of process synchronization was the development of *concurrent programming constructs*, which provided data abstraction and encapsulation features specifically suited to the construction of concurrent programs. They had well-defined semantics that were enforced by the language compiler. Effectively, concurrent programming constructs incorporated functions that were analogous to those provided by the synchronization primitives, but they also included features to ensure that these functions could not be used in a haphazard or indiscriminate manner. These properties helped in ensuring correctness of programs, which made construction of large applications practical. Most modern programming languages provide a concurrent programming construct called a *monitor*.

We discuss algorithmic approaches to process synchronization in Section 6.8, and semaphores and synchronization primitives for mutual exclusion in Section 6.9. Section 6.10 describes monitors.

6.6 STRUCTURE OF CONCURRENT SYSTEMS

A concurrent system consists of three key components:

- Shared data
- Operations on shared data
- Interacting processes

Shared data include two kinds of data—application data used and manipulated by processes, and synchronization data, i.e., data used for synchronization between processes. An operation is a convenient unit of code, typically a function or a procedure in a programming language, which accesses and manipulates shared data. A *synchronization operation* is an operation on synchronization data.

A *snapshot* of a concurrent system is a view of the system at a specific time instant. It shows relationships between shared data, operations and processes at that instant of time. We use the pictorial conventions shown in Figure 6.11 to depict a snapshot. A process is shown as a circle. A circle with a cross in it indicates a blocked process. A data item, or a set of data items, is represented by a rectangular box. The value(s) of data, if known, are shown inside the box.

Operations on data are shown as connectors or sockets joined to the data. An oval shape enclosing a data item indicates that the data item is shared. A dashed line connects a process and an operation on data if the process is currently engaged in executing the operation. Recall that a dashed rectangular box encloses code executed as a critical section. We extend this convention to operations on data. Hence mutually exclusive operations on data are enclosed in a dashed rectangular box. A queue of blocked processes is associated with the dashed box to show the processes waiting to perform one of the operations.

The execution of a concurrent system is represented by a series of snapshots.

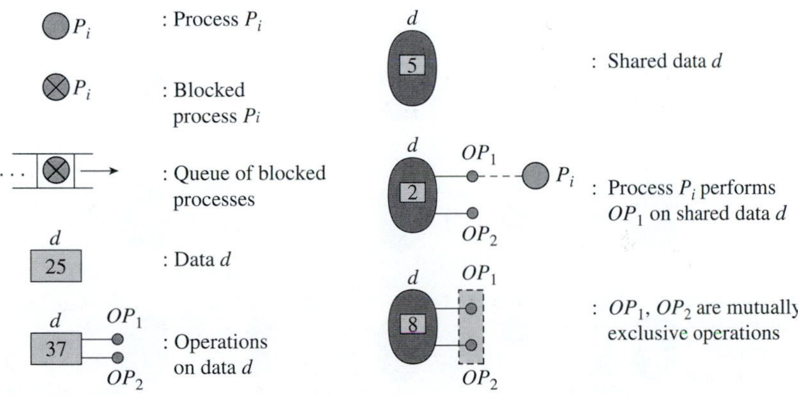

Figure 6.11 Pictorial conventions for snapshots of concurrent systems.

Example 6.3 Snapshots of a Concurrent System

Consider the system of Figure 6.5, where process P_i performs action a_i only after process P_j performs action a_j. We assume that operations a_i and a_j operate on shared data items X and Y, respectively. Let the system be implemented using the operations *check_aj* and *post_aj* of Figure 6.7. This system comprises the following components:

Shared data	Boolean variables *operation_aj_performed* and *pi_blocked*, both initialized to *false*, and data items X and Y.
Operations on application data	Operations a_i and a_j.
Synchronization operations	Operations *check_aj* and *post_aj*.
Processes	Processes P_i and P_j.

Figure 6.12 shows three snapshots of this system. T and F indicate values *true* and *false*, respectively. Operations *check_aj* and *post_aj* both use the boolean variables *operation_aj_performed* and *pi_blocked*. These operations are indivisible operations, so they are mutually exclusive. Accordingly, they are enclosed in a dashed box. Figure 6.12(a) shows the situation when process P_j is engaged in performing operation a_j and process P_i wishes to perform operation a_i, so it invokes operation *check_aj*. Operation *check_aj* finds that *operation_aj_performed* is *false*, so it sets *pi_blocked* to *true*, blocks process P_i and exits. When P_j finishes performing operation a_j, it invokes operation *post_aj* (see Figure 6.12(b)). This operation finds that *pi_blocked* is *true*, so it sets *pi_blocked* to *false*, activates process P_i, and exits. Process P_i now performs operation a_i (see Figure 6.12(c)).

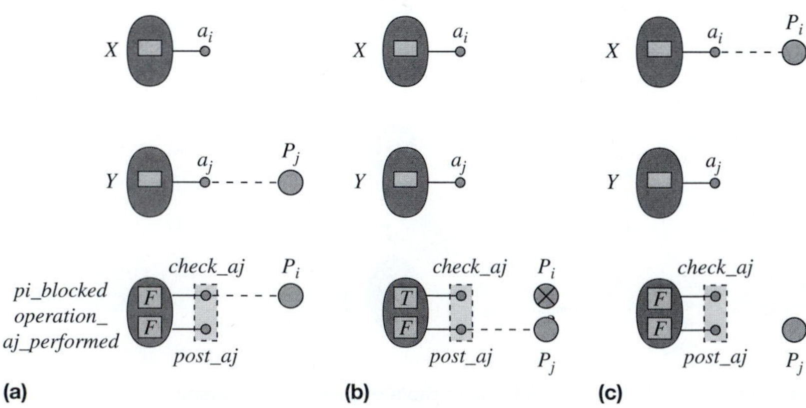

Figure 6.12 Snapshots of the system of Example 6.3.

6.7 CLASSIC PROCESS SYNCHRONIZATION PROBLEMS

A solution to a process synchronization problem should meet three important criteria:

- *Correctness:* Data access synchronization and control synchronization should be performed in accordance with synchronization requirements of the problem.
- *Maximum concurrency:* A process should be able to operate freely except when it needs to wait for other processes to perform synchronization actions.
- *No busy waits:* To avoid performance degradation, synchronization should be performed through blocking rather than through busy waits (see Section 6.5.1).

As discussed in sections 6.3 and 6.4, critical sections and signaling are the key elements of process synchronization, so a solution to a process synchronization problem should incorporate a suitable combination of these elements. In this section, we analyze some classic problems in process synchronization, which are representative of synchronization problems in various application domains, and discuss issues (and common mistakes) in designing their solutions. In later Sections we implement their solutions using various synchronization features provided in programming languages.

6.7.1 Producers—Consumers with Bounded Buffers

A *producers–consumers system with bounded buffers* consists of an unspecified number of *producer* and *consumer* processes and a finite pool of buffers (see Figure 6.13). Each buffer is capable of holding one item of information—it is said to become *full* when a producer writes a new item into it, and become *empty* when a consumer copies out an item contained in it; it is empty when the producers–consumers system starts its operation. A producer process produces one item of information at a time and writes it into an empty buffer. A consumer process consumes information one item at a time from a full buffer.

A producers–consumers system with bounded buffers is a useful abstraction for many practical synchronization problems. A print service is a good example

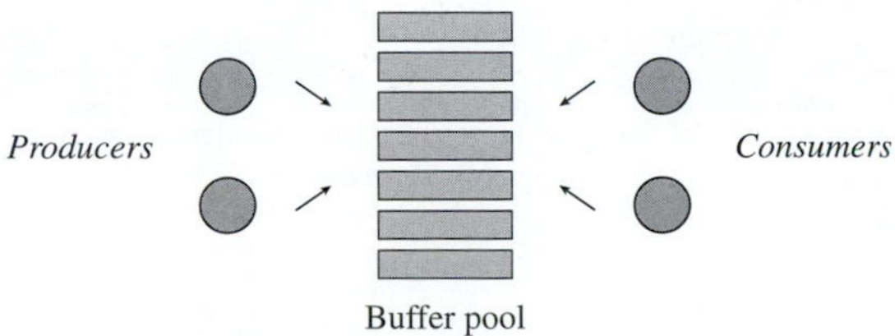

Figure 6.13 A producers–consumers system with bounded buffers.

in the OS domain. A fixed-size queue of print requests is the bounded buffer. A process that adds a print request to the queue is a producer process, and a print daemon is a consumer process. The data logging application of Example 5.1 would also be an instance of the producers–consumers problem if the *housekeeping* process is omitted—the *copy_sample* process is the producer since it writes a data sample into a buffer. The *record_sample* process is a consumer since it removes a data sample from the buffer and writes it into the disk file.

A solution to the producers–consumers problem must satisfy the following conditions:

1. A producer must not overwrite a full buffer.
2. A consumer must not consume an empty buffer.
3. Producers and consumers must access buffers in a mutually exclusive manner.

The following condition is also sometimes imposed:

4. Information must be consumed in the same order in which it is put into the buffers, i.e., in FIFO order.

Figure 6.14 shows an outline for the producers–consumers problem. Producer and consumer processes access a buffer inside a critical section. A producer enters its critical section and checks whether an empty buffer exists. If so, it produces into that buffer; otherwise, it merely exits from its critical section. This sequence is repeated until it finds an empty buffer. The boolean variable *produced* is used to break out of the **while** loop after the producer produces into an empty buffer. Analogously, a consumer makes repeated checks until it finds a full buffer to consume from.

This outline suffers from two problems—poor concurrency and busy waits. The pool contains many buffers, and so it should be possible for producers and consumers to concurrently access empty and full buffers, respectively. However,

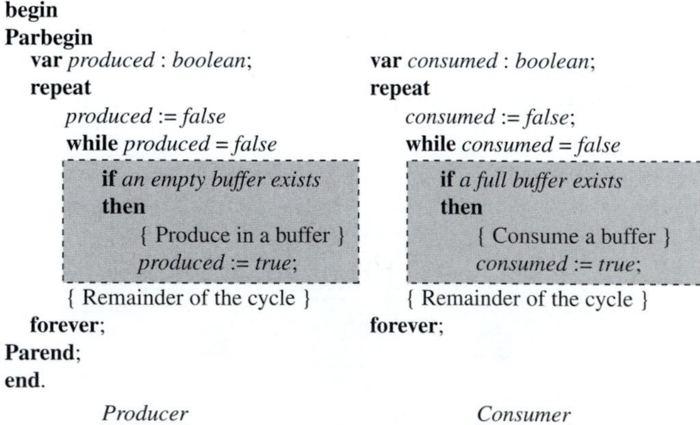

Figure 6.14 An outline for producers–consumers using critical sections.

both produce and consume actions take place in critical sections for the entire buffer pool, and so only one process, whether producer or consumer, can access a buffer at any time.

Busy waits exist in both producers and consumers. A producer repeatedly checks for an empty buffer and a consumer repeatedly checks for a full buffer. To avoid busy waits, a producer process should be blocked if an empty buffer is not available. When a consumer consumes from a buffer, it should activate a producer that is waiting for an empty buffer. Similarly, a consumer should be blocked if a full buffer is not available. A producer should activate such a consumer after producing in a buffer.

When we reanalyze the producers–consumers problem in this light, we notice that though it involves mutual exclusion between a producer and a consumer that use the same buffer, it is really a signaling problem. After producing an item of information in a buffer, a producer should signal a consumer that wishes to consume the item from that buffer. Similarly, after consuming an item in a buffer, a consumer should signal a producer that wishes to produce an item of information in that buffer. These requirements can be met by using the signaling arrangement discussed in Section 6.4.

An improved outline using this approach is shown in Figure 6.15 for a simple producers–consumers system that consists of a single producer, a single consumer, and a single buffer. The operation *check_b_empty* performed by the producer blocks it if the buffer is full, while the operation *post_b_full* sets *buffer_full* to *true* and activates the consumer if the consumer is blocked for the buffer to become full. Analogous operations *check_b_full* and *post_b_empty* are defined for use by the consumer process. The boolean flags *producer_blocked* and *consumer_blocked* are used by these operations to note whether the producer or consumer process

```
var
        buffer : . . . ;
        buffer_full : boolean;
        producer_blocked, consumer_blocked : boolean;
begin
        buffer_full := false;
        producer_blocked := false;
        consumer_blocked := false;
Parbegin
  repeat                                repeat
     check_b_empty;                        check_b_full;
     {Produce in the buffer}               {Consume from the buffer}
     post_b_full;                          post_b_empty;
     {Remainder of the cycle}              {Remainder of the cycle}
  forever;                              forever;
Parend;
end.
            Producer                              Consumer
```

Figure 6.15 An improved outline for a single buffer producers–consumers system using signaling.

```
procedure check_b_empty                 procedure check_b_full
begin                                   begin
    if buffer_full = true                   if buffer_full = false
    then                                    then
        producer_blocked := true;               consumer_blocked := true;
        block (producer);                       block (consumer);
end;                                    end;

procedure post_b_full                   procedure post_b_empty
begin                                   begin
    buffer_full := true;                    buffer_full := false;
    if consumer_blocked = true              if producer_blocked = true
    then                                    then
        consumer_blocked := false;              producer_blocked := false;
        activate (consumer);                    activate (producer);
end;                                    end;

     Operations of producer                  Operations of consumer
```

Figure 6.16 Indivisible operations for the producers–consumers problem.

is blocked at any moment. Figure 6.16 shows details of the indivisible operations. This outline will need to be extended to handle multiple buffers or multiple producer/consumer processes. We discuss this aspect in Section 6.9.2.

6.7.2 Readers and Writers

A *readers–writers system* consists of shared data, an unspecified number of *reader* processes that only read the data, and an unspecified number of *writer* processes that modify or update the data. We use the terms *reading* and *writing* for accesses to the shared data made by reader and writer processes, respectively. A solution to the readers–writers problem must satisfy the following conditions:

1. Many readers can perform reading concurrently.
2. Reading is prohibited while a writer is writing.
3. Only one writer can perform writing at any time.

Conditions **1**–**3** do not specify which process should be preferred if a reader and a writer process wish to access the shared data at the same time. The following additional condition is imposed if it is important to give a higher priority to readers in order to meet some business goals:

4. A reader has a nonpreemptive priority over writers; i.e., it gets access to the shared data ahead of a waiting writer, but it does not preempt an active writer.

This system is called a *readers preferred readers–writers system*. A *writers preferred readers–writers system* is analogously defined.

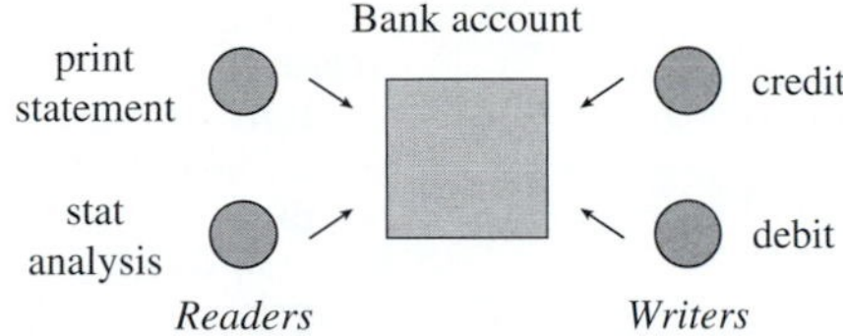

Figure 6.17 Readers and writers in a banking system.

Figure 6.17 illustrates an example of a readers–writers system. The readers and writers share a bank account. The reader processes *print statement* and *stat analysis* merely read the data from the bank account; hence they can execute concurrently. *credit* and *debit* modify the balance in the account. Clearly only one of them should be active at any moment and none of the readers should be concurrent with it. In an airline reservation system, processes that merely query the availability of seats on a flight are reader processes, while processes that make reservations are writer processes since they modify parts of the reservation database.

We determine the synchronization requirements of a readers–writers system as follows: Conditions **1**–**3** permit either one writer to perform writing or many readers to perform concurrent reading. Hence writing should be performed in a critical section for the shared data. When a writer finishes writing, it should either enable another writer to enter its critical section, or activate *all* waiting readers using a signaling arrangement and a count of waiting readers. If readers are reading, a waiting writer should be enabled to perform writing when the last reader finishes reading. This action would require a count of concurrent readers to be maintained.

Figure 6.18 is an outline for a readers–writers system. Writing is performed in a critical section. A critical section is not used in a reader, because that would prevent concurrency between readers. A signaling arrangement is used to handle blocking and activation of readers and writers. For simplicity, details of maintaining and using counts of waiting readers and readers reading concurrently are not shown in the outline; we shall discuss these in Section 6.9.3. The outline of Figure 6.18 does not provide bounded waits for readers and writers; however, it provides maximum concurrency. This outline does not prefer either readers or writers.

6.7.3 Dining Philosophers

Five philosophers sit around a table pondering philosophical issues. A plate of spaghetti is kept in front of each philosopher, and a fork is placed between each pair of philosophers (see Figure 6.19). To eat, a philosopher must pick up the two forks placed between him and the neighbors on either side, one at a time. The problem is to design processes to represent the philosophers such that each philosopher can eat when hungry and none dies of hunger.

Parbegin	
repeat	**repeat**
If *a writer is writing*	**If** *reader(s) are reading, or a writer is writing*
then	**then**
{ wait };	{ wait };
{ read }	{ write }
If *no other readers reading*	**If** *reader(s) or writer(s) waiting*
then	**then**
if *writer(s) waiting*	*activate either one waiting writer or all waiting readers*;
then	
activate one waiting writer;	
forever;	**forever**;
Parend;	
end.	
Reader(s)	*Writer(s)*

Figure 6.18 An outline for a readers–writers system.

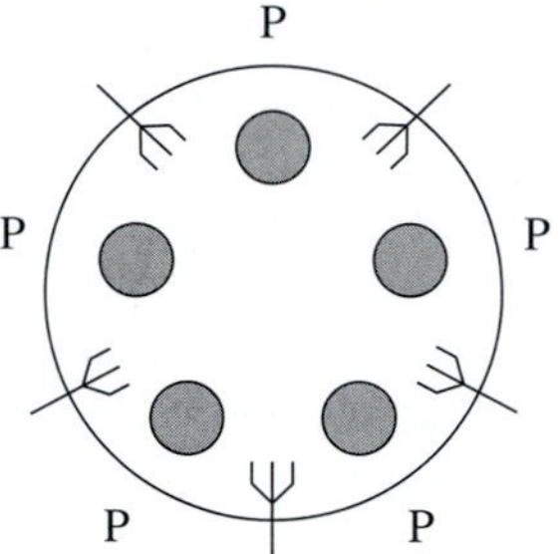

Figure 6.19 Dining philosophers.

The correctness condition in the dining philosophers system is that a hungry philosopher should not face indefinite waits when he decides to eat. The challenge is to design a solution that does not suffer from either *deadlocks*, where processes become blocked waiting for each other (see Section 1.4.2), or *livelocks*, where processes are not blocked but defer to each other indefinitely. Consider the outline of a philosopher process P_i shown in Figure 6.20, where details of process synchronization have been omitted. A philosopher picks up the forks one at a time, say, first the left fork and then the right fork. This solution is prone to deadlock, because if all philosophers simultaneously lift their left forks, none will be able to lift the right fork! It also contains race conditions because neighbors might fight over a shared fork. We can avoid deadlocks by modifying the philosopher process so that if the right fork is not available, the philosopher would defer to his left neighbor by putting down the left fork and repeating the attempt to take the forks sometime later. However, this approach suffers from livelocks because the same situation may recur.

```
repeat
    if left fork is not available
    then
        block (P_i);
    lift left fork;
    if right fork is not available
    then
        block (P_i);
    lift right fork;
    { eat }
    put down both forks
    if left neighbor is waiting for his right fork
    then
        activate (left neighbor);
    if right neighbor is waiting for his left fork
    then
        activate (right neighbor);
    { think }
forever
```

Figure 6.20 Outline of a philosopher process P_i.

```
var    successful : boolean;
repeat
    successful := false;
    while (not successful)
      if both forks are available then
         lift the forks one at a time;
         successful := true;
      if successful = false
      then
          block (P_i);
    { eat }
    put down both forks;
    if left neighbor is waiting for his right fork
    then
        activate (left neighbor);
    if right neighbor is waiting for his left fork
    then
        activate (right neighbor);
    { think }
forever
```

Figure 6.21 An improved outline of a philosopher process.

An improved outline for the dining philosophers problem is given in Figure 6.21. A philosopher checks availability of forks in a CS and also picks up the forks in the CS. Hence race conditions cannot arise. This arrangement ensures that at least some philosopher(s) can eat at any time and deadlocks cannot arise. A philosopher who cannot get both forks at the same time blocks himself. He gets activated when any of his neighbors puts down a shared fork, hence he has to check for availability of forks once again. This is the purpose of the **while** loop. However, the loop also causes a busy wait condition. Some innovative solutions to the dining philosophers problem prevent deadlocks without busy waits (see Exercise 6.14). Deadlock prevention is discussed in detail in Chapter 8.

6.8 ALGORITHMIC APPROACH TO IMPLEMENTING CRITICAL SECTIONS

The algorithmic approach to implementing critical sections did not employ either the process blocking and activation services of the kernel to delay a process, or indivisible instructions in a computer to avoid race conditions. Consequently, process synchronization implemented through this approach was independent of both the OS and the computer. However, these features required the approach to use a busy wait to delay a process at a synchronization point (see Section 6.5.1), and use a complex arrangement of logical conditions to ensure absence of race conditions, which complicated proofs of correctness. The algorithmic approach was not widely used in practice due to these weaknesses.

This section describes the algorithmic approach to implementing critical sections which, as we saw in Section 6.5.2, can be used for both data access synchronization and control synchronization. This study provides an insight into how to ensure mutual exclusion while avoiding both deadlocks and livelocks. We begin by discussing critical section implementation schemes for use by two processes. Later we see how to extend some of these schemes for use by more than two processes.

6.8.1 Two-Process Algorithms

Algorithm 6.1 *First Attempt*

```
var     turn : 1 .. 2;
begin
        turn := 1;
Parbegin
   repeat                                  repeat
      while turn = 2                          while turn = 1
          do { nothing };                         do { nothing };
      { Critical Section }                    { Critical Section }
      turn := 2;                              turn := 1;
      { Remainder of the cycle }              { Remainder of the cycle }
   forever;                                forever;
Parend;
end.
            Process P1                              Process P2
```

The variable *turn* is a shared variable. The notation 1 .. 2 in its declaration indicates that it takes values in the range 1–2; i.e., its value is either 1 or 2. It is initialized to 1 before processes P_1 and P_2 are created. Each process contains a critical section for some shared data d_s. The shared variable *turn* indicates which process can enter its critical section next. Suppose process P_1 wishes to enter its critical section. If $turn = 1$, P_1 can enter right away. After exiting its critical section, P_1 sets *turn* to 2 so that P_2 can enter its critical section. If P_1 finds $turn = 2$ when it wishes to enter its critical section, it waits in the **while** $turn = 2$ **do** { *nothing* } loop until P_2 exits from its critical section and executes the assignment $turn := 1$. Thus the correctness condition is satisfied.

Algorithm 6.1 violates the progress condition of critical section implementation described in Table 6.1 because of the way it uses shared variable *turn*. Let process P_1 be in its critical section and process P_2 be in the remainder of the cycle. When P_1 exits from its critical section, it would set *turn* to 2. If it finishes the remainder of its cycle and wishes to enter its critical section once again, it will encounter a busy wait until after P_2 uses its critical section and sets *turn* to 1. Thus, P_1 is not granted entry to its critical section even though no other process is interested in using its critical section. Algorithm 6.2 is an attempt to eliminate this problem.

Algorithm 6.2 *Second Attempt*

```
var    c1, c2 : 0 .. 1;
begin
       c1 := 1;
       c2 := 1;
Parbegin
   repeat                              repeat
       while c2 = 0                        while c1 = 0
           do { nothing };                     do { nothing };
       c1 := 0;                            c2 := 0;
       { Critical Section }                { Critical Section }
       c1 := 1;                            c2 := 1;
       { Remainder of the cycle }          { Remainder of the cycle }
   forever;                            forever;
Parend;
end.
            Process P1                          Process P2
```

The algorithm uses two shared variables c_1 and c_2, whose values are restricted to either a 0 or a 1. These variables can be looked upon as status flags for processes P_1 and P_2, respectively. P_1 sets c_1 to 0 while entering its critical section, and sets it back to 1 after exiting from its critical section. Thus $c_1 = 0$ indicates that P_1 is in its critical section and $c_1 = 1$ indicates that it is not in its critical section. Similarly, the value of c_2 indicates whether P_2 is in its critical section. Before entering its critical section, each process checks whether the other process is in its critical section. If not, it enters its own critical section right away; otherwise, it loops until the other process exits its critical section, and then enters its own critical section. The progress violation of Algorithm 6.1 is eliminated because processes are not forced to take turns using their critical sections.

Algorithm 6.2 violates the mutual exclusion condition when both processes try to enter their critical sections at the same time. Both c_1 and c_2 will be 1 (since none of the processes is in its critical section), and so both processes will enter their critical sections. To avoid this problem, the statements "**while** $c_2 = 0$ **do** { *nothing* };" and "$c_1 := 0$;" in process P_1 could be interchanged and the statements "**while** $c_1 = 0$ **do** { *nothing* };" and "$c_2 := 0$;" could be interchanged in process P_2. This way c_1 will be set to 0 before P_1 checks the value of c_2, and hence both processes will not be able to be in their critical sections at the same time. However, if both processes try to enter their critical sections at the same time, both c_1 and c_2 will be 0, and so both processes will wait for each other indefinitely. This is a *deadlock* situation (see Section 1.4.2).

Both—the correctness violation and the deadlock possibility—can be eliminated if a process defers to the other process when it finds that the other process also wishes to enter its critical section. This can be achieved as follows: if P_1 finds that P_2 is also trying to enter its critical section, it can set c_1 to 0. This will permit P_2 to enter its critical section. P_1 can wait for some time and make another attempt to enter its critical section after setting c_1 to 1. Similarly, P_2 can set c_2 to 0 if it finds that P_1 is also trying to enter its critical section. However, this approach may lead to a situation in which both processes defer to each other indefinitely. This is a *livelock* situation we discussed earlier in the context of dining philosophers (see Section 6.7.3).

Dekker's Algorithm Dekker's algorithm combines the useful features of Algorithms 6.1 and 6.2 to avoid a livelock situation. If both processes try to enter their critical sections at the same time, *turn* indicates which of the processes should be allowed to enter. It has no effect at other times.

Algorithm 6.3 *Dekker's Algorithm*

```
var    turn : 1 .. 2;
       c1, c2 : 0 .. 1;
begin
       c1 := 1;
       c2 := 1;
       turn := 1;
Parbegin
   repeat                           repeat
      c1 := 0;                         c2 := 0;
      while c2 = 0 do                  while c1 = 0 do
         if turn = 2 then                 if turn = 1 then
         begin                            begin
           c1 := 1;                         c2 := 1;
           while turn = 2                   while turn = 1
               do { nothing };                  do { nothing };
           c1 := 0;                         c2 := 0;
         end;                             end;
```

```
        { Critical Section }              { Critical Section }
        turn := 2;                        turn := 1;
        c1 := 1;                          c2 := 1;
        { Remainder of the cycle }        { Remainder of the cycle }
    forever;                          forever;
Parend;
end.
            Process P1                        Process P2
```

Variables c_1 and c_2 are used as status flags of the processes as in Algorithm 6.2. The statement **while** $c_2 = 0$ **do** in P_1 checks if it is safe for P_1 to enter its critical section. To avoid the correctness problem of Algorithm 6.2, the statement c_1 :=0 in P_1 precedes the **while** statement. If $c_2 = 1$ when P_1 wishes to enter a critical section, P_1 skips the **while** loop and enters its critical section right away. If both processes try to enter their critical sections at the same time, the value of *turn* will force one of them to defer to the other. For example, if P_1 finds $c_2 = 0$, it defers to P_2 only if *turn* = 2; otherwise, it simply waits for c_2 to become 1 before entering its critical section. Process P_2, which is also trying to enter its critical section at the same time, is forced to defer to P_1 only if *turn* = 1. In this manner the algorithm satisfies mutual exclusion and also avoids deadlock and livelock conditions. The actual value of *turn* at any time is immaterial to correctness of the algorithm.

Peterson's Algorithm Peterson's algorithm is simpler than Dekker's algorithm. It uses a boolean array *flag* that contains one flag for each process; these flags are equivalent to the status variables c_1, c_2 of Dekker's algorithm. A process sets its flag to *true* when it wishes to enter a critical section and sets it back to *false* when it exits from the critical section. Processes are assumed to have the ids P_0 and P_1. A process id is used as a subscript to access the status flag of a process in the array *flag*. The variable *turn* is used for avoiding livelocks; however, it is used differently than in Dekker's algorithm.

Algorithm 6.4 *Peterson's Algorithm*

```
var     flag : array [0 .. 1] of boolean;
        turn : 0 .. 1;
begin
        flag[0] := false;
        flag[1] := false;
Parbegin
    repeat                            repeat
      flag[0] := true;                  flag[1] := true;
      turn := 1;                        turn := 0;
      while flag[1] and turn = 1        while flag[0] and turn = 0
          do {nothing};                     do {nothing};
      { Critical Section }              { Critical Section }
      flag[0] :=false;                  flag[1] :=false;
      { Remainder of the cycle }        { Remainder of the cycle }
```

```
        forever;                              forever;
Parend;
end.
              Process P0                      Process P1
```

A process wishing to enter a critical section begins by deferring to another process by setting *turn* to point to the other process. However, it goes ahead and enters its critical section if it finds that the other process is not interested in using its own critical section. If both processes try to enter their critical sections at the same time, the value of *turn* decides which process may enter. As an example, consider process P_0. It sets *flag*[0] to *true* and *turn* to 1 when it wishes to enter its critical section. If process P_2 is not interested in using its critical section, *flag*[1] will be false, and so P_0 will come out of the **while** loop to enter its critical section right away. If P_1 is also interested in entering its critical section, *flag*[1] will be *true*. In that case, the value of *turn* decides which process may enter its critical section.

It is interesting to consider operation of Peterson's algorithm for different relative speeds of P_0 and P_1. Consider the situation when both P_0 and P_1 wish to use their critical sections and P_0 is slightly ahead of P_1. If both processes execute at the same speed, P_0 will enter its critical section ahead of P_1 because P_1 will have changed *turn* to 0 by the time P_1 reaches the **while** statement. P_1 now waits in the **while** loop until P_0 exits from its critical section. If, however, P_0 is slower than P_1, it will set *turn* to 1 sometime after P_1 sets it to 0. Hence P_0 will wait in the **while** loop and P_1 will enter its critical section.

6.8.2 *n*-Process Algorithms

In an algorithmic implementation of a critical section, the algorithm has to know the *number* of processes that use a critical section for the same data item. This awareness is reflected in many features of its code—the size of the array of status flags, the checks to determine whether any other process wishes to enter a critical section, and the arrangement for one process to defer to another. Each of these features has to change if the number of processes to be handled by the critical section implementation changes. For example, in a two-process critical section implementation, any process needs to check the status of only one other process, and possibly defer to it, to ensure correctness and absence of deadlocks and livelocks. In an *n*-process critical section implementation, a process must check the status of $n - 1$ other processes, and do it in a manner that prevents race conditions. It makes an *n*-process algorithm more complex. We see this in the context of the algorithm by Eisenberg and McGuire [1972], which extends the two-process solution of Dekker's algorithm to *n* processes.

Algorithm 6.5 *An n-Process Algorithm (Eisenberg and McGuire [1972])*

```
const   n = ...;
var     flag : array [0 .. n − 1] of (idle, want_in, in_CS);
```

```
        turn : 0 .. n − 1;
begin
        for j := 0 to n − 1 do
            flag[j] := idle;
Parbegin
    process Pi :
        repeat
            repeat
                flag[i] := want_in;
                j := turn;
                while j ≠ i
                    do if flag[j] ≠ idle
                        then j := turn { Loop here! }
                        else j := j + 1 mod n;
                flag[i] := in_CS;
                j := 0;
                while (j < n) and (j = i or flag[j] ≠ in_CS)
                    do j := j + 1;
            until (j ≥ n) and (turn = i or flag[turn] = idle);
            turn := i;
            { Critical Section }
            j := turn +1 mod n;
            while (flag[j] = idle) do j := j + 1 mod n;
            turn := j;
            flag[i] := idle;
            { Remainder of the cycle }
        forever
    process Pk : . . .
Parend;
end.
```

The variable *turn* indicates which process may enter its critical section next. Its initial value is immaterial to correctness of the algorithm. Each process has a 3-way status flag that takes the values *idle, want_in* and *in_CS*. It is initialized to the value *idle*. A process sets its flag to *want_in* whenever it wishes to enter a critical section. It now has to decide whether it may change the flag to *in_CS*. To make this decision, it checks the flags of other processes in an order that we call the modulo n order. The modulo n order is $P_{\text{turn}}, P_{\text{turn}+1}, \ldots, P_{n-1}, P_0, P_1, \ldots, P_{\text{turn}-1}$. In the first **while** loop, the process checks whether any process ahead of it in the modulo n order wishes to use its own critical section. If not, it turns its flag to *in_CS*.

Since processes make this check concurrently, more than one process may simultaneously reach the same conclusion. Hence another check is made to ensure correctness. The second **while** loop checks whether any other process has turned its flag to *in_CS*. If so, the process changes its flag back to *want_in* and repeats all the checks. All other processes that had changed their flags to *in_CS* also change their flags back to *want_in* and repeat the checks. These processes will not tie for entry to a critical section again because they have all turned their flags to *want_in*, and so only one of them will be able to get past the first **while** loop. This feature avoids the livelock condition. The process earlier in the modulo n order from P_{turn} will get in and enter its critical section ahead of other processes. It changes its flag to *idle* when it leaves its critical section. Thus the flag has the value *idle* whenever a process is in the remainder of its cycle.

This solution contains a certain form of unfairness since processes do not enter their critical sections in the same order in which they requested entry to a critical section. This unfairness is eliminated in the Bakery algorithm by Lamport [1974].

Bakery Algorithm When a process wishes to enter a critical section, it chooses a number that is larger than any number chosen by any process earlier. *choosing* is an array of boolean flags. *choosing*[*i*] is used to indicate whether process P_i is currently engaged in choosing a number. *number*[*i*] contains the number chosen by process P_i. *number*[*i*] = 0 if P_i has not chosen a number since the last time it entered the critical section. The basic idea of the algorithm is that processes should enter their critical sections in the order of increasing numbers chosen by them. We discuss the operation of the algorithm in the following.

Algorithm 6.6 *Bakery Algorithm (Lamport [1974])*

```
const  n = ... ;
var    choosing : array [0 .. n − 1] of boolean;
       number : array [0 .. n − 1] of integer;
begin
       for j := 0 to n − 1 do
           choosing[j] := false;
           number[j] := 0;
Parbegin
    process Pi :
       repeat
           choosing[i] := true;
           number[i] := max (number[0], .. ,number[n − 1])+1;
           choosing[i] := false;
           for j := 0 to n − 1 do
           begin
               while choosing[j] do { nothing };
               while number[j] ≠ 0 and (number[j], j) < (number[i],i)
                   do { nothing };
           end;
           { Critical Section }
           number[i] := 0;
           { Remainder of the cycle }
       forever;
    process Pj : . . .
Parend;
end.
```

A process wishing to enter a critical section defers to a process with a smaller number. However, a tie-breaking rule is needed because processes that choose their numbers concurrently may obtain the same number. The algorithm uses the pair (*number*[*i*], *i*) for this purpose—a process enters a critical section if its pair precedes every other pair, where the precedes relation $<$ is defined as follows:

$$(number[j], j) < (number[i], i) \text{ if}$$
$$number[j] < number[i], \text{ or}$$
$$number[j] = number[i] \text{ and } j < i.$$

Thus, if many processes obtain the same number, the process with the smallest process id enters its critical section first. In all other cases, processes enter critical sections in the order in which they raise their requests for entry to a critical section.

6.9 SEMAPHORES

As mentioned in Section 6.5.3, *synchronization primitives* were developed to overcome the limitations of algorithmic implementations. The primitives are simple operations that can be used to implement both mutual exclusion and control synchronization. A *semaphore* is a special kind of synchronization data that can be used only through specific synchronization primitives.

Definition 6.5 Semaphore A shared integer variable with nonnegative values that can be subjected only to the following operations:

1. Initialization (specified as part of its declaration)
2. The indivisible operations *wait* and *signal*

The *wait* and *signal* operations on a semaphore were originally called the P and V operations, respectively, by Dijkstra. Their semantics are shown in Figure 6.22. When a process performs a *wait* operation on a semaphore, the operation checks whether the value of the semaphore is > 0. If so, it decrements the value of the semaphore and lets the process continue its execution; otherwise, it blocks the process on the semaphore. A *signal* operation on a semaphore activates a process blocked on the semaphore, if any, or increments the value of the semaphore by 1. Due to these semantics, semaphores are also called *counting semaphores*. Indivisibility of the *wait* and *signal* operations is ensured by the programming language or the operating system that implements it. It ensures that race conditions cannot arise over a semaphore (see Section 6.9.4).

Processes use *wait* and *signal* operations to synchronize their execution with respect to one another. The initial value of a semaphore determines how many processes can get past the *wait* operation. A process that does not get past a *wait* operation is blocked on the semaphore. This feature avoids busy waits. Section 6.9.1 describes uses of semaphores. Sections 6.9.2 and 6.9.3 discuss implementation of the producers–consumers and readers–writers problems using semaphores.

```
procedure wait (S)
begin
    if S > 0
        then S := S–1;
        else block the process on S;
end;

procedure signal (S)
begin
    if some processes are blocked on S
        then activate one blocked process;
        else S := S+1;
end;
```

Figure 6.22 Semantics of the *wait* and *signal* operations on a semaphore.

Table 6.3 Uses of Semaphores in Implementing Concurrent Systems

Use	Description
Mutual exclusion	Mutual exclusion can be implemented by using a semaphore that is initialized to 1. A process performs a *wait* operation on the semaphore before entering a CS and a *signal* operation on exiting from it. A special kind of semaphore called a *binary semaphore* further simplifies CS implementation.
Bounded concurrency	Bounded concurrency implies that a function may be executed, or a resource may be accessed, by n processes concurrently, $1 \leq n \leq c$, where c is a constant. A semaphore initialized to c can be used to implement bounded concurrency.
Signaling	Signaling is used when a process P_i wishes to perform an operation a_i only after process P_j has performed an operation a_j. It is implemented by using a semaphore initialized to 0. P_i performs a *wait* on the semaphore before performing operation a_i. P_j performs a *signal* on the semaphore after it performs operation a_j.

6.9.1 Uses of Semaphores in Concurrent Systems

Table 6.3 summarizes three uses of semaphores in implementing concurrent systems. *Mutual exclusion* is useful in implementing critical sections. *Bounded concurrency* is important when a resource can be shared by up to c processes, where c is a constant ≥ 1. *Signaling* is useful in control synchronization. We discuss details of these uses in this section.

6.9.1.1 Mutual Exclusion

Figure 6.23 shows implementation of a critical section in processes P_i and P_j by using a semaphore named *sem_CS*. *sem_CS* is initialized to 1. Each process performs a *wait* operation on *sem_CS* before entering its critical section, and a *signal* operation after exiting from its critical section. The first process to perform *wait(sem_CS)* finds that *sem_CS* is > 0. Hence it decrements *sem_CS*

```
var sem_CS : semaphore := 1;
Parbegin
    repeat                              repeat
        wait (sem_CS);                      wait (sem_CS);
        { Critical Section }                { Critical Section }
        signal (sem_CS);                    signal (sem_CS);
        { Remainder of the cycle }          { Remainder of the cycle }
    forever;                            forever;
Parend;
end.
                Process P_i                         Process P_j
```

Figure 6.23 CS implementation with semaphores.

by 1 and goes on to enter its critical section. When the second process performs *wait*(*sem_CS*), it is blocked on *sem_CS* because its value is 0. It is activated when the first process performs *signal*(*sem_CS*) after exiting from its own critical section; the second process then enters its critical section. If no process is blocked on *sem_CS* when a *signal*(*sem_CS*) operation is performed, the value of *sem_CS* becomes 1. This value of *sem_CS* permits a process that is performing a *wait* operation at some later time to immediately enter its critical section. More processes using similar code can be added to the system without causing correctness problems. The next example illustrates operation of this system using snapshots.

Example 6.4

Critical Sections through Semaphores

Figure 6.24 shows snapshots taken during operation of the system shown in Figure 6.23. The *wait* and *signal* operations on *sem_CS* are enclosed in a dashed rectangular box because they are mutually exclusive (refer to the pictorial conventions of Figure 6.11). Let process P_i perform *wait*(*sem_CS*). Figure 6.24(a) illustrates the situation at the start of P_i's *wait* operation. Figure 6.24(b) shows the situation after P_i completes the *wait* operation and P_j executes a *wait* operation—P_i's *wait*(*sem_CS*) operation has reduced the value of *sem_CS* to 0, so P_j becomes blocked on the *wait* operation. Figure 6.24(c) shows the situation after process P_i performs a *signal* operation. The value of *sem_CS* remains 0, but process P_j has been activated. Process P_j performs a *signal* operation on exiting from its critical section. Since no process is currently blocked on *sem_CS*, P_j's signal operation simply results in increasing the value of *sem_CS* by 1 (see Figure 6.24(d)).

It is interesting to check which properties of critical section implementations mentioned in Table 6.1 are satisfied by the implementation of Figure 6.23. Mutual exclusion follows from the fact that *sem_CS* is initialized to 1. The implementation possesses the progress property because a process performing the *wait* operation gets to enter its critical section if no other process is in its critical

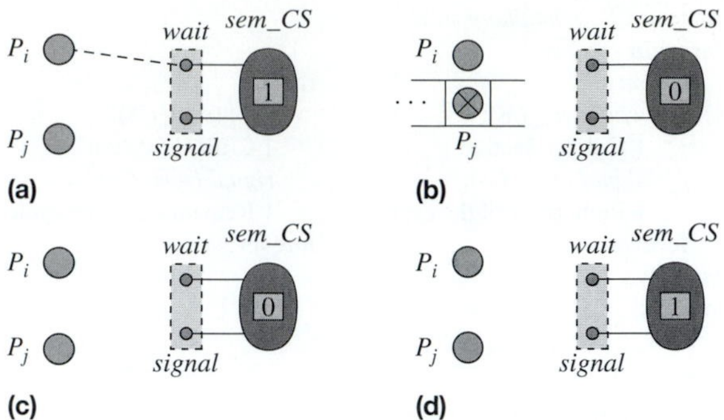

Figure 6.24 Snapshots of the concurrent system of Figure 6.23.

section. However, the bounded wait property does not hold because the order in which blocked processes are activated by *signal* operations is not defined in the semantics of semaphores. Hence a blocked process may starve if other processes perform *wait* and *signal* operations repeatedly.

Correctness problems can arise because the *wait* and *signal* operations are *primitives*, and so a program can use them in a haphazard manner. For example, process P_i of Figure 6.23 could have been erroneously written as

```
repeat
        signal(sem_CS);
        { Critical Section }
        signal(sem_CS);
        { Remainder of the cycle }
forever
```

where a *signal*(*sem_CS*) has been used instead of a *wait*(*sem_CS*) at P_i's entry to its critical section. Now the critical section would not be implemented correctly because many processes would be able to enter their critical sections at the same time. As another example, consider what would happen if the code of process P_i erroneously uses a *wait*(*sem_CS*) operation in place of the *signal*(*sem_CS*) operation following its critical section. When P_i executes its critical section, it will be blocked on the *wait* operation after exiting from its critical section because the value of *sem_CS* will be 0. Other processes wishing to enter the critical section will be blocked on the *wait* operation preceding their critical sections. Since no process performs a *signal* operation on *sem_CS*, all these processes will remain blocked indefinitely, which is a *deadlock* situation.

Binary Semaphores A *binary semaphore* is a special kind of semaphore used for implementing mutual exclusion. Hence it is often called a *mutex*. A binary semaphore is initialized to 1 and takes only the values 0 and 1 during execution of a program. The *wait* and *signal* operations on a binary semaphore are slightly different from those shown in Figure 6.22; the statement S := S−1 in the *wait* operation is replaced by the statement S := 0 and the statement S := S+1 in the *signal* operation is replaced by the statement S := 1.

```
var sync : semaphore := 0;
Parbegin
        ...                        ...
        wait (sync);               { Performaction a_j }
        { Performaction a_i }      signal (sync);
Parend;
end.
              Process P_i                Process P_j
```

Figure 6.25 Signaling using semaphores.

6.9.1.2 Bounded Concurrency

We use the term *bounded concurrency* for the situation in which up to c processes can concurrently perform an operation op_i, where c is a constant ≥ 1. Bounded concurrency is implemented by initializing a semaphore *sem_c* to c. Every process wishing to perform op_i performs a *wait*(*sem_c*) before performing op_i and a *signal*(*sem_c*) after performing it. From the semantics of the *wait* and *signal* operations, it is clear that up to c processes can concurrently perform op_i.

6.9.1.3 Signaling between Processes

Consider the synchronization requirements of processes P_i and P_j shown in Figure 6.6—process P_i should perform an operation a_i only after process P_j performs an operation a_j. A semaphore can be used to achieve this synchronization as shown in Figure 6.25. Here process P_i performs a *wait*(*sync*) before executing operation a_i and P_j performs a *signal*(*sync*) after executing operation a_j. The semaphore *sync* is initialized to 0, and so P_i will be blocked on *wait*(*sync*) if P_j has not already performed a *signal*(*sync*). It will proceed to perform operation a_i only after process P_j performs a *signal*. Unlike the solution of Figure 6.6, race conditions cannot arise because the *wait* and *signal* operations are indivisible. The signaling arrangement can be used repetitively, as the *wait* operation makes the value of *sync* 0 once again.

6.9.2 Producers—Consumers Using Semaphores

As discussed in Section 6.7.1, the producers–consumers problem is a signaling problem. After producing an item of information in a buffer, a producer signals to a consumer that is waiting to consume from the same buffer. Analogously, a consumer signals to a waiting producer. Hence we should implement producers–consumers using the signaling arrangement shown in Figure 6.25.

For simplicity, we first discuss the solution for the single buffer case shown in Figure 6.26. The buffer pool is represented by an array of buffers with a single element in it. Two semaphores *full* and *empty* are declared. They are used to indicate the number of full and empty buffers, respectively. A producer performs a *wait*(*empty*) before starting the produce operation and a consumer performs a *wait*(*full*) before a consume operation.

```
type    item = . . .;
var
        full  : Semaphore := 0; { Initializations }
        empty : Semaphore := 1;
        buffer : array [0] of item;
begin
Parbegin
   repeat                                  repeat
        wait (empty);                           wait (full);
        buffer [0] := . . .;                    x := buffer [0];
            { i.e., produce }                       { i.e., consume }
        signal (full);                          signal (empty);
        { Remainder of the cycle }              { Remainder of the cycle }
   forever;                                forever;
Parend;
end.
            Producer                                Consumer
```

Figure 6.26 Producers–consumers with a single buffer.

Initially the semaphore *full* has the value 0. Hence consumer(s) will be blocked on *wait*(*full*). *empty* has the value 1, and so one producer will get past the *wait*(*empty*) operation. After completing the produce operation it performs *signal*(*full*). This enables one consumer to enter, either immediately or later. When the consumer finishes a consume operation, it performs a *signal*(*empty*) that enables a producer to perform a produce operation. This solution avoids busy waits since semaphores are used to check for empty or full buffers, and so a process will be blocked if it cannot find an empty or full buffer as required. The total concurrency in this system is 1; sometimes a producer executes and sometimes a consumer executes. Example 6.5 describes the operation of this solution.

Example 6.5 Producers–Consumers with a Single Buffer through Semaphores

The snapshot of Figure 6.27(a) shows the initial situation in the producers–consumers system of Figure 6.26. Figure 6.27(b) shows the situation when the producer and consumer processes attempt to produce and consume, respectively. The producer process has got past its *wait* operation on *empty* since *empty* was initialized to 1. The value of semaphore *empty* becomes 0 and the producer starts producing in the buffer. The consumer process is blocked on the *wait* (*full*) operation because *full* is 0. When the producer performs a *signal*(*full*) after the produce operation, the consumer process is activated and starts consuming from the buffer. Figure 6.27(c) shows this situation.

Figure 6.28 shows how semaphores can be used to implement a solution of the n-buffer producers–consumers problem, $n \geq 1$, containing one producer and one

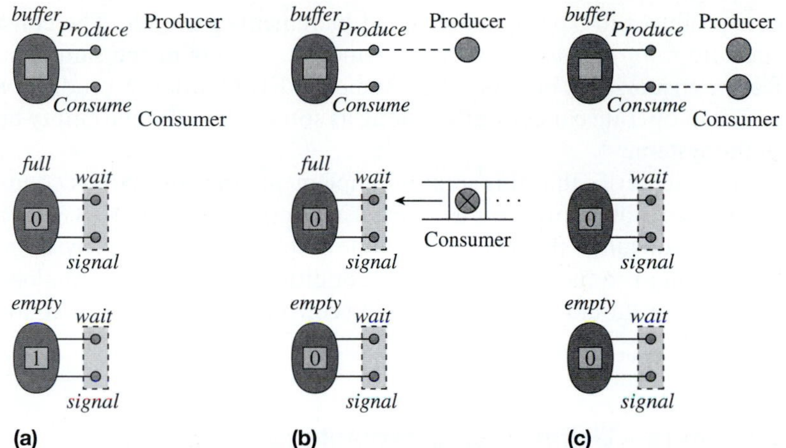

Figure 6.27 Snapshots of single buffer producers–consumers using semaphores.

```
const        n = . . .;
type         item = . . .;
var
             buffer : array [0..n – 1] of item;
             full : Semaphore := 0; { Initializations }
             empty : Semaphore := n;
             prod_ptr, cons_ptr : integer;
begin
             prod_ptr := 0;
             cons_ptr := 0;
Parbegin
  repeat                                  repeat
     wait (empty);                           wait (full);
     buffer [prod_ptr] := . . .;             x := buffer [cons_ptr];
        { i.e. produce }                        { i.e. consume }
     prod_ptr := prod_ptr + 1 mod n;         cons_ptr := cons_ptr + 1 mod n;
     signal (full);                          signal (empty);
     { Remainder of the cycle }              { Remainder of the cycle }
  forever;                                forever;
Parend;
end.
           Producer                               Consumer
```

Figure 6.28 Bounded buffers using semaphores.

consumer process. This solution is a simple extension of the single-buffer solution shown in Figure 6.26. The values of the semaphores *empty* and *full* indicate the number of empty and full buffers, respectively, hence they are initialized to *n* and 0, respectively. *prod_ptr* and *cons_ptr* are used as subscripts of the array *buffer*. The producer produces in *buffer*[*prod_ptr*] and increments *prod_ptr*. The consumer consumes from *buffer*[*cons_ptr*] and increments *cons_ptr* in the same manner. This feature ensures that buffers are consumed in FIFO order. A producer and a consumer can operate concurrently so long as some full and some empty buffers exist in the system.

It is easy to verify that this solution implements the correctness conditions of the bounded buffer problem described in Section 6.7.1. However, if many producer and consumer processes exist in the system, we need to provide mutual exclusion among producers to avoid race conditions on *prod_ptr*. Analogously, mutual exclusion should be provided among consumers to avoid race conditions on *cons_ptr*.

6.9.3 Readers—Writers Using Semaphores

A key feature of the readers–writers problem is that readers and writers must wait while a writer is writing, and when the writer exits, either all waiting readers should be activated or one waiting writer should be activated (see the outline of Figure 6.18). To implement this feature, we use four counters as follows:

runread	count of readers currently reading
totread	count of readers waiting to read or currently reading
runwrite	count of writers currently writing
totwrite	count of writers waiting to write or currently writing

With these counters, the outline of Figure 6.18 is refined as shown in Figure 6.29; we do not show details of how the counters are updated. A reader is allowed to begin reading when *runwrite* = 0 and a writer is allowed to begin writing when *runread* = 0 and *runwrite* = 0. The value of *totread* is used to activate all waiting readers when a writer finishes writing. This solution does not use an explicit critical section for writers. Instead writers are blocked until they can be allowed to start writing.

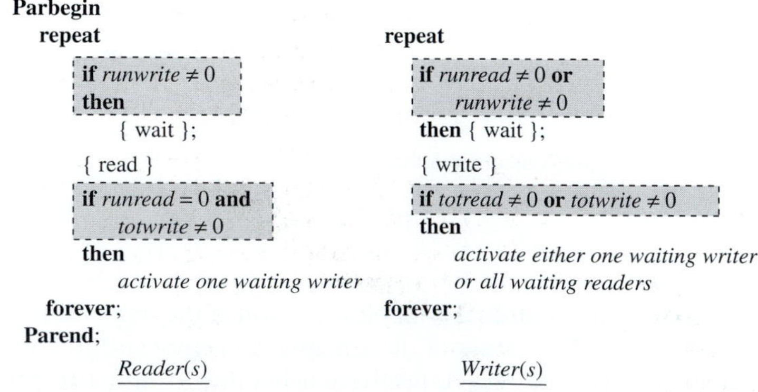

Figure 6.29 Refined solution outline for readers–writers.

Blocking of readers and writers resembles blocking of producers and consumers in the producers–consumers problem. Hence it is best handled by using semaphores for signaling. We introduce two semaphores named *reading* and *writing*. A reader process would perform *wait*(*reading*) before starting to read. This operation should block the reader process if conditions permitting it to read are not currently satisfied; otherwise, the reader should be able to get past it and start reading. Similarly, a writer process would perform a *wait*(*writing*) before writing and it would get blocked if appropriate conditions are not satisfied. The conditions on which readers and writers are blocked may change when any of the counter values change, i.e., when a reader finishes reading or a writer finishes writing. Hence the reader and writer processes should themselves perform appropriate *signal* operations after completing a read or a write operation.

This solution is implemented as follows (see Figure 6.30): To avoid race conditions all counter values are examined and manipulated inside critical sections implemented by using a binary semaphore named *sem_CS*. When a reader wishes to start reading, it enters a critical section for *sem_CS* to check whether *runwrite* = 0. If so, it increments *runread*, exits the critical section and starts reading. If not, it must perform *wait*(*reading*); however, performing a *wait*(*reading*) operation inside the critical section for *sem_CS* may cause a deadlock, so it performs a *wait*(*reading*) after exiting the critical section. If conditions permitting the start of a read operation were satisfied when it examined the counter values inside its critical section, it would have itself performed a *signal*(*reading*) inside the critical section. Such a reader will get past the *wait*(*reading*) operation. A writer will similarly perform a *signal*(*writing*) inside its critical section for *sem_CS* under the correct set of conditions and *wait*(*writing*) after exiting from the critical section.

Readers and writers that get blocked on their respective *wait* operations are activated as follows: When a reader finishes reading, it performs a *signal* operation to activate a writer if no readers are active and a writer is waiting. When a writer finishes writing, it performs *signal* operations to activate all waiting readers, if any; otherwise, it performs a *signal* operation to wake a waiting writer, if any. Hence the resulting system is a readers-preferred readers–writers system.

The solution appears to have two redundant features (see Exercise 6.10). First, it uses two semaphores, *reading* and *writing*, even though only one resource—the shared data—is to be controlled. Second, every reader performs a *wait*(*reading*) operation even though the operation is clearly redundant when some other readers are already engaged in reading. However, both features are needed to implement a writers-preferred readers–writers system (see Exercise 6.11).

6.9.4 Implementation of Semaphores

Figure 6.31 shows a scheme for implementing semaphores. A semaphore type is defined. It has fields for the value of a semaphore, a list that is used to store

```
var
        totread, runread, totwrite, runwrite : integer;
        reading, writing : semaphore := 0;
        sem_CS : semaphore := 1;
begin
        totread := 0;
        runread := 0;
        totwrite := 0;
        runwrite := 0;
Parbegin
  repeat
        wait (sem_CS);
        totread := totread + 1;
        if runwrite = 0 then
             runread := runread + 1;
             signal (reading);
        signal (sem_CS);
        wait (reading);
        { Read }
        wait (sem_CS);
        runread := runread–1;
        totread := totread–1;
        if runread = 0 and
             totwrite > runwrite
             then
                  runwrite := 1;
                  signal (writing);
        signal (sem_CS);
  forever;

  repeat
        wait (sem_CS);
        totwrite := totwrite + 1;
        if runread = 0 and runwrite = 0 then
             runwrite := 1;
             signal (writing);
        signal (sem_CS);
        wait (writing);
        { Write }
        wait (sem_CS);
        runwrite := runwrite–1;
        totwrite := totwrite–1;
        while (runread < totread) do
        begin
             runread := runread + 1;
             signal (reading);
        end;
        if runread = 0 and
        totwrite > runwrite then
             runwrite := 1;
             signal (writing);
        signal (sem_CS);
  forever;
Parend;
end.

          Reader(s)                       Writer(s)
```

Figure 6.30 A readers–preferred readers–writers system using semaphores.

ids of processes blocked on the semaphore, and a lock variable that is used to ensure indivisibility of the *wait* and *signal* operations on the semaphore. The *wait* and *signal* operations on semaphores are implemented as procedures that take a variable of the semaphore type as a parameter. A concurrent program declares semaphores as variables of the semaphore type, and its processes invoke the *wait* and *signal* procedures to operate on them.

To avoid race conditions while accessing the value of the semaphore, procedures *wait* and *signal* first invoke the function *Close_lock* to set the lock variable *sem.lock*. *Close_lock* uses an indivisible instruction and a busy wait; however, the busy waits are short since the *wait* and *signal* operations are themselves short. The procedures invoke the function *Open_lock* to reset the lock after completing

```
Type declaration for Semaphore
type
    semaphore =   record
                  value : integer;   { value of the semaphore }
                  list : . . .         { list of blocked processes }
                  lock : boolean;    { lock variable for operations on this semaphore }
                  end;

Procedures for implementing wait and signal operations

procedure wait (sem)
begin
    Close_lock (sem.lock);
    if sem.value > 0
        then
            sem.value := sem.value–1;
            Open_lock (sem.lock);
        else
            Add id of the process to list of processes blocked on sem;
            block_me (sem.lock);
end;

procedure signal (sem)
begin
    Close_lock (sem.lock);
    if some processes are blocked on sem
        then
            proc_id := id of a process blocked on sem;
            activate (proc_id);
        else
            sem.value := sem.value + 1;
    Open_lock (sem.lock);
end;
```

Figure 6.31 A scheme for implementing *wait* and *signal* operations on a semaphore.

their execution. Recall from Section 6.5.1 that a busy wait may lead to priority inversion in an OS using priority-based scheduling; we assume that a priority inheritance protocol is used to avoid this problem. In a time-sharing system, a busy wait can cause delays in synchronization, but does not cause more serious problems.

The *wait* procedure checks whether the value of *sem* is > 0. If so, it decrements the value and returns. If the value is 0, the *wait* procedure adds the id of the process to the list of processes blocked on *sem* and makes a *block me* system call with the lock variable as a parameter. This call blocks the process that invoked the *wait* procedure and also opens the lock passed to it as a parameter. Note that the *wait* procedure could not have performed these actions itself—race conditions would arise if it opened the lock before making a *block_me* call, and a deadlock would arise if it made made a *block_me* call before opening the lock!

The *signal* procedure checks whether any process is blocked on *sem*. If so, it selects one such process and activates it by making the system call *activate*. If no processes are waiting for *sem*, it increments the value of *sem* by 1. It is convenient to maintain the list of blocked processes as a queue and activate the first blocked process at a *signal* operation. This way, the semaphore implementation would also possess the bounded wait property. However, the semantics of the *signal* operation do not specify the order in which processes should be activated, so an implementation could choose any order it desired.

The *wait* operation has a very low failure rate in most systems using semaphores, i.e., processes performing *wait* operations are seldom blocked. This characteristic is exploited in some methods of implementing semaphores to reduce the overhead. In the following, we describe three methods of implementing semaphores and examine their overhead implications. Recall that we use the term *process* as a generic term for both processes and threads.

Kernel-Level Implementation The kernel implements the *wait* and *signal* procedures of Figure 6.31. All processes in a system can share a kernel-level semaphore. However, every *wait* and *signal* operation results in a system call; it leads to high overhead of using semaphores. In a uniprocessor OS with a noninterruptible kernel, it would not be necessary to use a lock variable to eliminate race conditions, so the overhead of the *Close_lock* and *Open_lock* operations can be eliminated.

User-Level Implementation The *wait* and *signal* operations are coded as library procedures, which are linked with an application program so that processes of the application can share user-level semaphores. The *block_me* and *activate* calls are actually calls on library procedures, which handle blocking and activation of processes themselves as far as possible and make system calls only when they need assistance from the kernel. This implementation method would suit user-level threads because the thread library would already provide for blocking, activation, and scheduling of threads. The thread library would make a *block_me* system call only when all threads of a process are blocked.

Hybrid Implementation The *wait* and *signal* operations are again coded as library procedures, and processes of an application can share the hybrid semaphores. *block_me* and *activate* are system calls provided by the kernel and the *wait* and *signal* operations make these calls only when processes have to be blocked and activated. Because of the low failure rate of the *wait* operation, these system calls would be made seldom, so a hybrid implementation of semaphores would have a lower overhead than a kernel-level implementation.

6.10 MONITORS

Recall from Section 6.5.3 that a concurrent programming construct provides data abstraction and encapsulation features specifically suited to the construction of concurrent programs. A *monitor type* resembles a class in a language like C++ or

Java. It contains declarations of shared data. It may also contain declarations of special synchronization data called *condition variables* on which only the built-in operations **wait** and **signal** can be performed; these operations provide convenient means of setting up signaling arrangements for process synchronization. Procedures of the monitor type encode operations that manipulate shared data and perform process synchronization through condition variables. Thus, the monitor type provides two of the three components that make up a concurrent system (see Section 6.6).

A concurrent system is set up as follows: A concurrent program has a monitor type. The program creates an object of the monitor type during its execution. We refer to the object as a monitor variable, or simply as a *monitor*. The monitor contains a copy of the shared and synchronization data declared in the monitor type as its local data. The procedures defined in the monitor type become operations of the monitor; they operate on its local data. The concurrent program creates processes through system calls. These processes invoke operations of the monitor to perform data sharing and control synchronization; they become blocked or activated when the monitor operations perform **wait** or **signal** operations.

The data abstraction and encapsulation features of the monitor assist in synchronization as follows: Only the operations of a monitor can access its shared and synchronization data. To avoid race conditions, the compiler of the programming language implements mutual exclusion over operations of a monitor by ensuring that at most one process can be executing a monitor operation at any time. Invocations of the operations are serviced in a FIFO manner to satisfy the bounded wait property.

Condition Variables A *condition* is some situation of interest in a monitor. A condition variable, which is simply a variable with the attribute **condition**, is associated with a condition in the monitor. Only the built-in operations **wait** and **signal** can be performed on a condition variable. The monitor associates a queue of processes with each condition variable. If a monitor operation invoked by a process performs a **wait** operation on a condition variable, the monitor blocks the process, enters its id in the process queue associated with the condition variable, and schedules one of the processes, if any, waiting to begin or resume execution of a monitor operation. If a monitor operation performs the **signal** operation on a condition variable, the monitor activates the first process in the process queue associated with the condition variable. When scheduled, this process would resume execution of the monitor operation in which it was blocked. The **signal** operation has no effect if the process queue associated with a condition variable is empty when the condition is signaled.

Implementation of a monitor maintains several process queues—one for each condition variable and one for processes waiting to execute monitor operations. To ensure that processes do not get stuck halfway through execution of an operation, the monitor favors processes that were activated by **signal** operations over those wishing to begin execution of monitor operations.

The following example describes use of a monitor to implement a binary semaphore. We discuss an interesting implementation issue after the example.

Example 6.6 Monitor Implementation of a Binary Semaphore

The upper half of Figure 6.32 shows a monitor type *Sem_Mon_type* that implements a binary semaphore, and the lower half shows three processes that use a monitor variable *binary_sem*. Recall from Section 6.9.1 that a binary semaphore takes only values 0 and 1, and is used to implement a critical section. The boolean variable *busy* is used to indicate whether any process is currently using the critical section. Thus, its values *true* and *false* correspond to the values 0 and 1 of the binary semaphore, respectively. The condition variable *non_busy* corresponds to the condition that the critical section is not busy; it is used to block processes that try to enter a critical section while *busy* = *true*. The procedures *sem_wait* and *sem_signal* implement the *wait* and *signal* operations on the binary semaphore. *Binary_sem* is a monitor variable. The initialization part of the monitor type, which contains the statement *busy* :=*false*; is invoked when *binary_sem* is created. Hence variable *busy* of *binary_sem* is initialized to *false*.

```
type Sem_Mon_type = monitor
    var
        busy : boolean;
        non_busy : condition;
    procedure sem_wait;
    begin
        if busy = true then non_busy.wait;
        busy := true;
    end;
    procedure sem_signal;
    begin
        busy := false;
        non_busy.signal;
    end;
    begin { initialization }
        busy := false;
end;

var binary_sem : Sem_Mon_type;
begin

Parbegin
repeat                          repeat                          repeat
   binary_sem.sem_wait;            binary_sem.sem_wait;            binary_sem.sem_wait;
   { Critical Section }            { Critical Section }            { Critica lSection }
   binary_sem.sem_signal;          binary_sem.sem_signal;          binary_sem.sem_signal;
   { Remainder of                  { Remainder of                  { Remainder of
      the cycle }                     the cycle }                     the cycle }
forever;                        forever;                        forever;
Parend;
end.
   Process P1                      Process P2                      Process P3
```

Figure 6.32 Monitor implementation of a binary semaphore.

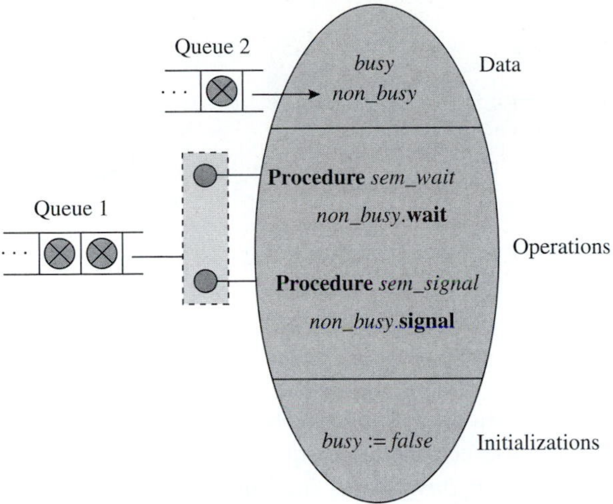

Figure 6.33 A monitor implementing a binary semaphore.

Figure 6.33 depicts the monitor *Sem_Mon_type*. The monitor maintains two queues of processes. Queue 1 contains processes waiting to execute operation *sem_wait* or *sem_signal* of the monitor, while queue 2 contains processes waiting for a *non_busy*.**signal** statement to be executed.

Let P_1 be the first process to perform *binary_sem.sem_wait*. Since *busy* is *false*, it changes *busy* to *true* and enters its critical section. If P_2 performs *binary_sem.sem_wait* while P_1 is still inside its critical section, it will be blocked on the statement *non_busy*.**wait**. It will wait in queue 2. Now let P_1 start executing *binary_sem.sem_signal* and let P_3 try to perform *binary_sem.sem_wait* before P_1 finishes executing *binary_sem.sem_signal*. Due to mutual exclusion over monitor operations, P_3 will be blocked and put in the queue associated with entry to the monitor, i.e., in queue 1. Figure 6.34 shows a snapshot of the system at this instant. When process P_1 executes the statement *non_busy*.**signal** and exits from the monitor, P_2 will be activated ahead of P_3 because queues associated with condition variables enjoy priority over the queue associated with entry to the monitor. Process P_3 will start executing *binary_sem.sem_wait* only when process P_2 completes execution of *binary_sem.sem_wait*, exits the monitor and enters its critical section. P_3 will now block itself on the condition *non_busy*. It will be activated when P_2 executes the *binary_sem.sem_signal* operation.

If procedure *sem_signal* of Example 6.6 contained some statements following the **signal** statement, an interesting synchronization problem would arise when process P_1 invokes *binary_sem.sem_signal* and executes the statement *non_busy*.**signal**. The **signal** statement is expected to activate process P_2, which

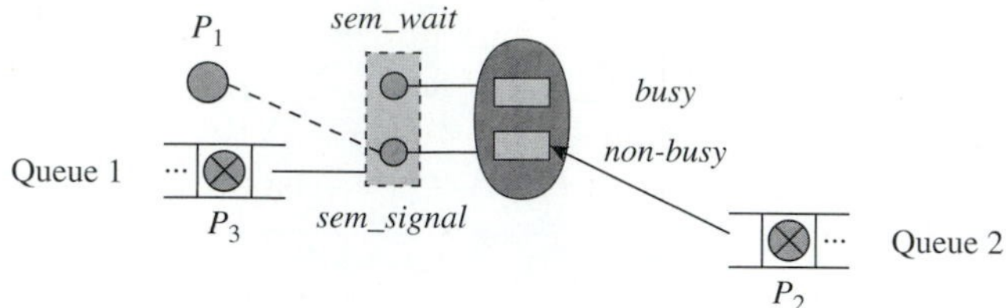

Figure 6.34 A snapshot of the system of Example 6.6.

should resume its execution of *binary_sem.sem_wait*. At the same time, process P_1 should continue its execution of *binary_sem.sem_signal* by executing statements that follow the *non_busy*.**signal** statement. Since monitor operations are performed in a mutually exclusive manner, only one of them can execute and the other one will have to wait. So which of them should be selected for execution?

Selecting process P_2 for execution would delay the signaling process P_1, which seems unfair. Selecting P_1 would imply that P_2 is not really activated until P_1 leaves the monitor. Hoare (1974) proposed the first alternative. Brinch Hansen (1973) proposed that a **signal** statement should be the last statement of a monitor procedure, so that the process executing **signal** exits the monitor procedure immediately and the process activated by the **signal** statement can be scheduled. We will follow this convention in our examples.

Example 6.7 Producers–Consumers Using Monitors

Figure 6.35 shows a solution to the producers–consumers problem that uses monitors. It follows the same approach as the solution of Figure 6.28, using semaphores. The upper half of Figure 6.35 shows a monitor type *Bounded_buffer_type*. Variable *full* is an integer that indicates the number of full buffers. In the procedure *produce*, a producer executes a *buffer_empty*.**wait** if $full = n$. It would be activated only when at least one empty buffer exists in the pool. Similarly, the consumer executes a *buffer_full*.**wait** if $full = 0$. Waiting consumers and producers are activated by the statements *buff_full*.**signal** and *buff_empty*.**signal** in the procedures *produce* and *consume*, respectively.

The lower half of Figure 6.35 shows a system containing two producer processes P_1, P_2 and a consumer process P_3. Operation of a single buffer system; i.e., $n = 1$ in Figure 6.35, can be depicted as shown in Figure 6.36. Let processes P_1 and P_2 try to produce and let process P_3 try to consume, all at the same time. Let us assume that process P_1 enters the procedure *produce*, gets past the **wait** statement and starts producing, while processes P_2

and P_3 are blocked on entry to the monitor (see Part (a) of the snapshot). P_1 executes *buff_full*.**signal** and exits. Process P_2 is now activated. However, it becomes blocked again on *buff_empty*.**wait** because *full* = 1. Process P_3 is activated when P_2 becomes blocked and starts consuming [see Figure 6.36(b)]. Process P_2 will be activated when P_3 exits after consuming.

6.10.1 Monitors in Java

A Java class becomes a monitor type when the attribute `synchronized` is associated with one or more methods in the class. An object of such a class is a monitor. The Java virtual machine ensures mutual exclusion over the synchronized methods in a monitor as follows: When a thread calls a synchronized method of an object, the Java virtual machine checks whether the object is currently locked. If it is unlocked, the lock is set now and the thread is permitted to execute the method; otherwise, the thread has to wait until the object is unlocked. When a thread exits a synchronized method, the object is unlocked and a waiting thread, if any, is activated.

Each monitor contains a single unnamed condition variable. A thread waits on the condition variable by executing the call `wait()`. The `notify()` call is like the **signal** operation described in Section 6.10. It wakes one of the threads waiting on the condition variable, if any. The Java virtual machine does not implement FIFO behavior for the wait and notify calls. Thus, wait and notify do not satisfy the bounded wait property. The `notifyall()` call activates all threads waiting on the condition variable.

Provision of a single condition variable in a monitor can lead to busy waits in an application. Consider the readers–writers system as an example. When a writer is active, all readers wishing to read and all writers wishing to write have to wait on the condition variable. When the writer finishes writing, it would have to use a `notifyall()` call to activate all waiting threads. If readers are preferred, all writer threads will have to perform `wait()` calls once again. If writers are preferred, all reader threads and some writer threads will have to perform `wait()` calls once again. Thus, a reader or writer thread may be activated many times before it gets an opportunity to perform reading or writing. A producers–consumers system with many producer and consumer processes would similarly suffer from busy waits.

6.11 CASE STUDIES OF PROCESS SYNCHRONIZATION

6.11.1 Synchronization of POSIX Threads

As mentioned in Section 5.3.1, POSIX threads provide mutexes for mutual exclusion and condition variables for control synchronization between processes. A mutex is a binary semaphore. An OS may implement POSIX threads

```
type Bounded_buffer_type = monitor
   const
      n = . . .;                          { Number of buffers }
   type
      item = . . .;
   var
      buffer : array [0..n–1] of item;
      full, prod_ptr, cons_ptr : integer;
      buff_full : condition;
      buff_empty : condition;
   procedure produce (produced_info : item);
   begin
      if full = n then buff_empty.wait;
      buffer [prod_ptr] := produced_info;          { i.e., Produce }
      prod_ptr := prod_ptr + 1 mod n;
      full := full + 1;
      buff_full.signal;
   end;
   procedure consume (for_consumption : item);
   begin
      if full = 0 then buff_full.wait;
      for_consumption := buffer[cons_ptr];         { i.e., Consume }
      cons_ptr := cons_ptr + 1 mod n;
      full := full–1;
      buff_empty.signal;
   end;
   begin { initialization }
      full := 0;
      prod_ptr := 0;
      cons_ptr := 0;
end;

begin
var B_buf : Bounded_buffer_type;

Parbegin
  var info : item;           var info : item;           var area : item;
  repeat                     repeat                     repeat
     info := . . .              info := . . .              B_buf.consume (area);
     B_buf.produce (info);      B_buf.produce (info);      { Consume area }
     { Remainder of             { Remainder of             { Remainder of
       the cycle }                the cycle }                the cycle }
  forever;                   forever;                   forever;
Parend;
end.
     Producer P1                Producer P2                Consumer P3
```

Figure 6.35 Producers–consumers using monitors.

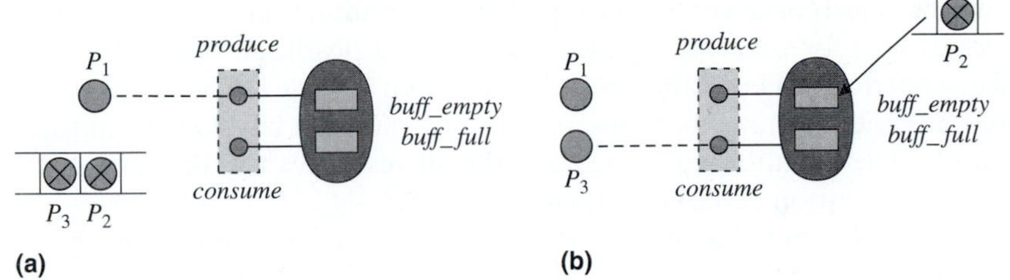

Figure 6.36 Snapshots of the monitor of Example 6.7 with a single buffer.

as kernel-level threads or user-level threads. Accordingly, mutexes would be implemented through either a kernel-level implementation or a hybrid implementation described in Section 6.9.4 when threads are implemented as kernel-level threads, and through the user-level implementation when threads are implemented through user-level threads. Analogously, condition variables are also implemented through a kernel-level, hybrid, or user-level implementation scheme.

6.11.2 Process Synchronization in Unix

Unix system V provides a kernel-level implementation of semaphores. The name of a semaphore is called a *key*. The key is actually associated with an array of semaphores, and individual semaphores in the array are distinguished with the help of subscripts. Processes share a semaphore by using the same key. A process wishing to use a semaphore obtains access to it by making a *semget* system call with a key as a parameter. If a semaphore array with matching key already exists, the kernel makes that array accessible to the process making the *semget* call; otherwise, it creates a new semaphore array, assigns the key to it and makes it accessible to the process.

The kernel provides a single system call *semop* for *wait* and *signal* operations. It takes two parameters: a key, i.e., the name of a semaphore array, and a list of (*subscript, op*) specifications where *subscript* identifies a semaphore in the semaphore array and *op* is a *wait* or *signal* operation to be performed. The entire set of operations defined in the list is performed in an atomic manner; that is, either all the operations are performed and the process is free to continue its execution, or none of the operations is performed and the process is blocked. A blocked process is activated only when all operations indicated in *semop* can succeed.

The semantics of *semop* can be used to prevent deadlocks. Consider the following example: Semaphores sem_1 and sem_2 are associated with resources R_1 and R_2, respectively. A process performs a $wait(sem_i)$ before using a resource R_i and a $signal(sem_i)$ after finishing with it. If each of processes P_1 and P_2 require both resources simultaneously, it is possible that P_1 will obtain access to R_1 but will become blocked on $wait(sem_2)$ and process P_2 will obtain access to R_2

but will become blocked on *wait*(sem_1). This is a deadlock situation because both processes wait for each other indefinitely. Such a deadlock would not arise if processes performed both *wait* operations through a single *semop*, since a process would be either allocated both resources or it would not be allocated any of the resources. The situation now resembles the all resources together approach to deadlock prevention described later in Section 8.5.1.

Unix SVR4 provides an interesting feature to make programs using semaphores more reliable. It keeps track of all operations performed by a process on each semaphore used by it, and performs an *undo* on these operations when the process terminates. This action helps to prevent disruptions in a concurrent application due to misbehavior of some process. For example, if a process P_i performed more *wait* operations than *signal* operations on semaphore sem_i and terminated, it could cause indefinite waits for other processes in the application. Performing an undo operation on all *wait* and *signal* operations performed by P_i might prevent such disasters. To perform undo operations efficiently, the kernel maintains a cumulative count of changes in the value of a semaphore caused by the operations in a process, and subtracts it from the value of the semaphore when the process terminates. If a process P_i performed more *wait* operations than *signal* operations on semaphore sem_i, its cumulative count for sem_i would be negative. Subtracting this count would nullify the effect of P_i on sem_i. P_i's cumulative count would be 0 if it had performed an equal number of *wait* and *signal* operations on sem_i. Thus the undo operation does not interfere with normal operation of processes using semaphores.

Unix 4.4BSD places a semaphore in memory areas shared by a set of processes, and provides a hybrid implementation of semaphores along the lines discussed in Section 6.9.4. This way, it avoids making system calls in cases where a *wait* operation does not lead to blocking of a process and a *signal* operation does not lead to activation of a process, which provides fast synchronization.

6.11.3 Process Synchronization in Linux

Linux provides a Unix-like semaphore (see Section 6.11.2) for use by user processes. It also provides two kinds of semaphores for use by the kernel—a conventional semaphore and a reader–writer semaphore. The conventional semaphore is implemented by a kernel-level scheme that is more efficient than the kernel-level scheme discussed in Section 6.9.4. It uses a data structure that contains the value of a semaphore, a flag to indicate whether any processes are blocked on it, and the actual list of such processes. Unlike the scheme of Section 6.9.4, a lock is not used to avoid race conditions on the value of the semaphore; instead, the *wait* and *signal* operations use indivisible instructions to decrement or increment the value of the semaphore. These operations lock the list of blocked processes only if they find that processes are to be added to it or removed from it—the *wait* operation locks the list only if the process that performed the *wait* operation is to be blocked, whereas the *signal* operation locks it only if the semaphore's flag indicates that the list is nonempty.

The reader–writer semaphore provides capabilities that can be used to implement the readers–writers problem of Section 6.9.3 within a kernel so that many processes can read a kernel data structure concurrently but only one process can update it at a time. Its implementation does not favor either readers or writers—it permits processes to enter their critical sections in FIFO order, except that consecutive readers can read concurrently. It is achieved by simply maintaining a list of processes waiting to perform a read or write operation, which is organized in the chronological order.

Kernels older than the Linux 2.6 kernel implemented mutual exclusion in the kernel space through system calls. However, as mentioned in Section 6.9.4, a *wait* operation has a low failure rate; i.e., a process is rarely blocked on a *wait* call, so many of the system calls are actually unnecessary. The Linux 2.6 kernel provides a fast user space mutex called *futex*. A *futex* is an integer in shared memory on which only certain operations can be performed. The *wait* operation on a futex makes a system call only when a process needs to be blocked on the futex, and the *signal* operation on a futex makes a system call only when a process is to be activated. The *wait* operation also provides a parameter through which a process can indicate how long it is prepared to be blocked on the *wait*. When this time elapses, the *wait* operation fails and returns an error code to the process that made the call.

6.11.4 Process Synchronization in Solaris

Process synchronization in the Sun Solaris operating system contains three interesting features—reader–writer semaphores and adaptive mutexes, a data structure called a turnstile, and use of the priority inversion protocol. The reader–writer semaphore is analogous to the reader–writer semaphore in Linux. An adaptive mutex is useful in a multiprocessor OS, hence it is discussed in Chapter 10; only an overview is included here.

Recall from Section 5.4.3 that the Solaris kernel provides parallelism through kernel threads. When a thread T_i performs a *wait* operation on a semaphore that is currently used by another thread T_j, the kernel can either block T_i or let it spin. The blocking approach involves the overhead of blocking thread T_i, scheduling another thread, and activating thread T_i when T_j releases the semaphore. Spinning, on the other hand, incurs the overhead of a busy wait until T_j releases the semaphore. If T_j is currently operating on another CPU, it may release the semaphore before either T_i or T_j is preempted, so it is better to let T_i spin. If T_j is not operating currently, T_i may spin for long, so it is better to conserve CPU time by blocking it. The adaptive mutex uses this method.

The Solaris kernel uses a data structure called a *turnstile* to hold information concerning threads that are blocked on a mutex or reader–writer semaphore. This information is used for both synchronization and priority inheritance. To minimize the number of turnstiles needed at any time, the kernel of Solaris 7 attaches a turnstile with every new thread it creates. It performs the following actions when a kernel thread is to be blocked on a mutex: If no threads are already blocked on the mutex, it detaches the turnstile from the thread, associates it with the mutex, and enters the thread's id in the turnstile. If a turnstile is already associated with the mutex, i.e., if some other threads are already blocked on it, the kernel detaches the turnstile of the thread and returns it to the pool of free turnstiles, and enters the thread's id into the turnstile that is already associated with the mutex. When a thread releases a mutex or a reader–writer semaphore, the kernel obtains information about threads blocked on the mutex or reader–writer semaphore, and decides which thread(s) to activate. It now attaches a turnstile from the pool of free turnstiles with the activated thread. A turnstile is returned to the pool of free turnstiles when the last thread in it wakes up.

The Solaris kernel uses a priority inheritance protocol to reduce synchronization delays. Consider a thread T_i that is blocked on a semaphore because thread T_j is in a critical section implemented through the semaphore. Thread T_i might suffer a long synchronization delay if T_j is not scheduled for a long time, which would happen if T_j has a lower priority than T_i. To reduce the synchronization delay for T_i, the kernel raises the priority of T_j to that of T_i until T_j exits the critical section. If many processes become blocked on the semaphore being used by T_j, T_j's priority should be raised to that of the highest-priority process blocked on the semaphore. It is implemented by obtaining priorities of the blocked processes from the turnstile associated with the semaphore.

6.11.5 Process Synchronization in Windows

Windows is an object-oriented system, hence processes, files and events are represented by objects. The kernel provides a uniform interface for thread synchronization over different kinds of objects as follows: A *dispatcher object* is a special kind of object that is either in the *signaled* state or in the *nonsignaled* state. A dispatcher object is embedded in every object over which synchronization may be desired, e.g., an object representing a process, file, event, mutex, or semaphore. Any thread that wishes to synchronize with an object would be put in the *waiting* state if the dispatcher object embedded in the object is in the nonsignaled state. Table 6.4 describes the semantics of various kinds of objects, which determine when the state of an object would change, and which of the threads waiting on it would be activated when it is signaled.

A thread object enters the signaled state when the thread terminates, whereas a process object enters the signaled state when all threads in the process terminate. In both cases, all threads waiting on the object are activated. The file object enters the signaled state when an I/O operation on the file completes. If any threads are waiting on it, all of them are activated and its synchronization state is changed back to nonsignaled. If no threads are waiting on it, a thread that waits on it sometime in future will get past the wait operation and the synchronization state of the file object would be changed to nonsignaled. The console input object has an analogous behavior except that only one waiting thread is activated when it

Table 6.4 Windows Objects Used for Synchronization

Object	Nonsignaled state	Signaled state	Signal time action
Process	Not terminated	Last thread terminates	Activate all threads
Thread	Not terminated	The thread terminates	Activate all threads
File	I/O request pending	I/O completed	Activate all threads
Console input	Input not provided	Input provided	Activate one thread
File change	No changes	Change noticed	Activate one thread
Notify event	Not yet set	Set event executed	Activate all threads
Synchronization event	Reset	Set event executed	Activate one thread and reset event
Semaphore	Successful wait	Released	Activate one thread
Mutex	Successful wait	Released	Activate one thread
Condition variable	Initially and after a `wake` or `wakeall` function call	`wake` or `wakeall` function is performed	Activate one thread or all threads
Timer	Reinitialization	Set time arrives or interval elapses	Same as notify and synchronization events

is signaled. The file change object is signaled when the system detects changes in the file. It behaves like the file object in other respects.

Threads use the event, semaphore, mutex, and condition variable objects for mutual synchronization. They signal these objects by executing library functions that lead to appropriate system calls. An event object is signaled at a *set event* system call. If it is a notification event, all threads waiting on it are activated. If it is a synchronization event, only one thread is activated and the event is reset. The timer object is also designed for use in the notification and synchronization modes. The kernel changes the state of the object to *signaled* when the specified time arrives or the specified interval elapses. Its signal time actions are similar to those of the notify and synchronization events.

The semaphore object implements a counting semaphore, which can be used to control a set of resources. The number of resources is specified as the initial value of the semaphore. A count in the semaphore object indicates how many of these resources are currently available for use by threads. The semaphore object is in the nonsignaled state when the count is 0, so any process performing a wait on it would be put in the *waiting* state. When a thread releases a resource, the kernel increments the number of available resources, which puts the semaphore in the signaled state. Consequently, some thread waiting on it would be activated.

A thread can specify a time interval in a wait call to indicate how long it is prepared to wait for an object. It would be activated before this interval elapses if the object is signaled; otherwise, its wait request would be withdrawn at the end of the interval and it would get activated. A mutex is implemented as a binary semaphore. The mutex object is signaled when a process executes the release function; the kernel releases one of the threads waiting on it.

The Windows kernel provides a variety of synchronization locks—a spinlock, a special lock called *queued spinlock* for multiprocessor configurations (see Section 10.6.3), and fast mutexes and push locks, which, like the *futex* of Linux, avoid system calls unless a thread has to wait on a synchronization object. Windows Vista provides a reader–writer lock.

6.12 SUMMARY

Process synchronization is a generic term for *data access synchronization*, which is used to update shared data in a mutually exclusive manner, and *control synchronization*, which is used to ensure that processes perform their actions in a desired order. Classic process synchronization problems such as producers–consumers, readers–writers, and dining philosophers represent important classes of process synchronization problems. In this chapter we discussed the fundamental issues in process synchronization, and the support for process synchronization provided by the computer, the kernel, and programming languages. We also analyzed classic process synchronization problems and demonstrated use of various synchronization facilities of programming languages and operating systems in implementing them.

A *race condition* is a situation in which actions of concurrent processes may have unexpected consequences, such as incorrect values of shared data or faulty interaction among processes. A race condition exists when concurrent processes update shared data in an uncoordinated manner. It is avoided through *mutual exclusion*, which ensures that only one process updates shared data at any time. A *critical section* on a shared data d is a section of code that accesses d in a mutually exclusive manner. A race condition may also exist in control synchronization—processes may not wait for each other's actions as expected. Hence avoidance of race conditions is a primary issue in process synchronization.

The computer provides *indivisible instructions*, which access memory locations in a mutually exclusive manner. A process may use an indivisible instruction on a lock variable to implement a critical section. However, this approach suffers from *busy waits* because a process that cannot enter the critical section keeps looping until it may do so, hence the kernel provides a facility to block such a process until it may be permitted to enter a critical section. Compilers of programming languages implement process synchronization primitives and constructs by using this facility. A *semaphore* is a primitive that facilitates blocking and activation of processes without race conditions. A *monitor* is a construct that provides two facilities—it implements operations on shared data as critical sections over the data and it provides statements for control synchronization.

Operating systems provide features for efficient implementation of process synchronization; e.g., Linux provides readers–writers semaphores, Solaris provides priority inheritance to avoid some of the problems related to busy waits, and Windows provides dispatcher objects.

TEST YOUR CONCEPTS

6.1 Classify each of the following statements as true or false:

a. An application can contain a race condition only if the computer system servicing the application contains more than one CPU.

b. Control synchronization is needed when processes *generate* and *analyze* of Figure 1.6(b) share the variable *sample*.

c. A process may be starved of entry to a critical section if the critical section implementation does not satisfy the bounded wait condition.

d. A process may be starved of entry to a critical section if the critical section implementation does not satisfy the progress condition.

e. A busy wait is unavoidable unless a system call is made to block a process.

f. Indefinite busy waits are possible in an OS using priority-based scheduling, but not possible in an OS using round-robin scheduling.

g. Algorithm 6.1 can be used to implement a single-buffer producers–consumers system if process P_1 is a producer and P_2 is a consumer.

h. When a lock variable is used, an indivisible instruction is not needed to implement a critical section.

i. In a producers–consumers system consisting of many producer processes, many consumer processes, and many buffers in the buffer-pool, it is possible for many producer processes to be producing and many consumer processes to be consuming at the same time.

j. In a writers-preferred readers–writers system, some reader processes wishing to read the shared data may become blocked even while some other reader processes are reading the shared data.

k. A deadlock cannot occur in the dining philosophers problem if one of the philosophers can eat with only one fork.

l. A critical section implemented using semaphores would satisfy the bounded wait property only if the *signal* operation activates processes in FIFO order.

m. A race condition can occur over forks if the outline of the dining philosophers problem in Figure 6.21 is modified to remove the action "lift the forks one at a time" from the **while** loop and put it following the **while** loop.

6.2 A semaphore is initialized to 1. Twelve wait operations and seven signal operations are performed on it. What is the number of processes waiting on this semaphore?

a. 12, **b.** 7, **c.** 4, **d.** 5

6.3 A binary semaphore is initialized to 1. 5 wait operations are performed on it in a row, followed by 8 signal operations. Now 5 more wait operations are performed on it. What is the number of processes waiting on this semaphore?

a. 1, **b.** 2, **c.** 4, **d.** 5

6.4 Ten processes share a critical section implemented by using a counting semaphore named x. Nine of these processes use the code $wait(x)$; {critical section} $signal(x)$. However, one process erroneously uses the code $signal(x)$; {critical section} $signal(x)$. What is the maximum number of processes that can be in the critical section at the same time?

a. 1, **b.** 2, **c.** 10, **d.** 3

6.5 In a readers–writers system, a read operation consumes 3 time units and a write operation consumes 5 time units. No readers or writers exist in the system at time $t_i - 1$. One reader arrives at time t_i, and 5 readers and 1 writer arrive at time $t_i + 1$. If no more readers or writers arrive, when will the writer finish writing?

a. $t_i + 8$,
b. $t_i + 20$,
c. $t_i + 9$,
d. none of a–c

6.6 A producer process produces a new item of information in 10 seconds and a consumer process consumes an item in 20 seconds. In a producers–consumers system consisting of a single producer process, a single consumer process, and a single buffer, both the producer and the consumer processes start their operation at time 0. At what time will the consumer process finish consuming 3 items?

a. 20, **b.** 60, **c.** 70, **d.** 90, **e.** none of a–d

EXERCISES

6.1 A concurrent program contains a few updates of a shared variable x, which occur inside critical sections. Variable x is also used in the following section of code which is not enclosed in a critical section:

> **if** $x < c$
>   **then** $y := x$;
> **else** $y := x + 10$;
> **print** x, y;

Does this program have a race condition?

6.2 Two concurrent processes share a data item `sum`, which is initialized to 0. However, they do not use mutual exclusion while accessing its value. Each process contains a loop that executes 50 times and contains the single statement `sum:=sum+1`. If no other operations are performed on `sum`, indicate the lower bound and upper bound on the value of `sum` when both processes terminate.

6.3 Analyze Algorithms 6.1 and 6.2 and comment on the critical section properties violated by them. Give examples illustrating the violations.

6.4 Answer the following in context of Dekker's algorithm:

a. Does the algorithm satisfy the progress condition?

b. Can a deadlock condition arise?

c. Can a livelock condition arise?

6.5 Is the bounded wait condition satisfied by Peterson's algorithm?

6.6 The following changes are made in Peterson's algorithm (see Algorithm 6.4): The statements *flag*[0] :=*true* and *flag*[0] :=*false* in process P_0 are interchanged, and analogous changes are made in process P_1. Discuss which properties of the implementation of critical sections are violated by the resulting system.

6.7 The statement **while** *flag*[1] **and** *turn* = 1 in Peterson's algorithm is changed to **while** *flag*[1] **or** *turn* = 1, and analogous changes are made in process P_1. Which properties of critical section implementation are violated by the resulting system?

6.8 Comment on the effect of deleting the statement **while** *choosing*[*j*] **do** { *nothing* }; on working of Lamport's Bakery algorithm.

6.9 The solution of the producers–consumers problem shown in Figure 6.37 uses kernel calls *block* and *activate* for process synchronization. It has a race condition. Describe how this race condition arises.

6.10 The readers–writers solution of Figure 6.30 uses two semaphores even though a single entity—the shared data—is to be controlled. Modify this solution to use a single semaphore *rw_permission* instead of semaphores *reading* and *writing*. (*Hint:* perform a *wait*(*rw_permission*) in the reader only if reading is not already in progress.)

6.11 Modify the readers–writers solution of Figure 6.30 to implement a writer-preferred readers–writers system.

6.12 Implement a critical section using the Test-and-set or Swap instructions of Section 6.5.2. Use ideas from Section 6.8.2 to ensure that the bounded wait condition is satisfied.

6.13 A resource is to be allocated to requesting processes in a FIFO manner. Each process is coded as

> **repeat**
>   ...
>   *request-resource*(*process_id*, *resource_id*);
>   { Use resource }
>   *release-resource*(*process_id*, *resource_id*);
>   { Remainder of the cycle }
> **forever**

Develop the procedures *request-resource* and *release-resource* using semaphores.

6.14 Can one or more of the following features eliminate deficiencies of the outline of the dining philosophers problem shown in Figure 6.20?

a. If n philosophers exist in the system, have seats for at least $n + 1$ philosophers at the dining table.

b. Make sure that at least one left-handed philosopher and at least one right-handed philosopher sit at the table at any time.

6.15 In Figure 6.35, producers and consumers always execute the statements *buf_full*.**signal** and *buf_empty*.**signal**. Suggest and implement a method of reducing the number of **signal** statements executed during the operation of the system.

```
type
        item = . . .;
var
        buffer : item;
        buffer_full : boolean;
        producer_blocked : boolean;
        consumer_blocked : boolean;
begin
        buffer_full := false;
        producer_blocked := false;
        consumer_blocked := false;
Parbegin
    repeat                                      repeat
      if buffer_full = false then                 if buffer_full = true then
          { Produce in buffer }                       { Consume from buffer }
          buffer_full := true;                        buffer_full := false;
          if consumer_blocked = true then             if producer_blocked = true then
              activate(consumer);                         activate(producer);
          { Remainder of the cycle }                  { Remainder of the cycle }
      else                                        else
          producer_blocked := true;                   consumer_blocked := true;
          block(producer);                            block(consumer);
          consumer_blocked := false;                  producer_blocked := false;
    forever                                     forever
Parend

            Producer                                    Consumer
```

Figure 6.37 The producer–consumer problem with a synchronization error due to a race condition.

6.16 Implement the dining philosophers problem using monitors. Minimize the number of executions of **signal** statements in your solution and observe its effect on the logical complexity of your solution.

6.17 A customer gives the following instructions to a bank manager: Do not credit any funds to my account if the balance in my account exceeds *n*, and hold any debits until the balance in the account is large enough to permit the debit. Design a monitor to implement the customer's bank account.

6.18 The synchronization problem called *sleeping barber* is described as follows: A barber shop has a single barber, a single barber's chair in a small room, and a large waiting room with *n* seats. The barber and the barber's chair are visible from the waiting room. After servicing one customer, the barber checks whether any customers are waiting in the waiting room. If so, he admits one of them and starts serving him; otherwise, he goes to sleep in the barber's chair. A customer enters the waiting room only if there is at least one vacant seat and either waits for the barber to call him if the barber is busy, or wakes the barber if he is asleep. Identify the synchronization requirements between the barber and customer processes. Code the barber and customer processes such that deadlocks do not arise.

6.19 A monitor is to be written to simulate a clock manager used for real-time control of concurrent processes. The clock manager uses a variable named *clock* to maintain the current time. The OS supports a signal called *elapsed_time* that is generated every 2 ms. The clock manager provides a signal handling action for *elapsed_time* (see Section 5.4.1) that updates *clock* at every occurrence of the signal. This action is coded as a procedure of the monitor. A typical request made to the clock manager is "wake me up at

9.00 a.m." The clock manager blocks the processes making such requests and arranges to activate them at the designated times. Implement this monitor.

6.20 Nesting of monitor calls implies that a procedure in monitor A calls a procedure of another monitor, say monitor B. During execution of the nested call, the procedure of monitor A continues to hold its mutual exclusion. Show that nested monitor calls can lead to deadlocks.

6.21 Write a short note on the implementation of monitors. Your note must discuss:

a. How to achieve mutual exclusion between the monitor procedures.

b. Whether monitor procedures need to be coded in a reentrant manner (see Section 11.3.3.2).

6.22 A large data collection D is used merely to answer queries, i.e., no updates are carried out on D, so queries can be processed concurrently. Because of the large size of D, it is split into several parts $D_1, D_2, \ldots, D_n$, and at any time only one of these parts, say D_1, is loaded in memory to handle queries related to it. If no queries are active on D_1, and queries exist on some other part of data, say D_2, D_2 is loaded in memory and queries on it are processed concurrently. When D is split into two parts D_1 and D_2, this system is called a readers–readers system. Implement this system, using any synchronization primitive or control structure of your choice. To prevent starvation of queries, it is proposed to handle a maximum of 10 queries on a part of the data at any time. Modify the monitor to incorporate this feature.

6.23 A bridge on a busy highway is damaged by a flood. One-way traffic is to be instituted on the bridge by permitting vehicles traveling in opposite directions to use the bridge alternately. The following rules are formulated for use of the bridge:

a. At any time, the bridge is used by vehicle(s) traveling in one direction only.

b. If vehicles are waiting to cross the bridge at both ends, only one vehicle from one end is allowed to cross the bridge before a vehicle from the other end starts crossing the bridge.

c. If no vehicles are waiting at one end, then any number of vehicles from the other end are permitted to cross the bridge.

Develop a concurrent system to implement these rules.

6.24 When vehicles are waiting at both ends, the rules of Exercise 23(a) lead to poor use of the bridge. Hence up to 10 vehicles should be allowed to cross the bridge in one direction even if vehicles are waiting at the other end. Implement the modified rules.

CLASS PROJECT 1: INTERPROCESS COMMUNICATION

An interprocess message communication system uses the *asymmetric naming* convention described later in Section 9.1.1, which uses the following rules: To send a message, a sender provides the id of the destination process to which it is to be delivered, and the text of the message. To receive a message, a process simply provides the name of a variable in which the message should be deposited; the system provides it with a message sent to it by *some* process.

The system consists of a monitor named *Communication_Manager* and four processes. The monitor provides the operations *send* and *receive*, which implement message passing using a *global* pool of 20 message buffers. The system is to operate as follows:

1. Each process has a cyclic behavior. Its operation is governed by commands in a command file that is used exclusively by it. In each iteration, it reads a command from the file and invokes an appropriate operation of the monitor. Three commands are supported:
   - **a.** *send <process_id>, <message_text>:* The process should send a message.
   - **b.** *receive <variable_name>:* The process should receive a message.
   - **c.** *quit:* The process should complete its operation.

2. When a process invokes a *send* operation, the monitor copies the text of the message in a free message buffer from the global pool of message buffers. If the destination process of the message is currently blocked on a *receive* operation, the message is delivered to it as described in Item 3 and the process is activated. In either case, control is returned to the process executing the *send* operation. If none of the message buffers in the global pool of 20 message buffers is free, the process performing the *send* operation is blocked until a message buffer becomes free.
3. When a process invokes a *receive* operation, it is given a message sent to it in FIFO order. The monitor finds the message buffer that contains the first undelivered message that was sent to the process, copies the text of the message into the variable mentioned by the process, and frees the message buffer. If a process executing the *send* operation was blocked as mentioned in Item 2, it is activated. The process performing the *receive* operation is blocked if no message exists for it. It would be activated when a message is sent to it.
4. After performing a *send* or *receive* operation, the monitor writes details of the actions performed by it in a log file.
5. The monitor detects a *deadlock* situation, in which some of the processes are blocked indefinitely. It writes details of the deadlock situation in the log file and terminates itself.
6. The interprocess message communication system terminates itself when all processes have completed their operation.

Write the monitor *Communication_Manager* and test its operation with several sets of sample command files for the processes that create various interesting situations in message passing, including some deadlock situations.

CLASS PROJECT 2: DISK SCHEDULER

A *disk scheduler* is that part of an OS which decides the order in which I/O operations should be performed on a disk to achieve high disk throughput (see Section 14.7). Processes that wish to perform I/O operations on the disk use a monitor named *Disk_scheduler* and the following pseudocode:

```
var Disk_scheduler : Disk_Mon_type;
Parbegin
    begin { User process P_i }
        var disk_block_address : integer;
        repeat
            {read a command from file F_i }
            Disk_scheduler . IO_request
                (P_i, IO_operation,
                disk_block_address);
            { Perform I/O Operation }
            Disk_scheduler . IO_complete (P_i);
            { Remainder of the cycle }
        forever
    end;
    ...                          { other user processes }
Parend;
```

Each process has cyclic behavior. Its operation is governed by commands in a command file that is used exclusively by it. Each command is for performing a read or write operation on a disk block. In each iteration, a process reads a command from its command file and invokes the monitor operation *IO_request* to pass details of the I/O operation to the monitor. *IO_request* blocks the process until its I/O operation is scheduled. When the process is activated, it returns from *IO_request* and performs its I/O operation. After completing the I/O operation, it invokes the monitor operation *IO_complete* so that the monitor can schedule the next I/O operation. The monitor writes details of its actions in a log file every time the *IO_request* or *IO_complete* operation is invoked.

Code the monitor type *Disk_Mon_type*. For simplicity, you may assume that I/O operations are scheduled in FIFO order, and that the number of processes does not exceed 10. (*Hint:* Note the process id of a process along with details of its I/O operation in a list in the monitor. Decide how many condition variables you would need to block and activate the processes.)

Modify *Disk_Mon_type* such that I/O operations would be performed by the monitor itself rather than by user processes. (*Hint:* Operation *I/O_complete* would no longer be needed.)

BIBLIOGRAPHY

Dijkstra (1965) discusses the mutual exclusion problem, describes Dekker's algorithm, and presents a mutual exclusion algorithm for *n* processes. Lamport (1974, 1979) describes and proves the Bakery algorithm. Ben Ari (1982) describes the evolution of mutual exclusion algorithms and provides a proof of Dekker's algorithm. Ben Ari (2006) discusses concurrent and distributed programming. Peterson (1981), Lamport (1986, 1991), and Raynal (1986) are other sources on mutual exclusion algorithms.

Dijkstra (1965) proposed semaphores. Hoare (1972) and Brinch Hansen (1972) discuss the critical and conditional critical regions, which are synchronization constructs that preceded monitors. Brinch Hansen (1973) and Hoare (1974) describe the monitor concept. Buhr et al. (1995) describes different monitor implementations. Richter (1999) describes thread synchronization in C/C++ programs under Windows. Christopher and Thiruvathukal (2001) describes the concept of monitors in Java, compares it with the monitors of Brinch Hansen and Hoare, and concludes that Java synchronization is not as well developed as the Brinch Hansen and Hoare monitors.

A synchronization primitive or construct is complete if it can be used to implement *all* process synchronization problems. The completeness of semaphores is discussed in Patil (1971), Lipton (1974), and Kosaraju (1975).

Brinch Hansen (1973, 1977) and Ben Ari (1982, 2006) discuss the methodology for building concurrent programs. Owicki and Gries (1976) and Francez and Pneuli (1978) deal with the methodology of proving the correctness of concurrent programs.

Vahalia (1996) and Stevens and Rago (2005) discuss process synchronization in Unix, Beck et al. (2002), Bovet and Cesati (2005), and Love (2005), discuss synchronization in Linux, Mauro and McDougall (2006) discusses synchronization in Solaris, while Richter (1999) and Russinovich and Solomon (2005) discuss synchronization features in Windows.

1. Beck, M., H. Bohme, M. Dziadzka, U. Kunitz, R. Magnus, C. Schroter, and D. Verworner (2002): *Linux Kernel Programming*, Pearson Education, New York.
2. Ben Ari, M. (1982): *Principles of Concurrent Programming*, Prentice Hall, Englewood Cliffs, N.J.
3. Ben Ari, M. (2006): *Principles of Concurrent and Distributed Programming,* 2nd ed., Prentice Hall, Englewood Cliffs, N.J.
4. Bovet, D. P., and M. Cesati (2005): *Understanding the Linux Kernel,* 3rd ed., O'Reilly, Sebastopol.
5. Brinch Hansen, P. (1972): "Structured multiprogramming," *Communications of the ACM*, **15** (7), 574–578.
6. Brinch Hansen, P. (1973): *Operating System Principles*, Prentice Hall, Englewood Cliffs, N.J.
7. Brinch Hansen, P. (1975): "The programming language concurrent Pascal," *IEEE Transactions on Software Engineering*, **1** (2), 199–207.
8. Brinch Hansen, P. (1977): *The Architecture of Concurrent Programs*, Prentice Hall, Englewood Cliffs, N.J.
9. Buhr, M., M. Fortier, and M. H. Coffin (1995): "Monitor classification," *Computing Surveys*, **27** (1), 63–108.
10. Chandy, K. M., and J. Misra (1988): *Parallel Program Design: A Foundation*, Addison-Wesley, Reading, Mass.
11. Christopher, T. W., and G. K. Thiruvathukal (2001): *Multithreaded and Networked Programming*, Sun Microsystems.
12. Courtois, P. J., F. Heymans, and D. L. Parnas (1971): "Concurrent control with readers and writers," *Communications of the ACM*, **14** (10), 667–668.
13. Dijkstra, E. W. (1965): "Cooperating sequential processes," Technical Report EWD-123, Technological University, Eindhoven.
14. Eisenberg, M. A., and M. R. McGuire (1972): "Further comments on Dijkstra's concurrent programming control problem," *Communications of the ACM*, **15**(11), 999.
15. Francez, N., and A. Pneuli (1978): "A proof method for cyclic programs," *Acta Informatica*, **9**, 133–157.
16. Hoare, C. A. R. (1972): "Towards a theory of parallel programming," in *Operating Systems Techniques*, C.A.R. Hoare and R.H. Perrot (eds.), Academic Press, London, 1972.

17. Hoare, C. A. R (1974): "Monitors: an operating system structuring concept," *Communications of the ACM*, **17**(10), 549–557.
18. Kosaraju, S. (1973): "Limitations of Dijkstra's semaphore primitives and petri nets," *Operating Systems Review*, **7**, 4, 122–126.
19. Lamport, L. (1974): "A new solution of Dijkstra's concurrent programming problem," *Communications of the ACM*, **17**, 453–455.
20. Lamport, L. (1979): "A new approach to proving the correctness of multiprocess programs," *ACM Transactions on Programming Languages and Systems*, **1**, 84–97.
21. Lamport, L. (1986): "The mutual exclusion problem," *Communications of the ACM*, **33** (2), 313–348.
22. Lamport, L. (1991): "The mutual exclusion problem has been solved," *ACM Transactions on Programming Languages and Systems*, **1**, 84–97.
23. Lipton, R. (1974): "On synchronization primitive systems," Ph.D. Thesis, Carnegie-Mellon University.
24. Love, R. (2005): *Linux Kernel Development,* 2nd ed., Novell Press.
25. Mauro, J., and R. McDougall (2006): *Solaris Internals,* 2nd ed., Prentice Hall, Englewood Cliffs, N.J.
26. Owicki, S., and D. Gries (1976): "Verifying properties of parallel programs: An axiomatic approach," *Communications of the ACM*, **19**, 279–285.
27. Patil, S. (1971): "Limitations and capabilities of Dijkstra's semaphore primitives for co-ordination among processes," Technical Report, MIT.
28. Peterson, G. L. (1981): "Myths about the mutual exclusion problem," *Information Processing Letters*, **12**, 3.
29. Raynal, M. (1986): *Algorithms for Mutual Exclusion*, MIT Press, Cambridge, Mass.
30. Richter, J. (1999): *Programming Applications for Microsoft Windows,* 4th ed., Microsoft Press, Redmond, Wash.
31. Russinovich, M. E., and D. A. Solomon (2005): *Microsoft Windows Internals,* 4th ed., Microsoft Press, Redmond, Wash.
32. Stevens, W. R., and S. A. Rago (2005): *Advanced Programming in the Unix Environment,* 2nd ed., Addison Wesley, Reading, Mass,.
33. Vahalia, U. (1996): *Unix Internals—The New Frontiers*, Prentice Hall, Englewood Cliffs, N.J.

7

Chapter

Scheduling

A scheduling policy decides which process should be given the CPU at the present moment. This decision influences both system performance and user service. In Chapter 3, we saw how *priority-based scheduling* provides good system performance, and how *round-robin scheduling* with *time-slicing* provides good response times to processes. The scheduling policy in a modern operating system must provide the best combination of user service and system performance to suit its computing environment.

A scheduling policy employs three fundamental techniques to achieve the desired combination of user service and system performance. *Assignment of priorities* to processes can provide good system performance, as in a multiprogramming system; or provide favored treatment to important functions, as in a real-time system. *Variation of time slice* permits the scheduler to adapt the time slice to the nature of a process so that it can provide an appropriate response time to the process, and also control its own overhead. *Reordering of processes* can improve both system performance, measured as throughput, and user service, measured as turnaround times or response times of processes. We discuss the use of these techniques and a set of scheduling heuristics in modern operating systems.

Performance analysis of a scheduling policy is a study of its performance. It can be used for comparing performance of two scheduling policies or for determining values of key system parameters like the size of a process queue. We discuss different approaches to performance analysis of scheduling policies.

7.1 SCHEDULING TERMINOLOGY AND CONCEPTS

Scheduling, very generally, is the activity of selecting the next request to be serviced by a *server*. Figure 7.1 is a schematic diagram of scheduling. The scheduler actively considers a list of pending requests for servicing and selects one of them. The server services the request selected by the scheduler. This request leaves the server either when it completes or when the scheduler preempts it and puts it back into the list of pending requests. In either situation, the scheduler selects the request that should be serviced next. From time to time, the scheduler admits one of the arrived requests for active consideration and enters it into the list of pending requests. Actions of the scheduler are shown by the dashed arrows

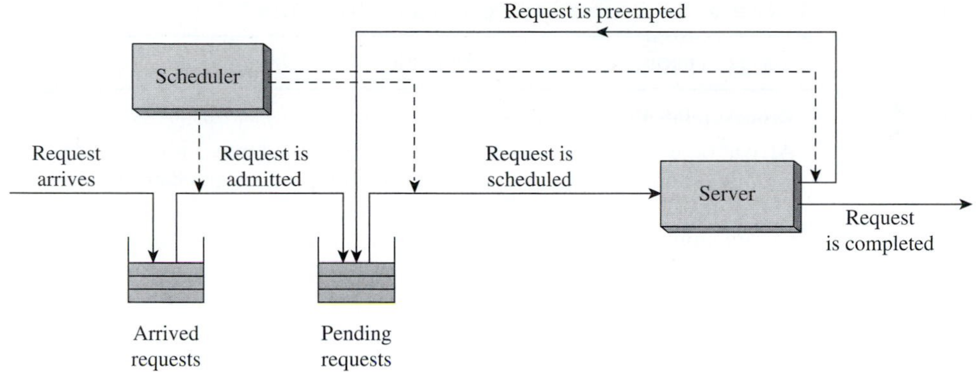

Figure 7.1 A schematic of scheduling.

in Figure 7.1. Events related to a request are its *arrival, admission, scheduling, preemption*, and *completion*.

In an operating system, a *request* is the execution of a job or a process, and the *server* is the CPU. A job or a process is said to *arrive* when it is submitted by a user, and to be *admitted* when the scheduler starts considering it for scheduling. An admitted job or process either waits in the list of pending requests, uses the CPU, or performs I/O operations. Eventually, it completes and leaves the system. The scheduler's action of admitting a request is important only in an operating system with limited resources; for simplicity, in most of our discussions we assume that a request is admitted automatically on arrival.

In Chapter 3 we discussed how use of priorities in the scheduler provides good system performance while use of round-robin scheduling provides good user service in the form of fast response. Modern operating systems use more complex scheduling policies to achieve a suitable combination of system performance and user service.

Table 7.1 lists the key terms and concepts related to scheduling. The *service time* of a job or a process is the total of CPU time and I/O time required by it to complete its execution, and the *deadline*, which is specified only in real-time systems (see Section 3.7), is the time by which its servicing should be completed. Both service time and deadline are an inherent property of a job or a process. The *completion time* of a job or a process depends on its arrival and service times, and on the kind of service it receives from the OS.

We group scheduling concepts into user-centric concepts and system-centric concepts to characterize the OS's concern for either user service or system performance.

User-Centric Scheduling Concepts In an interactive environment, a user interacts with a process during its operation—the user makes a *subrequest* to a process and the process responds by performing actions or by computing results. *Response time* is the time since submission of a subrequest to the time its processing is completed. It is an absolute measure of service provided to a subrequest. *Turnaround time* is an analogous absolute measure of service provided to a job or process.

Table 7.1 Scheduling Terms and Concepts

Term or concept	Definition or description
Request related	
Arrival time	Time when a user submits a job or process.
Admission time	Time when the system starts considering a job or process for scheduling.
Completion time	Time when a job or process is completed.
Deadline	Time by which a job or process must be completed to meet the response requirement of a real-time application.
Service time	The total of CPU time and I/O time required by a job, process or subrequest to complete its operation.
Preemption	Forced deallocation of CPU from a job or process.
Priority	A tie-breaking rule used to select a job or process when many jobs or processes await service.
User service related: individual request	
Deadline overrun	The amount of time by which the completion time of a job or process exceeds its deadline. Deadline overruns can be both positive or negative.
Fair share	A specified share of CPU time that should be devoted to execution of a process or a group of processes.
Response ratio	The ratio $\frac{\text{time since arrival} + \text{service time of a job or process}}{\text{service time of the job or process}}$
Response time (rt)	Time between the submission of a subrequest for processing to the time its result becomes available. This concept is applicable to interactive processes.
Turnaround time (ta)	Time between the submission of a job or process and its completion by the system. This concept is meaningful for noninteractive jobs or processes only.
Weighted turnaround (w)	Ratio of the turnaround time of a job or process to its own service time.
User service related: average service	
Mean response time ($\overline{rt}$)	Average of the response times of all subrequests serviced by the system.
Mean turnaround time ($\overline{ta}$)	Average of the turnaround times of all jobs or processes serviced by the system.
Performance related	
Schedule length	The time taken to complete a specific set of jobs or processes.
Throughput	The average number of jobs, processes, or subrequests completed by a system in one unit of time.

Turnaround time differs from the service time of a job or process because it also includes the time when the job or process is neither executing on the CPU nor performing I/O operations. We are familiar with these two measures from the discussions in Chapter 3.

Several other measures of user service are defined. The *weighted turnaround* relates the turnaround time of a process to its own service time. For example, a weighted turnaround of 5 indicates that the turnaround received by a request is 5 times its own service time. Comparison of weighted turnarounds of different jobs or processes indicates the comparative service received by them. *Fair share* is the share of CPU time that should be alloted to a process or a group of processes. *Response ratio* of a job or process is the ratio (time since arrival + service time)/service time. It relates the delay in the servicing of a job or process to its own service time; it can be used in a scheduling policy to avoid starvation of processes (see Section 7.2.3). The *deadline overrun* is the difference between the completion time and deadline of a job or process in a real-time application. A negative value of deadline overrun indicates that the job or process was completed before its deadline, whereas a positive value indicates that the deadline was missed. The *mean response time* and *mean turnaround time* are measures of average service provided to subrequests and processes or jobs, respectively.

System-Centric Scheduling Concepts Throughput and schedule length are measures of system performance. *Throughput* indicates the average number of requests or subrequests completed per unit of time (see Section 3.5). It provides a basis for comparing performance of two or more scheduling policies, or for comparing performance of the same scheduling policy over different periods of time. *Schedule length* indicates the total amount of time taken by a server to complete a set of requests.

Throughput and schedule length are related. Consider servicing of five requests $r_1, \ldots, r_5$. Let min_a and max_c be the earliest of the arrival times and the latest of the completion times, respectively. The schedule length for these five requests is $(max_c - min_a)$ and the throughput is $5/(max_c - min_a)$. However, it is typically not possible to compute schedule length and throughput in this manner because an OS may also admit and service other requests in the interval from min_a to max_c, to achieve good system performance. Nevertheless, schedule length is an important basis for comparing the performance of scheduling policies when the scheduling overhead is not negligible. Throughput is related to the mean response time and mean turnaround time in an obvious way.

7.1.1 Fundamental Techniques of Scheduling

Schedulers use three fundamental techniques in their design to provide good user service or high performance of the system:

- *Priority-based scheduling:* The process in operation should be the highest-priority process requiring use of the CPU. It is ensured by scheduling the highest-priority *ready* process at any time and preempting it when a process with a higher priority becomes *ready*. Recall from Section 3.5.1 that a multiprogramming OS assigns a high priority to I/O-bound processes; this assignment of priorities provides high throughput of the system.

- *Reordering of requests:* Reordering implies servicing of requests in some order other than their arrival order. Reordering may be used by itself to improve user service, e.g., servicing short requests before long ones reduces the average turnaround time of requests. Reordering of requests is implicit in preemption, which may be used to enhance user service, as in a time-sharing system, or to enhance the system throughput, as in a multiprogramming system.
- *Variation of time slice:* When time-slicing is used, from Eq. (3.2) of Section 3.6, $\eta = \delta/(\delta + \sigma)$ where η is the CPU efficiency, δ is the time slice and σ is the OS overhead per scheduling decision. Better response times are obtained when smaller values of the time slice are used; however, it lowers the CPU efficiency because considerable process switching overhead is incurred. To balance CPU efficiency and response times, an OS could use different values of δ for different requests—a small value for I/O-bound requests and a large value for CPU-bound requests—or it could vary the value of δ for a process when its behavior changes from CPU-bound to I/O-bound, or from I/O-bound to CPU-bound.

In Sections 7.2 and 7.3 we discuss how the techniques of priority-based scheduling and reordering of requests are used in classical nonpreemptive and preemptive scheduling policies. In Sections 7.4 and 7.5, we discuss how schedulers in modern OSs combine these three fundamental techniques to provide a combination of good performance and good user service.

7.1.2 The Role of Priority

Priority is a tie-breaking rule that is employed by a scheduler when many requests await attention of the server. The priority of a request can be a function of several parameters, each parameter reflecting either an inherent attribute of the request, or an aspect concerning its service. It is called a *dynamic priority* if some of its parameters change during the operation of the request; otherwise, it called a *static priority*.

Some process reorderings could be obtained through priorities as well. For example, short processes would be serviced before long processes if priority is inversely proportional to the service time of a process, and processes that have received less CPU time would be processed first if priority is inversely proportional to the CPU time consumed by a process. However, complex priority functions may be needed to obtain some kinds of process reorderings such as those obtained through time-slicing; their use would increase the overhead of scheduling. In such situations, schedulers employ algorithms that determine the order in which requests should be serviced.

If two or more requests have the same priority, which of them should be scheduled first? A popular scheme is to use round-robin scheduling among such requests. This way, processes with the same priority share the CPU among themselves when none of the higher-priority processes is ready, which provides better user service than if one of the requests is favored over other requests with the same priority.

Priority-based scheduling has the drawback that a low-priority request may never be serviced if high-priority requests keep arriving. This situation is called *starvation*. It could be avoided by increasing the priority of a request that does not get scheduled for a certain period to time. This way, the priority of a low-priority request would keep increasing as it waits to get scheduled until its priority exceeds the priority of all other pending requests. At this time, it would get scheduled. This technique is called *aging* of requests.

7.2 NONPREEMPTIVE SCHEDULING POLICIES

In *nonpreemptive scheduling*, a server always services a scheduled request to completion. Thus, scheduling is performed only when servicing of a previously scheduled request is completed and so preemption of a request as shown in Figure 7.1 never occurs. Nonpreemptive scheduling is attractive because of its simplicity—the scheduler does not have to distinguish between an unserviced request and a partially serviced one.

Since a request is never preempted, the scheduler's only function in improving user service or system performance is reordering of requests. We discuss three nonpreemptive scheduling policies in this section:

- First-come, first-served (FCFS) scheduling
- Shortest request next (SRN) scheduling
- Highest response ratio next (HRN) scheduling

We illustrate the operation and performance of various scheduling policies with the help of the five processes shown in Table 7.2. For simplicity we assume that these processes do not perform I/O operations.

7.2.1 FCFS Scheduling

Requests are scheduled in the order in which they arrive in the system. The list of pending requests is organized as a queue. The scheduler always schedules the first request in the list. An example of FCFS scheduling is a batch processing system in which jobs are ordered according to their arrival times (or arbitrarily,

Table 7.2 Processes for Scheduling

Process	P_1	P_2	P_3	P_4	P_5
Admission time	0	2	3	4	8
Service time	3	3	5	2	3

Time	Completed process *id*	*ta*	*w*	Processes in system (in FCFS order)	Scheduled process
0	–	–	–	P_1	P_1
3	P_1	3	1.00	P_2, P_3	P_2
6	P_2	4	1.33	P_3, P_4	P_3
11	P_3	8	1.60	P_4, P_5	P_4
13	P_4	9	4.50	P_5	P_5
16	P_5	8	2.67	–	–

$\overline{ta} = 6.40$ seconds

$\overline{w} = 2.22$

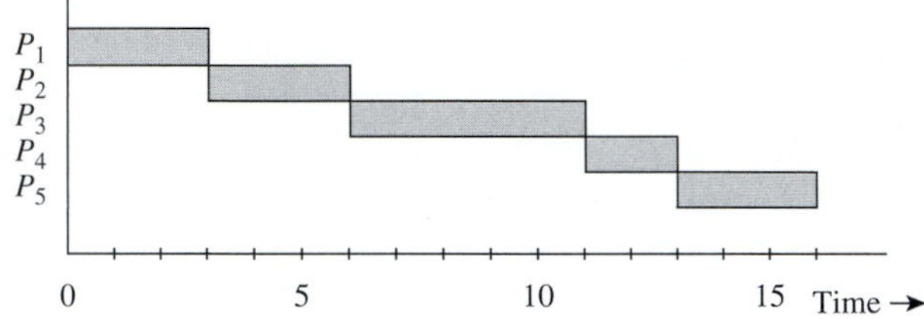

Figure 7.2 Scheduling using the FCFS policy.

if they arrive at exactly the same time) and results of a job are released to the user immediately on completion of the job. The following example illustrates operation of an FCFS scheduler.

Example 7.1 FCFS Scheduling

Figure 7.2 illustrates the scheduling decisions made by the FCFS scheduling policy for the processes of Table 7.2. Process P_1 is scheduled at time 0. The pending list contains P_2 and P_3 when P_1 completes at 3 seconds, so P_2 is scheduled. The *Completed* column shows the id of the completed process and its turnaround time (*ta*) and weighted turnaround (*w*). The mean values of *ta* and *w* (i.e., $\overline{ta}$ and $\overline{w}$) are shown below the table. The timing chart of Figure 7.2 shows how the processes operated.

From Example 7.1, it is seen that considerable variation exists in the weighted turnarounds provided by FCFS scheduling. This variation would have been larger if processes subject to large turnaround times were short—e.g., the weighted turnaround of P_4 would have been larger if its execution requirement had been 1 second or 0.5 second.

7.2.2 Shortest Request Next (SRN) Scheduling

The SRN scheduler always schedules the request with the smallest service time. Thus, a request remains pending until all shorter requests have been serviced.

Time	Completed process			Processes in system	Scheduled process
	id	*ta*	*w*		
0	–	–	–	$\{P_1\}$	P_1
3	P_1	3	1.00	$\{P_2, P_3\}$	P_2
6	P_2	4	1.33	$\{P_3, P_4\}$	P_4
8	P_4	4	2.00	$\{P_3, P_5\}$	P_5
11	P_5	3	1.00	$\{P_3\}$	P_3
16	P_3	13	2.60	$\{\}$	–

$\overline{ta} = 5.40$ seconds
$\overline{w} = 1.59$

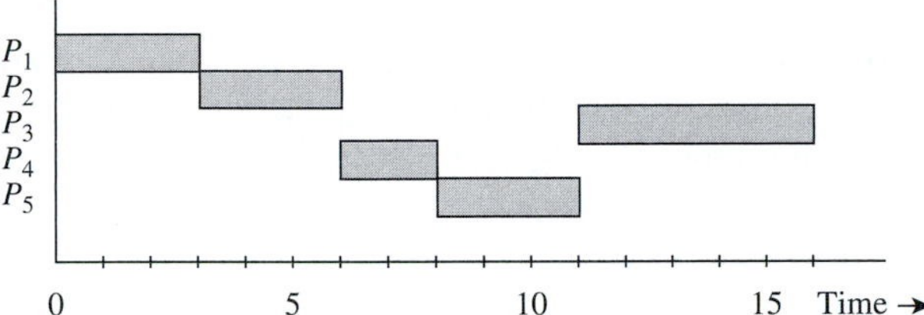

Figure 7.3 Scheduling using the shortest request next (SRN) policy.

Shortest Request Next (SRN) Scheduling

Example 7.2

Figure 7.3 illustrates the scheduling decisions made by the SRN scheduling policy for the processes of Table 7.2, and the operation of the processes. At time 0, P_1 is the only process in the system, so it is scheduled. It completes at time 3 seconds. At this time, processes P_2 and P_3 exist in the system, and P_2 is shorter than P_3. So P_2 is scheduled, and so on.

The mean turnaround time and the mean weighted turnaround are better than in FCFS scheduling because short requests tend to receive smaller turnaround times and weighted turnarounds than in FCFS scheduling. This feature degrades the service that long requests receive; however, their weighted turnarounds do not increase much because their service times are large. The throughput is higher than in FCFS scheduling in the first 10 seconds of the schedule because short processes are being serviced; however, it is identical at the end of the schedule because the same processes have been serviced.

Use of the SRN policy faces several difficulties in practice. Service times of processes are not known to the operating system *a priori,* hence the OS may expect users to provide estimates of service times of processes. However, scheduling performance would be erratic if users do not possess sufficient experience in estimating service times, or they manipulate the system to obtain better service by giving low service time estimates for their processes. The SRN policy offers poor service to long processes, because a steady stream of short processes arriving in the system can starve a long process.

7.2.3 Highest Response Ratio Next (HRN) Scheduling

The HRN policy computes the response ratios of all processes in the system according to Eq. (7.1) and selects the process with the highest response ratio.

$$\text{Response ratio} = \frac{\text{time since arrival} + \text{service time of the process}}{\text{service time of the process}} \tag{7.1}$$

The response ratio of a newly arrived process is 1. It keeps increasing at the rate (1/service time) as it waits to be serviced. The response ratio of a short process increases more rapidly than that of a long process, so shorter processes are favored for scheduling. However, the response ratio of a long process eventually becomes large enough for the process to get scheduled. This feature provides an effect similar to the technique of *aging* discussed earlier in Section 7.1.2, so long processes do not starve. The next example illustrates this property.

Example 7.3 Highest Response Ratio Next (HRN) Scheduling

Operation of the HRN scheduling policy for the five processes shown in Table 7.2 is summarized in Figure 7.4. By the time process P_1 completes, processes P_2 and P_3 have arrived. P_2 has a higher response ratio than P_3, so it is scheduled next. When it completes, P_3 has a higher response ratio than before; however, P_4, which arrived after P_3, has an even higher response ratio because it is a shorter process, so P_4 is scheduled. When P_4 completes, P_3 has a higher response ratio than the shorter process P_5 because it has spent a lot of time waiting, whereas P_5 has just arrived. Hence P_3 is scheduled now. This action results in a smaller weighted turnaround for P_3 than in SRN scheduling (see Figure 7.3). Thus, after a long wait, a long process gets scheduled ahead of a shorter one.

7.3 PREEMPTIVE SCHEDULING POLICIES

In *preemptive scheduling*, the server can be switched to the processing of a new request before completing the current request. The preempted request is put back into the list of pending requests (see Figure 7.1). Its servicing is resumed when it is scheduled again. Thus, a request might have to be scheduled many times before it completed. This feature causes a larger scheduling overhead than when nonpreemptive scheduling is used. We discussed preemptive scheduling in multiprogramming and time-sharing operating systems earlier, in Chapter 3.

Time	Completed process			Response ratios of processes					Scheduled process
	id	*ta*	*w*	P_1	P_2	P_3	P_4	P_5	
0	–	–	–	1.00					P_1
3	P_1	3	1.00		1.33	1.00			P_2
6	P_2	4	1.33			1.60	2.00		P_4
8	P_4	4	2.00			2.00		1.00	P_3
13	P_3	10	2.00					2.67	P_5
16	P_5	8	2.67						–

$\overline{ta}$ = 5.8 seconds
$\overline{w}$ = 1.80

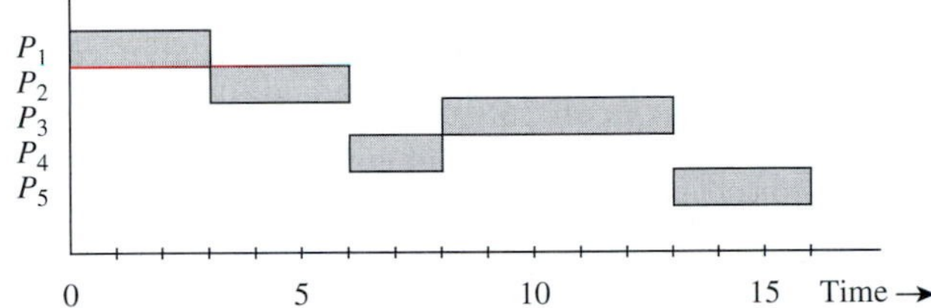

Figure 7.4 Operation of highest response ratio (HRN) policy.

We discuss three preemptive scheduling policies in this section:

- Round-robin scheduling with time-slicing (RR)
- Least completed next (LCN) scheduling
- Shortest time to go (STG) scheduling

The RR scheduling policy shares the CPU among admitted requests by servicing them in turn. The other two policies take into account the CPU time required by a request or the CPU time consumed by it while making their scheduling decisions.

7.3.1 Round-Robin Scheduling with Time-Slicing (RR)

The RR policy aims at providing good response times to all requests. The time slice, which is designated as δ, is the largest amount of CPU time a request may use when scheduled. A request is preempted at the end of a time slice. To facilitate this, the kernel arranges to raise a timer interrupt when the time slice elapses.

The RR policy provides comparable service to all CPU-bound processes. This feature is reflected in approximately equal values of their weighted turnarounds. The actual value of the weighted turnaround of a process depends on the number of processes in the system. Weighted turnarounds provided to processes that perform I/O operations would depend on the durations of their I/O operations. The RR policy does not fare well on measures of system performance like throughput because it does not give a favored treatment to short processes. The following example illustrates the performance of RR scheduling.

Example 7.4 Round-Robin (RR) Scheduling

A round-robin scheduler maintains a queue of processes in the *ready* state and simply selects the first process in the queue. The running process is preempted when the time slice elapses and it is put at the end of the queue. It is assumed that a new process that was admitted into the system at the same instant a process was preempted will be entered into the queue before the preempted process.

Figure 7.5 summarizes operation of the RR scheduler with $\delta = 1$ second for the five processes shown in Table 7.2. The scheduler makes scheduling decisions every second. The time when a decision is made is shown in the first row of the table in the top half of Figure 7.5. The next five rows show positions of the five processes in the ready queue. A blank entry indicates that the process is not in the system at the designated time. The last row shows the process selected by the scheduler; it is the process occupying the first position in the ready queue. Consider the situation at 2 seconds. The scheduling queue contains P_2 followed by P_1. Hence P_2 is scheduled. Process P_3 arrives at 3 seconds, and is entered in the queue. P_2 is also preempted at 3 seconds and it is entered in the queue. Hence the queue has process P_1 followed by P_3 and P_2, so P_1 is scheduled.

Time of scheduling		0	1	2	3	4	5	6	7	8	9	10	11	12	13	14	15	c	t_a	w
Position of	P_1	1	1	2	1													4	4	1.33
Processes in	P_2			1	3	2	1	3	2	1								9	7	2.33
ready queue	P_3				2	1	3	2	1	4	3	2	1	2	1	2	1	16	13	2.60
(1 implies	P_4					3	2	1	3	2	1							10	6	3.00
head of queue)	P_5									3	2	1	2	1	2	1		15	7	2.33
Process scheduled		P_1	P_1	P_2	P_1	P_3	P_2	P_4	P_3	P_2	P_4	P_5	P_3	P_5	P_3	P_5	P_3			

$\overline{t_a} = 7.4$ seconds, $\overline{w} = 2.32$

c: completion time of a process

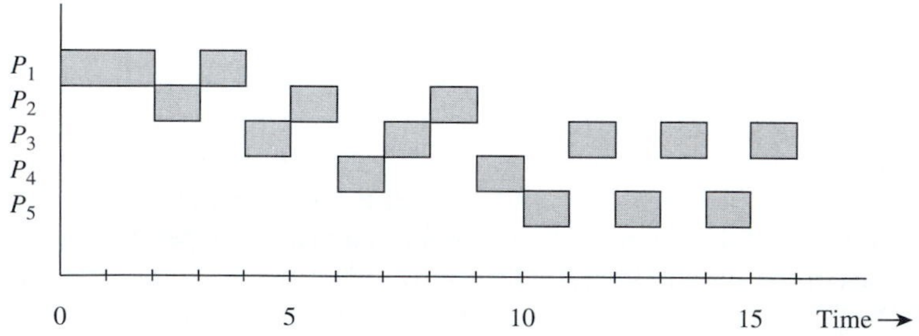

Figure 7.5 Scheduling using the round-robin policy with time-slicing (RR).

The turnaround times and weighted turnarounds of the processes are as shown in the right part of the table. The c column shows completion times. The turnaround times and weighted turnarounds are inferior to those given by the nonpreemptive policies discussed in Section 7.2 because the CPU time is shared among many processes because of time-slicing. It can be seen that processes P_2, P_3, and P_4, which arrive at around the same time, receive approximately equal weighted turnarounds. P_4 receives the worst weighted turnaround because through most of its life it is one of three processes present in the system. P_1 receives the best weighted turnaround because no other process exists in the system during the early part of its execution. Thus weighted turnarounds depend on the load in the system.

As discussed in Chapter 3, if a system contains n processes, each subrequest by a process consumes exactly δ seconds, and the overhead per scheduling decision is σ, the response time (rt) for a subrequest is $n \times (\sigma + \delta)$. However, the relation between δ and rt is more complex than this. First, some processes will be blocked for I/O or waiting for user actions, so the response time will be governed by the number of active processes rather than by n. Second, if a request needs more CPU time than δ seconds, it will have to be scheduled more than once before it can produce a response. Hence at small values of δ, rt for a request may be higher for smaller values of δ. The following example illustrates this aspect.

Variation of Response Time in RR Scheduling

Example 7.5

An OS contains 10 identical processes that were initiated at the same time. Each process receives 15 identical subrequests, and each subrequest consumes 20 ms of CPU time. A subrequest is followed by an I/O operation that consumes 10 ms. The system consumes 2 ms in CPU scheduling. For $\delta \geq 20$ ms, the first subrequest by the first process receives a response time of 22 ms and the first subrequest by the last process receives a response time of 220 ms. Hence the average response time is 121 ms. A subsequent subrequest by any process receives a response time of $10 \times (2+20) - 10$ ms $= 210$ ms because the process spends 10 ms in an I/O wait before receiving the next subrequest. For $\delta = 10$ ms, a subrequest would be preempted after 10 ms. When scheduled again, it would execute for 10 ms and produce results. Hence the response time for the first process is $10 \times (2 + 10) + (2 + 10) = 132$ ms, and that for the last process is $10 \times (2 + 10) + 10 \times (2 + 10) = 240$ ms. A subsequent subrequest receives a response time of $10 \times (2 + 10) + 10 \times (2 + 10) - 10 = 230$ ms. Figure 7.6 summarizes performance of the system for different values of δ. As expected, the schedule length and the overhead are higher for smaller values of δ. The graph in Figure 7.6 illustrates the variation of average response time to second and subsequent subrequests for different values of δ. Note that the response time is larger when δ is 5 ms than when it is 10 ms.

Time slice	5 ms	10 ms	15 ms	20 ms
Average *rt* for first subrequest (ms)	248.5	186	208.5	121
Average *rt* for subsequent subrequest (ms)	270	230	230	210
Number of scheduling decisions	600	300	300	150
Schedule length (ms)	4200	3600	3600	3300
Overhead (percent)	29	17	17	9

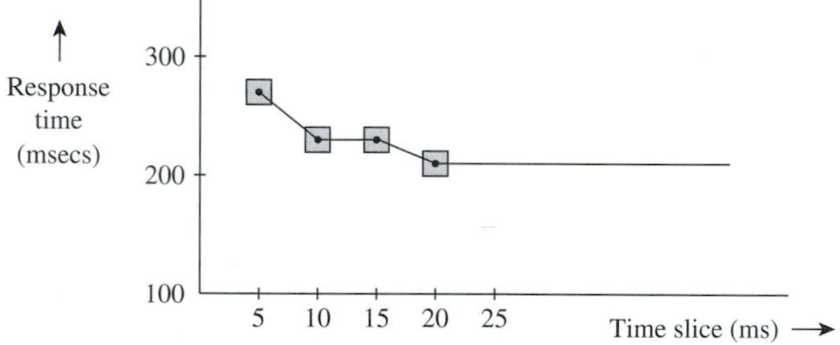

Figure 7.6 Performance of RR scheduling for different values of δ.

7.3.2 Least Completed Next (LCN) Scheduling

The LCN policy schedules the process that has so far consumed the least amount of CPU time. Thus, the nature of a process, whether CPU-bound or I/O-bound, and its CPU time requirement do not influence its progress in the system. Under the LCN policy, all processes will make approximately equal progress in terms of the CPU time consumed by them, so this policy guarantees that short processes will finish ahead of long processes. Ultimately, however, this policy has the familiar drawback of starving long processes of CPU attention. It also neglects existing processes if new processes keep arriving in the system. So even not-so-long processes tend to suffer starvation or large turnaround times.

Example 7.6 Least Completed Next (LCN) Scheduling

Implementation of the LCN scheduling policy for the five processes shown in Table 7.2 is summarized in Figure 7.7. The middle rows in the table in the upper half of the figure show the amount of CPU time already consumed by a process. The scheduler analyzes this information and selects the process that has consumed the least amount of CPU time. In case of a tie, it selects the process that has not been serviced for the longest period of time. The turnaround times and weighted turnarounds of the processes are shown in the right half of the table.

Time of scheduling		0	1	2	3	4	5	6	7	8	9	10	11	12	13	14	15
CPU time consumed by processes	P_1	0	1	2	2	2	2	2	2	2	2	2					
	P_2			0	1	1	1	2	2	2	2	2	2				
	P_3				0	1	1	1	2	2	2	2	2	2	3	4	5
	P_4					0	1	1	1								
	P_5									0	1	2	2	2	2		
Process scheduled		P_1	P_1	P_2	P_3	P_4	P_2	P_3	P_4	P_5	P_5	P_1	P_2	P_3	P_5	P_3	P_3

c	t_a	w
11	11	3.67
12	10	3.33
16	13	2.60
8	4	2.00
14	6	2.00

$\overline{t_a}$ = 8.8 seconds, $\overline{w}$ = 2.72

c: completion time of a process

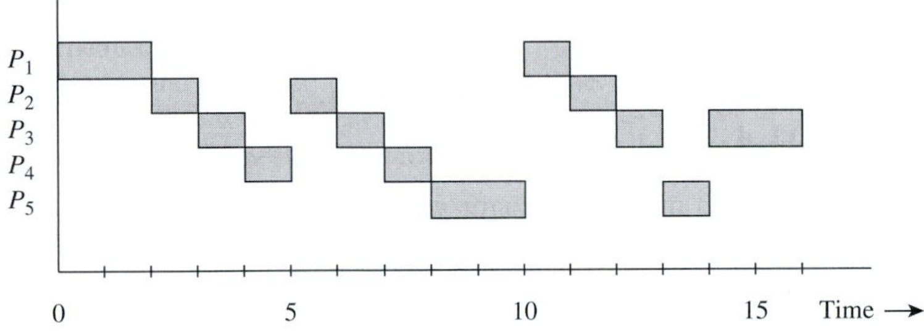

Figure 7.7 Scheduling using the least completed next (LCN) policy.

It can be seen that servicing of P_1, P_2, and P_3 is delayed because new processes arrive and obtain CPU service before these processes can make further progress. The LCN policy provides poorer turnaround times and weighted turnarounds than those provided by the RR policy (See Example 7.4) and the STG policy (to be discussed next) because it favors newly arriving processes over existing processes in the system until the new processes catch up in terms of CPU utilization; e.g., it favors P_5 over P_1, P_2, and P_3.

7.3.3 Shortest Time to Go (STG) Scheduling

The shortest time to go policy schedules a process whose remaining CPU time requirements are the smallest in the system. It is a preemptive version of the shortest request next (SRN) policy of Section 7.2, so it favors short processes over long ones and provides good throughput. Additionally, the STG policy also favors a process that is nearing completion over short processes entering the system. This feature helps to improve the turnaround times and weighted turnarounds of processes. Since it is analogous to the SRN policy, long processes might face starvation.

Time of scheduling		0	1	2	3	4	5	6	7	8	9	10	11	12	13	14	15	c	t_a	w
Remaining	P_1	3	2	1														3	3	1.00
CPU time	P_2			3	3	2	2	2	1									8	6	2.00
requirement	P_3				5	5	5	5	5	5	5	5	5	4	3	2	1	16	13	2.60
of a process	P_4					2	1											6	2	1.00
	P_5									3	2	1						11	3	1.00
Process scheduled		P_1	P_1	P_1	P_2	P_4	P_4	P_2	P_2	P_5	P_5	P_5	P_3	P_3	P_3	P_3	P_3			

$\overline{t_a}$ = 5.4 seconds, $\overline{w}$ = 1.52

c: completion time of a process

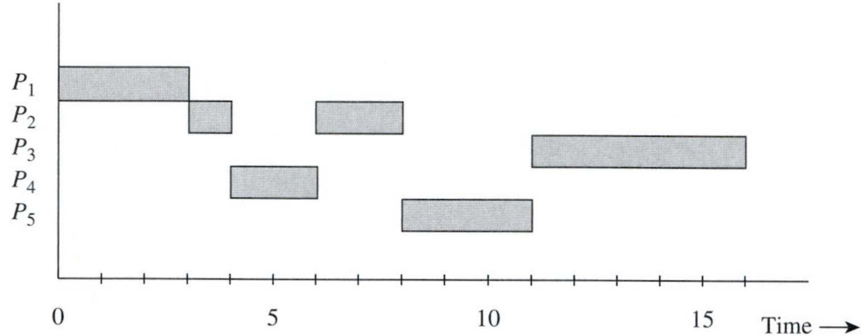

Figure 7.8 Scheduling using the shortest time to go (STG) policy.

Example 7.7 Shortest Time to Go (STG) Scheduling

Figure 7.8 summarizes performance of the STG scheduling policy for the five processes shown in Table 7.2. The scheduling information used by the policy is the CPU time needed by each process for completion. In case of a tie, the scheduler selects whatever process has not been serviced for the longest period of time. Execution of P_3 is delayed because P_2, P_4, and P_5 require lesser CPU time than it.

7.4 SCHEDULING IN PRACTICE

To provide a suitable combination of system performance and user service, an operating system has to adapt its operation to the nature and number of user requests and availability of resources. A single scheduler using a classical scheduling policy cannot address all these issues effectively. Hence, a modern OS employs *several* schedulers—up to three schedulers, as we shall see later—and some of the schedulers may use a *combination* of different scheduling policies.

7.4.1 Long-, Medium-, and Short-Term Schedulers

These schedulers perform the following functions:

- *Long-term scheduler:* Decides when to admit an arrived process for scheduling, depending on its nature (whether CPU-bound or I/O-bound) and on availability of resources like kernel data structures and disk space for swapping.
- *Medium-term scheduler:* Decides when to swap-out a process from memory and when to load it back, so that a sufficient number of *ready* processes would exist in memory.
- *Short-term scheduler:* Decides which *ready* process to service next on the CPU and for how long.

Thus, the *short-term scheduler* is the one that actually selects a process for operation. Hence it is also called the *process scheduler*, or simply the *scheduler*. Figure 7.9 shows an overview of scheduling and related actions. As discussed in Sections 2.3 and 5.2.2, the operation of the kernel is interrupt-driven. Every event that requires the kernel's attention causes an interrupt. The interrupt processing

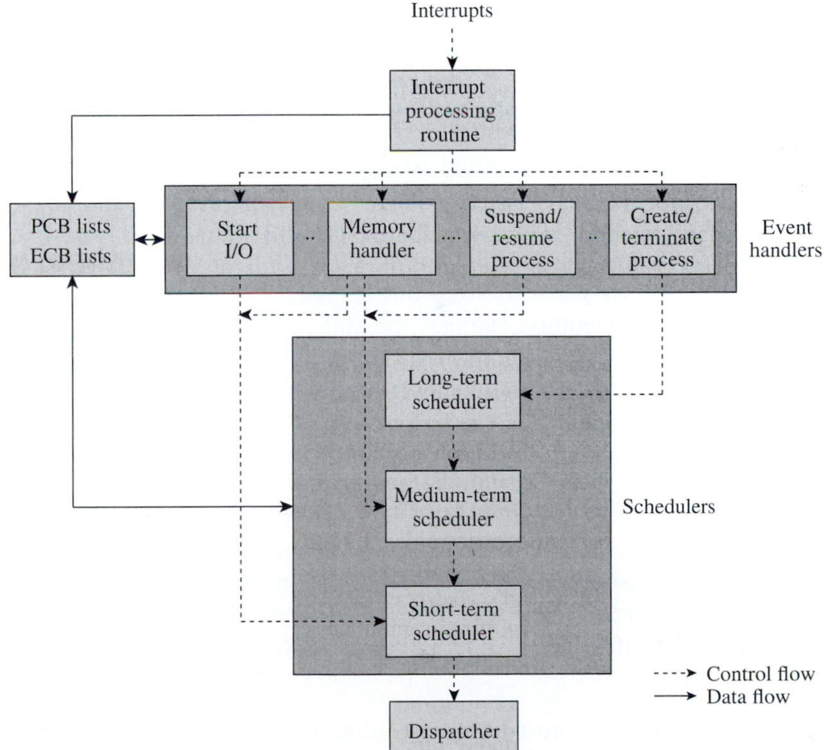

Figure 7.9 Event handling and scheduling.

routine performs a context save function and invokes an event handler. The event handler analyzes the event and changes the state of the process, if any, affected by it. It then invokes the long-term, medium-term, or short-term scheduler as appropriate. For example, the event handler that creates a new process invokes the long-term scheduler, event handlers for suspension and resumption of processes (see Section 5.2.1.1) invoke the medium-term scheduler, and the memory handler may invoke the medium-term scheduler if it runs out of memory. Most other event handlers directly invoke the short-term scheduler.

Long-Term Scheduling The long-term scheduler may defer admission of a request for two reasons: it may not be able to allocate sufficient resources like kernel data structures or I/O devices to a request when it arrives, or it may find that admission of a request would affect system performance in some way; e.g., if the system currently contained a large number of CPU-bound requests, the scheduler might defer admission of a new CPU-bound request, but it might admit a new I/O-bound request right away.

Long-term scheduling was used in the 1960s and 1970s for job scheduling because computer systems had limited resources, so a long-term scheduler was required to decide *whether* a process could be initiated at the present time. It continues to be important in operating systems where resources are limited. It is also used in systems where requests have deadlines, or a set of requests are repeated with a known periodicity, to decide *when* a process should be initiated to meet response requirements of applications. Long-term scheduling is not relevant in other operating systems.

Medium-Term Scheduling Medium-term scheduling maps the large number of requests that have been admitted to the system into the smaller number of requests that can fit into the memory of the system at any time. Thus its focus is on making a sufficient number of *ready* processes available to the short-term scheduler by suspending or reactivating processes. The medium-term scheduler decides when to swap out a process from memory and when to swap it back into memory, changes the state of the process appropriately, and enters its process control block (PCB) in the appropriate list of PCBs. The actual swapping-in and swapping-out operations are performed by the memory manager.

The kernel can suspend a process when a user requests suspension, when the kernel runs out of free memory, or when it finds that the CPU is not likely to be allocated to the process in the near future. In time-sharing systems, processes in *blocked* or *ready* states are candidates for suspension (see Figure 5.5). The decision to reactivate a process is more involved: The medium-term scheduler considers the position occupied by a process in the scheduling list, estimates when it is likely to be scheduled next, and swaps it in ahead of this time.

Short-Term Scheduling Short-term scheduling is concerned with effective use of the CPU. It selects one process from a list of *ready* processes and hands it to the dispatching mechanism. It may also decide how long the process should

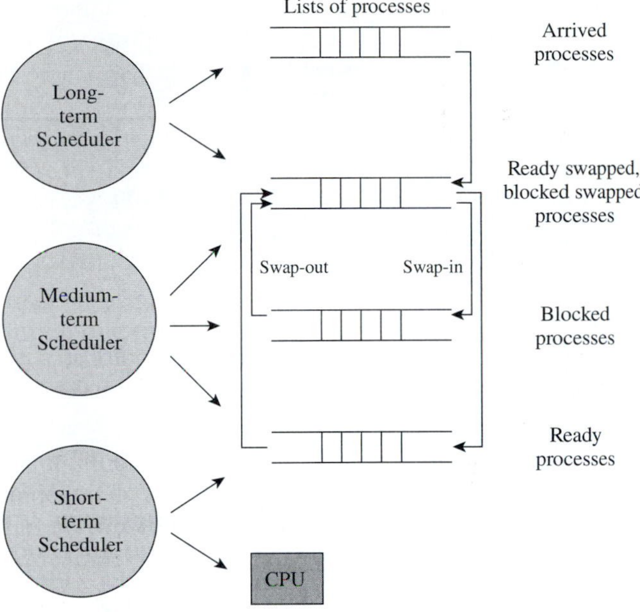

Figure 7.10 Long-, medium-, and short-term scheduling in a time-sharing system.

be allowed to use the CPU and instruct the kernel to produce a timer interrupt accordingly.

Example 7.8 illustrates long-, medium-, and short-term scheduling in a time-sharing OS.

Long-, Medium-, and Short-Term Scheduling in Time-Sharing — Example 7.8

Figure 7.10 illustrates scheduling in a time-sharing operating system. The long-term scheduler admits a process when kernel resources like control blocks, swap space on a disk, and other resources like I/O devices—whether real or virtual—can be allocated to it. The kernel copies the code of the process into the swap space, and adds the process to the list of swapped-out processes.

The medium-term scheduler controls swapping of processes and decides when to move processes between the *ready swapped* and *ready* lists and between the *blocked swapped* and *blocked* lists (see Figure 5.5). Whenever the CPU is free, the short-term scheduler selects one process from the *ready* list for execution. The dispatching mechanism initiates or resumes operation of the selected process on the CPU. A process may shuttle between the medium-, and short-term schedulers many times as a result of swapping.

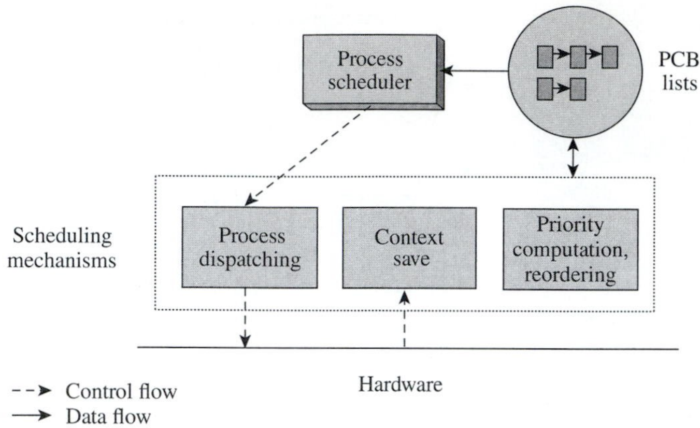

Figure 7.11 A schematic of the process scheduler.

7.4.2 Scheduling Data Structures and Mechanisms

Figure 7.11 is a schematic diagram of the process scheduler. It uses several lists of PCBs whose organization and use depends on the scheduling policy. The process scheduler selects one process and passes its id to the process dispatching mechanism. The process dispatching mechanism loads contents of two PCB fields—the program status word (PSW) and general-purpose registers (GPRs) fields—into the CPU to resume operation of the selected process. Thus, the dispatching mechanism interfaces with the scheduler on one side and the hardware on the other side.

The context save mechanism is a part of the interrupt processing routine. When an interrupt occurs, it is invoked to save the PSW and GPRs of the interrupted process. The priority computation and reordering mechanism recomputes the priority of requests and reorders the PCB lists to reflect the new priorities. This mechanism is either invoked explicitly by the scheduler when appropriate or invoked periodically. Its exact actions depend on the scheduling policy in use.

One question faced by all schedulers is: What should the scheduler do if there are no *ready* processes? It has no work for the CPU to perform; however, the CPU must remain alert to handle any interrupts that might activate one of the *blocked* processes. A kernel typically achieves it by executing an *idle loop*, which is an endless loop containing no-op instructions. When an interrupt causes a *blocked* → *ready* transition for some process, scheduling would be performed again and that process would get scheduled. However, execution of the idle loop wastes power. In Section 7.4.9, we discuss alternative arrangements that conserve power when there are no *ready* processes in the system.

7.4.3 Priority-Based Scheduling

Figure 7.12 shows an efficient arrangement of scheduling data for priority-based scheduling. A separate list of *ready* processes is maintained for each priority value;

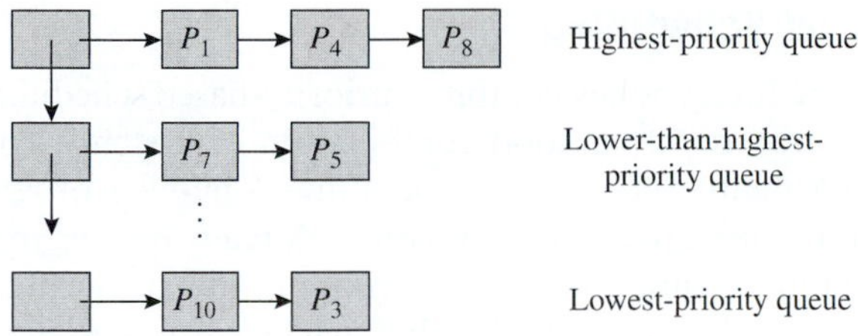

Figure 7.12 Ready queues in priority-based scheduling.

this list is organized as a queue of PCBs, in which a PCB points to the PCB of the next process in the queue. The header of a queue contains two pointers. One points to the PCB of the first process in the queue, and the other points to the header of the queue for the next lower priority. The scheduler scans the headers in the order of decreasing priority and selects the first process in the first nonempty queue it can find. This way, the scheduling overhead depends on the number of distinct priorities, rather than on the number of *ready* processes.

Priority-based scheduling can lead to starvation of low-priority processes. As discussed in Section 7.1.2, the technique of *aging* of processes, which increases the priority of a *ready* process if it does not get scheduled within a certain period of time, can be used to overcome starvation. In this scheme, process priorities would be *dynamic*, so the PCB of a process would be moved between the different ready queues shown in Figure 7.12.

Starvation in priority-based scheduling can also lead to an undesirable situation called *priority inversion*. Consider a high-priority process that needs a resource that is currently allocated to a low-priority process. If the low-priority process faces starvation, it cannot use and release the resource. Consequently, the high-priority process remains blocked indefinitely. This situation is addressed through the *priority inheritance protocol*, which temporarily raises the priority of the low-priority process holding the resource to the priority value of the high-priority process that needs the resource. The process holding the resource can now obtain the CPU, use the resource, and release it. The kernel changes its priority back to the earlier value when it releases the resource.

7.4.4 Round-Robin Scheduling with Time-Slicing

Round-robin scheduling can be implemented through a single list of PCBs of *ready* processes. This list is organized as a queue. The scheduler always removes the first PCB from the queue and schedules the process described by it. If the time slice elapses, the PCB of the process is put at the end of the queue. If a process starts an I/O operation, its PCB is added at the end of the queue when its I/O operation completes. Thus the PCB of a *ready* process moves toward the head of the queue until the process is scheduled.

7.4.5 Multilevel Scheduling

The multilevel scheduling policy combines priority-based scheduling and round-robin scheduling to provide a good combination of system performance and response times. A multilevel scheduler maintains a number of ready queues. A priority and a time slice are associated with each ready queue, and round-robin scheduling with time-slicing is performed within it. The queue at a high priority level has a small time slice associated with it, which ensures good response times for processes in this queue, while the queue at a low priority level has a large time slice, which ensures low process switching overhead. A process at the head of a queue is scheduled only if the queues for all higher priority levels are empty. Scheduling is preemptive, so a process is preempted when a new process is added to a queue at a higher priority level. As in round-robin scheduling with time-slicing, when a process makes an I/O request, or is swapped out, its PCB is removed from the ready queue. When the I/O operation completes, or the process is swapped in, its PCB is added at the end of that ready queue where it existed earlier.

To benefit from the features of multilevel scheduling, the kernel puts highly interactive processes in the queue at the highest priority level. The small time slice associated with this queue is adequate for these processes, so they receive good response times [see Eq. (3.1)]. Moderately interactive processes are put in a ready queue at a medium priority level where they receive larger time slices. Noninteractive processes are put in a ready queue at one of the low priority levels. These processes receive a large time slice, which reduces the scheduling overhead.

Example 7.9 Multilevel Scheduling

Figure 7.12 illustrates ready queues in a multilevel scheduler. Processes P_7 and P_5 have a larger time slice than processes P_1, P_4, and P_8. However, they get a chance to execute only when P_1, P_4, and P_8 are blocked. Processes P_{10} and P_3 can execute only when all other processes in the system are blocked. Thus, these two processes would face starvation if this situation is rare.

The multilevel scheduling policy uses static priorities. Hence it inherits the fundamental shortcoming of priority-based scheduling employed in multiprogramming systems: A process is classified *a priori* into a CPU-bound process or an I/O-bound process for assignment of priority. If wrongly classified, an I/O-bound process may receive a low priority, which would affect both user service and system performance, or a CPU-bound process may receive a high priority, which would affect system performance. As a result of static priorities, the multilevel scheduling policy also cannot handle a change in the computational or I/O behavior of a process, cannot prevent starvation of processes in low priority levels (see Example 7.9), and cannot employ the priority inheritance protocol to overcome priority inversion (see Section 7.4.3). All these problems are addressed by the multilevel adaptive scheduling policy.

Multilevel Adaptive Scheduling In multilevel *adaptive* scheduling, which is also called *multilevel feedback scheduling*, the scheduler varies the priority of a process such that the process receives a time slice that is consistent with its requirement for CPU time. The scheduler determines the "correct" priority level for a process by observing its recent CPU and I/O usage and moves the process to this level. This way, a process that is I/O-bound during one phase in its operation and CPU-bound during another phase will receive an appropriate priority and time slice at all times. This feature eliminates the problems of multilevel scheduling described earlier.

CTSS, a time-sharing OS for the IBM 7094 in the 1960s, is a well-known example of multilevel adaptive scheduling. The system used an eight-level priority structure, with the levels numbered 0 through 7, 0 being the highest-priority level and 7 being the lowest-priority level. Level number n had a time slice of 0.5×2^n CPU seconds associated with it. At initiation, each user process was placed at level 2 or 3 depending on its memory requirement. It was promoted or demoted in the priority structure according to the following rules: If a process completely used up the time slice at its current priority level (i.e., it did not initiate an I/O operation), it was demoted to the next higher numbered level, whereas if a process spent more than a minute in *ready* state in its current priority level without obtaining any CPU service, it was promoted to the next lower numbered level. Further, any process performing I/O on the user terminal was promoted to level 2. Subsequently, it would be moved to the "correct" priority level through possible demotions.

7.4.6 Fair Share Scheduling

A common criticism of all scheduling policies discussed so far is that they try to provide equitable service to processes, rather than to users or their applications. If applications create different numbers of processes, an application employing more processes is likely to receive more CPU attention than an application employing fewer processes.

The notion of a *fair share* addresses this issue. A fair share is the fraction of CPU time that should be devoted to a group of processes that belong to the same user or the same application; it ensures an equitable use of the CPU by users or applications. The actual share of CPU time received by a group of processes may differ from the fair share of the group if all processes in some of the groups are inactive. For example, consider five groups of processes, G_1–G_5, each having a 20 percent share of CPU time. If all processes in G_1 are *blocked*, processes of each of the other groups should be given 25 percent of the available CPU time so that CPU time is not wasted. What should the scheduler do when processes of G_1 become active after some time? Should it give them only 20 percent of CPU time after they wake up, because that is their fair share of CPU time, or should it give them all the available CPU time until their actual CPU consumption since inception becomes 20 percent? Lottery scheduling, which we describe in the following, and the scheduling policies used in the Unix and Solaris operating systems (see Section 7.6) differ in the way they handle this situation.

Lottery scheduling is a novel technique proposed for sharing a resource in a probabilistically fair manner. Lottery "tickets" are distributed to all processes sharing a resource in such a manner that a process gets as many tickets as its fair share of the resource. For example, a process would be given five tickets out of a total of 100 tickets if its fair share of the resource is 5 percent. When the resource is to be allocated, a lottery is conducted among the tickets held by processes that actively seek the resource. The process holding the winning ticket is then allocated the resource. The actual share of the resources allocated to the process depends on contention for the resource. Lottery scheduling can be used for fair share CPU scheduling as follows: Tickets can be issued to applications (or users) on the basis of their fair share of CPU time. An application can share its tickets among its processes in any manner it desires. To allocate a CPU time slice, the scheduler holds a lottery in which only tickets of *ready* processes participate. When the time slice is a few milliseconds, this scheduling method provides fairness even over fractions of a second if all groups of processes are active.

7.4.7 Kernel Preemptibility

Kernel preemptibility plays a vital role in ensuring effectiveness of a scheduler. A noninterruptible kernel can handle an event without getting further interrupted, so event handlers have a mutually exclusive access to the kernel data structures without having to use data access synchronization. However, if event handlers have large running times, noninterruptibility also causes a large kernel latency, as the kernel cannot respond readily to interrupts. This latency, which could be as much as 100 ms in computers with slow CPUs, causes a significant degradation of response times and a slowdown of the OS operation. When the scheduling of a high-priority process is delayed because the kernel is handling an event concerning a low-priority process, it even causes a situation analogous to priority inversion. Making the kernel preemptible would solve this problem. Now, scheduling would be performed more often, so a high-priority process that is activated by an interrupt would get to execute sooner.

7.4.8 Scheduling Heuristics

Schedulers in modern operating systems use many heuristics to reduce their overhead, and to provide good user service. These heuristics employ two main techniques:

- Use of a time quantum
- Variation of process priority

A *time quantum* is the limit on CPU time that a process may be allowed to consume over a time interval. It is employed as follows: Each process is assigned a priority and a time quantum. A process is scheduled according to its priority, provided it has not exhausted its time quantum. As it operates, the amount of CPU time used by it is deducted from its time quantum. After a process has exhausted its time quantum, it would not be considered for scheduling unless the kernel grants it another time quantum, which would happen only when all active processes have exhausted their quanta. This way, the time quantum of a process would control the share of CPU time used by it, so it can be employed to implement fair share scheduling.

Process priority could be varied to achieve various goals. The priority of a process could be boosted while it is executing a system call, so that it would quickly complete execution of the call, release any kernel resources allocated to it, and exit the kernel. This technique would improve response to other processes that are waiting for the kernel resources held by the process executing the system call. Priority inheritance could be implemented by boosting the priority of a process holding a resource to that of the highest-priority process waiting for the resource.

Process priority may also be varied to more accurately characterize the nature of a process. When the kernel initiates a new process, it has no means of knowing whether the process is I/O-bound or CPU-bound, so it assigns a default priority to the process. As the process operates, the kernel adjusts its priority in accordance with its behavior using a heuristic of the following kind: When the process is activated after some period of blocking, its priority may be boosted in accordance with the cause of blocking. For example, if it was blocked because of an I/O operation, its priority would be boosted to provide it a better response time. If it was blocked for a keyboard input, it would have waited for a long time for the user to respond, so its priority may be given a further boost. If a process used up its time slice completely, its priority may be reduced because it is more CPU-bound than was previously assumed.

7.4.9 Power Management

When no *ready* processes exist, the kernel puts the CPU into an *idle loop* (see Section 7.4.2). This solution wastes power in executing useless instructions. In power-starved systems such as embedded and mobile systems, it is essential to prevent this wastage of power.

To address this requirement, computers provide special modes in the CPU. When put in one of these modes, the CPU does not execute instructions, which conserves power; however, it can accept interrupts, which enables it to resume normal operation when desired. We will use the term *sleep mode* of the CPU generically for such modes. Some computers provide several sleep modes. In the "light" sleep mode, the CPU simply stops executing instructions. In a "heavy" sleep mode, the CPU not only stops executing instructions, but also takes other steps that reduce its power consumption, e.g., slowing the clock and disconnecting the CPU from the system bus. Ideally, the kernel should put the CPU into the deepest sleep mode possible when the system does not have processes in the *ready* state. However, a CPU takes a longer time to "wake up" from a heavy sleep mode than it would from a light sleep mode, so the kernel has to make a trade-off here. It starts by putting the CPU in the light sleep mode. If no processes become *ready* for some more time, it puts the CPU into a heavier sleep mode, and so on. This way, it provides a trade-off between the need for power saving and responsiveness of the system.

Operating systems like Unix and Windows have generalized power management to include all devices. Typically, a device is put into a lower power consuming state if it has been dormant at its present power consuming state for some time. Users are also provided with utilities through which they can configure the power management scheme used by the OS.

7.5 REAL-TIME SCHEDULING

Real-time scheduling must handle two special scheduling constraints while trying to meet the deadlines of applications. First, the processes within a real-time application are interacting processes, so the deadline of an application should be translated into appropriate deadlines for the processes. Second, processes may be periodic, so different instances of a process may arrive at fixed intervals and all of them have to meet their deadlines. Example 7.10 illustrates these constraints; in this section, we discuss techniques used to handle them.

Example 7.10 Dependences and Periods in a Real-Time Application

Consider a restricted form of the real-time data logging application of Example 5.1, in which the *buffer_area* can accommodate a single data sample. Since samples arrive at the rate of 500 samples per second, the response requirement of the application is 1.99 ms. Hence, processes *copy_sample* and *record_sample* must operate one after another and complete their operation within 1.99 ms. If process *record_sample* requires 1.5 ms for its operation, process *copy_sample* has a deadline of 0.49 ms after arrival of a message. Since a new sample arrives every 2 ms, each of the processes has a period of 2 ms.

7.5.1 Process Precedences and Feasible Schedules

Processes of a real-time application interact among themselves to ensure that they perform their actions in a desired order (see Section 6.1). We make the simplifying assumption that such interaction takes place only at the start or end of a process. It causes dependences between processes, which must be taken into account while determining deadlines and while scheduling. We use a *process precedence graph* (PPG) to depict such dependences between processes.

Process P_i is said to *precede* process P_j if execution of P_i must be completed before P_j can begin its execution. The notation $P_i \rightarrow P_j$ shall indicate that process P_i directly precedes process P_j. The precedence relation is transitive; i.e., $P_i \rightarrow P_j$ and $P_j \rightarrow P_k$ implies that P_i precedes P_k. The notation $P_i \xrightarrow{*} P_k$ is used to indicate that process P_i directly or indirectly precedes P_k. A *process precedence graph* is a directed graph $G \equiv (N, E)$ such that $P_i \in N$ represents a process, and an edge $(P_i, P_j) \in E$ implies $P_i \rightarrow P_j$. Thus, a path $P_i, \ldots, P_k$ in PPG implies $P_i \xrightarrow{*} P_k$. A process P_k is a descendant of P_i if $P_i \xrightarrow{*} P_k$.

In Section 3.7, we defined a *hard real-time system* as one that meets the response requirement of a real-time application in a guaranteed manner, even when fault tolerance actions are required. This condition implies that the time required by the OS to complete operation of all processes in the application does not exceed the response requirement of the application. On the other hand, a *soft real-time system* meets the response requirement of an application only in a probabilistic manner, and not necessarily at all times. The notion of a *feasible schedule* helps to differentiate between these situations.

Definition 7.1 Feasible Schedule A sequence of scheduling decisions that enables the processes of an application to operate in accordance with their precedences and meet the response requirement of the application.

Real-time scheduling focuses on implementing a feasible schedule for an application, if one exists. Consider an application for updating airline departure information on displays at 15-second intervals. It consists of the following independent processes, where process P_5 handles an exceptional situation that seldom occurs.

Process	P_1	P_2	P_3	P_4	P_5
Service time	3	3	2	4	5

A feasible schedule does not exist for completing all five processes in 15 seconds, so a deadline overrun would occur. However, several schedules are possible when process P_5 is not active. The scheduler in a soft real-time system can use any one of them.

Table 7.3 summarizes three main approaches to real-time scheduling. We discuss the features and properties of these scheduling approaches in the following.

Table 7.3 Approaches to Real-Time Scheduling

Approach	Description
Static scheduling	A schedule is prepared *before* operation of the real-time application begins. Process interactions, periodicities, resource constraints, and deadlines are considered in preparing the schedule.
Priority-based scheduling	The real-time application is analyzed to assign appropriate priorities to processes in it. Conventional priority-based scheduling is used during operation of the application.
Dynamic scheduling	Scheduling is performed when a request to create a process is made. Process creation succeeds only if response requirement of the process can be satisfied in a guaranteed manner.

Static Scheduling As the name indicates, a schedule is prepared before the system is put into operation. The schedule considers process precedences, periodicities, resource constraints, and possibilities of overlapping I/O operations in some processes with computations in other processes. This schedule is represented in the form of a table whose rows indicate when operation of different processes should begin. No scheduling decisions are made during operation of the system. The real-time OS simply consults the table and starts operation of processes as indicated in it. Static scheduling leads to negligible scheduling overhead during system operation. However, it is inflexible and cannot handle issues like fault tolerance.

The size of the scheduling table will depend on periods of processes. If all processes have the same period, or if processes are nonperiodic, the scheduling table will have only as many rows as the number of processes in the application. This schedule is used repeatedly during operation of the system. If periodicities of processes are different, the length of the schedule that needs to be represented in the scheduling table will be the least common multiple of periodicities of all processes in the application.

Priority-Based Scheduling A system analyst uses two considerations while assigning priorities to processes: criticality of processes and periodicity of processes. A process with a smaller period must complete its operation earlier than a process with a larger period, so it must have a higher priority. This approach has the benefits and drawbacks normally associated with the use of priorities. It provides graceful degradation capabilities because critical functions would continue to be performed even when failures occur. However, it incurs scheduling overhead during operation.

Dynamic Scheduling In systems using the dynamic scheduling approach, scheduling is performed during the system's operation. Multimedia systems like video on demand use a dynamic scheduling approach in which a scheduling decision is performed when a process arrives. A request to initiate a process contains information such as the process's resource requirement, service time, and a deadline or a specification of service quality. On receiving such a request, the scheduler checks whether it is possible to assign the resources needed by the process and meet its deadline or provide it the desired quality of service. It creates the process only if these checks succeed.

Another approach to dynamic scheduling is to optimistically admit processes for execution. In this approach, there is no guarantee that the deadline or service quality requirements can be met. Soft real-time systems often follow this approach.

7.5.2 Deadline Scheduling

Two kinds of deadlines can be specified for a process: a *starting deadline*, i.e., the latest instant of time by which operation of the process must begin, and a *completion deadline*, i.e., the time by which operation of the process must complete. We consider only completion deadlines in the following.

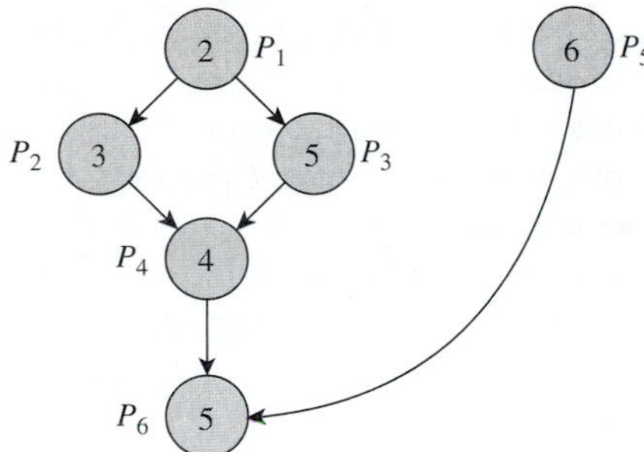

Figure 7.13 The process precedence graph (PPG) for a real-time system.

Deadline Estimation A system analyst performs an in-depth analysis of a real-time application and its response requirements. Deadlines for individual processes are determined by considering process precedences and working backward from the response requirement of the application. Accordingly, D_i, the completion deadline of a process P_i, is

$$D_i = D_{\text{application}} - \sum_{k \in descendant(i)} x_k \tag{7.2}$$

where $D_{\text{application}}$ is the deadline of the application, x_k is the service time of process P_k, and *descendant*(i) is the set of descendants of P_i in the PPG, i.e., the set of all processes that lie on some path between P_i and the exit node of the PPG. Thus, the deadline for a process P_i is such that if it is met, all processes that directly or indirectly depend on P_i can also finish by the overall deadline of the application. This method is illustrated in Example 7.11.

Determining Process Deadlines

Example 7.11

Figure 7.13 shows the PPG of a real-time application containing 6 processes. Each circle is a node of the graph and represents a process. The number in a circle indicates the service time of a process. An edge in the PPG shows a precedence constraint. Thus, process P_2 can be initiated only after process P_1 completes, process P_4 can be initiated only after processes P_2 and P_3 complete, etc. We assume that processes do not perform I/O operations and are serviced in a nonpreemptive manner. The total of the service times of the processes is 25 seconds. If the application has to produce a response in 25 seconds, the deadlines of the processes would be as follows:

Process	P_1	P_2	P_3	P_4	P_5	P_6
Deadline	8	16	16	20	20	25

A practical method of estimating deadlines will have to incorporate several other constraints as well. For example, processes may perform I/O. If an I/O operation of one process can be overlapped with execution of some independent process, the deadline of its predecessors (and ancestors) in the PPG can be relaxed by the amount of I/O overlap. (Independent processes were formally defined in Section 6.1.) For example, processes P_2 and P_3 in Figure 7.13 are independent of one another. If the service time of P_2 includes 1 second of I/O time, the deadline of P_1 can be made 9 seconds instead of 8 seconds if the I/O operation of P_2 can overlap with P_3's processing. However, overlapped execution of processes must consider resource availability as well. Hence determination of deadlines is far more complex than described here.

Earliest Deadline First (EDF) Scheduling As its name suggests, this policy always selects the process with the earliest deadline. Consider a set of real-time processes that do not perform I/O operations. If *seq* is the sequence in which processes are serviced by a deadline scheduling policy and $pos(P_i)$ is the position of process P_i in *seq*, a deadline overrun does not occur for process P_i only if the sum of its own service time and service times of all processes that precede it in *seq* does not exceed its own deadline, i.e.,

$$\sum_{k:pos(P_k)\leq pos(P_i)} x_k \leq D_i \tag{7.3}$$

where x_k is the service time of process P_k, and D_i is the deadline of process P_i. If this condition is not satisfied, a deadline overrun will occur for process P_i.

When a feasible schedule exists, it can be shown that Condition 7.3 holds for all processes; i.e., a deadline overrun will not occur for any process. Table 7.4 illustrates operation of the EDF policy for the deadlines of Example 7.11. The notation P_4 : 20 in the column *processes in system* indicates that process P_4 has the deadline 20. Processes P_2, P_3 and P_5, P_6 have identical deadlines, so three schedules other than the one shown in Table 7.4 are possible with EDF scheduling. None of them would incur deadline overruns.

The primary advantages of EDF scheduling are its simplicity and nonpreemptive nature, which reduces the scheduling overhead. EDF scheduling is a good policy for static scheduling because existence of a feasible schedule, which can be checked *a priori,* ensures that deadline overruns do not occur. It is also

Table 7.4 **Operation of Earliest Deadline First (EDF) Scheduling**

Time	Process completed	Deadline overrun	Processes in system	Process scheduled
0	–	0	$P_1 : 8, P_2 : 16, P_3 : 16, P_4 : 20, P_5 : 20, P_6 : 25$	P_1
2	P_1	0	$P_2 : 16, P_3 : 16, P_4 : 20, P_5 : 20, P_6 : 25$	P_2
5	P_2	0	$P_3 : 16, P_4 : 20, P_5 : 20, P_6 : 25$	P_3
10	P_3	0	$P_4 : 20, P_5 : 20, P_6 : 25$	P_4
14	P_4	0	$P_5 : 20, P_6 : 25$	P_5
20	P_5	0	$P_6 : 25$	P_6
25	P_2	0	–	–

a good dynamic scheduling policy for use in soft real-time system; however, the number of processes that miss their deadlines is unpredictable. The next example illustrates this aspect of EDF scheduling.

Problems of EDF Scheduling

Example 7.12

Consider the PPG of Figure 7.13 with the edge (P_5, P_6) removed. It contains two independent applications, one contains the processes P_1–P_4 and P_6, while the other contains P_5 alone. If all processes are to complete by 19 seconds, a feasible schedule does not exist. Now deadlines of the processes determined by using Eq. (7.2) are as follows:

Process	P_1	P_2	P_3	P_4	P_5	P_6
Deadline	2	10	10	14	19	19

EDF scheduling may schedule the processes either in the sequence $P_1, P_2, P_3, P_4, P_5, P_6$, which is the same as in Table 7.4, or in the sequence $P_1, P_2, P_3, P_4, P_6, P_5$. Processes P_5 and P_6 miss their deadlines in the first sequence, whereas only process P_5 misses its deadline in the second sequence. We cannot predict which sequence will be chosen by an implementation of EDF scheduling, so the number of processes that miss their deadlines is unpredictable.

7.5.3 Rate Monotonic Scheduling

When processes in an application are periodic, the existence of a feasible schedule can be determined in an interesting way. Consider three independent processes that do not perform I/O operations:

Process	P_1	P_2	P_3
Time period (ms)	10	15	30
Service time (ms)	3	5	9

Process P_1 repeats every 10 ms and needs 3 ms of CPU time. So the fraction of the CPU's time that it uses is $3/10$, i.e., 0.30. The fractions of CPU time used by P_2 and P_3 are analogously $5/15$ and $9/30$, i.e., 0.33 and 0.30. They add up to 0.93, so if the CPU overhead of OS operation is negligible, it is feasible to service these three processes. In general, a set of periodic processes $P_1, \ldots, P_n$ that do not perform I/O operations can be serviced by a hard real-time system that has a negligible overhead if

$$\Sigma_{i=1\ldots n} \frac{x_i}{T_i} \leq 1 \qquad \textbf{(7.4)}$$

where T_i is the period of P_i and x_i is its service time.

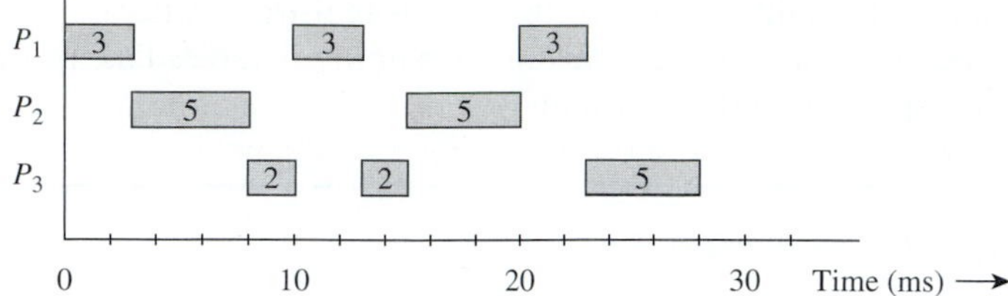

Figure 7.14 Operation of real-time processes using rate monotonic scheduling.

We still have to schedule these processes so that they can all operate without missing their deadlines. The *rate monotonic* (RM) scheduling policy does it as follows: It determines the *rate* at which a process has to repeat, i.e., the number of repetitions per second, and assigns the rate itself as the priority of the process. It now employs a priority-based scheduling technique to perform scheduling. This way, a process with a smaller period has a higher priority, which would enable it to complete its operation early.

In the above example, priorities of processes P_1, P_2, and P_3 would be $1/0.010$, $1/0.015$, and $1/0.025$, i.e., 100, 67, and 45, respectively. Figure 7.14 shows how these processes would operate. Process P_1 would be scheduled first. It would execute once and become dormant after 3 ms, because $x_1 = 3$ ms. Now P_2 would be scheduled and would complete after 5 ms. P_3 would be scheduled now, but it would be preempted after 2 ms because P_1 becomes *ready* for the second time, and so on. As shown in Figure 7.14, process P_3 would complete at 28 ms. By this time, P_1 has executed three times and P_2 has executed two times.

Rate monotonic scheduling is not guaranteed to find a feasible schedule in all situations. For example, if process P_3 had a time period of 27 ms, its priority would be different; however, relative priorities of the processes would be unchanged, so P_3 would complete at 28 ms as before, thereby suffering a deadline overrun of 1 ms. A feasible schedule would have been obtained if P_3 had been scheduled at 20 ms and P_1 at 25 ms; however, it is not possible under RM scheduling because processes are scheduled in a priority-based manner. Liu and Layland (1973) have shown that RM scheduling may not be able to avoid deadline overruns if the total fraction of CPU time used by the processes according to Eq. (7.4) exceeds $m(2^{1/m} - 1)$, where m is the number of processes. This expression has a lower bound of 0.69, which implies that if an application has a large number of processes, RM scheduling may not be able to achieve more than 69 percent CPU utilization if it is to meet deadlines of processes.

Liu and Layland also report a *deadline-driven scheduling algorithm* that dynamically assigns priorities to processes based on their current deadlines—a process with an earlier deadline is assigned a higher priority than a process with a later deadline. It can avoid deadline overruns even when the fraction of Eq. (7.4) has the value 1; that is, it can achieve 100 percent CPU utilization. However, its practical performance would be lower because of the overhead of dynamic priority assignment. Recall that EDF scheduling can avoid deadline overruns if a feasible schedule exists. Hence, it, too, can achieve 100 percent CPU utilization. If employed statically, it would suffer little overhead during operation.

7.6 CASE STUDIES

7.6.1 Scheduling in Unix

Unix is a pure time-sharing operating system. It uses a multilevel adaptive scheduling policy in which process priorities are varied to ensure good system performance and also to provide good user service. Processes are allocated numerical priorities, where a larger numerical value implies a lower effective priority. In Unix 4.3 BSD, the priorities are in the range 0 to 127. Processes in the user mode have priorities between 50 and 127, while those in the kernel mode have priorities between 0 and 49. When a process is blocked in a system call, its priority is changed to a value in the range 0–49, depending on the cause of blocking. When it becomes active again, it executes the remainder of the system call with this priority. This arrangement ensures that the process would be scheduled as soon as possible, complete the task it was performing in the kernel mode and release kernel resources. When it exits the kernel mode, its priority reverts to its previous value, which was in the range 50–127.

Unix uses the following formula to vary the priority of a process:

$$\begin{aligned}\text{Process priority} = &\ \text{base priority for user processes} \\ &+ f(\text{CPU time used recently}) + \text{nice value}\end{aligned} \quad \textbf{(7.5)}$$

It is implemented as follows: The scheduler maintains the CPU time used by a process in its process table entry. This field is initialized to 0. The real-time clock raises an interrupt 60 times a second, and the clock handler increments the count in the CPU usage field of the running process. The scheduler recomputes process priorities every second in a loop. For each process, it divides the value in the CPU usage field by 2, stores it back, and also uses it as the value of f. Recall that a large numerical value implies a lower effective priority, so the second factor in Eq. (7.5) lowers the priority of a process. The division by 2 ensures that the effect of CPU time used by a process *decays*; i.e., it wears off over a period of time, to avoid the problem of starvation faced in the least completed next (LCN) policy (see Section 7.3.2).

A process can vary its own priority through the last factor in Eq. (7.5). The system call "*nice(<priority value>);*" sets the *nice value* of a user process. It takes a zero or positive value as its argument. Thus, a process can only decrease its effective priority to be nice to other processes. It would typically do this when it enters a CPU-bound phase.

Table 7.5 Operation of a Unix-like Scheduling Policy When Processes Perform I/O

Time	P_1		P_2		P_3		P_4		P_5		Scheduled process
	P	T	P	T	P	T	P	T	P	T	
0.0	60	0									P_1
1.0		60									
	90	30									P_1
2.0		90		0							
	105	45	60	0							P_2
3.0		45		60		0					
	82	22	90	30	60	0					P_3
3.1	82	22	90	30	60	6					P_1
4.0		76		30		6					
	98	38	75	15	63	3					P_3
4.1	98	38	75	15	63	9					P_2
5.0		38		69		9		0			
	79	19	94	34	64	4	60	0			P_4
6.0		19		34		4		60			
	69	9	77	17	62	2	90	30			P_3

Example 7.13 Process Scheduling in Unix

Table 7.5 summarizes operation of the Unix scheduling policy for the processes in Table 7.2. It is assumed that process P_3 is an I/O bound process that initiates an I/O operation lasting 0.5 seconds after using the CPU for 0.1 seconds, and none of the other processes perform I/O. The T field indicates the CPU time consumed by a process and the P field contains its priority. The scheduler updates the T field of a process 60 times a second and recomputes process priorities once every second. The time slice is 1 second, and the base priority of user processes is 60. The first line of Table 7.5 shows that at 0 second, only P_1 is present in the system. Its T field contains 0, hence its priority is 60. Two lines are shown for the time 1 second. The first line shows the T fields of processes at 1 second, while the second line shows the P and T fields after the priority computation actions at 1 second. At the end of the time slice, the contents of the T field of P_1 are 60. The decaying action of dividing the CPU time by 2 reduces it to 30, and so the priority of P_1 becomes 90. At 2 seconds, the effective priority of P_1 is smaller than that of P_2 because their T fields contain 45 and 0, respectively, and so P_2 is scheduled. Similarly P_3 is scheduled at 2 seconds.

Since P_3 uses the CPU for only 0.1 second before starting an I/O operation, it has a higher priority than P_2 when scheduling is performed at 4 seconds; hence it is scheduled ahead of process P_2. It is again scheduled at 6 seconds. This feature corrects the bias against I/O-bound processes exhibited by pure round-robin scheduling.

Table 7.6 Operation of Fair Share Scheduling in Unix

	P_1			P_2			P_3			P_4			P_5			
Time	**P**	**C**	**G**	**P**	**C**	**G**	**P**	**C**	**G**	**P**	**C**	**G**	**P**	**C**	**G**	**Scheduled process**
0	60	0	0													P_1
1	120	30	30													P_1
2	150	45	45	105	0	45										P_2
3	134	22	52	142	30	52	60	0	0							P_3
4	97	11	26	101	15	26	120	30	30	86	0	26				P_4
5	108	5	43	110	7	43	90	15	15	133	30	43				P_3
6	83	2	21	84	3	21	134	37	37	96	15	21				P_1
7				101	1	40	96	18	18	107	7	40				P_3
8				80	0	20	138	39	39	83	3	20	80	0	20	P_5
9				100	0	40	98	19	19	101	1	40	130	30	40	P_3
10				80	0	20	138	39	39	80	0	20	95	15	20	P_2
11				130	30	40	98	19	19	100	0	40	107	7	40	P_3
12				95	15	20				80	0	20	83	3	20	P_4
13				107	7	40							101	1	40	P_5
14				113	3	50							110	0	50	P_5
15				116	1	55										P_2
16																

Fair Share Scheduling To ensure a fair share of CPU time to groups of processes, Unix schedulers add the term f (CPU time used by processes in the group) to Eq. (7.5). Thus, priorities of all processes in a group reduce when any of them consumes CPU time. This feature ensures that processes of a group would receive favored treatment if none of them has consumed much CPU time recently. The effect of the new factor also decays over time.

Fair Share Scheduling in Unix

Example 7.14

Table 7.6 depicts fair share scheduling of the processes of Table 7.2. Fields P, T, and G contain process priority, CPU time consumed by a process, and CPU time consumed by a group of processes, respectively. Two process groups exist. The first group contains processes P_1, P_2, P_4, and P_5, while the second group contains process P_3 all by itself.

At 2 seconds, process P_2 has just arrived. Its effective priority is low because process P_1, which is in the same group, has executed for 2 seconds. However, P_3 does not have a low priority when it arrives because the CPU time already consumed by its group is 0. As expected, process P_3 receives a favored treatment compared to other processes. In fact, it receives every alternate time slice. Processes P_2, P_4, and P_5 suffer because they belong to the same process group. These facts are reflected in the turnaround times and weighted turnarounds of the processes, which are as follows:

Process	P_1	P_2	P_3	P_4	P_5
Completion time	7	16	12	13	15
Turnaround time	7	14	9	9	7
Weighted turnaround	2.33	4.67	1.80	4.50	2.33

Mean turnaround time ($\overline{ta}$) = 9.2 seconds
Mean weighted turnaround ($\bar{w}$) = 3.15

7.6.2 Scheduling in Solaris

Solaris supports four classes of processes—time-sharing processes, interactive processes, system processes, and real-time processes. A time slice is called a *time quantum* in Solaris terminology. Time-sharing and interactive processes have priorities between 0 and 59, where a larger number implies a higher priority. System processes have priorities between 60 and 99; they are not time-sliced. Real-time processes have priorities between 100 and 159 and are scheduled by a round-robin policy within a priority level. Threads used for interrupt servicing have priorities between 160 and 169.

Scheduling of time-sharing and interactive processes is governed by a dispatch table. For each priority level, the table specifies how the priority of a process should change to suit its nature, whether CPU-bound or I/O-bound, and also to prevent starvation. Use of the table, rather than a priority computation rule as in Unix, provides fine-grained tuning possibilities to the system administrator. The dispatch table entry for each priority level contains the following values:

- `ts_quantum` The time quantum for processes of this priority level
- `ts_tqexp` The new priority of a process that uses its entire time quantum
- `ts_slpret` The new priority of a process that blocks before using its complete time quantum
- `ts_maxwait` The maximum amount of time for which a process can be allowed to wait without getting scheduled
- `ts_lwait` The new priority of a process that does not get scheduled within `ts_maxwait` time

A process that blocks before its time quantum elapses is assumed to be an I/O-bound process; its priority is changed to `ts_slpret`, which is a higher priority than its present priority. Analogously, a process that uses its entire time quantum is assumed to be a CPU-bound process, so `ts_tqexp` is a lower priority. `ts_maxwait` is used to avoid starvation, hence `ts_lwait` is a higher priority. In addition to these changes in priority effected by the kernel, a process can change its own priority through the *nice* system call with a number in the range −19 to 19 as a parameter.

Solaris 9 also supports a fair share scheduling class. A group of processes is called a project and is assigned a few shares of CPU time. The fair share of a project at any time depends on the shares of other projects that are active concurrently; it is the quotient of the shares of the project and the sum of the shares of all those projects that have at least one process active. In multiprocessor systems, shares are defined independently for each CPU. Solaris 10 added the notion of *zones* on top of projects. CPU shares are now assigned for both zones and projects to provide two-level scheduling.

7.6.3 Scheduling in Linux

Linux supports both real-time and non-real-time applications. Accordingly, it has two classes of processes. The real-time processes have static priorities between 0 and 100, where 0 is the highest priority. Real-time processes can be scheduled in two ways: FIFO or round-robin within each priority level. The kernel associates a flag with each process to indicate how it should be scheduled.

Non-real-time processes have lower priorities than all real-time processes; their priorities are dynamic and have numerical values between −20 and 19, where −20 is the highest priority. Effectively, the kernel has (100 + 40) priority levels. To start with, each non-real-time process has the priority 0. The priority can be varied by the process itself through the *nice* or *setpriority* system calls. However, special privileges are needed to increase the priority through the *nice* system call, so processes typically use this call to lower their priorities when they wish to be nice to other processes. In addition to such priority variation, the kernel varies the priority of a process to reflect its I/O-bound or CPU-bound nature. To implement this, the kernel maintains information about how much CPU time the process has used recently and for how long it was in the *blocked* state, and adds a bonus between 5 and −5 to the nice value of the process. Thus, a highly interactive process would have an effective priority of nice−5, while a CPU-bound process would have an effective priority of nice+5.

Because of the multilevel priority structure, the Linux kernel organizes its scheduling data as shown in Figure 7.12 of Section 7.4.3. To limit the scheduling overhead, Linux uses a scheduler schematic analogous to Figure 5.9. Thus, scheduling is not performed after every event handling action. It is performed when the currently executing process has to block due to a system call, or when the `need_resched` flag has been set by an event handling action. This is done while handling expiry of the time slice, or while handling an event that activates a process whose priority is higher than that of the currently executing process.

Non-real-time processes are scheduled by using the notion of a time slice; however, the Linux notion of a time slice is actually a time quantum that a process can use over a period of time in accordance with its priority (see Section 7.4.8). A process that exhausts its time slice would receive a new time slice only after all processes have exhausted their time slices. Linux uses time slices in the range of 10 to 200 ms. To ensure that a higher-priority process would receive more CPU attention than a lower-priority process, Linux assigns a larger time slice to a higher-priority process. This assignment of time slices does not affect response times because a high-priority process would be interactive in nature, hence it would perform an I/O operation before using much CPU time.

The Linux scheduler uses two lists of processes, an *active list* and an *exhausted list*. Both lists are ordered by priorities of processes and use the data structure described earlier. The scheduler schedules a process from the active list, which uses time from its time slice. When its time slice is exhausted, it is put into the exhausted list. Schedulers in Linux kernel 2.5 and earlier kernels executed a priority recomputation loop when the active list became empty. The loop computed a new time slice for each process based on its dynamic priority. At the end of the loop, all processes were transferred to the active list and normal scheduling operation was resumed.

The Linux 2.6 kernel uses a new scheduler that incurs less overhead and scales better with the number of processes and CPUs. The scheduler spreads the priority recomputation overhead throughout the scheduler's operation, rather than lump it in the recomputation loop. It achieves this by recomputing the priority of a process when the process exhausts its time slice and gets moved to the exhausted list. When the active list becomes empty, the scheduler merely interchanges the active and exhausted lists.

The scalability of the scheduler is ensured in two ways. The scheduler has a bit flag to indicate whether the list of processes for a priority level is empty. When invoked, the scheduler tests the flags of the process lists in the order of reducing priority, and selects the first process in the first nonempty process list it finds. This procedure incurs a scheduling overhead that does not depend on the number of ready processes; it depends only on the number of scheduling levels, hence it is bound by a constant. This scheduling is called $O(1)$, i.e., order 1, scheduling. Schedulers in older Linux kernels used a synchronization lock on the active list of processes to avoid race conditions when many CPUs were supported. The Linux 2.6 kernel maintains active lists on a per-CPU basis, which eliminates the synchronization lock and associated delays. This arrangement also ensures that a process operates on the same CPU every time it is scheduled; it helps to ensure better cache hit ratios.

7.6.4 Scheduling in Windows

Windows scheduling aims at providing good response times to real-time and interactive threads. Scheduling is priority-driven and preemptive. Scheduling within a priority level is performed through a round-robin policy with time-slicing. A time slice is called a *quantum* in Windows terminology. Priorities of non-real-time threads are dynamically varied to favor interactive threads. This aspect is analogous to multilevel adaptive scheduling (see Section 7.4.5).

Real-time threads are given higher priorities than other threads—they have priorities in the range 16–31, while other threads have priorities in the range 1–15. Priorities of non-real-time threads can vary during their lifetime, hence this class of threads is also called the *variable priority class*. The effective priority of a thread in this class at any moment is a combination of three factors—the base priority of the process to which the thread belongs; the base priority of the thread, which is in the range −2 to 2; and a dynamic component assigned by the kernel to favor interactive threads.

The kernel varies a thread's dynamic component of priority as follows: If the thread uses up its complete time slice when scheduled, its priority is reduced by 1. When a *waiting*, i.e., blocked, thread is activated, it is given a priority increase based on the nature of the event on which it was blocked. If it was blocked on input from the keyboard, its priority is boosted by 6. To deny an unfair advantage to an I/O-bound thread, the remaining time of its current quantum is reduced by one clock tick every time it makes an I/O request. To guard against starvation, the priority of a *ready* thread that has not received CPU time for more than 4 seconds is raised to 15 and its quantum is increased to twice its normal value. When this quantum expires, its priority and quantum revert back to their old values.

The scheduler uses a data structure resembling that shown in Figure 7.12, except for two refinements that provide efficiency. Since priority values lie in the range 0–31, with priority 0 reserved for a system thread, an array of 32 pointers is used to point at the queues of ready threads at different priority levels. A vector of 32 bit flags is used to indicate whether a ready thread exists at each of the priority levels. This arrangement enables the scheduler to speedily locate the first thread in the highest-priority nonempty queue. When none of the system or user threads is in the *ready* state, the scheduler schedules a special *idle thread* on the CPU that continually executes an *idle loop* until a thread is scheduled on it. In the loop, it activates functions in the hardware abstraction layer (HAL) at appropriate times to perform power management. In a multiprocessor system, the scheduler operating on one CPU may schedule a thread on another CPU that is idle (see Section 10.6.3). To facilitate such scheduling, the idle loop also examines the scheduling data structures to check whether a thread has been scheduled on the CPU that is executing the idle loop, and switches the CPU to the scheduled thread if this is the case.

To conserve power when the computer is idle, Windows provides a number of system states wherein the computer operates in a mode that consumes low power. In the *hibernate* state, the states of running applications are stored on the disk and the system is turned off. When the system is activated, application states are restored from the disk before operation is resumed. Use of the disk to store application states leads to slow resumption; however, it provides reliability because operation of the computer is immune to loss or depletion of power while the computer is in hibernation. In the *standby* state, states of running applications are saved in memory, and the computer enters a low-power mode of operation. Resumption using the application states stored in memory is faster. However, the state information would be lost if power is lost or depleted while the system is in the *standby* state, so computer operation is not reliable. Hence Windows Vista introduced a new hybrid state called the *sleep* state wherein the application states are stored both in memory and on the disk. System operation is resumed as in the *standby* state if application states are available in memory; otherwise, it is resumed as in the *hibernate* state using the application states stored on the disk.

7.7 PERFORMANCE ANALYSIS OF SCHEDULING POLICIES

Performance analysis of a scheduling policy is a study of its performance, using measures such as response time of a process, efficiency of use of the CPU, and throughput of the system. Performance analysis can be used to compare performance of alternative scheduling policies, and to determine "good" values of key system parameters like the time slice, number of active users, and the size of the list of *ready* processes.

Performance of a scheduling policy is sensitive to the nature of requests directed at it, and so performance analysis should be conducted in the environment in which the policy is to be put into effect. The set of requests directed at a scheduling policy is called its *workload*. The first step in performance analysis of a policy is to accurately characterize its typical workload. In the following, we discuss some issues involved in this step.

As mentioned in Section 7.2 in the context of the SRN policy, user estimates of service times are not reliable either because users lack the experience to provide good estimates of service time or because knowledgeable users may provide misleading estimates to obtain a favored treatment from the system. Some users may even resort to changes in their requests to obtain better service; for instance, a user who knows that the SRN policy is being used may split a long-running program into several programs with short service times. All these factors distort the workload. Hence the characterization of a typical workload should be developed without involving the users.

Three approaches could be used for performance analysis of scheduling policies:

- Implementation of a scheduling policy in an OS
- Simulation
- Mathematical modeling

Both simulation and mathematical modeling avoid the need for implementing a scheduling policy in an OS, thereby avoiding the cost, complexity, and delays involved in implementing the policy. However, to produce the same results as an implementation, these approaches require a very detailed characterization of requests in the workload, which is generally not feasible in practice. Hence, performance aspects like the scheduling overhead or service to individual requests are best studied through implementation, whereas simulation and mathematical modeling are well suited for studying performance of a scheduling policy and for determining "good" values of system parameters like the time slice, number of users, or the size of the list of *ready* processes.

7.7.1 Performance Analysis through Implementation

The scheduling policy to be evaluated is implemented in a real operating system that is used in the target operating environment. The OS receives real user

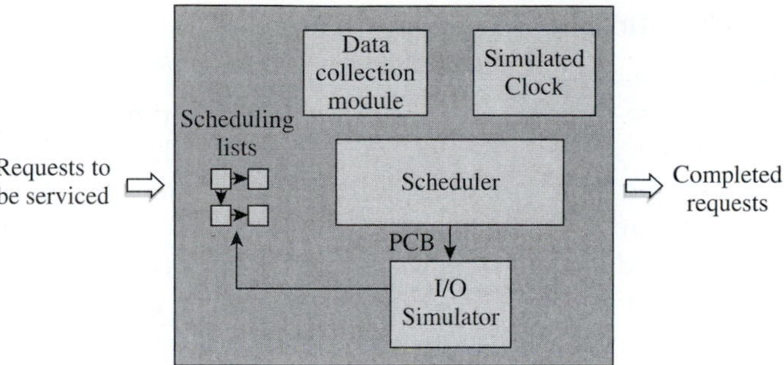

Figure 7.15 Simulation of a scheduling policy.

requests; services them using the scheduling policy; and collects data for statistical analysis of the policy's performance. This approach to performance analysis is disruptive, because a real OS has to be decommissioned, modified, and recommissioned for every scheduling policy that is to be analyzed. This disruption could be avoided by using virtual machine software, which permits a guest kernel to be modified without affecting operation of the host kernel; however, the overhead introduced by use of the virtual machine would cause inaccuracies in the performance measurement.

7.7.2 Simulation

Simulation is achieved by coding the scheduling policy and relevant OS functions as a program—the *simulator* program—and using a typical workload as its input. The workload is a recording of some real workload directed at the OS during a sample period. Analysis may be repeated with many workloads to eliminate the effect of variations across workloads.

Figure 7.15 shows a schematic of a simulator. The simulator operates as follows: It maintains the data structures that are used by the simulated scheduling policy, in which it puts information concerning user requests as they arrive in the system, get admitted, and receive service. It also maintains a clock to keep track of the *simulated time*. From time to time, it mimics the scheduling action and selects a request for processing. It estimates the length of time for which the request would use the CPU before an event like the initiation of an I/O operation or completion of a request, occurs. It now advances the simulated clock by the amount of time for which the request would have used the CPU before the event occurred, and moves the request out of the scheduling queue. It then performs scheduling once again, and so on. It may contain other modules like an I/O simulator module which would predict when the I/O operation initiated by a request would complete. When the simulated clock shows this time, it adds the request to a scheduling queue. The data collection module collects useful data for performance analysis. The level of detail handled in a simulator governs the cost of simulation and the quality of its results.

7.7.3 Mathematical Modeling

A *mathematical model* consists of two components—a model of the server and a model of the workload being processed. The model provides a set of mathematical expressions for important performance characteristics like service times of requests and overhead. These expressions provide insights into the influence of various parameters on system performance. The workload model differs from workloads used in simulations in that it is not a recording of actual workload in any specific time period. It is a statistical *distribution* that represents the workload; that is, it is a function that generates fictitious requests that have the same statistical properties as the actual workload during *any* period.

Queuing Theory Widespread use of mathematical models to analyze performance of various systems led to development of a separate branch of mathematics known as *queuing theory*. Performance analysis using queuing theory is called queuing analysis. The earliest well-known application of queuing analysis was by Erlang (1909) in evaluating the performance of a telephone exchange with the number of trunk lines as the controlling parameter.

The fundamental queuing theory model of a system is identical with the simple scheduler model discussed at the start of this Chapter (see Figure 7.1). This is known as the *single-server model*. Queuing analysis is used to develop mathematical expressions for server efficiency, mean queue length, and mean wait time.

A request arriving at time a_i with service time x_i is completed at time c_i. The elapsed time $(c_i - a_i)$ depends on two factors—arrival times and service times of requests that are either in execution or in the scheduling queue at some time during the interval $(c_i - a_i)$, and the scheduling policy used by the server. It is reasonable to assume that arrival times and service times of requests entering the system are not known in advance; i.e., these characteristics of requests are nondeterministic in nature.

Although characteristics of individual requests are unknown, they are customarily assumed to conform to certain statistical distributions. A computing environment is thus characterized by two parameters—a statistical distribution governing arrival times of requests, and a statistical distribution governing their service times. We give a brief introduction to statistical distributions and their use in mathematical modeling, using the following notation:

α Mean arrival rate (requests per second)
ω Mean execution rate (requests per second)
ρ α/ω

ρ is called the *utilization factor* of the server. When $\rho > 1$, the work being directed at the system exceeds its capacity. In this case, the number of requests in the system increases indefinitely. Performance evaluation of such a system is of little practical relevance since turnaround times can be arbitrarily large. When $\rho < 1$, the system capacity exceeds the total work directed at it. However, this is true only as a long-term average; it may not hold in an arbitrary interval of time.

Hence the server may be idle once in a while, and a few requests may exist in the queue at certain times.

Most practical systems satisfy $\rho < 1$. Even when we consider a slow server, ρ does not exceed 1 because most practical systems are self-regulatory in nature—the number of users is finite and the arrival rate of requests slackens when the queue length is large because most users' requests are locked up in the queue!

A system reaches a *steady state* when all transients in the system induced due to its abrupt initiation at time $t = 0$ die down. In the steady state, values of mean queue lengths, mean wait times, mean turnaround times, etc., reflect performance of the scheduling policy. For obtaining these values, we start by assuming certain distributions for arrival and servicing of requests in the system.

Arrival Times The time between arrival of two consecutive requests is called *interarrival time*. Since α is the arrival rate, the mean interarrival time is $1/\alpha$. A statistical distribution that has this mean interarrival time and that fits empirical data reasonably well can be used for workload characterization. Arrival of requests in the system can be regarded as random events totally independent of each other. Two assumptions leading to a Poisson distribution of arrivals are now made. First, the number of arrivals in an interval t to $t + dt$ is assumed to depend only on the value of dt and not on past history of the system during the interval $(0, t)$. Second, for small values of dt, probability of more than one arrival in the interval t to $(t + dt)$ is assumed to be negligible. The first assumption is known as the *memoryless property* of the arrival times distribution. An exponential distribution function giving the probability of an arrival in the interval 0 to t for any t has the form:

$$F(t) = 1 - e^{-\alpha.t}$$

This distribution has the mean interarrival time $1/\alpha$ since $\int_0^\infty t.dF(t) = 1/\alpha$. It is found that the exponential distribution fits the interarrival times in empirical data reasonably well. (However, a hyperexponential distribution with the same mean of $1/\alpha$ is found to be a better approximation for the experimental data (Coffman and Wood [1966]).

Service Times The function $S(t)$ gives the probability that the service time of a request is less than or equal to t.

$$S(t) = 1 - e^{-\omega.t}$$

As in the case of arrival times, we make two assumptions that lead to a Poisson distribution of service times. Hence the probability that a request that has already consumed t units of service time will terminate in the next dt seconds depends only on the value of dt and not on t. In preemptive scheduling, it applies every time a request is scheduled to run after an interruption.

The memoryless property of service times implies that a scheduling algorithm cannot make any predictions based on past history of a request in the system. Thus, any preemptive scheduling policy that requires knowledge of future behavior of requests must depend on estimates of service times supplied by a programmer. The scheduling performance will then critically depend on user inputs and may be manipulated by users. In a practical situation, a system must strive to achieve the opposite effect—that is, system performance should be immune to user specification (or misspecification) of the service time of a request. This requirement points toward round-robin scheduling with time-slicing as a practical scheduling policy.

Performance Analysis The relation between L, the mean queue length and W, the mean wait time for a request before its servicing begins is given by Little's formula,

$$L = \alpha \times W \tag{7.6}$$

This relation follows from the fact that while a request waits in the queue, $\alpha \times W$ new requests join the queue.

When a new request arrives, it is added to the request queue. In nonpreemptive scheduling, the new request would be considered only after the server completes the request it is servicing. Let W_0 be the expected time to complete the current request. Natually, W_0 is independent of a scheduling policy. $W_0 = \frac{\alpha}{2} \cdot \int_0^\infty t^2 dF(t)$, and has the value $\frac{\alpha}{\omega^2}$ for an exponential distribution $F(t) = 1 - e^{-\alpha . t}$. W, the mean wait time for a request when a specific scheduling policy is used, is computed from W_0 and features of the scheduling policy. We outline how the mean wait times for FCFS and SRN policies are derived. Derivations for HRN and round-robin policies are more complex and can be found in Brinch Hansen (1973). Table 7.7 summarizes the mean wait time for a request whose service time is t when different scheduling policies are used.

W, the waiting time for some request r', is the amount of time r' spends in the queue before its service begins. Hence in FCFS scheduling

$$W = W_0 + \Sigma_i x_i$$

Table 7.7 Summary of Performance Analysis

Scheduling policy	Mean wait time for a request with service time = t
FCFS	$\frac{W_0}{1-\rho}$
SRN	$\frac{W_0}{1-\rho_t}$, where $\rho_t = \int_o^t \alpha \cdot y \cdot dS(y)$
HRN	For small t: $W_0 + \frac{\rho^2}{1-\rho} \times \frac{t}{2}$
	For large t: $\frac{W_0}{(1-\rho)(1-\rho+\frac{2.W_0}{t})}$
Round-robin	$\frac{n}{\omega(1-P_0)} - \frac{1}{\alpha}$, where $P_0 = \frac{1}{\Sigma_{j=0}^{n} \frac{n!}{(n-j)!} \times (\alpha)^j}$
	(P_0 is the probability that no terminal awaits a response)

Note: $W_0 = \frac{\alpha}{2} \cdot \int_0^\infty t^2 dF(t)$. For an exponential distribution $F(t) = 1 - e^{-\alpha . t}$, it is $\frac{\alpha}{\omega^2}$.

where request i is ahead of request r' in the scheduling queue. Since the system is in the steady state, we can replace the Σ_i term by $n \times \frac{1}{\omega}$, where n is the number of requests ahead of r' and $\frac{1}{\omega}$ is the mean service time. Since n is the mean queue length, $n = \alpha \times W$ from Little's formula. Hence

$$W = W_0 + \alpha \times W \times \frac{1}{\omega}$$
$$= W_0 + \rho \times W.$$

Therefore, $W = \frac{W_0}{1-\rho}$. Thus, the mean wait time in FCFS scheduling rises sharply for high values of ρ.

In SRN scheduling, requests whose service times $< x_{r'}$, where $x_{r'}$ is the service time of r', are serviced before request r'. Hence the waiting time for request r' is

$$W = W_0 + \Sigma_i \, x_i, \text{ where } x_i < x_{r'}$$
$$= \frac{W_0}{1-\rho_{r'}}, \text{ where } \rho_{r'} = \int_0^{r'} \alpha \cdot y \cdot dS(y).$$

Capacity Planning Performance analysis can be used for capacity planning. For example, the formulae shown in Table 7.7 can be used to determine values of important parameters like the size of the list of *ready* processes used by the kernel.

As an example, consider an OS in which the mean arrival rate of requests is 5 requests per second, and the mean response time for requests is 3 seconds. The mean queue length is computed by Little's formula [Eq. (7.6)] as $5 \times 3 = 15$. Note that queues will exceed this length from time to time. The following example provides a basis for deciding the capacity of the ready queue.

Capacity Planning Using Queuing Analysis **Example 7.15**

A kernel permits up to n entries in the queue of *ready* requests. If the queue is full when a new request arrives, the request is rejected and leaves the OS. p_i, the probability that the ready queue contains i processes at any time, can be shown to be:

$$p_i = \frac{\rho^i \times (1-\rho)}{1-\rho^{n+1}} \tag{7.7}$$

For $\rho = 0.5$ and $n = 3, p_0 = \frac{8}{15}, p_1 = \frac{4}{15}, p_2 = \frac{2}{15}$, and $p_3 = \frac{1}{15}$. Hence 6.7 percent of requests are lost. A higher value of n should be used to reduce the number of lost requests.

7.8 SUMMARY

The scheduler of an OS decides which process should be serviced next by the CPU and for how long it should be serviced. Its decisions influence both user service and system performance. In this chapter, we discussed three techniques of process schedulers: *priority-based scheduling, reordering of requests, and variation of time slice;* and studied how schedulers use them to provide a desired combination of user service and system performance. We also studied real-time scheduling.

A nonpreemptive scheduling policy performs scheduling only when the process being serviced by the CPU completes; the policy focuses merely on reordering of requests to improve mean turnaround time of processes. The *shortest request next* (SRN) policy suffers from starvation, as some processes may be delayed indefinitely. The *highest response ratio next* (HRN) policy does not have this problem because the response ratio of a process keeps increasing as it waits for the CPU.

Preemptive scheduling policies preempt a process when it is considered desirable to make a fresh scheduling decision. The *round-robin* (RR) policy services all processes by turn, limiting the amount of CPU time used by each process to the value of the time slice. The *least completed next* (LCN) policy selects the process that has received the least amount of service, whereas the *shortest time to go* (STG) policy selects the process that is closest to completing.

In practice, an operating system uses an arrangement involving three schedulers. The *long-term scheduler* decides when a process should be admitted for servicing, whereas the *medium-term scheduler* decides when a process should be swapped out to a disk and when it should be reloaded in memory. The *short-term scheduler* selects one of the processes that is present in memory. The *multilevel adaptive* scheduling policy assigns different values of time slice to processes with different priorities and varies a process's priority in accordance with its recent behavior to provide a combination of good response time and low scheduling overhead. The *fair share* scheduling policy ensures that processes of an application collectively do not exceed a specified share of the CPU time.

Real-time scheduling focuses on meeting the time constraints of applications. *Deadline scheduling* considers deadlines of processes while performing scheduling decisions. *Rate monotonic* scheduling assigns priorities to processes based on their periods and performs priority-based scheduling.

Modern operating systems face diverse workloads, so schedulers divide processes into different classes such as real-time and non-real-time, and use an appropriate scheduling policy for each class.

Performance analysis is used to both study and tune performance of scheduling policies without implementing them in an OS. It uses a mathematical characterization of the typical workload in a system to determine system throughput or values of key scheduler parameters such as the time slice and sizes of scheduling lists.

TEST YOUR CONCEPTS

7.1 Classify each of the following statements as true or false:

a. If the scheduling overhead is negligible, the schedule length is identical in batch processing and multiprogramming systems.

b. If all requests arrive at the same time instant in a system using the shortest request next (SRN) scheduling policy and the system completes execution of these requests in the sequence $r_1, r_2, \ldots, r_n$, then weighted turnaround of $r_i >$ weighted turnaround of r_j if $i > j$.

c. The round-robin scheduling policy with time-slicing provides approximately equal response ratios to requests that arrive at the same time instant.

d. If processes do not perform I/O, the round-robin scheduling policy with time-slicing resembles the least completed next (LCN) scheduling policy.

e. When both CPU-bound and I/O-bound requests are present, the least completed next (LCN) scheduling policy provides better turnaround times for I/O-bound requests than provided by the round-robin scheduling policy with time-slicing.

f. The highest response ratio next (HRN) scheduling policy avoids starvation.

g. If a feasible schedule exists for a real-time application, use of the earliest deadline first (EDF) scheduling policy guarantees that no deadline overruns will occur.

h. An I/O-bound process is executed twice, once in a system using RR scheduling and again in a system using multilevel adaptive scheduling. The number of times it is scheduled by the RR scheduler and by the multilevel scheduler is identical.

i. A CPU-bound process cannot starve when multilevel adaptive scheduling is employed.

j. If processes do not perform I/O, the Unix scheduling policy degenerates to the RR scheduling policy.

7.2 Processes A, B, and C arrive at times 0, 1, and 2, respectively. The processes do not perform I/O and require 5, 3, and 1 second of CPU time. The process-switching time is negligible. At what time does process B complete if the scheduler uses the shortest time to go (STG) policy.

a. 8, **b.** 4, **c.** 5, **d.** 9.

7.3 Which of the following scheduling policies will provide the least turnaround time for an I/O-bound process? (Both I/O-bound and CPU-bound requests are present in the system.)

a. RR,
b. LCN,
c. multilevel adaptive scheduling,
d. None of these.

7.4 Which of the following scheduling policies will provide the least turnaround time for a CPU-bound process? (Both I/O-bound and CPU-bound requests are present in the system.)

a. RR,
b. LCN,
c. multilevel adaptive scheduling.

EXERCISES

7.1 Give examples of conflicts between user-centric and system-centric views of scheduling.

7.2 Study the performance of the nonpreemptive and preemptive scheduling policies on processes described in Table 7.2 if their arrival times are 0, 1, 3, 7, and 10 seconds, respectively. Draw timing charts analogous to those in Sections 7.2 and 7.3 to show operation of these policies.

7.3 Show that SRN scheduling provides the minimum average turnaround time for a set of requests that arrive at the same time instant. Would it provide the minimum average turnaround time if requests arrive at different times?

7.4 A program contains a single loop that executes 50 times. The loop includes a computation that lasts 50 ms followed by an I/O operation that consumes 200 ms. Ten independent executions of this program are started at the same time. The scheduling overhead of the kernel is 3 ms. Compute the response time of the first process in the first and subsequent iterations if

a. The time slice is 50 ms.
b. The time slice is 20 ms.

7.5 The kernel of an OS implements the HRN policy preemptively as follows: Every t seconds, response ratios of all processes are computed and the process with the highest response ratio is scheduled. Comment on this policy for large and small values of t. Also, compare it with the following policies

a. Shortest time to go (STG) policy.
b. Least completed next (LCN) policy.
c. Round-robin policy with time-slicing (RR).

7.6 A process consists of two parts that are functionally independent of one another. It is proposed to separate the two parts and create two processes to service them. Identify those scheduling policies under which the user would receive better user service through use of the two processes instead of the original single process.

7.7 For each of the scheduling policies discussed in Sections 7.2 and 7.3, a group of 20 requests is serviced with negligible overheads and the average turnaround time is determined. The requests are now organized arbitrarily into two groups of 10 requests each. These groups of requests are now serviced one after another through each of the scheduling policies used earlier and the average turnaround time is computed. Compare the two average turnaround times for each scheduling policy and mention conditions under which the two could be different.

7.8 A multilevel adaptive scheduler uses five priority levels numbered from 1 to 5, level 1 being the highest priority level. The time slice for a priority level is $0.1 \times n$, where n is the level number. It puts every process in level 1 initially. A process requiring 5 seconds of CPU time is serviced through this scheduler. Compare the response time of the process and the total scheduling overhead incurred if there are no other processes in the system. If the process is serviced through a round-robin scheduler using a time slice of 0.1 CPU seconds, what would be the response time of the process and the total scheduling overhead incurred?

7.9 A multilevel adaptive scheduling policy avoids starvation by promoting a process to a higher priority level if it has spent 3 seconds in its present priority level without getting scheduled. Comment on the advantages and disadvantages of the following methods of implementing promotion:

a. Promote a process to the highest priority level.

b. Promote a process to the next higher priority level.

7.10 The Houston Automatic Spooling system (HASP) was a scheduling subsystem used in the IBM/360. HASP assigned high priority to I/O-bound processes and low priority to CPU-bound processes. A process was classified as CPU-bound or I/O-bound based on its recent behavior vis-a-vis the time slice—it was considered to be a CPU-bound process if it used up its entire time-slice when scheduled; otherwise, it was an I/O-bound process. To obtain good throughput, HASP required that a fixed percentage of processes in the scheduling queue must be I/O-bound processes. Periodically, HASP adjusted the time slice to satisfy this requirement—the time slice was reduced if more processes were considered I/O-bound than desired, and it was increased if lesser number of processes were I/O-bound. Explain the purpose of adjusting the time slice. Describe operation of HASP if most processes in the system were (a) CPU-bound and (b) I/O-bound.

7.11 Comment on the similarities and differences between

a. LCN and Unix scheduling

b. HASP and multilevel adaptive scheduling (see Exercise 7.10).

7.12 Determine the starting deadlines for the processes of Example 7.11.

7.13 An OS using a preemptive scheduling policy assigns dynamically changing priorities. The priority of a process changes at different rates depending on its state as follows

α Rate of change of priority when a process is *running*

β Rate of change of priority when a process is *ready*

γ Rate of change of priority when a process is performing I/O

Note that the rate of change of priority can be positive, negative, or zero. A process has priority 0 when it is created. A process with a larger numerical value of priority is considered to have a higher priority for scheduling.

Comment on properties of the scheduling policies in each of the following cases:

a. $\alpha > 0, \beta = 0, \gamma = 0$.

b. $\alpha = 0, \beta > 0, \gamma = 0$.

c. $\alpha = \beta = 0, \gamma > 0$.

d. $\alpha < 0, \beta = 0, \gamma = 0$.

Will the behavior of the scheduling policies change if the priority of a process is set to 0 every time it is scheduled?

7.14 A *background* process should operate in such a manner that it does not significantly degrade the service provided to other processes. Which of the following alternatives would you recommend for implementing it?

a. Assign the lowest priority to a background process.

b. Provide a smaller quantum to a background process than to other processes (see Section 7.4.8).

7.15 Prepare a schedule for operation of the periodic processes P_1–P_3 of Section 7.5.3, using EDF scheduling.

7.16 If the response requirement of the application of Figure 7.13 is 30 seconds and service times of processes P_2–P_5 are as shown in Figure 7.13, what is the largest service time of P_1 for which a feasible schedule exists? Answer this question under two conditions:

a. None of the processes perform any I/O operations.

b. Process P_2 performs I/O for 3 seconds, 2 seconds of which can be overlapped with the processing of process P_3.

7.17 The service times of three processes P_1, P_2, and P_3 are 5 ms, 3 ms, and 10 ms, respectively; $T_1 =$ 25 ms and $T_2 = 8$ ms. What is the smallest value of T_3 for which the rate monotonic scheduling policy will be able to meet deadlines of all processes?

7.18 A system uses the FCFS scheduling policy. Identical computational requests arrive in the system at the rate of 20 requests per second. It is desired that the mean wait time in the system should not exceed 2.0 seconds. Compute the size of each request in CPU seconds.

7.19 Identical requests, each requiring 0.05 CPU seconds, arrive in an OS at the rate of 10 requests per second. The kernel uses a fixed-size ready queue. A new request is entered in the ready queue if the queue is not already full, else the request is discarded. What should be the size of the ready queue if less than 1 percent of requests should be discarded?

7.20 The mean arrival rate of requests in a system using FCFS scheduling is 5 requests per second. The mean wait time for a request is 3 seconds. Find the mean execution rate.

7.21 We define "small request" as a request whose service time is less than 5 percent of $\frac{1}{\omega}$. Compute the turnaround time for a small request in a system using the HRN scheduling policy when $\alpha = 5$ and $\omega = 8$.

BIBLIOGRAPHY

Corbato et al. (1962) discusses use of multilevel feedback queues in the CTSS operating system. Coffman and Denning (1973) reports studies related to multilevel scheduling. A fair share scheduler is described in Kay and Lauder (1988), and lottery scheduling is described in Waldspurger and Weihl (1994). Real-time scheduling is discussed in Liu and Layland (1973), Zhao (1989), Khanna et al. (1992), and Liu (2000). Power conservation is a crucial new element in scheduling. Power can be conserved by running the CPU at lower speeds. Zhu et al. (2004) discusses speculative scheduling algorithms that save power by varying the CPU speed and reducing the number of speed changes while ensuring that an application meets its time constraints.

Bach (1986), McKusick et al. (1996), and Vahalia (1996) discuss scheduling in Unix; O'Gorman (2003), Bovet and Cesati (2005), and Love (2005) discuss scheduling in Linux; Mauro and McDougall (2006) discusses scheduling in Solaris; while Russinovich and Solomon (2005) discusses scheduling in Windows.

Trivedi (1982) is devoted to queuing theory. Hellerman and Conroy (1975) describes use of queuing theory in performance evaluation.

1. Bach, M. J. (1986): *The Design of the Unix Operating System*, Prentice Hall, Englewood Cliffs, N.J.
2. Bovet, D. P., and M. Cesati (2005): *Understanding the Linux Kernel,* 3rd ed., O'Reilly, Sebastopol.
3. Brinch Hansen, P. (1972): *Operating System Principles*, Prentice Hall, Englewood Cliffs, N.J.

4. Coffman, E. G., and R. C. Wood (1996): "Interarrival statistics for time sharing systems," *Communications of the ACM*, **9** (7), 500–503.

5. Coffman, E. G., and P. J. Denning (1973): *Operating Systems Theory*, Prentice Hall, Englewood Cliffs, N.J.

6. Corbato, F. J., M. Merwin-Daggett, and R. C. Daley (1962): "An experimental time-sharing system," *Proceedings of the AFIPS Fall Joint Computer Conference*, 335–344.

7. Hellerman, H., and T. F. Conroy (1975): *Computer System Performance*, McGraw-Hill Kogakusha, Tokyo.

8. Kay, J., and P. Lauder (1988): "A fair share scheduler," *Communications of the ACM*, **31** (1), 44–55.

9. Khanna, S., M. Sebree, and J. Zolnowsky (1992): "Real-time scheduling in SunOS 5.0," *Proceedings of the Winter 1992 USENIX Conference*, San Francisco, January 1992, 375–390.

10. Love, R. (2005): *Linux Kernel Development,* 2nd ed., Novell Press.

11. Liu, C. L., and J. W. Layland (1973): "Scheduling algorithms for multiprogramming in a hard real-time environment," *Journal of the ACM*, **20**, 1, 46–61.

12. Liu, J. W. S. (2000): *Real-Time Systems*, Pearson Education, New York.

13. Mauro, J., and R. McDougall (2006): *Solaris Internals,* 2nd ed., Prentice Hall, Englewood Cliffs, N.J.

14. McKusick, M. K., K. Bostic, M. J. Karels, and J. S. Quarterman (1996): *The Design and Implementation of the 4.4BSD Operating System*, Addison-Wesley, Reading, Mass.

15. O'Gorman, J. (2003): *Linux Process Manager: The Internals of Scheduling, Interrupts and Signals*, John Wiley, New York.

16. Russinovich, M. E., and D. A. Solomon (2005): *Microsoft Windows Internals,* 4th ed., Microsoft Press, Redmond, Wash.

17. Trivedi, K. S. (1982): *Probability and Statistics with Reliability—Queuing and Computer Science Applications*, Prentice Hall, Englewood Cliffs, N.J.

18. Vahalia, U. (1996): *Unix Internals: The New Frontiers*, Prentice Hall, Englewood Cliffs, N.J.

19. Waldspurger, C. A., and W. E. Weihl (1994): "Lottery scheduling," *Proceedings of the First USENIX Symposium on Operating System Design and Implementation (OSDI)*, 1–11.

20. Zhao, W. (1989): Special issue on real-time operating systems, *Operating System Review*, **23**, 7.

21. Zhu, D., D. Mosse, and R. Melhem (2004): "Power-aware scheduling for AND/OR graphs in real-time systems," *IEEE Transactions on Parallel and Distributed Systems*, **15** (9), 849–864.

Chapter 8

Deadlocks

In real life, a deadlock arises when two persons wait for phone calls from one another, or when persons walking a narrow staircase in opposite directions meet face to face. A deadlock is characterized by the fact that persons wait indefinitely for one another to perform specific actions; these actions cannot occur.

Deadlocks in an operating system are analogous—processes wait for one another's actions indefinitely. Deadlocks arise in process synchronization when processes wait for each other's signals, or in resource sharing when they wait for other processes to release resources that they need. Deadlocked processes remain blocked indefinitely, which adversely affects user service, throughput and resource efficiency.

Deadlocks arise in resource sharing when a set of conditions concerning resource requests and resource allocations hold simultaneously. Operating systems use several approaches to handle deadlocks. In the *deadlock detection and resolution* approach, the kernel checks whether the conditions contributing to a deadlock hold simultaneously, and eliminates a deadlock by judiciously aborting some processes so that the remaining processes are no longer in a deadlock. In the *deadlock prevention* approach, the kernel employs resource allocation policies that ensure that the conditions for deadlocks do not hold simultaneously; it makes deadlocks impossible. In the *deadlock avoidance* approach, the kernel does not make resource allocations that may lead to deadlocks, so deadlocks do not arise.

We discuss these deadlock handling approaches and the practical resource allocation policies employed in operating systems.

8.1 WHAT IS A DEADLOCK?

A *deadlock* is a situation concerning a set of processes in which each process in the set waits for an event that must be caused by another process in the set. Each process is then waiting for an event that cannot occur. Example 8.1 illustrates how a deadlock could arise when two processes try to share resources.

Example 8.1 Two-Process Deadlock

A system contains one tape drive and one printer. Two processes P_i and P_j make use of the tape drive and the printer through the following programs:

Process P_i	*Process P_j*
Request tape drive; Request printer; Use tape drive and printer; Release printer; Release tape drive;	Request printer; Request tape drive; Use tape drive and printer; Release tape drive; Release printer;

As the two processes execute, resource requests take place in the following order:

1. Process P_i requests the tape drive
2. Process P_j requests the printer
3. Process P_i requests the printer
4. Process P_j requests the tape drive

The first two resource requests are granted right away because the system includes both a tape drive and a printer. Now, P_i holds the tape drive and P_j holds the printer. When P_i asks for the printer, it is blocked until P_j releases the printer. Similarly, P_j is blocked until P_i releases the tape drive. Both processes are blocked indefinitely because they wait for each other.

The deadlock illustrated in Example 8.1 is called a *resource deadlock*. Other kinds of deadlock can also arise in an OS. A *synchronization deadlock* occurs when the awaited events take the form of signals between processes. For example, if a process P_i decides to perform an action a_i only after process P_j performs action a_j, and process P_j decides to perform action a_j only after P_i performs a_i, both processes get blocked until the other process sends it a signal (see Section 6.4). Analogously, a *communication deadlock* occurs for a set of processes if each process sends a message only after it receives a message from some other process in the set (see Chapter 9). An OS is primarily concerned with resource deadlocks because allocation of resources is an OS responsibility. The other two forms of deadlock are seldom handled by an OS; it expects user processes to handle such deadlocks themselves.

Formally, we say that a deadlock arises if the conditions in the following definition are satisfied.

Definition 8.1 Deadlock A situation involving a set of processes D in which each process P_i in D satisfies two conditions:

1. Process P_i is blocked on some event e_j.
2. Event e_j can be caused only by actions of other process(es) in D.

In a deadlock, every process capable of causing the event e_j awaited by process P_i itself belongs to D. This property makes it impossible for event e_j to occur. Hence every process P_i in D waits indefinitely.

8.2 DEADLOCKS IN RESOURCE ALLOCATION

Processes use hardware resources, like memory and I/O devices, and software resources, such as files. An OS may contain several resources of a kind, e.g., several disks, tape drives, or printers. We use the term *resource unit* to refer to a resource of a specific kind, and use the term *resource class* to refer to the collection of all resource units of a kind; thus, a resource class contains one or more resource units; e.g., the printer class may contain two printers. We use the notation R_i for a resource class, and r_j for a resource unit in a resource class. Recall from Section 1.3.2 that the kernel maintains a resource table to keep track of the allocation state of a resource.

Resource allocation in a system entails three kinds of events—*request* for the resource, actual *allocation* of the resource, and *release* of the resource. Table 8.1 describes these events. A request event occurs when some process P_i makes a request for a resource r_l. Process P_i will be blocked on an allocation event for r_l if r_l is currently allocated to some process P_k. In effect, P_i is waiting for P_k to release r_l. A release event by P_k frees resource r_l, and the kernel may decide to allocate resource r_l to P_i. Thus, a release event by P_k may cause the allocation event for which P_i is waiting, in which case P_i will become the *holder* of the resource and enter the *ready* state. However, as we saw in Example 8.1, process P_i will face an indefinite wait if P_k's release of r_l is indefinitely delayed.

Table 8.1 Events Related to Resource Allocation

Event	Description
Request	A process requests a resource through a system call. If the resource is free, the kernel allocates it to the process immediately; otherwise, it changes the state of the process to *blocked*.
Allocation	The process becomes the *holder* of the resource allocated to it. The resource state information is updated and the state of the process is changed to *ready*.
Release	A process releases a resource through a system call. If some processes are blocked on the allocation event for the resource, the kernel uses some tie-breaking rule, e.g., FCFS allocation, to decide which process should be allocated the resource.

8.2.1 Conditions for a Resource Deadlock

By slightly rewording parts 1 and 2 of Definition 8.1, we can obtain the conditions under which resource deadlocks occur: (1) Each process P_i in D is blocked for an allocation event to occur and (2) the allocation event can be caused only by actions of some other process P_j in D. Since P_j is in D, parts 1 and 2 of Definition 8.1 apply to P_j as well. In other words, the resource requested by process P_i is currently allocated to P_j, which itself waits for some other resource to be allocated to it. This condition of each process, taken by itself, is called the *hold-and-wait* condition.

But parts 1 and 2 of Definition 8.1 also imply that processes in D must wait for each other. This condition is called the *circular wait* condition. A circular wait may be direct, that is, P_i waits for P_j and P_j waits for P_i, or it may be through one or more other processes included in D, for example P_i waits for P_j, P_j waits for P_k, and P_k waits for P_i.

Two other conditions must hold for a resource deadlock to occur. If process P_i needs a resource that is currently allocated to P_j, P_i must not be able to either (1) share the resource with P_j or (2) preempt it from P_j for its own use.

Table 8.2 summarizes the conditions that must be satisfied for a resource deadlock to exist. All these conditions must hold simultaneously: A circular wait is essential for a deadlock, a hold-and-wait condition is essential for a circular wait, and nonshareability and nonpreemptibility of resources are essential for a hold-and-wait condition.

Besides the conditions listed in Table 8.2, another condition is also essential for deadlocks:

- *No withdrawal of resource requests:* A process blocked on a resource request cannot withdraw its request.

This condition is essential because waits may not be indefinite if a blocked process is permitted to withdraw a resource request and continue its operation. However, it is not stated explicitly in the literature, because many operating systems typically impose the no-withdrawal condition on resource requests.

Table 8.2 Conditions for Resource Deadlock

Condition	Explanation
Nonshareable resources	Resources cannot be shared; a process needs exclusive access to a resource.
No preemption	A resource cannot be preempted from one process and allocated to another process.
Hold-and-wait	A process continues to hold the resources allocated to it while waiting for other resources.
Circular waits	A circular chain of hold-and-wait conditions exists in the system; e.g., process P_i waits for P_j, P_j waits for P_k, and P_k waits for P_i.

8.2.2 Modeling the Resource Allocation State

Example 8.1 indicated that we must analyze information about resources allocated to processes and about pending resource requests to determine whether a set of processes is deadlocked, All this information constitutes the *resource allocation state* of a system, which we simply call the *allocation state* of a system.

Two kinds of models are used to represent the allocation state of a system. A *graph model* can depict the allocation state of a restricted class of systems in which a process can request and use exactly one resource unit of each resource class. It permits use of a simple graph algorithm to determine whether the circular wait condition is satisfied by processes. A *matrix model* has the advantage of generality. It can model allocation state in systems that permit a process to request any number of units of a resource class.

8.2.2.1 Graph Models

A *resource request and allocation graph* (RRAG) contains two kinds of nodes—process nodes, and resource nodes. A *process node* is depicted by a circle. A *resource node* is depicted by a rectangle and represents one class of resources. The number of bullet symbols in a resource node indicates how many units of that resource class exist in the system. Two kinds of edges can exist between a process node and a resource node of an RRAG. An *allocation edge* is directed from a resource node to a process node. It indicates that one unit of the resource class is allocated to the process. A *request edge* is directed from a process node to a resource node. It indicates that the process is blocked on a request for one unit of the resource class. An allocation edge (R_k, P_j) is deleted when process P_j releases a resource unit of resource class R_k allocated to it. When a pending request of process P_i for a unit of resource class R_k is granted, the request edge (P_i, R_k) is deleted and an allocation edge (R_k, P_i) is added.

A *wait-for graph* (WFG) can represent the allocation state more concisely than an RRAG when every resource class in the system contains only one resource unit. The WFG contains nodes of only one kind, namely, process nodes. An edge (P_i, P_j) in the WFG represents the fact that process P_i is blocked on a request for a resource that is currently allocated to process P_j; i.e., process P_i is waiting for process P_j to release a resource. Hence the name *wait-for* graph. Representing the same information in an RRAG would have required two edges.

The next example illustrates and compares use of an RRAG and a WFG.

RRAG and WFG **Example 8.2**

Figure 8.1(a) shows an RRAG. The printer class contains only one resource unit, which is allocated to process P_1. Requests for a printer made by processes P_2 and P_3 are currently pending. The tape class contains two tape drives, which are allocated to processes P_2 and P_3. A request by process P_4 for one tape drive is currently pending.

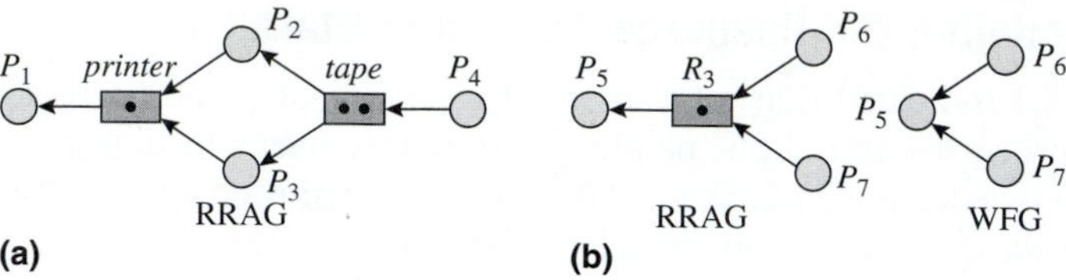

Figure 8.1 (a) Resource request and allocation graph (RRAG); (b) Equivalence of RRAG and wait-for graph (WFG) when each resource class contains only one resource unit.

Figure 8.1(b) shows both an RRAG and a WFG for a system that has a resource class R_3 that contains only one resource unit and three processes P_5, P_6, and P_7. The edges (P_6, R_3) and (R_3, P_5) in the RRAG together indicate that process P_6 is waiting for the resource currently allocated to P_5. Hence we have an edge (P_6, P_5) in the WFG. Edge (P_7, P_5) similarly indicates that process P_7 is waiting for the resource currently allocated to P_5.

Paths in an RRAG and a WFG We can deduce the presence of deadlocks from the nature of paths in an RRAG and a WFG. We define the following notation for this purpose:

Blocked_P	set of blocked processes
WF_i	The wait-for set of P_i, i.e., the set of processes that hold resources required by process P_i.

With this notation, Parts 1 and 2 of Definition 8.1 can be restated as follows:

$$D \subseteq Blocked\_P \qquad \textbf{(8.1)}$$

$$\text{For all } P_i \in D,\ WF_i \subseteq D. \qquad \textbf{(8.2)}$$

Consider a system in which each resource class contains only one resource unit. Let the system contain a single path $P_1 - R_1 - P_2 - R_2 \ldots P_{n-1} - R_{n-1} - P_n$ in its RRAG. Thus, process P_n is not blocked on any resource and no resource is currently allocated to P_1. The WFG of this system would contain the single path $P_1 - P_2 - \ldots - P_n$.

We can establish the absence of a deadlock in this system by showing that conditions (8.1) and (8.2) are not satisfied by any set of processes in the system. *Blocked_P* is $\{P_1, \ldots, P_{n-1}\}$. First, consider the set of processes $\{P_1, \ldots, P_n\}$. This set is not a subset of *Blocked_P*, which violates condition (8.1), and so this set of processes is not deadlocked. Now, consider the set $\{P_1, \ldots, P_{n-1}\}$. Here, $WF_{n-1} = \{P_n\}$ violates condition (8.2). Any other subset of $\{P_1, \ldots, P_n\}$ can similarly be shown to violate condition (8.2) for some process. Hence there is no deadlock in the system.

Now, if the unit of resource class R_{n-1} were to be allocated to P_1 instead of P_n, the path in the RRAG would be $P_1 - R_1 - P_2 - R_2 \ldots P_{n-1} - R_{n-1} - P_1$. This is a cyclic path, also called a *cycle*, because it ends on the same node on which it begins, i.e., node P_1. The WFG also contains a cycle, which is $P_1 - P_2 \ldots - P_1$. *Blocked_P* is $\{P_1, \ldots, P_{n-1}\}$, same as before. A deadlock exists because the set $\{P_1, \ldots, P_{n-1}\}$ satisfies both condition (8.1) and (8.2) since

- $\{P_1, \ldots, P_{n-1}\} \subseteq$ *Blocked_P*
- For all $P_i \in \{P_1, \ldots, P_{n-1}\}$, WF_i contains a single process P_l such that $P_l \in \{P_1, \ldots, P_{n-1}\}$.

From this analysis we can conclude that condition (8.2), which implies existence of mutual wait-for relationships between processes of D, can be satisfied only by cyclic paths. Hence a deadlock cannot exist unless an RRAG, or a WFG, contains a cycle.

RRAG Showing a Deadlock

Example 8.3

Figure 8.2 shows the RRAG for Example 8.1. The RRAG contains a cyclic path P_i–printer–P_j–tape–P_i. Here $WF_i = \{P_j\}$ and $WF_j = \{P_i\}$. $D = \{P_1, P_2\}$ satisfies both condition (8.1) and (8.2). Hence processes P_i and P_j are deadlocked.

Does presence of a cycle in an RRAG or a WFG imply a deadlock? In the system discussed so far, each resource class contained a single resource unit, so a cycle in the RRAG or WFG implied a deadlock. However, it may not be so in all systems. Consider a path $P_1 - R_1 \ldots P_i - R_i - P_{i+1} - \ldots P_n$ in a system in which a resource class R_i contains many resource units. A WFG cannot be used to depict the allocation state of this system; hence, we will discuss the RRAG for the system. If some process P_k not included in the path holds one unit of resource class R_i, that unit may be allocated to P_i when P_k released it. The edge (P_i, R_i) could thus vanish even without P_{i+1} releasing the unit of R_i held by it.

Thus, a cyclic path in an RRAG may be broken when some process not included in the cycle releases a unit of the resource. Therefore the presence of a cycle in an RRAG does not necessarily imply existence of a deadlock if a resource class contains more than one resource unit. (We draw on this knowledge

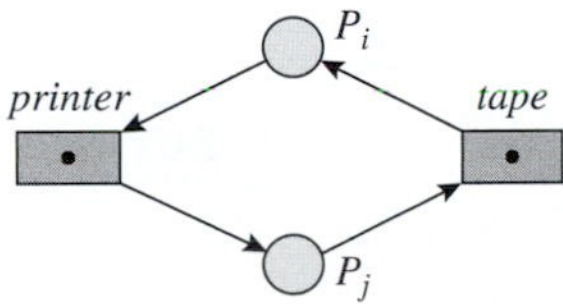

Figure 8.2 RRAG for the system of Example 8.1.

in Section 8.7 when we develop a formal characterization for deadlocks.) Example 8.4 illustrates such a situation.

Example 8.4 **A Cycle in RRAG Does Not Imply a Deadlock**

A system has one printer and two tape drives and three processes P_i, P_j, and P_k. The nature of processes P_i and P_j is the same as depicted in Example 8.1—each of them requires a tape drive and a printer. Process P_k requires only a tape drive for its operation. Let process P_k request for a tape drive before requests 1–4 are made as in Example 8.1.

Figure 8.3 shows the RRAG after all requests have been made. The graph has a cycle involving P_i and P_j. This cycle would be broken when process P_k completes because the tape drive released by it would be allocated to P_j. Hence there is no deadlock. We come to the same conclusion when we analyze the set of processes $\{P_i, P_j\}$ according to Definition 8.1 because $WF_j = \{P_i, P_k\}$ and $P_k \notin \{P_i, P_j\}$ violates condition (8.2).

8.2.2.2 Matrix Model

In the matrix model, the allocation state of a system is primarily represented by two matrices. The matrix *Allocated_resources* indicates how many resource units of each resource class are allocated to each process in the system. The matrix *Requested_resources* represents pending requests. It indicates how many resource units of each resource class have been requested by each process in the system. If a system contains n processes and r resource classes, each of these matrices is an $n \times r$ matrix. The allocation state with respect to a resource class R_k indicates the number of units of R_k allocated to each process, and the number of units of R_k requested by each process. These are represented as n-tuples ($Allocated\_resources_{1,k}, \ldots, Allocated\_resources_{n,k}$) and ($Requested\_resources_{1,k}, \ldots, Requested\_resources_{n,k}$), respectively.

Some auxiliary matrices may be used to represent additional information required for a specific purpose. Two such auxiliary matrices are *Total_resources* and *Free_resources*, which indicate the total number of resource units in each resource class and the number of resource units of each resource class that are free, respectively. Each of these matrices is a column matrix that has r elements in it. Example 8.5 is an example of a matrix model.

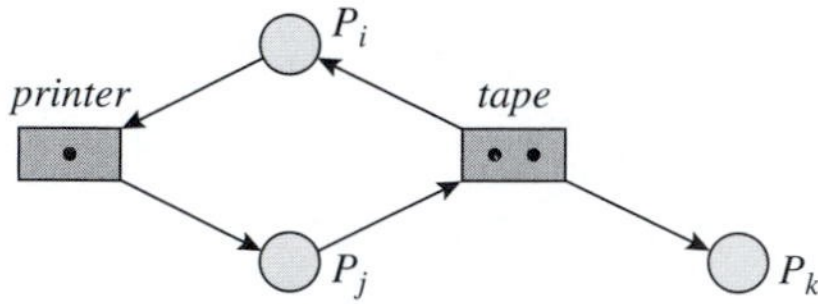

Figure 8.3 RRAG after all requests of Example 8.4 are made.

Matrix Model of Allocation State

Example 8.5

Using the matrix model, the allocation state of the system of Figure 8.3 is represented as follows:

Allocated resources

	Printer	Tape
P_i	0	1
P_j	1	0
P_k	0	1

Requested resources

	Printer	Tape
P_i	1	0
P_j	0	1
P_k	0	0

	Printer	Tape
Total resources	1	2
Free resources	0	0

The wait-for relationships in the system are not represented by the matrix model; they have to be deduced by an algorithm. Algorithms 8.1 and 8.2 discussed in later sections use the matrix model.

8.3 HANDLING DEADLOCKS

Table 8.3 describes the three fundamental approaches to deadlock handling. Each approach has different consequences in terms of possible delays in resource allocation, the kind of resource requests that user processes are allowed to make, and the OS overhead.

Under the *deadlock detection and resolution* approach, the kernel aborts some processes when it detects a deadlock on analyzing the allocation state. This action frees the resources held by the aborted process, which are now allocated to other processes that had requested them. The aborted processes have to be reexecuted. Thus, the cost of this approach includes the cost of deadlock detection and the cost of reexecuting the aborted processes. In the system of Example 8.1, the

Table 8.3 Deadlock Handling Approaches

Approach	Description
Deadlock detection and resolution	The kernel analyzes the resource state to check whether a deadlock exists. If so, it aborts some process(es) and allocates the resources held by them to other processes so that the deadlock ceases to exist.
Deadlock prevention	The kernel uses a resource allocation policy that ensures that the four conditions for resource deadlocks mentioned in Table 8.2 do not arise simultaneously. It makes deadlocks impossible.
Deadlock avoidance	The kernel analyzes the allocation state to determine whether granting a resource request can lead to a deadlock in the future. Only requests that cannot lead to a deadlock are granted, others are kept pending until they can be granted. Thus, deadlocks do not arise.

kernel would detect a deadlock sometime after processing the fourth request. This deadlock can be resolved by aborting either P_i or P_j and allocating the resource held by it to the other process.

In *deadlock prevention*, the kernel uses a resource allocation policy that makes deadlocks impossible and processes have to abide by any restrictions that the policy may impose. For example, a simple deadlock prevention policy would be to allocate all resources required by a process at the same time. This policy would require a process to make *all* its resource requests together. In Example 8.1, both processes would request both a printer and a tape drive at the same time. A deadlock would not arise because one of the processes would get both the resources it needed; however, the policy may force a process to obtain a resource long before it was actually needed.

Under the *deadlock avoidance* approach, the kernel grants a resource request only if it finds that granting the request will not lead to deadlocks later; otherwise, it keeps the request pending until it can be granted. Hence a process may face long delays in obtaining a resource. In Example 8.1, the kernel would realize the possibility of a future deadlock while processing the second request. Hence it would not grant the printer to process P_j until process P_i completed.

8.4 DEADLOCK DETECTION AND RESOLUTION

Consider a system that contains a process P_i, which holds a printer; and a process P_j that is blocked on its request for a printer. If process P_i is not in the *blocked* state, there is a possibility that it might complete its operation without requesting any more resources; on completion, it would release the printer allocated to it, which could then be allocated to process P_j. Thus, if P_i is not in the *blocked* state, P_j's wait for the printer is not indefinite because of the following sequence of events: process P_i completes–releases printer–printer is allocated to P_j. If some other process P_l waits for some other resource allocated to P_j, its wait is also not indefinite. Hence processes P_i, P_j, and P_l are not involved in a deadlock at the current moment.

From this observation, we can formulate the following rule for deadlock detection: A process in the *blocked* state is not involved in a deadlock at the current moment if the request on which it is blocked can be satisfied through a sequence of process completion, resource release, and resource allocation events. If each resource class in the system contains a single resource unit, this check can be made by checking for the presence of a cycle in an RRAG or WFG. However, more complex graph-based algorithms have to be used if resource classes may contain more than one resource unit (see Section 8.7), so we instead discuss a deadlock detection approach using the matrix model.

We check for the presence of a deadlock in a system by actually trying to construct fictitious but feasible sequences of events whereby *all* blocked processes can get the resources they have requested. Success in constructing such a sequence implies the absence of a deadlock at the current moment, and a failure to construct it implies presence of a deadlock. When we apply this rule to Examples 8.3 and 8.4, it correctly deduces that processes P_i and P_j of Example 8.3 are in a deadlock, whereas a deadlock does not exist in Example 8.4.

We perform the above check by simulating the operation of a system starting with its current state. We refer to any process that is not blocked on a resource request as a *running* process, i.e., we do not differentiate between the *ready* and *running* states of Chapter 5. In the simulation we consider only two events—completion of a process that is not blocked on a resource request, and allocation of resource(s) to a process that is blocked on a resource request. It is assumed that a *running* process would complete without making additional resource requests, and that some of the resources freed on its completion would be allocated to a *blocked* process only if the allocation would put that process in the *running* state. The simulation ends when all *running* processes complete. The processes that are in the *blocked* state at the end of the simulation are those that could not obtain the requested resources when other processes completed, hence these processes are deadlocked in the current state. There is no deadlock in the current state if no *blocked* processes exist when the simulation ends. Example 8.6 illustrates this approach.

Example 8.6

Deadlock Detection

The allocation state of a system containing 10 units of a resource class R_1 and three processes P_1–P_3 is as follows:

Allocated resources:

	R_1
P_1	4
P_2	4
P_3	2

Requested resources:

	R_1
P_1	6
P_2	2
P_3	0

	R_1
Total resources	10
Free resources	0

Process P_3 is in the *running* state because it is not blocked on a resource request. All processes in the system can complete as follows: Process P_3 completes and releases 2 units of the resource allocated to it. These units can be allocated to P_2. When it completes, 6 units of the resource can be allocated to P_1. Thus no *blocked* processes exist when the simulation ends, so a deadlock does not exist in the system.

If the requests by processes P_1 and P_2 were for 6 and 3 units, respectively, none of them could complete even after process P_3 released 2 resource units. These processes would be in the *blocked* state when the simulation ended, and so they are deadlocked in the current state of the system.

In our simulation, we assumed that a running process completes its execution without making further resource requests. This assumption has two consequences. First, our conclusions regarding existence of a deadlock are not sensitive to the order in which *blocked* processes are assumed to become *running* or the order in which *running* processes are assumed to complete. Second, even if a system is deadlock-free at the current moment, a deadlock could arise in the future. In Example 8.6, this could happen if P_3 makes a request for one more unit of R_1. As a consequence, deadlock detection has to be performed repeatedly during operation of the OS. It can be achieved by devoting a system process exclusively to deadlock detection, and activating it at fixed intervals. Alternatively, deadlock detection can be performed every time a process becomes blocked on a resource request. The overhead of deadlock detection would depend on several factors like the number of processes and resource classes in the system and how often deadlock detection is performed.

8.4.1 A Deadlock Detection Algorithm

Algorithm 8.1 performs deadlock detection. The inputs to the algorithm are two sets of processes *Blocked* and *Running*, and a matrix model of the allocation state comprising the matrices *Allocated_resources*, *Requested_resources*, and *Free_resources*.

The algorithm simulates completion of a running process P_i by transferring it from the set *Running* to the set *Finished* [Steps 1(a), 1(b)]. Resources allocated to P_i are added to *Free_resources* [Step 1(c)]. The algorithm now selects a *blocked* process whose resource request can be satisfied from the free resources [Step 1(d)], and transfers it from the set *Blocked* to the set *Running*. Sometime later the algorithm simulates its completion and transfers it from *Running* to *Finished*. The algorithm terminates when no processes are left in the *Running* set. Processes remaining in the set *Blocked*, if any, are deadlocked.

The complexity of the algorithm can be analyzed as follows: The sets *Running* and *Blocked* can contain up to n processes, where n is the total number of processes in the system. The loop of Step 1 iterates $\leq n$ times and Step 1(d) performs an order of $n \times r$ work in each iteration. Hence the algorithm requires an order of $n^2 \times r$ work. Example 8.7 illustrates the working of this algorithm.

Algorithm 8.1 *Deadlock Detection*

Inputs

n	:	Number of processes;
r	:	Number of resource classes;
Blocked	:	**set of** processes;
Running	:	**set of** processes;
Free_resources	:	**array** [1..r] **of** *integer*;
Allocated_resources	:	**array** [1..n, 1..r] **of** *integer*;
Requested_resources	:	**array** [1..n, 1..r] **of** *integer*;

Data structures

Finished	:	**set of** *processes*;

1. **repeat until** *set Running is empty*
   a. *Select a process P_i from set Running*;
   b. *Delete P_i from set Running and add it to set Finished*;

c. for $k = 1..r$

$Free\_resources[k] := Free\_resources[k] + Allocated\_resources[i,k]$;

d. while *set Blocked contains a process* P_l *such that*

for $k = 1..r$, $Requested\_resources[l,k] \leq Free\_resources[k]$

i. for $k = 1, r$

$Free\_resources[k] := Free\_resources[k] - Requested\_resources[l,k]$;

$Allocated\_resources[l,k] := Allocated\_resources[l,k]$
$+ Requested\_resources[l,k]$;

ii. *Delete* P_l *from set Blocked and add it to set Running*;

2. if *set Blocked is not empty* **then**

declare processes in set Blocked to be deadlocked.

Operation of a Deadlock Detection Algorithm

Example 8.7

A system has four processes P_1–P_4, and 5, 7, and 5 units of resource classes R_1, R_2, and R_3, respectively. It is in the following state just before process P_3 makes a request for 1 unit of resource class R_1:

Allocated resources

	R_1	R_2	R_3
P_1	2	1	0
P_2	1	3	1
P_3	0	1	1
P_4	1	2	2

Requested resources

	R_1	R_2	R_3
P_1	2	1	3
P_2	1	4	0
P_3			
P_4	1	0	2

Total resources

R_1	R_2	R_3
5	7	5

Free resources

R_1	R_2	R_3
1	0	1

One resource unit of resource class R_1 is allocated to process P_3 and Algorithm 8.1 is invoked to check whether the system is in a deadlock. Figure 8.4 shows steps in operation of the algorithm. Inputs to it are the sets *Blocked* and *Running* initialized to $\{P_1, P_2, P_4\}$ and $\{P_3\}$, respectively, and matrices *Allocated_resources*, *Requested_resources*, and *Free_resources* as shown in Figure 8.4(a). The algorithm transfers process P_3 to the set *Finished* and frees the resources allocated to it. The number of free units of the resource classes is now 1, 1 and 2, respectively. The algorithm finds that process P_4's pending request can now be satisfied, so it allocates the resources requested by P_4 and transfers P_4 to the set *Running* [see Figure 8.4(b)]. Since P_4 is the only process in *Running*, it is transferred to the set *Finished*. After freeing P_4's resources, the algorithm finds that P_1's resource request can be satisfied [see Figure 8.4(c)] and, after P_1 completes, P_2's resource request can be satisfied [see Figure 8.4(d)]. The set *Running* is now empty so the algorithm completes. A deadlock does not exist in the system because the set *Blocked* is empty.

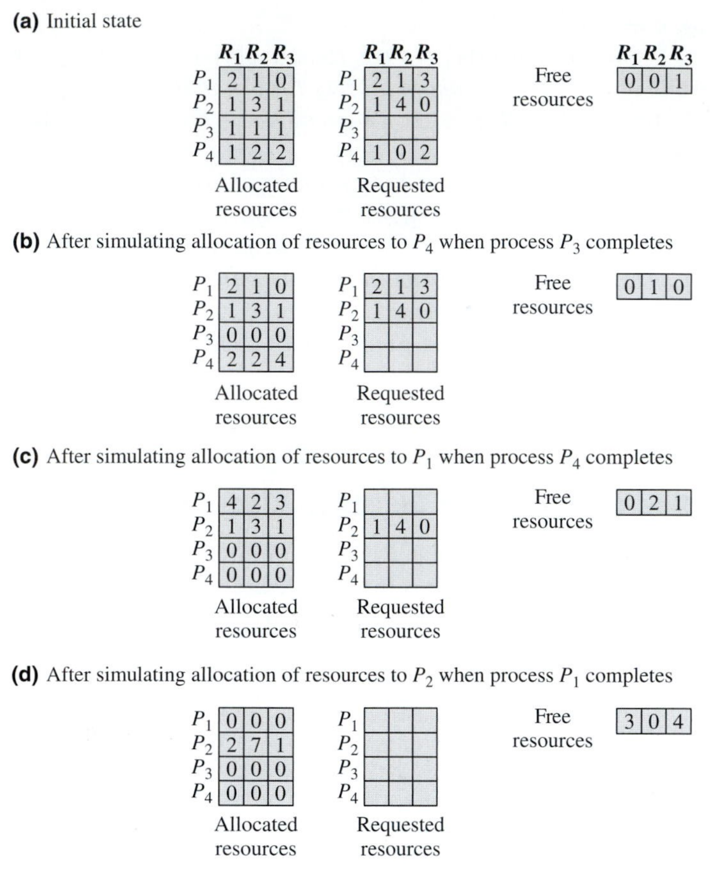

Figure 8.4 Operation of Algorithm 8.1, the deadlock detection algorithm.

8.4.2 Deadlock Resolution

Given a set of deadlocked processes D, *deadlock resolution* implies breaking the deadlock to ensure progress for some processes in D, that is, for processes in some set $D' \subset D$. It can be achieved by aborting one or more processes in set D, and allocating their resources to some processes in D'. Each aborted process is called a *victim* of deadlock resolution.

Thus, deadlock resolution can be seen as the act of splitting a set of deadlocked processes D into two sets such that $D = D' \cup D_v$, where

- Each process in D_v is a victim of deadlock resolution, and
- The set of processes D' is deadlock-free after the deadlock resolution actions are complete. That is, each process in D' can complete its operation through a sequence of process completion, resource release and resource allocation events.

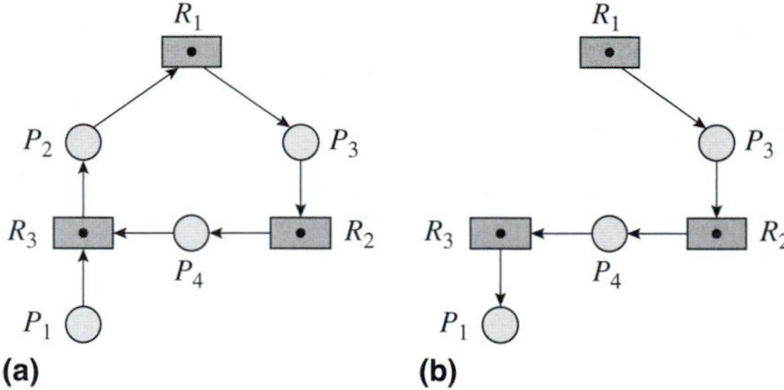

Figure 8.5 Deadlock resolution. (a) a deadlock; (b) resource allocation state after deadlock resolution.

The choice of the victim process(es) is made using criteria such as the priority of a process, resources already consumed by it, etc. The next example illustrates deadlock resolution.

Example 8.8

Deadlock Resolution

The RRAG of Figure 8.5(a) shows a deadlock situation involving processes P_1, P_2, P_3 and P_4. This deadlock is resolved by choosing process P_2 as the victim. Part (b) of the figure shows the RRAG after aborting process P_2 and allocating resource R_3 previously held by it to process P_1. Process P_4, which waited for the victim before deadlock resolution, now waits for P_1, the new holder of the resource. This fact is important for detection of future deadlocks. If the allocation state is represented by the matrix model, it is sufficient to delete the rows corresponding to P_2 in *Allocated_resources* and *Requested_resources*, modify the rows of process P_1, and modify *Free_resources* accordingly.

8.5 DEADLOCK PREVENTION

The four conditions described in Table 8.2 must hold simultaneously for a resource deadlock to arise in a system. To prevent deadlocks, the kernel must use a resource allocation policy that ensures that one of these conditions cannot arise. In this section, we first discuss different approaches to deadlock prevention and then present some resource allocation policies that employ these approaches.

Nonshareable Resources Wait-for relations will not exist in the system if all resources could be made shareable. This way paths in an RRAG would contain only allocation edges, so circular waits could not arise. Figure 8.6(a) illustrates the effect of employing this approach: the request edge (P_i, R_l) would be replaced by an allocation edge (R_l, P_i) because the resource unit of class R_l is shareable.

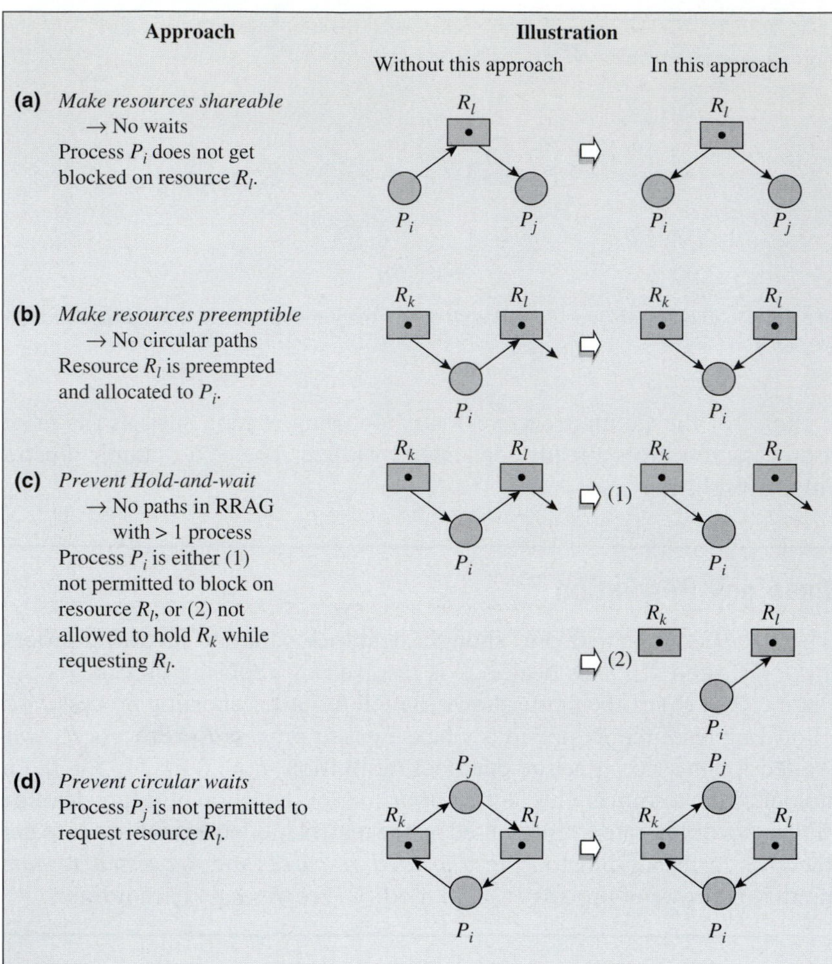

Figure 8.6 Approaches to deadlock prevention.

However, some resources such as printers are inherently nonshareable, so how can they be made shareable? OSs use some innovative techniques to solve this problem. An example is found in the THE multiprogramming system of the 1960s. It contained only one printer, so it buffered the output produced by different processes, formatted it to produce "page images," and used the printer to print one page image at a time. This arrangement mixed up the printed pages produced by different processes, and so the output of different processes had to be separated manually. (Interestingly, the reason the THE system performed page formatting was not to prevent deadlocks, but to improve printer utilization. In fact, the THE system made no provisions for handling resource deadlocks.) The nonshareability of a device can also be circumvented by creating virtual devices (see Section 1.3.2); e.g., virtual printers can be created and allocated to processes. However, this approach cannot work for software resources like shared files, which should be modified in a mutually exclusive manner to avoid race conditions.

Preemption of Resources If resources are made preemptible, the kernel can ensure that some processes have all the resources they need, which would prevent circular paths in RRAG. For example, in Figure 8.6(b), resource R_l can be preempted from its current holder and allocated to process P_i. However, nonpreemptibility of resources can be circumvented only selectively. The page formatting approach of the THE system can be used to make printers preemptible, but, in general, sequential I/O devices cannot be preempted.

Hold-and-Wait To prevent the hold-and-wait condition, either a process that holds resources should not be permitted to make resource requests, or a process that gets blocked on a resource request should not be permitted to hold any resources. Thus, in Figure 8.6(c), either edge (P_i, R_l) would not arise, or edge (R_k, P_l) would not exist if (P_i, R_l) arises. In either case, RRAG paths involving more than one process could not arise, and so circular paths could not exist. A simple policy for implementing this approach is to allow a process to make only one resource request in its lifetime in which it asks for all the resources it needs. We discuss this policy in Section 8.5.1.

Circular Wait A circular wait can result from the hold-and-wait condition, which is a consequence of the non-shareability and non-preemptibility conditions, so it does not arise if either of these conditions does not arise. Circular waits can be separately prevented by not allowing some processes to wait for some resources; e.g., process P_j in Figure 8.6(d) may not be allowed to wait for resource R_l. It can be achieved by applying a *validity constraint* to each resource request. The validity constraint is a boolean function of the allocation state. It takes the value *false* if the request may lead to a circular wait in the system, so such a request is rejected right away. If the validity constraint has the value *true*, the resource is allocated if it is available; otherwise, the process is blocked for the resource. In Section 8.5.2 we discuss a deadlock prevention policy taking this approach.

8.5.1 All Resources Together

This is the simplest of all deadlock prevention policies. A process must ask for all resources it needs in a single request; the kernel allocates all of them together. This way a blocked process does not hold any resources, so the hold-and-wait condition is never satisfied. Consequently, circular waits and deadlocks cannot arise. Under this policy, both processes of Example 8.1 must request a tape drive and a printer together. Now a process will either hold both resources or hold none of them, and the hold-and-wait condition will not be satisfied.

Simplicity of implementation makes "all resources together" an attractive policy for small operating systems. However, it has one practical drawback—it adversely influences resource efficiency. For example, if a process P_i requires a tape drive at the start of its execution and a printer only toward the end of its execution, it will be forced to request both a tape drive and a printer at the start. The printer will remain idle until the latter part of P_i's execution and any process requiring a printer will be delayed until P_i completes its execution. This situation also reduces the effective degree of multiprogramming and, therefore, reduces CPU efficiency.

8.5.2 Resource Ranking

Under this deadlock prevention policy, a unique number called a *resource rank* is associated with each resource class. When a process P_i makes a request for a resource, the kernel applies a validity constraint to decide whether the request should be considered. The validity constraint takes the value *true* only if the rank of the requested resource is larger than the rank of the highest ranked resource currently allocated to P_i. In this case, the resource is allocated to P_i if it is available; otherwise, P_i is blocked for the resource. If the validity constraint is *false*, the request is rejected and process P_i, which made the request, would be aborted.

Absence of circular wait-for relationships in a system using resource ranking can be explained as follows: Let $rank_k$ denote the rank assigned to resource class R_k, and let process P_i hold some units of resource class R_k. P_i can get blocked on a request for a unit of some resource class R_l only if $rank_k < rank_l$. Now consider a process P_j that holds some units of resource class R_l. Process P_j cannot request a unit of resource class R_k since $rank_k \not> rank_l$. Thus, if P_i can wait for P_j, P_j cannot wait for P_i! Hence two processes cannot get into a circular wait condition. An analogous argument holds for the absence of a circular wait involving a larger number of processes.

Example 8.9 illustrates operation of the resource ranking policy.

Example 8.9 Resource Ranking

In Example 8.1, let $rank_{printer} > rank_{tape}$. Request 1 leads to allocation of the tape drive to P_i and request 2 leads to allocation of the printer to P_j. Request 3, which is P_i's request for the printer, satisfies the validity constraint because $rank_{printer} > rank_{tape}$, but it remains pending because the printer is not available. Request 4 will be rejected since it violates the validity constraint and process P_j will be aborted. This action will release the printer, which will then be allocated to P_i.

The resource ranking policy works best when all processes require their resources in the order of increasing resource rank. However, difficulties arise when a process requires a resource having a lower rank. The only way it can get this resource is by first releasing the higher ranked resource. Thus, in Example 8.9, process P_j can get the tape by first releasing the printer, getting the tape allocated and then once again requesting the printer. However, it is difficult in practice since most resources are nonpreemptible. Processes may tend to circumvent such difficulties by acquiring lower ranked resources much before they are actually needed. For example, process P_j of Example 8.1 could acquire the tape drive before acquiring the printer. In the worst case, this policy may degenerate into the "all resources together" policy of resource allocation.

Despite these drawbacks, the resource ranking policy is attractive because of its simplicity. A kernel can use this policy for its own resource requirements when it needs the resources in a fixed order. We shall discuss this aspect in Section 8.8.

8.6 DEADLOCK AVOIDANCE

A deadlock avoidance policy grants a resource request only if it can establish that granting the request cannot lead to a deadlock either immediately or in the future. But it raises an obvious question: Algorithm 8.1 described in Section 8.4 can be used to check whether granting a resource request results in a deadlock immediately, but how would the kernel know whether a deadlock can arise in the future?

The kernel lacks detailed knowledge about future behavior of processes, so it cannot accurately predict deadlocks. To facilitate deadlock avoidance under these conditions, it uses the following conservative approach: Each process declares the maximum number of resource units of each class that it *may* require. The kernel permits a process to request these resource units in stages—that is, a few resource units at a time—subject to the maximum number declared by it, and uses a worst-case analysis technique to check for the possibility of future deadlocks. A request is granted only if there is no possibility of deadlocks; otherwise, it remains pending until it can be granted. This approach is conservative because a process may complete its operation without requiring the maximum number of units declared by it. Thus, the kernel may defer granting of some resource requests that it would have granted immediately had it known about future behavior of processes. This effect and the overhead of making this check at every resource request constitute the cost of deadlock avoidance. We discuss a well-known algorithm called the banker's algorithm that uses this approach.

Table 8.4 describes notation of the banker's algorithm. $Max\_need_{j,k}$ indicates the maximum number of resource units of resource class R_k that a process P_j may require. The kernel admits process P_j only if $Max\_need_{j,k} \leq Total\_resources_k$ for all k. The kernel may admit any number of processes satisfying this admission criterion. Thus Σ_j $Max\_need_{j,k}$ may exceed $Total\_resources_k$. $Allocated\_resources_{j,k}$ indicates the actual number of resource units of resource class R_k that are allocated to P_j, and $Total\_alloc_k$ indicates how many units of resource class R_k are allocated to processes at present. The banker's algorithm avoids deadlocks by

Table 8.4 Notation Used in the Banker's Algorithm

Notation	Explanation
$Requested\_resources_{j,k}$	Number of units of resource class R_k currently requested by process P_j
$Max\_need_{j,k}$	Maximum number of units of resource class R_k that may be needed by process P_j
$Allocated\_resources_{j,k}$	Number of units of resource class R_k allocated to process P_j
$Total\_alloc_k$	Total number of allocated units of resource class R_k, i.e., $\Sigma_j\ Allocated\_resources_{j,k}$
$Total\_resources_k$	Total number of units of resource class R_k existing in the system

ensuring that at every moment the system is in such an allocation state that all processes can complete their operation without the possibility of deadlocks. It is called the banker's algorithm because bankers need a similar algorithm—they admit loans that collectively exceed the bank's funds and then release each borrower's loan in installments.

The banker's algorithm uses the notion of a *safe allocation state* to ensure that granting of a resource request *cannot* lead to a deadlock either immediately or in future.

Definition 8.2 Safe Allocation State An allocation state in which it is possible to construct a sequence of process completion, resource release, and resource allocation events through which each process P_j in the system can obtain $Max\_need_{j,k}$ resources for each resource class R_k and complete its operation.

Deadlock avoidance is implemented by taking the system from one safe allocation state to another safe allocation state as follows:

1. When a process makes a request, compute the new allocation state the system would be in if the request is granted. We will call this state the *projected allocation state*.
2. If the projected allocation state is a safe allocation state, grant the request by updating the arrays *Allocated_resources* and *Total_alloc*; otherwise, keep the request pending.
3. When a process releases any resource(s) or completes its operation, examine all pending requests and allocate those that would put the system in a new safe allocation state.

The banker's algorithm determines the safety of a resource allocation state by trying to construct a sequence of process completion, resource release, and resource allocation events through which all processes can complete. It can be performed through simulation as in Section 8.4, except for one change: To complete, a process P_l, whether in the *running* or *blocked* state, may require $(Max\_need_{l,k} - Allocated\_resources_{l,k})$ more resource units of each resource class R_k, so the algorithm checks whether

$$\text{For all } R_k : Total\_resources_k - Total\_alloc_k \geq Max\_need_{l,k} - Allocated\_resources_{l,k} \quad \textbf{(8.3)}$$

When this condition is satisfied, it simulates completion of process P_l and release of all resources allocated to it by updating $Total\_alloc_k$ for each R_k. It then checks whether any other process can satisfy Eq. (8.3), and so on. The next example illustrates this method in a system having a single class of resources. Note that, as in deadlock detection, the determination of safety of an allocation state is not sensitive to the order in which processes are assumed to complete their operation.

Banker's Algorithm for a Single Resource Class

Example 8.10

A system contains 10 units of resource class R_k. The maximum resource requirements of three processes P_1, P_2, and P_3 are 8, 7, and 5 resource units, respectively, and their current allocations are 3, 1, and 3 resource units, respectively. Figure 8.7 depicts the current allocation state of the system. Process P_1 now makes a request for one resource unit. In the projected allocation state, $Total\_alloc = 8$, and so there will be two free units of resource class R_k in the system.

The safety of the projected state is determined as follows: P_3 satisfies condition (8.3) since it is exactly two units short of its maximum requirements. Hence the two available resource units can be allocated to P_3 if it requests them in the future, and it can complete. That will make five resource units available for allocation, so P_1's balance requirement of four resource units can be allocated to it and it can complete. Now all resource units in the system are available to P_2, so it, too, can complete. Thus the projected allocation state is safe. Hence the algorithm will grant the request by P_1.

The new allocation for the processes is 4, 1, and 3 resource units and $Total\_alloc_k = 8$. Now consider the following requests:

1. P_1 makes a request for 2 resource units.
2. P_2 makes a request for 2 resource units.
3. P_3 makes a request for 2 resource units.

The requests by P_1 and P_2 do not put the system in safe allocation states because condition (8.3) is not satisfied by any process, so these requests will not be granted. However, the request by P_3 will be granted.

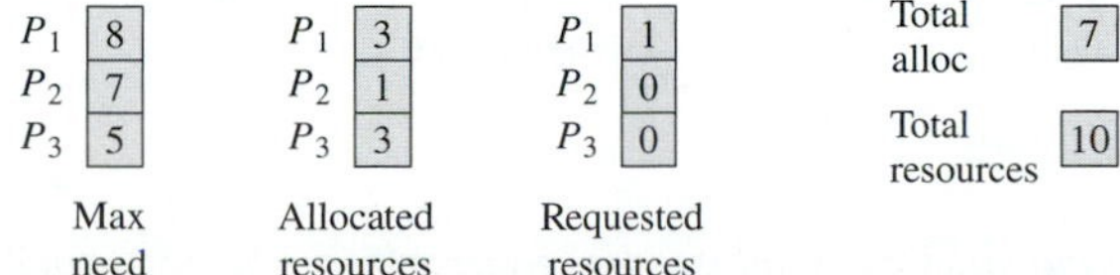

Figure 8.7 An allocation state in the banker's algorithm for a single resource class.

Algorithm 8.2 is the banker's algorithm. When a new request is made by a process, its request is entered in the matrix *Requested_resources*, which stores pending requests of all processes, and the algorithm is invoked with the id of the requesting process. When a process releases some resources allocated to it or completes its operation, the algorithm is invoked once for each process whose request is pending. The algorithm can be outlined as follows: After some initializations in Step 1, the algorithm simulates granting of the request in Step 2 by computing the projected allocation state. Step 3 checks whether the projected allocation state is feasible, i.e., whether sufficient free resources exist to permit granting of the request.

Step 4 is the core of the algorithm; it is executed only if the projected allocation state is feasible. To check whether the projected allocation state is a safe allocation state, it checks whether the maximum need of any active process, i.e., any process in the sets *Running* or *Blocked*, can be satisfied by allocating some of the free resources. If such a process exists, this step simulates its completion by deleting it from the set *Active* and releasing the resources allocated to it. This action is performed repeatedly until no more processes can be deleted from the set *Active*. If the set *Active* is empty at the end of this step, the projected state is a safe allocation state, so Step 5 deletes the request from the list of pending requests and allocates the requested resources. This action is not performed if the projected allocation state is either not feasible or not safe, so the request remains pending.

Note the similarity of Step 4 to the deadlock detection algorithm (Algorithm 8.1). Accordingly, the algorithm requires an order of $n^2 \times r$ work.

Algorithm 8.2 *Banker's Algorithm*

Inputs

n	:	Number of processes;
r	:	Number of resource classes;
Blocked	:	**set of** processes;
Running	:	**set of** processes;
$P_{requesting\_process}$	:	Process making the new resource request;
Max_need	:	**array** [1..*n*, 1..*r*] **of** *integer*;
Allocated_resources	:	**array** [1..*n*, 1..*r*] **of** *integer*;
Requested_resources	:	**array** [1..*n*, 1..*r*] **of** *integer*;
Total_alloc	:	**array** [1..*r*] **of** *integer*;
Total_resources	:	**array** [1..*r*] **of** *integer*;

Data structures

Active	:	**set of** *processes*;
feasible	:	*boolean*;
New_request	:	**array** [1..*r*] **of** *integer*;
Simulated_allocation	:	**array** [1..*n*, 1..*r*] **of** *integer*;
Simulated_total_alloc	:	**array** [1..*r*] **of** *integer*;

1. *Active* := *Running* $\bigcup$ *Blocked*;
 for $k = 1..r$
  New_request[*k*] := *Requested_resources*[*requesting_process*, *k*];

```
2. Simulated_allocation := Allocated_resources;
   for k = 1..r      /* Compute projected allocation state */
       Simulated_allocation[requesting_process, k] :=
               Simulated_allocation[requesting_process, k] + New_request[k];
       Simulated_total_alloc[k] := Total_alloc[k] + New_request[k];
3. feasible := true;
   for k = 1..r      /* Check whether projected allocation state is feasible */
       if Total_resources[k] < Simulated_total_alloc[k] then feasible := false;
4. if feasible = true
   then     /* Check whether projected allocation state is a safe allocation state */
       while set Active contains a process P_l such that
                   For all k, Total_resources[k] − Simulated_total_alloc[k]
                       ≥ Max_need[l, k] − Simulated_allocation[l, k]
           Delete P_l from Active;
           for k = 1..r
               Simulated_total_alloc[k] :=
                   Simulated_total_alloc[k] − Simulated_allocation[l, k];
5. if set Active is empty
   then     /* Projected allocation state is a safe allocation state */
       for k = 1..r      /* Delete the request from pending requests */
           Requested_resources[requesting_process, k] := 0;
           for k = 1..r      /* Grant the request */
               Allocated_resources[requesting_process, k] :=
                   Allocated_resources[requesting_process, k] + New_request[k];
               Total_alloc[k] := Total_alloc[k] + New_request[k];
```

Banker's Algorithm for Multiple Resource Classes

Example 8.11

Figure 8.8 illustrates operation of the banker's algorithm in a system containing four processes $P_1, \ldots, P_4$. Four resource classes contain 6, 4, 8, and 5 resource units, of which 5, 3, 5, and 4 resource units are currently allocated. Process P_2 has made a request (0, 1, 1, 0), which is about to be processed. The algorithm simulates the granting of this request in Step 2, and checks the safety of the projected allocation state in Step 4. Figure 8.8(b) shows the data structures of the Banker's algorithm at the start of this check. In this state, 1, 0, 2, and 1 resource units are available, so only process P_1 can complete. Hence the algorithm simulates its completion. Figure 8.8(c) shows the data structures after P_1 has completed. Resources allocated to P_1 have been freed so they are deducted from *Simulated_alloc*, and P_1 is deleted from set *Active*. Process P_4 needs 0, 1, 3, and 4 resource units to fulfill its maximum resource need, so it can be allocated these resources now, and it can complete. The remaining processes can complete in the order P_2, P_3. Hence the request made by process P_2 is granted.

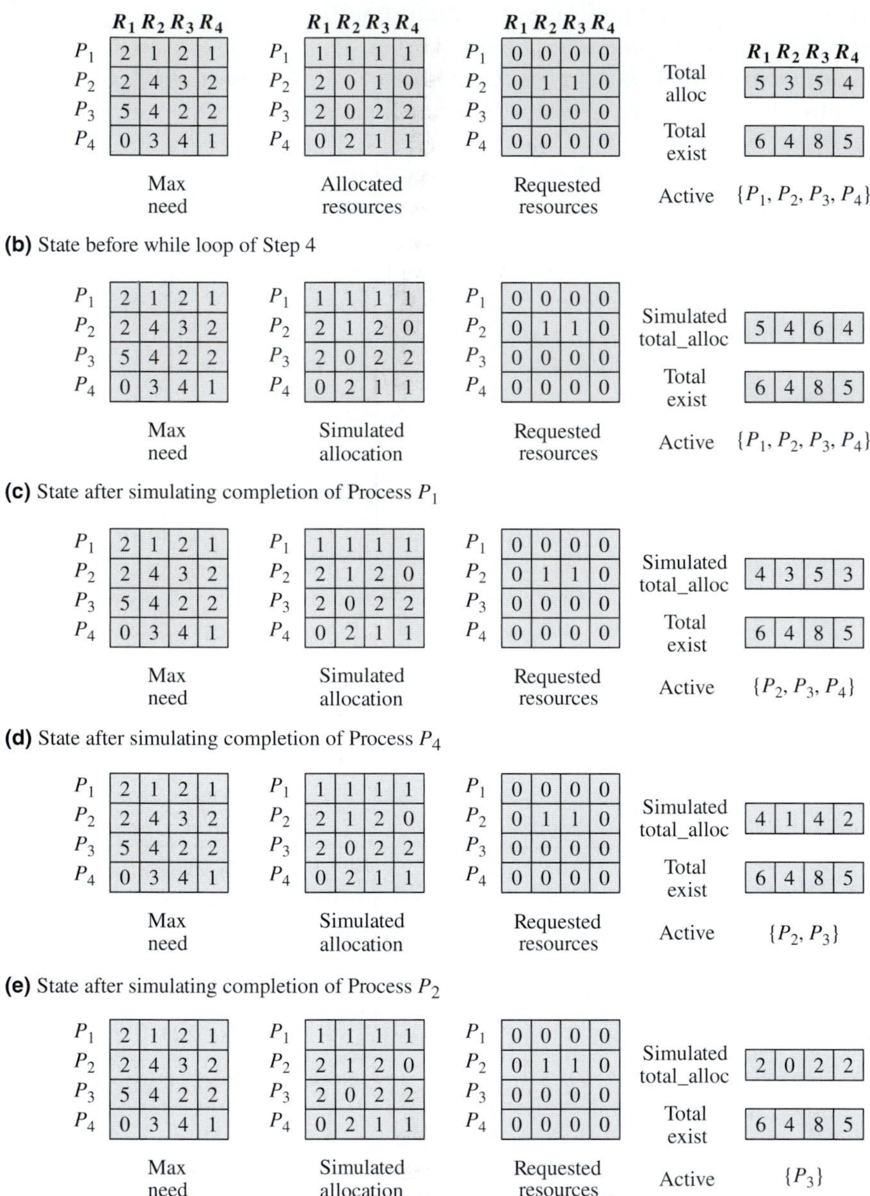

Figure 8.8 Operation of the banker's algorithm for Example 8.11.

8.7 CHARACTERIZATION OF RESOURCE DEADLOCKS BY GRAPH MODELS

A *deadlock characterization* is a statement of the essential features of a deadlock. In Section 8.4, we presented a deadlock detection algorithm using the matrix model of the allocation state of a system. Following that algorithm, we can characterize a deadlock as a situation in which we cannot construct a sequence of process completion, resource release, and resource allocation events whereby all processes in the system can complete.

In this section, we discuss characterization of deadlocks using graph models of allocation state and elements of graph theory. As we saw in Section 8.2.1, a circular wait-for relationship among processes is a *necessary* condition for a deadlock. It is manifest in a cycle in an RRAG or WFG. A cycle is a *sufficient* condition for a deadlock in some systems (see Example 8.3), but not in others (see Example 8.4). This difference is caused by the nature of resource classes and resource requests in the system, hence we first classify systems according to the resource classes and resource requests used in them and develop separate deadlock characterizations for different classes of systems. Later we point at a deadlock characterization that is applicable to all systems. We use an RRAG to depict the allocation state of a system all through this discussion.

Resource Class and Resource Request Models A resource class R_i may contain a single instance of its resource, or it may contain many instances. We refer to the two kinds of classes as *single instance* (SI) resource classes and *multiple instance* (MI) resource classes, respectively. We define two kinds of resource requests. In a *single request* (SR), a process is permitted to request one unit of only one resource class. In a *multiple request* (MR), a process is permitted to request one unit each of several resource classes. The kernel never partially allocates a multiple request; i.e., it either allocates *all* resources requested in a multiple request or does not allocate *any* of them. In the latter case, the process making the request is blocked until all resources can be allocated to it.

Using the resource class and resource request models, we can define four kinds of systems as shown in Figure 8.9. We name these systems by combining the name of the resource class model and the resource request model used by them. Accordingly, the SISR system is one that contains SI resource classes and SR requests.

8.7.1 Single-Instance, Single-Request (SISR) Systems

In an SISR system, each resource class contains a single instance of the resource and each request is a single request. As discussed in Section 8.2.2, existence of a cycle in an RRAG implies a mutual wait-for relationship for a set of processes. Since each resource class contains a single resource unit, each blocked process P_i in the cycle waits for exactly one other process, say P_k, to release the required resource. Hence a cycle that involves process P_i also involves process P_k. This fact

		Resource request models	
		Single request (SR) model	Multiple request (MR) model
Resource instance models	Multiple instance (MI) model	Multiple-instance, single-request (MISR)	Multiple-instance, multiple-request (MIMR)
	Single instance (SI) model	Single-instance, single-request (SISR)	Single-instance, multiple-request (SIMR)

Figure 8.9 Classification of systems according to resource class and resource request models.

satisfies condition (8.2) for all processes in the cycle. A cycle is thus a necessary as well as a sufficient condition to conclude that a deadlock exists in the system.

8.7.2 Multiple-Instance, Single-Request (MISR) Systems

A cycle is not a sufficient condition for a deadlock in MISR systems because resource classes may contain several resource units. The system of Example 8.4 in Section 8.2.2.1 illustrated this property, so we analyze it to understand what conditions should hold for a deadlock to exist in an MISR system. The RRAG of the system contained a cycle involving processes P_i and P_j, with P_j requiring a tape drive and P_i holding a tape drive (see Figure 8.3). However, process P_k, which did not belong to the cycle, also held a unit of tape drive, so the mutual wait-for relation between P_i and P_j ceased to exist when P_k released a tape drive. Process P_i would have been in deadlock only if processes P_j and P_k had both faced indefinite waits. Thus, for a process to be in deadlock, it is essential that all processes that hold units of a resource required by it are also in deadlock. We use concepts from graph theory to incorporate this aspect in a characterization of deadlocks in MISR systems.

A graph G is an ordered pair $G \equiv (N, E)$ where N is a set of *nodes* and E is a set of *edges*. A graph $G' \equiv (N', E')$ is a *subgraph* of a graph $G \equiv (N, E)$ if $N' \subseteq N$ and $E' \subseteq E$, i.e., if all nodes and edges contained in G' are also contained in G. G' is a nontrivial subgraph of G if $E' \neq \phi$, i.e., if it contains at least one edge. We now define a *knot* to characterize a deadlock in MISR systems.

Definition 8.3 Knot A nontrivial subgraph $G' \equiv (N', E')$ of an RRAG in which every node $n_i \in N'$ satisfies the following conditions:

1. For every edge of the form (n_i, n_j) in E: (n_i, n_j) is included in E' and n_j is included in N'.
2. If a path $n_i - \ldots - n_j$ exists in G', a path $n_j - \ldots - n_i$ also exists in G'.

Part 1 of Definition 8.3 ensures that if a node is included in a knot, all its out-edges, i.e., all edges emanating from it, are also included in the knot.

Part 2 of Definition 8.3 ensures that each out-edge of each node is included in a cycle. This fact ensures that each process in the knot is necessarily in the *blocked* state. Parts 1 and 2 together imply that all processes that can release a resource needed by some process in the knot are themselves included in the knot, which satisfies condition (8.2). Thus one can conclude that the presence of a knot in an RRAG is a necessary and sufficient condition for the existence of a deadlock in an MISR system.

Example 8.12

Deadlock in an MISR System

The RRAG of Figure 8.3 depicts the allocation state in Example 8.4 after requests 1–5 are made. It does not contain a knot since the path $P_i, \ldots, P_k$ exists in it but a path $P_k, \ldots, P_i$ does not exist in it. Now consider the situation after the following request is made:

6. P_k requests a printer.

Process P_k now blocks on the sixth request. The resulting RRAG is shown in Figure 8.10. The complete RRAG is a knot because Part 1 of Definition 8.3 is trivially satisfied, and every out-edge of every node is involved in a cycle, which satisfies Part 2 of Definition 8.3. It is easy to verify that processes $\{P_i, P_j, P_k\}$ are in a deadlock since $Blocked\_P = \{P_i, P_j, P_k\}$, $WF_i = \{P_j\}$, $WF_j = \{P_i, P_k\}$, and $WF_k = \{P_j\}$ satisfies conditions (8.1) and (8.2).

8.7.3 Single-Instance, Multiple-Request (SIMR) Systems

Each resource class in the SIMR system contains only one resource unit, and so it has exactly one out-edge in an RRAG. A process may make a multiple request, in which case it has more than one out-edge. Such a process remains blocked if even one of the resources requested by it is unavailable. This condition is satisfied when the process is involved in a cycle, so a cycle is a necessary and sufficient condition for a deadlock in an SIMR system. This property is illustrated by the system of Figure 8.11. The process node P_i has an out-edge (P_i, R_1) that is a part of a cycle, and an out-edge (P_i, R_3) that is not a part of any cycle. Process

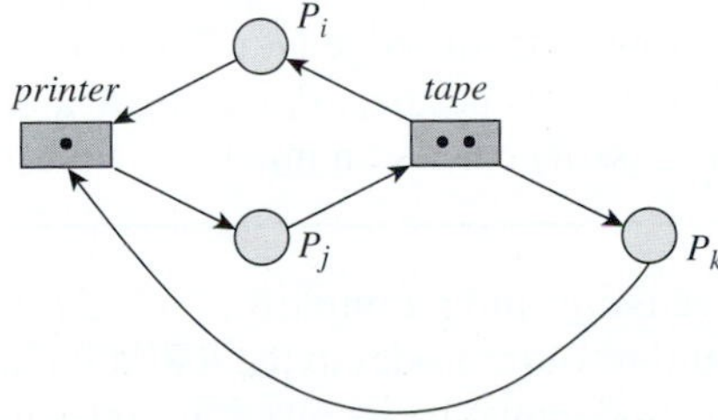

Figure 8.10 A knot in the RRAG of an MISR system implies a deadlock.

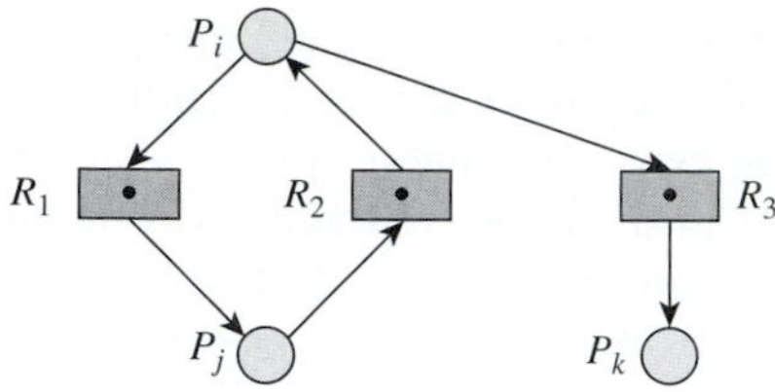

Figure 8.11 A cycle is a necessary and a sufficient condition for a deadlock in an SIMR system.

P_i remains blocked until a resource unit of R_1 can be allocated to it. Since the out-edge (P_i, R_1) is involved in a cycle, P_i faces an indefinite wait. P_j also faces an indefinite wait. Hence $\{P_i, P_j\}$ are involved in a deadlock.

8.7.4 Multiple-Instance, Multiple-Request (MIMR) Systems

In the MIMR model, resource classes contain several resource units and processes may make multiple requests, hence both process and resource nodes of an RRAG can have multiple out-edges. If none of the resource nodes involved in a cycle in the RRAG has multiple out-edges, the cycle is similar to a cycle in the RRAG of an SIMR system, and so it is a sufficient condition for the existence of a deadlock. However, if a resource node in a cycle has multiple out-edges, a cycle is a necessary condition but not a sufficient condition for a deadlock. In such cases every out-edge of the resource node must be involved in a cycle; this requirement is similar to that in the MISR systems. Example 8.13 illustrates this aspect.

Example 8.13 Deadlock in an MIMR System

The RRAG of Figure 8.12 contains the cycle $R_1 - P_i - R_2 - P_j - R_1$. Resource node R_1 contains an out-edge (R_1, P_k) that is not included in a cycle, hence process P_k may obtain resource R_3 and eventually release an instance of resource class R_1, which could be allocated to process P_j. It will break the cycle in the RRAG, hence there is no deadlock in the system. If the allocation edge of R_3 were to be (R_3, P_i), both out-edges of R_1 would be involved in cycles. Process P_j's request for R_1 would now face an indefinite wait, and so we would have a deadlock situation. Note that out-edge (P_i, R_4) of P_i is not involved in a cycle; however, a deadlock exists because P_i has made a multiple request and its request for resource class R_2 causes an indefinite wait for it.

From the above discussion and Example 8.13 it is clear that we must differentiate between process and resource nodes in the RRAG of an MIMR system—all out-edges of a resource node must be involved in cycles for a deadlock to arise, whereas a process node needs to have only one out-edge involved in a cycle.

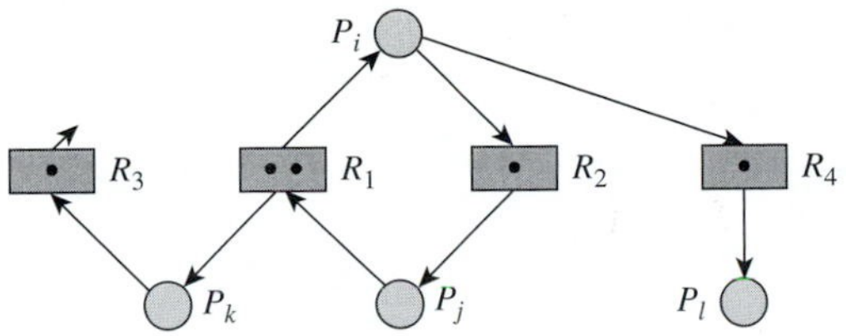

Figure 8.12 RRAG for an MIMR system.

We define a *resource knot* to incorporate this requirement, where a resource knot differs from a knot only in that Part 1 of Definition 8.4 applies only to resource nodes.

Definition 8.4 Resource Knot A nontrivial subgraph $G' \equiv (N', E')$ of an RRAG in which every node $n_i \in N'$ satisfies the following conditions:

1. If n_i is a resource node, for every edge of the form (n_i, n_j) in E: (n_i, n_j) is included in E' and n_j is included in N'.
2. If a path $n_i - \ldots - n_j$ exists in G', a path $n_j - \ldots - n_i$ also exists in G'.

Example 8.14

Resource Knot

Nodes $P_i, P_j, P_k, R_1, R_2,$ and R_3 of Figure 8.12 would be involved in a resource knot if the allocation edge of resource class R_3 is (R_3, P_i). Note that out-edge (P_i, R_4) of process P_i is not included in the resource knot.

Clearly, a resource knot is a necessary and sufficient condition for the existence of a deadlock in an MIMR system. In fact, we state here without proof that a resource knot is a necessary and sufficient condition for deadlock in all classes of systems discussed in this section (see Exercise 8.17).

8.7.5 Processes in Deadlock

D, the set of processes in deadlock, contains processes represented by process nodes in resource knots. It also contains some other processes that face indefinite waits. We use the following notation to identify all processes in D.

- RR_i The set of resource classes requested by process P_i.
- HS_k The *holder set* of resource class R_k, i.e., set of processes to which units of resource class R_k are allocated.
- KS The set of process nodes in resource knot(s) (we call it the *knot-set* of RRAG).
- AS An *auxiliary set* of process nodes in RRAG that face indefinite waits. These nodes are not included in a resource knot.

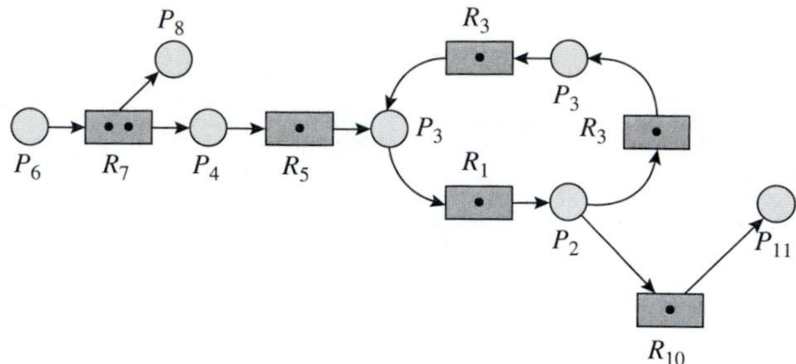

Figure 8.13 Processes in deadlock.

KS is the set of process nodes included in resource knots. Now a process $P_i \notin KS$ faces an indefinite wait if all holders of some resource class R_k requested by it are included in *KS*. Resource classes whose holders are included in $\{P_i\} \cup KS$ similarly cause indefinite waits for their requesters. Therefore we can identify *D*, the set of deadlocked processes, as follows:

$$AS = \{\, P_i \mid RR_i \text{ contains } R_k \text{ such that } HS_k \subseteq (KS \cup AS)\} \quad \textbf{(8.4)}$$

$$D = KS \cup AS \quad \textbf{(8.5)}$$

Example 8.15 Processes in Deadlock

Figure 8.13 shows an RRAG of an MIMR system. The cycle $P_1 - R_1 - P_2 - R_2 - P_3 - R_3 - P_1$ in the RRAG forms a resource knot because none of R_1, R_2, or R_3 have an out-edge leaving the cycle. Hence a deadlock exists in the system. We identify the processes in *D* as follows:

$$\begin{aligned} KS &= \{P_1, P_2, P_3\} \\ AS &= \{P_4\} \text{ since } RR_4 = \{R_5\},\ HS_5 = \{P_1\} \text{ and } \{P_1\} \subseteq \{P_1, P_2, P_3\} \\ D &= KS \cup AS = \{P_1, P_2, P_3, P_4\}. \end{aligned}$$

Process P_6 is not included in *AS* since $RR_6 = \{R_7\}$, $HS_7 = \{P_4, P_8\}$, and $HS_7 \not\subseteq (KS \cup AS)$.

8.8 DEADLOCK HANDLING IN PRACTICE

An operating system manages numerous and diverse resources—hardware resources such as memory and I/O devices, software resources such as files containing programs or data and interprocess messages, and kernel resources such as data structures and control blocks used by the kernel. The overhead of deadlock detection-and-resolution and deadlock avoidance make them unattractive deadlock handling policies in practice. Hence, an OS either uses the deadlock prevention approach, creates a situation in which explicit deadlock handling actions are unnecessary, or simply does not care about possibility of deadlocks. Further, since deadlock prevention constrains the order in which processes request their resources, operating systems tend to handle deadlock issues separately for each kind of resources like memory, I/O devices, files, and kernel resources. We discuss these approaches in the following.

Memory Memory is a preemptible resource, so its use by processes cannot cause a deadlock. Explicit deadlock handling is therefore unnecessary. The memory allocated to a process is freed by swapping out the process whenever the memory is needed for another process.

I/O Devices Among deadlock prevention policies, the "all resources together" policy requires processes to make one multiple request for *all* their resource requirements. This policy incurs the least CPU overhead, but it has the drawback mentioned in Section 8.5.1—it leads to underutilization of I/O devices that are allocated much before a process actually needs them. Resource ranking, on the other hand, is not a feasible policy to control use of I/O devices because any assignment of resource ranks causes inconvenience to some group of users. This difficulty is compounded by the fact that I/O devices are generally nonpreemptible. Operating systems overcome this difficulty by creating virtual devices. For example, the system creates a virtual printer by using some disk area to store a file that is to be printed. Actual printing takes place when a printer becomes available. Since virtual devices are created whenever needed, it is not necessary to preallocate them as in the "all resources together" policy unless the system faces a shortage of disk space.

Files and Interprocess Messages A file is a user-created resource. An OS contains a large number of files. Deadlock prevention policies such as resource ranking could cause high overhead and inconvenience to users. Hence operating systems do not extend deadlock handling actions to files; processes accessing a common set of files are expected to make their own arrangements to avoid deadlocks. For similar reasons, operating systems do not handle deadlocks caused by interprocess messages.

Control Blocks The kernel allocates control blocks such as process control blocks (PCBs) and event control blocks (ECBs) to processes in a specific order—a PCB is allocated when a process is created, and an ECB is allocated when the process becomes blocked on an event. Hence resource ranking can be a solution here. If a simpler policy is desired, all control blocks for a job or process can be allocated together at its initiation.

8.8.1 Deadlock Handling in Unix

Most operating systems simply ignore the possibility of deadlocks involving user processes, and Unix is no exception. However, Unix addresses deadlocks due to sharing of kernel data structures by user processes. Recall from Section 5.4.1 that a

Unix process that was running on the CPU executes kernel code when an interrupt or system call occurs, hence user processes could concurrently execute kernel code. The kernel employs the resource ranking approach to deadlock prevention (see Section 8.5.2) by requiring processes to set locks on kernel data structures in a standard order; however, there are exceptions to this rule, and so deadlocks could arise. We present simplified views of two arrangements used to prevent deadlocks.

The Unix kernel uses a buffer cache (see Section 14.13.1.2) to speed up accesses to frequently used disk blocks. It consists of a pool of buffers in memory and a hashed data structure to check whether a specific disk block is present in a buffer. To facilitate reuse of buffers, a list of buffers is maintained in least recently used (LRU) order—the first buffer in the list is the least recently used buffer and the last buffer is the most recently used buffer. The normal order of accessing a disk block is to use the hashed data structure to locate a disk block if it exists in a buffer, put a lock on the buffer containing the disk block, and then put a lock on the list of buffers to update the LRU status of the buffer. However, if a process merely wants to obtain a buffer for loading a new disk block, it directly accesses the list of buffers and takes off the first buffer that is not in use at the moment. To perform this action, the process puts a lock on the list. Then it tries to set the lock on the first buffer in the list. Deadlocks are possible because this order of locking the list and a buffer is different from the standard order of setting these locks.

Unix uses an innovative approach to avoid such deadlocks. It provides a special operation that tries to set a lock, but returns with a failure condition code if the lock is already set. The process looking for a free buffer uses this operation to check whether a buffer is free. If a failure condition code is returned, it simply tries to set the lock on the next buffer, and so on until it finds a buffer that it can use. This approach avoids deadlocks by avoiding circular waits.

Another situation in which locks cannot be set in a standard order is in the file system function that establishes a link (see Section 13.4.2). A link command provides path names for a file and a directory that is to contain the link to the file. This command can be implemented by locking the directories containing the file and the link. However, a standard order cannot be defined for locking these directories. Consequently, two processes concurrently trying to lock the same directories may become deadlocked. To avoid such deadlocks, the file system function does not try to acquire both locks at the same time. It first locks one directory, updates it in the desired manner, and releases the lock. It then locks the other directory and updates it. Thus it requires only one lock at any time. This approach prevents deadlocks because the hold-and-wait condition is not satisfied by these processes.

8.8.2 Deadlock Handling in Windows

Windows Vista provides a feature called *wait chain traversal* (WCT), which assists applications and debuggers in detecting deadlocks. A wait chain starts on a thread and is analogous to a path in the resource request and allocation graph (RRAG). Thus, a thread points to an object or lock for which it is waiting, and the object or lock points to the thread that holds it. A debugger can investigate the cause of a hang-up or freeze in an application by invoking the function `getthreadwaitchain` with the id of a thread to retrieve a chain starting on that thread. The function returns an array containing the ids of threads found on a wait chain starting on the designated thread, and a boolean value which indicates whether any subset of the threads found on the wait chain form a cycle.

8.9 SUMMARY

A *deadlock* is a situation in which a set of processes wait indefinitely for events because each of the events can be caused only by other processes in the set. A deadlock adversely affects user service, throughput and resource efficiency. In this chapter, we discussed OS techniques for handling deadlocks.

A resource deadlock arises when four conditions hold simultaneously: Resources are nonshareable and nonpreemptible, a process holds some resources while it waits for resources that are in use by other processes, which is called the *hold-and-wait* condition; and circular waits exist among processes. An OS can discover a deadlock by analyzing the *allocation state* of a system, which consists of information concerning allocated resources and resource requests on which processes are blocked. A *graph model* of allocation state can be used in systems where a process cannot request more than one resource unit of a resource class. A *resource request and allocation graph* (RRAG) depicts resource allocation and pending resource requests in the OS, whereas a *wait-for graph* (WFG) depicts wait-for relationships between processes. In both models, a circular wait condition is reflected in a circular path in the graph. A *matrix model* represents the allocation state in a set of matrices.

When a process completes its operation, it releases its resources and the kernel can allocate them to other processes that had requested them. When a matrix model of allocation state is used, a deadlock can be detected by finding whether every process currently blocked on a resource request can be allocated the required resource through a sequence of process completion, resource release, and resource allocation events. Deadlock detection incurs a high overhead as a result of this check, so approaches that ensure the absence of deadlocks have been studied. In the *deadlock prevention* approach, the resource allocation policy imposes some constraints on resource requests so that the four conditions for deadlock would not be satisfied simultaneously. In the *deadlock avoidance* approach, the resource allocator knows a process's maximum need for resources. At every resource request, it checks whether a sequence of process completion, resource release, and resource allocation events can be found through which all processes could satisfy their maximum need and complete their operation. It grants the resource request only if this check is satisfied.

When a graph model of allocation state is used, deadlocks can be characterized in terms of paths in the graph. However, the characterization becomes complex when a resource class can contain many resource units.

For reasons of convenience and efficiency, an OS may use different deadlock handling policies for different kinds of resources. Typically, an OS uses deadlock prevention approaches for kernel resources, and creates virtual resources to avoid deadlocks over I/O devices; however, it does not handle deadlocks involving user resources like files and interprocess messages.

TEST YOUR CONCEPTS

8.1 Classify each of the following statements as true or false:

a. A cycle in the resource request and allocation graph (RRAG) is a necessary and sufficient condition for a deadlock if each resource class contains only one resource unit.

b. Deadlock resolution guarantees that deadlocks will not occur in future.

c. The "all resources together" policy of deadlock prevention ensures that the circular wait condition will never hold in the system.

d. The resource ranking policy of deadlock prevention ensures that the hold-and-wait condition will never hold in the system.

e. If a set of processes D is deadlocked, the set *Blocked* of Algorithm 8.1 will contain some of these processes when execution of the algorithm completes; however, *Blocked* may not contain all of them.

f. If a process P_i requests r units of a resource class R_j and $\geq r$ units of R_j are free, then the banker's algorithm will definitely allocate r units to P_i.

g. The banker's algorithm does not guarantee that deadlocks will not occur in future.

h. An OS has a single resource class that is controlled by the banker's algorithm. 12 units of the resource have been currently allocated to processes, of which process P_i has been allocated 2 resources. If P_i has a max need of 5 resources, the system contains at least 15 resource units.

i. An OS employing a multiple-resource banker's algorithm has been in operation for some time with four processes. A new process arrives in the system. It is initially not allocated any resources. Is the new allocation state of the system safe?

j. If every resource class in a system has a single resource unit, every cycle in the RRAG of the system is also a resource knot.

8.2 An OS contains n resource units of a resource class. Three processes use this resource class, and each of them has a maximum need of 3 resource units. The manner and the order in which the processes request units of the resource class are not known. What is the smallest value of n for operation of the system to be free of deadlocks?

a. 3, **b.** 7, **c.** 6, **d.** 9

8.3 An OS employs the banker's algorithm to control allocation of 7 tape drives. Maximum need of three processes P_1, P_2, and P_3 are 7, 3, and 5 drives, respectively. How many drives can the OS allocate safely to process P_1, if the current allocation state is as follows:

a. 2, 1, and 1 tape drives are allocated to processes P_1, P_2, and P_3, respectively.

i. 0, **ii.** 1, **iii.** 2, **iv.** 3

b. 1, 2, and 1 tape drives are allocated to processes P_1, P_2, and P_3, respectively.

i. 0, **ii.** 1, **iii.** 2, **iv.** 3

EXERCISES

8.1 Clearly justify why deadlocks cannot arise in a bounded buffer producers–consumers system.

8.2 When resource ranking is used as a deadlock prevention policy, a process is permitted to request a unit of resource class R_k only if $rank_k > rank_i$ for every resource class R_i whose resources are allocated to it. Explain whether deadlocks can arise if the condition is changed to $rank_k \geq rank_i$.

8.3 A system containing preemptible resources uses the following resource allocation policy: When a resource requested by some process P_i is unavailable,

a. The resource is preempted from one of its holder processes P_j if P_j is *younger* than P_i. The resource is now allocated to P_i. It is allocated back to P_j when P_i completes. (A process is considered to be younger if it was initiated later.)

b. If condition (a) is not satisfied, P_i is blocked for the resource.

A released resource is always allocated to its oldest requester. Show that deadlocks cannot arise in this system. Also show that starvation does not occur.

8.4 Develop a matrix model for the allocation state of the system of Figure 8.13. Apply Algorithm 8.1 to find the processes involved in deadlock.

8.5 The system of Figure 8.13 is changed such that process P_6 has made a multiple request for resources R_7 and R_1. What are the processes involved in a deadlock? Process P_1 is aborted and process P_3 makes a request for resource R_5. Is the system in a deadlock now?

8.6 A system uses a deadlock detection-and-resolution policy. The cost of aborting one process is considered to be one unit. Discuss how to identify victim process(es) so as to minimize the cost of deadlock resolution in each of the following systems: (a) SISR systems, (b) SIMR systems, (c) MISR systems, and (d) MIMR systems.

8.7 Is the allocation state in which 6, 1, and 2 resource units are allocated to processes P_1, P_2, and P_3 in the system of Example 8.10 safe? Would the allocation state in which 3, 2, and 3 resource units are allocated be safe?

8.8 Would the following requests be granted in the current state by the banker's algorithm?

Max need:

	R_1	R_2
P_1	2	5
P_2	3	2

Allocated resources:

	R_1	R_2
P_1	1	3
P_2	2	1

	R_1	R_2
Total alloc	3	4
Total exist	4	5

a. Process P_2 requests $(1, 0)$
b. Process P_2 requests $(0, 1)$
c. Process P_2 requests $(1, 1)$
d. Process P_1 requests $(1, 0)$
e. Process P_1 requests $(0, 1)$

8.9 In the following system:

Max need:

	R_1	R_2	R_3
P_1	3	6	8
P_2	4	3	3
P_3	3	4	4

Allocated resources:

	R_1	R_2	R_3
P_1	2	2	3
P_2	2	0	3
P_3	1	2	4

	R_1	R_2	R_3
Total alloc	5	4	10
Total exist	7	7	10

a. Is the current allocation state safe?

b. Would the following requests be granted in the current state by the banker's algorithm?
   i. Process P_1 requests $(1, 1, 0)$
   ii. Process P_3 requests $(0, 1, 0)$
   iii. Process P_2 requests $(0, 1, 0)$

8.10 Three processes P_1, P_2, and P_3 use a resource controlled through the banker's algorithm. Two unallocated resource units exist in the current allocation state. When P_1 and P_2 request for one resource unit each, they become blocked on their requests; however, when P_3 requests for two resource units, its request is granted right away. Explain why it may be so.

8.11 A system using the banker's algorithm for resource allocation contains n_1 and n_2 resource units of resource classes R_1 and R_2 and three processes P_1, P_2, and P_3. The unallocated resources with the system are (1,1). The following observations are made regarding the operation of the system:

a. If process P_1 makes a (1,0) request followed by a (0,1) request, the (1,0) request will be granted but the (0,1) request will not be granted.

b. If, instead of making the resource requests in part (a), process P_1 makes a (0,1) request, it will be granted.

Find a possible set of values for the current allocations and maximum resource requirements of the processes such that decisions using the banker's algorithm will match the above observations.

8.12 Show that when the banker's algorithm is applied to a finite set of processes, each having a finite execution time, each resource request will be granted eventually.

8.13 Processes in a particular OS make multiple requests. This OS uses a banker's algorithm designed for a single resource class to implement deadlock avoidance as follows: When a process requests resource units of some n resource classes, the request is viewed as a set of n single requests; e.g., a multiple request $(2, 1, 3)$ would be viewed as three single requests $(2, 0, 0)$, $(0, 1, 0)$, and $(0, 0, 3)$. The multiple request is granted only if each single request would have been granted in the current allocation state of the system. Is this a sound approach to deadlock avoidance? Justify your answer, either by giving an argument about its correctness, or by giving an example where it will fail.

8.14 A single-resource system contains $Total\_resources_s$ units of resource class R_s. If the system contains n processes, show that a deadlock cannot arise if any one of the following conditions is satisfied (see the notation used in Algorithm 8.2):

a. For all i : $Max\_need_{i,s} \leq Total\_resources_s/n$

b. $\Sigma_i\ Max\_need_{i,s} \leq Total\_resources_s$

c. $\Sigma_i\ Max\_need_{i,s} \leq Total\_resources_s + n - 1$ and for all i, $1 \leq Max\_need_{i,s} \leq Total\_resources_s$

8.15 In a single-resource system containing $Total\_resources_s$ units of resource class R_s, set PA is defined as follows:

$$PA = \{P_i \mid P_i \text{ has been allocated some resources but all its resource requirements have not been met}\}$$

Which of the following statements are true (see the notation used in Algorithm 8.2)? Justify your answer.

a. "Processes in PA will definitely become deadlocked if $\Sigma_i\ Max\_need_{i,s} > Total\_resources_s$."

b. "Processes in PA may be deadlocked only if there exists some integer k such that $num\_proc(k) > Total\_resources_s/k$, where $num\_proc(k)$ is the number of processes in PA whose maximum requirement for the units of resource class R_s exceeds k."

8.16 The new allocation state of a system after granting of a resource request is not a safe allocation state according to the banker's algorithm.

a. Does it imply that a deadlock will definitely arise in future?

b. Can the system make a transition to a safe allocation state? If so, give an example showing such a transition.

8.17 Show that a resource knot in an RRAG is a necessary and sufficient condition for deadlocks in SISR, MISR, SIMR, and MIMR systems.

8.18 A WFG is used to represent the allocation state of a system in which resource classes may contain multiple units and processes can make multiple resource requests (an MIMR system). Develop a deadlock characterization using the WFG. (*Hint:* A node in the WFG would have more than one out-edge under two conditions: When a process requests a resource unit of a multiple-instance resource class, and when a process makes a multiple request. These are called OR out-edges and AND out-edges, respectively. To differentiate between the two kinds of out-edges, the AND out-edges of a process are joined by a straight line as shown in Figure 8.14(b). Figure 8.14(a) shows the out-edges for the RRAG of Figure 8.10, whereas Figure 8.14(b) shows the out-edges for the RRAG of Figure 8.11. These out-edges have different implications for deadlock detection!)

8.19 An OS uses a simple policy to deal with deadlock situations. When it finds that a set of processes is deadlocked, it aborts all of them and restarts them immediately. What are the conditions under which the deadlock will not recur?

8.20 An OS has a single disk, which it uses (a) to create user files and (b) to create a virtual printer for every process. Space is allocated for both uses on a demand basis, and a process is blocked if its disk space requirement cannot be granted. Print requests directed at a virtual

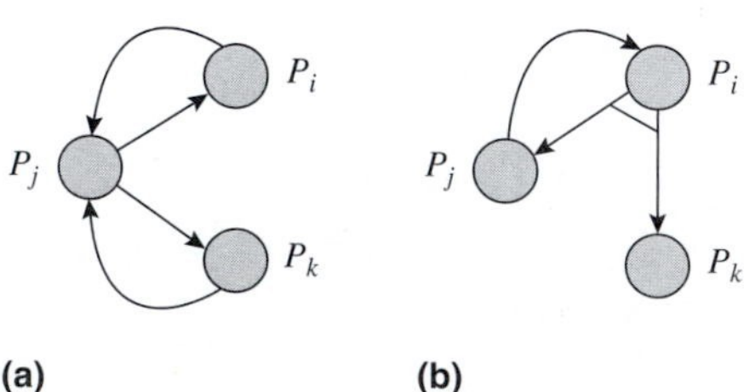

Figure 8.14 WFGs with multiple out-edges: (a) OR edges; (b) AND edges.

printer are sent to a real printer when a process finishes. Is there a possibility of deadlocks in this system? If so, under what conditions? Suggest a solution to the deadlock problem.

8.21 A *phantom deadlock* is a situation wherein a deadlock handling algorithm declares a deadlock but a deadlock does not actually exist. If processes are permitted to withdraw their resource requests, show that Algorithm 8.1 may detect phantom deadlocks. Can detection of phantom deadlocks be prevented?

8.22 A road crosses a set of railway tracks at two points. Gates are constructed on the road at each crossing to stop road traffic when a train is about to pass. Train traffic is stopped if a car blocks a track. Two way traffic of cars is permitted on the road and two-way train traffic is permitted on the railway tracks.

a. Discuss whether deadlocks can arise in the road-and-train traffic. Would there be no deadlocks if both road and train traffic are only one-way?

b. Design a set of simple rules to avoid deadlocks in the road-and-train traffic.

8.23 It is proposed to use a deadlock prevention approach for the dining philosophers problem (see Section 6.7.3) as follows: Seats at the dinner table are numbered from 1 to n, and forks are also numbered from 1 to n, such that the left fork for seat i has the fork number i. Philosophers are required to obey the following rule: A philosopher must first pick up the lower-numbered fork, then pick up the higher-numbered fork. Show that deadlocks cannot arise in this system.

8.24 A set of processes D is in deadlock. It is observed that

a. If a process $P_j \in D$ is aborted, a set of processes $D' \subset D$ is still in deadlock.

b. If a process $P_i \in D$ is aborted, no deadlock exists in the system.

State some possible reasons for this difference and explain with the help of an example. [*Hint:* Refer to Eqs. (8.4) and (8.5).]

8.25 After Algorithm 8.1 has determined that a set of processes D is in deadlock, one of the processes in D is aborted. What is the most efficient way to determine whether a deadlock exists in the new state?

BIBLIOGRAPHY

Dijkstra (1965), Havender (1968), and Habermann (1969) are early works on deadlock handling. Dijkstra (1965) and Habermann (1969) discuss the banker's algorithm. Coffman et al. (1971) discusses the deadlock detection algorithm for a system containing multiple-instance resources. Holt (1972) provided a graph theoretic characterization for deadlocks. Isloor and Marsland (1980) is a good survey paper on this topic. Zobel (1983) is an extensive bibliography. Howard (1973) discusses the practical deadlock handling approach described in Section 8.8. Tay and Loke (1995) and Levine (2003) discuss characterization of deadlocks.

Bach (1986) describes deadlock handling in Unix.

1. Bach, M. J. (1986): *The Design of the Unix Operating System*, Prentice Hall, Englewood Cliffs, N. J.
2. Coffman, E. G., M. S. Elphick, and A. Shoshani (1971): "System deadlocks," *Computing Surveys*, **3** (2), 67–78.
3. Dijkstra, E. W. (1965) : "Cooperating sequential processes," Technical report EWD–123, Technlogical University, Eindhoven.
4. Habermann, A. N. (1969): "Prevention of System deadlocks," *Communications of the ACM*, **12** (7), 373–377.
5. Habermann, A. N. (1973): "A new approach to avoidance of system deadlocks," in *Lecture notes in Computer Science*, Vol. 16, Springer-Verlag.
6. Havender, J. W. (1968): "Avoiding deadlock in multitasking systems," *IBM Systems Journal*, **7** (2), 74–84.
7. Holt, R. C. (1972): "Some deadlock properties of computer systems," *Computing Surveys*, **4** (3), 179–196.

8. Howard, J. H. (1973): "Mixed solutions to the deadlock problem," *Communications of the ACM*, **6** (3), 427–430.
9. Isloor, S. S., and T. A. Marsland (1980): "The deadlock problem—an overview," *Computer*, **13** (9), 58–70.
10. Levine, G. (2003): "Defining deadlock," *Operating Systems Review*, **37**, 1.
11. Rypka, D. J., and A. P. Lucido (1979): "Deadlock detection and avoidance for shared logical resources," *IEEE Transactions on Software Engineering*, **5** (5), 465–471.
12. Tay, Y. C., and W. T. Loke (1995): "On Deadlocks of exclusive AND-requests for resources," *Distributed Computing*, Springer Verlag, **9**, 2, 77–94.
13. Zobel, D. (1983): "The deadlock problem—a classifying bibliography," *Operating Systems Review*, **17** (4), 6–15.

Chapter 9

Message Passing

Message passing suits diverse situations where exchange of information between processes plays a key role. One of its prominent uses is in the *client–server* paradigm, wherein a *server* process offers a service, and other processes, called its *clients*, send messages to it to use its service. This paradigm is used widely—a microkernel-based OS structures functionalities such as scheduling in the form of servers, a conventional OS offers services such as printing through servers, and, on the Internet, a variety of services are offered by Web servers. Another prominent use of message passing is in higher-level protocols for exchange of electronic mails and communication between tasks in parallel or distributed programs. Here, message passing is used to exchange information, while other parts of the protocol are employed to ensure reliability.

The key issues in message passing are how the processes that send and receive messages identify each other, and how the kernel performs various actions related to delivery of messages—how it stores and delivers messages and whether it blocks a process that sends a message until its message is delivered. These features are operating system–specific.

We describe different message passing arrangements employed in operating systems and discuss their significance for user processes and for the kernel. We also describe message passing in Unix and in Windows operating systems.

9.1 OVERVIEW OF MESSAGE PASSING

In Section 5.2.5, we summarized four ways in which processes interact with one another—*data sharing, message passing, synchronization*, and *signals* (see Table 5.7). Of these, we discussed data sharing and synchronization in Chapter 6 and signals in Chapter 5. Data sharing provides means to access values of shared data in a mutually exclusive manner. Process synchronization is performed by blocking a process until other processes have performed certain specific actions. Capabilities of message passing overlap those of data sharing and synchronization; however, each form of process interaction has its own niche application area. We discuss this aspect after taking an overview of message passing.

Figure 9.1 shows an example of message passing. Process P_i sends a message to process P_j by executing the statement `send` (P_j, <*message*>). The compiled code of the `send` statement invokes the library module `send`. `send` makes a

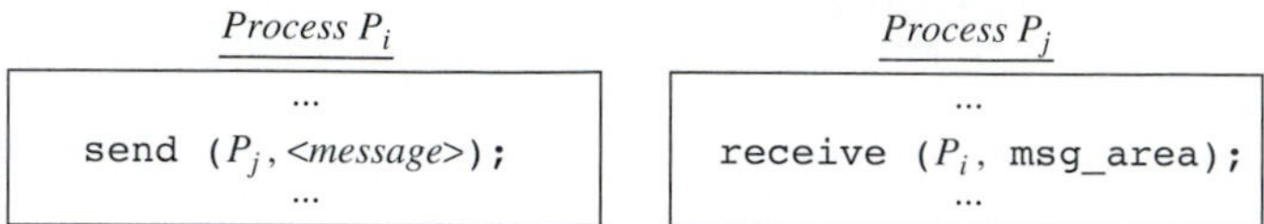

Figure 9.1 Message passing.

system call *send*, with P_j and the message as parameters. Execution of the statement `receive (`P_i`, msg_area)`, where `msg_area` is an area in P_j's address space, results in a system call *receive*.

The semantics of message passing are as follows: At a *send* call by P_i, the kernel checks whether process P_j is blocked on a *receive* call for receiving a message from process P_i. If so, it copies the message into `msg_area` and activates P_j. If process P_j has not already made a *receive* call, the kernel arranges to deliver the message to it when P_j eventually makes a *receive* call. When process P_j receives the message, it interprets the message and takes an appropriate action.

Messages may be passed between processes that exist in the same computer or in different computers connected to a network. Also, the processes participating in message passing may decide on what a specific message means and what actions the receiver process should perform on receiving it. Because of this flexibility, message passing is used in the following applications:

- Message passing is employed in the *client–server* paradigm, which is used to communicate between components of a microkernel-based operating system and user processes, to provide services such as the print service to processes within an OS, or to provide Web-based services to client processes located in other computers.
- Message passing is used as the backbone of higher-level protocols employed for communicating between computers or for providing the electronic mail facility.
- Message passing is used to implement communication between tasks in a parallel or distributed program.

In principle, message passing can be performed by using shared variables. For example, `msg_area` in Figure 9.1 could be a shared variable. P_i could deposit a value or a message in it and P_j could collect it from there. However, this approach is cumbersome because the processes would have to create a shared variable with the correct size and share its name. They would also have to use synchronization analogous to the producers–consumers problem (see Section 6.7.1) to ensure that a receiver process accessed a message in a shared variable only after a sender process had deposited it there. Message passing is far simpler in this situation. It is also more general, because it can be used in a distributed system environment, where the shared variable approach is not feasible.

The producers–consumers problem with a single buffer, a single producer process, and a single consumer process can be implemented by message passing as shown in Figure 9.2. The solution does not use any shared variables. Instead, process P_i, which is the producer process, has a variable called *buffer* and process

```
begin
  Parbegin
    var buffer : . . . ;                  var message_area : . . . ;
    repeat                                repeat
      { Produce in buffer }                 receive (P_i, message_area);
      send (P_j, buffer);                   { Consume from message_area }
      { Remainder of the cycle }            { Remainder of the cycle }
    forever;                              forever;
  Parend;
  end.
            Process P_i                             Process P_j
```

Figure 9.2 Producers–consumers solution using message passing.

P_j, which is the consumer process, has a variable called *message_area*. The producer process produces in *buffer* and sends the contents of *buffer* in a message to the consumer. The consumer receives the message in *message_area* and consumes it from there. The *send* system call blocks the producer process until the message is delivered to the consumer, and the *receive* system call blocks the consumer until a message is sent to it.

The producers–consumers solution of Figure 9.2 is much simpler than the solutions discussed in Chapter 6; however, it is restrictive because it permits a single producer and a single consumer process. In the general case, it is effective to use the process synchronization means discussed in Chapter 6 to implement a system containing producers and consumers.

Issues in Message Passing Two important issues in message passing are:

- *Naming of processes:* Whether names of sender and receiver processes are explicitly indicated in `send` and `receive` statements, or whether their identities are deduced by the kernel in some other manner.
- *Delivery of messages:* Whether a sender process is blocked until the message sent by it is delivered, what the order is in which messages are delivered to the receiver process, and how exceptional conditions are handled.

These issues dictate implementation arrangements and also influence the generality of message passing. For example, if a sender process is required to know the identity of a receiver process, the scope of message passing would be limited to processes in the same application. Relaxing this requirement would extend message passing to processes in different applications and processes operating in different computer systems. Similarly, providing FCFS message delivery may be rather restrictive; processes may wish to receive messages in some other order.

9.1.1 Direct and Indirect Naming

In *direct naming*, sender and receiver processes mention each other's name. For example, the `send` and `receive` statements might have the following syntax:

```
send (<destination_process>, <message_length>, <message_address>);
receive (<source_process>, <message_area>);
```

where *<destination_process>* and *<source_process>* are process names (typically, they are process ids assigned by the kernel), *<message_address>* is the address of the memory area in the sender process's address space that contains the textual form of the message to be sent, and *<message_area>* is a memory area in the receiver's address space where the message is to be delivered. The processes of Figure 9.2 used direct naming.

Direct naming can be used in two ways: In *symmetric naming*, both sender and receiver processes specify each other's name. Thus, a process can decide which process to receive a message from. However, it has to know the name of every process that wishes to send it a message, which is difficult when processes of different applications wish to communicate, or when a server wishes to receive a request from any one of a set of clients. In *asymmetric naming*, the receiver does not name the process from which it wishes to receive a message; the kernel gives it a message sent to it by *some* process.

In *indirect naming*, processes do not mention each other's name in `send` and `receive` statements. We discuss indirect naming in Section 9.3.

9.1.2 Blocking and Nonblocking Sends

A blocking *send* blocks a sender process until the message to be sent is delivered to the destination process. This method of message passing is called *synchronous message passing*. A nonblocking *send* call permits a sender to continue its operation after making a *send* call, irrespective of whether the message is delivered immediately; such message passing is called *asynchronous* message passing. In both cases, the *receive* primitive is typically blocking.

Synchronous message passing provides some nice properties for user processes and simplifies actions of the kernel. A sender process has a guarantee that the message sent by it is delivered before it continues its operation. This feature simplifies the design of concurrent processes. The kernel delivers the message immediately if the destination process has already made a *receive* call for receiving a message; otherwise, it blocks the sender process until the destination process makes a *receive* call. The kernel can simply let the message remain in the sender's memory area until it is delivered. However, use of blocking *send*s has one drawback—it may unnecessarily delay a sender process in some situations, for example, while communicating with a heavily loaded print server.

Asynchronous message passing enhances concurrency between the sender and receiver processes by letting the sender process continue its operation. However, it also causes a synchronization problem because the sender should not alter contents of the memory area which contains text of the message until the message is delivered. To overcome this problem, the kernel performs *message buffering*—when a process makes a *send* call, the kernel allocates a buffer in the system area and copies the message into the buffer. This way, the sender process is free to access the memory area that contained text of the message. However, this arrangement involves substantial memory commitment for buffers when many messages are awaiting delivery. It also consumes CPU time, as a message has to be copied twice—once into a system buffer when a *send* call is made, and later into the message area of the receiver at the time of message delivery.

9.1.3 Exceptional Conditions in Message Passing

To facilitate handling of exceptional conditions, the *send* and *receive* calls take two additional parameters. The first parameter is a set of flags indicating how the process wants exceptional conditions to be handled; we will call this parameter *flags*. The second parameter is the address of a memory area in which the kernel provides a condition code describing the outcome of the *send* or *receive* call; we will call this area *status_area*.

When a process makes a *send* or *receive* call, the kernel deposits a condition code in *status_area*. It then checks *flags* to decide whether it should handle any exceptional conditions and performs the necessary actions. It then returns control to the process. The process checks the condition code provided by the kernel and handles any exceptional conditions it wished to handle itself.

Some exceptional conditions and their handling actions are as follows:

1. The destination process mentioned in a *send* call does not exist.
2. In symmetric naming, the source process mentioned in a *receive* call does not exist.
3. A *send* call cannot be processed because the kernel has run out of buffer memory.
4. No message exists for a process when it makes a *receive* call.
5. A set of processes becomes deadlocked when a process is blocked on a *receive* call.

In cases 1 and 2, the kernel may abort the process that made the *send* or *receive* call and set its termination code to describe the exceptional condition. In case 3, the sender process may be blocked until some buffer space becomes available. Case 4 is really not an exception if *receive*s are blocking (they generally are!), but it may be treated as an exception so that the receiving process has an opportunity to handle the condition if it so desires. A process may prefer the standard action, which is that the kernel should block the process until a message arrives for it, or it may prefer an action of its own choice, like waiting for a specified amount of time before giving up.

More severe exceptions belong to the realm of OS policies. The deadlock situation of case 5 is an example. Most operating systems do not handle this particular exception because it incurs the overhead of deadlock detection. Difficult-to-handle situations, such as a process waiting a long time on a *receive* call, also belong to the realm of OS policies.

9.2 IMPLEMENTING MESSAGE PASSING

9.2.1 Buffering of Interprocess Messages

When a process P_i sends a message to some process P_j by using a nonblocking *send*, the kernel builds an *interprocess message control block* (IMCB) to store all information needed to deliver the message (see Figure 9.3). The control block contains names of the sender and destination processes, the length of the message, and the text of the message. The control block is allocated a buffer in the kernel area. When process P_j makes a *receive* call, the kernel copies the message from the appropriate IMCB into the message area provided by P_j.

The pointer fields of IMCBs are used to form IMCB lists to simplify message delivery. Figure 9.4 shows the organization of IMCB lists when blocking *sends* and FCFS message delivery are used. In symmetric naming, a separate list is used for every pair of communicating processes. When a process P_i performs a *receive* call to receive a message from process P_j, the IMCB list for the pair P_i–P_j is used to deliver the message. In asymmetric naming, a single IMCB list can be maintained per recipient process. When a process performs a *receive,* the first IMCB in its list is processed to deliver a message.

If blocking *sends* are used, at most one message sent by a process can be undelivered at any point in time. The process is blocked until the message is delivered. Hence it is not necessary to copy the message into an IMCB. The

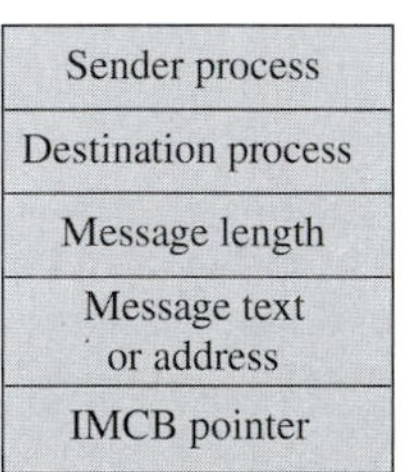

Figure 9.3 Interprocess message control block (IMCB).

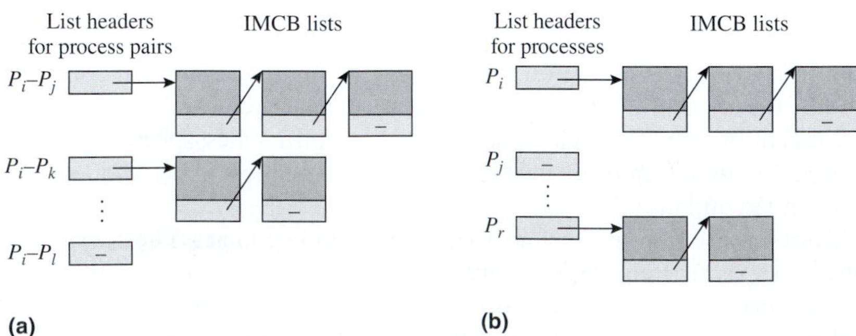

Figure 9.4 Lists of IMCBs for blocking *sends* in (a) symmetric naming; (b) asymmetric naming.

kernel can simply note the address of the message text in the sender's memory area, and use this information while delivering the message. This arrangement saves one copy operation on the message. However, it faces difficulties if the sender is swapped out before the message is delivered, so it may be preferable to use an IMCB. Fewer IMCBs would be needed than when *send*s are nonblocking, because at most one message sent by each process can be in an IMCB at any time.

The kernel may have to reserve a considerable amount of memory for interprocess messages, particularly if nonblocking sends are used. In such cases, it may save message texts on the disk. An IMCB would then contain the address of the disk block where the message is stored, rather than the message text itself.

9.2.2 Delivery of Interprocess Messages

When a process P_i sends a message to process P_j, the kernel delivers the message to P_j immediately if P_j is currently blocked on a *receive* call for a message from P_i, or from any process. After delivering the message, the kernel must also change the state of P_j to *ready*. If process P_j has not already performed a *receive* call, the kernel must arrange to deliver the message when P_j performs a *receive* call later. Thus, message delivery actions occur at both *send* and *receive* calls.

Recall from Section 5.2.4 that the kernel uses an *event control block* (ECB) to note actions that should be performed when an anticipated event occurs. The ECB contains three fields:

- Description of the anticipated event
- Id of the process that awaits the event
- An ECB pointer for forming ECB lists

Figure 9.5 shows use of ECBs to implement message passing with symmetric naming and blocking *send*s. When P_i makes a *send* call, the kernel checks whether an ECB exists for the *send* call by P_i, i.e., whether P_j had made a *receive* call and was waiting for P_i to send a message. If it is not the case, the kernel knows that the *receive* call would occur sometime in future, so it creates an ECB for the event "receive from P_i by P_j" and specifies P_i as the process that will be affected by the event. Process P_i is put into the *blocked* state and the address of the ECB is put in the event info field of its PCB [see Figure 9.5(a)]. Figure 9.5(b) illustrates

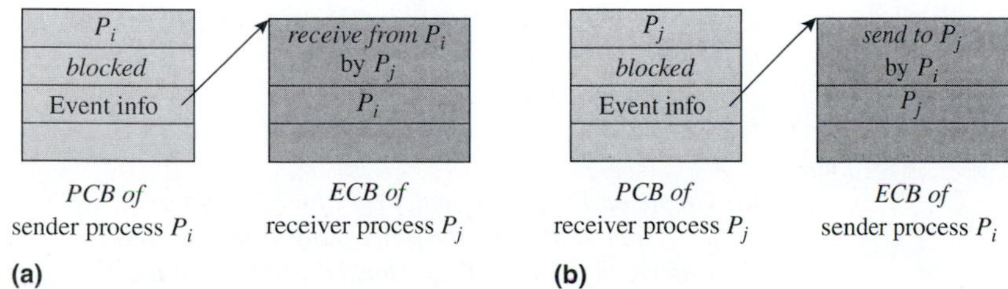

Figure 9.5 ECBs to implement symmetric naming and blocking *send*s (a) at *send*; (b) at *receive*.

the case when process P_j makes a *receive* call before P_i makes a *send* call. An ECB for a "send to P_j by P_i" event is now created. The id of P_j is put in the ECB to indicate that the state of P_j will be affected when the *send* event occurs.

Figure 9.6 shows complete details of the kernel actions for implementing message passing by using symmetric naming and blocking *sends*. For reasons mentioned earlier, the kernel creates an IMCB even though a sender process is blocked until message delivery. When process P_i sends a message to process P_j, the kernel first checks whether the *send* was anticipated, i.e., whether an ECB was created for the *send* event. It will have happened if process P_j has already made a *receive* call for a message from P_i. If this is the case, action S_3 immediately delivers the message to P_j and changes its state from *blocked* to *ready*. The ECB and the IMCB are now destroyed. If an ECB for *send* does not exist, step S_4 creates an ECB for a *receive* call by process P_j, which is now anticipated, blocks the sender process, and enters the IMCB in the IMCB list of process P_j. Converse actions are performed at a *receive* call: If a matching *send* has already occurred, a message is delivered to process P_j and P_i is activated; otherwise, an ECB is created for a *send* call and P_j is blocked.

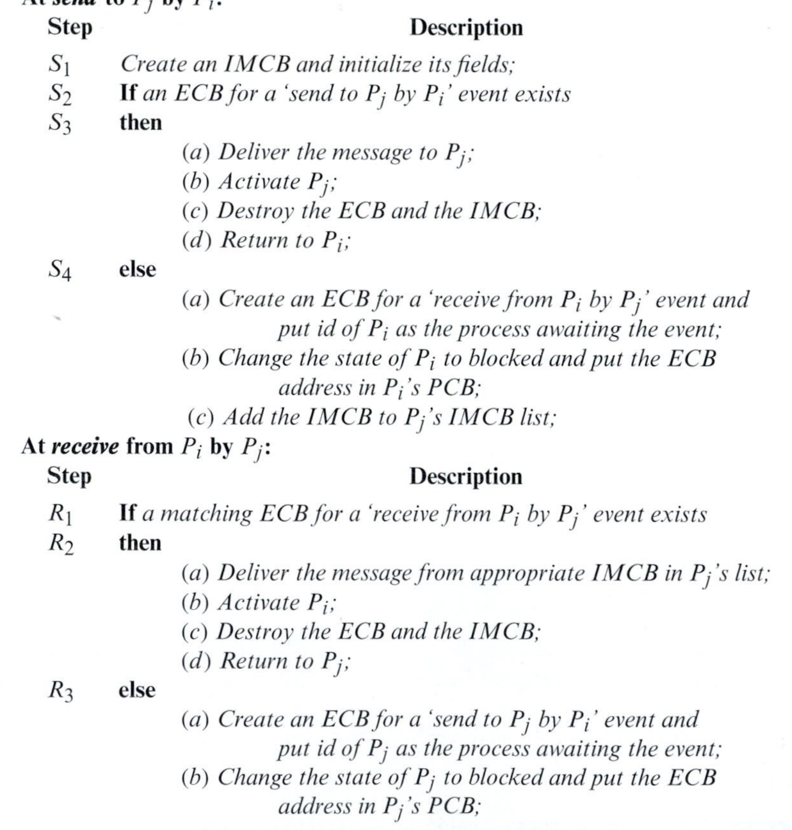

At *send* to P_j by P_i:

Step	Description
S_1	*Create an IMCB and initialize its fields;*
S_2	**If** *an ECB for a 'send to P_j by P_i' event exists*
S_3	**then**
	(*a*) *Deliver the message to P_j;*
	(*b*) *Activate P_j;*
	(*c*) *Destroy the ECB and the IMCB;*
	(*d*) *Return to P_i;*
S_4	**else**
	(*a*) *Create an ECB for a 'receive from P_i by P_j' event and put id of P_i as the process awaiting the event;*
	(*b*) *Change the state of P_i to blocked and put the ECB address in P_i's PCB;*
	(*c*) *Add the IMCB to P_j's IMCB list;*

At *receive* from P_i by P_j:

Step	Description
R_1	**If** *a matching ECB for a 'receive from P_i by P_j' event exists*
R_2	**then**
	(*a*) *Deliver the message from appropriate IMCB in P_j's list;*
	(*b*) *Activate P_i;*
	(*c*) *Destroy the ECB and the IMCB;*
	(*d*) *Return to P_j;*
R_3	**else**
	(*a*) *Create an ECB for a 'send to P_j by P_i' event and put id of P_j as the process awaiting the event;*
	(*b*) *Change the state of P_j to blocked and put the ECB address in P_j's PCB;*

Figure 9.6 Kernel actions in message passing using symmetric naming and blocking *sends*.

Actions when nonblocking *send*s are used are simpler. It is not necessary to block and activate the sender [see Steps $S_4(b)$ and $R_2(b)$ in Figure 9.6]. Creation of an ECB when a message being sent cannot be delivered immediately [see Step $S_4(a)$] is also unnecessary since a sender is not blocked until the message is delivered.

9.3 MAILBOXES

A mailbox is a repository for interprocess messages. It has a unique name. The owner of a mailbox is typically the process that created it. Only the owner process can receive messages from a mailbox. Any process that knows the name of a mailbox can send messages to it. Thus, sender and receiver processes use the name of a mailbox, rather than each other's names, in `send` and `receive` statements; it is an instance of *indirect naming* (see Section 9.1.1).

Figure 9.7 illustrates message passing using a mailbox named `sample`. Process P_i creates the mailbox, using the statement `create_mailbox`. Process P_j sends a message to the mailbox, using the mailbox name in its `send` statement. If P_i has not already executed a `receive` statement, the kernel would store the message in a buffer. The kernel may associate a fixed set of buffers with each mailbox, or it may allocate buffers from a common pool of buffers when a message is sent. Both `create_mailbox` and `send` statements return with condition codes.

The kernel may provide a fixed set of mailbox names, or it may permit user processes to assign mailbox names of their choice. In the former case, confidentiality of communication between a pair of processes cannot be guaranteed because any process can use a mailbox. Confidentiality greatly improves when processes can assign mailbox names of their own choice.

To exercise control over creation and destruction of mailboxes, the kernel may require a process to explicitly "connect" to a mailbox before starting to use it, and to "disconnect" when it finishes using it. This way it can destroy a mailbox

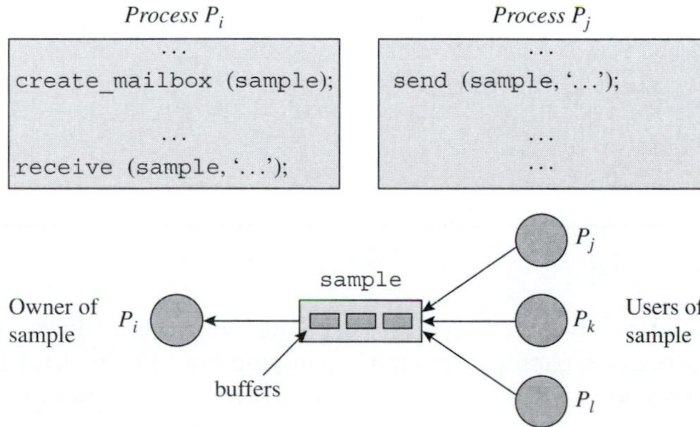

Figure 9.7 Creation and use of mailbox `sample`.

if no process is connected to it. Alternatively, it may permit the owner of a mailbox to destroy it. In that case, it has the responsibility of informing all processes that have "connected" to the mailbox. The kernel may permit the owner of a mailbox to transfer the ownership to another process.

Use of a mailbox has following advantages:

- *Anonymity of receiver:* A process sending a message to request a service may have no interest in the identity of the receiver process, as long as the receiver process can perform the needed function. A mailbox relieves the sender process of the need to know the identity of the receiver. Additionally, if the OS permits the ownership of a mailbox to be changed dynamically, one process can readily take over the service of another.
- *Classification of messages:* A process may create several mailboxes, and use each mailbox to receive messages of a specific kind. This arrangement permits easy classification of messages (see Example 9.1, below).

Anonymity of a receiver process, as we just saw, can offer the opportunity to transfer a function from one process to another. Consider an OS whose kernel is structured in the form of multiple processes communicating through messages. Interrupts relevant to the process scheduling function can be modeled as messages sent to a mailbox named *scheduling*. If the OS wishes to use different process scheduling criteria during different periods of the day, it may implement several schedulers as processes and pass ownership of the *scheduling* mailbox among these processes. This way, the process scheduler that currently owns *scheduling* can receive all scheduling-related messages. Functionalities of OS servers can be similarly transferred. For example, all print requests can be directed to a laser printer instead of a dot matrix printer by simply changing the ownership of a *print* mailbox.

Although a process can also remain anonymous when sending a message to a mailbox, the identity of the sender often has to be known. For example, a server may be programmed to return status information for each request. It can be achieved by passing the sender's id along with the text of the message. The sender of the message, on the other hand, might not know the identity of the server; then, it would have to receive the server's reply through an asymmetric *receive*. As an alternative, the compiler can implement the *send* call as a blocking call requiring a reply containing the status information; so, return of status information would be a kernel responsibility.

Example 9.1 Use of Mailboxes

An airline reservation system consists of a centralized data base and a set of booking processes; each process represents one booking agent. Figure 9.8 shows a pseudocode for the reservation server. It uses three mailboxes named *enquire*, *book*, and *cancel*, and expects a booking process to send enquiry, booking, and cancellation messages to these mailboxes, respectively. Values

repeat
  while `receive (book, flags1, msg_area1)` returns a message
    while `receive (cancel, flags2, msg_area2)` returns a message
      process the cancellation;
    process the booking;
  if `receive (enquire, flags3, msg_area3)` returns a message **then**
    while `receive (cancel, flags2, msg_area2)` returns a message
      process the cancellation;
    process the enquiry;
forever

Figure 9.8 Airline reservation server using three mailboxes: `enquire`, `book`, and `cancel`.

of flags in the *receive* calls are chosen such that a *receive* call returns with an error code if no message exists. For improved effectiveness, the server processes all pending cancellation messages before processing a booking request or an enquiry, and performs bookings before enquiries.

9.4 HIGHER-LEVEL PROTOCOLS USING MESSAGE PASSING

In this section, we discuss three protocols that use the message passing paradigm to provide diverse services. The *simple mail transfer protocol* (SMTP) delivers electronic mail. The *remote procedure call* (RPC) is a programming language facility for *distributed computing*; it is used to invoke a part of a program that is located in a different computer. *Parallel virtual machine* (PVM) and *message passing interface* (MPI) are message passing standards for parallel programming.

9.4.1 The Simple Mail Transfer Protocol (SMTP)

SMTP is used to deliver electronic mail to one or more users reliably and efficiently. It uses asymmetric naming (see Section 9.1.1). A mail would be delivered to a user's terminal if the user is currently active; otherwise, it would be deposited in the user's mailbox. The SMTP protocol can deliver mail across a number of interprocess communication environments (IPCEs), where an IPCE may cover a part of a network, a complete network, or several networks. SMTP is an applications layer protocol. It uses the TCP as a transport protocol and IP as a routing protocol. Details of these networking layers, and details of reliable delivery are, however, beyond the scope of this chapter; they are discussed later in Chapter 16.

SMTP consists of several simple commands. The relevant ones for our purposes are as follows: The MAIL command indicates who is sending a mail. It contains a reverse path in the network, which is an optional list of hosts and the name of the sender mailbox. The RCPT command indicates who is to receive the mail. It contains a forward path that is an optional list of hosts and a destination mailbox. One or more RCPT commands can follow a MAIL command. The DATA command contains the actual data to be sent to its destinations. After processing the DATA command, the sender host starts processing of the MAIL command to send the data to the destination(s). When a host accepts the data for relaying or for delivery to the destination mailbox, the protocol generates a timestamp that indicates when the data was delivered to the host and inserts it at the start of the data. When the data reaches the host containing the destination mailbox, a line containing the reverse path mentioned in the MAIL command is inserted at the start of the data. The protocol provides other commands to deliver a mail to the user's terminal, to both the user's terminal and the user's mailbox, and either to the user's terminal or the user's mailbox. SMTP does not provide a mailbox facility in the receiver, hence it is typically used with either the Internet Message Access Protocol (IMAP) or the Post Office Protocol (POP); these protocols allow users to save messages in mailboxes.

9.4.2 Remote Procedure Calls

Parts of a *distributed program* are executed in different computers. The *remote procedure call* (RPC) is a programming language feature that is used to invoke such parts. Its semantics resemble those of a conventional procedure call. Its typical syntax is

`call` *<proc_id>* (*<message>*);

where *<proc_id>* is the id of a remote procedure and *<message>* is a list of parameters. The call results in sending *<message>* to remote procedure *<proc_id>*. The result of the call is modeled as the reply returned by procedure *<proc_id>*. RPC is implemented by using a blocking protocol. We can view the caller–callee relationship as a client–server relationship. Thus, the remote procedure is the server and a process calling it is a client. We will call the computers where the client and the server processes operate as the *client node* and *server node*, respectively.

Parameters may be passed by value or by reference. If the architecture of the server node is different from that of the client node, the RPC mechanism performs appropriate conversion of value parameters. For reference parameters, the caller must construct systemwide capabilities for the parameters (see Chapter 15). These capabilities would be transmitted to the remote procedure in the message. Type checks on parameters can be performed at compilation time if the caller and the callee are integrated during compilation; otherwise, type checks have to be performed dynamically when a remote procedure call is made.

The schematic diagram of Figure 9.9 depicts the arrangement used to implement a remote procedure call. The server procedure is the remote procedure that is to be invoked. The client process calls the *client stub* procedure, which exists in the same node. The client stub marshals the parameters—collects the parameters, converts them into a machine-independent format, and prepares a message containing this representation of parameters. It now calls the *server stub*, which exists in the node that contains the remote procedure. The server stub converts the parameters into a machine-specific form and invokes the remote procedure. Results of the procedure call are passed back to the client process through the server stub and the client stub. Details concerning naming of the remote procedure and reliability of the remote procedure call are discussed later in Chapter 16.

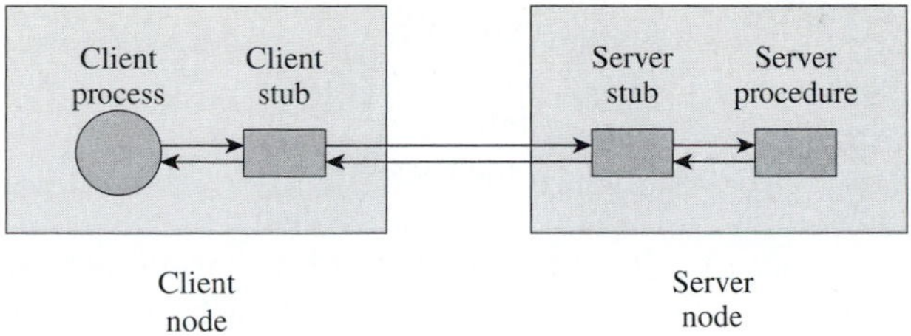

Figure 9.9 Overview of a remote procedure call (RPC).

Two standards for remote procedure calls—SunRPC and OSF/DCE—have emerged and are in use widely. Their use simplifies making of RPCs, and makes programs using RPCs portable across computers and their operating systems. These standards specify an *external representation* of data for passing parameters and results between the client and the server, and an interface compiler that handles the drudgery of marshaling of parameters.

The *remote method invocation* (RMI) feature of Java is an implementation of the remote procedure call that is integrated with the Java language. The remote method to be invoked is a method of some object. Parameters that are local objects are passed by value, while nonlocal objects are passed by reference. Integration with the Java language simplifies naming of the remote method and reliably passing parameters and results between the client and the server.

9.4.3 Message Passing Standards for Parallel Programming

A *parallel program* consists of a set of tasks that can be performed in parallel. Such programs can be executed on a heterogeneous collection of computers or on a *massively parallel processor* (MPP). Parallel programs use message passing libraries that enable parallel activities to communicate through messages. *Parallel virtual machine* (PVM) and *message passing interface* (MPI) are the two standards that are used in coding message passing libraries. Both standards provide the following facilities:

- Point-to-point communication between two processes, using both symmetric and asymmetric naming, and collective communication among processes, which includes an ability to broadcast a message to a collection of processes.
- *Barrier synchronization* between a collection of processes wherein a process invoking the barrier synchronization function is blocked until *all* processes in that collection of processes have invoked the barrier synchronization function.
- Global operations for scattering disjoint portions of data in a message to different processes, gathering data from different processes, and performing global reduction operations on the received data.

In the PVM standard, a collection of heterogeneous networked computers operates as a parallel virtual machine, which is a single large parallel computer. The individual systems can be workstations, multiprocessors, or vector supercomputers. Hence message passing faces the issue of heterogeneous representation of data in different computers forming the parallel virtual machine. After a message is received, a sequence of calls can be made to library routines that unpack and convert the data to a suitable form for consumption by the receiving process. PVM also provides signals that can be used to notify tasks of specific events.

MPI is a standard for a massively parallel processor. It provides a nonblocking send, which is implemented as follows: The message to be sent, which is some data, is copied into a buffer, and the process issuing the send is permitted to continue its operation. However, the process must not reuse the buffer before the previous send on the buffer has been completed. To facilitate it, a *request handle* is associated with every nonblocking send, and library calls are provided for checking the completion of a send operation by testing its request handle and for blocking until a specific send operation, or one of many send operations, is completed.

9.5 CASE STUDIES IN MESSAGE PASSING

9.5.1 Message Passing in Unix

Unix supports three interprocess communication facilities called *pipes, message queues*, and *sockets*. A pipe is a data transfer facility, while message queues and sockets are used for message passing. These facilities have one common feature—processes can communicate without knowing each other's identities. The three facilities are different in scope. Unnamed pipes can be used only by processes that belong to the same process tree, while named pipes can be used by other processes as well. Message queues can be used only by processes existing within the "Unix system domain," which is the domain of Unix operating on one computer system. Sockets can be used by processes within the Unix system domain and within certain Internet domains. Figure 9.10 illustrates the concepts of pipes, message queues, and sockets.

Pipes A pipe is a first-in, first-out (FIFO) mechanism for data transfer between processes called reader processes and writer processes. A pipe is implemented in the file system in many versions of Unix; however, it differs from a file in one important respect—the data put into a pipe can be read only once. It is removed from the pipe when it is read by a process. Unix provides two kinds of pipes, called named and unnamed pipes. Both kinds of pipes are created through the system call *pipe*. Their semantics are identical except for the following differences: A named pipe has an entry in a directory and can thus be used by any process, subject to file permissions, through the system call *open*. It is retained in the system until it is removed by an *unlink* system call. An unnamed pipe does not have an entry in a directory; it can be used only by its creator and its descendants

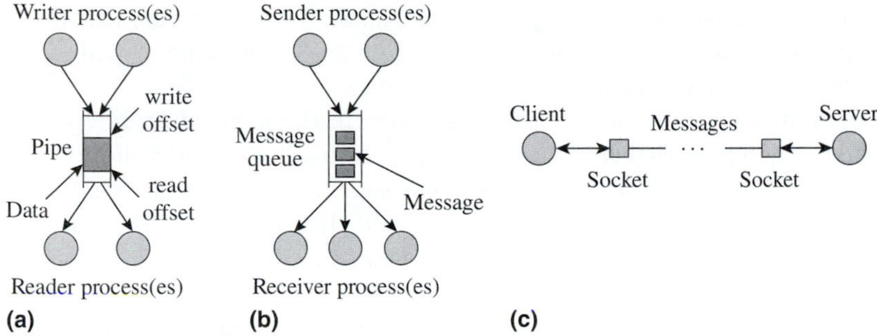

Figure 9.10 Interprocess communication in Unix: (a) pipe; (b) message queue; (c) socket.

in the process tree. The kernel deletes an unnamed pipe when readers or writers no longer exist for it.

A pipe is implemented like a file, except for two differences (see Section 13.14.1 for a discussion of file implementation in Unix). The size of a pipe is limited so that data in a pipe is located in the direct blocks of the inode. The kernel treats a pipe as a queue by maintaining two offsets—one offset is used for writing data into the pipe and the other for reading data from the pipe [see Figure 9.10(a)]. The read and write offsets are maintained in the inode instead of in the file structure. This arrangement forbids a process from changing the offset of a pipe through any means other than reading or writing of data. When data is written, it is entered into the pipe by using the write offset, and the write offset is incremented by the number of bytes written. Data written by multiple writers gets mixed up if their writes are interleaved. If a pipe is full, a process wishing to write data into it would be put to sleep. A read operation is performed by using the read offset, and the read offset is incremented by the number of bytes read. A process reading data from a pipe would be put to sleep if the pipe is empty.

Message Queues A message queue in Unix is analogous to a mailbox. It is created and owned by one process. Other processes can send or receive messages to or from a queue in accordance with access permissions specified by the creator of the message queue [see Figure 9.10(b)]. These permissions are specified by using the same conventions as file permissions in Unix (see Section 15.6.3). The size of a message queue, in terms of the number of bytes that it can buffer, is specified at the time of its creation.

A message queue is created by a system call *msgget* (*key, flag*) where *key* specifies the name of the message queue and *flag* indicates some options. The kernel maintains an array of message queues and their keys. The position of a message queue in this array is used as the message queue id; it is returned by the *msgget* call, and the process issuing the call uses it for sending or receiving messages. The naming issue is tackled as follows: If a process makes a *msgget* call with a key that matches the name of an existing message queue, the kernel simply returns its message queue id. This way, a message queue can be used by any process in the system. If the key in a *msgget* call does not match the name of an existing message queue, the kernel creates a new message queue, sets the key as its name, and returns its message queue id. The process making the call becomes the owner of the message queue.

Each message consists of a message type, in the form of an integer, and a message text. The kernel copies each message into a buffer and builds a message header for it indicating the size of the message, its type, and a pointer to the memory area where the message text is stored. It also maintains a list of message headers for each message queue to represent messages that were sent to the message queue but have not yet been received.

Messages are sent and received by using following system calls:

msgsnd (*msgqid, msg_struct_ptr, count, flag*)
msgrcv (*msgqid, msg_struct_ptr, maxcount, type, flag*)

The *count* and *flag* parameters of a *msgsnd* call specify the number of bytes in a message and the actions to be taken if sufficient space is not available in the message queue, e.g., whether to block the sender, or return with an error code. *msg_struct_ptr* is the address of a structure that contains the type of a message, which is an integer, and the text of the message; *maxcount* is the maximum length of the message; and *type* indicates the type of the message to be received.

When a process makes a *msgrcv* call, the type parameter, which is an integer, indicates the type of message it wishes to receive. When the type parameter has a positive value, the call returns the first message in the queue with a matching type. If the type value is negative, it returns the lowest numbered message whose type is smaller than the absolute value of the type. If the type value is zero, it returns with the first message in the message queue, irrespective of its type. The process becomes blocked if the message queue does not contain any message that can be delivered to it.

When a process makes a *msgsnd* call, it becomes blocked if the message queue does not contain sufficient free space to accommodate the message. The kernel activates it when some process receives a message from the message queue, and the process repeats the check to find whether its message can be accommodated in the message queue. If the check fails, the process becomes blocked once again. When it eventually inserts its message into the message queue, the kernel activates all processes blocked on a receive on the message queue. When scheduled, each of these processes checks whether a message of the type desired by it is available in the message queue. If the check fails, it becomes blocked once again.

Example 9.2 shows how these features can be used to code the reservation server of Example 9.1.

Example 9.3 Unix Message Queues

Figure 9.11 shows the reservation server coded using the system calls of Unix 5.4. The cancellation, booking, and enquiry messages are assigned the types 1, 2, and 3, respectively. The *msgrcv* call with *type* = –4 and *flag* = "*no wait*" returns a cancellation message, if one is present. If no cancellation

```
reservation_server()
{
   msgqid = msgget (reservation_data, flags);
    ...
   repeat
      msgrcv (msgqid, &msg_struct, 200, -4, "no wait");
      if ...          /* a message exists */
      then ...          /* process it */
   while(true);
}
```

Figure 9.11 A reservation server in Unix 5.4.

messages are present, it returns a bookings message if present, or an enquiry message. This arrangement results in processing of cancellations before bookings, and bookings before enquiries, as desired. It also obviates the need for the three mailboxes used in Figure 9.8.

Sockets A socket is simply one end of a communication path. Sockets can be used for interprocess communication within the Unix system domain and in the Internet domain; we limit this discussion to the Unix system domain. A communication path between a client and the server is set up as follows: The client and server processes create a socket each. These two sockets are then connected together to set up a communication path for sending and receiving messages [see Figure 9.10(c)]. The server can set up communication paths with many clients simultaneously.

The naming issue is tackled as follows: The server binds its socket to an address that is valid in the domain in which the socket will be used. The address is now widely advertised in the domain. A client process uses the address to perform a *connect* between its socket and that of the server. This method avoids the use of process ids in communication; it is an instance of indirect naming (see Section 9.1.1).

A server creates a socket *s* using the system call

$$s = socket\ (domain,\ type,\ protocol)$$

where *type* and *protocol* are irrelevant in the Unix system domain. The *socket* call returns a socket identifier to the process. The server process now makes a call *bind* (*s, addr*, ...), where *s* is the socket identifier returned by the *socket* call and *addr* is the address for the socket. This call binds the socket to the address *addr*; *addr* now becomes the 'name' of the socket, which is widely advertised in the domain for use by clients. The server performs the system call *listen* (*s*, ...) to indicate that it is interested in considering some connect calls to its socket *s*.

A client creates a socket by means of a *socket* call, e.g., *cs* = *socket* (...), and attempts to connect it to a server's socket using the system call

connect (*cs, server_socket_addr, server_socket_addrlen*)

The server is activated when a client tries to connect to its socket. It now makes the call *new_soc = accept (s, client_addr, client_addrlen)*. The kernel creates a new socket, connects it to the socket mentioned in a client's *connect* call, and returns the id of this new socket. The server uses this socket to implement the client–server communication. The socket mentioned by the server in its *listen* call is used merely to set up connections. Typically, after the *connect* call the server forks a new process to handle the new connection. This method leaves the original socket created by the server process free to accept more connections through *listen* and *connect* calls. Communication between a client and a server is implemented through *read* and *write* or *send* and *receive* calls. A *send* call has the format

count = send (s, message, message_length, flags)

It returns the count of bytes actually sent. A socket connection is closed by using the call *close (s)* or *shutdown (s, mode)*.

9.5.2 Message Passing in Windows

Windows provides several facilities for secure message passing within a host and within a Windows domain, which consists of a group of hosts. A *named pipe* is used for reliable bidirectional byte or message mode communication between a server and its clients. It is implemented through the file system interface and supports both synchronous and asynchronous message passing. The name of a pipe follows the Windows universal naming convention (UNC), which ensures unique names within a Windows network. The first *createnamedpipe* call for a named pipe is given by a server, which specifies its name, a security descriptor, and the number of simultaneous connections it is to support. The kernel notes this information and creates one connection to the pipe. The server now makes a *connectnamedpipe* call, which blocks it until a client connects to the pipe. A client connects to a pipe through a *createfile* or *callnamedpipe* function with the name of the pipe as a parameter. The call succeeds if the kind of access requested by it matches with the security descriptor of the pipe. Now the client can use *readfile* and *writefile* functions to access the pipe. The server can give additional *createnamedpipe* calls to create additional connections to the pipe. Windows provides a *mailslot* for unreliable unidirectional communication. It can be used for both point-to-point message passing and broadcasting of a short message across a Windows domain.

Local Procedure Call (LPC) The LPC facility performs message passing between processes located within the same host. It is used by components of the Windows OS for purposes such as invocation of the security authentication server, and by processes in user computations to communicate with environment subsystem processes. It is also invoked by the remote procedure call facility when the sender and receiver processes are located within the same host.

LPC provides a choice of three methods of message passing that suit passing of small and large messages, and special messages for use by Win32 GUI. The first two types of LPC use *port* objects to implement message passing. Each port object is like a mailbox. It contains a set of messages in a data structure called a *message queue*. To set up communication with clients, a server creates a port, publishes its name within the host, and awaits connection requests from clients. It is activated when a client sends a connection request to the port and gives a port handle to the client. The client uses this handle to send a message. The server can communicate with many clients over the same port. For small messages, the message queue contains the text of the message. As discussed in Section 9.1.2, such messages are copied twice during message passing. When a process sends a message, it is copied into the message queue of the port. From there, it is copied into the address space of the receiver. To control the overhead of message passing, the length of a message is limited to 256 bytes.

The second method of message passing is used for large messages. The client and server processes map a section object into their address spaces. When the client wishes to send a message, it writes the text of the message in the section object and sends a short message containing its address and size to the port. On receiving this message, the server views the message text in the section object. This way, the message is copied only once.

The third method of LPC is called *quick LPC*. It uses a section object to pass messages and an *event pair* object to perform synchronization between client and server processes. The server creates an event pair object for each client, which consists of two event objects. It also creates a thread for every client, which is devoted exclusively for handling requests made by the client. Message passing takes place as follows: The client process deposits a message in the section object, signals the event object on which the server thread is waiting and itself waits on the other event object of the pair. The server thread processes the message, signals the event object on which the client is waiting, and itself waits on the other event object. To facilitate message passing, the kernel provides a function that atomically signals one event object of the pair and issues a wait on the other event object.

Sockets and Remote Procedure Calls Windows *socket* (Winsock) was originally modeled on the Unix BSD socket but later included several extensions. Its features and implementation are analogous to those of Unix sockets described in Section 9.5. Winsock is integrated with Windows message passing. Hence a program can perform an asynchronous socket operation and receive a notification of completion of the operation through a Windows callback message.

The *remote procedure call* (RPC) facility of Windows is compatible with the OSF/DCE standard. It is implemented by using the LPC if the procedure being invoked exists on the same host as its client; otherwise, it is implemented along the lines discussed in Section 9.4.2. An *asynchronous RPC* is also supported, where the remote procedure operates concurrently with its client and at its completion the client is notified in the manner specified in the call—through an event synchronization object, through an asynchronous procedure call, through an I/O port, or through status information, which the client can poll.

9.6 SUMMARY

The message passing paradigm realizes exchange of information among processes without using shared memory. This feature makes it useful in diverse situations such as in communication between OS functionalities in a microkernel-based OS, in client–server computing, in higher-level protocols for communication, and in communication between tasks in a parallel or distributed program. In this chapter, we studied message passing facilities in programming languages and operating systems.

The key issues in message passing are naming of the sender and receiver processes in the *send* and *receive* calls, and delivery of messages. In *symmetric naming*, the sender and receiver processes name each other in *send* and *receive* calls. It permits a process to engage in multiple independent conversations simultaneously. In *asymmetric naming*, the receiver process does not name a sender in its *receive* call; the kernel considers messages sent by all processes to it for delivery. In *indirect naming*, sender and receiver processes mention the name of a *mailbox*, rather than names of receiver and sender processes, respectively. It permits the same sender and destination processes to engage in multiple independent conversations through different mailboxes. A mailbox contains a set of buffers in which messages can be stored pending their delivery. When mailboxes are not used, the kernel employs its own buffers to store undelivered messages.

Message passing is employed in higher-level protocols such as the *simple mail transfer protocol* (SMTP), the *remote procedure call* (RPC), and the *parallel virtual machine* (PVM) and *message passing interface* (MPI) standards for parallel programming. Operating systems provide many message passing facilities for use in diverse situations.

TEST YOUR CONCEPTS

9.1 Classify each of the following statements as true or false:

  a. When a process sends a message by using a blocking *send* call, the kernel has to copy the message into a buffer area.

  b. When a nonblocking *send* call is used, a message has to be copied two times before the receiver process can be allowed to examine it.

  c. In symmetric naming, a process that has become blocked on a *receive* call will be activated whenever any process sends it a message.

  d. When indirect naming is used, a process sending a message need not know the identity of the process to which the message will be delivered.

9.2 Select the appropriate alternative in each of the following questions:

  a. If an OS has n processes and uses blocking *send* calls and asymmetric *receive* calls,

    i. The OS may require up to $n-1$ buffers for each of the n processes at any time.

    ii. The OS may require upto $\frac{n}{2} \times \frac{n}{2}$ buffers at any time.

    iii. The OS may require upto n buffers at any time.

    iv. None of (i)–(iii).

  b. Answer question 9.2(a) if processes use blocking *send* calls and symmetric *receive* calls.

EXERCISES

9.1 In Figure 9.6, a process may be blocked because of lack of memory needed to create an IMCB or an ECB. Explain how these conditions should be handled.

9.2 Modify the scheme of Figure 9.6 to implement message passing with asymmetric naming and blocking *sends*.

9.3 The reservation system of Example 9.1 uses flags in a *receive* call to check for presence of pending messages. A hypothetical mailbox facility does not support flags. Hence a process uses the following approach to obtain an equivalent effect: When a process wishes to check whether messages exist in a mailbox, it sends a special message with the text "testing for messages" to the mailbox, and then performs a *receive* from the mailbox. If its own special message is delivered to it, it concludes that there are no other messages in the mailbox. Rewrite the reservation system using this approach. (*Hint:* Beware of outdated special messages!)

9.4 Modify the scheme of Figure 9.6 to implement Unix message queues.

9.5 It is proposed to introduce a time-out facility in message passing whereby a process performing a *receive* specifies the amount of time it is prepared to wait for a message. If this period elapses, a time-out occurs and the process is activated. Give a design to implement this facility using the event handling mechanism.

9.6 Processes in an OS use asymmetric and asynchronous message passing. The kernel reserves a limited amount of memory for use as message buffers and does not use disk space for this purpose. Analyze this system for deadlocks (see Chapter 8). How should the kernel detect such deadlocks?

9.7 Give a design to implement the asynchronous send of the *message passing interface* (MPI) standard described in Section 9.4.3.

BIBLIOGRAPHY

Interprocess communication in the RC4000 system is described in Brinch Hansen (1970). Accetta et al. (1986) discusses the scheme used in Mach. Bach (1986), McKusick et al. (1996), Vahalia (1996), and Stevens and Rago (2005) discusses message passing in Unix. Bovet and Cesati (2005) discusses message passing in Linux, while Russinovich and Solomon (2005) discusses message passing in Windows.

Geist et al. (1996) describes and compares the PVM and MPI message passing standards for parallel programming.

1. Accetta, M., R. Baron, W. Bolosky, D. B. Golub, R. Rashid, A. Tevanian, and M. Young (1986): "Mach: A new kernel foundation for Unix development," *Proceedings of the Summer 1986 USENIX Conference*, June 1986, 93–112.
2. Bach, M. J. (1986): *The Design of the Unix Operating System*, Prentice Hall, Englewood Cliffs, N. J.
3. Bovet, D. P., and M. Cesati (2005): *Understanding the Linux Kernel*, 3rd ed., O'Reilly, Sebastopol, Calif.
4. Brinch Hansen, P. (1970): "The nucleus of a multiprogramming system," *Communications of the ACM*, **13** (4), 238–241, 250.
5. Geist, G., J. A. Kohl, and P. M. Papadopoulos (1996): "PVM and MPI: a comparison of features," *Calculateurs Paralleles*, **8** (2).
6. McKusick, M. K., K. Bostic, M. J. Karels, and J. S. Quarterman (1996): *The Design and Implementation of the 4.4 BSD Operating System*, Addison Wesley, Reading, Mass.
7. Russinovich, M. E., and D. A. Solomon (2005): *Microsoft Windows Internals*, 4th ed., Microsoft Press, Redmond, Wash.
8. Stevens, W. R., and S. A. Rago (2005): *Advanced Programming in the Unix Environment*, 2nd ed., Addison Wesley Professional, Reading, Mass.
9. Tanenbaum, A. S. (2001): *Modern Operating Systems*, 2nd ed., Prentice Hall, Englewood Cliffs, N. J.
10. Vahalia, U. (1996): *Unix Internals—The New frontiers*, Prentice Hall, Englewood Cliffs, N. J.

10 Chapter

Synchronization and Scheduling in Multiprocessor Operating Systems

A multiprocessor system has the potential to provide three benefits—high throughput, computation speedup, and graceful degradation. *High throughput* can be obtained by using the CPUs to service many processes simultaneously. *Computation speedup* for an application can be obtained if many of its processes are serviced by the CPUs at the same time. *Graceful degradation* is the feature by which the system can continue to operate even if some of its CPUs fail. This way, the system can offer continuity of operation, though with reduced capabilities.

To realize the benefits of a multiprocessor system, the operating system exploits the presence of multiple CPUs through three special features: First, a *symmetric multiprocessor* kernel—*SMP kernel* for short—permits many CPUs to execute kernel code in parallel so that control functions of the kernel do not become a performance bottleneck. Second, special synchronization locks called *spin locks* and *sleep locks* reduce synchronization delays in processes that operate on different CPUs in parallel. Third, scheduling policies such as *affinity scheduling* and *coscheduling* ensure that processes of an application can operate efficiently on many CPUs.

We begin with an overview of the architecture of multiprocessor systems, which provides the background for a discussion of the three OS features described above.

10.1 ARCHITECTURE OF MULTIPROCESSOR SYSTEMS

Performance of a uniprocessor system depends on the performance of the CPU and memory, which can be enhanced through faster chips, and several levels of

Table 10.1 Benefits of Multiprocessors

Benefit	Description
High throughput	Several processes can be serviced by the CPUs at the same time. Hence more work is accomplished.
Computation speedup	Several processes of an application may be serviced at the same time, leading to a reduction in the duration, i.e., running time, of an application; it provides better response times.
Graceful degradation	Failure of a CPU does not halt operation of the system; the system can continue to operate with somewhat reduced capabilities.

caches. However, chip speeds cannot be increased beyond technological limits. Further improvements in system performance can be obtained only by using multiple CPUs.

As a result of the presence of multiple CPUs, multiprocessor architectures possess the potential to provide the three benefits summarized in Table 10.1. *High throughput* is possible because the OS can schedule several processes in parallel, and so several applications can make progress at the same time. The actual increase in throughput compared with a uniprocessor system may be limited by *memory contention* that occurs when several CPUs try to make memory accesses at the same time, which increases the effective memory access time experienced by processes. *Computation speedup* is obtained when processes of an application are scheduled in parallel. The extent of the speedup may be limited by the amount of parallelism within an application, that is, whether processes of the application can operate without requiring synchronization frequently. *Graceful degradation* provides continuity of operation despite CPU failures. This feature is vital for supporting mission-critical applications like online services and real-time applications.

A System Model Figure 10.1 shows a model of a multiprocessor system. The CPUs, the memory, and the I/O subsystem are connected to the interconnection network. Each CPU chip may contain level 1 and level 2 caches, i.e., L1 and L2 caches, that hold blocks of instructions and data recently accessed by the CPU. However, for simplicity, we assume that the CPU contains only an L1 cache. The memory comprises several memory units. We assume that an L3 cache is associated with each memory unit and holds blocks of instructions and data accessed recently from it. Every time a CPU or an I/O device wishes to make a memory access, the interconnection network establishes a path between it and the memory unit containing the required byte, and the access takes place over this path. Ignoring delays in the interconnection network, effective memory access time depends on hit ratios in the L1, L2, and L3 caches, and on the memory access time (see Section 2.2.3).

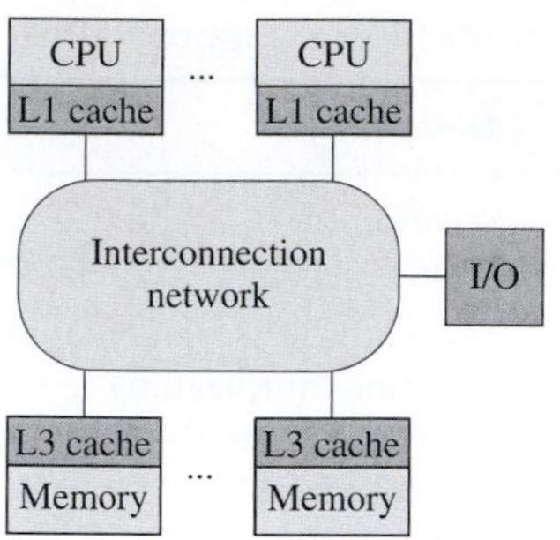

Figure 10.1 Model of multiprocessor system.

Cache and TLB Coherence When processes use shared data, several copies of a data item *d* may be present in the system at the same time. One of these copies would be in a memory unit and one may exist in the L3 cache associated with the memory unit, while the rest would exist in the L1 caches of CPUs where the processes were scheduled. When a process operating on one CPU updates a copy of *d*, the other copies of *d* become stale. Their use by processes would cause correctness and data consistency problems, so the system uses a *cache coherence protocol* to ensure that a stale copy is never used in a computation.

Cache coherence protocols are based on two fundamental approaches, several variants of which are applied in practice. The *snooping-based* approach can be used if the interconnection network is a bus. A CPU snoops on the bus to detect messages that concern caching, and eliminates stale copies from its L1 cache. In the *write-invalidate* variant of this approach, any process updating a copy of a shared data item *d* is required to update the copy of *d* existing in memory. Hence the memory never holds a stale copy. A CPU that updates *d* sends a "cache invalidate" message for *d* on the bus. On seeing this message, every snooping CPU discards the copy of *d*, if present, from its L1 cache. The next time such a CPU accesses *d*, the value is copied afresh into the CPU's L1 cache.

A *directory-based* cache coherence approach requires maintaining a directory of information about cached copies of data items in the system; the directory could indicate which CPUs contain cached copies of each data item. While updating a data item *d*, a CPU would send point-to-point cache invalidation signals to these CPUs. Alternatively, the dictionary could indicate the location of the most recently updated copy of each shared data item. When a CPU C_1 wishes to access a data item *d*, it would send a "read *d*" request to the directory. The directory would send the request to the memory unit or the CPU that has the most recent copy of *d* in its cache, which would forward the value of *d* to C_1. After the update, the directory entry of *d* would be set to point to C_1.

TLB coherence is an analogous problem, whereby information in some entries in a CPU's TLB becomes stale when other CPUs perform page replacements or change access privileges of processes to shared pages. A shared page p_i of a process has entries in the TLBs of many CPUs. If a page fault arises in a process operating on one of the CPUs, say, CPU C_1, and page p_i is replaced by a new page, the TLB entry of p_i in C_1 would be erased (see Section 12.2.2.2). The TLB entries of p_i in other CPUs are now stale, so they need to be erased too. It is achieved through a *TLB shootdown* action, in which CPU C_1 sends interprocessor interrupts to other CPUs with details of p_i's id, and the other CPUs invalidate p_i's entries in their TLBs. Similar actions are performed when access privileges of shared pages are changed. The overhead of a TLB shootdown is reduced in two ways. The page table entry of p_i indicates which CPUs have TLB entries for p_i, and C_1 sends the interrupts to only these CPUs. A CPU receiving the intimation for shootdown could implement it in a *lazy*, i.e., need-based, manner. If the shootdown concerns the currently operating process, it erases the TLB entry immediately; otherwise, it queues the intimation and handles it when the process that it concerns is next scheduled.

Classification of Multiprocessor Systems Multiprocessor systems are classified into three kinds of systems according to the manner in which CPUs and memory units are associated with one another.

- *Uniform memory access architecture* (*UMA architecture*): All CPUs in the system can access the entire memory in an identical manner, i.e., with the same access speed. Some examples of UMA architecture are the Balance system by Sequent and VAX 8800 by Digital. The UMA architecture is called the *tightly coupled multiprocessor architecture* in older literature. It is also called *symmetrical multiprocessor (SMP) architecture*.
- *Nonuniform memory access architecture* (*NUMA architecture*): The system consists of a number of *nodes*, where each node consists of one or more CPUs, a memory unit, and an I/O subsystem. The memory unit of a node is said to be *local* to the CPUs in that node. Other memory units are said to be *nonlocal*. All memory units together constitute a single address space. Each CPU can access the entire address space; however, it can access the local memory unit faster than it can access nonlocal memory units. Some examples of the NUMA architecture are the HP AlphaServer and the IBM NUMA-Q.
- *No-remote-memory-access architecture* (*NORMA architecture*): Each CPU has its local memory. CPUs can access remote memory units, but this access is over the network, and so it is very slow compared with access to local memory. The Hypercube system by Intel is an example of a NORMA architecture. A NORMA system is a distributed system according to Definition 3.8; therefore, we shall not discuss architecture of NORMA systems in this chapter.

Interconnection Networks CPUs in a multiprocessor system access memory units through an interconnection network. Two important attributes of an interconnection network are cost and effective access speed. Table 10.2 lists the characteristics and relative advantages of three popular interconnection networks. Figure 10.2 contains schematic diagrams of these networks.

A *bus* in a multiprocessor system is simply an extension of a bus in a uniprocessor system. All memory units and all CPUs are connected to the bus. Thus the bus supports data traffic between any CPU and any memory unit. However, only one CPU–memory conversation can be in progress at any time. The bus is simple

Table 10.2 Features of Interconnection Networks

Interconnection network	Features
Bus	Low cost. Reasonable access speed at low traffic density. Only one CPU–memory conversation can be in progress at any time.
Crossbar switch	High cost. Low expandability. CPUs and memory units are connected to the switch. A CPU–memory conversation is implemented by selecting a path between a CPU and a memory unit. Permits many CPU–memory conversations in parallel.
Multistage interconnection network (MIN)	A compromise between a bus and a crossbar switch. It consists of many stages of 2 × 2 crossbar switches. A CPU–memory conversation is set up by selecting a path through each stage. Permits some parallel conversations.

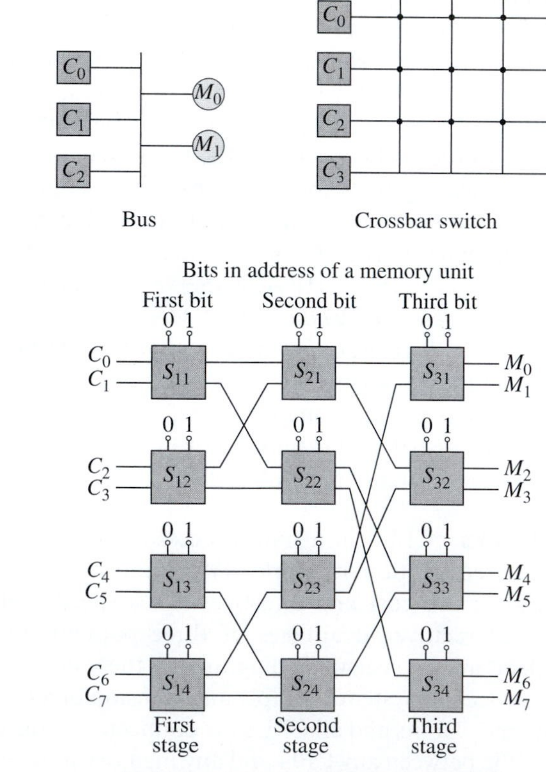

Figure 10.2 Bus, crossbar switch, and multistage interconnection network (MIN).

and inexpensive but it is slow because of bus contention at medium or high traffic densities because more than one CPU might wish to access memory at the same time. The bus may become a bottleneck when the number of CPUs is increased.

A *crossbar switch* reduces the contention problem by providing many paths for CPU–memory conversations. It uses a matrix organization wherein CPUs are arranged along one dimension and memory units along the other dimension (see Figure 10.2). Every CPU and every memory unit has its own independent bus. When a CPU, say CPU C_1, wishes to access a byte located in a memory unit, say memory unit M_3, the switch connects the bus of C_1 with the bus of M_3 and the CPU–memory conversation takes place over this path. This conversation does not suffer contention due to conversations between other CPUs and other memory units because such conversations would use different paths through the switch. Thus, the switch can provide a large effective memory bandwidth. Contention would arise only if two or more CPUs wish to converse with the same memory unit, which has a low probability of happening at low overall traffic densities between CPUs and memory units. However, a crossbar switch is expensive. It also suffers from poor expandability.

A *multistage interconnection network* (MIN) is a compromise between a bus and a crossbar switch in terms of cost and parallelism; it has been used in the BBN Butterfly, which has a NUMA architecture. Figure 10.2 shows an 8×8 Omega interconnection network, which permits 8 CPUs to access 8 memory units whose binary addresses range from 000 to 111. It contains three stages because memory units have three bits in their binary addresses. Each column contains 2×2 crossbar switches of one stage in the interconnection network. For each switch, a row represents a CPU and a column represents the value of one bit in the binary address of the memory unit to be accessed. If an address bit is 0, the upper output of the crossbar switch is selected. If the bit is 1, the lower output of the switch is selected. These outputs lead to switches in the next stage.

When CPU C_1 wishes to access memory unit M_4, the interconnection takes place as follows: The address of memory unit M_4 is 100. Because the first bit is 1, the lower output of switch S_{11} is selected. This leads to S_{22}, whose upper output is selected because the next address bit is 0. This leads to S_{33}, whose upper output is selected. It leads to M_4 as desired. Switches S_{13}, S_{24}, and S_{34} would be selected if CPU C_4 wishes to access memory unit 7. The interconnection network uses twelve 2×2 switches. The cost of these switches is much lower than that of an 8×8 crossbar switch. In general, an $N \times N$ multistage network uses $\log_2 N$ stages, and each stage contains $(N/2)$ 2×2 switches.

Other interconnection networks use combinations of these three fundamental interconnection networks. For example, the IEEE scalable coherent interface (SCI) uses a ring-based network that provides bus-like services but uses fast point-to-point unidirectional links to provide high throughput. A crossbar switch is used to select the correct unidirectional link connected to a CPU.

10.1.1 SMP Architecture

SMP architectures popularly use a bus or a crossbar switch as the interconnection network. As discussed earlier, only one conversation can be in progress over the bus at any time; other conversations are delayed. Hence CPUs face unpredictable delays while accessing memory. The bus may become a bottleneck and limit the performance of the system. When a crossbar switch is used, the CPUs and the I/O subsystem face smaller delays in accessing memory, so system performance would be better than when a bus is used. Switch delays are also more predictable than bus delays. Cache coherence protocols add to the delays in memory access in both of these variations of the SMP architecture. Hence SMP systems do not scale well beyond a small number of CPUs.

10.1.2 NUMA Architecture

Figure 10.3 illustrates the architecture of a NUMA system. Each dashed box encloses a node of the system. A node could consist of a single-CPU system; however, it is common to use SMP systems as nodes. Hence a node consists of CPUs, local memory units, and an I/O subsystem connected by a local interconnection network. Each local interconnection network also has a global port, and the global ports of all nodes are connected to a high-speed global interconnection network capable of providing transfer rates upward of 1 GB/s, i.e., 10^9 bytes per second. They are used for the traffic between CPUs and nonlocal memory units. A global port of a node may also contain a cache to hold instructions and data from nonlocal memories that were accessed by CPUs of the node. The global interconnection network shown in Figure 10.3 resembles the IEEE scalable coherent interface (SCI). It uses a ring-based network that provides fast point-to-point unidirectional links between nodes.

As in an SMP system, the hardware of a NUMA system must ensure coherence between caches in CPUs of a node. It must also ensure coherence between nonlocal caches. This requirement can slow down memory accesses and consume part of the bandwidth of interconnection networks. Ignoring delays in the local

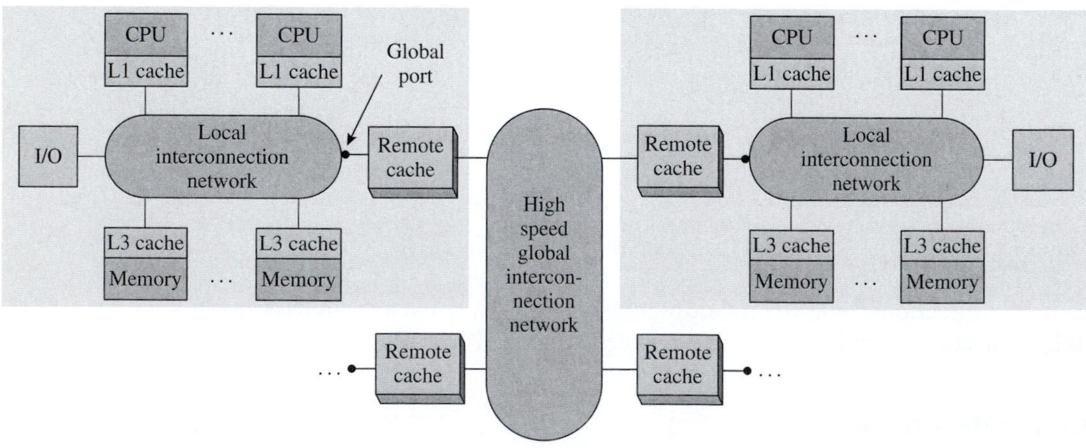

Figure 10.3 NUMA architecture.

and nonlocal interconnection networks, the effective memory access time to a local memory would depend on the hit ratios in the L1 and L3 caches, and the memory access time. The access time to a nonlocal memory would depend on hit ratios in the L1 cache and the remote cache in the global port, and on the memory access time.

The nodes in a NUMA system are typically high-performance SMP systems containing 4 or 8 CPUs. Because of the high speed nonlocal interconnection network, performance of such NUMA architectures is scalable as nodes are added. The actual performance of a NUMA system would depend on the nonlocal memory accesses made by processes during their execution. This is an OS issue, which we discuss in the next section.

10.2 ISSUES IN MULTIPROCESSOR OPERATING SYSTEMS

To realize the benefits of high throughput and computation speedup offered by a multiprocessor system, the CPUs must be used effectively and processes of an application should be able to interact harmoniously. These two considerations will, of course, influence process scheduling and process synchronization. They also affect the operating system's own methods of functioning in response to interrupts and system calls. Table 10.3 highlights the three fundamental issues raised by these considerations.

Early multiprocessor operating systems functioned in the *master–slave* mode. In this mode, one CPU is designated as the master, and all other CPUs operate as its slaves. Only the master CPU executes the kernel code. It handles interrupts and system calls, and performs scheduling. It communicates its scheduling decisions to other CPUs through *interprocessor interrupts* (IPIs). The primary advantage of the master–slave kernel structure is its simplicity. When a process makes a system call, the CPU on which it operated is idle until either the process resumes its operation or the master CPU assigns new work to the CPU. None of these can

Table 10.3 **Issues in Synchronization and Scheduling in a Multiprocessor OS**

Issue	Description
Kernel structure	Many CPUs should be able to execute kernel code in parallel, so that execution of kernel functions does not become a bottleneck.
Process synchronization	Presence of multiple CPUs should be exploited to reduce the overhead of switching between processes, and synchronization delays.
Process scheduling	The scheduling policy should exploit presence of multiple CPUs to provide computation speedup for applications.

happen until the master CPU handles the system call and performs scheduling. Hence execution of kernel functions by the master is a bottleneck that affects system performance. This problem can be solved by structuring the kernel so that many CPUs can execute its code in parallel.

Presence of multiple CPUs can be exploited to reduce synchronization delays. In a uniprocessor system, letting a process loop until a synchronization condition is met denies the CPU to other processes and may lead to priority inversion (see Section 6.5.1). Hence synchronization is performed through blocking of a process until its synchronization condition is met. However, in a multiprocessor system, synchronization through looping does not lead to priority inversion because the process holding the lock can execute on another CPU in parallel with the looping process. It would be preferable to let a process loop, rather than block it, if the amount of time for which it would loop is less than the total CPU overhead of blocking it and scheduling another process, and activating and rescheduling it sometime in future. This condition would be met if a process looping for entry to a critical section and the holder of the critical section are scheduled in parallel. Multiprocessor operating systems provide special synchronization techniques for exploiting this feature.

Scheduling of processes is influenced by two factors—cache performance during operation of a process, and synchronization requirements of processes of an application. Scheduling a process on the same CPU every time may lead to a high cache hit ratio, which would improve performance of the process and also contribute to better system performance. If the processes of an application interact frequently, scheduling them at the same time on different CPUs would provide them an opportunity to interact in real time, which would lead to a speedup of the application. For example, a producer and a consumer in a single-buffer producers–consumers system may be able to perform several cycles of producing and consuming of records in a time slice if they are scheduled to run in parallel.

Thus, kernel structure and the algorithms it uses for scheduling and synchronization together determine whether a multiprocessor OS will achieve high throughput. However, computer systems grow in size with advances in technology or requirements of their users, so another aspect of performance, called *scalability*, is equally important. Scalability of a system indicates how well the system will perform when its size grows. The size of a multiprocessor OS may grow through addition of more CPUs, memory units and other resources to the system, or through creation of more processes in applications. Two kinds of performance expectations arise when a system grows in size—the throughput of the system should increase linearly with the number of CPUs and delays faced by individual processes, due to either synchronization or scheduling, should not increase as the number of processes in the system increases.

Scalability is important in the design of both hardware and software. Interconnection technologies that work well when the system contains a small number of CPUs and memory units may not work as well when their number grows. To be scalable, the effective bandwidth of an interconnection network should increase linearly as the number of CPUs is increased. As we discussed in Section 10.1, the crossbar switch is more scalable than the bus as an interconnection network. In the software realm, special techniques are employed to ensure scalability of algorithms. We will discuss this aspect in Sections 10.4 and 10.5.

10.3 KERNEL STRUCTURE

The kernel of a multiprocessor operating system for an SMP architecture is called an *SMP kernel*. It is structured so that any CPU can execute code in the kernel, and many CPUs could do so in parallel. This capability is based on two fundamental provisions: The code of the SMP kernel is *reentrant* (see Section 11.3.3 for a discussion of reentrant code), and the CPUs executing it in parallel coordinate their activities through synchronization and interprocessor interrupts.

Synchronization The kernel uses binary semaphores to ensure mutual exclusion over kernel data structures (see Section 6.9)—we will refer to them as *mutex locks*. Locking is said to be *coarse-grained* if a mutex lock controls accesses to a group of data structures, and it is said to be *fine-grained* if a mutex lock controls accesses to a single data item or a single data structure. Coarse-grained locking provides simplicity; however, two or more of the data structures controlled by a lock cannot be accessed in parallel, so execution of kernel functionalities may become a bottleneck. Fine-grained locking permits CPUs to access different data structures in parallel. However, fine-grained locking may increase the locking overhead because a CPU executing the kernel code would have to set and release a larger number of locks. It may also cause deadlocks if all CPUs do not set the locks in the same order. Hence deadlock prevention policies such as the resource ranking policy (see Section 8.8) would have to be used—numerical ranks could be associated with locks and a CPU could set locks in the order of increasing ranks.

Good performance of SMP kernels is obtained by ensuring parallelism without incurring substantial locking overhead. It is achieved through two means:

- *Use of separate locks for kernel functionalities:* CPUs can perform different kernel functionalities in parallel without incurring high locking overhead.
- *Partitioning of the data structures of a kernel functionality:* CPUs can perform the same kernel functionality in parallel by locking different partitions of the data structures. Locking can be dispensed with altogether by permanently associating a different partition with each CPU.

Heap Management Parallelism in heap management can be provided by maintaining several *free lists*, i.e., lists of free memory areas in the heap (see Section 11.5.1). Locking is unnecessary if each CPU has its own free list; however, this arrangement would degrade performance because the allocation decisions would not be optimal. Forming separate free lists to hold free memory areas of different sizes and letting a CPU lock an appropriate free list would provide parallelism between CPUs that seek memory areas of different sizes. It would

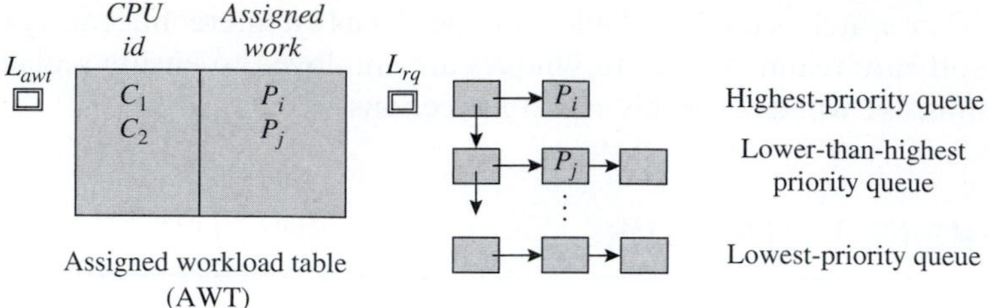

Figure 10.4 Scheduling data structures in an SMP kernel.

also avoid suboptimal performance caused by associating a free list permanently with a CPU.

Scheduling Figure 10.4 illustrates simple scheduling data structures used by an SMP kernel. CPUs C_1 and C_2 are engaged in executing processes P_i and P_j, respectively. The ready queues of processes are organized as discussed in Section 7.4.3—each ready queue contains PCBs of *ready* processes having a specific priority. The kernel maintains an additional data structure named *assigned workload table* (AWT) in which it records the workload assigned to various CPUs. Mutex locks called L_{rq} and L_{awt} guard the ready queues data structure and the AWT, respectively. Let us assume that CPUs set these locks in the order L_{rq} followed by L_{awt}.

However, use of the scheduling data structures shown in Figure 10.4 suffers from heavy contention for mutex locks L_{rq} and L_{awt} because every CPU needs to set and release these locks while scheduling. To reduce this overhead, some operating systems partition the set of processes into several subsets of processes, and entrust each subset to a different CPU for scheduling. In this arrangement, the ready queues and the assigned workload table get partitioned on a per-CPU basis. Now, each CPU would access the ready queues data structure that has only the *ready* processes in its charge. In a preemptible kernel, mutex locks would still be needed to avoid race conditions on each of the per-CPU data structures because the CPU may be diverted due to interrupts; however, these locks would rarely face contention, so the synchronization overhead would be low. The price for this reduction in the synchronization overhead is either poor system performance because some CPUs may be idle while others are heavily loaded, or the overhead of balancing the load across the CPUs by periodically transferring some processes from heavily loaded CPUs to lightly loaded CPUs.

An SMP kernel provides *graceful degradation* because it continues to operate despite failures, even though its efficiency may be affected. For example, failure of a CPU when it is not executing kernel code does not interfere with operation of other CPUs in the system. Hence they would continue to execute normally. Nonavailability of the failed CPU would affect the process whose code it was executing when the failure occurred. It would also affect throughput and response times in the system to some extent, as fewer processes can be scheduled in parallel.

NUMA Kernel CPUs in a NUMA system experience different memory access times for local and nonlocal memory. A process would operate more efficiently if instructions and operands accessed by it are found predominantly in local memory. In keeping with this principle, each node in a NUMA system has its own *separate kernel*, and exclusively schedules processes whose address spaces are in local memory of the node. This approach is analogous to the partitioning of processes across CPUs of an SMP system, hence it inherits the drawbacks of that arrangement.

Operating systems for most NUMA architectures generalize this concept of managing each node separately. They use the notion of an *application region* to ensure good performance of an application. An application region consists of a resource partition and an instance of the kernel. The resource partition contains one or more CPUs, some local memory units and a few I/O devices. The kernel of the application region manages processes of only one application. The advantage of this arrangement is that the kernel can optimize the performance of the application through clever scheduling. It can also ensure high hit ratios in the L1 cache by scheduling a process on the same CPU most of the time. Good hit ratios are obtained in the L3 cache as well because memory units in the application region contain address spaces of processes of only one application.

Use of a separate kernel for a node of a NUMA system or for an application region also has some disadvantages. Accesses to nonlocal memory units become more complex, since they span the domains of more than one kernel. The separate kernel arrangement also suffers from the generic problems associated with partitioning—underutilization of resources may result because idle resources in a partition cannot be used by processes of other partitions. Reliability is also poor because a computation has to be aborted or delayed if some resource (including a CPU) in one partition fails.

10.4 PROCESS SYNCHRONIZATION

Process synchronization involves use of critical sections or indivisible signaling operations. As discussed in Section 6.5.2, each of these is implemented by using a *lock variable* that has only two possible values—*open* and *closed*. A process cannot begin execution of a critical section or an indivisible operation if the lock variable associated with the critical section or indivisible operation has the value *closed*. If it finds the value of the lock variable to be *open*, it changes the value to *closed*, executes the critical section or indivisible signaling operation, and changes the value back to *open*. A process that finds the value of a lock variable to be *closed* must wait until the value is changed to *open*. We refer to this arrangement involving use of a lock variable as a *synchronization lock*, or simply a *lock*, and refer to the actions of closing and opening the lock as *setting* and *resetting* it.

Two qualities of synchronization locks are important for performance of a multiprocessor system. The first quality is *scalability* of a synchronization lock, which indicates the degree to which the performance of an application using the lock is independent of the number of processes in the application and the number

Table 10.4 Kinds of Synchronization Locks

Lock	Description
Queued lock	A process waiting for a queued lock becomes *blocked* and its id is entered into a queue of processes waiting for the lock. The process is activated when the lock is reset and it is the first process in the queue.
Spin lock	If a spin lock is already set when a process tries to set it, the process enters into a *busy wait* for the lock. The CPU on which the process is operating can handle interrupts during the busy wait.
Sleep lock	When a process waits for a sleep lock, the CPU on which it is running is put into a special *sleep* state in which it does not execute instructions or process interrupts. The CPU is activated when the CPU that resets the lock sends it an interprocessor interrupt.

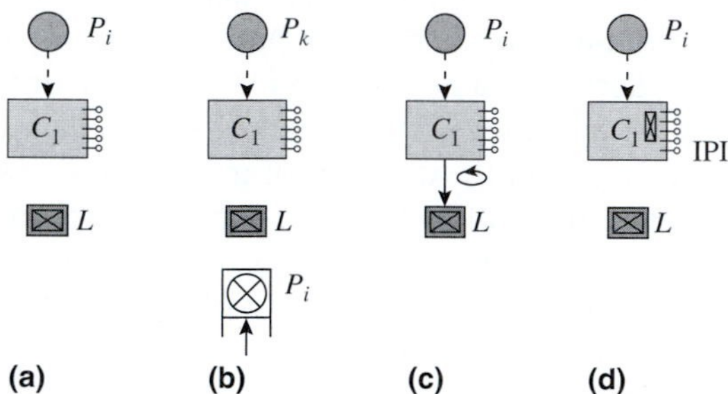

Figure 10.5 Synchronization locks in multiprocessor operating systems. (a) General schematic diagram of a lock guarding a mutual exclusion region; (b) Queued lock; (c) Spin lock; (d) Sleep lock.

of CPUs in the system. The second quality concerns ability of a CPU to handle interrupts while the process operating on the CPU is engaged in trying to set the synchronization lock. This ability helps the kernel in providing a quick response to events in the system.

Table 10.4 summarizes the features of three kinds of synchronization locks, the *queued*, *spin*, and *sleep* locks. Processes waiting for a queued lock become *blocked*; they are activated in FCFS order when the lock is opened. The spin lock is the synchronization lock we illustrated in Figures 6.9 and 6.10; it leads to a busy wait because a process that is trying to set it is not blocked. Interestingly, we had discarded the spin lock because of a busy wait, but it is useful in a multiprocessor system! The sleep lock is a new kind of lock. We discuss characteristics of all three kinds of locks in the following.

Figure 10.5 illustrates use of the three kinds of synchronization locks. Figure 10.5(a) shows a process P_i executing on CPU C_1 and a lock L that is used to guard a mutual exclusion region. The × mark inside the box representing the lock indicates that the lock is set. A similar mark inside a circle representing a process indicates that the process is in the *blocked* state. We discuss features of these synchronization locks in the following.

Queued Lock A queued lock is a conventional lock used for process synchronization. The kernel performs the following actions when process P_i executing on CPU C_1 requests a lock L: Lock L is tested. If it is not already set, the kernel sets the lock on behalf of P_i and resumes its execution. If the lock is already set by another process, P_i is blocked and its request for the lock is recorded in a queue. Figure 10.5(b) illustrates the situation after blocking of P_i. The id of P_i is entered in the queue of lock L and CPU C_1 has switched to execution of some other process P_k. When the process that had set lock L completes its use of the critical section, the process at the head of L's queue is activated and the lock is awarded to it.

A process that cannot set a queued lock relinquishes the CPU on which it is executing. Such a process will not be using a CPU and will not be accessing memory while it waits to set the lock. The average length of the queue for a lock determines whether the solution is scalable. If processes do not require lock L frequently, the queue length is bounded by some constant c (that is, it is never larger than c). Hence increasing the number of CPUs or processes in the system does not increase the average delay in acquiring the lock. The solution is scalable under these conditions. If processes require lock L frequently, the length of the queue may be proportional to the number of processes. In this case the solution is not scalable.

Spin Lock A spin lock differs from a queued lock in that a process that makes an unsuccessful attempt to set a lock does not relinquish the CPU. Instead it enters into a loop in which it makes repeated attempts to set the lock until it succeeds [see Figure 10.5(c)]. Hence the name *spin lock*. We depict the situation in which CPU C_1 spins on lock L by drawing an arrow from C_1 to L. CPU C_1 repeatedly accesses the value of the lock and tests it, using an indivisible instruction like a test-and-set instruction (see Section 6.9.4). This action creates traffic on the memory bus or across the network.

Use of spin locks may degrade system performance on two counts: First, the CPU remains with the process looping on the spin lock and so other processes are denied use of the CPU. Second, memory traffic is generated as the CPU spins on the lock. The latter drawback may not be significant if the memory bus or the network is lightly loaded, but it causes performance degradation in other situations. However, use of spin locks can be justified in two situations: (1) when the number of processes does not exceed the number of CPUs in the system, because there is no advantage in preempting a process, and (2) when a lock is used to control a critical section and the CPU time needed to execute the critical section is smaller than the total CPU time needed to block a process and schedule another one, and activate and reschedule the original process. In the first case blocking is unnecessary. In the second case it is counterproductive.

A spin lock has an interesting advantage over a queued lock. A CPU spinning on a lock can handle interrupts and the process operating on it can handle signals. This feature is particularly important in a real-time application as delays in servicing interrupts and signals can degrade response times. Nevertheless, spin locks are not scalable, because of the memory or network traffic that they generate.

In a NUMA system, a process using spin locks may face a situation called *lock starvation*, in which it might be denied the lock for long periods of time, possibly indefinitely. Consider a process P_i that is trying to set a spin lock that is in its nonlocal memory. Let processes P_j and P_k, which exist in the same node as the lock, try to set it. Since access to local memory is much faster than access to nonlocal memory, processes P_j and P_k are able to spin much faster on the lock than process P_i. Hence they are likely to get an opportunity to set the lock before P_i. If they repeatedly set and use the lock, P_i may not be able to set the lock for a long time. A scheme that we will see in Section 10.4.2 avoids lock starvation.

Sleep Lock When a process makes an unsuccessful attempt to set a sleep lock, the CPU on which it is operating is put into a special state called a *sleep* state. In this state it does not execute instructions and does not respond to any interrupts except interprocessor interrupts. In Figure 10.5(d) we depict this situation by putting a $\times$ mark against all interrupts except IPI. The CPU waiting for the lock does not spin on it, and so it does not cause memory or network traffic.

The CPU that releases the lock has the responsibility to send interprocessor interrupts to those CPUs that are sleeping on the lock. This feature leads to the overhead of generating and servicing interprocessor interrupts, both of which involve a context switch and execution of kernel code. The sleep lock will scale poorly if heavy contention exists for a lock; however, it will perform well if this is not the case. Use of sleep locks in a real-time application can also affect response times of the application. Nevertheless sleep locks may be preferred to spin locks if the memory or network traffic densities are high.

Scheduling Aware Synchronization As discussed earlier, some kinds of synchronization are effective only when processes involved in the synchronization are scheduled to run at the same time. The Solaris OS for Sun systems provides a synchronization lock called an *adaptive lock*. A process waiting for this lock spins on it if the holder of the lock is scheduled to run in parallel; otherwise, the process is preempted and queued as in a queued lock. Thus, implementation of a synchronization lock depends on scheduling decisions in the system.

10.4.1 Special Hardware for Process Synchronization

Some systems use special hardware to avoid the performance problems caused by queued, spin, and sleep locks. The Sequent Balance system uses a special bus called the *system link and interface controller* (SLIC) for synchronization. SLIC consists of a special 64-bit register in each CPU in the system. The registers of different CPUs are connected over the SLIC bus (see Figure 10.6). Each bit represents a spin lock. Thus SLIC can support 64 spin locks. When a CPU C_1 wishes to set a lock L_k, it tries to set the corresponding bit, say b_k, in its special

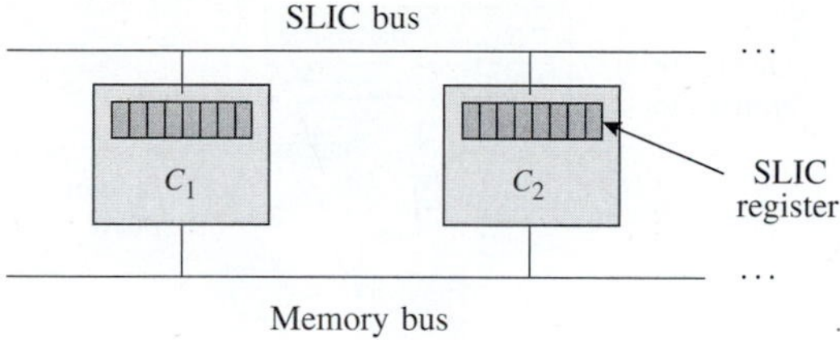

Figure 10.6 SLIC bus.

register. If the bit is not already set, an attempt to set it results in communication over the SLIC bus. If no other CPU is simultaneously trying to set the same bit, the lock is awarded to C_1 and bit b_k is set in the special registers of all CPUs. C_1 can now proceed with its execution. When it releases the lock, bit b_k is reset in special registers of all CPUs. If two or more CPUs simultaneously try to set the same lock, the hardware arbiter awards the lock to one CPU. The attempt to set lock L_k fails if bit b_k is already set on behalf of some other CPU. In this case, the CPU keeps spinning on this lock, i.e., on bit b_k of its special register.

The advantage of the SLIC approach is that a CPU spins on a lock located within the CPU. Therefore spinning does not generate memory or network traffic. Use of spinning rather than sleeping also avoids use of interprocessor interrupts for synchronization. Use of a special synchronization bus relieves pressure on the memory bus. This is a significant advantage when memory traffic density is high.

10.4.2 A Scalable Software Scheme for Process Synchronization

We describe a scheme for process synchronization in NUMA and NORMA architectures that achieves scalable performance by minimizing the synchronization traffic to nonlocal memory units in a NUMA architecture and over the network in a NORMA architecture. It does not require any special hardware and provides an effect that is analogous to the SLIC chip. It also avoids the lock starvation problem of spin locks.

The scheme uses two types of locks. A *primary lock* is like a conventional lock used for synchronization. When a process is unable to set a primary lock, it creates a *shadow lock* in the local memory of the node where it resides, associates the shadow lock with the primary lock, and spins on the shadow lock. This way spinning does not generate nonlocal memory traffic or network traffic. When a process wishes to reset a primary lock that it has set, it checks whether any shadow locks are associated with the primary lock. If so, it resets one of the shadow locks, which enables one of the processes waiting for the primary lock to proceed; otherwise, it resets the primary lock.

Figure 10.7 illustrates an implementation of this scheme, using the same notation as in Figure 10.5. A queue of shadow locks is maintained for each primary lock. Each entry in the queue contains the address of a shadow lock and a pointer to the next shadow lock in the queue. If a process fails to set the

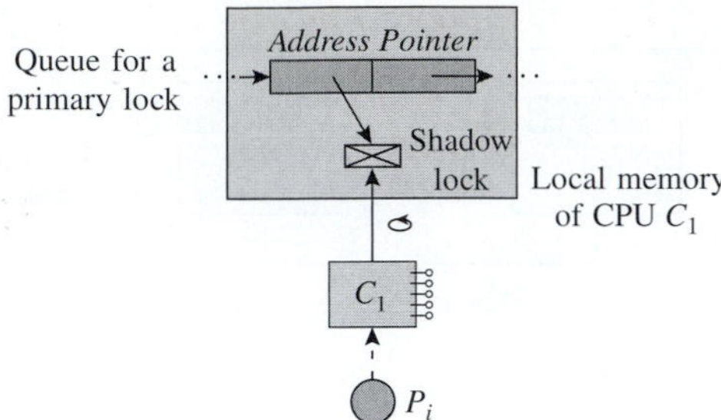

Figure 10.7 An efficient software solution for process synchronization.

primary lock, the process allocates a shadow lock in the local memory, enters its address in the primary lock's queue and starts spinning on it. The queue may span different memory units in the system; so the action of entering the shadow lock in the queue generates nonlocal memory traffic or network traffic. Resetting of a shadow lock also generates nonlocal memory traffic or network traffic. However, spinning does not generate such traffic. Needless to say, manipulation of the queue should itself be done under a lock.

10.5 PROCESS SCHEDULING

A process can be scheduled on any CPU in a multiprocessor system. However, its performance can be improved by making an intelligent choice of the CPU, i.e., by deciding *where* to schedule it. Performance of a group of processes that synchronize and communicate with one another can be improved by deciding *how* and *when* to schedule them. This section discusses issues involved in making these decisions.

Choice of the CPU When a process P_i operates on a CPU, say, CPU C_1, some parts of its address space are loaded into the L1 cache of the CPU. When the CPU is switched to another process, some of these parts are overwritten by parts of the address space of the new process, however some other parts of P_i's address space may survive in C_1's cache memory for some time. These parts are called the *residual address space* of a process. A process is said to have an *affinity* for a CPU if it has a residual address space in its cache. The process would have a higher cache hit ratio on this CPU than on a CPU for which it does not have affinity.

Affinity scheduling schedules a process on a CPU for which it has an affinity. This technique provides a good cache hit ratio, thereby speeding up operation of the process and reducing the memory bus traffic. Another way to exploit the affinity is to schedule the threads of a process on the same CPU in close succession. However, affinity scheduling interferes with load balancing across CPUs since processes and threads become tied to specific CPUs. Section 10.6.3 describes how it also leads to scheduling anomalies in the Windows system.

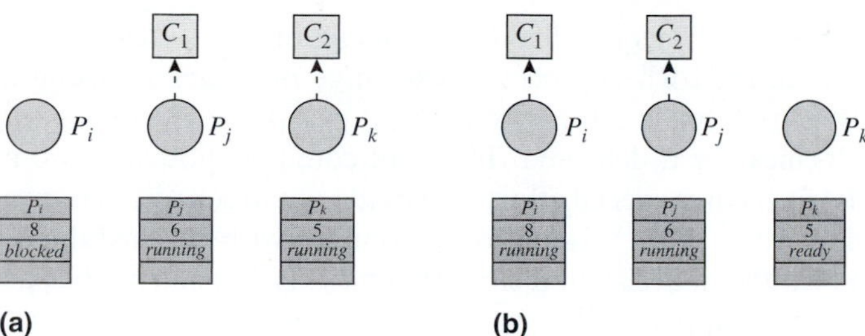

Figure 10.8 Process P_j is shuffled from CPU C_1 to CPU C_2 when process P_i becomes *ready*.

In Section 10.3, we discussed how the SMP kernel permits each CPU to perform its own scheduling. This arrangement prevents the kernel from becoming a performance bottleneck; however, it leads to scheduling anomalies in which a higher-priority process is in the *ready* state even though a low-priority process has been scheduled. Correcting this anomaly requires shuffling of processes between CPUs, as indicated in the next example.

Process Shuffling in an SMP Kernel

Example 10.1

An SMP system contains two CPUs C_1 and C_2, and three processes P_i, P_j, and P_k with priorities 8, 6, and 5, respectively. Figure 10.8(a) shows the situation in which process P_i is in the *blocked* state due to an I/O operation (see contents of its PCB fields) and processes P_j and P_k are executing using CPUs C_1 and C_2, respectively. When the I/O operation of P_i completes, the I/O interrupt is processed by CPU C_1, which changes P_i's state to *ready* and switches itself to service process P_i. So, process P_j, which is the process with the next higher priority, is in the *ready* state, and P_k, whose priority is the lowest, is in operation. To correct this situation, process P_k should be preempted and process P_j should be scheduled on CPU C_2. Figure 10.8(b) shows the situation after these actions are performed.

Process shuffling can be implemented by using the assigned workload table (AWT), discussed in Section 10.3, and the interprocessor interrupt (IPI). However, process shuffling leads to high scheduling overhead; this effect is more pronounced in a system containing a large number of CPUs. Hence some operating systems do not correct scheduling anomalies through process shuffling.

Synchronization-Conscious Scheduling Parts of a computation may be executed on different CPUs to achieve computation speedup. However, synchronization and communication among processes of an application influence the nature of parallelism between its processes, so a scheduling policy should take these into account as well. As commented earlier in Section 10.2, processes of an application should be scheduled on different CPUs at the same time if they use spin locks for synchronization. This is called *coscheduling*, or *gang scheduling*. A different approach is required when processes exchange messages by using a blocking protocol. When P_i sends a message to P_j, it can proceed with its computation only after its message is delivered. This wait could be quite long, so it is best to block P_i. In such cases special efforts are made *not* to schedule such processes in the same time slice. Since this approach conflicts with coscheduling, the kernel has to make a difficult decision. It can either base its decision on the past behavior of processes in the application or base it on user preference for a specific method of scheduling. The Mach operating system uses the latter approach.

10.6 CASE STUDIES

10.6.1 Mach

The Mach operating system, developed at Carnegie Mellon University, is an OS for multiprocessor and distributed systems. The multiprocessor Mach uses an SMP kernel structure. Figure 10.9 shows an overview of the scheduling arrangement used in Mach. The processors of the multiprocessor system are divided into *processor sets*. Each processor set is assigned a subset of threads for execution. Threads can have priorities between 0 and 31, where 0 is the highest priority. Each processor set has 32 ready queues to hold information about threads at each of the priority levels. These queues are common to all processors in the processor set. In addition, every processor has a local queue of threads. These are the threads that must be executed only on this processor. These threads have a higher priority than all threads in the thread queues. This feature provides for affinity scheduling. A thread is preempted at the end of a time slice only if some other ready thread exists in the thread queues, otherwise the thread is given another time slice. The time slice is varied according to the number of ready threads—a smaller time slice if many ready threads exist, and a larger time slice if few ready threads exist.

An interesting feature in the Mach operating system is the technique of *scheduling hints*. A thread issues a hint to influence processor scheduling

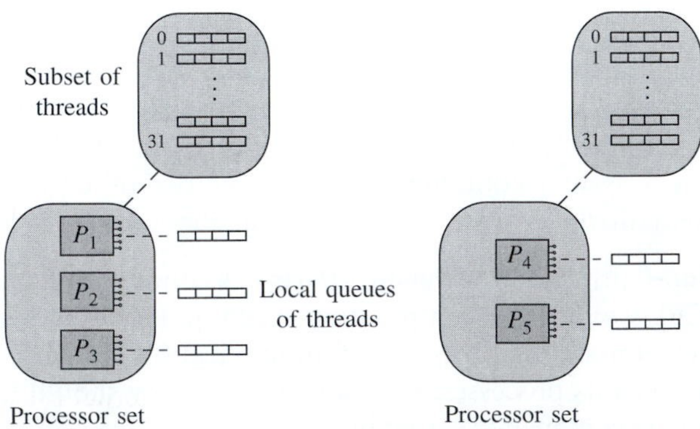

Figure 10.9 Scheduling in Mach.

decisions. It is presumed that a hint is based on the thread's knowledge of some execution characteristic of an application. A thread may issue a hint to ensure better scheduling when threads of an application require synchronization or communication. A discouragement hint reduces the priority of a thread. This type of hint can be issued by a thread that has to spin on a lock that has been set by some other process. A hands-off hint is given by a thread to indicate that it wishes to relinquish the processor to another thread: The thread can also indicate the identity of the thread to which it wishes to hand over the processor. On receiving such a hint, the scheduler switches the processor to execution of the named thread irrespective of its priority. This feature can be used effectively when a thread spins on a lock while the holder of the lock is preempted. The spinning thread can hand-off its processor to the preempted thread. This action will lead to an early release of the lock. It can also be used to implement the priority inheritance protocol discussed in Chapter 7.

10.6.2 Linux

Multiprocessing support in Linux was introduced in the Linux 2.0 kernel. Coarse-grained locking was employed to prevent race conditions over kernel data structures. Granularity of locks was made finer in later releases; however, the kernel was still nonpreemptible. With Linux 2.6 kernel, the Linux kernel became preemptible (see Section 4.8.2). The Linux 2.6 kernel also employs very fine-grained locking.

The Linux kernel provides spin locks for locking of data structures. It also provides a special *reader–writer spin lock* which permits any number of reader processes, that is, processes that do not modify any kernel data, to access protected data at the same time; however, it permits only one writer process to update the data at any time.

The Linux kernel uses another lock called the *sequence lock* that incurs low overhead and is scalable. The sequence lock is actually an integer that is used as a sequence counter through an atomic, i.e., *indivisible*, increment instruction. Whenever a process wishes to use a kernel data structure, it simply increments the integer in the sequence lock associated with the data structure, notes its new value, and performs the operation. After completing the operation, it checks whether the value in the sequence lock has changed after it had executed its increment instruction. If the value has changed, the operation is deemed to have failed, so it annuls the operation it had just performed and attempts it all over again, and so on until the operation succeeds.

Linux uses per-CPU data structures to reduce contention for locks on kernel data structures. As mentioned in Section 10.3, a per-CPU data structure of a CPU is accessed only when the kernel code is executed by that CPU; however, even this data structure needs to be locked because concurrent accesses may be made to it when an interrupt occurs while kernel code is being executed to service a system call and an interrupt servicing routine in the kernel is activated. Linux eliminates this lock by disabling preemption of this CPU due to interrupts while executing kernel code—the code executed by the CPU makes a system call to disable preemption when it is about to access the per-CPU data structures, and makes another system call to enable preemption when it finishes accessing the per-CPU data structures.

As described earlier in Section 7.6.3, Linux scheduling uses the ready queues data structure of Figure 7.12. Scheduling for a multiprocessor incorporates considerations of affinity—a user can specify a *hard affinity* for a process by indicating a set of CPUs on which it must run, and a process has a *soft* affinity for the last CPU on which it was run. Since scheduling is performed on a per-CPU basis, the kernel performs *load balancing* to ensure that computational loads directed at different CPUs are comparable. This task is performed by a CPU that finds that its ready queues are empty; it is also performed periodically by the kernel—every 1 ms if the system is idle, and every 200 ms otherwise.

The function `load_balance` is invoked to perform load balancing with the id of an underloaded CPU. `load_balance` finds a "busy CPU" that has at least 25 percent more processes in its ready queues than the ready queues of the underloaded CPU. It now locates some processes in its ready queues that do not have a hard affinity to the busy CPU, and moves them to the ready queues of the underloaded CPU. It proceeds as follows: It first moves the highest-priority processes in the *exhausted list* of the busy CPU, because these processes are less likely to have a residual address space in the cache of the busy CPU than those in the *active* list. If more processes are needed to be moved, it moves the highest-priority processes in the *active list* of the busy CPU, which would improve their response times.

10.6.3 SMP Support in Windows

The Windows kernel provides a comprehensive support for multiprocessor and NUMA systems, and for CPUs that provide hyperthreading—a hyperthreaded CPU is considered to be a single physical processor that has several logical processors. Spin locks are used to implement mutual exclusion over kernel data structures. To guarantee that threads do not incur long waits for kernel data structures, the Windows kernel never preempts a thread holding a spin lock if some other thread is trying to acquire the same lock.

The Windows Server 2003 and Windows Vista use several free lists of memory areas as described in Section 11.5.4, which permits CPUs to perform memory allocation in parallel. These kernels also use per-processor scheduling data structures as described in Section 10.3. However, CPUs may have to modify each other's data structures during scheduling. To reduce the synchronization overhead in this operation, the kernel provides a *queued spinlock* that follows the schematic of Section 10.4.2—a processor spins over a lock in its local memory, which avoids traffic over the network in NUMA systems and makes the lock scalable.

The Windows process and thread objects have several scheduling-related attributes. The *default processor affinity* of a process and *thread processor affinity* of a thread together define an affinity set for a thread, which is a set of processors. In a system with a NUMA architecture, a process can be confined to a single node in the system by letting its affinity set be a subset of processors in the node. The kernel assigns an *ideal processor* for each thread such that different threads of a process have different ideal processors. This way many threads of a process could operate in parallel, which provides the benefits of coscheduling. The affinity set and the ideal processor together define a *hard affinity* for a thread. A processor is assumed to contain a part of the address space of a thread for 20 milliseconds after the thread ceases to operate on it. The thread has a *soft affinity* for the processor during this interval, so its identity is stored in the *last processor* attribute of the thread.

When scheduling is to be performed for, say, CPU C_1, the kernel examines *ready* threads in the order of diminishing priority and selects the first *ready* thread that satisfies one of the following conditions:

- The thread has C_1 as its last processor.
- The thread has C_1 as its ideal processor.
- The thread has C_1 in its affinity set, and has been *ready* for three clock ticks.

The first criterion realizes soft affinity scheduling, while the other two criteria realize hard affinity scheduling. If the kernel cannot find a thread that satisfies one of these criteria, it simply schedules the first *ready* thread it can find. If no such thread exists, it schedules the *idle thread* (see Section 7.6.4).

When a thread becomes *ready* because of an interrupt, the CPU handling the interrupt chooses a CPU to execute this newly readied thread as follows: It checks whether there are idle CPUs in the system, and whether the ideal processor or the last processor of the newly readied thread is one of them. If so, it schedules the newly readied thread on this CPU by entering the thread's id in the scheduling data structure of the selected CPU. The selected idle CPU would be executing the *idle thread*, which would pick up the identity of the scheduled thread in the next iteration of its idle loop and switch to it. If the ideal processor or the last processor of the newly readied thread is not idle, the CPU handling the interrupt is itself idle, and it is included in the affinity set of the newly readied thread, it itself takes up the thread for execution. If this check fails and some CPUs in the affinity set of the thread are idle, it schedules the thread on the lowest numbered such CPU; otherwise, it schedules the thread on the lowest numbered idle CPU that is not included in the affinity set of the thread.

If no CPU is idle, the CPU handling the interrupt compares the priorities of the newly readied thread and the thread running on the ideal processor of the newly readied thread. If the newly readied thread has a higher priority, an interprocessor interrupt is sent to its ideal processor with a request to switch to the newly readied thread. If this is not the case, a similar check is made on the last processor of the newly readied thread. If that check also fails, the CPU handling the interrupt simply enters the newly readied thread in the ready queue structure. It would be scheduled sometime in future by an idle CPU. In this case, an anomalous situation may exist in the system because the priority of the newly readied thread may exceed the priority of some thread that is executing on some other CPU. However, correcting this anomaly may cause too much shuffling of threads between CPUs, so it is not attempted by the scheduling policy.

10.7 SUMMARY

A multiprocessor OS exploits the presence of multiple CPUs in the computer to provide *high throughput* of the system, *computation speedup* of an application, and *graceful degradation* of the OS capabilities when faults occur in the system. In this chapter we studied the architecture of multiprocessor systems and OS issues involved in ensuring good performance.

Multiprocessor systems are classified into three kinds based on the manner in which memory can be accessed by different CPUs. In the *uniform memory architecture* (UMA), the memory is shared between all CPUs. This architecture is also called the *symmetrical multiprocessor* (SMP) architecture. In the *nonuniform memory architecture* (NUMA), each CPU has some local memory that can be accessed faster than the rest of the memory which is accessible over an interconnection network.

A multiprocessor OS should exploit presence of multiple CPUs to schedule user processes in parallel, and also to ensure efficiency of its own functioning. Two issues are important in this context: kernel structure and delays caused by synchronization and scheduling. Many CPUs should be able to execute the kernel's code in parallel so that the kernel can respond to events readily and it does not become a performance bottleneck. Synchronization and scheduling of user processes should be performed in such a manner that processes do not incur large delays. The OS has to also ensure that its algorithms are *scalable*; that is, they perform well even when the size of the system increases because of an increase in the number of CPUs, memory units, or user processes.

Multiprocessor OSs employ special kinds of locks called *spin locks* and *sleep locks* to control the overhead of process synchronization. *Affinity scheduling* is employed to schedule a process on the same CPU so that it would obtain high cache hit ratios during its operation, and *coscheduling* is used to schedule processes of an application on different CPUs at the same time so that they can communicate efficiently among themselves. Operating systems employ *process shuffling* to ensure that the highest-priority ready processes are always in operation on its CPUs. We discussed features of Linux, Mach, and Windows operating systems in this context.

TEST YOUR CONCEPTS

10.1 Classify each of the following statements as true or false:

- **a.** Scheduling performed by one CPU in a symmetric multiprocessor system may result in shuffling of processes operating on many CPUs in the system.
- **b.** The interprocessor interrupt (IPI) is not used in process synchronization in a symmetric multiprocessor system.
- **c.** When a process spins on a lock, it affects performance of processes being serviced by other CPUs.
- **d.** When affinity scheduling is used, a process may require less CPU time to complete its operation.

10.2 What would be the consequence of not implementing cache coherence in a multiprocessor system?

- **a.** Results produced by a process that does not interact with any other process might be wrong.
- **b.** Results produced by a group of interacting processes that use the same CPU might be wrong.
- **c.** Results produced by a group of interacting processes that do not use the same CPU might be wrong.
- **d.** None of (a)–(c).

EXERCISES

10.1 Describe two situations in which an SMP kernel requires use of the interprocessor interrupt (IPI).

10.2 An OS assigns the same priority to all processes (or threads) of an application, but uses different priorities for different applications.

a. In a uniprocessor system, does this assignment of priorities provide an advantage that is similar to that provided by affinity scheduling?

b. In a multiprocessor system, does this assignment of priorities provide an advantage that is similar to that provided by coscheduling?

10.3 Can the hands-off feature of Mach be used to advantage in implementing the software scheme for process synchronization discussed in Section 10.4.2?

10.4 Can priority inversion occur when spin or sleep locks are used? (See Section 6.5.1 for a definition of priority inversion.)

10.5 Discuss suitability of various kinds of locks for synchronization of parallel activities within an SMP kernel.

10.6 Processes of an application interact among themselves very frequently. Among queued, spin, and sleep locks, which would you consider suitable for implementing this application on a multiprocessor system, and why?

BIBLIOGRAPHY

Most books on computer architecture discuss architecture of multiprocessors and interconnection networks, e.g., Hennessy and Patterson (2002), Hamacher et al. (2002), and Stallings (2003).

Mellor-Crummey and Scott (1991), Menasse et al. (1991), and Wisniewski et al. (1997) discuss synchronization of processes in a multiprocessor environment. The efficient software solution for process synchronization described in Fig. 10.7 is adapted from Mellor-Crummey and Scott (1991). Ousterhout (1982), Tucker and Gupta (1989), and Squillante (1990) discuss scheduling issues in multiprocessor operating systems.

Eykholt et al. (1992) discusses multithreading of the SunOS kernel to enhance effectiveness of its SMP structure. Accetta et al. (1986) describes the Mach multiprocessor operating system. Love (2005) discusses synchronization and scheduling in Linux 2.6, while Russinovich and Solomon (2005) describes synchronization and scheduling in Windows.

1. Accetta, M., R. Baron, W. Bolosky, D. B. Golub, R. Rashid, A. Tevanian, and M. Young (1986): "Mach: A new kernel foundation for Unix development," *Proceedings of the Summer 1986 USENIX Conference*, June 1986, 93–112.
2. Eykholt, J. R., S. R. Kleiman, S. Barton, S. Faulkner, A. Shivalingiah, M. Smith, D. Stein, J. Voll, M. Weeks, and D. William (1992): "Beyond multiprocessing: multithreading the SunOS kernel," *Proceedings of the Summer 1992 USENIX Conference*, 11–18.
3. Hamacher, C., Z. Vranesic, and S. Zaky (2002): *Computer Organization,* 5th ed., McGraw-Hill, New York.
4. Hennessy, J., and D. Patterson (2002): *Computer Architecture: A Quantitative Approach,* 3rd ed., Morgan Kaufmann, San Mateo, Calif.
5. Mellor-Crummey, and M. L. Scott (1991): "Algorithms for scalable synchronization on shared memory multiprocessor," *ACM Transactions on Computer Systems*, **9** (1), 21–65.
6. Karlin, A. R., K. Li, M. S. Menasse, and S. Owicki (1991): "Empirical studies of competitive spinning for shared memory multiprocessor," *Proceedings of 13th ACM Symposium on Operating System Principles*, 41–55.
7. Kontothanassis L. I., R. W. Wisniewski, and M. L. Scott (1997): "Scheduler conscious synchronization," *ACM Transactions on Computer Systems*, **15** (1), 3–40.
8. Love, R. (2005): *Linux Kernel Development,* 2nd ed., Novell Press.
9. Ousterhout, J. K. (1982): "Scheduling techniques for concurrent systems," *Proceedings of the 3rd International Conference on Distributed Computing Systems*, 22–30.

10. Russinovich, M. E., and D. A. Solomon (2005): *Microsoft Windows Internals,* 4th ed., Microsoft Press, Redmond, Wash.
11. Squillante, M. (1990): "Issues in shared-memory multiprocessor scheduling: A performance evaluation," Ph.D. dissertation, Dept. of Computer Science & Engineering, University of Washington.
12. Stallings, W. (2003): *Computer Organization and Architecture,* 6th ed., Prentice Hall, Upper Saddle River, N.J.
13. Tanenbaum, A. S. (2001): *Modern Operating Systems,* 2nd ed., Prentice Hall, Englewood Cliffs, N.J.
14. Tucker, A., and A. Gupta (1989): "Process control and scheduling issues for multiprogrammed shared memory multiprocessors," *Proceedings of 12th ACM Symposium on Operating System Principles*, 159–166.

part 3

Memory Management

The memory of a computer system is shared by a large number of processes, so memory management has traditionally been a very important task of an operating system. Memories keep becoming cheaper and larger every year; however, the pressure on memory as an OS resource persists because both the size of processes and the number of processes that an operating system has to service at any time also keep growing. The basic issues in memory management are efficient use of memory, protection of memory allocated to a process against illegal accesses by other processes, performance of individual processes, and performance of the system.

Efficient use of memory is important because it determines the number of processes that can be accommodated in memory at any time. This number, in turn, influences performance of the system because presence of too few processes in memory could lead to CPU idling. Both memory efficiency and system performance deteriorate when some memory areas remain unused because they are too small to accommodate a process. This situation is called *memory fragmentation*.

The technique of *noncontiguous memory allocation* enables efficient use of memory by countering memory fragmentation. When the OS does not find a memory area that is large enough to accommodate a process, it allocates several nonadjoining memory areas to the process. Special features exist in a computer's hardware to support operation of such a process. Operating systems exploit noncontiguous memory allocation to keep only some parts of a process, rather than the whole process, in memory. This technique permits the size of a process to exceed the size of memory, which creates an illusion that the memory of a computer is larger than it actually is. This illusion is called *virtual memory*.

Road Map for Part 3

Chapter 11: Memory Management

This chapter is devoted to the fundamentals of memory management. It begins by discussing how memory protection is implemented in the hardware by using special registers in the CPU. It then discusses how efficient use of memory is achieved by reusing memory released by a process while handling subsequent

Road Map for Part 3

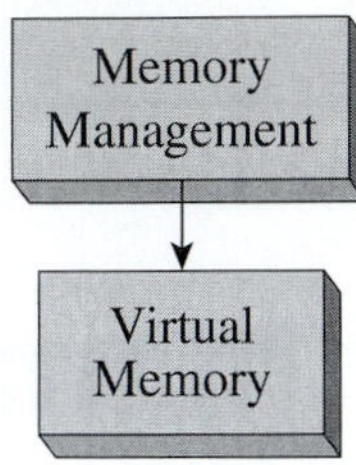

Schematic diagram showing the order in which chapters of this part should be covered in a course.

memory requests, and how techniques for fast memory allocation and deallocation may cause *memory fragmentation*. The noncontiguous memory allocation approaches called *paging* and *segmentation* are then described. The chapter also discusses the special techniques employed by the kernel to manage its own memory requirements efficiently.

Chapter 12: Virtual Memory

This chapter deals with virtual memory implementation using *paging* in detail. It discusses how the kernel keeps the code and data of a process on a disk and loads parts of it into memory when required, and how the performance of a process is determined by the rate at which parts of a process have to be loaded from the disk. It shows how this rate depends on the amount of memory allocated to a process, and the *page replacement algorithm* used to decide which pages of a process should be removed from memory so that new pages can be loaded. Page replacement algorithms that use clues from the empirical law of *locality of reference* are then discussed. Virtual memory implementation using segmentation is also described.

Chapter 11

Memory Management

As seen in Chapter 2, the memory hierarchy comprises the cache, the memory management unit (MMU), random access memory (RAM), which is simply called *memory* in this chapter, and a disk. We discuss management of memory by the OS in two parts—this chapter discusses techniques for efficient use of memory, whereas the next chapter discusses management of *virtual memory*, which is part of the memory hierarchy consisting of the memory and the disk.

Memory binding is the association of memory addresses with instructions and data of a program. To provide convenience and flexibility, memory binding is performed several times to a program—the compiler and linker perform it *statically*, i.e., before program execution begins, whereas the OS performs it *dynamically*, i.e., during execution of the program. The kernel uses a model of memory allocation to a process that provides for both static and dynamic memory binding.

The speed of memory allocation and efficient use of memory are the two fundamental concerns in the design of a memory allocator. To ensure efficient use, the kernel recycles the memory released by a process to other processes that need it. *Memory fragmentation* is a problem that arises in memory reuse, leading to inefficient use of memory. We will discuss practical techniques for reducing the amount of memory fragmentation in an OS, in particular, *noncontiguous memory allocation* using *paging* or *segmentation*.

The kernel creates and destroys data structures used to store control data—mainly, various control blocks such as PCBs—at a high rate. The sizes of these data structures are known *a priori*, so the kernel employs a set of techniques that exploit this foreknowledge for achieving fast allocation/deallocation and efficient use of memory.

11.1 MANAGING THE MEMORY HIERARCHY

As discussed earlier in Chapter 2, a memory hierarchy comprises cache memories like the L1 and L3 caches, the memory management unit (MMU), memory, and a disk. Its purpose is to create an illusion of a fast and large memory at a low cost. The upper half of Figure 11.1 illustrates the memory hierarchy. The

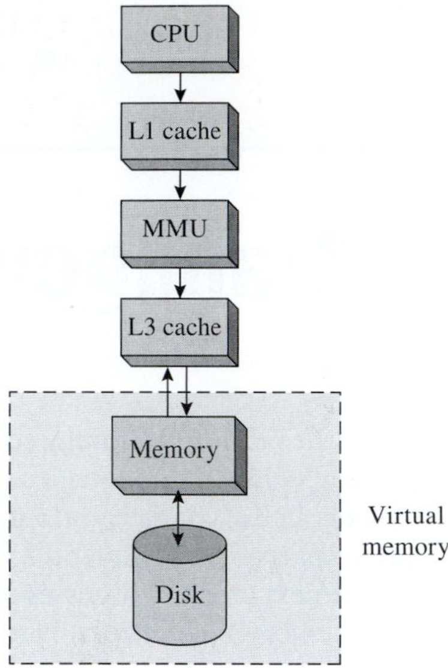

Levels	How managed	Performance issues
Caches	Allocation and use is managed by hardware	Ensuring high hit ratios
Memory	Allocation is managed by the kernel and use of allocated memory is managed by run-time libraries	(1) Accommodating more process in memory, (2) Ensuring high hit ratios
Disk	Allocation and use is managed by the kernel	Quick loading and storing of parts of process address spaces

Figure 11.1 Managing the memory hierarchy.

CPU refers to the fastest memory, the *cache*, when it needs to access an instruction or data. If the required instruction or data is not available in the cache, it is fetched from the next lower level in the memory hierarchy, which could be a slower cache or the random access memory (RAM), simply called *memory* in this book. If the required instruction or data is also not available in the next lower level memory, it is fetched there from a still lower level, and so on. Performance of a process depends on the *hit ratios* in various levels of the memory hierarchy, where the hit ratio in a level indicates what fraction of instructions or data bytes that were looked for in that level were actually present in it. Eq. (2.1) of Chapter 2 indicates how the effective memory access time depends on a hit ratio.

The caches are managed entirely in the hardware. The kernel employs special techniques to provide high cache hit ratios for a process. For example, the kernel switches between threads of the same process whenever possible to benefit from presence of parts of the process address space in the cache, and it employs affinity scheduling in a multiprocessor system (see Section 10.5), to schedule a process on the same CPU every time to achieve high cache hit ratios.

Memory is managed jointly by the kernel and the *run-time library* of the programming language in which the code of the process is written. The kernel allocates memory to user processes. The primary performance concern in this function is accommodating more user processes in memory, so that both system performance and user service would improve. The kernel meets this concern through efficient reuse of memory when a process completes. During operation, a process creates data structures *within* the memory already allocated to it by the kernel. This function is actually performed by the run-time library. It employs techniques that efficiently reuse memory when a process creates and destroys data structures during its operation. Thus some of the concerns and techniques employed by the kernel and the run-time libraries are similar.

As a sequel to the kernel's focus on accommodating a large number of processes in memory, the kernel may decide on keeping only a part of each process's address space in memory. It is achieved by using the part of the memory hierarchy called *virtual memory* that consists of memory and a disk (see the dashed box in Figure 11.1). The parts of a process's address space that are not in memory are loaded from the disk when needed during operation of the process. In this arrangement, the hit ratio of a process in memory determines its performance. Hence the kernel employs a set of techniques to ensure a high hit ratio for processes. The disk in the virtual memory is managed entirely by the kernel; the kernel stores different parts of each process's address space on the disk in such a manner that they can be accessed efficiently. It contributes to good execution performance of processes in a virtual memory.

We discuss management of the memory hierarchy by an operating system in two parts. This chapter focuses on the management of memory, and focuses on techniques employed for efficient use of memory and for speedy allocation and deallocation of memory. Later we discuss how presence of the memory management unit (MMU) simplifies both these functions. Chapter 12 discusses management of the virtual memory, particularly the techniques employed by the kernel to ensure high hit ratios in memory and limit the memory committed to each process.

11.2 STATIC AND DYNAMIC MEMORY ALLOCATION

Memory allocation is an aspect of a more general action in software operation known as *binding*. Two other actions related to a program—its linking and loading—are also aspects of binding.

Any entity in a program, e.g., a function or a variable, has a set of attributes, and each attribute has a value. Binding is the act of specifying the value of an attribute. For example, a variable in a program has attributes such as name, type, dimensionality, scope, and memory address. A name binding specifies the variable's name and a type binding specifies its type. Memory binding is the act of specifying the variable's memory address; it constitutes memory allocation for the variable. Memory allocation to a process is the act of specifying memory addresses of its instructions and data.

A binding for an attribute of an entity such as a function or a variable can be performed any time before the attribute is used. Different binding methods perform the binding at different times. The exact time at which binding is performed may determine the efficiency and flexibility with which the entity can be used. Broadly speaking, we can differentiate between early binding and late binding. Late binding is useful in cases where the OS or run-time library may have more information about an entity at a later time, using which it may be able to perform a better quality binding. For example, it may be able to achieve more efficient use of resources such as memory. Early and late binding are represented by the two fundamental binding methods of *static* and *dynamic* binding, respectively.

Definition 11.1 Static Binding A binding performed before the execution of a program (or operation of a software system) is set in motion.

Definition 11.2 Dynamic Binding A binding performed during the execution of a program (or operation of a software system).

Static memory allocation can be performed by a compiler, linker, or loader while a program is being readied for execution. *Dynamic memory allocation* is performed in a "lazy" manner during the execution of a program; memory is allocated to a function or a variable just before it is used for the first time.

Static memory allocation to a process is possible only if sizes of its data structures are known before its execution begins. If sizes are not known, they have to be guessed; wrong estimates can lead to wastage of memory and lack of flexibility. For example, consider an array whose size is not known during compilation. Memory is wasted if we overestimate the array's size, whereas the process may not be able to operate correctly if we underestimate its size. Dynamic memory allocation can avoid both these problems by allocating a memory area whose size matches the actual size of the array, which would be known by the time the allocation is performed. It can even permit the array size to vary during operation of the process. However, dynamic memory allocation incurs the overhead of memory allocation actions performed during operation of a process.

Operating systems choose static and dynamic memory allocation under different circumstances to obtain the best combination of execution efficiency and memory efficiency. When sufficient information about memory requirements is available a *priori*, the kernel or the run-time library makes memory allocation decisions statically, which provides execution efficiency. When little information is available a *priori*, the memory allocation decisions are made dynamically, which incurs higher overhead but ensures efficient use of memory. In other situations, the available information is used to make some decisions concerning memory allocation statically, so that the overhead of dynamic memory allocation can be reduced. We discuss an instance of this approach in Section 11.11, where the kernel exploits its knowledge of its own data structures to achieve efficient memory allocation for them.

11.3 EXECUTION OF PROGRAMS

A program P written in a language *L* has to be transformed before it can be executed. Several of these transformations perform memory binding—each one binds the instructions and data of the program to a new set of addresses. Figure 11.2 is a schematic diagram of three transformations performed on program P before it can be loaded in memory for execution.

- *Compilation or assembly:* A compiler or an assembler is generically called a *translator*. It translates program P into an equivalent program in the *object module* form. This program contains instructions in the machine language of the computer. While invoking the translator, the user specifies the *origin* of the program, which is the address of its first instruction or byte; otherwise, the translator assumes a default address, typically 0. The translator accordingly assigns addresses to other instructions and data in the program and uses these addresses as operand addresses in its instructions. The *execution start address* or simply the *start address* of a program is the address of the instruction with which its execution is to begin. It can be the same as the origin of the program, or it can be different.

  The addresses assigned by the translator are called *translated addresses*. Thus, the translator binds instructions and data in program P to translated addresses. An object module indicates the translated origin of the program, its translated start address, and size.
- *Linking:* Program P may call other programs during its execution, e.g., functions from mathematical libraries. These functions should be included in the program, and their start addresses should be used in the function call instructions in P. This procedure is called *linking*. It is achieved by selecting object modules for the called functions from one or more libraries and merging them with program P.

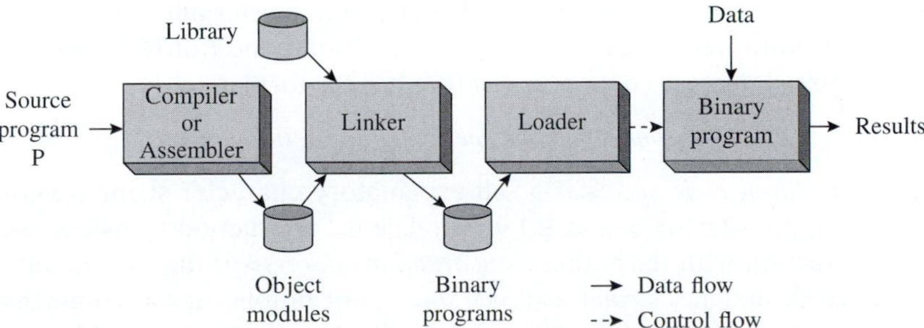

Figure 11.2 Schematic diagram of transformation and execution of a program.

- *Relocation:* Some object module(s) merged with program P may have conflicting translated time addresses. This conflict is resolved by changing the memory binding of the object module(s); this action is called *relocation* of object modules. It involves changing addresses of operands used in their instructions.

The relocation and linking functions are performed by a program called a *linker*. The addresses assigned by it are called *linked addresses*. The user may specify the linked origin for the program; otherwise, the linker assumes the linked origin to be the same as the translated origin. In accordance with the linked origin and the relocation necessary to avoid address conflicts, the linker binds instructions and data of the program to a set of linked addresses. The resulting program, which is in a ready-to-execute program form called a *binary program*, is stored in a library. The directory of the library stores its name, linked origin, size, and the linked start address.

A binary program has to be loaded in memory for execution. This function is performed by the *loader*. If the start address of the memory area where a program is to be loaded, which is called its *load origin*, differs from the linked origin of program, the loader has to change its memory binding yet again. A loader possessing this capability is called a *relocating loader*, whereas a loader without this capability is called an *absolute loader*. Note that translators, linkers, and loaders are *not* parts of the OS.

In this section we discuss different forms of programs and their properties concerning memory bindings, processing by the linker, and memory requirements during execution. We use programs written in a simple hypothetical assembly language to illustrate the relocation and linking actions performed by the linker.

A Simple Assembly Language An assembly language statement has the following format:

[Label] <*Opcode*> <*operand spec*> ,<*operand spec*>

The first operand is always a general-purpose-register (GPR)—`AREG`, `BREG`, `CREG` or `DREG`. The second operand is either a GPR or a symbolic name that corresponds to a memory byte. Self-explanatory opcodes like `ADD` and `MULT` are used to designate arithmetic operations. The `MOVER` instruction moves a value from its memory operand to its register operand, whereas the `MOVEM` instruction does the opposite. All arithmetic is performed in a register and sets a *condition code*. The condition code can be tested by a branch-on-condition (`BC`) instruction. The assembly statement corresponding to it has the format

`BC` <*condition code spec*>, <*instruction address*>

where <*condition code spec*> is a self-explanatory character string describing a condition, e.g., `GT` for > and `EQ` for =. The `BC` instruction transfers control to the instruction with the address <*instruction address*> if the current value of condition code matches <*condition code spec*>. For simplicity, we assume that all addresses and constants are in decimal, and all instructions occupy 4 bytes. The sign is not a part of an instruction. The opcode and operands of an instruction

Assembly statement			Generated code Address	Code
	START	500		
	ENTRY	TOTAL		
	EXTRN	MAX, ALPHA		
	READ	A	500)	+ 09 0 540
LOOP			504)	
	⋮			
	MOVER	AREG, ALPHA	516)	+ 04 1 000
	BC	ANY, MAX	520)	+ 06 6 000
	⋮			
	BC	LT, LOOP	532)	+ 06 1 504
	STOP		536)	+ 00 0 000
A	DS	1	540)	
TOTAL	DS	3	541)	
	END			

Figure 11.3 Assembly program P and its generated code.

occupy 2, 1, and 3 digits, respectively, and the GPRs AREG, BREG, CREG, and DREG are represented by 1, 2, 3, and 4, respectively, in an instruction.

11.3.1 Relocation

Figure 11.3 shows program P, an assembly program, and its generated code. The ENTRY and EXTRN statements have significance for linking; they are discussed later in Section 11.3.2. A DS statement merely reserves the number of bytes mentioned as its operand. The statement START 500 indicates that the translated origin of the program should be 500. The translated address of LOOP is therefore 504. The address of A is 540. The instructions in bytes with addresses 532 and 500 use these addresses to refer to LOOP and A, respectively. These addresses depend on the origin of the program in an obvious way. Instructions using such addresses are called *address-sensitive instructions*. A program containing address-sensitive instructions can execute correctly only if it is loaded in the memory area whose start address coincides with the origin of the program. If it is to execute in some other memory area, addresses in address-sensitive instructions have to be suitably modified. This action is called *relocation*. It requires knowledge of translated and linked origins and information about address-sensitive instructions. The next example illustrates relocation of P.

Relocation of a Program — Example 11.1

The translated origin of program P in Figure 11.3 is 500. The translated address of the symbol A is 540. The instruction corresponding to the statement READ A is an address-sensitive instruction. If the linked origin of P is 900, the linked address of A would be 940. It can be obtained by adding the difference between the translated and linked origins, i.e., 900 − 500, to its translated address. Thus, relocation can be performed by adding 400 to the address used in each address-sensitive instruction. Thus, the address in the `READ` instruction would be changed to 940. Similarly, the instruction in translated memory byte 532 uses the address 504, which is the address of `LOOP`. This address would be changed to 904. (Note that operand addresses in the instructions with addresses 516 and 520 also need to be "corrected." However, it is an instance of linking, which is discussed in the next section.)

Static and Dynamic Relocation of Programs When a program is to be executed, the kernel allocates it a memory area that is large enough to accommodate it, and invokes the loader with the name of the program and the load origin as parameters. The loader loads the program in the memory allocated to it, relocates it using the scheme illustrated in Example 11.1 if the linked origin is different from the load origin, and passes it control for execution. This relocation is static relocation as it is performed before execution of the program begins. Some time after the program's execution has begun, the kernel may wish to change the memory area allocated to it so that other programs can be accommodated in memory. This time, the relocation has to be performed during execution of the program, hence it constitutes dynamic relocation.

Dynamic relocation can be performed by suspending a program's execution, carrying out the relocation procedure described earlier, and then resuming its execution. However, it would require information concerning the translated origin and address-sensitive instructions to be available during the program's execution. It would also incur the memory and processing costs described earlier. Some computer architectures provide a *relocation register* to simplify dynamic relocation. The relocation register is a special register in the CPU whose contents are added to every memory address used during execution of a program. The result is another memory address, which is actually used to make a memory reference. Thus,

$$\text{Effective memory address} = \text{memory address used in the current instruction} \\ + \text{contents of relocation register}$$

The following example illustrates how dynamic relocation of a program is achieved by using the relocation register.

Example 11.2 Dynamic Relocation through Relocation Register

A program has the linked origin of 50000, and it has also been loaded in the memory area that has the start address of 50000. During its execution, it is to be shifted to the memory area having the start address of 70000, so it has to be relocated to execute in this memory area. This relocation is achieved simply

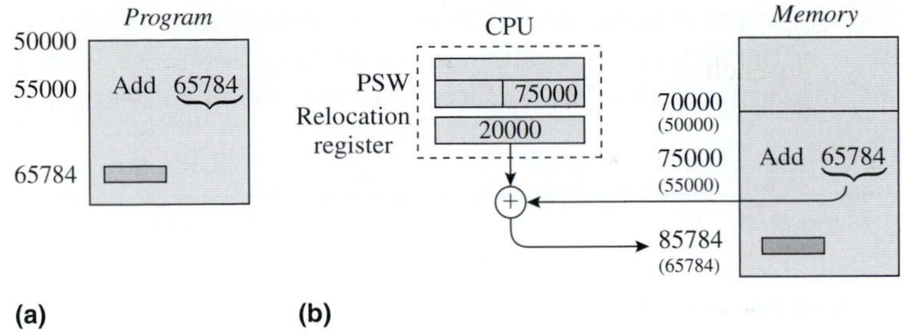

Figure 11.4 Program relocation using a relocation register: (a) program; (b) its execution.

by loading an appropriate value in the relocation register, which is computed as follows:

Value to be loaded in relocation register
= start address of allocated memory area – linked origin of program
= 70000 – 50000 = 20000

Consider execution of the Add instruction in the program shown in Figure 11.4(a). This instruction has the linked address 55000 in the program and uses an operand whose linked address is 65784. As a result of relocation, the program exists in the memory area starting with the address 70000. Figure 11.4(b) shows the load addresses of its instructions and data; the corresponding linked addresses are shown in parenthesis for easy reference. The Add instruction exists in the location with address 75000. The address of its operand is 65784 and the relocation register contains 20000, so during execution of the instruction, the effective address of its operand is 65784 + 20000 = 85784. Hence the actual memory access is performed at the address 85784.

11.3.2 Linking

An ENTRY statement in an assembly program indicates symbols that are defined in the assembly program and may be referenced in some other assembly programs. Such symbols are called *entry points*. An EXTRN statement in an assembly program indicates symbols that are used in the assembly program but are defined in some other assembly program. These symbols are called external symbols and uses of these symbols in the assembly program are called *external references*. The assembler puts information about the ENTRY and EXTRN statements in an object module for use by the linker.

Linking is the process of binding an external reference to the correct linked address. The linker first scans all object modules being linked together to collect the names of all entry points and their linked addresses. It stores this information in a table for its own use. It then considers each external reference, obtains the linked address of the external symbol being referenced from its table, and puts this address in the instruction containing the external reference. This action is called resolution of an external reference. The next example illustrates the steps in linking.

Example 11.3 Linking

The statement `ENTRY TOTAL` in program P of Figure 11.3 indicates that `TOTAL` is an entry point in the program. Note that `LOOP` and `A` are not entry points even though they are defined in the program. The statement `EXTRN MAX, ALPHA` indicates that the program contains external references to `MAX` and `ALPHA`. The assembler does not know the addresses of `MAX` and `ALPHA` while processing program P, so it puts zeroes in the operand address fields of instructions containing references to these symbols (see Figure 11.3).

Consider program Q shown below:

```
         Assembly statement          Generated code
                                   Address      Code

               START   200
               ENTRY   ALPHA
               - -
         ALPHA DC      25            232)    + 00 0 025
               END
```

The `DC` statement declares a constant 25. Symbol `ALPHA` is an entry point in Q; it has the translated address 232. Let the linked origin of program P of Figure 11.3 be 900. The size of P is 44 bytes, so the linker assigns the address 944 to the linked origin of Q. Therefore, the linked address of `ALPHA` is $232 - 200 + 944 = 976$. The linker resolves the external reference to `ALPHA` in program P by putting the address 974 in the operand address field of the instruction that uses `ALPHA`, i.e., in the instruction with the translated address 516 in P. This instruction has the linked address 916.

Static and Dynamic Linking/Loading The distinction between the terms linking and loading has become blurred in modern operating systems. However, we use the terms as follows: A *linker* links modules together to form an executable program. A *loader* loads a program or a part of a program in memory for execution.

In *static linking*, the linker links all modules of a program before its execution begins; it produces a binary program that does not contain any unresolved external references. If several programs use the same module from a library, each program will get a private copy of the module; several copies of the module might be present in memory at the same time if programs using the module are executed simultaneously.

Dynamic linking is performed during execution of a binary program. The linker is invoked when an unresolved external reference is encountered during its execution. The linker resolves the external reference and resumes execution of the program. This arrangement has several benefits concerning use, sharing, and updating of library modules. Modules that are not invoked during execution of a program need not be linked to it at all. If the module referenced by a program has already been linked to another program that is in execution, the same copy of the module could be linked to this program as well, thus saving memory. Dynamic linking also provides an interesting benefit when a library of modules is updated—a program that invokes a module of the library automatically starts using the new version of the module! Dynamically linked libraries (DLLs) use some of these features to advantage.

To facilitate dynamic linking, each program is first processed by the static linker. The static linker links each external reference in the program to a dummy module whose sole function is to call the dynamic linker and pass the name of the external symbol to it. This way, the dynamic linker is activated when such an external reference is encountered during execution of the program. It maintains a table of entry points and their load addresses. If the external symbol is present in the table, it uses the load address of the symbol to resolve the external reference. Otherwise, it searches the library of object modules to locate a module that contains the required symbol as an entry point. This object module is linked to the binary program through the scheme illustrated in Example 11.3 and information about its entry points is added to the linker's table.

11.3.3 Program Forms Employed in Operating Systems

Two features of a program influence its servicing by an OS:

- Can the program execute in any area of memory, or does it have to be executed in a specific memory area?
- Can the code of the program be shared by several users concurrently?

If the load origin of the program does not coincide with the start address of the memory area, the program has to be relocated before it can execute. This is expensive. A program that can execute in any area of memory is at an advantage in this context. Shareability of a program is important if the program may have to be used by several users at the same time. If a program is not shareable, each user has to have a copy of the program, and so several copies of the program will have to reside in memory at the same time.

Table 11.1 summarizes important programs employed in operating systems. An object module is a program form that can be relocated by a linker, whereas a binary program cannot be relocated by a linker. The dynamically linked program form conserves memory by linking only those object modules that are referenced during its execution. We discussed these three program forms in previous sections. A *self-relocating program* can be executed in any part of memory. This program form is not important when a computer provides either a relocation register or virtual memory. The *reentrant program* form avoids the need to have multiple copies of a program in memory. These two program forms are discussed in the following sections.

Table 11.1 Program Forms Employed in Operating Systems

Program form	Features
Object module	Contains instructions and data of a program and information required for its relocation and linking.
Binary program	Ready-to-execute form of a program.
Dynamically linked program	Linking is performed in a lazy manner, i.e., an object module defining a symbol is linked to a program only when that symbol is referenced during the program's execution.
Self-relocating program	The program can relocate itself to execute in any area of memory.
Reentrant program	The program can be executed on several sets of data concurrently.

11.3.3.1 Self-Relocating Programs

Recall from Section 11.3.1 that relocation of a program involves modification of its address-sensitive instructions so that the program can execute correctly from a desired area of memory. Relocation of a program by a linker requires its object module form to be available; it also incurs considerable overhead. The self-relocating program form was developed to eliminate these drawbacks; it performs its own relocation to suit the area of memory allocated to it.

A self-relocating program knows its own translated origin and translated addresses of its address-sensitive instructions. It also contains a *relocating logic*, i.e., code that performs its own relocation. The start address of the relocating logic is specified as the execution start address of the program, so the relocating logic gains control when the program is loaded for execution. It starts off by calling a dummy function. The return address formed by this function call is the address of its next instruction. Using this address, it obtains address of the memory area where it is loaded for execution, i.e., its load origin. It now has all the information needed to implement the relocation scheme of Section 11.3.1. After performing its own relocation, it passes control to its first instruction to begin its own execution.

11.3.3.2 Reentrant Programs

Programs can be shared in both static and dynamic manner. Consider two programs A and B that use a program C. We designate A and B as *sharing* programs and C as the *shared* program. Static sharing of C is performed by using static linking. Hence the code and data of C are included in both A and B; the identity of C is lost in the binary programs produced by the linker. If programs A and B are executed simultaneously, two copies of C will exist in memory [see Figure 11.5(a)]. Thus, static sharing of a program is simple to implement, but may waste memory.

When dynamic sharing is used, a single copy of a shared program's code is loaded in memory and used by all sharing programs in execution. Dynamic

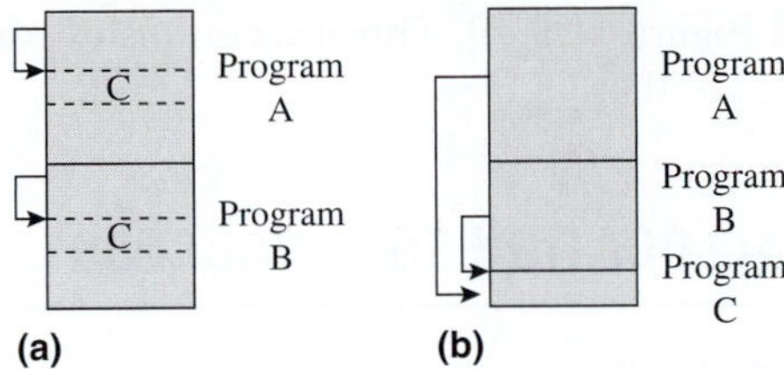

Figure 11.5 Sharing of program C by programs A and B: (a) static sharing; (b) dynamic sharing.

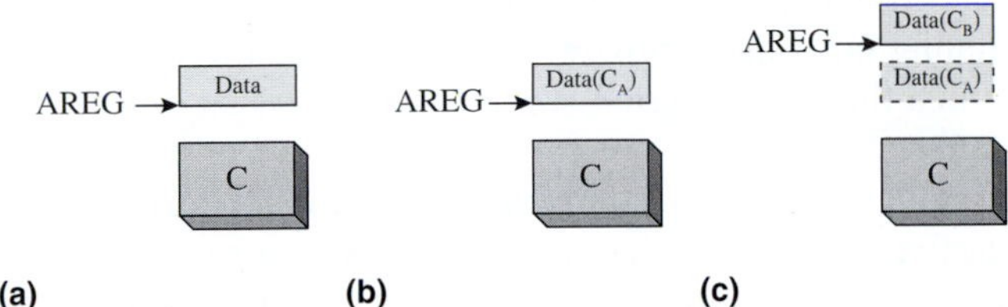

Figure 11.6 (a) Structure of a reentrant program; (b)–(c) concurrent invocations of the program.

sharing is implemented by using dynamic linking. The kernel keeps track of shared programs in memory. When a program wishes to use one of the shared programs, the kernel dynamically links the program to the copy of the shared program in memory. Figure 11.5(b) illustrates dynamic sharing. When program A needs to use program C in a shared mode, the kernel finds that C does not exist in memory. Hence it loads a copy of C in memory and dynamically links it to A. In Figure 11.5(b), this linking is depicted by the arrow from A to C. When program B needs to use program C, the kernel finds that a copy of C already exists in memory, so it merely links this copy to B. This arrangement avoids the need to have multiple copies of a program in memory, but we need to ensure that concurrent executions of a program do not interfere with one another.

A *reentrant program* is one that can be executed concurrently by many users without mutual interference. When invoked, the reentrant program allocates a new copy of its data structures and loads the memory address of this copy in a general-purpose register (GPR). Its code accesses its data structures through the GPR. This way, if the reentrant program is invoked concurrently by many programs, the concurrent invocations would use different copies of the data structure.

Figure 11.6 illustrates execution of program C coded as a reentrant program. Program C is coded so that it assumes AREG to point to the start of its data area [see Figure 11.6(a)]. Data items in this area are accessed by using different offsets from the address contained in AREG. When program A calls C, C allocates a data area for use during this invocation. It is depicted as Data(C_A) in Figure 11.6(b). When execution of A is preempted, the contents of AREG are stored in A's PCB; they would be loaded back in AREG when A is scheduled again. When C is called by B, a data area Data(C_B) is similarly allocated and AREG is set to point to the start of this area [see Figure 11.6(c)]. Thus executions of programs A and B do not interfere with one another.

11.4 MEMORY ALLOCATION TO A PROCESS

11.4.1 Stacks and Heaps

The compiler of a programming language generates code for a program and allocates its static data. It creates an object module for the program (see Section 11.3). The linker links the program with library functions and the run-time support of the programming language, prepares a ready-to-execute form of the program, and stores it in a file. The program size information is recorded in the directory entry of the file.

The run-time support allocates two kinds of data during execution of the program. The first kind of data includes variables whose scope is associated with functions, procedures, or blocks, in a program and parameters of function or procedure calls. This data is allocated when a function, procedure or block is entered and is deallocated when it is exited. Because of the last-in, first-out nature of the allocation/deallocation, the data is allocated on the stack. The second kind of data is dynamically created by a program through language features like the `new` statement of Pascal, C++, or Java, or the `malloc`, `calloc` statements of C. We refer to such data as *program-controlled dynamic data* (PCD data). The PCD data is allocated by using a data structure called a *heap*.

Stack In a *stack*, allocations and deallocations are performed in a last-in, first-out (LIFO) manner in response to *push* and *pop* operations, respectively. We assume each entry in the stack to be of some standard size, say, l bytes. Only the last entry of the stack is accessible at any time. A contiguous area of memory is reserved for the stack. A pointer called the *stack base* (SB) points to the first entry of the stack, while a pointer called the *top of stack* (TOS) points to the last entry allocated in the stack. We will use the convention that a stack grows toward the lower end of memory; we depict it as upward growth in the figures.

During execution of a program, a stack is used to support function calls. The group of stack entries that pertain to one function call is called a *stack frame*; it is also called an *activation record* in compiler terminology. A stack frame is pushed on the stack when a function is called. To start with, the stack frame contains either addresses or values of the function's parameters, and the *return address*, i.e., the address of the instruction to which control should be returned after completing the function's execution. During execution of the function, the run-time support of the programming language in which the program is coded creates local data of the function within the stack frame. At the end of the function's execution, the entire stack frame is popped off the stack and the return address contained in it is used to pass control back to the calling program.

Two provisions are made to facilitate use of stack frames: The first entry in a stack frame is a pointer to the previous stack frame on the stack. This entry facilitates popping off of a stack frame. A pointer called the *frame base* (FB) is

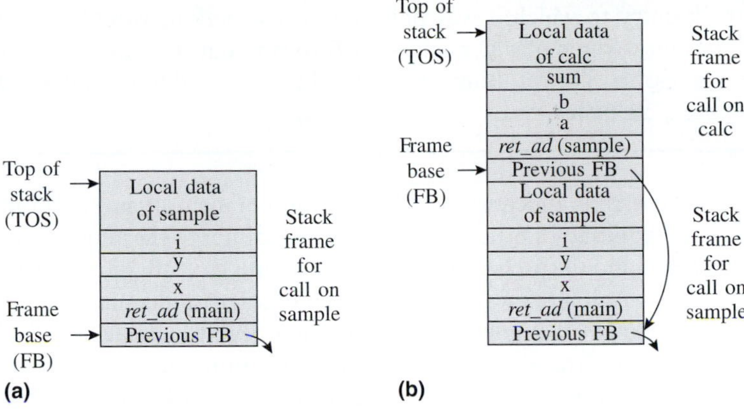

Figure 11.7 Stack after (a) `main` calls `sample`; (b) `sample` calls `calc`.

used to point to the start of the topmost stack frame in the stack. It helps in accessing various stack entries in the stack frame. Example 11.4 illustrates how the stack is used to implement function calls.

Use of a Stack

Example 11.4

Figure 11.7 shows the stack during execution of a program containing nested function calls. Figure 11.7(a) shows the stack after `main`, the primary function of the program, has made a function call `sample(x,y,i)`. A stack frame was pushed on the stack when the call was made. The first entry in the stack frame contains the previous value of the frame base, i.e., a pointer to the previous stack frame in the stack. The second entry is *ret_ad*(`main`), which is the return address into function `main`. The next three entries pertain to the parameters `x`, `y`, and `i`, while the entries following them pertain to the local data of function `sample`. The frame base (FB) points to the first entry in this stack frame. The TOS pointer points to the last local data in the stack frame. The code for function `sample` accesses the return address, information about the parameters, and its local data using displacements from the frame base (FB): Assuming each stack entry to be 4 bytes, the return address is at a displacement of 4 from the address in the frame base, the first parameter is at a displacement of 8, etc.

Figure 11.7(b) shows the stack after function `sample` has made a function call `calc(a, b, sum)`. A new stack frame has been pushed on the stack, the value of the FB has been saved in the first entry of this stack frame, the FB has been set to point at the start of the new stack frame, and the top of stack pointer now points at the last entry in the new stack frame. At the completion of the function, the TOS pointer would be set to point at the stack entry preceding the entry pointed to by FB, and FB would be loaded with the address contained in the stack entry to which it was pointing. These actions would effectively pop off the stack frame of `calc` and set FB to point at the start of the stack frame for `sample`. The resulting stack would be identical to the stack before function `sample` called `calc`.

Heap A *heap* permits allocation and deallocation of memory in a random order. An allocation request by a process returns with a pointer to the allocated memory area in the heap, and the process accesses the allocated memory area through this pointer. A deallocation request must present a pointer to the memory area to be deallocated. The next example illustrates use of a heap to manage the PCD data of a process. As illustrated there, "holes" develop in the memory allocation as data structures are created and freed. The heap allocator has to reuse such free memory areas while meeting future demands for memory.

Example 11.5 Use of a Heap

Figure 11.8 shows the status of a heap after executing the following C program:

```
float *floatptr1, *floatptr2;
int *intptr;
floatptr1 = (float *) calloc(5, sizeof(float));
floatptr2 = (float *) calloc(4, sizeof(float));
intptr = (int *) calloc(10, sizeof(int));
free(floatptr2);
```

The `calloc` routine is used to make a request for memory. The first call requests sufficient memory to accommodate 5 floating point numbers. The heap allocator allocates a memory area and returns a pointer to it. This pointer is stored in `floatptr1`. The first few bytes of each allocated memory area are assumed to contain a *length* field. This field is used during deallocation when the routine `free` is called with a pointer to an allocated memory area. Figure 11.8(a) shows the heap after all `calloc` calls have been processed. Figure 11.8(b) shows the heap after the `free` call. `free` has freed the memory area pointed to by `floatptr2`. This action has created a "hole" in the allocation.

11.4.2 The Memory Allocation Model

The kernel creates a new process when a user issues a command to execute a program. At this time, it has to decide how much memory it should allocate to the following components:

- Code and static data of the program
- Stack
- Program-controlled dynamic data (PCD data)

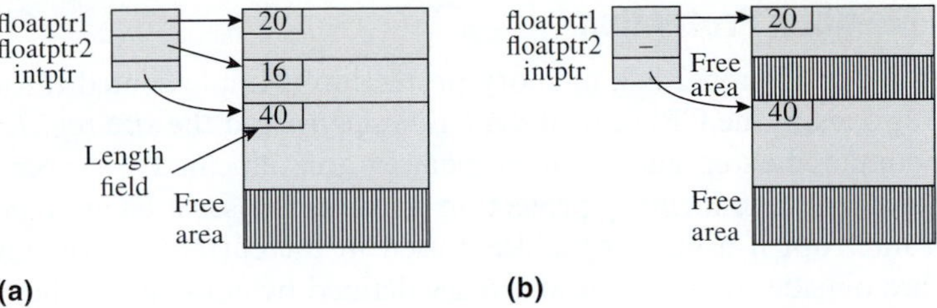

Figure 11.8 (a) A heap; (b) A "hole" in the allocation when memory is deallocated.

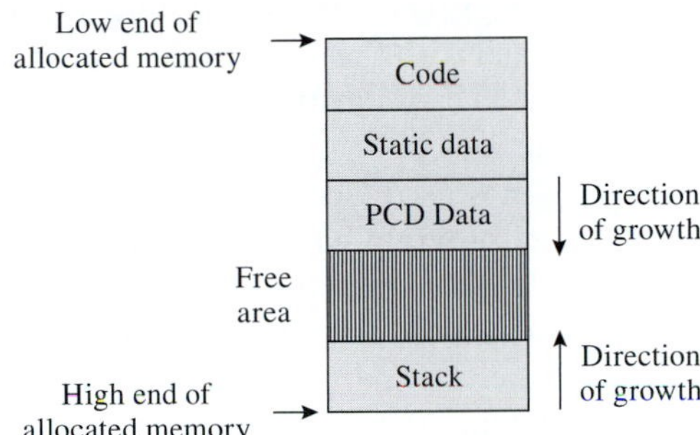

Figure 11.9 Memory allocation model for a process.

The size of the program can be obtained from its directory entry. Sizes of the stack and the PCD data vary during execution of a program, so the kernel does not know how much memory to allocate to these components. It can guess the maximum sizes the stack and the heap would grow to, and allocate them accordingly. However, this amounts to static allocation, which lacks flexibility. As discussed in Section 11.2, the allocated memory may be wasted or a process may run out of memory during its operation.

To avoid facing these problems individually for these two components, operating systems use the memory allocation model shown in Figure 11.9. The code and static data components in the program are allocated memory areas that exactly match their sizes. The PCD data and the stack share a single large area of memory but grow in opposite directions when memory is allocated to new data. The PCD data is allocated by starting at the low end of this area while the stack is allocated by starting at the high end of the area. The memory between these two components is free. It can be used to create new data in either component. In this model the stack and PCD data components do not have individual size restrictions.

A program creates or destroys PCD data by calling appropriate routines of the run-time library of the programming language in which it is coded. The library routines perform allocations/deallocations in the PCD data area allocated to the process. Thus, the kernel is not involved in this kind of memory management. In fact it is oblivious to it.

11.4.3 Memory Protection

As discussed in Section 2.2.3, memory protection is implemented through two control registers in the CPU called the *base register* and the *size register*. These registers contain the start address of the memory area allocated to a process and its size, respectively. The memory protection hardware raises a *memory protection violation* interrupt if a memory address used in the current instruction of the process lies outside the range of addresses defined by contents of the base and size registers (see Figure 2.5). On processing this interrupt, the kernel aborts the erring process. The base and size registers constitute the memory protection information (MPI) field of the program status word (PSW). The kernel loads appropriate values into these registers while scheduling a process for execution. A user process, which is executed with the CPU in the user mode, cannot tamper with contents of these registers because instructions for loading and saving these registers are privileged instructions.

When a *relocation register* is used (see Section 11.3.1), memory protection checks become simpler if every program has the linked origin of 0. In Figure 2.5, the comparison with the address contained in the base register can be omitted because the address used in an instruction cannot be < 0. The memory protection hardware merely checks whether an address is smaller than contents of the size register. The relocation register and the size register now constitute the MPI field of the PSW.

11.5 HEAP MANAGEMENT

11.5.1 Reuse of Memory

The speed of memory allocation and efficient use of memory are the two fundamental concerns in the design of a memory allocator. Stack-based allocation addresses both these concerns effectively since memory allocation and deallocation is very fast—the allocator modifies only the SB, FB, and TOS pointers to manage the free and allocated memory (see Section 11.4.1)—and released memory is reused automatically when fresh allocations are made. However, stack-based allocation cannot be used for data that are allocated and released in an unordered manner. Hence heap allocators are used by run-time support of programming languages to manage PCD data, and by the kernel to manage its own memory requirements.

In a heap, reuse of memory is not automatic; the heap allocator must try to reuse a free memory area while making fresh allocations. However, the size of a memory request rarely matches the size of a previously used memory area, so some memory area is left over when a fresh allocation is made. This memory area will be wasted if it is too small to satisfy a memory request, so the allocator must carefully select the memory area that is to be allocated to the request. This requirement slows down the allocator. Because of the combined effect of unusably small memory areas and memory used by the allocator for its own data

Table 11.2 Kernel Functions for Reuse of Memory

Function	Description
Maintain a free list	The *free list* contains information about each free memory area. When a process frees some memory, information about the freed memory is entered in the free list. When a process terminates, each memory area allocated to it is freed, and information about it is entered in the free list.
Select a memory area for allocation	When a new memory request is made, the kernel selects the most suitable memory area from which memory should be allocated to satisfy the request.
Merge free memory areas	Two or more adjoining free areas of memory can be merged to form a single larger free area. The areas being merged are removed from the free list and the newly formed larger free area is entered in it.

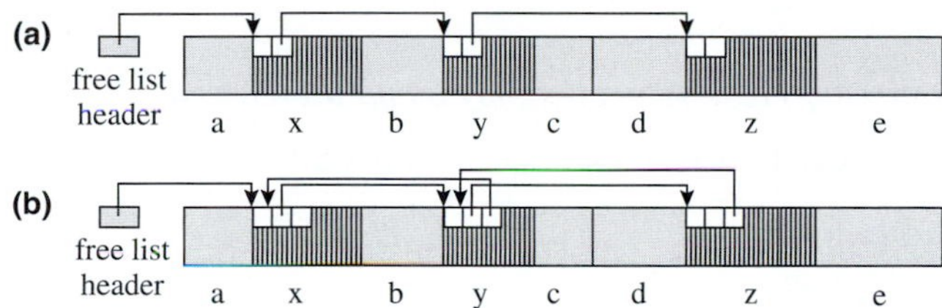

Figure 11.10 Free area management: (a) singly linked free list; (b) doubly linked free list.

structures, a heap allocator may not be able to ensure a high efficiency of memory utilization.

The kernel uses the three functions described in Table 11.2 to ensure efficient reuse of memory. The kernel maintains a *free list* to keep information about free memory areas in the system. A memory request is satisfied by using the free memory area that is considered most suitable for the request, and the memory left over from this memory area is entered in the free list. The allocation policy prevents free memory areas from becoming unusably small. The kernel tries to merge free areas of memory into larger free areas so that larger memory requests can be granted.

11.5.1.1 Maintaining a Free List

The kernel needs to maintain two items of control information for each memory area in the free list: the size of the memory area and pointers used for forming the list. To avoid incurring a memory overhead for this control information, the kernel stores it in the first few bytes of a free memory area itself. Figure 11.10(a) shows a *singly linked free list* in a heap that contains five areas marked a–e in active use and three free areas x–z. Each memory area in the free list contains its size and a pointer to the next memory area in the list. This organization is simple; however, it requires a lot of work when a memory area is to be inserted into the list or deleted from it. For example, deletion of a memory area from the list requires a change in the pointer stored in the previous memory area in the list. Insertion of a memory area at a specific place in the list also involves a similar operation. Therefore, insertion and deletion operations on a singly linked list are performed by processing the list from its start. It requires an order of m work, where m is the number of memory areas in the free list.

A *doubly linked free list* is used to facilitate faster insertion and deletion operations on memory areas. Each entry in this list contains two pointers—one points to the next memory area in the list, while the other points to the previous memory area [see Figure 11.10(b)]. If a memory area with a specific address is to be deleted from the list, the kernel can simply take the pointers to the previous and following memory areas in the list, and manipulate the pointers in these areas to perform the deletion. Analogous operations would suffice to add a new memory area at a specific place in the list. Thus the amount of work required to insert or delete a memory area is a constant, irrespective of the number of memory areas in the free list.

11.5.1.2 Performing Fresh Allocations by Using a Free List

Three techniques can be used to perform memory allocation by using a free list:

- First-fit technique
- Best-fit technique
- Next-fit technique

To service a request for n bytes of memory, the *first-fit* technique uses the first free memory area it can find whose size is $\geq n$ bytes. It splits this memory area in two parts. n bytes are allocated to the request, and the remaining part of the memory area, if any, is put back into the free list. This technique may split memory areas at the start of the free list repeatedly, so free memory areas become smaller with time. Consequently, the allocator may not have any large free memory areas left to satisfy large memory requests. Also, several free memory areas may become unusably small.

The *best-fit* technique uses the smallest free memory area with size $\geq n$. Thus, it avoids needless splitting of large memory areas, however it tends to generate a small free memory area at every split. Hence in the long run it, too, may suffer from the problem of numerous small free memory areas. The best-fit technique also incurs higher allocation overhead because it either has to process the entire free list at every allocation or maintain the free list in ascending order by size of free memory areas.

The *next-fit* technique remembers which entry in the free list was used to make the last allocation. To make a new allocation, it searches the free list starting from the next entry and performs allocation using the first free memory area of size $\geq n$ bytes that it can find. This way, it avoids splitting the same free area repeatedly as in the first-fit technique and also avoids the allocation overhead of the best-fit technique.

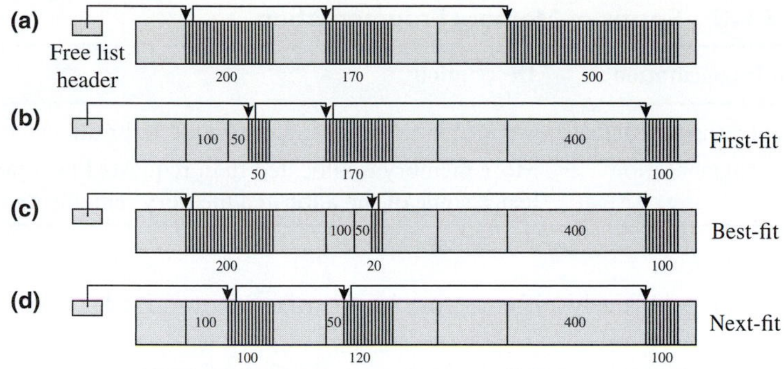

Figure 11.11 (a) Free list; (b)–(d) allocation using first-fit, best-fit and next-fit.

First, Best, and Next-Fit Allocation

Example 11.6

The free list in Figure 11.11(a) contains three free memory areas of size 200, 170, and 500 bytes, respectively. Processes make allocation requests for 100, 50, and 400 bytes. The first-fit technique will allocate 100 and 50 bytes from the first free memory area, thus leaving a free memory area of 50 bytes, and allocates 400 bytes from the third free memory area. The best-fit technique will allocate 100 and 50 bytes from the second free memory area, leaving a free memory area of 20 bytes. The next-fit technique allocates 100, 50, and 400 bytes from the three free memory areas.

Knuth (1973) presents experimental data on memory reuse and concludes that both first-fit and next-fit perform better than best-fit. However, next-fit tends to split *all* free areas if the system has been in operation long enough, whereas first-fit may not split the last few free areas. This property of first-fit facilitates allocation of large memory areas.

11.5.1.3 Memory Fragmentation

Definition 11.3 Memory Fragmentation The existence of unusable areas in the memory of a computer system.

Table 11.3 describes two forms of memory fragmentation. *External fragmentation* occurs when a memory area remains unused because it is too small to be allocated. *Internal fragmentation* occurs when some of the memory allocated to a process remains unused, which happens if a process is allocated more memory than it needs. In Figure 11.11(c), best-fit allocation creates a free memory area of 20 bytes, which is too small to be allocated. It is an example of external fragmentation. We would have internal fragmentation if an allocator were to allocate, say, 100 bytes of memory when a process requests 50 bytes; this would happen if an

Table 11.3 Forms of Memory Fragmentation

Form of fragmentation	Description
External fragmentation	Some area of memory is too small to be allocated.
Internal fragmentation	More memory is allocated than requested by a process, hence some of the allocated memory remains unused.

allocator dealt exclusively with memory blocks of a few standard sizes to limit its overhead.

Memory fragmentation results in poor utilization of memory. In this section, and in the remainder of this chapter, we discuss several techniques to avoid or minimize memory fragmentation.

11.5.1.4 Merging of Free Memory Areas

External fragmentation can be countered by merging free areas of memory to form larger free memory areas. Merging can be attempted every time a new memory area is added to the free list. A simple method would be to search the free list to check whether any adjoining area is already in the free list. If so, it can be removed from the free list and merged with the new area to form a larger free memory area. This action can be repeated until no more merging is possible, and the free memory area at hand can be added to the free list. However, this method is expensive because it involves searching of the free list every time a new memory area is freed. We now describe two generic techniques that perform merging more efficiently; in Section 11.5.2 we describe a special merging technique used in the buddy system allocator.

Boundary Tags A *tag* is a status descriptor for a memory area. It consists of an ordered pair giving allocation status of the area; whether it is free or allocated, represented by F or A, respectively; and its size. Boundary tags are identical tags stored at the start and end of a memory area, i.e., in the first and last few bytes of the area. If a memory area is free, the free list pointer can be put following the tag at its starting boundary. Figure 11.12 shows this arrangement.

When an area of memory becomes free, the kernel checks the boundary tags of its neighboring areas. These tags are easy to find because they immediately precede and follow boundaries of the newly freed area. If any of the neighbors are free, it is merged with the newly freed area. Figure 11.13 shows actions to be performed when memory areas X, Y, and Z are freed while a system using boundary tags is in the situation depicted in Figure 11.13(a). In Figure 11.13(b), memory area X is freed. Only its left neighbor is free, and so X is merged with it. Boundary tags are now set for the merged area. The left neighbor already existed in the free list, so it is enough to simply change its size field. Only the right neighbor of Y is free. Hence when Y is freed, it is merged with its right neighbor and boundary tags are set for the merged area. Now the free list has to be modified to remove the entry for the right neighbor and add an entry for the merged area [see Figure 11.13(c)]. Both neighbors of memory area Z are free. Hence when Z

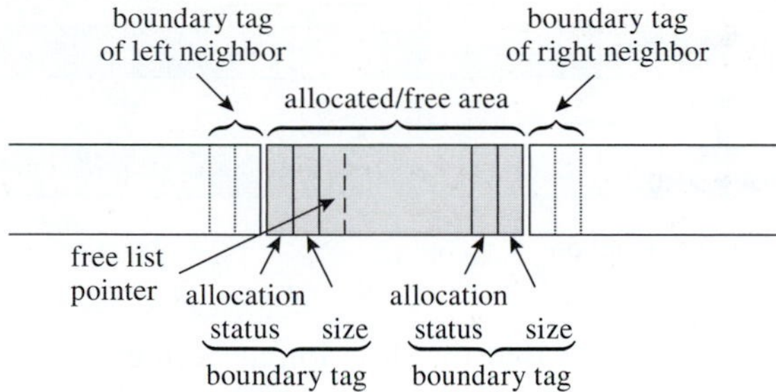

Figure 11.12 Boundary tags and the free list pointer.

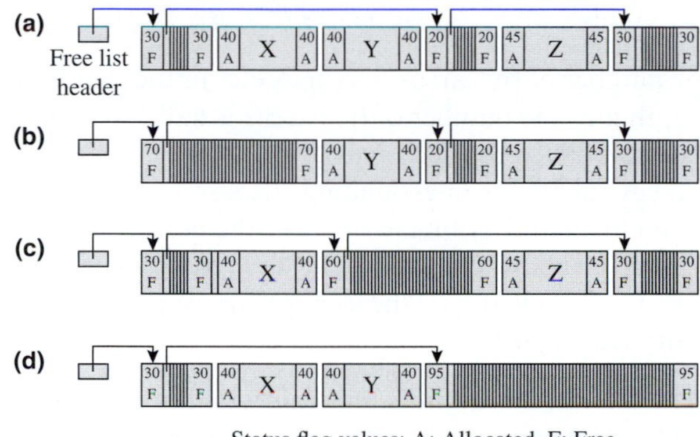

Figure 11.13 Merging using boundary tags: (a) free list; (b)–(d) freeing of areas X, Y, and Z, respectively.

is freed, it is merged with both of them to form a single free area. The size field of the left neighbor's entry in the free list is modified to reflect the merging. Since the right neighbor also had an entry in the free list, the free list is modified to remove this entry [see Figure 11.13(d)]. Whenever merging occurs with the right neighbor, management of the free list requires an order of m work, where m is the number of entries in the free list. As mentioned earlier in Section 11.5.1.1, maintaining the free list as a doubly linked list would enable this operation to be performed efficiently.

A relation called the *50-percent rule* holds when we use this method of merging. When an area of memory is freed, the total number of free areas in the system increases by 1, decreases by 1 or remains the same depending on whether the area being freed has zero, two, or one free areas as neighbors. These areas of memory are shown as areas of type C, A, and B, respectively, in the following:

When an allocation is made, the number of free areas of memory reduces by 1 if the requested size matches the size of some free area; otherwise, it remains unchanged since the remaining free area would be returned to the free list.

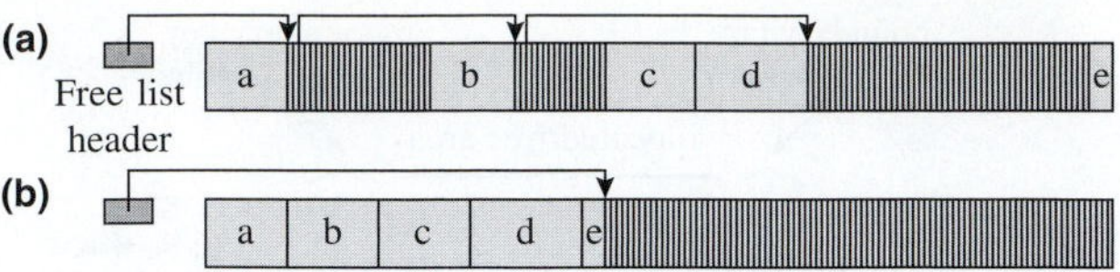

Figure 11.14 Memory compaction.

Assuming a large memory so that the situation at both ends of memory can be ignored, and assuming that each area of memory is equally likely to be released, we have

$$\text{Number of allocated areas, } n = \#\text{A} + \#\text{B} + \#\text{C}$$
$$\text{Number of free areas, } m = \tfrac{1}{2}(2 \times \#\text{A} + \#\text{B})$$

where #A is the number of free areas of type A etc. In the steady state #A = #C. Hence $m = n/2$, that is, the number of free areas is half the number of allocated areas. This relation is called the 50-percent rule.

The 50-percent rule helps in estimating the size of the free list and, hence, the effort involved in an allocation method like the best-fit method that requires the entire free list to be analyzed. It also gives us a method of estimating the free area in memory at any time. If s_f is the average size of free areas of memory, the total free memory is $s_f \times n/2$.

Memory Compaction In this approach memory bindings are changed in such a manner that all free memory areas can be merged to form a single free memory area. As the name suggests, it is achieved by "packing" all allocated areas toward one end of the memory. Figure 11.14 illustrates compaction to merge free areas.

Compaction is not as simple as suggested by this discussion because it involves movement of code and data in memory. If area b in Figure 11.14 contains a process, it needs to be relocated to execute correctly from the new memory area allocated to it. Relocation involves modification of all addresses used by a process, including addresses of heap-allocated data and addresses contained in general-purpose registers. It is feasible only if the computer system provides a relocation register (see Section 11.3.1); relocation can be achieved by simply changing the address in the relocation register.

11.5.2 Buddy System and Power-of-2 Allocators

The buddy system and power-of-2 allocators perform allocation of memory in blocks of a few standard sizes. This feature leads to internal fragmentation because some memory in each allocated memory block may be wasted. However, it enables the allocator to maintain separate free lists for blocks of different sizes. This arrangement avoids expensive searches in a free list and leads to fast allocation and deallocation.

Buddy System Allocator A buddy system splits and recombines memory blocks in a predetermined manner during allocation and deallocation. Blocks created by splitting a block are called *buddy blocks*. Free buddy blocks are merged to form the block that was split to create them. This operation is called *coalescing*. Under this system, adjoining free blocks that are not buddies are not coalesced. The *binary* buddy system, which we describe here, splits a block into two equal-size buddies. Thus each block b has a single buddy block that either precedes b in memory or follows b in memory. Memory block sizes are 2^n for different values of $n \geq t$, where t is some threshold value. This restriction ensures that memory blocks are not meaninglessly small in size.

The buddy system allocator associates a 1-bit tag with each block to indicate whether the block is *allocated* or *free*. The tag of a block may be located in the block itself, or it may be stored separately. The allocator maintains many lists of free blocks; each free list is maintained as a doubly linked list and consists of free blocks of identical size, i.e., blocks of size 2^k for some $k \geq t$. Operation of the allocator starts with a single free memory block of size 2^z, for some $z > t$. It is entered in the free list for blocks of size 2^z. The following actions are performed when a process requests a memory block of size m. The system finds the smallest power of 2 that is $\geq m$. Let this be 2^i. If the list of blocks with size 2^i is not empty, it allocates the first block from the list to the process and changes the tag of the block from *free* to *allocated.* If the list is empty, it checks the list for blocks of size 2^{i+1}. It takes one block off this list, and splits it into two halves of size 2^i. These blocks become buddies. It puts one of these blocks into the free list for blocks of size 2^i and uses the other block to satisfy the request. If a block of size 2^{i+1} is not available, it looks into the list for blocks of size 2^{i+2}, splits one of them to obtain blocks of size 2^{i+1}, splits one of these blocks further to obtain blocks of size 2^i, and allocates one of them, and so on. Thus, many splits may have to be performed before a request can be satisfied.

When a process frees a memory block of size 2^i, the buddy system changes the tag of the block to *free* and checks the tag of its buddy block to see whether the buddy block is also free. If so, it merges these two blocks into a single block of size 2^{i+1}. It now repeats the coalescing check transitively; i.e., it checks whether the buddy of this new block of size 2^{i+1} is free, and so on. It enters a block in a free list only when it finds that its buddy block is not free.

Operation of a Buddy System — Example 11.7

Figure 11.15 illustrates operation of a binary buddy system. Parts (a) and (b) of the figure show the status of the system before and after the block marked with the ⇩ symbol is released by a process. In each part we show two views of the system. The upper half shows the free lists while the lower half shows the layout of memory and the buddy blocks. For ease of reference, corresponding blocks in the two halves carry identical numbers. The block being released has a size of 16 bytes. Its buddy is the free block numbered 1 in Figure 11.15(a), and so the buddy system allocator merges these two blocks to form a new block of 32 bytes. The buddy of this new block is block 2, which is also free. So block 2 is removed from the free list of 32-byte blocks and merged with the new block to form a free block of size 64 bytes. This free block is numbered 4 in Figure 11.15(b). It is now entered in the appropriate free list.

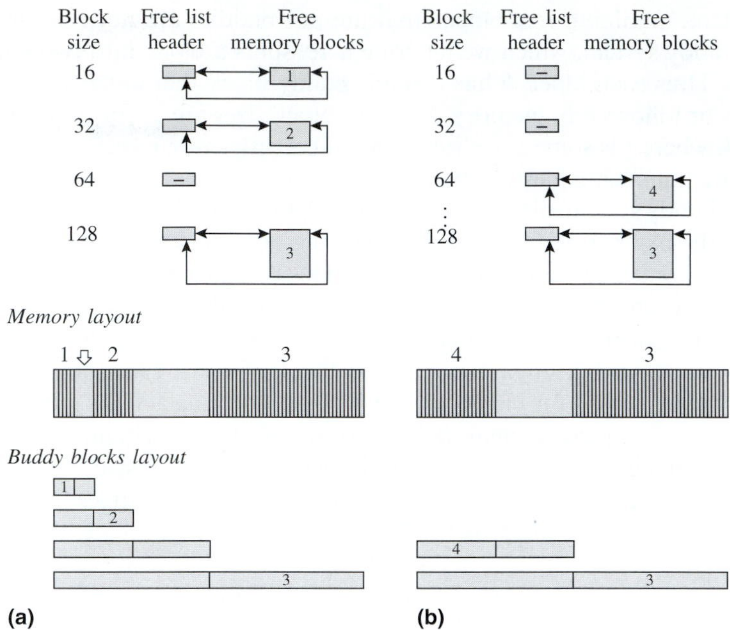

Figure 11.15 Buddy system operation when a block is released.

The check for a buddy's tag can be performed efficiently because block sizes are powers of 2. Let the block being freed have a size of 16 bytes. Since 16 is 2^4, its address is of the form $\ldots y0000$, where four 0s follow y, and y is 0 or 1. Its buddy block has the address $\ldots z0000$ where $z = 1 - y$. This address can be obtained simply by performing an exclusive or operation with a number ...10000, i.e., with 2^4. For example, if the address of a block is 101010000, its buddy's address is 101000000. In general, address of the buddy of a block of size 2^n bytes can be found by performing exclusive or with 2^n. This advantage is applicable even if the tags are stored separately in a bitmap (see Exercise 11.8).

Power-of-2 Allocator As in the binary buddy system, the sizes of memory blocks are powers of 2, and separate free lists are maintained for blocks of different sizes. Similarity with the buddy system ends here, however. Each block contains a header element that contains the address of the free list to which it should be added when it becomes free. When a request is made for m bytes, the allocator first checks the free list containing blocks whose size is 2^i for the smallest value of i such that $2^i \geq m$. If this free list is empty, it checks the list containing blocks that are the next higher power of 2 in size, and so on. An entire block is allocated to a request, i.e., no splitting of blocks takes place. Also, no effort is made to coalesce adjoining blocks to form larger blocks; when released, a block is simply returned to its free list.

System operation starts by forming blocks of desired size and entering them into the appropriate free lists. New blocks can be created dynamically either when the allocator runs out of blocks of a given size, or when a request cannot be fulfilled.

11.5.3 Comparing Memory Allocators

Memory allocators can be compared on the basis of speed of allocation and efficient use of memory. The buddy and power-of-2 allocators are faster than the first-fit, best-fit, and next-fit allocators because they avoid searches in free lists. The power-of-2 allocator is faster than the buddy allocator because it does not need to perform splitting and merging.

To compare memory usage efficiency in different memory allocators, we define a memory utilization factor as follows:

$$\text{Memory utilization factor} = \frac{\text{memory in use}}{\text{total memory committed}}$$

where *memory in use* is the amount of memory being used by requesting processes, and *total memory committed* includes memory allocated to processes, free memory existing with the memory allocator, and memory occupied by the allocator's own data structures. Memory in use may be smaller than memory allocated to processes because of internal fragmentation and smaller than total memory committed because of external fragmentation. The largest value of the memory utilization factor represents the best-case performance of an allocator and the smallest value at which the allocator fails to grant a memory request represents its worst-case performance.

Allocators using the first-fit, best-fit, or next-fit techniques do not incur internal fragmentation. However, external fragmentation limits their worst-case performance because free blocks may be too small to satisfy a request (see Exercise 11.4). The buddy and power-of-2 allocators allocate blocks whose sizes are powers of 2, so internal fragmentation exists unless memory requests match block sizes. These allocators also use up additional memory to store the free list headers and tags or header elements for blocks. In a power-of-2 allocator, the header element in a block cannot be used by a process. Thus the useful portion of a block is somewhat smaller than a power of 2. If a memory request is for an area that is exactly a power of 2 in size, this method uses up twice that amount of memory. A power-of-2 allocator fails to satisfy a request if a sufficiently large free block does not exist. Since it does not merge free blocks into larger blocks, this situation can arise even when the total free memory available in smaller-size blocks exceeds the size of the request. In a buddy system this situation can arise only if adjoining free blocks are not buddies. This is rare in practice. In fact, Knuth (1973) reports that in simulation studies the best-case performance of a buddy allocator was 95 percent.

11.5.4 Heap Management in Windows

The Windows operating system uses a heap management approach that aims at providing low allocation overhead and low fragmentation. By default, it uses a free list and a best-fit policy of allocation. However, this arrangement is not adequate for two kinds of situations: If a process makes heavy use of the heap, it might repeatedly allocate and free memory areas of a few specific sizes, so the overhead incurred by the best-fit policy and the merging of free areas is unnecessary. In a multiprocessor environment, the free list may become a performance bottleneck (see Section 10.3). So in such situations Windows uses an arrangement called the *low-fragmentation heap* (LFH).

The low-fragmentation heap maintains many free lists, each containing memory areas of a specific size. The sizes of memory areas are multiples of 8 bytes up to 256 bytes, multiples of 16 bytes up to 512 bytes, multiples of 32 bytes up to 1 KB, where 1 KB = 1024 bytes, etc., up to and including multiples of 1 KB up to 16 KB. When a process requests a memory area that is less than 16 KB in size, a memory area is taken off an appropriate free list and allocated. Neither splitting nor merging is performed for such memory areas. This arrangement is analogous to that used in the power-of-2 allocator, though the blocks are *not* powers of two, so it inherits its advantages and disadvantages—memory allocation is fast but internal fragmentation exists in an allocated area. For satisfying memory requests exceeding 16 KB in size, the heap manager maintains a single free list and allocates a memory area whose size exactly matches the request.

If the heap manager cannot find an appropriately sized memory area in a free list for a request <16 KB, it passes the request to the core heap manager. It also keeps statistics of the requests and the way they were satisfied, e.g., the rate at which memory areas of a specific size were requested and a count of the number of times it could not find memory areas of a specific size, and uses it to fine-tune its own performance by creating free memory areas of appropriate sizes ahead of the actual requests for them.

11.6 CONTIGUOUS MEMORY ALLOCATION

Contiguous memory allocation is the classical memory allocation model in which each process is allocated a single contiguous area in memory. Thus the kernel allocates a large enough memory area to accommodate the code, data, stack, and PCD data of a process as shown in Figure 11.9. Contiguous memory allocation faces the problem of memory fragmentation. In this section we focus on techniques to address this problem. Relocation of a program in contiguous memory allocation and memory protection were discussed earlier in Sections 11.3.1 and 11.4.3.

Handling Memory Fragmentation We discussed the causes of internal and external fragmentation earlier in Section 11.5.1.3. Internal fragmentation has no cure in contiguous memory allocation because the kernel has no means of estimating the memory requirement of a process accurately. The techniques of memory

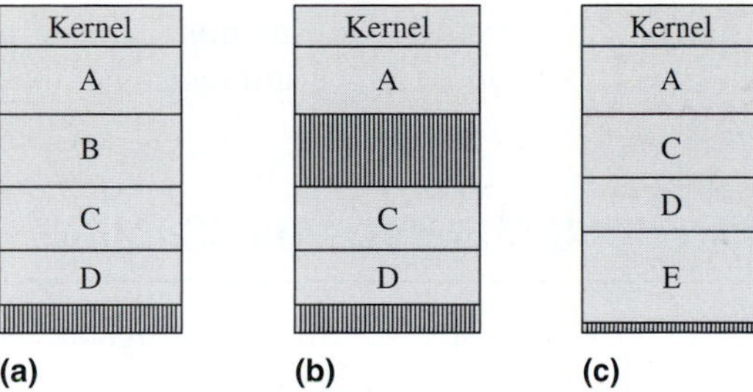

Figure 11.16 Memory compaction.

compaction and reuse of memory discussed earlier in Section 11.5 can be applied to overcome the problem of external fragmentation. Example 11.8 illustrates use of memory compaction.

Example 11.8

Contiguous Memory Allocation

Processes A, B, C, and D are in memory in Figure 11.16(a). Two free areas of memory exist after B terminates; however, neither of them is large enough to accommodate another process [see Figure 11.16(b)]. The kernel performs compaction to create a single free memory area and initiates process E in this area [see Figure 11.16(c)]. It involves moving processes C and D in memory during their execution.

Memory compaction involves *dynamic relocation*, which is not feasible without a relocation register (see Section 11.3.1). In computers not having a relocation register, the kernel must resort to reuse of free memory areas. However, this approach incurs delays in initiation of processes when large free memory areas do not exist, e.g., initiation of process E would be delayed in Example 11.8 even though the total free memory in the system exceeds the size of E.

Swapping The basic mechanism of swapping, and the rationale behind it, was described in Section 3.6.1. The kernel swaps out a process that is not in the *running* state by writing out its code and data space to a *swapping area* on the disk. The swapped out process is brought back into memory before it is due for another burst of CPU time.

A basic issue in swapping is whether a swapped-in process should be loaded back into the same memory area that it occupied before it was swapped out. If so, its swapping in depends on swapping out of some other process that may have been allocated that memory area in the meanwhile. It would be useful to be able to place the swapped-in process elsewhere in memory; however, it would amount to dynamic relocation of the process to a new memory area. As mentioned earlier, only computer systems that provide a relocation register can achieve it.

11.7 NONCONTIGUOUS MEMORY ALLOCATION

Modern computer architectures provide the *noncontiguous memory allocation* model, in which a process can operate correctly even when portions of its address space are distributed among many areas of memory. This model of memory allocation permits the kernel to reuse free memory areas that are smaller than the size of a process, so it can reduce external fragmentation. As we shall see later in this section, noncontiguous memory allocation using paging can even eliminate external fragmentation completely.

Example 11.9 illustrates noncontiguous memory allocation. We use the term *component* for that portion of the process address space that is loaded in a single memory area.

Example 11.9 Noncontiguous Memory Allocation

In Figure 11.17(a), four free memory areas starting at addresses 100K, 300K, 450K, and 600K, where K = 1024, with sizes of 50 KB, 30 KB, 80 KB and 40 KB, respectively, are present in memory. Process P, which has a size of 140 KB, is to be initiated [see Figure 11.17(b)]. If process P consists of three components called P-1, P-2, and P-3, with sizes of 50 KB, 30 KB and 60 KB, respectively; these components can be loaded into three of the free memory areas as follows [see Figure 11.17(c)]:

Process component	Size	Memory start address
P-1	50 KB	100K
P-2	30 KB	300K
P-3	60 KB	450K

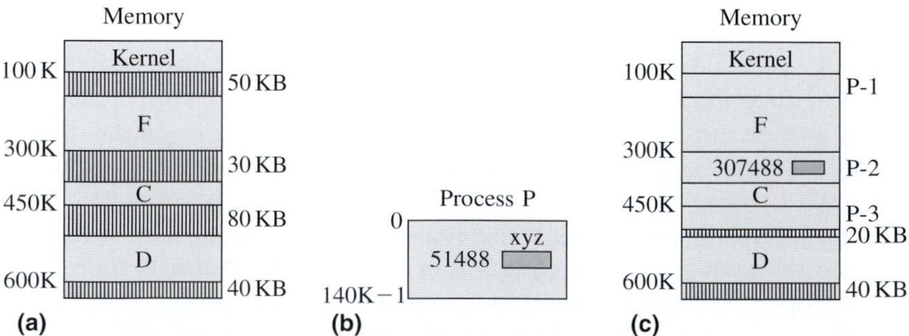

Figure 11.17 Noncontiguous memory allocation to process P.

11.7.1 Logical Addresses, Physical Addresses, and Address Translation

In Section 1.1, we mentioned that the abstract view of a system is called its *logical view* and the arrangement and relationship among its components is called the *logical organization*. On the other hand, the real view of the system is called its *physical view* and the arrangement depicted in it is called the *physical organization*. Accordingly, the views of process P shown in Figures 11.17(b) and Figures 11.17(c) constitute the logical and physical views of process P of Example 11.9, respectively.

A *logical address* is the address of an instruction or data byte as used in a process; it may be obtained using index, base, or segment registers. The logical addresses in a process constitute the *logical address space* of the process. A *physical address* is the address in memory where an instruction or data byte exists. The set of physical addresses in the system constitutes the *physical address space* of the system.

Example 11.10

Logical and Physical Address Spaces

In Example 11.9, the logical address space of P extends from 0 to 140K−1, while the physical address space extends from 0 to 640K−1. Data area xyz in the program of process P has the address 51488 [see Figure 11.17(b)]. This is the logical address of xyz. The process component P-1 in Figure 11.17 has a size of 50 KB , i.e., 51200 bytes, so xyz is situated in component P-2 and has the byte number 288. Since P-2 is loaded in the memory area with the start address 300 KB, i.e., 307200 bytes, the physical address of xyz is 307488 [see Figure 11.17(c)].

The schematic diagram of Figure 11.18 shows how the CPU obtains the physical address that corresponds to a logical address. The kernel stores information about the memory areas allocated to process P in a table and makes it available to the *memory management unit* (MMU). In Example 11.9, this

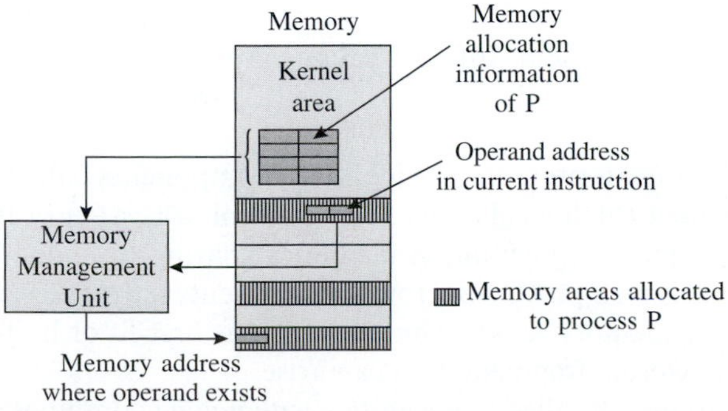

Figure 11.18 A schematic of address translation in noncontiguous memory allocation.

information would consist of the sizes and memory start addresses of P-1, P-2, and P-3. The CPU sends the logical address of each data or instruction used in the process to the MMU, and the MMU uses the memory allocation information stored in the table to compute the corresponding physical address. This address is called the *effective memory address* of the data or instruction. The procedure of computing the effective memory address from a logical address is called *address translation*.

A logical address used in an instruction consists of two parts—the id of the process component containing the address, and the id of the byte within the component. We represent each logical address by a pair of the form

$$(comp_i, byte_i)$$

The memory management unit computes its effective memory address through the formula

$$\begin{aligned}\text{Effective memory address of } (comp_i, byte_i) \\ = \text{start address of memory area allocated to } comp_i \\ + \text{ byte number of } byte_i \text{ within } comp_i \qquad \textbf{(11.1)}\end{aligned}$$

In Examples 11.9 and 11.10, instructions of P would refer to the data area `xyz` through the logical address (P-2, 288). The MMU computes its effective memory address as 307,200 + 288 = 307,488.

11.7.2 Approaches to Noncontiguous Memory Allocation

There are two fundamental approaches to implementing noncontiguous memory allocation:

- Paging
- Segmentation

In *paging*, each process consists of fixed-size components called *pages*. The size of a page is defined by the hardware of a computer, and demarcation of pages is implicit in it. The memory can accommodate an integral number of pages. It is partitioned into memory areas that have the same size as a page, and each of these memory areas is considered separately for allocation to a page. This way, any free memory area is exactly the same size as a page, so external fragmentation does not arise in the system. Internal fragmentation can arise because the last page of a process is allocated a page-size memory area even if it is smaller than a page in size.

In *segmentation*, a programmer identifies components called *segments* in a process. A segment is a logical entity in a program, e.g., a set of functions, data structures, or objects. Segmentation facilitates sharing of code, data, and program modules between processes. However, segments have different sizes, so the kernel has to use memory reuse techniques such as first-fit or best-fit allocation. Consequently, external fragmentation can arise.

A hybrid approach called *segmentation with paging* combines the features of both segmentation and paging. It facilitates sharing of code, data, and program

Table 11.4 Comparison of Contiguous and Noncontiguous Memory Allocation

Function	Contiguous allocation	Noncontiguous allocation
Memory allocation	The kernel allocates a single memory area to a process.	The kernel allocates several memory areas to a process—each memory area holds one component of the process.
Address translation	Address translation is not required.	Address translation is performed by the MMU during program execution.
Memory fragmentation	External fragmentation arises if first-fit, best-fit, or next-fit allocation is used. Internal fragmentation arises if memory allocation is performed in blocks of a few standard sizes.	In paging, external fragmentation does not occur but internal fragmentation can occur. In segmentation, external fragmentation occurs, but internal fragmentation does not occur.
Swapping	Unless the computer system provides a relocation register, a swapped-in process must be placed in its originally allocated area.	Components of a swapped-in process can be placed anywhere in memory.

modules between processes without incurring external fragmentation; however, internal fragmentation occurs as in paging. We discuss features of these three approaches in later sections.

Table 11.4 summarizes the advantages of noncontiguous memory allocation over contiguous memory allocation. Swapping is more effective in noncontiguous memory allocation because address translation enables the kernel to load components of a swapped-in process in any parts of memory.

11.7.3 Memory Protection

Each memory area allocated to a program has to be protected against interference from other programs. The MMU implements this function through a bounds check. While performing address translation for a logical address ($comp_i$, $byte_i$), the MMU checks whether $comp_i$ actually exists in the program and whether $byte_i$ exists in $comp_i$. A protection violation interrupt is raised if either of these checks fails. The bounds check can be simplified in paging—it is not necessary to check whether $byte_i$ exists in $comp_i$ because, as we shall see in the next section, a logical address does not have enough bits in it to specify a value of $byte_i$ that exceeds the page size.

11.8 PAGING

In the logical view, the address space of a process consists of a linear arrangement of pages. Each page has s bytes in it, where s is a power of 2. The value of s is specified in the architecture of the computer system. Processes use numeric logical addresses. The MMU decomposes a logical address into the pair (p_i, b_i), where p_i is the page number and b_i is the byte number within page p_i. Pages in a program and bytes in a page are numbered from 0; so, in a logical address (p_i, b_i), $p_i \geq 0$ and $0 \leq b_i < s$. In the physical view, pages of a process exist in nonadjacent areas of memory.

Consider two processes P and R in a system using a page size of 1 KB. The bytes in a page are numbered from 0 to 1023. Process P has the start address 0 and a size of 5500 bytes. Hence it has 6 pages numbered from 0 to 5. The last page contains only 380 bytes. If a data item `sample` had the address 5248, which is $5 \times 1024 + 128$, the MMU would view its address as the pair (5, 128). Process R has a size of 2500 bytes. Hence it has 3 pages, numbered from 0 to 2. Figure 11.19 shows the logical view of processes P and R.

The hardware partitions memory into areas called *page frames*; page frames in memory are numbered from 0. Each page frame is the same size as a page. At any moment, some page frames are allocated to pages of processes, while others are free. The kernel maintains a list called the *free frames list* to note the frame numbers of free page frames. While loading a process for execution, the kernel consults the free frames list and allocates a free page frame to each page of the process.

To facilitate address translation, the kernel constructs a *page table* (PT) for each process. The page table has an entry for each page of the process, which indicates the page frame allocated to the page. While performing address translation for a logical address (p_i, b_i), the MMU uses the page number p_i to index the page table of the process, obtains the frame number of the page frame allocated to p_i, and computes the effective memory address according to Eq. (11.1).

Figure 11.20 shows the physical view of execution of processes P and R. Each page frame is 1 KB in size. The computer has a memory of 10 KB, so page frames are numbered from 0 to 9. Six page frames are occupied by process P, and three page frames are occupied by process R. The pages contained in the page frames are shown as P-0, ..., P-5 and R-0, ..., R-2. Page frame 4 is free. Hence the free frames list contains only one entry. The page table of P indicates the page frame allocated to each page of P. As mentioned earlier, the variable `sample` of

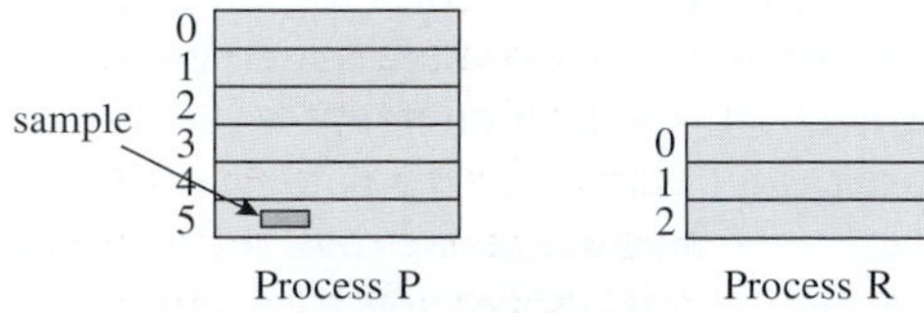

Figure 11.19 Logical view of processes in paging.

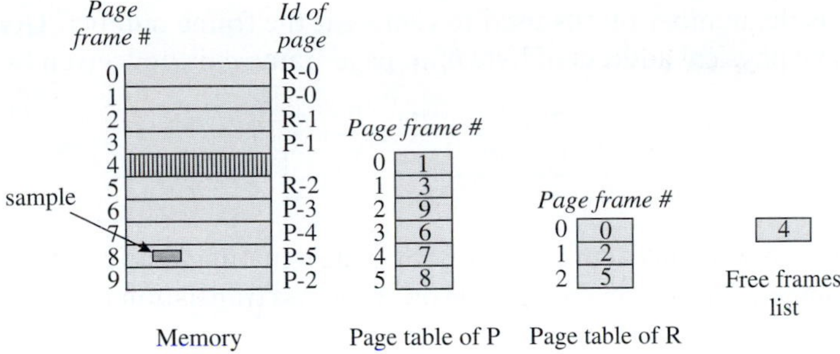

Figure 11.20 Physical organization in paging.

process P has the logical address (5, 128). When process P uses this logical address during its execution, it will be translated into the effective memory address by using Eq. (11.1) as follows:

$$\begin{aligned}\text{Effective memory address of } (5, 128) &= \text{start address of page frame \#8} + 128 \\ &= 8 \times 1024 + 128 \\ &= 8320\end{aligned}$$

We use the following notation to describe how address translation is actually performed:

s	Size of a page
l_l	Length of a logical address (i.e., number of bits in it)
l_p	Length of a physical address
n_b	Number of bits used to represent the byte number in a logical address
n_p	Number of bits used to represent the page number in a logical address
n_f	Number of bits used to represent the frame number in a physical address

The size of a page, s, is a power of 2. n_b is chosen such that $s = 2^{n_b}$. Hence the least significant n_b bits in a logical address give us b_i, the byte number within a page. The remaining bits in a logical address form p_i, the page number. The MMU obtains the values of p_i and b_i simply by grouping the bits of a logical address as follows:

← n_p →	← n_b →
p_i	b_i
← l_l	→

where $n_p = l_l - n_b$. Use of a power of 2 as the page size similarly simplifies construction of the effective memory address. Let page p_i be allocated page frame q_i. Since pages and page frames have identical sizes, n_b bits are needed to address the bytes in a page frame. The physical address of byte 0 of page frame q_i is therefore

← n_f →	← n_b →
q_i	0 · · · · · · 0
← l_p	→

where n_f is the number of bits used to represent the frame number. Hence $n_f = l_p - n_b$. The physical address of byte b_i in page frame q_i is now given by

← n_f →	← n_b →
q_i	b_i
← l_p	→

The MMU obtains this address simply by concatenating q_i and b_i to obtain an l_p bit number. The next example illustrates address translation in a system using paging.

Example 11.11 **Address Translation in Paging**

A hypothetical computer uses 32-bit logical addresses and a page size of 4 KB. 12 bits are adequate to address the bytes in a page. Thus, the higher order 20 bits in a logical address represent p_i and the 12 lower order bits represent b_i. For a memory size of 256 MB, l_p = 28. Thus, the higher-order 16 bits in a physical address represent q_i. If page 130 exists in page frame 48, p_i = 130, and q_i = 48. If b_i = 600, the logical and physical addresses look as follows:

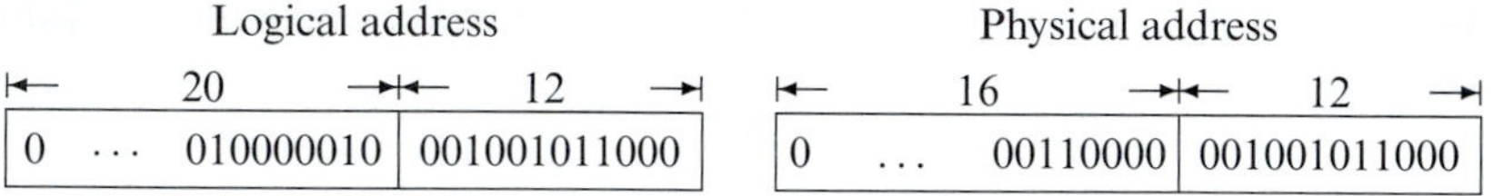

During address translation, the MMU obtains p_i and b_i merely by grouping the bits of the logical address as shown above. The 130th entry of the page table is now accessed to obtain q_i, which is 48. This number is concatenated with b_i to form the physical address.

11.9 SEGMENTATION

A *segment* is a logical entity in a program, e.g., a function, a data structure, or an object. Hence it is meaningful to manage it as a unit—load it into memory for execution or share it with other programs. In the logical view, a process consists of a collection of segments. In the physical view, segments of a process exist in nonadjacent areas of memory.

A process Q consists of five logical entities with the symbolic names `main`, `database`, `search`, `update`, and `stack`. While coding the program, the programmer declares these five as segments in Q. This information is used by the compiler or assembler to generate logical addresses while translating the program. Each logical address used in Q has the form (s_i, b_i) where s_i and b_i are the ids of a segment and a byte within a segment. For example, the instruction corresponding to a statement `call get_sample`, where `get_sample` is a procedure in

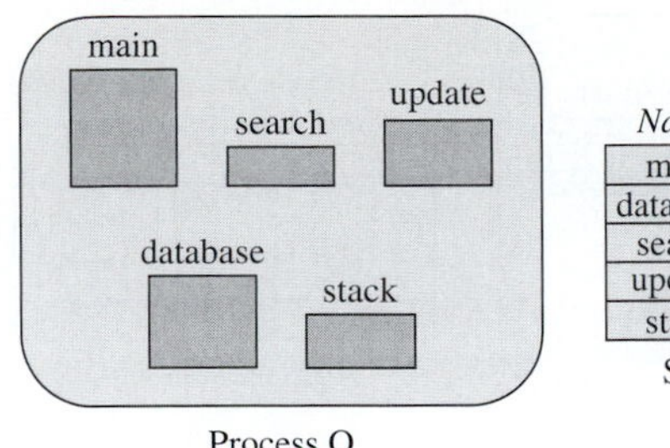

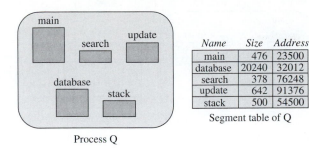

Name	*Size*	*Address*
main	476	23500
database	20240	32012
search	378	76248
update	642	91376
stack	500	54500

Segment table of Q

Figure 11.21 A process Q in segmentation.

segment `update`, may use the operand address (`update`, `get_sample`). Alternatively, it may use a numeric representation in which s_i and b_i are the segment number and byte number within a segment, respectively. For simplicity, we assume such a representation in this chapter.

Figure 11.21 shows how the kernel handles process Q. The left part of Figure 11.21 shows the logical view of process Q. To facilitate address translation, the kernel constructs a segment table for Q. Each entry in this table shows the size of a segment and the address of the memory area allocated to it. The size field is used to perform a bound check for memory protection. The MMU uses the segment table to perform address translation (see Figure 11.18). Segments do not have standard sizes, so address translation cannot be performed through bit concatenation as in paging. Calculation of the effective memory address for the logical address (s_i, b_i) therefore involves addition of b_i to the start address of segment s_i according to Eq. (11.1). In Figure 11.21, if `get_sample` has the byte number 232 in segment `update`, address translation of (`update`, `get_sample`) will yield the address $91376 + 232 = 91608$.

Memory allocation for each segment is performed as in the contiguous memory allocation model. The kernel keeps a free list of memory areas. While loading a process, it searches through this list to perform first-fit or best-fit allocation to each segment of the process. When a process terminates, the memory areas allocated to its segments are added to the free list. External fragmentation can occur because segments have different sizes.

11.10 SEGMENTATION WITH PAGING

In this approach, each segment in a program is paged separately. Accordingly, an integral number of pages is allocated to each segment. This approach simplifies memory allocation and speeds it up, and also avoids external fragmentation. A page table is constructed for each segment, and the address of the page table is kept in the segment's entry in the segment table. Address translation for a logical address (s_i, b_i) is now done in two stages. In the first stage, the entry of s_i is located in the segment table, and the address of its page table is obtained. The byte number b_i is now split into a pair (ps_i, bp_i), where ps_i is the page number in

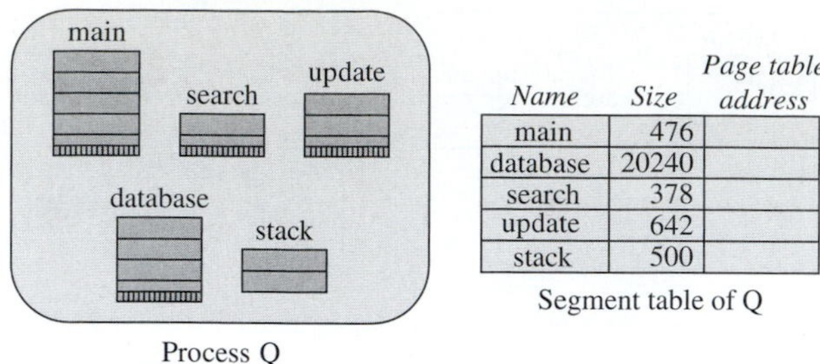

Figure 11.22 A process Q in segmentation with paging.

segment s_i, and bp_i is the byte number in page p_i. The effective address calculation is now completed as in paging, i.e., the frame number of ps_i is obtained and bp_i is concatenated with it to obtain the effective address.

Figure 11.22 shows process Q of Figure 11.21 in a system using segmentation with paging. Each segment is paged independently, so internal fragmentation exists in the last page of each segment. Each segment table entry now contains the address of the page table of the segment. The size field in a segment's entry is used to facilitate a bound check for memory protection.

11.11 KERNEL MEMORY ALLOCATION

The kernel creates and destroys data structures at a high rate during its operation. These are mostly *control blocks* that control the allocation and use of resources in the system. Some familiar control blocks are the process control block (PCB) created for every process and the event control block (ECB) created whenever the occurrence of an event is anticipated. (In Chapters 13 and 14, we will introduce two other frequently used control blocks: the I/O control block (IOCB) created for an I/O operation and the file control block (FCB) created for every open file.) The sizes of control blocks are known in the design stage of an OS. This prior knowledge helps make kernel memory allocation simple and efficient—memory that is released when one control block is destroyed can be reused when a similar control block is created. To realize this benefit, a separate free list can be maintained for each type of control block.

Kernels of modern operating systems use noncontiguous memory allocation with paging to satisfy their own memory requirements, and make special efforts to use each page effectively. Three of the leading memory allocators are:

- McKusick–Karels allocator
- Lazy buddy allocator
- Slab allocator

The McKusick–Karels and lazy buddy allocators allocate memory areas that are powers of 2 in size *within* a page. Since the start address of each page in memory is a larger power of 2, the start address of each allocated memory area of size 2^n is a multiple of 2^n. This characteristic, which is called boundary alignment on a power of 2, leads to a cache performance problem as follows: Some parts of an object are accessed more frequently than others. Because of boundary alignment on a power of 2, the frequently accessed parts of objects may be mapped into the same areas of a cache by the set-associative technique of cache lookup. Hence some parts of the cache face a lot of contention leading to poor cache performance of the kernel code. The slab allocator uses an interesting technique to avoid this cache performance problem.

Descriptions of these three allocators follow. In interest of consistency, we use the same terminology we used in previous sections; it differs from the terminology used in the literature on these allocators. The bibliography at the end of the chapter indicates which modern operating systems use these allocators.

McKusick--Karels Allocator This is a modified power-of-2 allocator; it is used in Unix 4.4 BSD. The allocator has an integral number of pages at its disposal at any time, and asks the paging system for more pages when it runs out of memory to allocate. The basic operating principle of the allocator is to divide each page into blocks of equal size and record two items of information—the block size, and a free list pointer—under the logical address of the page. This way, the address of the page in which a block is located will be sufficient for finding the size of the block and the free list to which the block should be added when it is freed. Hence, it is not necessary to have a header containing this information in each allocated block as in a conventional power-of-2 allocator.

With the elimination of the header element, the entire memory in a block can be used for the intended purpose. Consequently, the McKusick–Karels allocator is superior to the power-of-2 allocator when a memory request is for an area whose size is an exact power of 2. A block of identical size can be allocated to satisfy the request, whereas the conventional power-of-2 allocator would have allocated a block whose size is the next higher power of 2.

The allocator seeks a free page among those in its possession when it does not find a block of the size it is looking for. It then divides this page into blocks of the desired size. It allocates one of these blocks to satisfy the current request, and enters the remaining blocks in the appropriate free list. If no free page is held by the allocator, it asks the paging system for a new page to be allocated to it. To ensure that it does not consume a larger number of pages than necessary, the allocator marks any page in its possession as free when all blocks in it become free. However, it lacks a feature to return free pages to the paging system. Thus, the total number of pages allocated to the allocator at any given moment is the largest number of pages it has held at any time. This burden may reduce the memory utilization factor.

Lazy Buddy Allocator The buddy system in its basic form may perform one or more splits at every allocation and one or more coalescing actions at every release. Some of these actions are wasteful because a coalesced block may need to be split again later. The basic design principle of the lazy buddy allocator is to delay coalescing actions if a data structure requiring the same amount of memory as a released block is likely to be created. Under the correct set of conditions, this principle avoids the overhead of both coalescing and splitting.

The lazy buddy allocator used in Unix 5.4 works as follows: Blocks with the same size are considered to constitute a *class* of blocks. Coalescing decisions for a class are made on the basis of the rates at which data structures of the class are created and destroyed. Accordingly, the allocator characterizes the behavior of the OS with respect to a class of blocks into three states called *lazy, reclaiming*, and *accelerated*. For simplicity we refer to these as *states* of a class of blocks.

In the lazy state, allocations and releases of blocks of a class occur at matching rates. Consequently, there is a steady and potentially wasteful cycle of splitting and coalescing. As a remedy, excessive coalescing and splitting can both be avoided by delaying coalescing. In the reclaiming state, releases occur at a faster rate than allocations so it is a good idea to coalesce at every release. In the accelerated state, releases occur much faster than allocations, and so it is desirable to coalesce at an even faster rate; the allocator should attempt to coalesce a block being released, and, additionally, it should also try to coalesce some other blocks that were released but not coalesced in the past.

The lazy buddy allocator maintains the free list as a doubly linked list. This way both the start and end of the list can be accessed equally easily. A bit map is maintained to indicate the allocation status of blocks. In the lazy state, a block being released is simply added to the head of the free list. No effort is made to coalesce it with its buddy. It is also not marked free in the bit map. This way the block will not be coalesced even if its buddy is released in future. Such a block is said to be *locally free*. Being at the head of the list, this block will be allocated before any other block in the list. Its allocation is efficient and fast because the bit map does not need to be updated—it still says that the block is allocated.

In the reclaiming and accelerated states a block is both added to the free list and marked free in the bit map. Such a block is said to be *globally free*. Globally free blocks are added to the end of the free list. In the reclaiming state the allocator tries to coalesce a new globally free block transitively with its buddy. Eventually a block is added to some free list—either to a free list to which the block being released would have belonged, or to a free list containing larger-size blocks. Note that the block being added to a free list could be a locally free block or a globally free block according to the state of that class of blocks. In the accelerated state the allocator tries to coalesce the block being released, just as in the reclaiming state, and additionally tries to coalesce one other locally free block—the block found at the start of the free list—with its buddy.

The state of a class of blocks is characterized as follows: Let A, L, and G be the number of allocated, locally free, and globally free blocks of a class, respectively. The total number of blocks of a class is given by $N = A + L + G$. A parameter called *slack* is computed as follows:

$$slack = N - 2 \times L - G$$

A class is said to be in the lazy, reclaiming, or accelerated state if the value of *slack* is ≥ 2, 1, or 0, respectively. (The allocator ensures that slack is never < 0.)

The coalescing overhead is different in these three states. There is no overhead in the lazy state. Hence release and allocation of blocks is fast. In the reclaiming state the overhead would be comparable with that in the buddy system, whereas in the accelerated state the overhead would be heavier than in the buddy system. It has been shown that the average delays with the lazy buddy allocator are 10 to 32 percent lower than average delays in the case of a buddy allocator.

The implementation of the lazy buddy allocator in Unix 5.4 uses two kinds of blocks. Small blocks vary in size between 8 and 256 bytes. Large blocks vary in size between 512 and 16 KB. The allocator obtains memory from the paging system in 4 KB areas. In each area, it creates a pool of blocks and a bit map to keep track of the allocation status of the blocks. When all blocks in the pool are free, it returns the area to the paging system. This action overcomes the problem of nonreturnable blocks seen in the McKusick–Karels allocator.

Slab Allocator The slab allocator was first used in the Solaris 2.4 operating system; it has been used in Linux since version 2.2. A *slab* consists of many *slots*, where each slot can hold an active object that is a kernel data structure, or it may be empty. The allocator obtains standard-size memory areas from the paging system and organizes a slab in each memory area. It obtains an additional memory area from the paging system and constructs a slab in it when it runs out of memory to allocate, and it returns a memory area to the paging system when all slots in its slab are unused.

All kernel objects of the same class form a pool. For small objects, a pool consists of many slabs and each slab contains many slots. (Large objects are not discussed here.) The slabs of a pool are entered in a doubly linked list to facilitate addition and deletion of slabs. A slab may be full, partially empty, or empty, depending on the number of active objects existing in it. To facilitate searches for an empty slab, the doubly linked list containing the slabs of a pool is sorted according to the slab's status—all full slabs are at the start of the list, partially empty slabs are in the middle, and empty slabs are at the end of the list. Each slab contains a free list from which free slots can be allocated. Each pool contains a pointer to the first slab that contains a free slot. This arrangement makes allocation very efficient.

Figure 11.23 shows the format of a slab. When the allocator obtains a memory area from the paging system, it formats the memory area into a slab by creating an integral number of slots, a free list containing all slots, and a descriptor field

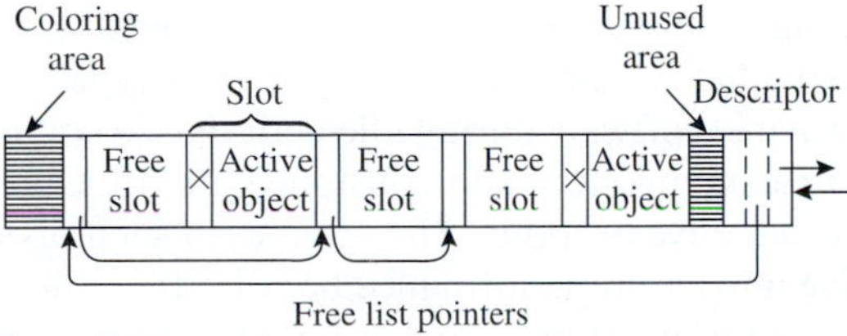

Figure 11.23 Format of a slab.

at the end of the slab that contains both the count of active objects in it and the free list header. Each slot in the slab is then initialized; this action involves initializing the various fields in it with object-specific information like fixed strings of constant values. When allocated, the slot can be used as an object straightaway. At deallocation time, the object is brought back to its allocation time status, and the slot is added to the free list. Since some fields of the objects never change, or change in such a manner that their values at deallocation time are the same as their values at allocation time, this approach eliminates the repetitive overhead of object initialization suffered in most other allocators. However, use of initialized objects has some implications for the memory utilization factor. If a free slot were simply free memory, a part of this memory itself could be used as the free list pointer; but a slot is an initialized object, and so the pointer field must be located outside the object's area even when the slot is free (see Figure 11.23).

The slab allocator provides improved cache behavior by avoiding the cache performance problem faced by power-of-2 allocators and their variants described at the start of this section. Each slab contains a reserved area at its start called the *coloring area* (see Figure 11.23). The allocator uses different-size coloring areas in the slabs of a pool. Consequently, objects in different slabs of a pool have different alignments with respect to the closest multiples of a power of 2, and so they map into different areas of a set-associative cache. This feature avoids excessive contention for certain areas of a cache, thus improving the cache performance.

The slab allocator also provides a better memory utilization factor because it allocates only the required amount of memory for each object. Thus, unlike the McKusick–Karels and lazy buddy allocators, no internal fragmentation exists on a per object basis; only external fragmentation exists in the form of an unused area in each slab. Bonwick (1994) has reported that fragmentation is only 14 percent in the slab allocator as against 45 and 46 percent in the McKusick–Karels and lazy buddy allocators, respectively. The average allocation times are also better than in the other allocators.

11.12 USING IDLE RAM EFFECTIVELY

A workstation or laptop has a large memory because it is needed for running specific applications. However, memory remains idle when the applications are not active. Operating system designers have long pondered the issue of how idle memory can be exploited for the benefit of the user. A typical solution is to run utilities such as antivirus software during idle periods of a computer so that their execution does not tie up memory and consume CPU time when the computer is being used for productive purposes. However, even such operation of utilities can have a negative impact on performance because the utilities might displace important applications from memory, so they have to be loaded back into memory before they can be used.

The Windows Vista operating system has a feature called *SuperFetch* which maintains prioritized information about frequently used applications and documents, and uses it to preload high-priority applications and documents in idle parts of memory. It also ensures that only idle low-priority applications would be removed from memory to run antivirus and other utilities. Vista also has another feature called *Readyboost* which uses a flash memory in a USB drive to boost system performance by copying applications on the USB drive, from where they can be loaded in memory faster than from the disk. When used in conjunction with SuperFetch, Readyboost effectively makes the USB drive a cache between memory and the disk, which enhances system performance through quick loading of applications.

11.13 SUMMARY

In this chapter, we discussed techniques of effective management of memory, which involves performing fast allocation and deallocation of memory to processes and ensuring efficient use of memory so that many processes can be accommodated in it simultaneously.

When a program is coded or compiled, it is not known which area of the memory would be allocated for its execution. However, instructions used in it need to use memory addresses for its operands. This dilemma is resolved as follows: A compiler assumes a specific memory area to be available to a program and generates a program form called *object module*. The *linker*, which is a system program, uses the procedure called *relocation*, which changes the operand addresses in a program's instructions such that the program can execute correctly in the allocated memory area. The linker also connects the program with library functions required by it to prepare a ready-to-execute program. *self-relocating* programs can perform their own relocation. Computer hardware assists in dynamic relocation of programs through a special register in the CPU called the *relocation register*. It permits the kernel to change the memory area allocated to a program during the program's execution.

Memory allocation can be performed in two ways: *Static memory allocation* is performed before execution of a program commences; however, it requires knowledge of the exact amount of memory required, failing which it may overallocate and waste memory. *Dynamic memory allocation* is performed during execution of a program, which incurs a memory management overhead during execution, but makes efficient use of memory by allocating only the required amount of memory. The kernel uses a model of memory allocation for a process that contains a statically allocated component for the code and data of the program, and dynamically allocated components for the *stack*, and for the *heap* in which a program can dynamically allocate memory through statements such as *new* or *alloc*.

When a process completes its execution, or releases the memory allocated to it, the kernel reuses the memory to satisfy the requirements of other processes. When static memory allocation is used, some of the memory allocated to a process may remain unused, which is called *internal fragmentation*. When dynamic memory allocation is used, unless new requests exactly match the sizes of released memory, some memory is left over when a new request is satisfied. It remains unused if it is too small to satisfy a request, which is called *external fragmentation*.

Two approaches can be used to tackle the fragmentation problem: In the first approach, the kernel minimizes fragmentation while reusing memory. Various techniques called *first-fit* allocation, *best-fit* allocation, etc. are used to minimize external fragmentation, while techniques called *buddy systems allocation* and *power-of-2 allocation* are used to eliminate external fragmentation. In the other approach, *noncontiguous memory allocation* is used, whereby a process can be executed even when it is allocated many small memory areas that add up to its total size requirement. This way external fragmentation is eliminated. *Paging* and *segmentation* are two such approaches. Noncontiguous memory allocation requires use of a *memory management unit* in the hardware.

The kernel creates and destroys control blocks such as the PCB at a very fast rate. Since the sizes of control blocks are known to the kernel, it minimizes the memory management overhead and the fragmentation problem by having many memory blocks of required size and allocating one of them when a new control block is to be created. The *lazy buddy allocator* and the *slab allocator* are some of the techniques used by the kernel.

TEST YOUR CONCEPTS

11.1 Classify each of the following statements as true or false:

- **a.** When a stack is used, reuse of a released memory area is automatic.
- **b.** PCD data can be allocated on a stack.
- **c.** The relocation register helps the kernel perform compaction of programs to avoid external fragmentation.
- **d.** Memory allocation performed by using a buddy system allocator does not suffer from internal fragmentation.
- **e.** When a memory area is released in a system employing a buddy system allocator, the number of free memory areas increases by 1, decreases by 1, or remains unchanged.
- **f.** External fragmentation can occur when either a buddy system allocator or a power-of-2 allocator is used.
- **g.** When dynamic linking and loading is employed, a routine that is not used in an execution of a program is not loaded in memory.
- **h.** In a paging system, it is not possible to swap in a process into a set of noncontiguous memory area(s) that is different from the set of noncontiguous memory areas from which it was swapped out.
- **i.** In a paging system, a programmer has to demarcate the pages in the code and data of a program.
- **j.** There would be no need for linkers if all programs were coded as self-relocating programs.

11.2 Select the correct alternative in each of the following questions:

- **a.** A *worst-fit* allocator always splits the largest free memory area while making an allocation. A free list contains three memory areas of sizes 6 KB, 15 KB and 12 KB. The next four memory requests are for 10 KB, 2 KB, 5 KB, and 14 KB of memory. The only placement strategy that would be able to accommodate all four processes is
  - **i.** First-fit,
  - **ii.** best-fit,
  - **iii.** worst-fit,
  - **iv.** next-fit.
- **b.** Three processes requiring 150 KB, 100 KB, and 300 KB of memory are in operation in an OS employing a paging system with a page size of 2 KB. The maximum internal memory fragmentation due to memory allocation to the three processes is
  - **i.** Approximately 2 KB
  - **ii.** Approximately 6 KB
  - **iii.** 275 KB
  - **iv.** None of (i)–(iii)
- **c.** A reentrant program is one that
  - **i.** Calls itself recursively
  - **ii.** Can have several copies in memory that can be used by different users
  - **iii.** Can have a single copy in memory that is executed by many users concurrently

EXERCISES

11.1 A hypothetical programming language permits one of the following three attributes to be associated with a variable in a program:

a. *Static:* Variables with this attribute are allocated memory at compilation time.

b. *Automatic:* When execution of a program is initiated or a function/subroutine is invoked, variables with the *automatic* attribute declared in the program, function, or subroutine are allocated memory. Memory is deallocated when the program completes or the invocation of the function/subroutine is exited.

c. *Controlled:* A variable x with the *controlled* attribute is allocated memory when the program executes the statement **new** x. Memory is deallocated when the program executes the statement **release** x.

Discuss the method used to allocate memory to variables with each of these attributes. Comment on (i) memory utilization efficiency and (ii) execution efficiency of these methods.

11.2 A memory allocator using the best-fit allocation policy organizes its free list in ascending order by sizes of free areas. This organization avoids having to scan the entire free list for making an allocation. However, while handling a request for n bytes, the allocator has to skip over the entries for memory areas that are $< n$ bytes in size. Propose a method of organizing the free list that would eliminate the overhead of examining and skipping over these entries.

11.3 The kernel of an OS uses a separate memory allocator for handling its own memory requirements. It is found that this memory allocator receives requests to grant and release memory areas of only two sizes, namely, 100 bytes and 150 bytes, at a high rate. Comment on memory utilization efficiency and speed of allocation if the memory allocator is

a. A first-fit allocator

b. A best-fit allocator

c. A slab allocator

11.4 A memory allocator uses the following policy to allocate a single contiguous area for requests of 1 KB and 2 KB: It sets apart a contiguous memory area of n KB for handling such requests, and splits this memory area into n areas of 1 KB each. To meet a request for 2 KB, it merges two adjoining free areas of 1 KB each, if present, and allocates the resulting contiguous area. When an area of 2 KB is released, it treats the freed area as two free areas of 1 KB each. Show that if the allocator has 22 KB available for allocation, it may not be able to honor requests for a total of 16 KB.

11.5 A buddy system allocator is allocated an area of 64 KB. Blocks of size 2 KB, 11 KB, 120 bytes, and 20 KB are allocated in that order.

a. Show the allocation status and free lists of the allocator. How many splits were performed?

b. Show the allocation status and free lists of the allocator after the block of 120 bytes is freed. How many coalesce operations were performed?

11.6 A power-of-2 allocator uses a minimum block size of 16 bytes and a maximum block size of 32 KB. It starts its operation with one free block each of sizes 512 bytes, 2 KB, 16 KB and 32 KB. Calculate the internal fragmentation if the allocator processes the same requests as in Exercise 11.5.

11.7 When a memory block is freed, a memory allocator makes an effort to merge it with one or both of its neighbors. Do you agree with the following statement? "If sizes of neighboring blocks are known, it is adequate to have a tag at only one boundary of each block. However, if sizes of neighboring blocks are not known, it is essential to have tags at both boundaries of each block."

11.8 A buddy system organizes tags of the blocks in a bitmap, which is a one-dimensional array of tags. Comment on how best the bitmap can be organized and used. (*Hint:* Note that blocks may be split and coalesced during operation of the buddy system.)

11.9 If a binary buddy system starts its operation with a single free block of size 2^z bytes.

a. Justify the statement : "When a block is released, the number of free blocks in the system may increase by 1, may remain unchanged, or may decrease by a number between 1 and n, both inclusive, where $n < z$."

b. Determine the value of n if the minimum block size in the buddy system is 16 bytes.

11.10 A Fibonacci buddy system uses blocks whose sizes are multiples of the terms of the Fibonacci series, for example 16, 32, 48, 80, 128, ... Hence the size of a block is the sum of the sizes of the two immediately smaller blocks. This formula governs the splitting and merging of blocks. Compare the execution efficiency and memory efficiency of the Fibonacci buddy system with the binary buddy system.

11.11 A memory allocator works as follows: Small memory areas are allocated by using a buddy system. Large memory areas are allocated by using a free list and a first-fit allocator. Comment on the efficiency and memory utilization achieved by this allocator.

11.12 An OS has 110 MB available for user processes. The maximum memory requirement of a process for its own code and data is 20 MB, while the average memory requirement of a process is 10 MB. If the OS uses contiguous memory allocation and does not know sizes of individual processes, what is the average internal and external fragmentation?

11.13 Does the 50-percent rule apply to the following allocators?

a. Buddy system
b. Power-of-2 allocator
c. Slab allocator

11.14 An OS receives requests for memory allocation at a high rate. It is found that a large fraction of the requests are for memory areas of size 100, 300, and 400 bytes (let us call these "standard" sizes). Other requests are for areas of various other sizes. Design a memory allocation scheme in which no fragmentation arises while allocating areas of standard sizes and no internal fragmentation arises while allocating areas of other sizes.

11.15 Compute the slack for each class of buffers if a lazy buddy allocator were to be used instead of the buddy allocator in Exercise 11.5.

11.16 If the OS of Exercise 11.12 employed paging with a page size of 2 KB, is it possible to compute the average internal fragmentation in the system?

BIBLIOGRAPHY

Linkers and Loaders are described in Dhamdhere (1999).

Knuth (1973) is the classical starting point for a study of contiguous memory management. He describes various techniques of memory allocation and efficient data structures to keep track of free memory. Hoare and Mckeag (1971) surveys various memory management techniques. Randell (1969) is an early paper on the motivation for virtual memory systems. Denning (1970) describes the fundamentals of virtual memory systems.

Vahalia (1996) describes the various kernel memory allocators used in Unix systems. McKusick and Karels (1988) describes the McKusick–Karels memory allocator. Lee and Barkley (1989) describes the lazy buddy allocator. Both these allocators are used in Unix. Bonwick (1994) and Bonwick and Adams (2001) describe the slab allocator. Mauro and McDougall (2006) describes use of the slab allocator in Solaris, while Beck et al. (2002), and Bovet and Cesati (2005) describe its implementation in Linux. The Windows kernel uses several memory allocation policies for its own memory requirements. It implements buddy-system-like allocation for medium-size blocks and heap-based allocation for small block sizes. Russinovich and Solomon (2005) describes heap allocation and kernel memory allocation in Windows.

1. Beck, M., H. Bohme, M. Dziadzka, U. Kunitz, R. Magnus, C. Schroter, and D. Verworner (2002): *Linux Kernel Programming*, 3rd ed., Pearson Education, New York.
2. Bonwick, J. (1994): "The slab allocator: An object-caching kernel memory allocator," *Proceedings of the Summer 1994 Usenix Technical Conference*, 87–98.
3. Bonwick, J., and J. Adams (2001): "Extending the slab allocator to many CPUs and arbitrary

resources," *Proceedings of the 2001 USENIX Annual Technical Conference*, 15–34.

4. Bovet, D. P., and M. Cesati (2005): *Understanding the Linux Kernel*, 3rd ed., O'Reilly, Sebastopol, Calif.
5. Denning, P. J. (1970): "Virtual Memory," *Computing Surveys*, **2** (3), 153–189.
6. Dhamdhere, D. M. (1999): *Systems Programming and Operating Systems*, 2nd revised ed., Tata McGraw-Hill, New Delhi.
7. Hoare, C. A. R., and R. M. Mckeag (1971): "A survey of store management techniques," in *Operating Systems Techniques*, by C.A.R. Hoare and R.H. Perrott (eds.) Academic Press, London.
8. Knuth, D. E. (1973): *The Art of Computer Programming*, 2nd ed., Vol. I : Fundamental Algorithms, Addison-Wesley, Reading, Mass.
9. Kuck, D. J., and D. H. Lowrie (1970): "The use and performance of memory hierarchies," in *Software Engineering*, **1**, J.T. Tou (ed.), Academic Press, New York.
10. Lee, T. P., and R. E. Barkley (1989): "A watermark-based lazy buddy system for kernel memory allocation," *Proceedings of the Summer 1989 USENIX Technical Conference*, 1–13.
11. Mauro, J., and R. McDougall (2006): *Solaris Internals*, 2nd ed., Prentice Hall, Englewood Cliffs, N. J.
12. McKusick, M. K., and M. J. Karels (1988): "Design of a general-purpose memory allocator for the 4.3 BSD Unix kernel," *Proceedings of the Summer 1988 USENIX Technical Conference*, 295–303.
13. Peterson, J. L., and T. A. Norman (1977): "Buddy systems,"*Communications of the ACM*, **20** (6), 421–431.
14. Randell, B.(1969): "A note on storage fragmentation and program segmentation," *Communications of the ACM*, **12** (7), 365–369.
15. Russinovich, M. E., and D. A. Solomon (2005): *Microsoft Windows Internals*, 4th ed., Microsoft Press, Redmond, Wash.
16. Vahalia, U. (1996): *Unix Internals—The New Frontiers*, Prentice Hall, Englewood Cliffs, N. J.

12 Chapter

Virtual Memory

Virtual memory is a part of the memory hierarchy that consists of memory and a disk. In accordance with the principle of memory hierarchies described in Chapter 2, only some portions of the address space of a process—that is, of its code and data—exist in memory at any time; other portions of its address space reside on disk and are loaded into memory when needed during operation of the process. The kernel employs virtual memory to reduce the memory commitment to a process so that it can service a large number of processes concurrently, and to handle processes whose address space is larger than the size of memory.

Virtual memory is implemented through the *noncontiguous memory allocation model* described earlier in Chapter 11 and comprises both hardware components and a software component called a *virtual memory manager*. The hardware components speed up *address translation* and help the virtual memory manager perform its tasks more effectively. The virtual memory manager decides which portions of a process address space should be in memory at any time.

Performance of virtual memory depends on the rate at which portions of a process address space have to be loaded in memory from a disk and removed from memory to make space for new portions. According to the empirical law of *locality of reference*, a process is likely to access recently referenced portions of its address space again. The virtual memory manager ensures good performance of virtual memory by allocating an adequate amount of memory to a process and employing a *replacement algorithm* to remove a portion that has not been referenced recently.

We start by discussing locality of reference and its importance for performance of a virtual memory. The techniques employed by the virtual memory manager to ensure good performance are then discussed.

12.1 VIRTUAL MEMORY BASICS

Users always want more from a computer system—more resources and more services. The need for more resources is satisfied either by obtaining more efficient use of existing resources, or by creating an illusion that more resources exist in the system. A *virtual memory* is what its name indicates—it is an illusion of a memory that is larger than the real memory, i.e., RAM, of the computer system. As we pointed out in Section 1.1, this illusion is a part of a user's abstract view of memory. A user or his application program sees only the virtual memory. The kernel implements the illusion through a combination of hardware and software means. We refer to real memory simply as memory. We refer to the software component of virtual memory as a *virtual memory manager*.

The illusion of memory larger than the system's memory crops up any time a process whose size exceeds the size of memory is initiated. The process is able to operate because it is kept in its entirety on a disk and only its required portions are loaded in memory at any time. The basis of virtual memory is the *noncontiguous memory allocation* model described earlier in Section 11.7. The address space of each process is assumed to consist of portions called *components*. The portions can be loaded into nonadjacent areas of memory. The address of each operand or instruction in the code of a process is a *logical address* of the form ($comp_i$, $byte_i$). The *memory management unit* (MMU) translates it into the address in memory where the operand or instruction actually resides.

Use of the noncontiguous memory allocation model reduces memory fragmentation, since a free area of memory can be reused even if it is not large enough to hold the entire address space of a process. More user processes can be accommodated in memory this way, which benefits both users and the OS. The kernel carries this idea further—even processes that can fit in memory are not loaded fully into memory. This strategy reduces the amount of memory that is allocated to each process, thus further increasing the number of processes that can be in operation at the same time.

Figure 12.1 shows a schematic diagram of a virtual memory. The logical address space of the process shown consists of five components. Three of these components are presently in memory. Information about the memory areas where these components exist is maintained in a data structure of the virtual memory manager. This information is used by the MMU during address translation. When an instruction in the process refers to a data item or instruction that is not in memory, the component containing it is loaded from the disk. Occasionally, the virtual memory manager removes some components from memory to make room for other components.

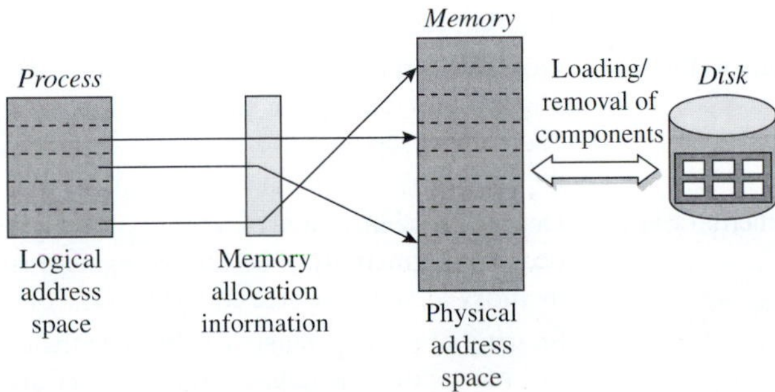

Figure 12.1 Overview of virtual memory.

The arrangement shown in Figure 12.1 is a memory hierarchy as discussed in Section 2.2.3 and illustrated in Figure 2.4. The hierarchy consists of the system's memory and a disk. Memory is fast, but small in size. The disk is slow, but has a much larger capacity. The MMU and the virtual memory manager together manage the memory hierarchy, so that the current instruction in a process finds its operands in memory.

We are now ready to define virtual memory.

Definition 12.1 Virtual Memory A memory hierarchy, consisting of a computer system's memory and a disk, that enables a process to operate with only some portions of its address space in memory.

Demand Loading of Process Components The virtual memory manager loads only one component of a process address space in memory to begin with—the component that contains the *start address* of the process, that is, address of the instruction with which its execution begins. It loads other components of the process only when they are needed. This technique is called *demand loading.* To keep the memory commitment to a process low, the virtual memory manager removes components of the process from memory from time to time. These components would be loaded back in memory when needed again.

Performance of a process in virtual memory depends on the rate at which its components have to be loaded into memory. The virtual memory manager exploits the law of *locality of reference* to achieve a low rate of loading of process components. We discuss this law in Section 12.2.1.1.

Table 12.1 Comparison of Paging and Segmentation

Issue	Comparison
Concept	A page is a fixed-size portion of a process address space that is identified by the virtual memory hardware. A segment is a logical entity in a program, e.g., a function, a data structure, or an object. Segments are identified by the programmer.
Size of components	All pages are of the same size. Segments may be of different sizes.
External fragmentation	Not found in paging because memory is divided into page frames whose size equals the size of pages. It occurs in segmentation because a free area of memory may be too small to accommodate a segment.
Internal fragmentation	Occurs in the last page of a process in paging. Does not occur in segmentation because a segment is allocated a memory area whose size equals the size of the segment.
Sharing	Sharing of pages is feasible subject to the constraints on sharing of code pages described later in Section 12.6. Sharing of segments is freely possible.

Paging and Segmentation In Chapter 11, we discussed how these two approaches to implementation of virtual memory differ in the manner in which the boundaries and sizes of address space components are determined. Table 12.1 compares the two approaches. In paging, each component of an address space is called a *page*. All pages have identical size, which is a power of two. Page size is defined by the computer hardware and demarcation of pages in the address space of a process is performed implicitly by it. In segmentation, each component of an address space is called a *segment*. A programmer declares some significant logical entities (e.g., data structures or objects) in a process as segments. Thus identification of components is performed by the programmer, and segments can have different sizes. This fundamental difference leads to different implications for efficient use of memory and for sharing of programs or data. Some systems use a hybrid segmentation-with-paging approach to obtain advantages of both the approaches.

12.2 DEMAND PAGING

As discussed earlier in Section 11.8, a process is considered to consist of pages, numbered from 0 onward. Each page is of size s bytes, where s is a power of 2. The memory of the computer system is considered to consist of *page frames*, where a page frame is a memory area that has the same size as a page. Page frames are numbered from 0 to $\#frames-1$ where $\#frames$ is the number of page frames of memory. Accordingly, the physical address space consists of addresses from 0 to $\#frames \times s - 1$. At any moment, a page frame may be free, or it may contain a page of some process. Each logical address used in a process is considered to be a pair (p_i, b_i), where p_i is a page number and b_i is the byte number in p_i, $0 \le b_i < s$. The effective memory address of a logical address (p_i, b_i) is computed as follows:

$$\begin{aligned}&\text{Effective memory address of logical address } (p_i, b_i)\\&\quad = \text{start address of the page frame containing page } p_i + b_i\end{aligned} \tag{12.1}$$

The size of a page is a power of 2, and so calculation of the effective address is performed through bit concatenation, which is much faster than addition (see Section 11.8 for details).

Figure 12.2 is a schematic diagram of a virtual memory using paging in which page size is assumed to be 1 KB, where 1 KB = 1024 bytes. Three processes P_1, P_2 and P_3, have some of their pages in memory. The memory contains 8 page frames numbered from 0 to 7. Memory allocation information for a process is stored in a *page table*. Each entry in the page table contains memory allocation information for one page of a process. It contains the page frame number where a page resides. Process P_2 has its pages 1 and 2 in memory. They occupy page frames 5 and 7 respectively. Process P_1 has its pages 0 and 2 in page frames 4 and 1, while process P_3 has its pages 1, 3 and 4 in page frames 0, 2 and 3, respectively. The free frames list contains a list of free page frames. Currently only page frame 6 is free.

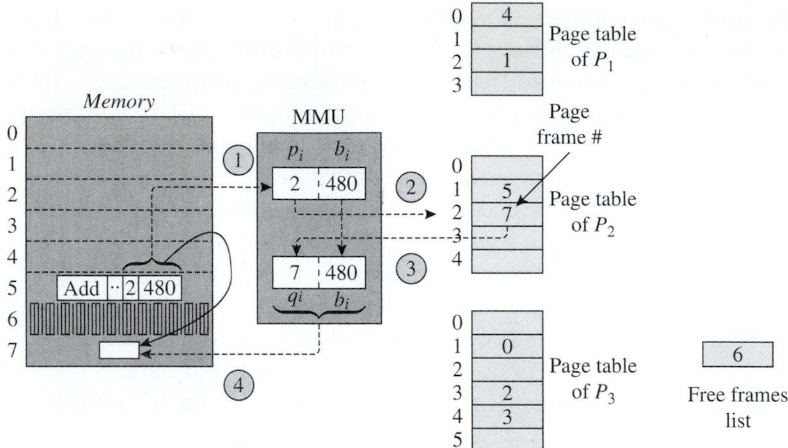

Figure 12.2 Address translation in virtual memory using paging.

Process P_2 is currently executing the instruction 'Add ·· 2528', so the MMU uses P_2's page table for address translation. The MMU views the operand address 2528 as the pair (2, 480) because $2528 = 2 \times 1024 + 480$. It now accesses the entry for page 2 in P_2's page table. This entry contains frame number 7, so the MMU forms the effective address $7 \times 1024 + 480$ according to Eq. (12.1), and uses it to make a memory access. In effect, byte 480 in page frame 7 is accessed.

12.2.1 Demand Paging Preliminaries

If an instruction of P_2 in Figure 12.2 refers to a byte in page 3, the virtual memory manager will load page 3 in memory and put its frame number in entry 3 of P_2's page table. These actions constitute demand loading of pages, or simply *demand paging*.

To implement demand paging, a copy of the entire logical address space of a process is maintained on a disk. The disk area used to store this copy is called the *swap space* of a process. While initiating a process, the virtual memory manager allocates the swap space for the process and copies its code and data into the swap space. During operation of the process, the virtual memory manager is alerted when the process wishes to use some data item or instruction that is located in a page that is not present in memory. It now loads the page from the swap space into memory. This operation is called a *page-in* operation. When the virtual memory manager decides to remove a page from memory, the page is copied back into the swap space of the process to which it belongs if the page was modified since the last time it was loaded in memory. This operation is called a *page-out* operation. This way the swap space of a process contains an up-to-date copy of every page of the process that is not present in memory. A *page replacement* operation is one that loads a page into a page frame that previously contained another page. It may involve a page-out operation if the previous page was modified while it occupied the page frame, and involves a page-in operation to load the new page.

In this section we describe the data structures used by the virtual memory manager, and the manner in which the virtual memory manager performs the page-in, page-out, and page replacement operations. We then discuss how the effective memory access time for a process depends on the overhead of the virtual memory manager and the time consumed by the page-in, page-out, and page replacement operations.

Page Table The page table for a process facilitates implementation of address translation, demand loading, and page replacement operations. Figure 12.3 shows the format of a page table entry. The *valid bit* field contains a boolean value to indicate whether the page exists in memory. We use the convention that 1 indicates "resident in memory" and 0 indicates "not resident in memory." The *page frame* # field, which was described earlier, facilitates address translation. The *misc info* field is divided into four subfields. Information in the *prot info* field is used for protecting contents of the page against interference. It indicates whether the process can read or write data in the page or execute instructions in it. *ref info* contains information concerning references made to the page while it is in memory. As discussed later, this information is used for page replacement decisions. The *modified* bit indicates whether the page has been modified, i.e., whether it is *dirty*. It is used to decide whether a page-out operation is needed while replacing the page. The *other info* field contains information such as the address of the disk block in the swap space where a copy of the page is maintained.

Page Faults and Demand Loading of Pages Table 12.2 summarizes steps in address translation by the MMU. While performing address translation for a logical address (p_i, b_i), the MMU checks the valid bit of the page table entry of p_i

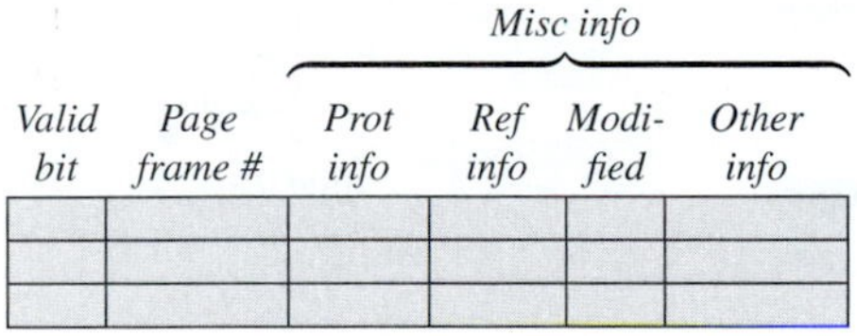

		Misc info			
Valid bit	*Page frame #*	*Prot info*	*Ref info*	*Modified*	*Other info*

Field	Description
Valid bit	Indicates whether the page described by the entry currently exists in memory. This bit is also called the *presence* bit.
Page frame #	Indicates which page frame of memory is occupied by the page.
Prot info	Indicates how the process may use contents of the page—whether read, write, or execute.
Ref info	Information concerning references made to the page while it is in memory.
Modified	Indicates whether the page has been modified while in memory, i.e., whether it is dirty. This field is a single bit called the *dirty* bit.
Other info	Other useful information concerning the page, e.g., its position in the swap space.

Figure 12.3 Fields in a page table entry.

Table 12.2 Steps in Address Translation by the MMU

Step	Description
1. Obtain page number and byte number in page	A logical address is viewed as a pair (p_i, b_i), where b_i consists of the lower order n_b bits of the address, and p_i consists of the higher order n_p bits (see Section 11.8).
2. Look up page table	p_i is used to index the page table. A page fault is raised if the *valid bit* of the page table entry contains a 0, i.e., if the page in not present in memory.
3. Form effective memory address	The *page frame #* field of the page table entry contains a frame number represented as an n_f-bit number. It is concatenated with b_i to obtain the effective memory address of the byte.

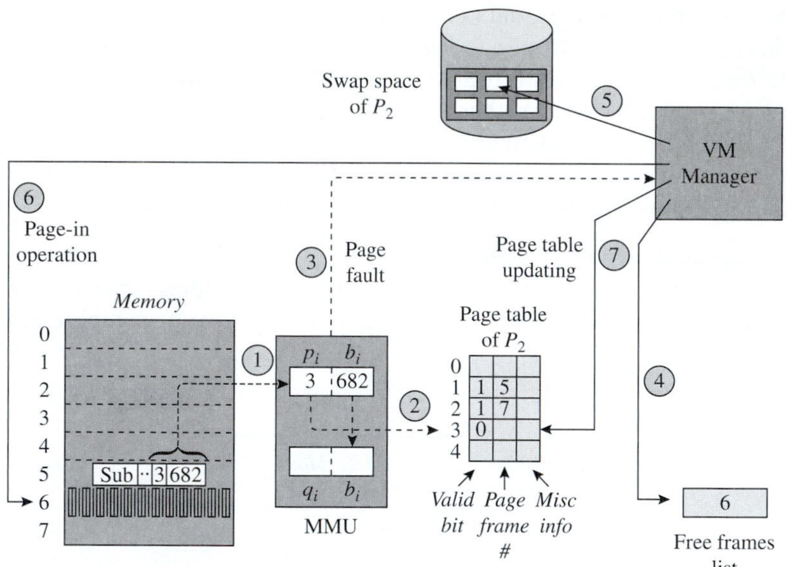

Figure 12.4 Demand loading of a page.

(see Step 2 in Table 12.2). If the bit indicates that p_i is not present in memory, the MMU raises an interrupt called a *missing page interrupt* or a *page fault*, which is a program interrupt (see Section 2.2.5). The interrupt servicing routine for program interrupts finds that the interrupt was caused by a page fault, so it invokes the virtual memory manager with the page number that caused the page fault, i.e., p_i, as a parameter. The virtual memory manager now loads page p_i in memory and updates its page table entry. Thus, the MMU and the virtual memory manager interact to decide *when* a page of a process should be loaded in memory.

Figure 12.4 is an overview of the virtual memory manager's actions in demand loading of a page. The broken arrows indicate actions of the MMU, whereas firm arrows indicate accesses to the data structures, memory, and the disk by the virtual memory manager when a page fault occurs. The numbers in circles indicate the steps in address translation, raising, and handling of the page fault—Steps 1–3 were described earlier in Table 12.2. Process P_2 of Figure 12.2 is in operation. While translating the logical address (3, 682), the MMU raises a page fault because the valid bit of page 3's entry is 0. When the virtual memory manager gains control, it knows that a reference to page 3 caused the page fault. The *Misc info* field of the page table entry of page 3 contains the address of the disk block in P_2's swap space that contains page 3. The virtual memory manager obtains this address. It now consults the free frames list and finds that page frame 6 is currently free, so it allocates this page frame to page 3 and starts an I/O operation to load page 3 in page frame 6. When the I/O operation completes, the virtual memory manager updates page 3's entry in the page table by setting the *valid* bit to 1 and putting 6 in the *page frame #* field. Execution of the instruction "Sub ·· (3, 682)", which had caused the page fault, is now resumed. The logical address (3, 682) is translated to the effective address of byte number 682 in page frame 6, i.e., $6 \times 1024 + 682$.

Page-in, Page-out, and Page Replacement Operations Figure 12.4 showed how a page-in operation is performed for a required page when a page fault occurs in a process and a free page frame is available in memory. If no page frame is free, the virtual memory manager performs a *page replacement operation* to replace one of the pages existing in memory with the page whose reference caused the page fault. It is performed as follows: The virtual memory manager uses a *page replacement algorithm* to select one of the pages currently in memory for replacement, accesses the page table entry of the selected page to mark it as "not present" in memory, and initiates a page-out operation for it if the *modified* bit of its page table entry indicates that it is a *dirty* page. In the next step, the virtual memory manager initiates a page-in operation to load the required page into the page frame that was occupied by the selected page. After the page-in operation completes, it updates the page table entry of the page to record the frame number of the page frame, marks the page as "present," and makes provision to resume operation of the process. The process now reexecutes its current instruction. This time, the address translation for the logical address in the current instruction completes without a page fault.

The page-in and page-out operations required to implement demand paging constitute *page I/O*; we use the term *page traffic* to describe movement of pages in and out of memory. Note that page I/O is distinct from I/O operations performed by processes, which we will call *program I/O*. The state of a process that encounters a page fault is changed to *blocked* until the required page is loaded in memory, and so its performance suffers because of a page fault. The kernel can switch the CPU to another process to safeguard system performance.

Effective Memory Access Time The effective memory access time for a process in demand paging is the average memory access time experienced by the process. It depends on two factors: time consumed by the MMU in performing address translation, and the average time consumed by the virtual memory manager in handling a page fault. We use the following notation to compute the effective memory access time:

pr_1 probability that a page exists in memory
t_{mem} memory access time
t_{pfh} time overhead of page fault handling

pr_1 is called the *memory hit ratio*. t_{pfh} is a few orders of magnitude larger than t_{mem} because it involves disk I/O—one disk I/O operation is required if only a page-in operation is sufficient, and two disk I/O operations are required if a page replacement is necessary.

A process's page table exists in memory when the process is in operation. Hence, accessing an operand with the logical address (p_i, b_i) consumes two memory cycles if page p_i exists in memory—one to access the page table entry of p_i for address translation, and the other to access the operand in memory using the effective memory address of (p_i, b_i). If the page is not present in memory, a page fault is raised after referencing the page table entry of p_i, i.e., after one memory cycle. Now the required page is loaded in memory and its page table entry is updated to record the frame number where it is loaded. When operation of the process is resumed, it requires two more memory references—one to access the page table and the other to actually access the operand. Accordingly, the effective memory access time is as follows:

$$\text{Effective memory access time} = pr_1 \times 2 \times t_{mem} + (1 - pr_1) \times (t_{mem} + t_{pfh} + 2 \times t_{mem}) \quad \textbf{(12.2)}$$

The effective memory access time can be improved by reducing the number of page faults. One way of achieving it is to load pages before they are needed by a process. The Windows operating system performs such loading speculatively—when a page fault occurs, it loads the required page and also a few adjoining pages of the process. This action improves the average memory access time if a preloaded page is referenced by the process. The Linux operating system permits a process to specify which pages should be preloaded. A programmer may use this facility to improve the effective memory access time.

12.2.1.1 Page Replacement

Page replacement becomes necessary when a page fault occurs and there are no free page frames in memory. However, another page fault would arise if the replaced page is referenced again. Hence it is important to replace a page that is not likely to be referenced in the immediate future. But how does the virtual memory manager know which page is not likely to be referenced in the immediate future?

The empirical law of *locality of reference* states that logical addresses used by a process in any short interval of time during its operation tend to be bunched together in certain portions of its logical address space. Processes exhibit this behavior for two reasons. Execution of instructions in a process is mostly sequential in nature, because only 10–20 percent of instructions executed by a process are branch instructions. Processes also tend to perform similar operations on several elements of nonscalar data such as arrays. Due to the combined effect of these two reasons, instruction and data references made by a process tend to be in close proximity to previous instruction and data references made by it.

We define the *current locality* of a process as the set of pages referenced in its previous few instructions. Thus, the law of locality indicates that the logical address used in an instruction is likely to refer to a page that is in the current locality of the process. As mentioned in Section 2.2.3, the computer exploits the law of locality to ensure high hit ratios in the cache. The virtual memory manager can exploit the law of locality to achieve an analogous effect—fewer page faults would arise if it ensures that pages that are in the current locality of a process are present in memory.

Note that locality of reference does not imply an absence of page faults. Let the *proximity region* of a logical address a_i contain all logical addresses that are in close proximity to a_i. Page faults can occur for two reasons: First, the proximity region of a logical address may not fit into a page; in this case, the next address may lie in an adjoining page that is not included in the current locality of the process. Second, an instruction or data referenced by a process may not be in the proximity of previous references. We call this situation a *shift in locality* of a process. It typically occurs when a process makes a transition from one action in its logic to another. The next example illustrates the locality of a process.

Current Locality of a Process

Example 12.1

In Figure 12.5, bullets indicate the last few logical addresses used during operation of a process P_i. Dashed boxes show the proximity regions of these logical addresses. Note that the proximity region of a logical address may extend beyond a page boundary. Proximity regions of logical addresses may also overlap; we show the cumulative proximity regions in Figure 12.5; e.g., the proximity regions of logical addresses referenced in page 4 cumulatively cover the entire page 4 and parts of pages 3 and 5. Thus, proximity regions are located in pages 0, 1, 3, 4, 5, 6, and 7; however, the current locality of P_i is the set of pages whose numbers are marked with the * marks in Figure 12.5, i.e., the set of pages $\{0, 1, 4, 6\}$.

The law of locality helps to decide which page should be replaced when a page fault occurs. Let us assume that the number of page frames allocated to a process P_i is a constant. Hence whenever a page fault occurs during operation of P_i, one of P_i's own pages existing in memory must be replaced. Let t_1 and t_2 be the periods of time for which pages p_1 and p_2 have not been referenced during the operation of P_i. Let $t_1 > t_2$, implying that some byte of page p_2 has been referenced or executed (as an instruction) more recently than any byte of page p_1. Hence page p_2 is more likely to be a part of the current locality of the process than page p_1; that is, a byte of page p_2 is more likely to be referenced or executed than a byte of page p_1. We use this argument to choose page p_1 for replacement

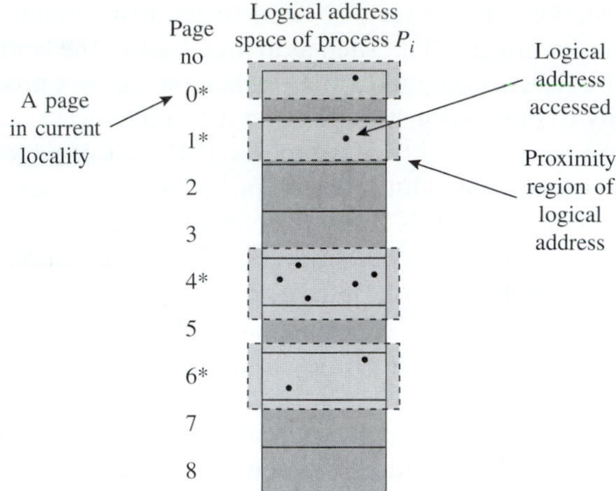

Figure 12.5 Proximity regions of previous references and current locality of a process.

when a page fault occurs. If many pages of P_i exist in memory, we can rank them according to the times of their last references and replace the page that has been least recently referenced. This page replacement policy is called *LRU page replacement*.

12.2.1.2 Memory Allocation to a Process

Figure 12.6 shows how the page fault rate of a process should vary with the amount of memory allocated to it. The page fault rate is large when a small amount of memory is allocated to the process; however, it drops when more memory is allocated to the process. This page fault characteristic of a process is desired because it enables the virtual memory manager to take corrective action when it finds that a process has a high page fault rate—it can bring about a reduction in the page fault rate by increasing the memory allocated to the process. As we shall discuss in Section 12.4, the LRU page replacement policy possesses a page fault characteristic that is similar to the curve of Figure 12.6 because it replaces a page that is less likely to be in the current locality of the process than other pages of the process that are in memory.

How much memory should the virtual memory manager allocate to a process? Two opposite factors influence this decision. From Figure 12.6, we see that an overcommitment of memory to a process implies a low page fault rate for the process; hence it ensures good process performance. However, a smaller number of processes would fit in memory, which could cause CPU idling and poor system performance. An undercommitment of memory to a process causes a high page fault rate, which would lead to poor performance of the process. The desirable operating zone marked in Figure 12.6 avoids the regions of overcommitment and undercommitment of memory.

The main problem in deciding how much memory to allocate to a process is that the page fault characteristic, i.e., the slope of the curve and the page

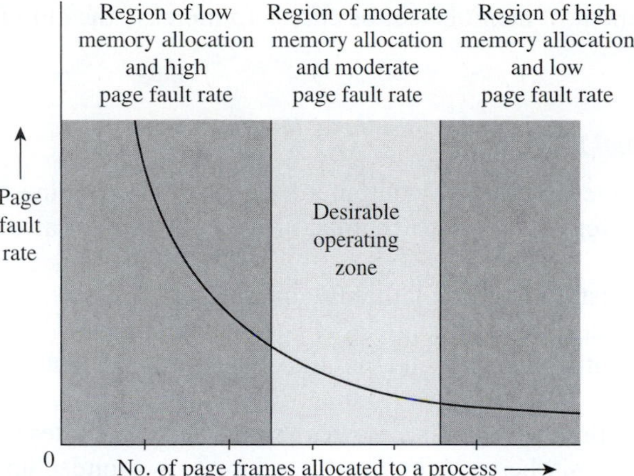

Figure 12.6 Desirable variation of page fault rate with memory allocation.

fault rate in Figure 12.6, varies among processes. Even for the same process, the page fault characteristic may be different when it operates with different data. Consequently, the amount of memory to be allocated to a process has to be determined dynamically by considering the actual page fault characteristic of the process. This issue is discussed in Section 12.5.

Thrashing Consider a process that is operating in the region of low memory allocation and high page fault rate in Figure 12.6. Due to the high page fault rate, this process spends a lot of its time in the *blocked* state. Such a process is not in a position to use the CPU effectively. It also causes high overhead due to high page fault rate and process switching caused by page faults. If all processes in the system operate in the region of high page fault rates, the CPU would be engaged in performing page traffic and process switching most of the time. CPU efficiency would be low and system performance, measured either in terms of average response time or throughput, would be poor. This situation is called *thrashing*.

Definition 12.2 Thrashing A condition in which high page traffic and low CPU efficiency coincide.

Note that low CPU efficiency can occur because of other causes as well, e.g., if too few processes exist in memory or all processes in memory perform I/O operations frequently. The thrashing situation is different in that *all* processes make poor progress because of high page fault rates.

From Figure 12.6, we can infer that the cause of thrashing is an under-commitment of memory to each process. The cure is to increase the memory allocation for each process. This may have to be achieved by removing some processes from memory—that is, by reducing the degree of multiprogramming. A process may individually experience a high page fault rate without the system thrashing. The same analysis now applies to the process—it must suffer from an undercommitment of memory, so the cure is to increase the amount of memory allocated to it.

12.2.1.3 Optimal Page Size

The size of a page is defined by computer hardware. It determines the number of bits required to represent the byte number in a page. Page size also determines

1. Memory wastage due to internal fragmentation
2. Size of the page table for a process
3. Page fault rates when a fixed amount of memory is allocated to a process

Consider a process P_i of size z bytes. A page size of s bytes implies that the process has n pages, where $n = \lceil z/s \rceil$ is the value of z/s rounded upward. Average internal fragmentation is $s/2$ bytes because the last page would be half empty on the average. The number of entries in the page table is n. Thus internal fragmentation varies directly with the page size, while page table size varies inversely with it.

Interestingly, page fault rate also varies with page size if a fixed amount of memory is allocated to P_i. This can be explained as follows: The number of pages of P_i in memory varies inversely with the page size. Hence twice as many pages of P_i would exist in memory if the page size were made $s/2$. Now let the proximity region of an instruction or data byte as defined in Section 12.2 be small compared with $s/2$, so that it can be assumed to fit within the page that contains the byte. When the page size is $s/2$, memory contains twice as many proximity regions of recent logical addresses as when the page size is s bytes. From the page fault characteristic of Figure 12.6, page fault rates would be smaller for smaller page sizes.

We can compute the page size that minimizes the total of memory penalty due to internal fragmentation and memory commitment to page tables. If $s \ll z$ and each page table entry occupies 1 byte of memory, the optimal value of s is $\sqrt{2z}$. Thus, the optimal page size is only 400 bytes for a process size of 80 KB, and it is 800 bytes for a process of 320 KB. However, computers tend to use larger page sizes (e.g., Pentium and MIPS use page sizes of 4 KB or more, Sun Ultrasparc uses page sizes of 8 KB or more and the PowerPC uses a page size of 4 KB) for the following reasons:

1. Page table entries tend to occupy more than 1 byte.
2. Hardware costs are high for smaller page sizes. For example, the cost of address translation increases if a larger number of bits is used to represent a page number.
3. Disks, which are used as paging devices, tend to operate less efficiently for smaller disk block sizes.

The decision to use larger page sizes than the optimal value implies somewhat higher page fault rates for a process. This fact represents a tradeoff between the hardware cost and efficient operation of a process.

12.2.2 Paging Hardware

Figure 12.7 illustrates address translation in a multiprogrammed system. Page tables for many processes are present in memory. The MMU contains a special register called the *page-table address register* (PTAR) to point to the start of a page table. For a logical address (p_i, b_i), the MMU computes $<$PTAR$>$ $+ p_i \times l_{PT\_entry}$ to obtain the address of the page table entry of page p_i, where l_{PT_entry} is the length of a page table entry and $<$PTAR$>$ denotes the contents of the PTAR. The PTAR has to be loaded with the correct address when a process is scheduled. To facilitate this, the kernel can store the address of the page table of a process in its process control block (PCB).

Table 12.3 summarizes the functions performed by the paging hardware. We describe the techniques used in implementing these functions, and name a few modern computer systems that use them.

12.2.2.1 Memory Protection

A *memory protection violation* interrupt should be raised if a process tries to access a nonexistent page, or exceeds its access privileges while accessing a page. The MMU provides a special register called the *page-table size register* (PTSR) to detect violations of the first kind. The kernel records the number of pages

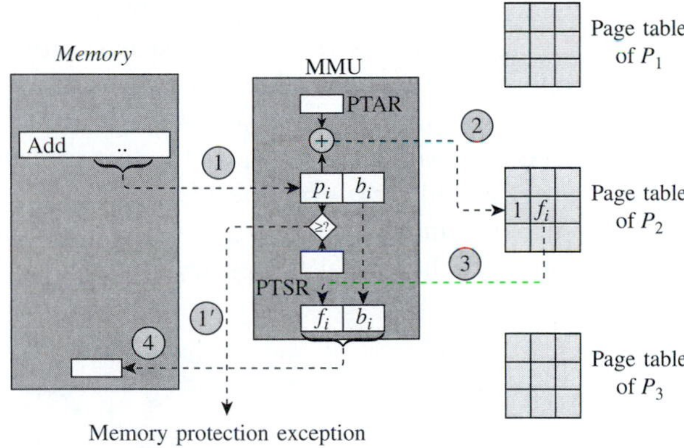

Figure 12.7 Address translation in a multiprogrammed system.

Table 12.3 Functions of the Paging Hardware

Function	Description
Memory protection	Ensure that a process can access only those memory areas that are allocated to it.
Efficient address translation	Provide an arrangement to perform address translation efficiently.
Page replacement support	Collect information concerning references made to pages. The virtual memory manager uses this information to decide which page to replace when a page fault occurs.

contained in a process in its *process control block* (PCB) and loads this number from the PCB in the PTSR when the process is scheduled. A memory protection violation is raised if the page number in a logical address is not smaller than contents of PTSR; this check is analogous to the one using the *size* register in the memory protection scheme of Chapter 2.

The access privileges of a process to a page are stored in the *prot info* field of the page's entry in the page table. During address translation, the MMU checks the kind of access being made to the page against this information and raises a memory protection violation if the two are not compatible. The information in the *prot info* field can be bit-encoded for efficient access—each bit in the field corresponds to one kind of access to the page (e.g., read, write, etc.); it is set "on" only if the process possesses the corresponding access privilege to the page.

12.2.2.2 Address Translation and Page Fault Generation

The MMU follows the steps of Table 12.2 to perform address translation. For a logical address (p_i, b_i), it accesses the page table entry of p_i by using $p_i \times l_{PT\_entry}$ as an offset into the page table, where l_{PT_entry} is the length of a page table entry. l_{PT_entry} is typically a power of 2, so $p_i \times l_{PT\_entry}$ can be computed efficiently by shifting the value of p_i by a few bits.

Address Translation Buffers A reference to the page table during address translation consumes one memory cycle because the page table is stored in memory. The *translation look-aside buffer* (TLB) is a small and fast associative memory that is used to eliminate the reference to the page table, thus speeding up address translation. The TLB contains entries of the form (page #, page frame #, protection info) for a few recently accessed pages of a program that are in memory. During address translation of a logical address (p_i, b_i), the TLB hardware searches for an entry of page p_i. If an entry is found, the page frame # from the entry is used to complete address translation for the logical address (p_i, b_i). Figure 12.8 illustrates

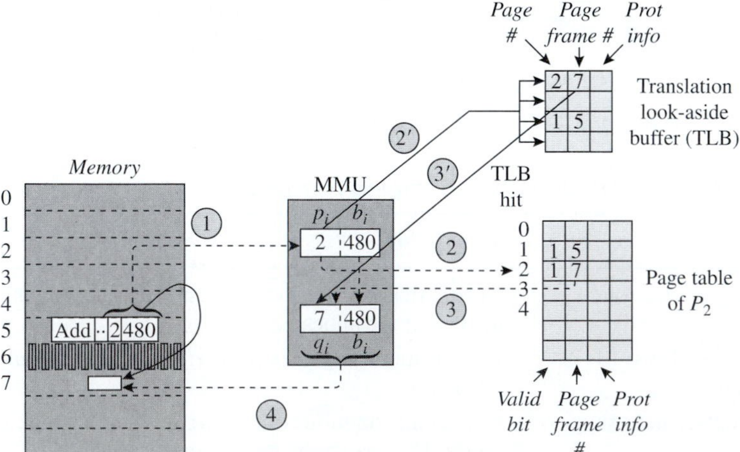

Figure 12.8 Address translation using the translation look-aside buffer and the page table.

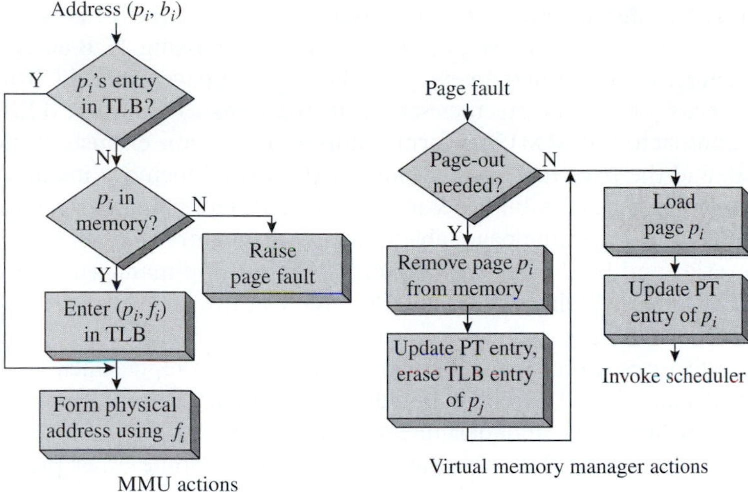

Figure 12.9 Summary of address translation of (p_i, b_i) (note: PT = page table).

operation of the TLB. The arrows marked 2′ and 3′ indicate TLB lookup. The TLB contains entries for pages 1 and 2 of process P_2. If p_i is either 1 or 2, the TLB lookup scores a hit, so the MMU takes the page frame number from the TLB and completes address translation. A TLB miss occurs if p_i is some other page, hence the MMU accesses the page table and completes the address translation if page p_i is present in memory; otherwise, it generates a page fault, which activates the virtual memory manager to load p_i in memory.

Figure 12.9 summarizes the MMU and software actions in address translation and page fault handling for a logical address (p_i, b_i). MMU actions concerning use of the TLB and the page table are as described earlier. The virtual memory manager is activated by a page fault. If an empty page frame is not available to load page p_i, it initiates a page-out operation for some page p_j to free the page frame, say page frame f_j, occupied by it. p_j's page table entry is updated to indicate that it is no longer present in memory. If p_j has an entry in the TLB, the virtual memory manager erases it by executing an "erase TLB entry" instruction. This action is essential for preventing incorrect address translation at p_j's next reference. A page-in operation is now performed to load p_i in page frame f_j, and p_i's page table entry is updated when the page-in operation is completed. Execution of the instruction that caused the page fault is repeated when the process is scheduled again. This time p_i does not have an entry in the TLB but it exists in memory, and so the MMU uses information in the page table to complete the address translation. An entry for p_i has to be made in the TLB at this time.

New entries in the TLB can be made either by the hardware or by the virtual memory manager. Hardware handling of the TLB is more efficient; the hardware can make a new entry in the TLB whenever it has to complete address translation through a reference to the page table. When the TLB is managed by the virtual memory manager, the MMU raises a "missing TLB entry" interrupt whenever it cannot find an entry for the required page in the TLB, and the virtual memory manager executes several instructions to make the TLB entry. In this approach, the MMU performs address translation exclusively through the TLB, and the page table is used only by the virtual memory manager. This arrangement provides flexibility because the virtual memory manager can use different organizations of the page table to conserve memory (see Section 12.2.3). The PowerPC and Intel 80x86 architectures use hardware-managed TLBs, while the MIPS, Sparc, Alpha, and PA-RISC architectures use software-managed TLBs.

A few features are common to both the approaches. A replacement algorithm is used to decide which TLB entry should be overwritten when a new entry is to be made. Use of the TLB can undermine protection if the MMU performs address translation through TLB entries that were made while some other process was in operation. This issue is analogous to the protection issue in a cache discussed earlier in Section 2.2.3. Hence the solutions are also analogous. Each TLB entry can contain the id of the process that was in operation when the entry was made—that is, each TLB entry can have the form (process id, page #, page frame #, protection info)—so that the MMU can avoid using it when some other process is in operation. Alternatively, the kernel must flush the TLB while performing process switching.

We use the following notation to compute the effective memory access time when a TLB is used:

pr_1	probability that a page exists in memory
pr_2	probability that a page entry exists in TLB
t_{mem}	memory access time
t_{TLB}	access time of TLB
t_{pfh}	time overhead of page fault handling

As mentioned earlier in Section 12.2.1, pr_1 is the memory hit ratio and t_{mem} is a few orders of magnitude smaller than t_{pfh}. Typically t_{TLB} is at least an order of magnitude smaller than t_{mem}. pr_2 is called the *TLB hit ratio.*

When the TLB is not used, the effective memory access time is as given by Eq. (12.2). The page table is accessed only if the page being referenced does not have an entry in the TLB. Accordingly, a page reference consumes $(t_{TLB} + t_{mem})$ time if the page has an entry in the TLB, and $(t_{TLB} + 2 \times t_{mem})$ time if it does not have a TLB entry but exists in memory. The probability of the latter situation is $(pr_1 - pr_2)$. When the TLB is used, pr_2 is the probability that an entry for the required page exists in the TLB. The probability that a page table reference is both necessary and sufficient for address translation is $(pr_1 - pr_2)$. The time consumed by each such reference is $(t_{TLB} + 2 \times t_{mem})$ since an unsuccessful TLB search would precede the page table lookup. The probability of a page fault is $(1 - pr_1)$. It occurs after the TLB and the page table have been looked up, and it requires $(t_{pfh} + t_{TLB} + 2 \times t_{mem})$ time if we assume that the TLB entry is made for the page while the effective memory address is being calculated. Hence the effective memory access time is

$$\begin{aligned}&\text{Effective memory access time} =\\ &pr_2 \times (t_{TLB} + t_{mem}) + (pr_1 - pr_2) \times (t_{TLB} + 2 \times t_{mem}) \quad \textbf{(12.3)}\\ &+ (1 - pr_1) \times (t_{TLB} + t_{mem} + t_{pfh} + t_{TLB} + 2 \times t_{mem})\end{aligned}$$

To provide efficient memory access during operation of the kernel, most computers provide *wired TLB entries* for kernel pages. These entries are never touched by replacement algorithms.

Superpages Sizes of computer memories and processes have grown rapidly since the 1990s. TLB sizes have not kept pace with this increase because TLBs are expensive as a result of their associative nature; their sizes have grown from about eight in the 1960s to only about a thousand in 2005. Hence *TLB reach*, which is the product of the number of entries in a TLB and the page size, has increased marginally, but its ratio to memory size has shrunk by a factor of over 1000. Consequently, TLB hit ratios are poor, and average memory access times are high [see Eq. (12.3)]. Processor caches have also become larger than the TLB reach, which affects performance of a cache that is searched by physical addresses because access to contents of the cache may be slowed down by TLB misses and lookups through the page table. A generic way of countering these problems is to use a larger page size, so that the TLB reach becomes larger. However, it leads to larger internal fragmentation and more page I/O. In the absence of a generic solution, techniques were developed to address specific problems created by the low TLB reach. Searching the cache by logical addresses took the TLB out of the path from the CPU to the cache, which avoided a slowdown of cache lookup due to limited TLB reach. However, poor TLB hit ratios continued to degrade virtual memory performance.

Superpages were evolved as a generic solution to the problems caused by low TLB reach. A *superpage* is like a page of a process, except that its size is a power-of-2 multiple of the size of a page, and its start address in both the logical and physical address spaces is aligned on a multiple of its own size. This feature increases the TLB reach without increasing the size of the TLB, and helps to obtain a larger TLB hit ratio. Most modern architectures permit a few standard superpage sizes and provide an additional field in a TLB entry to indicate the size of superpage that can be accessed through the entry.

The virtual memory manager exploits the superpages technique by adapting the size and number of superpages in a process to its execution characteristics. It may combine some pages of a process into a superpage of an appropriate size if the pages are accessed frequently and satisfy the requirement of contiguity and address alignment in the logical address space. This action is called a *promotion*. The virtual memory manager may have to move the individual pages in memory during promotion to ensure contiguity and address alignment in memory. A promotion increases the TLB reach, and releases some of the TLB entries that were assigned to individual pages of the new superpage.

If the virtual memory manager finds that some pages in a superpage are not accessed frequently, it may decide to disband the superpage into individual pages. This action, called *demotion*, frees some memory that can be used to load other pages. Thus, it has the potential to reduce page fault frequency.

12.2.2.3 Support for Page Replacement

The virtual memory manager needs two kinds of information for minimizing page faults and the number of page-in and page-out operations during page replacement:

1. The time when a page was last used.
2. Whether a page is *dirty*, i.e., whether a write operation has been performed on any byte in the page. (A page is *clean* if it is not dirty.)

The time of last use indicates how recently a page was used by a process; it is useful in selecting a candidate for page replacement. However, it is expensive to provide a sufficient number of bits in a page table entry for this purpose, so most computers provide a single bit called the *reference* bit. The *modified* bit in a page table entry is used to indicate whether a page is clean or dirty. If a page is clean, its copy in the swap space of the process is still current, so no page-out operation is needed; the page being loaded can simply overwrite such a page in memory. For a dirty page, a page-out operation must be performed because its copy in the swap space is stale. A page-in operation for the new page to be loaded can be started only after the page-out operation is completed.

12.2.3 Practical Page Table Organizations

A process with a large address space requires a large page table. Hence the virtual memory manager has to commit a large amount of memory for each page table. For example, in a computer system using 32-bit logical addresses and a page size of 4 KB, a process can have 1 million pages. If the size of a page table entry is 4 bytes, the page table has a size of 4 MB. Thus, the virtual memory manager might tie up a few hundred megabytes of memory for storing page tables of processes! The memory requirements would be even larger when 64-bit logical addresses are used. Two approaches are followed to reduce the size of memory committed to page tables:

- *Inverted page table*: The inverted page table (IPT) has one entry for each page frame in memory that indicates which page, if any, occupies the page frame; the table got this name because the information in it is the "inverse" of the information in a page table. The size of an inverted page table is governed by the size of memory, so it is independent of the number and sizes of processes. However, information about a page cannot be accessed directly as in a page table; it has to be searched for in the IPT.
- *Multilevel page table*: The page table of a process is itself paged; the entire page table therefore does not need to exist in memory at any time. A higher-level page table is used to access pages of the page table. If the higher-level page table is large, it could itself be paged, and so on. In this organization,

the page table entry of a page has to be accessed through relevant entries of the higher-level page tables.

In both approaches, the TLB is used to reduce the number of memory references needed to perform address translation.

12.2.3.1 Inverted Page Tables

Figure 12.10(a) illustrates address translation using an *inverted page table* (IPT). Each entry of the inverted page table is an ordered pair consisting of a process id and a page number. Thus a pair (R, p_l) in the f_lth entry indicates that page frame f_l is occupied by page p_l of a process R. While scheduling a process, the scheduler copies the id of the process from its PCB into a register of the MMU. Let this id be P. The MMU performs address translation for a logical address (p_i, b_i) in process P, using the following steps:

1. Separate the components p_i and b_i of the logical address.
2. Using the process id P, form the pair (P, p_i).
3. Search for the pair (P, p_i) in the IPT. Raise a page fault if the pair does not exist in the IPT.

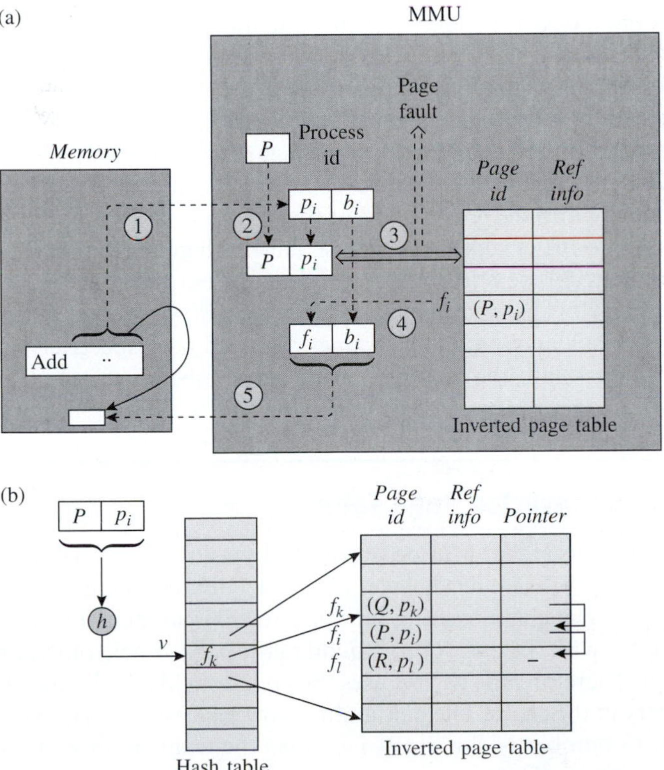

Figure 12.10 Inverted page table: (a) concept; (b) implementation using a hash table.

4. If the pair (P, p_i) exists in entry f_i of the IPT, copy the page frame number f_i for use in address translation.
5. Calculate the effective memory address using f_i and b_i.

These steps are shown as the circled numbers 1 to 5 in Figure 12.10(a).

The search for (P, p_i) in Step 3 should be conducted efficiently, otherwise it would slow down address translation. Accordingly, a *hash table* is used to speed up the search in the inverted page table. Figure 12.10(b) shows an arrangement called *hash-with-chaining*, which operates as follows: Each entry of the inverted page table contains an additional field *pointer*, which points to another entry in the same table. To hash a pair (P, p_i), we first concatenate the bit strings representing P and p_i to obtain a larger bit string. We now interpret this bit string as an integer number x, and apply the following hash function h to it:

$$h(x) = \text{remainder } (\tfrac{x}{a})$$

where a is the size of the hash table, which is typically some prime number. $h(x)$, which is in the range $0, \ldots, a-1$, is an entry number in the hash table. Let v designate its value. Hashing of many process id–page id pairs may produce the same value v, because the total number of pages of all processes in memory is much larger than the size of the hash table. Entries of all these pairs in the inverted page table are chained together by the *pointer* field.

The inverted page table is constructed and maintained by the virtual memory manager as follows: When page p_i of process P is loaded in page frame f_i in memory, the virtual memory manager stores the pair (P, p_i) in the f_ith entry of the inverted page table. It now hashes this pair to obtain an entry number, say v, and adds the f_ith entry of the inverted page table in the chain starting on the vth entry of the hash table as follows: It copies the value found in the vth entry of the hash table into the *pointer* field of the f_ith entry of the inverted page table, and enters f_i into the vth entry of the hash table. When this page is removed from memory, the virtual memory manager deletes its entry from the chain starting on the vth entry of the hash table. In Figure 12.10(b), the pages (R, p_l), (P, p_i) and (Q, p_k) were loaded into page frames f_l, f_i and f_k, respectively, and they all happened to hash into the vth entry of the hash table. Example 12.2 describes how the MMU uses the inverted page table during address translation.

Example 12.2 Search in the Inverted Page Table

The logical address (p_i, b_i) is to be translated by using the inverted page table of Figure 12.10(b). The pair (P, p_i) is hashed to obtain an entry number v in the hash table. The chain starting on this entry is searched. The pair (P, p_i) does not match with the pair (Q, p_k) found in the *page id* field of the first entry of the chain. Therefore, the MMU uses the *pointer* field of this entry to locate the next entry in the chain. The pair in this entry matches (P, p_i), so the MMU uses the entry number of this entry, i.e., f_i, as the frame number to form the physical address (f_i, b_i).

The average number of comparisons required to locate the entry of a pair (P, p_i) in the inverted page table depends on the average length of the chain starting on an entry of the hash table. Increasing the size of the hash table, a, reduces the average length of the chain. A value of $a > 2 \times \#frames$ ensures that the average number of entries in a linked list is less than 2. The inverted page table contains exactly $\#frames$ entries in it. Note that the inverted page table does not contain any information about pages that are not present in memory; a conventional page table would have to be maintained on disk to contain their information. Inverted page tables have been used in the IBM RS 6000 and AS 400 systems, and in the PowerPC and PA-RISC architectures. They have also been used in Solaris OSs for Sparc architectures.

12.2.3.2 Multilevel Page Tables

The memory requirement of the page table of a process is reduced by paging the page table itself and loading its pages on demand just like pages of processes. This approach requires a two-tiered addressing arrangement in which a higher-level page table contains entries that hold information about pages of the page table and the page table contains information concerning pages of the process. The information in each of these tables is similar to the information contained in a conventional page table. Figure 12.11 illustrates the concept of a two-level page table. Memory now contains two kinds of pages—pages of processes and pages of page tables of processes, which we shall call *PT pages*. Only three PT pages of a process P are currently in memory. For address translation of a logical address (p_i, b_i) in process P, page p_i of process P should exist in memory and the PT page that contains the entry for page p_i should also exist in memory.

As mentioned in Section 12.2, the page number and byte number in a logical address (p_i, b_i) are represented in n_p and n_b bits. The size of each page table entry is a power of 2, so the number of page table entries that fit in one PT page is also a power of 2. If the size of a table entry is 2^e bytes, the number of page table entries in one PT page is $2^{n_b}/2^e$, i.e., 2^{n_b-e}. Therefore, the page number p_i in the logical address itself consists of two parts—id of the PT page that contains the page table entry of p_i, and an entry number within the PT page. As shown in Figure 12.11, we call these two parts p_i^1 and p_i^2, respectively. From the preceding discussion, p_i^2 is contained in the lower order $n_b - e$ bits of p_i. Since the binary representation of p_i contains n_p bits, p_i^1 is contained in $n_p - (n_b - e)$ higher-order bits.

Figure 12.11 illustrates address translation for a logical address (p_i, b_i). It consists of the following steps:

1. The address (p_i, b_i) is regrouped into three fields

$n_p - (n_b - e)$	$n_b - e$	n_b
p_i^1	p_i^2	b_i

The contents of these fields are p_i^1, p_i^2 and b_i, respectively.

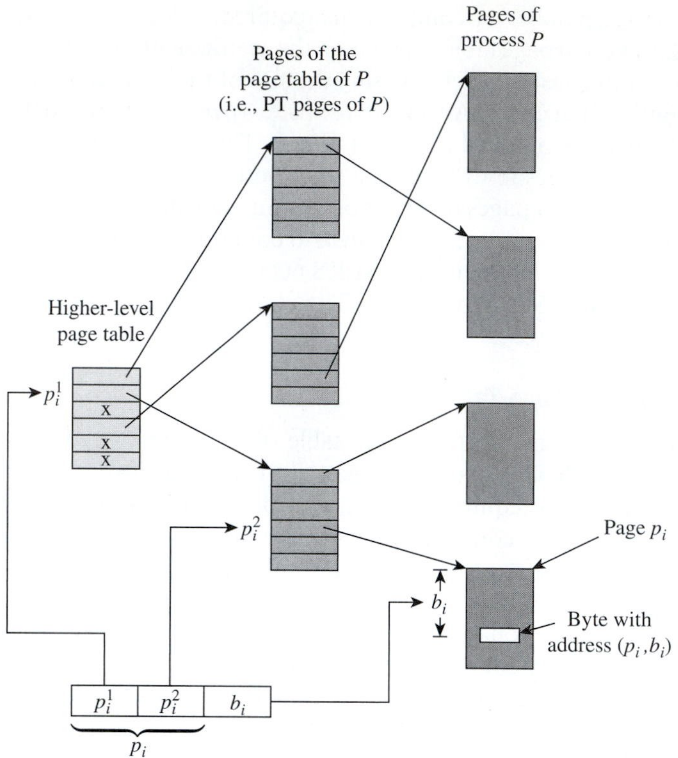

Figure 12.11 Two-level page table organization.

2. The PT page with the number p_i^1 contains the page table entry for p_i. The MMU checks whether this page exists in memory and raises a page fault if it does not. The page fault is serviced by the virtual memory manager to load the PT page in memory.
3. p_i^2 is the entry number for p_i in the PT page. The MMU uses information in this entry to check whether page p_i exists in memory and raises a page fault if it does not. The virtual memory manager services the page fault and loads page p_i in memory.
4. The contents of p_i's page table entry are used to perform address translation.

Thus, address translation requires two memory accesses—one to access the higher-level page table and another to access the page table of process P. It can be speeded up through the TLB by making two kinds of entries—entries of the form (P, p_i^1, frame number, protection info) help to eliminate accesses to the higher-level page table of process P and entries of the form (P, p_i^1, p_i^2, frame number, protection info) help to eliminate accesses to the page table of P.

When the size of the higher-level page table in a two-level page table organization is very large, the higher-level page table can itself be paged. This arrangement results in a three-level page table structure. Address translation using three-level page tables is performed by an obvious extension of address translation in two-level page tables. A logical address (p_i, b_i) is split into four components p_i^1, p_i^2, p_i^3, and b_i, and the first three components are used to address the three levels of the page table. Thus address translation requires up to three memory accesses. In computer systems using 64-bit addresses, even the highest-level page table in a three-level page table organization may become too large. Four-level page tables are used to overcome this problem.

The Intel 80386 architecture used two-level page tables. Three and four-level page tables have been used in the Sun Sparc and Motorola 68030 architectures, respectively.

12.2.4 I/O Operations in a Paged Environment

A process makes a system call for performing I/O operations. Two of its parameters are the number of bytes to be transferred and the logical address of the *data area*, which is the area of memory that participates in the data transfer. The call activates the *I/O handler* in the kernel. The I/O subsystem does not contain an MMU; it uses physical addresses to implement data transfer to and from the memory. Consequently, the I/O handler has to perform a few preparatory actions before initiating the I/O operation. The first of these is to replace the logical address of the data area with its physical address, using information from the page table of the process. It has to perform some more actions to address two more issues discussed in the following.

The data area in an I/O operation may span several pages of the process. A page fault while accessing a page of the data area would disrupt the I/O operation, so all these pages must remain in memory while I/O is being performed. The I/O handler satisfies this requirement by loading all pages of the data area into memory and putting an *I/O fix* on each page to instruct the virtual memory manager that these pages should not be replaced until the I/O fix is removed at the end of the I/O operation. It now starts the I/O operation. A simple way to implement I/O fixing of pages is to add an I/O fix bit in the *misc info* field of each page table entry.

Since the I/O subsystem operates without an MMU, it expects the data area to occupy a contiguous area of memory. However, the process is paged, hence pages of the data area may not have contiguous physical addresses. This situation can be addressed in two ways. Most I/O subsystems provide a *scatter/gather* feature, which can deposit parts of an I/O operation's data in noncontiguous areas of memory. For example, the first few bytes from an I/O record can be read into a page frame located in one part of memory and the remaining bytes can be read into another page frame located in a different part of memory. Analogously, a "gather write" can draw the data of the I/O operation from noncontiguous memory areas and write it into one record on an I/O device. Example 12.3 illustrates how a scatter-read operation is used to implement an I/O operation that spans two pages in a process. If an I/O subsystem does not provide the scatter/gather feature, the I/O handler can handle the situation in two ways. It can either instruct the virtual memory manager to put pages containing the data area contiguously in memory, or it can first read the data into a kernel area that has contiguous physical addresses and then copy it to the data area in the process. Analogous provisions can be made to support a write operation.

Example 12.3 I/O Operations in Virtual Memory

Page i_2 of a process P_i contains a system call "*perf_io* (`alpha`, read, 828, $(i_1, 520)$)," where `alpha` is a file, 828 is the count of data bytes to be read, and $(i_1, 520)$ is the logical address of the start of the data area. Figure 12.12 illustrates how the I/O operation is implemented. The page size is 1 KB, and so the data area is situated in pages i_1 and $i_1 + 1$ of the process. Before initiating the I/O operation, the I/O handler invokes the virtual memory manager to load pages i_1 and $i_1 + 1$ into memory. They are loaded into page frames 14 and 10 of memory. The I/O handler puts an I/O fix on these pages by setting the I/O fix bits in the *misc info* field of their page table entries. These pages are not replaced until the I/O fix is removed at the end of the I/O operation. The I/O handler now generates a scatter-read operation to read the first 504 bytes starting at byte number 520 in page frame 14, and the remaining 324 bytes starting at byte number 0 in page frame 10. It removes the I/O fix on pages 14 and 10 when the I/O operation completes.

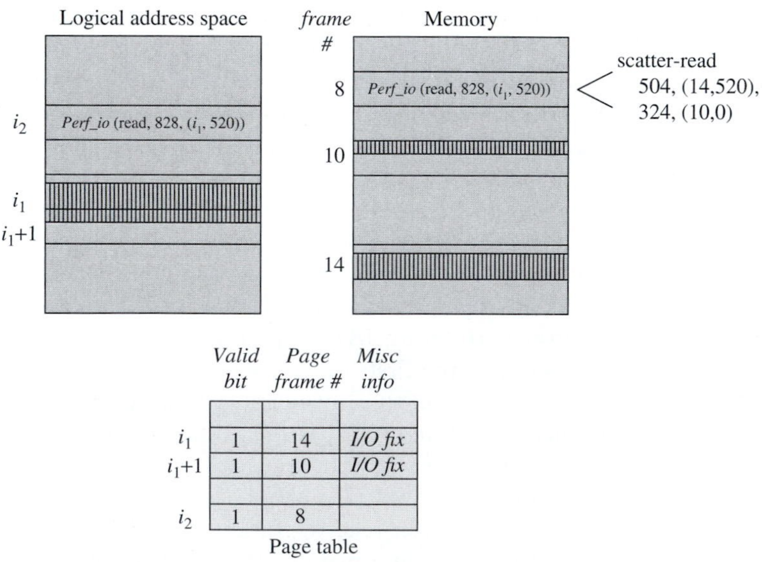

Figure 12.12 An I/O operation in virtual memory.

12.3 THE VIRTUAL MEMORY MANAGER

The virtual memory manager uses two data structures—the page table, whose entry format is shown in Figure 12.3, and the free frames list. The *ref info* and *modified* fields in a page table entry are typically set by the paging hardware. All other fields are set by the virtual memory manager itself. Table 12.4 summarizes the functions of the virtual memory manager. We discuss the first four functions in this section. Other functions—page replacement, allocation of memory to processes, and implementation of page sharing—are discussed in the next few sections.

Management of the Logical Address Space of a Process The virtual memory manager manages the logical address space of a process through the following subfunctions:

1. Organize a copy of the instructions and data of the process in its swap space.
2. Maintain the page table.
3. Perform page-in and page-out operations.
4. Perform process initiation.

As mentioned earlier in Section 12.2, a copy of the entire logical address space of a process is maintained in the swap space of the process. When a reference to a page leads to a page fault, the page is loaded from the swap space by using a page-in operation. When a dirty page is to be removed from memory, a page-out operation is performed to copy it from memory into a disk block in the swap

Table 12.4 Functions of the Virtual Memory Manager

Function	Description
Manage logical address space	Set up the swap space of a process. Organize its logical address space in memory through page-in and page-out operations, and maintain its page table.
Manage memory	Keep track of occupied and free page frames in memory.
Implement memory protection	Maintain the information needed for memory protection.
Collect page reference information	Paging hardware provides information concerning page references. This information is maintained in appropriate data structures for use by the page replacement algorithm.
Perform page replacement	Perform replacement of a page when a page fault arises and all page frames in memory, or all page frames allocated to a process, are occupied.
Allocate physical memory	Decide how much memory should be allocated to a process and revise this decision from time to time to suit the needs of the process and the OS.
Implement page sharing	Arrange sharing of pages be processes.

space. Thus the copy of a page in the swap space is current if that page is not in memory, or it is in memory but it has not been modified since it was last loaded. For other pages the copy in the swap space is stale (i.e., outdated), whereas that in memory is current.

One issue in swap space management is size of the swap space of a process. Most virtual memory implementations permit the logical address space of a process to grow dynamically during its operation. This can happen for a variety of reasons. The size of stack or PCD data areas may grow (see Section 11.4.2), or the process may dynamically link more modules or may perform memory mapping of files (see Section 12.7). An obvious approach to handling dynamic growth of address spaces is to allocate swap space dynamically and noncontiguously. However, this approach faces the problem that the virtual memory manager may run out of swap space during operation of a process.

To initiate a process, only the page containing its *start address*, i.e., address of its first instruction, need managers to be loaded in memory. Other pages are brought in on demand. Details of the page table and the page-in and page-out operations have been described earlier in Section 12.2.

Management of Memory The free frames list is maintained at all times. A page frame is taken off the free list to load a new page, and a frame is added to it when a page-out operation is performed. All page frames allocated to a process are added to the free list when the process terminates.

Protection During process creation, the virtual memory manager constructs its page table and puts information concerning the start address of the page table and its size in the PCB of the process. The virtual memory manager records access privileges of the process for a page in the *prot info* field of its page table entry. During dispatching of the process, the kernel loads the page-table start address of the process and its page-table size into registers of the MMU. During translation of a logical address (p_i, b_i), the MMU ensures that the entry of page p_i exists in the page table and contains appropriate access privileges in the *prot info* field.

Collection of Information for Page Replacement The *ref info* field of the page table entry of a page indicates when the page was last referenced, and the *modified* field indicates whether it has been modified since it was last loaded in memory. Page reference information is useful only so long as a page remains in memory; it is reinitialized the next time a page-in operation is performed for the page. Most computers provide a single bit in the *ref info* field to collect page reference information. This information is not adequate to select the best candidate for page replacement. Hence the virtual memory manager may periodically reset the bit used to store this information. We discuss this aspect in Section 12.4.1.

Example 12.4 Page Replacement

The memory of a computer consists of eight page frames. A process P_1 consists of five pages numbered 0 to 4. Only pages 1, 2, and 3 are in memory at the moment; they occupy page frames 2, 7, and 4, respectively. Remaining page

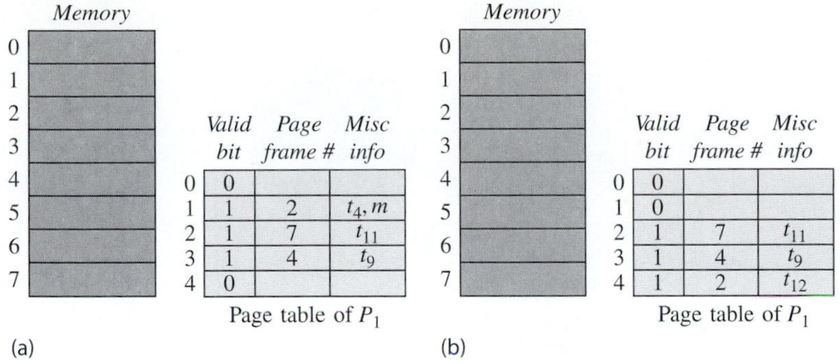

Figure 12.13 Data structures of the virtual memory manager: (a) before and (b) after a page replacement.

frames have been allocated to other processes and no free page frames are left in the system.

Figure 12.13(a) illustrates the situation in the system at time instant t_{11}^{+}, i.e., a little after t_{11}. Only the page table of P_1 is shown in the figure since process P_1 has been scheduled. Contents of the *ref info* and *modified* fields are shown in the *misc info* field. Pages 1, 2, and 3 were last referenced at time instants t_4, t_{11}, and t_9, respectively. Page 1 was modified sometime after it was last loaded. Hence the *misc info* field of its page table entry contains the information t_4, m.

At time instant t_{12}, process P_1 gives rise to a page fault for page 4. Since all page frames in memory are occupied, the virtual memory manager decides to replace page 1 of the process. The mark m in the *misc info* field of page 1's page table entry indicates that it was modified since it was last loaded, so a page-out operation is necessary. The *page frame #* field of the page table entry of page 1 indicates that the page exists in page frame 2. The virtual memory manager performs a page-out operation to write the contents of page frame 2 into the swap area reserved for page 1 of P_1, and modifies the *valid* bit in the page table entry of page 1 to indicate that it is not present in memory. A page-in operation is now initiated for page 4 of P_1. At the end of the operation, the page table entry of page 4 is modified to indicate that it exists in memory in page frame 2. Execution of P_1 is resumed. It now makes a reference to page 4, and so the page reference information of page 4 indicates that it was last referenced at t_{12}. Figure 12.13(b) indicates the page table of P_1 at time instant t_{12}^{+}.

12.3.1 Overview of Operation of the Virtual Memory Manager

The virtual memory manager makes two important decisions during its operation:

- When a page fault occurs during operation of some process $proc_i$, it decides which page should be replaced.

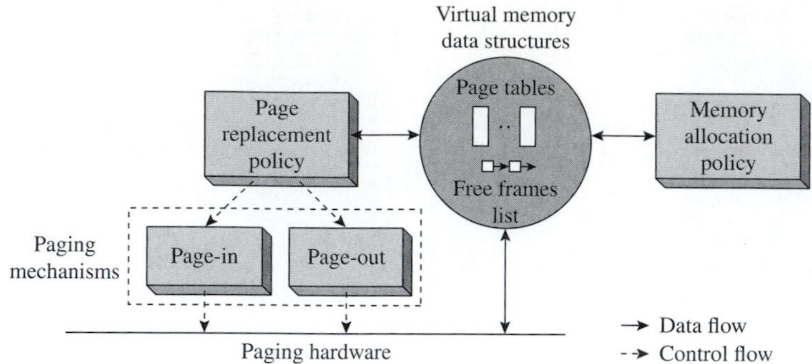

Figure 12.14 Modules of the virtual memory manager.

- Periodically it decides how much memory, i.e., how many page frames, should be allocated to each process.

As discussed in later sections, these decisions are taken independently of one another. When a page fault occurs, the virtual memory manager merely replaces a page of the same process if all page frames allocated to the process are occupied. When it decides to increase or decrease memory committed for a process, it merely specifies the new number of page frames that should be allocated to each process.

Figure 12.14 depicts the arrangement of policy and mechanism modules of the virtual memory manager. The page replacement policy uses the page reference information available in the virtual memory manager's data structures, and updates the page tables to reflect its decisions. It is implemented using page-in and page-out operations as mechanisms. The page-in and page-out mechanisms interact with the paging hardware to implement their functionalities. The paging hardware updates page reference information maintained in virtual memory manager's tables. The memory allocation policy uses the information in the page tables and the free frames list to periodically decide whether and how to vary the memory allocated to each process. We use the following notation for the memory allocated to each process:

$alloc_i$ Number of page frames allocated to process $proc_i$

We omit the subscript of $alloc_i$ when only one process is under consideration.

12.4 PAGE REPLACEMENT POLICIES

As discussed earlier in Section 12.2.1.1, a page replacement policy should replace a page that is not likely to be referenced in the immediate future. We evaluate the following three page replacement policies to see how well they fulfill this requirement.

- Optimal page replacement policy
- First-in, first-out (FIFO) page replacement policy
- Least recently used (LRU) page replacement policy

For our analysis of these page replacement policies, we rely on the concept of *page reference strings*. A page reference string of a process is a trace of the pages accessed by the process during its operation. It can be constructed by monitoring the operation of a process, and forming a sequence of page numbers that appear in logical addresses generated by it. The page reference string of a process depends on the data input to it, so use of different data would lead to a different page reference string for a process.

For convenience we associate a *reference time string* $t_1, t_2, t_3, \ldots$ with each page reference string. This way, the kth page reference in a page reference string is assumed to have occurred at time instant t_k. (In effect, we assume a *logical clock* that runs only when a process is in the *running* state and gets advanced only when the process refers to a logical address.) Example 12.5 illustrates the page reference string and the associated reference time string for a process.

Page Reference String

Example 12.5

A computer supports instructions that are 4 bytes in length, and uses a page size of 1 KB. It executes the following nonsense program in which the symbols A and B are in pages 2 and 5, respectively:

```
      START  2040
      READ   B
LOOP  MOVER  AREG, A
      SUB    AREG, B
      BC     LT, LOOP
      ...
      STOP
A     DS     2500
B     DS     1
      END
```

The page reference string and the reference time string for the process are as follows:

Page reference string	1, 5, 1, 2, 2, 5, 2, 1, ...
Reference time string	$t_1, t_2, t_3, t_4, t_5, t_6, t_7, t_8, \ldots$

The logical address of the first instruction is 2040, and so it lies in page 1. The first page reference in the string is therefore 1. It occurs at time instant t_1. B, the operand of the instruction is situated in page 5, and so the second page reference in the string is 5, at time t_2. The next instruction is located in page 1 and refers to A, which is located in page 2, and thus the next two page references are to pages 1 and 2. The next two instructions are located in page 2, and the instruction with the label LOOP is located in page 1. Therefore, if the value of B input to the READ statement is greater than the value of A, the next four page references would be to pages 2, 5, 2 and 1, respectively; otherwise, the next four page references would be to pages 2, 5, 2 and 2, respectively.

Optimal Page Replacement *Optimal* page replacement means making page replacement decisions in such a manner that the total number of page faults during operation of a process is the minimum possible; i.e., no other sequence of page replacement decisions can lead to a smaller number of page faults. To achieve optimal page replacement, at each page fault, the page replacement policy would have to consider all alternative page replacement decisions, analyze their implications for future page faults, and select the best alternative. Of course, such a policy is infeasible in reality: the virtual memory manager does not have knowledge of the future behavior of a process. As an analytical tool, however, this policy provides a useful comparison in hindsight for the performance of other page replacement policies (see Example 12.6, below, and Exercise 12.5).

Although optimal page replacement might seem to require excessive analysis, Belady (1966) showed that it is equivalent to the following simple rule: At a page fault, replace the page whose next reference is farthest in the page reference string.

FIFO Page Replacement At every page fault, the FIFO page replacement policy replaces the page that was loaded into memory earlier than any other page of the process. To facilitate FIFO page replacement, the virtual memory manager records the time of loading of a page in the *ref info* field of its page table entry. When a page fault occurs, this information is used to determine $p_{earliest}$, the page that was loaded earlier than any other page of the process. This is the page that will be replaced with the page whose reference led to the page fault.

LRU Page Replacement The LRU policy uses the law of locality of reference as the basis for its replacement decisions. Its operation can be described as follows: At every page fault the *least recently used* (LRU) page is replaced by the required page. The page table entry of a page records the time when the page was last referenced. This information is initialized when a page is loaded, and it is updated every time the page is referenced. When a page fault occurs, this information is used to locate the page p_{LRU} whose last reference is earlier than that of every other page. This page is replaced with the page whose reference led to the page fault.

Analysis of Page Replacement Policies Example 12.6 illustrates operation of the optimal, FIFO, and LRU page replacement policies.

Example 12.6 Operation of Page Replacement Policies

A page reference string and the reference time string for a process P are as follows:

Page reference string	0, 1, 0, 2, 0, 1, 2, ...	**(12.4)**
Reference time string	$t_1, t_2, t_3, t_4, t_5, t_6, t_7, \ldots$	**(12.5)**

Figure 12.15 illustrates operation of the optimal, FIFO and LRU page replacement policies for this page reference string with $alloc = 2$. For convenience, we show only two fields of the page table, *valid bit* and *ref info*. In the interval t_0

Time instant	Page ref	Optimal: Valid bit, Ref info	Optimal: Replacement	FIFO: Valid bit, Ref info	FIFO: Replacement	LRU: Valid bit, Ref info	LRU: Replacement
t_1	0	0 1 1 0 2 0	–	0 1 t_1 1 0 2 0	–	0 1 t_1 1 0 2 0	–
t_2	1	0 1 1 1 2 0	–	0 1 t_1 1 1 t_2 2 0	–	0 1 t_1 1 1 t_2 2 0	–
t_3	0	0 1 1 1 2 0	–	0 1 t_1 1 1 t_2 2 0	–	0 1 t_1 1 1 t_2 2 0	–
t_4	2	0 1 1 0 2 1	Replace 1 by 2	0 0 1 1 t_2 2 1 t_4	Replace 0 by 2	0 1 t_3 1 0 2 1 t_4	Replace 1 by 2
t_5	0	0 1 1 0 2 1	–	0 1 t_5 1 0 2 1 t_4	Replace 1 by 0	0 1 t_5 1 0 2 1 t_4	–
t_6	1	0 0 1 1 2 1	Replace 0 by 1	0 1 t_5 1 1 t_6 2 0	Replace 2 by 1	0 1 t_5 1 1 t_6 2 0	Replace 2 by 1
t_7	2	0 0 1 1 2 1	–	0 0 1 1 t_6 2 1 t_7	Replace 0 by 2	0 0 1 1 t_6 2 1 t_7	Replace 0 by 2

Figure 12.15 Comparison of page replacement policies with *alloc* = 2.

to t_3 (inclusive), only two distinct pages are referenced: pages 0 and 1. They can both be accommodated in memory at the same time because *alloc* = 2. t_4 is the first time instant when a page fault leads to page replacement.

The left column shows the results for optimal page replacement. Page reference information is not shown in the page table since information concerning past references is not needed for optimal page replacement. When the page fault occurs at time instant t_4, page 1 is replaced because its next reference is farther in the page reference string than that of page 0. At time t_6 page 1 replaces page 0 because page 0's next reference is farther than that of page 2.

The middle column of Figure 12.15 shows the results for the FIFO replacement policy. When the page fault occurs at time t_4, the *ref info* field shows that page 0 was loaded earlier than page 1, and so page 0 is replaced by page 2.

The last column of Figure 12.15 shows the results for the LRU replacement policy. The *ref info* field of the page table indicates when a page was last referenced. At time t_4, page 1 is replaced by page 2 because the last reference of page 1 is earlier than the last reference of page 0.

The total number of page faults occurring under the optimal, FIFO, and LRU policies are 4, 6, and 5, respectively. By definition, no other policy has fewer page faults than the optimal page replacement policy.

When we analyze why the LRU policy performed better than the FIFO policy in Example 12.6, we find that the FIFO policy removed page 0 at time t_4 but LRU did not do so because it had been referenced later than page 1. This decision is consistent with the law of locality of reference, which indicates that because page 0 was referenced more recently than page 1, it has a higher probability of being referenced again than page 1. The LRU policy performed better because page 0 was indeed referenced earlier after time t_4 than page 1 was. However, the LRU page replacement policy may not perform better than the FIFO policy if references in a page reference string do not follow the law of locality of reference. For example, for $alloc = 3$, the LRU and FIFO policies would perform identically for the page reference string $0, 1, 2, 3, 0, 1, 2, 3$, while the LRU policy would perform worse than the FIFO policy for the string $0, 1, 2, 0, 3, 1$. However, such situations are not encountered frequently.

To achieve the desirable page fault characteristic of Figure 12.6, a page replacement policy must possess the *stack property* (also called the *inclusion property*). It is defined by using the following notation:

$\{p_i\}_n^k$	Set of pages existing in memory at time instant t_k^+ if $alloc_i = n$ all through the operation of process $proc_i$ (t_k^+ implies a time after time instant t_k but before t_{k+1}).

Definition 12.3 Stack Property A page replacement policy possesses the *stack property* if

$$\{p_i\}_n^k \subseteq \{p_i\}_m^k \quad \text{for all } n, m \text{ such that } n < m.$$

Figure 12.16 illustrates $\{p_i\}_n^k$ for different values of n for a page replacement policy. We find that $\{p_i\}_n^k \subseteq \{p_i\}_{n+1}^k$ for $n = 1, \ldots, 4$. Hence the algorithm possesses the stack property.

To understand how the stack property ensures the desirable page fault characteristic of Figure 12.6, consider two runs of process $proc_i$, one with $alloc_i = n$ all through the execution, and another with $alloc_i = m$, such that $n < m$. If a

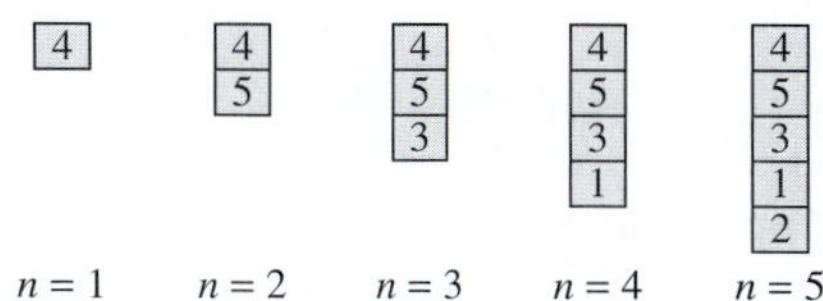

Figure 12.16 $\{p_i\}_n^k$ for different n for a page replacement policy processing the stack property.

page replacement policy exhibits the stack property, then at identical points during these operations of $proc_i$ (i.e., at identical time instants) all pages that were in memory when $alloc_i = n$ would also be in memory when $alloc_i = m$. In addition, memory also contains $m - n$ other pages of the process. If any of these pages are referenced in the next few page references of $proc_i$, page faults occur if $alloc_i = n$, but not if $alloc_i = m$. Thus the page fault rate is higher if $alloc_i = n$ than if $alloc_i = m$. This satisfies the page fault characteristic of Figure 12.6. The page fault rates will be identical if these $m - n$ pages are not referenced in the next few page references. However, in no case will the page fault rate increase when the memory allocation for a process is increased. If a page replacement policy does not exhibit the stack property, then $\{p_i\}_m^k$ may not contain some page(s) contained in $\{p_i\}_n^k$. References to these pages would result in page faults. Hence the page fault rate can increase when the memory allocation for a process is increased.

Example 12.7 illustrates that the FIFO page replacement policy does not exhibit the stack property. One can prove that the LRU page replacement policy exhibits the stack property (see Exercise 12.9).

Problems in FIFO Page Replacement

Example 12.7

Consider the following page reference and reference time strings for a process:

$$\text{Page reference string} \quad 5, 4, 3, 2, 1, 4, 3, 5, 4, 3, 2, 1, 5, \ldots \tag{12.6}$$

$$\text{Reference time string} \quad t_1, t_2, t_3, t_4, t_5, t_6, t_7, t_8, t_9, t_{10}, t_{11}, t_{12}, t_{13}, \ldots \tag{12.7}$$

Figure 12.17 shows operation of the FIFO and LRU page replacement policies for this page reference string. Page references that cause page faults and result in page replacement are marked with a * mark. A column of boxes is associated with each time instant. Each box is a page frame; the number contained in it indicates which page occupies it *after* execution of the memory reference marked under the column.

For FIFO page replacement, we have $\{p_i\}_4^{12} = \{2, 1, 4, 3\}$, while $\{p_i\}_3^{12} = \{1, 5, 2\}$. Thus, FIFO page replacement does not exhibit the stack property. This leads to a page fault at t_{13} when $alloc_i = 4$, but not when $alloc_i = 3$. Thus, a total of 10 page faults arise in 13 time instants when $alloc_i = 4$, while 9 page faults arise when $alloc_i = 3$. For LRU, we see that $\{p_i\}_3 \subseteq \{p_i\}_4$ at all time instants.

Figure 12.18 illustrates the page fault characteristic of FIFO and LRU page replacement for page reference string (12.6). For simplicity, the vertical axis shows the total number of page faults rather than the page fault frequency. Figure 12.18(a) illustrates an anomaly in behavior of FIFO page replacement—the number of page faults increases when memory allocation for the process is increased. This anomalous behavior was first reported by Belady and is therefore known as Belady's anomaly.

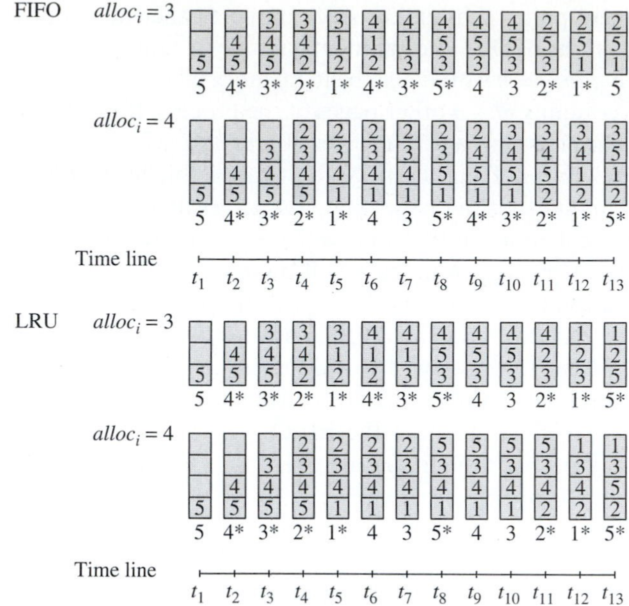

Figure 12.17 Performance of FIFO and LRU page replacement.

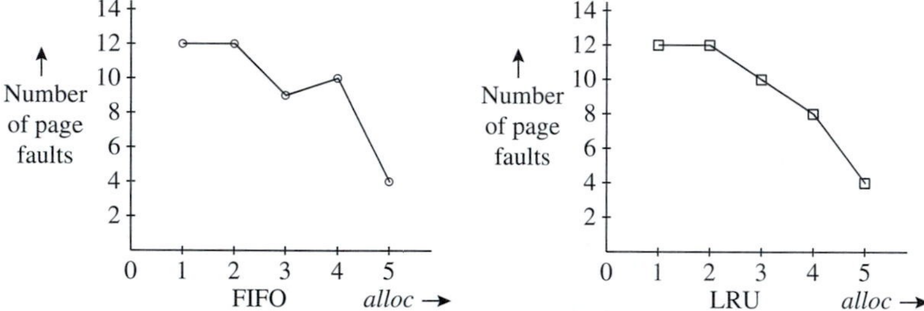

Figure 12.18 (a) Belady's anomaly in FIFO page replacement; (b) page fault characteristic for LRU page replacement.

The virtual memory manager cannot use FIFO page replacement because increasing the allocation to a process may increase the page fault frequency of the process. This feature would make it difficult to combat thrashing in the system. However, when LRU page replacement is used, the number of page faults is a nonincreasing function of *alloc*. Hence it is possible to combat thrashing by increasing the value of *alloc* for each process.

12.4.1 Practical Page Replacement Policies

Figure 12.19 shows a schematic diagram of a practical virtual memory manager. The virtual memory manager maintains a free frames list and tries to keep a few page frames in this list at all times. The virtual memory manager consists

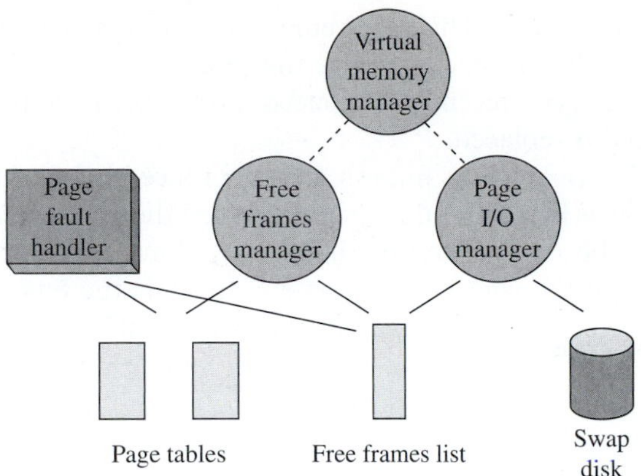

Figure 12.19 Page replacement in practice.

of two daemon threads. The thread called *free frames manager* is activated by the virtual memory manager when the number of free page frames drops below a threshold defined by the virtual memory manager. The free frames manager scans the pages present in memory to identify a few pages that can be freed, and adds the page frames occupied by these pages to the free frames list. If the page contained in a newly added page frame is dirty, it marks the page frame as *dirty* in the free frames list. It also resets the *valid* bit of this page in the page table of the process to which it belongs. The free frames manager puts itself to sleep when the number of free page frames exceeds another threshold of the virtual memory manager. The thread called *page I/O manager* performs page-out operations on dirty page frames in the free frames list; it resets the *dirty* bit of a page frame when its page-out operation is completed.

The page fault handler runs as an event handler of the kernel. It is activated when a page fault occurs. It first checks whether the required page exists in any of the page frames in the free frames list. If so, it simply reclaims the page by removing its page frame from the free frames list, setting the *valid* bit of the page in the page table of the process and copying the value of the *dirty* bit of the page frame into the *modified* bit of the page. This operation makes the required page available without having to perform a page-in operation. If the required page does not exist in any page frame, it takes a clean page frame off the free frames list and starts the page-in operation on it.

Effectively, the page replacement policy is implemented in the free frames manager of the virtual memory manager; however, in the following we will discuss page replacement as if it were done directly by the virtual memory manager. The LRU page replacement policy should be the automatic choice for implementation in a virtual memory manager because it exhibits the stack property. However, LRU page replacement is not feasible because computers do not provide sufficient bits in the *ref info* field to store the time of last reference—most computers provide a single reference bit for collecting information about references to a page. Therefore page replacement policies have to be implemented using only the reference bit. This requirement has led to a class of policies called *not recently used* (NRU) policies, where the reference bit is used to determine whether a page has been recently referenced, and some page that has not been recently referenced is replaced.

A simple NRU policy is as follows: The reference bit of a page is initialized to 0 when the page is loaded, and it is set to 1 when the page is referenced. When page replacement becomes necessary, if the virtual memory manager finds that the reference bits of all pages have become 1, it resets the bits of all pages to 0 and arbitrarily selects one of the pages for replacement; otherwise, it replaces a page whose reference bit is 0. Future page replacement would depend on which of the pages were referenced after the reference bits were reset. Page replacement algorithms called *clock algorithms* provide better discrimination between pages by resetting reference bits of pages periodically, rather than only when all of them become 1, so that it would be possible to know whether a page has been referenced in the immediate past, say within the past 100 instructions, rather than since the time when all reference bits were reset to 0.

Clock Algorithms In clock algorithms, pages of all processes in memory are entered in a circular list and pointers used by the algorithms move over the pages repeatedly. The algorithms get their name from the fact that movement of the pointers is analogous to movement of the hands of a clock over the clock dial. The page pointed to by a pointer is examined, a suitable action is performed on it, and the pointer is advanced to point to the next page. The clock algorithms can also be applied at the level of a single process when the memory allocation for a process is to be decreased. In this case, the virtual memory manager would maintain a separate list of pages for each process and the clock algorithm would scan only the list of the process whose memory allocation is to be decreased.

In the *one-handed clock algorithm*, a scan consists of two passes over all pages. In the first pass, the virtual memory manager simply resets the reference bit of the page pointed to by the pointer. In the second pass it finds all pages whose reference bits are still off and adds them to the free list. In the *two-handed clock algorithm*, two pointers are maintained. One pointer, which we will call the *resetting pointer* (RP), is used for resetting the reference bits and the other pointer, which we will call the *examining pointer* (EP), is used for checking the reference bits. Both pointers are incremented simultaneously. The page frame to which the checking pointer points is added to the free frames list if its reference bit is *off*. Example 12.8 describes operation of the two-handed clock algorithm.

Example 12.8 Two-Handed Clock Algorithm

Figure 12.20 illustrates operation of the two-handed clock algorithm when used by the free frames manager of Figure 12.19. The *ref* mark against a page implies that the reference bit of the page is set to 1; absence of this mark implies that the reference bit is 0. When the free frames manager is activated, it examines page 7, which is pointed to by the examining pointer [see Figure 12.20(a)]. Its reference bit is 1, so both the resetting and examining

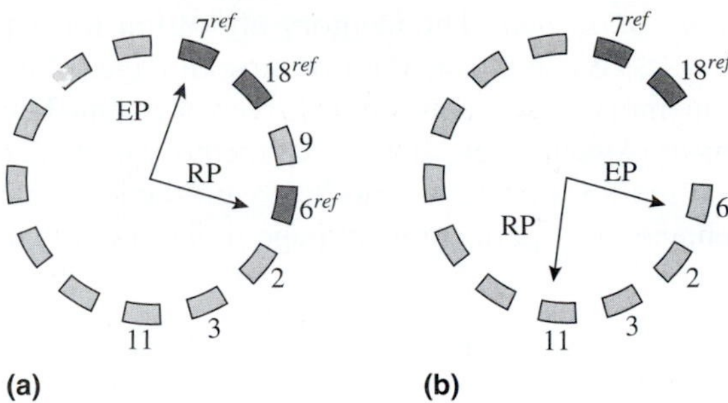

Figure 12.20 Operation of the two-handed clock algorithm.

pointers are advanced. At this time, the reference bit of page 6 is reset to 0 because RP was pointing to it. The examining pointer moves over page 18 (and the resetting pointer moves over page 2) because it, too, has its reference bit set to 1. It now rests on page 9. Page 9 has its reference bit 0, so it is removed from the list of pages in memory and added to the free frames list. The resetting and examining pointers now point to pages 6 and 11, respectively [see Figure 12.20(b)].

The distance between the resetting and examining pointers gives different properties to the page replacement algorithm. If the clock pointers are close together, a page will be examined very soon after its reference bit has been reset, hence only recently used pages will survive in memory. If the clock pointers are far apart, only pages that have not been used in a long time would be removed.

12.5 CONTROLLING MEMORY ALLOCATION TO A PROCESS

Section 12.2 described how an overcommitment of memory to processes affects system performance because of a low degree of multiprogramming, whereas an undercommitment of memory to processes leads to *thrashing*, which is characterized by high page I/O, low CPU efficiency, and poor performance of processes and the system. Keeping the memory allocation for a process within the desirable operating zone shown in Figure 12.6 avoids both overcommitment and undercommitment of memory to a process. However, it is not clear how the virtual memory manager should decide the correct number of page frames to be allocated to each process, that is, the correct value of *alloc* for each process.

Two approaches have been used to control the memory allocation for a process:

- *Fixed memory allocation:* The memory allocation for a process is fixed. Hence performance of a process is independent of other processes in the system. When a page fault occurs in a process, one of its own pages is replaced. This approach is called *local page replacement*.

- *Variable memory allocation:* The memory allocation for a process may be varied in two ways: When a page fault occurs, all pages of all processes that are present in memory may be considered for replacement. This is called *global page replacement*. Alternatively, the virtual memory manager may revise the memory allocation for a process periodically on the basis of its locality and page fault behavior, but perform local page replacement when a page fault occurs.

In fixed memory allocation, memory allocation decisions are performed statically. The memory to be allocated to a process is determined according to some criterion when the process is initiated. To name a simple example, the memory allocated to a process could be a fixed fraction of its size. Page replacement is always performed locally. The approach is simple to implement, and the overhead of page replacement is moderate, as only pages of the executing process are considered in a page replacement decision. However, the approach suffers from all problems connected with a static decision. An undercommitment or overcommitment of memory to a process would affect the process's own performance and performance of the system. Also, the system can encounter thrashing.

In variable memory allocation using global page replacement, the allocation for the currently operating process may grow too large. For example, if an LRU or NRU page replacement policy is used, the virtual memory manager will be replacing pages of other processes most of the time because their last references will precede references to pages of the currently operating process. Memory allocation to a blocked process would shrink, and so the process would face high page fault rates when it is scheduled again.

In variable memory allocation using local page replacement, the virtual memory manager determines the correct value of *alloc* for a process from time to time. In the following, we discuss how this can be done in practice.

Working Set Model The concept of a *working set* provides a basis for deciding how many and which pages of a process should be in memory to obtain good performance of the process. A virtual memory manager following the working set model is said to be using a *working set memory allocator*.

Definition 12.4 Working Set The set of pages of a process that have been referenced in the previous Δ instructions of the process, where Δ is a parameter of the system.

The previous Δ instructions are said to constitute the *working set window*. We introduce the following notation for our discussion:

$WS_i(t, \Delta)$	Working set for process $proc_i$ at time t for window size Δ
$WSS_i(t, \Delta)$	Size of the working set $WS_i(t, \Delta)$, i.e., the number of pages in $WS_i(t, \Delta)$.

Note that $WSS_i(t, \Delta) \leq \Delta$ because a page may be referenced more than once in a working set window. We omit (t, Δ) when t and Δ are either unimportant or obvious from the context.

A working set memory allocator either holds the complete working set of a process in memory, or suspends the process. Thus, at any time instant t, a process $proc_i$ either has WS_i in memory and $alloc_i = WSS_i$, or it has $alloc_i = 0$. This strategy helps in ensuring a good hit ratio in memory through the law of locality of reference. It also prevents undercommitment of memory to a process, thereby preventing thrashing.

The working set memory allocator must vary the degree of multiprogramming in accordance with changes in working set sizes of processes. For example, if $\{proc_k\}$ is the set of processes in memory, the degree of multiprogramming should be decreased if

$$\Sigma_k WSS_k > \#frames$$

where $\#frames$ is the total number of page frames in memory. The working set memory allocator removes some processes from memory until $\Sigma_k WSS_k \leq \#frames$. The degree of multiprogramming should be increased if $\Sigma_k WSS_k < \#frames$ and there exists a process $proc_g$ such that

$$WSS_g \leq (\#frames - \Sigma_k WSS_k)$$

$proc_g$ should now be allocated WSS_g page frames and its operation should be resumed.

Variations in the degree of multiprogramming are implemented as follows: The virtual memory manager maintains two items of information for each process—$alloc_i$ and WSS_i. When the degree of multiprogramming is to be reduced, the virtual memory manager selects the process to be suspended, say, process $proc_i$. It now performs a page-out operation for each modified page of $proc_i$ and changes the status of all page frames allocated to it to *free*. $alloc_i$ is set to 0; however, the value of WSS_i is left unchanged. When the degree of multiprogramming is to be increased and the virtual memory manager decides to resume $proc_i$, it sets $alloc_i = WSS_i$ and allocates as many page frames as the value of $alloc_i$. It now loads the page of $proc_i$ that contains the next instruction to be executed. Other pages would be loaded when page faults occur. Alternatively, the virtual memory manager loads all pages of WS_i when execution of $proc_i$ is resumed. However, this approach may lead to redundant loading of pages because some pages in WS_i may not be referenced again.

Performance of a working set memory allocator is sensitive to the value of Δ. If Δ is too large, memory will contain some pages that are not likely to be referenced again. This is overcommitment of memory to processes. Too large a value of Δ also forces the virtual memory manager to reduce the degree of multiprogramming, thereby affecting system performance. If Δ is too small, there is a danger of undercommitment of memory to processes, leading to an increase in page fault frequency and the possibility of thrashing.

Implementation of a Working Set Memory Allocator Use of a working set memory allocator suffers from one practical difficulty. It is expensive to determine $WS_i(t, \Delta)$ and $alloc_i$ at every time instant t. To address this difficulty, a virtual

Process	t_{100}		t_{200}		t_{300}		t_{400}	
	WSS	*alloc*	*WSS*	*alloc*	*WSS*	*alloc*	*WSS*	*alloc*
P_1	14	14	12	12	14	14	13	13
P_2	20	20	24	24	11	11	25	25
P_3	18	18	19	19	20	20	18	18
P_4	10	0	10	0	10	10	12	0

Figure 12.21 Operation of a working set memory allocator.

memory manager using a working set memory allocator can determine the working sets of processes periodically rather than at every time instant. Working sets determined at the end of an interval are used to decide values of *alloc* for use during the next interval. The next example illustrates this approach.

Example 12.9 Working Set Memory Allocator

A virtual memory manager has 60 page frames available for allocation to user processes. It recomputes the working sets of all processes at time instants $t^+_{j \times 100}, j = 1, 2 \ldots$. Following the computation of working sets, it handles each process P_i as follows: It sets $alloc_i = WSS_i$ if it can allocate WSS_i page frames to it, else it sets $alloc_i = 0$ and removes all pages of P_i from memory. The value of *alloc* assigned at $t^+_{j \times 100}$ is held constant until $t_{(j+1) \times 100}$.

Figure 12.21 illustrates operation of the working set memory allocator. It shows values of *alloc* and *WSS* for all processes at time instants t^+_{100}, t^+_{200}, t^+_{300}, and t^+_{400}. At t^+_{100}, $WSS_4 = 10$, $alloc_4 = 0$, and $\Sigma_{i=1,\ldots,3} WSS_i = 52$. It implies that the working set size of P_4 is 10 page frames, however, its operation has been suspended because only $60 - 52$, i.e., 8, page frames are free. At t^+_{200}, values of WSS_i, $i = 1, \ldots, 3$ are recomputed. The value of WSS_4 is carried over from t^+_{100} since P_4 has not been executed in the interval t_{100}–t_{200}. $alloc_i$, $i = 1, \ldots, 3$ are now assigned new values. P_4 still cannot be swapped in for lack of memory since $\Sigma_{i=1,\ldots,3} WSS_i = 55$, so only five page frames are free and $WSS_4 = 10$. At t_{300}, P_4 is swapped in; however, it is swapped out again at t_{400}. Note that during the interval $t_{100} - t_{400}$ the smallest allocation for P_2 is 11 page frames and the largest allocation is 25 page frames. This variation is performed to adjust the process's memory allocation to its recent behavior.

Expansion and contraction of *alloc* is performed as follows: At t_{200}, the virtual memory manager decides to reduce $alloc_1$ from 14 page frames to 12 page frames, so it uses an NRU-like policy to remove two pages of P_1. At t_{300}, it increases $alloc_1$ to 14 page frames, so it allocates two more page frames to $alloc_1$. These page frames will be used when page faults arise during operation of P_1.

The virtual memory manager can use the reference bits provided by the paging hardware to determine the working sets. Reference bits of all pages in memory can be turned off when working sets are determined. These bits will be turned on again as these pages get referenced during the next interval. While performing page replacements, the virtual memory manager can record which of the replaced pages had their reference bits *on*. The working set at the end of the next interval will consist of these pages and all pages in memory whose reference bits are on.

Implementation of working sets in this manner faces one problem. Resetting of reference bits at the end of an interval would interfere with page replacement decisions. If a page fault occurs in a process soon after working sets are determined, the reference bits of most of the process's pages in memory will be *off*. Hence the virtual memory manager cannot differentiate between these pages for page replacement. If some processes either remain blocked or do not get an opportunity to execute all through an interval, their allocations will shrink unnecessarily. This aspect makes it difficult to decide on the correct size of Δ, the working set window.

An alternative is to use a working set window for each process individually. However, it would complicate the virtual memory manager and add to its overhead. It would also not address the issue of interference with the page replacement decisions. For these reasons, operating systems do not actually determine working sets of processes according to Definition 12.4. In Section 12.8.4 we describe how the Windows operating systems use the notion of working set of a process.

12.6 SHARED PAGES

Sharing of programs was discussed in Section 11.3.3. *Static sharing* results from static binding performed by a linker or loader before execution of a program begins (see Section 11.3.3.2). Figure 12.22(a) shows the logical address space of program C. The `Add` (4,12) instruction in page 1 has its operand in page 4. With static binding, if two processes A and B statically share program C, then C is included in the code of both A and B. Let the 0th page of C become page i of process A [see Figure 12.22(a)]. The instruction `Add` (4,12) in page 1 of program C would be relocated to use the address $(i+4,12)$. If the 0th page of C becomes page j in process B, the Add instruction would be relocated to become `Add` $(j+4, 12)$ Thus, each page of program C has two copies in the address spaces of A and B. These copies may exist in memory at the same time if processes A and B are in operation simultaneously.

Dynamic binding (see Section 11.2) can be used to conserve memory by binding the same copy of a program or data to several processes. In this case, the program or data to be shared would retain its identity [see Figure 12.22(c)]. It is achieved as follows: The virtual memory manager maintains a *shared pages table* to hold information about shared pages in memory. Process A makes a system call to bind program C as a shared program starting at a specific page, say, page i, in its logical address space. The kernel invokes the virtual memory manager, which creates entries in the page table of A for pages of program C, and sets an s flag in each of these entries to indicate that it pertains to a shared page. It now checks whether the pages of program C have entries in the *shared pages table*. If not, it makes such entries now, sets up the swap space for program C, and invokes the dynamic linker, which dynamically binds program C to the code of process A. During this binding, it relocates the address-sensitive instructions of C. Thus, the `Add` instruction in page 1 of program C is modified to read `Add` $(i + 4, 12)$ [see Figure 12.22(c)]. When a reference to an address in program C page faults, the virtual memory manager finds that it is a shared page, so it checks the shared pages table to check whether the required page is already in memory, which would happen if another process had used it recently. If so, it copies the page frame number of the page from the shared pages table into the entry of that page in A's page table; otherwise, it loads the page in memory and updates its entry in A's page table and in the *shared pages table*. Similar actions are performed when process B dynamically binds program C to the start address of page i and references to C's pages in process B's instructions cause page faults. Figure 12.23 shows the resulting arrangement.

Two conditions should be satisfied for dynamic binding of programs to work. The program to be shared should be coded as a reentrant program so that it can be invoked by many processes at the same time (see Section 11.3.3.2). The program should also be bound to identical logical addresses in every process that

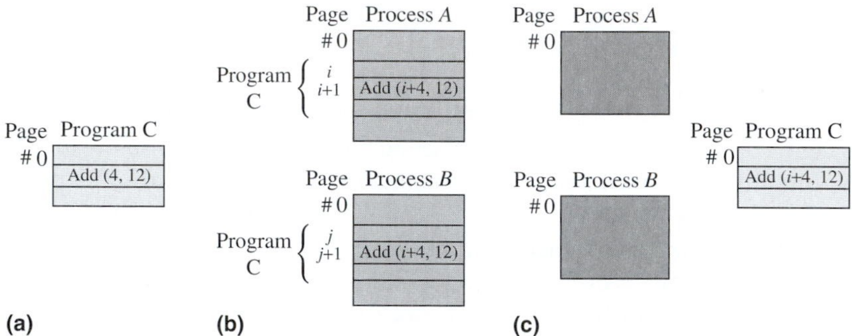

Figure 12.22 Sharing of program C by processes A and B: (a) program C; (b) static binding of C to the codes of processes A and B; and (c) dynamic binding of C.

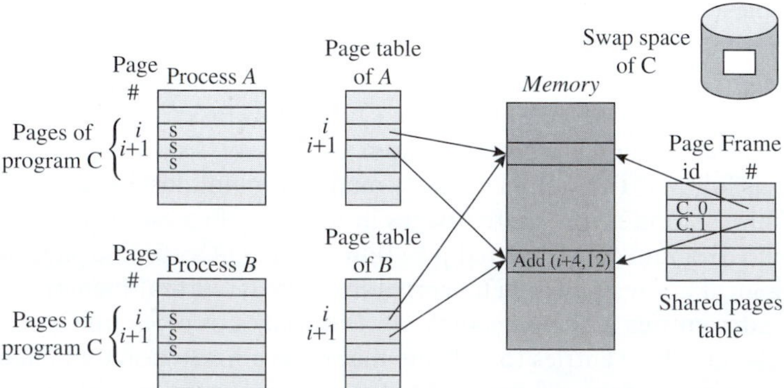

Figure 12.23 Dynamic sharing of program C by processes A and B.

shared it. It would ensure that an instruction like `Add (i+4, 12)` in page $i+1$ of Figure 12.23 will function correctly in each of the processes. These conditions are unnecessary when data, rather than a program, is dynamically bound to several processes; however, processes sharing the data would have to synchronize their accesses to the shared data to prevent race conditions.

When sharing of pages is implemented by making the page table entries of sharing processes point at the same page frame, page reference information for shared pages will be dispersed across many page tables. The page replacement algorithm will have to gather this information together to get the correct picture about references to shared pages. This is rather cumbersome. A better method would be to maintain information concerning shared pages in the *shared pages table* and collect page reference information for shared pages in entries in this table. This arrangement also permits a different page replacement criterion to be used for managing shared pages. In Section 12.8.4, we describe a related technique used in Windows operating systems.

12.6.1 Copy-on-Write

The copy-on-write feature is used to conserve memory when data in shared pages could be modified but the modified values are to be private to a process. When processes A and B dynamically bind such data, the virtual memory manager sets up the arrangement shown in Figure 12.24(a), which is analogous to the arrangement illustrated in Figure 12.23 except for a *copy-on-write* flag in each page table entry, which indicates whether the copy-on-write feature is to be employed for that page. The mark c in a page table entry in Figure 12.23 indicates that the *copy-on-write* flag is set for that page. If process A tries to modify page k, the MMU raises a page fault on seeing that page k is a copy-on-write page. The virtual memory manager now makes a private copy of page k for process A, accordingly changes the page frame number stored in page k's entry in the page table of A, and also turns off the *copy-on-write* flag in this entry [Figure 12.24(b)].

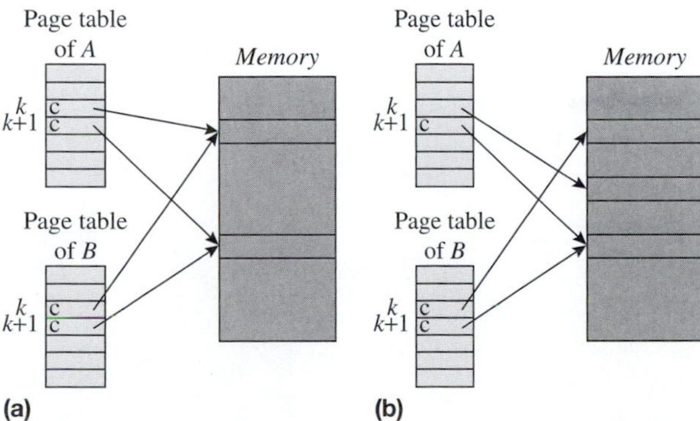

Figure 12.24 Implementing copy-on-write: (a) before and (b) after process A modifies page k.

Other processes sharing page k would continue to use the original copy of page k in memory; each of them would get a private copy of the page if they modified it.

In Unix systems, a child process starts off with the code and data of the parent process; however, it can modify the data and the modified values are private to it. The copy-on-write feature is used for the entire address spaces of the parent and child processes. It speeds up process creation. It also avoids copying of code pages because they are never modified; only data pages would be copied if they are modified.

12.7 MEMORY-MAPPED FILES

Memory mapping of a file by a process binds that file to a part of the logical address space of the process. This binding is performed when the process makes a *memory map* system call; it is analogous to dynamic binding of programs and data discussed earlier in Section 12.6. After memory mapping a file, the process refers to data in the file as if it were data located in pages of its own address space, and the virtual memory manager coordinates with the file system to load page-size parts of the file into memory on demand. When the process updates the data contained in such pages, the *modified* bits of the pages are set *on* but the data is not immediately written out into the file; dirty pages of data are written out to the file when the page frames containing them are to be freed. When the process makes a *memory unmap* call, the virtual memory manager writes out any dirty pages that still contain the file's data and deletes the file from the logical address space of the process.

Figure 12.25 shows the arrangement used for memory mapping of file `info` by process A. Note that the page-in and page-out operations on those pages of process A that do not belong to file `info` involve the swap space of the process and are performed by the virtual memory manager. Reading and writing of data from file `info` are performed by the file system in conjunction with the virtual memory manager. If several processes memory map the same file, we have an arrangement analogous to that shown in Figure 12.23; these processes would effectively share the memory-mapped file.

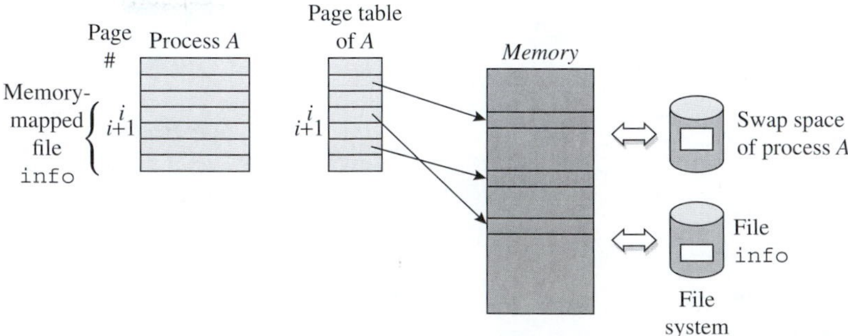

Figure 12.25 Memory mapping of file `info` by process A.

Table 12.5 Advantages of Memory-Mapped Files

Advantage	Description
File data as pages	Access to file data is looked upon as access to pages, which is inherently more efficient because of virtual memory hardware.
Avoids memory-to-memory copying	File data is a part of the process space. Hence the process does not have to copy it into a variable for processing.
Fewer read/write operations	File data is read in or written out one page at a time, rather than at every file operation, and so a single read/write operation may suffice for several file operations.
Prefetching of data	For sequential reads, data will already be in memory if the page that contains the data was read in during a previous file operation.
Efficient data access	File data can be accessed efficiently irrespective of file organization.

Table 12.5 summarizes the advantages of memory mapping of files. Memory-mapping makes file records accessible through the virtual memory hardware. This is inherently more efficient. Memory-to-memory copy operations are avoided as follows: When a process accesses some data in a non-memory-mapped input file, the file system first copies the record into a memory area used as a file buffer or disk cache (see Chapter 14). The process now copies the data from the buffer or the disk cache into its own address space (i.e., into some variables) for accessing it. Thus one disk-to-memory copy operation and one memory-to-memory copy operation are performed. When a file is memory-mapped, the memory-to-memory copy operation from the buffer to the process address space is not necessary since the data is already a part of the process address space. Similarly, fewer copy operations are performed when file data is modified. Data located in a page that was read in or written into during a previous file operation can be accessed without disk I/O, so memory mapping reduces the number of I/O operations performed during file processing.

The last advantage, efficient access to data in a file irrespective of its organization, arises from the fact that data in a memory-mapped file is accessed through the virtual memory hardware. Hence any part of the data can be accessed equally efficiently, whereas, as discussed in Chapter 13, efficiency of access to the same data through file operations would depend on the manner in which the data is organized in the file.

Memory mapping of files poses some performance problems. The *open* and *close* operations on a memory-mapped file incur more overhead than the *open* and *close* operations on normal files. It is caused by updating of page table and TLB entries while setting up and dismantling that part of the process address space where the file is mapped. The virtual memory manager also has to differentiate between memory-mapped pages and other pages in an address space—dirty data pages of the address space are written out to a disk only when a memory crunch exists, whereas the dirty pages of a memory-mapped file have to be written to the disk periodically for reasons of file reliability. Thus, the virtual memory manager has to create a special thread that keeps writing out dirty pages of memory-mapped files.

12.8 CASE STUDIES OF VIRTUAL MEMORY USING PAGING

12.8.1 Unix Virtual Memory

Unix has been ported on computer systems with diverse hardware designs. A variety of ingenuous schemes have been devised to exploit features of the paging hardware of different host machines. This section describes some features common to all Unix virtual memory implementations and some interesting techniques used in different versions of Unix. Its purpose is to provide a view of the practical issues in virtual memory implementations rather than to study the virtual memory manager of any specific Unix version in detail. Wherever possible, we are replacing the Unix terminology with terminology we used in previous sections of this chapter.

Logical Address Space and Swap Space The page table of a process differentiates among three kinds of pages—resident, unaccessed, and swapped-out pages. A resident page is currently in memory. An unaccessed page is one that has not been accessed even once during operation of the process and therefore has never been loaded in memory. It will be loaded when a reference to it causes a page fault. As described later, the page exists either in a file or in the swap space, depending on whether it is a text page, i.e., it contains instructions, or it is a data page. A swapped-out page is a page that is currently in the swap space; at a page fault, it is loaded back in memory from its location in the swap space.

An unaccessed page may be a text page or a data page. A text page is loaded from an executable file existing in the file system. Locating such a page in the file system may require reading of several disk blocks in the inode and the file allocation table (see Section 13.14.1). To avoid this overhead, the virtual memory manager maintains information about text pages in a separate table and refers to it when a page needs to be loaded. As described later, the 4.3BSD virtual memory manager maintains this information in the page table entry itself. This information gets overwritten by the page frame number when the page is loaded in memory, and so it is not available if the page gets removed from memory and has to be reloaded. To overcome this difficulty, the virtual memory manager writes out a text page into the swap space when it is removed from memory for the first time, and thereafter loads it from the swap space on demand. A data page is called a zero-fill page; it is filled with zeroes when its first use leads to a page fault. Thereafter, it is either a resident page or a swapped-out page.

A text page may remain in memory even if it is marked nonresident in its page table entry. This situation arises if some other process is using the page (or has used it in the past). When a page fault occurs for a text page, the virtual memory manager first checks whether the page already exists in memory. If so, it simply puts the page frame information in its page table entry and marks it as resident. This action avoids a page-in operation and also conserves memory.

To conserve disk space, an effort is made to allocate as little swap space as possible. To start with, sufficient swap space is allocated to accommodate the user stack and the data area. Thereafter swap space is allocated in large chunks whenever needed. This approach suffers from the problem that swap space in the system may become exhausted when the data area of a process grows; the process then has to be suspended or aborted.

Copy-on-Write The semantics of *fork* require that the child process should obtain a copy of the parent's address space. These semantics can be implemented by allocating distinct memory areas and a swap space for the child process. However, child processes frequently discard the copy of their parent's address space by loading some other program for execution through the *exec* call. In any case, a child process may not wish to modify much of the parent's data. Hence memory and swap space can be optimized through the copy-on-write feature (see Section 12.6.1).

Copy-on-write is implemented as follows: When a process is forked, the reference count of all data pages in the parent's address space is incremented by 1 and all data pages are made read-only by manipulating bits in the access privileges field of their page table entries. Any attempt at modifying a data page raises a protection fault. The virtual memory manager finds that the reference count of the page is > 1, so it realizes that this is not a protection fault but a reference to a copy-on-write page. It now reduces the count, makes a copy of the page for the child process and assigns the read and write privileges to this copy by setting appropriate bits in its page table entry. If the new reference count is $= 1$, it also enables the read and write privileges in the page table entry that had led to the page fault because the entry no longer pertains to a shared page.

Efficient Use of Page Table and Paging Hardware If a page is not present in memory, the *valid* bit of its page table entry is "off." Under these circumstances, bits in other fields of this entry, like the *ref info* field or the *page frame #* field, do not contain any useful information. Hence these bits can be used for some other purposes. Unix 4.3BSD uses these bits to store the address of a disk block in the file system that contains a text page.

The VAX 11 architecture does not provide a reference bit to collect page reference information. Its absence is compensated by using the *valid* bit in a novel manner. Periodically, the *valid* bit of a page is turned off even if the page is in memory. The next reference to the page causes a page fault. However, the virtual memory manager knows that this is not a genuine page fault, and so it sets the *valid* bit and resumes the process. In effect, the *valid* bit is used as the reference bit.

Page Replacement The system permits a process to fix a certain fraction of its pages in memory to reduce its own page fault rate and improve its own performance. These pages cannot be removed from memory until they are unfixed by the process. Interestingly, there is no I/O fixing of pages in Unix since I/O operations take place between a disk block and a block in the buffer cache rather than between a disk block and the address space of a process.

Unix page replacement is analogous to the schematic of Figure 12.19, including the use of a clock algorithm. To facilitate fast page-in operations, Unix virtual memory manager maintain a list of free page frames and try to keep at least 5 percent of total page frames on this list at all times. A daemon called the *pageout daemon* (which is labeled process 2 in the system) is created for this purpose. It is activated any time the total number of free page frames falls below 5 percent. It tries to add pages to the free list and puts itself to sleep when the free list contains more than 5 percent free page frames. Some versions of Unix use two thresholds—a high threshold and a low threshold—instead of a single threshold at 5 percent. The daemon goes to sleep when it finds that the number of pages in the free list exceeds the high threshold. It is activated when this number falls below the low threshold. This arrangement avoids frequent activation and deactivation of the daemon.

The virtual memory manager divides pages that are not fixed in memory into active pages, i.e., pages that are actively in use by a process, and inactive pages, i.e., pages that have not been referenced in the recent past. The virtual memory manager maintains two lists, the active list and the inactive list. Both lists are treated as queues. A page is added to the active list when it becomes active, and to the inactive list when it is deemed to have become inactive. Thus the least recently activated page is at the head of the active list and the oldest inactive page is at the head of the inactive list. A page is moved from the inactive list to the active list when it is referenced. The pageout daemon tries to maintain a certain number of pages, computed as a fraction of total resident pages, in the inactive list. If it reaches the end of the inactive list while adding page frames to the free list, it checks whether the total number of pages in the inactive list is smaller than the expected number. If so, it transfers a sufficient number of pages from the active list to the inactive list.

The pageout daemon is activated when the number of free page frames falls below the low threshold while the system is handling a page fault. It frees page frames in the following order: page frames containing pages of inactive processes, page frames containing inactive pages of active processes, and page frames containing active pages of active processes. The daemon finds inactive processes, if any, and activates the swapper to swap them out. It goes back to sleep if the number of free page frames now exceeds the high threshold.

If the number of free page frames after swapping out inactive processes is still below the high threshold, the pageout daemon scans the inactive list and decides whether and when to add page frames occupied by inactive pages to the free list. A page frame containing an inactive page is added to the free list immediately if the page is unreferenced and not dirty. If the page is dirty and not already being swapped out, the pageout daemon starts a page-out operation on the page and proceeds to examine the next inactive page. If a page is being swapped out, the daemon merely skips it. The *modified* bit of a page is reset when its page-out operation is completed. The page frame containing this page would be added to the free list in a subsequent pass if it is still inactive and the daemon finds that its page-out operation is complete. The daemon activates the swapper if it cannot add a sufficient number of page frames to the free list. The swapper swaps out one or more active processes to free a sufficient number of page frames.

To optimize page traffic, the virtual memory manager writes out dirty pages to the swap space in clusters. When the page daemon finds a dirty page during its scan, it examines adjacent pages to check if they are also dirty. If so, a cluster of dirty pages is written out to the disk in a single I/O operation. Another optimization concerns redundant page-in operations. When a page frame f_i occupied by some clean page p_i is added to the free list, the valid bit of p_i's page table entry is set to 0. However, the page is not immediately overwritten by loading another page in the page frame. This happens sometime later when the page's entry comes to the head of the free list and it is allocated to some process. The next reference to p_i would create a page fault since the valid bit in its page table entry has been set to 0. If p_i is still in f_i, i.e., if f_i is still in the free list, f_i can be simply taken out of the free list and p_i can be "reconnected" to the logical address space of the process. This saves a page-in operation and consequent delays to the page-faulting process.

Swapping The Unix virtual memory manager does not use a working set memory allocator because of the high overhead of such an allocator. Instead it focuses on maintaining needed pages in memory. A process is swapped out if all its required pages cannot be maintained in memory and conditions resembling thrashing exist in the system. An inactive process, i.e., a process that is blocked for a long time, may also be swapped out in order to maintain a sufficient number of free page frames. When this situation arises and a swap-out becomes necessary, the pageout daemon activates the swapper, which is always process 0 in the system. The swapper finds and swaps out inactive processes. If that does not free sufficient memory, it is activated again by the pageout daemon. This time it swaps out the process that has been resident the longest amount of time. When swapped out processes exist in the system, the swapper periodically checks whether sufficient free memory exists to swap some of them back in. A swap-in priority—which is a function of when the process was swapped out, when it was last active, its size and its *nice value*—is used for this purpose (see Section 7.6.1 for details of the nice value). This function ensures that no process remains swapped out indefinitely. In Unix 4.3BSD, a process was swapped-in only if it could be allocated as much memory as it held when it was swapped out. In Unix 4.4BSD this requirement was relaxed; a process is brought in if enough memory to accommodate its user structure and kernel stack can be allocated to it.

12.8.2 Linux Virtual Memory

Linux uses a page size of 4 KB. On 64-bit architectures, it uses a three-level page table (see Section 12.2.3.2). The three levels are the page global directory, the page middle directory and the page table. Accordingly, a logical address consists of four parts; three of these are for the three levels and the fourth one is the byte number within a page.

Linux uses an interesting arrangement to eliminate page-in operations for pages that were loaded previously in memory, but were marked for removal. This is achieved by using the following states for page frames: A *free* page frame is one that has not been allocated to a process, while an *active* page frame is one that is in use by a process to which it has been allocated. An *inactive dirty* page frame was modified by the process to which it was allocated but it is not in use by the process any more. An *inactive laundered* page is one what was *inactive dirty* and is therefore being written out to the disk. An *inactive laundered* page becomes *inactive clean* when its contents are copied to the disk. If a process page faults for a page that is in a page frame marked *inactive clean*, the page frame is once again allocated to the process, and the page is simply marked as present in memory. If the page is in a page frame marked *inactive laundered*, these actions are performed when its disk operation completes. Apart from saving on disk operations, this arrangement also prevents access to a stale copy of a page. An *inactive clean* page can also be allocated to another process straightaway.

Page replacement in Linux is based on a clock algorithm. The kernel tries to maintain a sufficient number of free page frames at all times so that page faults can be quickly serviced by using one of the free page frames. It uses two lists called *active list* and *inactive list*, and maintains the size of the active list to two-thirds the size of the inactive list. When the number of free page frames falls below a lower threshold, it executes a loop until a few page frames are freed. In this loop it examines the page frame at the end of the inactive list. If its reference bit is set, it resets the bit and moves the page frame to the head of the list; otherwise, it frees the page frame. When the balance between the active and inactive lists is to be maintained, it processes a few page frames from the end of the active list in a similar manner and either moves them to the head of the active list, or moves them to the head of the inactive list with their reference bits on. A page frame is moved from the inactive list to the active list if it is referenced by a process.

Linux uses a buddy system allocator for allocating page frames to processes (see Section 11.5.2). This method facilitates performing of I/O operations through older DMA buses that use physical addresses, because such I/O operations require memory to be contiguously allocated (see Section 12.2.4).

The logical address space of a process can consist of several virtual memory regions; each region can have different characteristics and is handled by using separate policies for loading and replacement of pages. A page in a *zero-filled memory region* is filled with zeroes at its first use. A *file-backed region* facilitates memory mapping of files. The page table entries of its pages point at the disk buffers used by the file system. This way, any update in a page of such a region is immediately reflected in the file and is visible to concurrent users of the file. A *private memory region* is handled in a different manner. When a new process is forked, the child process is given a copy of the parent's page table. At this time, pages of a private memory region are given a copy-on-write status. When a process modifies such a page, a private copy of the page is made for it.

12.8.3 Virtual Memory in Solaris

Solaris provides multiple page size support, whereby it uses both normal pages and superpages. Superpages are used automatically for processes with large address spaces; other processes can request use of superpages through the *memcntl* system call. Superpages are not used for memory-mapped files because a small change in a superpage requires the complete superpage to be written to the file, which poses a sizable performance penalty because dirty superpages of a memory-mapped file are written to the disk frequently to ensure reliability of the file (see Section 12.7).

A component of the virtual memory manager, called the *page scanner*, tries to keep a sufficient number of page frames on the *cyclic page cache*, which is like the *inactive clean* list of Linux, so that the virtual memory manager can allocate a page frame from the cyclic page cache straightaway when a page fault occurs. It selects a page for removal from memory, using a two-handed clock algorithm on a global basis; writes it out to the disk if it is dirty; and adds its page frame to the cyclic page cache. The page scanner is implemented as two kernel threads analogous to those shown in Figure 12.19. One thread identifies page frames for addition to the cyclic page cache, while the other thread writes out dirty pages from these page frames to the disk. If the page for which a process page faulted exists in a page frame included in the cyclic page cache, the virtual memory manager simply removes the page frame from the cyclic page cache and attaches it to the page table of the process. This arrangement saves on a page-in operation. To reduce page traffic, the page scanner does not put shared pages on the cyclic page cache if a sufficiently large number of processes are sharing them.

lotsfree is a parameter of the page scanner that indicates how many page frames should be free at any time. The page scanner starts scanning pages using the two-handed clock algorithm when the number of free page frames falls below *lotsfree*. The *scan rate*, which is the number of pages scanned per second, is varied according to the number of page frames that are actually free—it is smaller when this number is close to *lotsfree* and it is increased as the number falls below *lotsfree*. The spread between the two hands of the clock algorithm is calculated at boot time on the basis of the amount of memory in the system. This spread and the scan rate together determine the elapsed time between the resetting of a bit by one hand of the two-handed clock algorithm and its examination by the other hand of the algorithm. A smaller elapsed time implies that only most recently accessed pages will survive in memory, and a larger elapsed time means that only pages that have not been accessed for a long time will be removed from memory. To safeguard system performance, the virtual memory manager limits the amount of CPU overhead that the page scanner can cause. If the page scanner is not able to keep pace with the demand for free pages using the clock algorithm, the virtual memory manager swaps out inactive processes and frees all page frames occupied by them.

Solaris virtual memory manager has evolved into its present form through several design updates. Prior to Solaris 6, the page scanner maintained a free list that contained clean page frames allocated to both user processes and files. The file system took pages from the free list to accommodate data read from files. During periods of heavy file activity, the file system effectively stole pages from address spaces of user processes, which affected their performance. Solaris 6 introduced the feature called *priority paging*, which ensured that only those page frames in the free list that were allocated to file pages would be considered for allocation to data read from files. This way, file processing activity did not affect operation of processes; however, page frames were still allocated from the free list, which caused high scan rates and high overhead of the page scanner. Solaris 8 introduced the cyclic page cache described earlier and made the file system steal pages from itself directly, so that the file processing activity does not affect scan rates and overhead of the page scanner.

12.8.4 Virtual Memory in Windows

Windows operates on several architectures, hence it supports both 32-bit and 64-bit logical addresses. The page size is 4 KB. The address space of a process is either 2 GB or 3 GB. The remainder of the logical address space is reserved for OS use; the kernel is mapped into this part of every process's address space. On different architectures, Windows uses two-, three- or four-level page tables and various page table entry formats. The page table of a process is itself stored in the reserved part of the logical address space of the process.

On an Intel 80x86 architecture, Windows uses a two-level page table organization similar to the one shown in Figure 12.11. The higher-level page table is called a *page directory* (PD). The PD contains 1024 entries of 4 bytes each. Each entry in the PD points to a *page table* (PT). Each page table contains 1024 page table entries of 4 bytes each. Each 32-bit logical address is split into three components as shown below:

← 10 bits →	← 10 bits →	← 12 bits →
PD index	PT index	byte index

During address translation, the *PD index* field is used to locate a page table. The *PT index* field is used to select a 32-bit page table entry (PTE) in the page table, which contains a 20-bit address of the page frame that contains the page; the *byte index* is concatenated with this address to obtain the effective physical address. The virtual memory manager uses the remaining 12 bits in a page table entry to indicate how the process may access the page—whether read-only or read/write—and whether the page frame allocated to it is *dirty*, i.e., modified, or *accessed*, i.e., read from or modified. If the page is not in memory, the 20 address bits would specify the offset into the paging file, i.e., the swap space. If the page contains code, a copy of it would exist in a code file, hence 28 bits in the page table entry would point to a system data structure that indicates its position in the code file. Such a page is directly loaded from the code file, so it is not copied into a paging file.

A page frame can be in any one of eight states. Some of these states are:

- *valid*: the page is in active use,
- *free*: the page is not in active use,
- *zeroed*: the page is cleaned out and available for immediate use,
- *standby*: the page has been removed from the working set of the process to which it was allocated, but it could be "reconnected" to the process if it were referenced again,
- *modified*: the page is dirty and yet to be written out,
- *bad*: the page cannot be accessed because of a hardware problem.

A process cannot use the virtual address space available to it straightaway—it must first *reserve* it for use, and then actually *commit* it for accommodating specific entities like files and objects. Thus, only some portions of the logical address space of a process may have been reserved at any time, and only a part of the reserved logical address space may be in actual use. An access to a page that has not been reserved and committed leads to an access violation. When a thread in the process makes a system call to commit virtual memory to a region, the virtual memory manager constructs a *virtual address descriptor* (VAD) describing the range of logical addresses committed to it. To minimize the size of the page table of a process, the virtual memory manager builds it incrementally—the page table entry for a committed page is created only when an access to it leads to a page fault. To facilitate this operation, the VADs for committed portions of the logical address space are stored in an AVL tree, which is a balanced binary tree.

A *section* object represents a section of memory that can be shared. It can be connected to a file, in which case it provides memory-mapped files, or to memory, in which case it provides shared memory. A process maps a *view* of a section into its own address space by making a system call with parameters that indicate an offset into the section object, the number of bytes to be mapped, and the logical address in its address space where the object is to be mapped. When the process accesses a page in the view for the first time, the virtual memory manager allocates a page frame and loads it, unless it is already present in memory as a result of access by another process. If the memory section has the attribute *based*, the shared memory has the same virtual address in the logical address space of each sharing process. It facilitates sharing of code among processes (see Section 12.6).

A copy-on-write feature is used for sharing the pages (see Section 12.6.1). It is implemented by setting the protection field of a page to *read only*. A protection exception is raised when a process tries to modify the page. The virtual memory manager now makes a private copy of the page for use by the process.

Loading, accessing, and removal of shared pages is performed as follows: A *prototype PTE* is created for each shared page in an area of memory reserved for prototype PTEs. Each process that uses the shared page has a PTE for the page in its page table. When the shared page does not exist in memory, that is, it is either not yet loaded in memory or it has been removed from memory, it is marked invalid in the prototype PTE and in the PTEs in page tables of all sharing processes. In addition, the PTEs in the page tables of processes are set to point to the prototype PTE. When the shared page is referenced by one of the sharing processes, it is loaded in memory and the page frame number where it is loaded is stored in both the prototype PTE and the PTE of the process. When another process references this page, its PTE is updated by simply copying the page frame number information from the prototype PTE.

Translation look-aside buffers are employed to speed up address translation. In 32-bit architectures, they are managed entirely by the MMU hardware, while in 64-bit architectures they are managed by the virtual memory manager. When a memory access by a thread leads to a page fault, the thread is blocked until the page-in operation for the page completes. Several threads may page-fault for a shared page at the same time. These page faults are called *collided page faults*. The virtual memory manager ensures that all threads whose page faults collided become unblocked when the page-in operation is completed.

To reduce the number of page faults through page reference locality, the virtual memory manager always loads a few pages preceding and following a page-faulted page into memory. While booting the system or starting an application, the logical prefetcher loads a few pages into memory and monitors page faults that arise so that it could load a more effective set of pages in memory the next time the system is booted or the application is started.

The Windows kernel uses the notion of working sets to control the amount of memory allocated to a process. It defines a minimum and maximum working set size for each process; these sizes are determined by the memory configuration of the system, rather than by the size or nature of a process. For large memory configurations, the minimum and maximum working set sizes are 50 and 345 pages, respectively. At a page fault, the kernel considers the amount of free memory in the system, the current working set size of the process, and its minimum and maximum working set sizes. It allocates an additional page frame to the process if its current allocation is smaller than the maximum working set size and free memory exists; otherwise, it replaces one of the pages of the process in memory through a clock algorithm implemented by using the *accessed* bits in the page table. The *working set manager* is activated periodically, and when working sets of processes need to be adjusted. If the amount of free memory has fallen below a threshold due to allocation of page frames, it examines working sets whose sizes exceed the minimum working set size and removes from memory those pages that have not been used for a long time. This, too, is performed by using a clock algorithm.

The virtual memory manager maintains a number of page lists—a free list, a list of zero-initialized pages, a modified list, and a standby list. When a page is to be removed from memory, or when its process has terminated, it would be moved to the standby list if it were a clean page; otherwise, it would be moved to the modified list. (Recall that a standby page could be simply "reconnected" to a process that wished to use it.) The page writer writes out modified pages and changes their status to standby. It uses two thresholds—an upper threshold on the number of modified pages in the system and a lower threshold on the number of available pages—to decide when pages need to be written out.

12.9 VIRTUAL MEMORY USING SEGMENTATION

A segment is a logical entity in a program, such as a function, a data structure, or an object; or it is a module that consists of some or all of these. A program is composed of segments. During a program's execution, the kernel treats segments as the unit for memory allocation. This results in noncontiguous memory allocation for processes, which provides efficient use of memory by reducing memory fragmentation. Being a logical entity, a segment is also a convenient unit for sharing and protection. This feature is useful in constructing large software systems that comprise of a set of modules or objects.

A logical address in a segmented process is viewed as a pair (s_i, b_i) where s_i and b_i are the segment and byte ids, respectively. There are variations in the way s_i and b_i are indicated in a logical address. One method is to represent each of them numerically. The logical address thus consists of a segment number and a byte number. We shall discuss the second method separately later in this section. The logical address space of a process is two-dimensional in nature. One dimension is defined by the set of segments in the process. The number of segments can vary, subject to a maximum number that may be specified by the computer architecture or the virtual memory manager. The other dimension is defined by the set of bytes in a segment. The number of bytes in a segment can vary, subject to the maximum imposed by the number of bits available to represent b_i in a logical address. The two-dimensional nature of the address space implies that the last byte of a segment and the first byte of another segment are not logically adjoining bytes—if we add 1 to the address of the last byte in a segment, it does not spill over into the next segment; it is merely an invalid address. These are significant differences from paging. There are also significant similarities, which we now discuss in the context of address translation.

Figure 12.26 shows how address translation is performed in virtual memory using segmentation. Some parallels with paging are the existence of a *segment table* (ST) for a process, and a special hardware register called the *segment table address register* (STAR) that points to the segment table of a process. For a

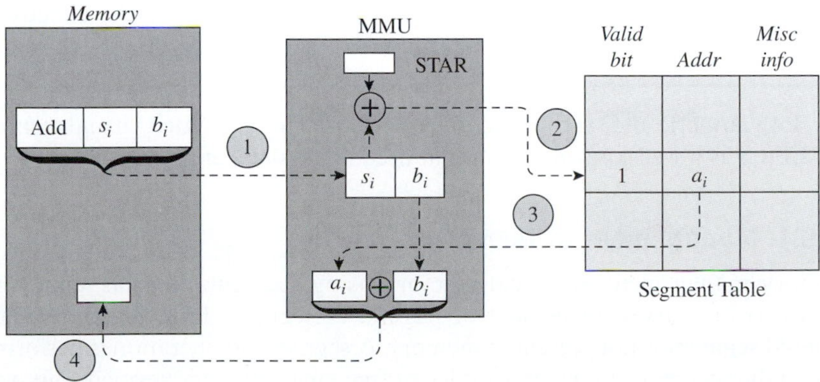

Figure 12.26 Virtual memory implementation using segmentation.

logical address (s_i, b_i), address translation is performed by using the memory address found in s_i's entry in the segment table and the byte number b_i in the segment. A missing segment fault is raised if segment s_i does not exist in memory. A difference with paging is that segments do not have a standard length. Hence address translation involves adding the byte number b_i to the start address of s_i; it cannot be performed by using bit concatenation as in paging. Address translation can be speeded up by using address translation buffers. An entry in the address translation buffer would contain a segment id and its address in memory, which is copied from its segment table entry.

In a logical address (s_i, b_i), s_i and b_i could also be specified in a symbolic form, i.e., as ids. In this case, a logical address is of the form (`alpha`, `beta`) where `alpha` is the name of a segment and `beta` is an id associated with a byte contained in segment `alpha`. Address translation of such logical addresses is performed as follows: While compiling a segment, the compiler builds a table showing byte ids defined in the segment and the byte numbers of corresponding bytes in the segment. This table is made available to the virtual memory manager for use during address translation. We will call it the *segment linking table* (SLT), and refer to the segment linking table for `alpha` as $\text{SLT}_{\texttt{alpha}}$. During address translation, the MMU obtains the start address of `alpha` from the segment table, picks up the address of $\text{SLT}_{\texttt{alpha}}$ from the *misc info* field of `alpha`'s entry and obtains the byte number of `beta` from $\text{SLT}_{\texttt{alpha}}$, and adds the two to obtain the effective memory address.

Example 12.10 Effective Address Calculation in Segmentation

Figure 12.27 illustrates effective address calculation for the logical address (`alpha`, `beta`). Part (a) of the figure shows segment `alpha`. `beta` and `gamma` are two ids associated with specific instructions or data in `alpha`. These ids are associated with the bytes numbered 232 and 478 in the segment, respectively. The segment linking table $\text{SLT}_{\texttt{alpha}}$ contains entries for `beta` and `gamma`, showing their byte numbers as 232 and 476, respectively. The segment table entry of `alpha` indicates that it exists in the memory area with the start address 23480. The byte number associated with `beta` is 232. Hence the effective address of (`alpha`, `beta`) would be computed as $23480 + 232 = 23712$.

Both numeric and symbolic ids have been used in segmented virtual memory. MULTICS is a well-known system that used symbolic identifiers.

12.9.1 Management of Memory

Memory management in virtual memory using segmentation has some similarities to memory management in paging. A segment fault indicates that a required segment is not present in memory. A segment-in operation is performed to load the segment. If there is insufficient free memory, some segment-out operations may have to precede loading of the required segment. The virtual memory

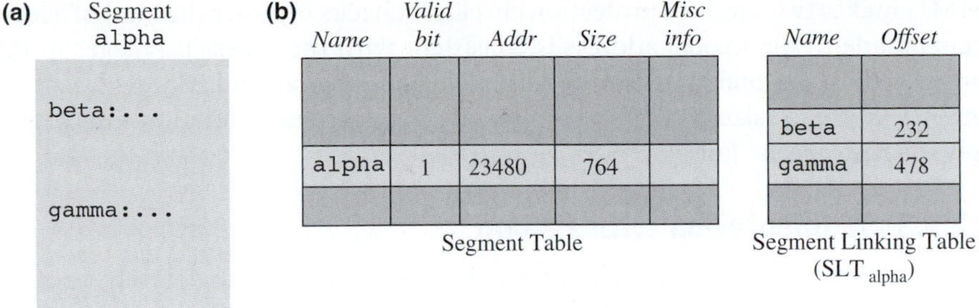

Figure 12.27 Use of symbolic segment and word ids.

manager can use a working set of segments to control memory allocation for a process. Segments could be replaced on an NRU basis by collecting segment reference information in each segment entry.

One difference from virtual memory using paging is that segments do not have a fixed size. The memory freed by removing one segment from memory may not suffice for loading another segment. Hence many segments may have to be removed before a new segment can be loaded. Differences in segment sizes can lead to external fragmentation, which can be tackled either through compaction or through memory reuse techniques such as first-fit or best-fit. Compaction is aided by presence of the MMU—only the address field of the segment table entry needs to be modified when a segment is moved in memory. However, the virtual memory manager should ensure that segments being moved are not involved in I/O operations.

The two-dimensional nature of the logical address space permits a segment to dynamically grow or shrink in size. Dynamic growth can be handled by allocating a larger memory area to a segment and releasing the memory area allocated to it earlier. A segment can be permitted to grow in its present location in memory if an adjoining free area exists.

12.9.2 Sharing and Protection

Two important issues in sharing and protection of segments are:

- Static and dynamic sharing of segments
- Detecting use of invalid addresses

A segment is a convenient unit for sharing because it is a logical entity in a process. It can be shared statically or dynamically by using the schemes described earlier in Section 12.6. If segment ids are numeric, segments must occupy identical positions in logical address spaces of sharing processes. This requirement is analogous to that concerning shared pages in virtual memory using paging (see Section 12.6 and Figure 12.23). It does not apply if segment ids are symbolic. Processes sharing a segment may have different access privileges to programs and data in it. The virtual memory manager puts the access privileges in the *misc info* field of a segment table entry. While translating a logical address (s_i, b_i), the

MMU makes two kinds of protection checks. It checks whether the kind of access being made to the logical address is consistent with the access privileges of the process for the segment. It also checks whether (s_i, b_i) is a valid address by checking whether $b_i <$ size of s_i. It raises a memory protection violation interrupt if any of these checks fails.

12.9.3 Segmentation with Paging

External fragmentation exists in a virtual memory using segmentation because segment sizes are different. This problem can be addressed by superimposing paging on a segment-oriented addressing scheme. A system using this approach retains the fundamental advantage of segmentation—the logical address space is two-dimensional, which permits dynamic changes in the size of a segment—while avoiding external fragmentation. Each segment contains an integral number of pages, and memory management is performed through demand paging. This arrangement may achieve more effective utilization of memory since only required pages of a segment need to be present in memory at any time. However, paging introduces internal fragmentation in the last page of a segment.

A logical address in such a system has the form (s_i, p_i, b_i). Since each segment consists of a number of pages, a page table is built for each segment. The segment table entry of a segment points to its page table. Figure 12.28 illustrates this arrangement. The *name* field of the segment table is needed only if symbolic segment ids are used. Address translation now involves an access to the segment table followed by an access to the page table of the segment. It requires two memory references if the segment and page tables are held in memory. To speed up address translation, address translation buffers would have to be employed for both the segment and page table references. A simple extension to the scheme described earlier in Section 12.2.2 can be used for this purpose. Alternatively, a single address translation buffer may be employed, each entry in the buffer containing a pair (s_i, p_i) and the corresponding page frame number.

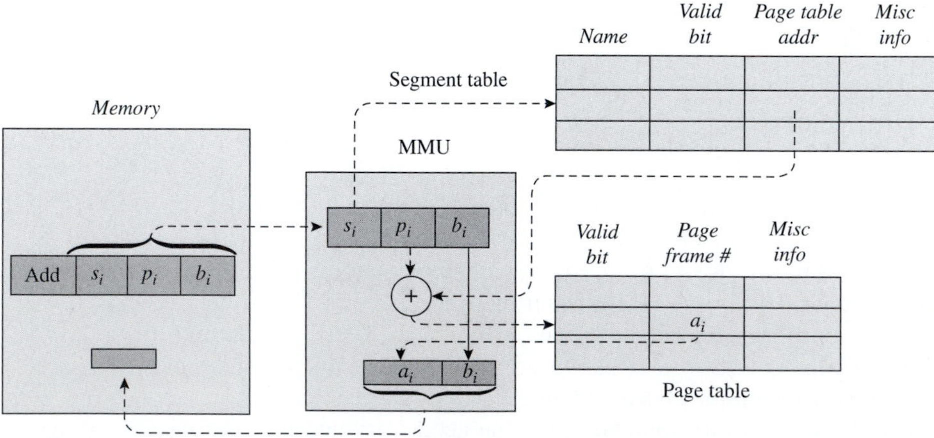

Figure 12.28 Address translation in segmentation with paging.

Memory protection can be performed at the level of segments through the scheme described in Section 12.9.2. Protection information for a segment can be put in its entry in the segment table, and it can be copied into its entry in the address translation buffer. Page level access validation is not needed.

12.10 SUMMARY

Virtual memory is a part of the memory hierarchy consisting of memory and a disk. During operation of a process, some components of its address space exist in memory, while others reside on a disk. This arrangement permits the total memory requirements of a process to exceed size of the system's memory. It also permits a larger number of processes to exist in memory simultaneously, because each of them occupies less memory than its own size. The performance of a process depends on the rate at which its parts have to be loaded in memory from the disk. In this chapter, we studied the techniques used by the kernel to ensure efficient operation of a process and good performance of the system.

Two basic actions in the operation of virtual memory using paging are *address translation* and *demand loading of pages*. The *memory management unit* (MMU), which is a hardware unit, and the *virtual memory manager*, which is a part of the kernel, jointly implement these two actions. The memory is divided into parts called *page frames*, whose size matches the size of pages. The virtual memory manager maintains a *page table* for each process to indicate which of its pages exist in which page frames of memory. When an operand in the current instruction in a process exists in one of the pages that is present in memory, the MMU obtains the page frame number where it exists from the page table and uses it to compute the effective memory address of the operand. If the page is not in memory, the MMU raises an interrupt called a *page fault*, and the virtual memory manager loads the page in memory. A fast *translation look-aside buffer* (TLB) is used to speed up address translation; it caches some entries of page tables of processes. The *inverted page table* and the *multilevel page table* are used in practice because they require less memory than the conventional page table.

The virtual memory manager has to make two key decisions that influence the performance of a process: Which page should it remove from memory to make space for a new page required by a process, and how much memory should it allocate to a process? It uses a *page replacement algorithm* to decide which page should be removed from memory. The empirical principle of *locality of reference* indicates that a recently accessed page is more likely to be accessed in future than a page that has not been recently accessed. Accordingly, the *least recently used* (LRU) page replacement algorithm removes the page that has been least recently used. It possesses the *stack property*, which guarantees that the page fault rate would not increase if the memory allocation to a process is increased. However, it is expensive to collect information about when a page was last referenced. Hence MMUs typically provide a single bit for collecting information about page references, and a class of page replacement algorithms called the *not recently used* (NRU) algorithms are used in practice. *Clock algorithms* are a widely used subclass of NRU algorithms.

The *working set* of a process is the collection of distinct pages referenced by it recently. Its size provides a useful pointer to how many pages of the process should be in memory to ensure good performance of the process. The virtual memory manager can use the notion of working sets to avoid the situation called *thrashing* in which most processes in the system have insufficient amounts of memory allocated to them, so they produce page faults at a high rate and little useful work gets done in the system.

An operating system uses special techniques that exploit the virtual memory to speed up operation of processes. The *copy-on-write* technique avoids keeping identical copies of shared pages in memory, while *memory mapping* of files enables a file to be treated as a part of the address space of a process, thereby speeding up accesses to its data.

TEST YOUR CONCEPTS

12.1 Classify each of the following statements as true or false:

- **a.** In a computer providing virtual memory, the number of bits in a logical address can exceed the number of bits in a physical address.
- **b.** A page-out operation is always needed in a page replacement operation, irrespective of whether the page being replaced is dirty.
- **c.** Loss of protection can result if an entry in the translation look-aside buffer (TLB) that was made during operation of one process is used during operation of another process.
- **d.** The inverted page table organization requires more accesses to memory during address translation than the conventional organization of page tables.
- **e.** The FIFO page replacement policy guarantees that allocating more page frames to a program would reduce its page fault rate.
- **f.** If the virtual memory hardware provides a single reference bit and the reference bits in the page table entries of all memory-resident pages are set, the LRU page replacement algorithm degenerates to FIFO replacement.
- **g.** Page faults would not occur during operation of a process if all pages included in the working set of a process are in memory at every instant.
- **h.** Heavy page traffic implies that thrashing has occurred.
- **i.** If a single copy of a program C is shared by two processes *A* and *B*, pages of C should occupy identical positions in the page tables of processes *A* and *B*.

12.2 Select the most appropriate alternative in each of the following questions:

- **a.** If the virtual memory hardware provides a single reference bit in an entry of a page table, the reference bit in the entry of page p_i of process P_k indicates:
  - **i.** Whether page p_i is likely to be referenced in the future
  - **ii.** Whether page p_i will be the next page to be referenced during operation of P_k
  - **iii.** Whether page p_i has been referenced since it was last loaded in memory
  - **iv.** Whether page p_i is the most recently referenced page of P_k
- **b.** During operation of a process P_k, the translation look-aside buffer contains:
  - **i.** Some arbitrary entries from the page table of P_k
  - **ii.** The most recently referenced entries of the page table of P_k
  - **iii.** The last few entries of the page table of P_k
  - **iv.** The least recently referenced entries of the page table of P_k
- **c.** The stack property of a page replacement algorithm implies that if more memory would have been allocated to a process:
  - **i.** Fewer page faults would have occurred
  - **ii.** More page faults would have occurred
  - **iii.** The number of page faults would have been smaller or the same
  - **iv.** None of (i)–(iii)
- **d.** If pfr_i and pfr_j are the page fault rates of processes P_i and P_j when process P_i has 5 percent of its pages in memory, process P_j has 10 percent of its pages in memory, and the page replacement policy possesses the stack property, then:
  - **i.** $pfr_i < pfr_j$
  - **ii.** $pfr_i \leq pfr_j$
  - **iii.** $pfr_i > pfr_j$
  - **iv.** Nothing can be said about the relative magnitudes of pfr_i and pfr_j

e. If pfr_i and pfr'_i are the page fault rates of process P_i when it is operated with 5 percent of its pages and 10 percent of its pages in memory, respectively, and the page replacement policy possesses the stack property, then:

i. $pfr_i < pfr'_i$
ii. $pfr_i \geq pfr'_i$
iii. $pfr_i > pfr'_i$
iv. Nothing can be said about the relative magnitudes of pfr_i and pfr'_i

f. Thrashing can be overcome if

i. The degree of multiprogramming is increased
ii. The I/O speed is increased
iii. Memory allocation for a process is controlled by its working set size
iv. None of (i)–(iii)

EXERCISES

12.1 Page tables are stored in a memory that has an access time of 100 nanoseconds. The translation look-aside buffer (TLB) can hold 64 page table entries and has an access time of 10 nanoseconds. During operation of a process, it is found that 85 percent of the time a required page table entry exists in the TLB and only 2 percent of the references lead to page faults. The average time for page replacement is 2 ms. Compute the effective memory access time.

12.2 Using the access speeds and hit ratios mentioned in Exercise 12.1, compute the effective memory access time in two-level, three-level, and four-level page table organizations.

12.3 Three approaches to paging of the kernel in virtual memory are:

a. Make the kernel permanently memory-resident.
b. Page the kernel in a manner analogous to the paging of user processes.
c. Make the kernel a compulsory part of the logical address space of every process in the system and manage its pages as shared pages.

Which approach would you recommend? Give reasons.

12.4 Execution performance of a process in virtual memory depends on locality of reference displayed during its operation. Develop a set of guidelines that a programmer can follow to obtain good performance of a process. Describe the rationale behind each guideline. (*Hint:* Consider array references occurring in nested loops!)

12.5 Give a sample page reference string for a process that produces more page faults when the LRU page replacement policy is used with $alloc = 5$ than when the optimal page replacement policy is used with $alloc = 5$.

12.6 A process makes r page references during its operation. The page reference string of the process contains d distinct page numbers in it. The size of the process is p pages and it is allocated f page frames all through its operation.

a. What is the least number of page faults that can occur during its operation?
b. What is the maximum number of page faults that can occur during its operation?

12.7 Prove the validity of the following statement if the page replacement policy uses a fixed memory allocation and local page replacement: "If a process does not modify any of its pages, then it is optimal to replace the page whose next reference is farthest in the page reference string." Show that this policy may not lead to the minimum number of page-in and page-out operations if the process modifies some of its pages.

12.8 What is Belady's anomaly? Show that a page replacement algorithm that possesses the stack property cannot exhibit Belady's anomaly.

12.9 Prove that the LRU page replacement policy possesses the stack property.

12.10 Optimal page replacement can be implemented by replacing the page whose next reference is farthest in the page reference string. Does this policy possess the stack property? Does the clock algorithm possess the stack property?

12.11 For the page reference string (12.6),

a. Show the working set at each time instant if the size of the working set window is (i) three instructions, (ii) four instructions.

b. Compare the operation and performance of the working set allocator with the FIFO and LRU allocators.

12.12 A working set allocator is used for a page reference string with two values of Δ, $\Delta_1 < \Delta_2$. pfr_1 and pfr_2 are page fault rates when Δ_1 and Δ_2 are used, respectively. Is $pfr_1 \geq pfr_2$ if working sets are recomputed (a) after every instruction and (b) after every n instructions for some n?

12.13 Describe the actions of a virtual memory manager using a working set memory allocator when it decides to reduce the degree of multiprogramming. Clearly indicate how it uses and manipulates its data structures for this purpose.

12.14 Explain, with the help of examples, why the working set size of a process may increase or decrease during its operation.

12.15 Justify the following statement: "Thrashing can arise when a working set memory allocator is used. However, it cannot last for long."

12.16 A virtual memory manager uses the following page replacement policy: When a combination of a high page fault rate in the system and low CPU efficiency is noticed, reduce the allocation for each process and load one more process. Comment on the effectiveness of this policy.

12.17 Explain why the two-handed clock algorithm for page replacement is superior to the one-handed clock algorithm (see Section 12.8.1).

12.18 A virtual memory manager implements a working set memory allocator and uses dynamic sharing of pages. Describe the housekeeping actions performed by it in the following situations.

a. When a page fault occurs.

b. When a shared page drops out of the working set of one of the sharing processes.

12.19 The amount of memory allocated to a process in a system using virtual memory is held constant and the page size is varied. (This action varies the number of pages of the process in memory.) Draw a graph of page size versus expected page fault rate.

12.20 The degree of multiprogramming in a system using virtual memory is varied by changing the memory allocation for processes. Draw a graph of degree of multiprogramming versus CPU efficiency. Explain the nature of the graph in the region of high degree of multiprogramming.

12.21 We refer to "instructions in the past" during operation of a process as follows: The most recently executed instruction is said to be "1 instruction in the past" of the process, the instruction before it is said to be "2 instructions in the past," etc. A memory allocator refers to the page reference in the instruction that is i instructions in the past as the $-i$ page reference. It uses a parameter w, and the following rules for memory allocation and page replacement:

a. Do nothing if the next page reference matches the $-w$ page reference.

b. Else, if the next page reference matches the $-i$ page reference for some $i < w$, do the following: if the $-w$ page reference does not match with the $-j$ page reference for some $j < w$, then reduce the memory allocation for the process by one page frame and remove the least recently used page, otherwise do nothing.

c. Else, if the next page reference causes a page fault and the $-w$ page reference does not match with the page reference in the $-j$ instruction for some $j < w$, then perform a page replacement using the LRU page replacement policy.

d. Else, increase the memory allocation for the process by one page frame and load the page contained in the next page reference.

Show that the actions of the memory allocator are equivalent to actions of the working set memory allocator with $\Delta = w$.

12.22 Compare the following memory management proposals in virtual memory using segmentation-with-paging.

a. Use the LRU policy within a process.

b. Use the LRU policy within a segment.

12.23 Comment on the validity of the following statement: "In virtual memory using segmentation-with-paging, the role of segmentation is limited to sharing. It does not play any role in memory management."

12.24 An I/O operation consists of the execution of a sequence of I/O commands. A *self-describing* I/O operation is an I/O operation some of whose I/O commands are read in by a previous I/O command of the same I/O operation. For example, consider the I/O operation

1. Read *d*, 6, *aaa*
2. Read *d*, *count*, *bbb*

where d is the id of the I/O device. The first I/O command reads 6 bytes into the memory area with address *aaa*. Let this be the area where the fields containing *count* (2 bytes) and *bbb* (4 bytes) of the second I/O command are stored. Thus, the first I/O command modifies the second I/O command. Let n and *ccc* be the values read into fields *count* and *bbb*, respectively, by the first I/O command. After I/O for the first I/O command is completed, the second I/O command reads n bytes into the memory area with address *ccc*. The data for this I/O operation would be

$$n,\ ccc,\ \underbrace{\qquad\qquad\qquad}_{n\text{ bytes of data}}$$

Can the methods of performing I/O in virtual memory described in Section 12.2.4 handle self-describing I/O operations correctly? Clearly justify your answer. In a simplified form of self-describing I/O, the first I/O command reads in only 2 bytes and stores them in the *count* field. Can the methods described in Section 12.2.4 handle such I/O operations correctly?

12.25 While initiating a process, the virtual memory manager copies the code of the process, which exists in a file, into the swap space reserved for the process. From the swap space, code pages are loaded into memory when needed. Explain the advantages of this arrangement. Why not load code pages directly from the file when needed? Some code pages may not be used during a run, hence it is redundant to copy them into the swap space. To avoid redundant copying, some virtual memory managers copy a code page into the swap space when it is used for the first time. Discuss the advantages and drawbacks of the optimization.

12.26 Performance of a virtual memory is determined by the interplay of three factors—CPU speed, size of memory, and peak throughput of the paging device. Possible causes of low or high efficiency of the CPU and the paging disk can be summarized as follows:

	High utilization	**Low utilization**
CPU	Processes are CPU-bound, or CPU is slow	Only few of the processes are CPU-bound, or thrashing is present
Paging disk	Thrashing is present, or disk is slow	Memory is overcommited to each process

Performance of virtual memory may improve if one or several of the following changes are made: the CPU is replaced by a faster CPU, the paging disk is replaced by a faster disk, the memory is increased, or the degree of multiprogramming is increased. In each of the following situations, which of the above changes would you recommend for improving system performance?

a. Low CPU efficiency, low disk efficiency
b. Low CPU efficiency, high disk efficiency
c. High CPU efficiency, low disk efficiency
d. High CPU efficiency, high disk efficiency

CLASS PROJECT: SIMULATION OF VIRTUAL MEMORY MANAGER

A virtual memory manager uses the two-thread arrangement shown in Figure 12.19, where the thread called *free frames manager* tries to maintain a sufficient number of free page frames at all times and the thread called *page I/O manager* performs page-out operations on dirty page frames. The virtual memory manager uses the *two-handed clock algorithm* discussed in Example 12.8 and illustrated in Figure 12.20. It performs page replacement on a *global* basis.

The working of this virtual memory manager is to be simulated. The simulation is controlled by commands in an input file, where each command has the format *<action>* *<parameters>*. Details of the actions are as follows:

Action name	Parameters and explanation
Memory_size	Number of page frames (integer)
Lower_threshold	Minimum number of free page frames (integer)
Upper_threshold	Maximum number of free page frames (integer)
Distance	Distance between clock hands, in terms of number of page frames (integer)
#processes	Number of processes (integer). Process id's are $P_0, P_1, \ldots$
Process_size	Process id, number of pages (both are integers)
Read	Process id, Page number : The indicated process reads the indicated page (both are integers)
Modify	Process id, Page number : The indicated process modifies the indicated page (both are integers)
Page_table	No parameters. Simulator displays the page tables of processes
IO_list	No parameters. Simulator displays the list of page frames on which page-out operations need to be performed
Hit_ratio	Simulator displays hit ratios for processes
Reset_counters	Simulator resets counters used for calculation of hit ratios

Develop a simulator of the virtual memory manager. The simulator must maintain page tables and swap spaces of the processes. It must also maintain a list of page frames on which page-out operations should be performed. The free frames manager puts page frame numbers in this list. The page I/O manager performs page-out operations on the page frames in a suitable order; it informs the free frames manager when the page-out operation of a page frame has been completed.

BIBLIOGRAPHY

Randell (1969) is an early paper on the motivation for virtual memory systems. Ghanem (1975) discusses memory partitioning in virtual memory systems for multiprogramming. Denning (1970) is a survey article on virtual memory. Hatfield (1971) discusses aspects of program performance in a virtual memory system.

Belady (1966) discusses the anomaly that carries his name. Mattson et al. (1970) discusses stack property of page replacement algorithms. Denning (1968a, 1968b) discusses thrashing and the fundamental working set model. Denning (1980) is a comprehensive discussion on working sets. Smith (1978) is a bibliography on paging and related topics. Wilson et al. (1995) discusses memory allocation in virtual memory environments. Johnstone and Wilson (1998) discusses the memory fragmentation problem.

Chang and Mergen (1988) describes the inverted page table, while Tanenbaum (2001) discusses the two-level page tables used in Intel 30386. Jacob and Mudge (1998) compares virtual memory features in MIPS, Pentium, and PowerPC architectures. Swanson et al. (1998) and Navarro et al. (2002) describe superpages.

Car and Hennessy (1981) discusses the clock algorithm. Bach (1986) and Vahalia (1996) describe Unix virtual memory, Beck et al. (2002), Gorman (2004), Bovet and Cesati (2005), and Love (2005) discuss Linux virtual memory, Mauro and McDougall (2006) discusses virtual memory in Solaris, while Russinovich and Solomon (2005) discusses Windows virtual memory.

Organick (1972) describes virtual memory in MULTICS.

1. Aho, A. V., P. J. Denning, and J. D. Ullman (1971): "Principles of optimal page replacement," *Journal of ACM*, **18** (1), 80–93.
2. Bach, M. J. (1986): *The Design of the Unix Operating System*, Prentice Hall, Englewood Cliffs, N.J.

3. Beck, M., H. Bohme, M. Dziadzka, U. Kunitz, R. Magnus, C. Schroter, and D. Verworner (2002): *Linux Kernel Programming*, 3rd ed., Pearson Education, New York.
4. Belady, L. A. (1966): "A study of replacement algorithms for virtual storage computers," *IBM Systems Journal*, **5** (2), 78–101.
5. Bensoussen, A., C. T. Clingen, and R. C. Daley (1972): "The MULTICS virtual memory—concepts and design," *Communications of the ACM*, **15** (5), 308–318.
6. Bryant, P. (1975): "Predicting working set sizes," *IBM Journal of R and D*, **19** (5), 221–229.
7. Bovet, D. P., and M. Cesati (2005): *Understanding the Linux Kernel*, 3rd ed., O'Reilly, Sebastopol, Calif.
8. Carr, W. R., and J. L. Hennessy (1981): "WSClock—a simple and effective algorithm for virtual memory management," *Proceedings of the ACM Symposium on Operating Systems Principles*, 87–95.
9. Chang, A., and M. Mergen (1988): "801 storage: architecture and programming," *ACM Transactions on Computer Systems*, **6**, 28–50.
10. Daley, R. C., and J. B. Dennis (1968): "Virtual memory, processes and sharing in MULTICS," *Communications of the ACM*, **11** (5), 305–322.
11. Denning, P. J. (1968a): "The working set model for program behavior," *Communications of the ACM*, **11** (5), 323–333.
12. Denning, P. J. (1968b): "Thrashing : Its causes and prevention," *Proceedings of AFIPS FJCC*, **33**, 915–922.
13. Denning, P. J. (1970): "Virtual Memory," *Computing Surveys*, **2** (3), 153–189.
14. Denning, P. J. (1980): "Working sets past and present," *IEEE Transactions on Software Engineering*, **6** (1), 64–84.
15. Ghanem, M. Z. (1975): "Study of memory partitioning for multiprogramming systems with virtual memory," *IBM Journal of R and D*, **19**, 451–457.
16. Gorman, M. (2004): *Understanding the Linux Virtual Memory Manager*, Prentice Hall, Englewood Cliffs, N.J.
17. Guertin, R.L.(1972): "Programming in a paging environment," *Datamation*, **18** (2), 48–55.
18. Hatfield, D. J., and J. Gerald (1971): "Program restructuring for virtual memory," *IBM Systems Journal*, **10** (3), 169–192.
19. Jacob, B., and T. Mudge (1998): "Virtual memory in contemporary microprocessors," *IEEE Micro Magazine*, **18**, 60–75.
20. Johnstone, M. S., and P. R. Wilson (1998): "The memory fragmentation problem: solved?," *Proceedings of the First International Symposium on Memory Management*, 26–36.
21. Love, R. (2005): *Linux Kernel Development*, 2nd ed. Novell Press.
22. Mauro, J., and R. McDougall (2006): *Solaris Internals,* 2nd ed., Prentice-Hall, Englewood Cliffs, N.J.
23. Mattson, R. L., J. Gecsei, D. R. Slutz, and I. L. Traiger (1970): "Evaluation techniques for storage hierarchies," *IBM Systems Journal*, **9** (2), 78–117.
24. Navarro, J., S. Iyer, P. Druschel, and A. Cox (2002): "Practical, transparent operating system support for superpages," *ACM SIGOPS Operating Systems Review*, **36**, issue SI, 89–104.
25. Organick, E. I. (1972): *The MULTICS System*, MIT Press, Cambridge, Mass.
26. Randell, B. (1969): "A note on storage fragmentation and program segmentation," *Communications of the ACM*, **12** (7), 365–369.
27. Rosell, J. R., and J. P. Dupuy (1973): "The design, implementation and evaluation of a working set dispatcher," *Communications of the ACM*, **16**, 247–253.
28. Russinovich, M. E., and D. A. Solomon (2005): *Microsoft Windows Internals*, 4th ed., Microsoft Press, Redmond, Wash.
29. Smith, A. J. (1978): "Bibliography on paging and related topics," *Operating Systems Review*, **12** (4), 39–56.
30. Swanson, M., L. Stoller, and J. Carter (1998): "Increasing TLB reach using superpages backed by shadow memory," *Proceedings of the 25th International Symposium on Computer Architecture*, 204–213.
31. Tanenbaum, A. S. (2001): *Modern Operating Systems*, 2nd ed., Prentice Hall, Englewood Cliffs, N.J.
32. Vahalia, U. (1996): *Unix Internals—The New Frontiers*, Prentice Hall, Englewood Cliffs, N.J.
33. Wilson, P. R., M. S. Johnstone, M. Neely and D. Boles (1995): "Dynamic storage allocation: a survey and critical review," *Proceedings of the International Workshop on Memory Management*, 1–116.

part 4

File Systems and I/O Management

Computer users expect convenience and efficiency while creating and manipulating files, and sharing them with other users of the system. They also expect a file system to possess protection, security and reliability features so that their files are not subjected to illegal accesses or tampering by other persons, or damage due to faults in the system. A system administrator expects a file system to ensure efficient use of I/O devices and contribute towards high performance of the system.

The file system uses a hierarchy of views and organizations to meet these diverse requirements. The *logical view* is employed to provide the features desired by users. In this view, a file is an entity that is owned by some user, shared by a group of users, and reliably stored over a period of time. The logical organization implements the logical view. It consists of different kinds of files and operations on files, *directory structures* and arrangements used for sharing and protection of files, and arrangements for reliable operation of the file system.

The *physical view* is employed to ensure speedy access to data, good performance of file operations in a process, and good performance of I/O devices. In this view, a file is a collection of data, which need to be accessed speedily, that is stored on I/O devices, which need to be used efficiently. The physical organization consists of arrangements using *buffers* and *caches* to implement the physical view.

We discuss the logical and physical views of a file system in separate chapters. The third chapter in this part discusses protection and security measures employed in an OS.

Chapter 13: File Systems

This chapter discusses a programmer's view of files and the file system. It describes fundamental *file organizations*, *directory structures*, operations on files and directories, and *file sharing semantics*, which specify the manner in which results of file manipulations performed by concurrent processes are visible to one another. Issues that compromise reliability of a file system are discussed. Fault tolerance using *atomic actions* and recovery using *backups* are described.

Road Map for Part 4

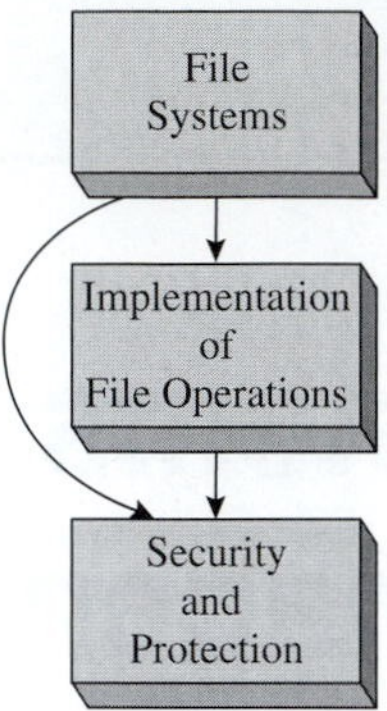

Schematic diagram showing the order in which chapters of this part should be covered in a course.

This chapter also discusses the role of the *file control block* as the interface between the logical and physical organizations used in a file system. Its use in implementing file operations and file sharing semantics is discussed.

Chapter 14: Implementation of File Operations

This chapter discusses the physical organization used in file systems. It starts with an overview of I/O devices and their characteristics, and discusses different *RAID organizations* that provide high reliability, fast access, and high data transfer rates. The arrangements used to implement device-level I/O are then discussed, including use of *buffers* and *caches* to speed up I/O operations and use of *disk scheduling* policies to improve throughput of disk devices.

Chapter 15: Security and Protection

Security and protection measures together ensure that only authorized users can access a file. This chapter discusses different kinds of security and protection threats in an operating system, measures used to thwart these threats, and the role played by the *encryption* technique in implementing these measures.

Chapter 13

File Systems

Computer users store programs and data in files so that they can be used conveniently and preserved across computing sessions. A user has many expectations when working with files, namely

- Convenient and fast access to files
- Reliable storage of files
- Sharing of files with collaborators

The resources used for storing and accessing files are I/O devices. As it must, the OS ensures both efficient performance of file processing activities in processes and efficient use of I/O devices.

Operating systems organize file management into two components called the *file system* and the *input-output control system* (IOCS) to separate the file-level concerns from concerns related to efficient storage and access of data. Accordingly, a file system provides facilities for creating and manipulating files, for ensuring reliability of files when faults such as power outages or I/O device malfunctions occur, and for specifying how files are to be shared among users. The IOCS provides access to data stored on I/O devices and good performance of I/O devices.

This chapter deals with the design of the file system. After discussing the basics of file organizations, directory structures and disk space management, we describe the *file sharing semantics* that govern concurrent sharing of files and *file system reliability*. Implementation of file operations by means of the IOCS is discussed in Chapter 14.

13.1 OVERVIEW OF FILE PROCESSING

We use the term *file processing* to describe the general sequence of operations of opening a file, reading data from the file or writing data into it, and closing the file. Figure 13.1 shows the arrangement through which an OS implements file processing activities of processes. Each *directory* contains entries describing some files. The directory entry of a file indicates the name of its owner, its location on a disk, the way its data is organized, and which users may access it in what manner.

The code of a process P_i is shown in the left part of Figure 13.1. When it opens a file for processing, the file system locates the file through the *directory*

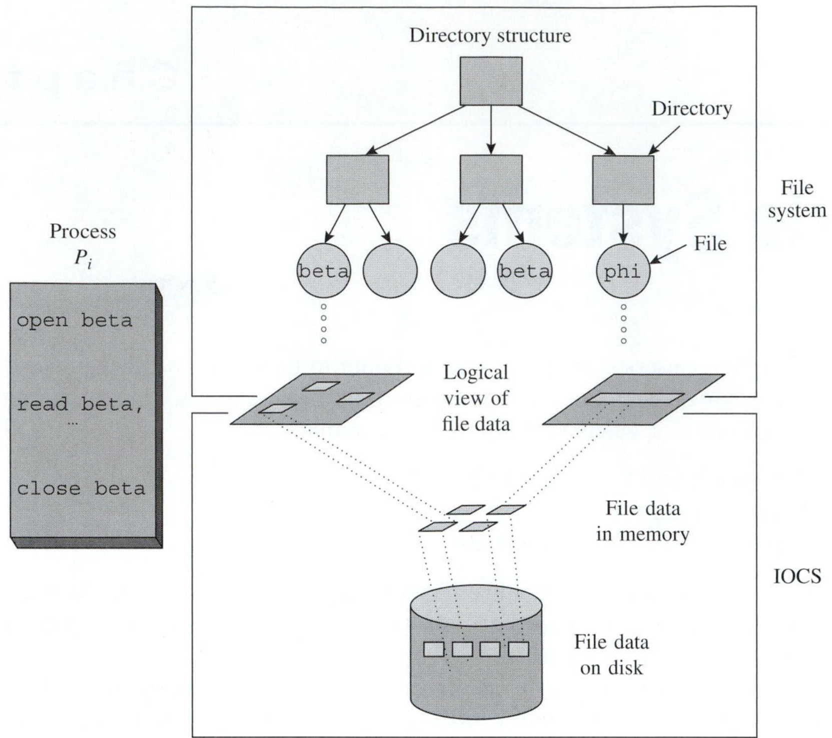

Figure 13.1 File system and the IOCS.

structure, which is an arrangement of many directories. In Figure 13.1, there are two files named `beta` located in different directories. When process P_i opens `beta`, the manner in which it names `beta`, the directory structure, and identities of the user who initiated process P_i will together determine which of the two files will be accessed.

A file system provides several *file types* (see Section 13.2). Each file type provides its own abstract view of data in a file—we call it a *logical view* of data. Figure 13.1 shows that file `beta` opened by process P_i has a *record*-oriented logical view, while file `phi` has a *byte stream*–oriented logical view in which distinct records do not exist.

The IOCS organizes a file's data on an I/O device in accordance with its file type. It is the *physical view* of the file's data. The mapping between the logical view of the file's data and its physical view is performed by the IOCS. The IOCS also provides an arrangement that speeds up a file processing activity—it holds some data from a file in memory areas organized as *buffers*, a *file cache*, or a *disk cache*. When a process performs a `read` operation to get some data from a file, the IOCS takes the data from a buffer or a cache if it is present there. This way, the process does not have to wait until the data is read off the I/O device that holds the file. Analogously, when a process performs a `write` operation on a file, the IOCS copies the data to be written in a buffer or in a cache. The actual I/O operations to read data from an I/O device into a buffer or a cache, or to write it from there onto an I/O device, are performed by the IOCS in the background.

13.1.1 File System and the IOCS

A file system views a file as a collection of data that is *owned* by a user, can be *shared* by a set of authorized users, and has to be *reliably stored* over an extended period of time. A file system gives users freedom in naming their files, as an aspect of ownership, so that a user can give a desired name to a file without worrying whether it conflicts with names of other users' files; and it provides privacy by protecting against interference by other users. The IOCS, on the other hand, views a file as a repository of data that need to be *accessed speedily* and are stored on an I/O device that needs to be *used efficiently*.

Table 13.1 summarizes the facilities provided by the file system and the IOCS. The file system provides directory structures that enable users to organize their data into logical groups of files, e.g., one group of files for each professional activity. The file system provides protection against illegal file accesses and ensures correct operation when processes access and update a file concurrently. It also ensures that data is reliably stored, i.e., data is not lost when system crashes occur. Facilities of the IOCS are as described earlier.

The file system and the IOCS form a hierarchy. Each of them has policies and provides mechanisms to implement the policies. In the language of Section 1.1, the IOCS and the file system provide different abstractions that lead to the following division of functions:

- The file system provides an interface through which a process can perform open, read/write, and close operations on files. Its policy modules handle protection and sharing of files during open and read/write operations. Its mechanism modules assist in the implementation of open and close operations by accessing directories. They also pass on read/write requests for file data to the IOCS.
- The IOCS policy modules ensure efficient operation of I/O devices and efficient file processing in each process through the IOCS mechanism modules. The mechanism modules in the IOCS, in turn, invoke the kernel through system calls to initiate I/O operations.

Table 13.1 **Facilities Provided by the File System and the Input-Output Control System**

File System
• Directory structures for convenient grouping of files
• Protection of files against illegal accesses
• File sharing semantics for concurrent accesses to a file
• Reliable storage of files
Input-Output Control System (IOCS)
• Efficient operation of I/O devices
• Efficient access to data in a file

Data and Metadata A file system houses two kinds of data—data contained within files, and data used to access files. We call the data within files *file data*, or simply *data*. The data used to access files is called *control data*, or *metadata*. In the logical view shown in Figure 13.1, data contained in the directory structure is metadata. As discussed later in this chapter and in Chapter 14, other metadata play a role in implementing file operations.

13.1.2 File Processing in a Program

At the programming language level, a file is an object that possesses *attributes* describing the organization of its data and the method of accessing the data. A program contains a declaration statement for a file, which specifies values of its attributes, and statements that open it, perform read/write operations on it, and close it (we call them file processing statements). During execution of the program, file processing is actually implemented by library modules of the file system and the IOCS.

Figure 13.2 illustrates how file processing is actually implemented. The program of Figure 13.2(a) declares `alpha` as a sequential-access file that contains records with a size of 60 bytes (see Section 13.2 for a discussion of records in a file). It also contains statements to open `alpha` and read a record from it. The compiler of the programming language processes the file declaration statement in the program and determines attributes of the file. It now replaces `open`, `close`, `read`, and `write` statements with calls on file system library modules `open`, `close`, `read`, and `write`, and passes the file attributes as parameters to the `open` call [see Figure 13.2(b)]. The file system modules invoke modules of the IOCS to actually perform I/O operations. The linker links the file system library

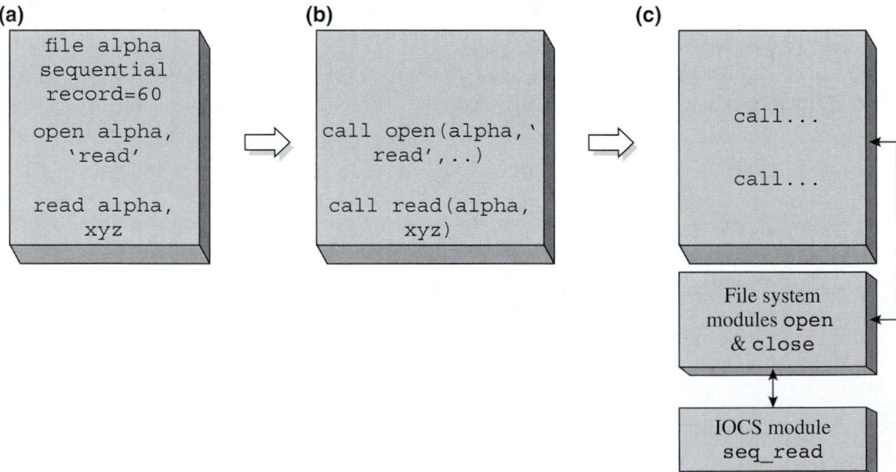

Figure 13.2 Implementing a file processing activity: (a) program containing file declaration statements; (b) compiled program showing calls on file system modules; (c) process invoking file system and IOCS modules during operation.

modules and the IOCS modules invoked by them to produce the program shown in Figure 13.2(c) (see Section 11.3.2 for a description of the linking function). When a process is created for execution of this program, it invokes the file system library modules during its operation to perform the `open` and `read` operations on the file, and these modules implement them with the help of appropriate IOCS library modules.

13.2 FILES AND FILE OPERATIONS

File Types A file system houses and organizes different types of files, e.g., data files, executable programs, object modules, textual information, documents, spreadsheets, photos, and video clips. Each of these file types has its own format for recording the data. These file types can be grouped into two classes:

- Structured files
- Byte stream files

A *structured file* is a collection of records, where a record is a meaningful unit for processing of data. A *record* is a collection of fields, and a *field* contains a single data item. Each record in a file is assumed to contain a *key* field. The value in the key field of a record is unique in a file; i.e., no two records contain an identical key. Many file types mentioned earlier are structured files. File types used by standard system software like compilers and linkers have a structure determined by the OS designer, while file types of user files depend on the applications or programs that create them.

A *byte stream file* is "flat." There are no records and fields in it; it is looked upon as a sequence of bytes by the processes that use it. The next example illustrates structured and byte stream files.

Structured and Byte Stream Files

Example 13.1

Figure 13.3(a) shows a structured file named `employee_info`. Each record in the file contains information about one employee. A record contains four fields: employee id, name, designation, and age. The field containing the employee id is the key field. Figure 13.3(b) shows a byte stream file `report`.

File Attributes A file attribute is a characteristic of a file that is important either to its users or to the file system, or both. Commonly used attributes of a file are: type, organization, size, location on disk, access control information, which indicates the manner in which different users can access the file; owner name, time of creation, and time of last use. The file system stores the attributes of a file in its directory entry. During a file processing activity, the file system uses the attributes of a file to locate it, and to ensure that each operation being performed on it is consistent with its attributes. At the end of the file processing activity, the file system stores changed values of the file's attributes, if any, in the file's directory entry.

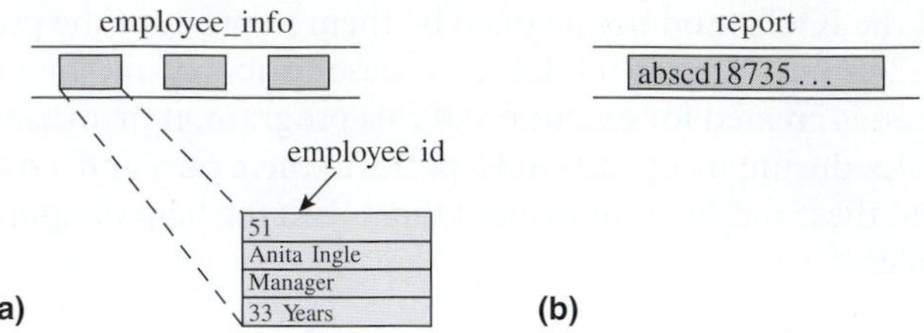

Figure 13.3 Logical views of (a) a structured file `employee_info`; (b) a byte stream file `report`.

Table 13.2 Operations on Files

Operation	Description
Opening a file	The file system finds the directory entry of the file and checks whether the user whose process is trying to open the file has the necessary access privileges for the file. It then performs some housekeeping actions to initiate processing of the file.
Reading or writing a record	The file system considers the organization of the file (see Section 13.3) and implements the read/write operation in an appropriate manner.
Closing a file	The file size information in the file's directory entry is updated.
Making a copy of a file	A copy of the file is made, a new directory entry is created for the copy and its name, size, location, and protection information is recorded in the entry.
File deletion	The directory entry of the file is deleted and the disk area occupied by it is freed.
File renaming	The new name is recorded in the directory entry of the file.
Specifying access privileges	The protection information in the file's directory entry is updated.

File Operations Table 13.2 describes operations performed on files. As mentioned earlier, operations such as open, close, rename, and delete are performed by file system modules. Actual access of files, i.e., reading or writing of records, is implemented by the IOCS modules.

13.3 FUNDAMENTAL FILE ORGANIZATIONS AND ACCESS METHODS

We use the term "record access pattern" to describe the order in which records in a file are accessed by a process. The two fundamental record access patterns are *sequential access*, in which records are accessed in the order in which they fall in a file (or in the reverse of that order), and *random access*, in which records may be accessed in any order. The file processing actions of a process will execute efficiently only if the process's record access pattern can be implemented efficiently in the file system. The characteristics of an I/O device make it suitable for a specific record access pattern. For example, a tape drive can access only the record that is placed immediately before or after the current position of its read/write head. Hence it is suitable for sequential access to records. A disk drive can directly access any record given its address. Hence it can efficiently implement both the sequential and random record access patterns.

A *file organization* is a combination of two features—a method of arranging records in a file and a procedure for accessing them. A file organization is designed to exploit the characteristics of an I/O device for providing efficient record access for a specific record access pattern. A file system supports several file organizations so that a process can employ the one that best suits its file processing requirements and the I/O device in use. This section describes three fundamental file organizations—sequential file organization, direct file organization and index sequential file organization. Other file organizations used in practice are either variants of these fundamental ones or are special-purpose organizations that exploit less commonly used I/O devices.

Accesses to files governed by a specific file organization are implemented by an IOCS module called an *access method*. An access method is a policy module of the IOCS. While compiling a program, the compiler infers the file organization governing a file from the file's declaration statement (or from the rules for default, if the program does not contain a file declaration statement), and identifies the correct access method to invoke for operations on the file. We describe the functions of access methods after discussing the fundamental file organizations.

13.3.1 Sequential File Organization

In *sequential file organization*, records are stored in an ascending or descending sequence according to the key field; the record access pattern of an application is expected to follow suit. Hence sequential file organization supports two kinds of operations: read the next (or previous) record, and skip the next (or previous) record. A sequential-access file is used in an application if its data can be conveniently presorted into an ascending or descending order. The sequential file organization is also used for byte stream files.

13.3.2 Direct File Organization

The *direct file organization* provides convenience and efficiency of file processing when records are accessed in a random order. To access a record, a read/write command needs to mention the value in its key field. We refer to such files as *direct-access files*. A direct-access file is implemented as follows: When a process provides the key value of a record to be accessed, the access method module for the direct file organization applies a transformation to the key value that generates the address of the record in the storage medium. If the file is organized on a disk, the transformation generates a (*track_no, record_no*) address. The disk heads are now positioned on the track *track_no* before a read or write command is issued on the record *record_no*.

Consider a file of employee information organized as a direct-access file. Let p records be written on one track of the disk. Assuming the employee numbers and the track and record numbers of the file to start from 1, the address of the record for employee number n is (*track number* (t_n), *record number* (r_n)) where

$$t_n = \left\lceil \frac{n}{p} \right\rceil \quad \textbf{(13.1)}$$

$$r_n = n - (t_n - 1) \times p \quad \textbf{(13.2)}$$

and $\lceil \ldots \rceil$ indicates a rounded-up integer value.

Direct file organization provides access efficiency when records are processed randomly. However, it has three drawbacks compared to sequential file organization:

- Record address calculation consumes CPU time.
- Disks can store much more data along the outermost track than along the innermost track. However, the direct file organization stores an equal amount of data along each track. Hence some recording capacity is wasted.
- The address calculation formulas (13.1) and (13.2) work correctly only if a record exists for every possible value of the key, so dummy records have to exist for keys that are not in use. This requirement leads to poor utilization of the I/O medium.

Hence sequential processing of records in a direct-access file is less efficient than processing of records in a sequential-access file. Another practical problem is that characteristics of an I/O device are explicitly assumed and used by the address calculation formulas (13.1) and (13.2), which makes the file organization device-dependent. Rewriting the file on another device with different characteristics, e.g., different track capacity, will imply modifying the address calculation formulas. This requirement affects the portability of programs.

Example 13.2 Sequential and Direct-Access Files

Figure 13.4 shows the arrangement of employee records in sequential and direct file organizations. Employees with the employee numbers 3, 5–9 and 11 have left the organization. However, the direct-access file needs to contain a record for each of these employees to satisfy the address calculation formulas (13.1) and (13.2). This fact leads to the need for dummy records in the direct-access file.

13.3.3 Index Sequential File Organization

An *index* helps to determine the location of a record from its key value. In a pure indexed file organization, the index of a file contains an index entry with

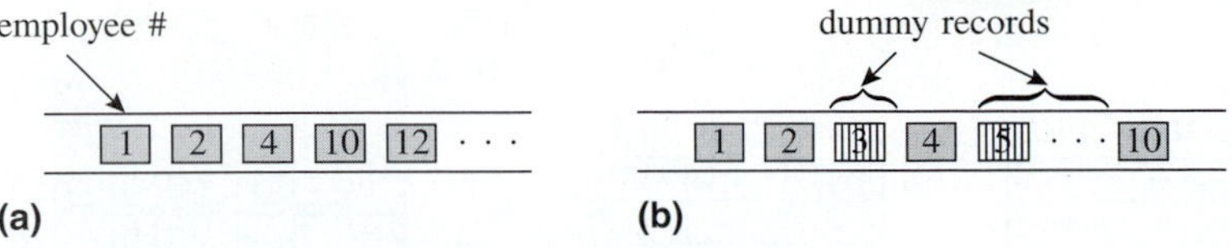

Figure 13.4 Records in (a) sequential file; (b) direct-access file.

the format (key value, disk address) for each key value existing in the file. To access a record with key *k*, the index entry containing *k* is found by searching the index, and the disk address mentioned in the entry is used to access the record. If an index is smaller than a file, this arrangement provides high access efficiency because a search in the index is more efficient than a search in the file.

The *index sequential* file organization is a hybrid organization that combines elements of the indexed and the sequential file organizations. To locate a desired record, the access method module for this organization searches an index to identify a section of the disk that *may* contain the record, and searches the records in this section of the disk sequentially to find the record. The search succeeds if the record is present in the file; otherwise, it results in a failure. This arrangement requires a much smaller index than does a pure indexed file because the index contains entries for only some of the key values. It also provides better access efficiency than the sequential file organization while ensuring comparably efficient use of I/O media.

For a large file the index would still contain a large number of entries, and so the time required to search through the index would be large. A higher-level index can be used to reduce the search time. An entry in the higher-level index points to a section of the index. This section of the index is searched to find the section of the disk that may contain a desired record, and this section of the disk is searched sequentially for the desired record. The next example illustrates this arrangement.

Index Sequential File Organization

Example 13.3

Figure 13.5 illustrates a file of employee information organized as an index sequential file. Records are stored in ascending order by the key field. Two indexes are built to facilitate speedy search. The track index indicates the smallest and largest key value located on each track (see the fields named *low* and *high* in Figure 13.5). The higher-level index contains entries for groups of tracks containing 3 tracks each. To locate the record with a key *k*, first the higher-level index is searched to locate the group of tracks that may contain the desired record. The track index for the tracks of the group is now searched to locate the track that may contain the desired record, and the selected track is searched sequentially for the record with key *k*. The search ends unsuccessfully if it fails to find the record on the track.

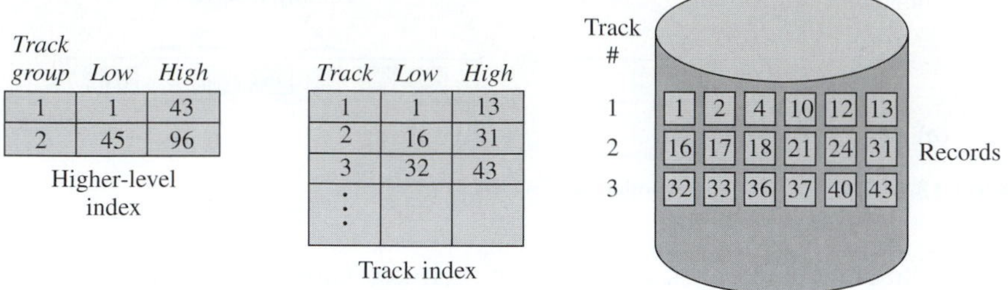

Figure 13.5 Track index and higher-level index in an index sequential file.

13.3.4 Access Methods

An *access method* is a module of the IOCS that implements accesses to a class of files using a specific file organization. The procedure to be used for accessing records in a file, whether by a sequential search or by address calculation, is determined by the file organization. The access method module uses this procedure to access records. It may also use some advanced techniques in I/O programming to make file processing more efficient. Two such techniques are *buffering* and *blocking* of records.

Buffering of Records The access method reads records of an input file ahead of the time when they are needed by a process and holds them temporarily in memory areas called *buffers* until they are actually used by the process. The purpose of buffering is to reduce or eliminate the wait for an I/O operation to complete; the process faces a wait only when the required record does not already exist in a buffer. The converse actions are performed for an output file. When the process performs a write operation, the data to be written into the file is copied into a buffer and the process is allowed to continue its operation. The data is written on the I/O device sometime later and the buffer is released for reuse. The process faces a wait only if a buffer is not available when it performs a write operation.

Blocking of Records The access method always reads or writes a large block of data, which contains several file records, from or to the I/O medium. This feature reduces the total number of I/O operations required for processing a file, thereby improving the file processing efficiency of a process. Blocking also improves utilization of an I/O medium and throughput of a device.

We discuss the techniques of buffering and blocking of records in Chapter 14.

13.4 DIRECTORIES

A directory contains information about a group of files. Each entry in a directory contains the attributes of one file, such as its type, organization, size, location, and the manner in which it may be accessed by various users in the system. Figure 13.6

File name	*Type and size*	*Location info*	*Protection info*	*Open count*	*Lock*	*Flags*	*Misc info*

Field	**Description**
File name	Name of the file. If this field has a fixed size, long file names beyond a certain length will be truncated.
Type and size	The file's type and size. In many file systems, the type of file is implicit in its extension; e.g., a file with extension .c is a byte stream file containing a C program, and a file with extension .obj is an object program file, which is often a structured file.
Location info	Information about the file's location on a disk. This information is typically in the form of a table or a linked list containing addresses of disk blocks allocated to a file.
Protection info	Information about which users are permitted to access this file, and in what manner.
Open count	Number of processes currently accessing the file.
Lock	Indicates whether a process is currently accessing the file in an exclusive manner.
Flags	Information about the nature of the file—whether the file is a directory, a link, or a mounted file system.
Misc info	Miscellaneous information like id of owner, date and time of creation, last use, and last modification.

Figure 13.6 Fields in a typical directory entry.

shows the fields of a typical directory entry. The *open count* and *lock* fields are used when several processes open a file concurrently. The *open count* indicates the number of such processes. As long as this count is nonzero, the file system keeps some of the metadata concerning the file in memory to speed up accesses to the data in the file. The *lock* field is used when a process desires exclusive access to a file. The *flags* field is used to differentiate between different kinds of directory entries. We put the value "D" in this field to indicate that a file is a directory, "L" to indicate that it is a link, and "M" to indicate that it is a mounted file system. Later sections in this chapter will describe these uses. The *misc info* field contains information such as the file's owner, its time of creation, and last modification.

A file system houses files owned by several users. Therefore it needs to grant users two important prerogatives:

- *File naming freedom:* A user's ability to give any desired name to a file, without being constrained by file names chosen by other users.
- *File sharing:* A user's ability to access files created by other users, and ability to permit other users to access his files.

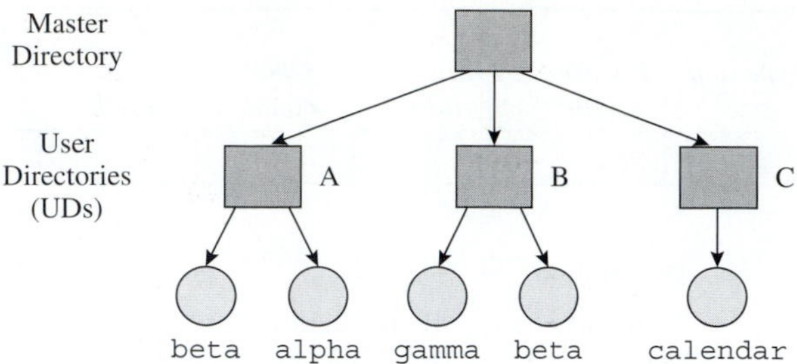

Figure 13.7 A directory structure composed of master and user directories.

The file system creates several directories and uses a *directory structure* to organize them for providing file naming freedom and file sharing. We include schematic diagrams to illustrate directory structures, using the convention that a directory is represented by a rectangle, while a file is represented by a circle. Figure 13.7 shows a simple directory structure containing two kinds of directories. A *user directory* (UD) contains entries describing the files owned by one user. The *master directory* contains information about the UDs of all registered users of the system; each entry in the master directory is an ordered pair consisting of a user id and a pointer to a UD. In the file system shown, users A and B have each created their own file named `beta`. These files have entries in the users' respective UDs. We describe the directory structure shown in Figure 13.7 as a *two-level* directory structure.

Use of separate UDs is what provides naming freedom. When a process created by user A executes the statement `open (beta, ...)`, the file system searches the master directory to locate A's UD, and searches for `beta` in it. If the call `open(beta, ...)` had instead been executed by some process created by B, the file system would have searched B's UD for `beta`. This arrangement ensures that the correct file is accessed even if many files with identical names exist in the system.

Use of UDs has one drawback, however. It inhibits users from sharing their files with other users. A special syntax may have to be provided to enable a user to refer to another user's file. For example, a process created by user C may execute the statement `open (A→beta, ...)` to open A's file `beta`. The file system can implement this simply by using A's UD, rather than C's UD, to search and locate file `beta`. To implement file protection, the file system must determine whether user C is permitted to open A's file `beta`. It checks the *protection info* field of `beta`'s directory entry for this purpose. Details of file protection are discussed in Section 13.6.

13.4.1 Directory Trees

The MULTICS file system of the 1960s contained features that allowed the user to create a new directory, give it a name of his choice, and create files and other directories in it up to any desired level. The resulting directory structure is a *tree*;

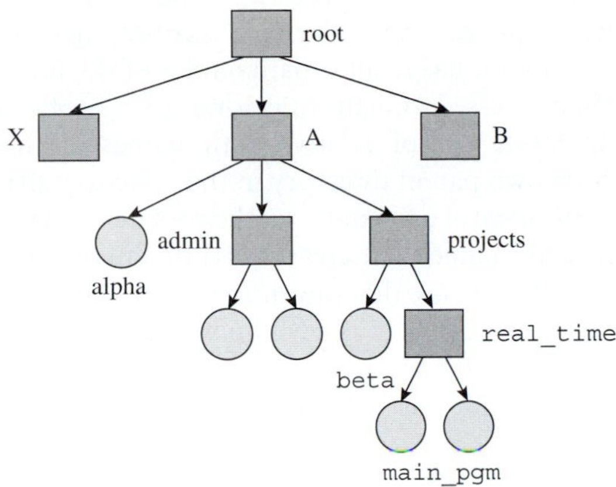

Figure 13.8 Directory trees of the file system and of user A.

we call it the *directory tree*. After MULTICS, most file systems have provided directory trees.

A user can create a file to hold data or to act as a directory. When a distinction between the two is important, we will call these files respectively *data files* and *directory files*, or simply *directories*. The file system provides a directory called `root` that contains the *home directory* for each user, which is a directory file that typically has the same name as the user's name. A user structures his information by creating directory files and data files in his home directory, creating files and other directories in a directory file, and so on. We will assume that the file system puts a "D" in the *flags* field of a file's entry if the file is a directory file. Figure 13.8 shows the directory tree of the file system. The root of this tree is the directory `root`, which contains a home directory for each user that bears the user's name. User A has created a file called `alpha` and directories called `admin` and `projects`. The `projects` directory contains a directory `real_time`, which contains a file `main_pgm`. Thus user A has a directory tree of his own; its root is his home directory.

At any time, a user is said to be "in" some specific directory, which is called his *current directory*. When the user wishes to open a file, the file name is searched for in this directory. Whenever the user logs in, the OS puts him in his home directory; the home directory is then the user's current directory. A user can change his current directory at any time through a "change directory" command.

A file's name may not be unique in the file system, so a user or a process uses a *path name* to identify it in an unambiguous manner. A path name is a sequence of one or more path components separated by a slash (/), where each path component is a reference through a directory and the last path component is the name of the file.

Path names for locating a file from the current directory are called *relative path names*. Relative path names are often short and convenient to use; however, they can be confusing because a file may have different relative path names when accessed from different current directories. For example, in Figure 13.8, the file alpha has the simple relative path name alpha when accessed from current directory A, whereas it has relative path names of the form ../alpha and ../../alpha when accessed from the directories projects and real_time, respectively. To facilitate use of relative path names, each directory stores information about its own parent directory in the directory structure.

The *absolute path name* of a file starts on the root directory of the file system's directory tree. Identically named files created in different directories differ in their absolute path names. We will use the convention that the first path component in an absolute path is a null symbol, and the home directory of a user A is specified as ~A. Thus, in Figure 13.8, the absolute path name of file alpha is /A/alpha. An alternative path name for it is ~A/alpha.

13.4.2 Directory Graphs

In a directory tree, each file except the root directory has exactly one parent directory. This directory structure provides total separation of different users' files and complete file naming freedom. However, it makes file sharing rather cumbersome. A user wishing to access another user's files has to use a path name that involves two or more directories. For example, in Figure 13.8, user B can access file beta using the path name ../A/projects/beta or ~A/projects/beta.

Use of the tree structure leads to a fundamental asymmetry in the way different users can access a shared file. The file will be located in some directory belonging to one of the users, who can access it with a shorter path name than can other users. This problem can be solved by organizing the directories in an *acyclic graph structure*. In this structure, a file can have many parent directories, and so a shared file can be pointed to by directories of all users who have access to it. Acyclic graph structures are implemented through links.

Links A *link* is a directed connection between two existing files in the directory structure. It can be written as a triple (*<from_file_name>*, *<to_file_name>*, *<link_name>*), where *<from_file_name>* is a directory and *<to_file_name>* can be a directory or a file. Once a link is established, *<to_file_name>* can be accessed as if it were a file named *<link_name>* in the directory *<from_file_name>*. The fact that *<link_name>* is a link in the directory *<from_file_name>* is indicated by putting the value "L" in its *flags* field. Example 13.4 illustrates how a link is set up.

Example 13.4 Link in a Directory Structure

Figure 13.9 shows the directory structure after user C creates a link using the command (~C, ~C/software/web_server, quest). The name of the link is quest. The link is made in the directory ~C and it points to the file ~C/software/web_server. This link permits ~C/software/web_server to be accessed by the name ~C/quest.

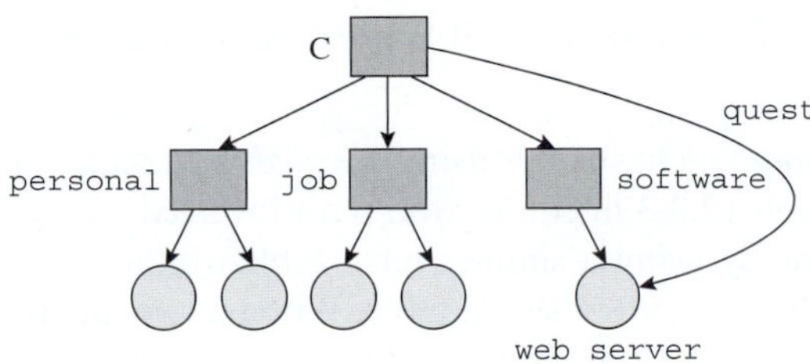

Figure 13.9 A link in the directory structure.

An unlink command nullifies a link. Implementation of the link and unlink commands involves manipulation of directories that contain the files *<from_file_name>* and *<to_file_name>*. Deadlocks may arise while link and unlink commands are implemented if several processes issue these commands simultaneously. The file system can use some simple policy to ensure absence of deadlocks (see Section 8.8.1).

13.4.3 Operations on Directories

A search is the most frequent operation on directories. Other operations on directories are maintenance operations like creating or deleting files, updating file entries when a process performs a close operation, listing a directory, and deleting a directory.

The deletion operation specifies a path name for the file to be deleted. It becomes complicated when the directory structure is a graph because a file may have multiple parents. A file is deleted only if it has a single parent; otherwise, it is simply made inaccessible from its parent directory in the path name specified in the delete command. To simplify the delete operation, the file system maintains a link count with each file. The count is set to 1 when the file is created, incremented by 1 whenever a link is set to point to it, and decremented by 1 at a delete command. The file can be deleted only when its link count becomes 0.

This simple strategy is not adequate if the directory structure contains cycles. A cycle develops when a link is set from a directory to one of its ancestor directories, e.g., if a link is set up from the directory `real_time` in Figure 13.8 to the directory `projects`. Now the link count of `projects` is 2, so its deletion by using the path name `~A/projects` would lead only to deletion of the entry of `projects` in `A`. However, there is no reason to retain directory `projects` and files reachable from it, since `projects` would not be accessible from the home directory of any user! This problem can be solved either by using a technique to detect cycles that are not reachable from any home directories, which can be expensive, or by preventing cycles from arising in the directory structure, which is equally expensive.

13.4.4 Organization of Directories

A directory could be a flat file that is searched linearly to find the required file entry. However, this organization is inefficient if the directory contains a large number of entries. Hash tables and B+ trees are used to provide greater search efficiency.

Hash Table Directory A hash table using the *hash with chaining* organization was discussed in Section 12.2.3 in connection with inverted page tables. A directory can be maintained by using a simpler hash table organization called *hash with open addressing* that requires a single table. When a new file is to be created in a directory, a hashing function h is applied to a bit string obtained from the file's name, which yields an entry number e. If the eth entry in the directory is already occupied by another file, the entry given by $(e + 1) mod(n)$, where n is the size of the hash table, is checked and so on until an unused entry is found, and the new file's details are entered in it. When a file is to be opened, a similar search is carried out to locate its entry in the directory. Hash table organizations that do not require more than two comparisons to locate a required file name are practical, so a hash table directory can be searched efficiently. However, use of a hash table directory organization has a few drawbacks—it is cumbersome to change the size of a directory, or to delete an entry from it.

B+ Tree Directory A B+ tree is an m-way search tree where $m \leq 2 \times d$, d being an integer called the *order* of the tree. The B+ tree is a balanced tree; i.e., the length of the path from the root to any leaf node is the same. This property has a useful implication for directory search—it takes approximately the same amount of time to find the information concerning any file name existing in the directory.

A B+ tree directory is organized as follows: Information about files is recorded only in leaf nodes of the tree; nonleaf nodes are used merely to direct search to appropriate parts of the tree. The nonleaf nodes of the tree contain *index entries*, where each index entry is an ordered pair consisting of a pointer to another node in the tree and a file name. The last index entry in a node does not contain a file name; it contains only a pointer to another node in the tree. The leaf nodes of the tree contain only *information entries* for files—each entry is an ordered pair consisting of a pointer to information associated with a file name and the file name itself.

The root node contains between 2 and $2 \times d$ entries, both inclusive, where d is the order of the tree. A nonroot node contains between d and $2 \times d$ entries, both inclusive. To facilitate search for a file name, the entries in a node—whether index entries or information entries—are lexicographically ordered on file names. Thus, a file name in an entry is "larger" than the file name in the preceding entry in the node, and "smaller" than the file name in the following entry in the node. A leaf node contains two extra pointers. These pointers point to tree nodes that are to its left and to its right in the tree, if any, respectively. These pointers are used to facilitate insertion and deletion of entries. We do not discuss their use here.

To locate a file in a directory, the directory B+ tree is searched, starting with its root node. The file's name is compared with the file name in the first index entry in the node. If it is lexicographically "smaller" than the file name in the entry, the pointer in the index entry is used to locate another tree node, where the search is continued; otherwise, the search is continued with the next index entry in the node, if any, and so on. If the next index entry is the last index entry in the

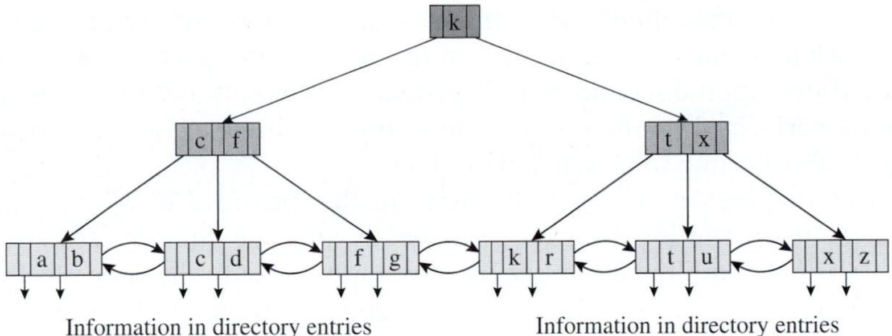

Figure 13.10 A directory organized as a B+ tree.

node, the search is simply continued with the tree node pointed to by the pointer in the index entry (note that the last index entry in a node does not contain a file name). This procedure is followed until a leaf node of the tree is encountered. Now, information entries in the leaf node are searched by using a convenient search technique like linear or binary search. If an information entry is found for the file name we are looking for, we use the pointer in the information entry to locate the information associated with the file name; otherwise, the file name does not exist in the directory.

Directory as a B+ Tree

Example 13.5

Figure 13.10 shows a directory organized as B+ tree of order 2. A down-arrow in a leaf node is a pointer to information associated with a file name. To search for file `c`, we compare `c` with `k`, the file name in the first index entry in the root. Since the file name `c` is "smaller" than `k`, we use the pointer in this index entry to locate the tree node where the search is to be continued. This is the node that contains index entries for file names `c` and `f`. Since `c` is not smaller than the file name in the first index entry, we compare it with the file name in the next index entry in the node, i.e., with `f`. It is smaller, hence we use the pointer in this index entry. This pointer points to a leaf node. Hence we search for `c` in the information entries in this node. We find a match in the first information entry, so we use the pointer in this entry to locate the directory information about file `c`.

The advantages of a B+ tree are its fast search capability and the efficiency of the methods for rebalancing the tree when insertions and deletions are made. Windows NTFS uses B+ trees for directories.

13.5 MOUNTING OF FILE SYSTEMS

There can be many file systems in an operating system. Each file system is constituted on a *logical disk*, i.e., on a partition of a disk. Files contained in a file system can be accessed only when the file system is *mounted.* The mount operation is what "connects" the file system to the system's directory structure. An unmount operation disconnects a file system. The mount and unmount operations are performed by the system administrator. These operations provide an element of protection to files in a file system.

Mounting creates an effect analogous to that provided by a link. The difference is that mounting does not permanently alter the directory structure. Its effect lasts only until the file system is unmounted or until the system is booted again. Mounting of file systems is useful when there are multiple file systems in the OS (see Section 13.14.1), or when a user of a distributed system wishes to access files located in a remote machine (see Chapter 20).

A *mount point* is a directory in which a file system can be mounted. A mount operation is performed by issuing the command `mount` (*<FS_name>*, *<mount_point_name>*), where *<FS_name>* and *<mount_point_name>*, both of which are path names, designate the root of the file system to be mounted and the mount point, respectively. When the mount operation is performed, the root of the mounted file system assumes the name *<mount_point_name>*. Thus, any file with the relative path name ap_i in the directory *<FS_name>* can be accessed by the path name *<mount_point_name>* / ap_i. If a file system is mounted in a directory that already contains some files, these files become invisible to the user until the file system is unmounted. The next example illustrates the effect of executing a *mount* command.

Example 13.6 Mounting of a File System

In Figure 13.11(a), `~A/admin` is a mount point in a directory structure, and `meeting` is the root directory of another file system. Figure 13.11(b) shows the effect of the command `mount (meeting,~A/admin)`. File `items` can now be accessed as `~A/admin/agenda/items`.

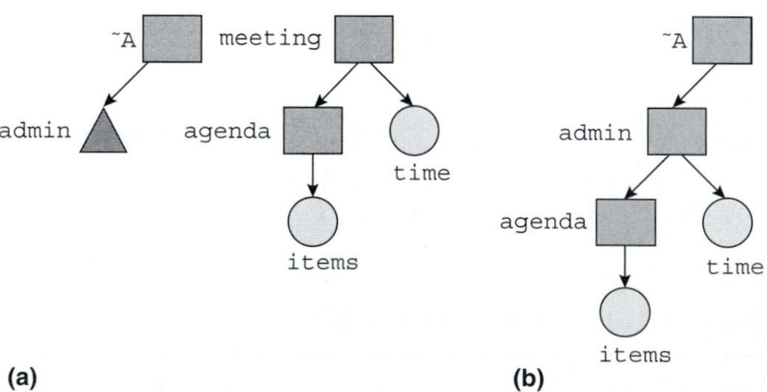

Figure 13.11 Directory structures (a) before a mount command; (b) after a mount command.

The effect of a mount operation is nullified by the corresponding command unmount (<*FS_name*>, <*mount_point_name*>). The unmount operation succeeds only if no files of the mounted file system are currently open. To check this condition easily, the file system keeps a count in the root of the mounted file system to indicate how many of its files have been opened.

13.6 FILE PROTECTION

A user would like to share a file with collaborators, but not with others. We call this requirement *controlled sharing* of files. To implement it, the owner of a file specifies which users can access the file in what manner. The file system stores this information in the *protection info* field of the file's directory entry (see Figure 13.6), and uses it to control access to the file.

Different methods of structuring the protection information of files are discussed in Chapter 15. In this section, we assume that a file's protection information is stored in the form of an *access control list*. Each element of the access control list is an access control pair of the form (<*user_name*>, <*list_of_access_privileges*>). When a process executed by some user X tries to perform an operation <*opn*> on file alpha, the file system searches for the pair with <*user_name*>= X, in the access control list of alpha and checks whether <*opn*> is consistent with the <*list_of_access_privileges*>. If it is not, the attempt to access alpha fails. For example, a write attempt by X will fail if the entry for user X in the access control list is (X, read), or if the list does not contain an entry for X.

The size of a file's access control list depends on the number of users and the number of access privileges defined in the system. To reduce the size of protection information, users can be classified in some convenient manner and an access control pair can be specified for each user class rather than for each individual user. Now an access control list has only as many pairs as the number of user classes. For example, Unix specifies access privileges for three classes of users—the file owner, users in the same group as the owner, and all other users of the system.

In most file systems, access privileges are of three kinds—*read*, *write*, and *execute*. A *write* privilege permits existing data in the file to be modified and also permits new data to be added: One can further differentiate between these two privileges by defining a new access privilege called *append*; however, it would increase the size of the protection information. The *execute* privilege permits a user to execute the program contained in a file. Access privileges have different meanings for directory files. The *read* privilege for a directory file implies that one can obtain a listing of the directory, while the *write* privilege for a directory implies that one can create new files in the directory. The *execute* privilege for a directory permits an access to be made through it—that is, it permits a file existing in the directory to be accessed. A user can use the execute privilege of directories to make a part of his directory structure visible to other users.

13.7 ALLOCATION OF DISK SPACE

As mentioned in Section 13.5, a disk may contain many file systems, each in its own partition of the disk. The file system knows which partition a file belongs to, but the IOCS does not. Hence disk space allocation is performed by the file system.

Early file systems adapted the contiguous memory allocation model (see Section 11.6) by allocating a single contiguous disk area to a file when it was created. This model was simple to implement. It also provided data access efficiency by reducing disk head movement during sequential access to data in a file. However, contiguous allocation of disk space led to external fragmentation. Interestingly, it also suffered from internal fragmentation because the file system found it prudent to allocate some extra disk space to allow for expansion of a file. Contiguity of disk space also necessitated complicated arrangements to avoid use of bad disk blocks: The file system identified bad disk blocks while formatting the disk and noted their addresses. It then allocated substitute disk blocks for the bad ones and built a table showing addresses of bad blocks and their substitutes. During a read/write operation, the IOCS checked whether the disk block to be accessed was a bad block. If it was, it obtained the address of the substitute disk block and accessed it.

Modern file systems adapt the noncontiguous memory allocation model (see Section 11.7) to disk space allocation. In this approach, a chunk of disk space is allocated on demand, i.e., when the file is created or when its size grows because of an update operation. The file system has to address three issues for implementing this approach:

- *Managing free disk space:* Keep track of free disk space and allocate from it when a file requires a new disk block.
- *Avoiding excessive disk head movement:* Ensure that data in a file is not dispersed to different parts of a disk, as it would cause excessive movement of the disk heads during file processing.
- *Accessing file data:* Maintain information about the disk space allocated to a file and use it to find the disk block that contains required data.

The file system can maintain a *free list* of disk space and allocate from it when a file requires a new disk block. Alternatively, it can use a table called the *disk status map* (DSM) to indicate the status of disk blocks. The DSM has one entry for each disk block, which indicates whether the disk block is free or has been allocated to a file. This information can be maintained in a single bit, and so a DSM is also called a *bit map*. Figure 13.12 illustrates a DSM. A 1 in an entry indicates that the corresponding disk block is allocated. The DSM is consulted every time a new disk block has to be allocated to a file.

To avoid dispersing file data to different parts of a disk, file systems confine the disk space allocation for a file either to consecutive disk blocks, which form an *extent*, also called a *cluster*, or consecutive cylinders in a disk, which form *cylinder groups* (see Section 14.3.2). Use of a disk status map, rather than a free

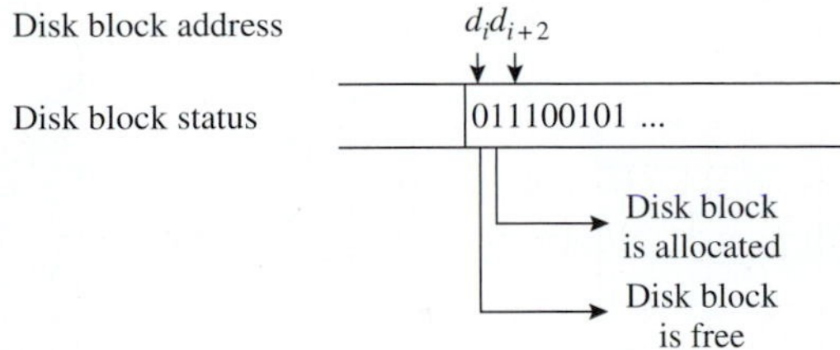

Figure 13.12 Disk status map (DSM).

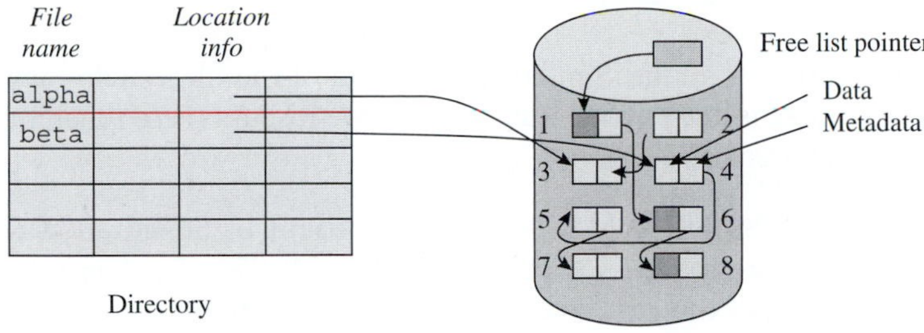

Figure 13.13 Linked allocation of disk space.

list, has the advantage that it allows the file system to readily pick disk blocks from an extent or cylinder group.

We discuss two fundamental approaches to noncontiguous disk space allocation. They differ in the manner they maintain information about disk space allocated to a file.

13.7.1 Linked Allocation

A file is represented by a linked list of disk blocks. Each disk block has two fields in it—*data* and *metadata.* The *data* field contains the data written into the file, while the *metadata* field is the link field, which contains the address of the next disk block allocated to the file. Figure 13.13 illustrates linked allocation. The *location info* field of the directory entry of file `alpha` points to the first disk block of the file. Other blocks are accessed by following the pointers in the list of disk blocks. The last disk block contains null information in its metadata field. Thus, file `alpha` consists of disk blocks 3 and 2, while file `beta` consists of blocks 4, 5, and 7. Free space on the disk is represented by a *free list* in which each free disk block contains a pointer to the next free disk block. When a disk block is needed to store new data added to a file, a disk block is taken off the free list and added to the file's list of disk blocks. To delete a file, the file's list of disk blocks is simply added to the free list.

Linked allocation is simple to implement, and incurs a low allocation/deallocation overhead. It also supports sequential files quite efficiently. However, files with nonsequential organization cannot be accessed efficiently. Reliability is also poor since corruption of the metadata field in a disk block may lead to

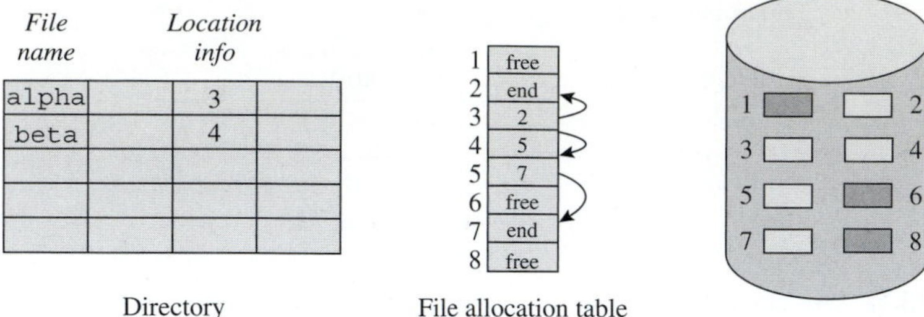

Figure 13.14 File Allocation Table (FAT).

loss of data in the entire file. Similarly, operation of the file system may be disrupted if a pointer in the free list is corrupted. We discuss these reliability issues in Section 13.11.

File Allocation Table (FAT) MS-DOS uses a variant of linked allocation that stores the metadata separately from the file data. A *file allocation table* (FAT) of a disk is an array that has one element corresponding to every disk block in the disk. For a disk block that is allocated to a file, the corresponding FAT element contains the address of the next disk block. Thus the disk block and its FAT element together form a pair that contains the same information as the disk block in a classical linked allocation scheme.

The directory entry of a file contains the address of its first disk block. The FAT element corresponding to this disk block contains the address of the second disk block, and so on. The FAT element corresponding to the last disk block contains a special code to indicate that the file ends on that disk block. Figure 13.14 illustrates the FAT for the disk of Figure 13.13. The file `alpha` consists of disk blocks 3 and 2. Hence the directory entry of `alpha` contains 3. The FAT entry for disk block 3 contains 2, and the FAT entry for disk block 2 indicates that the file ends on that disk block. The file `beta` consists of blocks 4, 5, and 7. The FAT can also be used to store free space information. The list of free disk blocks can be stored as if it were a file, and the address of the first free disk block can be held in a free list pointer. Alternatively, some special code can be stored in the FAT element corresponding to a free disk block, e.g. the code "free" in Figure 13.14.

Use of the FAT rather than the classical linked allocation involves a performance penalty, since the FAT has to be accessed to obtain the address of the next disk block. To overcome this problem, the FAT is held in memory during file processing. Use of the FAT provides higher reliability than classical linked allocation because corruption of a disk block containing file data leads to limited damage. However, corruption of a disk block used to store the FAT is disastrous.

13.7.2 Indexed Allocation

In indexed allocation, an index called the *file map table* (FMT) is maintained to note the addresses of disk blocks allocated to a file. In its simplest form, an

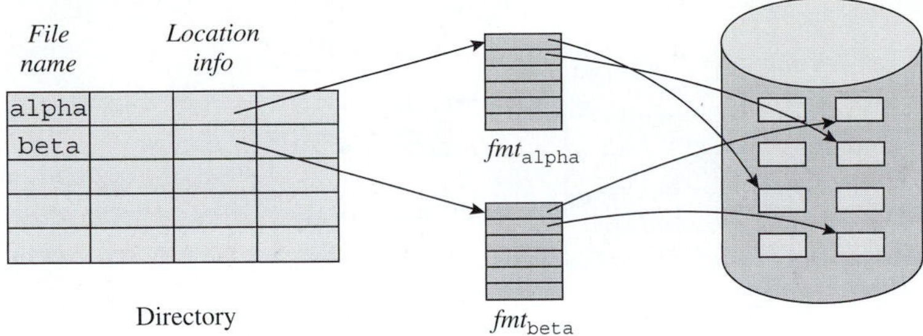

Figure 13.15 Indexed allocation of disk space.

FMT can be an array containing disk block addresses. Each disk block contains a single field—the data field. The *location info* field of a file's directory entry points to the FMT for the file (see Figure 13.15). In the following discussion we use the notation $fmt_{\texttt{alpha}}$ for the FMT of the file `alpha`. If the size of the file `alpha` grows, the DSM is searched to locate a free block, and the address of the block is added to $fmt_{\texttt{alpha}}$. Deallocation is performed when `alpha` is deleted. All disk blocks pointed to by $fmt_{\texttt{alpha}}$ are marked free before $fmt_{\texttt{alpha}}$ and the directory entry of `alpha` are erased.

The reliability problem is less severe in indexed allocation than in linked allocation because corruption of an entry in an FMT leads to only limited damage. Compared with linked allocation, access to sequential-access files is less efficient because the FMT of a file has to be accessed to obtain the address of the next disk block. However, access to records in a direct-access file is more efficient since the address of the disk block that contains a specific record can be obtained directly from the FMT. For example, if address calculation analogous to (13.1)–(13.2) shows that a required record exists in the ith disk block of a file, its address can be obtained from the ith entry of the FMT.

For a small file, the FMT can be stored in the directory entry of the file; it is both convenient and efficient. For a medium or large file, the FMT will not fit into the directory entry. A two-level indexed allocation depicted in Figure 13.16 may be used for such FMTs. In this organization, each entry of the FMT contains the address of an *index block*. An index block does not contain data; it contains entries that contain addresses of data blocks. To access the data block, we first access an entry of the FMT and obtain the address of an index block. We then access an entry of the index block to obtain the address of the data block. This arrangement resembles a multilevel page table (see Section 12.2.3). The index blocks resemble pages of a page table for the file, and the FMT resembles a higher-level page table. Such an FMT is compact; hence even FMTs of large files may fit into a directory entry. However, access to data blocks is slower since two levels of indirection are involved.

Some file systems use a hybrid FMT organization that includes some of the features of both classical and multilevel indexed allocation. Figure 13.17 shows such an organization. The first few entries in the FMT, say n entries, point to

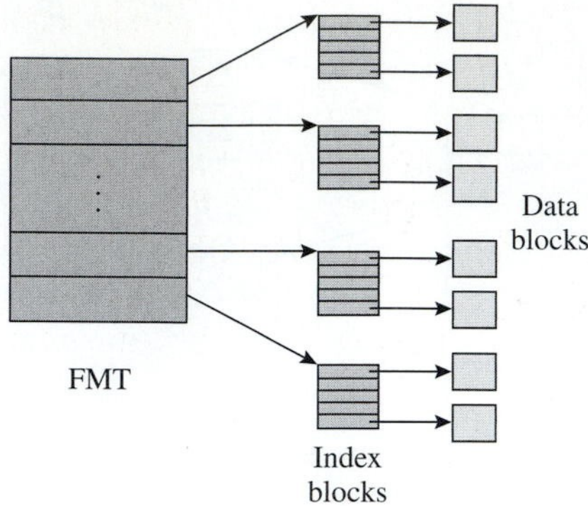

Figure 13.16 A two-level FMT organization.

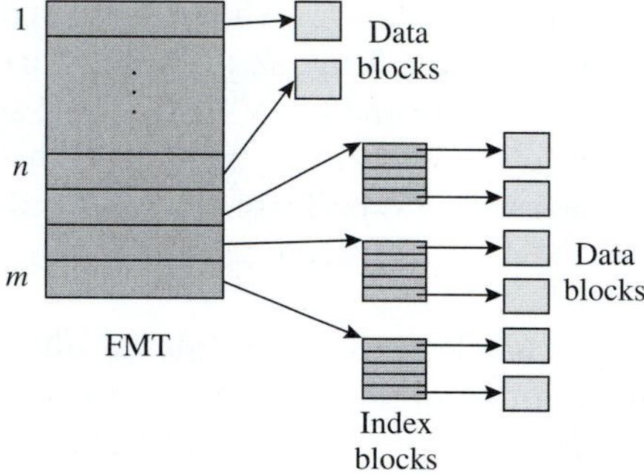

Figure 13.17 A hybrid organization of FMT.

data blocks as in the conventional indexed allocation. Other entries point to index blocks. The advantage of this arrangement is that small files containing *n* or fewer data blocks continue to be accessible efficiently, as their FMT does not use index blocks. Medium and large files suffer a marginal degradation of their access performance because of multiple levels of indirection. The Unix file system uses a variation of the hybrid FMT organization.

13.7.3 Performance Issues

Two performance issues are associated with the use of a disk block as the unit of disk space allocation—size of the metadata, i.e., the control data of the file system; and efficiency of accessing file data. Both issues can be addressed by using a larger unit of allocation of disk space. Hence modern file systems tend to use an *extent*, also called a *cluster*, as a unit of disk space allocation. An extent is a set of consecutive disk blocks. Use of large extents provides better access efficiency. However, it causes more internal fragmentation. To get the best of both worlds, file systems prefer to use variable extent sizes. Their metadata contains the size of an extent along with its address.

13.8 INTERFACE BETWEEN FILE SYSTEM AND IOCS

The file system uses the IOCS to perform I/O operations and the IOCS implements them through kernel calls. The interface between the file system and the IOCS consists of three data structures—the *file map table* (FMT), the *file control block* (FCB), and the *open files table* (OFT)—and functions that perform I/O operations. Use of these data structures avoids repeated processing of file attributes by the file system, and provides a convenient method of tracking the status of ongoing file processing activities.

As discussed earlier in Section 13.7.2, the file system allocates disk space to a file and stores information about the allocated disk space in the *file map table* (FMT). The FMT is typically held in memory during the processing of a file.

A *file control block* (FCB) contains all information concerning an ongoing file processing activity. This information can be classified into the three categories shown in Table 13.3. Information in the file organization category is either simply extracted from the file declaration statement in an application program, or inferred from it by the compiler, e.g., information such as the size of a record and number of buffers is extracted from a file declaration, while the name of the access method is inferred from the type and organization of a file. The compiler puts this information as parameters in the `open` call. When the call is made during execution of the program, the file system puts this information in the FCB. Directory information is copied into the FCB through joint actions of the file system and the IOCS when a new file is created. Information concerning the current state of processing is written into the FCB by the IOCS. This information is continually updated during the processing of a file.

The *open files table* (OFT) holds the FCBs of all open files. The OFT resides in the kernel address space so that user processes cannot tamper with it. When a

Table 13.3 Fields in the File Control Block (FCB)

Category	Fields
File organization	File name File type, organization, and access method Device type and address Size of a record Size of a block Number of buffers Name of access method
Directory information	Information about the file's directory entry Address of parent directory's FCB Address of the file map table (FMT) (or the file map table itself) Protection information
Current state of processing	Address of the next record to be processed Addresses of buffers

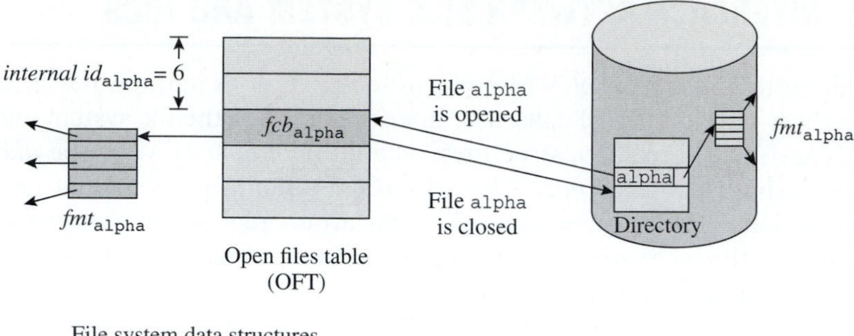

Figure 13.18 Interface between file system and IOCS—OFT, FCB and FMT.

file is opened, the file system stores its FCB in a new entry of the OFT. The offset of this entry in the OFT is called the *internal id* of the file. The internal id is passed back to the process, which uses it as a parameter in all future file system calls.

Figure 13.18 shows the arrangement set up when a file `alpha` is opened. The file system copies $fmt_{\texttt{alpha}}$ in memory; creates $fcb_{\texttt{alpha}}$, which is an FCB for `alpha`, in the OFT; initializes its fields appropriately; and passes back its offset in OFT, which in this case is 6, to the process as $internal\_id_{\texttt{alpha}}$.

The file system supports the following operations:

- `open` (*<file_name>*, *<processing_mode>*, *<file_attributes>*)
- `close` (*<internal_id_of_file>*)
- `read/write` (*<internal_id_of_file>*, *<record_info>*, *<I/O_area_addr>*)

<file_name> is an absolute or relative path name of the file to be opened. *<processing_mode>* indicates what kind of operations will be performed on the file—the values "input," "create," and "append" of it have obvious meanings, while "update" indicates that the process intends to update existing data in place. *<file_attributes>* is a list of file attributes, such as the file's organization, record size, and protection information. It is relevant only when a new file is being created—attributes from the list are copied into the directory entry of the file at this time. *<record_info>* indicates the identity of the record to be read or written if the file is being processed in a nonsequential mode. *<I/O_area addr>* indicates the address of the memory area where data from the record should be read, or the memory area that contains the data to be written into the record.

The IOCS interface supports the following operations:

- `iocs-open` (*<internal_id_of_file>*, *<directory_entry_address>*)
- `iocs-close` (*<internal_id_of_file>*, *<directory_entry_address>*)
- `iocs-read/write` (*<internal_id_of_file>*, *<record_info>*, *<I/O_area_addr>*)

Each of these operations is a generic operation for the various file organizations supported by the file system. It works in two parts: It performs some

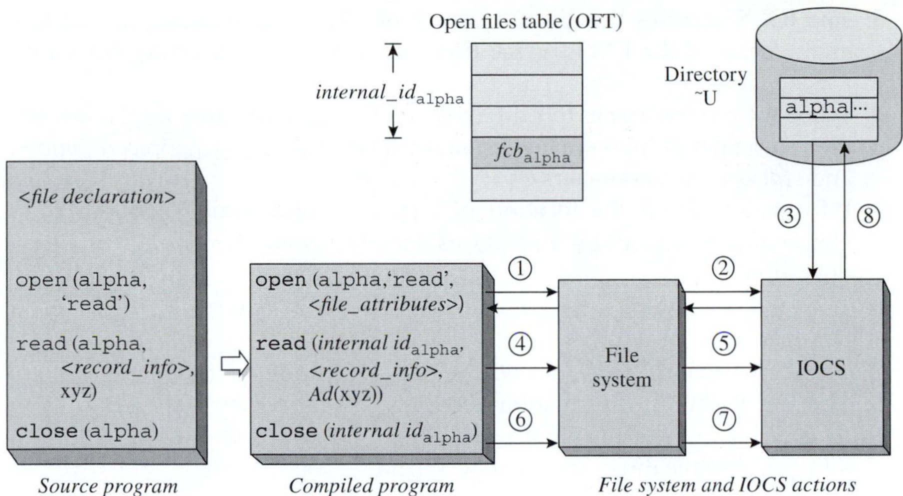

Figure 13.19 Overview of file processing.

actions that are common to all file organizations, and invokes a module of the access method mentioned in the FCB of the file for performing special actions required for specific file organizations.

The `iocs-open` and `iocs-close` operations are specialized read and write operations that copy information into the FCB from the directory entry or from the FCB into the directory entry. The `iocs-read/write` operations access the FCB to obtain information concerning the current state of the file processing activity, such as the address of the next record to be processed. When a write operation requires more disk space, `iocs-write` invokes a function of the file system to perform disk space allocation (see Section 13.7).

Figure 13.19 is a schematic diagram of the processing of an existing file `alpha` in a process executed by some user `U`. The compiler replaces the statements `open`, `read`, and `close` in the source program with calls on the file system operations `open`, `read`, and `close`, respectively. The following are the significant steps in file processing involving the file system and the IOCS, shown by numbered arrows in Figure 13.19:

1. The process executes the call `open` (`alpha`, '`read`,' *<file_attributes>*). The call returns with $internal\_id_{\texttt{alpha}}$ if the processing mode "read" is consistent with protection information of the file. The process saves $internal\_id_{\texttt{alpha}}$ for use while performing operations on file `alpha`.
2. The file system creates a new FCB in the open files table. It resolves the path name `alpha` as described later in Section 13.9.1, locates the directory entry of `alpha`, and stores the information about it in the new FCB for use while closing the file. Thus, the new FCB becomes $fcb_{\texttt{alpha}}$. The file system now makes a call `iocs-open` with $internal\_id_{\texttt{alpha}}$ and the address of the directory entry of `alpha` as parameters.

3. The IOCS accesses the directory entry of `alpha`, and copies the file size and address of the FMT, or the FMT itself, from the directory entry into $fcb_{\texttt{alpha}}$.
4. When the process wishes to read a record of `alpha` into area `xyz`, it invokes the `read` operation of the file system with $internal\_id_{\texttt{alpha}}$, *<record_info>*, and *Ad*(`xyz`) as parameters.
5. Information about the location of `alpha` is now available in $fcb_{\texttt{alpha}}$. Hence the `read/write` operations merely invoke `iocs-read/write` operations.
6. The process invokes the `close` operation with $internal\_id_{\texttt{alpha}}$ as a parameter.
7. The file system makes a call `iocs-close` with $internal\_id_{\texttt{alpha}}$.
8. The IOCS obtains information about the directory entry of `alpha` from $fcb_{\texttt{alpha}}$ and copies the file size and FMT address, or the FMT itself, from $fcb_{\texttt{alpha}}$ into the directory entry of `alpha`.

13.9 FILE PROCESSING

In this section we discuss the processing of structured files, in which read/write operations are performed on a record.

13.9.1 File System Actions at `open`

The purpose of a call `open` (*<path_name>*, *<processing_mode>*, *<file_attributes>*), where *<path_name>* is an absolute or relative path name for a file *<file_name>*, is to set up the processing of the file. As described in Section 13.8, `open` performs the following actions:

1. It aborts the process if *<processing_mode>* is not consistent with the protection information for the file. Otherwise, it creates an FCB for the file *<file_name>* in the OFT, and puts relevant information in its fields. If *<file_name>* is a new file, it also writes *<file_attributes>* into its directory entry.
2. It passes the internal id of the file *<file_name>* back to the process for use in file processing actions.
3. If the file *<file_name>* is being created or appended to, it makes provision to update the file's directory entry when a `close` call is made by the process.

The procedure called *path name resolution* traverses all path components in a path name and checks the validity of each component. It uses two pointers called the *file FCB pointer* and the *directory FCB pointer* during the traversal. It points the *file FCB pointer* at the FCB of the file corresponding to the current component in the path name, and the *directory FCB pointer* at the FCB of its parent directory. At the end of path name resolution, the *file FCB pointer* is used to determine the *internal id* of the file. Path name resolution consists of the following steps:

1. If an absolute path name is used, locate the FCB of the file system root directory in the OFT; otherwise, locate the FCB of the current directory. (This step assumes that the FCBs of these directories have already been created in the OFT. If not, they should be created in this step.) Set *directory FCB pointer* to point to this FCB.
2. **a.** Search for the next path component of the path name in the directory represented by *directory FCB pointer*. Indicate an error if the component does not exist or if the process owner lacks privileges to access it.
   b. Create an FCB for the file described by the path component. Store this FCB in a free entry of the OFT. Copy the *directory FCB pointer* in this FCB.
   c. Set the *file FCB pointer* to point to this FCB.
   d. If this is not the last path component in the path name, initialize the newly created FCB using information from the directory entry of the file. Set *directory FCB pointer* = *file FCB pointer*, and repeat step 2.
3. **a.** If the file already exists, copy the file size and the pointer to the FMT from the directory entry of the file into the FCB pointed to by *file FCB pointer*.
   b. If the file does not already exist, create the FMT of the file and store its address in the FCB. (This action may involve allocating a disk block for the FMT.)
4. Set *internal id* of the file to the offset of *file FCB pointer* in the OFT. Copy the *directory FCB pointer* into the FCB of the file. Return *internal id* to the process.

Apart from the actions described above, the file system may perform some other actions in the interest of efficiency. For example, while opening an existing file it may copy a part or all of the file's FMT into memory [see Step 3(a)]. This action ensures efficient access to data in the file. Also, only the FCBs pointed to by *directory FCB pointer* and *file FCB pointer* are needed during file processing, so other FCBs created during path name resolution may be destroyed.

The following example illustrates the data structures built by the file system when a file is opened.

Implementation of the `open` Operation — Example 13.7

Figure 13.20 shows the result of the file system actions after executing the call

```
open(/info/alpha,..);
```

The path name used in the `open` call is an absolute path name. The file system searches for the name `info` in the root directory, and creates an FCB

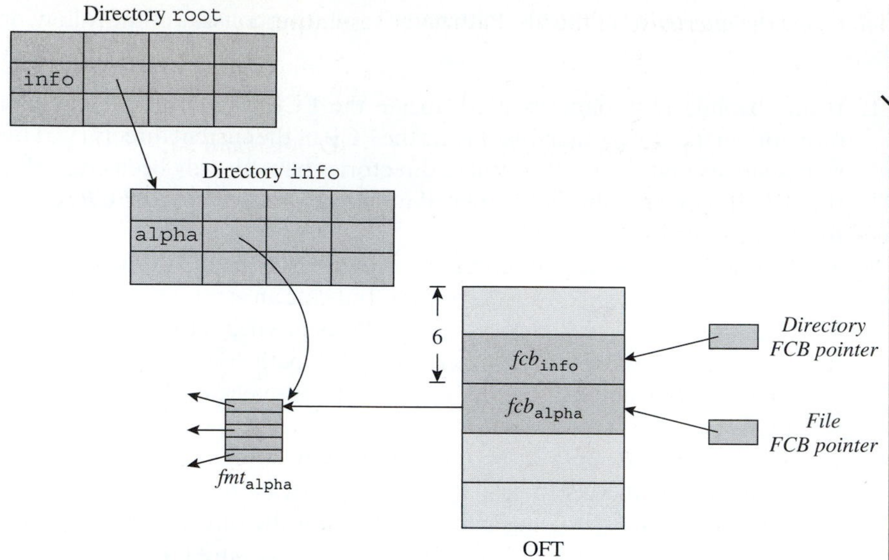

Figure 13.20 File system actions at `open`.

for `info` in the OFT. It now searches for the name `alpha` in `info` and creates an FCB for `alpha` in the OFT. *directory FCB pointer* points to $fcb_{\texttt{info}}$ and *file FCB pointer* points to $fcb_{\texttt{alpha}}$. Since `alpha` is an existing file, its FMT pointer is copied into $fcb_{\texttt{alpha}}$ from the directory entry of `alpha`. The call returns with the internal id of `alpha`, which is 6.

The mount command `mount` (<*FS_name*>, <*mount_point_name*>) mounts <*FS_name*> at the mount point (see Section 13.4). A simple way to implement mounting is to temporarily change the directory entry of <*mount_point_name*> in its parent directory to point to the directory entry of <*FS_name*>.

When a mount point is crossed during path name resolution, the file system has to switch from the directory structure of the mount point to the directory structure of the mounted file system, or vice versa. To facilitate this, while processing a mount command, the file system puts the value "M" in the *flags* field of the directory entry of <*FS_name*> and maintains a *mount table* to store pairs of the form (<*FS_name*>, <*mount_point_name*>). For example, when the call `mount (meeting,~A/admin)` of Section 13.4 is executed, the file system adds the pair (`meeting`, `~A/admin`) to the mount table. During path name resolution, this table is consulted when a mount point is encountered during traversal of the directory structure from parent to child (for the slash (/) operator in the path name) or child to parent (for the ".." operator). The file system also has to ensure that disk space allocation performed during the processing of a mounted file is in the mounted file system rather than in the host file system.

13.9.2 File System Actions during a File Operation

After opening a file *<file_name>*, a process executed by user U performs some read or write operations on it. Each such operation is translated into a call

<opn> (internal id, record id, <IO_area addr>);

where *internal id* is the internal id of *<file_name>* returned by the `open` call, and *record id* is absent if the operation is performed on a sequential-access file because the operation is necessarily performed on the *next* record in the file. The file system performs the following actions to process this call:

1. Locate the FCB of *<file_name>* in the OFT using *internal id.*
2. Search the access control list of *<file_name>* for the pair (`U`, ...). Give an error if the protection information found in the file's FCB does not permit user U to perform *<opn>* on the file.
3. Make a call on `iocs-read` or `iocs-write` with the parameters *internal id*, *record id* and *<IO_area addr>*. For nonsequential-access files, the operation is performed on the indicated record. For sequential-access files, the operation is performed on the record whose address is in the FCB field "address of the next record to be processed," and the contents of this field are updated to point to the next record in the file.

In Step 3, the IOCS and the access method invoked by it obtains the FMT of the file from its FCB and uses it to convert *record id* into a pair of the form (*disk block id, byte offset*). If it runs out of disk space during a write operation, it calls a module of the file system, which allocates a new disk block to the file and adds its address to the FMT.

Example 13.8

Implementation of read/write Operations

Following the `open` call of Example 13.7, a call `read (alpha, 25, ...)` by the process, where 25 is *record id*, would lead to the call `iocs-read (6, 25, ..)`. If disk blocks have a size of 1000 bytes each, and a record is 100 bytes in length, the IOCS will convert *record id* into disk block number 3 and record number 5 in the disk block, which implies a byte offset of 400. Now the address of the third disk block allocated to `alpha` is obtained from its FMT and this block is read to obtain the desired record.

13.9.3 File System Actions at `close`

The file system performs the following actions when a process executes the statement `close` (*internal id*, ...).

1. If the file has been newly created or appended to.
   a. If it is a newly created file, create an entry for the file in the directory pointed to by the *directory FCB pointer*. If the directory entry format

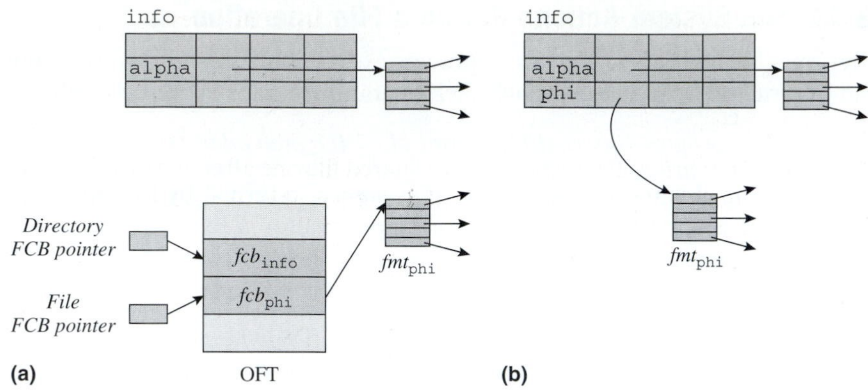

Figure 13.21 File system data structures (a) before; (b) after `close`.

contains a field where the complete FMT can be stored, copy the FMT into this field; otherwise, first write the FMT into a disk block and copy the address of this disk block into the directory entry.

b. If the file has been appended to, the directory entry of the file is updated by using *directory FCB pointer*.

c. If necessary, repeat Steps 1b and 1c to update other directories in the path name of the file after setting *file FCB pointer* := *directory FCB pointer* and *directory FCB pointer* := address of parent directory's FCB found in the FCB of the file. If their FCBs were deleted after `open`, the directory files would have to be opened and updated.

2. The FCB of the file and FCBs of its parent and ancestor directories are erased from the OFT.

Example 13.9 Implementation of File `close` Operation

Figure 13.21 illustrates the file system actions before and after executing the command `close phi` for a newly created file `phi` that was opened using the path name `/info/phi`. An entry is created for `phi` in directory `info` and a pointer to $fmt_{\texttt{phi}}$ is put in the *location info* field of this entry. Addition of this entry to `info` increases the size of `info`; hence an additional disk block may have to be allocated to `info`. It will involve updating the FMT of `info` and the size of `info` in its entry in the root directory [see Steps 1(b) and 1(c) of actions at `close`].

13.10 FILE SHARING SEMANTICS

As discussed in Section 13.6, the owner of a file may authorize some other users to access the file. Processes created by authorized users can read, write, or execute the file in accordance with access privileges granted to them. In essence they *share* the files to which they have access. The file system provides two methods of file sharing so that processes can choose the one that permits them to collaborate and build on each other's work effectively:

- *Sequential sharing:* Processes access a shared file one after another. Thus, file modifications made by one process, if any, are visible to processes that access the file afterwards.
- *Concurrent sharing:* Two or more processes access a file over the same period of time.

File sharing semantics is a set of rules that determine the manner in which results of file manipulations performed by concurrent processes are visible to one another.

Sequential sharing of a file can be implemented through the *lock* field in the file's directory entry (see Figure 13.6). If the *lock* field of the file's directory entry has the value "reset," an `open` operation would succeed and change the value to "set"; otherwise, the `open` operation would fail and would have to be repeated. A `close` operation would change the value in the *lock* to "reset."

To facilitate concurrent sharing of a file, the file system has to ensure that file processing activities of processes do not interfere. Accordingly, it creates a separate FCB for each process by simply following the procedure of Section 13.9.1 every time a file is opened. Several FCBs may thus be created for concurrent sharing of file `alpha`. We use the notation $fcb^{P_1}_{\texttt{alpha}}$ for the FCB of `alpha` created for process P1. Table 13.4 summarizes three modes of concurrent file sharing provided in file systems.

Sharing Immutable Files When the file `alpha` is shared as an *immutable file*, none of the sharing processes can modify it. Hence the processes sharing file `alpha` are independent of one another. Creation of an $fcb_{\texttt{alpha}}$ for each sharing process is adequate to implement this form of file sharing.

Table 13.4 Modes of Concurrent File Sharing

Mode	Description
Immutable files	The file being shared cannot be modified by any process.
Single-image mutable files	All processes concurrently sharing a file "see" the same image of the file, i.e., they have an identical view of file's data. Thus, modifications made by one process are immediately visible to other processes using the file.
Multiple-image mutable files	Processes sharing a file may "see" different images of the file. Thus, updates made by a process may not be visible to some concurrent processes. The file system may maintain many images of a file, or it may reconcile them in some manner to create a single image when processes close the file.

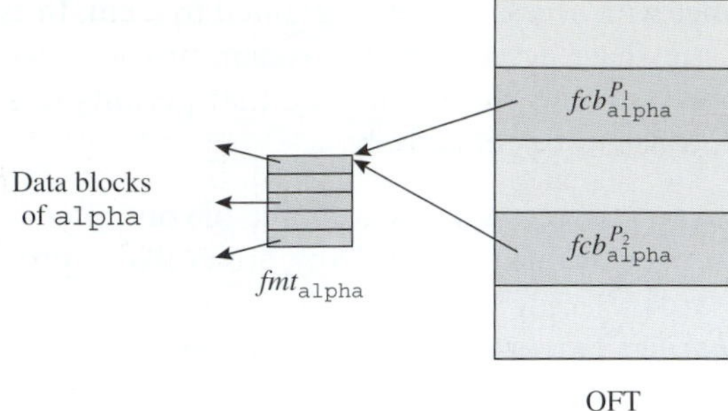

Figure 13.22 Concurrent sharing of a single-image mutable file by processes P_1 and P_2.

Sharing Single-Image Mutable Files A single copy of the file is shared by processes accessing it. Hence modifications made by one process are immediately visible to other processes. To implement this form of sharing, it is essential that a single copy of the FMT be used by all sharing processes. Hence it is best to keep a pointer to the FMT, rather than the FMT itself, in an FCB.

Figure 13.22 shows concurrent sharing of file `alpha` using such an arrangement. The FCBs $fcb^{P_1}_{\text{alpha}}$ and $fcb^{P_2}_{\text{alpha}}$ are created when `alpha` is opened by processes P_1 and P_2. Both FCBs point to the same copy of fmt_{alpha}. Each FCB contains the address of the next record to be accessed by a process. If the sets of records processed by P_1 and P_2 overlapped, their modifications would be visible to one another. Race conditions could also arise in such situations, and updates made by processes might be lost. A typical file system does not provide any means of tackling this problem; the processes have to evolve their own synchronization conventions for this purpose. The Unix file system supports single-image mutable files; we discuss *Unix file sharing semantics* in Section 13.14.1.

Sharing Multiple-Image Mutable Files When a multiple-image mutable file `alpha` is shared by several processes, each process that modifies the file creates a new version of `alpha` that is distinct from versions created by other concurrent processes. In this scheme, there has to be a distinct fmt_{alpha} for each FCB, and each FMT must point to an exclusive copy of the file. This requirement is best implemented by making a copy of `alpha` (and its FMT) for each process concurrently accessing it.

Figure 13.23 illustrates the arrangement for implementing multiple-image mutable files. Processes P_1 and P_2 are engaged in updating `alpha`. alpha^{P1} represents the copy of `alpha` made for process P_1. Processing by P_1 uses $fcb^{P_1}_{\text{alpha}}$ and $fmt^{P_1}_{\text{alpha}}$ to access alpha^{P_1}, while processing by P_2 uses $fcb^{\text{P2}}_{\text{alpha}}$ and $fmt^{P_2}_{\text{alpha}}$ to access alpha^{P_2}. alpha^{P_1} and alpha^{P_2} are thus two versions of `alpha`. To arrive at a unique implementation scheme, the file sharing semantics must specify how `alpha` would be accessed by processes that wish only to read it, i.e., which version of `alpha` they would access.

Sharing of multiple-image mutable files has special features that may not be valid or applicable in many applications. Hence it can be used only in applications

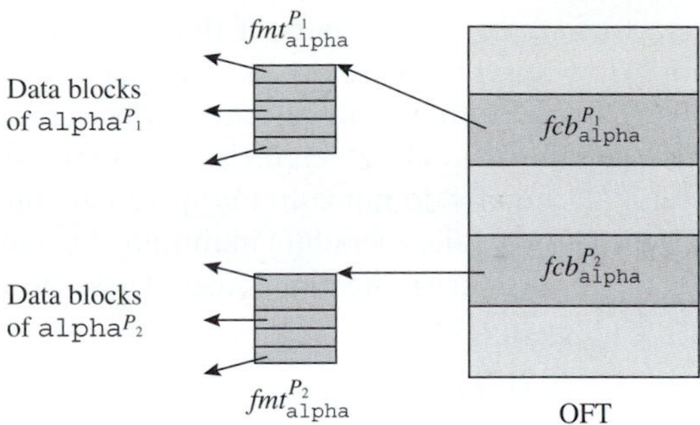

Figure 13.23 Concurrent sharing of a multiple-image mutable file by processes P_1 and P_2.

where existence of multiple versions due to concurrent updates is meaningful. We discuss one kind of semantics for multiple-image mutable files, called *session semantics*, in Section 20.3. Unfortunately, file sharing semantics for multiple-image mutable files are hard to understand and implement. Hence their use is not very common.

13.11 FILE SYSTEM RELIABILITY

File system reliability is the degree to which a file system will function correctly even when faults such as data corruption in disk blocks and system crashes due to power interruptions occur. The two principal aspects of file system reliability are:

- Ensuring correctness of file creation, deletion and updates.
- Preventing loss of data in files.

The former concerns consistency and correctness of metadata, i.e., the control data of the file system, while the latter concerns consistency and correctness of data stored in files.

Reliability literature distinguishes between the terms *fault* and *failure*. A fault is a defect in some part of the system. A failure is a system behavior that is erroneous, or that differs from its expected behavior. Occurrence of a fault causes a failure. Thus corruption of a disk block due to a damaged disk head or a power outage is a fault, whereas inability of the file system to read a faulty block is a failure. Chapter 19 discusses these terms formally.

13.11.1 Loss of File System Consistency

File system consistency implies correctness of metadata and correct operation of the file system. Loss of consistency arises if the metadata of the file system is lost or damaged. It is interesting to see how this can happen. Consider operation of a process that updates a file `alpha`. To ensure efficient operation, the file system maintains some of its metadata in memory. Thus, $fcb_{\texttt{alpha}}$ (which exists in the open files table), part of $fmt_{\texttt{alpha}}$, and part of the disk status map or free list would be in memory. Some of this metadata, like $fmt_{\texttt{alpha}}$, are written on a disk when `alpha` is closed. In addition, the file system may periodically copy the disk status map or free list on the disk. However, metadata is modified constantly, so disk copies of metadata generally do not contain up-to-date information during system operation. When power fails, metadata maintained in memory is lost, and when a disk fails metadata stored on the disk is lost. These situations may result in one or more of the following failures:

1. Some data from file `alpha` may be lost.
2. Part of file `alpha` may become inaccessible.
3. Contents of two files may get mixed up.

It is easy to visualize a situation of the first kind. For example, suppose a fault occurs after a new disk block has been added to the file `alpha`. The disk copy of $fmt_{\texttt{alpha}}$ will not contain this block's id, and so data in the newly added block will be lost when the fault occurs. The second and third kind of situation can arise in a file system that does not employ any reliability techniques. We illustrate these situations in a file system that uses linked allocation of disk space and employs Algorithm 13.1 to add a new disk block to a file. The third kind of situation can also arise in a file system that uses indexed allocation of disk space.

Algorithm 13.1 *Add Block d_j between Blocks d_1 and d_2*

Input :

d_1, d_2, d_j : **record**
    next : ...; { id of next block }
    data : ...;
  end

1. $d_j.next := d_1.next$;
2. $d_1.next :=$ address (d_j);
3. *Write d_1 to disk.*
4. *Write d_j to disk.*

Algorithm 13.1 adds a new disk block d_j between blocks d_1 and d_2 of the file. Figure 13.24 illustrates how parts of file `alpha` may become inaccessible due to a fault. Figures 13.24(a), (b) show the file before and after a normal execution of the algorithm. Figures 13.24(c) shows the file if a fault occurs between Steps 3 and 4 of Algorithm 13.1. New contents have been written into disk block d_1, but not into disk block d_j. Hence $d_1.next$ points to d_j, whereas d_j does not contain correct metadata in its *next* field. Disk blocks $d_2, d_3, \ldots$ would not be accessible as parts of the file any more.

Contents of two files may get mixed up if the file system writes metadata to the disk only while closing a file, and not after every file operation. Consider the following situation: A process P_1 deletes a disk block d_k from some file `beta`. d_k will be returned to the free list (or will be marked free in the disk status map). Now process P_2 adds a new record to file `alpha`. The file system allocates a new disk block d_j for this purpose and adds it ahead of disk block d_m in file `alpha`

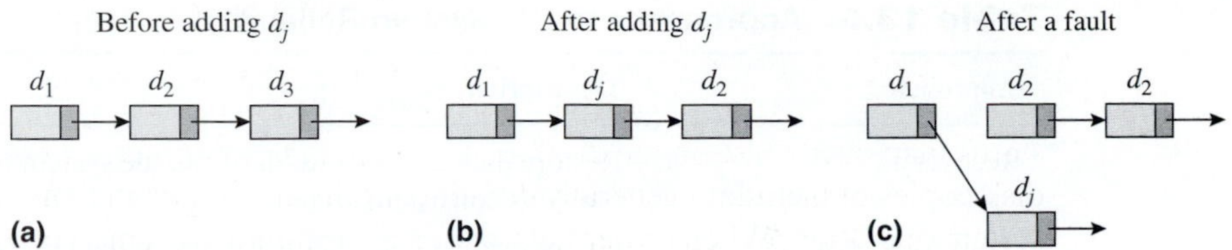

Figure 13.24 Inconsistencies in metadata due to faults: (a)–(b) before and after adding d_j during normal operation; (c) after a fault.

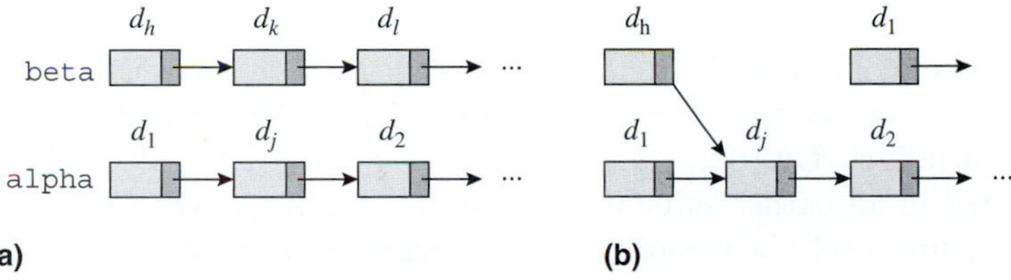

Figure 13.25 Files `alpha` and `beta`: (a) after adding d_j during normal operation; (b) if $d_j = d_k$, `alpha` is closed and a power outage occurs.

[see Figure 13.25(a)]. Now, consider the situation when $d_j = d_k$ and the following events occur in the system:

1. File `alpha` is closed.
2. The file system updates the disk copy of file `alpha`. It involves adding disk block d_j to `alpha`.
3. A power outage occurs.

Note that file `beta` was not closed before the power outage occurred, so the disk contains an old copy of `beta` that contains block d_k, and the new copy of `alpha` that contains block d_j. Since $d_j = d_k$, `alpha` and `beta` now share disk block d_j and all other blocks accessible through it [see Figure 13.25(b)]. All disk blocks of file `beta` that were previously accessible through d_k, i.e., block d_l and other blocks accessible through it, are now inaccessible. In effect, some data is common to files `alpha` and `beta`, while some data of `beta` has been lost.

13.11.2 Approaches to File System Reliability

By means of the two approaches described in Table 13.5, operating systems ensure that user files are reliably stored over a period of time. *Recovery* is a classic approach that is activated when a failure is noticed. It restores the data and metadata of the file system to some previous consistent state. The file system now resumes its operation from this state. Thus, deviations from correct behavior do occur, but system operation is rectified when deviations are noticed. *Fault tolerance*, on the other hand, provides correct operation of the file system at all times, i.e., it ensures that faults do not lead to failures. It achieves this ability through some special techniques.

Table 13.5 Approaches to File System Reliability

Approach	Description
Recovery	Restore data and metadata of the file system to some previous consistent state.
Fault tolerance	Guard against loss of consistency of data and metadata due to faults, so that system operation is correct at all times, i.e., failures do not occur.

To see the difference between the two approaches, consider the example of a disk block that becomes unreadable. Inability of the file system to read the block is a failure. Under the recovery approach, the data in the block would be restored to an earlier value when a failure is noticed. With fault tolerance, each data unit would be recorded in two blocks—a primary block and an alternative block. If a failure occurs while the primary block is being read, the file system would automatically read the alternative block. Of course, fault tolerance is not absolute. The system can tolerate only those faults that it is designed to. For example, when a data unit is recorded in two blocks, the system can tolerate a fault in the primary block, but not faults in both primary and alternative blocks.

13.11.2.1 Recovery Techniques

The *file system state* at some time instant t_i is the collection of all data and metadata in the file system at t_i. A *backup* of the file system is a recording of the file system state. To support recovery, the file system periodically produces backups during its operation. Let t_{lb} represent the time at which the latest backup was produced. In the event of a failure, say, at time t_f, the file system is restored to the state recorded in its latest backup. File updates performed between t_{lb} and t_f are lost; operations that performed these updates need to be reprocessed after recovery. Recovery using backups thus involves two kinds of overheads—overhead of creating backups, and overhead of reprocessing.

Reprocessing overhead in recovery can be reduced through a combination of backups and incremental backups of a file system. An *incremental backup* contains copies of only those files or disk blocks that were modified after the last backup or incremental backup was created. The file system creates backups at large intervals of time, e.g., a day, a few days, or a week. Incremental backups are created at shorter intervals and are discarded when the next backup is created. For example, an incremental backup may be created when a process closes a file after updating it; the incremental backup would contain a copy of only that file. Use of incremental backups increases the overhead of the backing up activity. The space overhead is also high because backups and incremental backups coexist and some files may exist in more than one incremental backup. However, the reprocessing overhead is low for the following reason: After a crash the system could be restored from the latest backup, and incremental backups would then be processed in the same order in which they were created. This action would restore all files whose modification was completed before the last of the incremental backups was created. Only the file processing activities that were in progress at the time of the failure would have to be repeated.

To reduce the recovery overhead, the file system could be restored by processing all incremental backups and the latest backup in the reverse order, taking care not to restore a file that has been already restored from a later incremental backup. This approach would reduce overhead by restoring each file exactly once. However, it would be effective only if the file system metadata is consistent at the time of a failure.

Recovery in a File System

Example 13.10

Figure 13.26 illustrates a system in which backups were taken at times t_1 and t_4, and incremental backups were taken at t_2 and t_3. The incremental backups contain 3 and 2 disk blocks, respectively, because 3 disk blocks were updated between t_1 and t_2 and 2 disk blocks were updated between t_2 and t_3. If a failure occurs after t_4, the system would be restored to the state recorded in the backup taken at t_4. However, if a failure occurred between t_3 and t_4, the system would have been restored by using the backup taken at t_1 and the incremental backups taken at t_2 and t_3.

Creating Backups The key issue in creation of backups is consistency of metadata recorded in a backup. Consider the following scenario during operation of a file system.

1. The free list data structure is written in the backup.
2. A record is added to a file `phi`, which requires a new disk block to be allocated to `phi` from the free list.
3. File `phi` is now written in the backup.

Here, recording of the free list and file `phi` in the backup would be mutually inconsistent. It could lead to a mix-up of data in files as discussed in Section 13.11.1. Similar problems would arise even if these three actions are performed in the reverse order. Inconsistencies of metadata could be prevented by freezing all activities in the file system while a backup is created; however, this method is intrusive and it would cause delays in processes. An alternative is to create a backup during normal operation of a system, but use some simplifications like not writing the free list in a backup. When the state of the file system is restored from such a backup, the file system could scan the complete disk and build the free list anew. However, in this scheme files would have been recorded in the backup at different times, so they would suffer loss of data to different extents if the file system is restored by using this backup. Another issue is the backing up of a file that is being processed when a backup is initiated—either its backing up should be delayed until its processing is complete, or the user would not precisely know how much of the file's processing would be lost if the file system is restored by

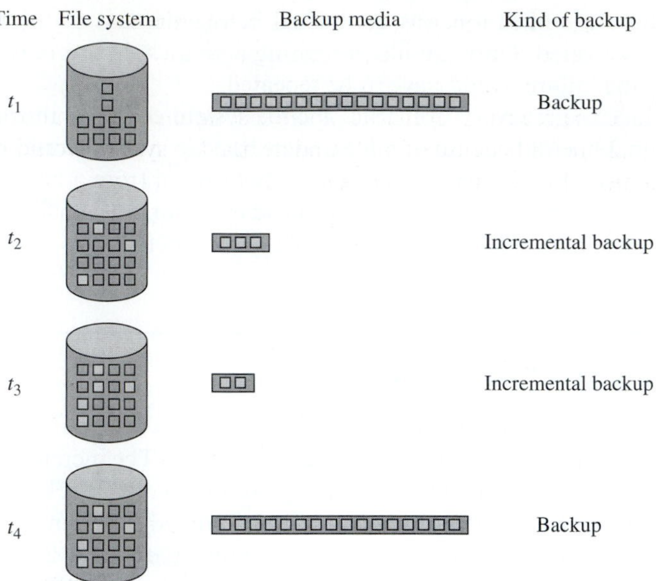

Figure 13.26 Backups and incremental backups in a file system.

using the backup. An incremental backup that is created when a file is closed does not face any of these consistency problems because only modified files are written into the backup, so file system metadata like free lists would not be written into it.

What about the overhead of creating a backup? When disk space was expensive, backups were typically created on slower I/O devices like tapes; however, disk space is affordable in modern computer systems, so it is possible to create backups on disks. When indexed allocation of disk space is used, it is possible to create an on-disk backup of a file cheaply by means of a technique that resembles the *copy-on-write* technique of virtual memory. Figure 13.27 illustrates this technique.

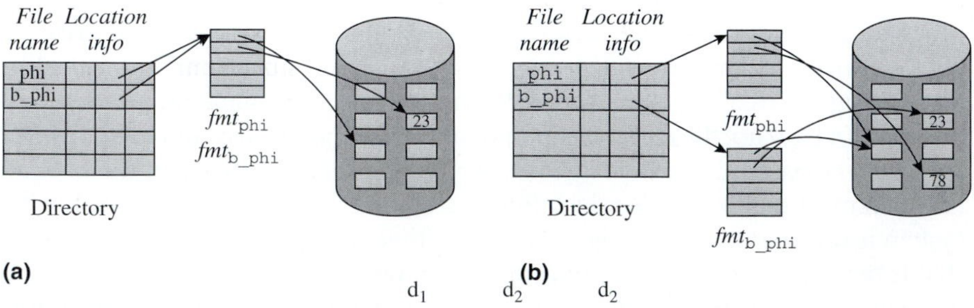

Figure 13.27 Creating a backup: (a) after backing up file `phi`; (b) when `phi` is modified.

When file phi is to be backed up, the file system creates a copy of the directory entry of phi and names the new file appropriately, say b_phi. Now, the FMT pointers of phi and b_phi are identical [see Figure 13.27(a)], so file b_phi is a copy of phi as desired. If contents of the second disk block allocated to phi change from 23 to 78 because of a file update, the file system would perform the following actions [see Figure 13.27(b)]:

1. If the FMT pointers of phi and b_phi are identical, make a copy of the FMT and make the directory entry of b_phi point to the copy.
2. Allocate a new disk block to file phi.
3. Change the appropriate pointer in $fmt_{\texttt{phi}}$ to point to the new disk block.
4. Write the new contents into the new disk block.

Thus, only the FMT and the disk block whose contents are updated after the backup is created would be copied. This arrangement conserves both disk space and time.

13.11.2.2 Fault Tolerance Techniques

File system reliability can be improved by taking two precautions—preventing loss of data or metadata due to I/O device malfunction, and preventing inconsistency of metadata due to faults. These precautions are implemented by using the fault tolerance techniques of stable storage and atomic actions, respectively.

Stable Storage Lampson (1981) proposed the technique of redundant recording of data to ensure reliability. It is called *stable storage* because it can tolerate one fault in the recording of a data item. Two copies of a record, called its *primary* and *secondary* copy, are maintained on a disk. A write operation updates both copies—the primary copy is updated first, followed by the secondary copy. A read operation accesses the disk block containing the primary copy. If it is unreadable, the block containing the secondary copy is accessed. Since only single faults are assumed to occur, one of the blocks is sure to contain readable data.

Figure 13.28 illustrates operation of the stable storage technique if faults occur at times t_1, t_2, t_3, or t_4, respectively, while a process P_i is executing an update operation on some data D. Parts (a)–(d) show timing charts and values in the primary and secondary copies of D when faults occur. In Part (a), a fault occurs at time t_1, i.e., before the primary copy is updated. Hence the primary copy, containing the old value of the data, is accessible after a fault. In Part (b), a fault occurs while the primary copy is being updated, so that the primary copy becomes unreadable. The old value of the data is accessible from the secondary copy. In Part (c), a fault occurs after the primary copy is updated but before the secondary copy is updated. New data is accessible in the primary copy after the fault occurs. In Part (d), a fault occurs after both copies have been updated. Hence both copies are accessible.

The stable storage technique can be applied to entire files. (Lampson called this technique disk mirroring; however, it is different from the *disk mirroring* we will come across in Section 14.3.) However, stable storage incurs high space and time overhead, which makes it unsuitable for general use in a file system,

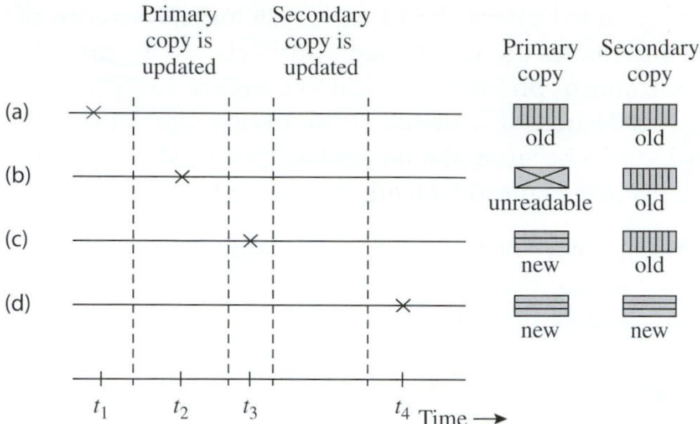

Figure 13.28 Fault tolerance using the stable storage technique.

so processes may use it selectively to protect some of their own data. Also, while stable storage guarantees that one copy of data will survive a single fault, it cannot indicate whether this value is old or new [see parts (a), (d) of Figure 13.28]. Hence the user does not know whether to reexecute the update operation in P_i when system operation is restored. An atomic action overcomes this problem.

Atomic Actions An action may involve manipulation of many data structures, e.g., consider Algorithm 13.1 of Section 13.11.1. These data structures may become inconsistent if a fault interrupts execution of the action. An *atomic action* is a method of avoiding such ill effects of faults.

Definition 13.1 Atomic Action An action that consists of a set of subactions and whose execution has the property that either

1. The effects of all of its subactions are realized, or
2. The effects of none of its subactions are realized.

Thus, an atomic action has an *all-or-nothing* property. This property avoids data inconsistency when faults occur. Consistency of file system metadata can be preserved by updating all file system data structures by using atomic actions. Database systems use a concept called an *atomic transaction* or a *database transaction* that ensures certain additional properties such as serializability; our discussion is restricted to atomic actions for file system reliability only.

The subactions in an atomic action are enclosed between the statements **begin atomic action** and **end atomic action**. Execution of the atomic action begins when the **begin atomic action** statement is executed. The action can end in two ways—it can either fail or succeed. It fails if it loses interest in continuing its execution and executes an **abort** statement, or if a fault occurs before the statement **end atomic action** is executed. If it fails, the state of each file or metadata used by it should be left as it was prior to execution of the **begin atomic action** statement. An atomic action succeeds when it executes the **end atomic action** statement. It is said to

```
begin atomic action add_a_block;
    d_j.next := d_1.next;
    d_1.next := address(d_j);
    write d_1;
    write d_j;
end atomic action add_a_block;
```

Figure 13.29 Atomic action *add_a_block*.

commit at this time. All updates made by it are guaranteed to survive any faults after it commits.

Figure 13.29 shows Algorithm 13.1 of Section 13.11.1 coded as an atomic action named *add_a_block*. It differs from Algorithm 13.1 only in the use of the statements **begin atomic action** and **end atomic action**. If the atomic action *add_a_block* commits, disk block d_j is added to file `alpha` and `alpha` now consists of disk blocks $\ldots d_1, d_j, d_2, \ldots$. If it fails, disk block d_j is not added to file `alpha`; i.e., `alpha` continues to consist of disk blocks $\ldots d_1, d_2, \ldots$. Thus it avoids the problem described in Section 13.11.1 and illustrated in Figure 13.24.

Atomic actions can be implemented in many ways. In one implementation approach, files or metadata are not updated during execution of the atomic action. They are updated only after the atomic action commits. This arrangement automatically tolerates faults that occur before an atomic action commits since no updates will have been made in files. Thus it implements the "nothing" part of the all-or-nothing property. To implement the "all" part of the all-or-nothing property, it is necessary to ensure that all updates will be made even if faults occur. Two data structures called *intentions list* and *commit flag* are maintained to ensure this. Both data structures are maintained in stable storage to protect them against data corruption and loss due to faults.

Every time the atomic action modifies a file or metadata, the file system makes an entry of the form (<*disk block id*>, <*new contents*>) in the intentions list to indicate that <*new contents*> should be written in the disk block with the id <*disk block id*>. The file system uses the information in the intentions list to update the files when the atomic action commits. This action is called *commit processing*. The commit flag contains two fields, *transaction id* and *value*. This flag is created when the statement **begin atomic action** of an atomic action A_i is executed and its fields are initialized to A_i and "not committed," respectively. The value in the commit flag is changed to "committed" when **end atomic action** is executed. The flag is destroyed after all updates described in the intentions list have been carried out.

If a failure occurs, the file system checks for the presence of commit flags when its operation is resumed. If a commit flag exists for A_i and has the value "not committed," the file system simply destroys the commit flag and the intentions list, and executes atomic action A_i again starting with the statement **begin atomic action**. Existence of a commit flag for A_i with the value "committed" implies that commit processing of A_i was in progress when occurrence of a fault led to

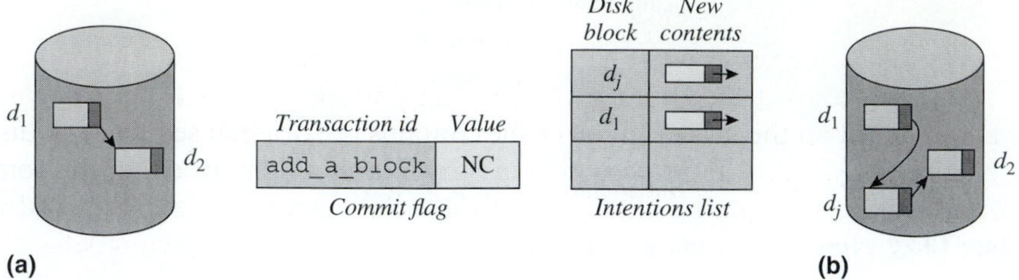

Figure 13.30 (a) Before and (b) after commit processing. (*Note:* NC means *not committed*.)

a failure. Since it is not known whether any entries of the intentions list were processed before the fault, the entire commit processing is now repeated.

If faults occur during commit processing, some entries of the intentions list may be processed many times. However, it does not pose any data consistency problems because the operation of writing *<new contents>* into *<disk block id>* is an *idempotent operation*, which has the property that executing it many times has the same effect as executing it once. The following algorithm summarizes all actions concerning implementation of an atomic action.

Algorithm 13.2 *Implementation of an Atomic Action*

1. *Execution of an atomic action A_i:*
   - **a.** When the statement **begin atomic action** is executed, create a *commit flag* and an *intentions list* in stable storage, and initialize them as follows:
     commit flag := (A_i, "not committed");
     intentions list := "empty";
   - **b.** For every file update made by a subaction, add a pair (d, v) to the intentions list, where d is a disk block id and v is its new content.
   - **c.** When the statement **end atomic action** is executed, set the value of A_i's *commit flag* to "committed" and perform Step 2.
2. *Commit processing:*
   - **a.** For every pair (d, v) in the intentions list, write v in the disk block with the id d.
   - **b.** Erase the commit flag and the intentions list.
3. *On recovering after a failure:*
   If the commit flag for atomic action A_i exists,
   - **a.** If the value in commit flag is "not committed": Erase the commit flag and the intentions list. Reexecute atomic action A_i.
   - **b.** Perform Step 2 if the value in commit flag is "committed."

Example 13.11 Implementation of an Atomic Action

Figure 13.30(a) shows the file `alpha`, the commit flag and the intentions list when Algorithm 13.2 is applied to the atomic action *add_a_block* of

Figure 13.29. The new contents of disk blocks d_j and d_1 are kept in the intentions list until commit processing. Atomicity of the action is ensured as follows: If a fault occurs during Step 13.2 of the algorithm, none of the file updates are reflected on the disk. Hence the file contains the original sequence of disk blocks $d_1, d_2, \ldots$. A fault occurring in Step 2 cannot damage either the commit flag or the intentions list because these data structures are recorded in stable storage. Thus, processing of the intentions list eventually completes; the file contains the sequence of disk blocks $d_1, d_j, d_2 \ldots$ at the end of commit processing, as shown in Figure 13.30(b).

13.12 JOURNALING FILE SYSTEM

As discussed in Section 13.11.1, a file system keeps some part of file data as well as metadata such as file control blocks, file map tables, and free lists of disk blocks in memory during its operation. When a file system's operation is shut down by a system administrator, the file system copies all the data and metadata held in memory onto the disk, so that the copy on disk is complete and consistent. However, when a power outage occurs, or when the system is switched off abruptly, the file system does not get an opportunity to copy the file data and metadata from memory to disk. Such a shutdown is called an *unclean* shutdown; it results in loss of file data and metadata that was held in memory.

Traditionally, file systems relied on recovery techniques to protect against loss of data and metadata because they were so simple to implement. Thus, backups were created periodically, and files were recovered from backups when failures were detected. Metadata was recovered by laborious searches to find and fix inconsistencies. Use of recovery techniques imposed little overhead during normal operation of the system. When a failure was detected, however, CPU overhead was incurred in checking consistency of metadata, and the system was unavailable during recovery, as well. As an example, consider what happened when a Unix system using the ext2 file system was shut down uncleanly. On rebooting, the file system would realize that it was shut down uncleanly, and hence its metadata was likely to be inconsistent. It would invoke the `fsck` program to recover the metadata. `fsck` would look through every file system data structure on the disk and try to fix any inconsistencies it could find. Operation of the OS was delayed while `fsck` executed.

A modern file system uses fault tolerance techniques so that it can resume its operation quickly after an unclean shutdown. A *journaling file system* implements fault tolerance by maintaining a *journal*, which resembles the intentions list used to implement atomic actions (see Section 13.11.2). The file system records actions that it is about to perform in the journal before actually performing them. When operation of a file system is restored after an unclean shutdown, it consults the journal to identify actions that were not performed as a result of the shutdown and performs them, thus ensuring correctness of file data and metadata. The ext3

Table 13.6 Journaling Modes

Mode	Description
Write behind	Protects only metadata. Does not provide any protection to file data.
Ordered data	Protects metadata. Limited protection is offered for file data as well—it is written to disk before metadata concerning it is written.
Full data	Journals both file data and metadata.

file system of Linux, XFS of Silicon Graphics, JFS of IBM, and VxFS of Veritas are some examples of journaling file systems.

Use of fault tolerance techniques to protect consistency of both metadata and file data causes high overhead—it amounts to performing every file update as an atomic action. Hence a journaling file system offers a menu of journaling modes, each mode providing a different kind of protection to metadata and file data. A system administrator can choose a journaling mode to suit the kind of reliability that is necessary in the computing environment. Table 13.6 describes three journaling modes.

In the *write behind* mode, metadata is protected but file data is not. When new data is added to a file, this mode ensures that the disk blocks allocated to hold the new data would be added in the disk copy of the file's FMT. However, it does not ensure that new data added to the file would be recorded in these blocks before a fault can occur. Consequently, if a fault occurs while the file is being processed, the disk copy of the file may contain junk data. The *ordered data* mode avoids this problem by ensuring that file data is written to disk before metadata is written. However, when this mode is used, we may have a situation where disk blocks in which the new file data have been written are not added to the file map table. The *full data* mode protects both metadata and file data.

13.13 VIRTUAL FILE SYSTEM

Users have diverse requirements of a file system, such as convenience, high reliability, fast response, and access to files on other computer systems. A single file system cannot provide all these features, so an operating system provides a *virtual file system* (VFS), which facilitates simultaneous operation of several file systems. This way each user gets to use the file system he prefers.

A virtual file system (VFS) is an abstraction that supports a generic file model. The abstraction is implemented by a VFS layer that is situated between a process and a file system (see Figure 13.31). The VFS layer has two interfaces—an interface with the file systems, and an interface with processes. Any file system that conforms to the specification of the VFS–file system interface can be installed to work under the VFS. This feature makes it easy to add a new file system. The VFS–process interface provides functionalities to perform generic open, close, read, and

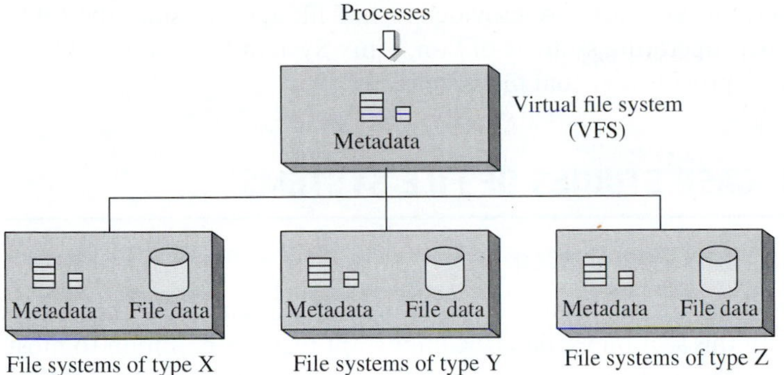

Figure 13.31 Virtual file system.

write operations on files, and mount, unmount operations on file systems. These functionalities are invoked through system calls. The VFS determines which file system a file actually belongs to and invokes the open, close, read, and write functionalities of the specific file system through the VFS–file system interface. It also invokes functions of the specific file system to implement mount and unmount operations.

All file systems operating under the VFS are available for use simultaneously. In the system of Figure 13.31, one process may use a file system of type X while another process simultaneously uses a file system of type Y. The virtual file system can also be used to compose a heterogeneous file system. For example, a user can mount a file system of type X in a directory of a file system of type Y. This feature is useful with removable media like CDs; it permits a user to mount the file system that exists in a CD in his current directory and access its files without any concern for the fact that file data is recorded in a different format. This feature is also useful in a distributed environment for mounting a remote file system into a file system of a computer. It is described in Section 20.6.1.

As shown in the schematic diagram of Figure 13.31, the virtual file system does not contain any file data. It merely contains data structures that constitute VFS metadata. Each file system contains its own metadata and file data. The key data structure used by the virtual file system is the *virtual node*, popularly called *vnode*, which contains the information needed for performing operations on a file. It can be looked upon as a file object with the following three parts:

- File-system-independent data such as a file id that is unique within the domain of the VFS, which may be the individual computer system or a network; the file type, e.g., directory, data file, or a special file; and other fields such as an open count, lock, and flags.
- File-system-specific data such as the file map table.
- Addresses of functions in the file system that contains this file. These functions implement the open, close, read, and write operations on files of this file type.

Operating systems have provided virtual file systems since the 1990s. Sun OS and Solaris operating systems of Sun, Unix System V version 4, Unix 4.2 BSD, and Linux provide a virtual file system.

13.14 CASE STUDIES OF FILE SYSTEMS

13.14.1 Unix File System

The design of the Unix file system is greatly influenced by the MULTICS file system. In this section we describe important features common to most versions of Unix, in the context of the generic description of file processing in Sections 13.4 and 13.8.

Inodes, File Descriptors, and File Structures The information that constituted the directory entry of a file in Figure 13.6 is split in Unix between the directory entry and the *inode* of the file. The directory entry contains only the file name and the inode number; the bulk of the information concerning a file is contained in its inode. Files are considered to be streams of characters and are accessed sequentially. The system administrator can specify a disk quota for each user. It prevents a user from occupying too much disk space.

The inode data structure is maintained on disk. Some of its fields contain the following information:

- File type, e.g., whether directory, link, or special file
- Number of links to the file
- File size
- Id of the device on which the file is stored
- Inode serial number
- User and group ids of the owner
- Access permissions
- Allocation information

The splitting of the conventional directory entry into the directory entry and the inode facilitates creation and deletion of links. A file can be deleted when its number of links drops to zero. Note the similarity between fields of the inode and those of the FCB (see Table 13.3).

Figure 13.32 illustrates the arrangement in memory during the processing of a file. It consists of inodes, *file structures*, and *file descriptors*. A file structure contains two fields—the current position in an open file, which is in the form of an offset from the start of the file; and a pointer to the inode for the file. Thus an inode and a file structure together contain all the information necessary to access the file. A file descriptor points to a file structure. File descriptors are stored in a per-process table. This table resembles the *open files table* (OFT) described in Section 13.8.

When a process opens a file `alpha`, the directory entry for `alpha` is located. A directory lookup cache is employed to speed up this operation. Once the entry of `alpha` is located, its inode is copied into memory, unless memory already

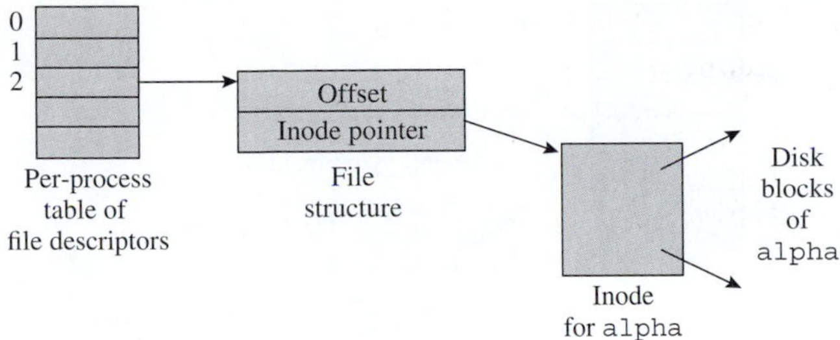

Figure 13.32 Unix file system data structures.

contains such a copy. The arrangement shown in Figure 13.32 is now set up and the index of the file descriptor in the file descriptors table, which is an integer, is passed back to the process that opened the file. The process can use it in a manner that resembles use of the internal id of a file in the generic arrangement of Sections 13.4 and 13.8.

When a process creates a child process, a table of descriptors is created for the child process, and the file descriptors of the parent process are copied into it. Thus more than one file descriptor may point to the same file structure. Processes owning these file descriptors share the offset into the file. A read or write by one process will modify the offset for the other processes as well.

File Sharing Semantics Several processes may independently open the same file. In that case, the arrangement of Figure 13.32 is set up for each process. Thus, two or more file structures may point to the same inode. Processes using these file structures have their own offsets into the file, so a read or write by one process does not modify the offset used by other processes.

Unix provides single-image mutable file semantics for concurrent file sharing. As shown in Figure 13.32, every process that opens a file points to the copy of its inode through the file descriptor and file structure. Thus, all processes sharing a file use the same copy of the file; changes made by one process are immediately visible to other processes sharing the file. Implementation of these semantics is aided by the fact that Unix uses a disk cache called *buffer cache* rather than buffers for individual file processing activities (see Section 14.13.1.2). To avoid race conditions while the inode of a shared file is accessed, a lock field is provided in the memory copy of an inode. A process trying to access an inode must sleep if the lock is set by some other process. Processes concurrently using a file must make their own arrangements to avoid race conditions on data contained in the file.

Disk Space Allocation Unix uses indexed disk space allocation, with a disk block size of 4 KB. Each file has a *file allocation table* analogous to an FMT, which is maintained in its inode. The allocation table contains 15 entries (see Figure 13.33). Twelve of these entries directly point to data blocks of the file. The next entry in the allocation table points to an indirect block, i.e., a block that itself contains pointers to data blocks. The next two entries point to double and triple indirect

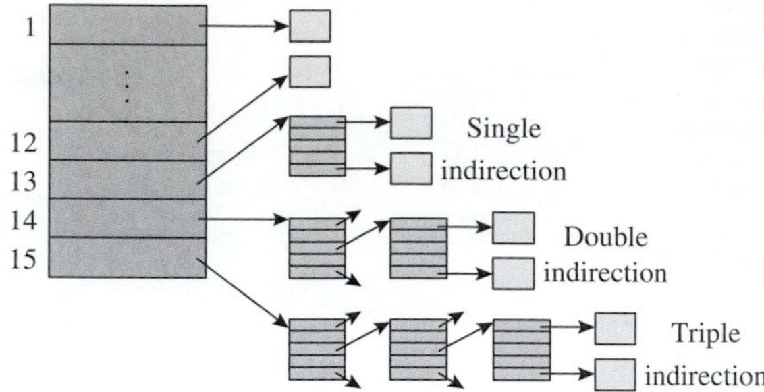

Figure 13.33 Unix file allocation table.

blocks, respectively. In this manner, the total file size can be as large as 2^{42} bytes. However, the file size information is stored in a 32-bit word of the inode. Hence file size is limited to $2^{32}-1$ bytes, for which the direct, single, and double indirect blocks of the allocation table are adequate.

For file sizes smaller than 48 KB, this arrangement is as efficient as the flat FMT arrangement discussed in Section 13.7. Such files also have a small allocation table that can fit into the inode itself. The indirect blocks permit files to grow to large sizes, although their access involves traversing the indirection in the file allocation table. A survey of Unix file sizes conducted in 1996 reported that the average file size in Unix was 22 KB, and over 93 percent of files had sizes smaller than 32 KB. Thus the Unix file allocation table is as efficient as the flat FMT for most files.

Unix maintains a *free list* of disk blocks. Each entry in the list is similar to an indirect block in an FMT—it contains addresses of free disk blocks, and the id of the next disk block in the free list. This arrangement minimizes the overhead of adding disk blocks to the free list when a file is deleted; only marginal processing is required for files that contain only direct and single indirect blocks. A lock field is associated with the free list to avoid race conditions when disk blocks are added and deleted from it. A file system program named `mkfs` is used to form the free list when a new file system is created. `mkfs` lists the free blocks in ascending order by block number while forming the free list. However, this ordering is lost as disk blocks are added to and deleted from the free list during file system operation. The file system makes no effort to restore this order. Thus blocks allocated to a file may be dispersed throughout a disk, which reduces the access efficiency of a file. BSD Unix uses *cylinder groups* to address this issue (see Section 13.7).

Multiple File Systems The root of a file system is called the *superblock*. It contains the size of the file system, the free list, and the size of the inode list. In the interest of efficiency, Unix maintains the superblock in memory but copies it onto the disk periodically. This arrangement implies that some part of file system state is lost in the event of a system crash. The file system can reconstruct some of this information, e.g., the free list, by analyzing the disk status. This is done as a part of the system booting procedure.

There can be many file systems in a Unix system. Each file system has to be kept on a single logical disk device; hence files cannot span different logical disks. A physical disk can be partitioned into many logical disks and a file system can be constructed on each of them. Such partitioning provides some protection across file systems, and also prevents a file system from occupying too much disk space. A file system has to be mounted before being accessed. Only a user with the root password, typically a system administrator, can mount a file system.

Mounting and unmounting of file systems works as follows: A logical disk containing a file system is given a device special file name. This name is indicated as *FS_name* in a *mount* command (see Section 13.5). When a file system is mounted, the superblock of the mounted file system is loaded in memory. Disk block allocation for a file in the mounted file system is performed within the logical disk device of the mounted file system. Files in a mounted file system are accessed as described in Section 13.9.1.

A file open call in Unix specifies three parameters—path name, flags, and mode. Flags indicate what kind of operations will be performed on the file—whether *read*, *write*, or *read/write*. The mode parameter is provided only when a file is being created. It specifies the access privileges to be associated with the file. This information is typically copied from the file creation mask of the user. The owner of a file can change the file protection information any time through a `chmod` command.

13.14.1.1 Berkeley Fast File System

The Berkeley fast file system (FFS) for Unix was developed to address the limitations of the file system s5fs. It supports a *symbolic link*, which is merely a file that contains a reference to another file. If the symbolic link is encountered during path name resolution, the path name resolution is simply continued at the referenced file. It also includes several innovations concerning disk block allocation and disk access, which we describe in the following.

FFS permits use of large disk blocks—blocks can be as large as 8 KB. Different file systems can use different block sizes; however, block size cannot vary within one file system. A large block size makes larger files accessible through the direct blocks in the file allocation table. A large block size also makes I/O operations more efficient and makes efficient use of the disk. However, a large block size leads to large internal fragmentation in the last disk block of a file. FFS counters this effect by allocating a part of a disk block to the last portion of a file. This way, a disk block may be shared by many files. To facilitate such allocation, a disk block is divided into equal-size parts called *fragments*. The number of fragments in a disk block is a parameter of a file system, and is either 1, 2, 4, or 8. FFS uses a bit map to keep track of free fragments of a block. File growth requires special attention in this scheme, because a file may need more fragments, which might not be available in the same disk block. In such cases, all its fragments are moved to another disk block and the previously allocated fragments are freed.

FFS uses the notion of *cylinder groups* to reduce the movement of disk heads (see Section 13.7). To reduce disk head movement further, it puts all inodes of a file system in the same cylinder group and tries to put the inode of a file and the file itself in the same cylinder group. It also prevents a file from filling up a cylinder group. If a file grows to a size that would violate this constraint, it relocates the entire file into a larger cylinder group. This technique increases the possibility that concurrently accessed files will be found within the same cylinder group, which would reduce disk head movement.

FFS tries to minimize rotational latency while reading a sequential file. As described later in Section 14.3.2, a certain period of time elapses between the end of a disk read operation and start of the next disk read operation. During this time, the next few disk blocks inevitably pass under the disk head. Even if a command to read the next disk block is issued immediately, the block can therefore be read only during the next revolution of the disk. To ensure that consecutively numbered blocks on a track can be read during the same disk revolution, FFS separates them by putting a few other disk blocks between them. This feature is similar to the technique of interleaving of sectors in a track discussed later in Section 14.3.2. As illustrated there, this technique has a significant impact on disk throughput.

13.14.2 Linux File System

Linux provides a virtual file system (VFS) which supports a common file model that resembles the Unix file model. This file model is implemented by using Unix-like data structures such as superblocks and inodes. When a file is opened, the VFS transforms its directory entry into a *dentry* object. This dentry object is cached so that the overhead of building it from the directory entry is avoided if the file is opened repeatedly during a computing session. The standard file system of Linux is called ext2. The file system ext3 incorporates journaling, which provides integrity of file data and metadata and fast booting after an unclean shutdown (see Section 13.12).

Ext2 provides a variety of file locks for process synchronization. *Advisory* locks are those that are supposed to be heeded by processes to ensure mutual exclusion; however, the file system does not enforce their use. Unix file locks belong to this category of locks. *Mandatory* locks are those that are checked by the file system; if a process tries to access data that is protected by a mandatory lock, the process is blocked until the lock is reset by its holder. A *lease* is a special kind of file lock that is valid for a specific amount of time after another process has tried to access the data protected by it. It is implemented as follows: If a process accesses some data that is protected by a lease, the holder of the lease is intimated by the file system. It now has a stipulated interval of time to finish accessing the file and release the lease. If it does not do so, its lease is broken and awarded to the process that tried to access the data protected by it.

Design of ext2 was influenced by BSD's fast file system (see Section 13.14.1). Ext2 uses the notion of a *block group*, which is a set of consecutive disk blocks, to reduce the movement of disk heads when a file is opened and its data is accessed. It uses a bit map to keep track of free disk blocks in a block group. When a file is created, it tries to allocate disk space for the inode of the file within the same block group that contains its parent directory, and also accommodates the file data within the same block group. Every time a file is extended through addition of new data, it searches the bit map of the block group to find a free disk block that is close to a target disk block. If such a disk block is found, it checks whether a few adjoining disk blocks are also free and preallocates a few of these to the file. If such a free disk block is not found, it preallocates a few contiguous disk blocks located elsewhere in the block group. This way it is possible to read large sections of data without having to move the disk head. When the file is closed, preallocated but unused disk blocks are freed. This strategy of disk space allocation ensures use of contiguous disk blocks for contiguous sections of file data even when files are created and deleted at a high rate; it contributes to high file access performance.

13.14.3 Solaris File System

The Solaris file system provides Unix-like file access permissions in which three access control pairs exist in each access control list—for the file owner, for other users in the file owner's group, and for all other users in the system (see Section 13.6). To provide flexibility that is lacking in this basic scheme, it also permits new pairs containing *<list_of_user_ids>* and *<list_of_access_privileges>* to be added to the access control list of a file; the system administrator specifies a new pair through the `setfacl` command.

Solaris offers convenience and flexibility in file processing, through a virtual file system as described in Section 13.13 and through a variety of file processing modes. An *exclusive open* operation on a file fails if the file already exists; otherwise, it creates the file and returns its descriptor in a single indivisible action. This operation avoids race conditions while a new file is created; it is used by processes that create a lock file to synchronize their activities. Record-level locking is provided to implement fine-grained synchronization between processes that concurrently access a file; when a process tries to access a record whose lock has been set by another process, it is blocked until the lock is reset. The *nonblocked I/O* mode is provided to avoid indefinite waits due to this feature. In this mode, an I/O operation that tries to access a record that is locked by another process simply fails. The process issuing the operation now has an opportunity to perform some other actions and retry the I/O operation later. An *asynchronous I/O* mode is provided in which a process is not blocked for its I/O operation to complete. This mode is useful in real-time applications. In the *direct I/O* mode, the file system does not buffer or cache file data; this mode facilitates applications such as database systems that wish to perform their own buffering or caching.

Data synchronization and file integrity flags can be set in the directory entry of a file to obtain reliable operation. When some of these flags are set for a file, I/O operations on the file ensure the integrity of metadata and/or the file data in a manner resembling the journaling modes summarized in Table 13.6.

13.14.4 Windows File System

The NTFS file system of Windows is designed to meet the requirements of servers and workstations. It provides support for client–server applications for file and database servers. A key feature of NTFS is recoverability of the file system, which we will discuss later in this section.

A *partition* is a large collection of contiguous sectors on a disk; A *volume* is a logical partition on a disk; i.e., it is a virtual disk. A simple volume contains a single partition, while a multipartition volume called a *spanned volume* may contain up to 32 partitions located on one or more disks. NTFS performs disk space allocation in units called *clusters*. Each cluster is a group of contiguous sectors; the number of sectors in a cluster is a power of 2. A cluster on a volume is assigned a *logical cluster number* (LCN), whereas that in a file is assigned a *virtual cluster number* (VCN).

An NTFS volume contains a boot sector, a *master file table* (MFT), some system files and user files. The presence of a boot sector makes every volume bootable. The MFT typically contains a 1 KB record for each file and directory on the volume, though large files may need multiple MFT records. The MFT also contains information about unused areas on the volume. Each file on a volume has a unique *file reference*, which consists of two components—a 48-bit *file number*, which is simply the record number of the MFT record occupied by it, and a 16-bit *sequence number*, which is a count of the number of times the MFT record has been used to date. The sequence number is used to prevent mix-ups between two files that have used the same MFT record at different times.

Each file has a set of attributes, where each attribute is an independent byte stream that can be edited. Some standard attributes are common to all files. In addition, a file may have special attributes required in an application. Each file has an MFT record called its *base file record*, which contains the file reference of the file, the time of its last update, and its attributes. An unnamed data attribute of a file contains file data. This arrangement permits the data in a small file or directory to be stored in its base file record itself, which provides high file access efficiency. If an attribute cannot fit in the file's base file record, it is stored as a *nonresident* attribute—it is stored in another MFT record and a pointer to it is put in its base file record. If the nonresident attribute itself cannot fit in one MFT record, it is stored in clusters on the disk and the MFT record pointed to by the file's base file record contains a VCN-to-LCN mapping for its clusters. When a process opens a file, NTFS sets up a *stream control block* (SCB) for each of its attributes. An SCB contains a pointer to a *file control block* for the file, which contains its file reference, and an offset into an attribute. When the process wishes to access an attribute of a file, NTFS uses the SCB to locate the file's base file record, finds information about location of the attribute, and then applies the offset to access the required portion of the attribute.

A directory is organized as a B+ tree with files as its leaf nodes, and it is implemented by using an index file. The B+ tree data structure has the property that the length of each path in the tree is the same. This feature facilitates efficient search for a file in a directory (see Section 13.4.4). NTFS provides hard links to set up multiple paths to a file. It also supports symbolic links, called *junctions*, that redirect path name translation from a directory to an alternative one. This feature provides an effect that is analogous to mounting of file systems.

NTFS employs two techniques to save disk space. If a file is sparse, it does not allocate disk space to that portion of the file into which either no data has been written, or the written data is such that one or more complete sectors contain zeroes. It performs data compression for nonsparse files, using 16 consecutive virtual clusters in a file as a unit. It replaces them by a compressed form only if that action would save at least one cluster, and notes this fact so that it can automatically perform decompression when the file is accessed.

NTFS stores its metadata also in files. Some of these files are as follows:

- The *MFT file* contains MFT records.
- The *log file* contains information used for recovery; its use is described later in this section.
- The *attribute definition table* contains information about attributes.
- A *bit map file* indicates which clusters in a volume are allocated and which are free.
- The *boot file* contains the boot sector.
- A *bad clusters* file keeps track of clusters that are unusable due to hardware problems.

NTFS provides robustness by ensuring consistency of the metadata when a crash occurs. It is achieved by treating every modification of the metadata as an atomic transaction. From the discussion of atomic actions in Section 13.11.2, it would appear that atomic transactions can be implemented simply by writing the "intentions" of a transaction in a write-ahead log file, and actually carrying out the intentions when the transaction commits. However, certain actions like creation of a new file's record in the MFT cannot be delayed until a transaction commits, so NTFS uses a combined redo/undo log that contains two kinds of records. The collection of *redo* records in the log resembles the intentions list of Section 13.11.2, while the *undo* records pertain to actions that have been already performed by transactions that are yet to commit. During normal operation, only the redo records are used—they are processed to actually perform modification of NTFS's metadata when a transaction commits. The undo records are used only during recovery from a crash, as described in the following.

NTFS performs recovery as follows: It modifies its metadata according to the redo entries in the log pertaining to transactions that had committed prior to the crash. It then processes the undo entries to undo the modifications performed by transactions that had not committed prior to the crash. The metadata is in a consistent state at the end of these actions, so NTFS now resumes normal operation. This feature provides the *write behind* capabilities of journaling file systems discussed in Section 13.12.

In principle, log entries pertaining to a transaction can be discarded after all of its actions are carried out during normal operation or recovery, or after all of its actions are undone during recovery. However, NTFS cannot discard log entries in this manner for two reasons—it stores its metadata in files, and it uses a *file cache* (see Section 14.13.3) to speed up file processing activities. Thus, changes made in a file containing metadata while processing the redo or undo entries in the log would remain in the file cache for a long time and may be lost if a crash occurred before they were written to the disk. To prevent indefinite growth of the log, NTFS takes a *checkpoint* every 5 seconds. It puts a checkpoint record into the log at this time, in which it writes contents of dirty blocks existing in the file cache. When a crash occurs, NTFS locates the latest checkpoint record in the log, restores values of disk blocks found there in the file cache, and then processes the redo/undo entries of transactions that were in progress at the time of the crash. This recovery procedure does not require the log entries of transactions that had committed or aborted before the checkpoint was taken, hence NTFS deletes these log entries while taking the checkpoint.

File data may be lost if a crash damages some disk blocks. The volume manager driver that runs under NTFS employs the RAID technology to tolerate such faults. *Disk mirroring* implies recording of identical data on disk blocks in two disks, so that one of the disk blocks would be accessible even if the other one is damaged because of a fault. (Disk mirroring and other RAID configurations are discussed in Section 14.3.5.)

Windows Vista has many new features for recovery. The *kernel transaction manager* implements transaction semantics over files and objects which can span several computer systems. The *backup and recovery center* permits a user to specify when and how frequently each file should be backed up, and to request recovery of a specific previous version of the file. To conserve disk space, it stores only the changes made in a file in a backup.

13.15 PERFORMANCE OF FILE SYSTEMS

File systems employ five techniques to provide high file access performance:

- *Use of efficient data structures:* Directories are organized by using data structures that facilitate fast search.
- *Effective disk space allocation:* Disk space is allocated to a file in such a manner that little disk head movement and rotational delays are involved in processing of a sequential file.
- *Caching:* Part of memory is used as a *cache* for data stored on an I/O device. As discussed in Section 2.2.3, caching speeds up accesses to information that exhibits either *temporal locality* or *spatial locality*—that is, data that is either repeatedly accessed or located in proximity of previously accessed data.
- *Buffering:* A *buffer* is a memory area that is used to store data temporarily. The file system loads data from an I/O device into a buffer before a process needs it, so that the process can access the data without having to wait for an I/O operation to complete. Converse actions are performed when a process wishes to write data in a file.
- *Disk scheduling:* I/O operations on a disk are performed in an order that reduces disk head movement; it ensures high throughput of a disk.

Figure 13.34 summarizes how a file system uses these techniques to speed up file processing. Hash tables and B+ trees enable fast searches in a directory (see Section 13.4.3). Disk space allocation of a file is confined to *extents* and *cylinder*

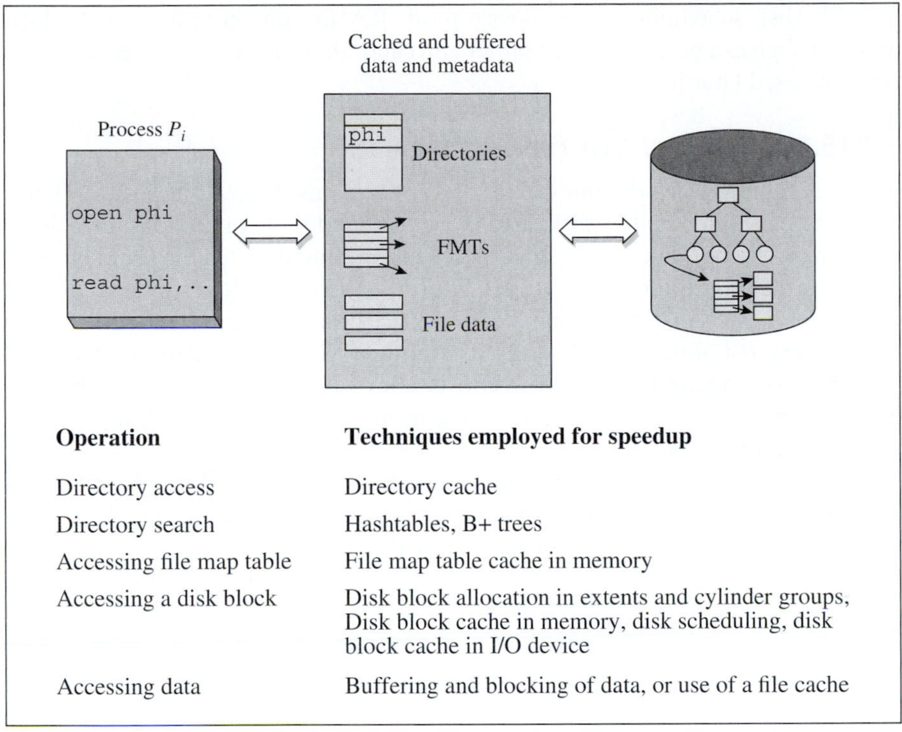

Operation	Techniques employed for speedup
Directory access	Directory cache
Directory search	Hashtables, B+ trees
Accessing file map table	File map table cache in memory
Accessing a disk block	Disk block allocation in extents and cylinder groups, Disk block cache in memory, disk scheduling, disk block cache in I/O device
Accessing data	Buffering and blocking of data, or use of a file cache

Figure 13.34 Techniques employed to provide high file access performance.

groups to reduce disk head movement and rotational delays (see Section 13.7). The other techniques provide fast access to file data and metadata of a file system, such as directory entries and file map tables.

Directories are cached in memory when accessed for the first time. Thus a directory used to resolve a path name is retained in the cache to speed up future references to files located in it. This cache is called a *directory names cache*. A file map table is buffered in memory when the file is opened, in anticipation of accesses to it. It may be cached after its first access. Buffering may not be feasible if a file map table is large in size. In that case, parts of it may be cached in memory when first referenced.

A *disk cache* stores disk blocks in memory following their first use in a file processing activity. Hit ratios better than 0.9 are possible in the disk cache. Hence its use reduces the number of I/O operations on a disk significantly. An access method uses *buffering* and *blocking* of file data or stores file data in a *file cache* to reduce the wait time involved in an I/O operation. *Disk scheduling* is used to reduce disk head movement and the average wait time for I/O operations. These techniques are employed by the IOCS; they are discussed later in Chapter 14.

As technology advances, techniques that were developed for use in software become implemented in the hardware. Modern I/O device technology incorporates some of the techniques mentioned in Figure 13.34. Thus SCSI disks provide disk scheduling in the device itself. RAID units contain a disk block buffer, which can be used to both buffer and cache disk blocks. These technologies are discussed later in Chapter 14.

13.15.1 Log-Structured File System

Disk caching reduces the number of read operations directed at a disk. Hence disk usage is dominated by disk head movement and write operations. Disk head movement can be reduced through disk scheduling and through the use of *cylinder groups* in disk space allocation for files. However, these techniques are less effective when files located in different parts of a disk are processed simultaneously, which is the case most of the time in a shared computer system. For example, in a Unix system, write operations to a disk consume only about 10 percent of the disk time; the rest of the time is spent in disk head movement, which leads to poor throughput of a disk.

A *log-structured file system* reduces disk head movement through a radically different file organization. It writes file data of *all* files together in a single sequential structure that resembles a journal. We call it the *log file*. When an update or write operation is performed on any file, the new data is simply added to the end of the log file. Hence little disk head movement is involved in this operation. The file system writes special *index blocks* into the log file to contain metadata about the location of each file's data in the log file. These index blocks are used when file data has to be read off the disk. Thus, little disk head movement is required for reading data that was written into a file recently; however, more disk head movement is involved for older data. Performance studies on the Sprite log-structured file system showed that disk head movement accounted for only 30 percent of the disk time consumed during file processing, and its performance was superior to the conventional file system for frequent small writes. Example 13.12 illustrates operation of a log-structured file system.

Example 13.12 Log-Structured File System

Figure 13.35(a) is a schematic diagram of the arrangement used in a log-structured file system. For simplicity, it shows the metadata and file data of a single file in the log file. The data blocks in the log file are numbered for convenience. The directory entry of a file points to an index block in the log file; we assume the index block to contain the FMT of the file. When file data residing in block 1 is updated, the new values are written into a new disk block, i.e., block 4. Similarly some file data is written into disk block 5 when the data in block 3 is updated. The file system now writes a new index block that contains the updated FMT of the file and sets the FMT pointer in the directory entry of the file to point to the new index block. The new FMT contains pointers to the two new data blocks and to data block 2 that has not been modified [see Figure 13.35(b)]. The old index block and disk blocks 1 and 3 are now free.

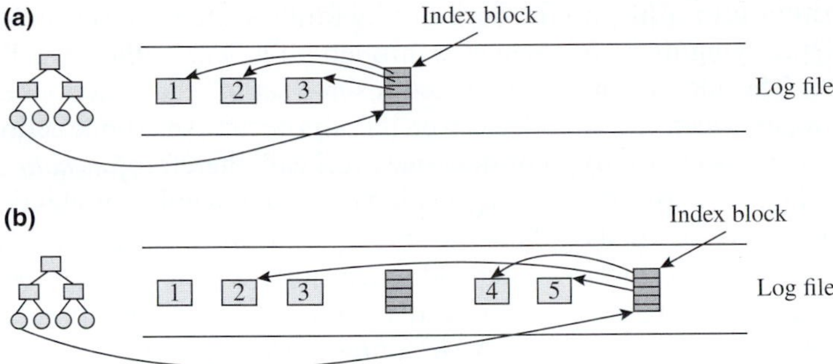

Figure 13.35 File update in a log-structured file system.

Since the log file is written as a sequential-access file, the file system has to ensure that a large-enough disk area is always available to write the log file. It achieves this by moving data blocks around on the disk to make a large free area available for the log file. This operation is analogous to memory compaction (see Section 11.5.1.4). It involves considerable disk head movement, which now dominates the disk usage; however, compaction is performed as a background activity so it does not delay file processing activities in processes.

13.16 SUMMARY

Computer users have many expectations of a file system—convenience, good performance of a file processing activity, and efficient use of I/O devices. To deal with these concerns effectively, the file system is structured into two layers: The file system layer deals with convenience issues such as sharing and protection of files and reliability; the *input-output control system* (IOCS) layer implements file operations and deals with efficiency issues. In this chapter, we discussed the techniques of file systems.

A file may be a structured file, i.e., it may contain records of data, or it may be an unstructured, or *byte stream*, file. A file system provides convenience to its users through three means. First, it provides different *file organizations*, where each organization suits a specific pattern of accessing records in a file—it provides a method of arranging records of a file on an I/O device and accessing them efficiently. The *sequential* and *direct* file organizations suit sequential and random access to records in a file, respectively. Several hybrid organizations, such as the *index sequential* organization, are also widely used. Second, a file system allows users to group related files logically and conveniently by creating files and directories to any desired level. Third, it allows a user to specify which other users may access his files in what manner, which facilitates *sharing* and *protection* of files.

The file system allocates disk space to a file such that fragmentation of disk space is avoided and file data can be accessed efficiently. *Indexed allocation* of disk space to a file uses a disk block or an *extent* as the unit of disk space for allocation. The disk blocks or extents allocated to a file are confined to *cylinder groups* to ensure efficient access to file data. Information concerning the disk space allocated to a file is stored in a *file map table* (FMT).

Before reading from or writing into a file, a process has to open the file by specifying its *path name* in the directory structure. The file system traverses the path name, determines which file is being opened, and sets up a *file control block* (FCB) to contain information such as the file's type and organization, address of its FMT, and address of its next record. When the process wishes to perform a read or write operation, the file system passes the FCB to the IOCS, and the IOCS implements the operation, using the information accessible through the FCB. The file system specifies the *file sharing semantics*, which determine how the results of a file update made by a process should be visible to other processes using the file concurrently.

The file system ensures reliability of operation by ensuring that the file data and metadata such as FMTs and FCBs are not lost or made inconsistent by faults such as power outages. It is achieved through an *atomic action*, which ensures that all actions in a set of related actions are completed even if faults occur. An atomic action incurs considerable overhead, therefore *journaling file systems* provide a menu of reliability modes that guard data and metadata to different extents, so that a system administrator can choose the mode that is cost-effective for a computing environment.

A *virtual file system* (VFS) is a software layer that permits several file systems to be in operation on a computer system simultaneously, so that a user can choose the file system that is most suitable for his application. The VFS provides a unified method of accessing different file systems. A process invokes the VFS layer using generalized commands to access files, and the VFS layer directs the commands to the appropriate file system.

TEST YOUR CONCEPTS

13.1 Classify each of the following statements as true or false:

- **a.** Allocation of contiguous disk space for a sequential-access file leads to more efficient file processing than allocation of noncontiguous disk space.
- **b.** Cycles in the directory structure create difficulties with the file deletion operation.
- **c.** Absolute path names for two different files cannot be identical, whereas their relative path names could be identical.
- **d.** The purpose of the file control block (FCB) is to facilitate a file open operation; the FCB can be deleted immediately after the file is opened.
- **e.** When a file is closed after updating, the directory containing the file may have to be updated as well.
- **f.** Maintaining a file's file map table (FMT) in memory while the file is being processed reduces the number of disk accesses during file processing.
- **g.** During creation of a new file in a mounted file system, the file is allocated disk space in the logical disk used by the mounted file system.
- **h.** The effect of mounting a file system is similar to that of setting up a link in the directory structure, except that the effect is obliterated when the file system is unmounted.
- **i.** When a user updates the data in a single-image mutable file, changes made to the file are not immediately visible to users concurrently using the file.
- **j.** When a fault occurs, a single incremental backup is adequate for restoring the entire file system to a previous consistent state.
- **k.** Journaling incurs overhead during operation of a file system.
- **l.** A virtual file system permits use of many file systems in a computer; however, these file systems cannot be used concurrently.

13.2 Select the appropriate alternative in each of the following questions:

a. The file control block (FCB) of a file `alpha`:
   i. Contains only information copied from the directory entry of `alpha`
   ii. Is used to avoid frequent accesses to the directory entry of `alpha`
   iii. Is used only to protect file `alpha` against invalid accesses

b. The stable storage technique is:
   i. A fault tolerance technique that is used to recover from two faulty blocks on a disk
   ii. A recovery technique used to recover the file system after a power failure
   iii. A fault tolerance technique that is used to recover from one faulty block on a disk
   iv. None of the above

EXERCISES

13.1 A file named `data` is frequently accessed by users in a system. The following alternatives are proposed to simplify access to `data`.

a. Set up links from every user's home directory to `data`.

b. Copy `data` into every user's home directory.

Compare the advantages and drawbacks of these approaches.

13.2 An index sequential file contains 10,000 records. Its index contains 100 entries. Each index entry describes an area of the file that contains 100 records. If all records in the file have the same probability of being accessed, calculate the average number of disk operations involved in accessing a record. Compare this number with the number of disk operations required if the same records were stored in a sequential file.

13.3 Consider the index sequential file of Figure 13.5. The following problem arises when a new record, say record for employee number 8 (we will call it record 8), is added to it. There is no space to store the new record on the track. Hence the access method takes out record 13 from the track and shifts records 10 and 12 to make space for the new record. Record 13 is now put into an *overflow area*. A new field called *overflow area pointer* is added to each entry in the track index. This field in the first entry of the track index is set to point to record 13 in the overflow area. If more records overflow out of the first track, they are put into a linked list and the overflow area pointer of the track index points to the head of the list. Similar linked lists may be formed for several tracks over a period of time.

If all records in the index sequential file have the same probability of being accessed, show that access efficiency of the file will be affected by the presence of records in the overflow area. Can access efficiency be restored by rewriting the file as a new file that does not contain any overflow records?

13.4 The Amoeba distributed operating system uses contiguous allocation of disk space. When a file is updated, it writes the updated file as a new file and deletes its old copy.

Comment on the advantages and drawbacks of this approach.

13.5 Does noncontiguous allocation of disk space influence the feasibility and effectiveness of the fundamental file organizations discussed in Section 13.3?

13.6 A file system uses indexed disk space allocation. The size of each disk block is 4 KB and each disk block address is 4 bytes in length. The size of the FMT is one disk block. It contains 12 pointers to data blocks. All other pointers point to index blocks.

A sequential file `info` contains 5000 records, each of size 4 KB. Characteristics of the disk and of a process that reads and processes all records in file `info` are as follows:

Average time to read a disk block = 3 ms
Average time to process a record = 5 ms

Calculate the elapsed time of the process under the following conditions:

a. The file system keeps the FMT in memory, but does not keep any index blocks in memory while processing `info`.

b. The file system keeps the FMT and one index block of `info` in memory.

13.7 A new record is to be added to the file `info` of Problem 13.15.1. What is the minimum number of disk operations required to reflect this change in `info` on the disk? What is the maximum number?

13.8 A file system uses indexed allocation of disk space; however, it permits a sequential file to contain partially full disk blocks. What are the advantages and disadvantages of this scheme?

13.9 A file system uses contiguous allocation of disk space. The sequential access method handles bad blocks on a disk as follows: If an error occurs while reading/writing a block, it consults the bad blocks table that is itself stored on the disk and accesses the alternative disk block assigned to the bad block. Assuming all disk accesses to require identical access times, calculate degradation in file access performance if 2 percent of the disk blocks allocated to a file are bad blocks. Suggest a method to improve the access performance.

13.10 To reduce the overhead of file access validation (see Step 2 of Section 13.9.2), an OS designer proposes to perform validation only at file "open" time. As mentioned in Section 13.9.1, the `open` statement specifies the kind of accesses which will be made to the file, e.g., `open (abc, 'read', ..)`. Is a single access validation check at file open time adequate? If not, explain why. In either case, suggest an implementation outline.

13.11 Step 2 of Section 13.9.1 creates an FCB for every directory appearing in a path name.

a. Is this arrangement adequate when a relative path name is used?

b. Are these entries necessary if a file is being opened for reading?

c. Can the number of FCBs created per file be reduced?

13.12 Explain how the following features can be incorporated in a file system:

a. *Cascaded mounts:* Directory `C` contains a file `D`. The directory structure rooted at `C` is mounted at mount point `X/B`. Later, the directory structure rooted at `X` is mounted in directory `Y/A`. It should be possible to access file `D` as `..Y/A/B/D`.

b. *Multiple mounts:* The directory structure rooted at some directory, say, W, is mounted at many mount points simultaneously.

13.13 When indexed allocation is used for files, explain how a disk block may occur in more than one file if a fault occurs.

13.14 Let Algorithm 13.1 be rewritten as follows:

1. $d_j.next := d_1.next$;
2. $d_1.next :=$ address (d_j);
3. *Write* d_j *to disk.*
4. *Write* d_1 *to disk.*

Does this modified algorithm prevent mix-up between files in the event of a fault?

13.15 Explain how the byte offset into a Unix file can be converted into the pair (*<disk block id>*, *<byte offset>*).

13.16 By default, Unix assigns the files *stdin* and *stdout* to the keyboard and terminal, respectively. A user can use the redirection operators $<$ and $>$ in a command to override the default assignments and use some other files for input and output. The "redirect and append" operator $>>$ appends the output of a process to the end of an existing file. The default assignments of the files are restored at the end of the command. These features can be implemented by permanently associating FCBs for *stdin* and *stdout* with each process.

a. Describe the file system actions involved in implementing the default assignments for *stdin* and *stdout* and the redirection operators $<$ and $>$.

b. Describe the file system actions involved in implementing the $>>$ operator.

13.17 Disk blocks allocated to a file are added to the free list when the file is deleted. Write an algorithm to perform this operation in Unix.

13.18 The Unix file system associates a lock field with the free list (see Section 13.14.1). Classify the following statement as true or false: "Locking of the free list is necessary due to the nature of Unix processes. Such locking is unnecessary in an OS using the conventional process model."

BIBLIOGRAPHY

Organick (1972) is historically the most important paper on directory structures, since the MULTICS directory structure has influenced most contemporary file systems like Unix, Linux, Solaris, and Windows. USENIX (1992) contains proceedings of a file system workshop. Grosshans (1986), Weiderhold (1987), and Livadas (1990) discuss file organizations and file systems.

McKusick et al. (1990) describes a memory-based file system, which provides memory-mapped files and directory structures implemented in pageable memory. Levy and Silberschatz (1990) discusses file sharing semantics. Lampson (1981) describes the stable storage technique for reliability of disk data, while Svobodova (1984) surveys how atomic actions are performed in various file servers. Florido (2000) discusses design of journaling file systems. Kleiman (1986) describes the virtual file system design. Vahalia (1996) describes the Unix virtual file system interface. Rosenblum and Ousterhout (1992) discusses design of the Sprite log-structured file system, while Matthews et al. (1997) discusses adaptive methods for improving the performance of log-structured file systems. McKusick et al. (1996) discusses the log-structured file system of Unix 4.4 BSD.

Bach (1986) and Vahalia (1996) describe the Unix file system. Kowalski (1978) describes the Unix program used to check file system integrity. This program looks through every file system data structure on disk. Bina and Emrath (1989) discusses how the file system integrity checks can be speeded up in the Unix file system. Beck et al. (2002) and Bovet and Cesati (2005) discuss the ext2 file system of Linux. Mauro and McDougall (2006) discusses the Solaris file system. Nagar (1997) and Russinovich and Solomon (2005) describe the NTFS file system of Windows.

1. Bach, M. J. (1986): *The Design of the Unix Operating System*, Prentice Hall, Englewood Cliffs, N.J.
2. Beck, M., H. Bohme, M. Dziadzka, U. Kunitz, R. Magnus, C. Schroter, and D. Verworner (2002): *Linux Kernel Programming*, Pearson Education, New York.
3. Bina, E. J., and P. A. Emrath (1989): "A faster *fsck* for BSD UNIX," *Proceedings of the Winter 1989 USENIX Technical Conference*, 173–185.
4. Bovet, D. P., and M. Cesati (2005): *Understanding the Linux Kernel,* 3rd ed., O'Reilly, Sebastopol, Calif.
5. Burrows, M., C. Jerian, B. Lampson, and T. Mann (1992): "On-line data compression in a log-structured file system," *ACM Sigplan Notices*, **27**, 9, 2–9.
6. Florido, J. I. S. (2000): "Journal file systems," *Linux Gazette*, issue 55.
7. Grosshans, D. (1986): *File Systems: Design and Implementation*, Prentice Hall, Englewood Cliffs, N.J.
8. Kleiman, S. R. (1986): "Vnodes: an architecture for multiple file system types in Sun Unix," *Proceedings of the Summer 1986 USENIX Technical Conference*, 238–247.
9. Kowalski, T. (1978): "Fsck—the Unix system check program," Bell Laboratories, Murray Hill, N.J.
10. Lampson, B. W. (1981): "Atomic transactions," in *Distributed systems—Architecture and Implementation: An Advanced Course, Goos, G., and J. Hartmanis* (eds), Springer Verlag, Berlin, 246–265.
11. Levy, H. M., and A. Silberschatz (1990): "Distributed file systems: concepts and examples," *ACM Computing Surveys*, **22**, 4, 321–374.
12. Livadas, P. (1990): *File Structures: Theory and Practice*, Prentice Hall, Englewood Cliffs, N.J.
13. Love, R. (2005): *Linux Kernel Development,* 2nd ed., Novell Press.
14. Matthews, J. N., D. Roselli, A. M. Costello, R. Y. Wang, and T. E. Anderson (1997): "Improving the performance of log-structured file systems with adaptive methods," *Proceedings of Sixteenth Symposium on Operating Systems Principles*, 238–251.
15. Mauro, J., and R. McDougall (2006): *Solaris Internals,* 2nd ed., Prentice-Hall, Englewood Cliffs, N.J.

16. McKusick, M. K., K. Bostic, M. Karels, and J. S. Quarterman (1996): *The Design and Implementation of the 4.4BSD Operating System*, Addison Wesley, Reading, Mass.
17. McKusick, M. K., M. Karels, and K. Bostic (1990): "A pageable memory based filesystem," *Proceedings of the Summer 1990 USENIX Technical Conference*, 137–144.
18. Nagar, R. (1997): *Windows NT File System Internals*, O'Reilly, Sebastopol, Calif.
19. Organick, E. I. (1972): *The MULTICS System*, MIT Press, Cambridge, Mass.
20. Rosenblum, M., and J. K. Ousterhout (1992): "The design and implementation of a log-structured file system," *ACM Transactions on Computer Systems*, **10**, 2, 26–52.
21. Russinovich, M. E., and D. A. Solomon (2005): *Microsoft Windows Internals,* 4th ed., Microsoft Press, Redmond, Wash.
22. Svobodova, L. (1984): "File servers for network-based distributed systems," *ACM Computing Surveys*, **16**, 4, 353–398.
23. USENIX (1992): *Proceedings of the File Systems Workshop*, Ann Arbor, Mich., May 1992.
24. Vahalia, U. (1996): *Unix Internals: The New Frontiers*, Prentice Hall, Englewood Cliffs, N.J.
25. Weiderhold, G. (1987): *File Organization for Database Design*, McGraw-Hill, New York.

Chapter **14**

Implementation of File Operations

As we saw in Chapter 13, a file processing activity is implemented through modules of the file system and the input-output control system (IOCS). The file system modules provide file-naming freedom, sharing and protection of files, and reliability. Operations on files are implemented by the IOCS.

The IOCS has two primary concerns—efficient implementation of a file processing activity in a process and high throughput of I/O devices. To address these concerns, the IOCS is organized into two layers called the *access method* and the *physical IOCS* layers. An access method module organizes reading and writing of file data to efficiently implement a file processing activity in a process. It invokes the physical IOCS to actually perform reading and writing of data. The physical IOCS performs input-output at the I/O device level and carries out scheduling policies to enhance throughput of an I/O device.

We first discuss the characteristics of I/O devices, and arrangements that provide high reliability, fast access and high data transfer rates of disks. We then discuss how I/O operations are performed at the level of I/O devices, what facilities are offered by the physical IOCS to simplify I/O operations, and how *disk scheduling* provides high disk throughput. Finally, we discuss how the techniques of *buffering*, *blocking*, and *caching* of data speed up a file processing activity.

14.1 LAYERS OF THE INPUT-OUTPUT CONTROL SYSTEM

The schematic of Figure 14.1 shows how the input-output control system (IOCS) implements file operations. Processes P_i and P_j are engaged in file processing activities and have already opened some files. When one of these processes makes a request to read or write data from a file, the file system passes on the request to the IOCS. Recall from Section 13.1 that the IOCS holds some file data in memory areas called *buffers*, the *file cache*, or the *disk cache* to speed up file processing activities. For a read operation, the IOCS checks whether the data required by the process is present in memory. If so, the process can access the data straightaway; otherwise, the IOCS issues one or more I/O operations to load the data into a file buffer or the disk cache, and the process has to wait until this I/O

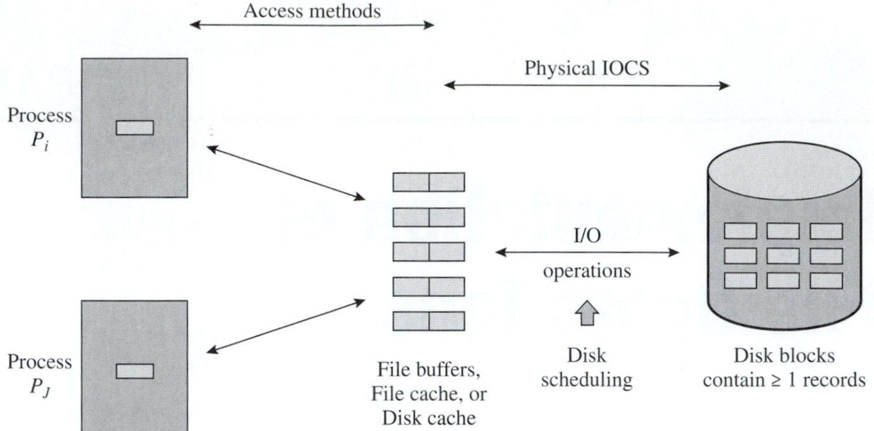

Figure 14.1 Implementation of file operations by the IOCS.

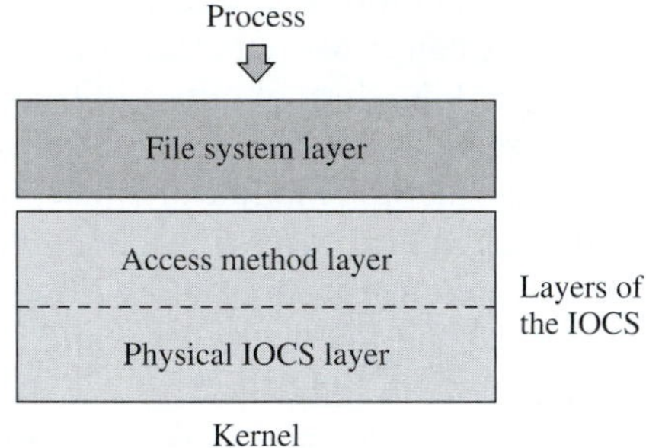

Figure 14.2 Layers of the file system and the IOCS.

operation completes. Since many processes perform I/O operations concurrently, the I/O operations are scheduled by a *disk scheduling* algorithm, which aims to provide high throughput of the disk. Thus the IOCS implements I/O operations in a manner that provides efficiency of file processing activities in processes and high throughput of I/O devices.

The IOCS is structured into two layers called the *access method* and the *physical IOCS*. The access method layer provides efficient file processing and the physical IOCS layer provides high device throughput. This structure of the IOCS separates process-level concerns in efficient implementation of file operations from device-level concerns.

Figure 14.2 shows the hierarchy of file system and IOCS layers. The number of IOCS layers and their interfaces vary across operating systems. In older operating systems, the physical IOCS was typically a part of the kernel; however, modern operating systems put it outside the kernel to enhance extensibility and reliability of the OS. We will assume that the physical IOCS is invoked through system calls, and it invokes other functionalities of the kernel also through system calls.

Table 14.1 Mechanisms and Policies in File System and IOCS Layers

Layer	Mechanisms and policies
Physical IOCS	• *Mechanisms:* I/O initiation, providing I/O operation status, I/O completion processing, error recovery. • *Policy:* Optimization of I/O device performance through a *disk scheduler* and a *disk cache*.
Access methods	• *Mechanisms:* File open and close, read and write. • *Policy:* Optimization of file access performance through *buffering* and *blocking* of file data and use of a *file cache*.
File System	• *Mechanisms:* Allocation of disk blocks, directory maintenance, setting and checking of file protection information. • *Policies:* Disk space allocation for access efficiency, sharing and protection of files.

Table 14.1 summarizes significant mechanisms and policies implemented by IOCS layers in a conventional two-layer IOCS design. The physical IOCS layer implements device-level I/O. Its policy modules determine the order in which I/O operations should be performed to achieve high device throughput. These modules invoke physical IOCS mechanisms to perform I/O operations. The access method layer has policy modules that ensure efficient file processing and mechanisms that implement file-level I/O by using physical IOCS policy modules. The file system layer implements sharing and protection of files, using the modules of the access method.

Note that Table 14.1 lists only those mechanisms that can be meaningfully accessed from a higher layer. Other mechanisms, which are "private" to a layer, are not listed here. For example, mechanisms for *buffering* and *blocking* of file data, and for managing a file cache exist in the access method layer. However, they are available only to access method policy modules; they are not accessed directly from the file system layer. Similarly, the physical IOCS has mechanisms for managing the disk cache, which cannot be accessed from outside the physical IOCS layer.

14.2 OVERVIEW OF I/O ORGANIZATION

Section 2.2.4 contained an overview of I/O organization. Three modes of performing I/O operations—programmed mode, interrupt mode, and direct memory access (DMA) mode—were summarized in Table 2.1. We focus on the DMA mode of I/O operations. Figure 2.1 showed how I/O devices are connected to device controllers, which are in turn connected to the DMA controller. Each device controller has a unique numeric id. Similarly, each device connected to it has a unique numeric device id. A device address is a pair of the form (*controller_id, device_id*).

An I/O operation involves the following details:

- Operation to be performed—read, write, etc.
- Address of the I/O device.
- Number of bytes of data to be transferred.
- Addresses of areas in memory and on the I/O device that are to participate in the data transfer.

When an I/O operation is performed in the DMA mode, the CPU initiates the I/O operation, but it is not involved in data transfer between an I/O device and memory. To facilitate this mode of I/O, an I/O operation is initiated by executing an *I/O instruction*. The CPU, the DMA controller, the device controller, and the I/O device participate to realize an I/O instruction. The I/O instruction points to a set of *I/O commands* that specify the individual tasks involved in the data transfer. Implementation of an I/O command requires participation of the DMA controller, the device controller, and the I/O device, but does not require participation of the CPU. This way, the CPU is free to execute other instructions while the I/O operation is in progress.

Typically, I/O commands are stored in memory and the address of the memory area containing I/O commands is used as an operand in the I/O instruction (in some computers, the address is picked up from a standard memory location when the I/O instruction is executed). When the I/O instruction is executed, the CPU passes this address to the DMA controller. The DMA controller now realizes the I/O commands. The next example provides details of this arrangement.

Example 14.1 I/O Operations

The I/O operation to read the data recorded in a disk block with the id (*track_id, block_id*) is performed by executing the following I/O instruction:

I/O-init (*controller_id, device_id*), *I/O_command_addr*

where *I/O_command_addr* is the start address of the memory area containing the following two I/O commands:

1. Position disk heads on track *track_id*
2. Read record *record_id* into the memory area with the start address *memory_addr*

The arrangement called *third party DMA* works as follows: Device controllers are connected to the DMA controller as shown in Figure 2.1. When an I/O instruction is executed, the DMA controller passes details of the I/O commands to the device controller of the I/O device. The device delivers the data to the device controller. Transfer of data between the device controller and memory is organized as follows: The device controller sends a DMA-request signal when it is ready to perform a data transfer. On seeing this signal, the DMA controller obtains control of the bus, puts address of the memory location that is to participate in the data transfer on the bus, and sends a DMA-acknowledgment signal to the device controller. The device controller now transfers the data to or from memory. At the end of data transfer, the DMA controller raises an I/O completion interrupt with the address of the device as the interrupt code. The interrupt servicing routine analyzes the interrupt code to find which device has completed its I/O operation, and takes appropriate actions.

Since the CPU continues to execute instructions while an I/O operation is in progress, the CPU and the DMA controller are in competition for use of the bus. The technique of *cycle stealing* ensures that both can use the bus without facing large delays. The CPU defers to the DMA controller for use of the bus at some specific points in its instruction cycle, typically when it is about to read an instruction or its data from memory. When the DMA wishes to transfer data to or from memory, it waits until the CPU reaches one of these points. It then steals a memory cycle from the CPU to implement its data transfer.

First party DMA is more efficient than third party DMA. In this arrangement, the device controller and the DMA controller are rolled into one unit. The combined unit obtains control of the bus when it is ready for a data transfer. This technique is called *bus mastering*. It achieves higher data transfer rates than third party DMA.

14.3 I/O DEVICES

I/O devices operate under a variety of principles, such as electromechanical signal generation and electromagnetic or optical data recording. I/O devices work with different I/O media, serve different purposes, and organize and access data in different ways, so they can be classified through the following criteria:

- *Purpose:* Input, print and storage devices
- *Nature of access:* Sequential and random-access devices
- *Data transfer mode:* Character and block mode devices

The information written (or read) in one I/O command is said to form a *record*. A sequential-access device uses its I/O medium in a sequential manner; hence an operation is always performed on a record that adjoins the record accessed in the previous operation. Access to any other record requires additional commands to skip over intervening records. A random-access device can perform a read or write operation on a record located in any part of the I/O medium. A keyboard, a mouse, a network and a tape drive are sequential-access devices. Disks can be accessed in both sequential and random manner.

A unit of I/O medium is called an *I/O volume*; thus, a tape cartridge and a disk can be called a tape volume and a disk volume, respectively. I/O volumes for some I/O devices are detachable, e.g., floppy disks, compact disks (CDs), or digital audiotape (DAT) cartridges; while those for other I/O devices like hard disks are permanently fixed in the device.

Data Transfer Modes The data transfer mode of a device depends on its speed of data transfer. A slow I/O device operates in the *character mode*; i.e., it transfers one character at a time between memory and the device. The device contains a buffer register that can store one character. The device controller raises an interrupt after an input device reads a character into the buffer or an output device writes a character from the buffer. Device controllers of such devices can be connected directly to the bus. The keyboard, mouse, and printer are character mode devices.

A device capable of a high data transfer rate operates in the *block mode* of data transfer. It is connected to a DMA controller. Tapes and disk drives are block mode devices. A block mode device needs to read or write data at a specific speed. Two kinds of problems would arise if a data transfer is delayed because of contention for the bus: Data would be lost during a read operation if the bus were unable to accept data from an I/O device at the required rate for transfer to memory. A write operation would fail if the bus were unable to deliver data to the I/O device at the required rate.

To prevent problems due to contention for the bus, data is not transferred over the bus during the operation; instead, it is transferred between an I/O device and a buffer. During an input operation, the data delivered by the I/O device is stored in a buffer in the DMA controller, which we will call the *DMA buffer*. It is transferred from the DMA buffer to memory after the I/O operation completes. To perform an output operation, data to be written onto the I/O device is first transferred from memory to the DMA buffer. During the I/O operation, it is transferred from the DMA buffer to the I/O device.

Data transfer between the CPU and an I/O device can also be realized by using *memory-mapped I/O*. In this approach, a set of memory addresses are reserved for an I/O device. These addresses are mapped into some of the registers of the I/O device such that when the CPU writes some data into a memory location with one of the reserved addresses, the data is actually written into the corresponding register of the I/O device. Similarly, when the CPU executes an instruction that reads data from a memory location with one of the reserved addresses, the data actually gets read from the corresponding register of the I/O device. This way the transfer of data takes place without a DMA yet it does not load the CPU much. Memory-mapped I/O is implemented as follows: An I/O device listens on the bus on which memory is connected. When one of its reserved addresses appears on the bus, it simply transfers data between the bus and the register corresponding to the reserved address. Memory-mapped I/O is popular on the PCs because a special I/O bus is not needed, and the CPU does not have to provide any special instructions for initiating I/O operations and for checking the status of I/O devices, which reduces the cost of the CPU. However, more hardware is needed on the memory bus to decode the reserved addresses.

Access Time and Transfer Time We use the following notation while discussing I/O operations.

- t_{io} *I/O time*, i.e., time interval between the execution of an instruction to initiate an I/O operation and completion of the I/O operation.
- t_a *access time*, i.e., time interval between the issue of a read or write command and the start of data transfer.
- t_x *transfer time*, i.e., time taken to transfer the data from/to an I/O device during a read or write operation. It is the time between start of transfer of the first byte to end of transfer of the last byte.

The I/O time for a record is the sum of its access time and transfer time, i.e.,

$$t_{io} = t_a + t_x \tag{14.1}$$

Figure 14.3 illustrates the factors influencing t_{io}. The access time in a sequential device is a constant because the device can only read or skip a record on either side of its current position. The access time in a random-access device varies because it can read or write *any* record in an I/O volume, so it must reposition either the read/write head or the I/O medium before commencing a read or write operation.

Error Detection and Correction Errors might arise during recording or reading of data or transferring it between an I/O medium and memory. To facilitate detection and correction of such errors, data being recorded or transmitted is viewed as a *bit stream*, i.e., as a stream of 1s and 0s, and special codes are used to represent the bit stream. We discuss some of these codes in the following.

Error detection is performed through recording of redundancy information with data. This information, which we will call error detection information, is derived from the data by using a standard technique. When data is read off an I/O medium, this information is also read off the medium. Now, error detection information is computed again from the read data, using the same technique, and it is compared with the error detection information read off the medium. A mismatch indicates some recording errors. Error correction is performed analogously, except that more powerful algorithms are used to generate the error correction information. This information can both detect an error and indicate

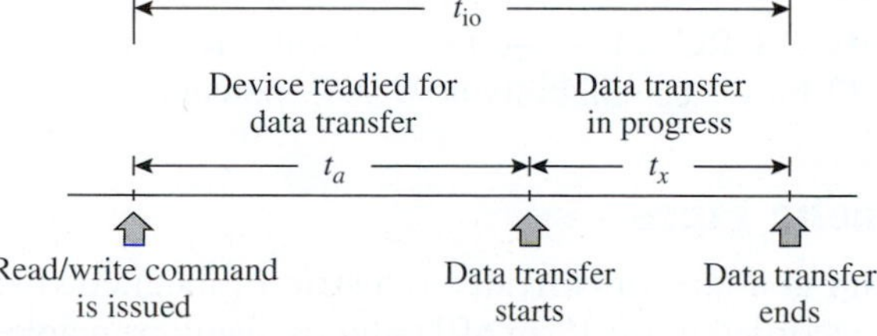

Figure 14.3 Access and transfer times in an I/O operation.

how it can be corrected. Recording and reading of redundant information causes an overhead. Error correction incurs more overhead than error detection.

Figure 14.4 describes two approaches to error detection and correction. In the *parity bits* approach, n_p parity bits are computed for n_d bits of data. The parity bits are put in fixed locations in a record. They are indistinguishable from data, except to the error detection/correction algorithm. In the *cyclic redundancy check* (CRC) approach, an n_c bit number called the CRC is recorded in the CRC field of a record. A key difference between the two approaches is that n_p depends on n_d, while n_c is independent of n_d.

Both approaches use modulo-2 arithmetic. This arithmetic is analogous to binary arithmetic, except that it ignores carries or borrows generated in any bit position. This property makes it very fast. A modulo-2 addition is represented as an exclusive-OR operation $\oplus$. It uses the following rules: $0 \oplus 0 = 0$, $1 \oplus 0 = 1$, $0 \oplus 1 = 1$, and $1 \oplus 1 = 0$.

A popular variant of the parity bits approach used in RAMs and older magnetic tapes associates a single parity bit with a byte of data. As described in Figure 14.4, it is generated from all bits of a byte by using the $\oplus$ operation. It can detect a single error in a byte, but fails if two errors occur. It also cannot correct any errors. The error detection overhead is 1 parity bit for 8 bits of data, i.e., 12.5 percent. A *Hamming code* can detect up to two errors in a record and can correct a single error. The correct technical name of the code is $(n_d + n_p, n_d)$ Hamming code. Comparison of the parity bit values in a record read off the medium with parity values computed from the read data by applying the rules of the code indicates which bit is in error. The value in this bit is inverted to correct the error. Figure 14.4 gives the rules for determining the number of parity bits and computing their values. A (12, 8) Hamming code can perform error detection and correction for 1 byte. It uses 12–8, i.e., 4, parity bits. Thus, the overhead is 50 percent. The overhead decreases with the number of data bits; e.g., 8 parity bits are adequate for 30 bytes of data.

The CRC is computed from data that is to be transmitted or recorded, and it is put into the CRC field of a record. It can indicate whether one or more errors have occurred in *any* byte of data, or if bytes have been swapped or reordered. When a record is read, a CRC is computed from its data field and compared with the number in its CRC field. An error exists if the two do not match. A practical value of n_c is 16 or 32 bits, irrespective of the value of n_d. With $n_c < n_d$, error detection is not foolproof because two bit streams, say s_1 and s_2, could generate the same CRC. If one of them is transformed into the other due to errors, the errors cannot be detected using CRC. The probability of this happening is $\frac{1}{2^{n_c}}$. Hence, reliability of CRC is $1 - \frac{1}{2^{n_c}}$. For a 16-bit CRC, the reliability is 99.9985 percent. For a 32-bit CRC, reliability is 99.9999 percent.

14.3.1 Magnetic Tapes

The I/O medium in a tape or cartridge is a strip of magnetic material on which information is recorded in the form of 1s and 0s, using principles of electromagnetic recording. The recording on a tape is multitrack; each track records a bit

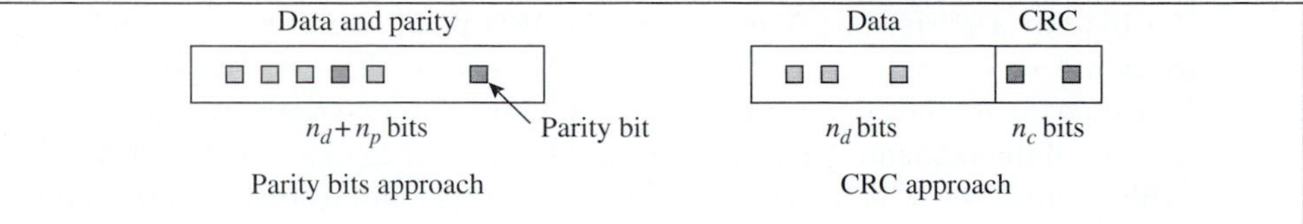

Calculating a parity bit

A parity bit is computed from a collection of data bits by modulo-2 arithmetic, i.e., by using the exclusive OR operator $\oplus$. For example, the parity bit for 4 data bits b_i, b_j, b_k and b_l is computed as follows: $p = b_i \oplus b_j \oplus b_k \oplus b_l \oplus c_1$, where c_1 is a constant which is 1 for *odd parity* and 0 for *even parity*.

Hamming code

Step 1: Determine the number of parity bits as the smallest value of n_p which satisfies $n_d + n_p + 1 \leq 2^{n_p}$. Fix parity bit positions as powers of 2, i.e., positions $b_1, b_2, b_4, b_8, \ldots,$ in a record, where bits are numbered as $b_1, b_2 \ldots$ from the start of the record.
Step 2: Compute the parity bit occupying the 2^nth position from the following bits, excepting itself: For each value of c_2, take 2^n consecutive bits starting on bit position $2^n + c_2 \times 2^{n+1}$, where c_2 has values $1, 2, 3, \ldots,$ etc. Thus, parity bit b_1 is computed from $b_3, b_5, \ldots$; b_2 is computed from $b_3, b_6, b_7, b_{10}, b_{11} \ldots$; and b_4 is computed from $b_5, b_6, b_7, b_{12}, b_{13}, b_{14}, b_{15}, \ldots$.
Step 3: When a record is received or read, compute parity bits and compare them with the parity bit values in the record. Form a binary number $e_1, e_2, e_4, \ldots$ as follows: e_i is 1 if the received and computed values of parity bit b_i are different; otherwise, it is 0. No error has occurred if this number is zero. If a single error exists, this number indicates the position of the bit which is in error.
Example: If 5-bit data 10110 is to be transmitted or recorded, 4 parity bits are used. They occupy positions $b_1, b_2, b_4,$ and b_8. The record contains $\underline{01}1\underline{0}011\underline{0}0$, where the parity bits have been underlined. If the record is read as $\underline{01}1\underline{0}011\underline{0}1$, the error word is 1001, indicating that the error has occurred in position 9.

Cyclic redundancy check (CRC)

Step 1: A bit stream is looked upon as a binary polynomial, i.e., a polynomial each of whose coefficients is either a 0 or a 1. For example, a bit stream 1101 is looked upon as a binary polynomial $1 \times x^3 + 1 \times x^2 + 0 \times x^1 + 1 \times x^0$, i.e., $x^3 + x^2 + 1$. Here a + is interpreted as modulo-2 addition, i.e., an exclusive-OR operation $\oplus$.
Step 2: The data in a received record is augmented by adding n_c zeroes at its end. The polynomial obtained from the augmented data is divided by a predefined polynomial of degree $n_c + 1$. The remainder of this division is a polynomial of degree n_c. Coefficients in this polynomial form the CRC. For example, the CRC for data 11100101 using a predefined 5-bit polynomial 11011 is 0100.
Step 3: When a record is received, the receiver computes the CRC from the data part of the record and compares it with the CRC part of the record. A mismatch indicates error(s). Alternatively, the receiver computes the CRC from the entire record. An error exists if the computed CRC is not 0.

Figure 14.4 Approaches to error detection and correction.

of a byte or a parity bit. A read–write head is positioned on each track. Tape drives are sequential-access devices. The operations that can be performed on these devices are: `read/write` a specified number of bytes, `skip`, and `rewind`. Because of the sequential nature, tapes and DAT cartridges are popularly used for archival purposes, which involve reading or writing of all records on the medium.

In older tape technologies, adjoining records on a tape are separated by an *interrecord gap*. This gap provides for the start–stop motion of the medium between the reading or writing of successive records. The *access time* (t_a) during a read or write operation is caused by both the need to achieve uniform-velocity motion of the I/O medium before the data transfer can be initiated and the need to position the next record under the read–write head. Total I/O time for a record of size s bytes is given by the formula

$$t_{io} = t_a + \frac{s}{d \times v}$$

where d recording density
v velocity of the I/O medium.

Interrecord gaps cause heavy penalties—they lead to poor use of the recording medium and slow down file processing activities. Despite the drawback of poor utilization of the recording medium, in the 1990s tapes offered a cost per megabyte that was one-tenth of that offered by disks. However, tapes lost this edge in the subsequent decade because disk technology made rapid progress and large disks became both practical and cheap. To regain the cost advantage, a streaming tape technology was developed.

A *streaming tape* contains a single record that is stored without a break irrespective of its size. Hence interrecord gaps do not exist even when a large volume of data is recorded on a tape. A streaming tape device contains a buffer. A write operation is started after putting some data in the buffer. The device writes the data from the buffer onto the tape. To keep the streaming tape operating at full speed, it is important to put new data into the buffer at a speed that matches the writing speed of the tape. The tape drive stops writing when it finds that the buffer is empty. When new data is put into the buffer, the tape drive resumes the write operation. To avoid creating an interrecord gap, the tape is first moved back and then moved forward again so that it can gather recording velocity by the time the head passes over the last bit it has written. It now resumes writing. Effectively, resumption of writing consumes a few milliseconds.

The streaming tape provides a high data transfer rate if the buffer is not allowed to become empty at any time. However, if the tape stops frequently, the effective writing speed can drop to a much smaller value. The physical IOCS has to ensure that this does not happen. The stop–start–resume operation of the tape also requires precise positioning and alignment, which makes streaming tapes expensive.

14.3.2 Magnetic Disks

The essential storage element of a magnetic disk is a flat circular object called a *platter*, which rotates on its axis. The circular surfaces of a platter are covered with magnetic material. A single read–write head records on and reads from a surface, so a byte is recorded serially along a circular *track* on the disk surface. The read–write head can move radially over the platter. For each position of the head, the recorded information forms a separate circular track. Parity information is not used in a disk; a CRC is written with each record to support error detection.

A start-of-track position is marked on each track, and records of a track are given serial numbers with respect to this mark. The disk can access any record whose address is specified by the pair (*track number, record number*). The access time for a disk record is given by

$$t_a = t_s + t_r \tag{14.2}$$

where t_s *seek time*, i.e., time to position the head on the required track
t_r *rotational latency,* i.e., time to access desired record on the track

The seek time is the time required for the mechanical motion of the head. Rotational latency arises because an I/O operation can start only when the required record is about to start passing under the head. The average rotational latency is the time taken for half a disk revolution. Representative values of the average rotational latency are 3–4 ms, seek times are in the range of 5–15 ms, and data transfer rates are of the order of tens of megabytes per second.

Variations in disk organization have been motivated by the desire to reduce the access time of a disk, increase its capacity and data transfer rate, and reduce its price. The cheapest disk is a floppy disk which is slow and has a small capacity. A hard disk has a higher capacity; still higher capacities are obtained mainly through mounting of many platters on the same spindle. One read–write head is provided for each circular surface of a platter—that is one above and one below each platter. All heads in the disk pack are mounted on a single access arm, which is called the *actuator*, and so at any moment all heads are located on identically positioned tracks of different surfaces. The set of such identically positioned tracks outlines a *cylinder* (see Figure 14.5), a form that can be exploited for data organization. All the tracks in a cylinder are accessible from the same position of the access arm; thus, cylinders make several disk tracks accessible without requiring any movement of the disk heads, and so I/O operations on records situated in the same cylinder can be performed without incurring seek times.

A hard disk can be looked upon as consisting of a set of concentric cylinders, from the innermost to the outermost. A record's address can thus be specified by the triple (*cylinder number, surface number, record number*). The necessary commands for operation of a disk device are `seek` (*cylinder number, surface number*) and `read`/`write` a specified record.

Disk capacity can be increased by increasing the number of platters. However, more platters require more disk heads, which in turn require a heavier actuator and impose more mechanical stresses. Hence disks tend to have only a few platters. When a very large capacity is desired, applications use multiple disk drives. (In Section 14.3.5, we discuss how arrangements using multiple disk

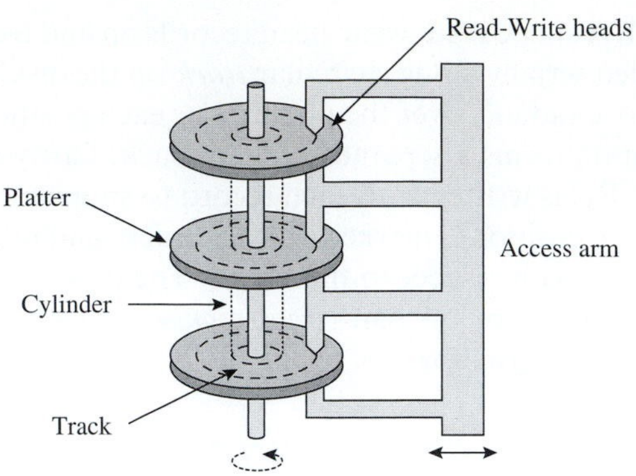

Figure 14.5 A disk pack.

drives can also be exploited to provide high data transfer rates and high reliability.) Seek times can be reduced by using higher rotational speeds, but high speeds increase the cost of mechanical components, and so fast disks tend to have smaller platters to compensate. PCs and desktop computers tend to use cheaper disks. These disks have large platters, which provide large capacity, and comparatively low rotational speeds. In contrast, servers tend to use costlier disks that are smaller and rotate faster.

To optimize use of disk surface, tracks are organized into *sectors*. A sector is a standard-sized "slot" in a track for a disk record. The sector size is chosen to ensure minimum wastage of recording capacity due to interrecord gaps on the surface. Sectoring can be made a part of the disk hardware (hard sectoring), or could be implemented by the software (soft sectoring).

14.3.3 Data Staggering Techniques

Recall from Section 14.3 that the data read off an I/O device during a read operation is stored in the DMA buffer, from where the DMA transfers it to memory as a single block. But while this transfer is under way, the disk continues to revolve and one or more following sectors may pass under the head by the time the transfer is completed. Hence if a read operation on the next consecutive sector is issued immediately after the previous one, the required sector may have passed under the head by the time the DMA can initiate the read operation. Such a read operation can be performed only in the next disk revolution. Analogously, during a write operation, recording of the data is initiated only after data is transferred from memory to the DMA buffer, so recording in the next sector cannot take place in the same revolution if the sector passes under the read–write head before the data transfer is completed. A similar problem is caused by *head switching time*, which is the time taken to switch operation between heads positioned on different platters. By this time a few sectors of the next platter have passed under the read–write head. The seek time to move the head to the next cylinder also causes a similar problem. All these problems adversely affect the throughput of a disk.

The techniques of sector interleaving, head skewing, and cylinder skewing address the problems caused by data transfer time, head switch time, and seek time, respectively. These techniques, collectively called *data staggering* techniques, ensure that the next consecutively numbered sector will not pass under the read–write head before the head will be in a position to perform a read/write operation on it, so that the operation can be performed in the current revolution of the disk. *Sector interleaving* staggers sectors along a track in such a way that consecutively numbered sectors are separated by a few other sectors. This arrangement permits the I/O operation for a sector to be completed by the time the sector with the next consecutive address passes under the head. *Head skewing* staggers the "start of track" positions on different platters of a cylinder so that the times when the last sector of a track and the first sector of the next track pass under their respective heads are separated by the head switch time. *Cylinder skewing* analogously staggers the "start of track" positions on consecutive cylinders to allow for the seek time after reading the last sector on a cylinder.

Figure 14.6 illustrates how the techniques of sector interleaving, head skewing, and cylinder skewing reduce rotational delays through data staggering. It is assumed that the disk has five sectors in a track and uses ten platters, so a cylinder has 50 sectors in it. For each data staggering technique, the left and right parts of the figure show operation of the disk without and with data staggering. The first line in each part shows which sectors pass under the read-write heads of the disk at different times. The next few lines show what activities involved in an I/O operation are in progress as the disk rotates—they constitute a timing diagram for the I/O operation.

Figure 14.6(a) illustrates sector interleaving. We assume the disk head is positioned immediately before the first sector on the first cylinder where a file is stored, so the command to read the first sector does not incur any seek or rotational latency. Reading of the sector into the DMA buffer completes a little before time t_1, and the transfer of this data to memory by the DMA controller completes a little after time t_1. The command to read the next sector is issued immediately after reading of the previous sector completes, i.e., a little after time t_1. By that time the head is positioned somewhere over sector 2, so sector 2 cannot be read immediately. A rotational delay now occurs that lasts until sector 2 passes under the head in the next revolution of the disk, i.e., until time t_6. The right part of the figure shows the arrangement of sectors when sector interleaving is employed; sectors 1 and 2 are separated by sector 4 on the track. When the command to read sector 2 is issued, the read–write head is located almost at the end of sector 4. Now, the rotational delay lasts only until time t_2, when sector 2 starts passing under the head.

Figure 14.6(b) illustrates head skewing. Here, we show the arrangement of sectors in the first two tracks allocated to a file. The read command on sector 5, which is the last sector on the first track, is issued at time t_{10}. The reading of this sector and transfer of the data to memory completes before time t_{11}, so the read command for sector 6 is issued some time before t_{11}. However, it involves head switching because t_{11} is located on a different track; head switching is not completed before time t_{11} when sector 6 starts passing under the head.

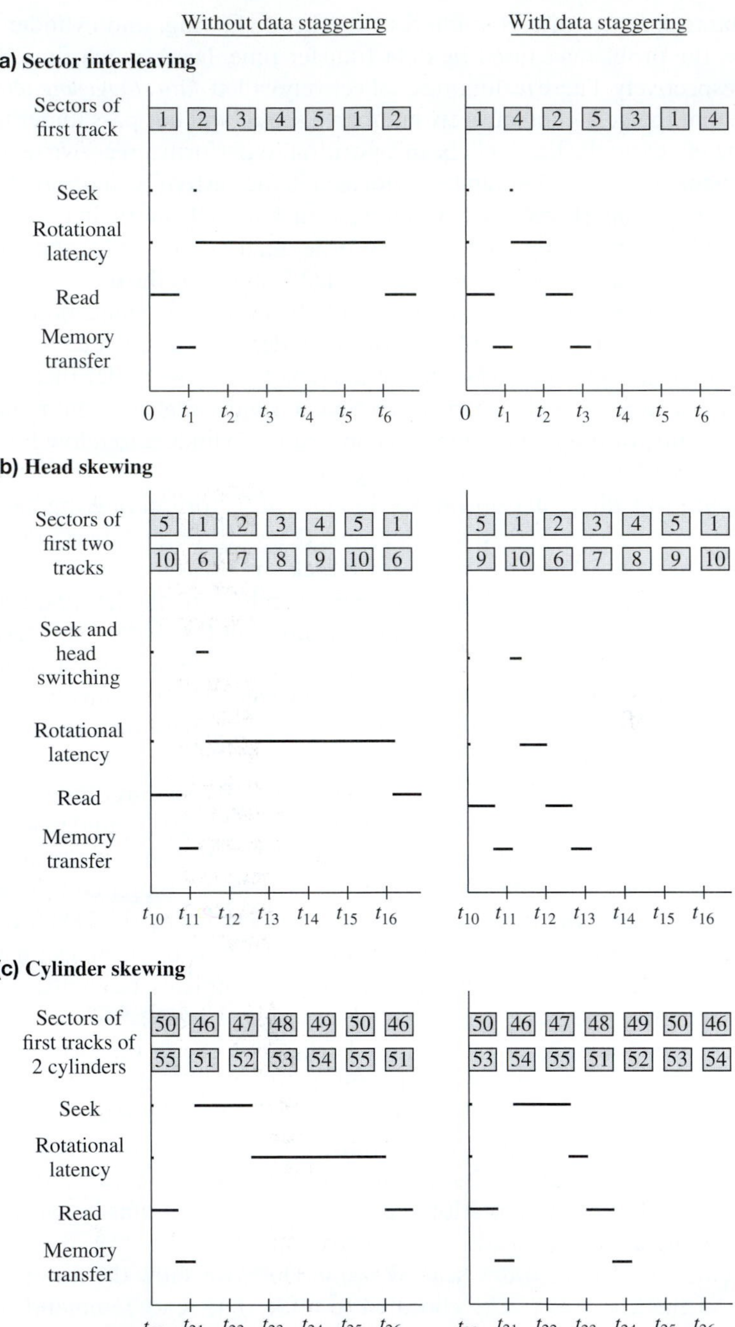

Figure 14.6 Effect of data staggering: (a) sector interleaving; (b) head skewing; and (c) cylinder skewing.

So reading of sector 6 cannot be commenced immediately; it has to wait until sector 6 starts passing under the head in the next revolution of the disk at time t_{16}. This rotational delay is reduced by staggering the recording on the second track by one sector position, as shown in the right half of the figure. Now, the reading of sector 6 can commence at time t_{12}, thus incurring a much smaller rotational delay. Figure 14.6(c) illustrates cylinder skewing. Here, we show the arrangement of sectors in the first track of the first two cylinders allocated to a file. The seek operation for reading sector 51 results in movement of the read–write head by one cylinder. The seek operation completes a little before t_{23}; however, sector 51 has passed under the read–write head by that time, hence a rotational delay is incurred until sector 51 passes under the head in the next revolution at time t_{26}. As shown in the right half of the figure, data staggering by two sector positions enables sector 51 to be read starting at time t_{23}.

Sector interleaving had a dramatic impact on the throughput of older disks. Modern disks have controllers that transfer data to and from memory at very high rates, so that sector interleaving is not needed. However, we discuss sector interleaving because it provides an insight into optimizing the peak disk throughput through data staggering. Head and cylinder skewing are still used to optimize the peak disk throughput.

Figure 14.7 illustrates sector interleaving. The interleaving factor (F_{int}) is the number of sectors that separate consecutively numbered sectors on the same disk track. Part (b) of Figure 14.7 illustrates the arrangement when $F_{int} = 2$, i.e., consecutively numbered sectors have two other sectors between them. Interleaving is uniform, that is, each pair of consecutively numbered sectors are separated by the same number of sectors, if either $n - 1$ or $n + 1$ is a multiple of $F_{int} + 1$, where n is the number of sectors on a track. The arrangement in the figure, where there are 8 sectors to a track, is uniform, whereas interleaving with $F_{int} = 1$ or 3 would not be uniform (see the second column in Table 14.2—some consecutive sectors are separated by more than F_{int} sectors). As we shall see in Example 14.2, a performance penalty is incurred when interleaving is not uniform.

Let t_{st} be the time taken to transfer one sector's data between the DMA controller and memory, and let t_{sect} be the time taken for one sector to pass under the disk head. Optimal performance is obtained if $t_{st} = F_{int} \times t_{sect}$, since I/O on the next sector can be started immediately after the DMA finishes transferring

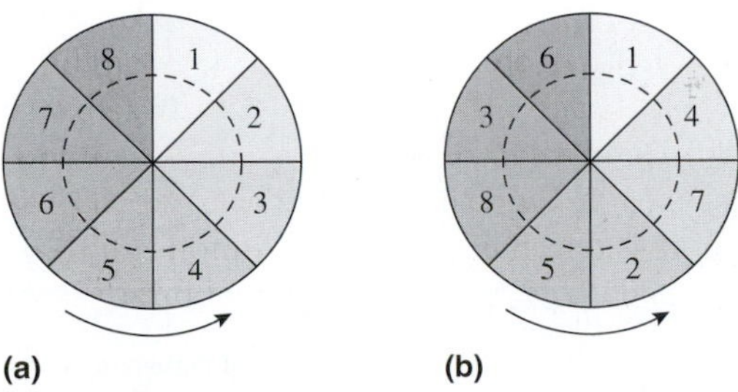

Figure 14.7 Sectors in a disk track: (a) without interleaving; (b) with interleaving factor = 2.

the previous sector's data. If $t_{st} > F_{int} \times t_{sect}$, the next sector would pass under the head before the DMA finishes data transfer for the previous sector. Hence the next sector can be accessed only in the next revolution of the disk. $t_{st} < F_{int} \times t_{sect}$ implies that the disk would be idle for some time before the next sector is accessed in the same revolution. Disk throughput suffers in both these cases. Analogously, throughput would suffer when other data staggering techniques are employed if data is staggered by too little or too much. The following example illustrates the variation of peak disk throughput with the sector interleaving factor.

Example 14.2 Sector Interleaving

A disk completes one revolution in 8 ms and has 8 sectors on a track, each containing 1000 bytes. The values of t_{st} and t_{sect} satisfy the relation $t_{sect} < t_{st} < 2 \times t_{sect}$. To obtain the peak disk throughput for a value of F_{int}, we read the sectors in the order $1, \ldots, 8$ over and over again and observe the number of bytes transferred in one second. Figure 14.8 shows variation of peak disk throughput for different values of F_{int}.

Table 14.2 shows the arrangement of sectors for different values of F_{int} and the corresponding disk throughput represented in units of kB/s where 1 kB/s is 1000 bytes per second. Interleaving with $F_{int} = 1$ or 3 is not uniform. For $F_{int} = 1$, the arrangement of sectors on the track is 1, 5, 2, 6, 3, 7, 4, 8. After reading sector 1, sector 2 cannot be read in the same revolution. Hence the disk takes 10 ms to read sector 2. Similarly, sectors 3 and 4 require 10 ms. Sectors 4 and 5 are separated by 2 sectors. Hence they can be read in the same revolution of the disk; the disk takes only 3 ms to read sector 5 after sector 4 has been read. Reading of sectors 6, 7, and 8 requires 10 ms each, while reading of sector 1 requires 9 ms.

Figure 14.8 shows the variation of throughput with different values of F_{int}. $F_{int} = 2$ is adequate to satisfy $t_{st} \leq F_{int} \times t_{sect}$, and so the throughput increases sharply. Values of $F_{int} > 2$ are counterproductive since the disk spends some idle time before the next sector passes under the head. Hence the throughput dips for $F_{int} > 2$.

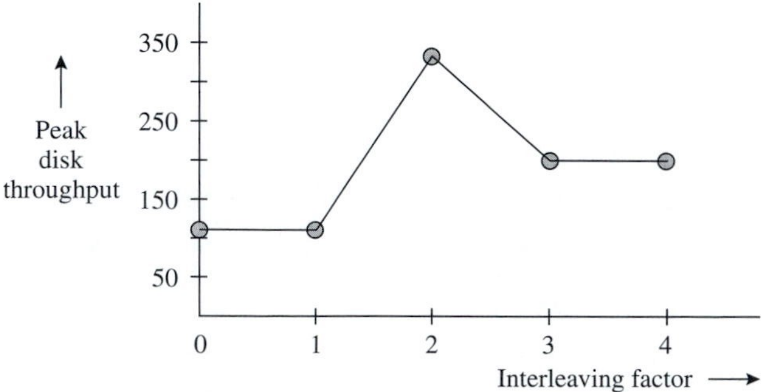

Figure 14.8 Variation of throughput with sector interleaving factor.

Table 14.2 Sector Arrangement and Performance in Sector Interleaving

F_{int}	Arrangement of sectors	t_{io} for sectors (ms)	Average t_{io} (ms)	Peak throughput (kB/s)
0	1, 2, 3, 4, 5, 6, 7, 8	9, 9, 9, 9, 9, 9, 9, 9	9	111.1
1	1, 5, 2, 6, 3, 7, 4, 8	9, 3, 10, 10, 10, 10, 10, 10	9	111.1
2	1, 4, 7, 2, 5, 8, 3, 6	3, 3, 3, 3, 3, 3, 3, 3	3	333.3
3	1, 3, 5, 7, 2, 4, 6, 8	9, 5, 5, 5, 4, 4, 4, 4	5	200.0
4	1, 6, 3, 8, 5, 2, 7, 4	5, 5, 5, 5, 5, 5, 5, 5	5	200.0

14.3.4 Disk Attachment Technologies

EIDE and SCSI Interfaces *Enhanced integrated device electronics* (EIDE) and *small computer system interconnect* (SCSI) are the leading disk interfaces for attaching disks to computers. Disks attached this way have come to be called *host-attached storage. Integrated device electronics* (IDE, also called advanced technology attachment, or ATA) was the predecessor of EIDE. Before EIDE was developed, the different features of IDE and SCSI made each of them ideal for specific applications. For example, IDE was considered to provide excellent performance for sequential I/O while SCSI was considered to be superior for random I/O. Accordingly, IDE disks were used in the low-cost PC and desktop environment while SCSI disks were used in the server environment. With EIDE, the gap in random-access performance has narrowed considerably. Both retain their traditional niche areas, but EIDE and SCSI now compete in some application segments, such as backup storage media. Both kinds of disks provide a large buffer of a few megabytes.

IDE disks primarily worked with programmed I/O modes, though they supported a DMA mode as well. EIDE supports new DMA modes including the first party, i.e., bus mastering, DMA mode; the ultra ATA mode of EIDE supports transfer rates of 33.3 MB per second, which is 8 times faster than the IDE data transfer rate. EIDE disks use larger platters, rotate relatively slowly, and are cheap. Up to two disks can be connected to EIDE; however, only one of them can operate at a time.

SCSI supports several DMA modes; the fastest of these provides a data transfer rate of 80 MB per second. SCSI permits up to 7 disks to be connected to it. SCSI is called an interface, but technically it is an I/O bus because it permits simultaneous operation of many disks connected to it. SCSI disks are smaller, rotate faster, and are more expensive. Accordingly, they provide smaller seek times and higher data transfer rates. A SCSI disk supports *scatter/gather* I/O wherein it can transfer data from a disk block into noncontiguous areas of memory or collect data from noncontiguous areas and write them into a disk block (see Section 12.2.4). It also provides several functionalities that were traditionally performed by the IOCS, including the following:

- *Disk scheduling:* A SCSI disk accepts several I/O requests concurrently and stores them into a queue of requests. It uses its knowledge of the current position of disk heads and the rotational position of the platters to select an I/O operation that involves the minimum delay due to seek and rotational latency. This feature is described in Section 14.7.
- *Bad block recovery:* A SCSI disk detects bad disk blocks and assigns substitute disk blocks for them. It maintains a table showing addresses of bad blocks and their substitutes. If an I/O command is directed toward a bad disk block, the disk automatically redirects it at the substitute block. This feature speeds up I/O operations by performing bad block management in the device rather than in the access method layer of IOCS.
- *Prefetching of data:* A SCSI disk contains a buffer. At every I/O operation, it reads the next few disk blocks into the buffer. This action speeds up subsequent read operations during processing of a sequential file.

Network-Attached Storage and Storage Area Networks Host attachment of disks suffers from poor scalability because disk sizes are limited by prevailing technologies and the number of disks that can be attached to a host is limited by the interface. Therefore, organizations have to constantly replace disks or add more servers to meet their requirements for more storage. This problem is addressed by facilitating use of remote disks through a network. This approach enables the storage capacity to be increased incrementally and seamlessly, and storage to be shared by applications operating on many servers.

A *network-attached storage* (NAS) is a disk or a redundant array of inexpensive disks (RAID), which is discussed in the next section, attached directly to a local area network (LAN) [see Figure 14.9(a)]. NAS is an inexpensive method of providing large disk capacities, because it employs the hardware and software existing in a LAN environment. Functionalities such as a file server or a distributed file system (see Chapter 20) can be provided by using the NAS. However, use of NAS faces some difficulties in practice: LANs use protocols that optimize application-to-application data transfers whereas the file server or distributed file system requires use of a file-based protocol like the Sun NFS protocol discussed in Section 20.6.1, or Microsoft's common interface file system (CIFS) protocol. The load created by the file-based protocol slows down networking applications.

A *storage area network* (SAN) is an alternative arrangement that avoids slowdown of networking applications. A SAN is a network composed of disks that provides a high bandwidth [see Figure 14.9(b)]. The network could be a dedicated fiber channel that uses the SCSI protocol, or an Internet protocol (IP) network that uses the iSCSI protocol. Several servers can be connected to a SAN; each server can access the entire storage. This feature facilitates formation of high-performance *clusters* of computer systems (see Section 16.2). Data integrity and availability is provided through the redundancy of disks and servers connected to the SAN.

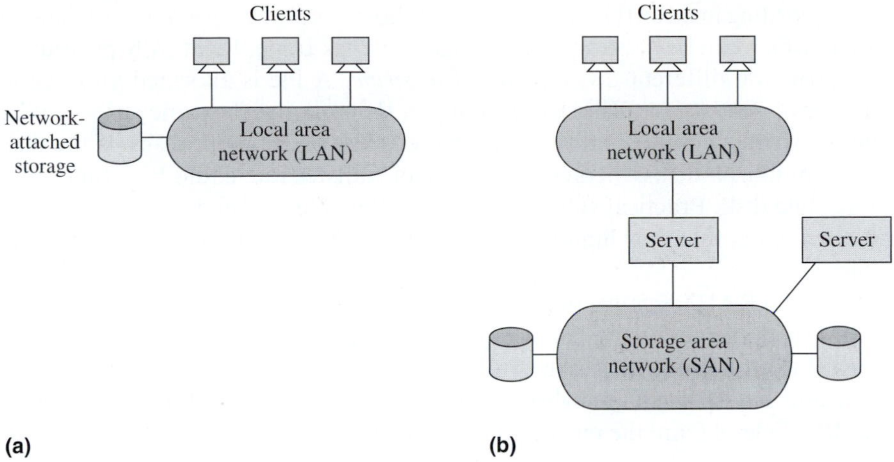

Figure 14.9 (a) Network-attached storage; (b) storage area network.

New technologies that employ the iSCSI protocol over an IP network to combine the features of the NAS and SAN technologies are emerging. These technologies support both block-accessed SAN devices and file-accessed NAS devices without incurring the cost of a fiber channel.

14.3.5 RAID

Computer users constantly clamor for disks with larger capacity, faster access to data, higher data transfer rate and higher reliability. All these issues are addressed through arrangements involving multiple disks. The *redundant array of inexpensive disks* (RAID) technology was originally employed for providing large disk capacities at a low cost through use of several inexpensive disks. However, the recent trend is to enhance disk capacities through network-attached storage and storage area networks (see Section 14.3.4). Hence today's RAID technology is used for providing fast access, high data transfer rates, and high reliability; it is more appropriately called *redundant array of independent disks*.

The RAID technology spreads the data involved in an I/O operation across several disks and performs I/O operations on these disks in parallel. This feature can provide either fast access or a high data transfer rate, depending on the arrangement employed. High reliability is achieved by recording redundant information; however, the redundancy employed in a RAID is qualitatively different from that employed in conventional disks: A conventional disk provides reliability only by writing a CRC at the end of every record (see Section 14.3), whereas redundancy techniques in a RAID employ extra disks to store redundant information so that data can be recovered even when some disks fail. Access to redundant information does not cost additional I/O time because both data and redundant information can be accessed in parallel.

Recording in a RAID is performed as follows: A *disk strip* is a unit of data on a disk, which can be a sector, a disk block, or a disk track. Identically positioned disk strips on different disks form a *disk stripe*. A file is allocated an integral number of disk stripes. The data residing in the strips of the same stripe can be read or written simultaneously because they exist on different disks. If the disk array contains n disks, theoretically the data transfer rate could be n times that of a single disk. Practical values of data transfer rates depend on overhead and on any factors that may limit the parallelism of I/O operations while processing a file.

Several RAID organizations using different redundancy techniques and disk striping arrangements have been proposed. These organizations are called RAID *levels*. Table 14.3 summarizes the properties of various RAID levels. RAID levels $0 + 1$ and $1 + 0$, which are hybrid organizations based on RAID levels 0 and 1, and RAID level 5 are the most popular RAID organizations.

RAID Level 0 Level 0 employs only disk striping; it is not really a RAID organization because it does not involve redundant recording of data. It provides high data transfer rates, particularly if each disk is under a separate disk controller. However, it suffers from low reliability. Data becomes inaccessible even if a single disk is inoperative. Also, lack of redundancy implies that data is lost if a disk fails, and so reliability still has to be achieved by means other than the RAID organization.

RAID Level 1 Level 1 RAID organization writes identical information on two disks; it is called *disk mirroring*. When a process writes or updates a record in a file, one copy of the record is written on each disk. This way, RAID 1 incurs 100 percent overhead; however, one copy of a record is guaranteed to be accessible even if a single fault occurs. During a read, the RAID simply reads the copy that can be accessed earlier. High data transfer rates can be achieved during read operations because both disks could operate in parallel when no errors arise.

Hybrid organizations that use the features of RAID levels 0 and 1 are often used in practice to obtain both high data transfer rates as in RAID level 0 and high reliability as in RAID level 1. RAID $0 + 1$ employs disk striping as in RAID 0, and mirrors each stripe as in RAID 1. RAID $1 + 0$ first mirrors each disk and then performs striping. These organizations provide different kinds of fault tolerance: In RAID $0 + 1$, a single error in a copy of a stripe makes the entire copy inaccessible, so errors in both copies of a stripe would make the stripe inaccessible. In RAID $1 + 0$, an error on one disk would be tolerated by accessing its mirror disk. A stripe would become inaccessible only if both a disk and its mirror disk have errors.

RAID Level 2 This RAID organization uses *bit striping*, i.e., it stores each bit of data or redundancy information on a different disk. When data is to be written, the ith data strip contains the ith bit of each byte and a parity strip contains one of the parity bits computed from corresponding bits in all strips of the stripe. An *error correcting code* is used to compute and store redundancy information for each byte (see Section 14.3). Thus, 8 disks are used to record the bits of a byte,

Table 14.3 RAID Levels

Level	Technique	Description
Level 0	Disk striping 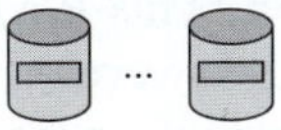	Data is interleaved on several disks. During an I/O operation, the disks are accessed in parallel. Potentially, this organization can provide an n-fold increase in data transfer rates when n disks are used.
Level 1	Disk mirroring  Disk 1 Disk 2	Identical data is recorded on two disks. During reading of data, the copy that is accessible faster is used. One of the copies is accessible even after a failure occurs. Read operations can be performed in parallel if errors do not arise.
Level 2	Error correction codes 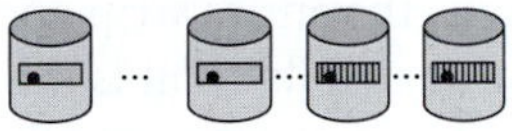 D D P P	Redundancy information is recorded to detect and correct errors. Each bit of data or redundancy information is stored on a different disk and is read or written in parallel. Provides high data transfer rates.
Level 3	Bit-interleaved parity  D D P	Analogous to level 2, except that it uses a single parity disk for error correction. An error that occurs while reading data from a disk is detected by its device controller. The parity bit is used to recover lost data.
Level 4	Block-interleaved parity 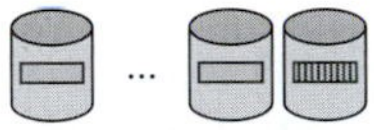 D D P	Writes a *block* of data, i.e., consecutive bytes of data, into a strip and computes a single parity strip for strips of a stripe. Provides high data transfer rates for large read operations. Small read operations have low data transfer rates; however, many such operations can be performed in parallel.
Level 5	Block-interleaved distributed parity 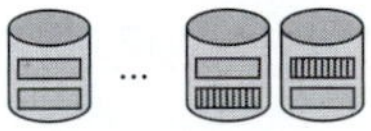	Analogous to level 4, except that the parity information is distributed across all disk drives. Prevents the parity disk from becoming an I/O bottleneck as in level 4. Also provides better read performance than level 4.
Level 6	P + Q redundancy 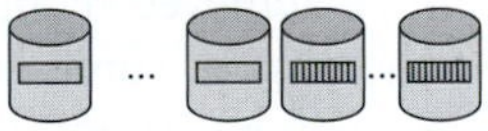 D D P P	Analogous to RAID level 5, except that it uses two independent distributed parity schemes. Supports recovery from failure of two disks.

Note: D and P indicate disks that contain only data and only parity information, respectively. ▭ indicates a strip. • Indicates bits of a byte that are stored on different disks, and their parity bits. ▥ indicates a strip containing only parity information.

and a few more disks are used to record redundancy information. For example, the (12, 8) Hamming code, which is adequate for recovery from a single failure, would require 4 redundancy bits. The RAID 2 arrangement employing this code would consist of 8 data disks and 4 disks containing redundancy information, each storing 1 bit of data or parity information. This RAID arrangement can read/write data 8 times faster than a single disk. However, it is expensive because several disks are needed to store redundancy information, hence it is not practical.

RAID Level 3 Level 3 employs disk striping with a *bit-interleaved parity* scheme; i.e., it employs *bit interleaving*—it writes the bits of a byte on different disks—and employs a single parity bit per byte. The data strips of a stripe are stored on 8 data disks and the parity strip is stored on the parity disk. Thus, RAID level 3 employs a significantly smaller amount of redundant information than RAID level 2. A read operation is performed as follows: The disk controller checks whether an error exists within a strip. If so, it ignores the entire strip and recovers the data in the strip using the parity strip—the value of a data bit is the modulo-2 difference between the parity bit and the modulo-2 sum of corresponding bits of other strips in the stripe.

All data disks participate in an I/O operation. This feature provides high data transfer rates. However, it also implies that only one I/O operation can be in progress at any time. Another drawback of RAID level 3 is that parity computation can be a significant drain of the CPU power. Hence parity computation is off-loaded to the RAID itself.

RAID Level 4 Level 4 is analogous to level 3 except that it employs *block-interleaved parity*. Each strip accommodates a *block* of data, i.e., a few consecutive bytes of data. If an I/O operation involves a large amount of data, it will involve all data disks as in RAID level 3, hence RAID level 4 can provide high data transfer rates for large I/O operations. A fault-free read operation whose data fits into one block will involve only a single data disk, so small I/O operations have small data transfer rates; however, several such I/O operations can be performed in parallel.

A write operation involves computation of parity information based on data recorded in all strips of a stripe. This can be achieved by first reading data contained in all strips of a stripe, replacing the data in some of the strips with new data that is to be written, computing the new parity information, and writing the new data and parity information on all disks. However, this procedure limits parallelism because all disks are involved in the write operation even when new data is to be written into a single block $block_i$ of stripe $stripe_i$. Hence, the parity information is computed by a simpler method that involves the exclusive OR of three items—the old information in the parity block, the old data in block $block_i$, and the new data to be written in block $block_i$. This way, only the disk(s) containing the block(s) to be written into and the parity block are involved in the write operation, and so several small fault-free read operations involving other disks can be performed in parallel with the write operation.

RAID Level 5 Level 5 uses block level parity as in level 4, but distributes the parity information across all disks in the RAID. This technique permits small write operations that involve a single data block to be performed in parallel if their parity information is located on different disks. Small fault-free read operations can be performed in parallel as in RAID level 4. Hence this organization is particularly suitable for small I/O operations performed at a high rate. Larger operations cannot be performed in parallel; however, the organization provides high data transfer rates for such operations. It also provides higher peak disk throughput for read operations than level 4 because one more disk can participate in read operations.

RAID Level 6 This organization uses two independent distributed parity schemes. These schemes support recovery from failure of two disks. Peak disk throughput is slightly higher than in level 5 because of the existence of one more disk.

14.3.6 Optical Disks

Data is recorded on an optical disk by creating changes in reflectivity of the disk, and it is read by a laser and a photosensitive assembly that picks up changes in reflectivity of the surface under the disk head. A compact disc (CD) is an optical disk. The disk writer stores a 1 by causing a change in reflectivity compared with the data bit in the preceding position, and stores a 0 by retaining the same reflectivity as the preceding bit.

Recording on a CD can be performed by various means. Mass-produced prerecorded CDs that contain music are produced by mechanical means. They are called *stamped CDs.* Recording can also be performed by using a laser beam. A laser-recorded CD contains three layers: a polycarbonate layer, a polymer dye, and a reflective metallic layer. When a strong laser beam is directed at a spot on the CD, it heats the dye and creates a permanent mark on the disk called a *pit*, which has a lower reflectivity. This is why the recording process is called "burning" a CD. Data is recorded in a shallow spiral groove on a CD that extends from the inside diameter of the disk to its outside diameter. A CD contains 22,188 spiral revolutions, which are about 1.6 microns apart. Each revolution is called a *track*. Speed control and absolute time information are prerecorded on a CD.

A CD contains several regions reserved for use by a CD recorder. The power calibration area is used to calibrate the power of the writing laser. The program memory area stores track information for all sessions in the CD. It is followed by lead-in, program, and lead-out areas for each session. A lead-in area is a table of contents of a session. It indicates the number of tracks, track start and stop points, and the length of the session. The program area contains data tracks of the session. The lead-out area indicates end of a session.

Two features of a CD are important from an operating system viewpoint—recording of data and creation of a file system. Data is recorded in the form of sectors on a track. A CD-ROM intended for computer use contains sectors of 2 KB. It has a capacity of about 650 MB. A DVD (digital versatile disk), on the other hand, has a capacity of about 5 GB. Data is recorded on either

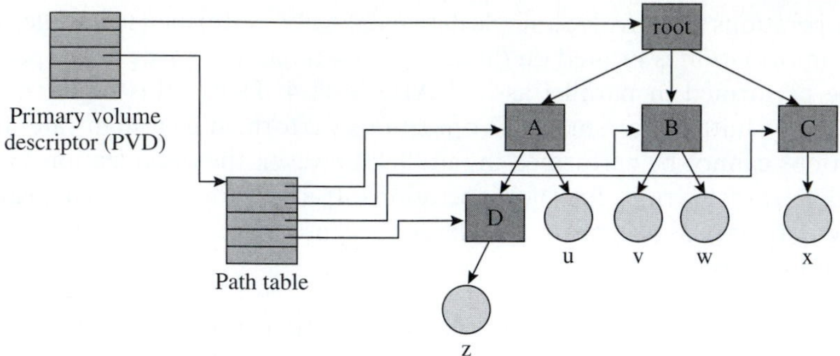

Figure 14.10 Primary volume descriptor of a CD.

type of disk by using the encoding method called CIRC (cross-interleaved Reed–Solomon code). CIRC encodes a unit of data that is 24 bytes, i.e., 192 bits, in size, to produce an encoded unit that is 588 bits in size. Apart from data, this unit contains information concerning relative and absolute timing, placement of tracks and indices; synchronization data, and error prevention and correction data. To make error correction reliable, data is scrambled while encoding. This way, if a few bytes of consecutively recorded data are lost, a large number of bytes may lose only 1 bit each. This data can be recovered by using the error correction information.

ISO Standard 9660 defines a common logical format for files and directories on a CD. It defines basic requirements for data interchange and also provides for optional extensions to Windows, Unix, and Macintosh environments. The Rockridge extension allows Unix-specific long filenames, multilevel directories, access privileges, and file types. The universal disk format (UDF) is also designed for a common logical, i.e., cross-platform, file system. UDF can coexist with ISO 9660, and many CD drives can write information in either format.

Figure 14.10 shows how a file system is implemented on a CD volume. The primary volume descriptor (PVD) is recorded in logical sector 16. It indicates the position of the root directory, and the position of a path table. Each entry in the path table contains information about the location of a directory. Its use to locate a required directory avoids searches through intermediate directories in a path name; in a Unix system, for example, it avoids searches through directories `root` and `A` for a pathname `~A/D/z`.

14.4 DEVICE-LEVEL I/O

Four functions are involved in implementing I/O at the level of an I/O device—initiating an I/O operation, performing read/write operations, checking the status of an I/O device, and handling interrupts raised by devices. The first three of these functions are performed through *I/O instructions* and *I/O commands* described in Section 14.2. Table 14.4 describes features in the computer system that support

Table 14.4 Computer System Features Supporting Functions in Device-Level I/O

Function	Description of computer system feature supporting it
Initiating an I/O operation	The I/O instruction *I/O-init (cu, d), command_address* initiates an I/O operation (see Example 14.1). The *I/O-init* instruction sets a condition code to indicate whether the I/O operation has been initiated successfully.
Performing read/write	Device-specific I/O commands implement tasks like positioning of read–write heads over a record and reading of a record.
Checking device status	The I/O instruction *I/O-status (cu, d)* obtains status information for an I/O device. The information indicates whether the device is busy, free, or in an error state, and cause of the error, if any.
Handling interrupts	The interrupt hardware implements the interrupt action described in Section 2.2. The CPU is switched to the physical IOCS when an I/O completion interrupt occurs.

these functions. We assume that I/O operations are performed in the DMA mode (see Section 2.2.4). In Section 14.4.1, we discuss details of device-level I/O and in Section 14.5, we discuss the facilities provided by the physical IOCS to simplify device-level I/O.

14.4.1 I/O Programming

We use the term *I/O programming* to describe all actions involved in performing an I/O operation. To understand two key aspects of I/O programming—namely, I/O initiation and I/O completion processing—we consider the program of Figure 14.11, which is an assembly language version of the following program in a higher-level language:

```
read a, b;
...
result := a + b;
```

The program uses a bare machine, i.e., a computer system that does not have any software layers between the program and the machine's hardware. The program uses the flag `IO_FLAG` to indicate whether the I/O operation is in progress. It sets the `IO_FLAG` to 1, initiates an I/O operation and loops until the I/O operation completes before performing its computations.

I/O Initiation When the *I/O-init* instruction of Figure 14.11 is executed, the CPU sends the device address to the DMA controller. The DMA controller finds whether the device is available for the I/O operation, and informs the CPU accordingly; the CPU sets an appropriate condition code in the *condition code* field (also called the *flags* field) of the PSW. If the device is available, the DMA also starts the I/O operation by accessing and decoding the first I/O command. The

```
              SET       IO_FLAG, '1'         To indicate that I/O is in progress
RETRY:        IO_init   (cu, d), COMMANDS    Read a, b
              BC        cc1, IN_PROGRESS     Branch if I/O initiation is successful
              BC        cc2, RETRY           Loop if the device is busy
              BC        cc3, ERROR           Error. Inform system administrator

IN_PROGRESS:  COMP      IO_FLAG, '1'         Check whether I/O is still in progress
              BC        EQ, IN_PROGRESS      Loop if I/O is in progress

              { Perform result := a+b; }

COMMANDS:     {I/O commands}
              ...

IO_INTRPT:    SET       IO_FLAG, '0'         Interrupt processing: I/O is complete
              ...
```

Figure 14.11 I/O programming.

I/O-init instruction is now complete. The I/O operation, if initiated, will proceed in parallel with the CPU's execution of instructions.

In the next few instructions, the program examines the condition code set by the *I/O-init* instruction to handle any exceptional situations that might have occurred when the *I/O-init* instruction was executed. The instruction `BC` cc_1, `IN_PROGRESS` is a conditional branch instruction. Condition code cc_1 would have been set if I/O initiation was successful. In that event the I/O operation would have already started, and so execution of the program is diverted to the instruction with the label `IN_PROGRESS`. Condition code cc_2 indicates that the device was busy, so the program would retry the I/O instruction until I/O initiation succeeds. Condition code cc_3 indicates that an I/O error occurred, so the program would report the error to the system administrator. These details are not shown in Figure 14.11.

I/O Completion Processing The program cannot perform the computation `result := a+b;` until the I/O operation completes. However, the program's execution cannot be suspended because it is executing on a bare machine. The program addresses this problem by using the flag `IO_flag` to indicate whether the I/O operation has completed. To start with, it sets the value of `IO_FLAG` to 1 to indicate that I/O is in progress. After starting the I/O operation, it enters a loop at `IN_PROGRESS` where it repeatedly checks this flag. This is a busy wait—see Section 6.5.1.

When an I/O interrupt occurs indicating the end of the I/O operation, control is transferred to the instruction with the label `IO_INTRPT` by the interrupt action (see Section 2.2). This is the start of the I/O interrupt servicing routine, which changes `IO_FLAG` to 0 and returns. This action ends the busy wait at `IN_PROGRESS`.

14.5 THE PHYSICAL IOCS

The purpose of physical IOCS is to simplify the code of user processes by hiding the complexity of I/O operations and to ensure high system performance. It is achieved through the following three functions:

- *Handling device-level I/O:* The physical IOCS provides an interface for device-level I/O that eliminates the complexity of I/O programming discussed earlier in Section 14.4.1.
- *Synchronizing a process with completion of an I/O operation:* This synchronization avoids the busy wait following I/O initiation in Figure 14.11 and releases the CPU for use by other processes.
- *I/O scheduling:* The physical IOCS schedules the I/O operations to be performed on a device in a suitable order to provide high device throughput.

Handling Device-Level I/O While requesting initiation of an I/O operation, a process needs to specify only the device address and details of the I/O operation. The physical IOCS initiates an I/O operation immediately if the I/O device is available; otherwise, it notes the request for I/O initiation and initiates it sometime later. In either case, control is returned to the process that made the I/O request. When an interrupt arises, the physical IOCS notes which I/O operation has completed, and initiates another operation on the I/O device, if one is pending.

Synchronizing a Process with Completion of an I/O Operation The physical IOCS provides an "await I/O completion" functionality to block a process until an I/O operation completes. Its parameters are the address of the I/O device and details of the I/O operation. When a process invokes this functionality, the physical IOCS checks whether the I/O operation has already completed. If it has not, it requests the kernel to block the process. This action avoids the busy wait of Figure 14.11. The state of the process is changed to *ready* when the I/O operation completes.

I/O Scheduling The throughput of an I/O device can be computed as the number of bytes of data transferred per unit time, or the number of I/O operations performed per unit time. Throughput can be optimized by minimizing the access times suffered during I/O operations. In disk devices it can be achieved by reducing the rotational latency and mechanical motion of disk heads by performing I/O operations in a suitable order. This function is called *I/O scheduling*. It is performed automatically by the physical IOCS; it is not explicitly invoked by a process.

14.5.1 Logical Devices

A *logical device* is an abstraction that is employed for a variety of useful purposes. In the simplest case, a logical device is merely a name for a physical I/O device. Use of a logical device in the code of a process solves a practical difficulty—the address of a physical device that a process will use is not known when its code is written. While creating a process that uses a logical device, the kernel assigns a physical device to the logical device. When the process performs an operation on the logical device, the physical IOCS implements the operation on the physical device assigned to the logical device.

A logical device can also be a virtual device as described in Section 1.3.2. In this case, the kernel has to map the logical device into a part of a physical device. Many logical disks may be mapped into a physical disk in this manner; the I/O operations directed at the logical disks would all be performed on the same physical disk.

14.5.2 Physical IOCS Data Structures

The physical IOCS uses the following data structures (see Figure 14.12):

- Physical device table (PDT)
- Logical device table (LDT)
- I/O control block (IOCB)
- I/O queue (IOQ)

The *physical device table* (PDT) is a systemwide data structure. Each entry in it contains information about one I/O device. The *IOQ pointer* field of an entry points to the queue of I/O operations that are to be performed on the device. Each entry in the queue is a pointer to an *I/O control block* (IOCB), which contains information concerning one I/O operation. The *current operation* field points to the I/O control block that contains information concerning the I/O operation

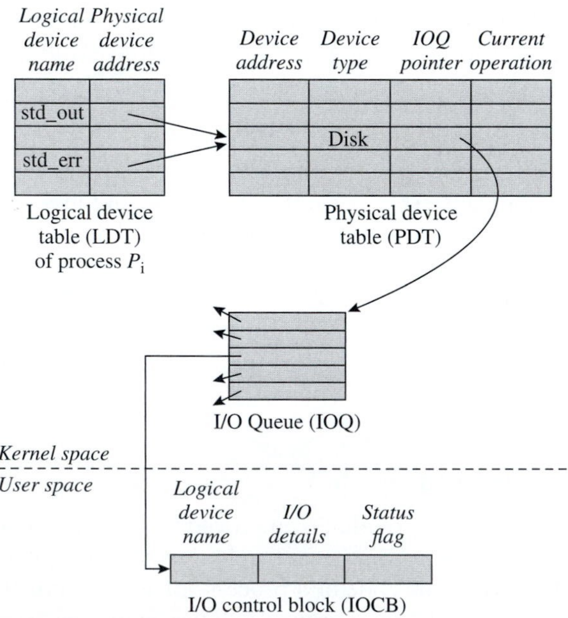

Figure 14.12 Data structures of the physical IOCS.

that has been initiated on the device. This information is useful in processing completion of the I/O operation.

The *logical device table* (LDT) is a per-process data structure. There is one copy of the LDT for every process in the system; this copy is accessible from the process control block (PCB) of the process. The LDT contains one entry for each logical device used by the process. The field *physical device address* in the entry contains information concerning the current assignment, if any, for the logical device. Note that many logical devices, possibly belonging to different user processes, may be assigned the same physical device such as a disk.

An *I/O control block* (IOCB) contains all information pertaining to an I/O operation. The important fields in an IOCB are *logical device name*, *I/O details*, and *status flag*. The I/O details field contains the address of the first I/O command. The status flag indicates whether an I/O operation is "in progress" or "completed"; it is the equivalent of `IO_FLAG` in Figure 14.11.

The *I/O queue* (IOQ) is a list of all I/O operations pending on a physical device. Each entry of the IOQ contains a pointer to an I/O control block. Information in the IOQ is used for I/O scheduling.

The PDT is formed at system boot time by obtaining details of all devices connected to the system. The size of the LDT is specified at boot time. An LDT is formed when a process is created. An I/O control block is allocated when an I/O operation is to be initiated. The IOQ is shown as an array of pointers in Figure 14.12. However, it is more practical to organize it as a linked list of IOCBs.

The PDT, LDT, and IOQ data structures are found within the kernel, whereas a process creates an IOCB in its own address space, initializes its fields, and uses it as a parameter in a call on a physical IOCS module. The IOCB's presence in the address space of the process permits the process to check the status of an I/O operation without having to invoke the kernel.

14.5.3 Organization of Physical IOCS

Figure 14.13 shows organization of the physical IOCS. Modules above the dashed line execute with the CPU in the user mode, while those below this line execute with the CPU in the kernel mode. The physical IOCS is activated in one of two ways:

- Through calls on the physical IOCS library modules `start-io` or `await-io` by a process, with an I/O control block as a parameter
- Through occurrence of an I/O completion interrupt

When a process invokes `start-io`, `start-io` invokes the I/O initiator through a system call. The I/O initiator obtains the address of the physical device on which the I/O operation is to be performed, enters the I/O operation in the IOQ of the physical device and passes control to the I/O scheduler. The I/O scheduler invokes the I/O initiator to start the I/O operation immediately if no other I/O operations exist in the IOQ of the device. Control is then passed to the process scheduler, which returns it to the process that had requested the I/O operation.

When the `await-io` module of the physical IOCS is invoked, it determines the status of the I/O operation from the status flag of the I/O control block. If

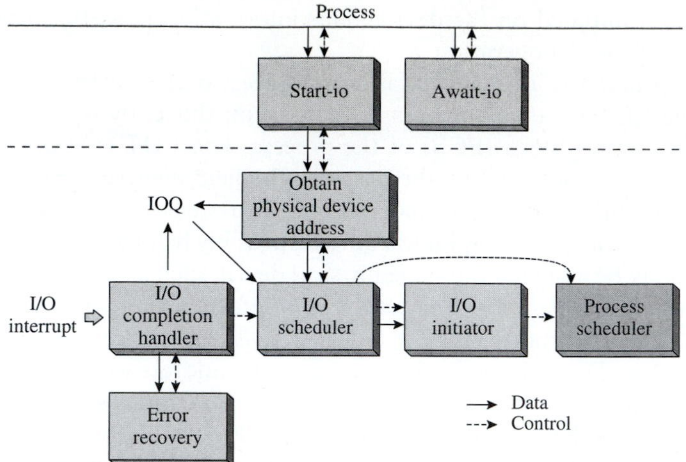

Figure 14.13 Organization of the physical IOCS.

the I/O operation is complete, control is immediately returned to the process; otherwise, the `await-io` module makes a system call to block the process. At an I/O completion interrupt from a device, an error recovery routine is invoked if an I/O error has occurred; otherwise, the status flag in the I/O control block describing the current operation on the device is set to "completed," the ECB-PCB arrangement of Example 5.4 is used to activate a process (if any) awaiting completion of the I/O operation, and the I/O scheduler is invoked. It selects one of the I/O operations pending on the device and hands it over to the I/O initiator. The I/O initiator initiates the I/O operation and passes control to the process scheduler.

14.5.4 Implementation of Physical IOCS

Recall from Section 13.1 that the compiler replaces the file processing statements in a program with calls on the file system operations `open`, `read`, and `close`. As seen in Section 13.8, the file system operation `read` makes a call on the IOCS library module `seq-read`. `seq-read` contains code that contributes to efficient processing of a file (more about it later in this chapter). This code makes a call on the physical IOCS library module `start-io` to perform device-level I/O. The linker links all these modules of the file system, IOCS, and the physical IOCS with the compiled program.

A process representing execution of the linked program makes a call on the file system operation `open` to open a file named `alpha`. `open` constructs a file control block (FCB) for `alpha`, i.e., $fcb_{\texttt{alpha}}$, in the open files table (OFT) and returns *internal* $id_{\texttt{alpha}}$, which is the offset of the FCB in the OFT (see Section 13.9.1). The following actions take place when the process wishes to read a record of `alpha` (see Figure 14.14):

1. The process calls the file system module `read`, which invokes the IOCS module `seq-read` with *internal* $id_{\texttt{alpha}}$ as a parameter.

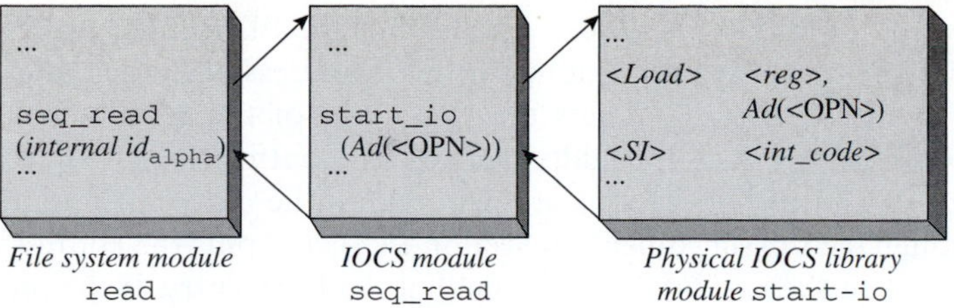

Figure 14.14 Invocation of the physical IOCS library module `start-io` in a process.

2. When `seq-read` decides to read a record of `alpha`, it uses *internal* $id_{\texttt{alpha}}$ to access $fcb_{\texttt{alpha}}$, obtains the address of $fmt_{\texttt{alpha}}$ and finds the address of the disk block that contains the desired record. It now forms an I/O control block for the I/O operation and calls `start-io` with the address of the I/O control block as a parameter. The I/O control block is named `OPN` in Figure 14.14.
3. `start-io` loads the address of the I/O control block in a general-purpose register and executes an SI instruction with an appropriate code to invoke the physical IOCS.

I/O Initiation When invoked through a system call, the physical IOCS obtains the address of the IOCB from the general-purpose register and performs the following actions:

1. Sets the *status flag* field of the IOCB to "in progress."
2. Enters the address of the I/O control block in the IOQ of the physical device.
3. Initiates the I/O operation, if the I/O device is not busy.
4. Returns control to the process.

To enter the I/O control block address in the correct IOQ, the physical IOCS extracts the logical device id from the IOCB, and accesses the logical device table (LDT) of the process to obtain the address of the physical device assigned to the logical device. It then obtains the address of the IOQ for the physical device from its entry in the physical device table (PDT) and adds the IOCB address at the end of the IOQ. The I/O operation can be initiated immediately if there are no other entries in the IOQ. If other entries exist, presumably one of the previous I/O operations is in progress, so the I/O operation cannot be initiated now.

I/O initiation is performed as described in Section 14.4.1. The *status flag* field of the I/O control block is used in a manner analogous to the use of IO_FLAG in Figure 14.11. Address of the I/O control block is stored in the *current operation* field of the device's entry in the physical device table.

I/O Completion Handling The I/O completion handler is implicitly invoked at the occurrence of an I/O completion interrupt. The interrupt hardware provides the address of the physical device raising the I/O interrupt. The I/O completion handler queries the device to obtain an I/O status code describing the cause of the interrupt. It now performs the following actions: If the I/O operation was unsuccessful, it consults the *device type* field of the PDT entry and invokes an appropriate I/O error recovery routine with the address of the I/O control block as a parameter. Otherwise, it sets the *status flag* of the I/O control block to "completed" and removes the address of the I/O control block from the IOQ of the device. If any I/O operations are pending on the device, it initiates one of them through the I/O scheduler (see Section 14.7), and puts the address of its I/O control block in the *current operation* field of the PDT entry. If the process that had issued the just-completed I/O operation is blocked awaiting completion of the I/O operation, it changes the state of the process to *ready*. The arrangement used for this purpose is described in the following.

Awaiting Completion of an I/O Operation A process invokes this function through the physical IOCS library call `await-io` (<*IOCB_address*>) where the I/O control block describes the awaited I/O operation. The physical IOCS merely tests the status flag in the I/O control block, and returns control to the process if the flag value is "completed." If not, the physical IOCS library routine makes a "block me" system call to block itself on the event "successful I/O completion." The kernel creates an event control block (ECB) for the I/O completion event and enters it in the list of event control blocks. This event control block contains the id of the process waiting for completion of the I/O operation. When the I/O completion event occurs, the I/O completion handler locates its event control block, extracts the id of the process, and marks an appropriate change in its state. This arrangement ensures that the process would be activated at the completion of the I/O operation and would return from the call on the physical IOCS library routine. (See Example 5.4 for an explanation of this arrangement.)

14.6 DEVICE DRIVERS

In the physical IOCS design described in previous sections, the physical IOCS handles I/O initiation, I/O completion and error recovery for all classes of I/O devices within the system. Consequently, addition of a new class of I/O devices requires changes to the physical IOCS, which can be both complex and expensive because the physical IOCS may be a part of the kernel. Modern operating systems overcome this problem through a different arrangement. The physical IOCS provides only generic support for I/O operations, and invokes a specialized *device driver* (DD) module for handling device-level details for a specific class of devices. Thus device drivers are not part of the physical IOCS. This arrangement enables new classes of I/O devices to be added to the system without having to modify the physical IOCS. Device drivers are loaded by the system boot procedure depending on the classes of I/O devices connected to the computer. Alternatively, device drivers can be loaded whenever needed during operation of the OS. This feature is particularly useful for providing a *plug-and-play* capability.

Figure 14.15 illustrates how device drivers are used by the physical IOCS. The entry of a device in the physical device table (PDT) shows the name of its

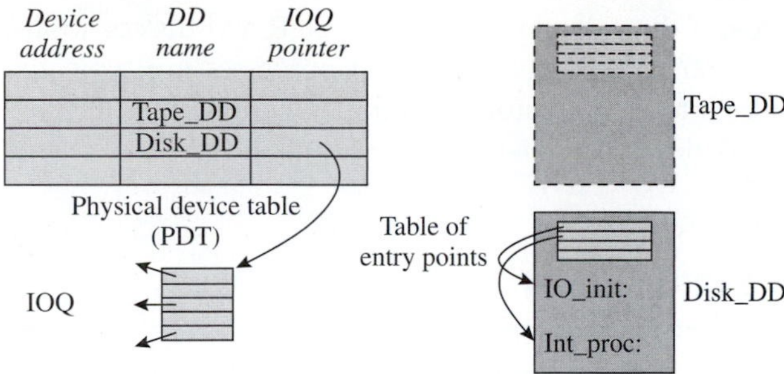

Figure 14.15 Use of device drivers.

device driver in the *DD name* field. The Disk_DD, the device driver for the system disk, has been loaded at system boot time. The Tape_DD would be loaded on demand, so it is shown as a dashed box. A device driver contains functionalities of the four physical IOCS modules shown in Figure 14.13, namely, I/O scheduler, I/O initiator, I/O completion handler, and error recovery. A table of entry points located at the start of its code contains start addresses of these functionalities.

When the physical IOCS is invoked for initiating an I/O operation, it locates the PDT entry of the device and performs the generic function of entering details of the I/O operation into the IOQ of the device. It now consults the *DD name* field of the PDT entry, obtains the identity of the device driver and loads the device driver in memory if it is not already in memory. It now obtains the address of the entry point for I/O initiator in the device driver by following the standard conventions and passes control to it. The device driver performs I/O initiation processing and returns control to the physical IOCS, which passes control to the process scheduler. When the physical IOCS is invoked implicitly at an I/O interrupt, it performs similar actions to identify the device driver entry point for handling interrupts and passes control to it. After servicing the interrupt, the device driver returns control to the physical IOCS, which passes it to the process scheduler.

Device-Level Optimization One important optimization is *disk scheduling* to ensure good throughput, which is discussed in the next section. Another optimization is reducing the number of seek operations in a disk. This optimization can be performed in various ways. One simple way is to read several adjoining disk blocks when a read operation is to be performed. It amounts to buffering of data, which is useful in sequential files. Device drivers for RAID units reduce the number of seek operations by combining several I/O operations into a single one.

A device driver can also support a novel or nonstandard I/O device. A good example of the former is a *RAM disk*, which is simply a virtual disk maintained in the RAM of a computer system: An area in RAM is reserved for use as a disk. All read and write operations directed at the disk are actually performed on relevant parts of the RAM. Operation of the RAM disk is extremely fast. However, data stored in it is lost if the system crashes or if the RAM disk is abolished. For this reason, only scratch files of compilers and processes are typically created in a RAM disk. Files intended for storage of data over a period of time are stored on conventional disk devices.

14.7 DISK SCHEDULING

The seek time of a disk block depends on its position relative to the current position of the disk heads. Consequently, the total seek time involved in performing a set of I/O operations depends on the order in which the operations are performed. The throughput of a disk defined as the number of I/O operations performed per second, also depends on the order in which I/O operations are performed. Hence the physical IOCS and device drivers for disks employ a *disk scheduling* policy to perform disk I/O operations in a suitable order. We shall discuss the following disk scheduling policies before describing disk scheduling in modern systems:

- *First-come, first-served (FCFS) scheduling:* Select the I/O operation that was requested earliest.
- *Shortest seek time first (SSTF) scheduling:* Select the I/O operation whose seek time from the current position of disk heads is the shortest.
- *SCAN scheduling:* This policy moves the disk heads from one end of the platter to the other, servicing I/O operations for blocks on each track or cylinder before moving on to the next one. It is called a *scan*. When the disk heads reach the other end of the platter, they are moved in the reverse direction and newly arrived requests are processed in a reverse scan. A variant called *look* scheduling reverses the direction of disk heads when no more I/O operations can be serviced in the current direction. It is also called the *elevator algorithm*.
- *Circular SCAN or CSCAN scheduling:* This policy performs a scan as in SCAN scheduling. However, it never performs a reverse scan; instead, it moves the heads back to that end of the platter from where they started and initiates another scan. The *circular look* variant (we will call it *C-look* scheduling) moves the heads only as far as needed to service the last I/O operation in a scan before starting another scan.

The FCFS disk scheduling policy is easy to implement but does not guarantee good disk throughput. To implement the shortest seek time first (SSTF) policy, the physical IOCS uses a model of the disk to compute the seek time of the disk block involved in an I/O operation given the current position of the disk heads. However, the SSTF policy is analogous to the *shortest request next* (SRN) scheduling policy, so while it achieves good disk throughput, it may starve some I/O requests. SSTF and the various scan policies can be efficiently implemented if the IOQs are maintained in sorted order by track number.

Example 14.3 describes the operation of various disk scheduling policies for a set of five I/O operations. The *look* policy completes all I/O operations of this example in the shortest amount of time. However, none of these policies is a clear winner in practice because the pattern of disk accesses cannot be predicted.

Disk Scheduling Policies

Example 14.3

Figure 14.16 summarizes the performance of the FCFS, SSTF, Look, and C-Look disk scheduling policies for five I/O operations on a hypothetical disk having 200 tracks. The requests are made at different instants of time. It is assumed that the previous I/O operation completes when the system clock reads 160 ms. The time required for the disk heads to move from track_1 to track_2 is assumed to be a linear function of the difference between their positions:

$$t_{hm} = t_{const} + |\ \text{track}_1 - \text{track}_2\ | \times t_{pt}$$

where t_{const} is a constant, t_{pt} is the per-track head movement time and t_{hm} is the total head movement time. We assume the rotational latency and data transfer times to be negligible, $t_{const} = 0$ ms and $t_{pt} = 1$ ms. A practical value of t_{const} is 2 ms. Also, the formula for t_{hm} is not linear in practice.

Figure 14.16 shows the following details for each decision: time at which the decision is made, pending requests and head position at that time, the scheduled I/O operation, and its seek time. The last column shows the total seek time for each policy. The plots in the lower half of the figure show the disk head movement for each policy. Note that the total seek times in different scheduling policies vary greatly. SSTF is better than FCFS; however *look* has the smallest total seek time in this example. It is better than *C-Look* because it can reverse the direction of disk-head traversal after completing the I/O operation on track 100, and service the operations on tracks 75, 40, and 12, whereas C-Look starts a new scan with the operation on track 12.

Scheduling in the disk itself can surpass scheduling in the physical IOCS because the disk uses a more precise model that considers the seek time as well as the rotational latency of a disk block. Hence it can make fine distinctions between two I/O commands that would appear equivalent to the physical IOCS. As an example, consider I/O commands that concern disk blocks that are $+n$ and $-n$ tracks away from the current position of the disk heads. Both commands have equal seek times; the physical IOCS would have to make a random choice between them. However, given the current rotational position of the platters and the position of the required disk block or sector, the disk may find that the block that is $+n$ tracks away may already be passing under the heads by the time the heads are positioned on that track. It would mean that the disk block can be read only in the next revolution of the disk. The disk block that is $-n$ tracks away, on the other hand, might pass under the heads sometime after the heads have been positioned on that track. Hence its rotational latency would be smaller than that of the disk block that is $+n$ tracks away. Such finer distinctions can contribute to higher throughput of the disk.

t_{const} and t_{pt}	=	0 ms and 1 ms, respectively
Current head position	=	Track 65
Direction of last movement	=	Toward higher numbered tracks
Current clock time	=	160 ms

Requested I/O operations:

Serial number	1	2	3	4	5
Track number	12	85	40	100	75
Time of arrival	65	80	110	120	175

Scheduling details:

Policy	**Details**	**Scheduling decisions**					**Σ Seek time**
		1	**2**	**3**	**4**	**5**	
FCFS	Time of decision	160	213	286	331	391	
	Pending requests	1, 2, 3, 4	2, 3, 4, 5	3, 4, 5	4, 5	5	
	Head position	65	12	85	40	100	
	Selected request	1	2	3	4	5	
	Seek time	53	73	45	60	25	256
SSTF	Time of decision	160	180	190	215	275	
	Pending requests	1, 2, 3, 4	1, 3, 4, 5	1, 3, 4	1, 3	1	
	Head position	65	85	75	100	40	
	Selected request	2	5	4	3	1	
	Seek time	20	10	25	60	28	143
Look	Time of decision	160	180	195	220	255	
	Pending requests	1, 2, 3, 4	1, 3, 4, 5	1, 3, 5	1, 3	1	
	Head position	65	85	100	75	40	
	Selected request	2	4	5	3	1	
	Seek time	20	15	25	35	28	123
C-Look	Time of decision	160	180	195	283	311	
	Pending requests	1, 2, 3, 4	1, 3, 4, 5	1, 3, 5	3, 5	5	
	Head position	65	85	100	12	40	
	Selected request	2	4	1	3	5	
	Seek time	20	15	88	28	35	186

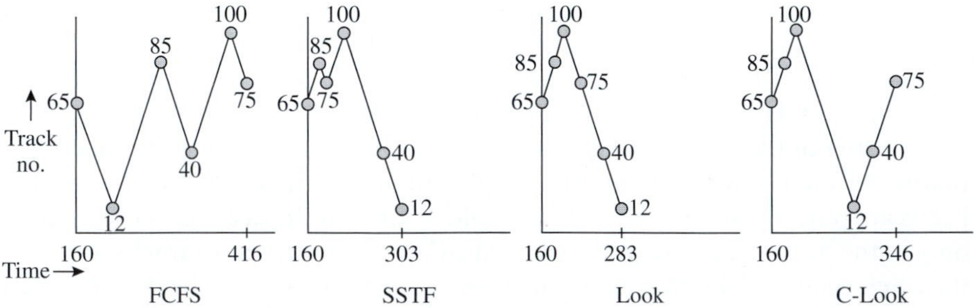

Figure 14.16 Disk scheduling summary using the FCFS, SSTF, Look, and C-Look policies.

Scheduling in SCSI Disks A SCSI disk can accept up to 32 commands concurrently from the physical IOCS. The physical IOCS associates a tag with each I/O command to indicate how it wants the disk to handle it. The disk stores the commands in a command table and uses their tags while making scheduling decisions. This feature is called *tagged command queuing*.

The tag in a command can be of three kinds—simple queue tag, ordered queue tag, and head-of-queue tag. A *simple queue tag* in a command indicates that the command can be reordered to optimize disk throughput. A command with an *ordered queue tag* indicates that all commands that were entered in the queue earlier should be scheduled before it is scheduled. Such a command should be issued periodically to ensure that I/O operations do not starve, i.e., do not remain indefinitely in the command table. A command with a *head-of-queue tag* should be performed immediately by the disk; i.e., it should be performed ahead of any other command. This feature may be used to ensure that file data are written to the disk before metadata (see the discussion of journaling file systems in Section 13.12).

Scheduling in the disk also has its drawbacks. Since the disk treats all I/O operations uniformly, it might interfere with file-level optimizations performed by access method modules. Consider processing of a sequential file through a few buffers, which we discuss later in Section 14.8. When the file is opened, the access method layer issues commands to read the first few records of the file in its buffers. To exploit the advantages of buffering, these read commands should be performed in the order in which they are issued. However, the disk might reorder them on the basis of their seek and rotational latencies. Hence a later record of the file may be read in while a process waits to access an earlier record! When a disk is used for both paging and user files, the OS may wish to perform paging operations at a higher priority. Scheduling in the disk may interfere with this requirement.

These drawbacks of disk scheduling lead to the obvious question—should disk scheduling be performed in the disk, in the physical IOCS or in both? Use of a more precise model to compute seek and rotational latencies indicates that scheduling should be performed in the disk. Command ordering requirements to support file-level access optimization imply that scheduling should also be performed in the physical IOCS. An OS designer has to use the tagged command queuing features to ensure that these schedulers work harmoniously.

14.8 BUFFERING OF RECORDS

To process the records in a sequential file using the physical IOCS, a process initiates a read operation on a record by invoking the `start-io` module and immediately invokes the `await-io` module to check whether the read operation has completed. The `await-io` module blocks the process until the I/O operation completes (see Section 14.5.4). Thus the process suffers a wait time for each record, which affects its performance. An access method for sequential files reduces the wait times faced by a process through the technique of *buffering of records*, which tries to overlap the I/O and CPU activities in the process. It is achieved through two means:

- *Prefetching* an input record into an I/O buffer, or
- *Postwriting* an output record from an I/O buffer

where an *I/O buffer*, or simply a *buffer*, is a memory area that is temporarily used to hold the data involved in an I/O operation.

In prefetching, the I/O operation to read the next record into a buffer is started sometime before the record is actually needed by the process—it may be started while the process is engaged in processing the previous record. This arrangement overlaps a part of the time spent in reading the next record with processing of the previous record, which reduces the wait time for the next record. In postwriting, the record to be written is simply copied into a buffer when the process issues a write operation and the process is allowed to continue. Actual writing is performed from the buffer sometime later. It can overlap with (a part of) processing of the next record.

We use the following notation while discussing the technique of buffering:

t_{io} *I/O time per record* [see Eq. (14.1)]

t_c *copying time per record* (i.e., the amount of CPU time required to copy a record from one memory area to another)

t_p *processing time per record* (i.e., the amount of CPU time consumed by the process in processing a record)

t_w *wait time per record* (i.e., the amount of time for which the process has to wait before the next record is available for processing)

t_{ee} *effective elapsed time per record* (i.e., the interval between the time when a process wishes to start processing a record and the time when the processing of the record is completed)

t_w and t_{ee} are analogously defined for an output file.

Consider a program that reads and processes 100 records from a sequential file F. We consider three versions of the program named *Unbuf_P*, *Single_buf_P*, and *Multi_buf_P* that use zero, one, and n buffers, $n > 1$, respectively. We assume $t_{\text{io}} = 75$ ms, $t_p = 50$ ms and $t_c = 5$ ms.

Figure 14.17 illustrates the operation and performance of processes that represent executions of *Unbuf_P*, *Single_buf_P*, and *Multi_buf_P*. For convenience, we assume a process to have the same name as the program it executes. Each column of the figure shows the code of a program, illustrates the steps involved in reading and processing a record and shows a timing chart depicting performance of the process executing it. The statements "start an I/O operation" and "await I/O completion" in the programs are translated into calls on the physical IOCS modules `start-io` and `await-io` with appropriate operands. The start I/O statement reads the next record of F, if any, into a memory area. If there are no more records in F, the *end_of_file* condition is set when an await I/O statement is executed. *Unbuf_P* uses a single area of memory named *Rec_area* to read and process a record of file F [see Figure 14.17(a)]. It issues a read operation and

Programs

Program *Unbuf_P*

```
start an I/O operation for
    read (F, Rec_area);
await I/O completion;
while (not end_of_file(F))
begin
    process Rec_area;
    start an I/O operation for
        read (F, Rec_area);
    await I/O completion;
end
```

Program *Single_buf_P*

```
start an I/O operation for
        read (F, Buffer);
await I/O completion;
while (not end_of_file(F))
begin
    copy Buffer into Rec_area;
    start an I/O operation for
        read (F, Buffer);
    process Rec_area;
    await I/O completion;
end
```

Program *Multi_buf_P*

```
for i := 1 to n
    start an I/O operation
        for read (F, Buf_i);
await I/O completion on
        Buf_1;
k := 1;
while (not end_of_file(F))
    copy Buf_k into Rec_area;
    start an I/O operation for
        read (F, Buf_k);
    process Rec_area;
    k := (k mod n) +1;
    await I/O completion on
        Buf_k;
end
```

I/O, Copying, and Processing activites (UP:*Unbuf_P*, SP:*Single_buf_P*, MP:*Multi_buf_P*)

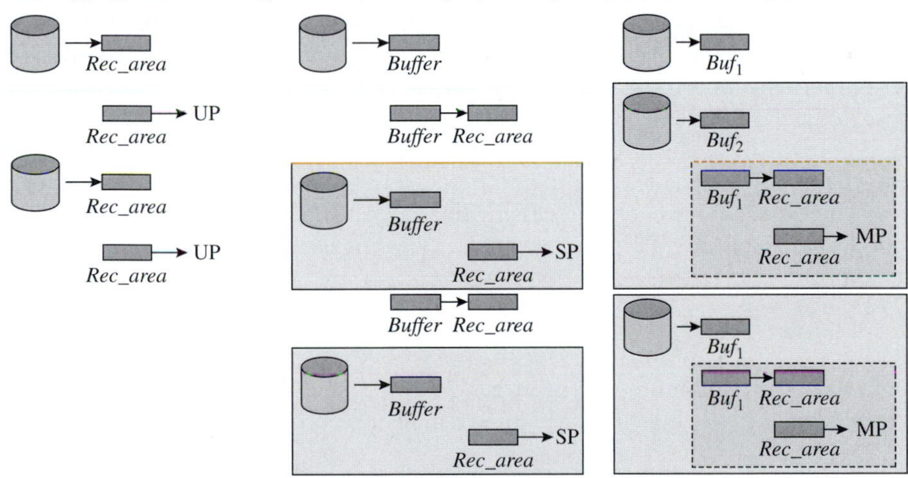

Timing Diagrams (I: I/O operation, C: Copying, P: Processing)

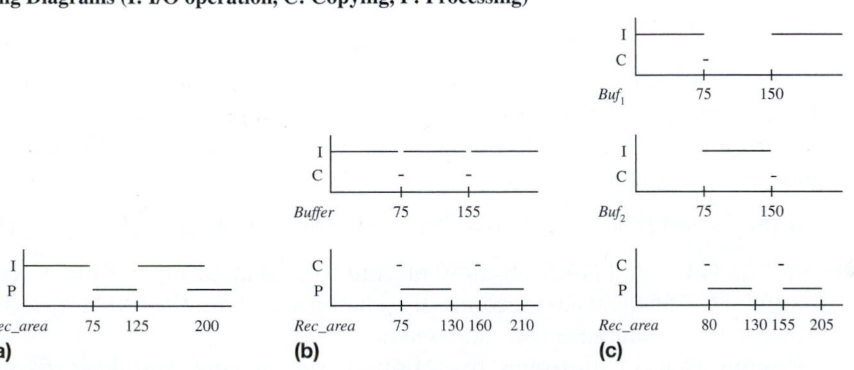

Figure 14.17 Unbuffered and buffered file processing. (*Note:* the *end_of_file* condition is set when the statement *await I/O completion* is executed for an operation that tried to read past the end of a file.)

awaits its completion before processing the record in *Rec_area* itself. The timing diagram shows that I/O is performed on *Rec_area* from 0 to 75 ms, and CPU processing of the record held in *Rec_area* occurs between 75 ms and 125 ms. Hence $t_w = t_{\text{io}}$ and $t_{\text{ee}} = t_{\text{io}} + t_p$. This sequence of operations repeats 100 times, hence the elapsed time of the process is $100 \times (75 + 50)$ ms = 12.5 seconds.

Figure 14.17(b) illustrates operation of *Single_buf_P*, which uses a single buffer area named *Buffer*. The process issues a read operation to read the first record into *Buffer* and awaits its completion. It now enters the main loop of the program, which repeats the following four-step procedure 99 times:

1. Copy the record from *Buffer* into *Rec_area*.
2. Initiate an I/O operation on *Buffer*.
3. Process the record held in *Rec_area*.
4. Await end of I/O operation on *Buffer*.

As shown in the timing diagram of Figure 14.17(b), the process faces an I/O wait in Step 1 until the read operation on *Buffer* completes. It now performs Steps 2–4. Hence after copying the record into *Rec_area*, it initiates a read operation for the second record and starts processing the first record. These two activities proceed in parallel, thus overlapping processing of the first record with I/O for the second record. We depict this parallelism by drawing a rectangular box to enclose these two actions in the activities part of Figure 14.17(b). Step 1, i.e., copying of the next record from *Buffer* to *Rec_area*, is performed only after both, reading of the next record and processing of the current record, complete. It is once again followed by processing of a record and reading of the next record in parallel. Hence, the wait time before processing each of records 2–99 is

$$\begin{aligned} t_w &= (t_{\text{io}} - t_p) + t_c, \quad \text{if } t_{io} > t_p \\ &= t_c, \qquad\qquad\qquad \text{if } t_{\text{io}} \le t_p \end{aligned} \tag{14.3}$$

and so buffering is more effective when $t_{io} \le t_p$.

For records 2–99, effective elapsed time per record (t_{ee}) is given by

$$\begin{aligned} t_{\text{ee}} &= t_w + t_p \\ &= t_c + \max(t_{\text{io}}, t_p) \end{aligned} \tag{14.4}$$

Thus the process goes through three distinct phases—the start-up phase when the first record is read, the steady state when a record is copied and processed while the next record is read in parallel, and the final phase when the last record is copied and processed. Accordingly, the total elapsed time of the process is given by

$$\text{Total elapsed time} = t_{\text{io}} + (\text{number of records} - 1) \times t_{\text{ee}} + (t_c + t_p) \tag{14.5}$$

From Eqs. (14.4) and (14.5), t_{ee} is 80 ms and total elapsed time of the process is $75 + 99 \times 80 + 55$ ms = 8.05 seconds. If t_{io} had been 50 ms, the total elapsed time of the process would have been 5.55 seconds.

Figure 14.17(c) illustrates operation of the process *Multi_buf_P*, which uses buffer areas named $Buf_1, Buf_2, \ldots, Buf_n$. At the start of file processing,

Multi_buf_P initiates I/O operations on all n buffers. Inside the file processing loop, it uses the buffers in turn, following the four steps of the program loop for processing a record in a buffer. The statement $k := (k \bmod n) + 1$; ensures that the buffers are used in a cyclic manner. The process waits for I/O to complete on the next buffer, copies the record from the buffer into *Rec_area*, invokes `start-io` for reading the next record in the buffer, and then processes the record in *Rec_area*.

Presence of multiple buffers causes one significant difference between operations of *Multi_buf_P* and *Single_buf_P*. Consider processing of the first two records by *Multi_buf_P* [see Figure 14.17(c)]. When I/O on Buf_1 completes, *Multi_buf_P* would copy the first record from Buf_1 into *Rec_area* and start processing it. A read operation on Buf_2 would have been requested earlier, so the physical IOCS would initiate this read operation when the I/O on Buf_1 completes. Hence this operation would overlap with the copying out of the first record from Buf_1. In Figure 14.17(c), we depict this parallelism as follows: The dashed rectangular box around copying and processing of the record from Buf_1 is meant to indicate that these actions are performed sequentially. The rectangular box enclosing this box and the I/O operation on Buf_2 indicates that these two activities are performed in parallel. Accordingly, the effective elapsed time per record is given by

$$\begin{aligned} t_w &= t_{io} - t_p & \text{if } t_{io} > t_c + t_p \\ &= t_c, & \text{if } t_{io} \le t_c + t_p \end{aligned} \tag{14.6}$$

$$t_{ee} = \max(t_{io}, t_c + t_p) \tag{14.7}$$

From Eq. (14.7), t_{ee} = 75 ms. The total elapsed time, which is governed by Eq. (14.5), is $75 + 99 \times 75 + 55$ ms = 7.555 seconds, which is marginally better than *Single_Buf_P*'s elapsed time of 8.05 seconds.

The ratio of the elapsed times of *Unbuf_P* and *Multi_buf_P* is the speedup factor due to use of multiple buffers. Considering the steady state, the speedup factor is approximately

$$\frac{t_{io} + t_p}{\max(t_{io}, t_c + t_p)}$$

From Eq. (14.7), it can be seen that its best value is obtained when $t_{io} = t_c + t_p$. This value has the upper bound of 2.

Consider the operation of *Multi_Buf_P* when more than one buffer is used. Figure 14.18 illustrates a typical situation during execution of *Multi_Buf_P*. The CPU has recently copied the record from Buf_{i-1} into *Rec_area* and started an I/O operation on Buf_{i-1}. Thus, I/O operations have been initiated on all n buffers. Some of the I/O operations, specifically, those on $Buf_i, \ldots, Buf_{j-1}$, are already complete. I/O is currently in progress for Buf_j, while $Buf_{j+1}, \ldots, Buf_n, Buf_1, \ldots, Buf_{i-1}$ are currently in the queue for I/O initiation. Thus $(j - i)$ buffers are full at the moment, I/O is in progress for one buffer, and $(n - j + i - 1)$ buffers are in the queue for I/O.

The value of $(j - i)$ depends on the values of t_{io} and t_p. If $t_{io} < t_p$, i.e., if the I/O operation for a record requires less time than its processing, we can see

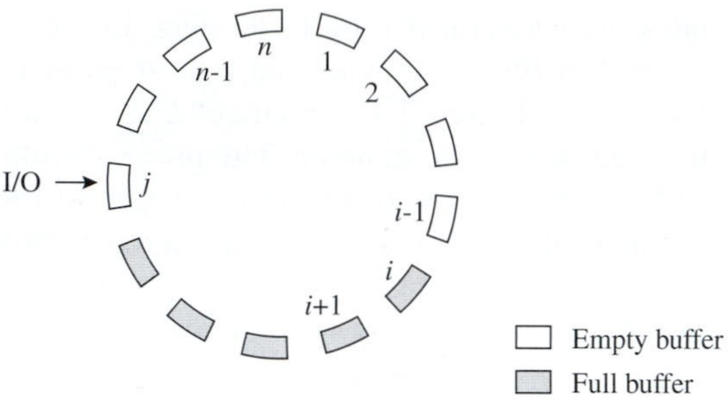

Figure 14.18 Use of buffers in *Buf_P*.

that buffers $Buf_{i+1}, \ldots, Buf_n, Buf_1, \ldots, Buf_{i-2}$ will be full, and Buf_{i-1} will be either under I/O or full when the CPU is processing the record copied out of Buf_{i-1}. If $t_{io} > t_p$, the steady-state situation will be that Buf_i is under I/O when the CPU is processing the record copied out of Buf_{i-1} and buffers $Buf_{i+1}, \ldots, Buf_n, Buf_1, \ldots, Buf_{i-1}$ are empty.

Use of multiple buffers is irrelevant if a process manipulates each record individually. However, it makes a significant difference if a process manipulates many records together. Using n buffers helps in such a case because many buffers may be full when the process needs a few records together. The next example illustrates this point.

Example 14.4 **Use of Multiple Buffers**

Each line of a program written in language L is stored in a record of file F. The compiler of L used to compile this program needs to read an entire statement into memory before starting its processing. A statement may contain up to l lines. The I/O wait for the compiler can be eliminated only if the following conditions hold:

1. $t_{io} \leq t_{pl}$, and
2. $l \leq n$

where t_{pl} is the average processing time for each line of a statement. Condition 1 ensures that in the steady state, all buffers will be full when the compiler finishes processing one statement. Condition 2 ensures that at least l buffers are full when the compiler finishes processing a statement. Hence the compiler will not face I/O waits. It would face I/O waits if $l > n$, e.g., if $l = 3$ and it used two buffers.

14.9 BLOCKING OF RECORDS

In unbuffered processing of a file by a process, the time spent in performing I/O operations may dominate the elapsed time of the process. Even in buffered processing of a file, $t_w > 0$ if $t_{io} > t_p$, or $t_{io} > t_c + t_p$ [see Eqs. (14.3) and (14.6)]. Thus both unbuffered and buffered processing of files would benefit from a reduction in t_{io}. The technique of *blocking of records* reduces the effective I/O time per record by reading or writing many records in a single I/O operation. From Eq. (14.1), $t_{io} = t_a + t_x$. Hence, a program that processes two records from a file that does not employ blocking would incur the total I/O time of $2 \times (t_a + t_x)$. If blocking is employed and a process reads or writes two records in a single I/O operation, the total I/O time would reduce to $t_a + 2 \times t_x$.

Logical and Physical Records When several records are read or written together, it is necessary to differentiate between how file data is accessed and processed in a process, and how it is written on an I/O device. A *logical record* is the unit of file data for accessing and processing in a process. A *physical record*, also called a *block*, is the unit of data for transfer to or from an I/O device. The *blocking factor* of a file is the number of logical records in one physical record. A file is said to employ *blocking* of records if the blocking factor is greater than 1. Figure 14.19 shows a file that uses a blocking factor of 3. Note that when blocking is employed, interrecord gaps on the I/O media separate physical records, i.e., blocks, rather than logical records.

Deblocking Actions A read operation on a file containing blocked records transfers m logical records to memory, where m is the blocking factor. Actions for extracting a logical record from a block for use in a process are collectively called *deblocking actions*.

Figure 14.20 shows a program that manipulates a file with blocked records in an unbuffered manner. The main loop of the program reads one physical record in each iteration. It contains an inner loop that extracts logical records from a physical record and processes them. Thus, an I/O operation is initiated only after

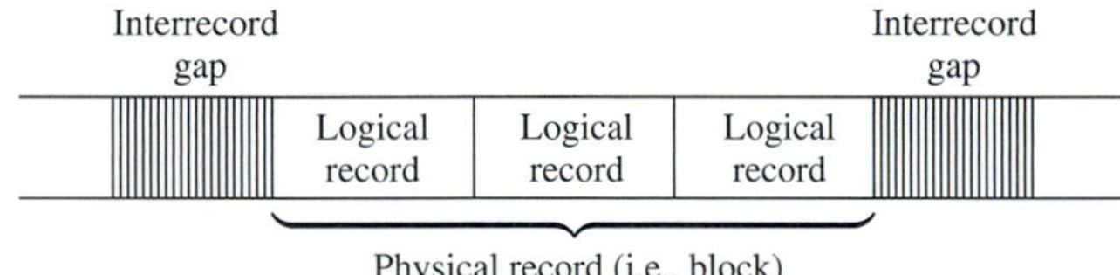

Figure 14.19 A file with blocking factor = 3.

```
start an I/O operation for read (F, Rec_area);
await I/O completion;
while (not end_of_file(F))
    for i := 1 to m
        { extract i^th record in Rec_area and process it }
    start an I/O operation for read (F, Rec_area);
    await I/O completion;
end
```

Figure 14.20 Processing of a file with blocked records in an unbuffered manner.

m records are processed. A similar logic can be incorporated into the programs of Figures 14.17(b), (c) to achieve buffered processing of a file containing blocked records.

Choice of Blocking Factor Generalizing on the previous discussion,we can say that if s_{lr} and s_{pr} represent the size of a logical and a physical record, respectively, $s_{pr} = m \times s_{lr}$. The I/O time per physical record, $(t_{io})_{pr}$, and the I/O time per logical record, $(t_{io})_{lr}$, are given by

$$(t_{io})_{pr} = t_a + m \times t_x \qquad \textbf{(14.8)}$$

$$(t_{io})_{lr} = \frac{t_a}{m} + t_x \qquad \textbf{(14.9)}$$

Thus blocking reduces the effective I/O time per logical record, which would benefit both buffered and unbuffered processing of a file. If $t_x < t_p$, with an appropriate choice of m it is possible to reduce $(t_{io})_{lr}$ such that $(t_{io})_{lr} \leq t_p$. Once it is achieved, from Eqs. (14.3) and (14.6) it follows that buffering can be used to reduce the wait time per record to t_c. The next example illustrates how $(t_{io})_{lr}$ varies with the blocking factor.

Example 14.5 Blocking of Records

Table 14.5 shows the variation of $(t_{io})_{lr}$ with m for a disk device with $t_a = 10$ ms, transfer rate of 800 kB/s, where 1 kB/s = 1000 bytes per second, and $s_{lr} = 200$ bytes. t_x, the transfer time per logical record, is $\frac{200}{800}$ ms, i.e., 0.25 ms. $(t_{io})_{pr}$ and $(t_{io})_{lr}$ are computed according to Eqs. (14.8) and (14.9). If $t_p = 3$ ms, $m \geq 4$ makes $(t_{io})_{lr} < t_p$.

The value of m is bounded on the lower side by the desire to make $(t_{io})_{lr} \leq t_p$. On the higher side, it is bounded by the memory commitment for file buffers, and the size of a disk track or sector. A practical value of the blocking factor is the smallest value of m that makes $(t_{io})_{lr} \leq t_p$. The next example illustrates processing of a file employing both blocking and buffering of records.

Table 14.5 Variation of $(t_{io})_{lr}$ with Blocking Factor

Blocking factor (m)	Block size	t_a ms	$m \times t_x$ ms	$(t_{io})_{pr}$ ms	$(t_{io})_{lr}$ ms
1	200	10	0.25	10.25	10.25
2	400	10	0.50	10.50	5.25
3	600	10	0.75	10.75	3.58
4	800	10	1.00	11.00	2.75

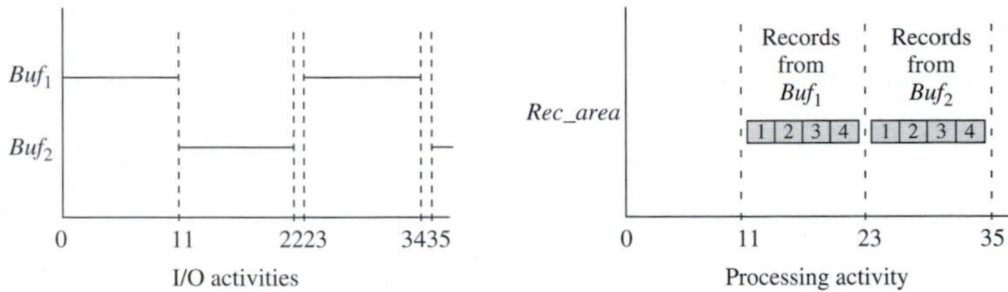

Figure 14.21 Buffered processing of blocked records with blocking factor = 4 and two buffers.

Example 14.6

Buffered Processing of a File Containing Blocked Records

Figure 14.21 shows the timing chart of processing the blocked file of Example 14.5 with a blocking factor of 4, using two buffers Buf_1 and Buf_2. We assume t_c to be negligible. When the file is opened at time 0 second, read operations are initiated on Buf_1 and Buf_2. The operation on Buf_1 completes at $t = 11$ ms. The process copies out one logical record from Buf_1 at a time and processes it. $t_p = 3$ ms, so processing of the four records of Buf_1 consumes 12 ms. This processing overlaps with the read operation on Buf_2, which consumes 11 ms. Hence the next physical record of the file has been read into Buf_2 before processing of records in Buf_1 is completed. The process starts processing of the logical records copied from Buf_2 at $t = 23$ ms. Thus, it does not suffer any waits after the start-up phase.

14.10 ACCESS METHODS

As mentioned in Section 13.3.4, an access method provides support for efficient processing of a class of files that use a specific file organization. For the fundamental file organizations discussed in Section 13.3, the IOCS may provide access methods for the following kinds of processing:

- Unbuffered processing of sequential-access files
- Buffered processing of sequential-access files
- Processing of direct-access files
- Unbuffered processing of index sequential-access files
- Buffered processing of index sequential-access files

Access methods for buffered processing of sequential-access and index sequential-access files incorporate the buffering technique illustrated in Figure 14.17(c). These access methods also optionally perform blocking of records, using the technique shown in Figure 14.20.

We assume that each access method module provides three entry points with the following parameters:

1. `AM-open` (<*internal_id*>)
2. `AM-close` (<*internal_id*>)
3. `AM-read/write` (<*internal_id*>, <*record_info*>, <*I/O_area addr*>)

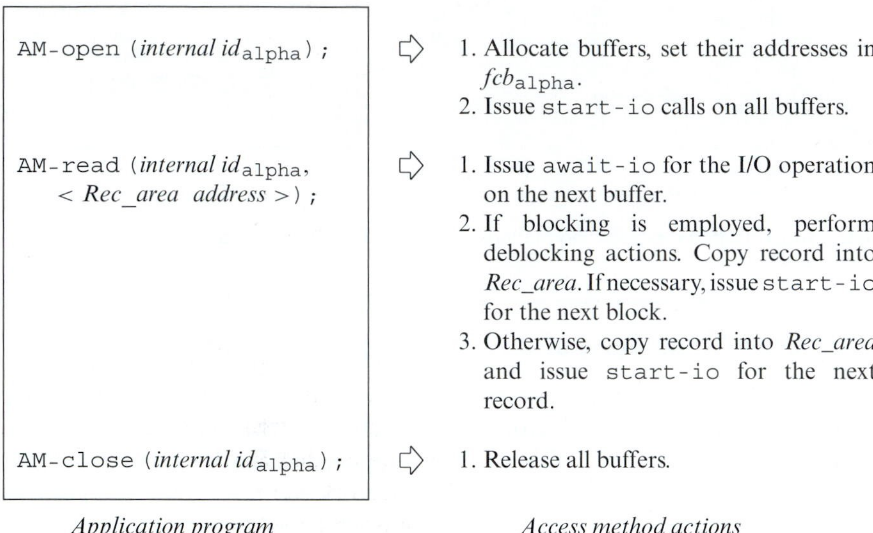

Figure 14.22 Actions of an access method for buffered reading of a file.

Modules of the file system and IOCS invoke these functionalities to implement file processing. `AM-open` is invoked after a file control block has been created for the file, using information from the directory entry of the file. Similarly, `AM-close` is invoked by `iocs-close`. `AM-read/write` are invoked by a file system module; the entry point `AM-read` is actually the start of the IOCS library module `seq-read` of Figure 14.14.

Figure 14.22 shows actions of the access method for buffered processing of a sequential-access file `alpha`. `AM-open` issues read operations on all buffers. `AM-read` uses the information in $fcb_{\texttt{alpha}}$, including $fmt_{\texttt{alpha}}$, to form a pair (*record id*, *byte id*) in Steps 2 and 3 for the next physical record in the file. A few actions of the access method would be different if `alpha` were an output file. `AM-write` would be invoked to perform write operations. In steps 2 and 3, it would invoke a module of the file system to allocate more disk space to `alpha` and enter its address into $fmt_{\texttt{alpha}}$.

14.11 DISK AND FILE CACHES

A generic technique of speeding up access to file data is to use a memory hierarchy consisting of a part of memory and files stored on a disk. Recall from the principles of memory hierarchies discussed in Section 2.2.3 that memory would contain some parts of the file data stored on the disk; other parts would be loaded in memory when required. In essence, memory would function as a *cache* between files on the disk and processes. Both physical IOCS and access methods use this principle. The physical IOCS uses a *disk cache*, which treats all files stored on a disk uniformly and holds *some* data of *some* files in memory at any time. An access method, on the other hand, uses a *file cache*, which focuses on keeping some part of the data in a specific file in memory. The access method maintains a separate file cache for each file.

The unit of data kept in a disk or file cache is typically a few consecutive disk blocks; for simplicity we assume it to be a single disk block. We will call the memory area used to store a unit of data a *buffer*. The cache is thus a collection of buffers managed in the software. Each buffer has two parts—the *header* part indicates what data is contained in it, and the data part actually contains data. The header contains the following information:

- Address of the disk blocks from where data has been loaded in the buffer
- A *dirty* flag
- Information needed for performing replacement of data in the buffer, such as the time of last reference made to it

When a process issues a read operation, it specifies the offset of the required data in the file. The IOCS determines the address of the disk block that contains the required data and searches the cache to check whether contents of that disk block are present in a buffer. If so, the required data is copied from the buffer into the address space of the process. Otherwise, an I/O operation is initiated to load the data from the disk block into a buffer in the cache and it is copied into the address space of the process when the I/O operation completes. When a process performs a write operation, the IOCS checks whether contents of the disk block that contains old values of the data are present in a buffer. If so, it copies the values to be written from address space of the process into the buffer and sets the dirty flag of the buffer to *true*. Otherwise, it copies the disk block address and values of the data to be written into a new buffer and sets its dirty flag to *true*. In either case, contents of the buffer would be written on the disk by the procedure described in the following.

To facilitate speedy search in the cache, the buffer headers are stored in an efficient data structure such as a hash table. For example, the *hash-with-chaining* organization used in the inverted page table of the virtual memory handler could be adapted for use in the cache (see Figure 12.10 in Section 12.2.3.1). In this organization, the address of a disk block whose data is contained in a buffer is hashed to obtain an entry number in the hash table. All buffers that contain disk blocks whose addresses hash into the same entry of the hash table are entered into a linked list, called a *chain*, and the hash table entry is made to point to the chain. To check whether data from a disk block is present in the cache, the address of the disk block is hashed to obtain an entry number in the hash table, and the chain pointed to by this entry is searched to check whether a copy of the disk block is contained in one of the buffers. If it is not present in the cache, it is loaded in a free buffer in the cache and the buffer is added to the chain. If the cache is full, a policy such as LRU replacement is employed to decide which buffer should be used to load the required data. If the *dirty* flag of the buffer is *true*, its contents would be written in the disk block whose address is contained in its header before new data is loaded in the buffer. Such an arrangement used in the Unix *buffer cache* is described later in Section 14.13.1.2.

Loading of whole disk blocks, which are a few KB in size, in the cache captures *spatial locality* because data that adjoins previously accessed data would exist in the cache. This effect is analogous to *blocking* of records discussed previously in Section 14.9. Studies mentioned in Section 14.13.1.2 indicate that disk cache hit ratios of 0.9 or more can be obtained by committing a small amount of memory to the disk cache. A file cache can exploit temporal locality further by preloading the next few disk blocks of a sequential-access file in the cache, which is analogous to *buffering* of records discussed in Section 14.8.

Use of a cache has some drawbacks too. An I/O operation involves two copy operations, one between the disk and the cache and the other between the cache and the address space of the process that initiated the I/O operation. Use of a cache also leads to poor reliability of the file system because modified data exists in a buffer in the cache until it is written to the disk. This data will be lost in the event of a crash.

File Cache A file cache is implemented in an access method and aims to provide efficient access to data stored in a file. As shown in Figure 14.23(a), the access method invokes the cache manager, which checks whether the required data is available in the file cache. It invokes the physical IOCS only if the file cache does not already contain the required data. The key advantage of a file cache over a disk cache is that the cache manager can employ file-level techniques to speed up accesses to file data. Such a technique exploits properties of a file's organization to speed up data accesses, e.g., it can perform prefetching of data for sequential-access files. However, a key disadvantage is that a separate file cache has to be implemented for each file, so the IOCS has to decide how much memory to commit to each individual file cache.

Disk Cache The disk cache is implemented in the physical IOCS or device driver of a disk. Its purpose is to speed up accesses to data stored on the disk. As shown in Figure 14.23(b), a request for an I/O operation is passed to the I/O scheduler only if the required data is not present in the disk cache. The key advantage of a

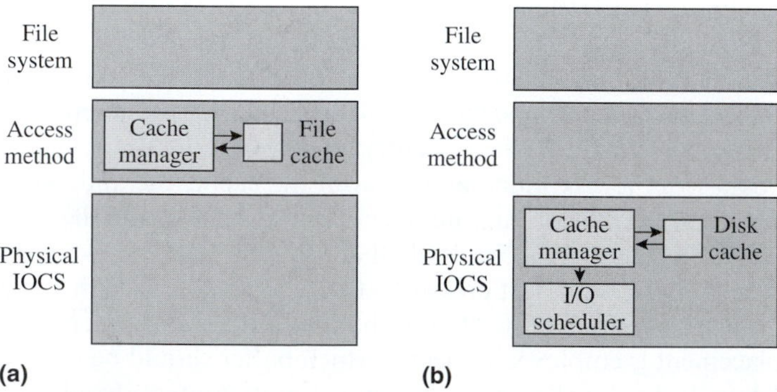

Figure 14.23 (a) File cache; (b) disk caches.

disk cache over a file cache is that it does not differentiate between files stored on a disk, so its use benefits all file processing activities in the system. It also does not have to determine cache size for each file individually. However, the hit ratio in the disk cache is sensitive to the file access behavior of processes. For example, if a process reads a large sequential file very rapidly, its data might occupy most of the buffers in the cache, which will degrade accesses to data in other files. Disk caches implemented in modern operating systems also incorporate some features of file caches to enhance hit ratios. Hence a disk cache may prefetch a few disk blocks in a sequential-access file to reduce wait times in processes.

14.12 UNIFIED DISK CACHE

Apart from disk or file caches, the OS also maintains, implicitly or explicitly, another cache called the *page cache* in the virtual memory handler. Use of several caches may increase the number of copy operations that have to be performed to access data stored on a disk. The time and memory overhead introduced by multiple copy operations motivates use of a unified disk cache.

Figure 14.24(a) is a schematic diagram showing use of the disk cache and the page cache. The page cache contains all code and data pages of processes that are presently in memory, including pages of any memory-mapped files. A new page is loaded into the page cache when a page fault occurs. Since the page size is typically a few disk blocks, this operation involves reading a few blocks from a program file or a swap file. This is file I/O. Hence the disk blocks get read into the disk cache, and they have to be copied into the page cache. When a modified page is to be removed from memory, it is first copied into the disk cache. From there, it is written to the disk sometime in the future. Thus, two copy operations are involved in each page-in and page-out operation—one copy operation between a disk and the disk cache, and another between the disk cache and the

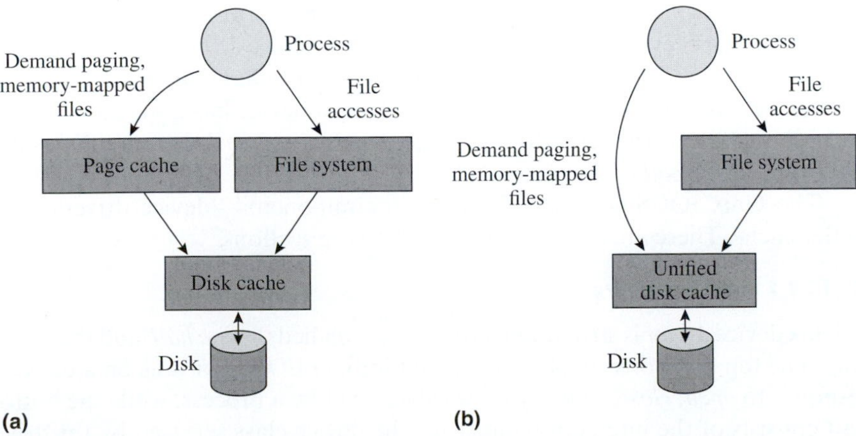

Figure 14.24 Disk caching: (a) separate disk and page caches; (b) unified disk cache.

page cache. After a page-in operation, two copies of the page would be present in memory until either of the copies is overwritten.

Multiple copy operations on pages and duplicate copies of pages cause performance problems. The amount of memory to be committed to each cache is also a difficult design decision; it can affect performance of the system because undercommitment of memory to the page cache could lead to either a reduced degree of multiprogramming or thrashing, while undercommitment to the disk cache would slow down file processing activities because of frequent accesses to the disk. Merging the two caches would solve these problems: duplicate copies and multiple copy operations would be eliminated, and portions of the cache committed to the two uses could be varied to adapt to changes in the system workload.

A *unified disk cache* is a single cache used for both paging and file I/O. Figure 14.24(b) is a schematic diagram of the unified disk cache. The file system looks upon files as paged objects on the disk. It decomposes the byte offset provided in a read or write statement into a page number and an offset into a page. It passes the page number to the unified disk cache to ensure that the page is loaded in memory and uses the offset into the page to copy the data between the unified disk cache and the address space of a process. Page I/O continues to be handled as in conventional systems because the unified disk cache is really a page cache.

The unified disk cache was introduced in the Sun OS 4.0. Later it was implemented in the Unix System 5 version 4. The Linux 2.4 kernel and its later versions also use a unified disk cache.

14.13 CASE STUDIES

14.13.1 Unix

Unix supports two types of devices—*block* devices and *character* devices. Block devices are random-access devices that are capable of reading or writing blocks of data, such as various kinds of disks, while character devices are serial-access devices such as keyboards, printers and mice. A block device can also be used as a serial device. Unix files are simply sequences of characters, and so are I/O devices, so Unix treats I/O devices as files. Thus a device has a file name, has an entry in the directory hierarchy, and is accessed by using the same calls as files, viz. *open, close, read* and *write*.

The Unix IOCS consists of two main components—device drivers and a buffer cache. These are described in the following sections.

14.13.1.1 Device Drivers

A Unix device driver is structured into two parts called the *top half* and the *bottom half*. The top half consists of routines that initiate I/O operations on a device in response to *open*, *close*, *read*, or *write* calls issued by a process, while the bottom half consists of the interrupt handler for the device class serviced by the driver. Thus the top half corresponds to the I/O scheduler and I/O initiator modules in

Figure 14.13, while the bottom half corresponds to the I/O completion handler and error recovery modules.

A device driver has an interface consisting of a set of predefined entry points into the device driver routines. Some of these are:

1. *<ddname>_init* : Device driver initialization routine
2. *<ddname>_read/write* : Routines to read or write a character
3. *<ddname>_int* : Interrupt handler routine

The *<ddname>_init* routine is called at system boot time. It initializes various flags used by the device driver. It also checks for the presence of various devices, sets flags to indicate their presence, and may allocate buffers to them. Character I/O is performed by invoking the *<ddname>_read* and *<ddname>_write* routines. The device driver has to provide a strategy routine for block data transfers, which is roughly equivalent to the I/O scheduler shown in Figure 14.13. A call on the strategy routine takes the address of an I/O control block as a parameter. The strategy routine adds this I/O control block to an IOQ, and initiates the I/O operation if possible. If immediate initiation is not possible, the I/O operation is initiated subsequently when an I/O completion interrupt occurs.

14.13.1.2 Buffer Cache

The buffer cache is a *disk cache* as described in Section 14.12. It is organized as a pool of buffers, where each buffer is the same size as a disk block. Each buffer has a header containing three items of information: A (*device address*, *disk block address*) pair gives the address of the disk block that is present in the buffer, a *status flag* indicates whether I/O is in progress for the buffer, and a *busy* flag indicates whether some process is currently accessing the contents of the buffer.

A hash table is used to speed up the search for a required disk block (see Figure 14.25). The hash table consists of a number of buckets, where each bucket points to a list of buffers. When a disk block with address *aaa* is loaded into a buffer with the address *bbb*, *aaa* is hashed with function h to compute a bucket number $e = h(aaa)$ in the hash table. The buffer is now entered in the list of buffers in the eth bucket. Thus, the list contains all buffers that hold disk blocks whose addresses hash into the eth bucket.

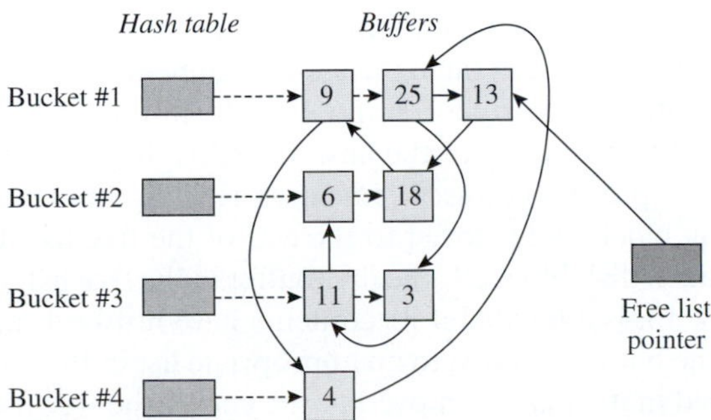

Figure 14.25 Unix buffer cache.

The following procedure is used when a process P_i performs a read operation on some file `alpha`:

1. Form the pair (*device address, disk block address*) for the byte required by P_i.
2. Hash *disk block address* to obtain a bucket number. Search the buffers in the bucket to check whether a buffer has a matching pair in its header.
3. If there is no buffer with a matching header, allocate a free buffer, put the (*device address, disk block address*) information in its header, enter the buffer in the list of the appropriate bucket, set its *status flag* to "I/O in progress," queue the buffer for I/O, and put P_i to sleep on completion of I/O.
4. If a buffer with matching header exists, return to P_i with its address if flags indicate that the I/O operation on the buffer is complete and the buffer is "not busy." Otherwise, put P_i to sleep on completion of a read operation on the buffer or buffer "not busy" condition.
5. If free buffers exist, check whether the next disk block allocated to `alpha` is already present in a buffer. If not, allocate a free buffer to it and queue it for a read operation.

This procedure does not allocate buffers on a per-process basis, so processes that concurrently access a file can share the file data present in a buffer. This arrangement facilitates Unix file sharing semantics (see Section 13.14.1). At the same time, prefetching of data is performed on a per-process basis by initiating an I/O for the next disk block of the file (see Step 5), which provides buffering on a per-process basis. The benefits of blocking of records are inherent in the fact that a complete disk block is read/written when any byte in it is accessed.

Buffers in the buffer pool are reused on an LRU basis as follows: All buffers are entered in a free list. A buffer is moved to the end of the list whenever its contents are referenced. Thus the least recently used buffers move toward the head of the free list. In Step 3, the buffer at the head of the free list is allocated unless it contains some modified data that is yet to be written into the disk block. In that case, a write operation for the buffer is queued and the next buffer in the list is allocated.

Example 14.7 Unix Buffer Cache

Figure 14.25 illustrates the Unix buffer cache. Disk blocks 9, 25 and 13 hash into the first entry of the hash table; hence they are entered in the linked list starting on this entry. Similarly 6, 18 and 11, 3 form the linked lists starting on the second and third entries of the hash table. All buffers are also entered in the free list. If a process accesses some data residing in disk block 18, the buffer containing block 18 is moved to the end of the free list. If the process now accesses data in disk block 21, the first buffer in the free list, i.e., the buffer containing block 13, is allocated if its contents have not been modified since it was loaded. The buffer is added to an appropriate list in the hash table after block 21 is loaded in it. It is also moved to the end of the free list.

The effectiveness of the Unix buffer cache has been extensively studied. A 1989 study reported that a 60 MB cache on an HP system provided a hit ratio of 0.99 and a 16 MB cache on another system provided a hit ratio of 0.9. Thus a comparatively small memory commitment to the buffer cache can provide a high hit ratio.

14.13.2 Linux

The organization of Linux IOCS is analogous to that of Unix IOCS. Thus, block- and character-type I/O devices are supported by individual device drivers, devices are treated like files, and a buffer cache is used to speed up file processing. However, many IOCS specifics are different. We list some of them before discussing details of disk scheduling in Linux 2.6.

1. Linux kernel modules—which include device drivers—are dynamically loadable, so a device driver has to be registered with the kernel when loaded and deregistered before being removed from memory.
2. For devices, the *vnode* data structure of the virtual file system (VFS) (see Section 13.13) contains pointers to device-specific functions for the file operations *open, close, read*, and *write*.
3. Each buffer in the disk cache has a buffer header that is allocated in a slab of the slab allocator (see Section 11.11).
4. Dirty buffers in the disk cache are written to the cache when the cache is too full, when a buffer has been in the cache for a long time, or when a file directs the file system to write out its buffers in the interest of reliability.

I/O scheduling in Linux 2.6 uses some innovations to improve I/O scheduling performance. A read operation needs to be issued to the disk when a process makes a *read* call and the required data does not already exist in the buffer cache. The process would get blocked until the read operation is completed. On the other hand, when a process makes a *write* call, the data to be written is copied into a buffer and the actual write operation takes place sometime later. Hence the process issuing a *write* call does not get blocked; it can go on to issue more *write* calls. Therefore, to provide better response times to processes, the IOCS performs read operations at a higher priority than write operations.

The I/O scheduler maintains a list of pending I/O operations and schedules from this list. When a process makes a *read* or a *write* call, the IOCS checks whether the same operation on some adjoining data is pending. If this check succeeds, it combines the new operation with the pending operation, which reduces the number of disk operations and the movement of disk heads, thereby improving disk throughput.

Linux 2.6 provides four I/O schedulers. The system administrator can choose the one that best suits the workload in a specific installation. The *no-op* scheduler is simply an FCFS scheduler. The *deadline* scheduler uses Look scheduling as its basis but also incorporates a feature to avoid large delays. It implements Look scheduling by maintaining a scheduling list of requests sorted by track numbers and selecting a request based on the current position of disk heads. However,

Look scheduling faces a problem when a process performs a large number of write operations in one part of the disk—I/O operations in other parts of the disk would be delayed. If a delayed operation is a read, it would cause considerable delays in the requesting process. To prevent such delays, the scheduler assigns a deadline of 0.5 second to a read operation and a deadline of 5 seconds to a write operation, and maintains two queues—one for read requests and one for write requests—according to deadlines. It normally schedules requests from the scheduling list; however, if the deadline of a request at the head of the read or write queue expires, it schedules this request, and a couple of more requests from its queue, out of sequence before resuming normal scheduling. The *completely fair queuing* scheduler maintains a separate queue of I/O requests for each process and performs round robin between these queues. This approach avoids large delays for processes.

A process that performs synchronous I/O is blocked until its I/O operation completes. Such a process typically issues the next I/O operation immediately after waking up. When Look scheduling is used, the disk heads would most probably have passed over the track that contains the data involved in the next I/O operation, so the next I/O operation of the process would get serviced only in the next scan of the disk. This causes delays in the process and may cause more movement of the disk heads. The *anticipatory* scheduler addresses this problem. After completing an I/O operation, it waits a few milliseconds before issuing the next I/O operation. This way, if the process that was activated when the previous I/O operation completed issues another I/O operation in close proximity to the previous operation that operation may also be serviced in the same scan of the disk.

14.13.3 File Processing in Windows

The schematic of Figure 14.26 shows the file processing arrangement used in Windows. The *cache manager* performs *file caching*. The *I/O manager* provides generic services that can be used to implement subsystem-specific I/O operations through a set of device drivers, and also performs management of I/O buffers. As described in Section 4.8.4, subsystem DLLs linked to a user application invoke functions in the I/O manager to obtain subsystem-specific I/O behavior. The *VM manager* was described in Section 12.8.4.

The file cache is organized as a set of cache blocks, each of size 256 KB. The part of a file held in a cache block is called a *view*. A *virtual address control block* (VACB) describes each view; it contains the virtual address associated with the view, the offset of its first byte in the file, and the number of read or write operations currently accessing the view. Presence of the virtual address and file offset information in the VACB helps in implementing file sharing semantics—it ensures that processes making concurrent accesses to a file would see the result of the latest update operation irrespective of whether the file was memory-mapped or accessed directly. The cache manager sets up a VACB index array for a file when the file is opened. For a sequential file, the index array would contain only one pointer that points to the VACB covering the current offset into the file. For

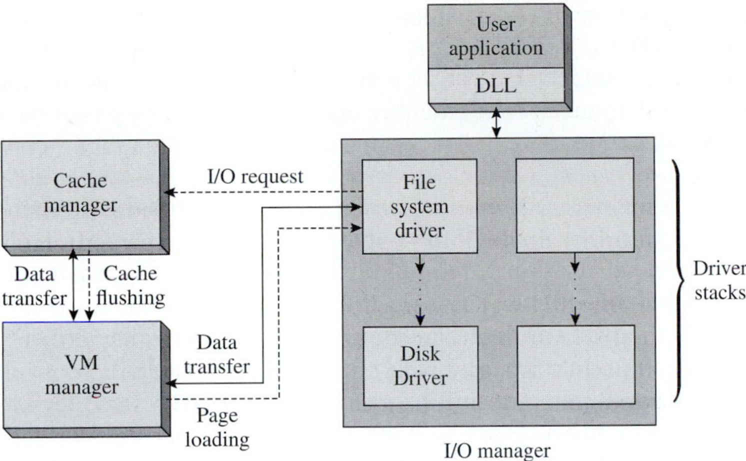

Figure 14.26 File processing in Windows.

a random file, the VACB index array would contain pointers to VACBs that cover several recent accesses made to the file.

An I/O operation is performed by a *layered device driver*. It is represented as a linked list of device drivers called a *driver stack*. When a thread requests an I/O operation, the I/O manager constructs an *I/O request packet* (IRP) for it and passes it to the first device driver in the appropriate driver stack. The device driver may perform the complete I/O operation itself, write a status code in the IRP, and pass it back to the I/O manager. Alternatively, it may decide on additional actions required to complete the I/O operation, write their information in the IRP, and pass the IRP to the next device driver in the stack, and so on, until the I/O operation actually gets implemented. This model permits device drivers to be added to provide additional features in the I/O subsystem. For example, a device driver could be added between the file system driver, which we discuss in the following, and the disk driver to perform disk mirroring. Such a driver is called a *filter driver*. Drivers such as the disk driver are called *function drivers*. They contain functionalities for initialization, scheduling, and initiation of I/O operations; interrupt servicing; and dynamic addition of new devices to facilitate the plug-and-play capability.

A file system is also implemented as a *file system driver* (FSD). It invokes other drivers that implement the functionalities of the access method and the device drivers. This arrangement permits many file systems to coexist in the host. The I/O manager thus provides the functionalities of a virtual file system (see Section 13.13). When a subsystem DLL linked to a thread requests a file operation, the I/O manager invokes an appropriate file system driver to handle the request. The request typically contains the byte offset of the file data involved in the I/O operation. The file system driver consults the file map table for the concerned file, which is accessible from the file's base file record in the master file table (MFT), to convert the byte offset within the file into a byte offset within a data block on a device and invokes the device driver for it. If the concerned device is a RAID, the device driver is actually a *volume manager*, which manages the RAID. It converts the byte offset within a data block into one or more units containing a disk number, sector number, and a byte offset and passes the request to the disk driver. Windows supports *striped volumes*, which are level 0 RAID systems, *mirrored volumes*, which are level 1 RAID systems, and level 5 RAID systems in this manner. It supports *spanned volumes* described in section 13.14.4 analogously.

When a thread makes a request to read from a file, the I/O manager passes this request to the file system driver, which passes it to the cache manager. The cache manager consults the VACB index array for the file and determines whether the required bytes of the file are a part of some view in the cache. If not, it allocates a cache block, creates a view that covers the required bytes from the file in the cache block, and constructs a VACB for it. This operation involves reading the relevant part of the file into the cache block. The cache manager now copies the required data from the cache block into the caller's address space. Converse actions are performed at a write request. If a page fault arises while copying data to or from the caller's address space, the virtual memory manager invokes the disk driver through the file system to read the required page into the memory. This operation is performed in a noncached manner. Thus, a file system must support both cached and noncached file I/O. To facilitate efficient manipulation of metadata, the file system driver uses kernel-level read/write operations, which access the data directly in the cache instead of first copying it to/from the logical address space of the file system driver.

The cache manager keeps information about the last few I/O requests on a file. If it can detect a pattern from them, such as sequential accesses to the file, it prefetches the next few data blocks according to this pattern. It also accepts *hints* from user applications concerning the nature of file processing activities and uses them for the same purpose. File updates take place in an asynchronous manner. The data to be written into a file is reflected into the view of the file held in the cache manager. Once every second, the *lazy writer*, which is a system thread created by the cache manager, queues one-quarter of the dirty pages in the cache for writing on a disk and nudges the virtual memory manager to write out the data.

Recall that an OS typically finds out the devices connected to it at boot time and builds its device data structures accordingly. This arrangement is restrictive, as it requires rebooting of the system when a device is to be connected to it or disconnected from it. Windows supports a plug-and-play (PnP) capability which permits devices to be connected and disconnected to the system dynamically. It is achieved by coordinating the operation of I/O hardware, the operating system and the concerned device driver. The hardware cooperates with the boot software to construct the initial list of devices connected to the system, and also coordinates with the PnP manager when devices are added or disconnected. The PnP manager loads a device driver for a new device if necessary, determines the resources such as specific interrupt numbers that may be required for its operation, and ensures the absence of conflicts by assigning or reassigning required resources. It now initializes the device driver for the new device and reinitializes any other devices that may have been affected by the reorganization.

Windows Vista has a new feature that addresses a problem area in disk scheduling: Disk scheduling treats all I/O operations uniformly while trying to improve the throughput of a disk. Thus, occasionally I/O operations of low-priority processes may be favored over other I/O operations, which would cause delays in high-priority processes and degrade responsiveness of applications that spawned them. The Vista feature called *prioritized I/O* provides a method of striking the correct balance between throughput and responsiveness. Using this feature, an application can specify a priority for its I/O operations. It can make a system call to lower its I/O priority to *background* so that its I/O operations would not have priority over those of nonbackground processes, and can revert to its original priority through another system call when desired. A device driver checks the priority of the process that issued an I/O operation and sets flags in an IRP to indicate whether the I/O operation should be treated at a low priority.

14.14 SUMMARY

During a file processing activity, the file system implements sharing and protection of files, while the *input output control system* (IOCS) actually implements file operations. The IOCS is itself structured into two layers called *access methods* and *physical IOCS* that ensure good performance of a file processing activity, and good throughput of I/O devices, respectively. In this chapter, we studied the techniques employed by the access methods and the physical IOCS.

Good throughput of an I/O device is achieved through joint actions of the I/O device and the IOCS. The I/O device is designed such that it is reliable, and I/O operations incur short *access time*—which is the time spent in positioning the I/O media or the read–write heads prior to data transfer—and achieve high data transfer rates. *Data staggering* techniques, *disk attachment technologies*, and *redundant arrays of inexpensive disks* (RAID) are relevant in this context.

Even with fast access and high data transfer rates of I/O devices, a process performing an I/O operation incurs considerable *wait time* until the I/O operation completes. The physical IOCS provides two basic capabilities to enhance system performance: It blocks a process until its I/O operation has completed, which enables the kernel to switch the CPU to another process. It uses *disk scheduling* to perform the I/O operations directed at a disk in an order that would reduce the movement of read–write heads of the disk, which increases the throughput of the disk and reduces the average wait time of I/O operations.

An *access method* improves the performance of a file processing activity within a process through the techniques of *buffering* and *blocking* of records. A *buffer* is a memory area used to temporarily hold data that has been read off a device or that is to be written on it. For an input file, the technique of buffering tries to prefetch the data so that it would be available to a process without having to perform an I/O operation, which reduces or eliminates the wait time. For an output file, it copies the data into the buffer and lets the process continue its operation; the actual writing is performed later. The technique of blocking reads more data off a device in a single I/O operation than required by a process at a time; it reduces the number of I/O operations to be performed.

Caching is the technique of keeping some of the file data in memory, so that it can be accessed without having to perform an I/O operation.

Caching reduces the number of I/O operations performed to access data stored in files, thereby improving performance of file processing activities in processes and also improving performance of the system. The physical IOCS implements a *disk cache* to reduce the number of I/O operations performed for accessing the files stored on a disk. An access method implements a *file cache* to reduce the number of I/O operations performed during the processing of an individual file in a process.

The virtual memory handler also uses a cache called a *page cache*, which contains pages of processes, to improve virtual memory performance. However, since the swap areas of processes are implemented on a disk, use of the page cache and the disk cache involves copying of pages between the two caches, which consumes CPU time and ties up memory because of multiple copies of a page. Operating systems therefore use a *unified disk cache* to reduce copying and eliminate the need for multiple copies of pages.

TEST YOUR CONCEPTS

14.1 Classify each of the following statements as true or false:

a. When parity bits are used for reliable recording/reading of data, an error correction code requires more parity bits than an error detection code.

b. Restricting the disk space allocation for a file to a *cylinder group*—which is a group of consecutive cylinders on a disk—reduces disk head movement while the file is processed.

c. RAID level 4, which uses block-interleaved parity, provides parallelism between small I/O operations.

d. Blocking of records speeds up processing of sequential files.

e. Buffering of records speeds up processing of direct-access files.

f. The SCAN disk scheduling policy suffers from starvation.

g. The physical IOCS provides a method to avoid the busy wait condition while a process awaits completion of its I/O operation.

h. If $t_x < t_p$, it is possible to reduce t_w to t_c through appropriate buffering and blocking.

i. Using a blocking factor of m reduces the effective I/O time per logical record by a factor of m.

14.2 Select the correct alternative in each of the following questions:

a. A disk cache is used to

i. Reduce the number of I/O operations on a disk

ii. Increase the capacity of a disk

iii. None of (i)–(ii)

b. Data staggering techniques are used to

i. Reduce the number of disk operations while a file is processed

ii. Reduce disk head movement between disk blocks having adjoining addresses

iii. Reduce rotational delays while disk blocks having adjoining addresses are accessed.

iv. Improve effectiveness of buffering and blocking of file records

c. Disk scheduling

i. Reduces the number of I/O operations performed on a disk

ii. Reduces the average disk head movement per I/O operation

iii. Aims at speeding up processing of a file

d. A program executes a read statement on a file `alpha` 100 times during its execution; however only 50 I/O operations are actually performed to read data from the file `alpha`. This is possible if

i. The access method used for the file `alpha` employs buffering without blocking

ii. The access method does not employ blocking and the physical IOCS does not employ a disk cache

iii. Either the access method employs blocking or the physical IOCS employs a disk cache

EXERCISES

14.1 Explain how (and whether) buffering and blocking of records is beneficial for the following kinds of files:
   a. A sequential-access file
   b. An index sequential-access file
   c. A direct-access file

14.2 An *update* file is one that is read and modified during processing—a program reads a record, modifies it in memory, and writes it back into the file.
   a. Which I/O device is best suited for recording an update file?
   b. Is buffering and blocking of records useful for an update file?
   Justify your answers.

14.3 Discuss how the throughput of a disk device can be optimized in a file system that performs noncontiguous allocation of disk blocks to files. (*Hint:* Think of organization of blocks in the free list, data staggering, and cylinder groups.)

14.4 A sectored disk has the following characteristics:

Time for 1 revolution	= 8 ms
t_{sect}	= 1 ms
t_{st}	= 3 ms
Sector size	= 1024 bytes

Plot the peak disk throughput against the sector interleaving factor (F_{int}).

14.5 Comment on the effectiveness of (a) a disk cache and (b) a RAM disk for speeding up processing of sequential-access and direct-access files.

14.6 Requests for I/O operations on the following tracks are pending at time = 160 ms.

$$7, 45, 98, 70, 68, 180$$

If the requests are made in the above order, construct a table analogous to Table 14.16 for the disk of Example 14.3.

14.7 A *biased disk* is a hypothetical disk device whose seek time for track n is a linear function in n (for example, seek time $= 0.1 \times n$). $\{seq_i\}$ is the set of I/O operations requested over a certain period of time. Is the order in which I/O operations are scheduled on a biased disk by the SSTF algorithm identical to the order in which the same I/O operations would be scheduled by a SCAN algorithm on the conventional disk described in Example 14.3?

14.8 A process manipulates a sequential-access file. The I/O and processing times for each record in the file are as follows:

Access time of device	= 10 ms
Transfer time per record	= 6 ms
Largest number of records required together	= 5 records
Processing time per record	= 10 ms

   a. If two buffers are used, find the value of the smallest blocking factor that can minimize the wait time per record.
   b. If two buffers and a blocking factor of 5 are used, what is the minimum number of records that are present in memory at any time? (Assume that a process initiates an I/O operation on a buffer after processing the last record in it—see Figure 14.20.)

14.9 A sequential file is recorded by using blocking. A process manipulates it by using two buffers. The I/O and processing times are as follows:

Access time (average)	= 20 ms
Transfer time per record	= 5 ms
Largest number of records required together	= 5 records
Processing time per record	= 10 ms

Determine optimal values of the blocking factor and the number of buffers. What changes, if any, would you make in your design if the largest number of records that the process is likely to require together is (i) 3 records, (ii) 8 records? (*Hint:* See Example 14.4.)

14.10 One buffer is used in processing the file `info` of Exercise 13.6. Calculate the elapsed time of the process if the copying time per record is 0.5 ms. Explain your calculations.

14.11 Classify the following statement as true or false: "By judicious selection of the blocking factor and the number of buffers, it is always possible to reduce the wait time to t_c."

14.12 A process is expected to open a file before accessing it. If it tries to access a file without opening, the file system performs an open before implementing the access. A system programmers' handbook warns all programmers to open a file before accessing it or suffer a performance penalty. Explain the nature and causes of the performance penalty.

14.13 How do different disk scheduling algorithms influence the effectiveness of I/O buffering?

14.14 A process manipulates an input file using many buffers. Which of the following statements are accurate? Explain your reasoning.

a. "Of all the disk scheduling algorithms, FCFS disk scheduling is likely to provide the best elapsed time performance for the process."

b. "Data staggering is effective only during reading of the first few records in the file; it is not effective during reading of other records in the file."

14.15 A magnetic tape has a recording density of 80 bits/cm along a track. The tape moves at a velocity of 2 meters per second while reading/writing data. The inter-record gap is 0.5 cm wide, and the access time of the tape is 5 ms. A sequential file containing 5000 records, each of size 400 bytes, is stored on this magnetic tape. Calculate the length of the magnetic tape occupied by the file and the total I/O time required to read the file if the file is recorded (a) without blocking and (b) with a blocking factor of 4.

14.16 A process uses many buffers while manipulating a file containing blocked records. A system failure occurs during its execution. Is it possible to resume execution of the process from the point of failure?

14.17 The *speedup factor* resulting from the use of a special I/O technique is the ratio of the elapsed time of a process without blocking or buffering of records to the elapsed time of the same process with the special I/O technique. In Section 14.8, the speedup factor due to buffering was shown to have an upper bound of 2. Develop a formula for speedup factor when a process does not use buffers while processing a file containing blocked records. Can the value of this speedup factor exceed 2? If so, give an example.

14.18 Develop a formula for *speedup factor* when a process uses two buffers while processing a file containing blocked records and $t_p \geq t_x$.

14.19 Describe the implications of a file or disk cache for file system reliability. Unix supports a system call *flush*() that forces the kernel to write buffered output onto the disk. Can a programmer use *flush*() to improve the reliability of his files?

14.20 The `lseek` command of Unix indicates the offset of the next byte in a sequential-access file to be read or written. When a process wishes to perform a read or write operation, it issues an `lseek` command. This command is followed by an actual read or write command.

a. What are the advantages of using the `lseek` command?

b. What is the sequence of actions the file system and the IOCS should execute when a process issues an `lseek` command.

14.21 Show that division of the binary polynomial formed from $n_d + n_c$ bits in a record, where n_d is the number of data bits and n_c is the number of CRC bits, by the CRC polynomial will yield a 0 remainder. (*Hint:* A term of x^i, $i = 1, \ldots, n_d - 1$, in the polynomial for the n_d bits of data is the term of x^{i+n_c} in the polynomial for the $n_d + n_c$ bits in the record. Also note that modulo-2 addition and subtraction produce identical results.)

BIBLIOGRAPHY

Tanenbaum (1990) describes I/O hardware. Ruemmler and Wilkes (1994) presents a disk drive model that can be used for performance analysis and tuning. Teorey and Pinkerton (1972) and Hofri (1980) compare various disk scheduling algorithms, while Worthington et al. (1994) discusses disk scheduling for modern disk drives. Lumb et al. (2000) discusses how background activities like disk reorganization can be performed during mechanical positioning of disk heads for servicing foreground activities, and the effect of disk scheduling algorithms on effectiveness of this approach.

Chen and Patterson (1990) and Chen et al. (1994) describe RAID organizations, while Wilkes et al. (1996) and Yu et al. (2000) discuss enhancements to RAID systems. Alvarez et al. (1996) discusses how multiple failures can be tolerated in a RAID architecture, while Chau and Fu (2000) discusses a new layout method to evenly distribute parity information for declustered RAID. Gibson et al. (1997) discusses file servers for network-attached disks. Nagle et al. (1999) discusses integration of user-level networking with network-attached storage (NAS). Curtis Preston (2002) discusses NAS and storage area networks (SANs), while Clark (2003) is devoted to the SAN technology. Toigo (2000) discusses modern disks and future storage technologies.

Disk caching is discussed in Smith (1985). Braunstein et al. (1989) discusses how file accesses are speeded up when virtual memory hardware is used to look up the file buffer cache.

McKusick et al. (1996) discusses the Berkeley fast file system for Unix 4.4BSD. Bach (1986) and Vahalia (1996) discuss other Unix file systems. Ruemmler and Wilkes (1993) presents performance studies concerning various characteristics of disk accesses made in the Unix file system. Beck et al. (2002) and Bovet and Cesati (2005) discuss the I/O schedulers of Linux. Love (2004, 2005) describes the I/O schedulers in Linux 2.6. Custer (1994) describes the Windows NT file system, while Russinovich and Solomon (2005) discusses NTFS for Windows.

1. Alvarez, G. A., W. A. Burkhard, F. Cristian (1996): "Tolerating multiple failures in RAID architectures with optimal storage and uniform declustering," *Proceedings of the 24th Annual International Symposium on Computer Architecture*, 62–72.
2. Bach, M. J. (1986): *The design of the Unix operating system*, Prentice-Hall, Englewood Cliffs, N.J.
3. Beck, M., H. Bohme, M. Dziadzka, U. Kunitz, R. Magnus, C. Schroter, and D. Verworner (2002): *Linux Kernel Programming*, Pearson Education, New York.
4. Bovet, D. P., and M. Cesati (2005): *Understanding the Linux Kernel,* 3rd ed., O'Reilly, Sebastopol, Calif.
5. Braunstein, A., M. Riley, and J. Wilkes (1989): "Improving the efficiency of Unix buffer caches," *ACM Symposium on OS Principles*, 71–82.
6. Chau, A., and A. W. Fu (2000): "A gracefully degradable declustered RAID architecture with near optimal maximal read and write parallelism," *Cluster Computing*, **5** (1), 97–105.
7. Chen, P. M., and D. Patterson (1990): "Maximizing performance in a striped disk array," *Proceedings of 17th Annual International Symposium on Computer Architecture*, May 1990.
8. Chen, P. M., E. K. Lee, G. A. Gibson, R. H. Katz, and D. A. Patterson (1994): "RAID—high performance, reliable secondary storage," *Computing Surveys*, **26** (2), 145–186.
9. Clark, T. (2003): *Designing Storage Area Networks: A Practical Reference for Implementing Fibre Channel and IP SANS*, 2nd ed., Addison Wesley Professional.
10. Curtis Preston, W. (2002): *Using SANs and NAS*, O'Reilly, Sebastopol,Calif.
11. Custer, H. (1994): *Inside the Windows NT File System*, Microsoft Press, Redmond,Wash.
12. Gibson, G. A., D. Nagle, K. Amiri, F. W. Chang, E. M. Feinberg, H. Gobioff, C. Lee, B. Ozceri, E. Riedel, D. Rochberg, and J. Zelenka (1997): "File server scaling with network-attached secure disks," *Measurement and Modeling of Computer Systems*, 272–284.
13. Hofri, M. (1980): "Disk scheduling: FCFS *vs.* SSTF revisited," *Communications of the ACM*, **23** (11), 645–53.
14. Iyer, S., and P. Druschel (2001): "Anticipatory scheduling: a disk scheduling framework to overcome deceptive idleness in synchronous I/O," *Proceedings of the 18th ACM Symposium on Operating Systems Principles*.
15. Lampson, B. (1981): "Atomic transactions," in *Distributed Systems—Architecture and Implementation: An Advanced Course*, Goos, G. and J. Hartmanis (eds.), Springer Verlag, Berlin, 246–265.
16. Love, R. (2004): "I/O schedulers," *Linux Journal*, **118**.
17. Love, R. (2005): *Linux Kernel Development,* 2nd ed., Novell Press.
18. Lumb, C. R., J. Schindler, G. R. Ganger, and D. F. Nagle (2000): "Towards higher disk head utilization: extracting free bandwidth from busy disk drives," *Proceedings of the 4th Symposium on Operating Systems Design and Implementation*.

19. McKusick, M. K., K. Bostic, M. J. Karels, and J. S. Quarterman (1996): *The Design and Implementation of the 4.4BSD Operating System*, Addison Wesley, Reading, Mass.
20. Nagle D., G. Ganger, J. Butler, G. Gibson, and C. Sabol (1999): "Network support for network-attached storage," *Proceedings of Hot Interconnects*.
21. Ruemmler, C., and J. Wilkes (1993): "Unix disk access patterns," *Proceedings of the Winter 1993 USENIX Conference*, 405–420.
22. Ruemmler, C., and J. Wilkes (1994): "An introduction to disk drive modeling," *IEEE Computer*, **27** (3), 17–29.
23. Russinovich, M. E., and D. A. Solomon (2005): *Microsoft Windows Internals,* 4th ed., Microsoft Press, Redmond, Wash.
24. Smith, A. J. (1985): "Disk cache-miss ratio analysis and design considerations," *ACM Transactions on Computer Systems*, **3** (3), 161–203.
25. Tanenbaum, A. S. (1990): *Structured Computer Organization*, 3rd ed., Prentice Hall, Englewood Cliffs, N. J.
26. Teorey, T. J., and T. B. Pinkerton (1972): "A comparative analysis of disk scheduling policies," *Communications of the ACM*, **15** (3), 177–184.
27. Toigo, J. (2000): "Avoiding a data crunch," *Scientific American*, **282** (5), 58–74.
28. Vahalia, U. (1996): *Unix Internals—The New Frontiers*, Prentice Hall, Englewood Cliffs, N. J.
29. Wilkes, J., R. Golding, C. Staelin, and T. Sullivan (1996): "The HP autoRAID hierarchical storage system," *ACM Transactions on Computer Systems*, **14** (1), 108–136.
30. Worthington, B. L., G. R. Ganger, and Y. N. Patt (1994): "Scheduling algorithms for modern disk drives," *Proceedings of the 1994 ACM Sigmetrics Conference on Measurement and Modeling of Computer Systems*, 241–251.
31. Yu, X., B. Gum, Y. Chen, R. Y. Wang, K. Li, A. Krishnamurthy, and T. E. Anderson (2000): "Trading capacity for performance in a disk array," *Proceedings of the 2000 Symposium on Operating Systems Design and Implementation*, 243–258.

Chapter 15

Security and Protection

Operating systems employ security and protection measures to prevent a person from illegally using resources in a computer system, or interfering with them in any manner. These measures ensure that data and programs are used only by authorized users and only in a desired manner, and that they are neither modified nor denied to authorized users. *Security* measures deal with threats to resources that come from outside a computer system, while *protection* measures deal with internal threats.

Passwords are the principal security tool. A password requirement thwarts attempts by unauthorized persons to masquerade as legitimate users of a system. The confidentiality of passwords is upheld by *encryption*.

Computer users need to share data and programs stored in files with collaborators, and here is where an operating system's *protection* measures come in. The owner of a file informs the OS of the specific *access privileges* other users are to have—whether and how others may access the file. The operating system's protection function then ensures that all accesses to the file are strictly in accordance with the specified access privileges.

We begin by discussing how different kinds of security breaches are carried out: *Trojan horses*, *viruses*, *worms*, and *buffer overflows*. Their description is followed by a discussion of encryption techniques. We then describe three popular protection structures called *access control lists*, *capability lists*, and *protection domains*, and examine the degree of control provided by them over sharing of files. In the end, we discuss how security classifications of computer systems reflect the degree to which a system can withstand security and protection threats.

15.1 OVERVIEW OF SECURITY AND PROTECTION

Ensuring noninterference with the computations and resources of users is one of the three fundamental goals of an OS mentioned in Section 1.2. A resource could be a hardware resource such as an I/O device, a software resource such as a program or data stored in a file, or a service offered by the OS. Several kinds of interference can arise during operation of a computer system; we call each of them a *threat*. Some of the threats depend on the nature of specific resources or services and the manner of their use, while others are of a generic nature.

Unauthorized access to resources is an obvious threat in an OS. Persons who are not registered users of a computer system may try to access its resources, while registered users may try to access resources that they have not been authorized to use. Such persons may maliciously try to corrupt or destroy a resource. This is a potent threat for programs and data stored in files. A less obvious threat is interference in legitimate access of resources and services by users. It tends to disrupt computational activities of users by preventing them from using resources and services of an OS. This threat is called *denial of service*. In this chapter, we discuss how an OS counters generic threats and threats concerning programs and data stored in files.

Operating systems use two categories of techniques to counter threats to data and programs:

- *Security* measures guard a user's data and programs against interference from persons or programs outside the operating system; we broadly refer to such persons and their programs as *nonusers*.
- *Protection* measures guard a user's data and programs against interference from other users of the system.

Table 15.1 describes two key methods used by operating systems for implementing security and protection. *Authentication*, which is aimed at security, consists of verifying the identity of a person. Computer-based authentication rests on either of two kinds of assumptions. One common assumption is that a person is the user he claims to be if he knows something that only the OS and the user are expected to know, e.g., a password. It is called *authentication by knowledge*. The other authentication method relies on things that only the user is assumed to possess. For example, *biometric authentication* is based on some unique and inalterable biological feature such as fingerprints, retina, or iris. *Authorization* is the key method of implementing protection. It consists of: (1) granting an *access*

Table 15.1 **Terminology Used in Security and Protection of Information**

Term	Explanation
Authentication	Authentication is verification of a user's identity. Operating systems most often perform authentication *by knowledge*. That is, a person claiming to be some user X is called upon to exhibit some knowledge shared only between the OS and user X, such as a password.
Authorization	Authorization has two aspects: **1.** Granting a set of access privileges to a user; for example, some users may be granted read and write privileges for a file, while others are granted read-only privileges, **2.** Verifying a user's right to access a resource in a specific manner.

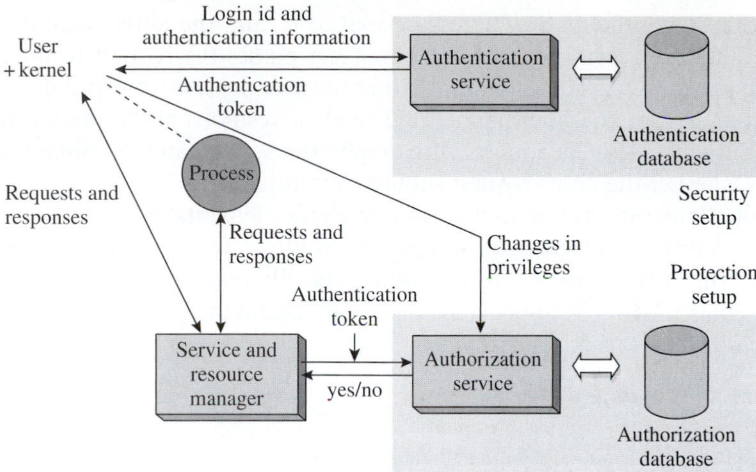

Figure 15.1 Generic security and protection setups in an operating system.

privilege for a resource to a user, which is a right to access the resource in the specified manner (see Chapter 13), and (2) determining whether a user possesses the right to access a resource in a specific manner.

Figure 15.1 shows a generic scheme for implementing security and protection in an operating system. The security setup is shown in the dashed box in the upper part of the figure. It consists of the *authentication service* and the *authentication database*. The authentication database contains a pair of the form (login id, validating information) for every registered user of the operating system, where the validating information is typically an encrypted form of a user's password. To log into the system, a person submits his login id and password to the kernel. The kernel passes this information to the authentication service, which encrypts the password and compares it with the validating information for the user stored in the authentication database. If the check succeeds, the authentication service generates an *authentication token* for the user and passes it back to the kernel. The authentication token is typically the user id assigned to the user. Whenever the user or a process initiated by the user makes a request to access a resource, the kernel appends the user's authentication token to the request to facilitate making of protection checks.

The protection setup is shown in the dashed box in the lower part of Figure 15.1. It consists of the *authorization service* and the *authorization database*. The *authorization database* contains triples of the form (authentication token, resource id, privileges). When a user wishes to grant access privileges for one of his files to some users, or withdraw some previously granted access privileges for the file, he makes a request to the kernel. As shown in Figure 15.1, the kernel passes on the request to the authorization service along with the authentication token for the user. The authorization service now makes appropriate changes in the authorization database. To access a resource, a user or his process makes a resource request to the *service and resource manager*. The request contains the id of a resource, the kind of access desired to it, and the authentication token of the user. The service and resource manager passes the request to the authorization service, which determines whether the user possesses the privilege to use the resource in the desired manner and sends a yes/no reply to the service and resource manager. Depending on this reply, the service and resource manager decides whether the user's request should be granted.

Not all operating systems incorporate all the elements shown in Figure 15.1 in their security and protection setups. For example, in most modern operating systems, the authorization information is typically maintained and used by the file system, so the operating system does not maintain the authorization database and does not perform authorization.

The distinction between security and protection provides a neat separation of concerns for the OS. In a conventional operating system, the security concern is limited to ensuring that only registered users can use the system. A security check is performed when a person logs in. It decides whether the person is a user of the OS and determines his user id. Following this check, all threats to information stored in the system are protection concerns; the OS uses the user id of a person to determine whether he can access a specific file in the OS. In a distributed system, however, security concerns are more complex because of the presence of the networking component (see Chapter 21). We confine the discussion in this chapter to conventional operating systems only.

Mechanisms and Policies Table 15.2 describes mechanisms and policies in security and protection. Security policies specify whether a person should be allowed to use a system. Protection policies specify whether a user should be allowed to access a specific file. Both these policies are applied outside the OS domain—a system administrator decides whether a person should be allowed to become a user of a system, and a user specifies what users may access his files. Security and protection mechanisms implement these policies by maintaining the authentication and authorization databases and using their contents to make specific checks during system operation.

Table 15.2 Policies and Mechanisms in Security and Protection

Security	• *Policy:* Whether a person can become a user of the system. The system administrator employs the policy while registering new users. • *Mechanisms:* Add or delete users, verify whether a person is a registered user (i.e., perform authentication), perform encryption to ensure confidentiality of passwords.
Protection	• *Policy:* The file owner specifies the authorization policy for a file. It decides which user can access a file and in what manner. • *Mechanisms:* Set or change authorization information for a file. Check whether a file processing request conforms to the user's privileges.

Table 15.3 Goals of Computer Security and Protection

Goal	Description
Secrecy	Only authorized users should be able to access information. This goal is also called *confidentiality*.
Privacy	Information should be used only for the purposes for which it was intended and shared.
Authenticity	It should be possible to verify the source or sender of information, and also verify that the information has been preserved in the form in which it was created or sent.
Integrity	It should not be possible to destroy or corrupt information, for example, by erasing a disk.

15.1.1 Goals of Security and Protection

Table 15.3 describes the four goals of security and protection, namely, *secrecy, privacy, authenticity*, and *integrity* of information.

Of the four goals, only *privacy* is exclusively a protection concern. An OS addresses privacy through the authorization service and the service and resource manager (see Figure 15.1). The authorization service verifies whether a user possesses the privilege to access a resource in a specific manner, and the service and resource manager disallows requests that do not conform to a user's privileges. It is up to users to ensure privacy of their information by using this setup. A user who wishes to share his data and programs with a few other users should set the authorization for his information according to the well-known *need-to-know* principle: Only those persons who need to use some information for a legitimate function should be authorized to access it.

Secrecy, authenticity, and *integrity* are both protection and security concerns. As protection concerns, secrecy, authenticity, and integrity are easy to satisfy because the identity of a user would have already been verified and the service and resource manager would use the authorization information, which is a part of the protection setup shown in Figure 15.1. However, elaborate arrangements are needed to satisfy secrecy, authenticity, and integrity as security concerns. These are discussed in Chapter 21.

15.1.2 Security and Protection Threats

To see how and when security and protection threats arise in an OS, first consider a conventional OS. Its authentication procedures ensure that only registered users can log into the system and initiate processes. Hence the OS knows which user has initiated a specific process, and with that knowledge it can readily check whether a process should be allowed to use a specific resource. When processes communicate with other processes, OS actions concerning communication are also confined to the same computer system. Hence an illegal access to a resource or a service by a process and an attempt to tamper with messages are both protection threats rather than security threats.

The situation is different when a system has an Internet connection and a user downloads data or programs from the Internet. Some person or programs external to the OS may be able to corrupt the data and programs being downloaded. Threats raised by such data and programs are, by definition, security threats.

Security threats can arise more easily in a distributed OS. An interprocess message may cross boundaries between nodes as it travels between a sender and a receiver. Communication between nodes takes place over open communication links, including public links. Hence it is possible for an external entity to tamper with messages. We discuss measures to counter such threats in Chapter 21.

15.2 SECURITY ATTACKS

Attempts to breach the security of a system are called *security attacks*, and the person or the program making the attack is called an *adversary* or *intruder*. Two common forms of security attacks are:

- *Masquerading:* Assuming the identity of a registered user of the system through illegitimate means.
- *Denial of service:* Preventing registered users of the system from accessing resources for which they possess access privileges.

In a successful *masquerading* attack, the intruder gains access to resources that the impersonated user is authorized to access, hence he can corrupt or destroy programs and data belonging to the impersonated user at will. The obvious way to launch a masquerading attack is to crack a user's password and use this knowledge to pass the authentication test at log in time. Another approach is to perform masquerading in a more subtle manner through programs that are imported into a software environment. We discuss this approach in Section 15.2.1.

A *denial-of-service* attack, also called a DoS attack, is launched by exploiting some vulnerability in the design or operation of an OS. A DoS attack can be launched through several means; some of these means can be employed only by users of a system, while others may be employed by intruders located in other systems. Many of these means are legitimate, which makes it easy to launch DoS attacks and hard for an OS to detect and prevent them. For example, a DoS attack can be launched by overloading a resource through phantom means to such an extent that genuine users of the resource are denied its use. If the kernel of an OS limits the total number of processes that can be created in order to control pressure on kernel data structures, a user may create a large number of processes so that no other users can create processes. Use of network sockets may be similarly denied by opening a large number of sockets. A DoS attack can also be launched by corrupting a program that offers some service, or by destroying some configuration information within the kernel, e.g., use of an I/O device can be denied by changing its entry in the physical device table of the kernel (see Section 14.5.2).

A *network DoS attack* may be launched by flooding the network with messages intended for a particular server so that network bandwidth is denied to genuine messages, and the server is so busy receiving messages that it cannot get around to responding to any messages. A *distributed DoS attack* is one that is launched by a few intruders located in different hosts in the network; it is even harder to detect and prevent than a nondistributed one.

Many other security attacks are launched through the message communication system. Reading of messages without authorization, which is also called *eavesdropping*, and tampering with messages are two such attacks. These attacks primarily occur in distributed operating systems, so we discuss them in Chapter 21.

15.2.1 Trojan Horses, Viruses, and Worms

Trojan horses, viruses, and *worms* are programs that contain some code that can launch a security attack when activated. Table 15.4 summarizes their characteristics. A Trojan horse or a virus enters a system when an unsuspecting user downloads programs over the Internet or from a disk. On the contrary, a worm existing in one computer system spreads to other computer systems by itself.

A *Trojan horse* is a program that has a hidden component that is designed to cause havoc in a computer system. For example, it can erase a hard disk in the computer, which is a violation of integrity; collect information for masquerading; or force a system to crash or slow down, which amounts to denial of service. A typical example of a Trojan horse is a spoof login program, which provides a fake login prompt to trick a user into revealing his password, which can be used later for masquerading. Since a Trojan horse is loaded explicitly by an unsuspecting user, it is not difficult to track its authorship or origin.

Table 15.4 **Security Threats through Trojan Horses, Viruses, and Worms**

Threat	Description
Trojan horse	A program that performs a legitimate function that is known to an OS or its users, and also has a hidden component that can be used later for nefarious purposes like attacks on message security or masquerading.
Virus	A piece of code that can attach itself to other programs in the computer system and spread to other computer systems when programs are copied or transferred.
Worm	A program that spreads to other computer systems by exploiting security holes in an OS like weaknesses in facilities for creation of remote processes.

A *virus* is a piece of code that infects other programs and spreads to other systems when the infected programs are copied or transferred. A virus called an *executable virus* or file virus causes infection as follows: The virus inspects the disk, selects a program for infection, and adds its own code, which we will call the *viral code*, to the program's code. It also modifies the program's code such that the viral code is activated when the program is executed. A simple way to achieve it is to modify the first instruction in the program's code, i.e., the instruction whose address is the execution start address of the program (see Section 11.3), to transfer control to the viral code. When the viral code gets activated, it inspects the disk looking for other programs to infect. After infecting these programs, it passes control to the genuine code of the program. Since the infection step does not consume much CPU time and the infected program's functioning is not affected, a user has no way of knowing whether a program has been infected. The way a virus attaches itself to another program makes it far more difficult to track than a Trojan horse.

A virus typically sets up a *back door* that can be exploited for a destructive purpose at a later date. For example, it may set up a daemon that remains dormant until it is activated by a trigger, which could be a specific date, time, or message, and performs some destructive acts when activated. Different categories of viruses infect and replicate differently. Apart from the file virus described above, a *boot-sector virus* plants itself in the boot sector of a hard or floppy disk. Such a virus gets an opportunity to execute when the system is booted, and gets an opportunity to replicate when a new bootable disk is made.

Executable and boot-sector viruses thrived when programs were loaded through floppies. Use of CDs that cannot be modified has curtailed their menace. However, newer viruses have switched to more sophisticated techniques to breach a computer's defenses. An *e-mail virus* enters a computer system through an e-mail and sends spurious mails to users whose e-mail ids can be found in an address book. The Melissa virus of 1999 used a viral code that was a Word document posted on an Internet newsgroup. The virus was triggered when a user opened a downloaded copy of the Word document, and it sent the document itself to 50 persons whose e-mail id's were found in the user's address book. The back door in this case was a tiny code fragment that was associated with the Word document using the language called Visual Basic Application (VBA). It was triggered by the autoexecute feature of Microsoft Word, which automatically executes the program associated with a Word document when the document is opened. The I LOVE YOU virus of year 2000 was an e-mail virus that attached viral code as an attachment in an e-mail. This code executed when some user double-clicked on the attachment. It sent e-mails containing its own copies to several others and then corrupted files on the disk of the host where it executed. Both Melissa and I LOVE YOU viruses were so powerful that they forced large corporations to completely shut off their e-mail servers until the viruses could be contained.

Viruses use various techniques to escape detection by antivirus software. These techniques include changing their form, compressing or encrypting their code and data, hiding themselves in parts of the OS, etc.

A *worm* is a program that replicates itself in other computer systems by exploiting holes in their security setup. It is more difficult to track than a virus because of its self-replicating nature. Worms are known to replicate at unimaginably high rates, thus loading the network and consuming CPU time during replication. The Code Red worm of 2001 spread to a quarter of a million hosts in 9 hours, using a buffer overflow attack. The Morris worm of 1988 spread to thousands of hosts through three weaknesses in the Unix system:

- The Unix remote login facility *rsh* enabled a user to set up an arrangement through which he could log into a remote host without having to supply a password. The worm searched for files that stored names of remote hosts that could be accessed through *rsh* and used these files to move to remote hosts.
- The *buffer overflow* technique, described later in Section 15.2.2, forces a daemon on an unprotected server to accept and execute a piece of code. The Morris worm used this attack on the `finger` daemon of a remote Unix host to send its own code to the remote host and achieve its execution on that host.
- It used the debug facility in the `sendmail` program of Unix to mail a copy of its code to another host and execute it there.

The security attacks launched through Trojan horses, viruses, or worms can be foiled through the following measures:

- Exercising caution while loading new programs into a computer
- Using antivirus programs
- Plugging security holes as they are discovered or reported

Loading programs from original disks on which they are supplied by a vendor can eliminate a primary source of Trojan horses or viruses. This approach is particularly effective with the compact disk (CD) technology. Since such disks cannot be modified, a genuine program cannot be replaced by a Trojan horse, or a vendor-supplied disk cannot be infected by a virus.

Antivirus programs analyze each program on a disk to see if it contains any features analogous to any of the known viruses. The fundamental feature it looks for is whether the execution start address of the program has been modified or whether the first few bytes of a program perform actions resembling replication, e.g., whether they attach code to any programs on a disk.

OS vendors post information about security vulnerabilities of their operating systems on their websites periodically and provide security patches that seal these loopholes. A system administrator should check such postings and apply security patches regularly. It would foil security attacks launched through worms.

15.2.2 The Buffer Overflow Technique

The *buffer overflow* technique can be employed to force a server program to execute an intruder-supplied code to breach the host computer system's security. It has been used to a devastating effect in mail servers and other Web servers. The basic idea in this technique is simple: Most systems contain a fundamental vulnerability—some programs do not validate the lengths of inputs they receive from users or other programs. Because of this vulnerability, a buffer area in which such input is received may overflow and overwrite contents of adjoining areas of memory. On hardware platforms that use stacks that grow downward in memory, e.g., the Intel 80x86 architecture, such overflows provide an opportunity to execute a piece of code that is disguised as data put in the buffer. This code could launch a variety of security attacks.

Figure 15.2 illustrates how an intruder can launch a security attack through the buffer overflow technique. A Web server is in operation. When one of its

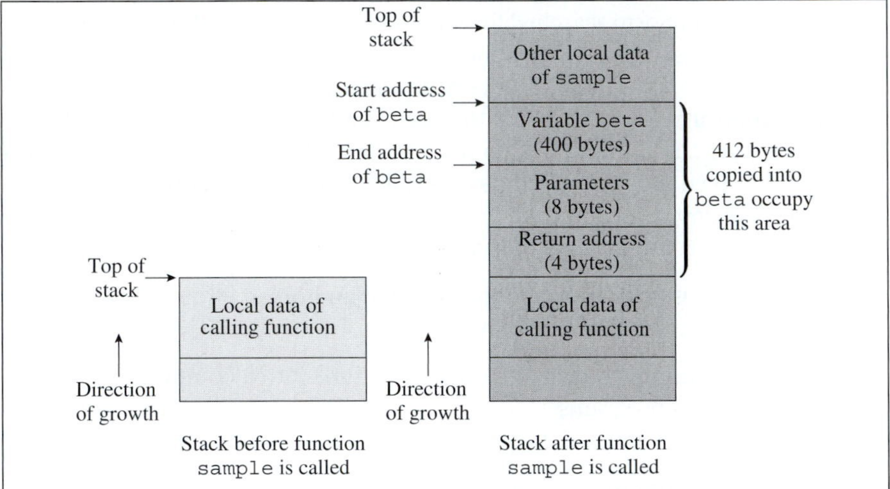

How a buffer overflow can be used to launch a security attack

1. The stack grows downward, i.e., toward smaller addresses in memory. It looks as shown on the left before the currently executing function calls function `sample`.
2. The code of the calling function pushes a return address and two parameters of `sample` onto the stack. Each of these occupies four bytes.
3. The code of `sample` allocates the variable `beta` and other variables on the stack. The stack now looks as shown on the right. Notice that the start address of `beta` is at the low end of the memory allocated to it. The end address of `beta` adjoins the last byte of the parameters.
4. The function `sample` copies 412 bytes into the variable `beta`. The first 408 bytes contain code whose execution would cause a security violation. Bytes 409–412 contain the start address of this code. These four bytes overwrite the return address in the stack.
5. The function `sample` executes a `return` statement. Control is transferred to the address found in the stack entry that is expected to contain the return address. Effectively, the code in variable `beta` is invoked. It executes with the privileges of the calling function.

Figure 15.2 Launching a security attack through the buffer overflow technique.

functions calls a function `sample` with two parameters, the stack is used for two purposes—to store a return address that would be used to resume execution of the calling function when `sample` completes its execution, and to pass the parameters to `sample`. We assume that the return address and each of the parameters occupy 4 bytes, and that the stack grows downward in memory, i.e., toward smaller addresses in memory. During execution, `sample` allocates space for its local variables on the stack. Thus a variable `beta`, which has a size of 400 bytes, adjoins the parameters on the stack. When invoked, `sample` accepts a message containing a request to the Web server and copies it into `beta`; however, it does not check to make sure that the message is not longer than 400 bytes. An intruder exploits this weakness by sending a message that is 412 bytes in length, such that the first 408 bytes contain some code and the last 4 bytes contain the start address of this code. When this message is copied into `beta`, its last 4 bytes would overwrite contents of the stack entry that holds the return address. When execution of `sample` completes, control would be passed to the address found in this stack entry. Thus, the intruder's code would be activated and would execute with the privileges of the Web server. This code could corrupt the Web server's code and files so that it does not respond to any requests, which would be a denial of service, or it could send out spurious mails.

How does an intruder know which Web server would fall prey to the buffer overflow technique and how many bytes should be provided so as to overwrite the return address? He could find out both these details through experimentation.

15.3 FORMAL ASPECTS OF SECURITY

To formally prove that a system can withstand all forms of security attacks, we need a security model comprising security policies and mechanisms, a list of threats, a list of fundamental attacks, and a proof methodology. The list of attacks must be provably complete in the sense that it should be possible to produce any threat in the list of threats through a combination of the fundamental attacks. The proof methodology should be capable of ascertaining whether the security model can withstand certain forms of attack.

Early work in security was performed along these lines. In the *take-grant model* of computer security (Landwehr [1981]), processes were given privileges for objects and for other processes. A privilege for an object entitled the holder of the privilege to access the object in a specific manner. A privilege for another process entitled the holder of the privilege to take an access privilege possessed by the other process (a *take* operation), or to transfer one of its own access privileges to the other process (a *grant* operation). The proof took the form of ascertaining whether a specific process could obtain a specific access privilege for a specific object through a series of take and grant operations. In the following example we discuss how a security flaw can be detected through the formal approach.

Example 15.1 Detection of a Security Flaw

In an organization employing military-like security, all documents are classified into three security levels—unclassified, confidential, and secret. Persons working in the organization are given security clearances called U (unclassified), C (confidential), and S (secret) with the proviso that a person can access all documents at his level of security classification and at lower levels of classification. Thus, a person with C classification can access confidential and unclassified documents, but is forbidden from accessing secret documents.

The organization uses a Unix system and persons in the organization use Unix features to access files containing documents. This way, it is expected that a program executed by a user can access a document at a specific security level only if the user possesses the appropriate security clearances. To check whether document security is foolproof, all operations in the system are modeled and a check is made to see whether a person can access a document that is at a higher level of classification than his security clearance. It is found that a combination of indiscriminate assignment of the "execute" privilege for programs to users and use of the *setuid* feature of Unix can enable a user to access a forbidden document. It can happen because the *setuid* feature permits a user to execute a program with the privileges of the program's owner (see Section 15.9.2), so if a user can execute a program owned by an individual with a higher security clearance, he can "take" the security clearance of the program's owner.

This security flaw can be eliminated by either forbidding use of the *setuid* feature or confining the "execute" privilege for a program only to users whose security clearance is not lower than that of the program's owner.

The security flaw in Example 15.1 could also have been discovered through manual procedures; however, manual procedures become less reliable as systems grow more complex. Formal methods construct feasible sequences of operations and deduce or verify their properties. This way they can discover sequences of operations that have disastrous consequences, or assert that such sequences of operations do not exist.

The formal approach also has some drawbacks. As the size of the system to be analyzed grows, the computing and storage requirements of formal methods exceed the capabilities of contemporary computer systems. The formal approach is also hard to apply because it requires a complete specification of a system and a comprehensive list of fundamental attacks; it is not possible to develop such a list for modern operating systems. It also requires a clear statement of security policies. This requirement is hard to meet because most security policies consist of rules that are informally stated so that everyone in an organization can understand them. However, this is where the formal approach contributes substantially to the field of security—it emphasizes the need for precise specifications.

15.4 ENCRYPTION

Encryption is application of an algorithmic transformation to data. When data is stored in its encrypted form, only a user or his process that knows how to recover the original form of data can use it. This feature helps in preserving *confidentiality* of data. Protection and security mechanisms use encryption to guard information concerning users and their resources; however, it could also be used to guard information belonging to users. *Cryptography* is the branch of science dealing with encryption techniques.

Table 15.5 summarizes key terms and definitions used in cryptography. The original form of data is called the *plaintext* form and the transformed form is called the *encrypted* or *ciphertext* form. We use the following notation:

P_d Plaintext form of data d
C_d Ciphertext form of data d

where $P_d \equiv d$. Encryption is performed by applying an encryption algorithm E with a specific encryption key k to data. Data is recovered by applying a decryption algorithm D with a key k'. In the simplest form of encryption called *symmetric encryption*, decryption is performed by using the same key k. In advanced encryption techniques called *asymmetric encryption*, a different key k' is used to decrypt a ciphertext.

Figure 15.3 illustrates symmetric encryption. We represent encryption and decryption of data by using algorithms E and D with key k as application of functions E_k and D_k, respectively. Thus,

$$C_d = E_k(d)$$
$$P_d = D_k(C_d)$$

Obviously the functions E_k and D_k must satisfy the relation

$$D_k(E_k(d)) = d, \text{ for all } d$$

Thus a process must be able to perform the transformation D_k in order to obtain the plaintext form of encrypted data.

In practice, encryption is performed by standard algorithms E and D. Hence, effectiveness of encryption depends on whether an intruder can determine the encryption key through trial and error. Later in this section, we see how it is impractical for an intruder to discover the encryption key because of the large number of trials involved; however, theoretically, it is not impossible to do so. This property makes encryption effective in a probabilistic sense, though not in an absolute sense. Confidentiality of encrypted data follows from this property.

Confidentiality provided through encryption also helps to verify integrity of data. If the encrypted form of data is tampered with by an intruder, its decryption by a process having the correct decryption algorithm and key would yield unintelligible data, which would reveal that it has been altered in an unauthorized manner. Because of this property of encrypted data, we use the term "decryption is unsuccessful" for the situation where decryption by the correct key yields unintelligible data.

Table 15.5 Cryptography Terms and Definitions

Term	Description
Encryption	Encryption is application of an algorithmic transformation E_k to data, where E is an *encryption algorithm* and k is an *encryption key*. It is used to protect confidentiality of data. The original data is recovered by applying a transformation $D_{k'}$, where D is a *decryption algorithm* and k' is a *decryption key*. A scheme using $k = k'$ is called *symmetric encryption*, and one using $k \neq k'$ is called *asymmetric encryption*.
Plaintext	Data to be encrypted.
Ciphertext	Encrypted form of plaintext.
Confusion	Shannon's principle of confusion requires that changes caused in a ciphertext due to a change in a plaintext should not be easy to find.
Diffusion	Shannon's principle of diffusion requires that the effect of a small substring in the plaintext should be spread widely in the ciphertext.
Attacks on cryptographic systems	An *attack* is a series of attempts by an intruder to find a decryption function D_k. In a *ciphertext only* attack, the intruder can examine only a set of ciphertexts to determine D_k. In a *known plaintext* attack, the intruder has an opportunity to examine the plaintext and ciphertext form of some data, whereas in a *chosen plaintext* attack the intruder can choose a plaintext and obtain its ciphertext form to perform the attack.
One-way function	A function, computation of whose inverse is expensive enough to be considered impractical. Its use as an encryption function makes cryptographic attacks difficult.
Block cipher	A block cipher technique substitutes fixed-size blocks of plaintext by blocks of ciphertext. It introduces some confusion, but does not introduce sufficient diffusion.
Stream cipher	Both a plaintext and the encryption key are considered to be bit streams. Bits in the plaintext are encrypted by using an equal number of bits in the encryption key. A stream cipher does not introduce confusion and introduces limited diffusion; however, some of its variants can introduce a high level of diffusion.
DES	The Data Encryption Standard of the National Bureau of Standards, adopted in 1976, uses a block cipher technique and provides cipher block chaining as an option. It contains 16 iterations, which perform complex transformations on the plaintext or the intermediate ciphertext.
AES	The Advanced Encryption Standard is the new standard adopted by the National Institute of Standards and Technology (formerly known as the National Bureau of Standards) in 2001. It performs between 10 and 14 rounds of operations, each involving only substitutions and permutations, on plaintext blocks of 128, 192, or 256 bits.

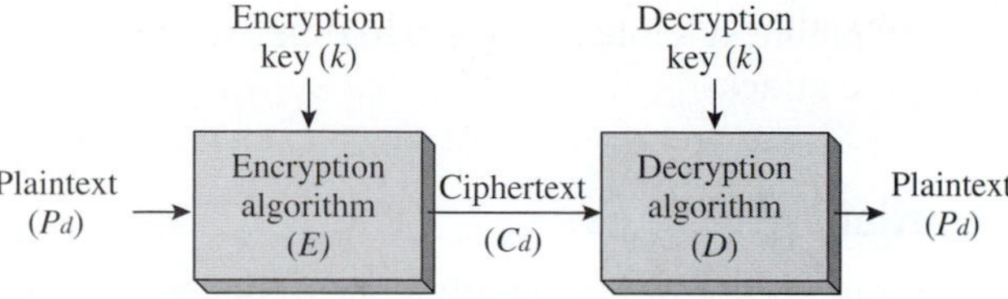

Figure 15.3 Symmetric encryption of data *d*.

15.4.1 Attacks on Cryptographic Systems

An attack on a cryptographic system consists of a series of attempts to find the decryption function D_k. Since $D_k(E_k(d)) = d$, D_k is the inverse of E_k. Hence an attack implies finding the inverse of E_k. If we define the *quality* of encryption to mean its ability to withstand attacks, the aim of an encryption technique is to perform high-quality encryption at a low cost. The encryption quality is best if the function E_k is a *one-way function*, i.e., if computation of its inverse through an attack involves an impractical amount of effort and time.

An intruder, who may be within an OS or outside it, can launch a variety of attacks on a cryptographic system. The nature of an attack depends on the position that an intruder can occupy within the system. If an intruder cannot invoke the encryption function and can only examine data in the ciphertext form, he has to depend on guesswork. This is a trial-and-error approach in which the function D_k is guessed repeatedly until its application to a ciphertext produces intelligible output. This attack is called an *exhaustive attack* because all possibilities for D_k may have to be tried out.

An exhaustive attack involves a very large number of trials. For example, 2^{55} trials would be needed to break an encryption scheme employing a 56-bit key by using an exhaustive attack. The huge number was believed to make such a scheme computationally secure, and the quality of encryption was believed to improve with an increase in the number of bits in an encryption key. However, powerful mathematical techniques like differential analysis may be employed to find D_k much more easily than in an exhaustive attack. Intruders may also employ the attacks described below that involve fewer trials than an exhaustive attack. We see examples of these attacks when we discuss password security in Section 15.5.

In the *ciphertext only attack*, an intruder has access only to a collection of ciphertexts. Consequently, to make the attack more efficient than an exhaustive attack, the intruder relies on clues extracted through analysis of strings in ciphertexts and information about features of plaintexts, such as whether they consist only of words in a dictionary. In the *known plaintext attack*, an intruder knows the plaintext corresponding to a ciphertext. This attack is feasible if an intruder can gain a position within the OS from which both a plaintext and the corresponding ciphertext can be observed. Collecting a sufficient number of plaintext–ciphertext pairs provides clues for determining D_k. In the *chosen plaintext attack*, an intruder is able to supply a plaintext and observe its encrypted form, i.e., choose a d and observe $E_k(d)$. It allows the intruder to systematically build a collection of plaintext–ciphertext pairs to support guessing and refinement of guesses during the attack.

15.4.2 Encryption Techniques

Encryption techniques differ in the way they try to defeat intruder attempts at finding D_k. The fundamental approach is to mask the features of a plaintext—i.e., ensure that a ciphertext does not reveal features of the corresponding plaintext—without incurring a very high cost of encryption.

Consider the simplest encryption technique, the classical *substitution cipher*, which substitutes each letter in a plaintext by some other letter of the alphabet. It does not mask features of a plaintext well enough; so *frequency analysis* provides a simple method for finding D_k : Arrange letters of the alphabet in the order of decreasing frequency of usage in a collection of ciphertexts. Take standard data for frequency of letters in English texts, and organize the letters in the order of decreasing frequency. Now, a good guess for D_k is a function that simply maps a letter of the first list into the corresponding letter of the second list.

So how to mask features of a plaintext during encryption? Shannon (1949) formulated two principles for design of high-quality encryption techniques. These principles are called *confusion* and *diffusion*. The confusion principle recommends that it should not be easy to find what changes would occur in the ciphertext due to a change in a plaintext. The diffusion principle recommends that the effect of a small substring in the plaintext should be spread throughout the ciphertext. These principles ensure that features of a plaintext are masked effectively, because individual parts of a plaintext and its ciphertext would not have a strong correlation between them. In the following, we describe four encryption schemes and discuss their confusion and diffusion properties.

Block Cipher The block cipher is an extension of the classical substitution cipher. It performs substitution of fixed-size blocks of a plaintext by ciphertext blocks of equal size. For example, a block consisting of, say, n bits is encrypted with a key k to obtain an n-bit block of the ciphertext (see Figure 15.4). These blocks are assembled to obtain the ciphertext. The block cipher technique is simple to implement. However, the confusion and diffusion introduced by it is confined to a block in the ciphertext. Hence identical blocks in a plaintext yield identical blocks in the ciphertext. This feature makes it vulnerable to an attack based on frequency analysis and known plaintext or chosen plaintext attacks. Larger values of n can be used to make such attacks less practical.

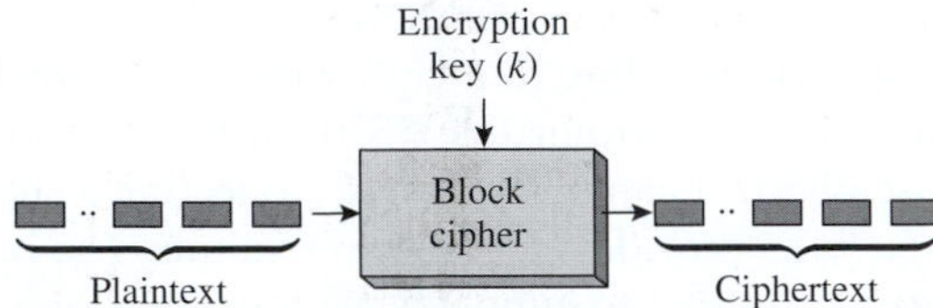

Figure 15.4 Block cipher.

Stream Cipher A stream cipher considers a plaintext as well as the encryption key to be streams of bits. Encryption is performed by using a transformation that involves a few bits of the plaintext and an equal number of bits of the encryption key. A popular choice of the transformation is a bit-by-bit transformation of a plaintext, typically by performing an operation like exclusive-OR on a bit of the plaintext and a bit of the encryption key.

A stream cipher is faster than a block cipher. It does not provide confusion or diffusion when a bit-by-bit transformation is used. A variant of this cipher, called a *vernam cipher*, uses a random stream of bits as the key stream, whose size exactly matches the size of the plaintext. Hence identical substrings in a plaintext do not lead to identical substrings in the ciphertext. The *one-time pad* that is famous for its use during the Second World War was actually a vernam cipher wherein a key stream was used to encode only one plaintext. It made the cipher unbreakable.

Variants of the stream cipher have been designed to introduce diffusion. Such a cipher operates as follows: An n-bit key stream is used to encrypt the first n bits of the plaintext. The next n bits of the key stream are the n bits of the ciphertext that were just produced, and so on until the complete plaintext is encrypted. Thus a substring in the plaintext influences encryption of the rest of the plaintext, which provides a high level of diffusion. This cipher is called a *ciphertext autokey* cipher (see Figure 15.5). If the key stream generator uses n bits of the plaintext that were just encrypted, instead of its ciphertext, the cipher is called a *self-synchronizing cipher*. The diffusion introduced by it is confined only to the next n bits of the ciphertext.

RC4 is a widely used stream cipher that uses a key stream that is a pseudorandom stream of bits. It uses a pseudorandom stream generator that is initialized by using a key generated by the key scheduling algorithm. It is fast, as it requires only between 8 and 16 machine operations to generate 1 byte in the key stream. It is used in the *Wired Equivalent Privacy* (WEP) protocol for security in wireless networks and its successor the *Wi-Fi Protected Access* (WPA) protocol, and in the *Secure Sockets Layer* (SSL) protocol for the Internet. The key scheduling algorithm of RC4 was shown to possess weaknesses, which led to breaking of the WEP and WPA protocols. However, its use in the SSL protocol is considered secure because the SSL protocol itself generates the key used to initialize the pseudorandom stream generator.

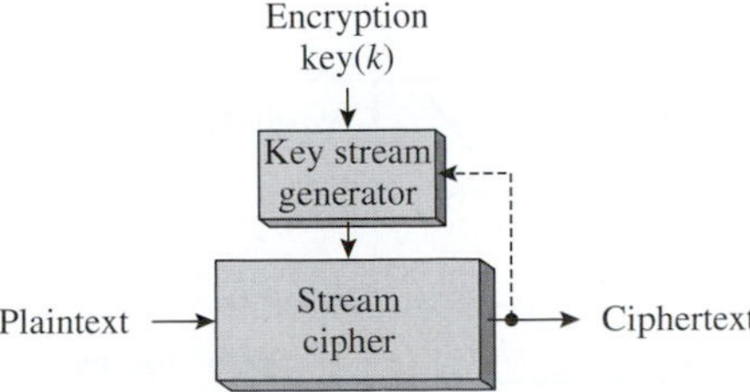

Figure 15.5 Ciphertext autokey cipher.

Data Encryption Standard (DES) DES was developed by IBM for the National Bureau of Standards. It uses a 56-bit key to encrypt 64-bit data blocks. Thus, it is a block cipher. However, to overcome the problem of poor diffusion, DES provides a *cipher block chaining* (CBC) mode. In this mode, the first block of plaintext is combined with an initial vector using an exclusive-OR operation and then enciphered. The resulting ciphertext is then combined with the second block of the plaintext using an exclusive-OR operation and then enciphered, and so on.

DES consists of three steps—the initial permutation step, the transformation step, and the final permutation step. The transformation step consists of 16 iterations. In each iteration the string input to the iteration is subjected to a complex transformation that involves a permutation operation on the string, which achieves diffusion, and a substitution operation through duplication and omission of some bits, which achieves confusion. Figure 15.6 illustrates operations performed in each iteration. In the first iteration, the input string is the plaintext. In all other iterations, the input string is the output of the previous iteration. The input string is split into two halves of 32 bits each. The right half of the input string becomes the left half of the result string, and a complex transformation involving the left and right halves is performed to obtain the right half of the result string.

Transformation of the right half of the input string consists of the following steps: The right half is first expanded to 48 bits by permuting its bits and duplicating some of them. It is combined with key K_i using an exclusive-OR operation (see the function f in Figure 15.6), where key K_i is derived by permuting the encryption key k, using the iteration number i. The result of this operation is split into eight groups of 6 bits each. Each 6-bit group is input to an S-box that substitutes a 4-bit group for it. The results of substitution are concatenated to obtain a 32-bit string that is permuted to obtain another 32-bit string. This string is combined with the left half of the input string, using an exclusive-OR operation to obtain the right half of the result string. The S-box introduces confusion. The permutation introduces diffusion, while the final exclusion-OR operation introduces confusion.

DES achieves both encryption and decryption by using the same sequence of steps, except that the keys are used in the reverse order during decryption; i.e., iteration i uses key K_{17-i} instead of key K_i. The 56-bit key length used in DES would have required 2^{55} trials in an exhaustive attack, which was considered a

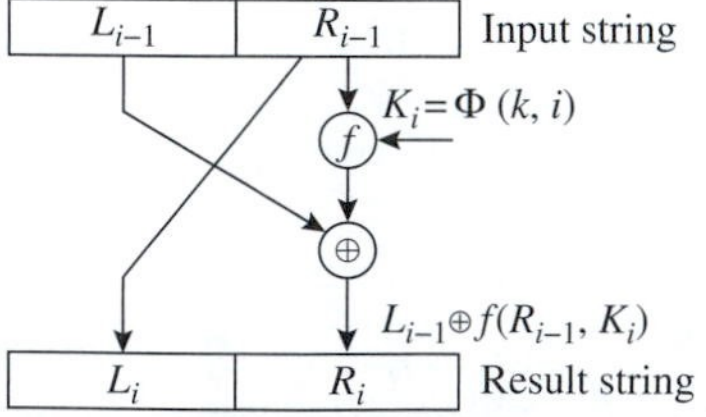

Figure 15.6 An iteration in DES ($\oplus$ indicates an exclusive-OR operation).

large enough number to defeat such attacks in the 1970s and 1980s. However, use of a small key length made DES vulnerable to attacks using modern technology. In 1998, a message encrypted through DES was broken in less than 3 days by a specially designed computer. In 1999, another message was broken in less than a day by using 100,000 PCs on the Internet. The *triple DES* algorithm was then endorsed as an interim standard until a new standard was adopted. It contained three iterations, where each iteration applied the DES algorithm, using a different key derived from the encryption key—the first and third iterations performed encryption using their keys, while the second iteration performed decryption using its key. Effectively it could use keys up to 168 bits in length, which was considered to make it secure against attacks for a few years. The new standard called the *Advanced Encryption Standard* (AES) was adopted in 2001.

Advanced Encryption Standard (AES) AES is a variant of *Rijndael*, which is a compact and fast encryption algorithm using only substitutions and permutations. AES uses a block size of 128 bits and keys of 128, 192, or 256 bits, whereas Rijndael can use any key and block sizes in the range 128 to 256 bits that are multiples of 32 bits. A plaintext block of 16 bytes is treated as a 4 byte $\times$ 4 byte array called a *state*. It is encrypted through many rounds of operations, where the number of rounds depends on the key length—10 rounds are performed for 128-bit keys, 12 rounds for 192-bit keys, and 14 rounds for 256-bit keys. Each round consists of the following operations:

1. *Byte substitution:* Each byte of the state is subjected to a nonlinear transformation applied by an S-box.
2. *Shifting of rows:* Rows in the state are shifted cyclically by 0, 1, 2, and 3 bytes, respectively.
3. *Mixing of columns:* The 4 bytes in a column are replaced such that each result byte is a function of all the 4 bytes in the column.
4. *Key addition:* A subkey, whose size is the same as the size of the state, is derived from the encryption key by using a key schedule. The subkey and the state are viewed as bit strings and combined by using the exclusive-OR operation. If this is the last round, the result of the exclusive-OR operation is a block of ciphertext; otherwise, it is used as the state for the next round of encryption.

To enable both encryption and decryption to be performed by the same sequence of steps, a key addition is performed before starting the first round, and the step of mixing of columns is skipped in the last round.

15.5 AUTHENTICATION AND PASSWORD SECURITY

Authentication is typically performed through passwords, using the scheme shown in Figure 15.1. For every registered user, the system stores a pair of the form (login id, <*validating_info*>) in a passwords table, where <*validating_info*>

$= E_k$(password). To authenticate a user, the system encrypts his password using E_k and compares the result with his validating information stored in the passwords table. The user is considered to be authentic if the two match.

If an intruder has access to the passwords table, he can launch one of the attacks described earlier in Section 15.4.1 to determine E_k. Alternatively, the intruder may launch an attack to crack the password of an individual user. In the scheme described above, if two users use identical passwords, the encrypted forms of their passwords would also be identical, which would facilitate an intruder's attempts at cracking of a password if the passwords table is visible to him. Hence the encryption function E takes two parameters. One parameter is the encryption key k, and the other parameter is a string derived from the user's login id. Now, identical passwords yield distinct encrypted strings.

Intruders may use password cracking programs to discover passwords of individual users. Their task is simplified by users' tendency to use passwords that are not difficult to guess, such as dictionary words and vehicle numbers, or use simple keyboard sequences. For infrequently used accounts, users often choose simple passwords that are easy to remember, the common refrain being that they do not have many important files in that account. However, a password is the proverbial weakest link in the security chain. Any password that is cracked provides an intruder with opportunities for launching further security attacks. Consequently, a large number of security problems relate to use of poor passwords.

Operating systems use a set of techniques to defeat attacks on passwords. Table 15.6 summarizes these techniques. *Password aging* limits the exposure of passwords to intruders, which is expected to make passwords more secure. System-chosen passwords ensure use of *strong* passwords, which cannot be cracked by

Table 15.6 OS Techniques for Defeating Attacks on Passwords

Technique	Description
Password aging	Encourage or force users to change their passwords frequently, at least once every 6 months. It limits the exposure of a password to intruder attacks.
System-chosen passwords	A system administrator uses a methodology to generate and assign *strong* passwords to users. Users are not allowed to change these passwords. An intruder would have to use an exhaustive attack to break such passwords.
Encryption of passwords	The encrypted form of passwords is stored in a system file; however, the ciphertext form of passwords is visible to all users in the system. An intruder can use one of the attacks described in Section 15.4.1 to find E_k, or launch an exhaustive attack to crack an individual user's password.
Encrypt and hide password information	The encrypted form of passwords is not visible to any person within or outside the system. Hence an intruder cannot use any of the attacks described in Section 15.4.1.

simple techniques like looking for parts of names or dictionary words in the passwords. Their use would force an intruder to use an exhaustive attack to crack a password, which is impractical.

When the encrypted passwords file is visible within and outside the system, a registered user can use a chosen plaintext attack to discover E_k by changing his own password repeatedly and viewing its encrypted form. However, an intruder would have to use a ciphertext-only attack to find E_k since he does not know any of the passwords. Hiding of the encrypted password file denies an intruder within or outside the system an opportunity to use any of the attacks described in Section 15.4.1, so he would have to rely on cracking of individual passwords, which has little chance of success if strong passwords are used.

The Unix operating system performs DES encryption of passwords. Linux employs a *message digest*, which is a 128-bit or 160-bit hash value obtained by applying a one-way hash function to a password. This technique has variants called MD2, MD4, and MD5. Linux uses MD5. Both Unix and Linux provide a shadow passwords file option. When this option is chosen, the ciphertext form of passwords is stored in a shadow file that is accessible only to the root.

15.6 PROTECTION STRUCTURES

A *protection structure* is the classical name for the authorization database discussed in Section 15.1 and illustrated in Figure 15.1. It contains information indicating which users can access which files in what manner. We begin by discussing the nature of information contained in a protection structure, and how the information is used to implement protection. Later in this section, we discuss the key issues in organization of the protection structure.

Recall from Section 15.1 that an *access privilege* for a file is a right to make a specific form of access to the file, e.g., a read access or a write access. A user may hold one or more access privileges for a file, e.g., he may be permitted to only read a file, or read and write a file but not execute it. An *access descriptor* is a representation of a collection of access privileges for a file. The *access control information* for a file is a collection of access descriptors; it represents access privileges for the file held by all users in the system.

We use the notations r, w, and x to represent access privileges to read, write, and execute the data or program in a file. An access descriptor can be represented as a set of access privileges, e.g., the set $\{r, w\}$ indicates privileges to both read and write a file. We will use a set representation in this chapter for simplicity; however, a set representation is expensive in terms of both memory requirements and access efficiency, so operating systems actually use a bit-encoding scheme for access descriptors. In this scheme, an access descriptor is a string of bits, where each bit indicates the presence or absence of a specific access privilege. For example, in an OS using only three access privileges r, w, and x, the access descriptor 110 could be used to indicate that the read and write privileges are present but the execute privilege is absent.

As discussed in Section 15.1, the access control information for a file `alpha` is created and used as follows:

1. When a user A creates file `alpha`, he specifies the access control information for it. The file system stores it in the protection structure.
2. When a user X logs in, he is authenticated. The authentication service generates an authentication token for him, which is typically a user id. When a process initiated by user X wishes to open or access file `alpha`, his authentication token is passed to the file system.
3. The file system uses the authentication token to find the access privileges of user X for file `alpha` in the protection structure, and checks whether the kind of access desired by the process is consistent with the access privileges.

Organization of the protection structure influences two key aspects of protection—how much discrimination the owner of a file can exercise in Step 1 while specifying which other users can access the file, and how efficiently the protection check of Step 3 can be implemented. We discuss these issues in the following sections.

15.6.1 Granularity of Protection

Granularity of protection signifies the degree of discrimination a file owner can exercise concerning protection of files. We define three levels of granularity in Table 15.7.

Coarse-grained protection implies that users are clubbed into groups and access privileges are specified for a group of users, whereas *medium-grained protection* implies that the owner of a file can specify access privileges individually for each user in the system. *Fine-grained protection* permits access privileges to be specified for a process or for different phases in operation of a process. This way, different processes created by the same user may possess different access privileges for a file, or the same process may possess different access privileges for the file at different times. It helps in ensuring privacy of information (see Section 15.1.1).

Table 15.7 Granularity of Protection

Granularity	Description
Coarse-grained protection	Access privileges for a file can be specified only for groups of users. Each user in a group has identical access privileges for the file.
Medium-grained protection	Access privileges for a file can be specified individually for each user in the system.
Fine-grained protection	Access privileges for a file can be specified for a process, or for a phase in operation of a process.

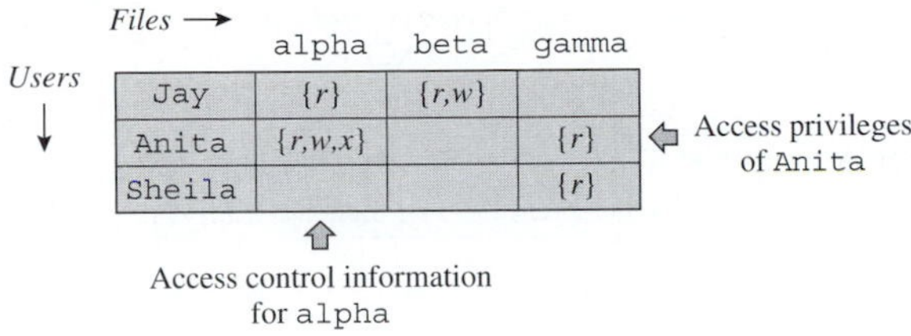

Figure 15.7 Access control matrix (ACM).

Users desire medium- or fine-grained protection. However, such protection leads to a large size of the protection structure. This is why operating systems resort to coarse-grained protection.

15.6.2 Access Control Matrix

An *access control matrix* (ACM) is a protection structure that provides efficient access to both access privileges of users for various files, and access control information for files. Each element of the ACM contains access privileges of one user for one file. Each user has a row in the ACM, while each file has a column in it. This way, a row in the ACM describes one user's access privileges for all files in the system, and each column describes the access control information for a file. When a user u_i wishes to access file f_k, the element ACM(u_i,f_k) can be accessed efficiently to validate the kind of access being made by u_i. Figure 15.7 shows an ACM. User Jay has {read, write} access privileges for beta but only a {read} privilege for alpha.

The ACM provides medium-grained protection. However, it is large in size because an OS has a large number of users and contains a large number of files. Accordingly, a large area of memory has to be committed to hold the ACM, or parts of it, in memory during system operation. Operating systems use two approaches to reduce the size of access control information. In the first approach, the number of rows is reduced by assigning access privileges to groups of users rather than to individual users. This approach retains the basic advantage of the ACM, namely efficient access to both access privileges of users and access control information of files. However, it leads to coarse-grained protection because all users in a group have identical access privileges for a file.

The second approach to reducing size of the protection structure exploits the fact that a typical user possesses access privileges for only a few files. Thus, most elements in an ACM contain null entries, so space can be conserved by organizing the protection information in the form of lists containing only nonnull access privileges. This approach does not affect the granularity of protection; however, it compromises access efficiency of the protection structure. We present two list-organized protection structures in the following sections.

15.6.3 Access Control Lists (ACLs)

The *access control list* (ACL) of a file is a representation of its access control information; it contains the non-null entries that the file's column would

File name	*Access control list* (ACL)
alpha	{(Jay, {*r*}), (Anita,{*r*, *w*, *x*})}
beta	{(Jay, {*r*, *w*})}
gamma	{(Anita, {*r*}), (Sheila, {*r*})}

Figure 15.8 Access control lists (ACLs).

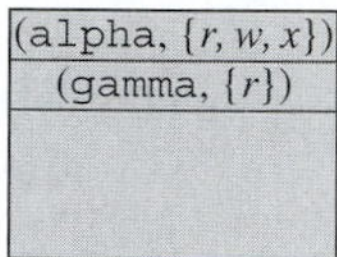

Figure 15.9 Capability list for user Anita.

have contained in the ACM. It is stored as a list of pairs of the form (*user_id, access_privileges*). Figure 15.8 shows access control lists for the files alpha, beta, and gamma of Figure 15.7. The ACL for alpha is {(Jay, {read}), (Anita, {read, write, execute})}, which indicates that user Jay can only read file alpha while Anita can read, write, or execute the file. User Sheila is not permitted any kind of access to alpha, since alpha's ACL does not contain an entry for Sheila.

Even though use of an ACL eliminates the need to store null access privileges, presence of a large number of users in a system leads to large ACL sizes, and thereby to large disk and memory overhead in the file system. The time overhead is also high because the ACL has to be searched for validating a file access. Both memory and CPU time can be conserved at the cost of using coarse-grained protection by specifying protection information for groups of users rather than for individual users. Such an ACL could be small enough to be stored in the directory entry of a file. For example, if users Jay and Anita belong to the same group of users, the ACL of file alpha would contain a single pair. It would now be easier to determine whether Jay can access alpha; however, both Jay and Anita would have identical access privileges.

15.6.4 Capability Lists (C-lists)

A *capability list* (C-list) represents access privileges of a user for various files in the system; it contains the non-null entries that the user's row in the ACM would have contained. Each entry in the C-list is a *capability*, which represents access privileges for one file; it is a pair of the form (*file_id, access_privileges*). Figure 15.9 shows a C-list for user Anita of Figure 15.7. Anita can read, write, or execute file alpha and can read file gamma. Anita has no access privileges for file beta, since no entry for beta exists in the C-list. C-lists are usually small in size; this feature limits the space and time overhead in using them for protection of files. We discuss how capabilities are used in a computer in Section 15.7.

15.6.5 Protection Domain

The access control matrix, access control list, or capability list is used to confer access privileges on users. This arrangement serves the *secrecy* goal of security and protection because only authorized users can access a file. However, the *privacy* goal of security and protection requires that information should be used only for intended purposes (see Section 15.1.1), and this requirement could be violated as follows: A user is granted an access privilege for a file because *some* process initiated by the user requires it. However, every other process initiated by the user also has the same access privilege for the file; some of these processes may access the file in an unintended manner, thus violating the privacy requirement. The next example illustrates how privacy of information may be jeopardized.

Example 15.2

Privacy Violation

A user u_i has an execute privilege for a program `invest` owned by another user u_j. When u_i executes `invest`, `invest` operates as a process initiated by user u_i. It can access any file for which user u_i holds an access privilege, including files that have nothing to do with investments. If u_j so wishes, he can code `invest` to obtain a listing of u_i's current directory and either copy or modify some of the files found in it.

Violation of privacy raises a major reliability concern, as the correctness of data would depend not only on correct manipulation by processes that are supposed to access it, but also on harmlessness of the accesses made by processes that are not supposed to access it. The concept of a *protection domain* is used to prevent privacy violations. We can think of a protection domain as a conceptual "execution environment": Access privileges are granted to a protection domain rather than to a user or his process. A process operates "within" a protection domain and can access those files for which the protection domain has access privileges. This arrangement facilitates implementation of the need-to-know principle with a fine granularity—a process should be allowed to operate within a protection domain only if it needs to access the files for which the protection domain has access privileges. The following example illustrates how this approach ensures privacy of information.

Example 15.3

Protection Domains

Figure 15.10 shows three protection domains. Domain D_1 has read and write privileges for the files `personal` and `finance`, while D_2 possesses only a read privilege for `finance`. Domain D_3 has read and write privileges for the files `memos` and `notes` and a read privilege for the file `project`. Thus domains D_1 and D_2 overlap while domain D_3 is disjoint with both of them.

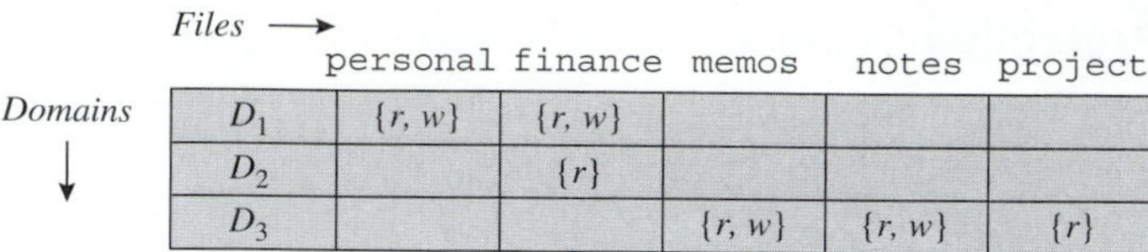

	personal	finance	memos	notes	project
D_1	$\{r, w\}$	$\{r, w\}$			
D_2		$\{r\}$			
D_3			$\{r, w\}$	$\{r, w\}$	$\{r\}$

Figure 15.10 Protection domains.

User u_i initiates three processes named `self`, `invest`, and `job_related` in domains D_1, D_2, and D_3, respectively. Thus `invest` can access only file `finance`, and can only read it.

If the OS did not use protection domains, user u_i would have needed read and write privileges for the files `personal`, `finance`, `memos`, and `notes` and a read privilege for the file `project`. When user u_i executed the program `invest` of Example 15.2, which is owned by user u_j, `invest` would have been able to modify files `personal`, `finance`, `memos`, and `notes` of user u_i.

Privacy can be enhanced by permitting a process to access some resources only during specific phases in its operation. It is facilitated by letting a process change its protection domain during operation, subject to some conditions. Using this domain change facility, user u_i of Example 15.3 would have been able to use a single process to perform some personal computing, make some investment decisions using program `invest` owned by user u_j, and write some memos and notes using a standard package. The process would be initiated in domain D_1. After performing personal computing in this domain, the process would change its domain to D_2 and call program `invest`, so that `invest` could only view u_i's financial details but not modify either those details or any of u_i's personal information. The process would later change to domain D_3 for writing memos and notes, using the standard package. We describe features for change of protection domain in the Unix and Multics operating systems in Section 15.9.

15.7 CAPABILITIES

Dennis and Van Horn (1966) proposed the concept of a *capability* for use in sharing and protection. A capability is a token representing some access privileges for an object, where an object is any hardware or software entity in the system, e.g., a laser printer, a CPU, a file, a program, or a data structure of a program. A capability is possessed by a process. Its possession gives the process a right to access the object in a manner that is consistent with the access privileges in the capability.

Figure 15.11 shows the format of a capability. It consists of two fields—*object id* and *access privileges*. Each object has an unique object id in the system. The

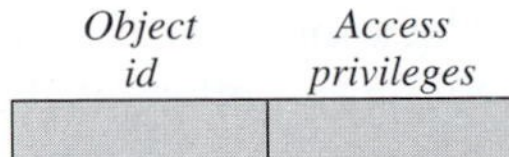

Figure 15.11 Format of a capability.

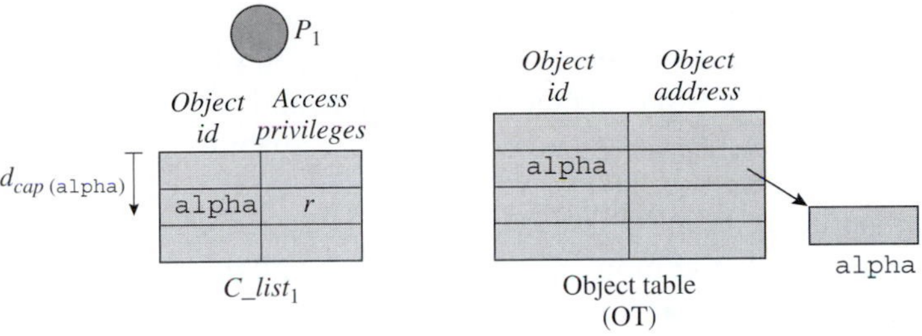

Figure 15.12 Capability-based addressing.

access privileges field typically contains a bit-encoded access descriptor. A process may possess many capabilities. These are stored in the *capability list* (C-list) discussed earlier in Section 15.6.4.

When some process P_i creates an object O_i, the OS forms a capability for O_i that contains the entire set of access privileges defined in the system, and passes this capability to P_i. Using this capability, P_i can request the OS to create *subset capabilities* for O_i that contain fewer access privileges. It can also make copies of the capability for O_i that it received from the OS. Thus, many capabilities for O_i may exist in the system. Process P_i can share the object O_i with other processes by passing capabilities for O_i to other processes. Thus, each process possesses capabilities for the objects it owns, and some capabilities passed to it by other processes. All these capabilities are obtained through legal means—none can be stolen or fraudulently created by a process. This is why a capability is often described as an unforgeable token that confers access privileges onto its holder.

We use the notation $Cap_k(obj_i)$ to refer to a capability for obj_i. The subscript of *Cap* is used simply to distinguish between different capabilities for an object. It does not have any other significance. For simplicity, we omit the subscript in contexts where a single capability of an object is involved.

15.7.1 Capability-Based Computer Systems

A capability-based computer system implements capability-based addressing and protection for *all* objects in the system, ranging from long-life objects like files to short-life objects like data structures and copies of programs in memory. Many capability-based systems were built for research; the Intel iapx-432 was a capability-based commercial system.

Figure 15.12 is a schematic diagram of capability-based addressing of objects. The system does not explicitly associate "memory" with processes; it associates C-lists with processes. Each object has an unique id. The *object table* (OT) is a systemwide table that contains location information for all objects in the system. The *object address* field of an OT entry indicates the address of the object in the computer's primary or secondary memory. Access to an object is implemented as follows: A process P_1 performs an operation $<op_i>$ on an object by using an instruction of the form

$$<op_i> \; d_{Cap(obj_i)} \qquad \textbf{(15.1)}$$

where $d_{Cap(obj_i)}$ is the displacement of $Cap(obj_i)$ in P_1's C-list. The CPU locates the capability in P_1's C-list using the displacement, and verifies that the operation $<op_i>$ is consistent with access privileges in the capability. The object id in the capability, that is, `alpha`, is now used to locate `alpha`'s entry in the OT and the object address found there is used to implement $<op_i>$. Capability-based addressing can be made more efficient by using buffers analogous to address translation buffers (see Section 12.2.2) and special cache memories for address translation.

The capabilities in a C-list may be used to access objects existing anywhere in the system, i.e., in memory or on disk; the location of an object is immaterial to a process. This feature permits the OS to move objects around in memory for better memory management, or move them between memory and disk for cost-effective access performance, without affecting the manner in which a program accesses the objects. Thus, long-life objects like files and short-life objects like data structures can be accessed in a uniform manner.

Operations on Objects and Capabilities A process may be given some capabilities by the OS by default when it is created. It may also inherit some capabilities from its parent process. When the process performs the operation "create a new object," the CPU creates a new object and creates a new entry in the OT for it. It puts the object id and address of the newly created object in the entry. It now creates a capability containing the entire set of access privileges for the object and puts it in the C-list of P_i. It also puts $d_{Cap(obj_i)}$ in a register of the CPU. Process P_i saves the contents of this register for use while accessing obj_i in future.

All operations performed by a process are subject to access privileges contained in its C-list. The operation of creating an object may itself be subject to an access privilege; if so, the OS would confer this access privilege through one of the default capabilities it gives to each process. Table 15.8 lists the operations a process can perform on objects and capabilities. Thus, a process can create, modify, destroy, copy, or execute an object if it possesses a capability with the appropriate access privileges.

Operations on a capability are also subject to access privileges in it. For example, a process may be able to create a subset capability of $Cap(obj_i)$ only if $Cap(obj_i)$ contains the access privilege "create subset capability." This feature controls the operations that processes can perform on capabilities. Sharing of objects occurs when a process passes a capability for an object to another process. The process receiving the capability enters it in its C-list. Sharing is implicit in the fact that both C-lists contain a capability for the object. Protection is implicit in the fact that these capabilities may confer different access privileges on the processes.

Table 15.8 Permissible Operations on Objects and Capabilities

Operations on objects	• Create an object • Read or modify the object • Destroy the object • Copy the object • Execute the object
Operations on capabilities	• Make a copy of the capability • Create a "subset" capability • Use the capability as a parameter in a function/procedure call • Pass the capability for use by another process • Delete the capability

Protection of Capabilities Protection using capabilities is based on the fundamental assumption that capabilities cannot be forged or tampered with. This assumption would be invalid if a process could access its C-list and modify the capabilities existing in it. For example, process P_1 of Figure 15.12 could alter the access privileges field of the capability for `alpha` to give itself a "write" access privilege, and then use the modified capability to modify object `alpha`. Such tampering of capabilities is prevented by ensuring that arbitrary operations cannot be performed on capabilities. It is implemented using two approaches—tagged architectures and capability segments.

In a computer with a *tagged architecture*, the run-time representation of an entity consists of two fields—a *tag* field and a value field. The tag field describes the type of the entity. The CPU is designed to perform only those operations on an entity that are consistent with its tag. This way, only the six operations on capabilities that are mentioned in Table 15.8 can be performed on a capability, which ensures that a capability cannot be tampered with. In a computer using *capability segments*, data objects and their capabilities are stored in different segments, and instructions in the CPU are designed to access their operands from an appropriate segment. Only the six operations on capabilities that are mentioned in Table 15.8 would take their operands from the capability segment. This way, arbitrary operations cannot be performed on a capability.

15.7.2 Software Capabilities

The OS for a non-capability-based computer can implement capabilities in the software. The arrangement of objects and capabilities can be analogous to the arrangement shown in Figure 15.12. However, manipulation and protection of objects cannot be performed by the CPU of the system; it is now performed by a component of the kernel called an *object manager* (OM). A program indicates its object manipulation requirements to the object manager by making a call

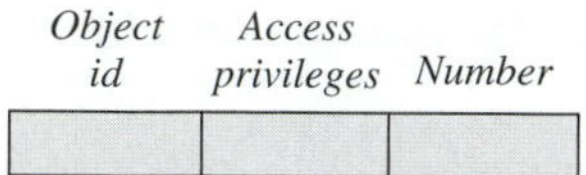

Figure 15.13 An Amoeba-like capability.

OM ($<op_i>$, $Cap(obj_i)$). This call has the same effect as instruction (15.1). The object manager implements $<op_i>$ only if $Cap(obj_i)$ contains the necessary access privileges for performing it.

Two important issues in software capabilities are: A process may be able to bypass the capability-based protection arrangement while accessing objects, and it may be able to tamper with or fabricate capabilities. How can we prevent a process from manipulating objects without going through the object manager? One way to achieve it is to hide objects from the view of user processes by encrypting the object table. Now processes will not know the locations of objects. Hence they will have to depend on the object manager to perform object manipulation. Tampering with capabilities can also be prevented by using encryption. As an example, we describe a simplified version of the capability protection scheme used in the distributed operating system Amoeba.

Capabilities in Amoeba An object obj_i, is assigned an encryption key key_i when it is created. The encryption key is stored in the object table entry of obj_i. The Amoeba capability has the format shown in Figure 15.13. The *number* field contains information that is used to protect the capability. A capability for obj_i is created using the following procedure:

1. The *object id* and *access privileges* fields of the capability are set appropriately.
2. The encryption key key_i is obtained from the object table entry of obj_i. Contents of the *access privileges* field are now concatenated with key_i and the resulting string is encrypted using key_i. We denote this operation as E_{key_i} (*access privileges* . key_i), where "." denotes concatenation. The result of the encryption step is stored in the *number* field of the capability.

To manipulate obj_i, a process must submit a capability for obj_i to the object manager. The object manager verifies the validity of this capability as follows:

1. The encryption key key_i is obtained from the object table entry of obj_i.
2. The string *access privileges* is obtained from the capability and E_{key_i} (*access privileges* . key_i) is compared with the *number* field in the capability.

The comparison in Step 2 would fail if the *object id* or *access privileges* field of a capability has been tampered with, so the object manager aborts the process if the comparison fails.

Comparison with Capability-Based Systems The major strength of software capabilities—their independence from the underlying hardware—is also their major weakness. Operations such as creation of subset capabilities, which are performed by the hardware of a capability-based system, need to be performed in the software. Each of these involves a system call to invoke the object manager. In addition, prevention of tampering requires validation of a capability before use. These requirements lead to substantial time overhead.

15.7.3 Problem Areas in the Use of Capabilities

Use of capabilities has three practical problems:

- *Need for garbage collection:* When can an object be destroyed?
- *Confinement of capabilities:* How to ensure that processes do not pass capabilities to other processes indiscriminately?
- *Revocation of capabilities:* How to cancel a capability or withdraw the access privileges conferred by it?

Garbage Collection The owner of an object may prepare subset capabilities for an object and pass them to other processes so that they can access the object. Before destroying such an object, the owner must know that no process is currently using the object. This information can be gained only through synchronization of the owner with all users of an object. This approach is impractical when objects are created and used at a high rate or when objects with long lifetimes are shared. Two problems can arise if objects are destroyed without collecting such information. Dangling pointers can exist—that is, an object may be destroyed while some capabilities still exist for it—or an object may exist long after capabilities for it have been destroyed. Preventing both these situations requires use of expensive garbage collection techniques.

Confinement of Capabilities Confinement implies restricting the use of a capability to a given set of processes. Lack of confinement implies proliferation of capabilities throughout the system due to indiscriminate passing of capabilities. It complicates garbage collection and prolongs the life of an object. It can also undermine protection by violating the need-to-know principle. Confinement can be achieved by making the passing of a capability itself an access right: If process P_i turns off the "pass" access right in a capability while passing it to P_j, P_j will not be able to pass the capability to any other process.

Revocation of Capabilities Revocation of all capabilities for an object is the most difficult problem in a capability-based system, since there is no way to know which processes hold capabilities for the object and there is no method of nullifying a capability. However, revocation is possible in the case of software capabilities because they are protected through encryption. In Amoeba, all existing capabilities of an object would be invalidated when the encryption key assigned to the object is changed. To selectively revoke some capabilities of an object, the owner can invalidate all capabilities of the object by changing the encryption key and then issue fresh capabilities to only some processes. However, it is an expensive and intrusive operation—every process holding a capability for the object is affected when *any* capability of the object is to be revoked.

15.8 CLASSIFICATIONS OF COMPUTER SECURITY

A security policy specifies the roles of entities—whether individuals or programs—in ensuring that resources of a computer system are used in a legitimate manner. In the terminology of Figure 15.1, a security policy would specify roles of system administrators and programs used by them to maintain the authentication and authorization databases and the roles of OS programs that constitute the authentication and authorization services.

Ideally, it should be possible to prove that the security policies cannot be undermined. However, such proofs are difficult for the reasons mentioned in Section 15.3, so system developers must use other means to inspire confidence in the security capabilities of systems. These means typically take the form of some evidence that the system implements *access control* to ensure that resources are used in a legitimate manner, and an *auditing capability*, which keeps information on how a security-related event has been handled by the relevant entity.

The U.S. Department of Defense evolved Trusted Computer System Evaluation Criteria (TCSEC) to determine how well a computer system conforms with the security and protection requirements. These criteria classify computer systems into four divisions and several levels within each division (see Table 15.9). The classification envisages that a computer system can be partitioned into two parts: The *trusted computing base* (TCB) is that part of its hardware, software,

Table 15.9 Trusted Computer System Evaluation Criteria

Division	Description and levels
Verified protection (division A)	A system must support formal methods for verification of security.
Mandatory protection (division B)	A system must associate sensitivity labels with data and programs and implement mandatory access control rules through a *reference monitor* (RM). • B1: Labeled security protection • B2: Structured protection • B3: Security domains
Discretionary protection (division C)	A system must implement need-to-know protection and provide audit capabilities for accountability of subjects and their actions. • C1: Discretionary security protection • C2: Controlled access protection
Minimal protection (division D)	A system that fails the requirements for a higher division.

and firmware that implements security-related functionalities in the system; the remainder of the system does not implement any security-related functions. The classification of a computer system depends on whether its TCB meets the requirements of a specific division in the classification and all lower divisions. Division D is the lowest security classification; it is awarded to systems that cannot meet the requirements of any of the other divisions.

The TCB of a division C computing system possesses three key capabilities. First, it permits a user to specify which other users can access the data or programs owned by him; it performs authentication of users to provide this capability. Second, it facilitates auditing of security-related events in the system by keeping a record of events such as authentication attempts, file open/close, actions of system administrators, etc. Third, it provides *object reuse protection* to ensure that a user's data cannot be accidentally accessed by another user. It is implemented by clearing the memory allocated to a data object before returning it to the TCB's pool of free objects or free memory. Levels C1 and C2 of division C correspond to the different protection granularities. A system satisfies level C2 of the classification if a user can identify each individual user who can access the files owned by him; otherwise, the system satisfies level C1. Thus, a system implementing coarse-grained protection would earn a level C1 classification (see Section 15.6.1).

To earn a division B classification, a computer system must assign sensitivity labels to all data and programs that reflect their security and protection levels, and must use these labels to validate every access of a data or program, which is called *mandatory access control*. It must also control the propagation of access rights. The system developer must furnish a security policy model on which the TCB is based. This model must employ a *reference monitor* (RM) to validate each reference to a data or program by a user or his process. The reference monitor should be tamper-proof and should be small so that its completeness can be analyzed and tested.

Division B consists of three levels, which differ in the extent of *mandatory protection*, resistance to penetration, support for trusted facility management, and structuring of the TCB into protection-critical and non-protection-critical elements. In level B1, mandatory access control must exist, and the system administrator should be able to audit the actions of select users or actions related to select programs or data objects. In level B2, mandatory access control should be extended to all users and all data and program objects. The system should be resistant to penetration, and should provide support for system administrator and operator functions. The system should also provide a *trusted path* between a user and the TCB. This path is typically used when a user wishes to log in. Its use eliminates masquerading attacks by a Trojan horse program (see Section 15.2). In level B3, the system should be highly resistant to penetration and must support a system administrator in collecting information on imminent security attacks and terminating events that could be parts of such attacks.

To qualify for the division A rating, a system has to have the capabilities of level B3, and its developer has to furnish a formal proof of its security policy.

15.9 CASE STUDIES IN SECURITY AND PROTECTION

15.9.1 MULTICS

MULTICS provides 64 protection domains that are organized as concentric rings. The rings are numbered from the innermost to the outermost (see Figure 15.14). The access privileges of a domain include access privileges of all higher-numbered domains. In addition, the domain may have a few other access privileges of its own. Each procedure of a program is assigned to a protection domain and can be executed only by a process that is in the same protection domain.

The code component of a process may consist of procedures in different protection domains. An interrupt is raised when a process executing in protection domain D_i invokes a procedure that is assigned to a protection domain D_j, where $D_j \neq D_i$. To execute the procedure, the protection domain of the process should be changed to D_j. The kernel checks whether this is permissible according to the rule for change of protection domain. A simplified view of this rule is as follows: Change of protection domain is permitted if a process running in some domain D_i invokes a procedure that exists in a higher-numbered domain. However, to enter a lower-numbered domain a process must invoke a specially designated procedure called a *gate*. An attempt to invoke any other procedure in a lower-numbered layer fails and the process is aborted. If a procedure call satisfies this rule, the protection domain of the process is temporarily changed to the domain in which the invoked procedure exists. The invoked procedure executes in this protection domain and accesses resources according to the access privileges of the domain. At return, the protection domain of the process is reset to its earlier value, i.e., to D_i.

The MULTICS protection structure is complex and incurs substantial execution overhead due to checks made at a procedure call. Because of the requirement that access privileges of a protection domain should include access privileges of all higher-numbered domains, it is not possible to use domains whose access privileges are disjoint. For example, domains D_1, D_2, and D_3 of Figure 15.10 cannot be implemented in MULTICS since domain D_3 is disjoint with domains D_1 and D_2. This feature restricts users' freedom in specifying protection requirements.

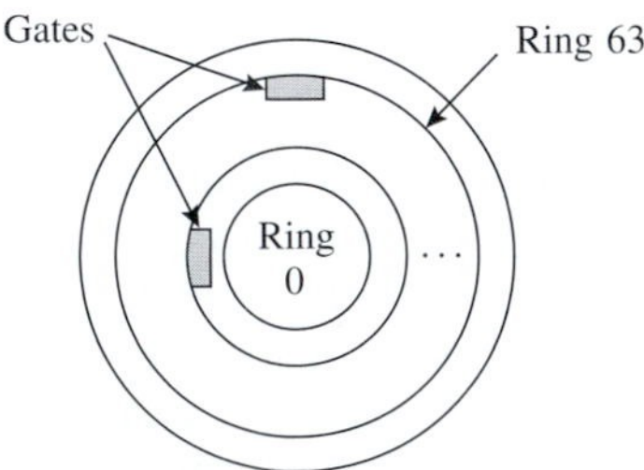

Figure 15.14 MULTICS protection rings.

15.9.2 Unix

As mentioned in Section 15.5, Unix employs encryption for password security. Under an option, it uses a shadow passwords file that is accessible only to the root, which forces an intruder to use an exhaustive attack to crack passwords. Each Unix user has an unique id in the system. The system administrator creates nonoverlapping groups of users and assigns a unique group id to each group. The credential of a user is composed of his user id and group id. It is stored in the passwords table and becomes the authentication token of the user after the user is authenticated.

Unix defines three user classes—file owner, user group, and other users—and provides only three access rights, *r*, *w*, and *x*, representing read, write, and execute, respectively. A 3-bit bit-encoded access descriptor is used for each user class and the access control list (ACL) contains access descriptors for three user classes in the sequence: file owner, user group, and other users. This way, the ACL requires only 9 bits; it is stored in the inode of a file (see Section 13.14.1). The identity of the file owner is stored in another field of the file's inode. Figure 15.15 shows the Unix ACLs as reported in a directory listing. The file `sigma` can be read by any user in the system, but can be written only by its owner. `delta` is a read-only file for all user classes, while `phi` has the read, write, and execute privileges only for its owner.

The access privileges of a Unix process are determined by its uid. When the kernel creates a process, it sets the uid of the process to the id of the user who created it. Thus the process operates in a protection domain determined by the id of the user who created it. Unix changes the protection domain of a process under two conditions—when the process makes a system call, and when the *setuid* or *setgid* feature is used. A process has two distinct *running* states—*user running* and *kernel running* (see Section 5.4.1). While in the user-running state, a process has access to the memory space and other resources allocated to it, and to files in the file system according to its uid. The process makes a transition to the kernel-running state through a system call. In this state, it can access kernel data structures and also contents of the entire memory. It returns to the user-running state when it returns from the system call. Thus, a change of protection domain occurs implicitly when a process makes a system call and when it returns from a system call.

The *setuid* feature can be used in two ways. A process can make a system call *setuid* <*id*> to change its uid to <*id*>, and another *setuid* system call with its own id to revert to its original uid. Alternatively, uid can be changed implicitly when a process performs an *exec* in order to execute a program. The latter usage

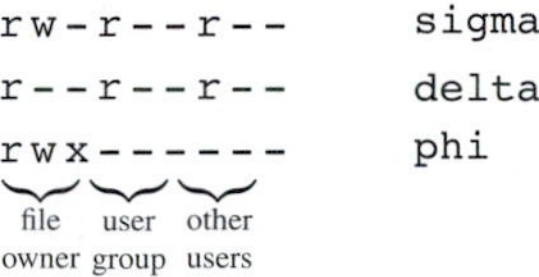

Figure 15.15 Unix access control list.

is realized as follows: Let a program P be stored in a file named P. If the owner of P requests the kernel that P be executed under the *setuid* feature, the kernel sets the *setuid* bit in the inode of file P. When P is *exec*'ed by some process that has an execute permission for it, the kernel notices that the *setuid* bit of file P is set, and temporarily changes the uid of the process executing P to the uid of P's owner. This action effectively puts the process into a protection domain whose access privileges are identical with the access privileges of P's owner. This feature can be used to avoid the privacy violation discussed in Example 15.2 as follows: User u_j sets the *setuid* bit of the program `invest`. User u_i provides u_j with a read access to the file `finance` before invoking `invest`. Now, the program `invest` executes with the uid of u_j. Thus, `invest` can access user u_i's file `finance`, but it cannot access any other files owned by u_i. The *setgid* feature analogously provides a method of temporarily changing the group id of a process.

15.9.3 Linux

Linux authenticates a user at login time by adding a "salt" value to his password and encrypting the result through MD5. Under an option, it employs a shadow passwords file that is accessible only to the root. Additionally, Linux provides *pluggable authentication modules* (PAMs), through which an application can authenticate a user at any time through a dynamically loadable library of authentication modules. This arrangement provides flexibility because the authentication scheme used in an application can be changed without having to recompile the application. An application developer can use PAMs to enhance application security in several ways—to employ a password encryption scheme of his own choice, to set resource limits to users so that they cannot consume an excessive amount of a resource to launch a denial-of-service attack, and to allow specific users to log in only at specific times from specific locations.

The system administrator maintains a PAM configuration file for each application that is authorized to employ PAM. Each PAM configuration file specifies how authentication is to be performed and what actions, such as mounting of home directories or logging of the authentication event, are to be taken after a user is authenticated. The configuration file also names the mechanism that is to be employed when a user wishes to change his password. PAM permits several authentication modules to be "stacked"; these modules are invoked one after another. An application can use this facility to authenticate a user through several means such as passwords and biometric identification, to enhance security.

Linux provides file access protection based on user id and group id of a process. When a server such as the NFS accesses a file on behalf of a user, file protection should be performed using the user id and group id of the user rather than those of the server. To facilitate this, Linux provides the system calls `fsuid` and `fsgid` through which a server can temporarily assume the identity of its client.

As described in Section 4.8.2, the Linux kernel supports loadable kernel modules. This feature has been employed to provide enhanced access controls through loadable kernel modules called the *Linux security modules* (LSM). Use of LSMs permits many different security models to be supported. The basic schematic of LSM is simple: The kernel invokes an access validation function before accessing an object. An LSM provides this function, which may permit or deny the access to go through. The Security Enhanced Linux (SELinux) of the U.S. National Security Agency has built additional access control mechanisms through LSM, which provide mandatory access control.

The Linux kernel provides the exec-shield patch, which enables protection against exploitation of buffer overflows and data structure overwriting to launch security attacks.

15.9.4 Security and Protection in Windows

The Windows security model has several elements of C2- and B2-class systems according to the TCSEC criteria (see Section 14.5.2). It provides discretionary access control, object reuse protection, auditing of security-related events, a security reference monitor (SRM) that enforces access control, and a trusted path for authentication that would defeat masquerading attacks launched through a Trojan horse. Among other notable features, it provides security for client–server computing through access tokens, which are analogous to capabilities (see Section 15.7).

Windows security is based around the use of *security identifiers* (SIDs); a security identifier is assigned to a user, a host, or a *domain*, which is composed of several hosts. The important fields in an SID are a 48-bit identifier authority value, which identifies the host or domain that issued the SID, and a few 32-bit subauthority or relative identifier (RID) values that are used primarily to generate unique SIDs for entities created by the same host or domain.

Each process and thread has an *access token* that identifies its security context. (Recall that we use the term *process* as being generic to both a process and a thread.) An access token is generated when a user logs on, and it is associated with the initial process created for the user. A process can create more access tokens through the *LogonUser* function. An access token contains a user account SID and a group account SID. These fields are used by the security reference monitor to decide whether the process holding the access token can perform certain operations on an object. An access token also contains a privilege array indicating any special privileges held by the process, such as a privilege for creating backups of files, impersonating a client, and shutting down a host. It may also contain a few superprivileges for loading and unloading drivers, taking ownership of objects, and creating new access tokens.

An object such as a file has a *security descriptor*, which contains the object owner's id, a *discretionary access control list* (DACL) and a *system access control list* (SACL). The DACL is used to specify which users can access the object in what manner, while the SACL is used to generate an audit log of operations performed on the object. Both DACL and SACL are lists of *access control entries*

(ACEs); however, an ACE plays different roles in these lists. An ACE in a DACL either indicates that the specified user is allowed to access the object, or indicates that the user is forbidden access to the object. This arrangement permits medium-grained protection and yet helps to make the DACL compact; however, the entire DACL has to be processed to determine whether a specific user is allowed to access the object in a specific manner. An object that can contain other objects, such as a directory, is called a *container* object; we will call the objects contained in it its "child objects". An ACE in the DACL of a container object contains flags to indicate how the ACE is to apply to a child object—identically, not at all, or in some other manner. An important option is that the ACE may be inherited by a child object that is itself a container object, but it may not be further inherited by objects that may be created within the child object. This feature helps to limit the propagation of access control privileges. An ACE in the SACL indicates which operation on the object by which users or groups of users should be audited. An entry is made in the audit log when any of these operations is performed.

The *impersonation* feature in the Windows security model provides security in client–server computing. When a server performs some operations on objects on behalf of a client, these operations should be subject to the access privileges of the client rather than those of the server; otherwise, the client may be able to realize operations on these objects that exceed its own access privileges. Analogously, the security audit log that is generated when the server accesses an object on behalf of a client should contain the identity of the client rather than that of the server. Both these requirements are satisfied by letting the server temporarily assume the identity of the client through impersonation.

Impersonation is implemented as follows: When a client invokes a server, it indicates the kind of impersonation it wishes the server to perform—the server cannot perform impersonation without the client's consent. If impersonation is enabled, an *impersonation token* is created from the client's token and given to the server. The server presents the impersonation token, rather than its own access token, while performing operations on objects. Effectively, the access token and the impersonation token act like the capabilities discussed in Section 15.7. Further, to ensure security, the server may create a restricted token from an impersonation token. Such a token would contain a subset of the privileges contained in the impersonation token—it is like a subset capability discussed in Section 15.7.

The following new security features were added in Windows Vista to make it a more secure OS:

- *Defeating buffer overflow attacks in Intel 80x86 architectures:* Recall from Section 15.2.2 that the stack grows downward in memory in processors with these architectures. Vista places the return pointers and parameters of a function call higher in the stack than local data to prevent their corruption by an overflow. Attempts at executing code smuggled in as data are defeated using the no-execute (NX) feature of processors by flagging parts of memory used to hold data as no-execute zones.
- *Detecting heap corruption:* An intruder can launch a buffer overflow attack in the heap as well. To prevent it, metadata such as pointers in the heap are

encoded by performing an exclusive-OR with a random number. Corruption of the heap, through overflow or otherwise, would change some of the metadata, hence its decryption would fail. The kernel aborts a process when this happens.

- *Preventing access to system code:* Parts of system code are loaded randomly in any one of 256 possible locations in memory, to make it difficult for an intruder to access them. Function pointers that exist in memory for long durations are obfuscated by performing an exclusive-OR with random numbers.
- *Preventing misuse of privileges:* System services do not run in the system account as they used to in earlier versions of Windows. They run in less privileged accounts. Processes initiated by system administrators also run in less privileged modes and the kernel prompts the administrator to authenticate himself when his process is about to execute a function that requires administrator privileges. If authentication is successful, other windows on the screen are blanked out to prevent spoofing of the user interface and mouse.
- *Network access protection:* Unless a computer conforms to the norms set by the administrator, it is either blocked from accessing the network or provided only limited access to it.

15.10 SUMMARY

A fundamental goal of an OS is to ensure noninterference in the computations and resources of users. However, users need to share some of their resources, such as programs and data stored in files, with collaborators. Hence an important aspect of implementing noninterference is knowing what accesses to a resource are legitimate and what accesses constitute interference. Threats of interference can arise outside a system or within it. Measures employed to counter such threats constitute *security* and *protection*, respectively. *Authentication* is the key technique of security; it determines whether a person is a registered user of a computer system. *Authorization* is the key technique of protection. It determines whether a user is permitted to access a resource. In this chapter we studied implementation of the authentication and authorization techniques.

A person or program posing a threat of interference is called an *intruder*. Intruders may employ various means that exploit security flaws in a computer system, either to masquerade as a user or to disrupt legitimate use of resources by users. These means include a *Trojan horse, virus*, or *worm* or use of a *buffer overflow*. Threats imposed by intruders are thwarted by exercising caution while loading unknown programs into a computer and by removing security flaws.

The authentication service of an OS keeps names of registered users, and information used to identify them, in a database. It uses *encryption*, which is an algorithmic transformation of data, to prevent intruders from accessing and misusing the authentication database. *Block cipher* and *stream cipher* are widely used encryption techniques; the encryption standards *digital encryption standard* (DES) and *advanced encryption standard* (AES) have been widely deployed.

The authorization service of an OS has a *protection structure*, which contains two kinds of information. An *access privilege* represents a user's right to access a specific file in a specific manner. The *protection information* of a file indicates which users can access the file in what manner.

Organization of the protection structure controls the amount of discrimination a user can exercise while specifying which users can access his files in what manner; it is called *granularity of protection*. *Access control lists, capability lists*, and *protection domains* are alternative protection structures.

A computer system is assigned a security classification based on how well it conforms to the security and protection requirements. Its ability to provide fine-grained protection and support the system administrator in implementing security policies are key determinants of its security classification.

TEST YOUR CONCEPTS

15.1 Classify each of the following statements as true or false:

- **a.** The authentication mechanism is used to distinguish between users and nonusers of a computer system.
- **b.** An authentication token contains the list of access privileges held by a user.
- **c.** The authorization database is used by security mechanisms.
- **d.** Encryption of information ensures its integrity.
- **e.** Masquerading is a security attack.
- **f.** A virus launches a security attack only if explicitly downloaded by a user.
- **g.** The buffer overflow technique can be used to launch a security attack.
- **h.** When encrypted by a stream cipher, identical substrings in a plaintext always lead to identical substrings in its ciphertext.
- **i.** To authenticate a user at login time, an OS decrypts the encrypted form of the user's password stored in the authentication database and compares the result with the password presented by the user.
- **j.** Password aging limits exposure of a password to attacks by an intruder.
- **k.** Two capabilities of an object may confer identical access privileges on their holders.
- **l.** Encryption is used to protect software capabilities.

15.2 Which of the following is a protection violation?

- **a.** User X who possesses a write privilege for file `alpha` of user Y writes invalid data into `alpha`.
- **b.** A nonuser manages to read the data stored in a file `beta` in a computer system.
- **c.** User X manages to read a file `alpha` of user Y even though he does not possess a read privilege for it.
- **d.** None of (a)–(c).

15.3 Pair the related items in each column:

i. Unix-style access control list	**i.** Fine-grained protection
ii. Access control matrix (ACM)	**ii.** Coarse-grained protection
iii. Protection domains	**iii.** Medium-grained protection

EXERCISES

15.1 Explain the procedure to be followed for making changes in the authentication and authorization databases of Figure 15.1.

15.2 List the security attacks that cannot be prevented by encryption.

15.3 Discuss whether encryption can ensure secrecy, privacy, and integrity of data.

15.4 Formulate a security rule that will eliminate the security flaw of Example 15.1.

15.5 Describe the conditions under which a chosen plaintext attack can be launched against passwords.

15.6 Comment on the impact of granularity of protection on sizes of various protection structures.

Suggest methods of reducing the size of the access control list (ACL) when medium-grained protection is to be implemented.

15.7 A file is encrypted by using an encryption function E and a key k. No other protection checks are made by the file system. If the user wishes to share the file with another user, he makes E and k available to the other user. Compare the above scheme for protecting files with a protection scheme using an access control list, on the basis of (a) ease of granting access privileges to users or withdrawing them, and (b) granting different kinds of access privileges to the same file.

15.8 Some old operating systems used to associate passwords with files and permit any program that presented a valid password for a file to access it. Compare this protection scheme with a capability-based protection scheme on the same criteria as in Exercise 15.7.

15.9 Capability review is the process by which an OS finds all processes that possess a capability for a specific object obj_i. Describe how a review operation can be performed in a system that uses hardware or software capabilities.

15.10 An OS performs validation of software capabilities as follows: When a new capability is created, the object manager stores a copy of the capability for its own use. When a process wishes to perform an operation on an object, the capability presented by it is compared with stored capabilities. The operation is permitted only if a matching capability exists with the object manager. Is this scheme foolproof? Does it permit selective revocation of access privileges?

15.11 An OS creates servers to offer various services to users. While handling a service request made by a user, a server may need to access resources on behalf of the user. Such resource accesses must be subject to access privileges of the user, rather than access privileges of the server.

a. The following scheme is proposed for this purpose: When a user invokes a service, he sends his own authentication token to the server. When the server requests access to a resource, it presents the user's authentication token, rather than its own authentication token, to the authorization service. This way, its use of resources would be subject to the user's access privileges. How to ensure that an intruder cannot exploit this arrangement to masquerade as a user? (*Hint:* Ensure that a user's authentication token cannot be forged.)

b. Design a scheme using capabilities.

15.12 Explain how buffers analogous to address translation buffers used in virtual memories (see Section 12.2.2.2) or a cache memory can be used in the schematic of Figure 15.12 to speed up object accesses.

15.13 Different nodes of a distributed system may concurrently create new objects. Describe a scheme that can ensure uniqueness of object ids in a distributed OS.

15.14 Study relevant Unix literature and describe the provisions in Unix for (a) finding the id of the user who owns a file, and (b) deciding whether a user belongs to the same user group as the owner of a file.

BIBLIOGRAPHY

Ludwig (1998) describes different kinds of viruses, while Ludwig (2002) discusses e-mail viruses. Spafford (1989) discusses the Morris Internet worm that caused havoc in 1988, and Berghel (2001) describes the Code Red worm of 2001.

Landwehr (1981) discusses formal models for computer security. Voydock and Kent (1983) discuss security issues in distributed systems and practical techniques used to tackle them.

Shannon (1949) is the classical work in computer security. It discusses the diffusion and confusion properties of cyphers. Denning and Denning (1979) and Lempel (1979) contain good overviews of data security and cryptology, respectively. Schneier (1996) and Ferguson and Schneier (2003) are texts on cryptography, while Pfleeger and Pfleeger (2003) is a text on computer security. Stallings (2003) discusses cryptography and network security.

Naor and Yung (1989) discusses one-way hash functions. Rivest (1991) describes the MD4 message digest function. The goal of MD4 is to make it computationally infeasible to produce two messages with an identical message digest, or to produce a message with a given message digest. MD4 is extremely fast and resists cryptanalysis attacks successfully. Rivest (1992) describes MD5, which is more conservative and a little slower than MD4. Preneel (1998) describes cryptographic primitives for information authentication.

Access matrix-based protection and protection domains are discussed in Lampson (1971) and Popek (1974). Organick (1972) discusses the MULTICS protection rings. The *setuid* feature of Unix is described in most books on Unix.

Dennis and Van Horn (1966) is a widely referenced paper on the concept of capabilities. Levy (1984) describes a number of capability-based systems. Mullender and Tanenbaum (1986) and Tanenbaum (2001) describe the software capabilities of Amoeba. Anderson et al. (1986) discusses software capabilities with a provision for containment.

The Trusted Computer System Evaluation Criteria (TCSEC) of the U.S. Department of Defense offers a classification of security features of computer systems. It is described in DoD (1985).

Spafford et al. (2003) discusses security in Solaris, Mac OS, Linux, and FreeBSD operating systems. Wright et al. (2002) discusses the Linux security modules. Russinovich and Solomon (2005) discusses security features in Windows.

1. Anderson, M., R. D. Pose, and C. S. Wallace (1986): "A password-capability system," *The Computer Journal*, **29** (1), 1–8.
2. Berghel, H. (2001): "The Code Red worm," *Communications of the ACM*, **44** (12), 15–19.
3. Denning, D. E., and P. J. Denning (1979): "Data security," *Computing Surveys*, **11** (4).
4. Dennis, J. B., and E. C. Van Horn (1966): "Programming semantics for multiprogrammed computations," *Communications of the ACM*, **9** (3).
5. DoD (1985): *Trusted Computer System Evaluation Criteria*, U.S. Department of Defense.
6. Ferguson, N., and B. Schneier (2003): *Practical Cryptography*, John Wiley, New York.
7. Fluhrer, S., I. Mantin, and A. Shamir (2001): "Weaknesses in the key scheduling algorithm of RC4," *Proceedings of 8th Annual Workshop on Selected Areas in Cryptography*.
8. Lampson, B. W. (1971): "Protection," *Operating Systems Review*, **8** (1), 18–24.
9. Landwehr, C. E. (1981): "Formal models for computer security," *Computing Surveys*, **13** (3), 247–278.
10. Lempel, A. (1979): "Cryptology in transition," *Computing Surveys*, **11** (4), 286–303.
11. Levy, H. M. (1984): *Capability-Based Computer Systems*, Digital Press, Burlington, Mass.
12. Ludwig, M. A. (1998): *The Giant Black Book of Computer Viruses,* 2nd ed., American Eagle, Show Low, Ariz.
13. Ludwig, M. A. (2002): *The Little Black Book of Email Viruses*, American Eagle, Show Low, Ariz.
14. Menezes, A., P. van Oorschot, and S. Vanstone (1996): *Handbook of Applied Cryptography*, CRC Press, Boca Raton, Fla.
15. Mullender, S. P., and A. Tanenbaum (1986): "The design of a capability-based distributed operating system," *Computer Journal*, **29** (4).
16. Nachenberg, C. (1997): "Computer virus–antivirus coevolution," *Communications of the ACM,* **40**, 46–51.
17. Naor, M., and M. Yung (1989): "Universal one–way hash functions and their cryptographic applications," *Proceedings of the 21st Annual ACM Symposium on Theory of Computing*, 33–43.
18. Oppliger, R. (1997): "Internet security: firewalls and beyond," *Communications of the ACM*, **40** (5), 92–102.
19. Organick, E. I. (1972): *The MULTICS System*, MIT Press, Cambridge, Mass.
20. Pfleeger, C. P., and S. Pfleeger (2003): *Security in computing*, Prentice Hall, Englewood Cliffs, N.J.
21. Popek, G. J. (1974): " Protection structures," *Computer*, **7** (6), 22–33.
22. Preneel, B. (1998): *Cryptographic primitives for Information Authentication—State of the art in applied cryptography*, LNCS 1528, Springer Verlag, 1998.
23. Rivest, R. (1991): "The MD4 message digest algorithm," *Proceedings of Advances in Cryptology—Crypto'90, Lecture Notes in Computer Science, volume 537*, Spinger-Verlag, 303–311.

24. Rivest, R. (1992): "The MD5 Message digest algorithm," Request for Comments, RFC 1321.
25. Russinovich, M. E., and D. A. Solomon (2005): *Microsoft Windows Internals,* 4th ed., Microsoft Press, Redmond, Wash.
26. Schneier, B. (1996): *Applied cryptography*, 2nd ed., John Wiley, New York.
27. Shannon, C. E. (1949): "Communication Theory of Secrecy Systems," *Bell System Technical Journal*, October 1949.
28. Spafford, E. H. (1989): "The Internet worm: crisis and aftermath," *Communications of the ACM*, **32** (6), 678–687.
29. Spafford, G., S. Garfinkel, and A. Schwartz (2003): *Practical UNIX and Internet Security*, 3rd ed., O'Reilly, Sebastopol, Calif.
30. Stallings, W. (2003): *Cryptography and Network Security: Principles and Practice,* 3rd ed., Prentice Hall, N.J.
31. Stiegler, H. G. (1979): "A structure for access control lists," *Software—Practice and Experience*, **9** (10), 813–819.
32. Tanenbaum, A. S. (2001): *Modern Operating Systems*, 2nd ed., Prentice Hall, Englewood Cliffs, N.J.
33. Voydock, V. L., and S. T. Kent (1983): "Security mechanisms in high level network protocols," *Computing Surveys*, **15** (2), 135–171.
34. Wofsey, M. M. (1983): *Advances in Computer Security Management*, John Wiley, New York.
35. Wright, C., C. Cowan, S. Smalley, J. Morris, and G. Kroah-Hartman (2002): "Linux Security modules: General security support for the Linux kernel," *Eleventh USENIX Security Symposium*.

part 5

Distributed Operating Systems

A distributed system consists of several nodes, where each node is a computer system with its own clock and memory, that can communicate among themselves through a network. A distributed operating system exploits these features as follows: It facilitates a user to structure his application as a *distributed computation*, which consists of several processes located in different nodes of the distributed system. To service all processes in the system efficiently, it balances computational loads in various computers by transferring processes between nodes, if necessary. This way, processes of an application can compete for CPUs in different nodes, which provides both *computation speedup* within an application and better performance of the system. Also, the OS uses the redundancy of resources and network links in the system to provide high reliability.

To realize these benefits of computation speedup, performance, and reliability, the OS has to perform control functions like scheduling and deadlock handling on a systemwide basis. Because of the distributed nature of the system, a distributed OS cannot use the notions of *time* and *state* to perform control functions the way a conventional OS uses them, so it performs its control functions in a distributed manner, i.e., through processes in several computers that work in close coordination to make decisions.

A fault in a distributed system does not halt the complete system. It may affect only some computations, or only some parts of a computation, so the distributed OS uses special reliability techniques to minimize the impact of a fault. Presence of the network has several implications for the distributed OS. Communication over the network is slow, so it can seriously erode system performance if processes access their files over the network. To prevent this, distributed file systems employ techniques that reduce network traffic during file processing. The networking component also makes the OS susceptible to security attacks, so it employs special techniques to provide security.

Road Map for Part 5

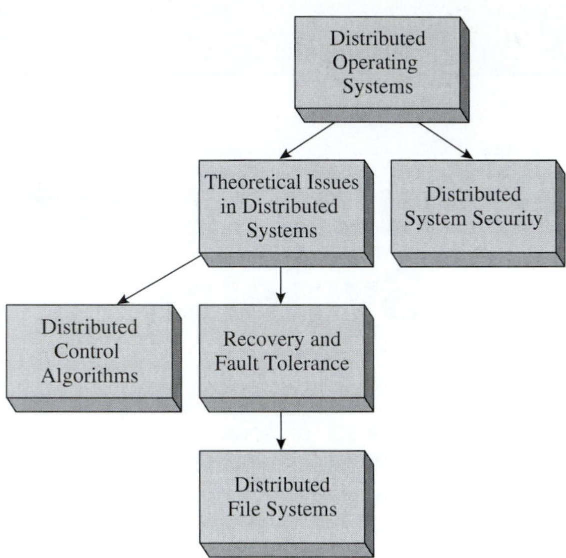

Schematic diagram showing the order in which chapters of this part should be covered in a course.

Chapter 16: Distributed Operating Systems

A distributed system consists of hardware components such as computer systems and the network, and software components such as *network protocols, distributed computations,* and the operating system. This chapter discusses important features of these components and the manner in which these features influence the *computation speedup, reliability,* and *performance* that can be achieved in a distributed system.

Chapter 17: Theoretical Issues in Distributed Systems

Time and *state* are two key notions used in a conventional OS. However, these notions cannot be used in the same manner in a distributed system because it contains several computer systems, each with its own clock and memory, that communicate through messages that incur unpredictable communication delays. This chapter discusses practical alternatives to the traditional notions of time and state. These alternative notions are used in the design of distributed control algorithms and recovery schemes used in a distributed OS.

Chapter 18: Distributed Control Algorithms

A distributed OS uses a distributed control algorithm to implement a control function. The algorithm involves actions in several nodes of the distributed system. This chapter describes the notions of correctness of a distributed control algorithm, and presents algorithms for performing five control functions in a distributed OS—*mutual exclusion, deadlock handling, leader election, scheduling,* and *termination detection*.

Chapter 19: Recovery and Fault Tolerance

A fault may disrupt operation in a system by damaging the states of some data and processes. The focus of *recovery* is to restore some data or process(es) to a consistent state such that normal operation can be restored. *Fault tolerance* provides uninterrupted operation of a system despite faults. This chapter discusses recovery and fault tolerance techniques used in a distributed operating system. *Resiliency*, which is a technique for minimizing the impact of a fault, is also discussed.

Chapter 20: Distributed File Systems

A distributed file system stores files in several nodes of a distributed system, so a process and a file used by it might be in different nodes of a system. Performance and reliability of a distributed file system are determined by the manner in which it organizes access to a required file. This chapter discusses different methods of organizing access to files and directories located in various nodes of a system, and techniques such as *file caching* and *stateless file servers* that are used to ensure good performance and reliability, respectively.

Chapter 21: Distributed System Security

Presence of the network makes a distributed system susceptible to security attacks such as tampering of messages and masquerading, which can be launched through interprocess messages. This chapter discusses *authentication* and *message security* measures used in distributed operating systems to thwart such attacks. Methods of verifying authenticity of data are also discussed.

Chapter 16

Distributed Operating Systems

A distributed system consists of many computer systems, each having its own clock and memory, connected to a network and operating under a distributed operating system. Its key benefits are sharing of resources located in different computers, reliability of operation through redundancy of CPUs and resources across the computer systems, and speedup of a user application achieved by operating its processes in different computers. Features of four hardware and software components are important for realizing these benefits—*computer systems* in the distributed system, the *network* connecting them, *distributed computations* performed in the system, and the *distributed operating system*.

The role of these four components can be described as follows: A computer system forms a *node* of a distributed system. Its architecture influences its ability to contribute to computation speedup and reliability of operation. The operating system integrates the operation of nodes of a distributed system to provide resource sharing, computation speedup, and reliability. To exploit the OS features for access to nonlocal resources and computation speedup, a user employs a distributed computation, whose actions are performed in several nodes of the system. Such a computation uses *interprocess communication protocols* to reliably transfer messages containing data and computations between nodes. These messages are actually sent over the network through *network protocols*.

In this chapter, we discuss important features of these four components of a distributed system to create the background for a study of distributed operating systems. We then identify design issues that arise in a distributed OS because of the distributed nature of its computing environment. We identify five such design issues. These issues are discussed in detail in subsequent chapters.

16.1 FEATURES OF DISTRIBUTED SYSTEMS

A distributed system can consist of two or more computer systems, each with its own clock and memory, some networking hardware, and a capability of

Table 16.1 Benefits of a Distributed System

Feature	Description
Resource sharing	An application may use resources located in different computer systems.
Reliability	A distributed system provides *availability*, i.e., continuity of services, despite occurrence of faults. It is achieved through redundancies in the network and resources, and in OS services.
Computation speedup	Parts of a computation can be executed in parallel in different computer systems, thus reducing duration of an application, i.e., its running time.
Communication	Users or their subcomputations located at different nodes can communicate reliably by using OS services.
Incremental growth	*Open system* standards permit new subsystems to be added to a distributed system without having to replace or upgrade existing subsystems. This way, the cost of enhancing a capability of a distributed system is proportional to the additional capability desired.

performing some of the control functions of the OS (see Definition 3.8). Benefits of a distributed system were discussed earlier in Section 3.8; these are summarized here in Table 16.1.

Use of distributed systems spread rapidly in 1990s when computer hardware prices dropped and use of the open system standard facilitated incremental growth of a system. An *open system* has well-defined and nonproprietary interfaces with its own components and with other systems. These interfaces are typically developed or approved by a standards body, so they have ready acceptance within the computer industry. Their use enables addition of new components and subsystems to a computer system, thereby facilitating incremental growth. The LAN is an excellent example of an open system. Computer systems ranging from supercomputers to cheap PCs can be connected to it because they all use a standard interface. When a distributed system is implemented by using a LAN, its computing capability can be enhanced incrementally by connecting new computer systems to the LAN.

The benefits of distributed systems listed in Table 16.1 are realized using the following hardware and software components:

- *Hardware components:* Individual computer systems and networking hardware such as cables, links, and routers.
- *Software components:* Operating system components that handle creation and scheduling of distributed computations and use of distant resources, OS and programming language features that support writing of distributed computations, and networking software, which ensures reliable communication.

Several terms are used for a computer system that is a part of a distributed system. We use the following convention: a *host* is a computer system in a physical sense, a *node* is a computer system in a logical sense, and a *site* is a location in a distributed system that contains one host. Entities, such as processes and resources, in the same site are said to be *local* entities and those in different sites are said to be *distant* entities.

16.2 NODES OF DISTRIBUTED SYSTEMS

A distributed system can contain different types of nodes. A *minicomputer* node has a single CPU that is shared to service applications of several users. A *workstation* node has a single CPU but services one or more applications initiated by a single user. A node that is a multiprocessor system is called a *processor pool* node. It contains several CPUs, and the number of CPUs may exceed the number of users whose applications are serviced in parallel.

A *cluster* is a group of hosts that work together in an integrated manner. A cluster constitutes a single node of a distributed system; each individual host is a node *within* the cluster. Figure 16.1 is a schematic diagram of a cluster. The cluster is shown to have two nodes; however, more nodes may be added to provide incremental growth. Each node is a computer system having its own memory and I/O devices. The nodes share disk storage, such as a multihost RAID, which offers both high transfer rate and high reliability (see Section 14.3.5), or a storage area network, which offers incremental growth (see Section 14.3.4). Each node is connected to two networks—a *private LAN* to which only the nodes in the cluster are connected, and a *public network* through which it can communicate with other nodes in the distributed system.

Cluster software controls operation of all nodes in a cluster. It can provide computation speedup by scheduling subtasks in an application on different nodes within the cluster, and reliability by exploiting redundancy of CPUs and resources within the cluster. Section 16.3 describes how these features are implemented in the Windows cluster server and the Sun Cluster.

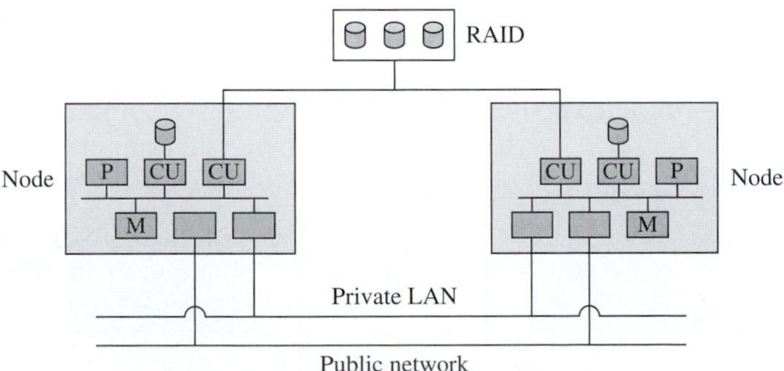

Figure 16.1 Architecture of a cluster.

16.3 INTEGRATING OPERATION OF NODES OF A DISTRIBUTED SYSTEM

To realize the benefits of resource sharing, reliability, and computation speedup summarized in Table 16.1, processes of an application should be scattered across various nodes in the system (1) whenever possible, to achieve computation speedup and efficiency of resources, and (2) whenever necessary to provide reliability. It is achieved by integrating the operation of various nodes in the system through interactions of their kernels. In this section, we sample features of a few systems to illustrate different ways in which operation of nodes is integrated. In Section 16.8, we discuss design issues in distributed operating systems.

Network Operating Systems A *network operating system* is the earliest form of operating system for distributed architectures. Its goal is to provide resource sharing among two or more computer systems that operate under their own OSs. As shown in the schematic of Figure 16.2, the network OS exists as a layer between the kernel of the local OS and user processes. If a process requests access to a local resource, the network OS layer simply passes the request to the kernel of the local OS. However, if the request is for access to a nonlocal resource, the network OS layer contacts the network OS layer of the node that contains the resource and implements access to the resource with its help. Many network operating systems have been developed on top of the Unix operating system. The *Newcastle connection*, also called *Unix United*, is a well-known network OS developed at the University of Newcastle upon Tyne. It provided access to remote files by using system calls that are identical with those used for local files.

A network OS is easier to implement than a full-fledged distributed OS. However, local operating systems retain their identities and operate independently, so their functioning is not integrated and their identities are visible to users. In some network OSs, a user had to log into a remote operating system before he could utilize its resources. This arrangement implies that a user must know where a resource is located in order to use it. A network OS cannot balance or optimize utilization of resources. Thus, some resources in a node may be heavily loaded while identical resources in other nodes may be lightly loaded or free. The network OS also cannot provide fault tolerance—a computation explicitly uses a resource id while accessing a resource, so it has to be aborted if the resource fails.

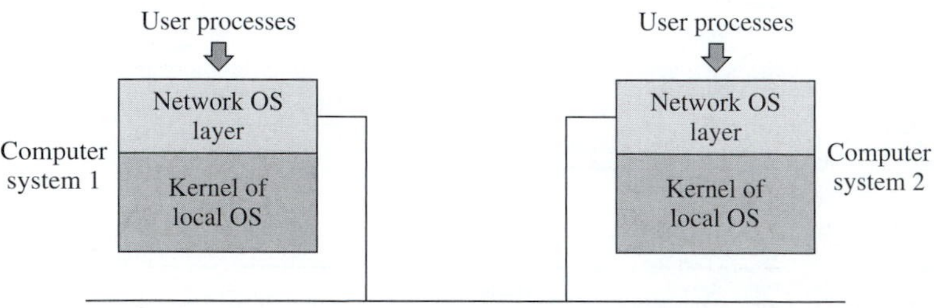

Figure 16.2 A network operating system.

Windows and Sun Cluster Software Cluster software is not a distributed operating system; however, it contains several features found in distributed operating systems—it provides availability through redundancy of resources such as CPUs and I/O devices and computation speedup by exploiting presence of several CPUs within the cluster.

The *Windows cluster server* provides fault tolerance support in clusters containing two or more server nodes. An application has to use a special application program interface (API) to access cluster services. Basic fault tolerance is provided through RAIDs of level 0, 1, or 5 (see Section 14.3.5) that are shared by all server nodes. In addition, when a fault or a shutdown occurs in one server, the cluster server moves its functions to another server without causing a disruption in its services.

A cluster is managed by *distributed control algorithms*, which are implemented through actions performed in all nodes (see Chapter 18). These algorithms require that all nodes must have a consistent view of the cluster, i.e., they must possess identical lists of nodes within the cluster. The following arrangement is used to satisfy this requirement: Each node has a *node manager*, which maintains the list of nodes in a cluster. The node manager periodically sends messages called *heartbeats* to other node managers to detect node faults. The node manager that detects a fault broadcasts a message containing details of the fault on the private LAN. On receiving this message, each node corrects its list of nodes. This event is called a regroup event.

A resource in the cluster server can be a physical resource, a logical resource, or a service. A resource is implemented as a dynamic link library (DLL), so it is specified by providing a DLL interface. A resource belongs to a *group*. A group is owned by one node in the cluster at any time; however, it can be moved to another node in the event of a fault. The resource manager in a node is responsible for starting and stopping a group. If a resource fails, the resource manager informs the *failover manager* and hands over the group containing the resource so that it can be restarted at another node. When a node fault is detected, all groups located in that node are "pulled" to other nodes so that resources in them can be accessed. Use of a shared disk facilitates this arrangement. When a node is restored after a failure, the failover manager decides which groups can be handed over to it. This action is called a *failback*; it safeguards resource efficiency in the system. The handover and failback actions can also be performed manually.

The network load balancing feature distributes the incoming network traffic among the server nodes in a cluster. It is achieved as follows: A single IP address is assigned to the cluster; however, incoming messages go to all server nodes in the cluster. On the basis of the current load distribution arrangement, exactly one of the servers accepts the message and responds to it. When a node fails, its load is distributed among other nodes, and when a new node joins, the load distribution is reconfigured to direct some of the incoming traffic to the new node.

The *Sun cluster framework* integrates a cluster of two or more Sun systems operating under the Solaris OS to provide availability and scalability of services.

Availability is provided through failover, whereby the services that were running at a failed node are relocated to another node. Scalability is provided by sharing the load across servers. Three key components of the Sun Cluster are global process management, distributed file system, and networking. Global process management provides globally unique process ids. This feature is useful in *process migration*, wherein a process is transferred from one node to another to balance the computational loads in different nodes, or to achieve computation speedup. A migrated process should be able to continue using the same path names to access files from a new node. Use of a distributed file system provides this feature.

Amoeba Amoeba is a distributed operating system developed at the Vrije Universiteit in the Netherlands during the 1980s. The primary goal of the Amoeba project is to build a transparent distributed operating system that would have the look and feel of a standard time-sharing OS like Unix. Another goal is to provide a testbed for distributed and parallel programming.

The Amoeba system architecture has three main components—X terminals, a processor pool, and servers such as file and print servers. The X terminal is a user station consisting of a keyboard, a mouse and a bit-mapped terminal connected to a computer. The processor pool has the features described in Section 16.2. The Amoeba microkernel runs on all servers, pool processors and terminals, and performs the following four functions:

1. Managing processes and threads
2. Providing low-level memory management support
3. Supporting communication
4. Handling low-level I/O

Amoeba provides kernel-level threads and two communication protocols. One protocol supports the client–server communication model through *remote procedure calls* (RPCs), while the other protocol provides group communication. For actual message transmission, both these protocols use an underlying Internet protocol called the *fast local Internet protocol* (FLIP), which is a network layer protocol in the ISO protocol stack (see Section 16.6.6).

Many functions performed by traditional kernels are implemented through servers that run on top of a microkernel. Thus actions like booting, process creation, and process scheduling are performed by servers. The file system is also implemented as a file server. This approach reduces the size of the microkernel and makes it suitable for a wide range of computer systems from servers to pool processors. The concept of objects is central to Amoeba. Objects are managed by servers and they are protected by using capabilities (see Section 15.7).

When a user logs in, a shell is initiated in some host in the system. As the user issues commands, processes are created in some other hosts to execute the commands. Thus a user's computation is spread across the hosts in the system; there is no notion of a home machine for a user. This disregard for machine boundaries shows how tightly all resources in the system are integrated. Amoeba uses the processor pool model of nodes in the system. When a user issues a command, the OS allocates a few pool processors to the execution of the command. Where necessary, pool processors are shared across users.

16.4 RELIABLE INTERPROCESS COMMUNICATION

In a conventional OS, processes that wish to communicate through messages exist in the same host, and have unique ids assigned by its kernel. However, in a distributed system, processes existing in different nodes may wish to communicate with one another, hence the distributed OS assigns globally unique names to processes. It also provides an arrangement through which a process with a given name can be located in the system, so that other processes can communicate with it. We discuss both these features in Section 16.4.1.

Once the location of a destination process is determined, a message meant for it can be sent to it over the network. However, message delivery may fail because of faults in communication links or nodes located in network path(s) to the destination process, hence processes must make their own arrangement to ensure reliable delivery of messages. This arrangement is in the form of an *interprocess communication protocol* (*IPC protocol*), which is a set of rules and conventions aimed at handling transient faults during message transmission. The sender and destination processes invoke *protocol routines* when they execute the `send` and `receive` statements. These routines perform necessary actions to ensure reliable delivery of messages.

Table 16.2 summarizes three key provisions in IPC protocols—*acknowledgments*, *time-outs*, and *retransmissions*. An acknowledgment informs the sender process that its message has been delivered to the destination process. A time-out is said to have occurred if the sender process does not receive an acknowledgment in an expected interval of time. The message is now retransmitted. These steps are repeated until the sender process receives an acknowledgment.

The protocol is implemented as follows: When a process sends a message, the protocol routine invoked by it makes a system call to request an interrupt at the end of a specific time interval. This interrupt is called a *time-out interrupt*. When the message is delivered to the destination process, the protocol routine invoked by the destination process sends an acknowledgment to the sender process to inform it that its message has been delivered. If the time-out interrupt occurs

Table 16.2 Provisions for Reliability in an IPC Protocol

Provision	Description
Acknowledgment	When a process receives a message, the protocol routine invoked by it sends an acknowledgment to the sender of the message.
Time-out	The protocol specifies an interval of time within which it expects a sender process to receive an acknowledgment. A *time-out* is said to have occurred if the acknowledgment is not received within this interval.
Retransmission of a message	If a time-out interrupt occurs before the sender receives an acknowledgment, the protocol routine invoked by the sender retransmits the message.

in the sender's site before an acknowledgment is received, the protocol routine retransmits the message and makes a system call to request another time-out interrupt. These actions are repeated until the sender receives an acknowledgment. A similar arrangement may be used to ensure that a reply, if any, sent by the destination process reaches the sender process. We discuss IPC protocols in Sections 16.4.2–16.4.3.

16.4.1 Naming of Processes

All entities in a distributed system, whether processes or resources, are assigned unique names as follows: Each host in a system is assigned a systemwide unique name, which can be either numeric or symbolic, and each process or resource in a host is assigned an id that is unique in the host. This way, the pair (*<host_name>*, *<process_id>*) is unique for each process and can be used as its name. A process that wishes to send a message to another process uses a pair like (`human_resources`, P_j) as the name of the destination process, where `human_resources` is the name of a host. This name should be translated into a network address for sending the message.

To easily locate a host in the Internet, the Internet is partitioned into a set of *domains* that have unique names, each domain is partitioned into smaller domains that have unique names in the domain, and so on. A host has a unique name in the immediately containing domain, but its name may not be unique in the Internet, so a unique name for a host is formed by adding names of all the domains that contain it, separated by periods, starting with the smallest domain and ending with the largest domain. For example, the host name Everest.cse.iitb.ac.in refers to the server Everest in the Computer Science and Engineering Department of IIT Bombay, which is in the academic domain in India.

The domain name space is hierarchically organized; the top level in the hierarchy is occupied by an unnamed root domain. This domain contains a small number of *top-level domains* that represent either organizations of a specific kind, or organizations within a country. In the host name Everest.cse.iitb.ac.in, "in" is the top-level domain representing India and "ac" is the name of a domain containing academic organizations. Hence "ac.in" contains academic organizations in India. "ac" is called a second-level domain because its name contains two domain names.

Each host connected to the Internet has a unique address known as the Internet protocol address (IP address). The *domain name system* (DNS) is a distributed Internet directory service that provides the IP address of a host with a given name. It has a *name server* in every domain, which contains a directory giving the IP address of each host in the domain. When a process operating in a host h_i wishes to send a message to another process with the name (*<host_name>*, *<process_id>*), host h_i performs *name resolution* to determine the IP address of *<host name>*. Host h_i is called the *resolver*. Name resolution proceeds as follows: The resolver knows the address of a name server for the root domain. To resolve the name *<host_name>*, the resolver sends it to the name server of the root domain. This name server responds by returning the IP address of a name server for the top-level domain in *<host_name>*. The resolver now sends *<host_name>* to this name server, which returns the address of a name server for the second-level domain, and so on, until a name server returns the address of the required host.

Name resolution using name servers can be slow, so each resolver can cache some name server data. This technique speeds up repeated name resolution the same way a directory cache speeds up repeated references to the directory entry of a file (see Section 13.15). An IP address can be kept in the cache for the amount of time specified as the *time to live*, which is 1 hour. The name server of a domain is replicated to enhance its availability and to avoid contention.

16.4.2 IPC Semantics

IPC semantics is the set of properties of an IPC protocol. IPC semantics depend on the arrangement of acknowledgments and retransmissions used in an IPC protocol. Table 16.3 summarizes three commonly used IPC semantics.

At-most-once semantics result when a protocol does not use acknowledgments or retransmission. These semantics are used if a lost message does not pose a serious threat to correctness of an application, or if the application knows how to recover from such situations. For example, an application that receives periodic reports from other processes knows when a message is not received as expected, so it may itself communicate with a sender whose message is lost and ask it to resend the message. These semantics provide high communication efficiency because acknowledgments and retransmissions are not used.

At-least-once semantics result when a protocol uses acknowledgments and retransmission, because a destination process may receive a message more than

Table 16.3 IPC Semantics

Semantics	Description
At-most-once semantics	A destination process either receives a message once, or does not receive it. These semantics are obtained when a process receiving a message does not send an acknowledgment and a sender process does not perform retransmission of messages.
At-least-once semantics	A destination process is guaranteed to receive a message; however, it may receive several copies of the message. These semantics are obtained when a process receiving a message sends an acknowledgment, and a sender process retransmits a message if it does not receive an acknowledgment before a time-out occurs.
Exactly-once semantics	A destination process receives a message exactly once. These semantics are obtained when sending of acknowledgments and retransmissions are performed as in at-least-once semantics; however, the IPC protocol recognizes duplicate messages and discards them so that the receiver process receives the message only once.

once if an acknowledgment is lost or delayed because of congestion in the network. A message received for the second or subsequent time is called a *duplicate message*. An application can use at-least-once semantics only if processing of duplicate messages does not pose any correctness problems such as updating of data many times instead of only once.

Exactly-once semantics result when a protocol uses acknowledgments and retransmission, but discards duplicate messages. These semantics hide transient faults from both sender and receiver processes; however, the IPC protocol incurs high communication overhead due to handling of faults and duplicate messages.

16.4.3 IPC Protocols

An IPC protocol specifies what actions should be performed at the sites of sender and destination processes so that a message is delivered to a destination process and its reply is delivered to the sender process. We describe how IPC protocols are classified and present a couple of examples.

Reliable and Unreliable Protocols A *reliable protocol* guarantees that a message, or its reply, is not lost. It achieves this through at-least-once or exactly-once semantics for both messages and their replies. An *unreliable protocol* does not guarantee that a message or its reply would not be lost—it provides at-most-once semantics either for messages or for their replies. As commented in the last section, a reliable protocol incurs substantial overhead due to acknowledgments and retransmission of messages and replies, whereas an unreliable protocol does not incur these overheads.

Blocking and Nonblocking Protocols As discussed in Chapter 9, it is common to block a process that executes a *receive* system call if no messages have been sent to it. There are no intrinsic reasons to block a process that executes a *send* system call; however, blocking of a sender process may simplify a protocol, reduce its overhead, and also add some desirable features to its semantics. For example, if a sender process is blocked until its message is delivered to a destination process, the message would never have to be retransmitted after the sender is activated, so the message need not be buffered by the protocol after the sender is activated. Also, blocking of the sender helps to provide semantics similar to the conventional procedure call.

A protocol is a *blocking protocol* if a sender process is blocked until it receives a reply to its message; otherwise, it is a *nonblocking protocol*. We assume that if a protocol does not block a sender process, interrupt(s) will be generated to notify the process of the arrival of a reply or an acknowledgment so that it can take appropriate actions. Blocking and nonblocking protocols are also called *process-synchronous* and *asynchronous* protocols, respectively.

16.4.3.1 The Request-Reply-Acknowledgment Protocol

The request-reply-acknowledgment (RRA) protocol is a reliable protocol for use by processes that exchange requests and replies. Receipt of the reply implies that the destination process has received the request, so a separate acknowledgment

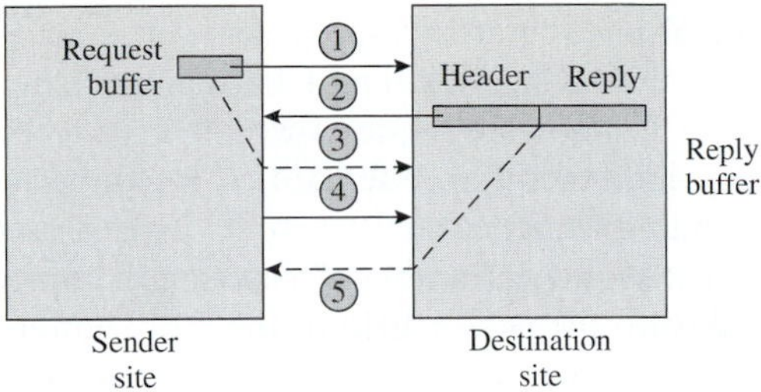

Figure 16.3 Operation of a blocking version of the request-reply-acknowledgment (RRA) protocol.

of the request is not needed. The sender, however, sends an an explicit acknowledgment of the reply. A blocking version of the RRA protocol is presented as Algorithm 16.1. Figure 16.3 depicts its operation.

Algorithm 16.1 *A Blocking Version of the RRA Protocol*

1. *When a process makes a request:* The request is copied in a buffer called the *request buffer* in its site and also sent to the destination process in the form of a message. A system call is made to request a time-out interrupt. The sender process is blocked until a reply is received from the destination process.
2. *When a destination process receives a message:* The destination process analyzes the request contained in the message and prepares a reply. The reply is copied in a buffer called the *reply buffer* in the destination site and also sent to the sender process. A system call is made to request a time-out interrupt.
3. *When a time-out occurs in the sender process:* The copy of the request stored in the request buffer is retransmitted.
4. *When the sender process receives a reply:* The sender process sends an acknowledgment to the destination process. It also releases the request buffer, if not already done.
5. *When a time-out occurs in the destination process:* The copy of the reply stored in the reply buffer is retransmitted.
6. *When the destination process receives an acknowledgment:* The destination process releases the reply buffer.

The sender process is blocked until it receives a reply, so a single request buffer in the sender site suffices irrespective of the number of messages a process sends out, or the number of processes it sends them to. The destination process is not blocked on an acknowledgment, so it could handle requests from other processes while it waits for an acknowledgment. Accordingly, the destination site needs one reply buffer for each sender process. The number of messages can be reduced through *piggybacking*, which is the technique of including the acknowledgment of a reply in the next request to the same destination process. Since a sender process is blocked until it receives a reply, an acknowledgment of a reply is actually implicit in the next request it makes. Hence only the reply to the last request would require an explicit acknowledgment message.

The RRA protocol has the at-least-once semantics because messages and replies cannot be lost; however, they might be delivered more than once. As mentioned in Table 16.3, duplicate requests would have to be discarded in the destination site to provide exactly-once semantics. It can be achieved as follows: A sender assigns ascending sequence numbers to its requests and includes them in its request messages. The sequence number of a message is copied into its reply and acknowledgment, and into the *header* field of the reply buffer in the destination site. The destination process also separately preserves the sequence number of the last request received from the sender process. If the sequence number in a request is not greater than the preserved sequence number, the request is a duplicate request so the destination process simply retransmits the reply if its copy is present in the reply buffer. Otherwise, either the copy of the reply in the reply buffer would have been discarded after receiving its acknowledgment, in which case the request is an outdated retransmission, or the destination process is still processing the request and would send its reply sometime in future. In either of these cases, the duplicate request is simply discarded.

16.4.3.2 The Request-Reply Protocol

The request-reply (RR) protocol simply performs retransmission of a request when a time-out occurs. A nonblocking version of the RR protocol that provides the exactly-once semantics is presented as Algorithm 16.4.3. Figure 16.4 depicts its operation.

Algorithm 16.2 *A Nonblocking Version of the RR Protocol*

1. *When a process makes a request:* The request is copied in a request buffer in the sender site and also sent to the destination process in the form of a message. A system call is made to request a time-out interrupt. The sender process proceeds with its computation.
2. *When the destination process receives a message:* If the message is not a duplicate request, the destination process analyzes the request contained in the message and prepares a reply, copies it in a reply buffer and also sends it to the sender process. Otherwise, it simply locates the reply of the message in a reply buffer and sends it to the sender process.

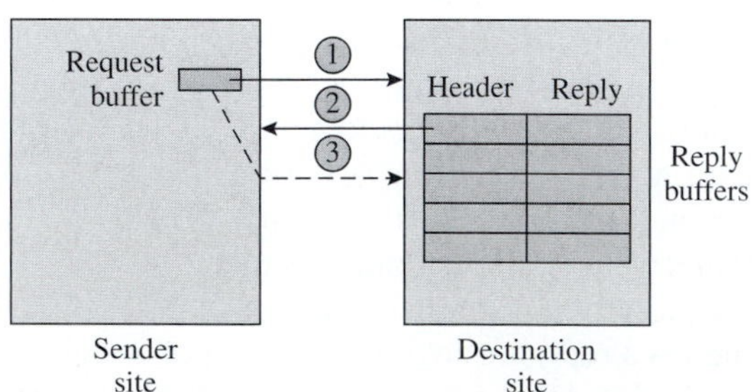

Figure 16.4 Operation of a nonblocking version of the request-reply (RR) protocol.

3. *When a time-out occurs in the sender site:* The copy of the request stored in the request buffer is retransmitted.
4. *When a reply is received at the sender site:* An interrupt is raised to notify the sender process of the arrival of a reply. The sender process releases the request buffer.

A sender does not explicitly acknowledge a reply. Also, unlike the RRA protocol of the previous section, an acknowledgment is not implicit in the sender's next request because the sender could have made the next request before receiving the reply to its previous request. Consequently, the destination process has to buffer its replies indefinitely, which leads to a very high buffer space requirement.

If requests made by a sender are delivered to the destination process in the same order, the duplicate recognition and discarding arrangement of the RRA protocol can be used with minor changes: A destination process preserves the sequence numbers and replies of *all* requests in a pool of buffers. When it recognizes a duplicate request through a comparison of sequence numbers, it searches for the reply of the request in the buffer pool using the sequence number, and retransmits the reply if found in a buffer; otherwise, it simply ignores the request, as a reply would be sent after processing the request. Exercise 16.5 addresses a refinement of this approach that is needed if the requests may be received out of order at the destination site.

This protocol can be simplified for use in applications involving *idempotent computations*. An idempotent computation has the property that it produces the same result if executed again. For example, the computation $i := 5$ is idempotent, whereas the computation $i := i+1$ is not. If the handling of a request involves only idempotent computations, data consistency would not be affected if a request is processed more than once, so it is possible to omit the arrangement for buffering of replies and discarding of duplicate requests. Read and write operations performed in a file are idempotent, so it is possible to employ the simplified RR protocol in using a remote file server. It has the additional advantage that the file server need not maintain information about which requests it has already processed, which helps to make it *stateless* and more reliable (see Section 20.4.3).

16.5 DISTRIBUTED COMPUTATION PARADIGMS

Data used in an application may be stored in different sites of a distributed system because of the following considerations:

- *Data replication:* Several copies of a data D may be kept in different sites of a distributed system to provide availability and efficient access.
- *Data distribution:* Parts of a data D may be kept in different sites of a system either because the data D is voluminous, or because its parts originate in different sites or are frequently used in different sites.

Table 16.4 Modes of Accessing Data in a Distributed System

Mode of access	Description
Remote data access	A computation accesses data over the network. This mode of access does not interfere with organization or access of data and does not require restructuring of a computation. However, computations are slowed down by communication delays.
Data migration	The data is moved to the site where a computation is located. Data migration provides efficient data access; however, it may interfere with replication and distribution of data.
Computation migration	A computation (or a part of it) is moved to the site where its data is located. It provides efficient data access without interfering with organization or access of data.

When data D is neither replicated nor distributed, the OS may position it such that the total network traffic generated by accesses to D by various applications is minimal.

Table 16.4 summarizes three modes of accessing data in a distributed system. In *remote data access*, the data is accessed *in situ*, i.e., where it exists. This mode of using data does not interfere with decisions concerning placement of the data; however, it is slow because of network latencies. *Data migration* involves moving data to the site of the computation that uses it. This mode faces difficulties if data is used by many computations or if it has been replicated to provide high availability. In the worst case, it may force the data to be used strictly by one computation at a time. *Computation migration* moves a computation to the site where its data is located. It does not interfere with replication or distribution of data.

Operating systems provide some support for each data access mode summarized in Table 16.4. As described in Section 16.3, a network OS supports remote data access. The File Transfer Protocol (FTP) is a facility for data migration; it performs transfer of files in an offline manner rather than during execution of a computation. *Process migration* is a feature for migrating a computation, or a part of it, while the computation is in progress. It is described later in Section 18.8.2.

A *distributed computation* is one whose parts can be executed in different sites for reasons of data access efficiency, computation speedup, or reliability. A *distributed computation paradigm* is a model of useful practices for designing distributed computations. The primary issues addressed by a distributed computation paradigm are manipulation of data and initiation of subcomputations in different sites of a distributed system. Table 16.5 summarizes three distributed computation paradigms. The *client–server computing* paradigm focuses on remote data access and manipulation, while the *remote procedure call* and *remote evaluation* paradigms provide different ways of performing computation migration.

Table 16.5 Distributed Computation Paradigms

Paradigm	Description
Client–server computing	A server process provides a specific service to its clients. A client process invokes its service by sending a message to it, and the server returns its results in another message. Applications use the client–server paradigm extensively to perform remote data access or remote data manipulation.
Remote procedure call (RPC)	A remote procedure resembles a conventional procedure except that it executes in a different node of the system. A remote procedure is installed in a node by a system administrator and it is registered with a name server. The remote procedure call has been used extensively for computation migration.
Remote evaluation	If a program uses the statement `at` *<node>* `eval` *<code_segment>*, the compiler of the language in which the program is written makes a provision to transfer *<code_segment>* to the node designated by *<node>*, execute it there and return its results. There is no need to install the code segment in the remote node. Java provides a facility for remote evaluation.

16.5.1 Client–Server Computing

A *server* is a process in a distributed system that provides a specific service to its clients. Typically, the name of a server and a specification of its service are widely advertised in a system. Any process can send a message to a server and become its client. A service may have a physical connotation like accessing or printing a file, or it may have a computational connotation like evaluating mathematical functions in a math server. Accordingly, the server's role ranges from mere data access to data manipulation; in the latter case the server may even play a computational role in a distributed computation.

A server may become a bottleneck if the rate at which clients make requests exceeds the rate at which the server can service them. Figure 16.5 depicts three methods of addressing this problem. Figure 16.5(a) shows many identical servers, each with its own request queue. The clients are partitioned in some way such that each client knows which server it should use. This arrangement inherits the drawbacks of partitioning—some servers may be heavily loaded while others are idle. In Figure 16.5(b) many servers dynamically share the same queue. This arrangement is more flexible than partitioning the clients to use different servers. Figure 16.5(c) shows a multithreaded server. A new thread is created to handle each request. The threads compete with one another for CPU and other resources. If the server function is I/O-bound, this arrangement can overlap servicing of several requests. Another way to eliminate the server bottleneck is to push most of the computational burden into a client process. Now the server can provide

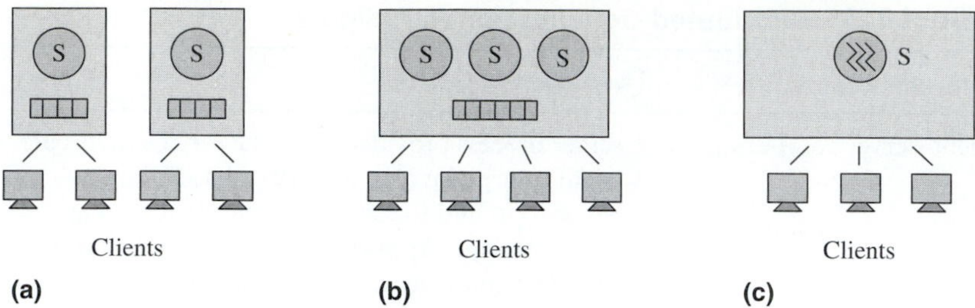

Figure 16.5 Servers with (a) independent and (b) shared queues; (c) a multithreaded server.

better response times to clients. Design methodologies have been evolved to design such client–server arrangements.

Client–server computing is a poor paradigm for distributed computing because methodologies for structuring a distributed computation in the form of a client–server configuration have not been evolved. The primary difficulty is that a distributed computation involves many entities with a symmetric relationship. This relationship is hard to model with the client–server paradigm. In practice, the client–server paradigm is used extensively for noncomputational roles in a LAN environment, such as accessing files, or handling simple database queries. To make its implementation efficient, simple protocols like the RR protocol are preferred over multilayered protocols like the ISO protocol, which is discussed in a later section.

16.5.2 Remote Procedure Calls

A *remote procedure call* (RPC) is a programming language feature designed for distributed computing. As discussed earlier in Section 9.4.2, its syntax and semantics resemble those of a conventional procedure call. In the remote procedure call

call <*proc_id*> (<*message*>);

<*proc_id*> is the id of a remote procedure, and <*message*> is a list of parameters. The call is implemented by using a blocking protocol. The result of the call may be passed back through one of the parameters, or through an explicit return value. We can view the caller–callee relationship as a client–server relationship. Thus, the remote procedure is the server and a process calling it is a client.

The schematic diagram of Figure 16.6 depicts the arrangement used to perform name resolution, parameter passing, and return of results during a remote procedure call. The *domain name system* (DNS) described in Section 16.4.1 is used to obtain the IP address of the called process. The functions of the client and server stubs are as described earlier in Section 9.4.2—the *client stub* converts the parameters into a machine-independent form and the *server stub* converts them into the machine-specific representation suitable for the server's host, whereas they play the converse roles for the results of the called procedure. The circled

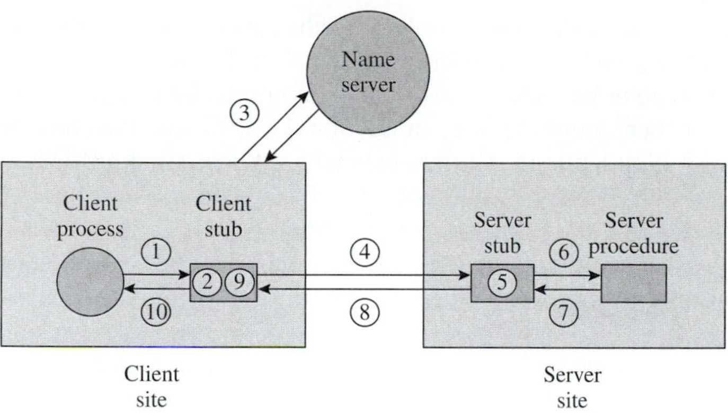

Figure 16.6 Implementation of a remote procedure call (RPC).

numbers in Figure 16.6 denote the steps in implementing the remote procedure call. Details of these steps are as follows:

1. The client process calls the client stub with parameters. This call is a conventional procedure call. Hence execution of the client process is suspended until the call is completed.
2. The client stub marshals the parameters and converts them into a machine-independent format. It now prepares a message containing this representation of parameters.
3. The client stub interacts with the name server to find the identity of the site at which the remote procedure exists.
4. The client stub sends the message prepared in Step 2 to the site where the remote procedure exists, using a blocking protocol. This send operation blocks the client stub until a reply to its message arrives.
5. The server stub receives the message sent by the client stub. It converts the parameters to the machine-specific format suitable for the server site.
6. The server stub now executes a call on the server procedure with these parameters. This is a conventional procedure call, hence execution of the server stub is suspended until the procedure call is completed.
7. The server procedure returns its results to the server stub. The server stub converts them into a machine-independent format and prepares a message containing the results.
8. The message containing the results is sent to the client site.
9. The client stub converts the results into the format suitable for the client site.
10. The client stub returns the results to the client process.

Step 10 completes execution of the remote procedure call. The client process is now free to continue its execution.

In Step 3, the client stub need not perform name resolution every time the RPC is executed. It can do so the first time, and save the information concerning site of the remote procedure in a name server cache for future use. Name resolution can even be performed statically, i.e., before operation of the client process begins.

Faults may occur during a remote procedure call—either in the communication link, in the server site, or in the client itself. If the client site crashes, the call becomes an *orphan* because its result is not going to be of any use. We discuss orphans and their handling later in Section 19.3. Communication and server faults can be handled using an arrangement involving acknowledgments and retransmissions (see Section 16.4). Ideally, RPCs should possess the exactly-once semantics; however, it is expensive to implement these semantics. At-least-once semantics are cheaper to implement; however, they require that either the actions of the remote procedure should be idempotent or that it must discard duplicate requests.

The remote procedure call feature can be used as a building block for distributed computations. Its advantages over the client–server paradigm are due to two factors. First, it may be possible to set up a remote procedure by simply intimating its name and location to the name server. It is much easier than setting up a server. Second, only those processes that know of the existence of a remote procedure can invoke it. So, use of remote procedures provides more privacy, and hence more security, than use of the client–server paradigm. Its primary disadvantage is a lack of flexibility—the remote procedure has to be registered with a name server, so its location cannot be changed easily.

16.5.3 Remote Evaluation

The remote evaluation paradigm was proposed by Stamos and Gifford (1990). The paradigm is implemented through the statement

`at` *<node>* `eval` *<code_segment>*

where *<node>* is an expression that evaluates to the identity of some node in the distributed system and *<code_segment>* is a segment of code, possibly a sequence of statements. When the `at` statement is encountered during operation of a process, *<node>* is evaluated to obtain the identity of a node, *<code_segment>* is executed in that node, and its results, if any, are returned to the process.

This paradigm has several advantages over the client–server and RPC paradigms. It requires minimal support from the OS. Most of the work is done by the compiler of the language in which the program is written. With the help of the OS, the compiler makes a provision to transfer *<code_segment>* to the target node and to execute it there. The OS of the target node creates a process to execute the code and to return its results. Prior installation of *<code_segment>* or an elaborate setup of stub procedures is not needed.

The issues of naming and binding are also much simpler than in an RPC environment. The decision about which node should be used to execute the code segment is taken dynamically. This decision could use information concerning computational loads at various nodes. *<code_segment>* can be any arbitrary section of code that can be executed remotely; it need not have the syntactic shape of a procedure. The remote evaluation paradigm can be used along with the client–server or RPC paradigms, i.e., the code segment could invoke procedures during its execution or it could itself be a procedure.

The remote evaluation paradigm can be used for computation speedup or for improving efficiency of a computation. For example, if a subcomputation involves considerable manipulation of data located at some specific node S_i, the subcomputation can itself be executed at S_i. It would reduce the amount of network traffic involved in remote data access. Similarly, if a user wishes to send an email to a number of persons at S_i, the mail sending command can itself be executed at S_i.

16.5.4 Case Studies

SUN RPC Sun RPC was designed for client–server communication in NFS, the Sun network file system. NFS models file processing actions as idempotent actions, so Sun RPC provides the at-least-once semantics. This feature makes the RPC efficient; however, it requires applications using RPC to make their own arrangements for duplicate suppression if exactly-once semantics are desired.

Sun RPC provides an interface language called XDR and an interface compiler called `rpcgen`. To use a remote procedure, a user has to write an interface definition for it in XDR, which contains a specification of the remote procedure and its parameters. The interface definition is compiled using `rpcgen`, which produces the following: a client stub, the server procedure and a server stub, a header file for use in the client and server programs, and two parameter handling procedures that are invoked by the client and server stubs, respectively. The client program is compiled with the header file and the client stub, while the server program is compiled with the header file and the server stub. The parameter handling procedure invoked by the client stub marshals parameters and converts them into a machine-independent format called the external data representation (XDR). The procedure invoked by the server stub converts parameters from the XDR format into the machine representation suitable for the called procedure.

The Sun RPC schematic has some limitations. The remote procedure can accept only one parameter. This limitation is overcome by defining a structure containing many data members and passing the structure as the parameter. The RPC implementation also does not use the services of a name server. Instead, each site contains a port mapper that is like a local name server. It contains names of procedures and their port ids. A procedure that is to be invoked as a remote procedure is assigned a port and this information is registered with the port mapper. The client first makes a request to the port mapper of the remote site to find which port is used by the required remote procedure. It then calls the procedure at that port. A weakness of this arrangement is that a caller must know the site where a remote procedure exists.

Java Remote Method Invocation (RMI) A server application running on a host creates a special type of object called a *remote object*, whose methods may be invoked by clients operating in other hosts. The server selects a name for the service that is to be offered by a method of the remote object, and registers it with a name server called the `rmiregistry`, which runs on the server's host. The `rmiregistry` typically listens on a standard port for registration and invocation requests. The prospective clients of the service know the IP address of the server's host. A client consults the `rmiregistry` in the server's host to locate the service with a given name. The `rmiregistry` returns an object handle for the remote object providing the service, and the client uses this object handle to invoke the method that provides the service. The syntax of this invocation resembles a similar operation on a local object. The invocation of the remote service resembles the familiar schematic described in section 16.5.2; the `javac` compiler is used to compile the source files containing the server and client programs, and the `rmic` compiler is used to generate client and server stubs.

A client can pass special types of objects called *serializable objects* as parameters of the remote method. The Java RMI passes the code and data of such objects to the invoked remote method. This code is loaded in the server's host while unmarshaling the parameters; it may be invoked by the object offering the remote service. This feature can be used to achieve an effect analogous to remote evaluation described in Section 16.5.3 as follows: A server registers a remote service `r_eval` that takes a serializable object `alpha` as a parameter and simply invokes the method `alpha.gamma()`. When a client creates a serializable object and passes it as a parameter in an invocation of `r_eval`, `r_eval` would load the code of the object and invoke its method `gamma`. In effect, the client would have achieved execution of some of its own code at the server's site. Different clients can use the same service `r_eval` to get different codes executed at the server's site.

16.6 NETWORKING

The term *networking* includes both network hardware and network software. Thus, it includes networking technology and design of computer networks, as also software aspects of implementing communication between a pair of processes. The basic issues in networking are summarized in Table 16.6. Network type, network topology, and networking technology concern the design of networks. All other issues concern message communication between processes—finding the IP address of the node where a destination process is located, deciding which route a message would follow to that node, and ensuring that the message is delivered efficiently and reliably. We discussed the *domain name system* (DNS) that determines the IP address of a host in Section 16.4.1. All other issues in networking are discussed in this section.

16.6.1 Types of Networks

A *wide area network* (WAN) connects resources and users that are geographically distant. When expensive mainframe computers were in use, it made good sense to make them accessible to a large number of users from different organizations and different locations. A WAN made this possible. The other motivation for WANs was to enable communication and data sharing between users.

Table 16.6 Issues in Networking

Issue	Description
Network type	The type of a network is determined by the geographical distribution of users and resources in the system. Two main types of networks are *wide area networks* (WANs) and *local area networks* (LANs).
Network topology	*Network topology* is the arrangement of nodes and communication links in a network. It influences the speed and reliability of communication, and the cost of network hardware.
Networking technology	Networking technology is concerned with transmission of data over a network. It influences network bandwidth and latency.
Naming of processes	Using the *domain name system* (DNS), the pair (*<host_name>*, *<process_id>*) for a destination process is translated into the pair (IP address, *<process_id>*).
Connection strategy	A connection strategy decides how to set up data paths between communicating processes. It influences throughput of communication links and efficiency of communication between processes.
Routing strategy	A routing strategy decides the route along which a message would travel through the system. It influences communication delays suffered by a message.
Network protocols	A *network protocol* is a set of rules and conventions that ensure effective communication over a network. A hierarchy of network protocols is used to obtain a separation of various concerns involved in data transmission and reliability.
Network bandwidth and latency	The *bandwidth* of a network is the rate at which data is transferred over the network. *Latency* is the elapsed time before data is delivered at the destination site.

When inexpensive personal computers became available, many organizations installed a large number of PCs within offices. Data used by PC users and resources like good-quality laser printers became critical resources, so *local area networks* (LANs) were set up to connect users and resources located within the same office or same building. Since all resources and users in a LAN belonged to the same organization, there was little motivation for sharing the data and resources with outsiders. Hence few LANs were connected to WANs, though the technology for making such connections existed. Advent of the Internet changed the scenario and most LANs and WANs are today connected to the Internet.

Figure 16.7 illustrates WANs and LANs. The LAN consists of PCs, printers, and a file server. It is connected to a WAN through a *gateway*, which is a computer that is connected to two (or more) networks and transfers messages between them.

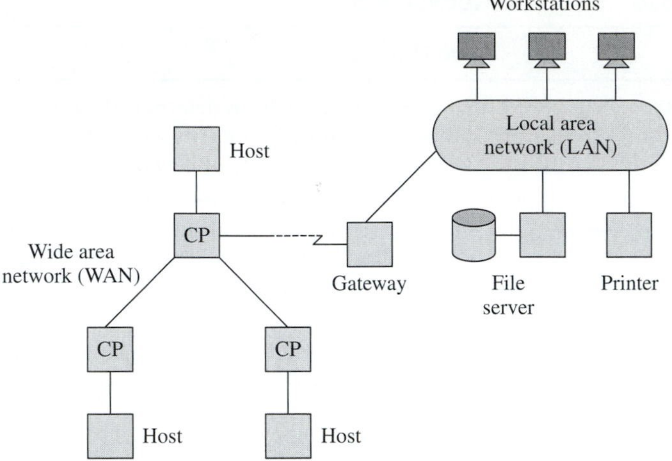

Figure 16.7 Types of networks.

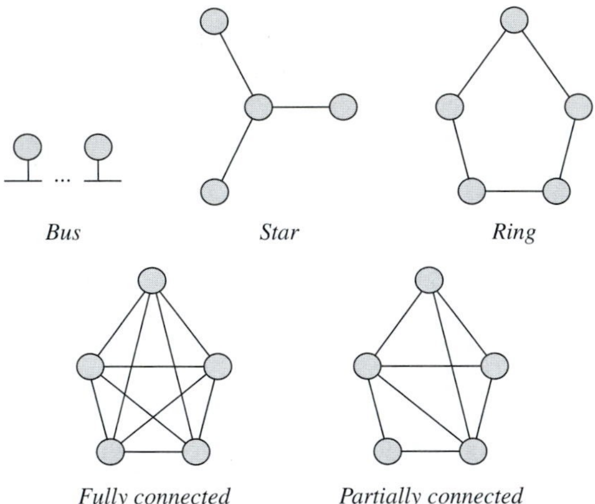

Figure 16.8 Network topologies.

Special-purpose processors called *communication processors* (CPs) are used in the WAN to facilitate communication of messages between distant hosts. LANs use expensive high-speed cables like Category 5 or fiber-optic cables to provide high data transfer rates. WANs often use public lines for data transfer because of cost considerations, so it is generally not possible to support high transfer rates.

16.6.2 Network Topology

Figure 16.8 illustrates five network topologies. These topologies differ in the cost of network hardware, speed of communication, and reliability. The *bus* topology is similar to the bus in a PC. All hosts are connected directly to the bus, so the cost of network hardware is low. Only one pair of hosts can communicate over the bus at any time. High transfer rates are achieved except when contention exists for the bus. The bus topology is used in Ethernet-based LANs.

In the *star* topology, each host is connected only to the host in the central site of the system. This topology is useful when the distributed system contains one server, and nodes contain processes that use this server. Reliability of a star network depends on reliability of the central host. Communication delays between a host and the central host, or between two hosts, depend on contention at the central host. Fast Ethernet uses a star topology.

In a *ring* network, each host has two neighbors. When a host wishes to communicate with another host, a message is passed along the ring until it reaches the destination host. Consequently, the communication load on a host is high even when none of its processes is communicating. In a unidirectional ring, a link carries messages in only one direction whereas in a bidirectional ring a link can carry messages in both directions. Naturally unidirectional and bidirectional rings have different reliability characteristics—a bidirectional ring network is immune to single host or link faults, whereas a unidirectional ring network is not.

In a *fully connected* network, a link exists between every pair of hosts. Consequently, communication between a pair of hosts is immune to crashes of other hosts, or faults in up to $(n - 2)$ links, where n is the number of hosts in the network. One or more hosts may become isolated if the number of faults exceeds $n - 2$. This situation is called *network partitioning*. A *partially connected* network contains fewer links than a fully connected network. It has a lower cost than a fully connected network; however, it may get partitioned with fewer host or link crashes than a fully connected network.

16.6.3 Networking Technologies

We discuss three networking technologies. The Ethernet and token ring technologies are used for local area networks and the Asynchronous Transfer Mode (ATM) technology is used for ISDN networks.

Ethernet Ethernet is a bus-like network (simple or branching bus) using a circuit that consists of cables linked by repeaters. Several entities, called *stations*, are connected to the same cable. Data is transmitted in units called *frames*. Each frame contains addresses of its source and destination, and a data field. Each station listens on the bus at all times. It copies a frame in a buffer if the frame is meant for it; otherwise, it ignores the frame. The original Ethernet operated at a transmission rate of 10 Mbits per second. Fast Ethernet, which operates at 100 Mbits per second, Gigabit Ethernet, and 10 Gigabit Ethernet are prevalent variants of Ethernet. A *bridge* is used to connect Ethernet LANs. It is a computer that receives frames on one Ethernet and, depending on the destination addresses, reproduces them on another Ethernet to which it is connected.

Since the basic Ethernet topology is that of a bus, only one conversation can be in progress at any time. The "carrier sense multiple access with collision detection" (CSMA/CD) technology ensures it as follows: A station that wishes to send a message listens to the traffic on the cable to check whether a signal is being transmitted. This check is called *carrier sensing*. The station starts transmitting its frame if it does not detect a signal. However, if many stations find no signal on the cable and transmit at the same time, their frames would interfere with one another, causing abnormal voltage on the cable. This situation is called a *collision*. A station that detects a collision emits a special 32-bit jam signal. On receiving the jam signal, any transmitting station that had not so far detected a collision becomes aware of a collision. All the transmitting stations now back off by abandoning their transmissions and waiting for a random period of time before retransmitting their frames. This procedure of recovering from a collision does not guarantee that the frames will not collide again; however, it helps in ensuring that eventually all frames will be transmitted and received without collisions. The frame size must exceed a minimum that facilitates collision detection. This size is 512 bits for the 10 Mbps and 100 Mbps Ethernets, where Mbps is an abbrevation of 2^{20} bits per second, and 4096 bits for the Gigabit Ethernet.

Token Ring A token ring is a network with a ring topology that uses the notion of a *token* to decide which station may transmit a message at any time. The token is a special message circulating over the network. It has a status bit, which can be either *free* or *busy*. The status bit value *busy* indicates that a message is currently being transmitted over the network, whereas the value *free* indicates that the network is currently idle. Any station that wishes to transmit a message waits until it sees the token with the status bit *free*. It now changes the status to *busy* and starts transmitting its message. Thus a message follows a *busy* token, so only one message can be in transit at any time. A message can be of any length. It need not be split into frames of a standard size.

Every station that sees a message checks whether the message is intended for it; only the destination station copies the message. When the station that transmitted a message sees the *busy* token over the network, it resets its status bit to *free*. This action releases the network for another message transmission. When early token release is supported, the destination station resets the status bit of the token to *free*. Operation of the token ring comes to a halt if the token is lost because of communication errors. One of the stations is responsible for recovering from this situation—it listens continuously to the traffic on the network to check for the presence of a token, and creates a new token if the token has been lost.

Asynchronous Transfer Mode (ATM) Technology ATM is a virtual-circuit–oriented packet-switching technology (see Sections 16.6.4 and 16.6.5). The virtual circuit is called a *virtual path* in ATM terminology, and a packet is called a *cell*. ATM implements a virtual path between sites by reserving specific bandwidth in physical links situated in a network path between the sites, that is, by reserving a specific portion of the capacity of each physical link for the virtual path. When a physical link is common to many virtual paths, it multiplexes the traffic of the various virtual paths on a statistical basis such that each virtual path receives the specified portion of the bandwidth of the physical link. This way, cells to be transmitted on a virtual path do not face delays due to traffic on other virtual paths.

The principle of reserving bandwidth is carried one step further by hosts in an ATM network. A virtual path may be set up between two hosts, say, hosts X and Y. When a process P_i in host X wishes to communicate with a process P_j in host Y, the hosts may set up a *virtual channel* between P_i and P_j by reserving some bandwidth of the virtual path between X and Y. This two-tier arrangement ensures that message traffic between a pair of processes does not incur delays due to message traffic between other pairs of processes.

The ATM technology aims to provide real-time transport capabilities for multimedia applications incorporating diverse traffics such as voice, video, and high-speed data. ATM uses a cell size of 53 bytes. This size is a compromise between a small cell size that is desired in voice communication to ensure small delays and a largish cell size desired in data communication to reduce the overhead of forming packets for a message and assembling them back to form a message. Each cell contains a header of 5 bytes and a data field of 48 bytes. The header contains two items of information: a *virtual path id* (VPI) and a *virtual channel id* (VCI).

Figure 16.9 is a schematic diagram illustrating functioning of an ATM switch. The switch contains a routing table, which has an entry for each virtual path defined in the switch. The entry contains two fields—the *VPI* field and the *port* field. In Figure 16.9, the virtual path identifier of the incoming cell is n, and the nth entry in the routing table contains m and p. The switch copies m in the VPI field of the cell and sends out the modified cell on port p. This simple arrangement ensures that the ids assigned to virtual paths need not be unique in the system; they only need to be unique in the switch. The switching actions are performed in the hardware of the switch; they provide extremely fast switching, of the order of low double digits of microseconds, which makes it possible to provide LAN-like transmission speeds over wide area networks.

While creating a new virtual path, an application specifies the desired bandwidth. The OS sets up a virtual path by reserving the bandwidth in individual links, choosing a unique virtual path identifier in each switch and updating its routing table. While managing the traffic in virtual channels of the same virtual path, hosts use statistical multiplexing to provide appropriate bandwidth to

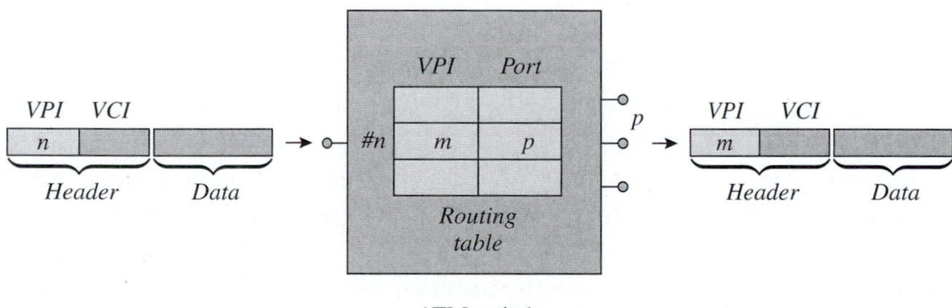

Figure 16.9 An ATM switch.

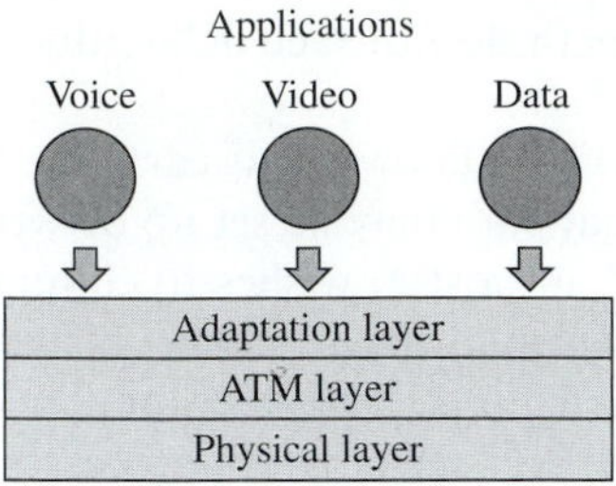

Figure 16.10 ATM protocol reference model.

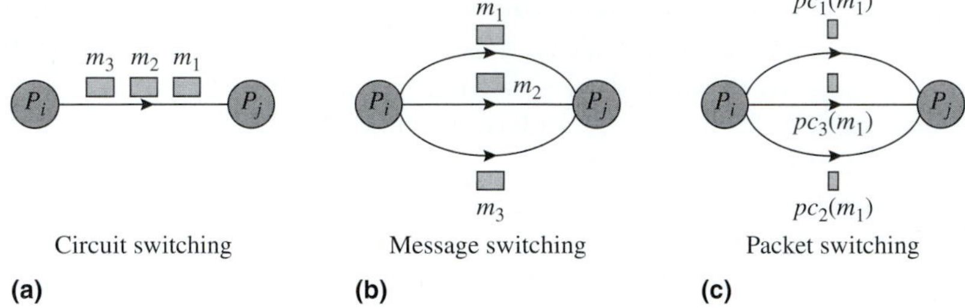

Figure 16.11 Connection strategies: circuit, message, and packet switching.

individual applications. Thus different applications can simultaneously transmit messages at different speeds over their virtual paths.

An ATM network has a mesh-star architecture. ATM switches are connected to one another in a mesh form. Hosts are connected to the ATM switches as in a star network. This strategy provides a path between every pair of nodes. Figure 16.10 shows the protocol layers in the ATM protocol reference model. The physical layer performs transfer of cells across the network. The ATM layer performs transmission of messages between ATM entities. It performs multiplexing and demultiplexing of virtual channels into virtual paths, cell scheduling, and cell routing. The ATM adaptation layer provides different kinds of services to different kinds of traffic such as voice, video, and data communication. It provides separate protocols for each kind of traffic.

16.6.4 Connection Strategies

A *connection* is a data path between communicating processes. A connection strategy, also called a *switching technique*, determines *when* a connection should be set up between a pair of processes, and *for how long* it should be maintained. Choice of the switching technique influences efficiency of communication between a pair of processes and throughput of communication links. Figure 16.11 illustrates three connection strategies. We use the notation m_i for a message and $pc_j(m_i)$ for the jth *packet* of message m_i, where a packet has the meaning defined later in this section.

Circuit Switching A *circuit* is a connection that is used exclusively by a pair of communicating processes and carries all messages between them [see Figure 16.11(a)]. A circuit is set up when processes decide to communicate, i.e., before the first message is transmitted, and is destroyed sometime after the last message has been transmitted. Circuit set up actions involve deciding the actual network path that messages will follow and reserving communication resources accordingly. Each circuit is given a unique id, and processes specify the circuit id while sending and receiving messages.

The advantage of circuit switching is that messages do not face delays once a circuit has been set up. However, a circuit ties up a set of communication resources and incurs set up overhead and delays, so use of circuit switching is justified only if the overall message density in the system is low but medium-to-heavy traffic is expected between a pair of processes.

Message Switching A connection is established for every message exchanged between a pair of processes. Thus messages between the same pair of processes may travel over different paths in the system [see Figure 16.11(b)]. Message switching incurs repetitive overhead and may cause delays due to the set up time of the connection, so its use is justified if light message traffic exists between a pair of processes. It does not tie up communication resources, so other processes can use the same connection, or some links in the connection, for their communication. Traffic in the network should be heavy enough to exploit this possibility.

Packet Switching In packet switching, a message is split into parts of a standard size, called *packets*. A connection is set up for each packet individually, so packets of a message may travel along different paths [see Figure 16.11(c)] and arrive out of sequence at a destination site. Use of packet switching incurs two kinds of overhead: A packet has to carry some identification information in its header—id of the message to which it belongs, sequence number within the message, and ids of the sender and destination processes—and packets have to be assembled into messages in the destination site. However, use of fixed-size packets reduces the cost of retransmission when an error arises. Also, links are not monopolized by specific pairs of processes, hence all pairs of communicating processes receive fair and unbiased service. These features make packet switching attractive for interactive processes.

Because of the cost of setting up connections, *connectionless protocols* are often used in practice for sending messages and packets. In such a protocol, the originating node simply selects one of its neighboring nodes and sends the message to it. If that node is not the destination node, it saves the message in its memory and decides which of the neighbors to send it to, and so on until the message reaches the destination node. This method is called the *store-and-forward* method of transmitting a message. A packet is transmitted similarly. Connectionless transmission can adapt better to traffic densities in communication links than message or packet switching, because a node can make the choice of the link when it is ready to send out a message or packet. It is typically implemented by exchanging traffic information among nodes and maintaining a table in each node that indicates which neighbor to send to in order to reach a specific destination node. However, each node should have a large memory for buffering messages and packets when its outgoing links are congested.

16.6.5 Routing

The routing function is invoked whenever a connection is to be set up. It decides which network path would be used by the connection. Choice of the routing strategy influences ability to adapt to changing traffic patterns in the system. Figure 16.12 illustrates three routing strategies.

Fixed Routing A path is permanently specified for communication between a pair of nodes [see Figure 16.12(a)]. When processes located in these nodes wish to communicate, a connection is set up over this path. Fixed routing is simple and efficient to implement—each node merely contains a table showing paths to all other nodes in the system; however, it lacks flexibility to deal with fluctuations in traffic densities and node or link faults. Hence its use can result in delays or low throughputs.

Virtual Circuit A path is selected at the start of a session between a pair of processes. It is used for all messages sent during the session [see Figure 16.12(b)]. Information concerning traffic densities and communication delays along different links in the system is used to decide the best path for a session. Hence this strategy can adapt to changing traffic patterns and node or link faults, and it ensures good network throughput and response times.

Dynamic Routing A path is selected whenever a message or a packet is to be sent, so different messages between a pair of processes and different packets of a message may use different paths [see Figure 16.12(c)]. This feature enables the routing strategy to respond more effectively to changes in traffic patterns and faults in nodes or links, and achieve better throughput and response times than when virtual circuits are used. In the Arpanet, which was the progenitor of the Internet, information about traffic density and communication delay along every link was constantly exchanged between nodes. This information was used to determine the current best path to a given destination node.

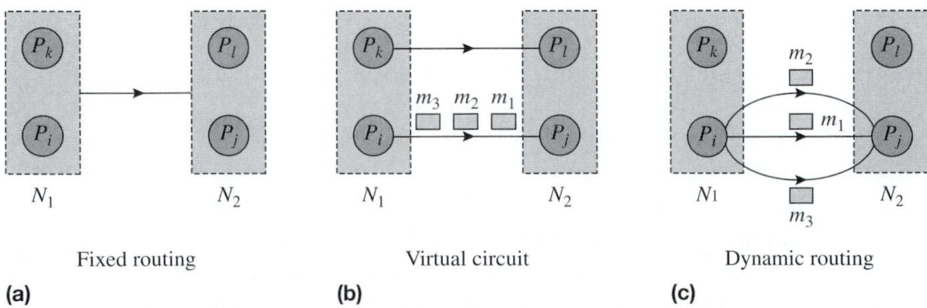

Figure 16.12 Routing strategies: fixed routing, virtual circuit, and dynamic routing.

16.6.6 Network Protocols

A *network protocol* is a set of rules and conventions used to implement communication over a network. Several concerns need to be addressed while implementing communication, such as ensuring confidentiality of data, achieving communication efficiency, and handling data transmission errors. Therefore, a hierarchy of network protocols is used in practice to provide a separation of concerns. Each protocol addresses one or more concerns and provides an interface to the protocols above and below it in the hierarchy. The protocol layers are like the layers of abstraction in a model (see Section 1.1). They provide the same benefits—an entity using a protocol in a higher layer need not be aware of details at a lower layer. Accordingly, lower-level protocols deal with data-transmission-related aspects such as detection of data transmission errors, middle-level protocols deal with formation of packets and routing, and higher-level protocols deal with semantic issues that concern applications, e.g., atomicity of actions and confidentiality of data.

ISO Procotol The International Organization for Standardization (ISO) developed an Open Systems Interconnection reference model (OSI model) for communication between entities in an open system. This model consists of seven protocol layers described in Table 16.7. It is variously called the *ISO protocol*, the *ISO protocol stack*, or the *OSI model*.

Figure 16.13 illustrates operation of the OSI model when a message is exchanged by two application processes. The message originates in an application, which presents it to the application layer. The application layer adds some control information to it in the form of a header field. The message now passes through the presentation and session layers, which add their own headers. The presentation layer performs change of data representation and

Table 16.7 Layers of the ISO Protocol Stack

Layer	Function
1. Physical layer	Provides electrical mechanisms for bit transmission over a physical link.
2. Data link layer	Organizes received bits into frames. Performs error detection on frames. Performs flow control.
3. Network layer	Performs switching and routing.
4. Transport layer	Forms outgoing packets. Assembles incoming packets. Performs error detection and retransmission and flow control.
5. Session layer	Establishes and terminates sessions. Provides for restart and recovery in applications.
6. Presentation layer	Implements data semantics by performing change of representation, compression, and encryption/decryption where necessary.
7. Application layer	Provides network interface for applications.

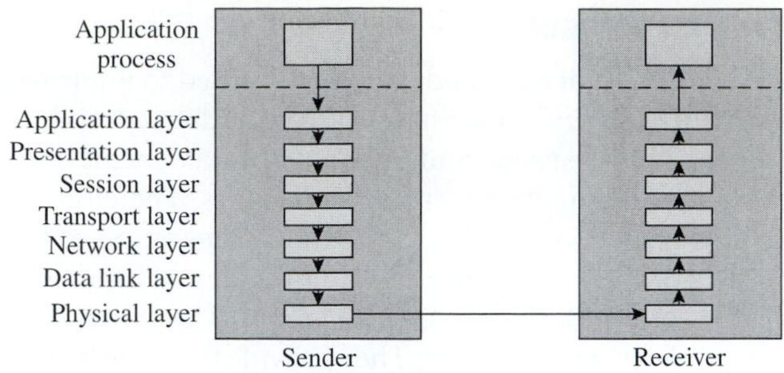

Figure 16.13 Operation of the ISO protocol stack.

encryption/decryption. The session layer establishes a connection between the sender and destination processes. The transport layer splits the message into packets and hands over the packets to the network layer. The network layer determines the link on which each packet is to be sent and hands over a link id and a packet to the data link layer. The data link layer views the packet as a string of bits, adds error detection and correction information to it, and hands it over to the physical layer for actual transmission. When the message is received, the data link layer performs error detection and forms frames, the transport layer forms messages, and the presentation layer puts the data in the representation desired by the application. The protocol layers are discussed in the following.

The *physical layer* is responsible for the mechanical, electrical, functional, and procedural aspects of transmitting bit streams over the network. It is implemented in the hardware of a networking device. RS-232C and EIA-232D are the common physical layer standards.

The *data link layer* provides error detection, error correction, and flow control facilities. It splits the bit stream to be sent into fixed-size blocks called *frames*, and adds a CRC to each frame (see Section 14.3). It provides flow control by sending frames at a rate that the receiver can handle. HDLC (high-level data link control) is a common protocol of this layer. Bridges and switches operate in this layer.

The *network layer* is responsible for providing connections and routes between two sites in a system; it also collects information for routing. Popular protocols of this layer are the X.25 protocol, which is a connection-oriented protocol using virtual circuits, and the Internet protocol (IP), which is a connectionless protocol. Thus, routing is the primary function of this layer, and connection is an optional one. Routers operate in this layer. The network layer is mostly redundant in LANs and in systems with point-to-point connections.

The *transport layer* provides error-free transmission of messages between sites. It splits a message into packets, and hands them over to the network layer. It handles communication errors like nondelivery of packets due to node or link faults. This feature resembles the reliability feature of IPC protocols, hence it is implemented analogously through time-outs and retransmissions (see Section 16.4). The transport layer also performs flow control so that data is transferred at a rate that the receiver can handle. The effective rate depends on the buffer space available in the receiver and the rate at which it can copy data out of the buffer. ISO has five classes of transport layer protocols, named TP0 through TP4. Other common transport layer protocols are the Transport Control Protocol (TCP), which is a connection-oriented reliable protocol, and User Datagram Protocol (UDP), which is a connectionless unreliable protocol.

The *session layer* provides means to control the dialog between two entities that use a connection-oriented protocol. It provides authentication, different types of dialogs (one-way, two-way alternate, or two-way simultaneous) and checkpoint–recovery facilities. It provides dialog control to ensure that messages exchanged using nonblocking *send* primitives arrive in the correct order (see Section 16.4). It also provides a quarantine service whereby messages are buffered at a receiver site until explicitly released by a sender. This facility is useful in performing atomic actions in a file (see Section 13.11.2) and in implementing atomic transactions (see Section 19.4).

The *presentation layer* supports services that change the representation of a message to address hardware differences between the sender and destination sites, to preserve confidentiality of data through encryption, and to reduce data volumes through compression.

The *application layer* supports application-specific services like file transfer, e-mail, and remote log in. Some popular protocols of this layer are FTP (File Transfer Protocol), X.400 (e-mail), and rlogin (remote log-in).

TCP/IP The *Transmission Control Protocol / Internet Protocol* (TCP/IP) is a popular protocol for communication over the Internet. It has fewer layers than the ISO protocol, so it is both more efficient and more complex to implement. Figure 16.14 shows details of its layers. The lowest layer is occupied by a data link protocol. The *Internet Protocol* (IP) is a network layer protocol in the ISO protocol stack; it can run on top of any data link protocol. The IP performs data transmission over the Internet using the 32-bit IP address of a destination host. It is a connectionless unreliable protocol; it does not guarantee that packets of a message will be delivered without error, only once, and in the correct order. These properties are provided by the protocols occupying higher levels in the hierarchy.

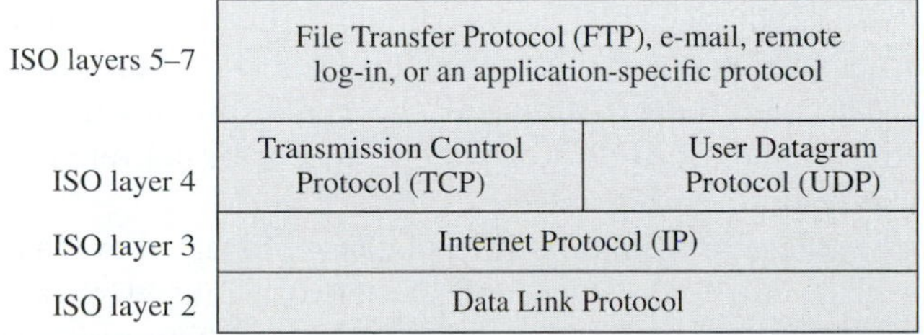

Figure 16.14 The Transmission Control Protocol/Internet Protocol (TCP/IP) stack.

Protocols in the next higher layers provide communication between processes—each host assigns unique 16-bit port numbers to processes, and a sender process uses a destination process address that is a pair (IP address, port number). Use of port numbers permits many processes within a host to send and receive messages concurrently. Some well-known services such as FTP, telnet, SMTP, and HTTP have been assigned standard port numbers by the Internet Assigned Numbers Authority (IANA); other port numbers are assigned by the OS in a host.

As shown in Figure 16.14, two protocols can be used in the layer above the IP, which corresponds to the transport layer, i.e., layer 4, in the ISO protocol stack. The *Transmission Control Protocol* (TCP) is a connection-oriented reliable protocol, It employs a virtual circuit between two processes and provides reliability by retransmitting a message that is not received in an expected time interval (see Section 16.4 for a discussion of acknowledgments and time-outs used to ensure reliable delivery of messages). The overhead of ensuring reliability is high if the speeds of a sender and a receiver mismatch, or if the network is overloaded; hence, the TCP performs *flow control* to ensure that a sender does not send packets faster than the rate at which a receiver can accept them, and *congestion control* to ensure that traffic is regulated so that a network is not overloaded.

The *User Datagram Protocol* (UDP) is a connectionless, unreliable protocol that neither guarantees delivery of a packet nor ensures that packets of a message will be delivered in the correct order. It incurs low overhead compared to the TCP because it does not have to set up and maintain a virtual circuit or ensure reliable delivery. The UDP is employed in multimedia applications and in video conferencing because the occasional loss of packets is not a correctness issue in these applications—it only leads to poor picture quality. These applications use their own flow and congestion control mechanisms such as reducing the resolution of pictures—and, consequently, lowering the picture quality—if a sender, a receiver, or the network is overloaded.

The top layer in the TCP/IP stack is occupied by an application layer protocol like the file transfer protocol, an e-mail protocol such as the SMTP, or a remote log-in protocol. This layer corresponds to layers 5–7 in the ISO protocol. When the UDP is used in the lower layer, the top layer can be occupied by an application-specific protocol implemented in an application process itself.

16.6.7 Network Bandwidth and Latency

When data is to be exchanged between two nodes, network hardware and network protocols participate in data transfer over a link, and communication processors (CPs) store and forward the data until it reaches the destination node. Two aspects of network performance are the rate at which data can be delivered and how soon data can reach the destination node.

Network bandwidth is the rate at which data is transferred over a network. It is subject to various factors such as capacities of network links, error rates and delays at routers, bridges, and gateways. Peak bandwidth is the theoretical maximum rate at which data can be transferred between two nodes. Effective bandwidth may be lower than the peak bandwidth because of data transmission errors, which lead to time-outs and retransmissions. *Latency* is the elapsed time between sending of a byte of data by a source node and its receipt at the destination node. It is typically computed for the first byte of data to be transferred. The processing time in the layers of a network protocol and delays due to network congestion contribute to latency.

16.7 MODEL OF A DISTRIBUTED SYSTEM

A system model is employed to determine useful properties of a distributed system, such as the impact of faults on its functioning and the latency and cost of message communication. A distributed system is typically modeled as a graph

$$S = (N, E)$$

where N and E are sets of nodes and edges, respectively. Each node may represent a host, i.e., a computer system, and each edge may represent a communication link connecting two nodes; however, as discussed later, nodes and edges may also have other connotations. The *degree* of a node is the number of edges connected to it. Each node is assumed to have an *import list* describing nonlocal resources and services that the node can utilize, and an *export list* describing local resources of the node that are accessible to other nodes. For simplicity, we do not include the *name server* (see Section 16.4.1) in the system model.

Two kinds of graph models of a distributed system are useful in practice. A *physical model* is used to represent the arrangement of physical entities in a distributed system. In this model, nodes and edges have the implications described earlier, i.e., a node is a computer system and an edge is a communication link. A *logical model* is an abstraction. Nodes in a logical model represent logical entities like processes and edges represent relationships between entities. A logical model may use undirected or directed edges. An undirected edge represents a symmetric relationship like two-way interprocess communication. A directed edge represents an asymmetric relationship like the parent–child relationship between processes or one-way interprocess communication. Note that nodes and edges in a logical model may not have a one-to-one correspondence with physical entities in a distributed system.

A system model is analyzed to determine useful properties of a system such as the ones described in Table 16.8. One important property is the *resiliency* of a system, which is its ability to withstand faults without facing disruption. A *k-resilient* system can withstand any combination of up to k faults. If n' is the smallest degree of a node, at least n' faults must occur for a node to get isolated; however, fewer faults may be able to partition a system (see Exercise 16.7). As illustrated in Example 16.1, analysis of the system model can be used as a network design technique as well.

Table 16.8 System Properties Determined by Analyzing a System Model

Property	Description
Impact of faults	Faults can isolate a node from the rest of the system or *partition* a system, i.e., split it into two or more parts such that a node in one part cannot be reached from a node in another part.
Resiliency	A system is said to be *k-resilient*, where k is a constant, if k is the largest number of faults that the system can withstand without disruption.
Latency between two nodes	The minimum latency of a communication path depends on the minimum latency of each communication link in it. The minimum latency between two nodes is the smallest of the minimum latencies across all paths between the nodes.
Cost of sending information to every node	The cost of this operation depends on topology of the system and the algorithm used for sending the information. In a fully connected system containing n nodes, the cost can be as low as $n - 1$ messages. The cost may be more if the system is not fully connected.

Example 16.1 Resiliency of a System

If it is expected that only one or two sites in a system may suffer faults simultaneously, and faults never occur in communication links, availability of a resource is guaranteed if three units of the resource exist in three different sites in the system. If communication links can also suffer faults but the total number of faults does not exceed two, three units of each resource must exist and each site must have at least three communication links connected to it. In such a system, a resource becomes unavailable only if three or more faults occur.

When a node wishes to send some information to all other nodes in the system, it can send the information to each of its neighbors in the form of a message and each neighbor receiving such a message for the first time can send similar messages to its neighbors, and so on. In this method, a node would receive the information as many times as the number of edges connected to it, so a total of e messages are required, where e is the number of edges in the system. However, because a node needs to receive a message only once, it is possible to use knowledge of the system's topology to manage with fewer messages. For example, if the system is fully connected, it is possible to use a simpler protocol in which only the originator node sends messages to its neighbors. This operation would require only $n - 1$ messages.

Both physical and logical models are used to determine useful properties. The latency between two nodes is determined by analyzing a physical model. Analyses on logical models are typically used to determine complexity of control algorithms used in a distributed OS. We shall see such usage in Chapter 18.

16.8 DESIGN ISSUES IN DISTRIBUTED OPERATING SYSTEMS

The user of a distributed system expects its operating system to provide the look and feel of a conventional OS and also provide the benefits of a distributed system summarized in Table 16.1. To meet these expectations, the OS must fully exploit the capabilities of all nodes by distributing data, resources, users, and their computations effectively among the nodes of the system. It gives rise to the following design issues.

Transparency of Resources and Services *Transparency* implies that names of resources and services do not depend on their locations in the system. It enables an application to access local and nonlocal resources identically. It also permits an OS to change the location of a resource freely because a change in location does not affect the name of the resource and hence does not affect the applications that use the resource. The OS can exploit transparency to perform data migration to speed up applications, reduce network traffic, or optimize use of disks. Transparency also facilitates computation migration because the computation can continue to access resources as it did before it was migrated. We discuss transparency in detail in Chapter 20.

Distribution of Control Functions A *control function* is a function performed by the kernel to control resources and processes in the system, e.g., resource allocation, deadlock handling, and scheduling. Centralized control functions face two problems in a distributed system: Because of network latency, it is not possible to obtain consistent information about the current state of processes and resources in all nodes of the system, so the centralized function may not be able to arrive at correct decisions. A centralized function is also a potential performance bottleneck and a single point of failure in the system. To handle these problems, a distributed OS performs a control function through a *distributed control algorithm*, whose actions are performed in several nodes of the system in a coordinated manner. We discuss distributed algorithms for performing control functions such as deadlock detection, scheduling, and mutual exclusion in Chapter 18.

System Performance In addition to techniques of conventional OSs, a distributed OS uses two new techniques to provide good system performance—data migration and computation migration. Data migration is employed to reduce network latencies and improve response times of processes. Computation migration is employed to ensure that nearly equal amounts of computational load are directed at all CPUs in the system. This technique is called *load balancing*.

A distributed system typically grows in size over time through addition of nodes and users. As the size of a system grows, process response times may degrade because of increased loading of resources and services of the OS, and increased overhead of OS control functions. Such degradation obstructs growth of a system, so the performance of a distributed system should be *scalable*; i.e., the delays and response times should not degrade with growth in system size, and the throughput should increase with growth in system size. An important scalability technique is to use self-sufficient clusters of hosts (see Section 16.3), so that network traffic does not grow as more clusters are added to the system. In Chapter 20, we discuss how the technique of *file caching* used in distributed file systems helps satisfy this requirement.

Reliability Fault tolerance techniques provide availability of resources and continuity of system operation when faults occur. Link and node faults are tolerated by providing redundancy of resources and communication links. If a fault occurs in a network path to a resource or in the resource itself, an application can use another network path to the resource or use another resource. This way, a resource is unavailable only when unforeseen faults occur.

Consistency of data becomes an issue when data is distributed or replicated. When several parts of distributed data are to be modified, a fault should not put the system in a state in which some parts of the data have been updated but others have not been. A distributed OS employs a technique called *two-phase commit protocol* to ensure that it does not happen (see Section 19.4.3).

Parts of a computation may be performed in different nodes of a system. If a node or link fault occurs during execution of such a computation, the system should assess the damage caused by the fault and judiciously restore some of the subcomputations to previous states recorded in backups. This approach is called *recovery*. The system must also deal with uncertainties about the cause of a fault. Example 16.2 illustrates these uncertainties.

Example 16.2 Uncertainties about Faults

A distributed computation consists of two subcomputations represented by processes P_i and P_j, executing in nodes N_1 and N_2, respectively (see Figure 16.15). Process P_i sends a request to P_j and waits for a response. However, a time-out occurs before it receives a reply. The time-out could have been caused by any one of the following situations:

1. Process P_j never received the request, so never started processing it.
2. The processing is taking longer than expected; i.e., process P_j is still processing the request.
3. Process P_j started processing the request but suffered a fault before completing it.
4. Process P_j completed the processing of the request but its reply to process P_i was lost.

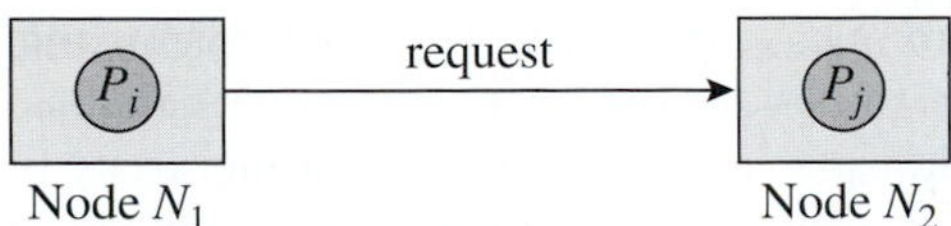

Figure 16.15 Recovery issues in a remote request.

In Example 16.2, the OS has to resolve the uncertainty and handle the situation that actually caused the time-out. If node N_2 had crashed, the subcomputation P_j would have to be repeated, possibly at some other node in the system. In other cases, the subcomputation P_j may have been completed, so reexecuting it elsewhere in the system may affect consistency of data (e.g., an update may be performed twice!) or waste CPU time. We discuss special recovery techniques designed for handling uncertainties in Chapter 19.

Security Security acquires a new dimension in a distributed system because interprocess messages may pass through a computer system called a communication processor, which may operate independently under its own OS. An intruder may gain control of such a computer system and either tamper with messages passing through it, or misuse them to perform masquerading. Special techniques for *message security* and *authentication* are used to prevent such attacks; we discuss them in Chapter 21.

16.9 SUMMARY

Resource sharing, reliability, and computation speedup are the key benefits of distributed systems. A distributed OS realizes these benefits by integrating operation of individual computer systems, ensuring reliable network communication, and effectively supporting operation of distributed computations. In this chapter we studied the relevant techniques of a distributed OS.

A distributed system consists of nodes connected to a network, where a *node* could be an individual computer system, or a *cluster*, which is a group of computers that share resources and operate in an integrated manner. A cluster can provide computation speedup and reliability within a node.

Parts of a *distributed computation* can be executed in different nodes to achieve resource sharing and computation speedup. Such a computation may use data located in a distant node in three ways: *Remote data access* uses the data over the network, *data migration* moves the data to the node where the computation exists, and *computation migration* moves a part of the computation to the node where the data is located. A *distributed computation paradigm* is a model of distributed computation that provides features for remote data access, data migration, or computation migration. The *client–server* paradigm provides remote data access, while the *remote procedure call* (RPC) and *remote evaluation* paradigms provide computation migration.

Processes located in different nodes of a distributed system communicate by using an *interprocess communication protocol* (IPC protocol), which is a set of rules for ensuring effective communication. The protocol uses the *domain name system* (DNS) to find the location of a destination process. *IPC semantics* describe the properties of an IPC protocol. A *reliable protocol* guarantees that a message would be delivered to the destination process in spite of faults in nodes and communication links. Reliability is achieved as follows: A process that receives a message returns an acknowledgment to the sender of the message. The sender process retransmits the message if an acknowledgment is not received within the expected time interval. In this protocol, a message may be received by the destination process more than once, hence it is called an *at-least-once* protocol. A protocol would be called an *exactly-once* protocol if it arranges to recognize and discard duplicate messages.

Network communication has to deal with transient faults in links and nodes of the system, and network traffic densities in different parts of the network. Hence apart from IPC semantics, the network software has to ensure reliability by detecting and tolerating faults, and ensure performance by finding an appropriate route for a message through the network and transmitting data at an appropriate rate. Effective network communication is implemented by a hierarchy of protocols called a *protocol stack*, in which each individual protocol addresses a different concern in network communication. The ISO protocol stack uses seven network protocols. The TCP and IP protocol stacks use fewer protocols. Network performance is measured either as effective *bandwidth*, which is the rate at which data can be transferred over the network, or as *latency*, which is the delay involved in the transfer of data.

A distributed system is modeled by a graph. In a *physical model*, nodes and edges of the graph are nodes and links of the distributed system, respectively; in a *logical model*, they are processes and relationships between processes, respectively. Graph models of a system are used to determine reliability properties of a system or as a basis for design of algorithms used by a distributed OS.

New design issues are faced by OS designers in providing resource sharing, reliability, and performance in the distributed environment. These issues are discussed in the next few chapters.

TEST YOUR CONCEPTS

16.1 Classify each of the following statements as true or false:

- **a.** Failure of a single node partitions a ring network.
- **b.** When message switching is used, all messages between a pair of processes travel over the same path in the network.
- **c.** Dynamic routing can adapt to link and node failures in a network.
- **d.** A message sent using a virtual path in an ATM network might face a delay in a link due to high traffic density.
- **e.** The at-least-once semantics are implemented by recognizing and discarding duplicate messages.
- **f.** The sequence number in a message plays a role in implementing semantics of interprocess communication.
- **g.** In a reliable, nonblocking interprocess communication protocol, a receiver process may maintain only one reply buffer per sender process.
- **h.** A remote procedure call is useful for performing data migration.
- **i.** Transferring n bytes between two nodes requires only 50 percent of the time required to transfer $2 \times n$ bytes.

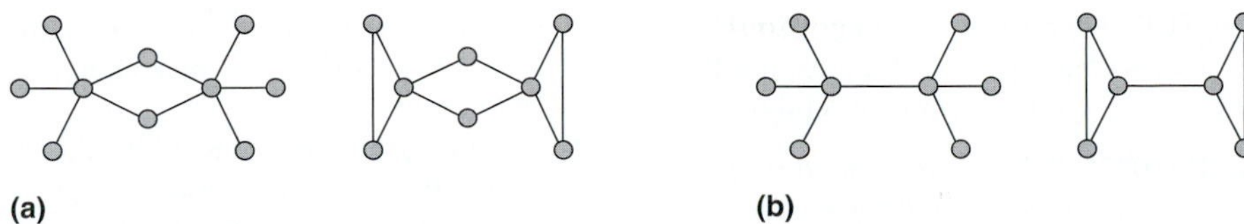

Figure 16.16 Exercises for determining resiliency of distributed systems.

EXERCISES

16.1 Discuss which process synchronization means used in symmetrical multiprocessor systems can be adapted for use in clusters (see Chapter 10).

16.2 Explore the possibility of implementing the blocking and nonblocking protocols through monitors. What are the difficulties in the implementation?

16.3 Write a short note on factors that influence the duration of the time-out interval in the RRA protocol of Section 16.4.3.1.

16.4 Develop schemes to discard duplicate replies received in the sender site in the blocking and nonblocking versions of the RRA protocol.

16.5 Requests made by nonblocking *send* calls may arrive out of sequence at the destination site when dynamic routing is used. Discuss how a nonblocking RR protocol should discard duplicate requests when this property holds (refer to Section 16.4.3.2).

16.6 One change is made in the RRA protocol of Section 16.4.3.1: A destination process blocks until it receives an acknowledgment of its reply. Analyze the properties of this protocol.

16.7 **a.** Determine the (i) site faults and (ii) link faults that the systems of Figure 16.16(a) can tolerate for interprocess communication.
b. Determine placement of copies of data D in the systems of Figure 16.16(b) if D is to be available despite two site/link faults in the system.

16.8 The *diameter* of a distributed system (d) is the largest number of links in any shortest path between nodes of the system. If the maximum communication delay along any link in the system is δ, what is the maximum communication delay in the system? Explain the conditions under which it occurs.

16.9 Compare the RPC and remote evaluation paradigms on the following basis
a. Flexibility
b. Efficiency
c. Security

BIBLIOGRAPHY

Tanenbaum and van Renesse (1985) is a survey article on distributed operating systems. It discusses blocking and nonblocking communication protocols. The texts by Sinha (1997), Tanenbaum and van Steen (2002), and Coulouris et al. (2005) discuss the topics included in this chapter.

Comer and Stevens (2000) discusses the client–server computing model. Birrell and Nelson (1984) discusses implementation of remote procedure calls. Tay and Ananda (1990) is a survey article on remote procedure calls. Lin and Gannon (1985) discusses a remote procedure call (RPC) schematic with exactly-once semantics. Stamos and Gifford (1990) discusses remote evaluation. Tanenbaum (2001) discusses the ISO protocol, the client–server model and the RPC. Birman (2005) discusses the client–server model and the RPC.

Tanenbaum (2003) is a text devoted to computer networks. It covers the ISO protocol in great detail. Comer (2004) is a broad introduction to networking.

It explains the TCP/IP protocol. Stallings (2004) discusses various networking protocols. Stevens and Rago (2005) describes network programming in Unix.

1. Birman, K. (2005): *Reliable Distributed Systems: Technologies, Web Services, and Applications*, Springer, Berlin.
2. Birrell, A. D., and B. J. Nelson (1984): "Implementing remote procedure calls," *ACM Transactions on Computer Systems*, **2**, 39–59.
3. Comer, D. (2004): *Computer Networks and Internets,* 4th ed., Prentice Hall, Englewood Cliffs, N.J.
4. Comer, D., and D. Stevens (2000): *Internetworking with TCP/IP,* Vol. III: *Client–Server Programming and Applications, Linux/POSIX Socket Version*, Prentice Hall, Englewood Cliffs, N.J.
5. Coulouris, G., J. Dollimore, and T. Kindberg (2005): *Distributed Systems—Concepts and Design,* 4th ed., Addison-Wesley, New York.
6. Lin, K. J., and J. D. Gannon (1985): "Atomic remote procedure call," *IEEE Transactions on Software Engineering*, **11** (10), 1126–1135.
7. Sinha, P. K. (1997): *Distributed Operating Systems*, IEEE Press, New York.
8. Stallings, W. (2004): *Computer Networking with Internet Protocols*, Prentice Hall, Englewood Cliffs, N.J.
9. Stamos, J. W., and D. K. Gifford (1990): "Remote evaluation," *ACM Transactions on Programming Languages and Systems*, **12** (4), 537–565.
10. Stevens, W. R., and S. A. Rago (2005): *Advanced Programming in the Unix Environment,* 2nd ed., Addison-Wesley Professional.
11. Tanenbaum, A. S. (2001): *Modern Operating Systems,* 2nd ed., Prentice Hall, Englewood Cliffs, N.J.
12. Tanenbaum, A. S. (2003): *Computer Networks,* 4th ed., Prentice Hall, Englewood Cliffs, N.J.
13. Tanenbaum, A. S., and M. van Steen (2002): *Distributed Systems: Principles and Paradigms*, Prentice Hall, Englewood Cliffs, N.J.
14. Tanenbaum, A. S., and R. Van Renesse (1985): "Distributed Operating Systems," *Computing Surveys*, **17** (1), 419–470.
15. Tay, B. H., and A. L. Ananda (1990): "A survey of remote procedure calls," *Operating Systems Review*, **24** (3), 68–79.

Chapter 17

Theoretical Issues in Distributed Systems

Time and *state* are two key notions used in an operating system—the OS needs to know the chronological order in which events such as resource requests occur, and it needs to know the states of resources and processes for performing resource allocation and scheduling. In a conventional computer system, presence of a single memory and a single CPU simplifies handling of time and state. Only one event can occur at any time, so the OS knows the chronological order of events implicitly, and it knows states of all processes and resources in the system.

A distributed system consists of several computer systems, each with a clock, memory, and one or more CPUs, that communicate through messages, which incur unpredictable communication delays. Consequently, the distributed OS cannot know the chronological order in which events occur, or the states of resources and processes in all nodes of the system at the same instant of time. Therefore, the key theoretical issues in distributed systems are to evolve practical alternatives to the traditional notions of time and state, develop algorithms to implement these alternatives, and show correctness of these algorithms.

We present the notion of *event precedence* which can be used to discover the chronological order in which *some* events occur in a distributed system. We then discuss two alternatives to the traditional notion of time, using the notions of *logical clocks* and *vector clocks*. We also present the notion of a *consistent recording of state* that can be used as an alternative to *global state* of a distributed system in several applications. These alternative notions of time and state are employed in the design of distributed control algorithms and recovery algorithms used in a distributed OS.

17.1 NOTIONS OF TIME AND STATE

Time is the fourth dimension; it indicates when an event occurred. The *state* of an entity is the condition or mode of its being. The state of an entity depends on its features; e.g., the state of a memory cell is the value contained in it. If an entity is composed of other entities, its state contains the states of its component entities. The *global state* of a system comprises the states of all entities in the system at a specific instant of time. An OS uses the notions of time and state for performing scheduling of resources and the CPU: It uses time to know when a request event occurred, or to find the *chronological order* in which request events occurred, and it uses the state of a resource to decide whether it can be allocated. A distributed OS also uses these notions in *recovery* to ensure that processes of a distributed computation would be in mutually consistent states after recovery from the crash of a node that contained some of the processes.

It is easy to handle time and state in a uniprocessor OS. The system has a clock and a single CPU, so the OS can find the times at which processes made their resource requests and use this information to determine their chronological order. However, a typical conventional operating system uses the notion of time only implicitly. When an event occurs, it adds information about the event to a queue, so the queue shows the chronological order of events. The OS also knows states of processes, and the states of all physical and logical resources.

In a distributed system, each node is a computer system with its own clock and a local memory, and nodes are connected by communication links which have unpredictable communication delays. Consequently, a node cannot precisely determine the time at which an event occurred in another node; its perception of the state of a remote process or resource may also be stale. Thus, a distributed OS cannot use the notions of time and state in the same manner as a uniprocessor OS.

In this chapter, we discuss some theoretical concepts in distributed systems and use them to develop practical alternatives to the notions of time and state as used in a uniprocessor system. These alternative notions of time and state are used in Chapter 18 in the design of distributed control algorithms, and in Chapter 19 in the design of recovery schemes.

17.2 STATES AND EVENTS IN A DISTRIBUTED SYSTEM

17.2.1 Local and Global States

Each entity in a system has its own state. The state of a memory cell is the value contained in it. The state of a CPU is the contents of its PSW and general-purpose registers. The state of a process is its state tag; state of the memory allocated to it; the CPU state if it is currently scheduled on the CPU, or contents of PCB fields if it is not scheduled on the CPU; and the state of its interprocess communication, which consists of information concerning the messages received and sent by it. The state of an entity is called a *local state*. The *global state* of a system at time instant t is the collection of local states of all entities in it at time t.

We denote the local state of a process P_k at time t as s_k^t, where the subscript is omitted if the identity of the process is implicit in the context. We denote the global state of a system at time t as S_t. If a system contains n processes $P_1, \ldots, P_n$, $S_t \equiv \{s_1^t, s_2^t, \ldots, s_n^t\}$.

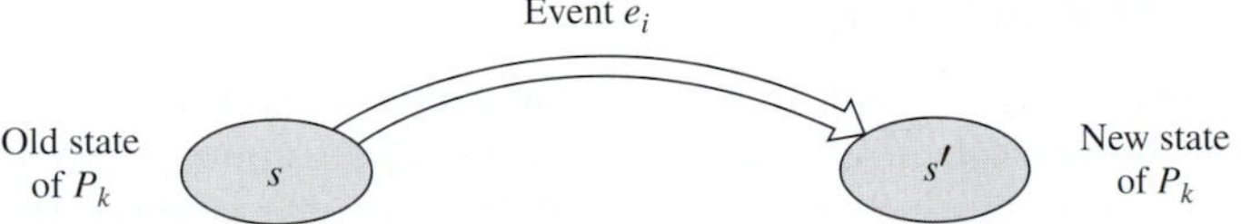

Figure 17.1 Change of state in process P_k on occurrence of event $(P_k, s, s', send, c, m)$.

17.2.2 Events

An *event* could be the sending or receiving of a message over a *channel*, which is an interprocess communication path, or some other happening that does not involve a message. The state of a process changes when an event occurs in it. We represent an event as follows:

(*process id, old state, new state, event description, channel, message*)

where *channel* and *message* are written as "–" if the event does not involve sending or receiving of a message. An event $e_i \equiv (P_k, s, s', send, c, m)$ can occur only when process P_k is in state s. The event is the sending of a message m over a channel c. When this event occurs, process P_k enters the new state s' (see Figure 17.1).

Certain events can occur only when some conditions are met, e.g., a receive event for message m on channel c can occur only if channel c contains message m. Thus, only some events may be feasible in the current state of a process.

17.3 TIME, CLOCKS, AND EVENT PRECEDENCES

Let a *global clock* be an abstract clock that can be accessed from different sites of a distributed system with identical results. If processes in two nodes of a distributed system perform the system call "give current time" at the same time instant, they would obtain identical time values. If they perform these system calls δ time units apart, they would obtain time values that differ by exactly δ time units. A global clock cannot be implemented in practice because of communication delays. Requests for current time made in two different nodes at the same time instant would face different communication delays to reach the site where the clock is maintained. Consequently, they would be given different time values. Similarly, requests that are made δ time units apart may get time values that do not differ by exactly δ time units.

Since a global clock cannot be implemented, we can explore an alternative arrangement that uses a clock in each process. Such a clock is called a *local clock*. The local clock of a process would be accessed whenever the process performs a "give current time" system call. To implement a practical timekeeping service using this idea, local clocks should be reasonably well synchronized. Section 17.3.2 discusses how clock synchronization can be achieved, using the notion of event precedence.

17.3.1 Event Precedence

The notation $e_1 \rightarrow e_2$ is used to indicate that event e_1 *precedes* event e_2 in time; i.e., event e_1 occurred before event e_2. *Event ordering* implies arranging a set of events in a sequence such that each event in the sequence precedes the next one. In essence, it implies determining the order in which events have occurred in a system. A *total order* with respect to the precedes relation "$\rightarrow$" is said to exist if all events that can occur in a system can be ordered. A *partial order* implies that some events can be ordered but not all events can be ordered—to be precise, at least two events exist that cannot be ordered.

Table 17.1 summarizes the fundamental rules used to order events. These rules can be explained as follows: The OS can readily determine precedence between events occurring within the same process. Events like execution of a "send P_3, <*message* m_i>" event in a process P_2 and a receive event in P_3 that receives message m_i have a *causal relationship*, i.e., a cause-and-effect relationship. Consequently, the send event in process P_2, which is the cause, precedes the receive event in process P_3, which is its effect. The precedes relation is transitive in nature, hence $e_1 \rightarrow e_3$ if $e_1 \rightarrow e_2$ and $e_2 \rightarrow e_3$. This property can be used to determine precedences between some events that neither have a causal relationship nor occur within the same process. For example, an event e_i preceding the send event for message m_i in P_2 precedes an event e_j that follows the receive event for message m_i in P_3, because e_i precedes the send event, the send event precedes the receive event, and the receive event precedes event e_j.

Using the rules of Table 17.1, precedence between any two events e_i and e_j can be classified as follows:

- *e_i precedes e_j:* If events e_k and e_l exist such that $e_k \rightarrow e_l$, $e_i \rightarrow e_k$ or $e_i \equiv e_k$, and $e_l \rightarrow e_j$ or $e_l \equiv e_j$.
- *e_i follows e_j:* If events e_g and e_h exist such that $e_g \rightarrow e_h$, $e_j \rightarrow e_g$ or $e_j \equiv e_g$, and $e_h \rightarrow e_i$ or $e_h \equiv e_i$.
- *e_i is concurrent with e_j:* If e_i neither precedes nor follows e_j.

A *timing diagram* is a plot of the activities of different processes against time—processes are marked along the vertical axis in the plot, and time is marked along

Table 17.1 Rules for Ordering of Events in a Distributed System

Category	Description of rule
Events within a process	The OS performs event handling, so it knows the order in which events occur within a process.
Events in different processes	In a *causal relationship*, i.e., a cause-and-effect relationship, an event that corresponds to the cause precedes an event in another process that corresponds to the effect.
Transitive precedence	The precedes relation is transitive; i.e., $e_1 \rightarrow e_2$ and $e_2 \rightarrow e_3$ implies $e_1 \rightarrow e_3$.

the horizontal axis. We use the notation e_{kn} for event e_n in process P_k. Example 17.1 demonstrates use of a timing diagram in determining event precedences by using transitiveness of the precedes relation. It also illustrates why a total order over events does not exist in a distributed system.

Event Precedence

Example 17.1

Figure 17.2 shows activities in processes P_1 and P_2. Event e_{23} is a "send" event while e_{12} is a "receive" event for message m_1. Hence $e_{23} \rightarrow e_{12}$. The transitive nature of "$\rightarrow$" leads to the precedence relations $e_{22} \rightarrow e_{12}$ and $e_{21} \rightarrow e_{12}$. Transitiveness also yields $e_{22} \rightarrow e_{13}$ and $e_{21} \rightarrow e_{13}$. Event e_{11} is concurrent with events e_{21} and e_{22}. It is also concurrent with events e_{23} and e_{24}!

17.3.2 Logical Clocks

An OS needs a practical method of event ordering for purposes related to scheduling and resource allocation. The method should be efficient, so it should perform event ordering directly, instead of working through causal relationships and transitivity. It should also provide a total order over events so that the OS can provide FCFS service to resource requests. Such an order can be obtained by

- Incorporating event precedences into the event order.
- Arbitrarily ordering events that are concurrent, e.g., the events e_{11} and e_{21} in Figure 17.2.

Timestamping of events provides a direct method of event ordering. Each process has a local clock that is accessible only to itself. The *timestamp* of an event is its occurrence time according to the local clock of the process. Let $ts(e_i)$ represent the timestamp of event e_i. Event ordering is performed in accordance with the timestamps of events, i.e., $\forall e_i, e_j : e_i \rightarrow e_j$ if $ts(e_i) < ts(e_j)$ and $e_j \rightarrow e_i$ if $ts(e_i) > ts(e_j)$. However, local clocks in different processes may show different times because of clock drift, which would affect reliability of timestamp-based event ordering. For example, if event e_i occurred before event e_j, $ts(e_i)$ should be $< ts(e_j)$; however, if the clock at the process where event e_i occurred is running faster than the clock at the process where e_j occurred, $ts(e_i)$ may be $> ts(e_j)$. To avoid such situations, it is necessary to synchronize the clocks of all processes.

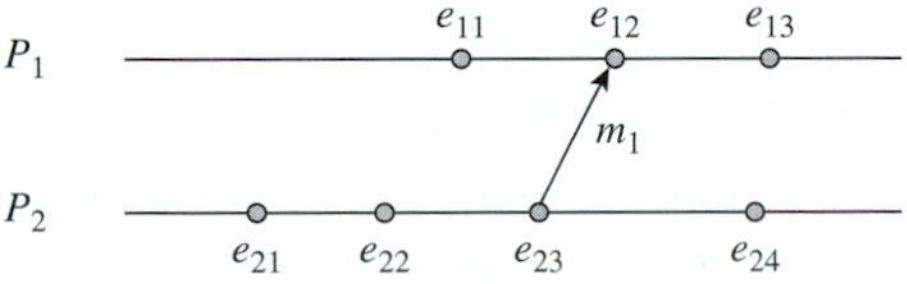

Figure 17.2 Event precedence via timing diagram.

Synchronization of local clocks is achieved by using the causal relationship found in interprocess message exchange. Consider a message m sent by process P_k to process P_l. Let timestamps of the send and receive events be t_k and t_l, respectively. The cause-and-effect relationship between the send and receive events implies that t_k must be smaller than t_l. If it is not, the situation can be corrected by increasing the time in the local clock of the receiver process to some value greater than t_k before timestamping the receive event. Algorithm 17.1 is the complete clock synchronization algorithm.

Algorithm 17.1 *Clock Synchronization*

1. *When a process P_k wishes to send a message m to process P_l:* P_k executes a command "send P_l, ($ts(send(m))$, m)," where $ts(send(m))$ is a timestamp obtained just prior to sending message m.
2. *When process P_l receives a message:* Process P_l performs the actions
   if $local\ clock(P_l) < ts(send(m))$ then
   $local\ clock(P_l) := ts(send(m)) + \delta$;
   timestamp the receive event.

   where $local\ clock(P_l)$ is the value in the local clock of process P_l and δ is the average communication delay in the network.

The clock synchronization achieved by Algorithm 17.1 is called loose synchronization because clocks of the two processes are mutually consistent at a message exchange, but can drift apart at other times (see Exercise 17.1). The quality of clock synchronization depends on the frequency of interprocess communication—a higher frequency of communication provides tighter synchronization. Synchronization can be improved by using special synchronization messages that are exchanged at short intervals simply to keep the clocks synchronized.

Note that clocks synchronized in this manner do not show "real" time. For example, if the clock at a sender process is fast, the clock at the receiver process would also be advanced. Once we accept that the local clocks do not show "real" time, there is no need to keep incrementing them all the time. A process may increment its local clock by 1 only when an event occurs in it, and synchronize the local clock, if necessary, when it receives a message. Such clocks are called *logical clocks*. We denote the logical clock of process P_k by LC_k. Logical clocks are implemented according to the following rules:

R1 A process P_k increments LC_k by 1 whenever an event occurs in it.

R2 When process P_k receives a message m containing $ts(send(m))$, P_k sets its clock by the rule $LC_k = \max(LC_k, ts(send(m))+1)$.

The next example illustrates synchronization of logical clocks by these rules.

Example 17.2 Synchronization of Logical Clocks

Figure 17.3 contains the timing diagram for a system consisting of three processes. The pair of numbers appearing in parentheses below an event indicate values in the logical clock of the process before and after the event. The logical

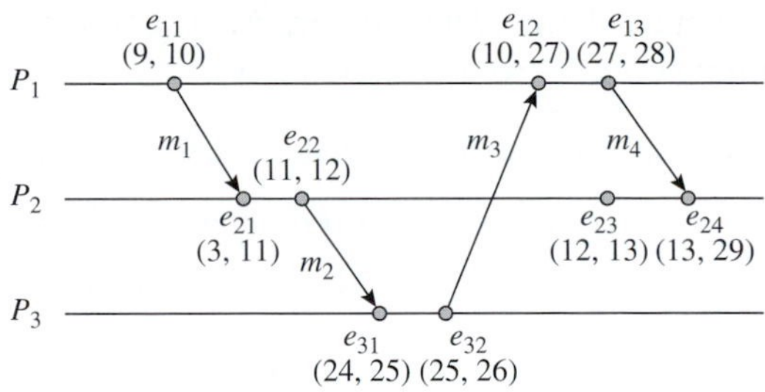

Figure 17.3 Synchronization of logical clocks.

clock in P_1 contains 9 when P_1 decides to send message m_1 to P_2. It is incremented by rule R1 and the send event is timestamped, so m_1 contains the timestamp 10. When P_2 receives the message, its clock reads 3. It first increments its clock to 4, using rule R1, and then synchronizes it, using rule R2. The clock now reads 11.

When P_2 decides to send message m_2, its logical clock is incremented to 12. m_2 thus contains the timestamp 12. When m_2 reaches P_3, P_3 applies rules R1 and R2. Rule R2 has no effect since P_3's logical clock value is much larger than the timestamp in the message. When P_3 sends m_3 to P_1, P_1's clock is synchronized to P_3's clock. Similarly P_2's clock gets synchronized to P_1's clock when P_1 sends m_4 to P_2.

Timestamps obtained by using logical clocks have the property that $ts(e_i) < ts(e_j)$ if $e_i \rightarrow e_j$. However, the converse is not guaranteed for events occurring in different processes; i.e., e_i may not precede e_j even if $ts(e_i) < ts(e_j)$. Such a situation may arise if e_i and e_j occur in processes X and Y, respectively, of the system, and there has been no direct synchronization of the clocks of X and Y either due to lack of message traffic between them or because the clock at process Y is running faster than that at process X (because more events occurred in process Y than in process X). We see this situation in Figure 17.3, where e_{32} occurs "earlier than" event e_{23} but has a larger timestamp than that of e_{23}.

Obtaining Unique Timestamps Events in different processes would obtain identical timestamps if the logical clocks in their processes happen to have identical time values when they occurred. Consequently, these timestamps cannot be used to obtain a total order over events. This problem can be overcome by using a pair $pts(e_i)$ as the timestamp of an event e_i, where

$$pts(e_i) \equiv (local\ time,\ process\ id)$$

This way, events cannot have identical timestamps. Event ordering is now performed by defining event precedence as follows:

$$e_i \text{ precedes } e_j \text{ iff } (i)\ pts(e_i).local\ time < pts(e_j).local\ time, \text{ or}$$
$$(ii)\ pts(e_i).local\ time = pts(e_j).local\ time \text{ and}$$
$$pts(e_i).process\ id < pts(e_j).process\ id \qquad \mathbf{(17.1)}$$

where $pts(e_i).local\ time$ and $pts(e_i).process\ id$ are the local time and process id in $pts(e_i)$, respectively. Note that this notion of event precedence would provide an identical ordering of events e_i and e_j as that obtained through logical clocks, if processes had different local times when events e_i and e_j occurred in them.

17.3.3 Vector Clocks

A *vector clock* is a vector containing n elements, where n is the number of processes in the distributed system. We denote the vector clock of process P_k by VC_k, and its lth element by $VC_k[l]$. Elements of the vector clock VC_k have the following significance:

$VC_k[k]$	The logical clock of process P_k
$VC_k[l], l \neq k$	The highest value in the logical clock of process P_l which is known to process P_k—that is, the highest value of $VC_l[l]$ known to it

The timestamp of an event e_i occurring in a process P_k is the value of VC_k when e_i occurred. Thus, the timestamp is a vector; we call it the *vector timestamp*. We denote the vector timestamp of event e_i by $vts(e_i)$, and the lth element of $vts(e_i)$ by $vts(e_i)[l]$. When process P_k sends a message m to process P_l, it includes $vts(send(m))$ in the message. Vector clocks are implemented according to the following rules:

R3 A process P_k increments $VC_k[k]$ by 1 whenever an event occurs in it.

R4 When process P_k receives a message m containing $vts(send(m))$, P_k sets its clock as follows:

For all l: $VC_k[l] = \max (VC_k[l], vts(send(m))[l])$.

From these rules, $VC_k[k] \geq VC_l[k]$ for all l. If e_i, e_j are two consecutive events in process P_k, $vts(e_j)[k] = vts(e_i)[k] + 1$ by rule R3. If e_i, e_j were *send* and *receive* events for a message in processes P_g and P_k, respectively, process P_k would increment $VC_k[k]$ by rule R3 when e_j occurs, and then update VC_k by rule R4 before timestamping e_j. Consequently, $vts(e_i)[l] \leq vts(e_j)[l]$, for all l and $vts(e_i)[k] < vts(e_j)[k]$. We represent this condition as $vts(e_i) < vts(e_j)$.

The precedence between events e_i and e_j is obtained as follows:

- *e_i precedes e_j:* For all l: $vts(e_i)[l] \leq vts(e_j)[l]$, but for some k: $vts(e_i)[k] \neq vts(e_j)[k]$.

- *e_i follows e_j:* For all l: $vts(e_i)[l] \geq vts(e_j)[l]$, but for some k: $vts(e_i)[k] \neq vts(e_j)[k]$.
- *e_i, e_j are concurrent:* For some k, l: $vts(e_i)[k] < vts(e_j)[k]$ and $vts(e_i)[l] > vts(e_j)[l]$.

Timestamping through vector clocks has two important properties: Every event has a unique timestamp as a result of rules R3 and R4, and $vts(e_i) < vts(e_j)$ if and only if $e_i \rightarrow e_j$. The next example illustrates these properties.

Example 17.3

Synchronization of Vector Clocks

Figure 17.4 shows synchronization of vector clocks for the system of Figure 17.3. The vector timestamp after the occurrence of an event is shown below it. When message m_1 is received, $VC_2[2]$ is incremented by 1 and $VC_2[1]$ is updated to 10. Analogously, when message m_2 is received by process P_3, $VC_3[3]$ is incremented by 1 and $VC_3[1]$ and $VC_3[2]$ are updated. Events e_{32} and e_{23} are concurrent events because $vts(e_{32})[2] < vts(e_{23})[2]$ and $vts(e_{32})[3] > vts(e_{23})[3]$.

The property that $vts(e_i) < vts(e_j)$ if and only if $e_i \rightarrow e_j$ implies that vector clocks do not provide a total order over events. Total order can be obtained by using a pair $pvts(e_i) \equiv (local\ time, process\ id)$ as the timestamp of an event e_i and the following event ordering relation:

$$\begin{aligned} e_i \text{ precedes } e_j \text{ iff } & (i)\ pvts(e_i).local\ time < pvts(e_j).local\ time, \text{ or} \\ & (ii)\ e_i, e_j \text{ are concurrent events and} \\ & \quad pvts(e_i).process\ id < pvts(e_j).process\ id \end{aligned} \tag{17.2}$$

where $pvts(e_i).local\ time$ and $pvts(e_i).process\ id$ are the local vector time and process id in $pvts(e_i)$, respectively.

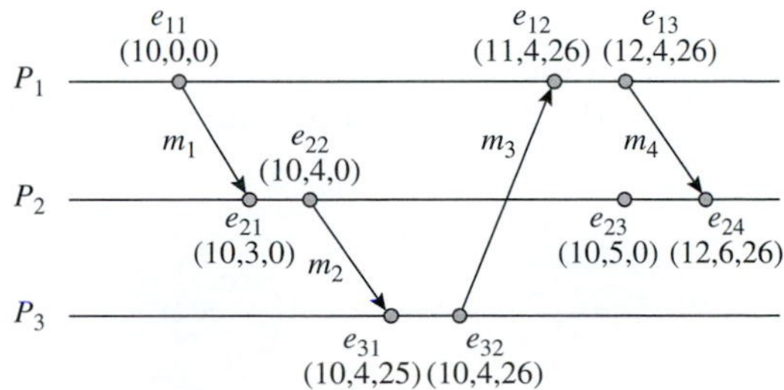

Figure 17.4 Synchronization of vector clocks.

17.4 RECORDING THE STATE OF A DISTRIBUTED SYSTEM

As discussed in Section 17.2.1, the global state of a distributed system at a time instant t is the collection of local states of all entities in the system at time t. However, it is not possible to get all nodes to record their states at the same time instant because local clocks are not perfectly synchronized. Any other collection of local states may be inconsistent. Consider the distributed system shown in Figure 17.5. A banking application has a process P_1 in node N_1 and a process P_2 in node N_2, which perform the following actions:

1. Process P_1 debits \$100 to account A.
2. Process P_1 sends a message to process P_2 to credit \$100 to account B.
3. Process P_2 credits \$100 to account B.

The recorded states of nodes N_1 and N_2 would be inconsistent if the balance in account A is recorded before Step 1 and that in account B is recorded after Step 3. A distributed OS cannot use such a state to perform its control functions.

In this section we present an algorithm for obtaining a consistent collection of local states. Such a collection of states is not a substitute for the global state; however, it has properties that facilitate some of the control functions in a distributed OS.

Consistent State Recording A *state recording* is a collection of local states of entities in a system obtained through some algorithm. A *consistent state recording* is one in which process states of every pair of processes in the system are consistent according to Definition 17.1.

Definition 17.1 Mutually Consistent Local States Local states of processes P_k and P_l are mutually consistent if

1. Every message recorded as "received from P_l" in P_k's state is recorded as "sent to P_k" in P_l's state, and
2. Every message recorded as "received from P_k" in P_l's state is recorded as "sent to P_l" in P_k's state.

In the state recording mentioned at the start of this section, the state of P_2 indicates that it has received the message from P_1 concerning credit of \$100 in account B, but the state of P_1 does not indicate that it has sent such a message.

Figure 17.5 A funds transfer system.

Hence the state recording is inconsistent. A state recording that shows any of the following situations would have been consistent:

1. Accounts A and B contain \$900 and \$300, respectively.
2. Accounts A and B contain \$800 and \$400, respectively.
3. Accounts A and B contain \$800 and \$300, respectively.

In case 1, none of the processes had received a message before its state was recorded, so the process states are consistent. In case 2, the message recorded as received from P_1 in P_2's state is recorded as sent in P_1's state. In case 3, again none of the process states records receipt of a message. The message from P_1 to P_2 is in transit. It will be delivered to process P_2 sometime in future, and process P_2 will add \$100 to account B when it receives the message. This is why mutual consistency of process states requires that every message recorded as received should be recorded as sent, but not vice versa.

17.4.1 Properties of a Consistent State Recording

Figure 17.6 shows a model of a distributed computation. The computation consists of four processes P_1–P_4 that communicate among themselves through messages. An edge (P_i, P_j) represents a *channel* Ch_{ij}, i.e., an interprocess communication path that is used by process P_i to send messages to process P_j. Note that a channel is unidirectional—a process either sends or receives messages along a channel, but not both. Channels Ch_{23} and Ch_{32} together indicate that processes P_2 and P_3 send messages to one another.

Figure 17.7 shows the timing diagram of the computation. Table 17.2 shows states of processes P_1–P_4 recorded at time instants t_{P_1}, t_{P_2}, t_{P_3}, and t_{P_4}, respectively. These time instants are marked with the symbol ▫ in the figure. The state of process P_1 shows that it has received message m_{21}, but not sent out any messages, while the state of process P_2 shows that it has sent out messages m_{21} and m_{23} before t_{P_2} but not received any messages. These states are mutually consistent according to Definition 17.1. However, the states of P_3 and P_4 are not mutually consistent because the state of process P_3 records message m_{43} as received but process P_4's state does not record it as sent. Hence the state recording of Table 17.2 is not a consistent state recording.

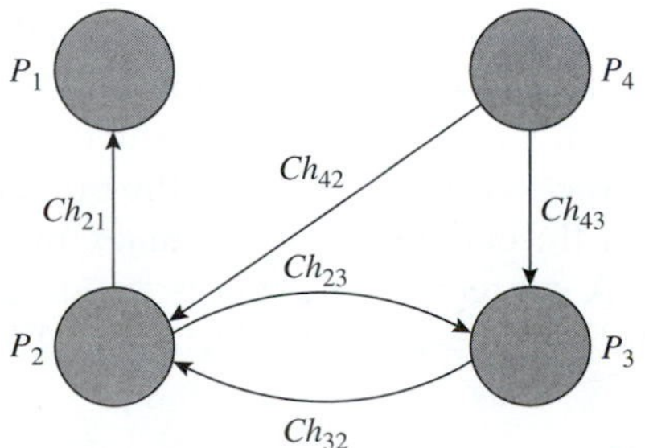

Figure 17.6 A distributed computation for state recording.

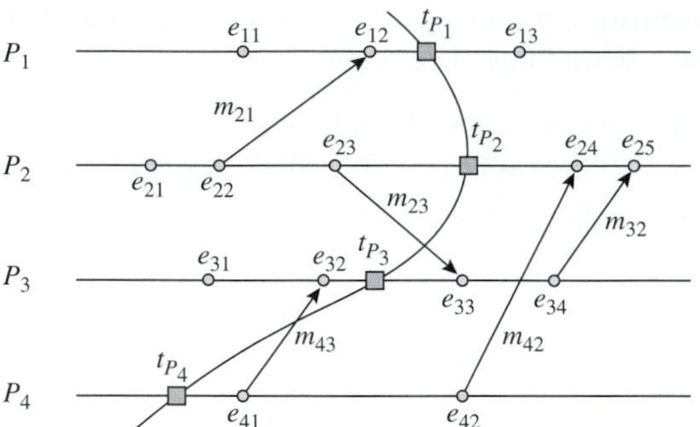

Figure 17.7 A timing diagram for the distributed computation of Figure 17.6.

Table 17.2 Local States of Processes

Process	Description of recorded state
P_1	No messages have been sent. Message m_{21} has been received.
P_2	Messages m_{21} and m_{23} have been sent. No messages have been received.
P_3	No messages have been sent. Message m_{43} has been received.
P_4	No messages have been sent. No messages have been received.

Cut of a System The notion of a *cut* of a system helps in determining the consistency of a state recording. Let t_{P_i} be the point in a timing diagram at which the state of a process P_i is recorded.

Definition 17.2 Cut of a System A curve that connects the points in a timing diagram at which states of processes are recorded, in increasing order by process number.

The cut of the distributed computation shown in Figure 17.7 represents the recorded state shown in Table 17.2. The term "a cut is taken" means that a collection of local states is recorded. An event that had occurred in a process before the state of the process was recorded is said to occur "to the left of the cut" in the timing diagram. Such an event belongs in the *past of the cut*. An event that would occur in a process after the state of the process was recorded is said to occur "to the right of the cut" in the timing diagram. Such an event belongs to the *future of the cut*. A cut represents a consistent state recording of a system if the states of each pair of processes satisfy Definition 17.1.

State of a Channel The state of a channel Ch_{ij} is the set of messages contained in Ch_{ij}, i.e., the messages sent by process P_i that are not yet received by process P_j. We use the following notation to determine the state of a channel Ch_{ij}:

$Recorded\_sent_{ij}$	The set of messages recorded as sent over channel Ch_{ij} in the state of P_i
$Recorded\_recd_{ij}$	The set of messages recorded as received over channel Ch_{ij} in the state of P_j

$Recorded\_sent_{ij} = Recorded\_recd_{ij}$ implies that all messages sent by P_i have been received by P_j. Hence the channel is empty. $Recorded\_sent_{ij} - Recorded\_recd_{ij} \neq \phi$, where "$-$" represents the set difference operator, implies that some messages sent by P_i have not been received by P_j. These messages are still contained in channel Ch_{ij}. $Recorded\_recd_{ij} - Recorded\_sent_{ij} \neq \phi$, implies that process P_j has recorded as received at least one message that is not recorded as sent by process P_i. This situation indicates inconsistency of the recorded local states of P_i and P_j according to Definition 17.1.

A cut in the timing diagram may intersect with a message m_k sent by process P_i to process P_j over channel Ch_{ij}. The manner of the cut indicates whether the recorded states of P_i and P_j are consistent with respect to the sending and receipt of the message. It also indicates the state of the channel. Three possibilities are:

- *No intersection with a message:* The message send and receive events are either both located to the left of the cut or both located to the right of the cut. In either case, the message did not exist in channel Ch_{ij} when the cut was taken.
- *Forward intersection with a message:* The message send event is located to the left of the cut and the message receive event is located to the right of the cut. Hence, the message existed in channel Ch_{ij} when the cut was taken. The cut in the timing diagram of Figure 17.7 has a forward intersection with message m_{23}.
- *Backward intersection with a message:* The message send event is located to the right of the cut and the message receive event is located to the left of the cut. Hence, the message had been received but had not been sent when the cut was taken. Such a message indicates an inconsistency in the recorded state. The cut in the timing diagram of Figure 17.7 has a backward intersection with message m_{43}.

From these observations, we can formulate a consistency condition for a cut as follows:

CC	A cut C represents a consistent state recording of a distributed system if the future of the cut is closed under the precedes relation on events, i.e., closed under "$\rightarrow$".

Condition CC can be explained as follows: A set of items I is said to be *closed under a relation R*, if using the relation on any item in I yields an item that is also in I. Let I be the set of events in the future of a cut. Applying the relation "$\rightarrow$" to an event $e_i \in I$ gives us an event e_j such that $e_i \rightarrow e_j$, i.e., e_i precedes e_j. If I is closed under "$\rightarrow$", this event also belongs to I. That is, it does not belong to the past of the cut. This condition is equivalent to the restriction that a cut should

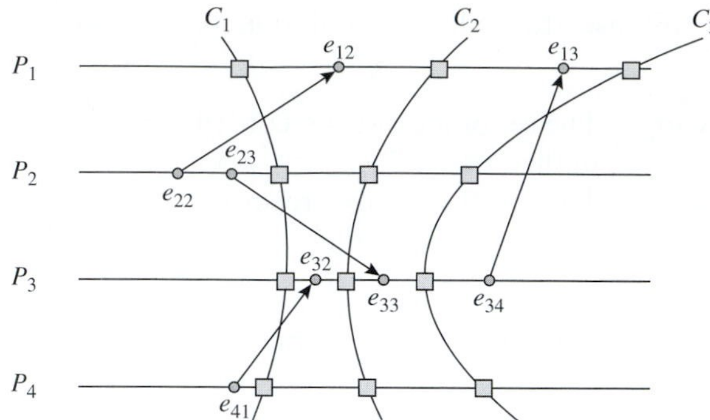

Figure 17.8 Consistency of cuts—cuts C_1, C_2 are consistent while C_3 is inconsistent.

not have a backward intersection with a message. A forward intersection does not violate condition CC since its send event is in the past and its receive event is in the future.

Example 17.4 **Consistency of a Cut**

In Figure 17.8, cuts C_1 and C_2 are consistent cuts because there is no event e_j belonging to the past of the cut that follows an event e_i in the future of the cut. Cut C_3 is inconsistent because event e_{13} follows event e_{34} because of the cause-and-effect relationship between a send and a receive; however, e_{34} is in the future of C_3 while e_{13} is in its past.

17.4.2 An Algorithm for Consistent State Recording

This section describes the state recording algorithm by Chandy and Lamport (1985). The algorithm makes the following assumptions:

1. Channels are unidirectional.
2. Channels have unbounded capacities to hold messages.
3. Channels are FIFO.

The assumption of FIFO channels implies that messages received by a destination process must be the first few messages sent by a sender process, and messages contained in a channel must be the last few messages sent by a process.

To initiate a state recording, a process records its own state and sends a state recording request called a *marker* on every outgoing channel. When a process receives a marker, it records the state of the channel over which it received the marker. If the marker is the first marker it received from any process, it also records its own state and sends a marker on every outgoing channel. We use the following notation to discuss how the state of a channel is determined:

Received$_{ij}$	The set of messages received by process P_j on channel Ch_{ij} before it received the marker on channel Ch_{ij}.
Recorded_recd$_{ij}$	The set of messages recorded as received over channel Ch_{ij} in the state of process P_j.

Algorithm 17.2 *Chandy–Lamport Algorithm*

1. *When a process P_i initiates the state recording:* P_i records its own state and sends a marker on each outgoing channel connected to it.
2. *When process P_j receives a marker over an incoming channel Ch_{ij}:* Process P_j performs the following actions:
   a. If P_j had not received any marker earlier, then
      i. Record its own state.
      ii. Record the state of channel Ch_{ij} as *empty*.
      iii. Send a marker on each outgoing channel connected to it.
   b. Otherwise, record the state of channel Ch_{ij} as the set of messages $Received_{ij} - Recorded\_recd_{ij}$.

Rules of Algorithm 17.2 are executed atomically, i.e., as indivisible operations. Recording of the channel state by the algorithm can be explained as follows: Let a process P_i send messages $m_{i_1}, m_{i_2}, \ldots m_{i_n}$ on channel Ch_{ij} before recording its own state and sending a marker on Ch_{ij}. Let process P_j have two incoming channels Ch_{ij} and Ch_{kj}. If the marker on channel Ch_{ij} is the first marker P_j received, it would record its own state, which would show $Recorded\_recd_{ij}$ and $Recorded\_recd_{kj}$ as the messages received by it. P_j would also record the state of Ch_{ij} as *empty*. Because channels are FIFO, process P_j would have received the marker after receiving messages $m_{i_1}, m_{i_2}, \ldots, m_{i_n}$ on Ch_{ij}, so it is correct to record the state of channel Ch_{ij} as *empty*.

Let P_j receive two more messages m_{k_1} and m_{k_2} on Ch_{kj} before it received the marker. Hence $Received_{kj} = Recorded\_recd_{kj} \cup \{m_{k_1}, m_{k_2}\}$ and the state of channel Ch_{kj} would be recorded as the set of messages $Received_{kj} - Recorded\_recd_{kj}$ i.e., $\{m_{k_1}, m_{k_2}\}$. It is correct because process P_k would have sent messages m_{k_1}, m_{k_2} before it recorded its own state and sent the marker on channel Ch_{kj}, so if these messages were not received by P_i by the time it recorded its own state, they must have been in the channel.

Example 17.5 illustrates operation of the Chandy–Lamport algorithm.

Operation of the Chandy–Lamport Algorithm — Example 17.5

Figure 17.9(a) shows a distributed system at time 0. Process P_1 has sent message m_1 to P_3. The message currently exists in Ch_{13}. At time 1, process P_3 sends message m_2 to process P_2. At time 2, P_1 decides to record the state of the system, so it records its own state and sends markers on its outgoing channels.

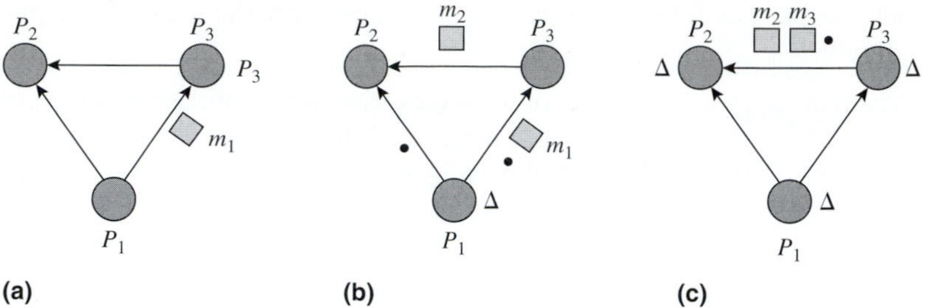

Figure 17.9 Example of the Chandy–Lamport algorithm: system at times $0, 2^+$, and 5^+.

Table 17.3 Recorded States of Processes and Channels in Figure 17.9

Entity	Description of recorded state
P_1	Message m_1 has been sent. No messages have been received.
P_2	No messages have been sent or received.
P_3	Messages m_2 and m_3 have been sent. Message m_1 has been received.
Ch_{12}	Empty
Ch_{13}	Empty
Ch_{23}	Contains the messages m_2 and m_3

Figure 17.9(b) shows the situation at time 2^+. Message m_1 is still in channel Ch_{13} and m_2 is in Ch_{32}. The bullets indicate markers. The symbol Δ indicates that the state of a process has been recorded.

Process P_2 receives the marker on Ch_{12} at time 3, records its own state and records the state of Ch_{12} as empty. Process P_3 sends message m_3 to process P_2 at time 4 and receives the marker on Ch_{13} at time 5. It now records its own state, records the state of Ch_{13} as empty, and sends a marker on Ch_{32}. Figure 17.9(c) shows the situation at time 5^+. States of all processes have been recorded. States of channels Ch_{12} and Ch_{13} have also been recorded; however, the state of Ch_{32} is yet to be recorded.

When the marker on Ch_{32} reaches process P_2, P_2 will record the state of Ch_{32} according to step 2(b) of Algorithm 17.2. It is recorded as messages $\{m_2, m_3\}$ because these messages are in $Received_{32}$ but not in $Recorded\_recd_{32}$. Table 17.3 shows the state recording of the system.

Properties of the Recorded State Let t_b and t_e be the time instants when the state recording of system S begins and ends. Let RS be the recorded state of the system. One would expect that system S would have been in the state RS at some time instant t_i such that $t_b < t_i < t_e$. However, this may not be so! That is, the recorded state *RS* may not match any global state of the system. Example 17.6 illustrates this fact.

Recorded State versus Global State

Example 17.6

Figure 17.7 shows the timing diagram of the distributed system of Figure 17.6. Let P_4 initiate state recording at time instant t_1. The timing diagram of Figure 17.10 shows how the markers are sent and received by processes during state recording. The markers are shown as dotted arrows.

Table 17.4 shows channel and process states recorded by the Chandy–Lamport algorithm. Only message m_{21} is recorded as sent by P_2 and received by P_1. No other messages are recorded as sent or received. However, because the timing diagram of Figure 17.7 is drawn to scale, it is clear that the system never existed in a state in which message m_{21} had been sent and received but no other messages had been sent—the message-send and message-receive events e_{23}, e_{32}, and e_{41} had occurred before event e_{12}, the message-receive event for message m_{21}. Thus any global state that recorded message m_{21} as received would have also recorded message m_{43} as sent and received, and message m_{23} as sent.

Even though the system may not have existed in the recorded state at any point in time, the recorded state is useful for applications that require only mutual

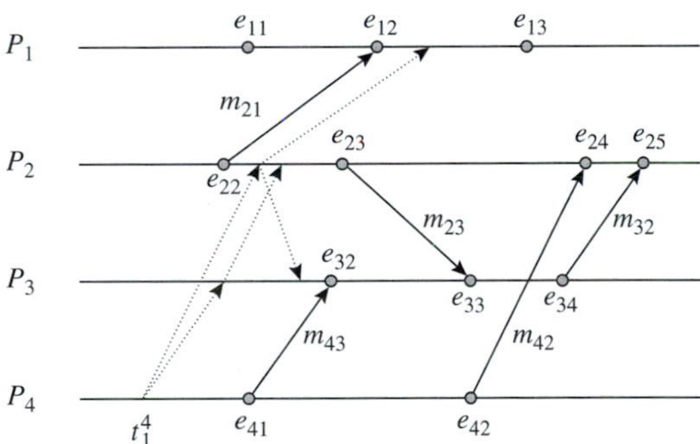

Figure 17.10 State recording of the system of Figures 17.6 and 17.7.

Table 17.4 A Recorded State that Does Not Match Any Global State

Entity*	Description of recorded state
P_1	No messages have been sent. Message m_{21} has been received.
P_2	Message m_{21} has been sent. No messages have been received.
P_3	No messages have been sent or received.
P_4	No messages have been sent or received.

* States of all channels are recorded as empty.

consistency of local states. Consider the problem of finding the total funds in a banking system. When $100 is transferred from account A to account B, it is irrelevant whether the recorded state shows this amount to be in account A or account B or in the channel connecting the two, so long as it shows exactly one of these three possibilities. The state recorded by Algorithm 17.2 meets this requirement.

Chandy and Lamport (1985) shows that Algorithm 17.2 can be used to detect a class of properties called *stable properties*. A stable property is one that, if it holds in the global state of a system at time instant t_i, it would hold in the global state of the system at all time instants $t_j > t_i$. Algorithm 17.2 is executed periodically to obtain a state recording and the recorded state is analyzed to detect presence of the stable property. This scheme may fail to capture the stable property in the first state recording that completes at a time instant $> t_i$. However, this failure is not disastrous because the property would continue to hold and some later execution of the scheme would capture it. A useful stable property is existence of a cycle, knot, or resource knot in a WFG or an RRAG, which can be used for deadlock detection (see Chapter 8). Another useful stable property is the *distributed termination condition*, which is defined as a situation in which all processes participating in a distributed computation are passive and no messages between the processes are in transit (see Section 18.6).

17.5 SUMMARY

An operating system uses the notions of time and state for controlling operation of user processes and for organizing its own functioning. However, each node in a distributed system has its own clock and memory, so these notions cannot be employed as simply as in a conventional operating system. In this chapter, we developed alternative notions of time and state for use in a distributed system.

An OS uses the notion of time to know the order in which events occurred, so that it can service events in time-dependent orders such as FCFS and LIFO. The notion of *precedence* of events, which indicates which event occurred before which other event, is *transitive*, that is, if event e_i occurred before e_j and event e_j occurred before e_k, then e_i must have occurred before e_k. The OS can determine precedence of events as follows: If two events occurred in the same node, the OS knows which of them occurred earlier. For events occurring in different nodes, the OS uses transitivity of events and the notion of a *causal relationship* between events—that is, cause-and-effect relationship—to find which of the events occurred earlier. For example, in interprocess message communication, the sending of a message is a cause and its receipt is the effect. Hence the receive event of a message is known to occur *after* its send event. Using transitivity, it follows that an event that preceded a send event of a message must have occurred before an event that followed its receipt. However, for some pairs of events, it is not possible to know which of the events occurred earlier. Such events are called *concurrent events*.

It is laborious to deduce the precedence of events by using transitivity. Hence an OS associates a *timestamp*, i.e., occurrence time, with each event and compares the timestamps of two events to know which of them occurred earlier. To facilitate timestamping, the OS maintains a clock in each process, which is called the *local clock* of the process, and keeps the local clocks of processes well synchronized. It performs clock synchronization by using the causal relationship governing interprocess messages as follows: Each message contains the timestamp of its send event. The local clock in the process receiving the message must show a time larger than the timestamp in the message. If it is not so, the local clock in the receiving process is incremented to a time that is larger than the timestamp in the message. Since local clocks do not show the real time, they are called *logical clocks*. Timestamps using logical clocks have the property that if t_i, t_j are the timestamps of events e_i, e_j, respectively, $t_i < t_j$ if event e_i precedes e_j. An alternative system of clocks called *vector clocks* has the additional property that $t_i < t_j$ implies that event e_i occurred before e_j. For concurrent events, it is immaterial how we order them. Hence a pair (*process id, timestamp*) is used to obtain a total order on events.

The state of a node is called its *local state*. The *global state* of a system is a collection of local states of its nodes obtained at exactly the same instant of time. It is not possible to record the global state by asking each node to record its local state at a specific time instant, because clocks in the nodes are not perfectly synchronized. An arbitrary collection of local states of nodes may be inconsistent. For example, if nodes record their states spontaneously, the local state of node N_i may be recorded before it sent a message m to node N_j and the local state of N_j may be recorded after it received message m. This problem was overcome by Chandy and Lamport (1985) by using special messages called *markers* to instruct individual nodes to record their local states. They showed that if interprocess communication is FIFO, the local states of processes recorded by their algorithm were mutually consistent. The collection of these local states can be used to detect *stable properties*, which are properties that do not change with time, such as presence of cycles in wait-for graphs.

TEST YOUR CONCEPTS

17.1 Classify each of the following statements as true or false:

a. Events e_i and e_j are concurrent events only if $ts(e_i) = ts(e_j)$, where $ts(e_i)$, $ts(e_j)$ are the timestamps of e_i, e_j using logical clocks.

b. Even if $ts(e_i) > ts(e_j)$, event e_i could have occurred earlier than event e_j.

c. Even if $vts(e_i) > vts(e_j)$, event e_i could have occurred earlier than event e_j.

d. A message from process P_i to process P_j that intersects with a cut of a system is a message that has been sent by P_i but not received by P_j in the states of processes P_i and P_j represented by the cut.

e. In a state recorded by the Chandy–Lamport algorithm, the state of channel Ch_{ij} is likely to be nonempty only if process P_j receives a marker on some other channel before receiving the marker on channel Ch_{ij}.

17.2 Select the appropriate alternative in each of the following questions:

a. If process P_i sends messages to process P_j, but process P_j does not send messages to process P_i, states of processes P_i, P_j are mutually consistent local states only if

i. All messages sent by process P_i to process P_j have been received by process P_j.

ii. Some messages sent by process P_i to process P_j have not been received by process P_j.

iii. All messages received by process P_j from process P_i have been sent by process P_i.

iv. None of (i)–(iii).

b. If event e_i in process P_i is in the past of a cut C_k,

i. All events in the system that precede event e_i are in the past of the cut C_k.

ii. Some of the events that precede event e_i may be in the past of the cut C_k.

iii. All events that occur after event e_i are in the future of the cut C_k.

iv. None of (i)–(iii).

EXERCISES

17.1 In Example 17.2, P_3's time is much larger than that of P_1 or P_2. List all conditions under which this can happen.

17.2 The following events occur in a system consisting of three processes:

process P_1	*process P_2*	*process P_3*
event e_1;	*event e_3*;	*event e_5*;
--	--	--
Send message to P_2;	Receive message from P_3;	Send message to P_2;
event e_2;	Receive message from P_1;	*event e_6*;
	--	Receive message from P_2;
	event e_4;	--
	Send message to P_3;	*event e_7*;

a. Draw a timing diagram for the system.
b. Show event precedences in this system.
c. List the concurrent events.

17.3 $Synch(P_i, P_j, t_k) = true$ if the logical clocks of P_i and P_j are reasonably consistent at time instant t_k; i.e., if the difference between their values is $<\delta$, for some small value δ. If $RP(i,k)$ is the set of processes from whom P_i has received a message before t_k and $SP(i,k)$ is the set of processes to which P_i has sent a message before t_k, determine whether $Synch(P_i, P_j, t_k)$ would be *true* in the following situations:
a. $RP(i,k) \bigcap RP(j,k) \neq \phi$
b. There exists a $P_g \in SP(i,k)$ such that $P_j \in SP(g,k)$
c. $P_j \in SP(i,k)$
d. $P_j \in RP(i,k)$ but $P_j \notin RP(i,k-1)$
e. $P_j \in SP(i,k)$ and $P_i \in SP(j,k)$
f. $P_j \in RP(i,k)$ but $P_j \notin RP(i,k-1)$ and P_i has not received any message from any process after the time it sent a message to P_j.

17.4 Relation (17.1) imposes a total order even if events can be only partially ordered by using causal relationships. Give an example of a system showing such events. Comment on the advantages and drawbacks of using relation (17.1).

17.5 Instead of using relation (17.2) to obtain a total order using vector timestamps, it is proposed to use the following relation:
e_i precedes e_j iff

$$(i)\ pvts(e_i).local\ time < pvts(e_j).local\ time, \text{ or}$$

$$(ii)\ pvts(e_i).local\ time = pvts(e_j).local\ time \text{ and}$$

$$pvts(e_i).process\ id < pvts(e_j).process\ id$$

Comment on the correctness of this proposal.

17.6 t_i and t_j are timestamps of events e_i and e_j.
a. Give an example of a system in which $t_i < t_j$ when logical clocks are used but $t_i \not< t_j$ when vector clocks are used.
b. If $t_i < t_j$ when vector clocks are used, show that $t_i < t_j$ when logical clocks are used.
c. If $t_i < t_j$ when logical clocks are used, show that $t_i \not> t_j$ when vector clocks are used.

17.7 Vector timestamps of concurrent events e_i and e_j are such that $vts(e_i)[k] < vts(e_j)[k]$. Show that events e_i and e_l are concurrent if $vts(e_l)[g] = vts(e_j)[g]$ for all $g \neq k$ and $vts(e_l)[k] > vts(e_j)[k]$.

17.8 Explain, with the help of an example, why the Chandy–Lamport algorithm requires channels to be FIFO.

17.9 A transitless state of a system is a state in which no messages are in transit. (See Table 17.4 for an example.) Give an example of a system in which all states recorded by the Chandy–Lamport algorithm are necessarily transitless.

17.10 A system consists of processes P_i, P_j and channels Ch_{ij} and Ch_{ji}. Each process sends a message to the other process every δ seconds. Every message requires σ seconds to reach P_j. Prove that if $\delta < \sigma$, the state recording initiated by P_i using the Chandy–Lamport algorithm cannot be transitless.

17.11 Give an example of a system in which the state recorded by the Chandy–Lamport algorithm is one of the states in which the system existed sometime during the execution of the algorithm.

17.12 What will be the state recording in Example 17.6, if the state recording request in channel Ch_{42} is delayed and delivered to process P_2 immediately after event e_{23} occurs?

17.13 The Chandy–Lamport algorithm works correctly if more than one node in a distributed system spontaneously initiates a state recording. Describe working of the algorithm if processes P_2 and P_4 of Figure 17.6 initiate state recording (a) before sending any messages, (b) after one message has been sent on each of Ch_{21}, Ch_{32} and Ch_{43} and no other messages are sent.

17.14 The assumption concerning FIFO channels can be removed from Algorithm 17.2 as follows: A *flag* field is added to each message. This field contains the values *before token* or *after token* depending on whether the message is sent before or after sending a token on the same channel. If a process receives a message with the flag value *after token* before it receives a token on the same channel, it performs the same actions as it would have performed on receiving a token, and ignores the token when it is received later. Formulate rules for recording the state of a channel using this scheme.

BIBLIOGRAPHY

Lamport (1978) discusses ordering of events in a distributed system and defines a partial order on events. Mattern (1989), Garg (2002), and Attiya and Welch (2004) discuss vector clocks and consistency of cuts. Consistency of cuts is also discussed in Chandy and Lamport (1985) and Knapp (1987).

Chandy and Lamport (1985) developed the distributed snapshot problem described in Section 17.2, which requires FIFO channels. Li, Radhakrishnan, and Venkatesh (1987), Lai and Yang (1987), and Mattern (1989) describe algorithms that do not require channels to be FIFO. Lynch (1996) and Tel (2000) discuss algorithms for global snapshots.

1. Attiya, H., and J. Welch (2004): *Distributed Computing: Fundamentals, Simulations and Advanced Topics*, John Wiley, New York.
2. Chandy K. M., and L. Lamport (1985): "Distributed snapshots: Determining global states of distributed systems," *ACM Transactions on Computer Systems*, **3**, 1 (Feb. 1985), 63–75.
3. Garg, V. K. (2002): *Elements of Distributed Computing*, Wiley-IEEE, New York.
4. Knapp, E. (1987): "Distributed deadlock Detection," *Computing Surveys*, **19**, 4 (Dec. 1987), 303–328.
5. Lai, T. H., and T. H. Yang (1987) : "On distributed snapshots," *Information Processing Letters*, **25**, 153–158.
6. Lamport L. (1978): "Time, clocks, and the ordering of events in a distributed system," *Communications of the ACM*, **21**, 7 (July 1978), 558–565.
7. Li, H. F., T. Radhakrishnan, and K. Venkatesh (1987) : "Global state detection in non-FIFO networks," *Proceedings of the 7th International Conference on Distributed Computing Systems*, 364–370.
8. Lynch, N. (1996): *Distributed Algorithms*, Morgan Kaufmann.
9. Mattern, F. (1989) : "Virtual time and global states of distributed systems," M. Cosnard et al. (eds.), *Parallel and Distributed Algorithms*, Elsevier Science, North Holland.
10. Spezialetti, M., and P. Kearns (1986) : "Efficient distributed snapshots," *Proceedings of the 6th International Conference on Distributed Computing Systems*, 382–388.
11. Tel, G. (2000): *Introduction to Distributed Algorithms*, 2nd ed. Cambridge University Press, Cambridge.

18 Chapter

Distributed Control Algorithms

A distributed operating system performs several control functions. Of these control functions, the *mutual exclusion* and *deadlock handling* functions are similar to those performed in a conventional OS. The *scheduling* function performs *load balancing* to ensure that computational loads in all nodes of the system are comparable. The *election* function elects one among a group of processes as the coordinator for an activity. The *termination detection* function checks whether processes of a distributed computation operating in different nodes of the system have all completed their tasks.

To respond speedily and reliably to events occurring in the system, a distributed operating system performs a control function using a *distributed control algorithm*, whose actions are performed in several nodes of the distributed system. Distributed control algorithms avoid using the global state of a system. Instead, they depend on local states of different nodes, and use interprocess messages to query the states and make decisions. Their correctness depends on how they use the local states and interprocess messages for arriving at correct decisions, and for avoiding wrong decisions. These two aspects of correctness are called *liveness* and *safety*, respectively.

We present distributed control algorithms for the different control functions and discuss their properties such as overhead and effect on system performance.

18.1 OPERATION OF DISTRIBUTED CONTROL ALGORITHMS

A distributed operating system implements a control function through a *distributed control algorithm*, whose actions are performed in several nodes of the system and whose data is also spread across several nodes. This approach has the following advantages over a centralized implementation of control functions:

- The delays and overhead involved in collecting the global state of a system are avoided.
- The control function can respond speedily to events in different nodes of the system.
- Failure of a single node does not cripple the control function.

Table 18.1 Overview of Control Functions in a Distributed OS

Function	Description
Mutual exclusion	Implement a critical section (CS) for a data item d_s for use by processes in a distributed system. It involves synchronization of processes operating in different nodes of the system so that at most one process is in a CS for d_s at any time.
Deadlock handling	Prevent or detect deadlocks that arise from resource sharing within and across nodes of a distributed system.
Scheduling	Perform *load balancing* to ensure that computational loads in different nodes of a distributed system are comparable. It involves transferring processes from heavily loaded nodes to lightly loaded nodes.
Termination detection	Processes of a distributed computation may operate in several nodes of a distributed system. Termination detection is the act of determining whether such a computation has completed its operation. It involves checking whether any of the processes is active and whether any interprocess message is in transit between them.
Election	A *coordinator* (also called a *leader* process) is the one that performs some privileged function like resource allocation. An election is performed when a coordinator fails or is terminated. It selects one of the active processes to become the new coordinator and informs the identity of the new coordinator to all other processes.

A distributed control algorithm provides a service whose clients include both user applications and the kernel. Table 18.1 describes control functions in a distributed OS. *Mutual exclusion* and *election* are services provided to user processes, *deadlock handling* and *scheduling* are services offered to the kernel, while the *termination detection* service may be used by both user processes and the kernel. In OS literature, names of these functions are generally prefixed with the word "distributed" to indicate that the functions are performed in a distributed manner. Note that fault tolerance and recovery issues are not discussed here; they are discussed separately in Chapter 19.

A distributed control algorithm operates in parallel with its clients, so that it can respond readily to events related to its service. The following terminology is used to distinguish between actions of a client and those of a control algorithm.

- *Basic computation:* Operation of a client constitutes a *basic computation*. A basic computation may involve processes in one or more nodes of the system. The messages exchanged by these processes are called *basic messages*.

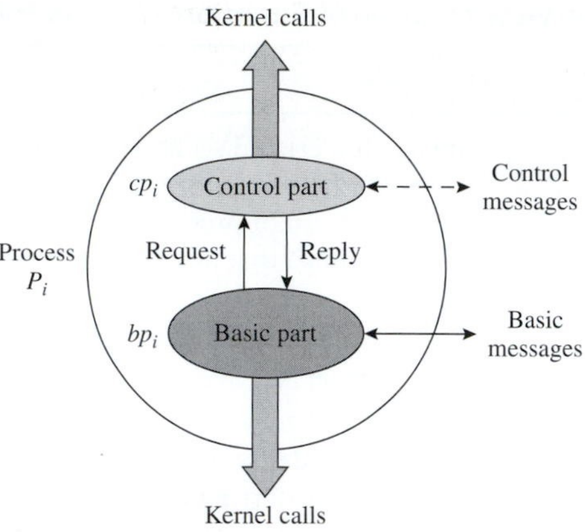

Figure 18.1 Basic and control parts of a process P_i.

- *Control computation:* Operation of a control algorithm constitutes a *control computation*. Messages exchanged by processes of a control computation are called *control messages*.

To understand operation of a distributed control algorithm, we visualize each process to consist of two parts that operate in parallel—a basic part and a control part. Figure 18.1 illustrates the two parts of a process P_i. The *basic part* of a process participates in a basic computation. It exchanges basic messages with basic parts of other processes. When it requires a service offered by a control algorithm, it makes a request to the control part of the process. All other requests are made directly to the kernel. The *control part* of a process participates in a control computation. It exchanges control messages with control parts of other processes, and may interact with the kernel to implement its part in the control function. The basic part of a process may become blocked when it makes a resource request; however, the control part of a process never becomes blocked—this feature enables it to respond to events related to its service in a timely manner.

Example 18.1 Basic and Control Parts of a Process

A distributed application consists of four processes P_1–P_4. Let process P_2 be currently in a CS for shared data d_s. When process P_1 wishes to enter a CS for d_s, bp_1 makes a request to cp_1, which is a part of some distributed mutual exclusion algorithm discussed later in Section 18.3. To decide whether P_1 may be allowed to enter a CS for d_s, cp_1 exchanges messages with cp_2, cp_3, and cp_4. From their replies, it realizes that some other process is currently in a CS for d_s, so it makes a kernel call to block bp_1. Note that cp_2 participates in this decision even while bp_2 was executing in a CS. When process P_2 wishes to exit the CS, bp_2 makes a request to cp_2, which interacts with control parts of other processes and decides that process P_1 may enter a CS for d_s. Accordingly, cp_1 makes a kernel call to activate bp_1.

18.2 CORRECTNESS OF DISTRIBUTED CONTROL ALGORITHMS

Processes of a distributed control algorithm exchange control data and coordinate their actions through control messages. However, message communication incurs delays, so the data used by the algorithm may become stale and inconsistent, and the algorithm may either miss performing correct actions or perform wrong actions. Accordingly, correctness of a distributed control algorithm has two facets:

- *Liveness:* An algorithm will *eventually* perform correct actions, i.e., perform them without indefinite delays.
- *Safety:* An algorithm does not perform wrong actions.

Lack of liveness implies that an algorithm would fail to perform correct actions. For example, a distributed mutual exclusion algorithm might fail to satisfy the *progress* and *bounded wait* properties of Section 6.3.1, or a deadlock detection algorithm might not be able to detect a deadlock that exists in the system. Note that the amount of time needed to perform a correct action is immaterial for the liveness property; the action must be performed *eventually*. Lack of safety implies that an algorithm may perform wrong actions like permitting more than one process to be in CS at the same time. Table 18.2 summarizes the liveness and safety properties of some distributed control algorithms.

Assuming a distributed control algorithm to consist of a set of distinct actions and a set of distinct conditions, we can represent the algorithm as a set of rules of the form <*condition*> : <*action*>, where a rule specifies that the algorithm should perform <*action*> if and only if <*condition*> is true. Using

Table 18.2 **Liveness and Safety of Distributed Control Algorithms**

Algorithm	Liveness	Safety
Mutual exclusion	(1) If a CS is free and some processes have requested entry to it, one of them will enter it in finite time. (2) A process requesting entry to a CS will enter it in finite time.	At most one process will be in a CS at any time.
Deadlock handling	If a deadlock arises, it will be detected in finite time.	Deadlock will not be declared unless one actually exists.
Termination detection	Termination of a distributed computation will be detected within a finite time.	Termination will not be declared unless it has occurred.
Election	A new coordinator will be elected in a finite time.	Exactly one process will be elected coordinator.

the notation "$\mapsto$" for the words "eventually leads to," we define the notion of correctness as follows:

- *Liveness:* For all rules, *<condition>* $\mapsto$ *<action>*, i.e., *<action>* will be eventually performed if *<condition>* holds.
- *Lack of safety:* For some rule, $\neg$ *<condition>* $\mapsto$ *<action>*, i.e., *<action>* may be eventually performed even if *<condition>* does not hold.

Proving correctness of a distributed algorithm is a complex task. *<condition>* and *<action>* should be specified to correctly represent the algorithm, and formal techniques must be employed to demonstrate that an algorithm possesses the liveness and safety properties. Theoretical foundations needed for formal proofs of distributed algorithms did not exist until the early 1990s. This is why many distributed algorithms developed earlier contained bugs.

It should be noted that liveness and safety are concerned only with correctness of an algorithm. Other desirable properties of an algorithm, e.g., FCFS service in distributed mutual exclusion algorithms, must be stated and proved separately.

18.3 DISTRIBUTED MUTUAL EXCLUSION

18.3.1 A Permission-Based Algorithm

The algorithm by Ricart and Agrawala (1981) grants entry to a critical section in FCFS order. The algorithm is *fully distributed* in that all processes participate equally in deciding which process should enter a CS next. A process that wishes to enter a CS sends timestamped request messages to all other processes and waits until it receives a "go ahead" reply from each of them. If the system contains n processes, $2 \times (n - 1)$ messages have to be exchanged before a process can enter the critical section. Safety of mutual exclusion follows from the fact that at most one process can obtain $(n - 1)$ replies at any time. Entry is granted in FCFS order, hence every process gains entry to CS in finite time. This feature satisfies the liveness property.

Algorithm 18.1 *Ricart-Agrawala Algorithm*

1. *When a process P_i wishes to enter a CS:* P_i sends request messages of the form ("request", P_i, *<timestamp>*) to all other processes in the system, and becomes blocked.
2. *When a process P_i receives a request message from process P_r:*
   - **a.** If P_i is not interested in using a CS, it immediately sends a "go ahead" reply to P_r.
   - **b.** If P_i itself wishes to enter a CS, it sends a "go ahead" reply to P_r if the timestamp in the received request is smaller than the timestamp of its

own request; otherwise, it adds the process id found in the request to the pending list.

c. If P_i is in a CS, it simply adds the request message to the pending list.

3. *When a process P_i receives $n - 1$ "go ahead" replies:* The process becomes active and enters a CS.

4. *When a process P_i exits a CS:* The process sends a "go ahead" reply to every process whose request message exists in its pending list.

Table 18.3 shows how steps of Algorithm 18.1 are implemented in the control part of a process. The first column shows steps in the basic computation performed by a process. It consists of a loop in which the process requests entry to a CS, performs some processing inside the CS, and exits from it. The other columns show actions of the control part of the algorithm.

Table 18.3 Basic and Control Actions of P_i in a Fully Distributed Mutual Exclusion Algorithm

	Algorithm steps executed by the control part	
Actions of basic part	**Steps**	**Details**
repeat forever		
{ Request CS entry }	1, 2(b), 3	i. Send request messages ("request", P_i, <*timestamp*>) to all other processes and request the kernel to block the basic part. ii. When a request message is received from another process, send a "go ahead" reply if the request has a smaller timestamp; otherwise, add the process id found in the request to the pending list. iii. Count the "go ahead" replies received. Activate the basic part of the process after receiving $(n - 1)$ replies.
{ Critical Section }	2(c)	Enter all received requests in the pending list.
{ Perform CS exit }	4	Send a "go ahead" reply to every process whose request message exists in its pending list.
{ Rest of the cycle }	2(a)	When a request is received, send a "go ahead" reply immediately.
end		

The number of messages required per CS entry can be reduced by requiring a process P_i to obtain permissions from a subset R_i of processes in the system. R_i is called the *request set* of P_i. Safety must be ensured by forming request sets carefully. The algorithm by Maekawa (1985) uses request sets of size $\sqrt{n}$, and uses the following rules to ensure safety (see Exercise 18.3):

1. For all P_i : $P_i \in R_i$.
2. For all P_i, P_j : $R_i \cap R_j \neq \phi$.

18.3.2 Token-Based Algorithms for Mutual Exclusion

A *token* represents the privilege to use a CS; only a process possessing the token can enter the CS. Safety of a token-based algorithm follows from this rule. When a process makes a request to enter a CS, the mutual exclusion algorithm ensures that the request reaches the process possessing the token and that the token is eventually transferred to the requesting process. This feature ensures liveness. Logical complexity and cost of a mutual exclusion algorithm depend on properties of the system model. Hence token-based algorithms use *abstract system models* in which edges represent the paths used to pass control messages, and the graph formed by nodes and these edges has certain nice properties. We discuss two algorithms that use abstract *ring* and *tree* topologies.

An Algorithm Employing the Ring Topology Figure 18.2 shows the logical model of a distributed computation and its abstract unidirectional ring model. The token is an object, i.e., a data structure, containing a request queue. In Figure 18.2(b), the token is currently with process P_4, P_4 is in a CS, and the request queue in the token contains P_2 and P_5. The algorithm works as follows: A process that wishes to enter a CS sends a message containing its request and becomes blocked. The message is routed along the ring until it reaches the token holder. If the token holder is currently in a CS, its control part enters the requester's id in the request queue contained in the token. When the token holder finishes using the CS, it removes the first process id from the request queue in the token and sends a message containing the token and the process id. This message is routed along the ring until it reaches the process whose id matches the process id in the message. The control part of this process extracts and keeps the token for future use, and activates its basic part, which enters a CS. In Figure 18.2(b),

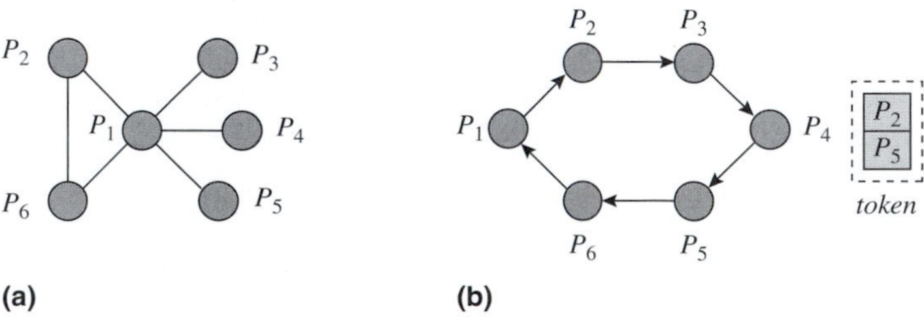

Figure 18.2 (a) System model; (b) abstract system model.

process P_2 would receive the token when P_4 exits from its CS. The algorithm is shown as Algorithm 18.2. The number of messages exchanged per CS entry is order of n, where n is the number of processes.

Algorithm 18.2 *Token-Based Mutual Exclusion Algorithm for a Ring Topology*

1. *When a process P_i wishes to enter a CS:* The process sends a request message ("request", P_i) along its out-edge and becomes blocked.
2. *When a process P_i receives a request message from process P_r:* If P_i does not possess the token, it forwards the message along its out-edge. If P_i possesses the token and it is currently not in a CS, it forms the message ("token", P_r) and sends it along its out-edge. If P_i is in a CS, it merely enters P_r in the request queue in the token.
3. *When a process P_i completes execution of a CS:* It checks whether the request queue is empty. If not, it removes the first process id from the queue. Let this id be P_r. It now forms a message ("token", P_r) and sends it along its out-edge.
4. *When a process P_i receives the message ("token", P_j):* P_i checks whether $P_i = P_j$. If so, it creates a local data structure to store the token, becomes active and enters its CS. If $P_i \neq P_j$, it merely forwards the message along its out-edge.

Raymond's Algorithm Raymond's algorithm uses an *abstract inverted tree* as the system model. The inverted tree differs from a conventional tree in that a tree edge points from a node to its parent in the tree. P_{holder} designates the process in possession of the token. Raymond's algorithm has four key features—invariants that ensure that a request reaches P_{holder}, a local queue of requesters in each node, features to reduce the number of request messages and provisions to ensure liveness.

Figure 18.3 depicts the model of a distributed computation and its abstract inverted tree model. Process P_5 holds the token, so it is at the root of the tree. Processes P_1 and P_3, which are its children, have out-edges pointing to P_5. Similarly, out-edges (P_6, P_1), (P_2, P_3), and (P_4, P_3) point from a process to its parent. The algorithm maintains three invariants concerning the abstract inverted tree:

1. Process P_{holder} is the root of the tree.
2. Each process in the system belongs to the tree.

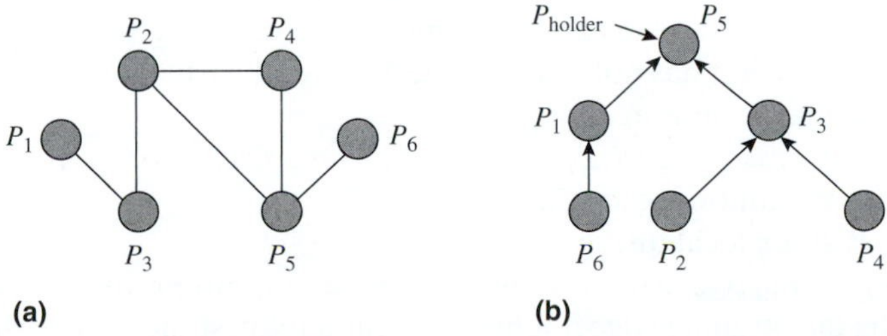

Figure 18.3 (a) System model; (b) abstract system model.

3. Each process $P_i \neq P_{\text{holder}}$ has exactly one out-edge (P_i, P_j), where P_j is its parent in the tree.

These invariants ensure that the abstract system model contains a path from every process $P_i \neq P_{\text{holder}}$ to P_{holder}. This property is useful for ensuring that a request made by P_i would reach P_{holder}. These invariants are maintained by changing edges in the abstract inverted tree when a process P_k sends the token to another process, say process P_j—the edge (P_j, P_k) is reversed. These actions reverse the direction of the tree edges along which the token is sent, and establish a path from previous holder of the token to the new holder. For example, edge (P_3, P_5) in Figure 18.3(b) would be reversed when P_5 sends the token to P_3.

Each process maintains a local queue of requesters. A request message contains a single field *requester_id*. A process wishing to enter a CS puts its own id in its local queue and also sends a request message along its out-edge. When a process P_i receives a request message, it enters the requesting process's id in its local queue. It now forms a request message in which it puts its own id, i.e., P_i, and sends it along its out-edge. Thus the request reaches P_{holder} along a path ensured by invariant **3**; however, the requester id is different in each edge of the path. To reduce the number of request messages, a process does not originate or send a request if a request sent earlier by it has not been honored yet. (It knows this because it would have received the token if its request had been honored.)

P_{holder} enters all requests it receives in its local queue. On exiting the CS, it removes the first process id from its local queue and sends the token to that process. The process receiving the token sends it to the first process in its local queue, unless its own id is at the head of the local queue. This action is repeated until the token reaches a process that is at the head of its own local queue. The control part of this process keeps the token with itself. Its basic part becomes active and enters a CS.

Liveness requires that every process that requests entry to a CS gets to enter it in finite time. To ensure this property, a process transferring the token to another process checks whether its local queue is empty. If the local queue still contains some requests, it forms a new request with its own id in the *requester_id* field and sends it to the process to which it has sent the token. This action ensures that it will receive the token sometime in future for servicing other requests in its local queue.

Algorithm 18.3 *Raymond's Algorithm*

1. *When a process P_i wishes to enter a CS:* Process P_i enters its own id in its local queue. It also sends a request message containing its own id along its outgoing edge if it has not sent a request message earlier, or if its last request has been already honored.
2. *When a process P_i receives a request message from process P_r:* Process P_i performs the following actions:
   a. Put P_r in its local queue.
   b. If $P_i \neq P_{\text{holder}}$, send a request message containing its own id, i.e., P_i, along its outgoing edge if it has not sent a request message earlier or if its last request has been already honored.

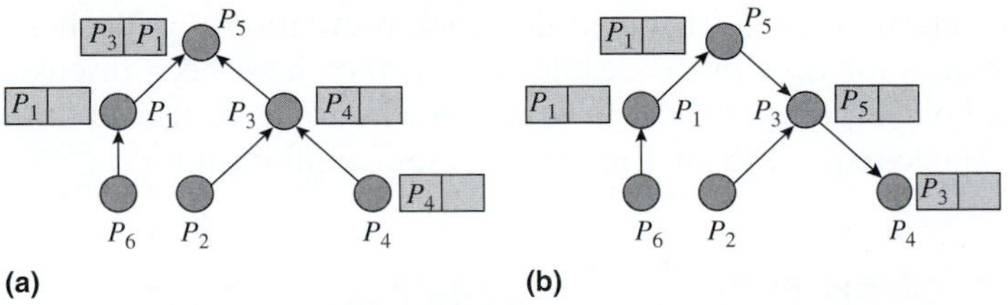

Figure 18.4 An example of Raymond's algorithm.

3. *When a process P_i completes execution of a CS:* P_i performs following actions:
   a. Remove the process id at the head of the local queue. Let it be P_j.
   b. Send the token to P_j.
   c. Reverse the tree edge (P_j, P_i).
   d. If the local queue is not empty, send a request message containing its own id, i.e., P_i, to P_j.
4. *When a process P_i receives the token:*
   a. If its own id is at the top of the local queue, it removes the request from the queue. Its basic part now becomes active and enters a CS.
   b. Otherwise, it performs Steps 3(a)–(d).

The algorithm requires an order of *log n* messages for each request. It does not ensure FIFO entry to a critical section [see Step 2(b)]. Example 18.2 illustrates operation of the algorithm.

Example 18.2

Raymond Algorithm

Figure 18.4(a) shows the situation in the system of Figure 18.3 after the requests made by P_4 and P_1 have reached P_5, which is P_{holder} (see Steps 1 and 2 of Algorithm 18.3). When process P_5 exits its CS, it removes P_3 from its local queue, passes the token to P_3, and reverses the edge (P_3, P_5). P_5 now sends a request to P_3 since its local queue is not empty [see Step 3(d)]. P_3 performs similar actions (see Step 4), which result in sending the token to process P_4, reversal of the edge (P_4, P_3), and sending of a request by P_3 to P_4.

Figure 18.4(b) shows the resulting abstract inverted tree. P_4 now enters its CS. After P_4 completes the CS, the token is transferred to process P_1 via P_3 and P_5 in an analogous manner, which enables P_1 to enter its CS. Note that this action would not have been possible if Step 3(d) did not exist in the algorithm.

18.4 DISTRIBUTED DEADLOCK HANDLING

The deadlock detection, prevention, and avoidance approaches discussed in Section 8.3 make use of state information. This section illustrates problems in extending these approaches to a distributed system, and then describes distributed deadlock detection and distributed deadlock prevention approaches. No special techniques for distributed deadlock avoidance have been discussed in OS literature. For simplicity, the discussion in this section is restricted to the single-instance, single-request (SISR) model of resource allocation (see Section 8.3).

18.4.1 Problems in Centralized Deadlock Detection

Distributed applications may use resources located in several nodes of the system. Deadlocks involving such applications could be detected by collecting the wait-for graphs (WFGs) of all nodes at a central node, superimposing them to form a merged WFG, and employing a conventional deadlock detection algorithm to check for deadlocks. However, this scheme has a weakness. It may obtain WFGs of individual nodes at different instants of time, so the merged WFG may represent a misleading view of wait-for relationships in the system. This could lead to detection of *phantom deadlocks*, which is a violation of the safety property in deadlock detection. Example 18.3 illustrates such a situation.

Example 18.3 Phantom Deadlock

The sequence of events in a system containing three processes P_4, P_5, and P_6 is as follows:

1. Process P_5 requests and obtains resource r_5 in node N_3.
2. Process P_6 requests and obtains resource r_4 in node N_3.
3. Process P_5 requests and obtains resource r_6 in node N_4.
4. Process P_4 requests resource r_5 in node N_3.
5. Process P_5 requests resource r_4 in node N_3.
6. Node N_3 sends its local WFG to the coordinator node.
7. Process P_6 releases resource r_4 in node N_3.
8. Process P_6 requests resource r_6 in node N_4.
9. Node N_4 sends its local WFG to the coordinator node.

Figures 18.5(a) and (b) show WFGs of the nodes at Steps 6 and 9, respectively. It can be seen that no deadlock exists in the system at any of these times. However, the merged WFG is constructed by superimposing the WFG of node N_3 taken at Step 6 and WFG of node N_4 taken at Step 9 [see Figure 18.5(c)], so it contains a cycle $\{P_5, P_6\}$ and the coordinator detects a phantom deadlock.

18.4.2 Distributed Deadlock Detection

Recall from Chapter 8 that a cycle is a necessary and sufficient condition for a deadlock in an SISR system, whereas a *knot* is a necessary and sufficient

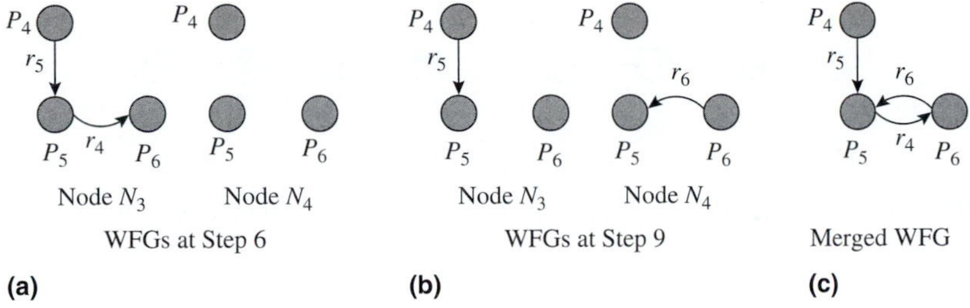

Figure 18.5 Phantom deadlock in Example 18.3: Node WFGs at Steps 6, 9 and the merged WFG.

condition for a deadlock in an MISR system. In the distributed deadlock detection approach, cycles and knots are detected through joint actions of nodes in the system, and every node in the system has the ability to detect and declare a deadlock. We discuss two such algorithms.

Diffusion Computation-Based Algorithm The *diffusion computation* was proposed by Dijkstra and Scholten (1980) for termination detection; they called it the diffusing computation. The diffusion computation contains two phases—a diffusion phase and an information collection phase. In the diffusion phase, the computation originates in one node and spreads to other nodes through control messages called *queries* that are sent along all edges in the system. A node may receive more than one query if it has many in-edges. The first query received by a node is called an *engaging query*, while queries received later are called *nonengaging queries*. When a node receives an engaging query, it sends queries along all its out-edges. If it receives a nonengaging query subsequently, it does not send out any queries because it would have already sent queries when it received the engaging query. In the information collection phase, each node in the system sends a reply to every query received by it. The reply to an engaging query contains information pertaining to the node to which the engaging query was directed, and about some other nodes connected to that node. The reply to a nonengaging query typically does not contain any information. It is called a *dummy* reply. If the initiator receives its own query along some edge, it sends a dummy reply immediately. The Chandy–Lamport algorithm for consistent state recording of a distributed system discussed in Section 17.4.2 actually uses the first phase of a diffusion computation (see Exercise 18.5).

Algorithm 18.4 uses a diffusion computation to perform deadlock detection. It was proposed by Chandy, Misra, and Haas (1983), and works for both SISR and MISR systems. The diffusion computation spreads through edges in the WFG. All steps in the algorithm are performed atomically, so if a process receives two messages at the same time, they will be processed one after another. It is assumed that diffusion computations initiated by different processes are assigned distinct ids, and that their queries and replies carry these ids. This way, different diffusion computations do not interfere with one another.

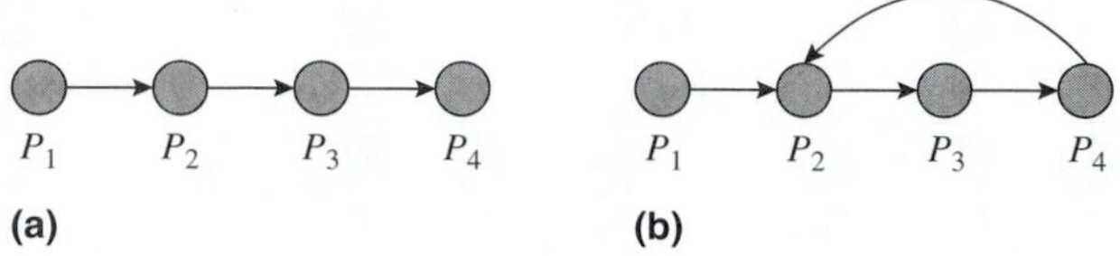

Figure 18.6 System for illustrating diffusion computation-based distributed deadlock detection.

Algorithm 18.4 *Diffusion Computation-Based Distributed Deadlock Detection*

1. *When a process becomes blocked on a resource request:* The process initiates a diffusion computation through the following actions:
   a. Send queries along all its out-edges in the WFG.
   b. Remember the number of queries sent out, and await replies to them.
   c. If replies are received for all the queries sent out and it has been in the blocked state continuously since it initiated the diffusion computation, declare a deadlock.
2. *When a process receives an engaging query:* If the process is blocked, it performs the following actions:
   a. Send queries along all its out-edges in the WFG.
   b. Remember the number of queries sent out, and await replies to them.
   c. If replies are received for all the queries sent out and it has been in the blocked state continuously since it received the engaging query, send a reply to the node from which it received the engaging query.
3. *When a process receives a nonengaging query:* If the process has been in the blocked state continuously since it received the engaging query, send a dummy reply to the node from which it received the nonengaging query.

Consider an SISR system that contains four processes P_1–P_4. The WFG of Figure 18.6(a) shows the system state immediately after process P_1 requests a resource that is currently allocated to P_2. P_1, P_2, and P_3 are now in the *blocked* state, whereas P_4 is not. P_1 initiates a diffusion computation when it becomes blocked. When P_2 receives its query, it sends a query to P_3, which sends a query to P_4. However, P_4 is not in the blocked state, so it does not reply to P_3's query. Thus, P_1 does not receive a reply and consequently does not declare that it is in a deadlock. Let P_4 now request the resource allocated to P_2 and get blocked [see the WFG of Figure 18.6(b)]. P_4 would now initiate a diffusion computation that would spread to processes P_2 and P_3. Since these processes are blocked, P_4 will get the reply to its query and declare that it is involved in a deadlock. The condition that a process should be continuously in the blocked state since the time it initiated the diffusion computation or since the time it received the engaging query ensures that a phantom deadlock would not be detected.

Edge Chasing Algorithm In this algorithm, a control message is sent over a *wait-for* edge in the WFG to facilitate detection of cycles in the WFG, hence the name *edge chasing* algorithm. It was proposed by Mitchell and Merritt (1982). Each

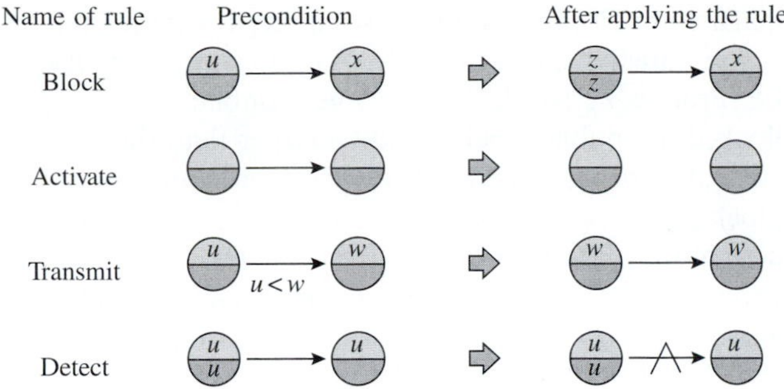

Figure 18.7 Rules of Mitchell–Merritt algorithm.

process is assigned two numerical labels called a *public label* and a *private label*. The public and private labels of a process are identical when the process is created. These labels change when a process gets blocked on a resource. The public label of a process also changes when it waits for a process having a larger public label. A wait-for edge that has a specific relation between the public and private labels of its start and end processes indicates existence of a deadlock.

Figure 18.7 illustrates rules of the Mitchell–Merritt algorithm. A process is represented as $\frac{u}{v}$ where u and v are its public and private labels, respectively. Figure 18.7 illustrates rules of the Mitchell–Merritt algorithm. A rule is applied when the public and private labels of processes at the start and end of a wait-for edge satisfy the pre-condition. It changes the labels of the processes as shown to the right of "⇨". Details of the four rules are as follows:

1. *Block:* The public and private labels of a process are changed to a value z when it becomes blocked because of a resource request. The value z is generated through the statement $z := inc(u, x)$, where u is the public label of the process, x is the public label of the process for which it waits, and function *inc* generates a unique value larger than both u and x.
2. *Activate:* The out-edge of a process is removed from WFG when it is activated following a resource allocation. Its labels remain unchanged.
3. *Transmit:* If the public label of the process at the start of a wait-for edge (u) is smaller than the public label of the process at the end of the edge (w), then u is replaced by w.
4. *Detect:* A deadlock is declared if the public and private labels of a process at the start of a wait-for edge are identical and also equal to the public label of the process at the end of the edge.

Operation of the algorithm can be explained as follows: Consider a path in the WFG from P_i to P_k. Let labels of process P_i be $\frac{u_i}{v_i}$ and let those of P_k be $\frac{u_k}{v_k}$. According to the *transmit* rule applied to all edges in the path from P_i to P_k, u_i is greater than or equal to the public label of every process on the path from P_i to P_k. Let P_k make a resource request that results in a wait-for edge (P_k, P_i). According to the *block* rule, public and private labels of P_k assume a value given by $inc(u_k, u_i)$. Let this be n. Hence $n > u_i$. According to the *transmit* rule, n is propagated to P_i through processes along the path from P_i to P_k. The edge (P_k, P_i) now satisfies the *detect* rule. As an example, consider the system of Figure 18.6. Process P_4 would be given new public and private labels when it becomes blocked. Its public label would be larger than the public labels of P_2 and P_3, so it would be propagated to P_2 via P_3. Consequently, process P_4 would detect a deadlock.

Correctness of the algorithm follows from the fact that the public label of a process P_i at the start of a wait-for edge gets propagated to another process P_j only if a path exists from P_j to P_i (see the transmit step). Thus, if the wait-for edge from P_i to P_j satisfies the detect rule, it completes a cycle in the WFG, so a deadlock exists. Safety follows trivially if processes are not permitted to withdraw their requests spontaneously.

18.4.3 Distributed Deadlock Prevention

Deadlock prevention approaches discussed in Section 8.5 prevent cycles from arising in a resource request and allocation graph (RRAG) or a wait-for graph (WFG) through restrictions on resource requests. Deadlocks in a distributed system can be prevented analogously: Each process creation event is timestamped by a pair (local time, node id), and the timestamp is associated with the newly created process. Circular waits in the RRAG or WFG are prevented by disallowing certain kinds of wait-for relationships through a comparison of process timestamps using relation (17.1). We discuss two such schemes.

- *Wait-or-die:* When a process P_{req} makes a request for some resource currently held by P_{holder}, P_{req} is permitted to wait for the resource if it is older than P_{holder}; otherwise, it is aborted. Circular waits cannot arise because an older process may wait for a younger process, but a younger process cannot wait for an older process.
- *Wound-or-wait:* If P_{req} is younger than P_{holder}, it is allowed to wait for the resource held by P_{holder}; otherwise, P_{holder} is aborted and the requested resource is allocated to P_{req}. Thus, a younger process can wait for an older process, but an older process cannot wait for a younger process.

In both approaches, the younger process is aborted and has to be reinitiated sometime in future. To avoid starvation due to repeated aborts, a process may be permitted to retain its old timestamp when it is reinitiated. The wait-or-die scheme may be preferred in practice because it does not involve preemption of a resource, whereas the wound-or-wait scheme does.

18.5 DISTRIBUTED SCHEDULING ALGORITHMS

Both system performance and computation speedup in applications would be adversely affected if computational loads in the nodes of a distributed system are uneven. A distributed scheduling algorithm balances computational loads in the nodes by transferring some processes from a heavily loaded node to a

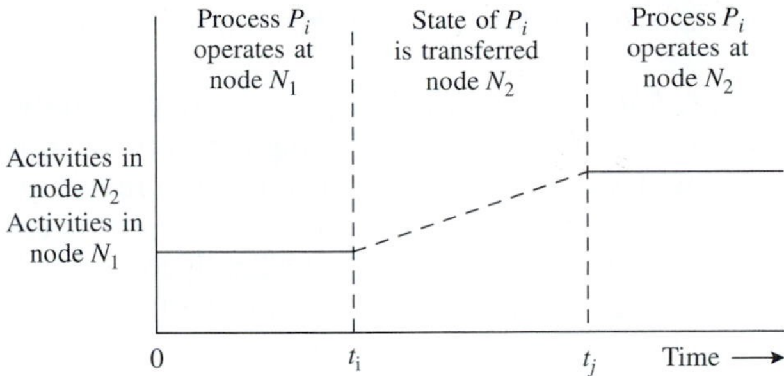

Figure 18.8 Migration of process P_i from node N_1 to node N_2.

lightly loaded node. Figure 18.8 illustrates this technique, which is called *process migration*. Process P_i is created in node N_1 at time $t = 0$. At time t_i the scheduling function decides to transfer the process to node N_2, so operation of the process is halted in node N_1 and the kernel starts transferring its state to node N_2. At time t_j the transfer of state is complete and the process starts operating in node N_2.

To perform load balancing through process migration, a scheduling algorithm needs to measure the computational loads in nodes, and apply a *threshold* to decide which ones are heavily loaded and which ones are lightly loaded. At appropriate times, it transfers processes from heavily loaded nodes to lightly loaded nodes. These nodes are called *sender nodes* and *receiver nodes*, respectively. CPU utilization is a direct indicator of the computational load serviced in a node; however, monitoring of CPU utilization incurs high execution overhead. Hence operating systems prefer to use the number of processes in a node or the length of the *ready* queue of processes, as measures of computational loads. These measures possess a good correlation with the average response time in a node, and their use incurs a low overhead.

Actual migration of a process can be performed in two ways. *Preemptive migration* involves suspending a process, recording its state, transferring it to another node and resuming operation of the process in the new node (see Figure 18.8); it requires extensive kernel support. In *nonpreemptive migration*, the load balancing decision is taken during creation of a new process. If the node in which a "create process" call is performed is heavily loaded, the process is simply created in a remote node. Nonpreemptive migration does not require any special support in the kernel.

Stability is an important issue in the design of a distributed scheduling algorithm. An algorithm is unstable if, under some load conditions, its overhead is not bounded. Consider a distributed scheduling algorithm that transfers a process from a heavily loaded node to a randomly selected node. If the node to which the process is sent is itself heavily loaded, the process would have to be migrated once again. Under heavy load conditions, this algorithm would lead to a situation that resembles thrashing—the scheduling overhead would be high because process migration is frequent, but processes being transferred would not make much progress.

A *sender-initiated algorithm* transfers a process nonpreemptively, i.e., from a sender node to a receiver node. While creating a process in a heavily loaded node, it polls other nodes to find a lightly loaded node so that it can migrate the process to that node. This action makes the scheduling algorithm unstable at high system loads because a sender that cannot find a lightly loaded node would poll continuously and waste a considerable fraction of its CPU's time. Instability can be prevented by limiting the number of attempts a sender is allowed to make to find a receiver. If this number is exceeded, the sender would abandon the process migration attempt and create the new process locally. Instability may also result if several processes are sent to the same receiver node, which now becomes a sender node and has to migrate some of the processes it received. This situation can be avoided by using a protocol whereby a node accepts a process only if it is still a receiver node (see Exercise 18.10).

A *receiver-initiated algorithm* checks whether a node is a receiver node every time a process in the node completes. It now polls other nodes in the system to find a node that would not become a receiver node even if a process is transferred out of it, and transfers a process from such a node to the receiver node. Thus, process migration is necessarily preemptive. At high system loads, the polling overhead would be bounded because the receiver would be able to find a sender quickly. At low system loads, continuous polling by a receiver would not be harmful because idle CPU times would exist in the system. Unbounded load balancing overhead can be prevented by abandoning a load balancing attempt if a sender cannot be found in a fixed number of polls; however, a receiver must repeat load balancing attempts at fixed intervals of time to provide the liveness property.

We discuss a *symmetrically initiated algorithm* that contains features of both sender-initiated and receiver-initiated algorithms. It behaves like a sender-initiated algorithm at low system loads and like a receiver-initiated algorithm at high system loads. Each node maintains a status flag to indicate whether it is presently a sender, a receiver, or an OK node, i.e., neither a sender nor a receiver. It also maintains three lists, called senders list, receivers list, and OK list, to contain ids of nodes that are known to be senders, receivers, and OK nodes, respectively.

Algorithm 18.5 *Symmetrically Initiated Load Balancing Algorithm*

1. *When a node becomes a sender as a result of creation of a process:* Change the status flag to "sender." If the receivers list is nonempty, poll the nodes included in it, subject to the limit on number of nodes that can be polled.
   a. If the polled node replies that it is a receiver node, transfer a process to it. Examine local load and set the status flag accordingly.
   b. Otherwise, move the polled node to the appropriate list, based on its reply.
2. *When a node becomes a receiver as a result of completion of a process:* Change the status flag to "receiver." Poll the nodes included in the senders list,

followed by those in the receivers list and OK list, subject to the limit on number of nodes that can be polled.

   a. If the polled node replies that it is a sender node, transfer a process from it. Examine local load and set the status flag accordingly.
   b. Otherwise, move the polled node to the appropriate list, based on its reply.

3. *When a node is polled by a receiver node:* Move the polling node to the receivers list. Send a reply containing own current status.
4. *When a node is polled by a sender node:* Move the polling node to the senders list. Send a reply containing own current status.
5. *When a process is transferred from or to a node:* Examine local load and set the status flag accordingly.

Instability would arise in this algorithm if too many processes are transferred to a receiver node simultaneously. To prevent it, a receiver node should change its flag in Step 3 by anticipating a transfer, rather than in Step 5 as at present.

Figure 18.9 depicts comparative performance of distributed scheduling algorithms. A sender-initiated algorithm incurs low overhead at low system loads because few senders exist in the system. Hence, the system can provide good response times to processes. As the load increases, the number of senders increases and the overhead of the algorithm increases. At high system loads the algorithm is unstable because a large number of senders exists in the system and few, if any, receivers exist. Consequently, the response time increases sharply. A receiver-initiated algorithm incurs a higher overhead at low system loads than a sender-initiated algorithm because a large number of receivers exists at low system loads. Hence the response time is not as good as when a sender-initiated algorithm is used. At high system loads, few receivers exist in the system, so a receiver-initiated algorithm performs distinctly better than a sender-initiated algorithm. The performance of a symmetrically initiated algorithm would resemble that of

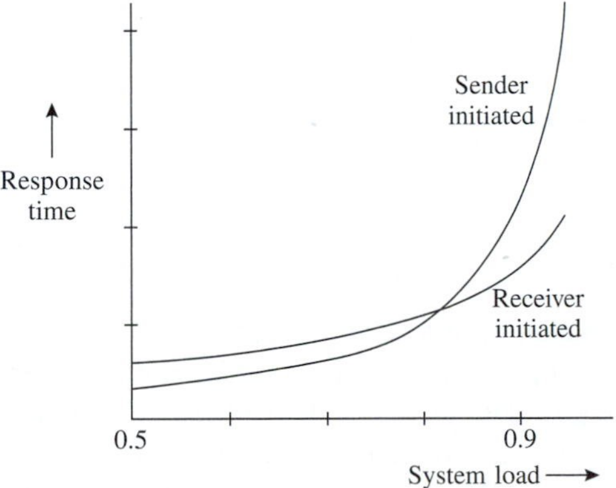

Figure 18.9 Performance of distributed scheduling algorithms.

a sender-initiated algorithm at low system loads and that of receiver-initiated algorithms at high system loads.

18.6 DISTRIBUTED TERMINATION DETECTION

A process ties up system resources such as kernel data structures and memory. The kernel releases these resources either when the process makes a "terminate me" system call at the end of its operation, or when it is killed by another process. This method is not adequate for processes of a distributed computation because they may not be able to decide when they should terminate themselves or kill other processes. For example, consider a distributed computation whose processes have a client–server relationship. A server would not know whether any more requests would be made to it, because it would not know who its clients are and whether all of them have completed their operation. In such cases, the kernel employs methods of *distributed termination detection* to check whether the entire distributed computation has terminated. If so, it winds up all processes of the computation and releases the resources allocated to them.

We define two process states in our system model to facilitate termination detection. A process is in the *passive state* when it has no work to perform; such a process is dormant and waits for some other process to send it some work through an interprocess message. A process is in the *active state* when it is engaged in performing some work. It can be performing I/O, waiting for a resource, waiting for the CPU to be allocated to it, or executing instructions. The state of a process changes several times during its execution. A passive process becomes active immediately on receiving a message, sends an acknowledgment to the sender of the message, and starts processing the message. An active process acknowledges a message immediately, though it may delay its processing until a convenient time. An active process becomes passive when it finishes its current work and does not have other work to perform. It is assumed that both control and basic messages travel along the same interprocess channels.

A distributed computation is said to have terminated if it satisfies the *distributed termination condition* (DTC). The DTC comprises two parts:

1. All processes of a distributed computation are passive.
2. No basic messages are in transit. **(18.1)**

The second part is needed because a message in transit will make its destination process active when it is delivered. We discuss two approaches to determining whether DTC holds for a distributed computation.

Credit-Distribution-Based Termination Detection In this approach by Mattern (1989), every activity or potential activity in a distributed computation is assigned a numerical weightage called *credit*. A distributed computation is initiated with a known finite amount of credit C. This credit is distributed among its processes. The manner of its distribution is immaterial so long as each process P_i receives a nonzero credit c_i. When a process sends a basic message to another process, it puts a part of its credit into the message—again, it is immaterial how much credit is put into a message, so long as it is neither zero nor the entire credit of the process. A process receiving a message adds the credit from the message to its own credit before processing the message. When a process becomes passive, it sends its entire credit to a special system process called the *collector process*, which accumulates all credit it receives. The distributed computation is known to have terminated when the credit accumulated by the collector process equals C. This algorithm is simple and elegant; however, credit may be distributed indefinitely, so a convenient representation of credit should be used in its implementation.

Diffusion Computation-Based Termination Detection Each process that becomes passive initiates a diffusion computation to determine whether the DTC holds. Thus, every process has the capability to detect termination. We discuss detection of the DTC in a system where the following three rules hold:

1. Processes are neither created nor destroyed dynamically during execution of the computation; i.e., all processes are created when the distributed computation is initiated, and remain in existence until the computation terminates.
2. Interprocess communication channels are FIFO.
3. Processes communicate with one another through synchronous communication; i.e., the sender of a message becomes blocked until it receives an acknowledgment for the message.

Rule 3 simplifies checking for the DTC as follows: The sender of a basic message becomes blocked; it resumes its operation after it receives the acknowledgment. It may enter the passive state only after finishing its work. Thus, the basic message sent by a process cannot be in transit when it becomes passive and the system cannot have any basic messages in transit when all processes are passive. Hence it is sufficient to check only the first part of the DTC condition, i.e., whether all processes are passive. Algorithm 18.6 performs this check through a diffusion computation over a graph whose nodes represent processes and edges represent interprocess communication. Example 18.4 illustrates operation of Algorithm 18.6.

Algorithm 18.6 *Distributed Termination Detection*

1. *When a process becomes passive:* The process initiates a diffusion computation through the following actions:
   - **a.** Send "Shall I declare distributed termination?" queries along all edges connected to it.
   - **b.** Remember the number of queries sent out, and await replies.
   - **c.** After replies are received for all of its queries, declare distributed termination if all replies are *yes*.
2. *When a process receives an engaging query:* If the process is in the *active* state, it sends a *no* reply; otherwise, it performs the following actions:
   - **a.** Send queries along all edges connected to it excepting the edge on which it received the engaging query.

b. Remember the number of queries sent out, and await replies.

c. After replies are received for all of its queries: If all replies are *yes*, send a *yes* reply to the process from which it received the engaging query; otherwise, send a *no* reply.

3. *When a process receives a nonengaging query:* The process immediately sends a *yes* reply to the process from which it received the query.

Example 18.4 Distributed Termination Detection

Figure 18.10 shows a distributed computation. Only processes P_1 and P_2 are active; all other processes are passive. Now the following events occur:

1. Process P_2 becomes passive, initiates termination detection and sends a query to process P_1.
2. Process P_1 sends a basic message to process P_5 along the edge (P_1, P_5) and becomes passive at the earliest opportunity.

The receive event in P_5 for the basic message of P_1, and events concerning sending and receipt of queries and their replies by the processes could occur in several different sequences. Two sequences of interest are as follows: If process P_1 received the query from P_2 before it became passive, it would send a *no* reply to P_2, so P_2 would not declare termination. If process P_1 received the query from P_2 after it became passive, according to Rule 3, it would have already received an acknowledgment to the basic message it had sent to process P_5 in Step 2, so process P_5 must have become active after receiving P_1's message before P_1 became passive. Now, when P_1 receives the query from P_2, it would send a query to each of P_3–P_7. P_5 would send a *no* reply to P_1, which would send a *no* reply to P_2, so P_2 would not declare termination. If Rules 2 and 3 of the system are removed, the algorithm would suffer from safety problems in some situations.

Distributed termination detection algorithms become complex when they try to remove Rules 1–3 of the system. Papers cited in the Bibliography discuss details of such algorithms.

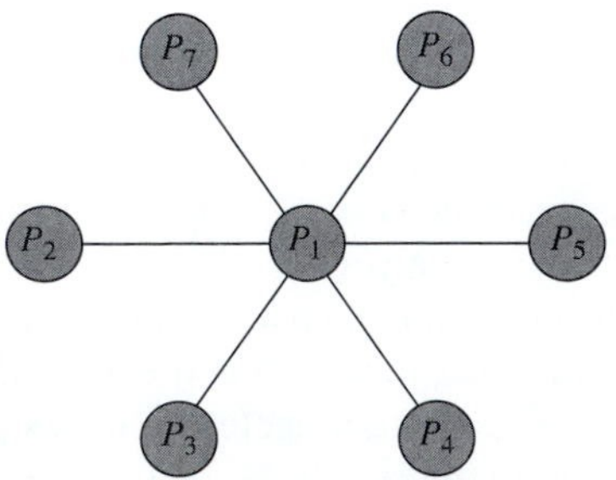

Figure 18.10 Illustration of distributed termination detection.

18.7 ELECTION ALGORITHMS

A critical function like replacing the lost token in a token-based algorithm is assigned to a single process called the *coordinator* for the function. Typically, priorities are assigned to processes and the highest-priority process among a group of processes is chosen as the coordinator for a function. Any process that finds that the coordinator is not responding to its request assumes that the coordinator has failed and initiates an *election algorithm*. The election algorithm chooses the highest-priority nonfailed process as the new coordinator and announces its id to all nonfailed processes.

Election Algorithms for Unidirectional Ring Topologies All links in the ring are assumed to be FIFO channels. It is further assumed that the control part of a failed process continues to function and simply forwards each received message along its out-edge. The election is performed by obtaining ids of all nonfailed processes in the system and electing the highest-priority process. It is achieved as follows: A process P_i initiates an election by sending out an ("elect me", P_i) message along its out-edge. A process P_j that receives this message performs two actions—it sends out an ("elect me", P_j) message of its own and also forwards the ("elect me", P_i) message immediately after its own message. These messages reach process P_i such that the ("elect me", P_i) message follows all the other messages. Process P_i examines process ids contained in all these messages and elects the highest priority process, say P_{high}, as the new coordinator. It now sends a ("new coordinator", P_{high}) message along the ring to inform all processes about the outcome of the election. It is assumed that failures do not occur during an election. This assumption ensures identical results even if two or more processes initiate elections in parallel. The algorithm requires an order of n^2 messages per election.

The number of messages per election can be reduced as follows: A process P_j that receives an ("elect me", P_i) message sends out only one message—it sends an ("elect me", P_j) message to start a new election if its own priority is higher than that of P_i; otherwise, it simply forwards the ("elect me", P_i) message. This way, only the highest-priority nonfailed process P_{high} would get back its own "elect me" message. It would send a ("new coordinator", P_{high}) message to announce its election. All other processes abandon their elections, if any, when they receive the ("new coordinator", P_{high}) message. When this refinement is used, the number of messages per election can be a maximum of $3n - 1$ as follows: The ("elect me", P_i) message sent by the process that initiates an election needs a maximum of $n - 1$ messages to reach the highest-priority process. The election initiated by the highest-priority process requires n messages to complete, and another n messages are required to inform every process about the outcome of the election. The time consumed by the election could be as high as $(3n - 1) \times t_{wc}$, where t_{wc} is the worst-case message delivery time over a link.

Bully Algorithm A process P_i that initiates an election sends an ("elect me", P_i) message to all higher-priority processes and starts a time-out interval T_1. If it does not hear from any of them before the time-out occurs, it assumes that all of them have failed, sends a ("new coordinator", P_i) message to all lower-priority processes, and becomes the new coordinator. If its "elect me" message reaches a higher-priority process P_j, process P_j sends a "don't you dare!" message to it. On receiving this message, process P_i abandons its claim to become the new coordinator. It now expects process P_j or another higher-priority process to announce itself the new coordinator, so it starts another time-out interval to wait for such a message. If it does not receive such a message before a time-out occurs, it assumes that a higher-priority process that should have become the coordinator has failed during the interval. It now initiates another election by once again sending ("elect me", P_i) messages. A process P_j that receives an "elect me" message from a lower-priority process responds by sending a "don't you dare!" message to the lower-priority process. Immediately following this, P_j itself initiates an election, unless it has already initiated one, by sending ("elect me", P_j) messages to all higher priority processes.

The total number of messages per election is an order of n^2. If the system graph is fully connected and no nodes fail or recover during an election, the time consumed by the election could be as high as $T_1 + T_2$, where T_1, T_2 are the two time-out intervals. $T_1 \geq 2 \times t_{wc}$, where t_{wc} is the worst-case message delivery time over a link. $T_2 \geq 3 \times t_{wc}$; however, $T_2 \geq 2 \times t_{wc}$ would suffice since transmission of the "elect me" message sent by a higher-priority process would overlap with transmission of the "don't you dare!" message sent by it. Hence the time consumed by the algorithm can be less than $5 \times t_{wc}$.

Example 18.5 Election Algorithms

A system contains 10 processes $P_1, P_2, \ldots, P_{10}$, with the priorities $1, \ldots, 10$, 10 being the highest priority. Process P_{10} is the coordinator process. Its failure is detected by process P_2. P_2 sends ("elect me", P_2) messages to P_3–P_{10}. Each of P_3–P_9 respond by sending a "don't you dare!" message to P_2, and start their own elections by sending "elect me" messages to higher-priority processes. Eventually processes P_2–P_8 receive "don't you dare!" messages from all higher-priority processes excepting P_{10}, which has failed. Process P_9 does not receive any "don't you dare!" message, so it elects itself as the coordinator and sends a ("new coordinator", P_9) message to P_1–P_8. During the election, 36 "elect me" messages, 28 "don't you dare!" messages and 8 "new coordinator" messages are sent. The total number of messages for this election is thus 72.

If the same system had been organized as a unidirectional ring with edges (P_i, P_{i+1}) $\forall i < 10$ and edge (P_{10}, P_1), a total of 27 messages would have been needed to complete the election.

18.8 PRACTICAL ISSUES IN USING DISTRIBUTED CONTROL ALGORITHMS

18.8.1 Resource Management

When a process requests access to a resource, the resource allocator must find the location of matching resources in the system, determine their availability,

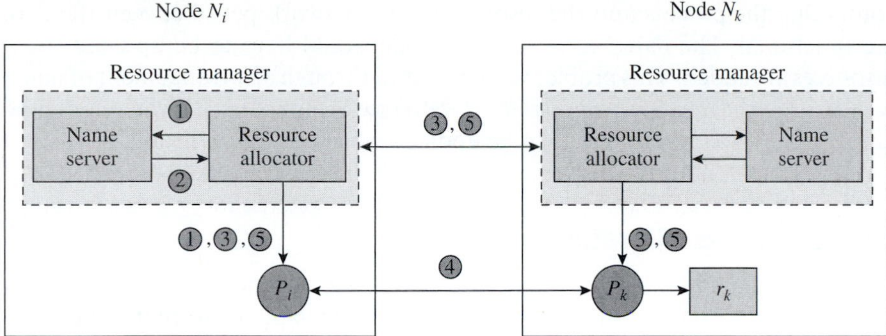

Figure 18.11 Resource allocation in a distributed system.

and allocate one of the resources. Figure 18.11 contains a schematic of resource allocation. A *resource manager* exists in each node of the system. It consists of a name server and a resource allocator. The numbered arcs in the schematic correspond to steps in the following resource allocation procedure:

1. When process P_i wishes to use a resource named res_j, it constructs a pair (res_j, P_i) and forwards it to the resource manager in its node. The resource manager forwards the request to the name server.
2. The name server locates res_j, using its name and attributes, and constructs the triple (r_k, N_k, P_i), where res_j is resource r_k at node N_k. It forwards the triple to the resource allocator.
3. The resource allocator finds whether resource r_k of node N_k is available. If so, it passes P_k, the id of the resource controller process for the resource, to P_i. It also sends an allocation message containing the id of P_i to P_k. If the resource is not available, it stores the request in a queue of pending requests. The request would be honored sometime in future when the resource becomes available.
4. Process P_k interacts with process P_i to fulfill P_i's service requests.
5. After completing its use of the resource, process P_i makes a release request. The resource manager sends a release message to P_k and allocates the resource to a pending request, if any.

The important issue in Step 3 is ensuring noninterference of resource allocators of different nodes. It could be achieved either through a distributed mutual exclusion algorithm or through an election algorithm to elect a coordinator that would perform all allocations in the system. Use of a mutual exclusion algorithm would incur overhead at every allocation. Use of an election algorithm would avoid this overhead. However, it would require a protocol to ensure that resource status information would be accessible to a new coordinator if the present coordinator failed. A simpler arrangement would be to entrust allocation of resources in a node to the resource allocator of that node. This scheme would avoid the overhead of mutual exclusion, election, and fault tolerance. It would also be more robust because a resource could be allocated to a process so long as the nodes containing the process and the resource, and a network path between the two, are functional. The name server in each node would have to be updated when resources are added. This problem can be solved through an arrangement of name servers as in the *domain name service* (DNS) (see Section 16.4.1), where only the name server of a domain needs to be updated when a resource is added.

18.8.2 Process Migration

The process migration mechanism is used to transfer a process between nodes in a distributed system. It is used to achieve load balancing, or to reduce network traffic involved in utilizing a remote resource. It may also be used to provide availability of services when a node has to be shut down for maintenance. The schematic Figure 18.8 made process migration look deceptively simple; however, in reality, it is quite complex for several reasons. The state of a process comprises the following:

- Process identifier and ids of its child processes
- Pending signals and messages
- Current working directory and internal ids of files (see Section 13.8)

Two kinds of problems are faced in transferring process state: Process state is often spread across many data structures in the kernel, so it is difficult to extract it from kernel data structures. Process ids and internal ids of files have to be unique in the node where a process operates; such information may have to be changed when a process is migrated. This requirement creates difficulties in process synchronization and in I/O. Providing globally unique process ids as in the Sun Cluster (see Section 16.3) and transparency of resources and services (see Section 16.8) are important in this context.

When a message is sent to a process, the DNS converts the process name (*<host_name>*, *<process_id>*) into the pair (IP address, *<process_id>*). Such a message may be in transit when its destination process is migrated, so arrangements have to be made to deliver the message to the process at its new location. Each node could maintain the *residual state* of a process that was migrated out of it. This state would contain the id of the node to which it was migrated. If a message intended for such a process reaches this node, the node would simply redirect the message to its new location. If the process had been migrated out of that node in the meanwhile, the node would similarly redirect the message, using the residual state maintained by it. In this manner a message would reach the process irrespective of its migration. However, the residual state causes poor reliability because a message would not be delivered if the residual state of its destination process in some node has been lost or has become inaccessible because of a fault. An alternative scheme would be to inform the changed location of a process (as also a change in the process id, if any) to all processes that communicate with it. This way, a message could be sent to the process directly at its new location. If a message that was in transit when a process was migrated reached the old node where the process once existed, the node would return a "no longer here" reply to the sender. The sender would then resend the message to the process at its new location.

18.9 SUMMARY

A *distributed control algorithm* is an algorithm for use in an OS, whose actions are performed in many nodes of the distributed system. An OS uses distributed control algorithms so that it can avoid the overhead of collecting state information about all entities in the system in one place, be responsive to events occurring in its nodes, and provide reliable operation in the presence of node and link faults. In this chapter, we discussed distributed control algorithms for mutual exclusion, deadlock handling, scheduling, electing coordinators for functions and services, and detecting termination of a distributed computation.

Parts of a distributed control algorithm executing in different nodes of a distributed system reach a decision by interacting among themselves through interprocess messages. This method of operation may delay decisions; however, the algorithm must make the correct decision eventually. Since distributed algorithms do not have access to states of all relevant entities at the same time, they must also ensure that they would not perform a wrong action. These two aspects of their correctness are called *liveness* and *safety*, respectively. They have to be interpreted in the context of the function performed by a distributed control algorithm. For example, in mutual exclusion, liveness implies that the progress and bounded wait conditions of Section 6.3.1 are satisfied, while safety implies that at most one process is in the CS at any time. Performance of a distributed control algorithm is measured in terms of the number of messages exchanged by the algorithm, and the delay incurred until a required action is performed.

A distributed control algorithm uses a system model that is either a *physical model* of the system or a *logical model* in which nodes are processes and an edge indicates that two processes exchange messages. Each node in the model is aware of its own local state, and interacts with other nodes to convey state information. The correctness of the algorithm depends on how state information is conveyed among nodes and how decisions are made, while performance depends on the nature of the system model used by the algorithm.

Mutual exclusion is performed by using either a fully connected logical model and *timestamping* of requests, or a *token* to represent the privilege to enter a critical section. The former incurs small decision times, while the latter requires fewer messages. Distributed deadlock detection algorithms use a logical model in which edges represent wait-for relationships between processes, and special messages are sent over the edges for deadlock detection. Either a special algorithm called *diffusion computation* is used to collect state information from all relevant processes, or presence of a cycle is inferred when a sender process receives back its own deadlock detection message. Distributed scheduling is performed by exchanging state information among nodes of the system to decide whether processes should be transferred between nodes to balance the execution loads among nodes.

A distributed computation terminates only when all its processes are idle and no messages are in transit between them. Distributed termination detection can be performed by using a diffusion computation to check whether any process is active or any interprocess message is in transit. Alternatively, some known amount of credit can be distributed among processes and some of it can be put on every interprocess message. Termination has occurred if the total credit with idle processes equals the amount of credit with which the system started. Election algorithms use logical models and special messages to find the highest-priority nonfailed process.

TEST YOUR CONCEPTS

18.1 Classify each of the following statements as true or false:
   a. The control part of a process never blocks.
   b. The Ricart–Agrawala algorithm is deadlock-free if timestamps are distinct.
   c. In a token-based algorithm for mutual exclusion, a requesting process sends its request to every other process.
   d. In a diffusion computation model, a process does not send a reply to a nonengaging query.
   e. A centralized deadlock detection algorithm may detect phantom deadlocks.
   f. A sender-initiated distributed scheduling algorithm is unstable at high system loads.
   g. A distributed computation is said to have terminated if all processes in the computation are in the passive state.

18.2 Select the appropriate alternative in each of the following questions:
   a. Which of the following properties of a critical section implementation will ensure liveness of a distributed mutual exclusion algorithm (refer to Table 6.1)?
      i. The progress property
      ii. The bounded wait property
      iii. The progress and bounded wait properties
      iv. None of (i)–(iii).
   b. A process P_i initiates a diffusion computation by sending out queries. A process P_k in the system
      i. Receives the query initiated by P_i exactly once.
      ii. May not receive the query even once.
      iii. Receives the query at least once, but may receive it several times
      iv. None of (i)–(iii).

EXERCISES

18.1 State and compare the liveness properties of (a) a distributed mutual exclusion algorithm, and (b) an election algorithm.

18.2 Step 2 of the Ricart–Agrawala algorithm is modified such that a process wishing to enter a CS does not send a "go ahead" reply to any other process until it has used its CS. Prove that this modified algorithm is not deadlock-free.

18.3 Prove the safety property of Maekawa's algorithm, which uses request sets of size $\sqrt{n}$.

18.4 Construct an example where Raymond's algorithm does not exhibit FCFS behavior for entry to a CS. (*Hint:* Consider the following situation in Example 18.2: Process P_2 makes a request for CS entry while P_5 is still in CS.)

18.5 Identify the engaging and nonengaging queries in the Chandy–Lamport algorithm for consistent state recording (Algorithm 17.2). Extend the algorithm to collect the recorded state information at the site of the node that initiated a state recording.

18.6 Prove that a resource allocator using the wait-or-die and wound-or-wait scheme for deadlock detection does not possess the liveness property if a killed process is given a new timestamp when it is reinitiated.

18.7 It is proposed to use an edge chasing deadlock detection algorithm for deadlocks arising in interprocess communication. When a process gets blocked on a "receive message" request, a query is sent to the process from which it expects the message. If that process is blocked on a "receive message" request, it forwards the query to the process for which it is waiting, and so on. A process declares a deadlock if it receives its own query. Comment on the suitability of this algorithm for
   a. Symmetric communication.
   b. Asymmetric communication.

18.8 If use of the *inc* function in the *block* rule is omitted from the Mitchell–Merritt algorithm, show that the modified algorithm violates the liveness requirement.

18.9 Prove correctness of the credit distribution-based distributed termination detection algorithm.

18.10 A sender-initiated distributed scheduling algorithm uses the following protocol to transfer a process from one node to another:

a. A sender polls all other nodes in the system in search of a receiver node.

b. It selects a node as the prospective receiver, and sends it a "lock yourself for a process transfer" message.

c. The recipient of the message sends a *no* reply if it is no longer a receiver. Else it increases the length of its CPU queue by 1 and sends a *yes* reply.

d. The sender transfers a process when it receives a *yes* reply.

e. If it receives a *no* reply, it selects another node and repeats Steps 10(b)–10(e).

Does this protocol avoid instability at high system loads?

18.11 Define the liveness and safety properties of a distributed scheduling algorithm. (*Hint:* Will imbalances of computational load arise in a system if its scheduling algorithm possesses liveness and safety properties?)

BIBLIOGRAPHY

Dijkstra and Scholten (1980) and Chang (1982) discuss the diffusion computation model of distributed algorithms. Andrews (1991) discusses broadcast and token passing algorithms.

Raymond (1989) and Ricart and Agrawala (1981) discuss distributed mutual exclusion algorithms. Dhamdhere and Kulkarni (1994) discusses a fault-tolerant mutual exclusion algorithm. The diffusion computation-based distributed deadlock detection algorithm (Algorithm 18.4) is adapted from Chandy et al. (1983). Knapp (1987) discusses several distributed deadlock detection algorithms. Sinha and Natarajan (1984) discuss an edge chasing algorithm for distributed deadlock detection. Wu et al. (2002) describes a distributed deadlock detection algorithm for the AND model.

Distributed termination detection is discussed in Dijkstra and Scholten (1980), Mattern (1989), and Dhamdhere et al. (1997). The bully algorithm for distributed elections is discussed in Garcia-Molina (1982). Smith (1988) discusses process migration techniques.

Singhal and Shivaratri (1994) and Lynch (1996) describe many distributed control algorithms in detail. Tel (2000) and Garg (2002) discuss election and termination detection algorithms. Attiya and Welch (2004) discusses algorithms for the election problem.

1. Andrews, G. R. (1991): "Paradigms for process interaction in distributed programs," *Computing Surveys*, **23**, 1, 49–40.
2. Attiya, H. and J. Welch (2004): *Distributed Computing: Fundamentals, Simulations and Advanced Topics*, John Wiley, New York.
3. Chandy, K. M., J. Misra, and L. M. Haas (1983): "Distributed deadlock detection," *ACM Transactions on Computer Systems*, **1** (2), 144–152.
4. Chang, E. (1982): "Echo algorithms: depth parallel operations on general graphs," *IEEE Transactions on Software Engineering*, **8** (4), 391–401.
5. Dhamdhere, D. M., and S. S. Kulkarni (1994): "A token based k-resilient mutual exclusion algorithm for distributed systems," *Information Processing Letters*, **50** (1994), 151–157.
6. Dhamdhere, D. M., S. R. Iyer, and E. K. K. Reddy (1997): "Distributed termination detection of dynamic systems," *Parallel Computing*, **22** (14), 2025–2045.
7. Dijkstra, E. W., and C. S. Scholten (1980): "Termination detection for diffusing computations," *Information Processing Letters*, **11** (1).
8. Garg, V. K. (2002): *Elements of Distributed Computing*, Wiley-IEEE, New York.
9. Garcia-Molina, H. (1982): "Elections in distributed computing systems," *IEEE Transactions on Computers*, **31** (1).
10. Knapp, E. (1987): "Deadlock detection in distributed databases," *Computing Surveys*, **19**, (4), 303–328.
11. Lynch, N. (1996): *Distributed Algorithms*, Morgan Kaufmann.
12. Mattern, F. (1989): "Global quiescence detection based on credit distribution and recovery," *Information Processing Letters*, **30** (4), 195–200.

13. Mitchell, D. P., and M. J. Merritt (1982): "A distributed algorithm for deadlock detection and resolution," *Proceedings of the ACM Conference on Principles of Distributed Computing*, August 1984, 282–284.
14. Obermarck, R. (1982): "Distributed deadlock detection algorithm," *ACM Transactions on Database Systems*, **7** (2), 187–202.
15. Raymond, K. (1989): "A tree-based algorithm for distributed mutual exclusion," *ACM Transactions on Computer Systems*, **7**, 61–77.
16. Ricart, G., and A. K. Agrawala (1981): "An optimal algorithm for mutual exclusion in computer networks," *Communications of the ACM*, **24** (1), 9–17.
17. Singhal, M., and N. G. Shivaratri (1994): *Advanced Concepts in Operating Systems*, McGraw-Hill, New York.
18. Sinha, M. K., and N. Natarajan (1984): "A priority based distributed deadlock detection algorithm," *IEEE Transactions on Software Engineering*, **11** (1), 67–80.
19. Smith, J. M. (1988): "A survey of process migration mechanisms," *Operating Systems Review*, **22** (3), 28–40.
20. Tel, G. (2000): *Introduction to Distributed Algorithms*, 2nd ed., Cambridge University Press, Cambridge.
21. Wu, H., W. Chin, and J. Jaffer (2002): "An efficient distributed deadlock avoidance algorithm for the AND model," *IEEE Transactions on Software Engineering*, **28**, 1, 18–29.

Chapter 19

Recovery and Fault Tolerance

A fault may damage the state of some data or processes. Several things could go wrong if a fault occurs during operation of a system—data consistency could be lost, a server could malfunction, resources and services could become unavailable, or the system could cease operation. To provide reliable operation, an OS avoids such consequences of faults using three approaches called *recovery*, *fault tolerance*, and *resiliency*.

Recovery in a distributed system uses the notion of rollbacks, discussed earlier in Chapter 13. When a fault occurs, some data or processes would be rolled back to states that were recorded before the fault. However, a rollback of one of the processes of a distributed computation may force rollbacks of a few of its other processes to ensure mutual consistency of process states. This requirement is called the *domino effect*. Normal operation of a computation would be resumed after recovery is completed; however, the computation may have to reexecute some actions it had performed before the fault occurred.

Fault tolerance provides uninterrupted operation of a system by *repairing* the states of data or processes affected by a fault, rather than by rolling them back to recorded states. The *resiliency* approach tries to minimize the cost of reexecution when faults occur. Resiliency is achieved through special techniques for (1) remembering useful results computed in a subcomputation and using them directly, i.e., without reexecution, after a fault and (2) reexecuting a subcomputation, rather than a complete computation, when a fault occurs.

We begin this chapter with an overview of different classes of faults and various ways of dealing with them. Subsequent sections discuss recovery, fault tolerance and resiliency.

19.1 FAULTS, FAILURES, AND RECOVERY

A fault like a power outage or a memory read error may damage the state of a system. For reliable operation, the system should be restored to a consistent state, and its operation should be resumed. *Recovery* is the generic name for all approaches used for this purpose.

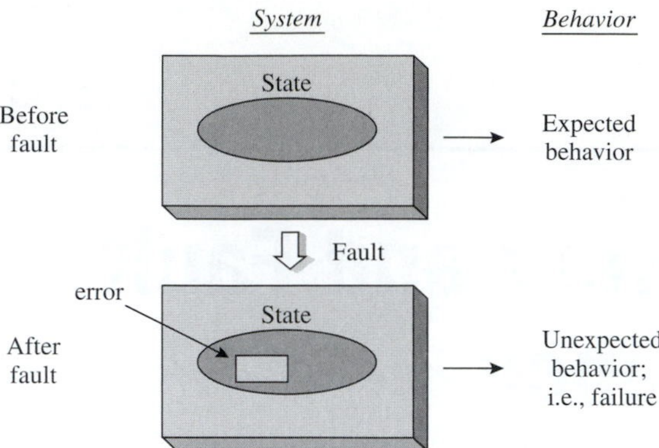

Figure 19.1 Fault, error, and failure in a system.

A fault like a power outage is noticed readily, whereas a fault like a damaged disk block becomes noticeable only when the resulting loss of data causes an unexpected behavior of the system or an unusual situation in it. Such unexpected behavior or situation is called a *failure*. Figure 19.1 illustrates how a failure arises. A fault causes an *error*, which is a part of the system state that is erroneous. An error causes unexpected behavior of the system, which is a failure. Example 19.1 discusses a fault, an error and a failure in a banking system.

Example 19.1 Fault, Error, and Failure

Bank accounts A and B contain \$1000 and \$250, respectively. A banking application transfers \$100 from account A to account B. A power outage occurs after it deducts \$100 from the balance in account A, but before it adds \$100 to the balance in account B. The power outage is a fault. The error is that \$100 has been deducted from account A but has not been added to account B. The failure is that \$100 has vanished!

A recovery is performed when a failure is noticed. Figure 19.2 illustrates the state of a system during normal operation, after a fault, and after recovery. The system is initiated in state S_0 at time 0. A fault occurs at time t_1. The consequent failure is detected at t_i. The system would have been in state S_i at time t_i if the fault had not occurred; however, it is actually in state S'_i. A recovery procedure applies a correction ΔS to the state and makes the system ready to resume its operation. The resulting state would depend on the recovery procedure employed. Let the resulting state be called S_{new}. It would be ideal if $S_{\text{new}} = S_i$; however, the nature of a fault, the failure caused by it, and the recovery approach would determine whether it could be so.

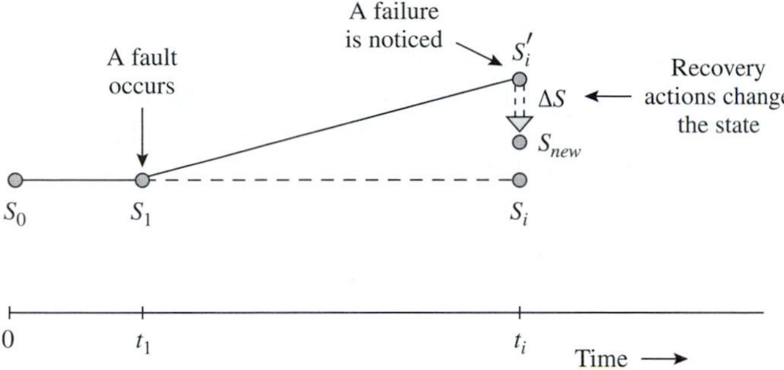

Figure 19.2 Recovery after a fault.

19.1.1 Classes of Faults

A fault may affect a computer system, affect only a process in the system, or affect hardware components such as memory and the communication hardware. Accordingly, faults are classified into system, process, storage, and communication faults. Within a class of faults, a *fault model* describes those properties of a fault that determine the kinds of errors and failures that might result from a fault.

A *system fault* is a system crash caused by a power outage or by component faults. System faults are classified into *amnesia* and *partial amnesia* faults, depending on how much state information is lost when a fault occurs. In an *amnesia fault*, the system completely "forgets" the state it was in when the fault occurred. In a *partial amnesia* fault, the system "forgets" some components of its state when the fault occured. File servers typically suffer partial amnesia faults because they lose the data or metadata that was stored in memory or on a disk that failed. A *fail-stop* system fault is one that brings a system to a halt. This characteristic is convenient in practice because it permits an external observer, whether a person or a computer system, to know when a fault has occurred. It also provides an opportunity to recover or repair the system state before putting the system back into operation.

A process that suffers a *Byzantine* fault may perform malicious or arbitrary actions. It is not possible to undo such actions when a failure is noticed. Hence Byzantine faults are handled by using redundant processes and agreement protocols. In this approach, several processes are created to perform the same computation. If their results do not match, the system uses an agreement protocol to decide which of them is the correct result. Processes producing incorrect results are identified and aborted before they perform any data updates; others are permitted to perform updates and continue their operation.

A typical *storage fault* occurs because of a bad block on a storage medium. It makes some data unreadable. The occurrence of a storage fault may be detected by error checking techniques (see Section 14.3), or it may be noticed when data is accessed. Storage faults are basically partial amnesia faults, however they could be made nonamnesia faults by using software techniques such as disk mirroring.

Communication faults are caused by link or transmission faults. These faults are nonamnesia faults because the networking software includes sufficient buffering and error handling capability to ensure that messages are not lost.

In Section 19.2, we discuss how Byzantine faults are handled in practice. The rest of this chapter assumes faults to be non-Byzantine.

19.1.2 Overview of Recovery Techniques

For non-Byzantine faults, recovery involves restoring a system or an application to a consistent state. It involves reexecuting some actions that were performed before the fault occurred. Recovery techniques can be classified into data recovery, process recovery, fault tolerance, and resiliency. These techniques have different implications for reliability, response times to computations, and the cost of recovery. Table 19.1 summarizes their features.

Data recovery techniques guard against loss of data in a file through *backups*. Backups are created periodically during normal operation. When a fault occurs, a file is restored to the state found in its latest backup (see Section 13.11). Data recovery techniques incur substantial reexecution overhead if backups are created at large intervals and high overhead during normal operation if they are created frequently. So deciding the frequency of backups involves a trade-off.

Process recovery techniques employ *checkpoints* to record the state of a process and its file processing activities. This operation is called *checkpointing*. When a fault occurs, the recovery procedure sets the state of a process to that found in a checkpoint. This operation is called a *rollback* of the process. It incurs the cost of reexecuting the actions that were performed after the checkpoint was taken. The tradeoff between the cost of a rollback and the overhead of checkpointing during normal operation is analogous to that in data recovery techniques.

Table 19.1 Recovery Techniques

Technique	Description
Data recovery	A *backup* is a recording of the state of a file. When a fault occurs, the state of the file is set to that found in its latest backup (see Section 13.11).
Process recovery	A *checkpoint* is a recording of the state of a process and its file processing activities. A process is recovered by setting its state to that found in a checkpoint that was taken before a fault occurred. This action is called a *rollback*.
Fault tolerance	The error in state caused by a fault is corrected without interrupting the system's operation.
Resiliency	Special techniques are employed to reduce the cost of fault tolerance—fewer results that were produced in a computation before a fault occurred are recomputed after the fault.

Fault tolerance techniques enable a system or an application to continue its operation despite the occurrence of a fault. A fault tolerance technique recovers the system or the application to a consistent state that differs only marginally, if at all, from the state the system would have been in if the fault had not occurred. Results of some computations that were in progress at the time when a fault occurred may be lost. These computations have to be reexecuted.

Resiliency techniques ensure that some of the results that were produced by a computation that was in progress when a fault occurred would be used in the computation after the fault. It reduces reexecution costs and degradation of response times due to a fault.

Backward and Forward Recovery Recovery approaches are classified into two broad classes. *Backward recovery* implies *resetting* the state of an entity or an application affected by a fault to some prior state and resuming its operation from that state. It involves reexecution of some actions that were performed before a fault. *Forward recovery* is based on *repairing* the erroneous state of a system so that the system can continue its operation. The repair cost depends on the nature of the computation and may involve a certain amount of reexecution.

Backward recovery is simpler to implement than forward recovery. However, it requires a practical method of producing a consistent state recording of a system. This aspect poses obvious difficulties in a distributed system. Another weakness of the backward recovery technique is that an application may not make any progress if faults occur frequently. A major advantage of forward recovery is that the operation of a system or an application continues from the repaired state rather than from some previous state as in backward recovery. This feature guarantees forward progress of a computation with time for certain classes of faults.

19.2 BYZANTINE FAULTS AND AGREEMENT PROTOCOLS

Because of the difficulty in undoing wrong actions, recovery from Byzantine faults has been studied only in the restricted context of agreement between processes. The agreement problem is motivated by the *Byzantine generals* problem where a group of generals have to decide whether to attack the enemy. The generals and their armies are located in different geographical locations, hence generals have to depend on exchange of messages to arrive at a decision. Possible faults are that messages may get lost, or some generals may be traitors who deliberately send out confusing messages. An agreement protocol is designed to arrive at an agreement in spite of such faults.

Three agreement problems have been defined in literature. In the *Byzantine agreement problem* one process starts the agreement protocol by broadcasting a single value to all other processes. A process that receives the value broadcasts it to other processes. A nonfaulty process broadcasts the same value that it receives. A faulty process may broadcast an arbitrary value; it may even send different values to different processes. Processes may have to perform many rounds of broadcasts before an agreement is reached. The problem requires all nonfaulty processes to agree on the same value. This value should be the same as the value broadcast by the initiator if the initiator is a nonfaulty process; otherwise, it could be any value. In the *consensus problem*, each process has its own initial value and all nonfaulty processes have to agree on a common value. In the *interactive consistency problem*, nonfaulty processes have to agree on a set of values. We discuss only the Byzantine agreement problem.

Lamport et al. (1982) developed an agreement protocol for use when processes may fail but messages are delivered without fail. It involves $m + 1$ rounds of information exchange, where the number of faulty processes is $\leq m$. However, there are some restrictions on the value of m. Agreement is possible only if the total number of processes exceeds 3 times the number of faulty processes. An impossibility result states that a group of three processes containing one faulty process cannot reach agreement.

The impossibility result is easy to prove if the initiator is a faulty process. Let process P_1, the initiator, send values 0 and 1 to processes P_2 and P_3. Process P_2 will send 0 to process P_3. Now, process P_3 has received two different values from two processes. It cannot decide which of the two is the correct value. A similar situation arises if P_1 is a nonfaulty initiator and sends 1 to P_2 and P_3, but process P_2 is faulty and sends 0 to process P_3. Agreement would have been possible if the system contained n processes, $n \geq 4$, and the following algorithm was used:

1. The initiator sends its value to every other process.
2. A process receiving the value from the initiator sends it to all processes other than itself and the initiator.
3. Each process forms a collection of $n - 1$ values containing one value received from the initiator in Step 1 and $n - 2$ values received from other processes in Step 2. If it did not receive a value from the initiator or from some other process, it would assume an arbitrary value 0. It uses the value appearing the majority of times in this collection.

This is the algorithm followed for a single Byzantine fault, i.e., for $m = 1$. The algorithm for $m > 1$ is quite complex, hence we do not discuss it here.

19.3 RECOVERY

A recovery scheme consists of two components. The *checkpointing algorithm* decides when a process should take a checkpoint. We will use the notation C_{ij} to denote the jth checkpoint taken by process P_i. The *recovery algorithm* rolls back some processes to their states recorded in checkpoints such that the new process states are mutually consistent. Example 19.2 illustrates the fundamental issue in the design of checkpointing and recovery algorithms.

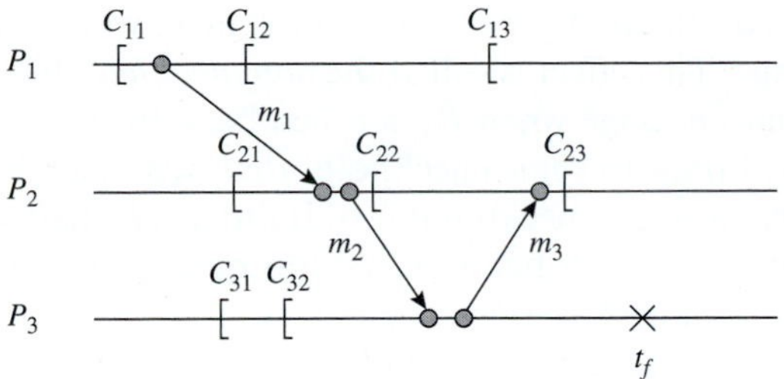

Figure 19.3 Checkpoints of processes in a distributed system.

Checkpointing and Recovery

Example 19.2

Figure 19.3 shows the timing diagram of a distributed computation whose processes $P_1 - P_3$ operate in nodes $N_1 - N_3$, respectively. C_{11}, C_{12} and C_{13} are the checkpoints taken by process P_1. Similarly C_{21}, C_{22}, C_{23}, and C_{31}, C_{32} are the checkpoints taken by processes P_2 and P_3, respectively. We denote the state recorded in *<checkpoint>* as *state*(*<checkpoint>*). Let processes P_1, P_2 and P_3 be in the states s_1, s_2 and s_3, respectively, at time instant t_f. Hence the distributed computation is in the state $S \equiv \{s_1, s_2, s_3\}$. Let a failure occur in node N_3 at time instant t_f. A naive recovery algorithm simply rolls back process P_3 to its latest checkpoint, i.e., C_{32}. However, the new state of the computation, $\{s_1, s_2, state(C_{32})\}$, is not a consistent state because P_2 has received message m_3 in state s_2 but P_3 has not sent m_3 in $state(C_{32})$, which is its new state (see Definition 17.1).

From Example 19.2 it is clear that the state of a process cannot be recovered in isolation. A recovery algorithm should restore the state of the computation to a state S' in which states of all pairs of processes are mutually consistent according to Definition 17.1. Hence the goal of a recovery algorithm is to make the following decisions for each process P_i in a distributed computation:

1. Decide whether process P_i should be rolled back.
2. If so, identify a checkpoint C_{ij} to which P_i should be rolled back.

In Example 19.2, the distributed computation could be recovered to the state $\{s_1, state(C_{22}), state(C_{32})\}$. We discuss a basis for such recovery in the following.

Definition 19.1 Orphan Message A message m_k sent by process P_i to process P_j is an *orphan message* in the state $S \equiv \{s_1, \ldots, s_i, \ldots, s_j, \ldots, s_n\}$ of a system if s_j, the state of process P_j, records m_k as received but s_i, the state of process P_i, does not record it as sent.

An orphan message is a message that has been received by its destination process, but it is disowned by its sender because of recovery. Hence the states of its sender and destination processes are inconsistent. This inconsistency is removed by rolling back its destination process to some state in which it had not received the orphan message. This effect is called the *domino effect*. In Example 19.2, m_3 becomes an orphan message when P_3 is rolled back to the state in C_{32}. Hence P_2 should be rolled back to some checkpoint that was taken before P_2 received message m_3, for example, to checkpoint C_{22}. If process P_2 had sent a message m_4 to P_1 after C_{22} and process P_1 had received this message in state s_1, the domino effect would force a rollback of process P_1 as well.

Using these ideas, checkpointing and recovery can be performed in one of two ways. The checkpointing algorithm would permit individual processes to take checkpoints at will. This method is called *asynchronous checkpointing*. At a fault, the recovery algorithm would roll back processes one by one in accordance with the domino effect. Alternatively, the checkpointing algorithm would coordinate the checkpointing actions of processes to ensure that the process states in the checkpoints are mutually consistent. This method is called *synchronous checkpointing*, and the collection of process checkpoints produced by it is called a *synchronous checkpoint*. When applied to the system of Figure 19.3, a synchronous checkpointing algorithm would produce either the synchronous checkpoint $\{C_{11}, C_{21}, C_{31}\}$ or the synchronous checkpoint $\{C_{12}, C_{22}, C_{32}\}$. The recovery algorithm would simply roll back each process to its individual checkpoint in the latest synchronous checkpoint.

19.4 FAULT TOLERANCE TECHNIQUES

The basic principle in fault tolerance is to ensure that a fault either does not cause an error, or the error can be removed easily. In some earlier chapters and sections, we saw how fault tolerance techniques ensure that no error in state would arise due to process, storage, and communication faults: Section 19.2 described how process faults of a Byzantine nature can be tolerated, Section 13.11.2.2 discussed how the stable storage technique tolerates storage faults, and Section 16.4 discussed an arrangement involving acknowledgment and retransmission of messages to tolerate communication faults.

In this section, we discuss two facets of the tolerance of system faults that follow the fail-stop model.

- *Fault tolerance for replicated data:* Despite a fault, data should be available and applications should see values resulting from the latest update operation.
- *Fault tolerance for distributed data:* Despite a fault, mutual consistency of different parts of the data should not be affected.

19.4.1 Logs, Forward Recovery, and Backward Recovery

A *log* is a record of actions or activities in a process. Two kinds of logs are used in practice:

- *Do logs:* A *do log* records those actions that should be performed to ensure correctness of state of an entity or a system. A do log is also called a *redo log* because actions recorded in it may be performed more than once if a fault occurs. Do logs are used to implement *forward recovery*.

- *Undo logs:* An *undo log* contains a record of those actions that should be undone to remove an error in state caused by occurrence of a fault. Undo logs are used to implement *backward recovery*.

A *write-ahead logging* principle is used to construct a log—a process writes information concerning an action it intends to take into a log before performing the action. This way, the log would contain all information necessary to achieve the correct state should a fault occur before the action is completed. A log could be an *operation log*, which contains a list of actions to be performed so that entities in the system would achieve correct states, or a *value log*, which contains a list of values or data images that should be assigned to entities.

The implementation scheme for an *atomic action* discussed in Section 13.11.2.2 used an *intentions list.* The intentions list is a value log that is used as a redo log. Being a value log, recovery actions that use it are idempotent; this property is needed because entries in the log would be processed more than once if faults occur during commit processing. Recovery using the intentions list constitutes forward recovery. If the subactions in an atomic action directly updated data, an undo log would have to be maintained so that the actions could be undone if a fault occurred before the atomic action could commit. The undo log would contain data images taken before updates were performed. Its use to undo data updates constitutes backward recovery.

The idea of atomic execution of a sequence of operations on a file can be extended to operations involving several files. A language construct called the *atomic transaction* is provided in a programming language or a database query language for this purpose. It has the following syntax:

```
begin transaction <transaction id>
    {Access and modify files}
    if <condition>
        then abort transaction;
    {Access and modify files}
end transaction <transaction id>
```

An atomic transaction has an all-or-nothing property like an atomic action. Its execution commences when a process executes the **begin transaction** statement. The atomic transaction is said to *commit* if the process executes the **end transaction** statement. All files modified by the atomic transaction would be updated consistently at this time. If the process executes the **abort transaction** statement, or if a fault occurs before the transaction commits, execution of the transaction would be aborted and no file updates would be made. In this case, all files would remain in their original states.

19.4.2 Handling Replicated Data

Availability of data D can be provided through replication. We can make n copies of D, $n > 1$ and locate them strategically in the system such that at least one copy of D would be accessible from any node despite anticipated faults in the system.

If data D may be modified, it is essential to use rules that would ensure correctness of data access and updates. We use the following rules:

1. Many processes can concurrently read D.
2. Only one process can write a new value into D at any time.
3. Reading and writing cannot be performed concurrently.
4. A process reading D must see the latest value of D.

Rules 1–3 are analogous to rules of the readers and writers problem of Section 6.7.2. Rule 4 addresses a special issue in data replication.

Quorum Algorithms A *quorum* is the number of copies of D that must be accessed to perform a specific operation on D. Quorum algorithms ensure adherence to Rules 1–4 by specifying a *read quorum* Q_r and a *write quorum* Q_w. Two kinds of locks are used on D. A *read lock* is a shared lock, and a *write lock* is an exclusive lock. A process requesting a read lock is granted the lock if D is presently unlocked or if it is already under a read lock. Request for a write lock is granted only if D is presently unlocked. Processes use read and write quorums while accessing D, so a process can read D after putting a read lock on Q_r copies of D, and can write D after putting a write lock on Q_w copies of D.

Since a read lock is a shared lock, any value of Q_r would satisfy Rule **1**. For implementing Rules 2 and 3, we choose Q_r and Q_w such that

$$2 \times Q_w > n \qquad \textbf{(19.1)}$$

$$Q_r + Q_w > n \qquad \textbf{(19.2)}$$

Equation (19.2) also ensures that a reader will always lock at least one copy that participated in the latest write operation. This copy contains the latest value of D, so Eq. (19.2) also satisfies Rule 4.

A choice of values that satisfies Eqs. (19.1) and (19.2) is $Q_r = 1$ and $Q_w = n$. With these quorums, a read operation is much faster than a write operation. It would be appropriate if read operations are more frequent than write operations. Many other quorum values are also possible. If write operations are more frequent, we could choose values of Q_r and Q_w such that Eqs. (19.1) and (19.2) are satisfied and Q_w is as small as possible. If $Q_w \neq n$, a writer would not update all copies of D, so a reader would access some copies of D that contain its latest value, and some copies that contain its old values. To be able to identify the latest value, we could associate a timestamp with each copy of D to indicate when it was last modified.

The choice of $Q_r = 1$ and $Q_w = n$ is not fault tolerant. $Q_w = n$ implies that a process would have to put locks on all n copies of D in order to perform a write operation. Hence a writer would be unable to write if even one node containing a copy of D failed or became inaccessible to it. If a system is required to tolerate faults in up to k nodes, we could choose

$$Q_r = k + 1$$
$$Q_w = n - k$$
$$n > 2 \times k$$

These quorum sizes are large, however it is unavoidable because Eq. (19.1) is essential to ensure consistency of data and Eq. (19.2) is essential to ensure that reading and writing are not performed concurrently.

19.4.3 Handling Distributed Data

A *distributed transaction* (also called a *multisite transaction*) is a facility for manipulating files located in different nodes of a distributed system in a mutually consistent manner. Each node participating in a distributed transaction T_i contains a transaction manager. It maintains information about data updates to be made on behalf of the transaction, which could be similar to the *intentions list* of atomic actions (see Section 13.11.2.2). In addition, it also maintains a log that is local to it. The node where the transaction was initiated contains a *transaction coordinator*. The coordinator implements the all-or-nothing property of transactions through the *two-phase commit protocol*, also called the *2PC protocol*. It initiates this protocol when the application executes the statement **end transaction** T_i. In the first phase the protocol checks whether each participating node can commit the updates of the transaction. Depending on responses from participating nodes, it decides whether to commit or abort the transaction. In the second phase, it informs its decision to each participating node, so that it could commit or abort accordingly. The 2PC protocol is presented as Algorithm 19.1.

Algorithm 19.1 *Two-Phase Commit Protocol*

Phase 1:

1. *Actions of the transaction coordinator:* Write the record *prepare* T_i in the log. Set a time-out interval δ and send a *prepare* T_i message to each participating node. Wait until either each participating node replies, or a time-out occurs.
2. *Actions of a participating node:* On receiving a *prepare* T_i message, the participating node decides whether it is ready to commit. If so, it writes information about data updates to be made, followed by the record *prepared* T_i in its log and sends a *prepared* T_i reply to the coordinator. Otherwise, it writes the record *abandoned* T_i in its log and sends an *abandoned* T_i reply to the coordinator.

Phase 2:

1. *Actions of the transaction coordinator:* If each participating node sent a *prepared* T_i reply, write the record *commit* T_i in its log and send a *commit* T_i message to each participating node. If a participating node sent an *abandoned* T_i message, or a time-out occurred, write the record *abort* T_i in its log and send an *abort* T_i message to each participating node. In either case, wait until an acknowledgment is received from each participating node, and write a *complete* T_i record in its log.

2. *Actions of a participating node:* Write the record *commit* T_i or *abort* T_i in the log in accordance with the coordinator's message and send an acknowledgment to the coordinator. Perform either commit processing or abort processing accordingly, and release locks on the data.

The 2PC protocol handles failure of a participating node as follows: If a participating node fails before the 2PC protocol was initiated by the coordinator, on recovery it would not find a *prepared* or *abandoned* record for the transaction in its log. It would assume that the first phase of the 2PC protocol would have timed out and the coordinator would have aborted the transaction. Hence it would abandon the transaction. This action is safe because a participating node can unilaterally withdraw from a transaction any time before sending a *prepared* reply in the first phase. The coordinator would abort the transaction because the failed node would not send a *prepared* T_i message even if it has recovered by the time the coordinator starts the 2PC protocol.

If the participating node fails after sending a *prepared* or *abandoned* reply to the coordinator, it would find a *prepared* or *abandoned* record in its log when it recovers. This record may be followed by a *commit* or *abort* record, in which case the node would perform commit or abort processing. Otherwise, the node would have to query the coordinator to find whether the transaction had been committed or aborted, and accordingly perform commit or abort processing. If the node fails while it was performing commit processing, it would find a *commit* record in its log when it recovered. So it would repeat commit processing. Recall from Section 13.11.2.2 that repeated commit processing would not cause data consistency problems because the data update operations performed during commit processing are idempotent.

If the coordinator fails after writing the *commit* record in its log, but before writing the *complete* record in the log, it would see the *commit* record in its log when it recovers. It would now resend *commit* T_i messages to all participating nodes, because it would not know whether it had sent such messages before it crashed. However, this requirement constitutes a weakness in the 2PC protocol: If the coordinator had failed before sending *commit* T_i messages, participating nodes would not know whether the coordinator decided to commit or abort the transaction. Any participating node that had sent an *abandoned* T_i reply in the first phase would know that the decision could not be to commit the transaction; however, a node that had sent a *prepared* T_i reply would be blocked until the coordinator recovered and sent it a *commit* T_i or *abort* T_i message. A *three-phase commit protocol* has been designed to avoid this blocking situation; however, it is not discussed here.

19.5 RESILIENCY

Resiliency techniques focus on minimizing the cost of reexecution when faults occur. The basis for resiliency is the property that failures in a distributed system are *partial*, rather than total, so some parts of a distributed computation, or the results computed by them, may survive a failure. Use of such results after recovery would reduce reexecution, and may even avoid it. Consider a distributed transaction that is initiated in node N_i and involves computations in nodes N_j and N_k. It has a *transaction manager* in each of these nodes. The transaction would be aborted if the transaction manager in node N_j does not respond to the *prepare* message from the coordinator in node N_i because of the failure of node N_j or link (N_i, N_j). The aborted transaction would have to be reexecuted at some other time. Much of the reexecution would be wasteful if node N_j had already completed the computation, but was simply unable to participate in commit processing because of a link fault.

A *nested transaction* T_{ik} is an atomic transaction that is a part of another transaction T_i. Transactions T_i and T_{ik} have a parent–child relationship; the transaction controller of T_i initiates T_{ik} and assigns it a unique id. The nested transaction can commit or abort just like an atomic transaction, except for one difference—when it reaches the commit point, a *tentative commit* is performed for it. A tentative commit is an intermediate stage between *not committed* and *committed*. The log of the nested transaction is written in stable storage; however, it is not processed at this time. The actual commit of the nested transaction, which involves processing of the log, is held in abeyance until the parent transaction commits. When a parent transaction reaches its commit point, it is committed by using a two-phase commit protocol to ensure that all its child transactions can commit.

Resiliency using nested transactions is implemented as follows: Consider a transaction T_i that executes in node N_i and initiates a nested transaction T_{ik} in node N_j. Let node N_j crash and recover sometime after T_{ik} has performed a tentative commit. The transaction coordinator, which is in node N_i, may find that the nested transaction T_{ik} is taking too long to complete, or that the transaction manager in node N_j is not responding to its *prepare* message, so it may decide to initiate T_{ik} once again—either in node N_j itself, or in another node. If it reinitiates T_{ik} in node N_j, the transaction manager in node N_j would check whether T_{ik} was initiated there in the past and had performed a tentative commit. If so, it would not reinitiate T_{ik} because it already has T_{ik}'s results in the log; it would simply use T_{ik}'s results when the parent transaction T_i commits. Thus, reexecution of T_{ik} would be avoided.

If the transaction coordinator of T_i decided to reinitiate the nested transaction in another node, it would assign another id to the new nested transaction, say, T_{il}. Now, transaction T_{ik} of node N_j has become an *orphan* because its parent transaction is no longer interested in it. If it has not performed a tentative commit, it should be prevented from performing it in future. If it has performed a tentative commit, care should be taken not to include it in the 2PC when the results of T_i are committed so that data consistency is not harmed through duplicate actions. To implement this aspect, the transaction coordinator for T_i maintains a list of ids of nested transactions in which it is currently interested. When it initiates nested transaction T_{ik}, it would add T_{ik}'s id to the list, and when it reinitiates the nested transaction with the id T_{il}, it would delete T_{ik} from this list and add T_{il} to it. When T_{ik} wishes to perform a tentative commit, its transaction manager would check with the transaction coordinator whether T_{ik}'s id is present in the list of nested transactions. Since it is not the case, the transaction manager would disallow a tentative commit of T_{ik} to take place. When T_i commits, T_{ik} would not participate in the 2PC because its id is not present in the list of nested transactions.

19.6 SUMMARY

Recovery and *fault tolerance* are two approaches to reliability of a computer system. These approaches are generically called *recovery*. The cost of a recovery approach is determined by its overhead during normal operation and the amount of reprocessing which becomes necessary when a fault occurs. In a distributed system, a fault typically affects the operation of a single link or node, hence special techniques are employed to minimize the cost of a recovery. It gives rise to a third recovery approach called *resiliency*. In this chapter we studied the recovery techniques of distributed operating systems.

A *fault* like an I/O device malfunction or a power outage causes an *error* in the state of the system. It leads to an unexpected behavior of the system, which is called a *failure*. Recovery is initiated when a failure is noticed. It puts the system into a new state from which its operation can be resumed. The nature of a fault determines what kind of recovery is possible. A *fail-stop* fault brings the system to a halt, a *partial amnesia* fault makes it lose a part of its state, while a *Byzantine* fault makes it behave in an unpredictable manner and perform wrong actions. It may not be possible to undo the effect of wrong actions performed because of a Byzantine fault in a process, hence recovery is implemented as follows: Several processes are created to perform the same computation in parallel. When a failure results from a Byzantine fault, the state in which majority of the processes exist is considered to be the correct state. Processes in the wrong state are aborted and others resume their operation.

Recovery from non-Byzantine faults can be performed by using two approaches. In *backward recovery*, recovery is performed by rolling back the system to a previous consistent state and resuming its operation, whereas in *forward recovery* the error is removed from the system's state and its operation is resumed. Backward recovery is implemented as follows: The states of processes are recorded periodically. When a node fails, a process that was executing in it, say process P_i, is rolled back to a previous state. If P_i had sent a message m that was received by another process P_j, P_i's rollback makes message m an *orphan message* and causes an inconsistency in the states of P_i and P_j. To remove this inconsistency, P_j has to be rolled back to some previous state in which it had not received message m. This effect is called the *domino effect*. Recovery is performed by rolling back processes in accordance with the domino effect until all processes assume mutually consistent states.

A system implements fault tolerance by maintaining a *log* in which it writes information for recovery. An *undo* log contains information useful for backward recovery, while a *do* log, which is also called a *redo* log, contains information for forward recovery. Fault tolerance is implemented through an *atomic transaction*, which ensures that if a fault occurs, either all actions in a specified sequence of actions would be performed or none of them would be performed. This way, the system will never be in a state in which only some of the actions have been performed. An atomic transaction can be implemented by using a do log and forward recovery if a fault occurs while implementing its actions; it can also be implemented by using an undo log and backward recovery. The *two-phase commit protocol* (2PC protocol) is used to implement atomic transactions that involve data existing in different nodes of the system. It ensures that actions of the transaction are implemented only if all nodes containing its data can carry out the required updates.

An atomic transaction that involves data in many nodes of the system can be implemented by using *nested transactions*, which are its parts that execute in different nodes. If an atomic transaction is unable to complete because of a node fault, it may be reinitiated. The *resiliency* technique reduces the cost of reprocessing as follows: A nested transaction of the failed transaction may have completed its operation in some other node. Hence it is not reinitiated even if its parent transaction is reinitiated; instead, its results are simply reused in the reinitiated parent transaction.

TEST YOUR CONCEPTS

19.1 Classify each of the following statements as true or false:

a. A power outage is a partial amnesia fault if no recovery techniques are used.

b. Use of a recovery technique incurs overhead even during normal operation of a system, i.e., even when no faults occur.

c. Backward recovery is performed by using backups and checkpoints.

d. An orphan message is a message that has been sent but has not been received by its destination process.

e. The domino effect may be observed while recovering a system by using asynchronous checkpoints.

f. Quorum algorithms are used for fault tolerance while updating distributed data.

19.2 Select the appropriate alternative(s) in each of the following questions:

a. A fault occurs when a system is in state S, and a process P_i is in state s_i. Process P_i is rolled back to a state s'_i contained in a checkpoint that was taken at time t. A domino effect arises if

i. P_i had received a message m' some time after time t.

ii. P_i had sent a message m^* to a process P_k some time after time t, and in state S the message is still in transit.

iii. P_i had sent a message m^* to a process P_k some time after time t, and in state S process P_k has received the message.

b. An atomic transaction can be implemented by using

i. A do log and backward recovery

ii. A do log and forward recovery

iii. An undo log and backward recovery

iv. An undo log and forward recovery

EXERCISES

19.1 A checkpoint is said to be strongly consistent if (i) states of all pairs of processes are mutually consistent, and (ii) every message recorded as sent by a sender process is recorded as received by a receiver process. Discuss whether a synchronous checkpoint is both consistent and strongly consistent.

19.2 Processes in a distributed computation perform asynchronous checkpointing as follows: Each process takes a checkpoint immediately after sending a message. Prove that recovery using such checkpoints can be performed without encountering the domino effect.

19.3 Can orphan messages arise if a process takes a checkpoint before receiving each message?

19.4 When asynchronous checkpointing is used, several checkpoints for each process need to be preserved to support rollbacks in the presence of orphan messages. To preserve disk space, it is useful to know *when* (if ever) a specific checkpoint can be deleted without affecting recovery. Comment on the following proposals:

a. Delete a checkpoint C_{ij} when another checkpoint is taken for process P_i.

b. Delete a checkpoint C_{ij} if another checkpoint C_{ij+1} is taken for process P_i and no messages were sent by P_i between the two checkpoints.

c. Delete a checkpoint C_{ij} if another checkpoint C_{ij+1} is taken for process P_i and no messages were received by P_i between the two checkpoints.

d. Delete all checkpoints for process P_i taken prior to checkpoint C_{ij} if for every message m_k recorded as received in C_{ij}, the process that sent message m_k has taken a checkpoint after sending it.

19.5 The node in a distributed system in which a process P_i operates fails. What are the processes that need to be rolled back due to recovery of P_i? Give an algorithm to recover from P_i's failure. While recovery from P_i's failure is in progress, the node in which another process P_j operates fails. State the conditions under which recovery from these two failures would be independent of one another. How should recovery from these failures be performed if these conditions are not satisfied?

19.6 Give a scheme to implement an atomic transaction using an undo log. In what order should entries in the undo log be processed if a transaction is aborted?

19.7 Can use of read and write quorums determined by Eq.(19.2) lead to deadlocks? If so, design a scheme to avoid deadlocks.

19.8 Because of large quorum sizes in handling replicated data, it is proposed to use an approach based on the notion of *request sets* of Maekawa (see Section 18.3.1). Comment on whether all four rules of Section 19.4.2 would be satisfied by this approach.

19.9 Comment on correctness of the following scheme for mutual exclusion of readers and writers over replicated data:

a. Set $Q_r = 1$ and $Q_w = n$, where n is the number of copies of data.

b. When a writer wishes to update the data, it tries to set a write lock on each copy.

i. If the copy is already locked, it waits for the copy's lock to be released by the process which had set it.

ii. If it cannot access the copy, it assumes that the node containing the copy has failed, and reduces Q_w by 1.

iii. It proceeds to update the data when it finds that it has set a write lock on as many copies as the current value of Q_w.

BIBLIOGRAPHY

Lamport et al. (1982) discusses the Byzantine generals problem. Barborak et al. (1993) surveys approaches that can be used to obtain agreement on a system status by the fault-free segment of the processor population. Lynch (1996), Tel (2000), and Garg (2002) discuss consensus in synchronous and asynchronous systems.

The two-phase commit protocol is discussed in Gray (1981). The three-phase commit protocol avoids the blocking problem of the two–phase commit protocol when the coordinator fails. It permits participating nodes to roll forward such a transaction to completion, or to roll it back to an abort. The three-phase commit protocol is discussed in Skeen (1983). Svobodova (1984) discusses resiliency in distributed computing.

Venkatesh et al. (1987) discusses optimal checkpointing and domino-free recovery. This topic continues to be much researched even today. Tel (2000) discusses fault tolerance in distributed systems. Garg (2002) discusses recovery based on checkpointing and message logging.

1. Barborak, M., M. Malek, and A. Dahbura (1993): "The consensus problem in fault tolerant computing," *Computing Surveys*, **25**, 2, 171–220.
2. Garg, V. K. (2002): *Elements of Distributed Computing*, Wiley-IEEE, New York.
3. Gray, J. N. (1981): "The transaction concept: virtues and limitations," *Proceedings of the International Conference on Very Large Data Bases*, 144–154.
4. Lamport, L., R. Shostak, and M. Pease (1982): "The Byzantine generals problem," *ACM Transactions on Programming Languages and Systems*, **4** (3), 382–401.

5. Lynch, N. (1996): *Distributed Algorithms*, Morgan Kaufmann.

6. Skeen, D. (1983): "A formal model of crash recovery in a distributed system," *IEEE Transactions on Software Engineering*, **9** (3), 219–228.

7. Svobodova, L. (1984): "Resilient Distributed computing," *IEEE Transactions on Software Engineering*, **10** (3), 257–267.

8. Tel, G. (2000): *Introduction to Distributed Algorithms*, 2nd ed., Cambridge University Press, Cambridge.

9. Venkatesh, K., T. Radhakrishnan, and H. F. Li (1987): "Optimal checkpointing and local recording for domino-free rollback recovery," *Information Processing Letters*, **25** (5), 295–304.

20 Chapter

Distributed File Systems

Users of a distributed file system (DFS) expect it to provide the convenience, reliability, and performance provided by conventional file systems. The convenience of using a distributed file system depends on two key issues. *Transparency* of a distributed file system makes users oblivious to the location of their files in the nodes and disks in the system. *File sharing semantics* specify the rules of file sharing—whether and how the effect of file modifications made by one process are visible to other processes using the file concurrently.

A process and a file accessed by it may exist in different nodes of a distributed system, so a fault in either node or in a path between the two can affect the file processing activity. Distributed file systems ensure high reliability through *file replication*, and through use of a *stateless file server* design to minimize the impact of file server crashes on ongoing file processing activities.

Response time to file system operations is influenced by network latencies in accessing remote files, so the technique of *file caching* is used to reduce network traffic in file processing. Another aspect of performance is *scalability*—response times should not degrade when the distributed system grows in size. It is addressed through techniques that localize a file processing activity to a *cluster*, which is a group of computer systems having a high-speed LAN.

This chapter discusses the DFS techniques for achieving user convenience, reliability, and high performance. Case studies of distributed file systems illustrate their operation in practice.

20.1 DESIGN ISSUES IN DISTRIBUTED FILE SYSTEMS

A distributed file system (DFS) stores user files in several nodes of a distributed system, so a process and a file being accessed by it often exist in different nodes of the distributed system. This situation has three likely consequences:

- A user may have to know the topology of the distributed system to open and access files located in various nodes of the system.
- A file processing activity in a process might be disrupted if a fault occurs in the node containing the process, the node containing the file being accessed, or a path connecting the two.

- Performance of the file system may be poor because of the network traffic involved in accessing a file.

The need to avoid these consequences motivates the three design issues summarized in Table 20.1 and discussed in the following.

Transparency A file system finds the location of a file during path name resolution (see Section 13.9.1). Two relevant issues in a distributed file system are: How much information about the location of a file should be reflected in its path name, and can a DFS change the location of a file to optimize file access performance? The notion of transparency has two facets that address these issues.

- *Location transparency:* The name of a file should not reveal its location.
- *Location independence:* The file system should be able to change the location of a file without having to change its name.

Location transparency provides user convenience, as a user or a computation need not know the location of a file. Location independence enables a file system to optimize its own performance. For example, if accesses to files stored at a node cause network congestion and result in poor performance, the DFS may move some of those files to other nodes. This operation is called *file migration*. Location independence can also be used to improve utilization of storage media in the system. We discuss these two facets of transparency in Section 20.2.

Fault Tolerance A fault disrupts an ongoing file processing activity, thereby threatening consistency of file data and *metadata*, i.e., control data, of the file system. A DFS may employ a journaling technique as in a conventional file

Table 20.1 Design Issues in Distributed File Systems

Design issue	Description
Transparency	High transparency of a file system implies that a user need not know much about location of files in a system. Transparency has two aspects. *Location transparency* implies that the name of a file should not reveal its location in the file system. *Location independence* implies that it should be possible to change the location of a file without having to change its name.
Fault tolerance	A fault in a computer system or a communication link may disrupt ongoing file processing activities. It affects availability of the file system and also impairs consistency of file data and *metadata*, i.e., control data, of the file system. A DFS should employ special techniques to avoid these consequences of faults.
Performance	*Network latency* is a dominant factor of file access times in a DFS; it affects both efficiency and scalability of a DFS. Hence a DFS should use techniques that reduce network traffic generated by file accesses.

system to protect consistency of metadata, or it may use a *stateless file server* design, which makes it unnecessary to protect consistency of metadata when a fault occurs. To protect file data, it may provide *transaction semantics*, which are useful in implementing *atomic transactions* (see Section 19.4.1), so that an application may itself achieve fault tolerance if it so desires. We discuss fault tolerance issues in Section 20.4.

Performance Performance of a DFS has two facets—efficiency and scalability. In a distributed system, *network latency* is the dominant factor influencing efficiency of a file processing activity. Network latency typically exceeds the processing time for a file record so, unlike I/O device latency, it cannot be masked by blocking and buffering of records (see Sections 14.8 and 14.9). A DFS employs the technique of *file caching*, which keeps a copy of a remote file in the node of a process that accesses the file. This way accesses to the file do not cause network traffic, though staleness of data in a file cache has to be prevented through *cache coherence* techniques. *Scalability* of DFS performance requires that response times should not degrade when system size increases because of addition of nodes or users. A distributed system is composed of *clusters*, which are groups of computer systems having high-speed LANs (see Section 16.2), so caching a single copy of a file in a cluster ensures that file access performance for accesses from a computer system within a cluster would be independent of system size. It also reduces network traffic. Both these effects help in enhancing scalability of DFS performance. When several processes access the same file in parallel, *distributed locking* techniques are employed to ensure that synchronization of the file processing activities scales well with an increase in system size. We discuss DFS performance enhancement techniques in Section 20.5.

20.1.1 Overview of DFS Operation

Figure 20.1 shows a simplified schematic of file processing in a DFS. A process in node N_1 opens a file with path name ... alpha. We call this process a *client process* of this file, or simply a *client* of this file, and call node N_1 the *client node*. Through path name resolution, the DFS finds that this file exists in node N_2, so it sets up the arrangement shown in Figure 20.1. The file system component in node N_2 is called a *file server*, and node N_2 is called the *server node*. Other nodes that were involved in path name resolution or that would be involved in transferring file data between nodes N_1 and N_2 are called *intermediate nodes*.

We refer to this model as the *remote file processing* model. An arrangement analogous to RPC is used to implement file accesses through stub processes called *file server agent* and *client agent* (see Section 16.5.2). When the client opens the file, the request is handed over to the client agent. The client agent communicates the request to the file server agent in node N_2, which hands over the request to the file server. The file server opens alpha and builds $fcb_{\texttt{alpha}}$. When file caching is not employed, a read or write operation on alpha is implemented through a

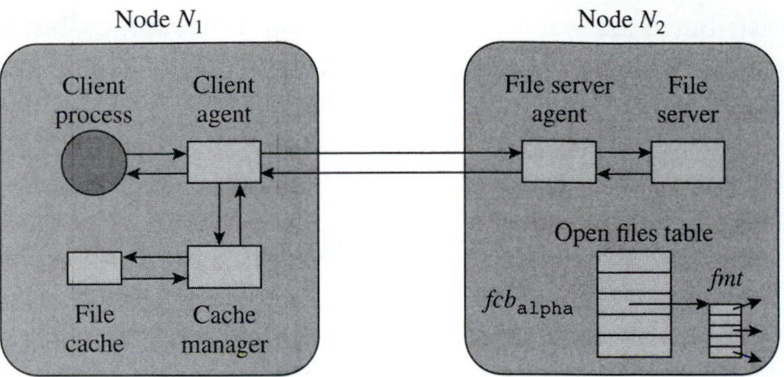

Figure 20.1 Basics of file processing in a distributed file system.

message between the client agent and the file server agent. I/O buffers for the file exist at node N_2, and only one record at a time gets passed to the client.

When *file caching* is employed, a read or write request is routed to the *cache manager*, which checks whether the required data can be accessed from or deposited in the *file cache*. The cache manager interacts with the file server agent through messages when it needs to transfer data between the file cache and the file. For efficiency reasons, the client agent and the cache manager are typically rolled into a single unit.

20.2 TRANSPARENCY

In a conventional file system, a user identifies a file through a path name. He is aware that the file belongs in a specific directory; however, he is not aware of its location in the system. The *location info* field of the file's directory entry indicates the file's location on disk. This arrangement would be adequate to provide *location transparency* in a DFS as well—a user would use a path name to access a file, and the DFS would obtain the location of the file from its directory entry. The DFS may choose to keep all files of a directory in the same node of the distributed system, or disperse them to different nodes. In the former case, its metadata would be identical with that of a conventional file system. In the latter case, the *location info* field of the directory entry of a file would contain a pair (node id, location).

Providing *location independence* would require the information in the *location info* field of a directory entry to change dynamically. Now, the DFS could change the location of a file at will, so long as it puts information about the new location in the *location info* field of the directory entry. It should similarly change information in all links to the file (see Section 13.4.2). To simplify these changes, a DFS may use the following arrangement: Each file is assigned a globally unique file id. The directory entry of the file contains this file id. DFS maintains a separate data structure to hold (file id, file location) pairs. This way, the DFS needs to change only one pair in this data structure when the location of a file is changed, irrespective of the number of links to the file.

Most distributed file systems provide location transparency, but not location independence. Hence files cannot be migrated to other nodes. This restriction deprives the DFS of an opportunity to optimize file access performance.

20.3 SEMANTICS OF FILE SHARING

Semantics of file sharing determine the manner in which the effect of file manipulations performed by concurrent users of a file are visible to one another. Recall from the discussion in Section 13.10 that all clients concurrently processing a *single-image mutable file* have the same view of its contents, so modifications made by one client are immediately visible to other clients processing the file. Clients processing a *multiple-image mutable file* can have different views of its contents. When their file processing activities complete, the file system can either reconcile these views in some manner to create a single image, or support existence of many versions of the file. In the latter case, it has to ensure that any client that opens the file subsequently gets access to the correct version of the file. Table 20.2, summarizes key features of three file sharing semantics—*Unix semantics*, *session semantics*, and *transaction semantics*.

Unix Semantics Recall from Section 13.10 that Unix file sharing semantics support a single-image mutable file. Thus, updates made by one client are visible to other clients immediately. Clients may optionally share the offset into a file. This feature is useful if clients process a file jointly. The Unix semantics are easy and efficient to implement in a conventional file system; however, as discussed later in Section 20.5.2, they incur the overhead of cache coherence in a DFS that uses file caching.

Table 20.2 Features of File Sharing Semantics

Semantics	Description
Unix semantics	A *single-image mutable file* is implemented. The effect of a write operation in a file by one client is visible immediately to other clients of the file. Clients may optionally share the file offset, i.e., pointer to the next record in a file.
Session semantics	A *multiple-image mutable file* is implemented. Only clients in a *session* share the same image of a file. Updates made by a client are visible to other clients in the same session immediately; they are visible to other clients only after the file is closed.
Transaction semantics	File processing performed by a client is implemented as an atomic transaction, so either all file operations are performed or none of them are performed. This property simplifies fault tolerance.

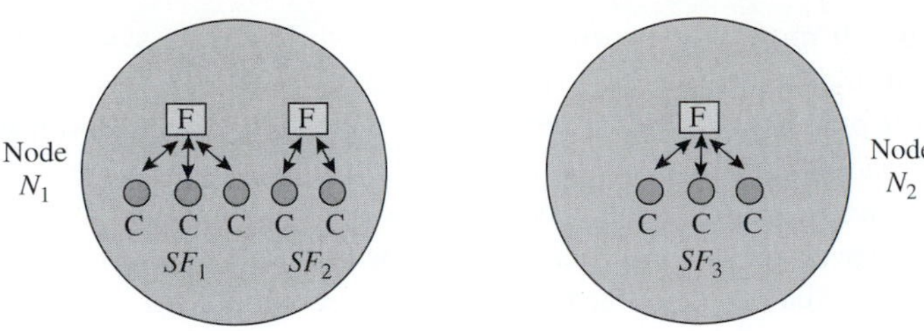

Figure 20.2 Three sessions in a DFS using session semantics.

Session Semantics A *session* consists of some of the clients of a file that are located in the same node of a system. Clients in one session share a single mutable image of the file. Thus, result of a write operation performed by a client process is visible to other clients in the same session immediately, but not to clients in other sessions.

Formation of sessions and visibility of file images is governed by the following rules: Let SF_i be a session involving a set of clients processing file F. When another client located in the same node opens file F, the DFS would let it join session SF_i if none of the clients in SF_i had closed F after performing a write operation; otherwise, the DFS would start a new session. When a client located in another node opens file F, the DFS always starts a new session. Figure 20.2 illustrates three sessions SF_1, SF_2, and SF_3 on a file F. Two of these sessions are in node N_1 for the reasons mentioned above. A new version of the file would be created every time a client closes a file after modifying it. However, session semantics do not specify the rules for deciding which version of a file should be opened when a new session is started, so file systems may implement this aspect differently. Consequently, applications that use session semantics may not be portable. Session semantics are easy to implement in a DFS employing file caching because changes made in a file are not to be visible to clients in other nodes.

Transaction Semantics The file processing activity of each client is performed as an atomic transaction. Transaction semantics can be implemented by treating the `open` and `close` operations on a file as the beginning and end of a transaction, providing a mutually exclusive access to a file by setting a lock on the file, and performing file updates as discussed in Section 19.4.1. Thus, only one client can access a file at any time and either all updates made by it are reflected in the file or none are. The all-or-nothing property of transaction semantics always maintains a file in a consistent state. Consequently, a client can simply reexecute a file processing activity that is disrupted by a fault. Locking of a file also implies that the DFS does not have to handle concurrent accesses to a file by clients.

20.4 FAULT TOLERANCE

File system reliability has several facets. A file must be *robust*, i.e., it must survive faults in a guaranteed manner. It must be *recoverable* to an earlier state when a failure occurs. It must also be *available* despite faults in the system, i.e., a copy of the file should be accessible at all times and a client process should be able to open it for processing. Robustness and recoverability depend on how files are stored and backed up, respectively, while availability depends on how files are opened and accessed. All these facets are independent of one another. Thus a file may be recoverable without being robust or available, recoverable and robust without being available, available without being recoverable or robust, and so on. Robustness is achieved by using techniques for reliable storage of data, e.g., the disk mirroring technique used in RAID level 1 (see Section 14.3.5). Recoverability and availability are achieved through special techniques discussed in this Section.

Faults in the server or intermediate nodes during a file `open` operation disrupt path name resolution. Such faults are tolerated through availability techniques. The DFS maintains many copies of the information required for path name resolution, and many copies of a file. If a copy is inaccessible because of a fault, the DFS uses another copy. However, availability techniques become very complex and expensive if faults that occur *during* file processing are to be tolerated (see Section 19.4.2 for the quorum-based fault tolerance techniques to handle replicated data). Hence few, if any, distributed file systems handle such faults.

Faults in the server or client nodes during file processing may result in loss of state. As we shall see in Section 20.4.3, a file server can be designed such that its operation is not disrupted if state information is lost because of a fault. However, clients may not use special design techniques to protect against loss of state, so client node crashes can be messy. The only defense against client node crashes is the use of *transaction semantics* in the file server, whereby the file would be restored to its state before the failed client had started its processing. A fault in an intermediate node does not affect file processing if the communication system has sufficient resiliency, i.e., if it can tolerate a few link and node faults. Hence file systems do not address these faults.

Table 20.3 summarizes fault tolerance techniques used in distributed file systems. File replication and cached directories address faults in a file server and in intermediate nodes during an `open` operation. The stateless file server design addresses faults in a file server during file processing. Following sections describe these techniques.

20.4.1 Availability

A file is said to be available if a copy of the file can be opened and accessed by a client. Ability to open a file depends on whether path name resolution can be completed, i.e., whether the server node and all nodes involved in path name resolution are functional. Ability to access a file requires only the client and server nodes to be functional, because a path between the two is guaranteed by resiliency of the network.

Consider a path name `a/b/c/d`, where directory files `a`, `b`, `c` and file `d` exist in nodes A, B, C, and D, respectively. Two approaches can be employed to resolve this path. When the DFS finds that file `b` exists in node B, it would send the path

Table 20.3 Fault Tolerance Techniques of Distributed File Systems

Technique	Description
Cached directories	A *cached directory* is a copy of a directory that exists at a remote site. It helps the DFS to tolerate faults in intermediate nodes involved in path name resolution.
File replication	Several copies of a file are maintained in the interest of availability. Special techniques are used to avoid inconsistencies between the copies. The *primary copy* technique permits client programs to read-access any copy of a file but restricts file updates only to a special copy called the primary copy. The results of these updates are propagated to other copies. This method simplifies concurrency control.
Stateless file server	A conventional file server maintains information concerning state of a file processing activity in the metadata, for example, in file control blocks and file buffers. A *stateless file server* does not maintain such information, so it is immune to faults that lead to loss of state information.

name suffix `b/c/d` to node B. At node B, it would look up `c` in directory `b` and find that it exists at node C, so it would send `c/d` to node C, and so on. In an alternative approach, the DFS would perform resolution of all path components in the client node itself. When it finds that a path name component is the name of a directory in a remote node, it would copy the directory from the remote node and continue path name resolution using it. This way, all directories would be copied into the client node during path name resolution. As we shall see later, these approaches have different implications for availability. In either approach, an access to file data does not involve the intermediate nodes involved in path name resolution. File processing would not be affected if any of these nodes failed after the file was opened.

Cached Directories An anomalous situation may arise when path names span many nodes. In the previous example, let node `c` fail after file `d` was opened using path name `a/b/c/d` and its processing was underway. If another client in node A tries to open `a/b/c/z`, where file `z` also exists in node D, it would fail because node `c` has failed. So file `z` cannot be processed even though its processing involves the same client and server nodes as file `d`.

The only way to avoid this anomaly is to cache remote directories accessed during path name resolution at the client node. For the path name `a/b/c/d`, it implies that the DFS would cache the directories `a/b` and `a/b/c` at node A. While resolving path names involving the prefixes `a/b` and `a/b/c`, the DFS would directly use the cached directories. Thus, it would be able to resolve the path name `a/b/c/z` without having to access nodes B or C. However, information in cached directories may be outdated because of creation or deletion of files in some of the intermediate nodes, so a cache updating protocol would have to be used. We discuss a related issue in the next section.

File Replication The DFS performs replication in such a way that it is transparent to clients. Replication of a file that is likely to be updated involves a trade-off between cost and complexity of the protocol for updating and its implications for efficient use of the file. A two-phase commit protocol could be used to update all copies of a file at the same time. This way, stale and updated copies of a file would not coexist, so a client would need only one copy of the file to implement a read access. However, an update operation may be delayed if some copies are in use by other processes or are inaccessible because of faults. Alternatives to this approach focus on speeding up the update operation by reducing the number of copies that need to be updated.

In the *primary copy* approach, updates are directed at a single copy—the primary copy. Other copies are invalidated when the primary copy is updated; they would be replicated afresh when they are referenced. Alternatively, the DFS can use a protocol similar to the readers-and-writers protocol for replicated data (see Section 19.4.2). To provide efficiency and fault tolerance, it would make the read and write quorums as small as possible. A timestamp would be associated with each copy to indicate when it was last updated. These timestamps would be compared to identify the most recent copy of data in a read quorum.

File replication works best if the use of a stale copy is also meaningful, because changes need not be propagated to all copies of a file immediately. Directories can be replicated in this manner. All updates are made in the primary copy. Staleness of a directory's copy can cause two kinds of failures—a file does not have an entry in the directory even though it has been created, or an entry for a file exists in the directory even though the file has been deleted. If the first kind of failure occurs, the file server can immediately consult the primary copy to check whether the file actually exists, and abort the process only if it does not. The second kind of failure would occur when a read or write operation is attempted on the file. The process would be aborted if it occurs.

20.4.2 Client and Server Node Failures

As described in Section 13.8, a conventional file system stores information concerning the state of a file processing activity in metadata such as the file control block (FCB) of the file. This state information provides an implicit context between the file system and a client, using which a read or write operation on the file can be performed efficiently. For example, to read the next record or byte from a sequential file, the file system simply accesses its FCB to obtain the id of the next record or byte to be read, and accesses the file map table (FMT) to obtain the disk address of the next record or byte; it does not have to access the directory entry of the file to obtain address of its FMT. We refer to this design of a file system as a *stateful* design. In a distributed file system, the server node can maintain FCBs and the open files table (OFT) in memory, just as in a conventional file system. This arrangement provides good performance. However, use of a stateful DFS design poses problems in the event of client and server crashes.

When a client crashes, the file processing activity would have to be abandoned and the file would have to be restored to its previous state so that the client can restart its file processing activity. The server would have committed resources like the FCB and I/O buffers to service the file processing activity. These resources would have to be released, otherwise they would remain committed to the aborted file processing activity indefinitely. These issues can be addressed as follows: The client and the file server share a virtual circuit (see Section 16.6.5). The virtual circuit "owns" the file processing actions and resources like file server metadata. These actions and resources become orphans when a client or server crash breaks the virtual circuit, so the actions would have to be rolled back and the metadata would have to be destroyed. A client–server protocol implementing transaction semantics may be used to ensure this. If a DFS does not provide transaction semantics, a client would have to make its own arrangements to restore the file to a previous consistent state.

When a file server crashes, state information stored in server metadata is lost, so an ongoing file processing activity has to be abandoned and the file has to be restored to its previous state. The stateless file server design described in the next section can be used to avoid both these problems.

20.4.3 Stateless File Servers

A stateless file server does not maintain any state information about a file processing activity, so there is no implied context between a client and the file server. Consequently, a client must maintain state information about a file processing activity and provide all relevant information in a file system call. For example, a client reading from a sequential file has to keep track of the id of the next record or byte to be read from the file so that it can issue the following call:

`read` ("`alpha`", <*record/byte id*>, <*io_area address*>);

At this call, the file server opens file `alpha`, locates its file map table, and uses it to convert <*record/byte id*> into the pair (*disk block id, byte offset*) (see Section 13.9.2). It then reads the disk block and provides the required record or byte to the client. Thus, many actions traditionally performed only at file open time are repeated at every file operation. If a file server crashes, time-outs and retransmissions occur in the client. The file server processes a retransmitted request when it recovers, and provides a reply to the client. Thus the client perceives only a delayed response to a request and is unaware of a file server crash.

Use of a stateless file server provides fault tolerance, but it also incurs a substantial performance penalty for two reasons. First, the file server opens a file at every file operation, and passes back state information to the client. Second, when a client performs a write operation, reliability considerations require that data should be written into the disk copy of a file immediately. Consequently, a stateless file server cannot employ buffering, file caching (see Section 20.5.2), or disk caching (see Section 14.12) to speed up its own operation. In Section 20.5.1, we discuss a hybrid design of file servers that avoids repeated file `open` operations.

A stateless file server is oblivious of client failures because it does not possess any state information for a client or its file processing activity. If a client fails, recovers and resends some requests to the file server, the file server would simply reprocess them. For the same reason, it cannot detect and discard duplicate requests, so it may process a request more than once. An individual read or write operation is idempotent, so its reprocessing does not pose any problem. However, directory-related requests like creation and deletion of files are not idempotent. Consequently, a client may receive ambiguous or misleading warnings if a stateless file server crashes and recovers during a file processing activity. A sequence of read and write operations may also not be idempotent. For example, a sequence of operations involving reading of a record from a file, searching for a string `xyz` in the record, insertion of a string S before string `xyz`, and writing of the modified record back into the file, is not idempotent. If a failed client has performed such a nonidempotent sequence, it must restore the file to a previous state before reissuing the sequence of operations.

20.5 DFS PERFORMANCE

Inherent efficiency of file access mechanisms determines peak performance of a DFS measured as either average response time to client requests or throughput of client requests. The DFS can achieve peak performance when all data accesses are local to client nodes, i.e., when clients and file servers are located in the same node. However, network latencies can completely overshadow the efficiency of access mechanisms even when only a small fraction of file accesses cause network traffic. This fact motivates measures to reduce network traffic caused by file processing activities.

A DFS design is *scalable* if DFS performance does not degrade with an increase in the size of a distributed system. Scalability is important for avoiding a situation in which a DFS that used to perform well in a user's organization becomes a bottleneck when the organization becomes large. Scalability is achieved through special techniques that ensure that network traffic does not grow with size of the distributed system.

Table 20.4 summarizes techniques used to achieve high DFS performance. These techniques are discussed in the following sections.

20.5.1 Efficient File Access

Inherent efficiency of file access depends on how the operation of a file server is structured. We discuss two server structures that provide efficient file access.

Multithreaded File Server The file server has several threads; each thread is capable of servicing one client request. Operation of several of these threads can be overlapped because file processing is an I/O-bound activity. This arrangement provides fast response to client requests and a high throughput. The number of threads can be varied in accordance with the number of client requests that are active at any time, and the availability of OS resources such as thread control blocks.

Table 20.4 Performance Techniques of Distributed File Systems

Technique	Description
Multithreaded file server design	Each thread in the file server handles one client request. File processing is an I/O-bound activity, hence several threads can make progress in parallel, thereby contributing to higher throughput.
Hint-based file server design	A *hint* is some information related to an ongoing file processing activity that *may* be maintained by a file server. When a suitable hint is available, the file server behaves like a stateful file server so that it can perform a file operation efficiently; otherwise, it behaves like a stateless file server.
File caching	Some part of a file located in a remote node is copied into the *file cache* in the client node. File caching reduces network traffic during file processing by converting data transfers over the network into data transfers that are local to a client node.
Semi-independent clusters of nodes	A *cluster of nodes* is a section of the distributed system that contains sufficient hardware and software resources such that processes operating in a cluster rarely need resources located elsewhere in the system.

Hint-Based File Server A hint-based file server is a hybrid design in that it has features of both a stateful and a stateless file server. In the interest of efficiency, it operates in a stateful manner whenever possible. At other times, it operates in a stateless manner. A *hint* is some information concerning an ongoing file processing activity, e.g., id of the next record in a sequential file that would to be accessed by a file processing activity (see Section 13.8). The file server maintains a collection of hints in its volatile storage. When a client requests a file operation, the file server checks for presence of a hint that would help in its processing. If a hint is available, the file server uses it to speed up the file operation; otherwise, it operates in a stateless manner—it opens the file and uses the record/byte id provided by the client to access the required record or byte. In either case, after completing the file operation, it inserts a part of the state of the file processing activity in its volatile storage as a hint and also returns it to the client as in a stateless file server. The overall efficiency of the file server depends on the number of file operations that are aided by the presence of hints.

Operation of a hint-based file server is fault tolerant because it would not be disrupted even if all hints in the server's volatile storage are lost because of a crash. Users will notice only a degradation of response times until the file server recovers and builds up a useful set of hints.

20.5.2 File Caching

The technique of *file caching* speeds up operation of a DFS by reducing network traffic. It holds some data from a remote file in a buffer in a client node called the *file cache*. The file cache and the copy of the file on a disk in the server node form a memory hierarchy (see Section 2.2.3), so operation of the file cache and its benefits are analogous to those of a CPU cache. *Chunks* of file data are loaded from the file server into the file cache. To benefit from spatial locality, each chunk is large enough to service a few file accesses made by a client. Studies of file size distributions indicate small average file size, so even an entire file can be copied into the file cache, which is called *whole-file caching*. Studies by Tanenbaum and others reported that 79 percent of files in their system were smaller than 4 KB in size and 94 percent were smaller than 16 KB. In the Andrew file system, where the chunk size was varied on a per-client basis, chunk size was frequently 8 KB and contained an entire file, and file cache hit ratios exceeded 0.98. A DFS may use a separate *attributes cache* to cache information about file attributes.

Figure 20.3 contains a schematic diagram of file caching. The *cache manager* exists on the path between a client and a file server. It loads chunks of file data into the file cache; supplies data from the cache to clients; maintains the file cache, using a replacement algorithm for chunks; and writes modified chunks into the file copy in the server node. Key issues in the design of a file cache are:

- Location of the file cache
- File updating policy
- Cache validation policy
- Chunk size

The file cache can be maintained in memory of a client node, or on a disk attached to the client node. Organizing the file cache in memory would provide faster access to file data; however, it would result in low reliability because a crash of the client node would lead to loss of the file cache, including any modified file data that is yet to be written to the file copy in the server. Locating the cache on the disk would slow down access to file data, but would provide reliability as the file cache and the modified data contained in it would survive client

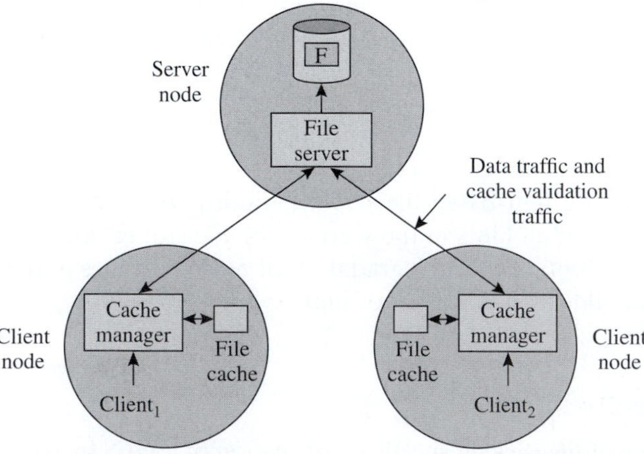

Figure 20.3 A schematic of file caching.

node crashes. Redundancy-based techniques like disk mirroring could be used to further enhance reliability of the file cache organized on a disk.

When a client performs a write operation on a disk, the modified file data would have to be written into the file copy in the server. The decision of whether to update the file copy immediately or at a later time involves a trade-off between delay in the client and reliability of the DFS. It is simplest to use the *write-through policy*, which updates the file cache in the client node and the file copy in the server node at the same time. This method is reliable, because the write-through could be implemented as a transaction to ensure that it completes; however, it delays the client that performed the write operation. To avoid delaying the client, the update of the file copy could be performed at a later time provided arrangements are made to ensure that the modified data would not be lost if the client node failed in the meanwhile. This policy is called the *delayed write policy*. Its variations perform the write operation at different times—when the modified chunk is deleted from the file cache due to replacement, or when the client closes the file.

When a file is processed by many clients in parallel, copies of its data would exist in several file caches at the same time. If one client performs a write operation, copies in other clients' caches become *invalid*, i.e., stale. The *cache validation* function identifies invalid data and deals with it in accordance with the file sharing semantics of the DFS. For example, when Unix semantics are used, file updates made by a client should be immediately visible to other clients of the file, so the cache validation function either refreshes invalid data or prevents its use by a client.

Chunk size in the file cache should be large so that spatial locality of file data contributes to a high hit ratio in the file cache. However, use of a large chunk size implies a higher probability of data invalidation due to modifications performed by other clients, hence more delays and more cache validation overhead than when a small chunk size is used. So the chunk size used in a DFS is a trade-off between these two considerations. A fixed chunk size may not suit all clients of a DFS, so some distributed file systems, notably the Andrew file system, adapt the chunk size to each individual client.

Cache Validation A simple method to identify invalid data is through timestamps. A timestamp is associated with each chunk in a file and with each of its cached chunks. The timestamp of a chunk indicates when it was last modified. When a chunk of the file is copied into a cache, its timestamp is also copied as the timestamp of the cached chunk. At any time, the cached chunk is invalid if its timestamp is smaller than the timestamp of the corresponding chunk in the file. This way a write operation in some chunk x of a file by one client invalidates all copies of x in other clients' caches. Data in such a chunk is refreshed, i.e., reloaded, at its next reference.

Two basic approaches to cache validation are *client-initiated validation* and *server-initiated validation*. Client-initiated validation is performed by the cache manager at a client node. At every file access by a client, it checks whether the required data is already in the cache. If so, it checks whether the data is valid. If the check succeeds, the cache manager provides the data from the cache to the client; otherwise, it refreshes the data in the cache before providing it to the client. This approach leads to cache validation traffic over the network at every access to the file. This traffic can be reduced by performing validation periodically rather than at every file access, provided such validation is consistent with the file sharing semantics of the DFS. Sun NFS uses this approach (see Section 20.6.1).

In the server-initiated approach, the file server keeps track of which client nodes have which file data in their caches and uses this information as follows: When a client updates data in some part x of a file, the file server finds the client nodes that have x in their file cache, and informs their cache managers that their copies of x have become invalid. Each cache manager now has an option of deleting the copy of x from its cache, or of caching it afresh either immediately or at the next reference to it.

Cache validation is an expensive operation, hence some file sharing semantics like the session semantics do not require that updates made by one client should be visible to clients in other nodes. This feature avoids the need for validation altogether. Another way to avoid the cache validation overhead is to disable file caching if some client opens a file in the update mode. All accesses to such a file are directly implemented in the server node.

20.5.3 Scalability

DFS scalability is achieved through techniques that localize most data traffic generated by file processing activities within small sections of a distributed system called *clusters of nodes* or, simply, *clusters* (see Section 16.2). There are two reasons why this approach is effective. First, clusters typically represent subnets like high-speed LANs, which provide high data transfer rates, so both response time and throughput improve when data traffic is confined to a cluster. Second, an increase in the number of clusters does not lead to degradation of performance because it does not add much network traffic. When a client of a DFS possessing both location transparency and location independence accesses a remote file, the file could be simply moved to the cluster where the client is located. If the DFS does not possess location independence, an analogous effect can be achieved for read-only files by replicating or caching a file in the client's node. For files that are updated, use of session semantics eliminates cache validation traffic, so locating a file version in the client node would suffice to reduce network traffic.

20.6 CASE STUDIES

20.6.1 Sun Network File System

The Sun network file system (NFS) provides sharing of file systems in nodes operating under the SunOS operating system, which is a version of Unix. Figure 20.4 shows a schematic diagram of the NFS. It uses a two-level architecture consisting of the *virtual file system* (VFS) layer (see Section 13.13) and the NFS layer. The VFS layer implements the *mount protocol* and creates a systemwide unique

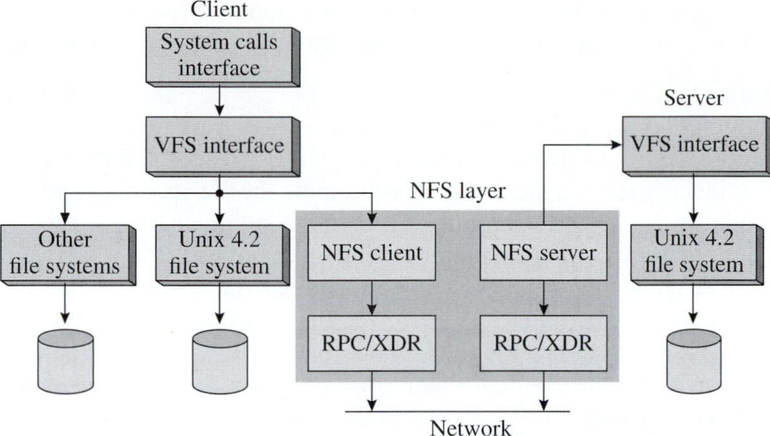

Figure 20.4 Architecture of the Sun network file system (NFS).

designator for each file, called the *vnode*. If the file on which an operation is to be performed is located in one of the local file systems, the VFS invokes that file system; otherwise, it invokes the NFS layer. The NFS layer interacts with the remote node containing the file through the *NFS protocol*. This architecture permits a node to be both a client and a server at the same time.

Mount Protocol Each node in the system contains an export list that contains pairs of the form (*<directory>*, *<list_of_nodes>*). Each pair indicates that *<directory>*, which exists in one of the local file systems, can be remotely mounted only in the nodes contained in *<list_of_nodes>*. When the superuser of a node makes a request to mount a remote directory, the NFS checks the validity of the request, mounts the directory, and returns a file handle, which contains the identifier of the file system that contained the remote directory, and the inode of the remote directory in that file system. Users in the node see a directory hierarchy constructed through such mount commands.

NFS permits cascaded mounting of file systems, i.e., a file system could be mounted at a mount point in another file system, which is itself mounted inside another file system, and so on. However, the NFS design carefully avoids transitivity of the mount mechanism. For example, consider the following situation:

1. The superuser in node N_1 of the system mounts the file system `C` of node N_3 at mount point `y` in the local file system `B`.
2. The superuser in node N_2 mounts the file system `B` of node N_1 at mount point `x` in the local file system `A`.

The NFS does not permit users in node N_2 to access the file system C that was mounted over some part of file system B. This way, each host's view of the directory hierarchy is the result of the mounts performed by its own superuser only, which enables the file server to operate in a stateless manner. If this restriction were not imposed, each file server would have to know about all mounts performed by all clients over its file system, which would require the file server to be stateful.

NFS Protocol The NFS protocol uses the remote service paradigm (i.e., remote file processing—see Section 20.1.1) through a client–server model employing remote procedure calls (RPC). A file server is stateless, so each RPC has parameters that identify the file, the directory containing the file, record id and the data to be read or written. The NFS provides calls for looking up a file within a directory; reading directory entries; manipulating links and directories; accessing file attributes, i.e., inode information; and performing a file read/write operation.

Since a file server is stateless, it performs an implicit open and close for every file operation, and does not use the Unix buffer cache (see Section 14.13.1.2 for a description of the Unix buffer cache). An NFS server does not provide locking of files or records; users must use their own means for concurrency control.

Path Name Resolution Let a user U1 located in node N_1 use a path name `x/y/z/w` where `y` is the root directory of a mounted file system. To start with, host node N_1 creates $vnode_{\mathtt{x}}$, the vnode for `x`. The NFS uses the mount table of N_1 while looking up the next component of the path name, so it knows that `y` is a mounted directory. It creates $vnode_{\mathtt{y}}$ from the information in the mount table. Let $vnode_{\mathtt{y}}$ be for a file in node N_2, so the NFS makes a copy of directory `y` in node N_1. While looking for `z` in this copy `y`, the NFS again uses the mount table of N_1. This action would resolve `z` properly even if `z` were a file system that was mounted by the superuser of node N_1 over some point in the remote file system `y`. The file server in node N_2, which contains `y`, does not need to have any knowledge of this mounting. Instead of using this procedure, if the path name `y/z/w` were to be handed over to the file server in node N_2, it would have to know about all mounts performed by all clients over its file system. It would require the file server to be stateful.

A *directory names cache* is used in each client node to speed up path name resolution. It contains remote directory names and their vnodes. New entries are added to the cache when a new path name prefix is resolved, and entries are deleted when a lookup fails because of mismatch between attributes returned by the file server and those of the cached vnodes.

File Operations and File Sharing Semantics The NFS uses two caches to speed up file operations. A *file attributes cache* caches inode information. This cache is used because it was found that a large percentage of requests made to a file server concerned file attributes. The cached attributes are discarded after 3 seconds for files and after 30 seconds for directories.

The *file blocks cache* is the conventional file cache. It contains data blocks from the file. The file server uses large (8 Kbytes) data blocks, and uses read-ahead and delayed-write techniques (i.e. buffering techniques, see Section 14.8) for improving file access performance. Cache validation is performed through timestamps associated with each file, and with each cache block. Contents of a cached block are assumed to be valid for a certain period of time. For any access after this time, the cached block is used only if its timestamp is larger than the timestamp of the file. A modified block is sent to the file server for writing into the file at an unspecified time during processing of a file, or when the file is closed. This policy is used even if clients concurrently access the same file block in conflicting modes. As a result of this policy and the cache validation scheme, visibility of a file modification made by one client to concurrent clients is unpredictable and the file sharing semantics are neither Unix semantics nor session semantics.

20.6.2 Andrew and Coda File Systems

Andrew, the distributed computing environment developed at the Carnegie Mellon University, is targeted at gigantic distributed systems containing 5000 workstations. Each workstation has a local disk, which is used to organize the local name space. This name space contains system programs for booting and operation of the workstation, and temporary files which are accommodated there for performance reasons. All clients have an identical shared name space, which is location transparent in nature. It is implemented by dedicated servers which are collectively called *Vice*.

Scalable performance is obtained as follows: Clusters localize file processing activities as much as possible so that file accesses do not cause traffic on the system backbone network. Traffic within a cluster is reduced by caching an entire file on the local disk of a workstation when it is opened for processing. These two techniques ensure that network traffic in the system does not grow as system size grows.

Shared Name Space Andrew uses the concept of a *volume*. A volume typically contains files of a single user. Many volumes may exist on a disk. Andrew treats a volume in much the same way Unix treats a disk partition, though a volume can be substantially smaller than a disk partition. A volume can be mounted. This fact provides a much finer granularity for mounting than in Unix. The file identifier used by *Vice* contains volume number of the volume which contains a file, and an index into the array of inodes contained in the volume.

A volume location database (VLDB) contains information about each volume in the system. This database is replicated on every server. Volumes are migrated from one disk to another in order to balance the utilization of disks in the system. The server that previously contained a migrated volume maintains some forwarding information until all servers update their volume location databases. This arrangement simplifies volume migration by eliminating the need to update all volume location databases at the same time. Actual migration of a volume is performed with minimum disruption of file processing activities by the following procedure: A copy of a volume is made at the new server. While this operation is in progress, its original server continues to service requests. Once the copying is completed, the volume is made off-line, recent updates performed after the copy operation was initiated are made on the copy at the new server, and the new copy is made operational.

File Operations and File Sharing Semantics When a client opens a file, Andrew caches the file on the local disk of the client's workstation using 64 KB *chunks*.

However, it adapts the chunk size on a per-client basis to suit the client's file access pattern. As mentioned earlier in Section 20.5.2, studies conducted in the mid-1990s have reported that chunks of 8 KB were widely used, and the hit ratio in the file cache typically exceeded 0.98. File open/close calls are directed to a user-level process called *Venus*. Venus caches a file when a client opens it, and updates the server's copy when the client closes the file. File read and write operations are performed on the cached copy without involving Venus. Consequently, changes made to a file are not immediately reflected on the server's copy and they are not visible to other clients accessing the file. These file sharing semantics have some features of session semantics; however, Andrew does not maintain multiple versions of a file.

The file copy cached by the Venus process in a node is considered to be valid unless the Venus process is told otherwise. This way, a cached copy of a file may persist across the close operation on the file and the next open operation on it in the same workstation. Cache validation is performed in a server-initiated manner using a mechanism called *callback*. When some file F is cached at client node N_1 because of an open, the server notes this fact in its table. As long as this entry remains in the table, node N_1 is said to have a callback on F. When the copy of F in the server is updated because some client closed F, the server removes N_1's entry from its table and notifies the Venus process in node N_1 that its callback on F has been broken. If some client in N_1 tried to open F in the future, Venus would know that N_1 does not have a callback on F, so it would cache file F once again. Venus maintains two caches—a data cache and a status cache. The status cache is used to service system calls that query file status information. Both caches are managed on an LRU basis.

Path name resolution is performed on a component-by-component basis. Venus maintains a mapping cache, which contains information concerning volumes which have been accessed recently. Since volumes may be migrated, Venus treats this information as a hint and discards it if it turns out to be wrong. During path name resolution, Venus also copies each directory involved in the path name in its cache. Presence of these cached copies may speed up path name resolution in the future.

File servers are multithreaded to prevent them from becoming a bottleneck. A lightweight process package is used to spawn new lightweight processes to handle file requests. Client–server communication is organized by using RPCs.

Features of Coda Coda, which is a successor of the Andrew file system version 2, added two complementary features to achieve high availability—replication and disconnected operation. Coda supports replication of volumes. The collection of servers that have a copy of a volume is known as the volume storage group (VSG). Coda controls use of replicated files through the *read one, write all* policy—only one of the copies needs to be available for reading; however, all copies must be updated at the same time. A multicasting RPC called multiRPC is used for this purpose.

A node enters the disconnected mode of operation when the subset of VSG accessible to it is null. Andrew already supported whole-file caching in a client's node, so a client in the disconnected mode of operation could operate on a file in isolation. The file updates made by this client would be reflected in the file when the client's node is able to connect to the server. Any conflicts with file versions created by other file processing activities in the meanwhile would have to be resolved at this time. This step can be automated in an application-specific manner; however, it may require human intervention in some cases.

Having a single file in cache may not be adequate for disconnected operation, so Coda provides *hoarding* of files. A user can provide a *hoarding database*, which contains path names of important files, to Coda. During a session initiated by the user, Coda uses a prioritized cache management policy to hold some recently accessed files and files named in the hoarding database in the cache of the user's node. This set of files is refined by recomputing their priorities periodically. This way, the cache in the node may contain an adequate set of files when the node becomes disconnected, which would enable meaningful disconnected operation.

20.6.3 GPFS

The *general parallel file system* is a high-performance shared-disk file system for large computing clusters operating under Linux. GPFS uses data striping (see Section 14.3.5) across all disks available in a cluster. Thus, data of a file is written on several disks, which can be read from or written to in parallel. A large-size block, i.e., strip, is used to minimize seek overhead during a file read/write; however, a large disk block may not provide high data transfer rates for small files that would occupy only a small number of strips, so a smaller subblock, which could be as small as $\frac{1}{32}$ of a block, is used for small files.

Locking is used to maintain consistency of file data when processes in several nodes of the cluster access a common file. High parallelism in accessing a common file requires fine-grained locking, whereas low locking overhead requires coarse-grained locking. So GPFS uses a composite approach that works as follows: The first process that performs a write operation on a file is given a lock whose byte range covers the entire file. If no other process accesses the same file, this process does not have to set and reset locks while processing the file. If another process wishes to write into the same file, that process is given a lock with a byte range that covers the bytes it wishes to write, and the byte range in the lock already held by the first process is reduced to exclude those bytes. This way the lock granularity is as coarse as possible, but as fine as necessary, subject to the restriction that the byte range in a lock cannot be smaller than a data block on a disk. Whenever the byte range in a lock is narrowed, updates made on the bytes that are not covered by the new byte range in the lock are flushed to the file. This way, a process acquiring a lock for these bytes would see their latest values.

The locking scheme of GPFS involves a centralized lock manager and a few distributed lock managers, and employs the notion of *lock tokens* to reduce the latency and overhead of locking. The first time some process in a node accesses a file, the centralized lock manager issues a lock token to that node. This token authorizes the node to locally issue locks on the file to other processes in that node, until the lock token is taken away from it. This arrangement avoids repeated traffic between a node and the centralized lock manager for acquiring locks on a file. When a process in some other node wishes to access the same file, the centralized lock manager takes away the lock token from the first node and gives it to the second node. Now, this node can issue locks on that file locally. The data bytes covered by byte ranges in the locks issued by a node can be cached locally at that node; no cache coherence traffic would be generated when these bytes are accessed or updated because no process in another node is permitted to access these bytes.

Race conditions may arise over the metadata of a file, such as the index blocks in the FMT, when several nodes update the metadata concurrently. For example, when two nodes add a pointer each to the same index block in the FMT, one client's update of the block would be lost when another client updates it. To prevent inconsistencies due to race conditions, one of the nodes is designated as the metanode for the file, and all accesses and updates to the file's metadata are made only by the metanode. Other nodes that update the file send their metadata to the metanode and the metanode commits them to the disk.

The list of free disk space can become a performance bottleneck when file processing activities in many nodes need more disk space. The central allocation manager avoids it by partitioning the free space map and giving one partition of the map to each node. A node makes all disk space allocations, using its partition of the map. When the free space in that partition is exhausted, it requests the allocation manager for another partition.

Each node writes a separate journal for recovery. This journal is located in the file system to which the file being processed belongs. When a node fails, other nodes can access its journal and carry out the pending updates. Consistency of the data bytes updated in this manner is implicit because the failed node would have locked the data bytes; these locks are released only after the journal of the failed node is processed.

Communication failures may partition the system. However, file processing activities in individual nodes may not be affected because nodes may be able to access some of the disks. Such operation of the file system can lead to inconsistencies in the metadata. To prevent such inconsistencies, only nodes in one partition should continue file processing and all other nodes must cease file processing. GPFS achieves it as follows: Only nodes in the majority partition, i.e., the partition that contains a majority of the nodes, are allowed to perform file processing at any time. GPFS contains a group services layer that uses heartbeat messages to detect node failures; it notifies a node when the node has fallen out of the majority partition or has become a part of the majority partition once again. However, this notification may itself be delayed indefinitely because of communication failures, so GPFS uses features in the I/O subsystem to prevent those nodes that are not included in the majority partition from accessing any disks. GPFS uses a replication policy to protect against disk failures.

20.6.4 Windows

The file system of the Windows Server 2003 provides two features for data replication and data distribution:

- *Remote differential compression* (RDC) is a protocol for file replication that reduces the file replication and file coherence traffic between servers.
- *DFS namespaces* is a method of forming a virtual tree of folders located on different servers, so that a client located in any node can access these folders.

Replication is organized by using the notion of a *replication group*, which is a group of servers that replicates a group of folders. If a client wishes to access several of these folders, it is made to access them off the same server. The RDC protocol is used to synchronize copies of a replicated folder across servers in its replication group. This protocol transmits only changes made to a file, or only the differences between copies of a file, among different members of a replication group, thereby conserving bandwidth between servers. Copies of a file are synchronized periodically. When a new file is created, cross-file RDC identifies existing files that are similar to the new file, and transmits only differences of the new file from one of these files to members of the replication group. This protocol reduces the bandwidth consumed by the replication operation.

The DFS namespace is created by a system administrator. For every folder in the namespace, the administrator specifies a list of servers that contain a copy of the folder. When a client refers to a shared folder that appears in the namespace, the namespace server is contacted to resolve the name in the virtual tree. It sends back a *referral* to the client, which contains the list of servers that contain a copy of the folder. The client contacts the first server in this list to access the folder. If this server does not respond and client failback is enabled, the client is notified of this failure and goes on to contact the next server in the list. Thus, if the list of servers contains two servers, the second server acts as a *hot standby* for the first server.

20.7 SUMMARY

A distributed file system (DFS) stores user files in several nodes of a distributed system, hence a process and a file being accessed by it may exist in different nodes. This situation requires a distributed file system to use special techniques so that a user (1) need not know where a file is located, (2) can perform file processing even when link and node failures occur in the system, and (3) can process files efficiently. In this chapter we discussed how distributed file systems fulfill these requirements.

The notion of *transparency* concerns the association between the path name of a file and location of the file—whether a user must know a file's location in order to access it and whether the system can change the location without affecting the file's name. High transparency provides user convenience and also enables a DFS to reduce network traffic by moving a file to a node where it is accessed very frequently. *File sharing semantics* represent another aspect of user convenience. They specify whether the file updates made by a process would be visible to other processes accessing the file concurrently. Three popular file sharing semantics are as follows: In *Unix semantics*, file updates made by a process are visible immediately to all other processes using the file. In *session semantics*, the updates made by a process are visible to only some processes in the same node. In *transaction semantics*, a complete file processing activity is treated as a single *atomic transaction* so that either all file updates made during the activity are reflected in the file or none of them are, and the updates made by a file processing activity are visible to other processes only after the activity completes.

High availability of a file system requires that a file processing activity in a process should not be affected by a transient fault in the node holding the file, which is called the *server node*. The DFS uses a *stateless server* design to provide high availability. The stateless server does not maintain any state information about an ongoing file processing activity. Consequently, a crash of the server node does not disrupt the file processing activity—it can be resumed when the server's operation is restored. However, the stateless design of the server implies that every time a file is accessed, the file server would have to access the directory entry of the file to find its location. The notion of a *hint* is used to improve performance of a stateless file server. A hint is simply a part of DFS state; however, the server is designed in such a manner that it uses a hint if one is available, but proceeds in a stateless manner if a hint is not available.

Performance of a DFS is affected by network latencies when a process and the file processed by it exist in different nodes. A DFS uses the technique of *file caching* to improve its performance. It maintains a copy of a file's data in the node where the process exists, so that accesses to file data are implemented locally in the node rather than over the network. If processes located in different nodes update the same file concurrently, copies of the file would exist in caches in many nodes, so a process may not see the latest value of the data that was updated by another process. This problem is overcome by using *cache coherence* techniques, which prevent accesses to stale file data. However, it causes network traffic for refreshing stale copies of a file's data in caches, which reduces the benefit of file caching. Session semantics eliminate the cache coherence traffic because updates made by a process are not visible outside its node.

TEST YOUR CONCEPTS

20.1 Classify each of the following statements as true or false:

- **a.** Location independence in a distributed file system provides user convenience.
- **b.** The session semantics use multiple-image mutable files.
- **c.** Robustness of a file can be achieved through disk mirroring.
- **d.** File caching has exactly the same effect as file migration, i.e., movement of files among nodes in the system.
- **e.** Directory caching improves file access performance in a distributed file system.
- **f.** Faults that occur in a file server during a file processing activity can be tolerated by using a stateless file server.

20.2 Select the appropriate alternative in each of the following questions:

- **a.** A distributed file system uses file caching to ensure good file access performance. Which file sharing semantics cause the least cache validation overhead?
  - **i.** Session semantics
  - **ii.** Unix semantics
  - **iii.** Transaction semantics.
- **b.** File replication improves
  - **i.** Robustness of a file system
  - **ii.** Recoverability of a file system
  - **iii.** Availability of a file system
  - **iv.** None of (i)–(iii).

EXERCISES

20.1 Discuss how session semantics can be implemented.

20.2 Should a DFS maintain file buffers at a server node or at a client node? What is the influence of this decision on Unix file sharing semantics (see Section 13.10) and session semantics?

20.3 Justify the following statement: "File caching integrates well with session semantics, but not so with Unix semantics."

20.4 Discuss the various techniques discussed in this chapter and in Chapters 13 and 19 that can be used to ensure robustness of a file.

20.5 Discuss how a client should protect itself against failures in a distributed file system using (a) a stateful file server design, (b) a stateless file server design.

20.6 What are the benefits and limitations of spawning multiple threads in a file server to handle file processing activities of different clients? Describe the synchronization requirements of these threads.

20.7 Discuss important issues to be handled during recovery of a failed node in a system that uses file replication to provide availability.

20.8 Discuss how locking can be used to reduce cache validation overhead and enhance scalability of a distributed file system.

BIBLIOGRAPHY

Svobodova (1986) and Levy and Silberschatz (1990) are survey papers on distributed file systems. Comer and Peterson (1986) discusses concepts in naming and discusses name resolution mechanisms in many systems.

Lampson (1983) and Terry (1987) discuss use of hints to improve performance of a distributed file system. Makaroff and Eager (1990) discusses effect of cache sizes on file system performance.

Brownbridge et al. (1982) discusses the Unix United system, which is an early network file system. Sandberg (1987) and Callaghan (2000) discuss the Sun NFS. Satyanarayanan (1990) discusses the Andrew distributed file system, while Kistler and Satyanarayanan (1992) describes the Coda file system. Braam and Nelson (1999) discusses the performance bottlenecks in Coda and Intermezzo, which is a sequel to Coda that incorporates journaling. Russinovich and Solomon (2005) discusses data replication and data distribution features of the Windows file system.

Application processes running in different nodes of a cluster of computer systems may make parallel accesses to files. Thekkath et al. (1997) discusses a scalable distributed file system for clusters of computer systems. Preslan et al. (2000) describes fault tolerance in a cluster file system through journaling. Carns et al. (2000) discusses a parallel file system that provides high bandwidth for parallel file accesses to data in shared files. Schmuck and Haskin (2002) discusses use of shared disks in a parallel file system and describes distributed synchronization and fault tolerance techniques.

1. Braam, P. J., and P. A. Nelson (1999): "Removing bottlenecks in distributed file systems: Coda and InterMezzo as examples," *Proceedings of Linux Expo, 1999*.
2. Brownbridge, D. R., L. F. Marshall, and B. Randell (1982): "The Newcastle Connection or UNIXes of the World Unite!," *Software—Practice and Experience*, **12** (12), 1147–1162.
3. Callaghan, B. (2000): *NFS Illustrated*, Addison-Wesley, Reading, Mass.
4. Carns, P. H., W. B. Ligon III, R. B. Ross, and R. Thakur (2000): "PVFS: A parallel file system for Linux Clusters," *2000 Extreme Linux Workshop*.
5. Comer, D., and L. L. Peterson (1986): "A model of name resolution in distributed mechanisms," *Proceedings of the 6th International Conference on Distributed Computing Systems*, 509–514.
6. Ghemawat, S., H. Gobioff, and S. T. Leung (2003): "The Google file system," *Proceedings of the 19th ACM Symposium on Operating System Principles*, 29–43.

7. Gray, C. G., and D. R. Cheriton (1989): "Leases: an efficient fault-tolerant mechanism for distributed file cache consistency," *Proceedings of the 12th ACM Symposium on Operating Systems Principles*, 202–210.
8. Kistler, J. J., and M. Satyanarayanan (1992): "Disconnected operation in the Coda file system," *ACM Transactions on Computer Systems*, **10**, 1, 3–25.
9. Lampson, B. W. (1983): "Hints for computer system designers," *Proceedings of the 9th Symposium of Operating Systems Principles*, 33–48.
10. Levy, E., and A. Silberschatz (1990): "Distributed File Systems: Concepts and Examples," *Computing Surveys*, **22** (4), 321–374.
11. Melamed, A. S. (1987): "Performance analysis of Unix-based network file systems," *IEEE Micro*, 25–38.
12. Makaroff, D. J., and D. L. Eager (1990): "Disk cache performance for distributed systems," *Proceedings of the 10th International Conference on Distributed Computing Systems*, 212–219.
13. Preslan, K. W., A. P. Barry, J. Brassow, R. Cattelan, A. Manthei, E. Nygaard, S. V. Oort, D. Teigland, M Tilstra, M. O'Keefe, G. Erickson, and M. Agarwal (2000): "Implementing journaling in a Linux shared disk file system," *Proceedings of the 7th IEEE Symposium on Mass Storage Systems*, 351–378.
14. Russinovich, M. E., and D. A. Solomon (2005): *Microsoft Windows Internals,* 4th ed., Microsoft Press, Redmond, Wash.
15. Sandberg, R. (1987): *The Sun Network File System: Design, Implementation, and experience*, Sun Microsystems, Mountain View, Calif.
16. Satyanarayanan, M. (1990): "Scalable, secure, and highly available distributed file access," *Computer*, **23** (5), 9–21.
17. Schmuck, F., and R. Haskin (2002): "GPFS: A shared-disk file system for large computing clusters," *Proceedings of the First USENIX Conference on File and Storage Technologies*, 231–244.
18. Svobodova, L. (1986): "File servers for network-based distributed systems," *Computing Surveys*, **16** (4), 353–398.
19. Terry, D. B. (1987): "Caching hints in distributed systems," *IEEE Transactions on Software Engineering*, **13** (1), 48–54.
20. Thekkath, C. A., T. Mann, and E. K. Lee (1997): "Frangipani: A scalable DFS," *Proceedings of the 16th ACM symposium on Operating System Principles*, 224–237.

Chapter 21

Distributed System Security

Processes in a distributed OS use the network for accessing distant resources and for communicating with other processes. The network may include public communication channels or computer systems called *communication processors* that are not under control of the distributed OS. Hence an intruder located in a communication processor may be able to corrupt interprocess messages to disrupt operation of processes or fabricate messages to masquerade as a user and access his resources.

A distributed OS employs *message security* techniques to prevent intruders from tampering with interprocess messages. *Encryption* forms the backbone of these techniques; however, use of encryption implies that cryptographic attacks must be prevented and processes must know what encryption keys to use while communicating with other processes. These issues are tackled either through use of *public key encryption* or through use of *session keys*, which are securely distributed to communicating processes by *key distribution centers*. To prevent masquerading, the distributed OS provides trusted third-party authentication means for use while sending messages or using resources.

In this chapter, we discuss message security and authentication techniques of distributed systems. We also discuss how integrity and authenticity of data is ensured through *message authentication codes* and *digital signatures*, respectively.

21.1 ISSUES IN DISTRIBUTED SYSTEM SECURITY

We term the nodes that are directly under control of the distributed OS as *secure nodes*. They contain resources and offer services to users and their processes. As shown in Figure 21.1, a user process accesses a remote resource through a message sent to the resource coordinator process. Such a message may travel over public networks and pass through computer systems called *communication processors*, which operate under local operating systems. Communication processors employ a *store-and-forward* model to route a message to its destination. Thus, messages between processes are exposed to observation and interference

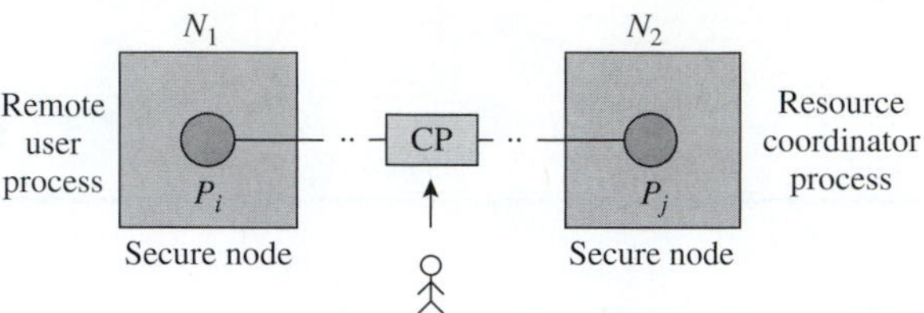

Figure 21.1 Security threats in a network.

by external entities. This situation raises new security threats that do not arise in a conventional system.

Security threats in distributed operating systems are of four kinds:

1. *Leakage:* Release of message contents to unauthorized user(s).
2. *Tampering:* Modification of message contents.
3. *Stealing:* Use of system resources without authorization.
4. *Denial of service to authorized users:* This threat can be in the form of willful destruction of system resources not amounting to stealing, i.e., destruction without any gain to the perpetrator, or disruption of access to resources.

Leakage and tampering are termed threats to *message security*. Tampering may be employed to modify the text of a message, which is a threat to its *integrity*, or modify the identity of its sender, which is a threat to its *authenticity*. An intruder can perform stealing by masquerading through tampering. Denial of service can be achieved by tampering with the text of a message or ids of its source and destination processes, or by masquerading. These security threats are addressed through two means:

- *Message security techniques:* Special techniques are employed to thwart attacks on messages.
- *Authentication of remote users:* Trusted means are provided to authenticate remote users.

Attacks on integrity and authenticity are addressed through a combination of these two means.

21.1.1 Security Mechanisms and Policies

Figure 21.2 shows an arrangement of security mechanisms and policies. *Authentication* in conventional systems has been described earlier in Chapter 15. Authentication in a distributed system has two new facets: The authentication service must be trustworthy and available to all nodes in a system. *Encryption* is used to ensure secrecy and integrity of the authentication and authorization databases. It is also used to implement message security by encoding the text of messages. Processes need to know what encryption keys to use while communicating with other processes. The lower-level mechanism called *key distribution* generates and

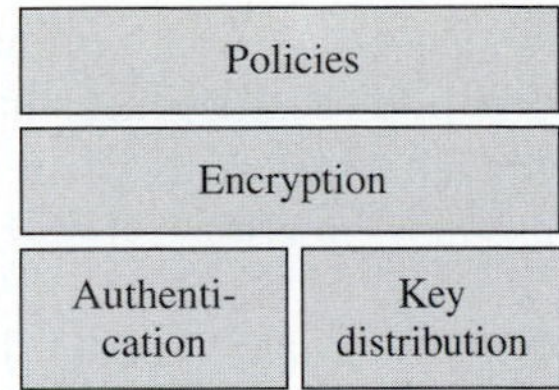

Figure 21.2 Mechanisms and policies for distributed system security.

Table 21.1 Classes of Security Attacks in Distributed Systems

Attack	Description
Eavesdropping	An intruder listens to interprocess messages over the network to obtain information concerning message content or statistical features of messages.
Message tampering	An intruder intercepts messages, alters their contents, and reinserts them into the communication stream.
Message replay	An intruder makes copies of messages exchanged by communicating processes and inserts the copies into the communication stream at a later time as if they were genuine messages being sent at that time.
Masquerading	An intruder is able to pass off as an authorized user of the system while consuming resources, and while sending and receiving messages.

distributes encryption keys for use by communicating processes; it is discussed in Section 21.2.1.

21.1.2 Security Attacks in Distributed Systems

Security attacks in distributed systems, which are typically launched through messages, can be classified into the four classes summarized in Table 21.1. *Eavesdropping* can take various forms like obtaining the content of a message or collecting information about messages exchanged by specific nodes or passing over specific links. In a police or military information system, the latter analyses can be used to reveal or guess identities of communicating entities. *Message tampering* can be used to mislead the recipient of a message. This attack is feasible in a store-and-forward network.

Message replay can be used to achieve a variety of nefarious ends. The recipient of a replayed message may be misled into thinking that messages are being exchanged in real time. If the recipient is a user process, it might be fooled into taking actions that are unnecessary, absurd, or wasteful in terms of resources. It may also be misled into revealing confidential information. If the recipient is a server process, a replayed message may lead to wrong authentication, leading to opportunities for masquerading or stealing of resources.

In *masquerading*, an intruder is able to pass off as an authorized user of the system. The intruder could corrupt or destroy information belonging to the user, or communicate with other processes and trick them into believing that they are communicating with the user.

Passive and Active Attacks Security attacks can be classified into *passive* attacks and *active* attacks. A passive attack does not interfere with the system's functioning in any manner. It neither fabricates messages nor destroys genuine messages. Eavesdropping is an example of a passive attack. An active attack interferes with a system's functioning. Replay, fabrication, modification, and destruction of messages are examples of active attacks. Passive attacks are harder to detect or thwart than active attacks.

21.2 MESSAGE SECURITY

Approaches to message security can be classified into *link-oriented approaches* and *end-to-end approaches*. In a link-oriented approach, security measures are applied at every link of a communication path. This approach tends to be expensive since its cost depends on the number of links over which a message travels. For example, if a message between process P_i located at node N_1 and process P_j located at node N_3 passes along the path N_1-N_2-N_3, it has to incur security overhead for links N_1-N_2 and N_2-N_3. In the end-to-end approach, security measures can be employed selectively by nodes or processes in the system. This feature permits users to employ security measures with varying degrees of cost and sophistication. In the following discussion, we will assume that end-to-end measures are used.

We describe three approaches to message security. They involve encryption using public keys, private keys, and session keys, respectively. Table 21.2 summarizes their features.

Private Key Encryption Private key encryption (also called *secret key encryption*) is the classical approach based on symmetric keys. Each process P_i has a *private key* V_i known to itself and to a few other processes in the system. A process sending a message to P_i must encrypt it by using V_i. On receiving a message, P_i decrypts it by using V_i. The main advantage of private key encryption is that the number of encryption keys in the system is limited to n, where n is the number of communicating entities in the system. Since all messages intended for process P_i are encrypted with the same key, P_i need not know the identity of the sender of a message in order to read the message.

Private key encryption suffers from a few drawbacks. Each sender process needs to know the private key of P_i. Thus, many processes know the private key of a process, and an intruder may discover it as a result of somebody's negligence. The private key is exposed to intruder attacks over a long period of time, so chances of a successful attack on the private key increase with time; however, it is not possible to change the private key of a process because it is known to many other processes in the system.

Table 21.2 Encryption Techniques Used for Message Security

Technique	Description
Private key encryption	Employs symmetric encryption. A process P_i has a unique encryption key V_i called the *private key*. All messages sent to P_i must be encrypted by using V_i. Process P_i decrypts them by using V_i. The private key of a process is exposed to intruder attacks over the entire lifetime of a process.
Public key encryption	Employs asymmetric encryption. A process P_i has a pair of unique keys (U_i, V_i). U_i is the *public key*, which can be made known to all processes in the system, whereas V_i is the *private key*, which is kept secret. Messages to P_i are encrypted by using U_i, but P_i decrypts them by using V_i. The Rivest–Shamir–Adelman (RSA) algorithm is widely used to generate the pair of keys for a process. The private key of a process is not exposed to intruder attacks.
Session key encryption	A pair of communicating processes (P_i, P_j) is assigned a *session key* SK_{ij} when they begin a communication session. The session key is used for symmetric encryption of all messages exchanged during the session. The session key has a smaller lifetime than a private or public key, so it suffers less exposure to intruder attacks.

User processes do not know each other's private keys, so private key encryption is not useful for security of interprocess messages in general. OS processes know private keys of user processes, so they use private key encryption while communicating with user processes. As discussed in Section 21.2.1, this feature is used in the implementation of key distribution centers. User processes need to use some other encryption scheme while communicating with one another.

Public Key Encryption Each process P_i has a pair of keys (U_i, V_i). U_i is the *public key* of P_i, which can be made known to all processes in the system. V_i is the *private key* known only to process P_i. U_i and V_i are chosen such that

- V_i cannot be guessed from U_i, and
- For any message m

$$D_{V_i}(E_{U_i}(P_m)) = P_m \quad \forall i \qquad \textbf{(21.1)}$$

where P_m is the plaintext form of message m and E, D are the encryption and decryption functions, respectively (see Section 15.4).

When P_j wishes to send a message to P_i, it obtains P_i's public key from the OS. Transmission of the message takes place as follows:

1. Process P_j encrypts the message with the public key of the destination process P_i, i.e., with U_i.
2. The encrypted message, i.e., $E_{U_i}(P_m)$, is transmitted over the network and is received by process P_i.

3. Process P_i decrypts the received message with its own private key, i.e., with V_i. Thus, it performs $D_{V_i}(E_{U_i}(P_m))$, which yields P_m.

The Rivest–Shamir–Adelman (RSA) encryption algorithm is used to generate pairs of keys (U_i, V_i) that satisfy Eq. (21.1). Let (u, v) be such a pair of keys. Given two numbers x and y, both smaller than a chosen integer number n, encryption and decryption using u and v, respectively, are performed as follows:

$$E_u(x) = x^u \bmod n$$

$$D_v(y) = y^v \bmod n$$

To encrypt and decrypt a message m, the RSA algorithm is used as a block cipher with a block size s, which is chosen such that $2^s < n$, the chosen number. x is now the number formed by the bit string found in a block of P_m, the plaintext form of message m, and y is the number formed by the bit string in the corresponding block of C_m, the ciphertext form of message m. This way, $x < 2^s$ and $y < 2^s$, so each of them is smaller than n, as required.

The RSA algorithm chooses n as the product of two large prime numbers p and q. Typically, p and q are 100 digits each, which makes n a 200-digit number. Assuming u and v to be the public and private keys, to satisfy Eq. (21.1) v should be relatively prime to $(p-1) \times (q-1)$ [i.e., v and $(p-1) \times (q-1)$ should not have any common factors except 1], and u should satisfy the relation

$$u \times v \bmod [(p-1) \times (q-1)] = 1$$

Choice of u and v as the public and private keys implies that a standard value of n is used in the system. Alternatively, the pair (u, n) can be used as the public key and the pair (v, n) can be used as the private key of a process. It will permit different values of n to be used for different pairs of processes.

An attack on the RSA cipher can succeed if n can be factored into p and q. However, it is estimated that factorization of a 200 digit number, which would be needed to break the cipher, would need 4 billion years on a computer that can perform 1 million operations per second.

Public key encryption suffers from some drawbacks when compared with private key encryption. Keys used in public key encryption are approximately an order of magnitude larger in size than private keys. This is unavoidable since public keys have to be large to make factorization prohibitively expensive. The encryption and decryption operations are also very expensive when compared with symmetric encryption; in many situations, these operations are up to 1000 times slower. Therefore it is not practical to use public key encryption for interprocess messages. Instead, it is used to securely communicate a session key to a pair of processes that intend to start a communication session. This aspect is discussed in the next section.

Session Keys Processes P_i and P_j obtain a *session key*, also called a *conversation key*, for one session of communication. This key is used for symmetric encryption during the session and is discarded at the end of the session. If the processes wish to enter into another session sometime in the future, they obtain a fresh session key. This approach limits exposure of an encryption key to an intruder, thereby reducing the risk of a successful attack on the cryptographic system.

21.2.1 Distribution of Encryption Keys

A process needs to know what encryption key to use while communicating with another process. The OS contains an interactive service called a *key distribution center* (KDC) to provide this information. Figure 21.3 shows a schematic of a key distribution center. A process P_i makes a request to the KDC for an encryption key to communicate with a process P_j. The KDC returns a key k. P_i uses this key to encrypt a message m to be sent to process P_j. If processes use public keys to communicate with one another, the KDC maintains a directory containing public keys of all entities in the system. If processes use session keys, the KDC does not posses a directory; it generates a new session key on demand.

An important issue in the KDC schematic is the protocol used for securely passing the keys. When a public key is requested, it needs to be passed only to the requester. When a session key is requested by a process P_i to communicate with a process P_j, the key has to be passed to both P_i and P_j. However, P_j is unaware that P_i is interested in setting up a session with it, so the KDC does not send the session key directly to P_j. Instead, P_i can send the session key to P_j along with its first message. These key transmission protocols are described in the following.

Distribution of Public Keys The following messages are exchanged between P_i, the requesting process, and the KDC:

$$\begin{aligned} &1.\ P_i \rightarrow \text{KDC} &:& \quad E_{U_{kdc}}(P_i, P_j) \\ &2.\ \text{KDC} \rightarrow P_i &:& \quad E_{U_i}(P_j, U_j) \end{aligned} \qquad \textbf{(21.2)}$$

P_i sends its own id and P_j, the id of the intended destination process, to the KDC. This message is encrypted with U_{kdc}, the public key of KDC. The KDC replies by sending U_j, the public key of P_j, encrypted with the public key of P_i. Here, the encryption is not used to protect confidentiality of P_j's key, because an intruder can legitimately obtain this key by itself by making a request to the KDC; the purpose of encryption is to prevent an intruder from tampering with messages

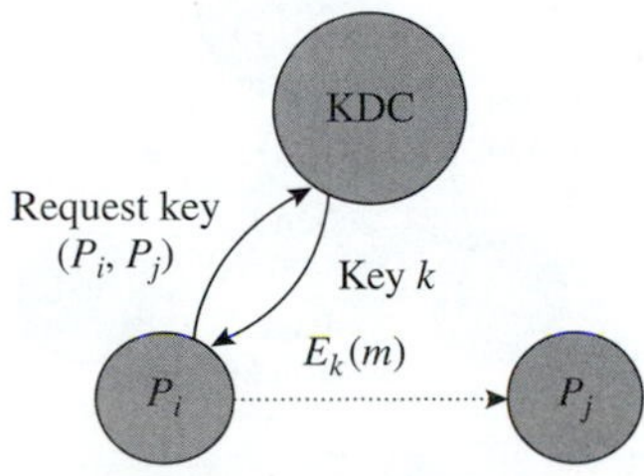

Figure 21.3 Key distribution center (KDC) in a distributed OS.

between P_i and the KDC to perpetrate a denial-of-service attack. In the absence of encryption, an intruder could have tampered with P_i's message to the KDC and changed P_j to some P_k, so that P_i would not obtain P_j's key, or the intruder could have tampered with the KDC's message to P_i and changed P_j's key that is being passed to P_i. When encryption is used, both the KDC and P_i would recognize tampered messages and discard them.

Distribution of Session Keys When P_i wishes to obtain a session key to communicate with P_j, the session key should be made known to both P_i and P_j. Figure 21.4 illustrates how it is achieved in three steps. In the first step, P_i sends a request message containing its own id and the id of P_j to the KDC. The KDC allocates a session key $SK_{i,j}$ for the session between P_i and P_j and sends it to P_j. Its reply to P_j also contains an encrypted unit containing $SK_{i,j}$, which can be decrypted only by P_j. P_i passes this encrypted unit to P_j in its first message, or in a special message intended for this purpose. P_j obtains $SK_{i,j}$ by decrypting this unit, and keeps it for use during the session with P_i.

In a private key system, this exchange can be implemented as follows:

$$\begin{array}{lll} 1.\ P_i \rightarrow \text{KDC} & : & P_i,\ P_j \\ 2.\ \text{KDC} \rightarrow P_i & : & E_{V_i}(P_j,\ SK_{i,j},\ E_{V_j}(P_i, SK_{i,j})) \\ 3.\ P_i \rightarrow P_j & : & E_{V_j}(P_i, SK_{i,j}), E_{SK_{i,j}}(<message>) \end{array} \quad \textbf{(21.3)}$$

In the second step, the KDC sends a reply to P_i, which is encrypted with P_i's private key. The reply contains the session key $SK_{i,j}$ and $E_{V_j}(P_i,\ SK_{i,j})$, which is the session key encrypted by using P_j's private key. P_i decrypts the KDC's message with its own private key to obtain the session key $SK_{i,j}$. Decryption also yields $E_{V_j}(P_i,\ SK_{i,j})$. P_i copies this unit in the first message it sends to P_j. When P_j decrypts this unit, it obtains $SK_{i,j}$, which it uses to decrypt all messages from P_i.

In a public key system, session keys need not be distributed by the KDC—a sender process can itself choose a session key. It merely has to communicate the session key securely to the destination process, which can be achieved through encryption by using the public key of the destination process. Thus a process P_i

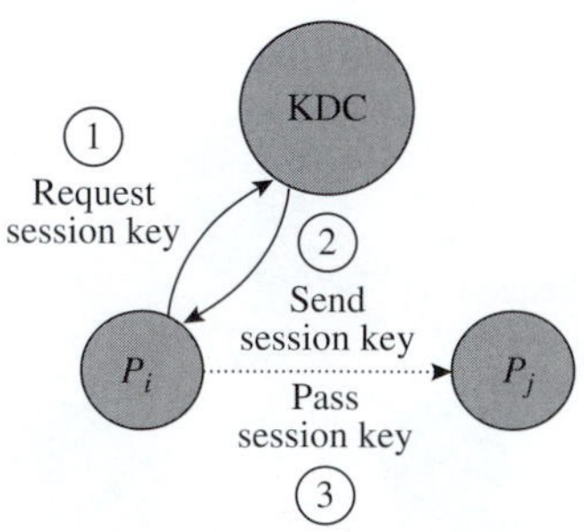

Figure 21.4 Distribution of session keys.

can employ the following protocol to communicate a session key to process P_j:

$$\begin{array}{lll} 1.\ P_i \rightarrow \text{KDC} & : & E_{U_{kdc}}(P_i,\ P_j) \\ 2.\ KDC \rightarrow P_i & : & E_{U_i}(P_j,\ U_j) \\ 3.\ P_i \rightarrow P_j & : & E_{U_j}(P_i, SK_{i,j}),\ E_{SK_{i,j}}(<message>) \end{array} \quad \textbf{(21.4)}$$

The first two steps of this protocol are identical with the first two steps of protocol (21.2); they provide P_i with the public key of P_j. Now, P_i itself generates a session key $SK_{i,j}$ and passes the session key and its first message to P_j in Step 3.

21.2.2 Preventing Message Replay Attacks

In a *message replay attack*, an intruder simply copies messages passing over the network and "plays them back" in the future. A replayed message may mislead its recipient into taking wrong or duplicate actions which may affect data consistency or reveal confidential information. For example, in a system using session keys, an intruder could replay the message of Step 3 in Protocol (21.3) or Protocol (21.4). When P_j receives the replayed message, it would be tricked into thinking that P_i is communicating with it using the session key $SK_{i,j}$. When process P_j responds to this message, the intruder would replay the next copied message. In this manner, it could replay an entire session.

The recipient of a message can employ the *challenge–response protocol* to check whether the message exchange is taking place in real time. Steps of the challenge–response protocol are as follows:

- *Challenge:* When a process P_j receives a message originated by a process P_i, it throws a challenge to P_i to prove that it is engaged in a message exchange with it in real time. The challenge is in the form of a message containing a *challenge string*, which is encrypted in such a manner that only process P_i can decrypt it.
- *Response:* On receiving the challenge message, process P_i is expected to decrypt it, obtain the challenge string, transform it in a manner expected by P_j, encrypt the result so that only P_j can decrypt it, and send it back to P_j.
- *Detect:* On receiving a reply message, process P_j decrypts the message and checks whether the decrypted contents match its expectations. A mismatch indicates that it is subject to a replay attack.

A challenger could send a number as the challenge string, and expect a reply that is the result of some simple tranformation of that number, like adding 1 to it; however, the challenger should use a different number in every challenge so that a replay of an old conversation would not provide the expected reply. Two choices of the challenge string are a random number or the current time of the day. The actual value of a challenge string is immaterial, so it is called a *nonce*.

The challenge–response protocol should be used in every situation where a message replay attack would be meaningful. As an example, consider the distribution of session keys through Protocol (21.3). An intruder could save the message of Step 3, and replay it sometime in the future to trick process P_j into starting a conversation with it using $SK_{i,j}$. So, before using the session key obtained in Step 3, process P_j would use the challenge–response protocol to ensure that the conversation is taking place in real time:

$$4.\ P_j \rightarrow P_i \quad : \quad E_{SK_{i,j}}(n)$$

$$5.\ P_i \rightarrow P_j \quad : \quad E_{SK_{i,j}}(n+1)$$

Here n is a nonce. P_i is expected to obtain n through decryption, using the session key $SK_{i,j}$, add 1 to it, encrypt the result by using $SK_{i,j}$, and send it back to P_j. An intruder would not be able to perform these actions correctly, since it does not know $SK_{i,j}$. In fact, P_i's ability to extract n from P_j's message implicitly verifies its identity. This property is useful in mutual authentication discussed in the next session.

21.2.3 Mutual Authentication

To defeat masquerading attacks, processes involved in a communication session should validate each other's identity at the start of the session. Recall from the previous section that the challenge–response protocol implicitly verifies the identity of the process that responds to a chellenge, so it can be employed for this purpose. Consider protocol (21.4), which is used to select session keys in a public key system. In Step 3, P_i sends the session key to P_j in a message that is encrypted by using the public key of P_j. In principle, any process could fabricate such a message and trick process P_j into thinking that it is engaging in a session with process P_i. So P_j must authenticate P_i before it engages in a session with it. P_j can achieve it as in the following protocol, whose first three steps are identical with protocol (21.4):

$$1.\ P_i \rightarrow \text{KDC} \quad : \quad E_{U_{kdc}}(P_i,\ P_j)$$

$$2.\ \text{KDC} \rightarrow P_i \quad : \quad E_{U_i}(P_j,\ U_j)$$

$$3.\ P_i \rightarrow P_j \quad : \quad E_{U_j}(P_i,\ SK_{i,j})$$

$$4.\ P_j \rightarrow P_i \quad : \quad E_{U_i}(P_j,\ n)$$

$$5.\ P_i \rightarrow P_j \quad : \quad E_{U_j}(n+1)$$

$$6.\ P_i \rightarrow P_j \quad : \quad E_{SK_{i,j}}(<message>)$$

In Step 4, P_j sends a nonce n encrypted with the public key of P_i. The identity of P_i is verified by its ability to decrypt this message, extract the nonce, and transform it in the expected manner. Note that in Step 4, P_j must not encrypt its message by using the session key $SK_{i,j}$, as the intruder would be able to decrypt such a message if he had fabricated the message in Step 3!

21.3 AUTHENTICATION OF DATA AND MESSAGES

Authenticity of data requires that a process should be capable of verifying that data was originated or sent by a claimed person or process and that it has not been tampered with by an intruder. The latter aspect implies *integrity* of data.

Integrity of data is ensured as follows: When data d is originated or is to be transmitted, a special one-way hash function h is used to compute a hash value v. This hash value, also called a *message digest*, has a fixed length irrespective of the size of data. Apart from the properties of one-way functions described earlier in Section 15.4.1, this special one-way hash function has the property that a *birthday attack* is infeasible; i.e., given the hash value v of data d, it is impractical to construct another data d' whose hash value would also be v. The data and the hash value are stored and transmitted as a pair $<d, v>$. To check the authenticity of d, its hash value is computed afresh by using h, and it is compared with v. Following from the special property of h mentioned above, data d is considered to be in its original form if the two match; otherwise, d has been tampered with. For this scheme to work, the value v should itself be protected against tampering or substitution by an intruder; otherwise, an intruder could substitute a pair $<d, v>$ by another pair $<d', v'>$ and mislead other processes into thinking that data d' is genuine. Accordingly, the person or process originating or transmitting d encrypts v or the pair $<d, v>$, using its own encryption key, so that tampering or substitution of v can be detected. Note that it is less expensive to encrypt v rather than $<d, v>$.

Authenticity requires one more check—verify whether v or $<d, v>$ was encrypted by the claimed person or process. This check is made by using a *certification authority*, which provides information concerning encryption keys used by persons or processes in a secure manner. Details of this check are described in the following.

21.3.1 Certification Authorities and Digital Certificates

A certification authority (CA) assigns public and private keys to an entity, whether a person or a process, after ascertaining its identity by using some means of physical verification. The keys are valid for a specific period of time. The certification authority also acts like a key distribution center discussed in Section 21.2.1: It keeps a record of all keys assigned by it, and when a process requests it for the public key of some person or process, it issues a *public key certificate* which includes the following information:

- Serial number of the certificate
- Owner's distinguished name (DN), which consists of the DNS name of the owner and the owner's name, unit, locality, state, and country in a textual form.
- Identifying information of owner, such as address
- Owner's public key

- Date of issue and date of expiry, and the issuer's distinguished name
- Digital signature on the above information by the certification authority

A number of certification authorities could operate in parallel. A server would obtain a certificate from one of these. If a client knows which certification authority a server is registered with, it can request the certification authority for the server's public key certificate. Alternatively, if it knows the IP address of the server, it can request the server to forward its own public key certificate.

The purpose of asking for the certificate of an entity is to obtain its public key for communicating with it. However, before the receiver of the certificate uses the key to communicate with the entity, it has to ensure that the certificate is genuine and belongs to the entity with which it wishes to communicate; i.e., it is not subject to a security attack called the *man-in-the-middle* attack. In this attack, an intruder masquerades as a server. When a client requests the server for the server's digital certificate, the intruder intercepts the message and sends a forged certificate containing its own public key to the client. Now, if it can intercept subsequent messages from the client to the server, it can read those messages by using its own private key. If it so desires, it can initiate a conversation with the genuine server, this time masquerading as the client, and pass on the client's messages to the server after reading them. Neither the client nor the server would be able to discover that they are subject to a successful man-in-the-middle attack.

The public key certificate contains many items of information that are used to prevent such attacks. The certificate is digitally signed by the certification authority. The client can use this digital signature to ensure that the certificate has not been tampered with or forged. (We discuss details of digital certificates in Section 21.3.2.) For this, it requires the public key of the certification authority that issued the certificate. If it does not already know this key, it can request a higher-order certification authority for a certificate of this certification authority. Once genuineness of the certificate has been established, it can check whether the certificate is valid by checking whether the current date falls within the validity period of the certificate. If it knows the IP address of the server, it can check that against the IP address information mentioned in the certificate. It begins exchanging messages with the server only if all these checks succeed.

21.3.2 Message Authentication Codes and Digital Signatures

A *message authentication code* (MAC) is used to check the integrity of data. A process that originates or transmits data d obtains MAC_d, the message authentication code of d, as follows: It generates a message digest v for d through a one-way hashing function. It encrypts v by using an encryption key that is known only to itself and to the intended recipient of d. The result is MAC_d. It now stores or transmits the pair $<d, MAC_d>$. Only the intended recipient of d can check and verify the integrity of d.

A *digital signature* is used to verify authenticity of data. A person or process that originates or transmits data d obtains v from d as mentioned above. It now obtains DS_d, the digital signature of d, by encrypting v and, optionally, a timestamp, by using its own private key. The pair $< d, DS_d >$ is now stored or transmitted. Any process that wishes to check the authenticity of d decrypts DS_d by using the public key of the originator of d. Successful decryption validates the integrity of d and also identifies its originator or sender. This identification is nonrepudiable; i.e., the identified originator or sender cannot deny having created or sent the data, because the data was encrypted by using the private key of the originator or sender, which is known only to itself. The digital signature can also be used to detect any modifications of data after the data was created or sent by a process.

Figure 21.5 illustrates steps in the use of a digital signature. The sender applies a one-way hash function to the text of a message to obtain a message digest. He signs the message digest by encrypting it with his private key. This digital signature is added at the end of the message text before sending the message. The recipient applies the same one-way hash function to the message text received by it to obtain its message digest. It now obtains a public key certificate of the sender of the message, and uses the public key contained in it to decrypt the digital signature. This step yields the message digest that was computed by the sender. The recipient compares this message digest with its own message digest. The message is authentic only if the two match and the timestamp in the digital signature is within the validity period of the public key certificate.

21.4 THIRD-PARTY AUTHENTICATION

An open system uses standard, well-specified interfaces with other systems. A process in any node with matching interfaces can request access to resources and services of an open system. This fact gives rise to an obvious problem in authentication—how does a server know whether a process wishing to act as its client was created by an authorized user? One solution is to require each server to authenticate every user through a password. This approach is inconvenient since each server would have to possess a systemwide authentication database and each user would be authenticated several times while using the system. An alternative is to use a third-party authenticator and a secure arrangement by which the authenticator can introduce an authorized user to a server. This way each server does not have to authenticate each user.

We discuss two protocols for third-party authentication in a distributed system. The Kerberos protocol employs an authentication database, whereas the *secure sockets layer* (SSL) protocol performs authentication in a decentralized manner.

21.4.1 Kerberos

Kerberos is a third-party authenticator developed in project Athena at MIT for use in an open system environment. It enables a user to prove his identity to the

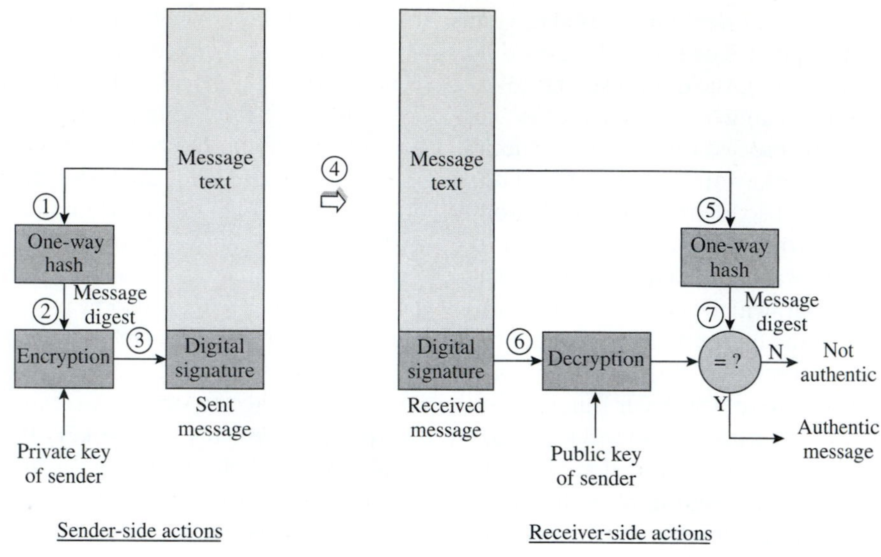

Step	Action	Description
1.	Message digest of message text	A one-way hash function is applied to the message text to produce a *message digest*, which is a bit string of a standard length.
2.	Create digital signature	The message digest and a timestamp are encrypted by using the private key of the sender. The result of encryption is the digital signature.
3.	Append signature	The digital signature is added at the end of the message text.
4.	Transmission	The message consisting of the message text and the digital signature is transmitted to the destination.
5.	Message digest of received text	The same one-way hash function as used in the sender is applied to the message text to produce a message digest.
6.	Decryption of digital signature	The digital signature at the end of the message is extracted and decrypted by using the public key of the sender.
7.	Authenticity check	The message digest produced in Step 5 and the result of decryption in Step 6 are compared. The message is authentic if the two are identical.

Figure 21.5 Message authenticity through digital signature.

servers in an open system without being subject to repeated authentication. A user is authenticated at log in time using a password. The authentication service issues *tickets* to an authenticated user; each ticket is like a capability—it grants a privilege to access one server. The user presents a ticket to a server whenever it wishes to use its service. The server provides the service if the ticket is valid. Private keys are assigned to users and servers. A user's key is used to encrypt messages from Kerberos to the user's processes, while a server's key is used to encrypt the tickets for the server. Session keys are used to ensure message security. They are generated by using a schematic similar to Figure 21.4. To limit exposure of a session key to intruders, it is valid for only a limited amount of time. Timestamps are used to implement this aspect and to foil message replay attacks. Hence nodes in the system must contain loosely synchronized clocks.

A *client* is a process that operates on a user's computer and requests remote services on behalf of the user. When a client C wishes to use the services of a server S_j, it creates a new *authenticator* and presents a *ticket* for S_j and the authenticator to S_j. The ticket is used to communicate the session key to the server in a secure manner, while the authenticator is used to prevent message replay attacks. The ticket contains the client and server ids, i.e., C and S_j; the session key assigned to the communication session between C and S_j; a *timestamp* indicating when the ticket was created; and the *lifetime* of the ticket, i.e., its expiry time. It is valid only during the time period starting at *timestamp* and ending at *lifetime*. Typically this period is about 8 hours. This arrangement limits exposure of the session key to intruder attacks. The authenticator presented by C contains C's id and address, and a timestamp encrypted by using the session key.

The server decrypts the ticket by using its own key. It checks the timestamp and lifetime of the ticket to ensure that the ticket is valid. It now extracts the session key and uses it to decrypt the authenticator. It checks the timestamp in the authenticator to ensure that the request has originated in real time and within the validity period of the ticket. It performs the service requested by the client only if all these checks succeed. Thus, an intruder cannot replay authenticators and tickets to obtain a service.

Working of Kerberos The Kerberos system has two main components: *Kerberos authentication server* (KAS), and *ticket granting server* (TGS). KAS authenticates a user at log in time, using an authentication database and provides him with a ticket to TGS. TGS enables a client to obtain tickets to other servers in the system. A user achieves use of servers through a three-stage protocol. Figure 21.6 illustrates various steps in the protocol. n_1, n_2, and n_3 are nonces.

1. *Initial authentication:* The user is authenticated at log in time as follows:

1.1	User $\rightarrow$ C	:	U, *password*
1.2	C $\rightarrow$ KAS	:	U, TGS, n_1
1.3	KAS $\rightarrow$ C	:	$E_{V_U}(n_1, SK_{U,TGS}, T_{TGS})$

The user submits his id and password to the client in Step 1.1. In Step 1.2, the client forwards the user id to KAS. It also encloses a nonce n_1 to authenticate KAS. This message is a request for a ticket to TGS. Note that the user's password is not passed to KAS. This fact avoids its exposure over the network. It also implies that authentication is not performed by KAS; it is actually performed by C in an interesting manner described later. In Step 1.3, KAS uses the user id U to retrieve V_U, the private key of U, from the authentication database and uses it to encrypt its reply to C. $SK_{U,TGS}$ is a session key for the session between the user and TGS, and T_{TGS} is a ticket for TGS encrypted with the key of TGS. T_{TGS} is also called a *ticket granting ticket* (TGT).

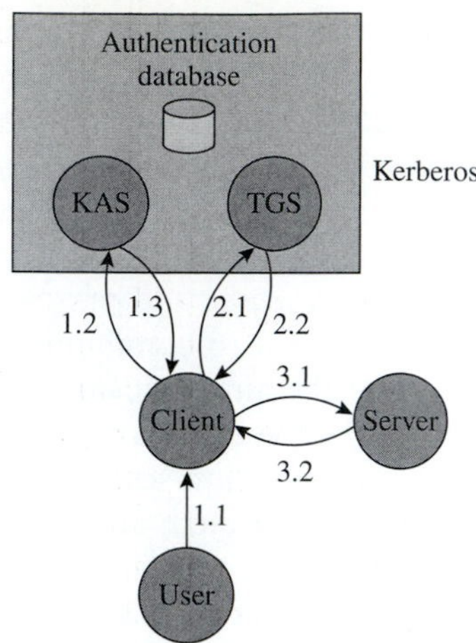

Figure 21.6 Kerberos.

C has to decrypt the reply from KAS by using the key V_U to obtain $SK_{U,TGS}$ and T_{TGS}. This step authenticates the user as follows: V_U, the private key of the user, satisfies the relation $V_U = f(password)$, where f is a one-way function known to C. C obtains V_U by applying f to *password*. It now decrypts the reply received from KAS by using this key. Decryption would be unsuccessful if the password supplied by the user is invalid. In this case C cannot extract T_{TGS} from the reply sent by KAS, so the user cannot use any services or resources in the system.

2. *Obtaining a ticket for a server:* When a user wishes to use a server, C obtains a ticket for the server, using the following protocol:

2.1	C → TGS	:	$<Server\_id>, T_{TGS}$, AU, n_2
2.2	TGS → C	:	$E_{SK_{U,TGS}}(n_2, T_{<Server\_id>}, SK_{U,<Server\_id>}, <Server\_id>)$

where <*Server_id*> is the name of the server that C wishes to use, AU is an authenticator, $SK_{U,Server\_id}$ is a session key for the session between the client and the desired server, and T_{Server_id} is the ticket for the desired server, encrypted by using the key of the server. Before replying to the client, TGS verifies that the ticket presented by the client is valid and that the request has originated in real time and within the validity period of the ticket.

3. *Obtaining a service:* When user U makes a service request, C generates an authenticator and a nonce and exchanges the following messages with the server:

3.1	C → Server	:	$T_{<Server\_id>}, AU, E_{SK_{U,<Server\_id>}}(<service\ request>, n_3)$
3.2	Server → C	:	$E_{SK_{U,<Server\_id>}}(n_3)$

The server performs the service if it finds that the ticket is valid, and the request originated in real time and within the validity period of the ticket. It returns the nonce n_3 to the client so that the client can authenticate it, if it so desires.

21.4.2 Secure Sockets Layer (SSL)

SSL is a message security protocol providing authentication and communication privacy. It works on top of a reliable transport protocol such as the TCP/IP. Its successor, the *transport layer security* (TLS) protocol, is based on SSL 3.0; we discuss features that are common to both. When a client wishes to communicate with a server, the *SSL handshake protocol* is used before message exchange can start. It uses RSA public key encryption to authenticate the server and optionally authenticate the client, and generates symmetric session keys for message exchange between the client and the server. Actual message exchange is performed through the *SSL record protocol*, which performs symmetric encryption of messages and transmits them over the network. Thus, message communication between the client and the server is reliable because of the transport protocol, secure because of authentication performed by the handshake protocol, and private because of encryption performed by the record protocol. Authenticity of data is ensured through a *digital signature* on a message. If mere integrity checking is desired, it is provided through a *message authentication code* (MAC). Higher-level application protocols such as HTTP and FTP can be implemented on top of the SSL.

The SSL handshake protocol performs the following functions:

1. It performs authentication of the server.
2. It allows the client and the server to select the cryptographic algorithms to be used during the session from among RC2, RC4, DES, triple-DES, and a few other algorithms; and digital signature and hash algorithms from among DSA, MD5, and SHA-1.
3. It optionally performs authentication of the client.
4. It enables the client and the server to generate a shared secret, which would be used to generate the session keys.

A simplified overview of the SSL handshake protocol is as follows: The client sends a *client_hello* message to the server. This message contains a specification of the cryptographic and compression options, and a 28-byte random number that we will call n_{client}. The server responds with a *server_hello* message, which contains another random number n_{server}. Immediately following the *server_hello* message, the server sends its certificate. SSL has a list of certificate authorities (CAs) on the client side, using which it ensures that the server's certificate is from one of the listed CAs, and verifies the server's authenticity by using public key cryptography. The server, if it so wishes, asks for the client's certificate and verifies the client's identity in a similar manner. Following this, the client sends the *encrypted premaster secret* message, which contains a 48-byte *premaster secret* string encrypted by the public key of the server.

Both client and server now generate a 48-byte *master secret* string from n_{client}, n_{server}, and *premaster secret*, using a standard one-way function. Use of n_{client} and n_{server}, which are randomly chosen values, ensures that the master secret would be different for different sessions between the same client–server pair. The *master secret* string is used to obtain four symmetric session keys using a standard algorithm. These keys are used as follows: Keys $k_{c \to s}^{crypt}$ and $k_{s \to c}^{crypt}$ are used for encryption and decryption of messages sent by the client to the server, and by the server to the client, respectively, and keys $k_{c \to s}^{mac}$ and $k_{s \to c}^{mac}$ are used to generate message authentication codes for messages sent by the client and by the server, respectively. Following key generation, both client and server send *finished* messages to one another. At this time, the SSL handshake protocol is complete.

Exchange of messages is performed by the SSL record protocol using the session keys generated during the handshake. The steps in sending a message m from the client to the server are as follows:

1. The client generates MAC_m, which is a message authentication code for message m, using the key $k_{c \to s}^{mac}$.
2. The pair $< m, MAC_m >$ is encrypted by using the key $k_{c \to s}^{crypt}$, and the encrypted string is sent to the server.
3. The server decrypts the string by using the key $k_{c \to s}^{crypt}$ to obtain the pair $< m, MAC_m >$. It accepts m if its MAC computed using the key $k_{c \to s}^{mac}$ matches MAC_m.

The SSL protocol could be subverted by a *man-in-the-middle* attack, where an intruder intercepts a client's messages to a server in the SSL handshake protocol and masquerades as the server in all subsequent message exchanges. It may analogously masquerade as the client and set up a secured SSL connection with the server. The client and server processes must take precautions to defeat the man-in-the-middle attack during the initial handshake. When the server provides its certificate to the client in the SSL handshake protocol, the client must verify that the distinguished name and IP address mentioned in the server's certificate match those of the server with which it is attempting to set up the SSL connection. A mismatch would indicate that it is subject to a man-in-the-middle attack, so it should abort the handshake protocol if this is the case.

The server does not know the IP address where a client resides, so it has to use a different approach to authenticate the client. If the server requires client authentication in the SSL handshake protocol, the client is required to provide a certificate and also a piece of random data known to the server which it digitally signs using its private key to authenticate itself. The server obtains the public key of the client from the client certificate and validates the client's digital signature. A failure in this step would indicate that it is subject to a man-in-the-middle attack, so it aborts the handshake protocol. This step is analogous to that in the challenge–response protocol described earlier in Section 21.2.2.

21.5 SUMMARY

Interprocess messages in a distributed system may pass through links and nodes that are not under control of the distributed OS. It provides an opportunity for an intruder to launch a variety of attacks such as unauthorized reading of messages, tampering with messages, masquerading as a registered user, or interfering with use of resources or services by users, which is called *denial of service*. In this chapter we discussed how a distributed OS deals with these threats.

The threats of leakage or tampering are called threats to *message security*. They are countered through *encryption*. In *private key encryption*, messages sent to a process must be encrypted with the key assigned to the process. This arrangement is convenient for communication between system entities and user processes because the system entities can readily find a user's key; however, it is not suitable for communication between user processes. In *public key encryption*, each process P_i has a pair of keys (u_i, v_i), where u_i is the public key which is made known to all processes in the system and v_i is a private key known only to P_i. These keys have the property that a message encrypted by using u_i can be decrypted by using v_i, and vice versa. The Rivest–Shamir–Adelman (RSA) algorithm is used to generate the pairs of keys for processes. Public key encryption has the disadvantage that the keys are an order of magnitude larger than the keys used in private key encryption, so encryption is an expensive operation. Because of these drawbacks, processes are assigned *session keys* for use during a communication session. A *key distribution center* (KDC) is used to provide public keys of processes or to generate session keys on demand by communicating processes.

An intruder can launch a *message replay* attack to masquerade as another user. In this attack, the intruder records messages to or from a process and plays them back at a later time to fool the OS or the KDC. A *challenge-response* protocol is used to thwart such attacks by authenticating the sender of a message. This protocol is included in the protocol for communicating with the KDC. Processes can also use it for mutual authentication. However, mutual authentication in this manner is cumbersome and expensive. Hence third-party authenticators such as Kerberos and SSL are employed in practice.

When processes exchange data, it is important to know that the data is authentic, that is, it was originated or sent by the claimed process and it has not been tampered with by anyone. A *digital signature* is used to verify authenticity of data. It consists of a hash code generated from the data, which is encrypted using the private key of the originator or sender of the data. Authenticity of the data is verified as follows: A *public key certificate* of the originator or sender of the data is obtained from a certification authority. The digital signature of the data is decrypted by using the public key of the originator or sender found in the certificate. A successful decryption establishes that the originator or sender had indeed originated or sent the data. The data is genuine if a hash code generated from it matches the decrypted form of its digital signature.

TEST YOUR CONCEPTS

21.1 Classify each of the following statements as true or false:

a. Message replay is an active security attack.

b. Encryption prevents eavesdropping, but cannot prevent tampering with messages.

c. In a distributed system using public key encryption, a message being sent by process P_i to process P_j should be encrypted with the private key of process P_i.

d. Public key encryption incurs higher overhead than private key encryption.

e. Session keys are used to limit exposure of encryption keys to intruder attacks.
f. A challenge–response protocol can be used to prevent a masquerading attack.
g. A key distribution center is used to distribute private keys of processes.

21.2 Select the appropriate alternative in each of the following questions:

a. A message contains the id of its sender process, the id of the receiver process, and a ciphertext form of the message text. An intruder can eavesdrop on the message readily
  i. If the message text is encrypted by using a session key
  ii. If the message text is encrypted by using the public key of the receiver process
  iii. If the message text is encrypted by using the private key of the sender process
  iv. None of (i)–(iii)

b. In a public key system, a key distribution center is used
  i. To ensure confidentiality of the private key of a process
  ii. To distribute information about private keys of processes
  iii. To ensure confidentiality of the public key of a process
  iv. To distribute information about public keys of processes

c. A digital signature
  i. Is a string that uniquely identifies the person who sent a message
  ii. Consists of the text of a message and the name or id of its sender
  iii. Consists of the encrypted form of a message and the name or id of its sender
  iv. None of (i)–(iii)

EXERCISES

21.1 Devise a public key cipher for $n = 77$ using the RSA approach.

21.2 Comment on the following statement : "There is no danger of masquerading if the message sent by a client to a key distribution center requesting a session key for a server is exposed to an intruder."

21.3 It is proposed to distribute session keys in a public key system as follows:

1. $P_i \rightarrow$ KDC : $E_{U_{kdc}}(P_i, P_j)$
2. KDC $\rightarrow P_i$: $E_{U_i}(P_j, SK_{i,j}, E_{U_j}(P_i, SK_{i,j}))$
3. $P_i \rightarrow P_j$: $E_{U_j}(P_i, SK_{i,j})$
4. $P_j \rightarrow P_i$: $E_{SK_{i,j}}(n)$
5. $P_i \rightarrow P_j$: $E_{SK_{i,j}}(n+1)$
6. $P_i \rightarrow P_j$: $E_{SK_{i,j}}(<message>)$

Does this protocol suffer from any weaknesses? If so, suggest ways to overcome them.

21.4 Can tampering of messages lead to denial of service? (*Hint:* Think of key distribution centers.)

21.5 Explain how Kerberos avoids transmitting password information over the network when a user logs in. What actions should be performed when a user changes his password?

21.6 Describe use of the lifetime field in a Kerberos ticket. How is the lifetime guessed? Comment on the advantages and disadvantages of using the lifetime field.

21.7 Comment on validity of the following statement: "Message replay attacks are possible in Kerberos until a ticket expires."

21.8 The challenge–response protocol for detecting message replay attacks described in Section 21.2.2 consists of the following steps:

$$P_j \rightarrow P_i : E_{SK_{i,j}}(n)$$
$$P_i \rightarrow P_j : E_{SK_{i,j}}(n+1)$$

However, in Step 3.2 of the Kerberos protocol, the server returns the nonce n_3 to the client without performing any operation on it. Explain why this is adequate.

21.9 The challenge–response protocol mentioned in Exercise 21.8 assumes that an intruder would not be able to guess or obtain $SK_{i,j}$. It fails if this assumption is not valid. An intruder can use this fact to subvert security of session key distribution in a private key system as follows: The intruder obtains an

$SK_{i,j}$ by some means. Now it replays the message in Step 3 of (21.3), namely.

$$3.\ P_i \rightarrow P_j : E_{V_j}(P_i, SK_{i,j}), E_{SK_{i,j}}(\textit{<message>})$$

This way it would be able to set up a spurious association with P_j, i.e. set up an association in which P_j believes that it is interacting with P_i. It would enjoy this ability to set up spurious associations indefinitely. Design a protocol to prevent this threat. (*Hint:* Would it help if, instead of using the challenge–response protocol, P_j tries to initiate a fresh session with P_i by obtaining a session key from the KDC?)

BIBLIOGRAPHY

Rivest (1978) and Pfleeger and Pfleeger (2003) describe the theory behind RSA encryption. Woo and Lam (1992) discusses authentication protocols in distributed systems. Steiner et al. (1988) describes the Kerberos protocol.

Denning and Denning (1998) is a collection of articles on cyberspace attacks and Internet security. Khare (1997) is a similar collection of articles that covers trust issues on the Web, including digital signatures and public key infrastructures. Cheswick et al. (2003) discusses security attacks, firewalls, and authentication.

1. Cheswick, W. R., S. M. Bellovin, and A. D. Rubin (2003): *Firewalls and Internet Security,* 2nd ed., Addison-Wesley Professional, Reading, Mass.
2. Denning, D. E., and P. J. Denning (eds.) (1998): *Internet Besieged: Countering Cyberspace Scofflaws,* Addison-Wesley, Reading, Mass.
3. Khare, R. (ed.) (1997): *Web Security: A Matter of Trust*, O'Reilly, Sebastopol, Calif.
4. Lampson, B., M. Abadi, M. Burrows, and E. Wobbler (1992): "Authentication in distributed systems: theory and practice," *ACM Transactions on Computers*, **10**, 4, 265–310.
5. Pfleeger, C. P., and S. Pfleeger (2003): *Security in computing*, Prentice Hall, Englewood Cliffs, N.J.
6. Rivest, R. L., A. Shamir, and L. Adelman (1978): "On digital signatures and public key cryptosystems," *Communications of the ACM*, **21**, 2, 120–126.
7. Steiner, J. G., C. Newman and J. I. Schiller (1988): "Kerberos: an authentication service for open network system", *Proceedings of the Winter USENIX conference*.
8. Woo, T. Y. C. and S. S. Lam (1992): "Authentication for distributed systems," *IEEE Computer*.

Index

A

D

E

G

H

I

M

N

O

P

S

T

U

V

W

X

Z